HANDBOOK OF GLOBAL FINANCIAL MARKETS

Transformations, Dependence, and Risk Spillovers

HANDBOOK OF GLOBAL FINANCIAL MARKETS

Transformations, Dependence, and Risk Spillovers

edited by

Sabri Boubaker
EM Normandie, France

Duc Khuong Nguyen
IPAG Business School, France & Indiana University, USA

World Scientific

NEW JERSEY • LONDON • SINGAPORE • BEIJING • SHANGHAI • HONG KONG • TAIPEI • CHENNAI • TOKYO

Published by

World Scientific Publishing Co. Pte. Ltd.
5 Toh Tuck Link, Singapore 596224
USA office: 27 Warren Street, Suite 401-402, Hackensack, NJ 07601
UK office: 57 Shelton Street, Covent Garden, London WC2H 9HE

National Library Board, Singapore Cataloguing in Publication Data
Names: Boubaker, Sabri, editor. | Nguyen, Duc Khuong, 1978– editor.
Title: Handbook of global financial markets : transformations, dependence, and risk spillovers / edited by Sabri Boubaker, Duc Khuong Nguyen.
Description: Singapore : World Scientific Publishing Co. Pte. Ltd., [2019]
Identifiers: OCN 1096380273 | 978-981-32-3664-6 (hardcover)
Subjects: LCSH: Capital market. | International finance. | Globalization--Economic aspects.
Classification: DDC 332.042--dc23

For any available supplementary material, please visit
https://www.worldscientific.com/worldscibooks/10.1142/10893#t=suppl

Desk Editor: Daniele Lee

Typeset by Stallion Press
Email: enquiries@stallionpress.com

Preface

The world financial system has witnessed profound changes in the aftermath of the successive crises in the late 2000s. National governments worldwide have been obligated to adopt unconventional policy measures such as asset repurchases, banking bailouts and tax cuts to stimulate economic growth. Many emerging markets, led by China, have also been facing economic slowdowns and exporting uncertainties to the rest of the world with a serious potential threat to growth, prosperity and economic and financial stability. The challenge is huge because these markets are now large and play an increasing role in the global economic activities and growth. On another ground, developed economies are not immune either from such contagious risks, to the extent that many of their large firms have built their strategies and planned their growth and development around the rise of emerging markets. What is also important to note is that at the firm level, corporations were required to carefully review not only their business models but also their risk management and corporate governance practices.

There is no doubt that the global economy is approaching a critical juncture. Growth slowdowns, low commodity prices, and relative price stability are dragging down the profits of the world's largest firms. Negative economic fundamentals in many countries, low interest rates, volatile financial markets and threat of another financial crash are prompting investors to become more cautious. They are also dumping equity, more than ever before, for safer havens such as cash, bonds, and commodity futures (in particular gold), creating new concerns about the increased systematic risk of the financial markets in the case of adverse and extreme events.

Ten years after the global financial crisis (GFC) of 2008–2009, the economic, financial and policy uncertainty even tends to increase. The monthly global economic policy uncertainty index is particularly high since July 2011.[1] It hits a record of 341.22 points in November 2018, which is 72% higher than the highest level of 198.19 points at the heart of the GFC. The same pattern of uncertainty is followed at the national level. Other events such as the Brexit, threats to the burst of China and other emerging market debt bubbles following recent credit booms to finance growth, and the up and down movements of oil prices have been significantly affecting growth opportunities and the performance of stock markets.

With a rich collection of 29 exceptional contributions, the Handbook "Handbook of Global Financial Markets: Transformations, Dependence, and Risk Spillovers" provides the readers with up-to-date insights about the ongoing transformations of global financial markets as well as the perspectives of their future development. Part I (Chapters 1 to 6) gives a dedicated assessment of cross-market dynamic linkages, shock transmission, and contagion at the global scale with some concrete examples of specific market areas. Part II (Chapters 7 to 9) addresses the issues of volatility, integration and spillovers in the global foreign exchange market — one of the most important financial markets nowadays with more than 5 trillion of trading volume per day. Part III (Chapters 10 to 14) looks closely at the transformations of financial markets from the risk management and portfolio allocation perspectives. Part IV (Chapters 15 to 18) dedicates attention to the evaluation of policy effectiveness, liquidity and volatility during the European debt crisis. Part V (Chapters 19 to 25) delivers insights about the so-called fundamental relationship between growth and finance as well as the macroeconomic effects on financial markets. Part VI (Chapters 26 to 29) enlightens new stylized facts in asset pricing and the way to take them into account when making investment and financing decisions.

All in all, this Handbook is particularly helpful for academics, research students, businesses and regulatory bodies as it addresses the state of art, current issues and new trends in global financial markets. It also brings insights about adaptation strategies and adjustments by firms and investors to secure their investments during times of crisis.

Sabri Boubaker & Duc Khuong Nguyen

[1]This index is constructed from the information contained in: i) newspaper coverage of policy-related economic uncertainty; ii) federal tax code provisions set to expire in future years; and iii) disagreement among economic forecasters. For more details, the readers can refer to http://www.policyuncertainty.com.

About the Editors

Sabri Boubaker is Professor of Finance at EM Normandie (France) and Research Fellow at the Institut de Recherche en Gestion (University of Paris Est). He holds a Ph.D. in Finance from University of Paris Est (2006) and a HDR degree (Habilitation for Supervising Doctoral Research) in 2010 from the same university. He has recently published several academic papers in international refereed journals including *Journal of Corporate Finance, Journal of Banking and Finance*, *Journal of International Money and Finance, Financial Management, International Review of Financial Analysis, European Financial Management Journal, Review of Quantitative Accounting and Finance*, and *Journal of International Financial Markets, and Institutions and Money*. Dr. Boubaker has also edited several books on corporate finance and financial markets and serves as subject and associate editors on editorial boards of many peer-reviewed finance journals. He is the co-founder (with Duc Khuong Nguyen) of the Paris Financial Management Conference (2013-) and Vietnam Symposium in Banking and Finance (2016-).

Duc Khuong Nguyen is Professor of Finance and Deputy Director for Research at IPAG Business School (France). He holds a PhD in Finance from the University of Grenoble Alpes (France) and a HDR (Habilitation for Supervising Scientific Research) degree in Management Science from University of Cergy-Pontoise (France), and completed an executive education program in "Leadership in Development" at Harvard Kennedy School (United States). He is also a Non-Resident Research Fellow at the School of Public and Environmental Affairs, Indiana University. His research articles are published in various refereed journals such as *European Journal of Operational Research, Journal of Banking and Finance, Journal of Economic Dynamics and Control, Journal of Empirical Finance, Journal of International Money* *and Finance*, *Journal of Macroeconomics*, *Macroeconomic Dynamics*, and *Review of International Economics*. Dr. Nguyen has edited many books on corporate finance and financial markets issues and serves as subject and associate editors of several finance journals. He is the co-founder (with Sabri Boubaker) of the Paris Financial Management Conference (2013-) and Vietnam Symposium in Banking and Finance (2016-).

About the Authors

Marcelle Chauvet is a Professor of Economics at University of California, Riverside and Director of the International Association for Applied Econometrics. She is also associate editor of the journals *Macroeconomic Dynamics* and *Journal of Applied Econometrics*. Before joining UC Riverside, Professor Chauvet received her Ph.D. from the University of Pennsylvania. Her research interests are in macroeconomics and finance, including application of time series analysis to modeling and predicting business cycles, forecasting macro and financial cycles, and the interactions between the economy and financial markets. Her research has been published in several reputable refereed journals.

Bo-Yu Chen is a Ph.D. candidate at the University of California, Riverside. His research interests include international macroeconomics, financial markets, and empirical macroeconomics. His recent research focuses on the interaction and dynamics of international financial markets and the business cycle.

Thomas Flavin is a Senior Lecturer in Financial Economics at Maynooth University. Thomas holds a Ph.D. in Finance from the University of York (UK). His main research interests are in the financial market linkages and shock transmission, financial contagion, and asset allocation. He has been a visiting scholar at the Federal Reserve Bank of Atlanta, University of Cambridge, and University of York. He has published his research in leading peer-reviewed journals such as *Journal of International Money and Finance*, *Journal of Forecasting*, *Emerging Market Review*, *International Review of Finance*, *Economics Letters* and *Journal of Financial Markets, Institutions and Money*, amongst others.

K. Thomas Liaw is a Professor of Finance in the Economics and Finance Department at St. John's University, New York. He was chairman of the department. Professor Liaw is Editor-in-Chief of *International Journal of Financial Research*. He has published articles in Treasury coupon rolls, repurchase agreements, emerging markets smart beta ETFs, and market risks. His book publications include investment banking, investment banking in China, and capital markets. His principal areas of teaching and research are capital markets, investment management, and investment banking. Professor Liaw was president of Chinese American Academic and Professional Society and was director at State Bank of Long Island. In addition, he has received corporate assignments in asset management and capital markets. Professor Liaw has a Ph.D. from Northwestern University.

Mohamed Zaki is a Research Associate at Cambridge Service Alliance, University of Cambridge. His research lies in the field of Information Governance, Business Intelligence, and Big Data Analytics. His Ph.D. investigated the impact of employing different business intelligence techniques to detect frauds in the stock exchange markets. The research proposed an ontological approach for financial fraud. The proposed ontology brings together existing domain knowledge from previous efforts together with new knowledge derived from the analysis of unstructured sources based on existing fraud cases reported by Security Exchange Commission (SEC). Currently, he is leading the performance and Information analytics research theme at the Cambridge Service Alliance. The research investigates "*How big data could play a role in improving and optimising services within complex service network organisation*": In particular, understand how data could play role in creating new business opportunities either in improving existing services or creating new business model within complex service organisations.

Babis Theodoulidis is an Associate Professor in Information Management at Alliance Manchester Business School, University of Manchester. His research has been published in both engineering and social science journals such as *Journal of Information Systems*, *Knowledge Management Research & Practice*, *Expert Systems with Applications*, *International Journal of Information Management*, *International Journal of Data Warehousing and Mining*, *International Journal Services Technology and Management*, and *Journal of Visual Languages and Computing*. His most recent research interests focus on the design of service-based information systems, the temporal and spatial aspects of information, the analysis of information using data and text mining techniques, the visualization of information, and service information management issues within organizations.

David Díaz is an Assistant Professor at the Facultad de Economía y Negocios of Universidad de Chile. As an academic staff, he performs educational activities in undergraduate, postgraduate, MBA, and other executive education programmes. Díaz is also a full-time researcher, counting with a trajectory of academic publications related to the use of data mining techniques and information systems in the business context. His research has been published in prestigious journal and professional magazines in Latin America, the United States, and Europe. His main line of research relates to the modelling of financial data and the environmental profile of companies, from a Business Intelligence and Service Analytics perspectives. He is a strong advocate of innovation through the use of Information Technologies as a main tool for competitive advantage and entrepreneurship competitive edge.

Besma Hkiri is Assistant Professor in Accounting and Finance at College of Business, University of Jeddah, Saudi Arabia. She obtained her Ph.D. in Finance from the Faculty of Economic Sciences and Management of Tunis, University Tunis El Manar. Besma Hkiri is also member of the International Finance Group-Tunisia (IFGT) Research (University Tunis El Manar). Dr. Besma HKIRI has published many papers in peer-reviewed journals such as *Economic Modeling*, *Pacific-Basin Finance Journal*, and *Applied Economics*. Her research interests include risk management, financial markets comovements, financial economics, comovement analysis, dynamic volatility analysis, and energy economics. Dr. Besma Hkiri also participated in many international conferences.

Azza Bejaoui is Assistant Professor in Accounting and Finance at Higher Institute of Management of Tunis, Tunis University. She received her Ph.D. in Finance in 2013 and Master in Finance in 2008 from Higher Institute of Management of Tunis, Tunisia. Her research interest includes risk management, financial markets, behavioral finance, portfolio management, and econometrics. She has published several papers in peer-referred journals. She has published two books (in French): Adaptive Markets Hypothesis: Reconciliation between Efficient Markets and Behavioral Finance & Market Risk — Attempt of Operationalization in the Tunisian Context. She also contributed with a book chapter entitled "Integrated Model of Perceived Risk and Risk-Reducing Strategies in the Tunisian Stock Market" to *Ethical and Social Perspectives on Global Business in Emerging Markets*, IGI Global, E-Editorial Discovery.

Sondes Ben Salem is Assistant in Accounting and Finance at the Faculty of Economics and Management Sciences of Sousse, Sousse University, Tunisia. She obtained her Ph.D. Thesis from the Higher Institute of Management of Tunis, Tunis University, Tunisia. Her research interests include markets microstructure and financial crises impact on stock exchange markets.

Igor Alexandre Clemente de Morais holds a Ph.D. in Economics from UFRGS. He served for 12 years as an economist at FIERGS. He is currently a partner and chief economist at Vokin Investments, as well as at BP Consultoria and is Professor in Economics at Unisinos. Also acts as economic adviser to the SINBORSUL (Union of Rubber Artifact Industries in Rio Grande do Sul) and the SIMECAN (Union of Metal Industries Mechanical and Electro Electronic Canoas and Nova Santa Rita). Also, he is director of studies and economic research ILADES (Latin American Institute for Sustainable Economic Development). He assumed the Chair of the Economics and Statistics Foundation — FEE in February 2015.

Guilherme Ribeiro de Macêdo holds a Ph.D. in Accounting and Finance at the UFRGS Business School since 2012. He graduated in Electrical Engineering from IME (Instituto Militar de Engenharia) in 2005 and worked for two years at BNDES in Investment Analysis area during 2003 until 2005. He is a researcher/risk consultant with several articles published in this area and is a professor at UFRGS.

Marcia Regina Godoy holds a Ph.D. in Economics at UFRGS since 2008. She is senior scientific advisor in pharmacoeconomics and senior researcher at Brazilian Institute of Health Technology Assessment. From 2011 until 2016, she was postdoctoral fellow at Universidade do Vale do Rio dos Sinos. She has 15 years of experience in health economics, pharmacoeconomics, market access, pricing strategies to drugs, and econometric methods. Her research interests are in following areas: health economics, econometric methods, pharmacoeconomics, economic of crime, public finance, healthcare finance, and international economics.

Leonardo Berteli Piveta graduated in Mechanical Engineering from Lutheran University of Brazil (ULBRA) and holds a Master in Economics from University of the Sinos Valley (Unisinos). He is a lecturer at University Center of the Serra Gaúcha, where he teaches graduate courses of Engineering and Architecture. He has experience in the field of Mechanical Engineering in Machines Projects and in Economics in International Economics mainly with econometrics models as deterministic and stochastic models.

Also, he is a lecturer at the Catholic University of Pelotas (UCPEL) where he teaches Financial Mathematic for the MBA in Controlling and Finance.

Walid Ben Omrane is an Associate Professor of Finance and holds Ph.D. and Master of Financial Economics from University of Louvain (Belgium). His research interests are in the area of financial market microstructure, international finance, and financial econometrics. Dr. Ben Omrane's research has been published in top-tier finance and statistics journals such as the *Journal of Banking and Finance*, the *Journal of International Money and Finance*, *Journal of International Financial Markets, Institutions and Money*, and *Computational Statistics and Data Analysis*. His research has been supported by the Social Sciences and Humanities Research Council of Canada (SSHRC) through the standard research grant program. He is an *ad hoc* reviewer for several Finance and Economics journals. He received several Research distinctions and Awards, including two external prestigious research grants from SSHRC and IFM2, and 4 Best Paper Awards, such as the Best Paper Award in Investments, Financial Markets, and Valuation at the Global Finance Association conference held in Dubai 2014.

Robert Welch is a Professor of Finance, has a Ph.D. from SUNY at Buffalo, and M. A. (statistics) and M.B.A. from the University of Western Ontario. He has published in the *Journal of Futures Markets*, *Journal of Derivatives*, *International Review of Economics and Finance*, *Review of Quantitative Finance and Accounting*, and *Advances in Futures and Options Research* concerning constant variance option pricing and fractionally cointegrated time series. Some of this work was supported by the Social Sciences and Humanities Research Council of Canada (SSHRC). He has also published in the Canadian Tax Journal (RRSPs and RESPs), Applied Economic Letters (cost of capital), and Research in International Business and Finance (tick test). He is currently involved with foreign exchange response to macroeconomic news announcements. His hobbies include windsurfing and guitar. He has been a department chair for several terms as well as served on the University pension, and promotion and tenure committees.

Xinyao Zhou is currently a Ph.D. student in Administration (Finance) at Schulich School of Business in York University. He holds an M.Sc. in Management (Finance) from the Goodman School of Business at Brock University and BBA from Harbin Institute of Technology. Xinyao's research interest includes financial econometrics, corporate finance, and international finance. Prior to joining academia, Xinyao Zhou worked as a Management Trainee at Unilever (China).

Dave Allen is a Honorary Chair Professor in the Department of Finance, Asia University, Taiwan, an Honorary Professor in the School of Mathematics and Statistics at the University of Sydney, and an Honorary Professor at Edith Cowan University. He was previously located in the Faculty of Business at Edith Cowan University where he was Foundation Professor of Finance from 1996 to 2013, and prior to this held the Challenge Bank Professorship of Finance at Curtin University of Technology. He has an Honours degree in economics from St. Andrews University in Scotland, an M.Phil in the history of economic thought completed at Leicester University in England and a Ph.D in Finance from the University of Western Australia. He has published several books, and monographs; 42 chapters in books in business economics, finance, and econometrics plus over 100 refereed journal publications. These have covered a wide range of topics including corporate financial policy decisions, asset pricing, business economics, funds management and performance bench-marking, volatility modeling and hedging, and market microstructure and liquidity. His recent work has been mainly focused on risk modeling.

Petko S. Kalev is a Professor in Finance at La Trobe Business School, La Trobe University, Melbourne, Victoria, and was previously the Director of the Centre for Applied Financial Studies (CAFS) in the School of Commerce, at the University of South Australia Business School. Professor Kalev holds a Ph.D. in Financial Econometrics from Monash University, a Master of Science in Statistics from the University of Melbourne and, a Bachelor of Science Degree in Mathematics from the University of Plovdiv. Prior to joining the University of South Australia in February 2010, Professor Kalev worked at the Department of Accounting and Finance, Monash University (1999–2010). Professor Kalev has several research interests ranging from Asset Pricing, Capital Markets and Market Microstructure, Market Efficiency, Corporate Finance, Assets Management, and Quantitative Finance Behavioural Finance. Professor Kalev is most known and recognised for his empirical research contributions to the field of Market Microstructure: Asymmetric Information and Informed Trading, Market Quality, Price Discovery, and Volatility Modelling.

Shelton Peiris did his Ph.D. at Monash University, Melbourne, Victoria. After graduation from Monash in 1987, he tutored at the Department of Econometrics (Monash University), and lectured at the University of Melbourne before joining what was then the Statistics Department at the University of Sydney in 1990. He has been there ever since except for various visiting appointments. Shelton was the chair of the international program committee for international conference in Colombo, December 2011. He was a council member and treasurer of the SSAI (Statistical Society of Australia Inc.) NSW branch (2003–2006). He has organised a number of workshops and invited paper sessions in Australia and overseas. He is an elected member of ISI. He has been the Director of Statistics Teaching Program (2005–2006) and from 2011. He is a SubDean (Student Affairs) of the Faculty of Science. His research interests include statistical analysis of stationary and non-stationary time series data, theory and applications of estimating functions, financial time series modelling, saddle point, and Edgeworth type approximations related to time series problems. Currently, his interests are in developing methods in Financial Econometrics and for modelling, financial time series data, ACD and Log-ACD modelling and volatility modelling.

Abhay Kumar Singh is a Senior Lecturer in Finance and Director of the Finance Decision Lab at the Department of Applied Finance in the Faculty of Business and Economics, Macquarie University, Sydney. He obtained his Ph.D. in 2011 from Edith Cowan University in Western Australia with a thesis evaluating extreme Financial Market Risk. He was the co-recipient of the prestigious Edith Cowan University Research Medal for his Ph.D. research work. His research interests include financial market risk modelling using stock market data and multivariate dependence using Vine Copula. Recently, he has also developed an interest in the field of big data analytics, particularly in financial network modelling, text mining, and related sentiment analysis.

Somar Almohamad obtained his Ph.D. from Western Sydney University, Australia. His doctoral thesis research focuses on financial integration in the MENA region.

Anil V. Mishra is an Associate Professor in Finance at the Western Sydney University, Australia. His research primarily focuses on home bias, asset pricing and behavioural finance. He has published in top tier finance journals including *Journal of Empirical Finance*, *Journal of International Money and Finance*, *Pacific Basin Finance Journal*, *Economic Modelling*, *International Review of Economics and Finance*, and *Emerging Markets Review*, among others. He is a recipient of the Early Career Researcher Award from the Western Sydney University for his specialist contribution in the research area of cross border investment.

Mazin A. M. Al Janabi is Full Professor of Finance at EGADE Business School, Tecnológico de Monterrey, Mexico City, Mexico. Professor Al Janabi holds a Ph.D. degree from the University of London, UK, and has over 30 years of real-world experience in diverse academic institutions and financial markets in many different roles. He has worked for top international financial groups (e.g., ING-Barings and BBVA-Bancomer) where he held several senior management positions. Professor Al Janabi has strong interest for research, publications, and developments within emerging economies. He has written extensively on contemporary topics in trading, market and counterparty risk management besides modern portfolio management. Professor Al Janabi has published in top-tier journals such as: *International Review of Financial Analysis, European Journal of Operational Research, Annals of Operations Research, Applied Economics, Economic Modelling, Review of Financial Economics, Service Industries Journal, Emerging Markets Finance and Trade*, among others.

Julien Chevallier is a Full Professor of Economics (Professeur des Universités) and Director of the MSc Money, Banking, Finance & Insurance. He undertakes research and lectures on empirical finance, applied time-series econometrics, and commodity markets. Dr. Chevallier is the author of *Econometric Analysis of Carbon Markets* (Springer), as well as the co-author of *The Economics of Commodity Markets* (Wiley Finance). He has published articles in leading refereed journals, including the *Journal of Empirical Finance*; *International Review of Financial Analysis*; *Quantitative Finance*; *Journal of Forecasting*; *Journal of International Financial Markets, Institutions & Money*, and *Annals of Operations Research*. Furthermore, Dr. Chevallier currently serves as Associate Editor at *Energy Economics* among other appointments. His latest book (co-authored) is entitled *Pricing and Forecasting Carbon Markets* (Springer, 2017).

Guldem Gokcek has been an Associate Professor at New York University, Honorary Lecturer/faculty member at the Management School, University of Liverpool/Laureate Online Education, and teaches regularly in the MBA and MSc, Programs. She has received her doctorate degree in the areas of Financial Economics and Econometrics from Pace University, New York, completed studies in Ph.D. in Economics (A.B.D) at the City University of New York, and in MA in Economics at Bosphorus University after graduating with BA in Economics from Marmara University, Istanbul. Prof.Gokcek taught at Columbia University, Pace University, and Fashion Institute of Technology, lectured and served as a consultant/advisor at companies including U.S Trust Company, Backer Spielvogel Bates, Inc., Creamer Dickson Basford, Inc., and Young and Rubicam brands in New York City, contributed to the research on education at New York City Board of Education, engaged in specialized and confidential research and statistical analysis related to the judicial system at the Office of Court Research, New York State Office of Court Administration, and served as a Senior Correspondent for the publication "Middle East Business and Banking," for three years. She was listed in the 'International Who's Who of professionals.' Guldem's research interests are in the areas of Financial Economics, Entrepreneurial Finance, Econometrics, Corporate Finance, Law, and banking. She has authored numerous articles, reviews, and book chapters. She is a member of many professional organizations, including the American Economic Association, Financial Management Association, and Society for Institutional & Organizational Economics.

Peter Julian Cayton is an Assistant Professor of Statistics at the University of Philippines Diliman. His research interests are in financial econometrics, time series analysis, and extreme value statistics. He has published in journals of various disciplines such as *The Philippine Statistician* (Scopus indexed), *The Philippine Review of Economics* (ABDC: C), and *Water International* (ISI indexed). He has a Bachelor of Science (magna cum laude, 2009) and a Master of Science (2011) degree in Statistics from the University of the Philippines Diliman. He completed his Ph.D. in Statistics at the Australian National University in 2018.

Kin-Yip Ho joined the Australian National University (ANU) in 2010 as an academic specializing in topics in actuarial studies, economics, econometrics, finance, and statistics. His current research and teaching interests are the actuarial applications of financial and economic models, financial econometrics, international finance, and time-series analysis. He has published his research findings in various journals, such as *Annals of Actuarial Science* (ABDC: A), *China Economic Review* (ABDC: A), *Economic Modelling* (ABDC: A), *International Review of Economics and Finance* (ABDC: A), *Journal of Applied Econometrics* (ABDC: A*), *Journal of Banking and Finance* (ABDC: A*), *Journal of Empirical Finance* (ABDC: A), *Scottish Journal of Political Economy* (ABDC: A), and *World Economy* (ABDC: A). He completed his Ph.D. program in Economics at Cornell University and undergraduate degree at the National University of Singapore (NUS). As an amateur pianist, he has an Associate Diploma in Piano Performance from London College of Music (University of West London).

Muhammad Shahbaz is Chair Professor at Energy and Sustainable Development (ESD), Montpellier Business School (France). He received his Ph.D. in Economics from National College of Business Administration and Economics, Lahore, Pakistan. His research focuses on development economics, energy economics, environmental and tourism economics, etc. He has widely published in peer-reviewed international journals. He has published more than 203 research papers so far in the national and international referred publications, having a cumulative impact factor of 250 so far. He is among world's top 31 authors in Economics category as compiled by IDEAS, and among Pakistan's top 1 authors in Economics category in Pakistan as compiled by IDEAS.

Syed Jawad Hussain Shahzad is Post Doc Fellow at Energy and Sustainable Development (ESD) of the Montpellier Business School France. After graduating with a degree in Finance at the COMSATS Institute of Information Technology Islamabad, Pakistan, Jawad received his doctoral degree in Finance from University of Malaysia Terengganu, Malaysia. Jawads research crosses several disciplines: in the business and finance area, he has published in a number of journals used by the Financial Times for ranking business schools (e.g., *Tourism Management, Journal of Banking and Finance, International Review of Economics and Finance, Economic Modelling*). His core area of research is applied financial econometric with application of probability theory for financial risk management, In addition, he has also published work in leading journals in applied mathematics (e.g., Physica A), in resources economics (Renewable and Sustainable Energy Reviews, Resources Policy, Economic Change and Restructuring), and in policy journals (e.g., Energy Policy), in social economics (e.g., Social Indicators Research, Quality and Quantity).

Sandrine Kablan is Associate Professor at the University of East Paris Créteil, France, and a researcher at the research laboratory ERUDITE. She received her Msc and Ph.D. in Economics at, respectively, the University of Cergy Pontoise and University of Nanterre, in France. She specialized in finance and development economics. She wrote several articles in well-known journals such as *Energy Economics*, *Emerging Market Review*, *African Development Review*, *Savings and Development*, *Applied Economics* and *Economics Bulletin*. The topics on which she works are the following: commodities and financial markets, efficiency of financial institutions, microfinance, banks in developing and emerging economies, natural resources management, and climate finance.

Shawkat Hammoudeh is a Palestinian American citizen with a Ph.D. in Economics from University of Kansas, USA. He also had done post-doctorate courses in Finance at Drexel University, USA, during 1989–1990. After graduation from the University of Kansas, he joined Kuwait Institute for Scientific Research as an Associate Research Scientist in 1981. He then worked for OAPEC in Kuwait from 1983 to 1989 and was part of the Arab team that worked on the OAPEC/ENI Interdependence Model in Rome, Italy during the period 1983–1985. He also served on the Steering Committee of the Euro Arab Dialogue Project which was sponsored by OAPEC and the European Union in 1986–1987, and the Steering Committee for the project on exploring the future of the Arab Home Land executed by the Arab Unity Studies Center in Cairo, Egypt. During 1988–1989, he worked as a consultant with the World Bank working on Jordan's Melody Energy-Economy in Amman, Jordan. Since then he has been a faculty member at Drexel University, where he was promoted from Associate Professor to Professor in 2004. His fields of specialization include OPEC oil pricing strategies, commodity markets, exchange rates, and business cycles in the GCC bloc; stock markets in the GCC region and the MENA area; and financial risk management for Islamic and conventional stock and sukuk markets. He serves as editor and special editor of refereed journal and edited books, and a referee for many journals. He is an associate editor of Energy Economics and Global Review of Economics and Business Research and Brazilian Journal of Business Administration.

Dr. Hammoudeh is a prolific researcher who has produced more than 100 articles in quality, refereed journals. SSNR ranks him among the top 10% economics researchers in its program. His RG score is above 34. Dr. Hammoudeh has cooperated on joint projects with researchers from many countries arnound the world. He is also active in participating, organizing and chairing secessions for the Middle East Economics Association (MEEA) Chapter of ASSA and the Western Economics Association International (WEAI). He is regularly interviewed by newspapers and radio and TV stations on current issues related to oil and commodities.

Conall O'Sullivan is an Assistant Professor of Finance at the Michael Smurfit Graduate Business School, University College Dublin. His primary research interests are in numerical methods for derivatives pricing, option implied information from derivatives markets, and fixed income securities markets. His published works have appeared in journals such as *Quantitative Finance*, the *International Journal of Theoretical and Applied Finance*, and the *Journal of Computational Finance*. He has presented papers at international conferences including the European Finance Association, Bachelier World Congress and Computational Financial Econometrics. He is the director of the M.Sc. in Quantitative Finance at the Michael Smurfit Graduate Business School, University College Dublin (UCD). He was a recipient of a UCD College of Business Teaching & Learning Award for Teaching Excellence in 2017.

Vassilios G. Papavassiliou is an Assistant Professor of Finance at the Michael Smurfit Graduate Business School, University College Dublin. He is also a research fellow at the Rimini Centre for Economic Analysis (RCEA). His research interests span the areas of market microstructure, high-frequency finance, liquidity, financial contagion, banking and risk management and energy economics. His work has been published in international refereed journals, such as *Energy Economics*, *Journal of International Financial Markets, Institutions and Money*, *European Journal of Finance*, and *Economics Letters*. He is currently the Banking and Finance Subject Area Head of Teaching and Learning at Michael Smurfit Graduate Business School. He brings multi-year experience in investment banking and has held senior management positions in multinational banking institutions, including Citibank. Dr. Papavassiliou earned his Ph.D. in Finance from the Queen's University of Belfast, United Kingdom.

Tobias Basse is currently working as economist and equity strategist for Norddeutsche Landesbank Girozentrale (NORD/LB) in Hannover. He received his doctoral degree (Dr. rer. pol.) in Economics from University of Paderborn, Department of Economics, and joined Norddeutsche Landesbank in 2001. In addition to that, Dr. Basse teaches Corporate Finance at Touro College in Berlin and Financial Risk Management at the Leibniz University Hannover. He published in peer-reviewed journals (e.g., *Journal of Banking and Finance, Economics Letters*, and *European Journal of Political Economy*). His main fields of research are issues in the fields of corporate finance and international economics.

Thomas S. Bürkle is Chief Executive Officer (CEO) of Norddeutsche Landesbank Girozentrale (NORD/LB) in Hannover since January 2017. Until December 2016, Mr. Bürkle was NORD/LB's Chief Risk Officer (CRO). Before joining the board of NORD/LB, he was *inter alia* CEO of Deutsche Hypothekenbank AG in Hannover as well as DnB NORD A.S. in Copenhagen. He completed his graduate studies in economics at the Free University of Berlin before starting his professional career as economist at Berliner Bank. Mr. Bürkle is honorary consul of the United Kingdom. He has published several chapters in books and papers in journals with a strong focus on applied financial risk management.

Frederik Kunze is working as economist for Norddeutsche Landesbank (NORD/LB) in Hannover since 2011. He joined NORD/LB in 2009 as Senior Credit Portfolio Manager. Before that, he worked as risk manager at DZ BANK in Frankfurt am Main. His main fields of research are the evaluation of financial market forecasts, the analysis of commodity markets, and issues on the Chinese economy. Frederik Kunze published various articles and book chapters focusing on crisis events and is working as lecturer for risk management, corporate finance, portfolio theory, and economics.

Christoph Wegener is an Assistant Professor at IPAG Business School in Paris and a Senior Research Associate at the Center for Risk and Insurance in Hannover. He received his doctoral degree (Dr. rer. pol.) in Economics (summa cum laude) from Leibniz University Hannover. Christoph Wegener published in peer-reviewed journals (e.g., *Journal of Banking and Finance, Journal of Forecasting*, and *Quantitative Finance*). His main research interests are rooted in the field of financial econometrics with applications to energy, housing, and bond markets.

Franck Martin is a full professor of economics at the University of Rennes 1, meanwhile a permanent researcher at CREM UMR CNRS 6211. He is in charge with Professor Jean-Laurent Viviani of the Rennes 1 Foundation Chair "New Challenges for the Bank". He has been the director of the MSc Economics and Financial Engineering at University of Rennes 1 for nearly 15 years. He was also a quantitative financial researcher at Caisse des Dépôts et Consignations and INDOCAM (now AMUNDI asset Management). He is the author of several articles in national and international journals and co-author of the manual *Económétrie Appliquée*.

Jiangxingyun Zhang has obtained a Ph.D. at the Faculty of Economic Sciences of University of Rennes 1, under the supervision of Prof. Franck Martin. He has been a temporary researcher at CREM UMR CNRS 6211. He received his bachelor degree from Shandong University. His research interests include Financial Markets, Financial Econometrics, and Macroeconomics.

Angela Armakolla is a mathematician specializing in CCP risk management and CCP regulation. She is a Ph.D. candidate at the Université Paris 1 Panthéon-Sorbonne and research assistant at the Laboratory of Excellence on Financial Regulation (Labex ReFi). Prior to her Ph.D., Angela worked as a risk management analyst on projects for major banks and CCPs.

Raphael Douady is a French mathematician and economist specializing in financial mathematics and chaos theory. He holds the Robert Frey endowed chair of quantitative finance at Stony Brook University (SUNY) and is also the academic director of the Laboratory of Excellence on Financial Regulation (Université Paris 1 Panthéon-Sorbonne and ESCP-Europe) and affiliated with the French National Centre for Scientific Research (CNRS). He co-founded fin-tech firms Riskdata (1999) and Datacore (2015). He has more than twenty years of experience in the banking industry (risk management, option models, trading strategies) and 35 years of research in pure and applied mathematics.

Jean-Paul Laurent is a Professor of Finance at Université Paris 1 Panthéon — Sorbonne and member of the Laboratory of Excellence on Financial Regulation (Labex ReFi). Prior to this, he has been within ISFA actuarial school at University of Lyon and research professor at CREST, a leading academic institution in Paris. He has been a long time scientific consultant to BNP Paribas research teams. Jean-Paul has extensively published in academic and professional journals. He is known for contributions in the modelling and management of financial risks. He currently investigates the changes induced in this field by new banking and market regulations.

Imad Moosa is currently a Professor of Finance at RMIT, Melbourne. Before taking on the present position, he was a Professor of Finance at Monash University and La Trobe University, and a Lecturer in Economics and Finance at the University of Sheffield. Prior to becoming an academic in 1991, he was a professional economist and a financial journalist for over 10 years, and he also worked as an economist at the Financial Institutions Division of the Bureau of Statistics, the International Monetary Fund (Washington DC). Professor Moosa has published 21 books and over 200 papers in scholarly journals. His most recent books are "*Econometrics as a Con Art*" and "*Publish or Perish: Perceived Benefits versus Unintended Consequences*" (Macmillan). He has served in a number of advisory positions, including as an economic advisor to the U.S. Treasury.

Sumru Altug received her B.A. in Economics from the University of Pittsburgh in 1978 and her Ph.D. in Economics from Carnegie-Mellon University in 1985. She has held permanent and visiting positions at the University of Minnesota, University of Wisconsin, Duke University, and Virgina Tech in the US, and at the University of Durham and the University of York in the UK. She is currently Professor and Chair at the Department of Economics at the American University of Beirut in Lebanon, and has been a Research Fellow at the Centre for Economic Policy Research, London, U.K. since 1997. She served as Associate Editor at the *Economic Journal* and a member of the ESRC Politics, Economics and Geography College in the UK. Her research interests are in the areas of dynamic macroeconomic modeling, business cycles, and growth. She has published papers in the *International Economic Review, Econometrica, The Review of Economic Studies, Economic Theory, Journal of Money, Credit, and Banking, The Journal of Macroeconomics, Macroeconomic Dynamics, European Review of Economic History, Journal of Economic Dynamics and Control, International Finance, International Journal of Forecasting*, among others. She has also coauthored or edited books from Academic Press, Cambridge University Press, and Routledge Publishers. Her most recent book is a monograph entitled *Business Cycles: Fact, Fantasy, and Fallacy*, published by World Scientific (2009).

Cem Çakmaklı graduated from the Tinbergen Institute at Erasmus University Rotterdam in 2011. He worked at the University of Amsterdam as an Assistant Professor of Econometrics until 2013. In 2013, he received a prestigious AXA post-doctoral research grant and, currently, he is an Assistant Professor at Koç University. He has published in the *International Journal of Forecasting, Journal of Applied Econometrics, Journal of Economic Dynamics and Control*, and *EoconomiA*. His main research interests include time-series econometrics and its applications in macroeconomics and finance.

Rüveyda Nur Gözen received her B.A. in Economics from Middle East Technical University and her M.A. in Economics from Koç University. In the fall of 2016, Gözen began her Ph.D. studies in Economics at the University of Illinois at Chicago. Her research interests are applied macroeconomics, econometrics, and development economics.

Arindam Bandopadhyaya is Professor of Finance at UMass Boston, where he was the Chair of the Accounting and Finance Department for fifteen years and is currently the Interim Dean of the College of Management. He has published in leading academic journals like the *Journal of International Money and Finance, Journal of Empirical Finance, Journal of Banking and Finance*, and *Review of Economics and Statistics*. He has presented his research in national and international conferences and in venues like the Boston Federal Reserve and the Boston Stock Exchange.

Jinglin Yang is a Finance Associate at Providence Equity Partners. She received her bachelor's degree in Accounting from Ohio Wesleyan University and worked as an Audit Assistant in Deloitte & Touché. While working at Deloitte, she was fascinated by the financial market and decided to pursue an MSF degree at UMass Boston. Jinglin is a CPA and has passed all 3 levels of the CFA Exam. Previously, she worked as an Equity Research Intern focusing on emerging technology at Oppenheimer & Co. Inc. and also worked as a Financial Analyst at Providence Specialty Product.

Boopen Seetanah is an Associate Professor at the University of Mauritius and the Faculty Research Advisor at the Faculty of Law and Management. He is currently the Director of Research International Centre for Sustainable Tourism and Hospitality at UoM and the WTO Chair Programme Co-chair. His research interests are transport and tourism economics, development, trade, and applied financial economics. Boopen has published several articles in the above fields and in leading journals. He also is a reviewer for a number of world-leading academic journals as well as an editorial board member for a few journals. He has been consulting with both the government of Mauritius and with international organization including UNCTAD, World Bank, UNDP, UNEP, African Development Bank, ILO, and COMESA among others.

Shashi Jeevita Matadeen is currently a Lecturer at the University of Mauritius in the Faculty of Law and Management. She has completed the CFA program and has recently completed her Ph.D. Her research interests include economic development, financial development, and stock markets.

İlkay Şendeniz-Yüncü obtained B.S. and M.S. degrees in civil engineering as well as an MBA from Middle East Technical University. She received a Ph.D. in finance from Bilkent University in 2007 and subsequently conducted postdoctoral research at the University of California, Berkeley and Tilburg University. She taught at Bilkent University and Tilburg University before joining IÉSEG School of Management as an Assistant Professor of Finance in 2008. Currently, she is an Assistant Professor of Finance at Middle East Technical University. Her research interests are banking, finance–growth relationships, and financial markets.

Levent Akdeniz obtained a Ph.D. in economics from the University of Houston in 1996. He joined the Bilkent University Faculty of Business Administration in the same year. His research interests include asset pricing and computational methods in economics. He teaches courses in microeconomics, macroeconomics, money and banking, and corporate finance.

Kürşat Aydoğan obtained a B.S. in management and an MBA in general management from Middle East Technical University, following which he received a Ph.D. in finance from Syracuse University in 1986. Before joining Bilkent University the same year, he taught at Ball State University and Middle East Technical University. Currently, he is a Professor of Finance and vice rector in charge of finance and administration at Bilkent, where he also served as dean of the Faculty of Business Administration until 2004. He has worked as a consultant in the Research Department of the Central Bank of Turkey (1988–1993) and taught at Michigan State University in spring 2000. His research interests are investments, capital markets, and corporate finance.

Maria Lucia Passador is currently a Research Fellow in Business, Angelo Sraffa Department of Legal Studies, at Bocconi University (Milan), inter alia, she was Visiting Scholar at Columbia Law School (New York, NY) and Visiting Researcher at Harvard Law School (Cambridge, MA). Her active research interests and publications relate to corporate law, financial exchanges and securities regulation, especially in a comparative perspective.

Luis Alfonso Dau is an Associate Professor of international business and strategy at the D'Amore-McKim School of Business, Northeastern University (see luisdau.com for detailed CV). His work operates at the intersection of political economy and international business. Cited over five hundred times, his award-winning research has appeared in the top journals in the field including the *Journal of International Business Studies, Academy of Management Journal, Journal of Business Venturing, Entrepreneurship: Theory & Practice, Journal of World Business, Journal of International Management*, and *Global Strategy Journal.* His research focuses on the effects of country-level institutional factors on the performance, global strategy, and corporate social responsibility of emerging market firms. Dau is a John Dunning Visiting fellow at Henley Business School at the University of Reading as well as an associate fellow at the Center for Emerging Markets at Northeastern University.

Elizabeth M Moore is a Visiting Assistant Professor at the D'Amore-McKim School of Business and the Global Resilience Institute, Northeastern University. Elizabeth's research interests include emerging markets and the interplay between systematic political actors and economic development with a specific focus on the determinants and benefits of entrepreneurship within emerging markets amidst a globalizing world. Her research has been recognized at several international conferences as a finalist for best overall paper and best thematic fit. While affiliated with the D'Amore McKim School of Business and the Global Resilience Institute, Elizabeth's research will focus on firm resilience corporate social responsibility, the dichotomy between formal and informal entrepreneurship, firm performance, and international strategy amidst a changing normative environment.

Katharine Petrich is a doctoral candidate in Political Science at Northeastern University in Boston, Massachusetts. Her academic interests center on issues of international security, gray area conflict, and the impact of violent transnational non-state actors in a globalizing world. Her tentative doctoral dissertation will focus on transnational crime and terrorism and the subsequent impact it has on states. During her tenure at Northeastern, Katharine has participated in several research clusters and served on research teams to contribute to a better understanding of the implications of non-state actor conflict and violence. She has an upcoming research appointment with a research branch of the United States military, where she will seek to understand the determinants and outcomes of politically charged violence and non-state actors throughout Latin America.

Max Abrahms is an Assistant Professor of political science and public policy whose research focuses on the consequences of terrorism (see tinyurl.com/jmn6t4x for detailed CV). Abrahms is also affiliated with the Council on Foreign Relations, the Observer Research Foundation in India, and the Center for Cyber and Homeland Security. Abrahms has published in the top international relations journals such as *International Organization, International Security, International Studies Quarterly, Foreign Affairs, Comparative Political Studies, Security Studies*, and *Harvard Business Review*. Abrahms fields daily interviews on the effects of terrorism with international media outlets such as the BBC. Previously, he has been awarded fellowships and financial backing from Stanford University, Princeton University, Dartmouth College, West Point Military Academy, Tel Aviv University, Bar Ilan University, Johns Hopkins University, and Harvard University.

Marc Desban has been a Ph.D. student at the Institut de Recherche en Gestion (IRG) at the University Paris-Est since 2015. He is a graduate of the Eiffel School of Management (IAE Gustave Eiffel), where he was awarded his Master's [2015] in portfolio management. He is also a graduate of the University of Cergy-Pontoise, where he received a double Master's in market and corporate finance [2014]. His current research is related to asset pricing models, market anomalies, socially responsible investment, and corporate social responsibility. Marc teaches courses on finance.

Souad Lajili Jarjir is Assistant Professor of finance at the Eiffel School of Management (IAE Gustave Eiffel) and has been a researcher at the Institut de Recherche en Gestion (IRG) at the University Paris-Est since 2008. She graduated from the University Paris Dauphine (France), where she obtained her Ph.D. [2003] and MBA [2000]. Souad has published in various international academic journals, including the *European Journal of Finance*, the *International Journal of Economics and Finance, Quality & Quantity International Journal of Methodology, Revue des Sciences de Gestion*, and *Bankers Markets & Investors.* Her current research deals with issues related to asset pricing models, financial markets, socially responsible investment, and corporate social responsibility. Souad teaches postgraduate courses on Portfolio Management, Risk Management, Financial engineering, and Socially Responsible Investment, and a graduate course on Portfolio Management and Financial Analysis Case studies.

Juan Arismendi Zambrano is Lecturer in Finance in the University of Maynooth, National University of Ireland and is Visiting Research Fellow of the ICMA Centre, University of Reading. In the past, he was Assistant Professor and Director of the Department of Economics, Accountancy, and Finance at the Business School of the University of Monterrey (UDEM), Senior Visiting Professor at the Technological Institute for Superior Studies of Monterrey (ITESM) — Campus Leon, and Assistant Professor at the Federal University of Bahia, Brazil. He was Research Fellow of the University of Brasilia under the supervision of Prof. Herbert Kimura. He has a Ph.D. in Finance (Mathematica Finance) from the ICMA Centre, Henley Business School (AACSB, AMBA, EQUIS) in the University of Reading, UK. He is certified as PRM (Professional Risk Manager — PRMIA), FRM (Financial Risk Manager-GARP), CQF (Certificate in Quantitative Finance, 7city, Wilmott), Series 65 Investment Advisor Law Examination, and as Investment Advisor by the Certificate of Investment Management from the Chartered Institute of Securities and Investment (Unit 6 FSA Principles of Financial Regulation+Unit 5 Investment Management) from the United Kingdom. He has published in Finance, Numerical Algebra, Statistics, and Physics journals such as: 'Journal of Banking and Finance', 'International Review of Financial Analysis', 'Applied Mathematical Finance', 'Numerical Linear Algebra with Applications', 'Journal of Multivariate Analysis', and 'Chaos Solitons & Fractals'.

Evren Arik is a graduate from the Department of Economics at Middle East Technical University. He earned an MA degree in history from Ankara University in 2010. Following his career at PriceWaterhouseCoopers and Central Bank of The Republic of Turkey during 2004–2008, he started to work as an assistant specialist at Borsa Istanbul, in 2008. He is currently working as a senior specialist in the Research and Business Development Department of Borsa İstanbul. He is currently a Ph.D. candidate in finance at Galatasaray University. His areas of research interest include financial markets, derivatives, and behavioral finance.

Ömür Süer is Professor at Galatasaray University, Department of Business Administration. She received her Ph.D. in finance from Sorbonne University (Paris) in 2002, and from Boğaziçi University (Istanbul) in 2005. She is the author or co-author of several articles and has published in different journals including *The Singapore Economic Review, North American Journal of Economics and Finance*, and *Emerging Markets Finance and Trade*. Her research interests concentrate on the following topics: Bank management, credit risk management, and behavioral finance.

Silvia Grandi holds a Ph.D. in Economic Geography from the University of Bologna (Italy). She is Associate Professor in Geography (Italian ASN). She has been specializing at the Vrije Universiteit Brussel (VUB), University of Newcastle, and at the University of Sussex (SPRU). She is Adjunct Professor in many Italian universities in geography and applied economics, such as University of Bologna, University of Modena and Reggio Emilia, University of Naples "Federico II", University of Salento, and International University Uninettuno. She is a tenure director of the Italian Ministry of Economic Development and an expert in economic development policy, public finance, international relations, and geopolitics. She has extensively participated in international, European and national research networks in economic policies and, lately, in finance geography.

Fabio Massimo Parenti, Ph.D., is Associate Professor in Geography (Italian ASN). He teaches at the Italian International Institute Lorenzo de Medici in Florence. He has been Visiting Professor at the China Foreign Affairs University, Beijing; Southern New Hampshire University, USA and the Tecnológico de Monterrey, Mexico City and Monterrey campuses. He teaches the following courses: Global Financial Markets, China's Development and the Global Shift, Globalization and Social Change, and War and Media. For further information about academic appointments and publications see: http://ldminstitute.academia.edu/FabioMassimoParenti.

Contents

Part I

Global Stock Markets: Dynamic Linkages, Shock Transmission, and Contagion

Chapter 1

International Stock Markets Linkages: A Dynamic Factor Model Approach

Marcelle Chauvet and Bo-Yu Chen

University of California Riverside

Abstract

This chapter investigates international stock market dynamics and their linkages. It uses factor models to extract stock market indicators from common cyclical stock components of industrialized countries, emerging markets, the BRICT, and global stock markets. We find that the stock market indicators for these groups are correlated with each other and with the global market factor. The BRICT display the highest average stock return and are the least correlated with the others. The stock return indicators as well as the global stock market factor show close relationship with economic downturns, entering in bear phases around the beginning of recessions, and in bull phases mid-way through recessions, anticipating future economic recovery. We also find that the stock return indicators are more persistent and, therefore, more predictable than the stock market of individual countries. We study international linkages across these stock market groups through impulse response analysis and find that economic development levels play and important role in shock propagation. In particular, all stock market indicators respond positively to global factor shocks, with the least reactive group being the BRICT, and the most responsive being the emerging markets. Interestingly, the BRICT respond negatively to positive shocks to industrialized countries stock markets, indicating that the BRICT may have a role in hedging risk.

1. Introduction

In recent decades, global markets have become increasingly more integrated, with less international capital and trade restrictions and stronger financial linkages across countries. Some of the reasons are the establishment and development of the Euro Area, which unified major industrialized countries, the increased pool of countries that evolved as emerging economies, and the advances of the BRICT, which have become powerhouses of recent economic growth.[1]

Progressive globalization has led to a worldwide interest from governments and the private sector in conducting their activities in light of both national and international economic and financial conditions. Changes in economic fundamentals in different parts of the world can influence the competitive position of businesses and the effectiveness of local government policies, even of those not directly related to international operations. This integration impacts the performance of firms, and therefore their stock returns. Thus, there is a strong connection between international business cycles and stock markets.

This chapter investigates the dynamics of international stock markets and their linkages. The performance of international stock markets is not directly observable, but it can be evaluated through the construction of indicators. We use dynamic factor models to extract common cyclical components from stock markets across countries as stock market indicators. We first model stock markets of group countries according to their economic development. We consider 24 of the most prominent markets, and group them as industrialized countries, emerging markets, and the BRICT. We then model each group of country as a function of an unobserved common factor and an idiosyncratic term. The unobserved dynamic factor summarizes underlying information common to the stock returns of the countries within the group, and separate out idiosyncratic movements that are specific to each country. Thus, as an outcome of the first approach we obtain three stock market indicators for the groups considered. We next use the framework to obtain a global stock market indicator based on data from all countries considered, and to examine the international linkages across country groups.

A large strand of literature traditionally uses correlation approach to study financial market linkages and contagion.[2] However, complex economic and financial systems cannot be appropriately described using only pairwise correlation between countries. The comovement among markets might be driven by several factors hitting countries simultaneously or by common cyclical factors, which cannot be captured using pairwise correlation.

[1]The countries included in the BRICT are Brazil, Russia, India, China and Turkey. The selection of these countries and those studied as emerging markets is discussed in Sec. 2.1.
[2]A more recent literature uses conditional dependence via copula-based framework or wavelet-based coherence measures, which circumvents some of the problems with pairwise correlation approach.

Additionally, in order to study global linkages, the number of pair-wise correlation increases exponentially with the number of countries considered, which poses estimation difficulty.

The proposed dynamic factor model extracts common components of international economic movements and circumvent several problems faced by this traditional approach. The common factors representing stock market for groups of countries and global financial markets enable examination of their dynamics and interactions among a multitude of financial markets in a parsimonious way.

There is a vast literature studying comovements of business and financial cycles across countries starting with the earlier work of Mitchell (1927) and Morgenstern (1959). Theoretical approaches were pioneered by Backus, Kehoe, and Kydland (1992, 1993) and Baxter and Crucini (1993), which propose international real business cycle models. The models generated some counterfactual results (e.g. negative output correlation), but served as background for later developments, such as in Kehoe and Perri (2002), Heathcote and Perri (2004), Iacoviello and Minettib (2006). The results in these papers are divergent and the dynamics of international business cycles and crisis propagation are, thus, not conclusive.

Recent empirical literature on the relationship between international financial markets and business cycles also reaches divergent results. Forbes and Rigobon (2001, 2002) study mechanisms of financial contagion, and find evidence of international interdependence but not contagion. Imbs (2004, 2006) and Davis (2014) study the relationship between financial integration and business cycle comovements and find a positive effect of the former on the latter. On the other hand, Kalemli-Ozcan, Papaioannou, and Perri (2013) and Kalemli-Ozcan, Papaioannou, and Peydro (2013) find a negative effect instead. Cheung, He, and Ng (1997) study the predictability of regional common components of stock markets for North America, Pacific Rim, and Europe, and find that only North America has some predictability over the other regions. Bekaert *et al.* (2009) study comovements in international stock return focusing at the country and industry sector levels and find an increase in return correlations for European stock markets but not for other countries. Bekaert *et al.* (2014) use factor model to study the dynamics of global stock markets during the 2008–2009 financial crisis, focusing on country and industry portfolios. They find small contagion effects from the U.S. or global markets but stronger contagion from equity markets to equity portfolios for countries with weak fundamentals. Kose, Otrok, and Whiteman (2003) use dynamic factor model to investigate global, regional, and country-specific business cycles and their comovements. They find that the world factor has a significant effect on the volatility of most countries, but regional business cycles do not.

More recently, Kose, Otrok, and Prasad (2012) argue that categorizing countries according to their geographic location has many pitfalls as countries within the same region might have very different fundamentals and, therefore, not share similar economic dynamics. These authors propose, instead, to categorize country groups according to their development level as industrialized, emerging markets, and other developing countries. They investigate the economic performance of these three groups and find that although country groups have become more integrated, global business cycles have become less important in contributing to the groups' business cycles.

In this paper we also classify stock returns into groups according to their economic development. However, as found in Bekaert *et al.* (2014) for international financial markets, and Kose, Otrok, and Prasad (2012) for global business cycles, there is recent evidence of decoupling of emerging economies from international global markets. We find evidence that this is primarily driven by the fact that the BRICT countries are considered together with other emerging economies, as discussed below. In our approach, we model separately stock markets for emerging economies and the BRICT, in addition to considering industrialized countries. This allows analysis of potential changes in the interactions of these different groups and international stock markets.

Our findings suggest that country specific stock markets are more correlated with their common group factor than with the countries within their group. We also find that the stock market factors from the group countries are correlated with each other, but a lot less than they are with the global market. The BRICT are the least correlated with the other groups and with the global markets. The stock market of these countries reflect their fundamentals, which seem to march to the beat of their own drums.

All stock return indicators as well as the global stock market index show a close relationship with recessions in the U.S. and Europe, usually decreasing substantially around the beginning of recessions — when income and earnings fall, and increasing mid-way through recessions, anticipating future economic recovery. Extensive empirical literature also finds evidence of systematic movements in stock returns related to business cycles. See for example, Whitelaw (1994), Hamilton and Lin (1996), Chauvet (1998/1999), Perez-Quiros and Timmermann (1998), Fama and French (1999), Chauvet and Potter (2000, 2001), Chauvet and Sun (2014), Chauvet, Senyuz and Yoldas (2015), etc.

The dynamic factors representing stock returns for the country groups and for the global market are more persistent and, therefore, more predictable than the stock market of individual countries. Idiosyncratic noise makes it difficult to detect the presence of predictable stock return components, as found in extensive literature. By construction, the dynamic factor model separates idiosyncratic noise from a common component underlying the observable stock returns, which is more predictable and more stable than country-specific stock market movements.

Further, BRICT stock returns are on average substantially higher than those from emerging markets and industrialized countries, while the stock return indicator for industrialized countries displays the lowest mean rate.

We study the lead-lag relationship across international markets through impulse response analysis. We find that countries with different economic development levels play different roles in shock propagation. In particular, all stock market indicators respond positively to a shock to the global stock market factor. The least reactive group to the global market is the BRICT, and the most responsive group is the emerging markets. Interestingly, the BRICT respond negatively (positively) to a positive (negative) shock to the stock market of industrialized countries. This indicates that stock market of the BRICT may have a role in hedging risk in the stock market of industrialized countries.

The rest of the chapter is organized as the follows. Sections 2 discusses the data and the proposed models, while Sec. 3 describes the estimation procedure. Section 4 reports the results for each of the country groups and for the global stock market. Section 5 discusses the linkages between these markets based on impulse response analysis, and Sec. 6 reports sensitivity tests. The last section concludes.

2. Modeling Stock Market Clusters and Global Stock Markets using Dynamic Factor Structures

2.1. *Data*

The dynamics of financial markets are examined using monthly stock returns from 24 countries. The representative market index selected for each country is the one with the largest market capitalization and longest time span. The countries selected can be categorized into three groups: 10 industrialized countries, the 4 BRIC countries with the addition of Turkey, and 9 emerging market economies. The sample studied was determined by the availability of data. The longest sample for which data are available for all countries is from September 1997 to August 2015. The data were obtained from Global Financial Data.[3] The complete list of data is described on Table 1.

The acronym BRIC was coined in the early 2000s by Jim O'Neil, former chairman of Goldman Sachs, to represent Brazil, Russia, India, and China, as those countries were developing at a fast pace, and were predicted to soon become global economic powers. The BRIC became a formal institution during its first Summit in 2009. In 2011 South Africa was considered as

Table 1. List of Variables: Stock Market Indices

Country	Representative Index
Industrialized	
Canada	S&P Toronto Stock Exchange 300 Composite
France	France Continuous Assisted Quotation All-tradable Index
Greece	Athens Stock Exchange General Index
Germany	Composite Deutscher Aktienindex
Italy	Banca Commerciale Italiana Index
Japan	Nikkei 225
Portugal	Oporto Portuguese Stock Index-20
Spain	Madrid Stock Exchange General Index
UK	Financial Times-Actuaries All-Share Index
USA	Dow Jones Industrial Average
BRIC	
Brazil	Ibovespa Brasil Sao Paulo Stock Exchange Index
China	Shanghai Stock Exchange Composite
India	Bombay Stock Exchange Sensitive Index
Russian	Moscow Interbank Currency Exchange Composite
Turkey	Istanbul Menkul Krymetler Borsas Index
Emerging Markets	
Chile	General Stock Price Index
Hong Kong	Hong Kong Hang Seng Composite Index
Korea	Korea Stock Exchange Stock Price Index
Malaysia	Kuala Lumpur Stock Exchange Composite
Mexico	Price and Quotes Index
Peru	Indice General de la Bolsa de Valores de Lima
Singapore	Singapore FTSE Straits-Times Index
Taiwan	Taiwan Stock Exchange Weighted Index
Thailand	Thailand Stock Exchange of Thailand General Index

[3]See https://www.globalfinancialdata.com/

a member, although O'Neil and many others criticized the move since South Africa's economy and population are too small to be part of the group. Emerging countries that have largest potential future GDP PPP (in purchasing power parity terms) and the highest predicted long run growth have been named N-11, the Next Eleven countries.[4] Notice that South Africa is not included in this group. From these 11 countries, South Korea and Turkey have the highest GDP per capita and Human Development Index (HDI) as of 2016.[5] We have initially considered South Korea and Turkey to extend the group of BRIC but the economic development of South Korea took place a lot earlier than those in the group (in the 1980s), and the cyclical movements of this country are not coincident with the ones in BRIC. For this reason, we include only Turkey with the BRIC and coined it BRICT.

We selected emerging markets according to their level of economic development in terms of GDP PPP per capita, HDI, trade openness, and development of financial markets.[6] We considered several other emerging economies but their inclusion or exclusion did not alter the results. We chose then a parsimonious representation, with the top 9 emerging countries according to these metrics (Table 1).[7]

The series studied are one hundred times the first difference of the log of the stock price index for each country, which yield stationary stock returns (based on Dickey-Fuller tests).

2.2. *The dynamic factor models*

We use unobserved dynamic factor structures to model international stock market dynamics. The model extracts common cyclical movements across stock market indices from several different countries. We propose two approaches: first, we categorize stock markets into three groups, according

[4]The N-11 are Bangladesh, Egypt, Indonesia, Iran, Mexico, Nigeria, Pakistan, Philippines, South Korea, Turkey, and Vietnam.

[5]The data for GDP per capita are obtained from the World Bank: World Development Indicators http://databank.worldbank.org/data/reports.aspx?source=2&country=MEX&series=&period=. The data for HDI are obtained from the United Nations Development Programme — Human Development Index http://hdr.undp.org/en/content/human-development-index-hdi-table.

[6]These metrics are obtained from the World Bank http://wits.worldbank.org/openness-to-trade-visualization.html; https://data.worldbank.org/

[7]The emerging countries are: Chile, Hong Kong, Korea, Malaysia, Mexico, Peru, Singapore, Taiwan, Thailand. Note that although Hong Kong and Singapore have developed stock markets, they are still considered as emerging economies based on their economic development level.

to their economic development levels as industrialized countries, emerging market countries, and the BRICT (Model 1). We then model each group of country as a function of an unobserved common factor and an idiosyncratic term. The unobserved dynamic factor summarizes underlying information common to the stock returns of the countries within the group, and separate out idiosyncratic movements that are specific to each country. We repeat this for each of the three groups. Thus, as an outcome of the first approach we obtain three stock return factors, which are estimated indicators of stock markets for the three country group considered. Next, we model the global stock market factor by extracting a common factor from stock returns of all 24 countries considered all at once (Model 2).

2.2.1. *Model 1 — Stock market clusters*

We first extract common factors representing stock market dynamics of the three country groups h = industrialized, the BRICT, and emerging markets. The stock market of each country within the group shares a common group-specific factor, f_t^h, and displays idiosyncratic movements that are country specific, $\varepsilon_{i,t}^h$. The model is cast in state-space form, with the measurement equations relating the observed stock market indices for each country to the unobserved common factor, representing the country groups h as:

$$y_{i,t}^h = \lambda_i^h f_t^h + \varepsilon_{i,t}^h \tag{1}$$

where $y_{i,t}^h$ are the observed monthly stock market return of country i at time t belonging to the group h, and f_t^h is the unobserved stock return group factor. λ_i^h are the factor loadings, which represent the sensitivity of the stock market factor to the observed variable i. The country-specific idiosyncratic term is assumed to be normally distributed, $\varepsilon_{i,t}^h \sim i.i.d.\, N(0, \sigma_{i,h}^2)$.

The factors are assumed to follow an $AR(1)$ process, according to the transition equation:

$$f_t^h = \mu^h + \varphi^h f_{t-1}^h + u_t^h \tag{2}$$

where $u_t^h \sim N(0,1)$ is the common group factor shock. We set the variance of the factor to one as a normalization to provide a scale for the factor. Thus, the units of the data do not affect the factor or the model parameters.

2.2.2. *Model 2 — Global stock market*

We obtain the global dynamic common factor representing stock returns of all countries considered by modeling:

$$y_{i,t}^g = \lambda_i^g f_t^g + \varepsilon_{i,t}^g \tag{3}$$

where $y_{i,t}^g$ are the observed monthly stock market return of country i at time t, f_t^g is the unobserved global stock return factor. λ_i^g are the factor loadings, and the country-specific innovations are $\varepsilon_{i,t}^g \sim i.i.d.\, N(0, \sigma_{j,g}^2)$. The global factor follows an $AR(1)$ process, with transition equation:

$$f_t^g = \mu^g + \varphi^g f_{t-1}^g + u_t^g \tag{4}$$

where $u_t^g \sim N(0, 1)$ is the common global stock market factor shock.

Since the factors obtained in Model 1 and Model 2 summarize information common to different variables and cannot be directly observed, a scale must be provided to allow for their interpretation as a normalization. We assign a scale to the stock return factors by setting its variance to unity. Notice that none of the time series properties of the dynamic factor or the correlation with its components is affected by the choice of the parameter scale.

3. Estimation

The factors are constructed using the Kalman filter, which allows estimation of the unobserved state vector and parameters. The filter calculates the course of the state vector (the common dynamic factors), using only observations on $y_{i,t}$. It computes recursively one-step-ahead predictions and updating equations of the dynamic factors and the associated mean squared error matrices. The filter provides the conditional mean and variance of the state vector at time t, and based on them evaluates the conditional likelihood of the observable variable. The filter evaluates this likelihood function, which can be maximized with respect to the model parameters using an optimization algorithm. Based on information available through time t, the algorithm yields as outputs predictions of the stock market common factors, $E(f_t|I_t)$, where I_t is the information set at t. That is, the filter computes the maximum likelihood estimate of the unobserved factor at t, given information at t.[8]

4. Results

We estimate the stock market factors for the three groups of countries and the global stock market factor at the monthly frequency from 1997.09 to 2015.08.

[8]The estimation procedure is described in more detail in the appendix available upon request.

The adequacy of the model specifications is examined through tests of the idiosyncratic errors. We use Brock, Dechert, and Scheinkman's (1987) BDS test to check their *i.i.d.* assumption. The diagnostic tests indicate that the specification selected is adequate for all equations in both models 1 and 2. The BDS test fails to reject the *i.i.d.* hypothesis for the residuals. In addition, the autocorrelation functions for the disturbances in the measurement equations are within the limit of two times their asymptotic standard deviation, and the pairwise covariance between the disturbances is close to zero.

These results imply that all common cyclical information underlying stock returns from the countries considered are captured by the dynamic factors, and the peculiarities of each individual market are the residual noise captured by the idiosyncratic errors.

4.1. *International stock returns — Contemporaneous relationship*

The estimates of the models obtained through numerical maximization of the conditional log likelihood function are presented in Tables 2 and 3, which report results for the dynamic factor model for each group of countries, and for the global stock market factor, respectively. The tables also show the correlation of each of the components with the factors.

As it can be observed, the mean growth rate of stocks for the BRICT ($\mu^{BRICT} = 0.138$) is substantially higher than emerging markets ($\mu^{EMK} = 0.047$) and industrialized countries ($\mu^{IND} = 0.032$). This is consistent with the opening and development of these countries' financial markets and accelerated economic growth they experienced until the late 2000s.

Idiosyncratic noise makes it difficult to detect the presence of predictable stock return components, as found in extensive literature. By construction, the dynamic factor model separates idiosyncratic noise from a common component underlying the observable stock returns. The dynamic factors representing stock returns for the country groups and for the global market are persistent — the first-order autoregressive coefficients of the factors are statistically significant and higher in magnitude than the ones of their components. Thus, the stock return common factors are more predictable than the stock market of individual countries. One of the reasons for their higher persistence is their lower variance compared to the variance of the individual countries' return, as the model extracts the signals (factors) from the noise in the observed stock return series.

The BRICT stock return indicator is the most persistence of all groups ($\varphi^{BRICT} = 0.276$), and even more persistent than the global stock market indicator ($\varphi^{Global} = 0.200$). Thus, surprisingly, these countries have the most predictable stock market factor among all the other groups.

All markets display relatively high correlations with their group stock market factor,[9] and they are generally even more correlated with the common factor than with each other. This indicates that the structure of the common stock market indicator is not merely imposed on the financial variables by assuming large idiosyncratic noise terms. On the contrary, the dynamic factor captures an underlying common cyclical movements highly correlated with stock returns of all countries considered (Tables 2 and 3).

Table 4 reports the pairwise contemporaneous correlation of stock market factors. The global stock market is highly correlated with stock returns of all groups, but particularly with the stock market of industrialized countries.

Interestingly, the stock market indicator for the group countries are correlated with each other, but a lot less than they are with the global market indicator. The BRICT are the least correlated with the other groups and with global markets. The stock market of these countries reflect their fundamentals, which seem to march to the beat of their own drums. In fact, some recent studies show that the BRICT economic movements are negative related with those of industrialized countries. This is particularly the case since the Great Recession in 2008–2009, in which most countries had a subsequent sluggish recovery. The BRICT, on the other hand, experienced a deep but shorter economic contraction, and a stronger recovery. As a result, the stock markets in these countries received a large inflow of capital as investors were hedging against the slow recovery in industrialized countries.

Figure 1 shows shaded areas representing recessions in the U.S. as dated by the NBER Business Cycle Dating Committee, and recessions in the Euro Area as dated by the Center for Economic Policy Research (CEPR).[10] The U.S. and the Euro Area experienced two economic recessions each in the period studied, in which one was common to both. The 2001 U.S. recession had as some of the culprits a slowdown in manufacturing production and a crash in the stock market in 2000. Although the Euro Area did not experience a recession in 2001, their economy had a low growth during this period. The second recession in the U.S. — the Great Recession in 2008–2009, spread

[9]The one exception is Brazil. The main reason is that Brazil stock market factor shows a stronger correlation at leads rather than contemporaneously with the BRICT stock market factor.

[10]The recession dating by these institutions is considered as the official beginning and ending of recessions in the U.S. and Euro Area.

Table 2. Maximum Likelihood Estimates for Model 1: Stock Market Factors for Industrialized Countries, Emerging Market Countries, and the BRICT 1997:09–2015:08

	Industrialized Countries		**Emerging Markets**		**BRICT**	
Factor Mean	0.03243		0.04732		0.13759	
φ_1	0.17042		0.24206		0.27586	
Factor Loading	USA	3.742	Hong Kong	6.024	China	2.796
	Japan	3.593	Singapore	5.931	Russia	8.280
	UK	3.725	Taiwan	4.842	India	4.147
	Germany	5.605	South Korea	5.725	Brazil	1.080
	France	5.170	Malaysia	4.432	Turkey	7.190
	Italy	5.397	Thailand	6.052		
	Canada	3.354	Mexico	4.682		
	Spain	5.113	Chile	2.952		
	Portugal	4.586	Peru	4.959		
	Greece	6.044				
Standard Deviation-Idiosyncratic Terms	USA	2.479	Hong Kong	4.055	China	7.491
	Japan	4.484	Singapore	2.862	Russia	8.355
	UK	1.789	Taiwan	5.003	India	5.762
	Germany	2.332	South Korea	6.274	Brazil	8.560
	France	1.404	Malaysia	4.935	Turkey	9.840
	Italy	2.791	Thailand	5.576		
	Canada	2.995	Mexico	4.456		
	Spain	2.990	Chile	3.333		
	Portugal	3.887	Peru	7.051		
	Greece	7.752				
Correlation with Factor	USA	0.8482	Hong Kong	0.8676	China	0.4330
	Japan	0.6397	Singapore	0.9398	Russia	0.8564
	UK	0.9159	Taiwan	0.7337	India	0.7150
	Germany	0.9375	South Korea	0.7079	Brazil	0.0824
	France	0.9788	Malaysia	0.7037	Turkey	0.7213
	Italy	0.9033	Thailand	0.7721		
	Canada	0.7603	Mexico	0.7614		
	Spain	0.8777	Chile	0.6984		
	Portugal	0.7804	Peru	0.6071		
	Greece	0.6326				

internationally affecting the Euro Area, which also experienced a recession during this period. This recession is associated with a severe crisis in the housing market and financial markets. The Euro Area had and additional recession, in 2011–2013, related with the European sovereign debt crisis, particularly resulting from structural economic problems in Greece, Spain, Italy, and Portugal.

Even though most of the individual countries studied do not have 'official' recession dating, extensive literature shows that most of them also

Table 3. Maximum Likelihood Estimates for Model 2: Global Stock Return Estimated from All Country Data 1997:09–2015:08

	Global Factor					
Factor Mean	0.0460					
φ_1	0.1998					
Factor Loading	USA	3.915	Hong Kong	5.375	China	2.519
	Japan	3.808	Singapore	4.943	Russia	6.972
	UK	3.707	Taiwan	4.509	India	4.255
	Germany	5.324	South Korea	5.219	Brazil	0.919
	France	4.820	Malaysia	3.428	Turkey	6.903
	Italy	5.037	Thailand	4.743		
	Canada	3.633	Mexico	4.514		
	Spain	4.934	Chile	2.627		
	Portugal	4.324	Peru	4.562		
	Greece	6.044				
Standard Deviation-Idiosyncratic Terms	USA	2.140	Hong Kong	4.985	China	7.631
	Japan	4.276	Singapore	4.480	Russia	9.787
	UK	1.779	Taiwan	5.359	India	5.792
	Germany	2.869	South Korea	6.765	Brazil	8.585
	France	2.297	Malaysia	5.741	Turkey	10.244
	Italy	3.366	Thailand	6.822		
	Canada	2.605	Mexico	4.678		
	Spain	3.237	Chile	3.629		
	Portugal	4.156	Peru	7.358		
	Greece	7.722				
Correlation with Factor	USA	0.894	Hong Kong	0.751	China	0.3215
	Japan	0.684	Singapore	0.759	Russia	0.595
	UK	0.919	Taiwan	0.663	India	0.608
	Germany	0.898	South Korea	0.627	Brazil	0.101
	France	0.919	Malaysia	0.527	Turkey	0.573
	Italy	0.850	Thailand	0.587		
	Canada	0.830	Mexico	0.712		
	Spain	0.854	Chile	0.602		
	Portugal	0.743	Peru	0.541		
	Greece	0.639				

experienced either a slowdown or a recession in 2001 and in 2008–2009.[11] This is in line with our findings that all stock return factors as well as the global stock market factor show a close relationship with recessions in the U.S. and Europe, usually decreasing substantially around the beginning of recessions — when income and earnings fall, and increasing mid-way through recessions, anticipating future economic recovery.

[11] Brazil has its own Business Cycle Dating Committee (CODACE), which has established that this country experienced recessions in 2001, 2003, 2008–2009, and 2014–2016.

Table 4. Contemporaneous Correlation between Stock Return Common Factors

Stock Return Common Factors	Global	Industrialized	Emerging Markets	BRICT
Global	1.000	0.973	0.834	0.703
Industrialized	0.973	1.000	0.699	0.631
Emerging Markets	0.834	0.699	1.000	0.637
BRICT	0.702	0.631	0.637	1.000

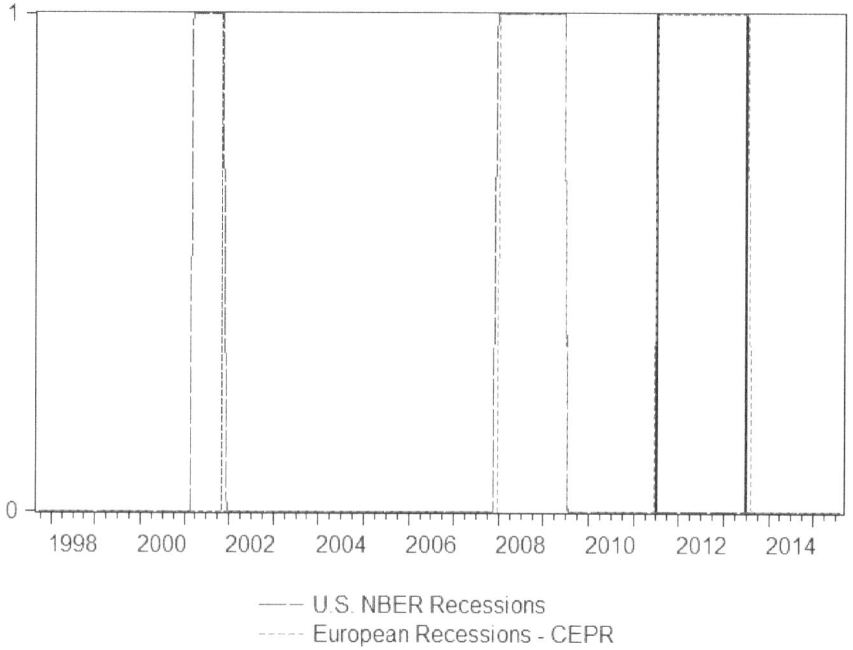

Figure 1. U.S. Recessions as Dated by the NBER (Solid Line, and Europe Recessions as Dated by the CEPR (Dash Line)

Periods in which stock returns are substantially negative (bear markets) are generally related to economic recessions. However, they also take place during economic expansions, possibly reflecting weak economic growth, economic or political instability, wars, sectoral contractions, negative sentiment, etc.

Figure 2 plots the global stock indicator factor, which is obtained from all the 24 countries considered, Fig. 3 plots the industrialized stock

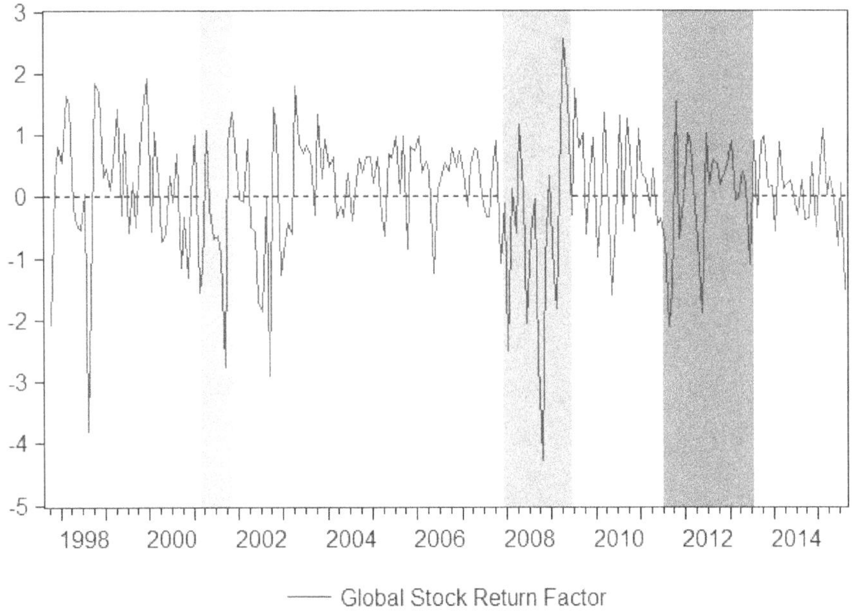

Figure 2. Global Stock Return Common Factor for All 24 Countries, U.S. Recessions as Dated by the NBER (Lighter and Medium Shaded Areas), and Euro Area Recessions as Dated by the CEPR (Medium and Darker Shaded Areas)

return indicator, emerging market return indicator, and the BRICT return indicator, while Fig. 4 compares the global stock market factor with the group factors. The international movements in stock returns are highly correlated with the ones from industrialized countries, displaying similar mean rate. Emerging market average returns were above the global returns in the late 1990s and slightly below since. The BRICT factor returns, on the other hand, are above the global returns throughout the sample, but particularly so until the 2008 recession.

Global stock market returns experienced five bear markets in the period studied, as did the industrialized countries. Global returns fell substantially during the U.S. and Euro Area recessions in 2001, 2008–2009 and in 2011–2013. International markets also crashed in 1998, related to the contagion of the Asian currency crisis to the BRICT in mid-1998, and the losses of the giant U.S. hedge fund Long-Term Capital Management (LTCM). Global returns also fell substantially in 2002, during the slow recovery from the 2001 recession.

The countries with the highest correlation with the global stock market are Singapore, Hong Kong, U.S. and Canada, while the ones with the lowest

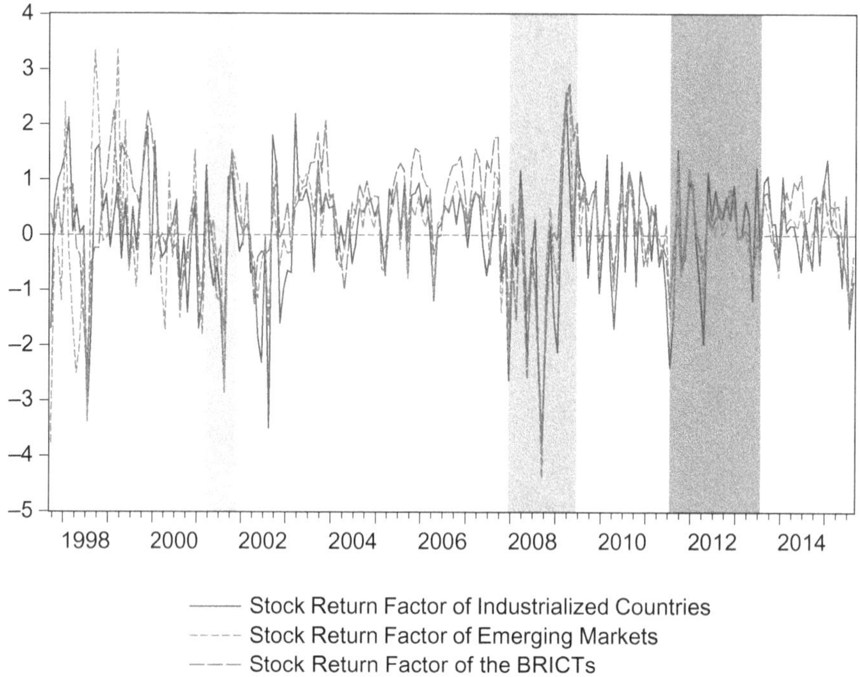

Figure 3. Stock Return Common Factors of Industrialized Countries, Emerging Markets, and the BRICT, U.S. Recessions as Dated by the NBER (Lighter and Medium Shaded Areas), and Europe Recessions as Dated by the CEPR (Darker and Medium Shaded Areas)

correlation are Greece, China, Russia, and Brazil. The latter are some of the ones with the largest volatility as measured both by their total variance and by the variance of their idiosyncratic errors. This will be discussed in more detail for each factor in the next sections.

4.2. *Stock market clusters — Country groups*

Table 2 shows the maximum likelihood estimates of the factor loadings and standard deviation of the idiosyncratic noises for the country groups. The factor loadings characterize the direct structural relation between the unobservable variable f_t and the observable variables y_t. The parameter λ_t can be interpreted as a reverse regression coefficient since it measures the sensitivity of f_t to changes in y_t. The variance of the stock return factor is set to one for normalization, as explained above. Thus, the sign of the factor loadings indicates the direction of the relation between the stock return of each country with their respective stock return group indicator.

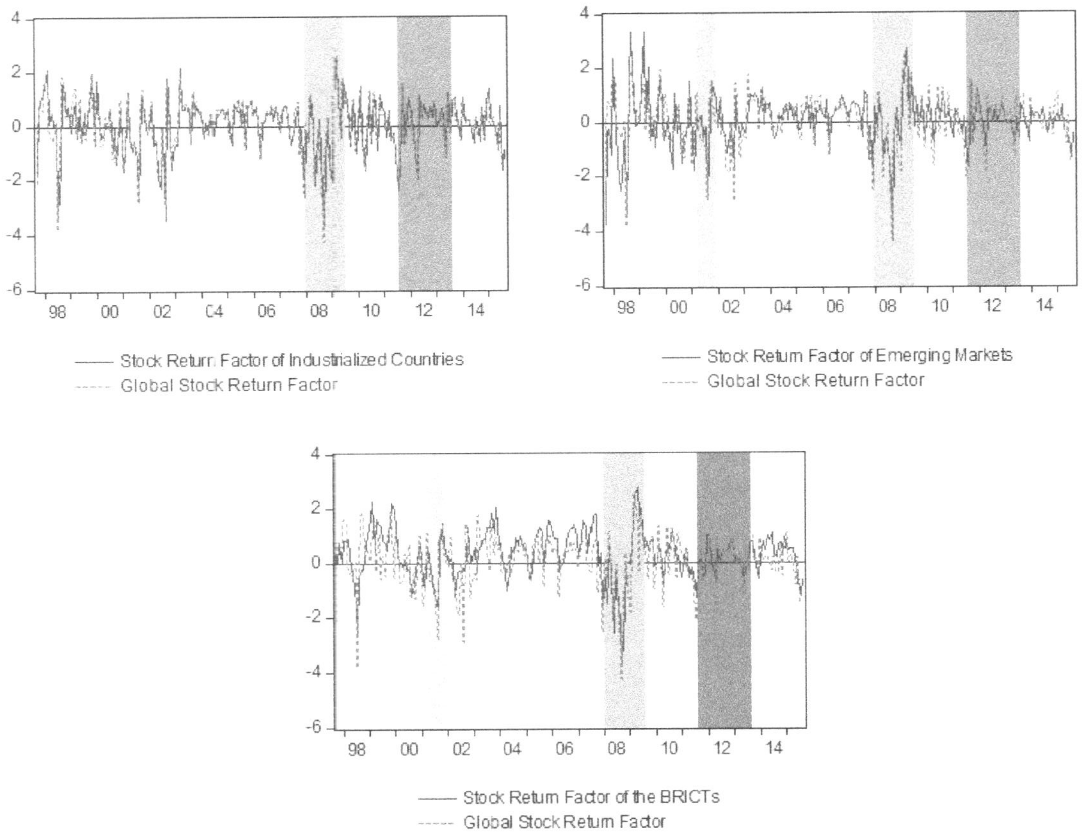

Figure 4. Stock Return Factor of Industrialized Countries, Stock Return Factor of Emerging Markets, and Stock Return Factor of the BRICT Compared with the Global Stock Return Common Factor, U.S. Recessions as Dated by the NBER (Lighter and Medium Shaded Areas), and Europe Recessions as Dated by the CEPR (Medium and Darker Shaded Areas)

Additionally, from Eqs. (1)–(4), it can be derived that the factor loading of the observed series i is directly proportional to the difference between the variance of series i and the variance of its idiosyncratic term. Thus, the higher the total variance of the stock markets of a country compared to its estimated country specific variance, the higher is its factor loading. The intuition is that the common factor separates the signal — the common correlation across the different countries, from their idiosyncratic noise.

4.2.1. *Stock market factor of industrialized countries*

Figure 5 shows the stock return indicator of the industrialized countries, together with U.S. recessions and Euro Area recessions, while Fig. 6 displays the stock return indicator of industrialized countries contrasted with each of its 10 country components. The stock return indicator of industrialized countries falls in the beginning of recessions and increases a couple of months before its end. It decreases during economic expansions as well. In particular, it falls below 2%[12] during the U.S. stock crash in 1998, and during the

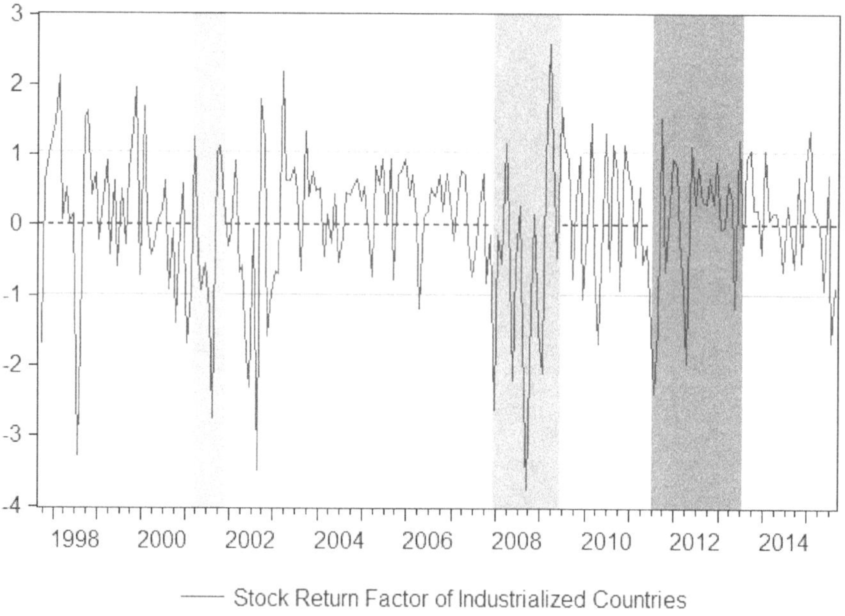

Figure 5. Stock Return Common Factor of Industrialized Countries, U.S. Recessions as Dated by the NBER (Lighter and Medium Shaded Areas), and Europe Recessions as Dated by the CEPR (Medium and Darker Shaded Areas)

[12]This corresponds to a fall below its mean minus two standard deviations.

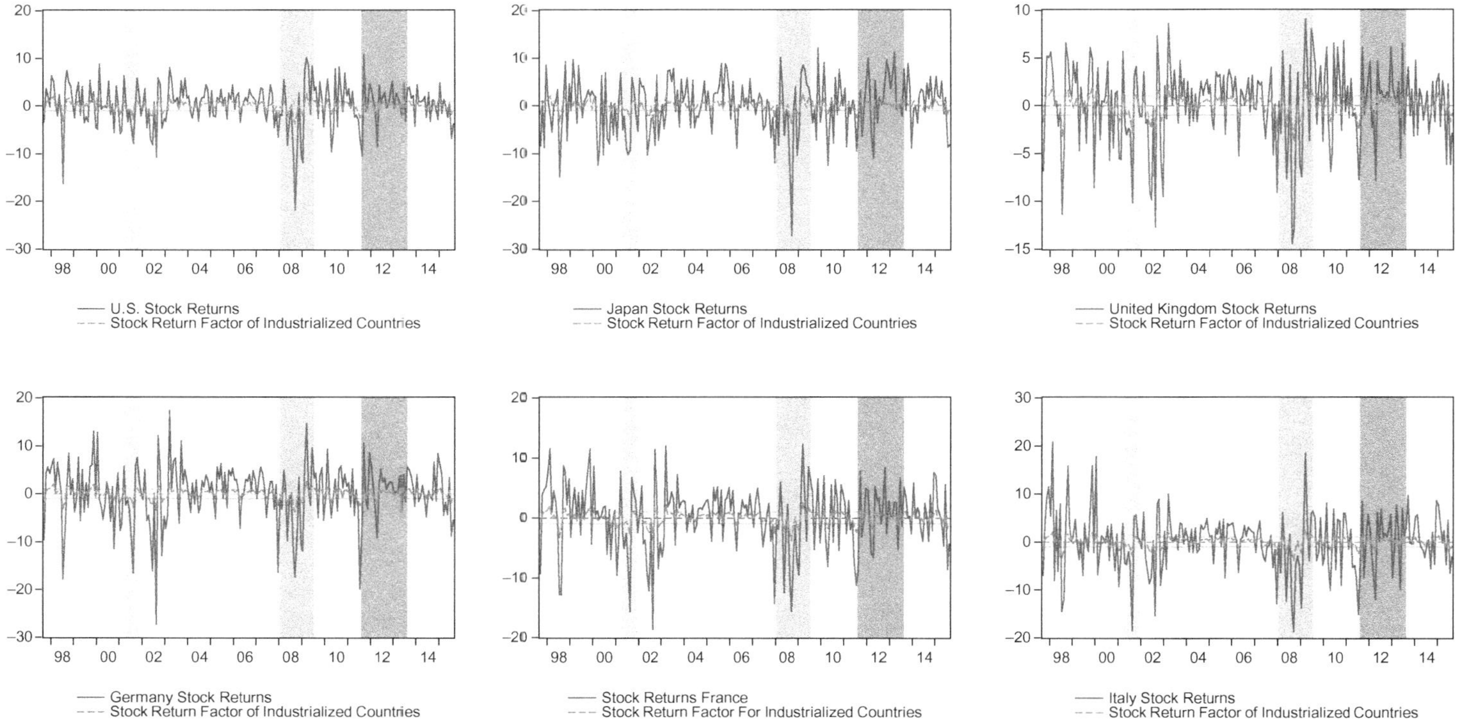

Figure 6. Industrialized Countries: Stock Return Common Factor and Country Specific Stock Returns, U.S. Recessions as Dated by the NBER (Lighter and Medium Shaded Areas), and Europe Recessions as Dated by the CEPR (Medium and Darker Shaded Areas)

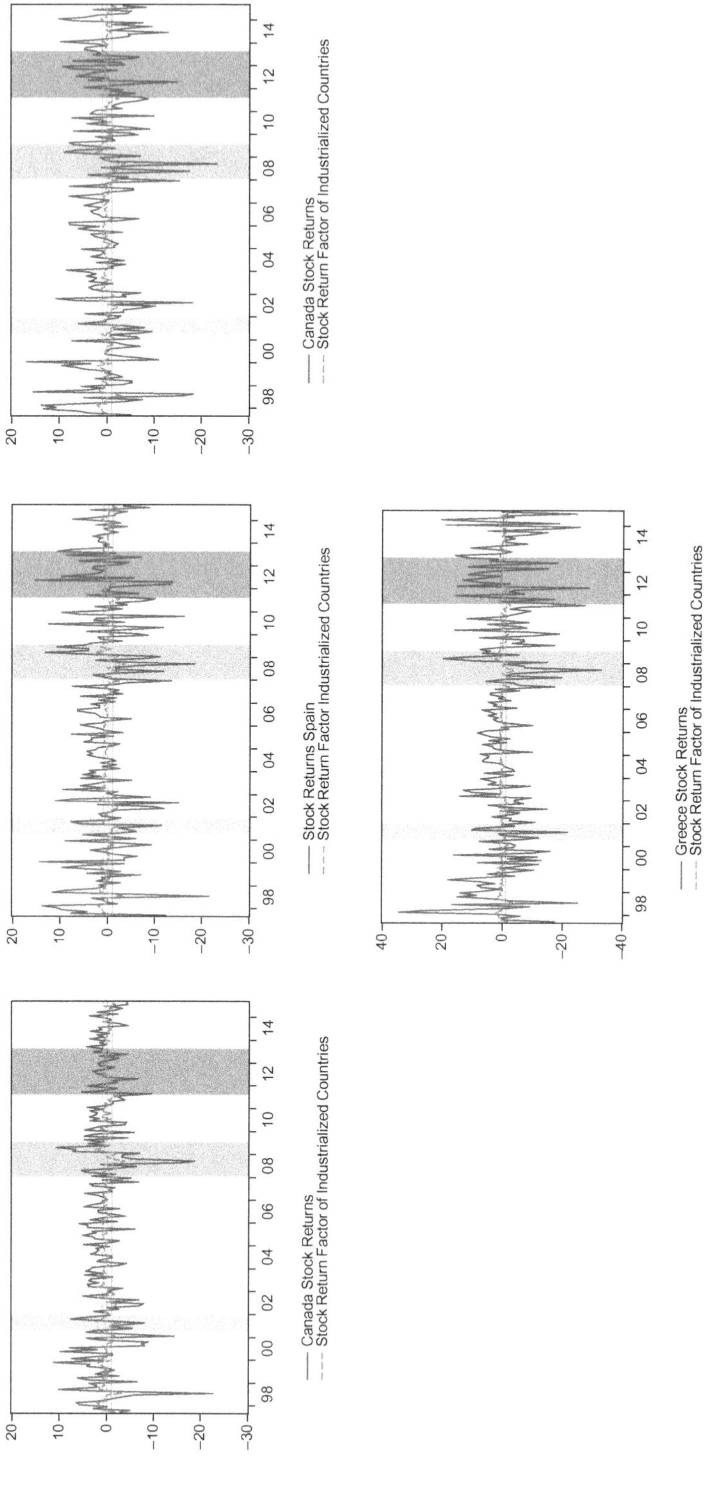

Figure 6. *(Continued)*

slow recovery of the U.S. economy in 2002. During this time Europe also displayed weak economic growth, but not sufficiently low to be classified as a recession.

As seen in Table 2, the country with the largest estimated factor loading is Greece (6.044), which implies that changes in Greece's stock market affect the most the stock market of industrialized countries, as represented by the common dynamic factor. This is partially related to the high Greece's country risk and volatility. The volatility of Greece's idiosyncratic stock return ($\sigma^h_{Greece} = 7.752$) is almost 8 times higher than the volatility of the common stock return factor of industrialized countries ($\sigma^h_u = 1$) (Table 2, Fig. 6). Germany' market also strongly contributes to movements in the common stock market factor of the industrialized countries, with a factor loading of 5.606 and idiosyncratic stock return volatility, $\sigma^h_{Germany} = 2.332$.

All markets display relatively high correlations with the stock market of industrialized countries, ranging from 0.63 to 0.98 — and generally they are even more correlated with the industrialized stock indicator than with each other. The highest correlated markets with the stock market of industrialized countries are France (0.98), followed by Germany (0.94), U.K. (0.92), and Italy (0.90). On the other hand, Greece and Japan's markets have the lowest correlation with the common factor. That is, contemporaneously, Greece is the market that most affect the stock market of industrialized countries, but Greece's market idiosyncratic movements dominate its own dynamics. This is also the case for Portugal and Japan.

The dynamic factor representing stock returns for all industrialized countries have a higher significant first-order autocorrelation coefficient ($\hat{\rho}(1) = 0.170$), than the individual countries.[13] That is, although the estimated industrialized stock return factor is highly correlated with all industrializes countries, it is also more persistent and, therefore, more predictable than the stock return for each country itself. The country specific stock returns of most industrialized countries show low persistence, with a first order autocorrelation, $\hat{\rho}(1)$, not statistically significant at the 10% level. Interestingly, the exceptions are the stock returns for France ($\hat{\rho}(1) = 0.131$), the U.S. ($\hat{\rho}(1) = 0.141$), and Portugal ($\hat{\rho}(1) = 0.219$), which are more persistent than the other countries, with first order correlations statistically significant at the 5% level.

[13]The only exception is Portugal, which has an autoregressive coefficient slightly higher.

4.2.2. *Stock market factor of emerging markets*

Figure 7 shows the stock return factor of the emerging markets together with recessions in the U.S. (NBER) and recessions in Europe (CEPR). A feature that stands out is that the stock market of emerging economies displays high volatility in the late 1990s. There was a sharp drop in 1997–1998 related to the currency crisis experienced by the Asian Tigers (Thailand, Malaysia, Korea, and Hong Kong).[14] This was followed by a substantial recovery in 1999. Since then, stock returns in emerging markets became much less volatile. Interestingly, it has since been more stable, displaying less bear phases than the other groups, including industrialized countries and the overall global stock markets. In fact, emerging market stock factor did not enter any bear market phases outside recessions, in contrast with industrialized countries and the BRICT, and it did not fall much during the Euro Area recession in 2011–2103.

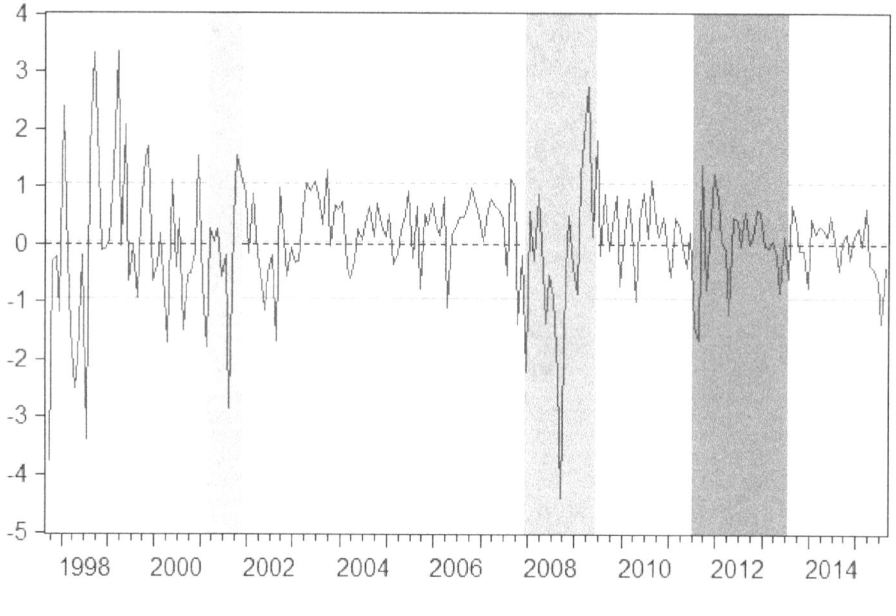

Figure 7. Stock Return Common Factor of Emerging Markets, U.S. Recessions as Dated by the NBER (Lighter and Medium Shaded Areas), and Europe Recessions as Dated by the CEPR (Medium and Darker Shaded Areas)

---

[14]Singapore and Taiwan were the least affected countries by the currency crisis.

The countries with the largest factor loadings are Thailand, Hong Kong, and Singapore, which are also the countries with the largest correlation with the common factor (Table 2). The country with the lowest factor loading is Chile, which as expected, has also the lowest difference between the total variance of returns and the variance of its idiosyncratic term. Chile's market has responded more to internal strong economic fundamentals than to the common cyclical movements in other emerging stock markets (Fig. 8).

4.2.3. *Stock market of the BRICT*

Figure 9 shows the stock return factor of the BRICT, recessions in the U.S. (NBER) and recessions in Europe (CEPR), and Fig. 10 shows the BRICT factor compared with each of the stock returns of its 4 components. The BRICT are the group of countries with the largest average stock return (0.138), which is four times higher than stock returns in industrialized countries and three times higher than in emerging markets.

As the emerging markets, the BRICT stock return factor was also very volatile in the late 1990s. Although the BRICT stock markets were not contemporaneously affected by the 1997 Asian currency crisis, there was a contagion effect later in most of the BRICT, starting with Russia. The Asian crisis severely impacted Russia foreign exchange reserves, which together with other political and structural economic problems led Russia to have a currency crisis a year later, in mid 1998. As a result, Russia stock market crashed in 1998, which increased the country risk of the other BRICT members. Brazil and Turkey's stock market also crashed in mid-1998, which was the largest fall for these countries in the whole sample. China and India markets were less affected by this early crisis.

Subsequently, the BRICT stock factor experienced a strong bull market in 1999–2000, when both the stock factor and the country specific stock markets had the largest rate of returns in the sample studied. China also had a strong bull market between 2006–2008. The BRICT factor had a mild bear market in 2001 and a strong fall during the Great Recession in 2008–2009. In particular, China and India were strongly affected by both recessions. Stock returns in the BRICT have shown a strong recovery right after the crisis, but the average return has been lower than its past record since the Great Recession, in spite of the fact that the BRICT did not experience a bear market during the Euro Area recession in 2011–2013.

The country with the largest factor loading in the BRICT factor is Russia, while Brazil has the lowest. This is consistent with the fact

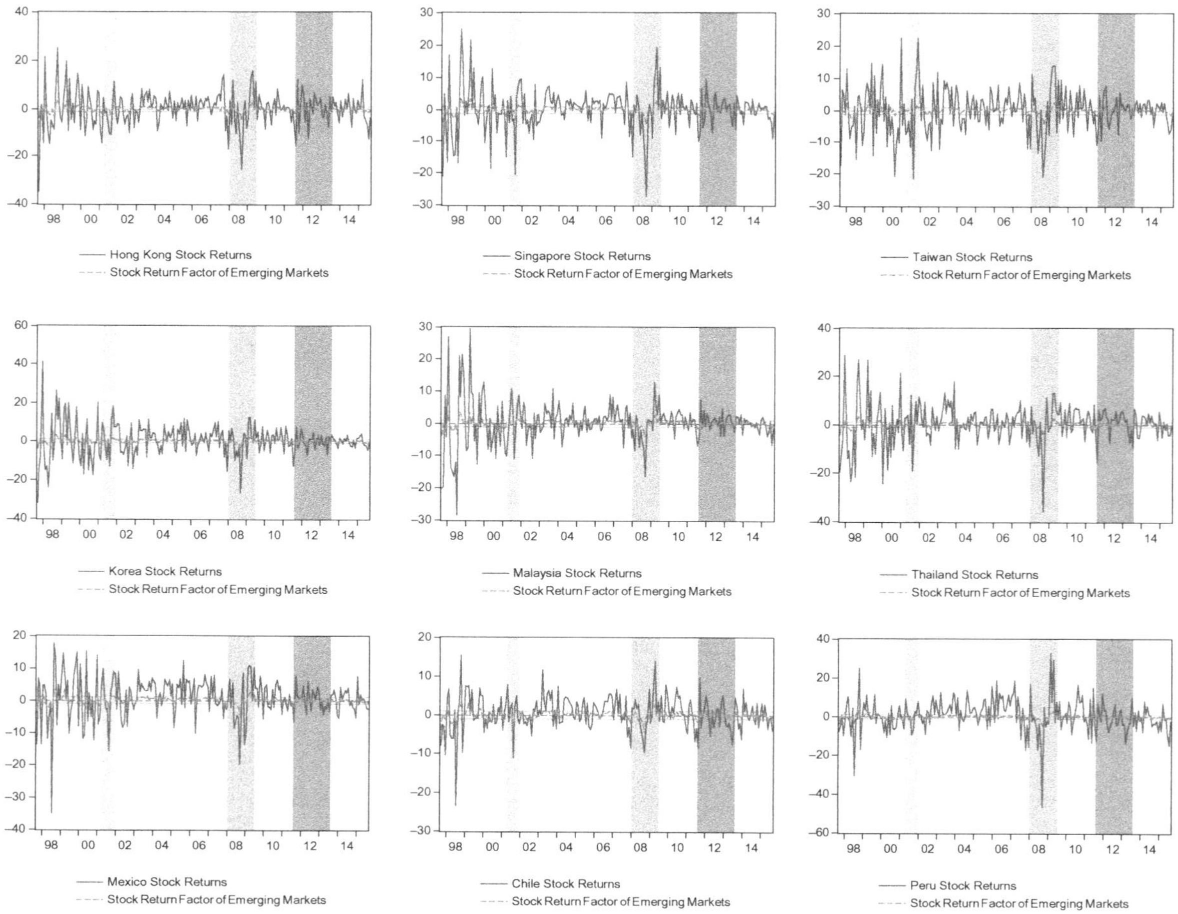

Figure 8. **Emerging Markets: Stock Return Common Factor and Country Specific Stock Returns, U.S. Recessions as Dated by the NBER (Lighter and Medium Shaded Areas), and Europe Recessions as Dated by the CEPR (Medium and Darker Shaded Areas)**

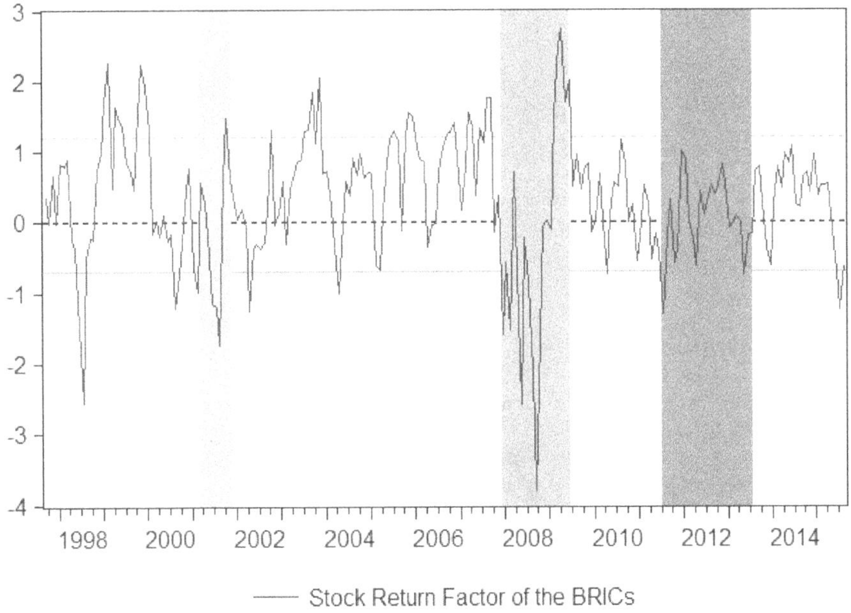

Figure 9. Stock Return Common Factor of The BRICT, U.S. Recessions as Dated by the NBER (Lighter and Medium Shaded Areas), and Europe Recessions as Dated by the CEPR (Medium and Darker Shaded Areas)

that Russia has the largest difference between its total variance and its idiosyncratic variance, while Brazil has the lowest.

A feature that stands out from the BRICT factor is that it has a lot higher correlation with its country components than the BRICT countries have with each other. In fact, the stock returns of the BRICT countries are not very correlated with each other, as their markets strongly respond to their idiosyncratic movements. Finally, the BRICT factor is surprisingly more persistent than the industrialized factors and emerging market factors and, therefore, more predictable.

5. International Stock Market Linkages — Lead-Lag Relationship

5.1. *Vector autoregressive model*

In order to study the linkages across international stock markets, we consider a parsimonious VAR model that includes the variables whose dynamic interrelationship we want to investigate. The relationship across markets is represented by the pth-order vector autoregression (VAR-p):

$$\mathbf{Z}_t = \mathbf{a} + \mathbf{A}_1\mathbf{Z}_{t-1} + \cdots + \mathbf{A}_p\mathbf{Z}_{t-p} + \mathbf{v}_t \tag{5}$$

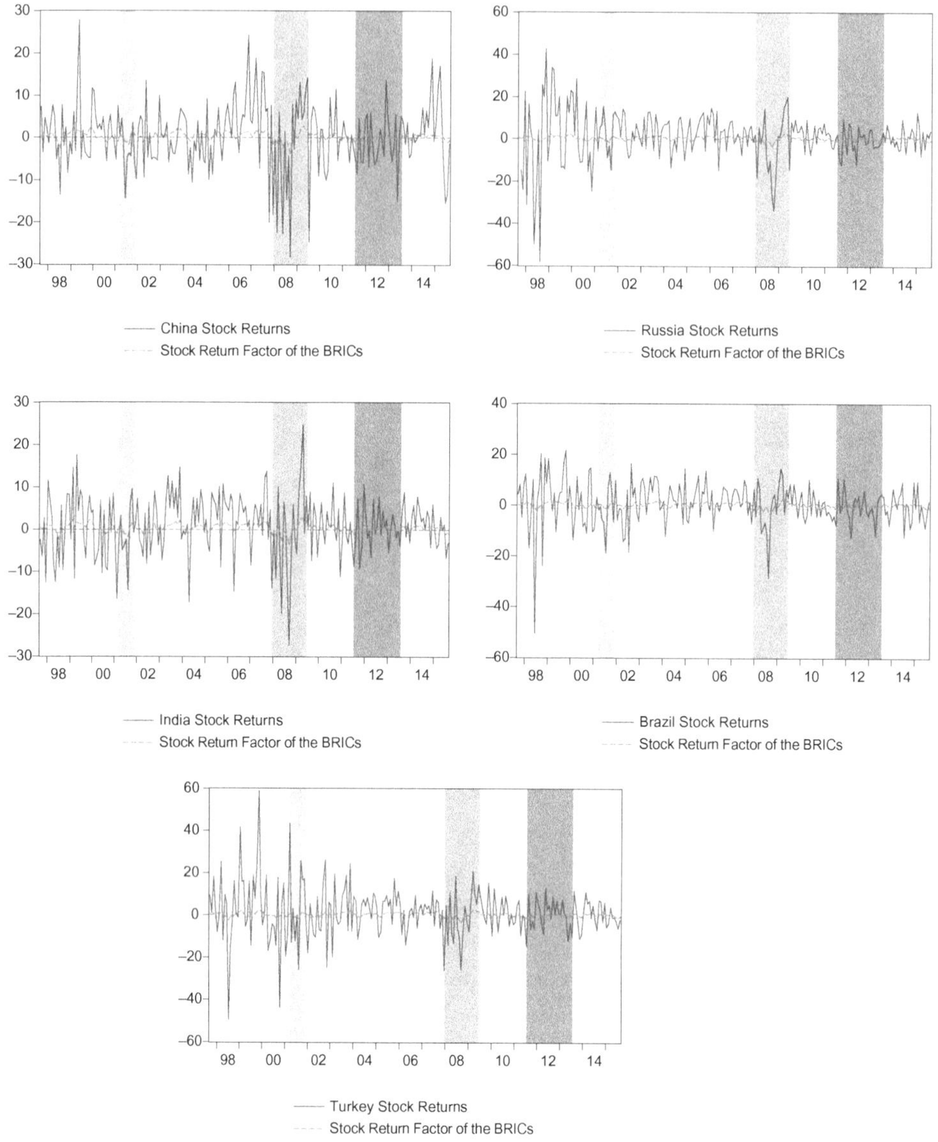

Figure 10. The BRICT: Stock Return Common Factor and Country Specific Stock Returns, U.S. Recessions as Dated by the NBER (Lighter and Medium Shaded Areas), and Europe Recessions as Dated by the CEPR (Medium and Darker Shaded Areas)

with $\mathbf{v}_t \sim (0, \Theta)$, where $\mathbf{Z}_t$ is an $n \times 1$ vector containing the values that the n stock return factors take at date t, $\mathbf{A}_j$ is the $n \times n$ coefficient matrices with $j = 1, \ldots, p$, $\mathbf{a}'$ is the $n \times 1$ vector of constants, and $\mathbf{u_t}$ is the $n \times 1$ vector of disturbances. Equation (5) describes the response of each of the stock return factors to changes in the other variables in the system.

The model identification conditions are formulated based on Swanson and Granger's (1997) method, which uses the notion of 'instantaneous causality' [see e.g. Lütkepohl 1990] to identify the causal structure for the innovations. Assume that the innovations of the VAR can be arranged as follows:

$$\mathbf{u}_{1t} = \mathbf{v}_{1t}; \mathbf{u}_{2t} = \gamma_2 \mathbf{u}_{1t} + \mathbf{v}_{2t}; \cdots ; \mathbf{u}_{nt} = \gamma_n \mathbf{u}_{n-1,t} + \mathbf{v}_{nt}.$$

This structure can be represented by a causal graph as:[15]

$$\begin{array}{ccccccc} \mathbf{u}_{1t} & \rightarrow & \mathbf{u}_{2t} & \rightarrow & \cdots & \rightarrow & \mathbf{u}_{nt} \\ \uparrow & & \uparrow & & & & \uparrow \\ \mathbf{v}_{1t} & & \mathbf{v}_{2t} & & \cdots & & \mathbf{v}_{nt} \end{array}$$

This graph means, for example, that $\mathbf{u}_{2t}$ may be expressed as a function of $\mathbf{u}_{1t}$, $\mathbf{u}_{3t}$ as a function of $\mathbf{u}_{2t}$, etc. Swanson and Granger (1997) show that this causal ordering implies that $E(\mathbf{u}_{ht}\mathbf{u}_{kt}|\mathbf{u}_{lt}) = 0$ for $h < l < k$, with $h < n$, and suggest testing the partial correlation between $\mathbf{u}_{ht}$ and $\mathbf{u}_{kt}$ conditional on $\mathbf{u}_{lt}$ in order to recover the causal ordering empirically. For example, given $\mathbf{u}_{3t} = \gamma_3 \mathbf{u}_{2t} + \mathbf{v}_{3t}$ and $E(\mathbf{u}_{2t}\mathbf{v}_{3t}) = 0$, the condition $E(\mathbf{u}_{1t}\mathbf{u}_{3t}|\mathbf{u}_{2t}) = 0$ implies that given $\mathbf{u}_{2t}$ the variable $\mathbf{u}_{1t}$ does not help to predict $\mathbf{u}_{3t}$. Conversely, if $\gamma_3 \neq 0, E(\mathbf{u}_{2t}\mathbf{u}_{3t}|\mathbf{u}_{1t}) \neq 0$ and the variable $\mathbf{u}_{2t}$ helps to predict ('cause') $\mathbf{u}_{3t}$.

The method suggests that the best specification is the one in which global stock market and stock returns of industrialized countries respond with a lag to shocks to stock markets in emerging markets and in the BRICT. Emerging markets and the BRICT, on the other hand, respond to all contemporaneous and lagged variables in the system.

5.2. *Impulse response functions*

We first estimate a VAR system that includes the stock market factors representing the three country groups: industrialized countries, emerging markets, and the BRICT. The BIC and AIC tests indicate that the best lag structure for this specification is $p = 2$. The relative short lag is due to the fact that stock markets react promptly to shocks and do not display high dependency with the past.

The impulse response functions are shown in Fig. 11. We find that the stock market of industrialized countries has a strong positive response to a

[15] Note that the causal graph with the arrows pointed forward implies the same restriction on the conditional expectation as the arrows pointed backward, and, therefore, the direction of the graph is not identified.

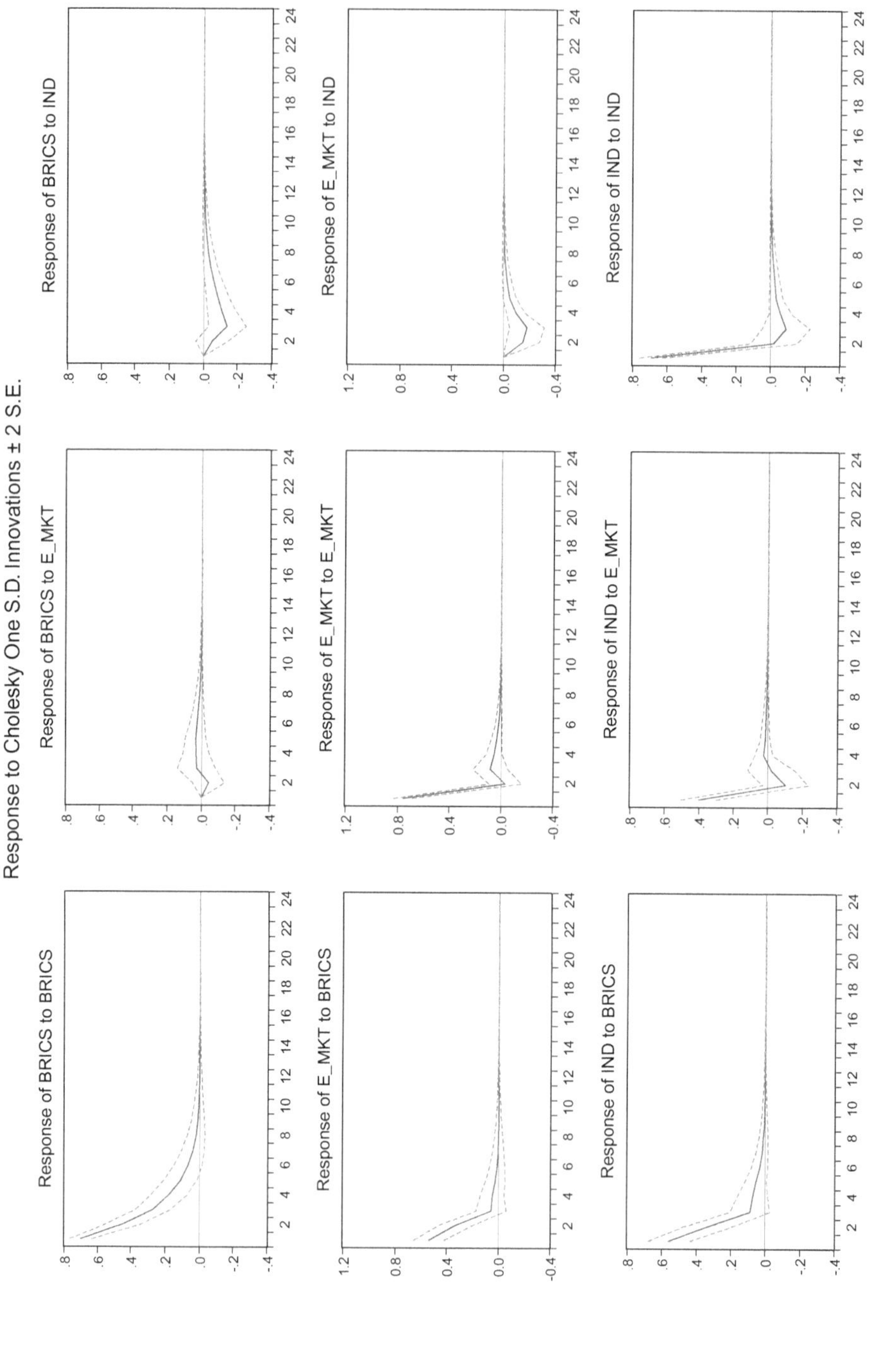

Figure 11. Impulse Response Functions for Industrialized Countries Stock Return Factor, Emerging Markets Stock Return Factor, BRICT Stock Return Factor — Full Sample

positive shock in stock returns of emerging markets and of the BRICT. A shock to the BRICT has a higher impact on industrialized countries in terms of magnitude and duration compared to shocks to emerging markets (third row).

The dynamic impacts of a positive shock in the stock market of industrialized countries are shown in Column 3. Interestingly, emerging markets and the BRICT show a statistically significant stronger negative response, particularly 3 months after the shock. This support evidence that stock market of the BRICT has some hedge component to industrialized countries, as capital flows from industrialized countries to the BRICT when the former is hit by negative shocks and vice versa.

We investigate this finding further by estimating the VAR system for expansion and recession phases in the U.S. and Europe. The responses during recession phases are not statistically significant as there are not enough recession observations ($t = 18$).[16] However, there is statistically significant response during expansions (Fig. 12). The negative response of BRICT and emerging markets to a positive shock in stock returns in industrialized countries is stronger for the full sample (including both expansions and recession phases) than during expansions phases. This indicates that some of the negative response is due to movements during recession phases.

We extend the analysis to examine the effect of global stock markets on the group country factors by estimating a VAR with four variables. Swanson and Granger (1997) method suggests that global stock return factor responds with a lag to shocks to all market. The BIC and AIC tests also indicates a lag structure $p = 2$ for this specification.

Figure 13 shows the impulse response function of the variables in the system to a shock to global stock market returns.

All stock markets show an immediate rise in the first period with a positive shock to global stock returns. The effect is short-lived, with the rise lasting only one period, and returning to zero after 3 or 4 periods. The least reactive group to the global market is the BRICT, and the most responsive is the emerging markets.

[16]Results for recession are not shown for parsimony but available upon request.

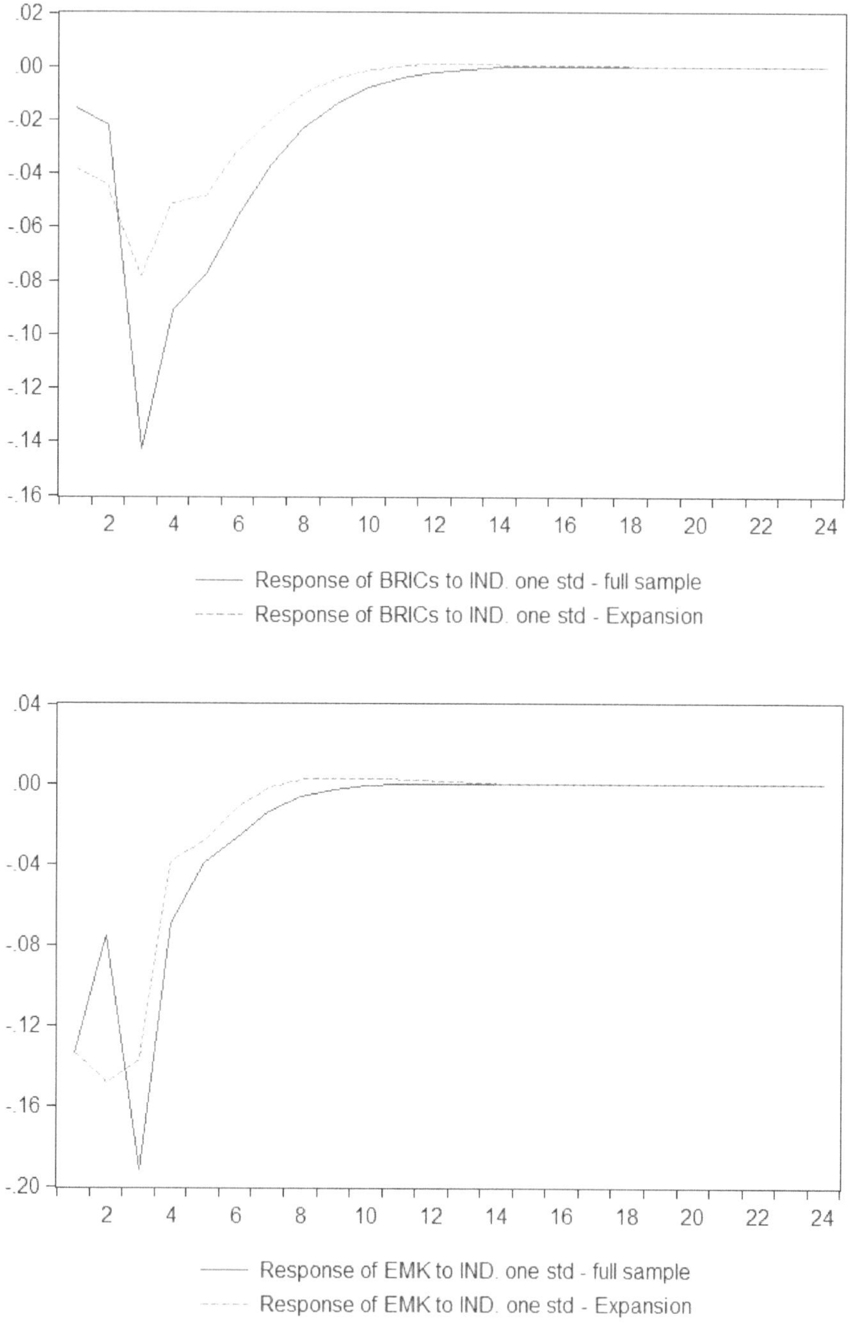

Figure 12. Impulse Response Functions for Industrialized Countries Stock Return Factor, Emerging Markets Stock Return Factor, BRICT Stock Return Factor — Expansion Phases in the U.S. and Euro Area

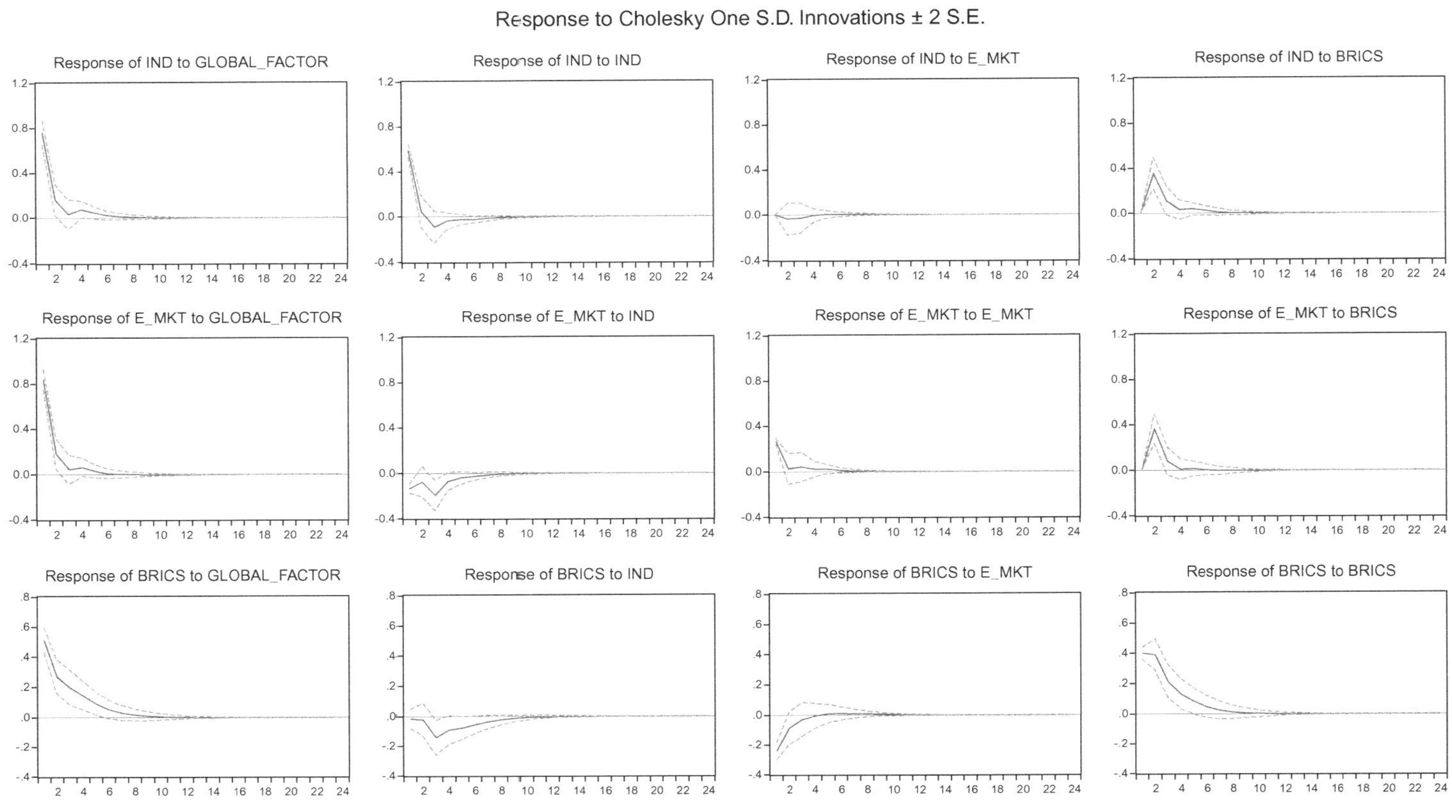

Figure 13. Impulse Response Functions — VAR with Global Stock Returns, Industrialized Countries Stock Return Factor, Emerging Markets Stock Return Factor, BRICT Stock Return Factor

6. Sensitivity Analysis

We have estimated several different specifications. The most relevant are discussed in this section.

First, we have estimated VAR specifications including different lags. Although the impulse response functions show more oscillations, the overall results are qualitatively very similar to the ones presented in the previous sections.

Second, we have estimated the factor models for different samples as there is availability of longer sample for some countries. We have not chosen them for our primary analysis because it would preclude inclusion of several countries that only have shorter sample spams. In particular, we estimated all dynamic factor models starting in 1994. In this case, Russia data are dropped because it is available only after 1997. We find that the results are striking similar, and not sample dependent, as shown in Figs. 14 and 15.

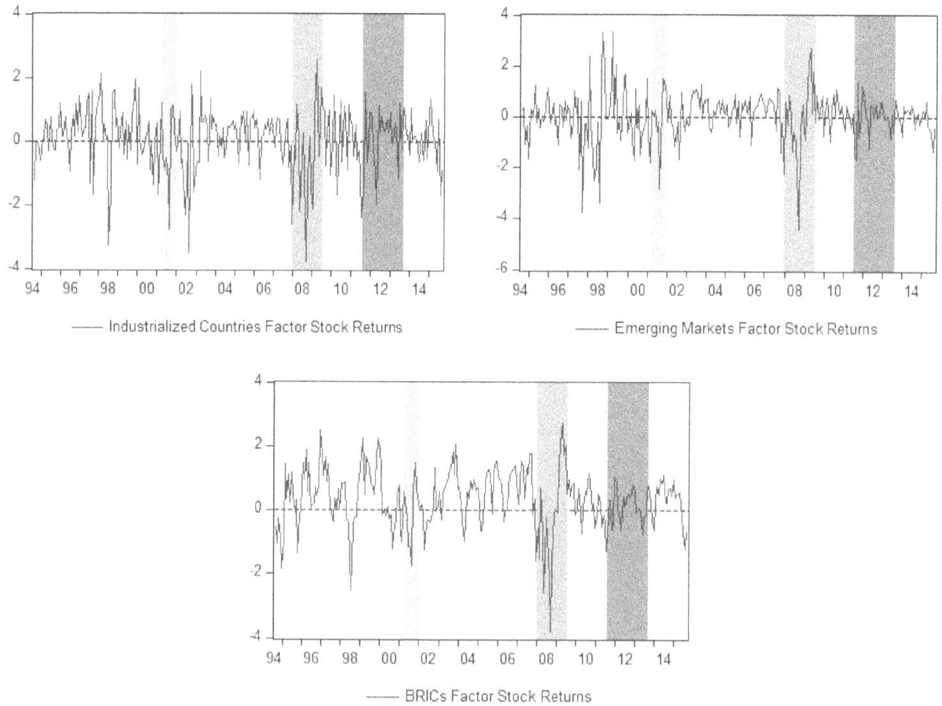

Figure 14. Industrialized Countries Stock Return Factor, Emerging Markers Stock Returns Factor, BRICT Stock Return Factor for the Extended Sample: 1994:08–2015:08

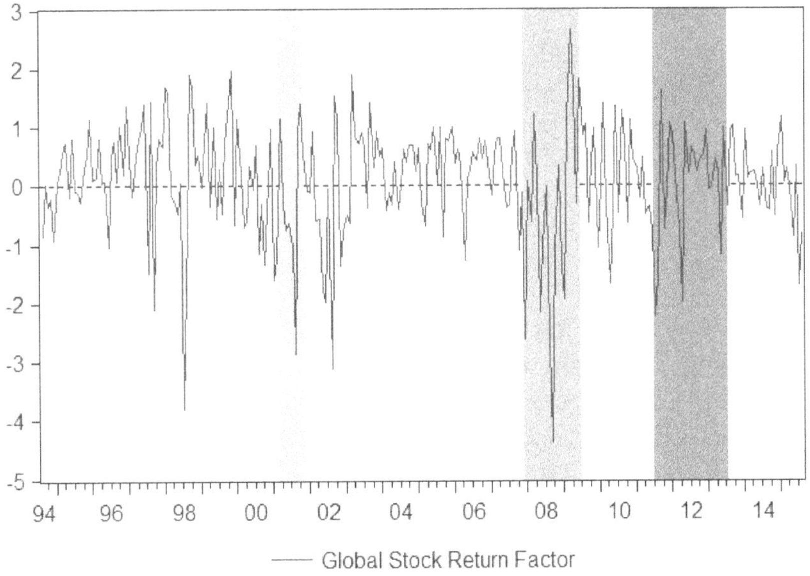

Figure 15. **Global Stock Return Common Factor for All 24 Countries, Global Stock Return Common Factor for Group Factors for the Extended Sample:1994:08–2015:08**

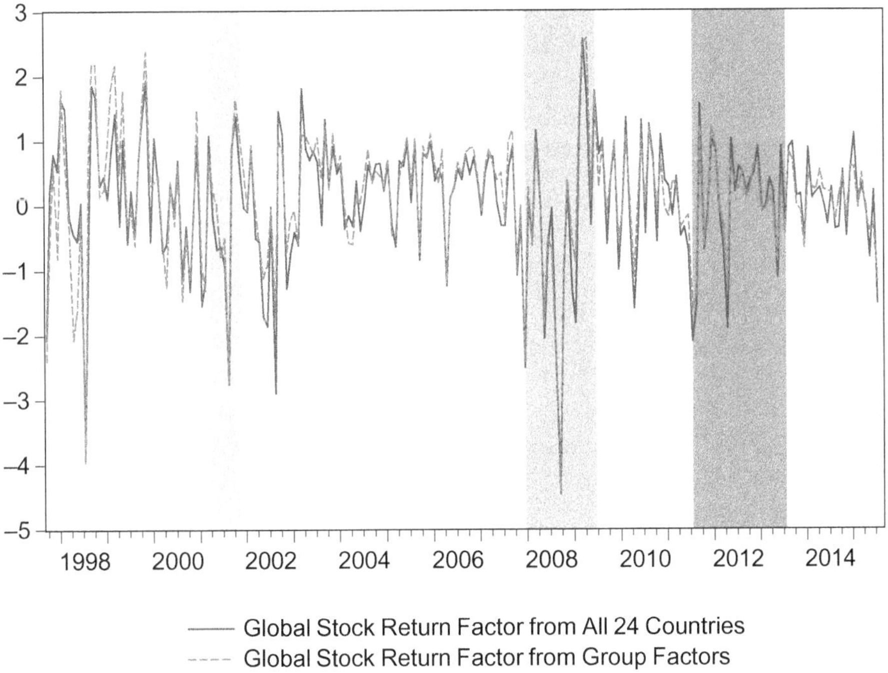

Figure 16. **Global Stock Return Common Factor obtained from the Stock Return Common Group Factors**

Finally, we have also estimated the global stock return factors from the factors obtained in equations (2.1) to (2.4), instead of extracting them from each of the 24 individual countries. As it can be seen in Fig. 16, the global market factors obtained from these distinct methods are strikingly similar, indicating that the results are robust across different specifications.

7. Conclusions

This chapter uses dynamic factor structure to model and investigate the linkages of country group stock returns and global financial markets. In particular, we group countries according to their development level and extract indicators of stock markets in industrialized countries, emerging economies, and the BRICT. We also build a global stock market factor.

The results indicate that stock market of country groups are correlated with each other and with the global stock market, much more so than individual countries are with each other. We also find that all markets respond to major economic recessions, entering in a bear phase around their beginning and entering a bull phase towards the middle of the economic contraction, predicting its end.

Further, although we find that the BRICT countries are correlated with the other markets, they tend to have more distinct features. In particular, the BRICT stock returns display the highest mean and are the most persistent — therefore, most predictable compared to the other country groups and to the global market factor.

We examine international linkages through impulse response analysis. We find that the stock market of country groups with different development levels play distinct roles in the propagation of shocks. In particular, the BRICT tend to respond less to global stock market shocks, while emerging economies are the most sensitive to changes in the world markets. Finally, we find that positive (negative) shocks to stock returns of industrialized countries have a negative (positive) impact on the BRICT. That is, the stock market of BRICT countries might attract capital hedging against conditions in the stock markets of industrialized countries.

Overall, the results indicate that the BRICT show some distinct dynamics compared to other emerging economies and industrialized countries. We find that some of the evidence in the literature of decoupling or decreasing in market integration arises from not considering separately the peculiarities of the BRICT compared to other emerging economies.

References

Backus, D. K., Kehoe, P. J., and Kydland, F. E. (1992). International real business cycles. *J. Polit. Econ.*, 100(4), pp. 745–775.

Backus, D. K., Kehoe, P. J., and Kydland, F. E. (1993). International business cycles: Theory and evidence (No. w4493), NBER.

Baxter, M. and Crucini, M. J. (1993). Explaining Saving-Investment Correlations. *Am. Econ. Rev.*, 83, pp. 416–436.

Bekaert, G., Hodrick, R. J., and Zhang, X. (2009). International stock return comovements. *J. Finance*, 64(6), pp. 2591–2626.

Bekaert, G., Ehrmann, M., Fratzscher, M., and Mehl, A. (2014). The global crisis and equity market contagion. *J. Finance*, 69(6), pp. 2597–2649.

Brock, W. A., Dechert, W., and Scheinkman, J. (1987). A test for independence based on the correlation dimension. Working paper, University of Wisconsin at Madison, University of Houston, and University of Chicago.

Chauvet, M. (1998/1999). Stock market fluctuations and the business cycle. *J. Econ. Soc. Meas.*, 25(3,4), pp. 235–257.

Chauvet, M. and Potter, S. (2000). Coincident and leading indicators of the stock market. *J. Empirical Fin.*, 7(1), pp. 87–111.

Chauvet, M., and Potter, S. (2001). Nonlinear risk. *Macroecon. Dynam.*, 5(4), pp. 621–646.

Chauvet, M., Senyuz, Z., and Yoldas, E. (2015). What does financial volatility tell us about macroeconomic fluctuations? *J. Econ. Dyn. Control*, 52, pp. 340–360.

Chauvet, M. and Sun, C. (2014). Monetary policy regimes and the stock market. In *Business Cycles in Economics: Types, Challenges and Impacts on Monetary Policies.* Ed. Jason Hsu. Nova Science Publisher, Chapter 6, 87–116.

Cheung, Y.-W., He, J., and Ng, L. K. (1997). Common predictable components in regional stock markets. *J. Bus. Econ. Stat.*, 15(1), pp. 35–42.

Davis, J. S. (2014). Financial integration and international business cycle comovement. *J. Monetary Econ.*, 64, pp. 99–111.

Fama, E. F. and French, K. R. (1989). Business conditions and expected returns on stocks and bonds. *J. Financ. Econ.*, 25(1), pp. 23–49.

Forbes, K. J. and Rigobon, R. (2001). *International financial contagion*, "Measuring contagion: Conceptual and empirical issues," (Springer US) pp. 43–66.

Forbes, K. J. and Rigobon, R. (2002). No contagion, only interdependence: Measuring stock market comovements. *J. Finance*, 57(5), pp. 2223–2261.

Imbs, J. (2004). Trade, finance, specialization, and synchronization. *Rev. Econ. Stat.*, 86, pp. 723–734.

Imbs, J. (2006). The real effects of financial integration. *J. Int. Econ.*, 68, pp. 296–324.

Kalemli-Ozcan, S., Papaioannou, E., and Perri, F. (2013). Global banks and crisis transmission. *J. Int. Econ.*, 89, pp. 495–510.

Kalemli-Ozcan, S., Papaioannou, E., and Peydró, J. L. (2013). Financial regulation, financial globalization, and the synchronization of economic activity. *J. Fin.*, 68(3), pp. 1179–1228.

Kehoe, P. J. and Perri, F. (2002). International business cycles with endogenous incomplete markets. *Econometrica*, 70, pp. 907–928.

Kose, M. A., Otrok, C., and Whiteman, C. H. (2003). International business cycles: World, region, and country-specific factors. *Am. Econ. Rev.*, 93(4), pp. 1216–1239.

Kose, M. A., Otrok, C., and Prasad, E. (2012). Global business cycles: Convergence or decoupling. *Int. Econ. Rev.*, 53(2), pp. 511–538.

Hamilton, J. D. and Lin, G. (1996). Stock market volatility and the business cycle. *J. App. Econ.*, 11(5), pp. 573–593.

Heathcote, J. and Perri, F. (2004). Financial globalization and real regionalization. *J. Econ. Theory*, 119(1), pp. 207–243.

Iacoviello, M. and Minetti, R. (2006). International business cycles with domestic and foreign lenders. *J. Monetary Econ.*, 53(8), pp. 2267–2282.

Mitchell, W. C. (1927). *Business Cycles: The Problem and its Setting,* New York: National Bureau of Economic Research.

Morgenstern, O. (1959). *International Financial Transactions and Business Cycles*, Vol. **8**. (Princeton University Press, Princeton, NJ).

Pérez-Quiros, G. and Timmermann, A. (2001). Business cycle asymmetries in stock returns: Evidence from higher order moments and conditional densities. *J. Econometrics*, 103(1), pp. 259–306.

Pérez-Quiros, G. and Timmermann, A. (1998). Variations in the mean and volatility of stock returns around turning points of the business cycle. In: Knight, J., Satchell, S. (Eds.), Forecasting Volatility in the Financial Markets. Butterworth-Heinemann, Oxford, pp. 287–306.

Whitelaw, R. (1994), Time variations and covariations in the expectation and volatility of stock market return. *J. Fin.*, 2, pp. 515–541.

Chapter 2

From Bulls to Bears: Stock–Bond Comovements in European Markets

Thomas J. Flavin

Department of Economics, Finance & Accounting
Maynooth University, Maynooth, Co. Kildare, Ireland
thomas.flavin@nuim.ie

Abstract

We analyze the stock–bond relationship across different market conditions for a number of European countries, separately investigating the impact of stock and bond market shocks. We find key differences between 'core' and 'periphery' countries. For the 'core' countries, stocks and long-term bond returns are always negatively related regardless of the shock source or the prevailing market conditions, while in the 'periphery' countries, this relationship is reversed during stock market downturns and can depend on whether the shock originated in the stock or bond market. This limits the portfolio diversification benefits of holding domestic sovereign bonds in these countries.

1. Introduction

The relationship between the returns on stocks and long-term sovereign bonds has received a great deal of attention in the financial literature. Many studies focus on the ability of such bonds to hedge against equity market risk and whether or not they provide a safe haven for equity market investors during stock market downturns and crashes. The early literature concentrated on U.S. financial markets and, in general, the consensus was that long-term sovereign bonds delivered diversification benefits to equity investors during stock market downturns, with the returns of the two asset classes exhibiting negative correlation during periods of stock market turbulence. For example, Fleming *et al.* (1998) concludes that, during crisis periods, government bonds provide a safe alternative to equity investors, while Scruggs and Glabadanidis (2003) finds that bond market variances are largely unresponsive to stock market shocks. Both De Goeij and Marquering (2004) and Cappiello *et al.* (2006) report asymmetries in conditional correlations in the response to adverse financial shocks, with the former finding that comovements between the asset classes tend to be low following bad (good) news in the stock (bond) market and the latter showing that equities are more sensitive than bonds to joint bad-news events.

Baele *et al.* (2010) documents that the stock–bond relationship exhibits substantial time variation, and this is borne out in the extant literature. Regime-switching studies of the stock–bond relationship produce interesting findings. Connolly *et al.* (2005) finds evidence of two well-defined regimes: one with low financial uncertainty and a positive cross-asset correlation, while the other is characterized by high volatility and negative correlation between stock and bond returns. Extending the number of regimes, Guidolin and Timmermann (2006) shows that a negative correlation prevails during 'crash' regimes. Flavin *et al.* (2014) distinguishes between common and idiosyncratic shocks but show that the relationship is consistently negative following an adverse stock market shock regardless of the conditions prevailing in the bond market.

Initially, the international evidence told a similar story. Steely (2006) reports that over a 20-year sample of UK asset returns, the correlation between stock and bond returns went from being positive to significantly negative. Kim *et al.* (2006) found a similar trend in the relationship for European, Japanese, and U.S. markets. Baur and Lucey (2009) analyzes the stock–bond relationship across eight international markets and find evidence of a flight-to-safety during periods of stock market turbulence with bond markets providing diversification benefits when most needed by equity investors. Likewise, Ciner *et al.* (2013) finds that bonds continue to deliver such benefits in major markets right up to the global financial crisis. Interestingly, Mensi *et al.* (2015) reports that the diversification benefits of holding U.S. Treasuries do not extend to equity investors in the emerging markets of the Gulf Cooperation Council (GCC) members. Overall, the majority view was that sovereign bonds provide an effective hedge against domestic equity market risk during periods of high-volatility financial shocks. However, this consensus has been challenged following the recent financial crisis, especially for Eurozone countries. For example, Papavassiliou (2014) for Greece, Acosta-Gonzàlez *et al.* (2015) for Italy and Spain, and Jammazi *et al.* (2015) for Greece, Ireland, Portugal, and Spain, all report positive relationships between stock and bond returns for these crisis-ridden countries during the

Eurozone sovereign debt crisis. For investors, the diversification benefits of holding bonds appear to decline when most desired in these markets.

We revisit this issue and concentrate on a sample of European countries, representing large, developed markets and smaller, crisis-hit countries. We contribute to the literature in a number of ways. First, we study the transmission of both stock and bond market shocks across different market conditions and analyze the induced comovement. Therefore, we can distinguish between changes in correlation due to a shock arising in the stock market as opposed to one originating in the sovereign bond market. This allows us to shed more light on the driving forces behind the recent literature documenting increased correlation between domestic stock and bond markets. Second, we do not exclusively focus on market downturns but examine the stock–bond relationship across three regimes — 'Bull', 'Bear', and 'Normal' markets — enabling us to assess the robustness of the relationship across different states of the world. Third, we study the impact of a shock on the dynamics of the stock–bond relationship and not just its contemporaneous effect. This is potentially important as Blatt *et al.* (2015) demonstrates that it may be the dynamics of cross-market relationships that are changed following an adverse shock.

The results of our analysis reveal a number of interesting findings. First, the stock–bond relationship is always negative in larger, developed markets irrespective of market conditions. Second, for a subset of crisis-hit countries, the stock and bond returns are positively related during crisis regime, regardless of whether the shock originates in the stock or bond market, and thus limiting the potential for portfolio diversification. Finally, for Ireland and Italy, the sign of the correlation during periods of market turbulence depends upon the source of the shock. Bond market shocks induce negative comovement as in the larger markets but equity market shocks cause positive comovement.

The remainder of this chapter is structured as follows. Section 2 presents our econometric framework and data. Section 3 reports and discusses our results, while Section 4 concludes.

2. Data and Methodology

2.1. *Methodology*

We estimate a bivariate Markov-switching VAR model for each country. We allow for up to three regimes and find that the three-regime specification better characterizes the evolution of financial market conditions over our sample compared to a more parsimonious two-regime model. The identified regimes correspond to 'Bull', 'Bear', and 'Normal' market conditions. The model is specified as follows:

$$y_t = \lambda(s_t) + \sum_{1}^{p} \beta_p(s_t) y_{t-p} + \varepsilon_t^{\mathrm{st}}, \tag{1}$$

$$\varepsilon_t^{\mathrm{st}} \sim \text{i.i.d.}(0, \sigma_s^2), \tag{2}$$

$$S_t \in \{1, 2, 3\}, \tag{3}$$

where y is the time series vector of dependent variables containing the stock and bond returns of country i, λ is a matrix of state-dependent intercepts, $\beta_1, \ldots, \beta_p$ are matrices of the state-dependent autoregressive coefficients, and ε_{it} is a state-dependent noise vector, which has a zero mean and constant variance within each regime. S_t is an unobserved latent variable, and we assume that it follows a first-order Markov process, which determines the regime path. It takes on a value of unity in the 'Bull' regime, 2 in the 'Normal' regime, and 3 in the 'Bear' regime.

The matrix of conditional probabilities for transition between the regimes is given by

$$\Pr[s_t = i | s_{t-1} = j] = p_{ij}. \tag{4}$$

We use Gibbs sampling within a Bayesian Markov-chain Monte Carlo (MCMC) approach, with a flat prior distribution for the mean coefficients (α and β), a Wishart distribution for the variance parameters (σ), and a weak Dirichlet distribution for the transition parameters. The following sequence describes the estimation procedure:

(1) Draw sigmas given the mean coefficients and regimes.
(2) Draw mean coefficients given sigmas and regimes.
(3) Draw regimes given the mean coefficients and sigmas.
(4) Draw the transition parameters.

The parameters of the model are based on 10,000 replications of the model after discarding the initial 'burn-in' set of 2000. From the estimated parameters, we generate regime-dependent impulse response functions (IRFs) (see Ehrmann *et al.*, 2003) and their associated 95% confidence bands. The IRFs are the Choleski factors standardized to unit variances. This facilitates a comparison of the differences in dynamics rather than the differences in variances, since we are predominantly interested in the direction (sign) of the response and how it varies across regimes.

The identification of the structural parameters requires the imposition of a restriction on the covariance matrix which, most often, means that one variable has a zero contemporaneous response to a shock to the other. Since there is no theory to indicate which variable to restrict, we estimate the MS-VAR twice, allowing each variable in turn to be unrestricted. The graphs included in this chapter are the unrestricted cross-asset responses.

2.2. *Data*

We analyze daily returns on stock and 10-year sovereign bonds for seven Eurozone countries and the UK. The countries included represent the 'core' states with the largest stock markets (Germany, France, and UK) and the 'periphery' countries (Greece, Ireland, Italy, Portugal, and Spain). During the crisis, many commentators referred to the latter group using the acronym, GIIPS. As the largest stock market and financial center in Europe, we include the UK as a benchmark case even though it is not a Eurozone member. All data are sourced from Datastream. Our sample covers the period from January 1, 2004 to December 31, 2015. We begin in 2004 to avoid contamination from earlier crises e.g., the collapse of the Dot.com bubble and the Russian bond crisis.

Table 1 presents summary statistics for all of the return series employed in this study. Panels (a) and (b) refer to stock and bond returns, respectively. Interestingly, over our sample period, bonds outperform stocks in terms of mean return in every country, with Greece and Portugal recording negative average stock returns. Furthermore, stock returns are more volatile. All series display skewness and kurtosis, with the bond returns of the 'periphery' countries having fatter tails than their stock market counterparts. This feature of the data appears to be associated with the recent crisis as earlier studies generally find stronger evidence of kurtosis in stock rather than bond markets e.g., Cappiello *et al.* (2006). The Jacque–Bera test for normality is reported in the final column, and all series exhibit strong evidence of non-normality, especially the bond returns of the Eurozone 'periphery' countries. This strong rejection of normality in the univariate series suggests that a single-state model is unlikely to capture the features of the data and that a mixture model or regime-switching approach may be more applicable.

3. Discussion of Results

We estimate the model as described above for each country. The three-regime specification is adopted for all countries with the three regimes being

Table 1. Summary Statistics

	Mean	Variance	Skewness	Kurtosis	JB
Panel A: Stock market returns					
France	0.0135	1.7585	−0.0530	4.5611	3620.07
Germany	0.0133	1.6147	0.2221	9.7814	16673.99
Greece	−0.0606	3.6626	−0.4554	9.5150	15889.80
Ireland	0.0174	1.8399	−0.5803	7.1643	9160.80
Italy	0.0046	1.8567	−0.1549	4.6243	3735.75
Portugal	−0.0009	1.2672	−0.2692	7.1702	8991.80
Spain	0.0149	1.8066	0.0333	4.4811	3493.09
UK	0.0141	1.3492	−0.2071	6.1797	6671.47
Panel B: Bond market returns					
France	0.0249	0.1201	−0.1967	2.8935	1482.95
Germany	0.0238	0.1176	−0.2030	2.1303	817.97
Greece	0.0134	2.6057	1.3742	120.1947	2513845.94
Ireland	0.0269	0.2572	0.4869	32.7254	186421.01
Italy	0.0274	0.1943	0.6219	19.2840	64944.13
Portugal	0.0279	0.4931	−0.5756	52.4175	478083.49
Spain	0.0267	0.8864	0.8864	16.1961	46167.58
UK	0.0232	0.1444	−0.0050	1.8933	623.45

Notes: This table presents summary statistics for the stock market returns (Panel A) and bond market returns (Panel B) of each country. The reported statistics include the full sample mean, variance, skewness, kurtosis, as well as Jacque–Bera (JB) test for normality.

identified as a 'Bull' regime with high stock returns and low volatility; a 'Normal' regime with returns close to and not statistically distinguishable from zero coupled with an intermediate level of volatility; and a 'Bear' regime with negative stock returns and high volatility. Table 2 shows the expected returns (ER) and standard deviations (σ) of returns, generated by our model, for all assets across countries. The magnitude of stock returns is greatest in the 'Bear' regime for all countries, with Greek returns being approximately double those of its European neighbors within this regime. Bond market volatility is generally increasing as we move from 'Bull' to 'Bear' regimes, and most often the expected returns are not statistically different from zero. Differences in bond returns across regimes are relatively muted compared to the stock market. Given the relative dominance of the stock market volatility, it appears that the stock market returns have a relatively stronger influence on the determination of the regime.

As an indicator of stock and bond market comovements within each regime, we first compute the regime-specific correlations for each country

Table 2. Regime-Specific Expected Returns and Volatilities

	Bull Regime		Normal Regime		Bear Regime	
	ER	σ	ER	Σ	ER	σ
Panel A: Stock market						
France	0.150	0.373	−0.022	1.486	−0.215	5.692
Germany	0.162	0.271	−0.005	1.178	−0.257	5.943
Greece	0.063	1.056	−0.111	3.953	−0.493	16.274
Ireland	0.130	0.569	0.003	2.177	−0.216	5.158
Italy	0.164	0.673	−0.059	1.749	−0.230	1.892
Portugal	0.101	0.352	−0.027	1.461	−0.256	6.045
Spain	0.161	0.370	−0.034	1.571	−0.213	6.274
UK	0.103	0.268	−0.001	1.169	−0.274	6.364
Panel B: Bond market						
France	0.014	0.063	0.039	0.096	0.016	0.351
Germany	0.014	0.066	0.032	0.108	0.005	0.367
Greece	0.013	0.069	0.033	0.901	−0.329	25.016
Ireland	0.035	0.061	−0.015	1.479	0.026	0.153
Italy	0.020	0.257	0.013	0.865	0.052	0.438
Portugal	0.013	0.061	0.020	0.300	0.101	4.832
Spain	0.016	0.055	0.028	0.160	0.013	0.879
UK	0.020	0.083	0.025	0.169	0.070	0.403

Notes: This table presents the regime-specific expected returns (ER) and standard deviation of returns (σ) for the stock markets (Panel A) and the bond markets (Panel B) of each country in the sample.

and these are reported in Table 3. Within the 'Bull' regime, the correlation is uniformly negative across countries. Thus during periods of positive stock market performance, stock and bond returns move in opposite directions, presumably due to investors selling off bonds to finance greater investment in equities. 'Normal' regimes see this correlation turn positive for the 'periphery' financial markets. This positive correlation limits the effectiveness of a hedging strategy during this period of stagnant returns and intermediate volatility, in these European markets. However, the correlation remains negative in the larger markets of France, Germany, and the UK. Finally, 'Bear' markets continue to generate negative correlation for the three large markets, and they are joined by Italy and Ireland. For each of these countries, the domestic government bond is an effective hedge against stock market risk. However for Greece, Portugal, and Spain the correlation is positive, suggesting that the diversification benefits of holding the long bond are not delivered when most needed by investors. Interestingly, even

Table 3. Regime-Specific Stock–Bond Correlations by Country

	Bull	Normal	Bear
France	−0.092	−0.376	−0.254
Germany	−0.080	−0.506	−0.412
Greece	−0.127	0.293	0.312
Ireland	−0.041	0.230	−0.304
Italy	−0.007	0.589	−0.176
Portugal	−0.088	0.118	0.293
Spain	−0.096	0.091	0.234
UK	−0.174	−0.368	−0.446

Notes: This table reports the regime-specific stock–bond correlation generated by our model for each country.

though the magnitude of the correlations varies across regimes, the asset classes are always negatively correlated in the 'core' countries regardless of the prevailing market condition.

3.1. *Bond market response to a stock market shock*

Of course, the regime-specific correlations do not provide conclusive statistical evidence as they are subject to the bias due to changes in variance across regimes as described by Forbes and Rigobon (2002). To overcome this problem, we recover the structural shocks from our model and generate the regime-specific IRFs to capture the cross-market effects of a shock sourced in either market. We first analyze the response of the bond market of country i following a shock in the domestic stock market. These IRFs are presented in Fig. 1. We group the countries by size of their stock markets, so responses for Italy are presented alongside the 'core' countries. The 'periphery' countries, Greece, Ireland, Portugal, and Spain, have smaller stock markets and also experienced more bond market turbulence in the recent crisis. Rows refer to the indicated country, while the columns represent the condition of the market. For each regime, we apply the same scale to all graphs (in a given panel) to get a sense of the relative importance of the response in each country. There is a marked difference in the magnitude of responses across countries in the 'Bear' regime which is not apparent in the 'Bull' regime.

First, we focus on the relationship during 'Bull' market conditions. For all countries, the contemporaneous reaction is zero or negative. A positive shock in the domestic equity market tends to produce a negative response in the domestic bond market, and hence lower comovement between the two

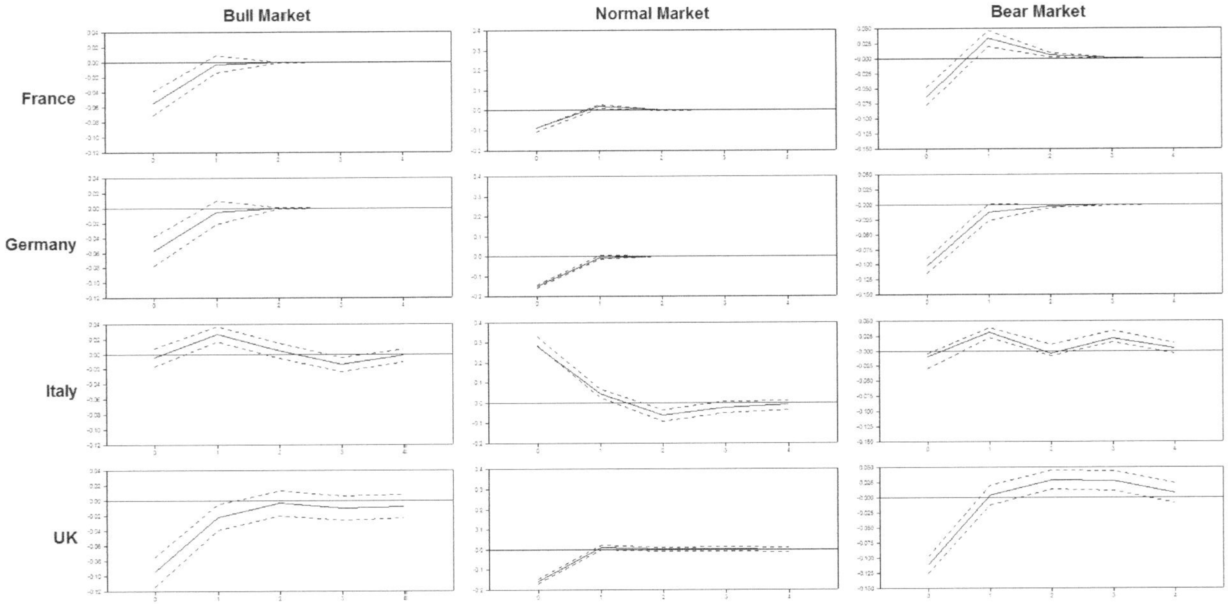

(a)

Figure 1. Bond Market Responses to a Stock Market Shock

Notes: Figure (a) presents the regime-specific impulse response functions (IRFs) of the bond markets of France, Germany, Italy, and the UK in response to a stock market shock. Each column presents the IRFs for a given regime across countries. Each row presents the IRFs of a given country across regimes. The solid line is the IRF and dashed lines are the 95% confidence bands. Within each regime, the scale of the graph is the same across countries to facilitate easier comparison of cross-country responses within a regime. Figure (b) presents the regime-specific impulse response functions (IRFs) of the bond markets of Greece, Ireland, Portugal, and Spain in response to a stock market shock. Each column presents the IRFs for a given regime across countries. Each row presents the IRFs of a given country across regimes. The solid line is the IRF and dashed lines are the 95% confidence bands. For each panel and within each regime, the scale of the graph is the same across countries to facilitate easier comparison of cross-country responses within a regime.

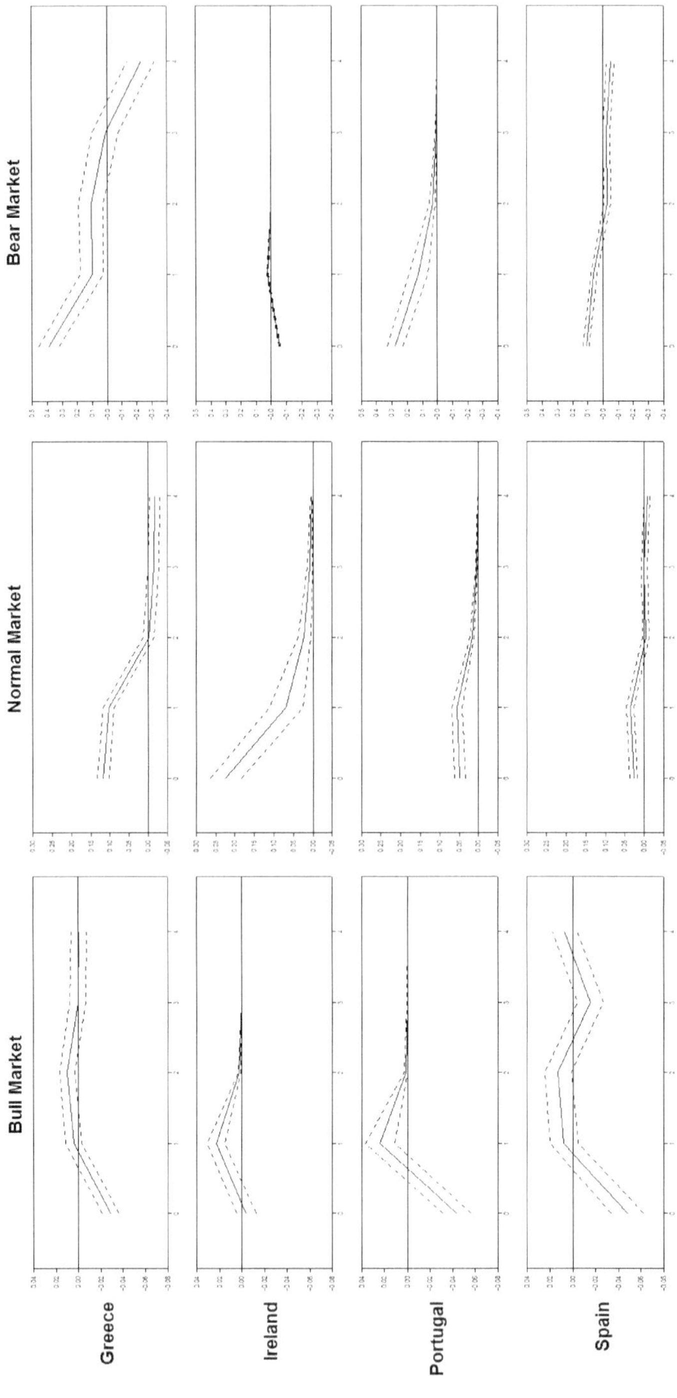

(b)

Figure 1. *(Continued)*

markets. This is consistent with investors rebalancing their portfolios in chase of higher yield, by liquidating bond positions and increasing their exposure to equity assets in response to good news about the stock market, causing prices to increase (fall) in equity (bond) markets. Only in Ireland and Italy is the contemporaneous effect not statistically significant. The dynamics of the IRFs are also interesting. In the larger markets of France, Germany, and the UK, the reaction always remains negative, but for other countries it oscillates about zero before dying out.

Second, we analyze the effect of a stock market shock during 'normal' financial market conditions. France, Germany, and the UK again exhibit a negative reaction to stock market events. For all other markets, the contemporaneous response is positive and statistically different from zero. There is little persistence in the shock for any country. For the 'core' markets, equity market shocks continue to reduce cross-market comovements, but all the 'periphery' markets experience increased correlation during this stagnant regime.

Finally, we focus on 'Bear' markets, which is arguably the most important regime to analyze since it is when investors most desire the potential diversification benefits from their bond investment. The scale is dominated by the relatively large response in Greece and, to a lesser extent, Portugal. The bond markets of all three 'core' financial markets continue to respond negatively to a stock market shock. This is comforting for investors and is consistent with much of the previous literature that domestic stocks and bonds are negatively correlated during stock market downturns. It provides further evidence of a 'flight-to-safety' with investors reducing their equity exposure and investing the proceeds in the relatively safer asset class. The Irish bond market behaves like the big three, while the response of the Italian bond market cannot be statistically distinguished from zero. Thus, holding a position in domestic long-term sovereign bonds can provide an effective hedge against equity market shocks in these countries. The other three markets from the group of 'periphery' countries, Greece, Portugal, and Spain, all exhibit positive contemporaneous reaction to a stock market shock. The Greek reaction is the strongest in relative terms and probably reflects the high sensitivity of Greek financial markets during the crisis. The response also shows the most persistence, oscillating from positive to negative and remaining an influence in the system for up to two weeks. Thus investors who hold portfolios of domestic stocks and bonds in these countries are likely to be disappointed at the time when diversification benefits are most needed.

3.2. *Stock market response to a bond market shock*

To assess the response of the stock market to a bond market shock, we change the required restriction as outlined above and generate a new set of IRFs. These are presented in Fig. 2.

In general, bond market shocks exert a significant contemporaneous effect on the domestic stock market, but their effects are relatively short-lived and exhibit little persistence. For six markets, the contemporaneous reactions tend to reinforce the relationship already discussed for the bond market response to a stock market shock. Across all regimes, bond market shocks have an oppositely signed impact on the stock markets of France, Germany, and the UK, producing a consistently negative stock–bond relationship in these countries. Neither the source of the shock nor the condition of the markets affect the stock–bond relationship in the 'core' set of countries. The relationship is also unambiguous for Greece, Portugal, and Spain, with the two-way feedback effects reinforcing each other. Shocks to either market generate a similarly signed response in the other market, within each regime. Thus the correlation is negative during 'Bull' markets and positive during both 'Normal' and 'Bear' markets.

However, our analysis of Irish and Italian markets shows how ambiguity might arise regarding the stock–bond relationship and demonstrates the benefit of separately investigating the effects of stock and bond market shocks. The relationship during 'Bull' markets is unchanged (from our analysis of a stock market shock), but for both 'Normal' and 'Bear' regimes, the reactions to a cross-market shock differ in sign. For example, in the 'Bear' regime, a stock market shock elicits a negative response in the bond market (Fig. 1), but a bond market shock generates a positive response in the stock market (Fig. 2). Overall, this leaves the relationship ambiguous and dependent on the source and strength of the shock in these countries. Finally, it is noteworthy that in the 'Bear' regime, bond market shocks generate positive stock market reactions in the five countries that faced the greatest funding difficulties during the Eurozone sovereign bond crisis. Bad news in these sovereign bond markets appears to have propagated the shock to domestic stock markets, perhaps due to fears of a protracted recession or even fears of an exit from the Eurozone.

3.3. *Linking our results to other literature*

In summary, we find evidence of a positive stock–bond correlation in the crisis-hit, 'periphery' Eurozone states. For Greece, Portugal, and Spain,

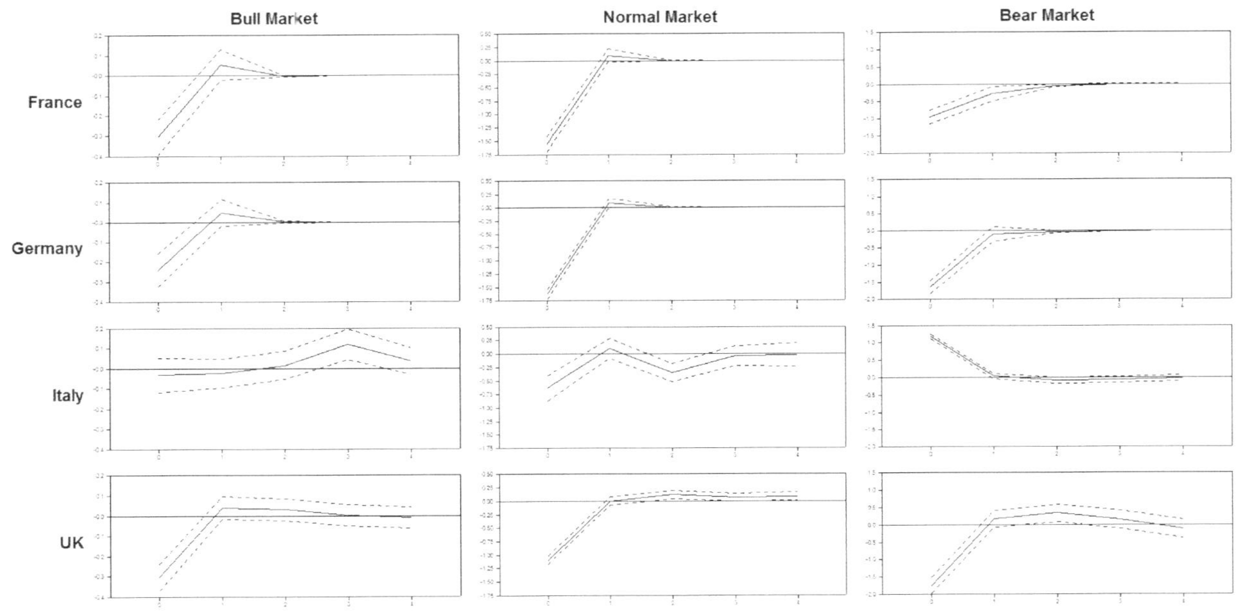

(a)

Figure 2. Stock Market Responses to a Bond Market Shock

Notes: Figure (a) presents the regime-specific impulse response functions (IRFs) of the stock markets of France, Germany, Italy, and the UK in response to a bond market shock. Each column presents the IRFs for a given regime across countries. Each row presents the IRFs of a given country across regimes. The solid line is the IRF and dashed lines are the 95% confidence bands. Within each regime, the scale of the graph is the same across countries to facilitate easier comparison of cross-country responses within a regime. Figure (b) presents the regime-specific impulse response functions (IRFs) of the stock markets of Greece, Ireland, Portugal, and Spain in response to a bond market shock. Each column presents the IRFs for a given regime across countries. Each row presents the IRFs of a given country across regimes. The solid line is the IRF and dashed lines are the 95% confidence bands. For each panel and within each regime, the scale of the graph is the same across countries to facilitate easier comparison of cross-country responses within a regime.

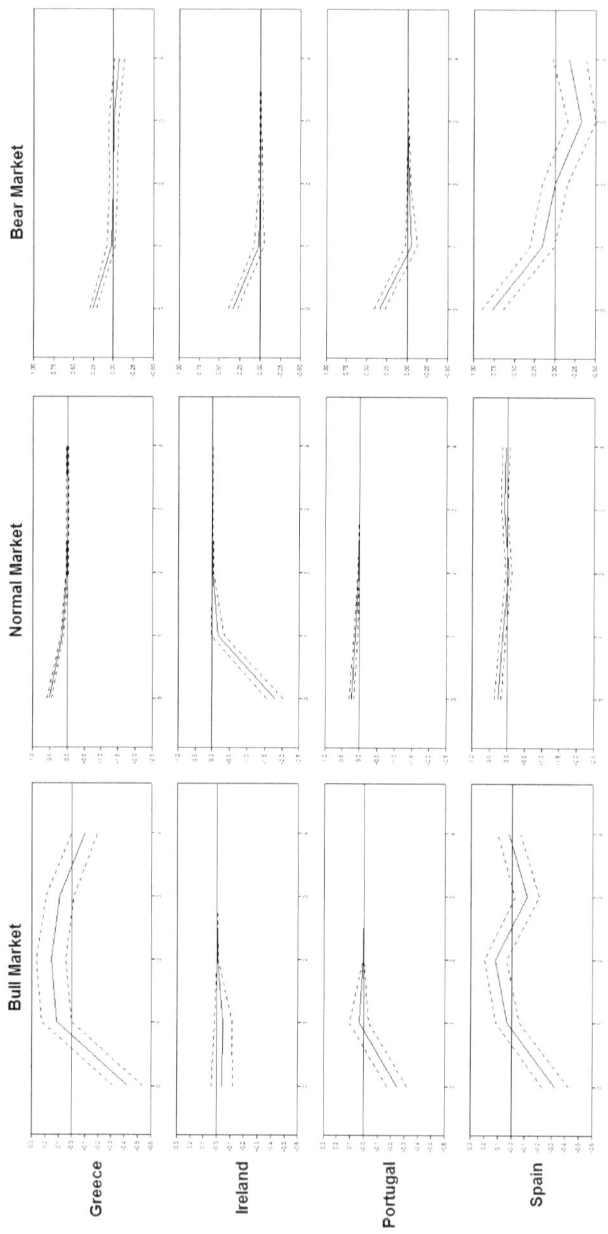

(b)

Figure 2. *(Continued)*

shocks to both equity and bond markets elicit the same response and reinforce each other. In Italy and Ireland, the increased cross-asset correlation appears to be driven by bond market shocks. Perego and Vermuelen (2016) investigates the underlying causes of the increased cross-market dependencies and find that most of the increase can be attributed to cross-country variation in macroeconomic fundamentals. In a similar vein, Caggiano and Greco (2012) demonstrates the link between fiscal variables and Eurozone bond spreads but also find an increased role for financial variables during the crisis in explaining sovereign bond spreads. Flavin and Lagoa (2016) examines the stock–bond relationship for Spain and dis-aggregate the overall stock market index into ten sectors. They find that it is mainly the financial sector that drives the increased correlation between Spanish stocks and bonds. This finding suggests that the 'doom-loop' of negative bi-directional effects between the financial sectors and sovereign bond markets in crisis countries is a driving force behind this amplified comovement. The pressure on governments to provide rescue packages for the domestic banking sector to ensure their survival created a strong link between the two sectors (see among others, Acharya *et al.*, 2014 and Mody and Sandri, 2012).

4. Conclusion

We analyze the relationship between domestic stock and long-term sovereign bond returns for a sample of Eurozone countries and the UK. There are a number of noteworthy findings. First, in the 'core' financial markets of France, Germany, and the UK, the relationship is always negative regardless of market conditions or the origin of the shock. Second, during market downturns, both stock and bond market shocks generate positive market comovement in Greece, Spain, and Portugal. Therefore, diversification benefits are limited in these countries. The 'flight-to-safety' frequently observed does not appear to occur in these markets. Investors may not believe the sovereign bonds to be safe and may have sought alternative non-domestic 'safe' assets. Third, the sign of the stock–bond relationship for Ireland and Italy depends upon the source of the shock. Bond markets react negatively to stock market shocks as in the larger financial markets, but bond market shocks tend to spillover to stock markets and generate positive comovement. Therefore, accounting for bond and stock market shocks provides a greater understanding of the driving forces behind the increased correlation documented in some recent papers.

Finally, for countries experiencing funding difficulties, bond shocks generate positive comovement between the assets. Domestic stock markets offer limited diversification benefits, possibly due to fears of a prolonged economic recession or even an exit from the common currency. In many of these crisis countries, the sovereign bond market shock transmitted to the stock market via the financial sector whose reliance on domestic governments for funding and resolution programs created a strong dependence between the two sectors — the so-called 'doom loop' whereby adverse news in either sector tended to worsen the plight of the other sector.

References

Acharya, V. V., Drechsler, I., and Schnabl, P. (2014). A pyrrhic victory? Bank bailouts and sovereign credit risk. *J. Fin.*, 69(6), pp. 2689–2739.

Acosta-González, E., Andrada-Félix, J., and Fernández-Rodríguez, F. (2015). Stock-bond decoupling before and after the 2008 crisis. *Appl. Econ. Lett.*, 23(7), pp. 465–470.

Baele, L., Bekaert, G., and Inghelbrecht, K. (2010). The determinants of stock and bond return comovements. *Rev. Financ. Stud.*, 23(6), pp. 2374–2428.

Blatt, D., Candelon, B., and Manner, H. (2015). Detecting contagion in a multivariate time series system: An application to sovereign bond markets in Europe. *J. Bank. Fin.*, 59, pp. 1–13.

Baur, D. and Lucey, B. (2009). Flights and contagion — An empirical analysis of stock–bond correlations. *J. Fin. Stab.*, 5, pp. 339–352.

Caggiano, G. and Greco, L. (2012). Fiscal and financial determinants of Eurozone sovereign spreads. *Econ. Lett.*, 117(3), pp. 774–776.

Cappiello, L., Engle, R. F., and Sheppard, K. (2006). Asymmetric dynamics in the correlations of global equity and bond returns. *J. Fin. Econom.*, 4, pp. 537–572.

Ciner, C., Gurdgiev, C., and Lucey, B. (2013). Hedges and safe havens: An examination of stocks, bonds, gold, oil and exchange rates. *Int. Rev. Fin. Anal.*, 29, pp. 202–211.

Connolly, R., Stivers, C., and Sun, L. (2005). Stock market uncertainty and the relation between stocks and bond returns. *J. Fin. Quant. Anal.*, 40, pp. 161–194.

De Goeij, P. and Marquering, W. (2004). Modelling the conditional covariance between stock and bond returns: A multivariate GARCH approach. *J. Fin. Econom.*, 2(4), pp. 531–564.

Ehrmann, M., Ellison, M., and Valla, N. (2003). Regime-dependent impulse response functions in a Markov-switching vector autogression model. *Econ. Lett.*, 78, pp. 295–299.

Flavin, T. J. and Lagoa-Varela, D. (2016). Do long-term bonds hedge equity risk? Evidence from Spain. Working paper N268-16, Maynooth University.

Flavin, T. J., Morley, C. E., and Panopoulou, E. (2014). Identifying safe haven assets for equity investors through an analysis of the stability of shock transmission. *J. Int. Fin. Markets, Inst. Money*, 33, pp. 137–154.

Fleming, J., Kirby, C., and Ostdiek, B. (1998). Information and volatility linkages in the stock, bond, and money markets. *J. Fin. Econ.*, 49(1), pp. 111–137.

Forbes, K. J. and Rigobon, R. (2002). No contagion, only interdependence: Measuring stock market comovements. *J. Fin.*, 57(5), pp. 2223–2261.

Guidolin, M. and Timmermann, A. (2006). An econometric model of nonlinear dynamics in the joint distribution of stock and bond returns. *J. Appl. Econom.*, 21(1), pp. 1–22.

Jammazi, R., Tiwari., A., Ferrer, R., and Moya, P. (2015). Time-varying dependence between stock and government bond returns: International evidence with dynamic copulas. *N. Amer. J. Econ. Fin.*, 33, pp. 74–93.

Kim, S. J., Moshirian, F., and Wu, E. (2006). Evolution of international stock and bond market integration: Influence of the European Monetary Union. *J. Bank. Fin.*, 30, pp. 1507–1534

Mensi, W., Hammoudeh, S., Reboredo, J. C., and Nguyen, D. K. (2015). Are Sharia stocks, gold U.S. Treasury hedges and/or safe havens for the oil-based GCC markets? *Emerging Mkt. Rev.*, 24, pp. 101–121.

Mody, A. and Sandri, D. (2012). The Eurozone crisis: How banks and sovereigns came to be joined at the hip. *Econ. Policy*, 27(70), pp. 199–230.

Papavassiliou, V. G. (2014). Cross-asset contagion in times of stress. *J. Econ. Bus.*, 76, pp. 133–139.

Perego, E. R. and Vermeulen, W. N. (2016). Macro-economic determinants of European stock and government correlations: A tale of two regions. *J. Empir. Fin.*, 37, pp. 214–232.

Scruggs, J. T. and Glabadanidis, P. (2003). Risk premia and the dynamic covariance between stock and bond returns. *J. Fin. Quant. Anal.*, 38(2), pp. 295–316.

Steeley, J. (2006). Volatility transmission between stock and bond markets. *J. Int. Fin. Markets, Inst. Money*, 16, pp. 71–86.

Chapter 3

Brexit and Contagion in Global Financial Markets

K. Thomas Liaw

Department of Economics and Finance,
Tobin College of Business, St. John's University,
8000 Utopia Parkway, Queens, NY 11439, USA
Liawk@stjohns.edu

Abstract

The shock of the Brexit referendum on June 23, 2016 drove a dramatic reaction in global financial markets. The chapter examines volatility and contagion in three important segments of the global capital markets: stock, government bond, and currency markets. The chapter documents the price/rate behavior pre- and post-referendum and discusses the implication for international diversification. The global stock markets lost trillions of capitalizations the day after Britain's surprise vote to withdraw from the European Union. The government bond yields dropped to record lows in countries where investors sought flight-to-safety. The British Sterling depreciated to a low level. The stock markets rebounded to higher than the pre-referendum levels by July, government bond yields went lower, and the British Sterling continued to slide. The results also show evidence of contagion from Brexit vote to the Japanese and US stock markets. Furthermore, the results show correlations of yields on government securities in UK with those in PIIGS countries increased significantly.

1. Introduction

The Brexit referendum is over. On June 23, 2016, British people voted to leave the European Union (EU). It was a rejection of open borders and free trade. During the day of the polls and before the results were known, it was business as usual in the financial markets. After the votes were counted, the surprise outcome of a retreat to globalization sent a shock wave in the global financial markets. The day after the referendum, volatilities spiked and new records were set in global financial markets. The initial shock in the United Kingdom (UK) was rapidly transmitted to markets around the globe and there was fear of another global financial crisis. Fortunately, many stock markets started to rebound within a few days. The prolonged risk spillovers experienced in recent financial crises did not reoccur. However, many were still concerned about the greater uncertainty leading to slower economic growth.

There is extensive literature on the studies of contagion effects or risk spillovers from one market to another during periods of crisis. For example, Calvo and Reinhart (1996) showed that during the Mexico's crisis there was increased comovement across weekly equity and Brady bond returns in Latin America. They also showed that the regional patterns of the contagion in Asia and in Latin America were different. Baig and Goldfajn (1998) examined the contagion effects from Asian crisis on Thailand, Malaysia, Indonesia, Korea, and the Philippines. They found that correlations among currencies and sovereign spreads increased during the crisis. Chiang *et al.* (2007) used nine Asian daily stock returns data series covering time period from 1990 to 2003 and showed a contagion effect. They reviewed the correlation coefficients and identified two phases of the crisis, first an increase in correlation (contagion) and then a continued high correlation (herding). Khan and Park (2009) also presented evidence of the herding contagion in the stock markets during the Asian financial crisis.

For Russian default, Baig and Goldfajn (2001) discussed the contagion of Russian crisis to Brazil. They observed that risk spillover was via the debt market and that there was a sudden halt in capital flows to Brazil and Russia. The more recent US subprime crisis spread immediately to other markets. Dodd and Mills (2016) observed that the outright losses from subprime mortgages themselves would have been relatively small, but the risks coalesced and spread to many key sectors of the global financial system. Longstaff (2010) used data for the ABX indices of subprime CDO prices and found strong evidence of contagion effects. Longstaff (2010) also showed that financial contagion was spread through liquidity and risk premium channels.

The chapter contributes to the literature by extending the financial contagion research to a recent consequential event — the Brexit referendum. This was an historic event that signaled the democratic will of the British people to withdraw from the EU. There are significant implications for the economies, financial markets, and political environments in UK and Europe. This chapter examines three important segments of the global financial markets including stock, government bond, and currency markets.

Understanding the correlations of markets before and after the polls has implications in investment strategy. If financial markets in different countries display relatively low correlations and do not increase after a crisis, international diversification reduces risk. Conversely, benefits of portfolio diversification across countries diminish when financial markets move more closely together after a negative shock.

Our results showed that global financial markets experienced large swings. In equities, global stock markets suffered large declines the day after the referendum and then gradually recovered. There were increases in comovements in UK, US, and Japan. But, the correlations between the London stock market and other stock markets in Europe and China decreased slightly. In the government bond markets, yields in UK, France, Germany, and US declined, while those in PIIGS countries (Portugal, Ireland, Italy, Greece, and Spain) rose initially. In foreign exchange, the Sterling's depreciation against USD, Euro, and Yen did not reverse.

The chapter is organized as follows. The remainder of this section reviews the pre-referendum discussions of potential impacts, documents financial market reactions after the voting results were in, and discusses the predicted economic consequences of Brexit. Section 2 covers the uncertainties in the upcoming negotiations between UK and the EU. The section discusses the potential impacts on the costs of debt and equity for low-risk and high-risk corporates as well. In addition, the section provides a brief description of data. Section 3 examines the volatility of the stock markets and the correlations pre- and post-referendum. Section 4 covers the government bond markets, and Sec. 5 examines the foreign exchange rates. The last section provides a concluding summary.

1.1. *The pre-referendum discussions of potential impacts on European markets*

Before the referendum, most observers believed that UK would remain in the EU. But, an exit, if it were to occur, would have significant adverse impacts on the UK markets and spillover to the global financial markets. In addition, there are political implications as well. The outcome of the referendum would shape the direction of Europe's capital markets and would impact on the political landscape of Europe for years to come. As an example, Irwin (2015) discussed the impact of Brexit on the UK and other European countries. After Brexit, it is likely that regulatory divergence and trade barriers would increase. Such a development would have adverse impacts on trade volume and investments in the UK. In financial services, London would probably still remain as Europe's leading financial center. The resulting net economic consequences would be negative for the UK, leading to slower economic growth.

Clifford Chance LLP (2016) assessed the impacts of the exit on EU's capital markets and on the emerging UK's relationships with other countries in the EU (EU27, indicating EU excluding UK). The report documented the historical development of the EU's single market and reviewed the regulatory schemes for the integration of the wholesale capital markets in the EU. Companies of the EU member states have passporting right to provide services and conduct businesses anywhere in the single market. In the event of UK's decision to leave the EU, global businesses and financial institutions based in the UK would lose the passporting to do business in the single market under existing legislation. The new relationships would have to be renegotiated, creating uncertainties for businesses.

Wright (2016) reported the survey results on the potential impacts of the exit on capital markets in Europe. The capital markets in the UK and EU27 countries are highly connected. The single market has enabled firms based in the UK to conduct EU-wide business. Over three quarters of EU firms that use passporting in the single market are based in the UK. Companies operating under this consistent regulatory framework in the single market enjoy more certainty over regulation. Many respondents expressed concerns that in the event of Brexit there could be divergence in regulations between UK and EU27. Other uncertainties include the rising protectionism resulting in barriers to free movement of labor, goods, and capital. On the other hand, several respondents indicated the potential positive effect of Brexit in democracy, less regulation, UK's global outlook, and its strong negotiating position.

The report by Capital Economics (2016) suggested a plausible net positive consequence on economic growth and job creation. Other likely positive areas include a more tailored immigration policy, more freedom to re-negotiate trade agreements, lower levels of regulation, and savings of union dues. Financial services would lose even if the passporting rights were reserved. A period of weak foreign direct investment inflows to UK is plausible.

In summary, market participants had different views. The concerns included possible tariffs on exports to EU27, loss of access to the single market, London losing its financial center status, and a decline in foreign investments. On the other hand, the possible benefits were less regulation, savings on EU dues, chances to negotiate new trade agreements, and skills-based immigration policy.

1.2. *The referendum and market reactions*

In January 2013, Prime Minister David Cameron indicated that if the Conservatives won the next election they would renegotiate UK's relationship with the EU and that the British people would vote before the end of 2017 to stay or to leave the EU. He won re-election in May 2015. He started discussions with other EU leaders to renegotiate the terms. He also worked with European Council, referendum task force, and EU summit in Brussels.

After meetings in February 18–19, 2016 in Brussels, Prime Minister Cameron reached an agreement with the EU27 member states for a package of reforms. But, opponents claimed the deal did not tackle the high level of immigration and did not take powers back from Brussels. They claimed that Prime Minister Cameron failed to achieve the objectives he originally set out in his 2013 statement.

Prime Minister Cameron announced on February 20, 2016 that the referendum vote was to be held on June 23, 2016. The official campaign kicked off on April 15. The proponents campaigned to remain in the EU and the opponents to leave. On June 23, 2016, British people went to the polls to cast their votes. During the day, trading activities in the financial markets seemed to indicate the "Remain" would carry the majority. At the end of the day, however, the vote count surprised most — the "Leave" won. The votes for "Leave" were 17,410,742 (52%) and those for "Remain" were 16,141,241 (48%).

The shock of the Brexit vote drove a risk-off reaction in global financial markets. Observers feared for a contagion effect and the worsening backlash against globalization. The day after the vote, the global stock markets lost trillions of capitalizations and the government bond yields dropped to record lows in UK and several flight-to-safety markets. But, the uncertainty pushed the government yields higher in PIIGS countries. This was because risk-adverse investors flocked to the perceived safety of government bonds in UK, France, Germany, and US. Volatility in the foreign exchange rates spiked during the trading day and GBP/USD sank to 1.3679. Many records were set on June 24, as the markets feared the risk contagion might lead to another global meltdown.

Fortunately, within a few days, many stock markets recovered and volatility declined (JPMorgan, 2016). The negative comovements reacting to the unexpected results of the referendum were short lived in many segments of the financial markets. The observations were different from the experiences of previous crises. The objectives of the chapter are to examine the volatilities and correlations in select stock markets, government bond markets, and the foreign exchange markets in pre- and post-referendum periods. The empirical results will have implications for investment strategy.

1.3. *Predicted economic consequences of Brexit*

Capital Economics (2016) reported that Brexit could produce modest benefits in the areas of immigration policy, trade deals, lower levels of regulation, and savings from EU contributions. But it could have a negative impact on foreign direct investments, financial services, and London property value. It is possible to experience a slower economic growth as a result of the Brexit. But it is also plausible that the net impacts are modestly positive.

In contrast to the optimistic assessment by Capital Economics (2016), others forecasted a slower economic growth rate. After the Brexit vote, the IMF lowered UK's economic growth rate in 2016 by 0.3%, from 2.2% to 1.9%. JPMorgan (2016) reported that before the referendum the median of analyst estimates on UK economic growth rates for 2017 was 2.1%. After the vote on June 24, the median forecast was down to 0.6%. PWC (2016) projected UK growth rate at 1.6% in 2016 and to slow to 0.6% in 2017. The main cause of the slowdown is the increased political and economic uncertainty following the vote to leave the EU.

AllianceBernstein (2016) showed the forecasted UK economic growth rate in 2017 was 1.1%, slower than the 1.9% in 2016. The decline in growth was modest because the near-term hit to the economy from Brexit would be smaller than initially feared. The report pointed out that recent data showed consumer confidence was back at pre-referendum levels in September. The composite PMI rose to 53.9 in September, from 53.6 in August and a low of 47.6 in July. A recent release of the economic growth rate indicated the economy grew by 0.5% in the three months after the Brexit vote. This was 0.2% slower than the previous quarter, but better than analysts' estimates of about 0.3% [BBC News, 10/27/2016].

Based on data from Consensus Economics, Hakkio and Sly (2016) observed that uncertainty about UK's growth in 2017 increased dramatically. The range of forecasts for UK growth widened to 4 percentage points, while that of forecasts for other nations increased by less than a half of a percentage point. The medium-term effects are difficult to estimate, as the upcoming negotiations between UK and EU27 will significantly affect the outcome. In the long run, Brexit will result in structural shifts in the European economy. Barriers to trade can reduce competition, and limits on worker flows between countries can affect the performance of UK and EU27 economies. The long-term growth in the UK will slow upon Brexit. The median forecast in February 2016 (before the Brexit vote) for UK growth over the 2024–2028 period was 2.2%, while the forecast declined to 2.0% in August 2016 (after the vote).

2. Brexit and Risk Contagion in Global Financial Markets

The reactions in the financial markets were dramatic immediately following the results of the vote. Thereafter, many stock markets rebounded to pre-referendum levels or higher. The shock did not lead to the repeat of the downward spiral of contagious markets as experienced in Mexico's devaluation of peso in 1994 (Musacchio, 2012), Russian default in 1998 (Chiodo and Owyang, 1998), Asian currency crisis in 1997–1998 (Moreno, 1998; Baig and Golfajn, 1998; Chiang *et al.*, 2007), or US subprime crisis in 2008 (Dodd and Mills, 2008; Holt, 2009; Longstaff, 2010). However, the volatilities and correlations of markets might have changed as a result of the event.

2.1. *Uncertainties after Brexit*

The new Prime Minister Theresa May decided not to trigger Article 50 of the Lisbon Treaty (that governs the withdrawal of a member state) right away. She sent formal notice of UK's intention to withdraw from the EU on March 29, 2017. Thereafter, the UK and the EU have to negotiate the arrangements for the withdrawal and future relationships. Britain can withdraw from the EU after two years (in March 2019). The negotiations for the new relationships will have direct impact on UK, EU27, and also to a certain degree other parts of the world. Some of the new arrangements include financial regulations, trade, passporting, foreign direct investments, and labor markets.

Financial regulations are not expected to change. It is unlikely that the vote will alter UK's international commitments or change financial regulations to weaken its competitive position. In international trade, the UK and EU27 will be two separate markets. Leaving the EU will create barriers to trade with EU27. On the other hand, UK will have the freedom to negotiate new trade agreements with other non-EU countries.

Within the single market, the high level of trade between UK and EU27 means that there are high levels of investments in each other. For example, Wright (2016) reported that EU27 accounted for 48% of the stock of foreign direct investments in the UK. In the recent 5-year period, EU27 companies accounted for more than one third of acquisitions of UK companies by foreign buyers. The foreign investments in UK would likely be impacted as a result of the Brexit.

The passporting rules permit a firm in one EU state to establish branches or to engage in business across the EU without additional local authorizations. Many UK-based firms are taking advantage of these passporting rights. Some of those UK-based firms are branches of EU27-owned financial services firms. The main concern after the Brexit is that firms might not continue to have their automatic passporting rights. If this were to happen, it could cause significant disruption to UK-based companies and their customers. Similarly, clients and counterparties in EU27 could also face uncertainty and disruption. UK firms may have to set up separately capitalized subsidiaries in EU27, resulting in a higher cost of business.

Another area of uncertainty is the free movement of labor. Currently, companies have the ability to employ talents from across the EU without the need for visas or work permits. It is not clear whether EU27 nationals living in UK would automatically retain that right or there would be some kind of application process involved.

2.2. *Financial markets post referendum*

The big swings in the financial markets immediately following the results of the referendum were due to the fear of greater uncertainty and slower growth. In major financial markets, equity indices suffered large declines, government bond yields lowered, and the Sterling depreciated against major currencies. A day after the referendum, the FTSE 100 dropped almost 200 points (more than 3%), GBP/USD suffered the largest intraday decline and to 1.32, a level not seen since 1985. The yield on 10-year gilt fell to an all-time low, closed at 1.084%.

The perceived increases in uncertainty might lead to lower equity valuation in general. However, as JPMorgan (2016) pointed out global flight to quality pushed the risk-free rate lower and market risk premium higher. As such, it is possible that the net impact is to reduce the cost of equity capital or required rate of return for low beta companies while the high beta companies pay a higher cost of capital. As an example, assume that the risk-free rate is 0.5% and the market risk premium is 8.5% before the referendum. The risk-free rate dropped to 0.3% and the market risk premium widened to 8.7% post-referendum. Based on the security market line formula without any adjustment, the cost of equity capital for a low-risk firm with a beta of 0.5 will be 4.75% pre-Brexit and 4.65% post-Brexit. The corresponding costs of equity for high-risk firm with a beta of 1.5 are 13.25% and 13.35%. Thus, the low-risk firm will enjoy a lower cost of equity while the high-risk firm has to pay more.

The bond markets could experience similar results if the decline in benchmark government bond yield is more than the increase in spread for high quality corporate. For example, if the benchmark government yield decreased by 30 basis points while the spread for high quality corporate widened by 10 basis points, in the flight to quality environment, the spread for high yield might widen more than the decline in government yield, say 60 basis points. The end results are high-quality companies enjoy a lower yield while the high-yield market will see a rate increase of 30 basis points.

In the foreign exchange market, most viewed the depreciation of Sterling (against USD) the natural outcome of the uncertainty. The GBP/USD suffered a big loss the day after the vote and continued to trend downward.

2.3. *Description of data*

The next three sections will examine the volatilities and correlations in select stock, government debt, and currency markets. Daily data covering the period from the first trading day of 2016 to the last trading day in July 2016 (January 4 to July 29, 2016) are obtained from Bloomberg. The equity markets cover FTSE 100, EURO STOXX 50, DAX, CAC, DJIA and S&P 500, Shanghai Stock Market Index (SSMI), and Nikkei 225. The government debt markets include UK, France, Germany, US, Portugal, Ireland, Italy, Greece, and Spain (the PIIGS countries). In addition, we will examine the foreign exchange rates GBP/USD, GBP/Euro, and GBP/Yen.

3. Stock Markets

This section examines stock market behavior to determine if the volatility in each market or the correlations between markets changed due to the Brexit vote. The focus is on the European and US markets. But we also include Japanese and Chinese stock markets to examine the impacts, if any, of the vote on the two markets that seem less related to the UK market.

Table 1 lists the stock market index levels in major markets at close of the day before the vote (Wednesday, June 22), the day of the vote (Thursday, June 23), the day after the vote (Friday, June 24), and several days after the vote (the following Monday, June 27; Tuesday, June 28; and Friday, July 1). Table 1 also shows changes of the index levels from June 23 to June 24 and from June 23 to July 1.

Table 1. Summary Statistics of Stock Market Indices

	FTSE 100	EURO STOXX 50	DAX	CAC	DJIA	S&P 500	SSMI	Nikkei 225
6/22	6,261.19	2,978.31	10,071.06	4,380.03	17,780.83	2,085.45	3,041.36	16,065.72
6/23	6,338.10	3,037.86	10,257.03	4,465.90	18,011.07	2,113.32	3,027.08	16,238.35
6/24	6,138.69	2,776.09	9,557.16	4,106.73	17,400.75	2,037.41	2,987.58	14,952.02
Change from 6/23	−199.41 (−3.15%)	−261.77 (−8.62%)	−699.87 (−6.82%)	−359.17 (−8.04%)	−610.32 (−3.39%)	−75.91 (−3.59%)	−39.50 (−1.30%)	−1,286.33 (−7.92%)
6/27	5,982.20	2,697.44	9,268.66	3,984.72	17,140.24	2,000.54	3,030.98	15,309.21
6/28	6,140.39	2,758.67	9,447.28	4,088.85	17,409.72	2,036.09	3,048.62	15,323.14
7/1	6,577.83	2,883.06	9,776.12	4,273.96	17,949.37	2,102.95	3,069.50	15,682.48
Change from 6/23	239.73 3.78%	−154.80 (−5.10%)	−480.91 (−4.69%)	−191.94 (−4.30%)	−61.70 (−0.34%)	−10.37 (−0.49%)	42.42 1.40%	−555.87 (−3.42%)
7/29	6724.43	2990.76	10337.50	4439.81	18432.24	2173.60	3118.90	16569.27

Note: SSMI denotes Shanghai Stock Market Index.
Source: Bloomberg.

Most people expected the referendum to be a non-event, that is UK to remain in the EU. Early polls indicated voters would choose to stay in the EU. The financial markets showed no large movements or any detected pattern that gave hint to the surprise results. Most markets advanced modestly on the day of the vote while the Shanghai Stock Market experienced a slight decline (declined by 14.28 points or 0.47%). Business went on as usual on the referendum day.

The shock came in after the votes were counted. Voters used the referendum to express their discontent toward globalization and immigration. The "Leave" won the majority of the votes. As Table 1 shows, the surprise sank the FTSE 100 index 3.15%, and the negative event spilled over to other markets. The DAX lowered by 6.82%, EURO STOXX 50 lost 8.62%, and CAC dropped 8.04%. The DJIA and S&P 500 each dropped by more than 3% and Japan lost almost 8% of market capitalizations. China, a different type of economy and more isolated, still suffered a loss of 1.30%. The global stock markets lost trillions of dollars in market capitalizations.

The following Monday (June 27), the stock markets in Asia (Shanghai and Tokyo) bounced back while other major markets in Europe and US continued to lose grounds. However, the downward spiral financial crisis similar to the one following the bankruptcy of Lehman Brothers in 2008 did not reoccur. This is because banks are now much better capitalized and central banks are providing ample liquidity. Thus, the US and European markets rebounded and the two Asian markets continued to move up the next day (June 28). By July 1, the London and Shanghai stock markets were higher than the pre-referendum levels. The FTSE 100 was up 3.78% and the SSMI was higher by 1.40%. The other markets had rebounded from the lows but were still down. As Table 1 shows, all markets rose to higher than the pre-referendum levels by the last trading day in July (July 29).

It is of interest to review the volatility of each market and the correlation between markets after the referendum. The daily data cover the period from January 4 to July 29, 2016. The analyses of volatility and correlation are performed for the periods before the vote (January 4 to June 22, 2016), after the vote (June 24 to July 29, 2016), and the entire sample period. Table 2 lists the volatility and correlation of stock index daily returns. Panel (a) of Table 2 shows the standard deviation for each market in each time period. The volatility for each market increased after the referendum, except the Chinese market that behaved differently. The stock markets in UK, US, and Japan experienced modest increases in volatilities after the vote (the

Table 2. Volatility and Correlation of Stock Index Daily Returns

	FTSE 100	EURO STOXX 50	DAX	CAC	DJIA	S&P 500	SSMI	Nikkei 225
Panel (a): Standard deviation of stock index daily returns (in %)								
1/4–6/22	1.193	1.500	1.472	1.450	0.885	0.913	1.892	1.906
6/24–7/29	1.399	2.185	1.884	2.103	0.994	1.071	0.850	2.112
1/4–7/29	1.229	1.634	1.547	1.577	0.904	0.942	1.752	1.933
5/1–6/22	0.974	1.266	1.219	1.178	0.597	0.583	1.155	1.346
5/1–7/29	1.159	1.689	1.515	1.609	0.786	0.819	1.032	1.678

	FTSE 100 and EURO STOXX 50	FTSE 100 and DAX	FTSE 100 and CAC	FTSE 100 and DJIA	FTSE 100 and S&P500	FTSE 100 and SSMI	FTSE 100 and NIKKEI 225
Panel (b): Correlation coefficient of stock index daily returns							
1/4–6/22	0.910	0.882	0.923	0.608	0.619	0.186	0.310
6/24–7/29	0.805	0.776	0.823	0.818	0.819	−0.022	0.413
1/4–7/29	0.878	0.857	0.893	0.655	0.666	0.161	0.336
5/1–6/22	0.876	0.851	0.894	0.491	0.503	0.049	0.402
5/1–7/29	0.827	0.807	0.842	0.698	0.707	0.019	0.417

Note: SSMI denotes Shanghai Stock Market Index.
Source: Bloomberg.

period from June 24 to July 29). The volatilities in EURO STOXX 50, DAX, and CAC indices rose even more. China, on the other hand, experienced a lower volatility. The standard deviation of the Shanghai Stock Market Index decreased from 1.892% to 0.850%.

We also used a shortened time period, from May 1 to July 29, to examine the market behavior. The standard deviations for the pre-referendum period of May 1 to June 22 were generally lower than those for the period from January 4 to June 22. As a reference, the standard deviations for the shorter time period (May 1 to July 29) and the whole sample period (January 4 to July 29) are included in Panel (a) of Table 2 as well.

We next review the correlation coefficients of daily returns in Panel (b) of Table 2. Before the referendum, FTSE 100 was highly correlated with EURO STOXX 50, DAX, and CAC. The correlation coefficients were at close to 0.90 or higher. The comovements in UK and US stock markets were modest. The correlation coefficients with DJIA and S&P 500 were 0.608 and 0.619, respectively. The markets in London, Shanghai, and Tokyo were not closely cointegrated. The pre-referendum correlation coefficients were relatively low at 0.186 and 0.310, respectively.

Examination of post-referendum correlation coefficients indicates that there were contagion effects from Brexit vote to US stock markets (both DJIA and S&P 500) and a lesser degree to Japan's NIKKEI 225. As a result, the benefits of international diversification in those markets were reduced after the vote. On the other hand, other correlation coefficients declined slightly, indicating there were no contagion effects in other stock markets. The reduction in portfolio risk from investment diversification in those countries did not diminish after the negative event.

The comovement pattern is similar when the pre-referendum period is shortened from (January 4–June 22, 2016) to (May 1–June 22, 2016). In general, the observations showed that the contagion effects were not global. The phenomenon that 'during a financial crisis, correlation becomes one' happened only one day in global stock markets during this event. Thereafter, the regional patterns differed.

4. Government Bond Markets

At a time of uncertainty, the yields on government securities tend to decline as investors seek a safe haven for their money. The daily yield data cover 10-year government securities in UK, France, Germany, US, and PIIGS countries (Portugal, Ireland, Italy, Greece, and Spain). The fluctuations in those yields indicated how investors reacted to the outcome of the referendum. As Panel (a) of Table 3 shows, there was little change in yields in each of the markets during the day of the referendum (the change from close of June 22 to close of June 23). Large swings in yields occurred the day after the vote. The 10-year UK gilt yield sank to 1.084%, a record low. Yield in France closed lower to 0.381%, in Germany to −0.049%, and in US to 1.561%. However, the opposites happened with higher yields in PIIGS countries. The observations indicate that risk aversion drove investors to the perceived safety markets (UK, France, Germany, and US). Note that the 10-year bund yield dropped to negative territory.

Investors were initially concerned about the PIIGS government securities, pushing rates higher. The 10-year yields in Portugal increased from 3.072% to 3.331%, in Ireland from 0.763% to 0.816%, in Italy from 1.397% to 1.552%, in Greece from 7.659% to 8.476%, and in Spain from 1.463% to 1.626%. But, soon yields in four of the PIIGS countries reversed to decline. The exception was in Greece where the 10-year government yield was much higher than in other countries pre-referendum and remained high thereafter. In other developed countries, yields continued to move lower. This could

Table 3. **Yields on Government Securities and Correlations**

	UK	France	Germany	US	Portugal	Ireland	Italy	Greece	Spain
Panel (a): Yields on government securities (in %)									
6/22	1.311	0.421	0.061	1.686	3.129	0.761	1.431	7.866	1.494
6/23	1.372	0.453	0.093	1.747	3.072	0.763	1.397	7.659	1.463
6/24	1.084	0.381	−0.049	1.561	3.331	0.816	1.552	8.476	1.626
6/27	0.933	0.290	−0.117	1.439	3.282	0.729	1.506	8.593	1.451
6/28	0.959	0.240	−0.113	1.467	3.126	0.631	1.397	8.494	1.311
7/1	0.861	0.156	−0.127	1.445	2.997	0.456	1.228	7.779	1.147
7/29	0.684	0.101	−0.121	1.454	2.917	0.405	1.166	8.068	1.015

	UK and France	UK and Germany	UK and US	UK and Portugal	UK and Ireland	UK and Italy	UK and Greece	UK and Spain
Panel (b): Correlation coefficients between yields on government securities								
1/4–6/22	0.906	0.939	0.929	−0.616	0.683	0.294	0.125	0.546
6/24–7/29	0.887	0.182	0.285	0.709	0.905	0.895	0.649	0.852

Source: Bloomberg.

be because the Brexit uncertainly would push the central banks to adopt additional expansionary monetary policies.

Panel (b) of Table 3 shows interesting changes. The correlations between UK and France, Germany, and US were all more than 0.90 pre-referendum. Government yields moved in sync in those countries. The correlations decreased post-referendum, and the decreases were large with Germany and US. Conversely, the UK's correlations with all PIIGS countries increased post-referendum. Note that a negative correlation (−0.616) was observed for yields between UK gilts and Portugal governments before the vote.

5. Currency Markets

In the foreign exchange markets, we examine the Sterling against three major currencies including the US dollar (GBP/USD), the Euro (GBP/Euro), and the Japanese Yen (GBP/Yen). Table 4 lists the exchange rates and standard deviations. As Panel (a) of Table 4 shows, the British Sterling experienced a sharp depreciation on June 24. The Sterling depreciated 8.05% against the USD (from 1.4877 to 1.3679), 5.75% against the Euro (from 1.3072 to 1.2320), and 11.44% against the Japanese Yen (from 157.865 to 139.801). The Sterling depreciation did not reverse course. The downward path persisted. By the last trading in July, the GBP/USD continued to slide to 1.3230, GBP/Euro to 1.1841, and GBP/Yen to 134.974. From the close of the referendum to the close of July 29, GBP/USD depreciated

Table 4. Volatility in Currency Markets

	GBP/USD	GBP/Euro	GBP/Yen
Panel (a): Exchange rates			
6/22	1.4707	1.3019	153.579
6/23	1.4877	1.3072	157.865
6/24	1.3679	1.2320	139.801
6/27	1.3255	1.1998	134.898
6/28	1.3344	1.2063	137.113
7/1	1.3267	1.1918	136.084
7/29	1.3230	1.1841	134.974
Panel (b): Standard deviation of exchange rates			
1/4–6/22	0.0192	0.0257	6.2595
6/24–7/29	0.0164	0.0139	3.2200

Source: Bloomberg.

11.07%, GBP/Euro dropped 9.42%, and GBP/Yen lowered 14.50%. During this time period, the British Sterling depreciated, even though the volatility declined (Panel (b) of Table 4). The standard deviation of GBP/USD lowered modestly from 0.0192 to 0.0164. The standard deviation of GBP/Euro declined almost by half to 0.0139 from 0.0257, and similarly the standard deviation of GBP/Yen dropped to 3.2200 from 6.2595. Thus, the value of Sterling continued to slide with smaller ups and downs from day to day.

The Sterling weakness benefitted the FTSE 100 index, as the index is made up of global companies that are now more competitive in international markets and enjoy stronger revenues as the Sterling weakened. As discussed in the section on stock markets, the FTSE 100 rebounded quickly and to higher than the pre-referendum level.

6. Conclusions

This chapter reviewed the market reactions to the Brexit referendum in global stock, government debt, and foreign exchange markets. Daily data from the first trading day of the year to the last trading day in July 2016 were used for the study. The objectives are to examine if there were risk contagion effects following the results of the vote and if volatilities in those three market segments changed. The first day after the vote, the global financial markets experienced large swings. In the stock markets, the initial losses were large. Yields on government securities in UK, France, Germany, and US declined, while those in PIIGS countries rose. The British Sterling depreciated against the three major currencies. The Brexit result was unexpected, and thus the market reactions were dramatic immediately following the results of the vote.

Stock markets gradually recovered. By the end of July, all markets had risen to higher levels. Other than the Chinese stock market, all other market indices experienced higher volatilities after the vote. The correlation between FTSE 100 and SSMI was low pre-referendum (0.186) but turned negative after the referendum (−0.022). Also, UK's correlation with Japanese market increased slightly but still was at a low level, compared to those between FTSE 100 and other indices in Europe and US. International diversification in China and Japan reduces portfolio risk. Such diversification benefits are much more limited in other countries examined in this chapter. In government bond markets, most yields declined and continued on this path. The Sterling's depreciation against USD, Euro, and Yen did not reverse.

The sample period was up to the last trading day in July 2016 (July 29). It is difficult at this time to predict how those markets will behave in the long run. Future research could examine the market behavior in those market segments for an expanded period of time. The negotiations between UK and other countries in Europe will take up to two years. The new relationships and the new policies are not known yet. It is possible that, in the longer time period, the data may show different observations in global financial markets.

Acknowledgement

I thank the editors for their helpful comments and suggestions. I also thank Allen Qu for assistance in data collection.

References

AllianceBernstein (2016). Global economic outlook. *Global Econom. Res.*, pp. 4–11.

Baig, T. and Goldfajn, I. (1998). Financial market contagion in the Asian crisis. *IMF Staff Papers*, 46(2), pp. 167–195.

Baig, T. and Goldfajn, I. (2001). The Russian Default and the Contagion to Brazil. In Claessens, S. and Forbes, K. J. (eds.), Chapter 11, *International Financial Contagion*, US, New York: Springer, pp. 267–299.

BBC News (10/27/2016). Brexit Britain: What has actually happened so far? http://www.bbc.com/news/business-36956418.

Calvo, S. and Reinhart, C. (1996). Capital flows to Latin America: Is there evidence of contagion effects?. The World Bank Policy Research Working Paper #1619.

Capital Economics (2016). *The Economic Impact of Brexit*. London, UK: Capital Economics.

Chiang, T. C., Jeon, B. N., and Li, H. (2007). Dynamic correlation analysis of financial contagion: Evidence from Asian markets. *J. Int. Money Fin.*, 26(7), pp. 1206–1228.

Chiodo, A. J. and Owyang, M. T. (2002). A case study of a currency crisis: The Russian default of 1998. *Review*, Federal Reserve of St. Louis, Nov/Dec, pp. 7–18.

Clifford Chance LLP (2016). *The UK Referendum-Challenges for Europe's Capital Markets*. London, UK: Association for Financial Markets in Europe.

Dodd, R. and Mills, P. (2008). Outbreak: US subprime contagion. *Finance and Development*, 45(2), International Monetary Fund.

Hakkio, C. S. and Sly, N. (2016). Global uncertainty in the wake of Brexit. *The Macro Bulletin*, Federal Reserve Bank of Kansas City, pp. 1–3.

Holt, J. (2009). A summary of the primary causes of the housing bubble and resulting credit crisis: A non-technical paper. *J. Business Inquiry*, pp. 120–129.

Irwin, G. (2015). Brexit: The impact on UK and the EU. *Global Counsel*, pp. 1–42.

JPMorgan (2016). *Corporate Finance Post-Brexit*, pp. 1–16.

Khan, S. and Park, K. W. (2009). Contagion in the stock markets: The Asian financial crisis revisited. *J. Asian Econom.*, 20(5), pp. 561–569.

Longstaff, F. A. (2010). The subprime credit crisis and contagion in financial markets. *J. Fin. Econom.*, 97(3), pp. 436–450.

Moreno, R. (1998). What caused East Asia's financial crisis. *Econom. Lett.*, Federal Reserve Bank of San Francisco.

Musacchio, A. (2012). Mexico's financial crisis of 1994–1995. Harvard Business School Working Paper, No. 12–101.

PWC (2016). *UK Economic Outlook*.

Wright, W. (2016). *The Potential Impact of Brexit on European Capital Markets: A Quantitative Survey of Market Participants*. London, UK: New Financial.

Chapter 4

Ontology-Driven Framework for Stock Market Monitoring and Surveillance

Mohamed Zaki*

*Institute for Manufacturing,
Department of Engineering,
University of Cambridge, Cambridge, UK

Babis Theodoulidis† and David Diaz‡

†Alliance Manchester Business School,
The University of Manchester,
Manchester, UK
‡Escuela de Economía y Negocios,
Departamento de Administración,
Universidad de Chile
Santiago, Chile

Abstract

Ontologies are used to define concepts shared within application domains, and thus they play a key role in all aspects of information management providing a common, agreed, and, significantly, usable representation of the domain knowledge. In the context of financial securities and trading, there is a lack of work developing an ontology for stock markets and episodes of fraud and manipulation. This chapter attempts to address this gap by proposing a systematic framework for the development and management of an ontology for stock markets. It demonstrates the proposed framework through the development of a comprehensive domain ontology for stock market monitoring and surveillance. To achieve this, the chapter presents the use of techniques to bring together and integrate domain knowledge from existing sources alongside new knowledge derived from the analysis of unstructured sources based on 'stock market' fraud cases reported by the Securities Exchange Commission. The proposed framework and domain ontology are evaluated through six case studies that validate and evaluate the work in different types of 'stock market' monitoring and surveillance applications.

1. Introduction

Since the early 1990s, ontologies have become a popular research topic studied by several research communities such as knowledge management (Dotsika, 2009; Mikroyannidis and Theodoulidis, 2007) and e-commerce (Kayed *et al.*, 2010). The most widely quoted definition of ontology is provided by Gruber (1993), *ontology is a formal, explicit specification of a shared conceptualization*. Simply, ontology can be defined as a set of concepts concerning a domain of knowledge and a specification of the relationships between these concepts enabling computers to process the content. Furthermore, various studies have deployed various techniques as ontology learning mechanisms, including interviews, focus groups, process tracing, and conceptual methods (Brewster 2008).

Financial communities have access to repositories of enormous volumes of unstructured and semi-structured texts from various sources. In practice, manual techniques for extracting and organizing such sources are challenging and increasingly unviable in satisfying the required analysis tasks (Brewster, 2008). Moreover, financial knowledge is rapidly evolving, making it difficult to keep any knowledge base current. In particular, the growth of financial fraud stock markets exemplifies how a current and up-to-date knowledge base could help to facilitate investigation and reduce the massive losses due to fraud (Kingston *et al.*, 2004).

The recent financial crisis has revealed structural problems with the monitoring and surveillance aspects of the stock markets (Katika *et al.*, 2011). In response, regulators in various regions have been developing new regulatory frameworks, such as MiFID II (European Commission, 2010), which increase the level of information disclosure and monitoring and surveillance requirements (Theodoulidis and Diaz, 2012). The increased information disclosure requirements add to the complexity of monitoring and surveillance issues for all stakeholders (market operators, regulators, investors, etc.). Given the complexity of the issue around stock markets nowadays, the solution to the 'stock market' fraud problem still depends on people's cognitive and social abilities to make decisions, and regulatory changes, to perform surveillance and detect market manipulations. There are no 'right' or 'wrong' solutions; only 'good enough' solutions. However, the continuous improvement and development of financial market monitoring and surveillance systems with high analytical capabilities to identify fraud are essential to guaranteeing and preserving an efficient market. This chapter argues that market surveillance and monitoring systems require a systematic framework and comprehensive financial ontology for several reasons: (i) to efficiently manage the vast quantities of financial data; (ii) to foster better communication and knowledge-sharing among analysts; (iii) to provide a mechanism to demonstrate knowledge of the processes of financial fraud; (iv) to understand and share financial fraud logic operations (practices of different manipulation types); (v) to manage relevant facts gathered for case investigations; (vi) to provide early detection techniques of fraudulent activities and develop proactive prevention practices; and (vii) to allow the reuse of these knowledge resources in other related financial contexts.

This research contributes to the development of an ontology-driven framework for stock markets, which aims to provide a knowledge base enabling the proactive prevention of fraud and manipulations in the stock market. The developed domain ontology is integrated and aligned with other ontologies from different sources, as well as being manageable through a systematic ontology framework that uses a multi-layer architecture (Mikroyannidis and Theodoulidis, 2012) for managing the different ontology layers (lexical, domain, data source, and application). The ontology-driven framework adds value in financial fraud monitoring and helps in open investigations by acting as a knowledge management system that manages the amount of data that can be gathered during monitoring and surveillance of stock market fraud, and shares existing manipulation patterns from prosecuted cases among investigators and relevant users.

The remainder of this chapter is organized as follows. Section 2 provides a review of the existing literature on ontologies for stock markets and financial ontologies. The concept of financial fraud ontology is established and gaps in the literature highlighted. Section 3 discusses the research methodology and describes the development of the domain ontology, including the coding and analysis process. In Sec. 4, ontology development and management are elaborated. Section 5 discusses the evaluation of the domain ontology through six cases studies. Finally, Sec. 6 concludes the chapter, points out limitations, and suggests follow-on research.

2. Background

Ontologies are widely perceived to play a vital role in fields such as, business intelligence and information/knowledge management (Mikroyannidis and Theodoulidis, 2010). Previous literature on ontology-related work refers to a diverse range of domains, such as intelligent information integration, collaborative information systems, information retrieval, electronic commerce, and knowledge management (Mikroyannidis and

Theodoulidis, 2007; Rubin and Rubin, 2013; Chen *et al.*, 2013). In relation to the financial domain and, more specifically, stock markets, the literature discusses the development of financial ontologies for specific applications such as stock predictions (Nassirtoussi *et al.*, 2014).

For example, Wang *et al.* (2008) proposed domain ontology for financial news in the context of an application that examined the impact of financial news on stock prices. It further analyzed the impact of different types of financial news to primitives such as price, risk, and earnings through casual map techniques. In follow-up research by the same authors (2011), the domain ontology was extended with news sentiment categories ('positive', 'neural', and 'negative') and an analysis carried out using classification techniques to examine the impact of news on 'stock market' movements. Mellouli *et al.* (2010) proposed domain ontology for various types of financial headline news. The domain ontology classified news into four categories: social, economic, financial, and environmental. The evaluation of the domain ontology was carried out for a limited number of sources as part of a virtual stock exchange system that demonstrated the use of headline news in trading decisions by intelligent agents representing traders. Novalija and Mladenić (2010) proposed a methodology for ontology evolution based on news. The evolution aspects are related to the ontology content and structure, and they used text analysis techniques to extract relevant keywords from news, check them against the ontology, and decide how to incorporate them into the ontology content or revise the ontology structure with the new knowledge. More recently, Chung (2014) developed an intelligent system (BizPro) to extract and categorize qualitative evidence influencing market reactions on a company. BizPro consists of novel text-mining procedures and business intelligence (BI) factor modelling and categorization and was used to profile BI factors of four major IT companies based on 6,859 sentences extracted from 231 news articles published in major news sources.

The main drawback of these efforts is their specific focus on developing ontologies and BI systems for analyzing financial news without considering manipulations or fraud scenarios and related concepts. Furthermore, these domain ontologies and BI systems are evaluated on a limited part of the domain (usually three or four case studies), and thus its applicability is restricted to the specific context of their development. In this sense, arguably these works were not aimed at the development of a systematic and comprehensive framework for use in related contexts, as well as supporting not only the construction and specific application of an ontology or BI System, but also its management, evaluation, and evolution.

Attempts have been made to provide an ontology framework for financial markets. Gottschalk *et al.* (2011) present a stage of growth model for knowledge-management systems to support the investigation and prevention of white-collar crime in business organizations; however, they do not consider specific concepts associated with market manipulation and fraud on stock markets. Cheng *et al.* (2009) proposed an ontology-based approach for BI applications in financial knowledge-management systems. The domain ontology developed covers a part of the 'stock market' domain and, furthermore, includes concepts related to the management of the domain knowledge in order to support decision-making. In that respect, it is similar to this work; however, their domain ontology is limited, as it does not cover concepts relating to fraud and does not provide an ontology framework for management of the domain ontology.

Similarly, the DIP project (Alonso *et al.*, 2005) developed a 'stock market' ontology using the on-to-knowledge methodology for ontology construction. The domain ontology developed includes concepts aimed at explaining the operational aspects of the European stock markets to individual investors. However, it does not contain concepts relevant to fraud and, furthermore, the methodology proposed only covers ontology construction. In contrast, the FF POIROT project (Kingston *et al.*, 2004) proposed a financial fraud ontology to explain the legal frameworks and processes involved in a European context and complemented this ontology with knowledge from published fraud cases. The focus of this work was fraud on cross-border VAT within the EU and investment fraud on the Internet and thus it did not cover fraud concepts on the stock markets. The FIORD project (McCarthy *et al.*, 2013), developed a collaborative networks environment and toolset to support the detection of systemic risk in financial markets. It is aimed at regulators and related bodies requiring real-time monitoring. The domain ontology is based on the Financial Industry Business Ontology (FIBO) (OMG, 2014), an industry initiative to define a financial industry ontology. It focuses on modeling risk and regulations only in a European context and, thus, is limited in scope. Furthermore, it does not contain concepts on fraud.

A domain taxonomy for fraud and manipulation on stock markets was preliminarily developed in previous work by the authors (Diaz *et al.*, 2011a, 2011b). Its aim was to support monitoring and surveillance in stock markets and thus shares the same domain context. However, this work did not propose a systematic ontology framework and was based on a top-down approach for ontology development, which implies that ontology management and evolution is not supported adequately. This work extends the domain taxonomy developed in Diaz *et al.* (2011a, 2011b) in a number of additional dimensions including concepts derived from existing lexical resources (top-down) and 'stock market' fraud cases (bottom-up). Furthermore, the work uses as the basis for the lexical ontology the INVESTOPEDIA online financial dictionary (www.investopedia.com). This is, perhaps, one of the most comprehensive sets of financial term definitions, including taxonomy, plain English interpretations, and examples of the concepts. These are discussed later in this chapter.

In relation to ontology frameworks, the approach adopted in most information management systems, such as SHOE (SHOE, 2003), OntoView (Klein *et al.*, 2002), Sesame (Broekstra *et al.*, 2003), OMM (Sure *et al.*, 2003), PROMPT [Noy and Musen, 2000], and KAON (Bozsak *et al.*, 2002), is simplistic and reveals certain shortcomings because they follow a flat ontology layering architecture (Mikroyannidis and Theodoulidis, 2012). The disadvantage of such ontologies is that their layers are managed independently, making them challenging to integrate, especially when multiple ontologies are introduced. Furthermore, there is a lack of an ontology evolution that can capture and enhance the temporal information contained in ontologies (Mikroyannidis and Theodoulidis, 2012).

On the contrary, this work adopts and extends the multi-layer architecture presented by Mikroyannidis and Theodoulidis (2012). The advantage of using a multi-layer ontology framework is facilitation of ontology lifecycle management by building and maintaining several layers containing ontologies for different purposes developed by various author groups. The architecture helps to improve the manageability of the technologies and demonstrates integration between the different ontologies presented through intra-layer (same layer) or inter-layer (different layer) ontology mapping (Mikroyannidis and Theodoulidis, 2012).

Therefore, we argue that there is a gap in the existing literature in relation to comprehensive domain ontologies to support monitoring and surveillance for stock markets. Furthermore, it argues that the need for comprehensive domain ontology for stock markets and a systematic framework would provide support for the efficient and effective monitoring and surveillance of stock markets across the world. Recent developments in regulatory frameworks, including developments in the USA (US Securities and Exchange Commission, Commission, and Commission, 2010) and Europe (European Commission, 2010) have identified the need for the introduction of extensive information disclosure and reporting requirements

(European Commission, 2012; FSA, 2012). This adds to the complexity of monitoring and surveillance issues and necessitates a cross-market and cross-border perspective of information management. We argue that a systematic ontology framework and comprehensive ontology would help with the complexity of monitoring and surveillance aspects.

3. Methodology

The methodology followed in this work to develop a systematic framework for stock markets is based, first, on using a top-down and bottom-up approach for ontology construction, as shown in Fig. 1, and, second, on adopting and extending the multi-layer architecture presented by Mikroyannidis and Theodoulidis (2012) to meet the needs of monitoring and surveillance of the stock markets.

As shown in Fig. 1, the methodology includes: ontology construction, discussed in Sec. 3, ontology development and management, discussed in Sec. 4, and ontology evaluation, discussed in Sec. 5. Furthermore, the ontology construction uses a combination of top-down and bottom-up approaches that correspond to the initial construction of the domain ontology discussed

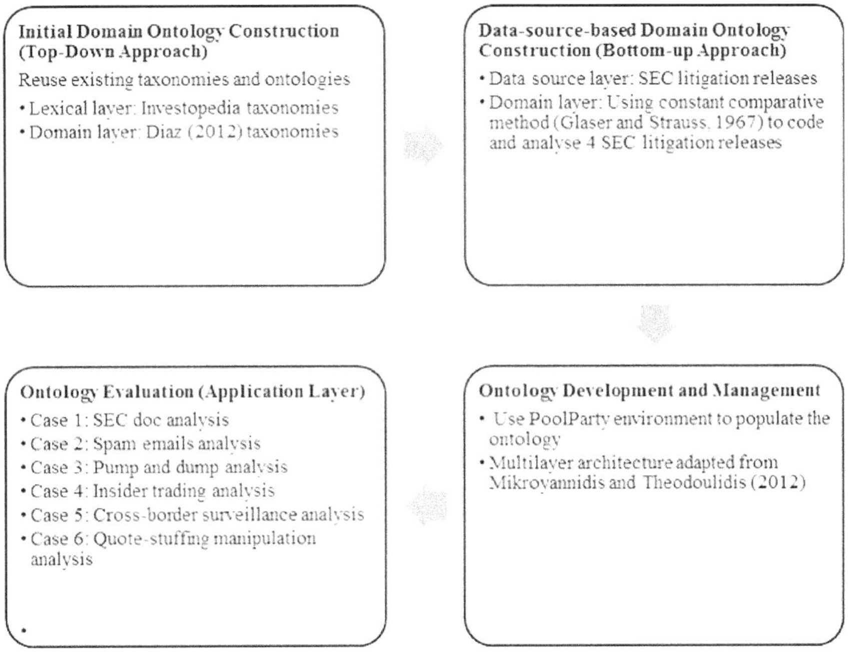

Figure 1. Ontology Construction

in Sec. 3.1 and the data-source-based ontology construction discussed in Sec. 3.2.

The initial domain ontology construction is based on the reuse of existing ontologies or taxonomies for a domain (Brewster 2008). The INVESTOPEDIA dictionary (www.investopedia.com) is used as the lexical layer for the developed domain ontology. Furthermore, the taxonomies of 'stock market' concepts proposed by Diaz *et al.* (2011a, 2011b) have been used.

The data-source-based domain ontology construction followed a bottom-up approach to ontology construction. The domain ontology extended the initial domain ontology with refined and additional concepts from the SEC litigation releases[1] data source. This data source was chosen because it provides a full list of fraud cases investigated and concluded by SEC. The information included in these documents is provided by the court that investigated the case and describes in detail all the evidence and facts that informed its decisions. This means that the level of information provided is sufficiently detailed and thus suitable for ontology construction purposes.

For the data-source-based ontology construction, a focus group was used as a method of knowledge elicitation from financial domain experts, who were asked to identify interesting financial concepts in SEC litigation releases that helped populate the domain ontology with relevant financial fraud concepts. The constant comparative method (Glaser and Strauss 1967; Lincoln and Cuba, 1985) was used to analyze the focus group data. The methodology suggests four distinct stages, *unitizing, categorizing, filing in patterns*, and *member checking*, and the whole process was evaluated by an external auditor (Grove 1988). Finally, the domain ontology was developed using the PoolParty thesaurus management system (http://poolparty.biz/) and was evaluated through six case studies to show the applicability of the domain ontology.

3.1. *Initial domain ontology construction*

The top-down ontology construction used the INVESTOPEDIA dictionary and the taxonomies proposed by Diaz *et al.* (2011a, 2011b). We used INVESTOPEDIA as a starting-point to develop a lexical layer providing the definitional context for the concepts in the domain ontology, as well as providing plain English explanations and associated examples. The INVESTOPEDIA dictionary has 28 main concept categories (for example, accounting, stock and taxes). Each category has relevant concepts including

[1]See http://www.sec.gov/litigation/litreleases.shtml.

their definition, plain English explanation and examples. INVESTOPEDIA has some limitations in relation to this work. It does not consider fraud as a separate category, and thus the relevant fraud concepts are distributed unevenly across the other categories. For example, the concept 'pump and dump' is classified under 'financial BuzzWords'.

Furthermore, many are duplicated and classified under more than one category. For example, 'Securities and Exchange Commission, SEC' is classified into three separate categories: 'acronyms', 'investor relations' and 'stocks'. Finally, INVESTOPEDIA is not up-to-date, with many manipulation concepts, such as 'front running research', 'scalping', and 'commodity flow at delivery points', not present or improperly defined.

To increase the richness and relevance of the concepts, we also considered the reuse of a group of taxonomies proposed by Diaz *et al.* (2011a, 2011b). These adapted a simple taxonomy proposed by Putnins (2009) following a 'top-down' approach based on a comprehensive literature review undertaken to construct a domain taxonomy containing concepts for understanding market monitoring and surveillance systems. Concepts are organized into three main categories of taxonomy: (1) the basic concepts present in different manipulation scenarios; (2) the interacting agents in financial market systems; and (3) the sub-systems, components, and information-management concepts of a fraud detection engine. Fig. 2 shows an overview of the taxonomy, including in total 274 sub-concepts under the eight concepts.

For example, 'agent' represents the fraudster that performs a manipulation by taking an action. The 'action' could be classified as *information-based action* (related to the release of false information or rumors to tempt investors and mislead their trading decisions); *trade-based action* (attempt

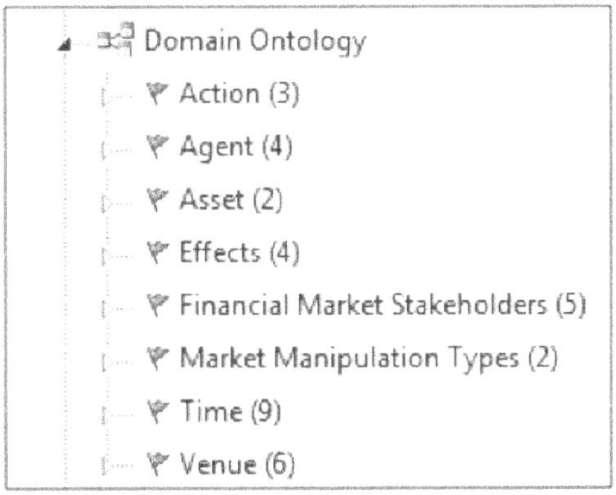

Figure 2. Overview of the Domain Taxonomy (Diaz, 2012)

to manipulate stock by buying and selling stocks, misleading the markets by moving the price artificially to levels that are convenient to the manipulator); or *action-based action* (changing the actual or perceived value of the assets by performing actions that occur outside the stock markets, for example, selling a branch of a company and failing to inform stockholders).

Furthermore, 'venue' describes where investors and manipulators organize their trade manipulations. Agents could target any type of asset, such as stocks, penny stocks, money manipulations, bonds, derivatives, or structured notes. The taxonomy also included a temporal dimension to describe the 'time' of manipulation. The consequences of the manipulation are described in the 'effects' concept to show the patterns that could be identified in the behavior of agents, or in trading, orders of trade and executions of the former. 'Market manipulation types' describes the different manipulation types existing in the financial market.

The work of Diaz *et al.* (2011a, 2011b) helped to build an organized body of knowledge from the literature; however, the study has not been extended to construct a comprehensive domain ontology. Thus, this research contributes to building a financial ontology for fraud purposes with general concepts containing a large set of financial concepts and definitions. In particular, the developed domain ontology contains 317 sub-concepts under nine concepts. As shown in Table 3, two main concepts have been added to the domain ontology, namely, 'laws and regulations' and 'manipulation participants'. Furthermore, many sub-concepts have been added and many existing concepts renamed based on expert recommendations. Furthermore, the intra-layer links between concepts in the same layer and the inter-layer links between concepts in different layers have been defined.

3.2. *Data-source-based domain ontology construction*

The bottom-up approach to ontology construction relies on a suitable and comprehensive data source corpus (SEC litigation releases) relevant to financial fraud to propose additions and alterations to the initial ontology. Domain experts were invited to act as coders and to identify the knowledge within the texts to populate the ontology with the relevant financial fraud concepts. Specifically, the focus group was used as a method of knowledge elicitation from financial domain experts. All participants have a finance background, studying for either a Masters or a PhD in Finance. The focus group aimed to identify interesting financial concepts within the SEC litigation releases and to populate the domain ontology with the relevant financial fraud concepts. They helped to build a dictionary of financial concepts for fraud purposes and map these instances to the relevant ontology concepts. Moreover, they were allowed to add, merge, and modify concepts and suggest better naming for existing concepts. The output of the focus group was to produce a domain ontology that met the saturation criterion, as discussed later, and, thus, was considered satisfactory.

Four litigation releases were selected based on the four main manipulation types identified in the initial domain ontology construction; these are *insider trading*, *pump and dump*, *front running*, and *marking the close*. In relation to group sizes of domain experts working in the elicitation stage, Morgan (1998) recommends using small groups when participants are likely to have a lot to contribute and when topics are complex and controversial. Accordingly, the total size of the chosen focus group was ten participants. The coding process started with two participants who analyzed one of the releases (a 'pump and dump' case) as a pilot test. A following second round involved eight participants divided into four groups of two; each pair shared and analyzed one litigation release and recorded their annotation directly in the NVIVO software (QSR, 2014). Two facilitators guided the session. Table 1 shows the focus group agenda for the two rounds.

This work used the constant comparative method to analyze the focus group data in order to build the domain ontology. The method was first introduced by Glaser and Strauss (1967) and expanded by Lincoln and Cuba (1985). Originally, the method was developed for use in grounded theory methodology, but it is now widely used to analyze qualitative data. In particular, the methodology explains the process of organizing data such as words, sentences, and paragraphs into existing or unidentified categories [Grove 1988].

As shown in Fig. 3, the methodology uses four distinct stages: *unitizing, categorizing, filing in patterns,* and *member checking.*

3.2.1. *Unitizing*

This stage analyses the process of annotation by the participants. In the first round, participants analyzed the 'pump and dump' case as a pilot. In total, participant A annotated 99 concepts and participant B 78 concepts. The main finding of this stage was that participants were not consistent in some parts of their annotation. A second observation was that neither participant paid attention to the specific terms requiring annotation as they were annotating a whole sentence. Moreover, in general, participants were not interested in the legal side of the litigation release, perhaps because of their backgrounds. Finally, there were many terms and concepts of which

Table 1. **Focus Group Process Overview**

Items	1st Round	2nd Round
Number of participants	2	8
Number of facilitators	2	2
Number of analysed cases	1	4
Manipulation type	Pump and dump	Pump and dump, insider trading, marking the close, front running
Stock names involved in the manipulation	Mobile Ready Entertainment Corp.	Pump and dump (Mobile Ready Entertainment Corp), insider trading (Bio-Medicus, Inc.), marking the close (Avicena Group, Inc., Neutron Enterprises, Inc., Hydrogen Hybrid Technologies, Inc., and Northern Ethanol, Inc.,) front running (Creswell Equities, Inc)
Length of the case	34 pages	By order: 35,18,37,14 pages
Cases web link	http://www.sec.gov/litigation/complaints/2008/comp20644.pdf	By Order: http://www.sec.gov/litigation/complaints/2008/comp20644.pdf, http://www.sec.gov/litigation/complaints/2006/comp19929.pdf, http://www.sec.gov/litigation/complaints/2009/comp20899.pdf, http://www.sec.gov/litigation/complaints/2010/comp21446.pdf
Litigation release number	21024	By order: 21024, 19929, 20899, 21446
Number of sessions	1 session (5 hours)	**Session 1**: 20 minutes (recorded and analysed) **Session 2:** average 4.30 hours (recorded and analysed)
Session agenda	A presentation demonstrates the research and focus group objectives. Focus group tasks. Some guidelines about the coding and mapping to the ontology classes.	**Session 1:** A presentation demonstrates the research and focus group objectives Focus group tasks. Some guidelines about the coding and mapping to the ontology classes. Present a summary of the case to the participants to save time. Provide participants with a hard copy of the litigation release and ontology classes. Arrange for the second session. **Session 2:** A quick presentation about the ontology classes providing examples of mapping process. A quick demonstration about how to use NVIVO.
Session tasks	Read the given document (SEC litigation release) to obtain an overview of the document structure	**Session 1:** Read the given document (SEC litigation release) to obtain an overview of the document structure in their own time. Annotate interesting concepts in their own time.

(*Continued*)

Table 1. (*Continued*)

Items	1st Round	2nd Round
	Annotate interesting concepts Every 2 participants had a hard copy of the SEC litigation releases. Discuss with your colleague the annotated concept Map the annotated concepts to ontology classes Adding new ontology classes if necessary or providing better naming for the existing ontology concepts Load the annotated concepts and ontology mapping to the NVIVO 9:0	**Session 2:** Discuss with your colleague the annotated concept. Map the annotated concepts to ontology classes. Adding new ontology classes if necessary or providing better naming for the existing ontology concepts. Load the annotated concepts and ontology mapping to the NVIVO.

participants had no previous knowledge despite their financial background; therefore, researchers suggested the use of INVESTOPEDIA to discover and explore the meaning. These findings were taken into consideration and explained to second-round participants.

The second round was organized as follows. First, participants read the cases and annotated the interesting concepts in their own time. At the second meeting, each pair of participants discussed their case and the annotated concepts to agree which concepts should be recorded in NVIVO and later mapped to the ontology concepts. From the different cases, these annotated concepts were used to build a financial dictionary for fraud purposes. Table 2 shows the number of concepts annotated and agreed per case. The participants considered the ontology concepts and annotated those that could describe the case and the patterns that could help the ontology to explain similar manipulation types in future. The number of concepts varies for many reasons, including case size, different views between participants in analyzing the case, the nature of the manipulation scheme, and background information provided for each case.

In the 'pump and dump' case, participants C and D largely agreed with the annotations from the first-round participants. However, they considered adding the financial laws and regulations aspects referred to by courts in the manipulators' cases. Furthermore, participants were eager to annotate

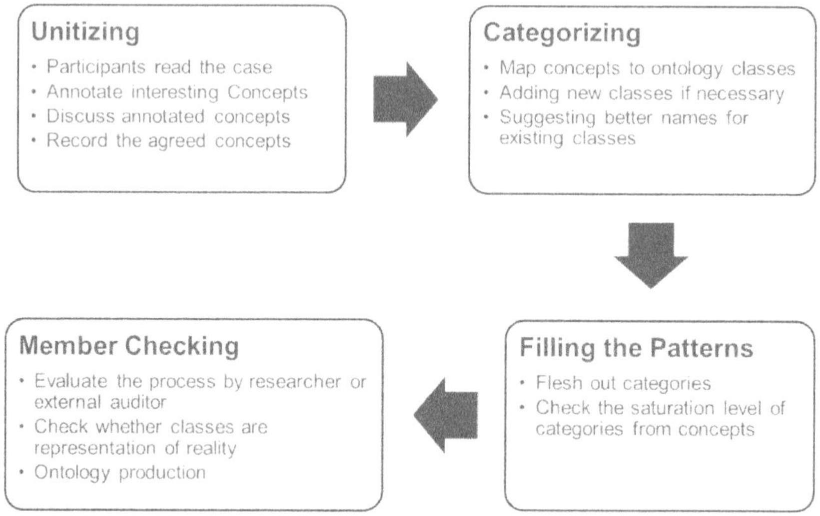

Figure 3. Constant Comparative Method (Grove, 2010)

Table 2. Total Number of Annotated Concepts Per Case

Case	Participant	Total Number of Annotated Concepts
Pump and dump	C, D	144
Insider trading	E, F	111
Marking the close	G, H	129
Front running	I, J	87

the description of agents through individual profiles such as agent's name or address. Furthermore, both participants considered the description of the corporation involved in the case. Overall, participants C and D annotated 144 concepts.

In the 'insider trading' case, participants E and F were more concerned in identifying not only the manipulators but also other participants involved in the manipulation, such as intermediaries who facilitated the process or victims of the scheme. Participants noted that the agent had been involved in different manipulation cases and suspended from the Commission for 12 months, prohibiting work with any brokers, dealers, or investment. Thus, they annotated all related background concepts about the agent's history so that ontology users could avoid dealing with this agent in future. Interestingly, the participants decided to highlight the timeline of the manipulation before, during and after. Overall, participants E and F annotated 111 concepts.

Participants G and H annotated 129 concepts from the 'marking the close' case. They were concerned with identifying the evidence and facts about patterns that could be used in the ontology to identify potential wash sale, matched order, and marking the close manipulation cases. In particular, structured evidence was more dominant in this case as participants annotated how manipulators artificially inflate stock prices, which later decline. Furthermore, participants tried to annotate concepts to show the means of manipulation and different beneficiaries from the scheme. Interestingly, participants differentiated the methods used by the agent, either to provide clients with false or misleading information or to conceal information about his/her association with nominee accounts. Furthermore, the participants considered the agent's different ways of communication in directing his/her manipulative schemes when colluding with other participants.

Participants I and J analyzed the 'front running' case and annotated 87 concepts. They were concerned with describing the evidence and patterns used by the agent to manipulate the trading system. The case was not officially classified by the court as front-running litigation, so the participants annotated equivalent concepts to describe the manipulation scheme. Participants were concerned with fully describing the orders handled by the agent.

3.2.2. *Categorizing*

The participants were asked to map annotated concepts to ontology concepts considering adding/merging concepts if necessary or suggesting better names for existing concepts. The facilitator presented the different concepts and their definitions and descriptions.

For example, in a selected 'pump and dump' litigation case (see Table 1 for litigation reference) the SEC filed a complaint against 'Magolnic and Mora', the cochief executive officers of Mobile Ready Entertainment Corp (SYMBOL: MRDY), a publicly traded company quoted on the Pink OTC Markets, Inc. ('Pink Sheets'). They were involved in a fraudulent 'pump and dump' stock scheme in addition to insider trading and securities registration violations of MRDY. This was achieved through distribution of false and misleading press releases after December 2006, and possibly through distribution of spam emails in March 2007. The investigation found that several press releases contained disingenuous revenue projections and mentioned indistinct business relationships. Nonetheless, they each sold substantial amounts of restricted shares held in the company in transactions that were not exempt from registration. In particular, following completion of Form 144, a number of misleading press releases were issued on consecutive days towards the middle of July 2007. Collectively these false and misleading press releases, spam emails, and securities registration violations impacted the market for Mobile Ready's stock.

When analyzing this litigation case, participants mapped mostly annotated concepts to the following: 'actions (what)', 'agent (who)', and 'financial market stakeholders', as shown in Table 3. 'Actions (what)' had the highest percentage, 6.36%, 'agent (who)' had 1.28% of the concepts describing the manipulators in the case, and 'financial market stakeholders' had 0.54% of concepts describing different stakeholders such as 'investors', 'shareholders seeking to obtain exemptions under Rule 144', and 'market', such as 'over-the-counter securities market'.

For instance, analysis of 'actions (what)' shows that participants wanted to map the different manipulation actions explained in this litigation. A first action was when manipulators disseminated false information to investors. Concepts such as 'identified contracts for future business that did not exist' and 'issued materially false and misleading press releases' were mapped to the 'information-based\false information' class. The second action was when manipulators used a company called '144opinions' to manage their legal letters. This company helped the manipulators to fraudulently facilitate the sale of securities in violation of the registration provisions of federal securities laws. The participants, therefore, suggested adding the concepts 'opinion mill', and 'legal opinion letters' to describe any legal violation evidence. A third identified action was when the manipulators hyped stock and then sold shares to gain profit. Thus, in the 'trade-based' class, participants mapped concepts such as 'dump more than two million restricted shares of Mobile Ready for approximately $70,000 in profits' and 'issuing shares of complete identity to themselves and to friends, family, and persons' to 'trade-based\trade\sell'. A fourth action related to the securities registration violation. Participants could not find a class to explain it; therefore, they suggested adding a new class called 'other related trade activities' with sub-concepts 'non-registered offering' and 'registered offering' to map concepts such as 'never registered any of the offering'.

As with insider trading and front-running litigation cases, participants suggested adding a class to describe the means of manipulation through 'means', but in this litigation, they suggested 'regulation specific actions'.

Table 3. **Pump and Dump Categories Analysis**

Main Classes	Node	Percentage Coverage	Total
	Nodes\\Financial Ontology\FinancialFraud\Actions (What)\Action-Based\Regulation specific actions	1.57%	
	Nodes\\Financial Ontology\FinancialFraud\Actions (What)\Information-Based\False Information	0.99%	
	Nodes\\Financial Ontology\FinancialFraud\Actions (What)\Information-Based\Legal Opinion Letters	1.05%	
Actions (What)	Nodes\\Financial Ontology\FinancialFraud\Actions (What)\Information-Based\Misleading Information	1.73%	6.36%
	Nodes\\Financial Ontology\FinancialFraud\Actions (What)\Information-Based\Opinion Mill	0.04%	
	Nodes\\Financial Ontology\FinancialFraud\Actions (What)\Trade-Based\Other Related Trade Activity\Non-registered Offerings	0.08%	
	Nodes\\Financial Ontology\FinancialFraud\Actions (What)\Trade-Based\Trade\sell	0.88%	
Financial Regulation	Nodes\\Financial Ontology\FinancialFraud\Financial Regulation	1.88%	1.88%
	Nodes\\Financial Ontology\FinancialFraud\Agent (Who)\Benefit\Third party	0.07%	
Agent (Who)	Nodes\\Financial Ontology\FinancialFraud\Agent (Who)\Characteristics\Corporation	0.29%	1.28%
	Nodes\\Financial Ontology\FinancialFraud\Agent (Who)\Characteristics\Individual	0.69%	
	Nodes\\Financial Ontology\FinancialFraud\Agent (Who)\Membership\Insider	0.23%	
	Nodes\\Financial Ontology\FinancialFraud\Effects (Consequences)\Benefit\Direct	0.24%	
Effects (Consequences)	Nodes\\Financial Ontology\FinancialFraud\Effects (Consequences)\Benefit\Indirect	0.07%	1.00%
	Nodes\\Financial Ontology\FinancialFraud\Effects (Consequences)\Evidence and Patterns\Legal	0.69%	
	Nodes\\Financial Ontology\FinancialFraud\Financial Market Stakeholders\Investors	0.07%	
	Nodes\\Financial Ontology\FinancialFraud\Financial Market Stakeholders\Market	0.22%	

(Continued)

Table 3. (*Continued*)

Main Classes	Node	Percentage Coverage	Total
Financial Market Stakeholders	Nodes\\Financial Ontology\FinancialFraud\Financial Market Stakeholders\Regulators	0.04%	0.54%
	Nodes\\Financial Ontology\FinancialFraud\Financial Market Stakeholders\Support Organizations\Services\Financial\Data Provision\Structured	0.21%	
Time (When)	Nodes\\FinancialOntology\FinancialFraud\Time (When)\Time of Year	0.06%	0.06%
Asset (Target)	Nodes\\FinancialOntology\FinancialFraud\Asset (Target)\Financial\Equity\Pink sheet	0.07%	0.07%
Market manipulation (Types)	Nodes\\Financial Ontology\Marketmanipulation(types)\Runs and Raids\Hype and Dump	0.06%	0.06%

They also added 'financial regulation' to include all the laws and regulations used by courts against manipulators.

3.2.3. *Filing in patterns*

This stage aims to flesh out the categories after extensive data collection and unitizing. All annotated concepts are checked to see whether they have been classified into relevant categories and whether these categories have become saturated (Livingstone and Lunt, 1994). Table 4 shows how many concepts were categorized under the main concepts of the ontology.

As shown in Table 4, participants were concerned about describing the agent's 'action', which represents the highest percentage of categorization in the ontology — 27.78%. Furthermore, the litigation releases have different sections describing the various actions taken by manipulators, especially in the summary and facts sections. Thus, participants saturated this class with 27.78% of concepts from manipulator actions related to being information-, trade-, or action-based. Generally, these actions are associated with timeline events to describe the temporal dimension of the manipulation activity. Therefore, participants decided to categorize concepts describing when the manipulators took action to execute the manipulation. Thus, the 'time (when)' class has the second highest percentage, with 23.02% of concepts annotated by participants. In order to describe the consequences and effects of these actions on the efficiency of the market, participants classified 20.41%

Table 4. Analysis of the Main Classes of the Financial Ontology

Main Classes	Insider Trading Case	Marking the Close Case	Front Running Case	Pump and Dump Case	Total
Actions (What)	6.73%	4.86%	9.83%	6.36%	27.78%
Agent (Who)	4.40%	0.48%	2.44%	1.28%	8.60%
Asset (Target)	1.58%	0.18%	0.58%	0.07%	2.41%
Effects (Consequences)	7.63%	1.15%	10.63%	1.00%	20.41%
Financial Market Stakeholders	0.26%	0.44%	5.37%	0.54%	6.61%
Market Manipulation (Types)	2.94%	0.16%	2.87%	0.06%	6.03%
Time (When)	12.01%	0.25%	10.70%	0.06%	23.02%
Venue (Where)	0.00%	0.22%	1.60%	0.00%	1.82%
Laws and Regulations	0.21%	0.58%	0.00%	1.88%	2.67%
Manipulation Participants	0.53%	0.00%	0.00%	0.00%	0.53%

of patterns and evidence describing the effect of agents' behavior, or trading orders and actions on market integrity.

As in the previous stage, a similar process and analysis were followed for the remaining concepts: 'agent (who)', 'asset (target)', 'market manipulation types', 'effects (consequences)', 'financial market stakeholders', 'venues (where)', 'laws and regulations' and 'time (when)'.

3.2.4. *Member checking*

This stage enables the researcher to reconstruct the data to check whether it is a reasonable representation of reality. Accordingly, the researcher proposes the current version of the domain ontology, which includes nine concepts: action, asset, effects, financial market stakeholders, laws and regulations, manipulation participants, market manipulation types, time, and venue. The complete developed ontology is shown in Fig. 4.

4. Ontology Development and Management

The domain ontology was developed using the PoolParty thesaurus management system. In the literature, there are many ontology editors, such as Protégé (Stanford, 2009). This work uses PoolParty because it supports the

Figure 4. The Developed Financial Ontology

multi-layer architecture shown in Fig. 5. More specifically, it helps to build and maintain ontologies using a web-based environment integrated with text-mining and linked-data technologies. It is designed for use by domain experts to collaboratively author the ontology, and it provides functionality for data integration from different sources (structured and unstructured), semantic search, similarity search, annotation and tag recommender, auto-complete, SPARQL queries, and a semantic index builder. As shown in Fig. 4, the financial ontology has four main layers of concept: application ontology, data source ontology, domain ontology, and lexical ontology. Each layer has its

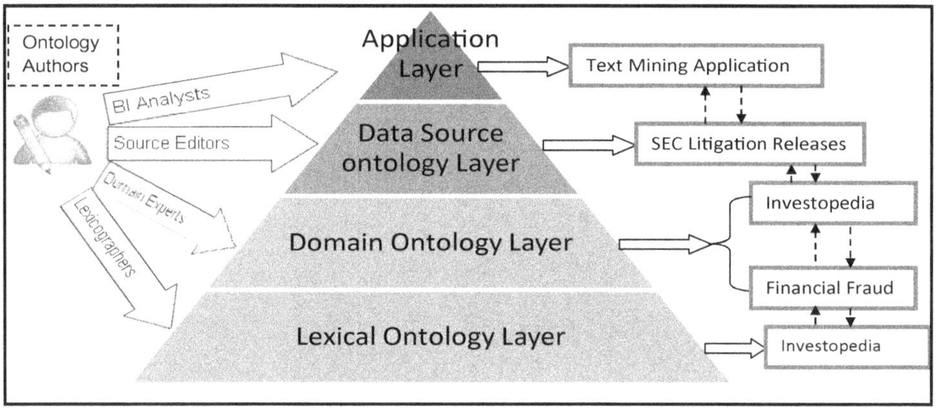

Figure 5. Ontology Architecture (Mikroyannidis and Theodoulidis, 2012)

own hierarchical concepts. The total number of ontology concepts is 721 with 36 alternative labels.

The ontology layers are presented in a multi-layer framework (pyramid), as shown in Fig. 5, demonstrating a range of basic and generic financial concepts in the lower layer to the more specific concepts of the upper layers. Each layer is developed and maintained in PoolParty by a different group of authors, using the different tools offered for ontology management. From bottom to top, the lexical layer was built, as explained in Sec. 3.1 (initial domain ontology construction). The domain ontology layer has been constructed following the constant comparative method, as explained in Sec. 3.2. The data source ontology layer contains the set of concepts necessary to describe the sources used to build the domain ontology. Finally, the application ontology layer contains the text-mining application that automates the process of extracting financial concepts from texts and provides an appropriate knowledge-base about 'stock market' fraud.

The different layers of the developed ontology framework were linked through inter-layer links in order to integrate them into the ontology architecture shown in Fig. 5. The main linking mechanism used was concept mapping. In each ontology layer, a number of concepts were linked to concepts of other layers via semantic relationships, resulting in inter-layer links. Furthermore, each layer includes relationships between concepts in the same layer called intra-layer links. Inter-layer and intra-layer links were implemented using the PoolParty semantic relationship called '*related* (R)', which is called an associative relationship and can be used to indicate any kind of semantic relation between concepts.

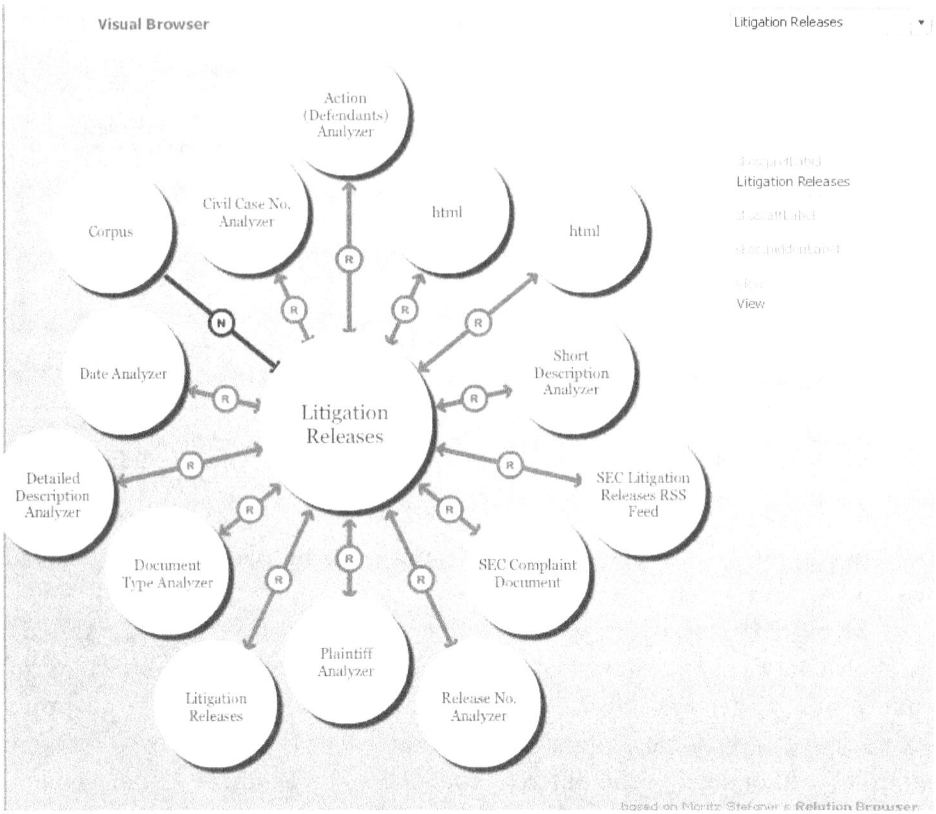

Figure 6. Litigation Release Relationships

The number of broader/narrower relationships is 683 and of related relations is 36. For example, Fig. 6 shows the data source used in the domain ontology and how it is linked to different concepts within or between layers. The navigation in PoolParty is intuitive; for example, selecting the 'releases' concept shows instantly what relationships are associated with it. Similarly, the intra-layer mapping of the 'litigation release' concept is the 'IE_Application\DocumentFormat\TextualFormat\SEC Litigation Releases RSS Feed' and 'IE_Application\DocumentFormat\TextualFormat\html', which represents the document format used to evaluate the ontology. Given that some litigation releases have an SEC complaints document, another semantic relationship is added. Furthermore, the litigation releases were analyzed through a text-mining application using different analyzers, such as 'action (defendant)', 'date', 'document type', 'plaintiff', 'release no.', 'short description', 'detailed description', and 'civil case no.'. In terms of inter-layer mappings, the concept 'litigation releases' has relationships with 'SEC Website\Enforcement\litigation releases' and 'DocumentFormat\DocumentType\html' in the data source ontology layer.

5. Ontology Evaluation

The domain ontology is evaluated through six case studies to show the applicability of the domain ontology. All of the cases used INVESTOPEDIA as the lexical layer. Through the cases, the domain ontology layer played a vital role in providing the underlying framework for the extraction process and capturing information related to 'stock market' fraud. Concepts such as asset, action, manipulation type, manipulation participant, venue, time, and effects were used to capture fraud concepts.

For instance, the first case study demonstrated an application of text mining that extracts information from the SEC enforcement portal in the appropriate knowledge base format to facilitate users' acquisition, maintenance, and access to knowledge and to improve search results (Zaki and Theodoulidis, 2013). Instantiation of the proposed ontology framework was linked to the data source layer that had the SEC litigation releases. The fraud concepts in these litigations were mapped to the domain ontology layer concepts using a text-mining application. For example, as shown in Fig. 7, the text-mining application automatically captured Robert J. Gallivan, the 'manipulation participant' who breached a duty of trust and confidence of his company *C&B consulting Firm,* and as insider trading 'action' through *recommending the purchase of different stocks to his relatives, friend, and cousin.* This 'manipulation type' is called *insider trading* and violates the *Harbour, Mid Valley and Valencia* securities 'assets'. The manipulation happened in *OTC* 'venue' from *09/09/2003 to September 2008.* In this case, the 'effects' of the manipulation included gaining unlawful and combined profits reaching $58,453. Overall, the proposed ontology framework can answer questions such as 'what', 'where', 'when', 'how', and 'which' in the case, and on the basis of these answers it can construct a storyline.

The other five case studies cover various 'stock market' manipulation activities such as 'insider trading', 'pump and dump', 'high-frequency quote stuffing', 'marking the close', and 'cross-border fraud'. A similar process and analysis were followed for the other cases. For example, the second case study sought to automatically extract key attributes and characteristics of different unstructured sources generated as part of 'touting campaigns' (Zaki *et al.*, 2010, 2011). In relation to the data source ontology, Case 2 extended it with concepts related to emails, the lexical layer with the OTC securities list, and,

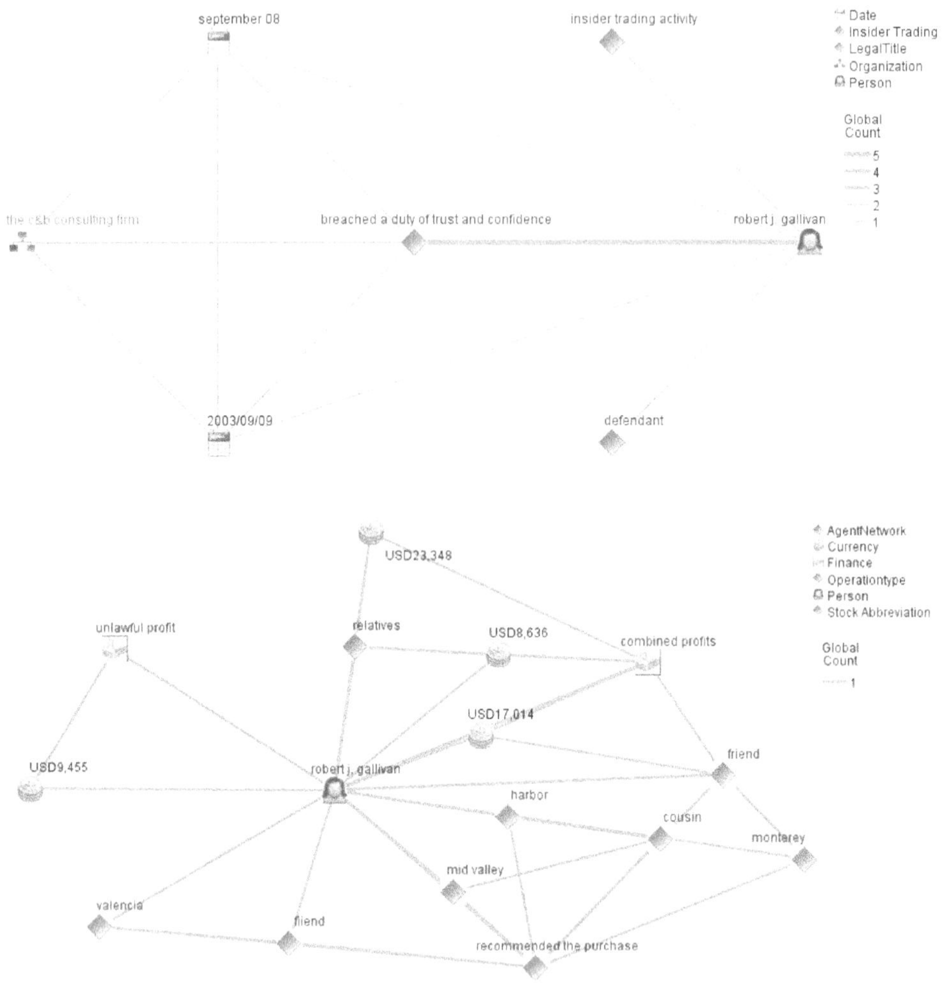

Figure 7. Case 1 Text Mining Analyzers

in relation to the domain ontology, instantiated it with concepts related to 'pump and dump' manipulation type and OTC venue.

The third case proposed a business intelligence (BI) service system for financial market monitoring and surveillance in order to produce alarms for possible securities fraud cases (Zaki *et al.*, 2012). Regarding the data source ontology, Case 3 extended it with concepts related to press releases and Form 144 data from SEC, and, in relation to the domain ontology, instantiated it with concepts related to the 'opinion mill' manipulation type and 'Pink Sheets' venue.

The fourth case investigated the insider trading manipulation case study from the NASDAQ market. The case study used real trading data as well as a collection of unstructured sources related to a case of market manipulation that occurred in the NASDAQ venue (Diaz *et al.*, 2011a). In relation to the data source ontology, Case 4 extended it with concepts related to news from FACTIVA, company financial information from COMPUSTAT and Form 4 data from SEC, and, in relation to the domain ontology, instantiated it with concepts related to 'insider trading' manipulation and 'NASDAQ' venue.

The fifth case study investigated cross-border market surveillance activities. The case study used real trading data for one of four microcap stocks (Diaz *et al.*, 2012). In relation to the data source ontology, Case 5 used the same as in Case 4, and, in relation to the domain ontology, instantiated it with concepts related to the various 'cross-border' manipulation types and 'FRANKFURT' venue.

Finally, the sixth case study presented high-frequency trading analysis of a particular trading scenario and discussed how quote stuffing can affect the function of trading systems (Diaz and Theodoulidis, 2012). In relation to the data source ontology, Case 6 extended it with concepts related to the FIX format for trades and quotes and the NASDAQ On-Demand data source, and, in relation to the domain ontology, instantiated it with concepts related to the 'ETF' asset, the 'HFT quote stuffing' manipulation type and 'NYSE' and 'BATS' venues. Furthermore, this case extended the time-modelling parts of the domain ontology, considering timescales to be more appropriate to the high-frequency trading context.

Overall, the different cases substantially extended the data source ontology and domain ontology with a wide range of concepts from various venues, manipulation types, and assets. More importantly, the six case studies demonstrate the applicability of the proposed framework and its use in a wide range of applications, while concurrently providing evidence for the flexibility of expanding and modifying the existing domain ontology with new concepts (ontology evolution).

6. Conclusions

This work proposed a systematic framework for the development and management of 'stock market' ontologies based on a multi-layering architecture that supports ontology construction and management. Furthermore, the chapter discussed the construction of the domain ontology using top-down and bottom-up approaches and demonstrated the deployment of the proposed framework through the development of domain ontology using the PoolParty platform.

A key contribution of the work is the use of techniques to bring together and integrate domain knowledge from existing sources with new knowledge derived from the analysis of unstructured sources based on 'stock market' fraud cases reported by the Securities Exchange Commission. The implications for this contribution are significant in many respects. This process could be extended to support intelligent search queries on the SEC enforcement portal and easier access to existing information. In addition, this process is sufficiently generic to be applied to other parts of the domain and to integrate the resulting knowledge with the domain ontology. Finally, the domain ontology was evaluated through six case studies that demonstrate and evaluate deployment of the framework and domain ontology in different types of 'stock market' monitoring and surveillance applications.

Nonetheless, the work has several limitations. The domain ontology provides limited semantic reasoning on its structure. This needs to be extended in order to facilitate automatic reasoning and to support enhanced ontology evolution. Furthermore, the six cases, although a substantial undertaking, do not represent the entirety of the possible fraud cases. In terms of future work, regarding construction of the ontology, it is still possible to enhance and expand it with semantic reasoning and, in addition, to expand the cases to include new manipulation schemes and corresponding concepts on the basis of the SEC and other possible sources. For example, high-frequency trading and stuff-quoting examples of possible stock market manipulation cases should be included (Katika *et al.*, 2011).

Given the dynamics of the domain and the never-ending need to support ontology evolution, future work should also examine the suitability of the proposed multi-layer architecture, as financial knowledge and concepts are rapidly evolving, making it difficult to keep any knowledgebase up-to-date. It might be appropriate to introduce mechanisms such as time stamping (valid/transaction time) to deal with concept evolution and the resulting ontology structure evolution. Finally, another possible direction for future work is evaluation of the framework and domain ontology through involvement of domain experts from the stock market and other stakeholders, such as lawyers, investigators, and analysts, in order to cater for different perspectives and views of ontology.

References

Alonso, S. L., Bas, J. L., Bellido, S., Contreras, J., Benjamins, R., and Gomez, J. M. (2005). Financial Ontology: WP10: Case study eBanking. DIP deliverable D. Retrieved from http://dip.semanticweb.org/documents/D10-7-Stock-Market-Ontology.pdf [Accessed: 30 April 2017].

Bozsak E., Ehrig, M., and Handschuh, S. (2002). KAON — Towards a large scale semantic web. In Bauknecht K., Tjoa A.M. and Quirchmayr G. (eds.), *E-Commerce and Web Technologies. EC-Web 2002*. Lecture Notes in Computer Science, Vol 2455. Berlin, Heidelberg: Springer.

Brewster, C. (2008). *Mind the Gap: Bridging from Text to Ontological Knowledge*. Retrieved from http://ethos.bl.uk/OrderDetails.do?uin=uk.bl.ethos.544561.

Broekstra, J., Kampman, A., and Van Harmelen, F. (2003). Sesame: An architecture for storing and querying RDF data and schema information. In *Proc. First Int. Semantic Web Conference on The Semantic Web* (ISWC '02), Ian Horrocks and James A. Hendler (eds.). London, UK: Springer-Verlag, pp. 54–68.

Chen, Y.-J., Chu, H.-C., Chen, Y.-M., and Chao, C.-Y. (2013). Adapting domain ontology for personalized knowledge search and recommendation. *Inform. Management*, 50(6), pp. 285–303.

Cheng, H., Lu, Y.-C., and Sheu, C. (2009). An ontology-based business intelligence application in a financial knowledge management system. *Expert Syst. Appl.*, 36(2), pp. 3614–3622.

Chung, W. (2014). BizPro: Extracting and categorizing business intelligence factors from textual news articles. *Int. J. Inform. Management*, 34(2), pp. 272–284.

Diaz, D., Theodoulidis, B., and Sampaio, P. (2011a). Analysis of stock market manipulations using knowledge discovery techniques applied to intraday trade prices. *Expert Syst. Appls.* 38(10), pp. 12757–12771.

Diaz, D., Zaki, M., Theodoulidis, B., and Sampaio, P. (2011b). A systematic framework for the analysis and development of financial market monitoring systems. In *2011 Annual SRII Global Conference*, pp. 145–153.

Diaz, D. and Theodoulidis, B. (2012). Financial markets monitoring and surveillance: A quote stuffing case study. Available at SSRN http://dx.doi.org/10.2139/ssrn.2193636.

Diaz, D., Theodoulidis, B., and Abioye, E. (2012). Cross-border challenges in financial markets monitoring and surveillance: A case study of customer-driven service value networks. In *2012 Annual SRII Global Conference*, pp. 146–157.

Dotsika, F. (2009). Uniting formal and informal descriptive power: Reconciling ontologies with folksonomies. *Int. J. Inform. Management*, 29(5), pp. 407–415.

European Commission. (2010). Investment Services Directive — Markets in Financial Instruments Directive (MiFID). Retrieved from https://ec.europa.eu/info/business-economy-euro/banking-and-finance/financial-markets/securities-markets/investment-services-and-regulated-markets-markets-financial-instruments-directive-mifid_en [Accessed: 30 April 2017].

FSA. (2012). Summary of the MiFID II proposals. Retrieved from http://www.fsa.gov.uk/about/what/international/mifid/summary [Accessed: 30 April 2017].

Glaser, R. and Strauss, R. (1967). *The Discovery of Grounded Theory*. Chicago, Aldine.

Gottschalk, P., Filstad, C., Glomseth, R., and Solli-Sæther, H. (2011). Information management for investigation and prevention of white-collar crime. *Int. J. Inform. Management*, 31(3), pp. 226–233.
Grove, R. W. (1988). An analysis of the constant comparative method. *Qualitative Stud. Educ.* (3), pp. 273–279.
Gruber, T. R. (1993). A translation approach to portable ontology specifications. *Knowledge Acquisition*, 5(2), pp. 199–220.
Katika, A., Theodoulidis, B., and Diaz, D. (2011). Investigating financial fraud in high frequency trading: Context and drivers. Available at SSRN: http://dx.doi.org/10.2139/ssrn.1974911.
Kayed, A., El-Qawasmeh, E., and Qawaqneh, Z. (2010). Ranking web sites using domain ontology concepts. *Inform. and Management*, 47(7–8), pp. 350–355.
Kingston, J., Schafer, B., and Vandenberghe, W. (2004). Towards a financial fraud ontology: A legal modelling approach. *Artif. Intelli. Law*, 12(4), pp. 419–446.
Klein, M., Fensel, D., Kiryakov, A., and Ognyanoff, D. (2002). Ontoview: Comparing and versioning ontologies. *Collected Posters of First Int. Semantic Web Conf. In (ISWC 2002).*
Lincoln, Y. S. and Cuba, E. G. (1985). *Naturalistic Inquiry.* New York: Sage.
Livingstone, S. and Lunt, P. (1994). *Talk on Television: Audience Participation and Public Debate.* London: Routledge.
McCarthy, J., Vasiliu, L., Grody, A. D., Muckley, C., Lawrence, D., Zervoudakis, F., Tabet, S., van Grondelle, J. Bouras, T., Fernandes, K., Krintas, T., Xidonas, P., Chourdakis, K., and Koumpis A. (2013), Financial industry ontologies for risk and regulation data (FIORD) a position paper. In Luis, M. Camarinha-Matos, and Raimar J. Scherer (eds.), *14th IFIP Working Conference on Virtual Enterprises PRO-VE 13 Collaborative Systems for Reindustrialization.* Dresden, Germany.
Mellouli, S., Bouslama, F., and Akande, A. (2010). An ontology for representing financial headline news. *Web Semantics*, 8(2–3), pp. 203–208.
Mikroyannidis, A. and Theodoulidis, B. (2007). H E R A C L I T U S I I?: A framework for semantic web adaptation, *IEEE Internet Comput*, 11(3), pp. 45–52.
Mikroyannidis, A. and Theodoulidis, B. (2010). Ontology management and evolution for business intelligence. *Inte. J. Inform. Management*, 30(6), pp. 559–566.
Mikroyannidis, A. and Theodoulidis, B. (2012). A framework for ontology-based temporal modelling of business intelligence. *Knowledge Management Res. Practice,* 10(2), pp. 188–199.
Morgan, D. L. (1998). *Planning Focus Groups.* Thousand Oaks, Calif: SAGE Publications.
Nassirtoussi, A. K., Wah, T. Y., Aghabozorgi, S. R., and Ling, D. N. C. (2014). Text mining for market prediction: A systematic review. *Expert Syst. Appl.*, 41(16), pp. 7653–7670.
Novalija, I. and Mladenić, D. (2010). Ontology extension towards analysis of business news existing approaches to ontology extension. *Finance*, 34, pp. 517–522.
Noy, N. F. and Musen, M. (2000). PROMPT: Algorithm and tool for automated ontology merging and alignment. In *Proc. Seventeenth Natl. Conf. Artificial Intelligence and Twelfth Conference on Innovative Applications of Artificial Intelligence.*
OMG (2014). Financial industry business ontology (FIBO). Retrieved from http://www.omg.org/hot-topics/fibo.htm [Accessed: 30 April 2017].
Putnins, T. J. (2009). Closing price manipulation and integrity of stock exchanges. *Discipline of Finance, Faculty of Economics and Business.* Sydney: University of Sydney.
QSR (2014). NVIVO. Retrieved from http://www.qsrinternational.com/products_nvivo.aspx [Accessed: 30 April 2017].

Rubin, E. and Rubin, A. (2013). The impact of Business Intelligence systems on stock return volatility. *Information & Management*, 50(2–3), pp. 67–75.

SHOE (2003). Simple HTML ontology extensions. Available from: https://en.wikipedia.org/wiki/Simple_HTML_Ontology_Extensions.

Stanford. (2009). Protege. Retrieved from http://protege.stanford.edu/.

Sure, Y., Akkermans, H., Broekstra, J., Davies, J., Ding, Y., Duke, A., and van Harmelen, F. (2003). On-to-knowledge: Semantic web-enabled knowledge management. In N. Zhong, J. Liu, and Y. Yao (eds.), *Web Intelligence*, pp. 277–300.

Theodoulidis, B. and Diaz, D. (2012). Financial markets and high frequency trading: An information management perspective. Available at SSRN: http://dx.doi.org/10.2139/ssrn.2178944.

U.S. Securities and Exchange Commission, Commission, U. S. C. F. T. U. S. S. & E., & Commission (2010). Preliminary findings regarding the market events of May 6, 2010. Retrieved from http://www.sec.gov/sec-cftc-prelimreport.pdf [Accessed: 30 April 2017].

Wang, S., Zhe, Z., Kang, Y., Wang, H., and Chen, X. (2008). An ontology for causal relationships between news and financial instruments. *Expert Syst. Appl.*, 35(3), pp. 569–580.

Wang, S., Xu, K., Liu, L., Fang, B., Liao, S., and Wang, H. (2011). An ontology based framework for mining dependence relationships between news and financial instruments. *Expert Syst. Appl.*, 38(10), pp. 12044–12050.

Zaki, M., Diaz, D., and Theodoulidis, B. (2010). Using text mining to analyze quality aspects of unstructured data: A case study for "stock-touting" spam emails. In *16th Americas Conference on Information Systems (AMCIS 2010)*. Lima, Peru.

Zaki, M., Theodoulidis, B., and Díaz, D. (2011). "Stock-touting" through spam e-mails: A data mining case study. *J. Manufactur. Technol. Management*, 22(6), pp. 770–787.

Zaki, M., Diaz, D., and Theodoulidis, B. (2012). Financial market service architectures: A "pump and dump" Case Study. In *2012 Annual SRII Global Conference*, pp. 554–563.

Zaki, M., and Theodoulidis, B. (2013). Analyzing financial fraud cases using a linguistics-based text mining approach. Available at SSRN:http://papers.ssrn.com/sol3/papers.cfm?abstract_id=2353834.

Chapter 5

Volatility Spillovers and Comovements between MENA Markets during Political Turbulent Times

Besma HKIRI*, Azza BEJAOUI† and Sondes BEN SALEM‡

*Department of Finance and Economics, College of Business, University of Jeddah, Saudi Arabia
†Higher Institute of Management of Tunis
‡Higher Institute of Management of Tunis, Tunisia

Abstract

This chapter explores the relationship between MENA indices during political crisis periods. In other words, we attempt to analyze the comovements and the volatility spillovers during the onset of dramatic country-specific events. For this end, we use daily data of 11 selected indices over the period spanning from March 18, 2005 to March 18, 2016. Methodologically, we assess the extent of volatility transmission among MENA markets indices using the generalized vector autoregressive framework proposed by Diebold and Yilamaz (2012). For the comovements among MENA indices, the wavelet coherence analysis tools and the overlap wavelet cross-correlation approach are proposed. Some interesting findings emerged from this analysis. First, our results reveal moderate comovement behavior between the selected MENA indices at different frequency bands and over time. This result indicates that the emerging markets are more feigned by local political and economic crisis rather than international political unrests. Second, the comovement behavior is more pronounced during the financial turmoil and the direction of volatility transmission seems to be affected by political events.

1. Introduction

A careful investigation of international financial markets movements reveals that there exists a considerable linkage among national and international financial markets. Investors, portfolio managers, and regulators want to understand the dynamic interactions between financial markets to assess market risk and hedging strategies. That is why many scholars have examined different aspects of intertwining of financial markets such as interdependence, contagion, cointegration, comovement, and volatility spillovers (Adrangi *et al.*, 2014). A large body of financial literature has been concerned with the volatility spillovers effect in different markets contexts (e.g., Syriopoulos *et al.*, 2015; Mensi *et al.*, 2015; Jin and An, 2016; Yarovaya and Lau, 2016). For instance, Hamao *et al.* (1990) used GARCH models to examine the reaction of UK and Japan stock markets to the 1987 US stock market crash. They pointed out significant volatility spillovers from New York to Tokyo, from London to Tokyo, and from New York to London. Aloui *et al.* (2011) employed a multivariate copula approach to study the interdependence of four emerging markets (China, Russia, India and Brazil) with the US during the period 2004–2009. They found a significant time-varying dependence between the US and the selected emerging markets during the 2007–2009 global financial turmoil.

Concerns about the spread of financial crises and the emergence of extreme events from emerging markets have increased the exposure of these economies to the risk. According to Adrangi *et al.* (2014), events during the decades of 1999s and 2000, as well as financial turmoil of Ireland, Greece, Portugal, and Spain in 2012–2013 show how economies of even small size play a crucial role in transmitting banking and stock market crises through world economies. These events, among others, have reignited interest in this line of research. On the other hand, political events such as the dissolution of governments, changes in the composition of governments, the formation of new governments, elections, coup d'etat, terrorist acts, revolutions, etc., as well as economic events, are sometimes responsible for stock prices' fluctuations and the transmission of volatility shocks among economies (Robbani and Anantharaman, 2002; Vuchelen, 2003). In this regard, several studies have focused on the impact of news announcements and political events on the domestic and international financial markets (e.g., Chen and Siems, 2003; Drakos, 2010b; Suleman, 2012; Kollias *et al.*, 2012; El-Chaarani, 2015). For example, Chen and Siems (2003) investigated the influence of political news on the stock market volatility in Hong Kong during the period January 1, 1990 to May 31, 1993. The results showed that the political news increase the volatility of the stock market indices. Kollias *et al.* (2012) studied the cross-market transmission of the London stock market' reaction to the July 7, 2005 London bomb attacks. The results displayed the existence of contagion effect from the London market to the Paris market. Moreover, there was a significant influence of FTSE volatility on the DAX and CAC indices volatilities. The authors also confirmed that the correlation between CAC and FTSE indices was significantly raised during the crisis period, implying the decrease of diversification's benefits between the two stock markets. Yi *et al.* (2013) found that international news significantly affected the volatility interdependence between BRICS and CIVETS markets.

The existing literature on the reaction of financial markets to different political events provides convenient evidence on the cross-border effects of unexpected and shock news of these events on the behavior and interconnectedness of international financial markets. Overall, literature on the political events clearly agrees that these events negatively influence the behavior of financial markets in terms of return and volatility. For example, Abadie and Gardeazabal (2008), Barth *et al.* (2006), Gul *et al.* (2010), and Karolyi and Martell (2010), among others, revealed negative effects of terrorist attacks on financial markets. Also, the political uncertainty contributes to financial instability (Gamba-Santamaria *et al.*, 2016). The effects of political events can make varied influence on international stock markets. For instance, Mousavi and Oueniche (2014) reported that the civil uprisings highly affected the returns' volatility of developed, developing, and Europe regions rather than the MENA region. As reported by Mnasri and Nechi (2016), the main empirical findings of many studies indicate that stock returns in all sample stock markets are negatively influenced by terrorist attacks, but the extent and duration of this impact vary across countries. A negative albeit short-lived impact of the terrorist attacks characterizes the reaction of the well-developed markets to such events. A rebound of stock markets after the political event (especially terrorist attacks) can be attributed to the fact that the markets incorporate news about violence in an efficient way (Wisniewski, 2016) or investors believe that such events are unrepeatable. Nevertheless, the occurrence of the political events is considered as bad news that shakes the national and international investors' confidence. This study belongs to a line of research on stock price comovements between the MENA stock markets. We attempt to examine if such political events have an impact on the MENA region markets' comovements and the direction of volatility spillovers transmission across these markets.

In this context, the MENA markets can be considered as a good example given that they have experienced many events such as civil uprisings (e.g., Arab Spring in Tunisia and Egypt), political assassinations (e.g. Assassination of the former Prime Minister of Lebanon Rafik Hariri), and terrorist attacks (e.g., terrorist attacks in Iraq). As matter of fact, Mousavi and Oueniche (2014, p. 21) report that "it would not be an overstatement that one of the most critical areas in the world is the MENA [...] Political conflicts in the MENA region can have an impact not only on the financial markets of the MENA countries but also on the global financial market".

Analyzing if the interconnectedness between markets is strengthened during the onset of dramatic country-specific events enables us to determine and assess if the stock markets are exposed to market-wide shocks. One of contributions of this study is the use of various models to investigate comovements and spillovers amongst stock markets. More precisely, and from an empirical standpoint, we adopt the Diebold and Yilmaz (2012) approach to study the volatility spillovers between indices. The volatility spillovers allow for identifying which market has perceived and incorporated the arrival of new information during turbulent periods. Unlike many studies employed the GARCH models to examine the impact of political events, we attempt to identify the comovements between MENA indices by using the wavelet coherence analysis and the maximal overlap wavelet cross correlation analysis. The wavelet analysis permits to study the behavior of time series jointly in both frequency and time domains. More importantly, the multi-resolution decomposition of the wavelet transform allows us to identify linkages between markets at time-frequency space. The maximal overlap wavelet is able to sufficiently enclose the dynamic interplays between indices time series across time scales. We apply the aforementioned tools to stock markets indices of 11 MENA markets (Tunisia, Egypt, Morocco, Saudi Arabia, United Arab Emirates (Dubai and Abu Dhabi), Bahrain, Israel, Jordan, Oman, and Lebanon) and compute directional spillovers for these market indices for the period spanning from March 18, 2005 to March 18, 2016.

Overall, foreshadowing the main results, we document that the selected MENA markets exhibit moderate changes in comovements. Precisely, the wavelet coherency analysis indicates that the highest comovement level is particularly localized at low and at medium frequencies, implying a cointegration relationship between the selected markets during crisis period. Thereby, the countries have, to varying degrees, been affected by recent episodes of 'Arabic crisis'. Also, our findings reveal significant time-varying patterns in the volatility spillovers for the majority of MENA indices. Furthermore, the volatility spillovers among MENA region indices increase significantly during the distress period. The direction of volatility transmission appears to be affected by the political events. The robustness test confirms our previous findings.

The remainder of the chapter is given as follows. Section 2 reviews the relevant literature and defines important terminologies. In Section 3, we present literature on the impact of political events on the international financial markets. Section 4 exposes different used approaches and data. Empirical results are reported in Section 5 and Section 6 provides the results of the robustness test analysis. Section 7 summarizes and gives some concluding remarks.

2. Terminology and Related Literature Review

A glance thrown at the literature on transmission mechanisms between international financial markets revealed the existence of some confusion on the terminology used. That is why we propose to clarify some notions before presenting the literature review linked to the topic of this chapter.

2.1. *Interdependence versus contagion*

Fobes and Rigobon (2002), among others, argue that the market relations can be subdivided into 'interdependence' and 'contagion'. The interdependence refers to a situation of continuous 'calm-period' relations between markets which are due to common fundamentals driven by financial market integration or real linkages. According to Fobes and Rigobon (2002), if the comovement did not significantly heighten after a crisis, then any continued high-level of market correlation is a prima facie evidence of interdependence between markets. As opposed to interdependence, Fobes and Rigobon (2002) defined contagion as 'a significant increase in cross-market linkages after a shock to one country (or group of countries)'. Contagion is also characterized by relevant and sudden shift in measured market linkages during crisis period. It tends to arise rapidly and dissipates in a short-term period (e.g., Ait-Shahalia *et al.*, 2010).

Many approaches are used to test how shocks are transmitted across markets such as testing for returns correlation between two markets during stable and turmoil periods (e.g., Calvo and Reinhart, 1996) and also using ARCH and GARCH models to estimate the variance–covariance propagation mechanisms across markets (e.g., Arouri *et al.*, 2013) or the impulsive response function and a variance decomposition to test for the shifts in the cointegration vector across markets over long horizon (Boubaker *et al.*, 2015). Another approach used in the contagion literature is the wavelet analysis which examines the dynamic markets comovements across several time horizons by decomposing any observed variable on scale by scale basis (Bodart and Candelon, 2009).

2.2. *Literature review on volatility spillover*

Empirical literature on the volatility spillover shows that this topic has been investigated in different markets contexts (Mensi *et al.*, 2015; Ben Rjeb and Boughrara, 2015; Jin and An, 2016; Yarovaya and Lau, 2016). In this regard, many researchers focus on the developed countries. For example, Theodossiou and Lee (1993) employed a GARCH-M model to study the nature and the degree of comovement for five developed stock markets (US, Japan, UK, Canada, and Germany). Their results showed a strong time varying conditional volatility in the return time series of all markets. Panopoulou and Pantelidis (2009) studied the volatility spillover between the US and the rest of the G7 countries. Their volatility impulsive response analysis demonstrated an increase in the amplitude and duration of the volatility spillovers compared to those over the pre-1995 period. More recently, Karanasos *et al.* (2014) applied the AR-DCC-FIAPARCH model on eight developed stock market indices (US, Canada, UK, Germany, France, Hong Kong, Japan, and Singapore) during the period 1988–2010. They revealed that, during both global financial crisis and Asian crisis, the financial liberalization caused contagion effects. They also noted much higher conditional correlation estimates for the global crisis than for the Asian one.

Due to the development of the BRICS and MENA stock markets and the rise of the 1997 Asian financial crises, another body of the empirical literature investigated the linkages between developed and emerging markets. For instance, Aloui *et al.* (2011) examined the extent of the 2008 financial crisis using a multivariate copula approach. The findings reveal a significant time-varying dependence between the US market and the selected emerging markets. Chiang *et al.* (2013) analyzed the spillover effects of returns and volatility from the US stock market to the BRICV stock markets (Brazil, Russia, India, China, and Vietnam). They revealed that Vietnam was the receiver of the most intense spillover effects after the 2008 financial crisis, whereas Russia received the highest contagious effects of returns and volatility from the US market before the crisis. The results also demonstrated that China and Brazil exhibited the highest risk while the lowest long-run total risk was found for India.

Other studies focus on the MENA stock markets' context. Using GARCH, threshold ARCH and ARCH-M models, and a VAR analysis, Neaime (2012) studied how the 2007 US financial crisis affected the MENA region during the period 2007–2010. They show that the degree of the contagion of the 2008 financial crisis to MENA stock markets depended on their level of integration with developed financial markets. Giovannetti and

Velucchi (2013) examined the volatility dynamics among three developed financial markets (US, UK, and China) and some emerging African markets (Botswana, Kenya, Nigeria, South Africa, Egypt, and Tunisia) over the period 2005–2012. Using a multiplicative error approach and the impulsive response functions, they reveal that South Africa, US, UK, and China markets had a relevant role in all African markets. Moreover, they showed that the shock of the Arab Spring seemed to have less global effect and to be limited to North African countries. Results from computation of synthetic index (volatility spillover balance) showed that US, Kenya, and Tunisia were net 'creators' of volatility while South Africa and China were net 'absorbers'. Adrangi *et al.* (2014) examined the volatility spillovers between the US market and three emerging markets of America (Brazil, Argentina, and Mexico) from August 2007 to August 2012. Using a battery of GARCH models, they found evidence of bi-directional spillovers and asymmetric market reactions to shocks in all markets. Moreover, the nonlinear Granger causality test results confirmed the existence of bi-directional spillovers among markets of America.

3. The Stock Markets' Reactions to Political Events

The emergence and increasing frequency of political events worldwide such as wars (e.g., Iraq invasion of Kuwait), military invasions, armed conflicts, parliament and presidential elections, terrorism (e.g., the 9/11 New York attacks, the March 2004 and July 2005 bombings in Madrid and London, respectively; the terrorist attacks of Paris in November 2015 and Brussels in March 2016), civil uprisings (e.g., Arab Spring), political assassinations (e.g., assassination of the former Prime Minister of Lebanon Rafik Hariri) have both real and delusional impacts on the performance stability and efficiency of financial markets. Cognizant of this fact and the importance of financial markets to the overall performance to the economy, a stream of research is focused on the influential effects of political events on the behavior of financial markets. This research focuses not only on short-term effects of political events on the national stock markets but also the spillover effects of these events by injecting sudden shocks to financial markets.

Even though political events are generally unprecedented and uncommon, it is well documented that the national financial markets (i.e., in countries where political events have taken place) react quickly to these events (e.g. Brounen and Derwall, 2010; Mnif, 2017; Apergis and Apergis,

2016). For instance, Brounen and Derwall (2010) investigated the impact of terrorist attacks on the behavior of national stock market indices. They found that the abnormal return amounted to −0.92% on the event day, which is more pronounced compared to that caused by earthquakes. Kollias *et al.* (2011b) analyzed the London and Spanish stock markets' behavior during the Madrid and London bomb attacks. They displayed that the price effect was transitory and the London stock market recovered much faster. According to Kollias *et al.* (2011b), the dissimilarity in speed of recovery is due to the differences in structure, size, and liquidity of the markets. Apergis and Apergis (2016) explore the effect of the Paris terrorist attacks on the stock returns of 24 global defense companies. Their results displayed the significant reaction on the terrorist attacks days and on the days following the event. Mnif (2017) examines the link between the political instability caused by the Arab Spring and the behavior and features of Tunisian stock cycle over time. The results show that such events lead to unstable financial market and more pronounced stock market cycles. Arguably, the financial effects of political events are not constrained by national boundaries and provide impetus for research in the ramifications on international markets. According to Kollias *et al.* (2010), unforeseen political events can be considered as external shocks to stock markets, which can negatively influence the investment decisions and portfolio allocation and increase the market volatility.

Along same lines of thought, Diamonte *et al.* (1996) examined the spillover effect of 1990 Gulf war on 21 developed and 24 emerging markets. They revealed a significant influence of such an event on the market returns in the emerging markets. They also recognized that the effect of the Gulf war on developing markets was more intense compared to that on developed markets. Using daily returns data from Karachi Stock Exchange, Ahmed and Farooq (2008) analyzed the impact of 9/11 attacks by studying the KSE100 index returns during the pre- and post-9/11 periods. They primarily found that the volatility behavior significantly varied after the 9/11 terrorist attacks. The same results are reported by Johnston and Nedelescu (2006). On the other hand, Karolyi and Martell (2010) investigated the influence of 75 terrorist attacks on stock prices during the period 1995–2002. They found a statistically significant negative stock price reaction of −0.83%, which corresponds to an average loss per firm per attack of $million 401 in firm market capitalization. Hobbs *et al.* (2016) investigate the impact of 28 terrorist and military events on stock returns during the period 1963–2012. Their empirical findings reveal that stocks significantly perform worse on the days of terrorist events than on the days of military events, but the opposite happens the day after.

Nguyen and Enomoto (2009) attempted to determine the effects of acts of terrorism on market returns in the Tehran and Karachi stock markets. Their empirical findings indicated that (i) the attacks against the USS Cole and the start of the Iraq war had an impact on market returns in the Karachi stock market, 5 days after the occurrence of the attacks; (ii) the attacks of the World Trade Center and the bombing in London decreased the market returns in the Tehran and Karachi stock markets, 5 days after the occurrence of attacks; (iii) the bombing of the Golden Mosque decreased market returns in the Tehran stock market within 10 days of the initial attacks; and (iv) the volatility of returns was decreased due to a reduction in trading activity among investors. Chesney *et al.* (2011) documented that Russian and Madrid bombings in 2004 negatively affected the European, Swiss, and the US stock markets. Essaddam and Karagianis (2014) investigated the influence of 44 terrorist attacks on return volatility of American companies over the period 1995–2010. They showed that the influence of terrorist attacks on American firms' stock return volatility lasts for at least 15 days.

More recently, Mousavi and Ouenniche (2014) investigated the impact of Arab Spring on the movements of several stock markets in developed, developing, MENA, European and Latin America countries. Using GARCH models, the results indicated that the uprising events of MENA region had more influence on return volatility of developed, developing, and European regions than MENA region. Chau *et al.* (2014) also found that the Arab Spring had an impact on the volatility of Islamic stock indices of the stock markets in Lebanon, Egypt, Jordan, Oman, Kuwait, and Bahrain. Their empirical findings revealed that the conventional indices of Lebanon, Kuwait, and Egypt displayed significant impact on volatility while the volatility of the indices in Jordan, Oman, and Bahrain have not been affected by such event. Alsharairi and Abubaker (2016) study the Arab Spring (especially, February 2011 Egyptian revolution) spillover effect on Dubai Financial Market (DFM) which is a relatively stable neighboring country. Using the daily returns of seven indices during January 1, 2008 to December 31, 2012, their empirical findings show that the volatility of the overall DFM has not been influenced, except for two indices at DFM (transportation and telecommunication). They also find that the Arab Spring has not affected the returns of overall DFM indices.

Other researchers have examined the impact of terrorist attacks on companies' stock prices. For instance, Kolaric and Schiereck (2016) investigate the influence of Paris 13/11 and Brussels 22/03 terrorist attacks on stock prices of 27 North American and European companies. They find that these events have strong short-term effects on the valuation of the sample airline companies. Aslam *et al.* (2016) examine the impact of terrorist attacks on stock returns in five Asian countries. They find that these events significantly affect the stock returns, but the magnitude of this influence depends on the severity of the attacks. Several other studies examine the change in market volatility during the period of the occurrence of political events. Recently, Bentes (2016) investigates the effects of crises such as the 9/11 terrorist attacks on the long memory behavior in the volatility of gold returns during the period 1985–2009. The author displays long memory in the conditional variance during the overall sample period.

A significant amount of research documents that significant terrorist attacks increase correlations between financial markets (Hon *et al.*, 2004). Major political event spillover effects can spread in international markets through financial market linkages (Pritsker, 2001), and specially trading partners (Kumar and Liu, 2013). When a bigger economy is attacked, the terrorist attack spillover is prominent for economically small trading partners. Terrorist attacks on non-trading partners do not propagate to national countries (Suleman, 2012). According to Kumar and Liu (2013), the increasing economic integration across countries can make international markets influence each other's performance. Also, the weak institutions and unstable financial markets lead to overreaction of the stock markets to terrorist attacks (Mnasri and Nechi, 2016).

4. Methodology Design and Data

4.1. *Methodology*

In this chapter, we attempt to investigate the volatility spillovers between selected MENA indices by adopting the Diebold and Yilmaz (2012) approach. In this regard, the volatility spillover index based on forecast error-variance decomposition from vector autoregression proposed by Diebold and Yilmaz (2009) is used to assess the extent of volatility transfer among stock markets indices. Diebold and Yilmaz (2012) have subsequently improved this approach by employing a generalized vector autoregression framework. Compared to the previous approach, the generalized vector autoregression framework provides the time-dependent analysis of the relationship between steadily changing volatility indices.

4.1.1. *Computation of volatility proxy*

The EGARCH conditional variance is used as a proxy of daily volatility for our sample. The EGARCH model does not require any restriction on the estimated parameters given that the positivity of variance is automatically satisfied (as the equation is expressed on log variance instead of variance). The EGARCH model also takes into account the so-called volatility clustering; a perceived shock at time $t-1$ impacts variance at time t. For a return time-series, given that r_t equals $\mu+\varepsilon_t$(μ is the expected return and ε_t is a zero-mean white noise), the conditional variance specified by an EGARCH(1,1) model can be expressed as follows:

$$\ln(\sigma_t^2) = w + \alpha(|z_{t-1}| - \mathrm{E}[|z_{t-1}|]) + \gamma z_{t-1} + \beta \ln(\sigma_{t-1}^2), \qquad (1)$$

4.1.2. *Measuring volatility spillovers*

In this section, we subsequently exhibit the three main concepts in the Diebold and Yilmaz (2012) approach (henceforth DY (2012)): the total volatility spillovers index, the directional spillovers, and net volatility spillovers.

4.1.2.1. Total spillovers index

The total volatility spillovers index is based on the KPSS variance decomposition. DY (2012) consider two variance shares (*own variance shares and cross-variance shares*). Initially, the assets' own variance shares are expressed as the fraction of the H-step-ahead error variances in forecasting the variable x_i (for $i = 1, 2 \ldots, N.$), due to the same variable shocks. The cross-variance (the spillovers) is calculated as the H-step-ahead error variances in forecasting the variable x_i, due to another variable shocks x_j (for $i, j = 1, 2, \ldots, N$, where $i \neq j$). For $H = 1, 2 \ldots$, the KPSS H-step-ahead forecast error decomposition is given as follows:

$$\theta_{ij}^{g}(H) = \frac{\sigma_{jj}^{-1} \sum_{h=0}^{H-1} \left(e_i' A_h \sum e_j\right)^2}{\sum_{h=0}^{H-1} \left(e_i' A_h \sum A_h' e_j\right)}, \qquad (2)$$

where $\sum$ is the variance matrix for the error vector ε. σ_{jj} is the standard error for the jth equation, and e_i is the selection vector, with one as the ith element and zeros otherwise.

In the generalized VAR framework, the shocks to each asset variable are not orthogonalized. As a result, the sum of each row of the variance decomposition matrix does not equal to one. Hence, each element of the decomposition matrix can be normalized by the row sum:

$$\tilde{\theta}_{ij}^{g}(H) = \frac{\theta_{ij}^{g}(H)}{\sum_{j=1}^{N} \theta_{ij}^{g}(H)}. \tag{3}$$

By construction, $\sum_{j=1}^{N} \tilde{\theta}_{ij}^{g}(H) = 1$ and $\sum_{i,j=1}^{N} \tilde{\theta}_{ij}^{g}(H) = N$

Based on the beyond input, the total volatility spillover index is given as follows:

$$S^{g}(H) = \frac{\sum_{i,j=1,i\neq j}^{N} \tilde{\theta}_{ij}^{g}(H)}{\sum_{j=1}^{N} \tilde{\theta}_{ij}^{g}(H)}.100 = \frac{\sum_{i,j=1,i\neq j}^{N} \tilde{\theta}_{ij}^{g}(H)}{N}.100. \tag{4}$$

The total spillover index permits to know how much the shocks to volatility spill over across variables.

4.1.2.2. Directional spillovers

The directional spillover is computed using the normalized elements of the generalized variance decomposition matrix. Using the directional spillover allows to decompose the total spillovers to those pending from or coming to a particular asset. The directional spillovers received (transmitted) by index i from all indices (to another index) j are conceptualized in Eq. (5a) (Eq. (5b)):

$$S_{i.}^{g}(H) = \frac{\sum_{j=1,j\neq i}^{N} \tilde{\theta}_{ij}^{g}(H)}{\sum_{i,j=1}^{N} \tilde{\theta}_{ij}^{g}(H)}.100 = \frac{\sum_{j=1,j\neq i}^{N} \tilde{\theta}_{ij}^{g}(H)}{N}.100, \tag{5a}$$

$$S_{.i}^{g}(H) = \frac{\sum_{j=1,j\neq i}^{N} \tilde{\theta}_{ji}^{g}(H)}{\sum_{i,j=1}^{N} \tilde{\theta}_{ji}^{g}(H)}.100 = \frac{\sum_{j=1,j\neq i}^{N} \tilde{\theta}_{ji}^{g}(H)}{N}.100 \tag{5b}$$

4.1.2.3. The net spillovers

The net volatility spillover from index i to all other indices j is specified as the difference between the gross volatility shocks broadcasted to and those received from all other indices. The corresponding equation is written as follows:

$$S_{i}^{g}(H) = S_{.i}^{g}(H) - S_{i.}^{g}(H) \tag{5c}$$

Net spillovers have the ability to specify how much each index contributes to the volatility in other indices in net terms.

4.1.2.4. Net pairwise spillovers

The net pairwise volatility spillover is inspired from the previous equation. It is defined as the difference between the gross shocks transmitted from index i to index j and shocks broadcasted from j to i. According to DY (2012), the net pairwise volatility spillovers are computed as follows:

$$S_{ij}^{g}(H) = \left(\frac{\tilde{\theta}_{ji}^{g}(H)}{\sum_{i,k=1}^{N} \tilde{\theta}_{ik}^{g}(H)} - \frac{\tilde{\theta}_{ij}^{g}(H)}{\sum_{j,k=1}^{N} \tilde{\theta}_{ik}^{g}(H)} \right) .100$$

$$= \left(\frac{\tilde{\theta}_{ji}^{g}(H) - \tilde{\theta}_{ij}^{g}(H)}{N} \right) .100. \qquad (6)$$

4.1.3. *Wavelet analysis*

The wavelet approach is a suitable tool to investigate the behavior of time series jointly in both frequency and time spaces. Distinctively, the wavelet coherence is employed under Morlet's specification. The wavelet is defined as:

$$\cdot\, \psi_{t,s}(t) = \frac{1}{\sqrt{s}} \psi \left(\frac{t-s}{s} \right).$$

Recall that a wavelet is a real-valued or a complex valued function $\psi(.)$ defined over the real axis. It is also assumed that the wavelet is the square integrable function $\psi(.) \in L^2(R)$. In the above equation, $\frac{1}{\sqrt{s}}$ is the normalization factor ensuring the unit variance of the wavelet $\|\psi_{u,s}\|^2 = 1$. u is the location parameter providing the exact position of the wavelet and s is the scale dilatation parameter of the wavelet which defines how the wavelet is stretched or dilated. In this regard, a higher scale implies a more stretched wavelet which is appropriate for detection of lower frequencies. Formally, the Morlet's wavelet is given by

$$\psi^{M}(t) = \frac{1}{\pi^{1/4}} e^{iw_0 t} e^{-t^2/2},$$

where w_0 is the central frequency of the wavelet.

4.1.3.1. The continuous wavelet transform

Following Rua and Nunes (2009) and Barunik *et al.* (2015), the continuous wavelet transform is given by

$$w_x(u,s) = \int_{-\infty}^{\infty} x(t)\frac{1}{\sqrt{s}}\overline{\psi\left(\frac{t-u}{s}\right)}.$$

Specifically, $w_x(u,s)$ is acquired by projecting the specific wavelet $\psi(.)$ on the selected time series. The main wavelet transform allows to decompose and then consequently reconstruct the function $x(t) \in L^2(R)$:

$$x(t) = \frac{1}{C_\Psi}\int_0^{\infty}\left[\int_{-\infty}^{\infty} W_x(u,s)\Psi_{u,s}(t)du\right]\frac{ds}{s^2} \quad s > 0. \tag{7}$$

The power spectrum analysis specifies the variance as follows:

$$\|x\|^2 = \frac{1}{C_\Psi}\int_0^{\infty}\left[\int_{-\infty}^{\infty} |W_x(u,s)^2|du\right]\frac{ds}{s^2}.$$

(a) Wavelet power spectrum

As reported by Torrence and Compo (1998) and Aguiar-Conraria *et al.* (2008), the wavelet power spectrum can be simply defined as $|W_n^x|^2$, and it assesses the local variance of each variable.[1] Based on Monte Carlo simulations through computing the white-noise and red-noise wavelet powers, Torrence and Compo (1998) show that, at each time n and scale s, the corresponding distribution for the local wavelet power spectrum can be written as

$$D\left(\frac{\left|W_n^X(s)\right|^2}{\sigma_X^2} < p\right) \Rightarrow \frac{1}{2}P_f\chi_v^2 \tag{8}$$

where P_k is the mean of spectrum at the Fourier frequency f that corresponds to the wavelet scale s ($s \approx 1/f$), and v takes the values of 1 or 2 for real or complex wavelets, respectively.

(b) Cross-wavelet power, wavelet coherence, and phase difference

The cross-wavelet power shows the area in the time-scale space where the time series exhibits high common power. The cross-wavelet power

[1] The statistical significance can be assessed based on the null hypothesis that the variable under consideration has a significant power spectrum, i.e. the signal is generated by an AR(0) or AR(1) stationary process with mean background power spectrum (P_f).

captures the local covariance of two time series in each frequency and shows the quantitative similarities of the power between them (Aguiar-Conraria *et al.*, 2008). According to Hudgins *et al.* (1993), for each signal X and Y, the individual wavelet spectra are specified as $W_n^X(s)$ and $W_n^Y(s)$, respectively. In the time-frequency analysis, the cross-wavelet between two signals is represented by the cross-wavelet spectrum $W_n^{XY}(s)$ in Eq. (9)[2]

$$W_n^{XY}(s) = W_n^X(s)W_n^{Y^*}(s), \tag{9}$$

where $W_n^{Y^*}(s)$ is the complex conjugate of $W_n^Y(s)$ and * denotes the complex conjugation. The cross-wavelet power is therefore given by $|W_n^{XY}|$ and measures the local covariance of two variables at each scale. Torrence and Compo (1998) show that the theoretical distribution of the cross-wavelet power of two signals with background power spectra P_k^X and P_k^Y acquires the following form:

$$D\left(\frac{|W_n^X(s)W_n^{Y^*}(s)|}{\sigma_X \sigma_Y} < p\right) = \frac{Z_v(p)}{v}\sqrt{P_k^X P_k^Y},$$

where σ_X and σ_Y are the standard deviations of x and y, respectively. $Z_v(p)$ is the confidence level related to the probability p for a (pdf) probability density function defined by the square root of the product of two χ^2 distributions.

On the other hand, the wavelet coherency of two time series $x = \{x_n\}$ and $y = \{y_n\}$ is defined as the localized correlation coefficient between these series in the time-frequency space (Torrence and Compo, 1998). Thus, it is a very useful tool for detecting time series comovements. Following Torrence and Webster (1999), the wavelet coherence is computed as the squared absolute value of the smoothed cross-wavelet spectra normalized by the product of the smoothed individual wavelet power spectra of each time series

$$R^2(u, s) = \frac{|S(s^{-1}W_{xy}(u, s))|^2}{S(s^{-1}|W_x(u, s)|^2)S(s^{-1}|W_y(u, s)|^2)}, \tag{10}$$

[2]See Torrence and Compo (1998) for more details about the cross-wavelet spectrum hypothesis and confidence levels.

where S denotes the smoothing parameter. In the no-smoothing case, the wavelet coherence will be equal to one. Additionally, the squared wavelet coherence coefficient satisfies this inequality $0 \leq R^2(u, s) \leq 1$. A value close to zero (one) indicates a weak (high) correlation.

Finally, the phase difference, given as $\phi_{x,y}$, provides information about the lateness of the oscillations between two variables as a function of frequency. This provides information about the time series positions in the pseudo-cycle. The phase difference is given as:

$$\phi_{x,y} = \tan^{-1}\left(\frac{I\{W_n^{xy}\}}{R\{W_n^{xy}\}}\right) \quad \text{with } \phi_{x,y} \in [-\pi, \pi]. \tag{11}$$

4.1.4. *Maximal overlap discrete wavelet transform*

The DWT of a time series X is a suitable method which enables the analysis of its multi-scale features. This analysis decomposes a time series into a set of equally orthogonal wavelet basis functions. The MODWT is a slight variation of the DWT. This approach is defined as a linear filtering process that is able to transform a time series into coefficients which are linked to deviations over different scales. For the MODWT cross-correlation analysis formulas, we adopt the same annotations used by Gallegati (2008). The MODWT wavelet and scaling coefficient $\tilde{w}_{j,t}$ and $\tilde{v}_{j,t}$ are given as follows:

$$\tilde{w}_{j,t} = \frac{1}{2^{1/2}} \sum_{l=0}^{L-1} \tilde{h}_{j,l} X_{t-l} \quad \text{and} \quad \tilde{v}_{j,t} = \frac{1}{2^{1/2}} \sum_{l=0}^{L-1} \tilde{g}_{j,l} X_{t-l}, \tag{12}$$

where $h_{j,t}$ and $g_{j,l}$ denote the level wavelet and scaling filters, respectively. The MODWT wavelet and scaling filters (Eq. (9)) are directly generated from the DWT filter and are, respectively, given as:

$$\tilde{h}_{j,l} = \frac{h_{j,l}}{2^{j/2}} \quad \text{and} \quad \tilde{g}_{j,l} = \frac{g_{j,l}}{2^{j/2}}. \tag{13}$$

In our study, we use the MODWT covariance analysis[3] as a robustness test to study the wavelet cross-correlation between MENA indices. This approach determines the magnitude of the connection between the selected indices. According to Gençay *et al.* (2001a), the covariance of two stochastic processes X and Y at wavelet scale j is specified as $\gamma_{XY,j} = \text{Cov}[\tilde{w}_{j,t}^X \tilde{w}_{j,t}^Y]$. Using the MODWT, an unbiased estimator of wavelet covariance after

[3]For more details about the MODWT variance analysis, see for example Serroukh *et al.* (2000), Gallegati (2008), and Saiti *et al.* (2014).

removing all wavelet coefficients affected by periodic boundary conditions is obtained. Using MODWT, the estimator of wavelet covariance is given by the following equation:

$$\tilde{\gamma}_{XY,j} = \frac{1}{\tilde{N}_j} N - 1 \sum_{t=L_{J-1}}^{N-1} \tilde{w}_{j,t}^{X} \tilde{w}_{j,t}^{Y}. \tag{14}$$

For scale τ and lag π, the MODWT estimator of wavelet cross-correlation coefficients is computed using the wavelet cross-covariance (Eq. 11) and the squared root of the two time series wavelet variances $\tilde{\sigma}_X(\tau_j)$ and $\tilde{\sigma}_Y(\tau_j)$;

$$\tilde{\rho}_{XY,\pi}(\tau_j) = \frac{\tilde{\gamma}_{XY,\pi}(\tau_j)}{\tilde{\sigma}_X(\tau_j)\tilde{\sigma}_Y(\tau_j)}. \tag{15}$$

From Eq. (15), the wavelet cross-correlation coefficients provide the lead/lag wavelet analysis between two time series on a scale-by-scale basis and are between 0 and 1.

4.2. *Data and preliminary statistics*

4.2.1. *Context description and preliminary statistics*

4.2.1.1. MENA region description

The selected MENA stock markets were established around the mid-1970s. The Egyptian Exchange is one of the oldest stock markets in the Middle East and Africa (Alexandria Stock Exchange and Cairo Stock Exchange began in 1883 and 1903, respectively). In 1929, the Casablanca Stock Exchange was created in Morocco and, in 1953, the Tel-Aviv Stock Exchange was launched. Similarly, the Tunis Stock Exchange was established in 1969. Newcomers include the Beirut Stock Exchange (Lebanon) in 1980, Saudi Stock Market in 1984, Muscat Stock Exchange (Oman) in 1988, and Bahrain Stock Exchange in 1989. However, the most recent markets are those in Jordan (Amman Stock Exchange) in 1999 and United Arab Emirates (Dubai Exchange and Abu Dhabi Exchange) in 2000.

Table 1 reports the performance indicators for the 11 selected MENA stock markets. The number of publicly listed firms in the selected MENA stock markets generally increased from 2010 to 2015 (except for Lebanon, Israel, and Jordan), which shows the attractiveness of stock market financing for companies. The market capitalization varies broadly across the 11 examined stock markets. In 2015, the Saudi Stock Exchange had the highest market capitalization ($421,060 million) while the less important equity

Table 1. Selected MENA Stock Market Performance Indicators-2015

Country	Number of Firms		Market Capitalization ($millions)		Market Capitalization (% of GDP)		Value of Shares Traded (% GDP)		Turnover Ratio (%)		Number of Transactions	Number of Day Traded
	2010	2015	2010	2015	2010	2015	2010	2015	2010	2015		
United Arab Emirates	104	125	131,491	195,874	46	52.9	9.7	15.6	21.1	29.4	2016709	498
Bahrain	44	44	20,060	19,251	78	59.7	1.1	0.9	1.4	1.5	9593	243
Egypt	227	250	84,277	55,192	38.5	16.7	17	4.5	44.2	26.7	—	—
Morocco	73	74	69,152	45,928	74.2	45.8	6.5	2.9	8.8	6.4	130733	241
Tunisia	58	78	10,652	—	24.2	—	4.2	1.9	17.2	—	393095	235
Israel	596	440	227,614	243,904	97.1	82.4	46.2	19	47.6	23.1	—	—
Oman	114	116	28,316	41,123	48.3	58.5	5.6	5.1	11.7	8.7	250799	2237
Jordan	277	228	30,864	25,452	116.8	67.8	32.5	9.5	27.9	14	872366	239
Lebanon	10	10	12,697	—	33.4	—	4.9	1.4	14.8	—	9434	235
Saudi Arabia	146	171	353,410	421,060	67.2	65.2	38.2	67.6	56.9	103.8	12331593	241

Notes: The main market indicators for the selected MENA markets are reported in this table. From this table, the market capitalization changes widely among the 11 emerging stock markets. Indeed, the Bahraini market seems to be one of the less important stock markets, whereas the Saudi Exchange appears to be one of the most important markets. In this respect, the highest ratio of the market capitalization of the listed companies to the Gross Domestic Product (GDP) was seen for Israel (82.4%) followed by Jordan (67.8%) and Saudi Arabia (65.2%) in 2015. The increasing number of publicly listed firms in the selected MENA stock markets generally rose from 2010 to 2015, displaying the attractiveness of stock market financing for companies, except for Lebanon, Israel, and Jordan.
Source: World Bank and Arab Monetary Fund.

market in our sample was the Bahrain Exchange. The ratio of the market capitalization of the listed companies to the Gross Domestic Product (GDP) is by far the greatest for Israel (82.4%) followed by Jordan (67.8%) and Saudi Arabia (65.2%) in 2015.

4.2.1.2. Data and elementary statistics

The selected daily MENA indices[4] are obtained from DataStream. It is interesting to mention that we excluded Yemen, Iraq, Algeria, Libya, Palestine, Kuwait, Qatar, and Syria indices due to the unavailability of market index data.

The sample period spans from March 18, 2005 to March 18, 2016 for a total of 2871 daily prices. The continuously compounded daily returns for each stock market are expressed in percentage computed by multiplying the first difference of the logarithm of stock market indices by 100:

$$R_t = \mathrm{Ln}\left(\frac{P_t}{P_{t-1}}\right) * 100,$$

where P_t and P_{t-1} are the closing prices in market i at time t and $t-1$.

From Fig. 1, the time series plots of the eleven stock indices appear to exhibit cyclical movements over the sample period. Many interesting facts emerge from Fig. 2 corresponding to daily returns: (i) all return series tend to fluctuate over time; (ii) Abu Dhabi, Jordan, and Lebanon seem to be less volatile than others and (iii) All daily indices returns seem to have volatility clustering behavior.

Table 2 reports the elementary statistics of the selected MENA region indices. From Table 2, we show that the average return ranges from −0.0206% for Bahrain to 0.1772% for Lebanon. The Tunis Stock Exchange seems to be the least risky as it records the lowest standard deviation (0.559) among all the MENA markets, while the Dubai market is the most risky one with the highest standard deviation (1.883). The skewness coefficient is

[4]The markets under consideration are three stock markets from North Africa: Tunis Stock Exchange (TUNINDEX), Egyptian Stock Exchange (EGX30), and Casablanca Stock Exchange (MADEX); the six stock markets of the GCC region: Saudi Stock Exchange (TADAWUL ALL SHARE), Bahrain Stock Market (BB All Share Index), Dubai Financial Market (DFM General Index), Abu Dhabi Securities Exchange (ADX), Oman Stock Market (MSM-30 Index), Amman Stock Exchange (ASE General Index), and two stock markets in the Middle East: Beirut Stock Exchange (BLOM) and Israel (TA100 Index).

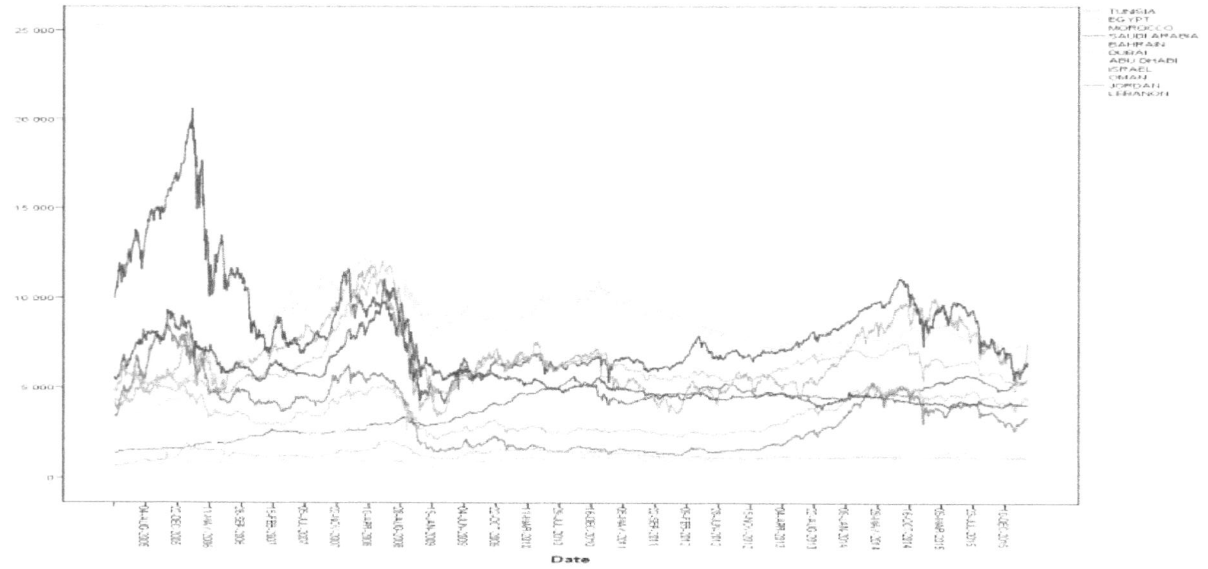

Figure 1. Price Indices for all Eleven Countries

Notes: This figure plots the stock price indices for all region indices. As shown in this figure, the time series plots of the eleven emerging stock indices seem to exhibit cyclical irregular fluctuations during the sample period.

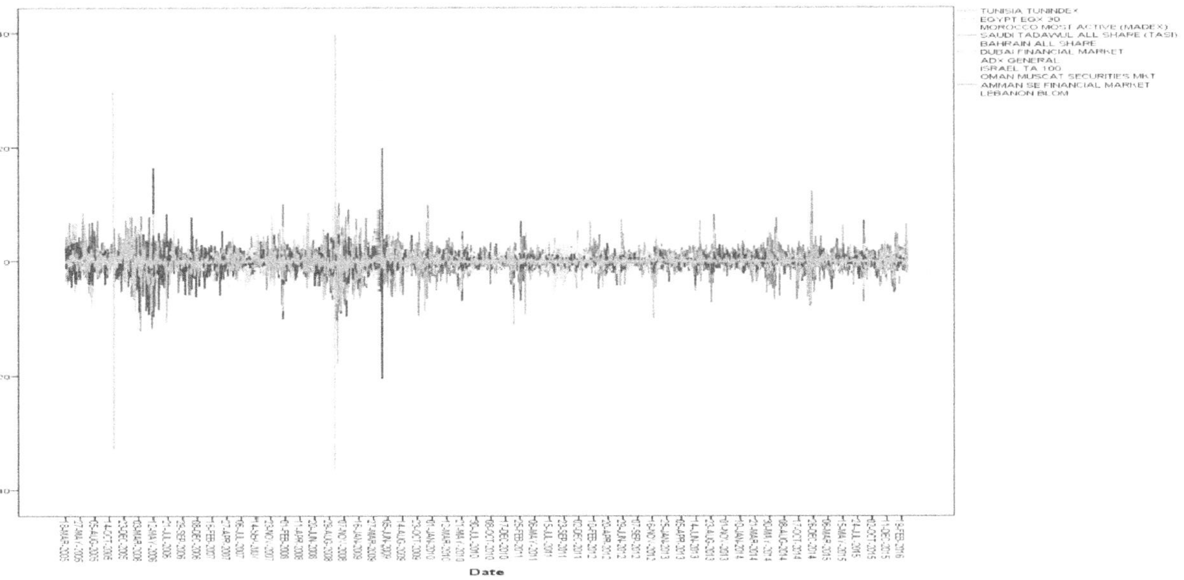

Figure 2. Daily Indices Returns for all Eleven Markets

Notes: This figure illustrates daily returns for our sample. Clearly, all stock returns series vary during the sample period. The less volatile stock markets are markets in Jordan, Abu Dhabi, and Lebanon. As well, the sample indices returns show the volatility clustering behavior.

Table 2. **Descriptive Statistics of the Selected MENA Markets**

Country	N	Mean	Min	Max	Var.	S.D	Skewness	Kurtosis
Tunisia	2870	0.0488	−5.0037	4.1086	0.312	0.559	−0.569	12.084
Morocco	2870	0.0199	−17.9916	7.314	2.932	1.712	−0.977	7.805
Egypt	2870	0.0276	−5.0935	4.5593	0.684	0.8268	−0.324	5.512
Saudi Arabia	2870	−0.0151	−11.6816	16.3995	2.841	1.6855	−0.605	6.719
Bahrain	2870	−0.0206	−4.9200	3.6132	0.326	0.571	−0.605	6.719
Dubai	2870	−0.0009	−12.157	12.2045	3.548	1.883	−1.03	5.500
Abu Dhabi	2870	−0.0034	−36.4920	39.818	2.626	1.620	1.063	218.409
Israel	2870	0.02231	−7.4708	9.7815	1.345	1.160	−0.390	15.579
Oman	2870	0.0095	−8.6990	8.0388	1.140	1.0679	−0.903	15.579
Jordan	2870	−0.0099	−20.5406	19.8740	1.405	1.1851	−0.324	61.996
Lebanon	2870	0.1772	−32.8276	30.0221	1.648	1.2836	−1.138	259.397

Notes: This table provides the descriptive statistics of the data used in this study for the whole period. As shown in this table, the mean return varies from −0.0206% to 0.1772% for Bahrain and Lebanon, respectively. The lowest standard deviation (0.559) is recorded for the Tunisian market, whereas the Dubai market seems to be the most risky given that its standard deviation equals 1.883. Expect for the Abu Dhabi market, other emerging stock markets exhibit negative skewness coefficient. Also, the distribution for all MENA daily returns is leptokurtic. As a result, we reject the normality distribution.
The sample period amounts to a total of 2871 daily observations.

negative for all returns series proving that the return distribution has a long left tail, except for the Abu Dhabi market (positive skewness coefficient). The kurtosis coefficient is highly significant (exceeding three), showing that the distribution of all MENA daily return is leptokurtic. We argue in favor of the rejection of the normality distribution of returns given the excess kurtosis and skewness statistic measures.

The correlation matrix is reported in Table 3. More precisely, we determine the Pearson correlation coefficients of all pairs of the eleven index returns, as depicted in matrix correlation coefficients. In general, the matrix correlation coefficients are statistically significant, implying the existence of the relationship between return series. The unconditional correlation estimates between the TUNINDEX, the GCC markets' indices, the Middle East markets' indices, and the North Africa markets' indices (EGX30 and MADEX) are on average 0.0813, 0.05, and 0.0485, respectively. The average estimated unconditional correlation is much higher between EGX30 and the GCC markets' indices (0.216), the Middle East markets' indices (0.131), and the North Africa markets' indices (0.048). The estimation of unconditional correlation between BLOM (resp., TA100) and the North Africa markets' indices, the GCC markets' indices and the Israel Stock Exchange (resp.,

Table 3. Unconditional Correlation Matrix for Index Returns

	TU	EG	MO	SAR	BAH	DUB	ABH	ISR	OM	JOR	LEB
TU	1	0.05 **	0.04 *	0.09 **	0.05 **	0.09 **	0.06 **	0.05 *	0.11 **	0.09 **	0.05 **
EGX		1	0.10 *	0.22 **	0.12 **	0.31 **	0.22 **	0.18 **	0.24 **	0.18 **	0.08 **
MO			1	0.08 **	0.08 **	0.09 **	0.04 *	0.07 **	0.08 **	0.10 **	0.04 **
SAR				1	0.09 **	0.32 **	0.27 **	0.16 **	0.21 **	0.13 **	0.11 **
BAH					1	0.22 **	0.18 **	0.04 *	0.26 **	0.17 **	0.02
DUB						1	0.53 **	0.21 **	0.36 **	0.22 **	0.04 **
ABH							1	0.09 **	0.29 **	0.16 **	0.04 *
ISR								1	0.15 **	0.1 **	0.04 *
OM									1	0.28 **	0.11 **
JOR										1	0.05 **
LEB											1

Notes: This table provides the unconditional correlation matrix based on the Pearson Correlation coefficients. The matrix correlation coefficients are statistically significant, involving the presence of the relationship between return series. For instance, the unconditional correlation estimates between the TUNINDEX, the GCC markets' indices, the Middle East markets' indices, and the North Africa markets' indices (EGX30 and MADEX) are on average 0.0813, 0.05, and 0.0485, respectively.
TUN: Tunisia; EGX: Egypt; MO: Morocco; SAR: Saudi Arabia; BAH: Bahrain; DUB: Dubai; ABH: Abu Dhabi; ISR: Israel; OM: Oman; JOR: Jordan; LEB: Lebanon;
** Significance level at 5%; * Significance level at 10%.

Beirut Stock Exchange) averages 0.06 (resp., 0.1), 0.061 (resp., 0.148), and 0.044.

5. Empirical Results

5.1. *Volatility and co-movement analysis of MENA indices*

Figures 3(a)–3(k) correspond to the individual wavelet spectra of all selected MENA indices.[5] In general, the wavelet individual spectra enable the

[5]According to Aguiar-Conraria *et al.* (2008), Grinsted *et al.* (2004), and Torrence and Compo (1998), the statistical significance of wavelet power is measured against the null

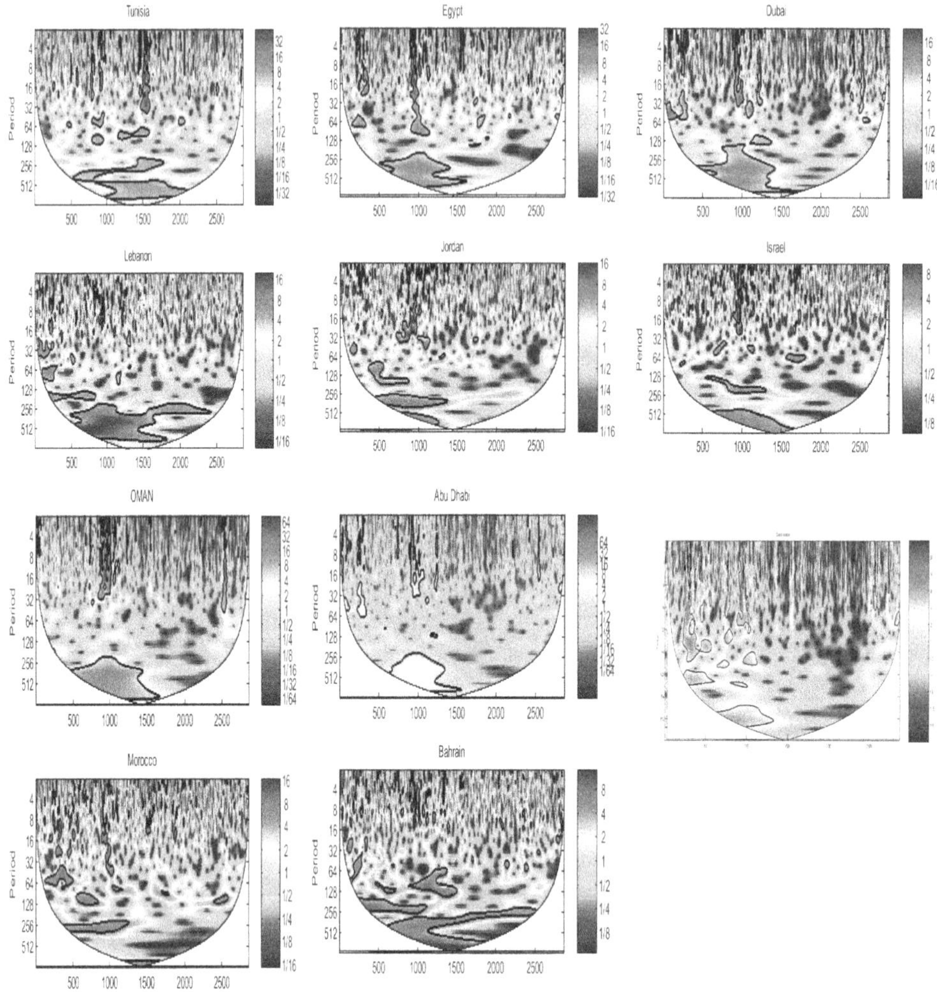

Figure 3. Continuous Wavelet Power Spectra of MENA Indices

Notes: This figure shows continuous wavelet power spectra of the selected MENA indices. The black contour identifies the regions in which the spectrum is significant at the 5% level against red noise. The Cone Of Influence (COI) is indicated by the lighter shade which delimits the high power regions. Time and frequency (years) are represented by the horizontal and vertical axes, respectively.

---

hypothesis of a stationary process with a background power spectrum, estimated from the Monte Carlo simulations using phase-randomized surrogate series. The significance level of the wavelet power spectrum at the 5% level against red noise is indicating by the black hardy contour. The Cone Of Influence (COI), which is designated by a lighter shade, splits visualization of the local variance of the index returns in the frequency-time space. From Fig. 3, some interesting facts are revealed. During the studied period, the most volatile indices are those of Tunisia, Lebanon, Egypt, and Bahrain. For the aforementioned indices, high levels of local variance are often localized both at high- and low-frequencies spending, especially in the period 2007–2013. Obviously, this result is not surprising given that the period of excessive volatility corresponds to the 'Arab Spring' age. During the period of the political turmoil of Arab world, the indices experience amplified levels of volatility, reflecting a lack of investors' confidence, and different market assessments (Chau and Wang, 2014).

Nonetheless, during the same period, indices of Jordan, Morocco, Abu Dhabi, Dubai, and Saudi Arabia were not influenced by the Arab Spring event as evidenced by the yellow areas. These findings corroborate those of Aggarwal *et al.* (1999), who show that the local political and economic events increasingly alter the volatility in emerging stock markets rather than global political unrests. However, unlike Hammoudeh and Li (2008), our results show that GCC and Jordan indices (except for Bahrain index) do not experience high volatility during global political turmoil.

The cross-wavelet transformation allows not only to identify the lead-lag relationship between time series but also it ascertains the localization of the co-movement between markets, if it exists, in the time-frequency domain. Figures 4(a)–4(j) show the cross-wavelet power spectrum[6] between Tunisian index returns and all MENA indices returns. A close look at Fig. 4 clearly shows common regions of co-movement, for all pairwises, at high and low frequencies over the period 2007–2013. During the period 2007–2011 and at high frequency (256–512 days of year), the Tunisian index exhibits high co-movements with all other selected MENA indices, except for Morocco and Saudi Arabia cases. More interestingly, the comovements between markets become less important or disappear after 2011, implying a lack of dynamic relationship between Tunisian index and the selected MENA indices over

the high power regions from the rest. There is the region of the wavelet spectrum in which edge effects become important.

[6]For the corresponding figures, the same interpretations of color ranging were kept, and we interpret the phase difference in terms of the arrows direction. Recall that arrows localized in the right (left) indicates that variables are in phase (out of phase). If arrows move to the right and up (down), the first variable x is leading (lagging). However, when arrows switch to the left and up (down), the variable x is lagging (leading).

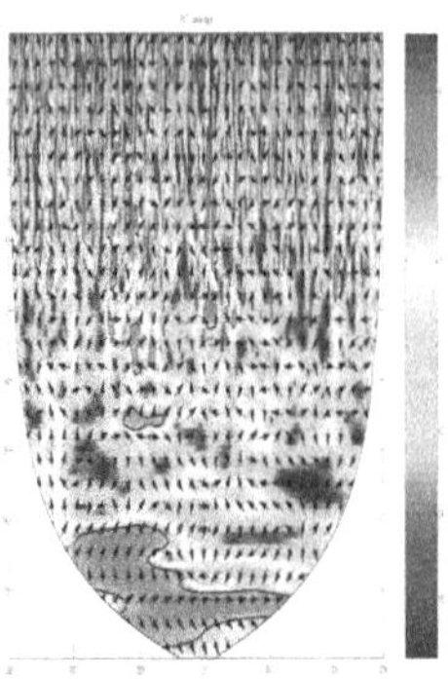

(a) Tunisia vs. Egypt

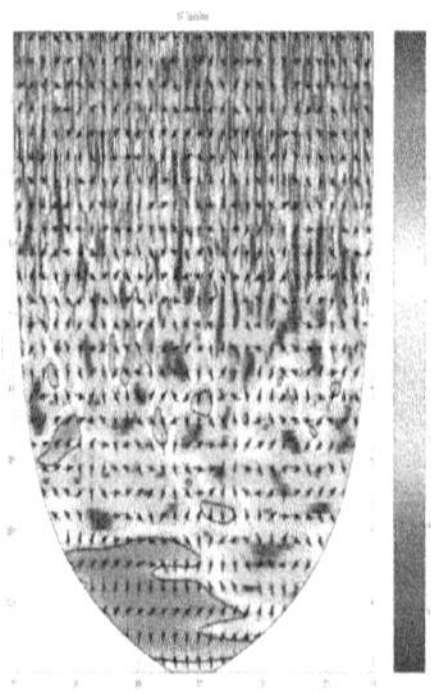

(b) Tunisia vs. Dubai

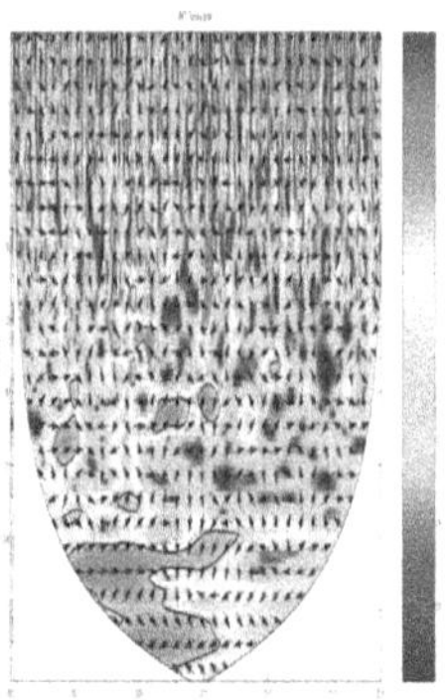

(c) Tunisia vs. Jordan

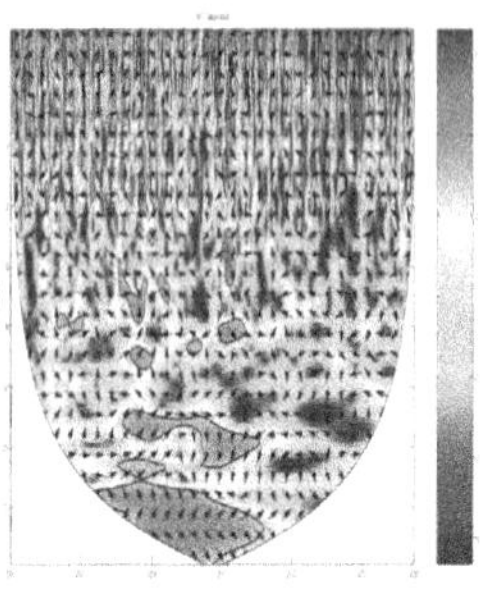

(d) Tunisia vs. Israel

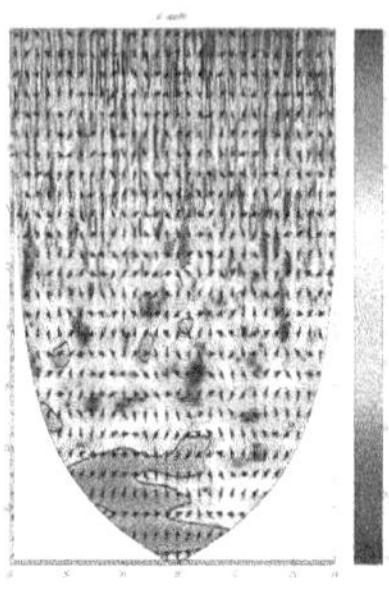

(e) Tunisia vs. Oman

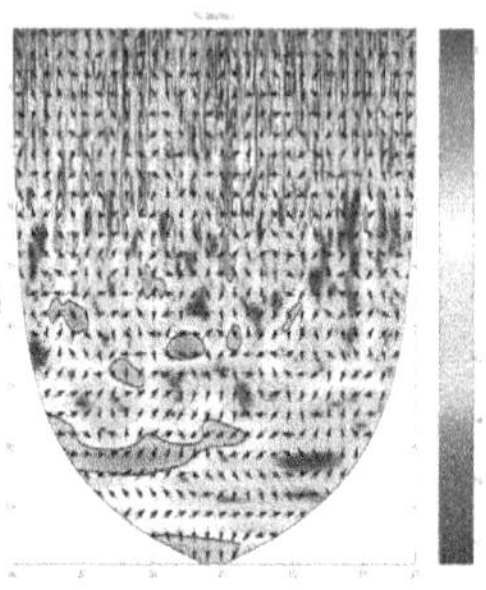

(f) Tunisia vs. Morocco

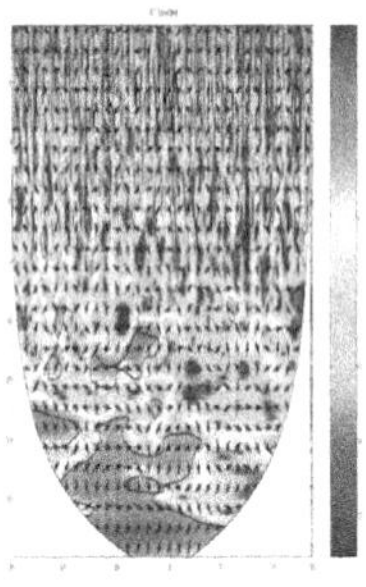

(g) Tunisia vs. Bahrain

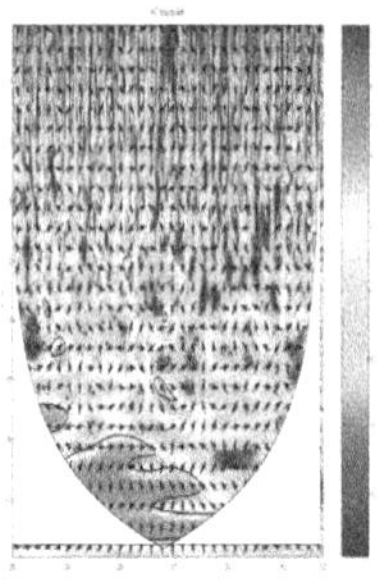

(h) Tunisia vs. Abu Dhabi

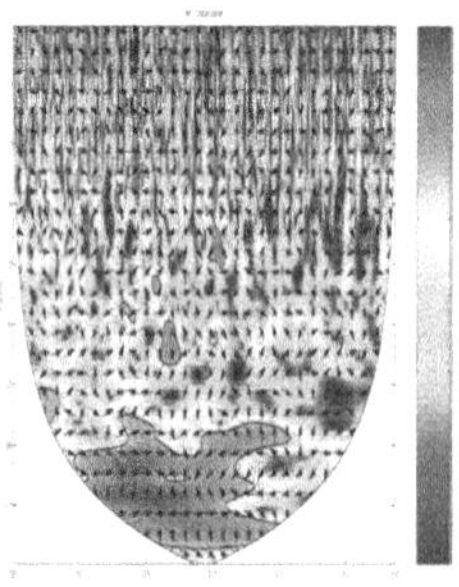

(i) Tunisia vs. Lebanon

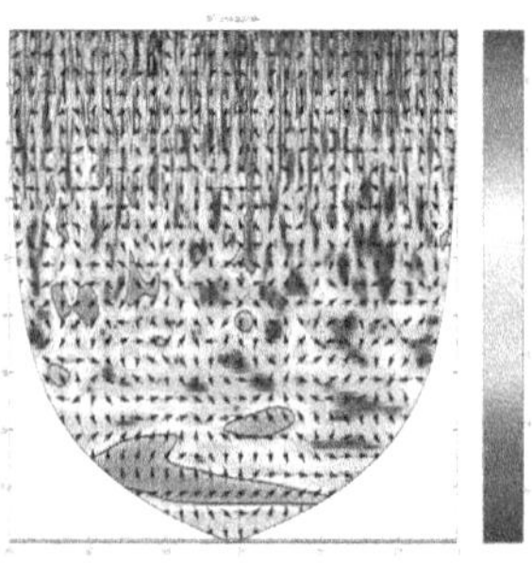

(j) Tunisia vs. Saudi Arabia

Figure 4. Cross-Wavelet Power Spectra of MENA Indices

Notes: This figure illustrates the cross-wavelet power spectra between MENA indices. The thick black contour encloses regions where cross-wavelet power spectra is significant at the 5% level against the red noise estimated from Monte Carlo simulations using phase randomized surrogate series. The Cone Of Influence (COI) is indicated by the lighter shade which delimits the important power regions. The arrows indicate the phase difference between the two time series. The direction of arrows captures the phase difference between two time series. Arrows pointing to the right (left) indicate that variables are in phase (anti-phase), to the right and up (down), the first variable is leading (lagging), and to the left and up (down), the first variable is lagging (leading). Time and frequency (day) are represented by the horizontal and the vertical axis, respectively.

the post-'Arab Spring' period.[7] This finding is also proved by the difficulty to interpret the lead–lag relationship between indices as the arrows change direction rapidly for the same scale and time interval.

For the low-frequency bands and all of the pairwises, small red areas are scattered at 4–64 days of year over the period 2008–2011. After this period, the comovements between Tunisian index and selected MENA indices are fictional.

The wavelet coherence can be used to find out correlation estimates across diverse frequencies and times. While comovements at higher frequencies indicate short-run causalities between selected MENA indices, high degree of comovements at low frequencies exhibits a long-term comovement (cointegration) between indices.

From Figs. 5(a)–5(j), we clearly see a moderate co-movement between Tunisian index and the chosen MENA indices given that little regions of coherency are dispersed over the sample period at high frequency band (8–32 days of scale). The highest power coherency is shown for the Tunisian versus Jordan pairwise, as evidenced by Fig. 5(b). The results display the short-run dynamic relationship between Tunisia and selected MENA indices. A look at Tunisia vs. MENA indices pairwises reveals the difficulty in understanding the direction of causality between indices based on arrow direction.[8]

---

[7]The dates about political events are collected from the Global Terrorism Database. The Global Terrorism Database documents all incidents of terrorism across the globe since 1970.

[8]For the other couples, all figures are available upon request. For the Egyptian case some interesting facts emerge: A remarkable powerful coherency between time series is seen at both at medium and low frequencies over the sample period. Even though the powerful coherences are dispersed at medium frequencies over the entire the sample period, the powerful coherences are concerted at 256–512 frequency bands and over the

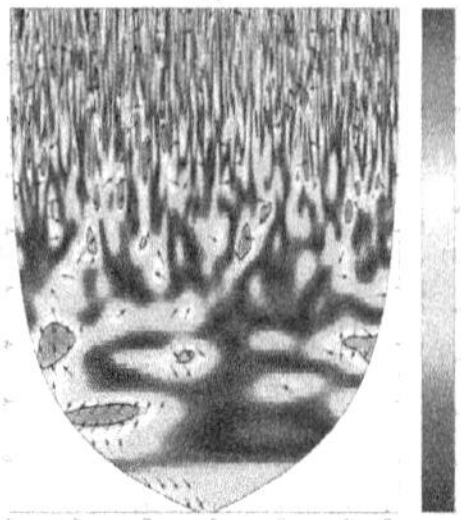

(a) Tunisia vs. Egypt

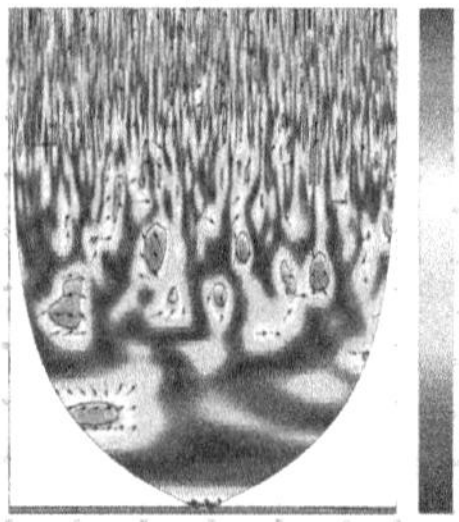

(b) Tunisia vs. Jordan

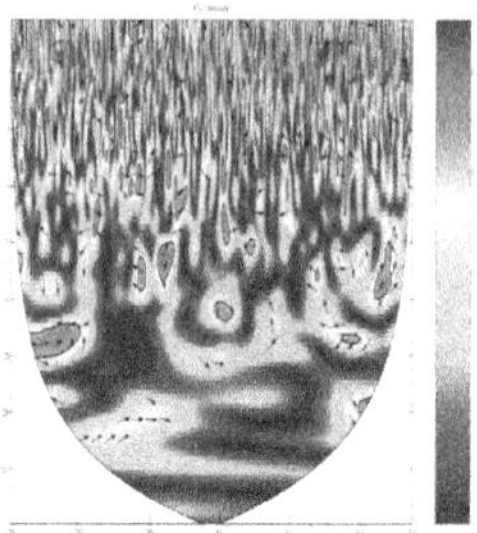

(c) Tunisia vs. Israel

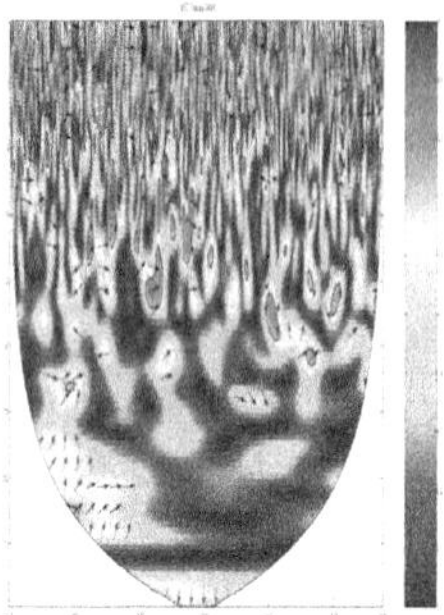

(d) Tunisia vs. Oman

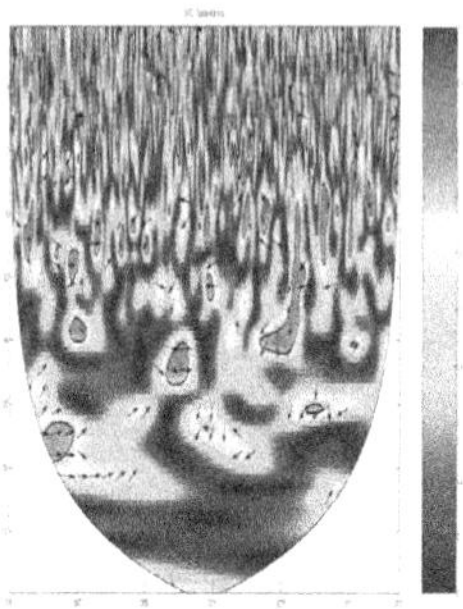

(e) Tunisia vs. Morocco

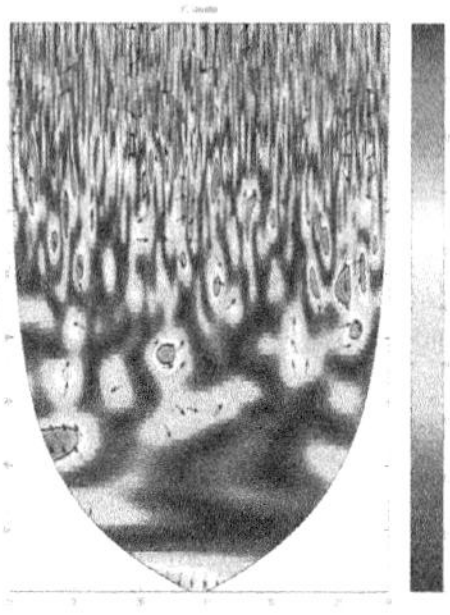

(f) Tunisia vs. Bahrain

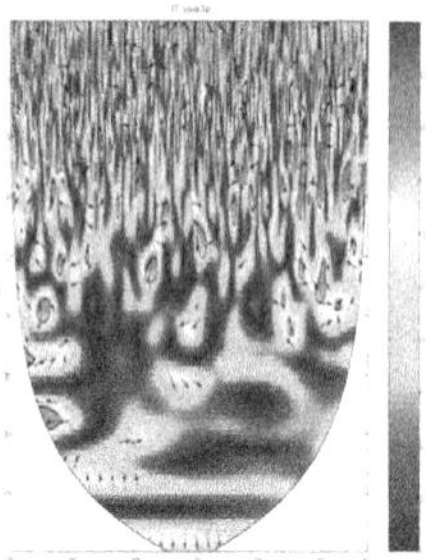

(g) Tunisia vs. Abu Dhabi

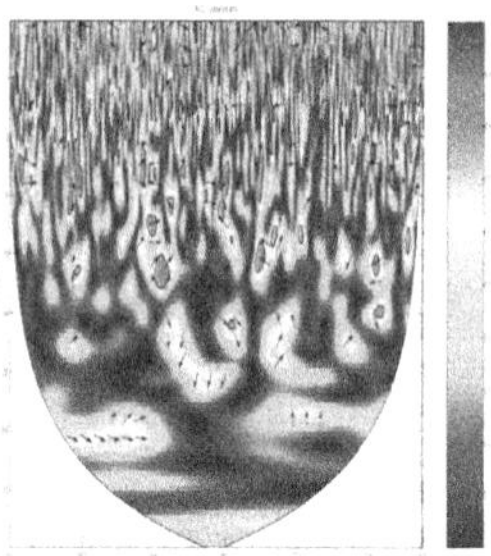

(h) Tunisia vs. Lebanon

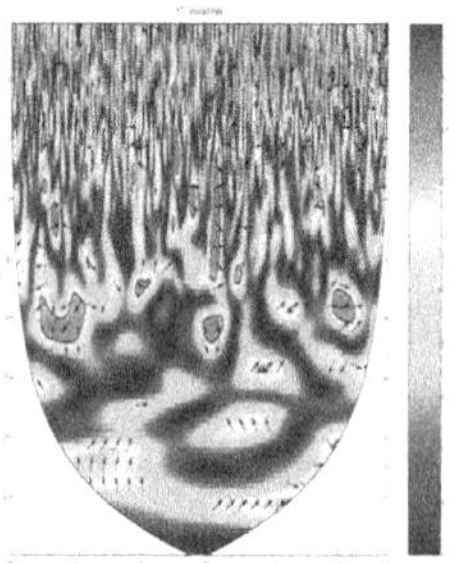

(i) Tunisia vs. Saudi Arabia

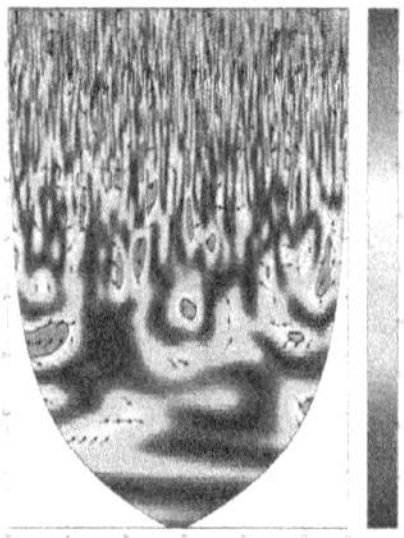

(j) Tunisia vs. Dubai

Figure 5. Wavelet Coherence of the MENA Indices

Notes: The thick black contour encloses regions where the wavelet coherence is significant at the 5% level against the red noise estimated from Monte Carlo simulations using phase randomized surrogate series. The Cone Of Influence (COI) is indicated by the lighter shade which delimits the important power regions. The arrows indicate the phase difference between the two time series. The direction of arrows captures the phase difference between two time series. Arrows pointing to the right (left) indicate that variables are in phase (out of phase), to the right and up (down), the first variable is leading (lagging), and to the left and up (down), the first variable is lagging (leading). Time and frequency (year) are represented by the horizontal and the vertical axis, respectively.

5.2. *Volatility spillover among MENA region indices*

As previously indicated, we extract the daily conditional volatility from EGARCH model. To inspect the volatility spillover patterns between the MENA indices, we run a rolling window of 10 daily volatility observations. Table 4 reports the results of the degree and direction of volatility spillovers within and across the selected MENA stock markets. The $ijth$ entry is the estimated contribution to the forecast error variance of market i, ensuing from innovations to market j. When i is equal $j(i \neq j)$, the diagonal elements (the off-diagonal elements) assess own-market (cross-market) within (between) volatility spillovers markets. Each element of the 'contribution to others' (corresponding to the sum of each off-diagonal columns) refers to the total 'to' volatility spillovers in each market. In contrast, the sum of each off-diagonal rows (i.e., 'Contribution from others') provides the 'from' volatility spillovers of each market in our sample. It is

period 2007–2013 for most pairwises. These findings are not surprising given that 2008 geo-political events, such as bombing at North of Sina (Egypt) and Northern Bahrain and the assassination in Beirut (Lebanon), seem to influence the dynamic relationship between these markets. All of these findings clearly show that terror incidents (or political instability) in Middle-East countries can affect the comovement behavior between stock market indices. The Jordan index exhibits high level of comovements with selected MENA indices at medium- and low-frequency bands over the whole sample period. For the Dubai stock market, the results reveal high coherency between Dubai and MENA selected countries. For most of pairwises, higher coherencies are displayed at low frequencies especially over the period 2007–2013. In addition, our results show integration and causality relationship between Dubai and Abu Dhabi stock market indices. Our findings also reveal a cointegration relationship between the Israel market and the selected MENA indices. In addition, the common features of the region make the comovement between the GCC indices more pronounced. All of the aforementioned findings clearly show that terror incidents (or political instability) in Middle-East countries can affect the comovement behavior between stock market indices.

worth noting that the sum of the variances in a row is 100%.[9] The difference between 'from' and 'to' is the so-called net volatility spillovers from market index i to all other markets j. The total volatility spillover is computed as the average of the spillovers from all the other markets.

From Table 4, there is moderate cross-MENA market volatility spillover. The rows sums (labeled 'contribution from others') reveal that Saudi Stock Exchange and Israel Stock Exchange are the most affected by the contribution of others. Also, the total volatility spillover index averages 31.6% across all the MENA indices, indicating that 31.6% of the volatility forecast error variance in all selected MENA markets comes from spillovers.

Figure 6 plots the total volatility spillovers between the selected MENA region indices. This graph allows us to assess the extent and the nature of the time-varying behavior of the volatility spillovers among MENA indices over the whole sample period. It is clearly seen that there is a substantial volatility spillover among MENA indices over the sample period. More precisely, we observe two increasing volatility spillover stages. Whereas the first phase is observed between the end of 2007 and the beginning of 2009 (ranging between 46% and 92% level), the second one is seen during the whole year of 2010 (the volatility reaches a level of 90%). Not surprisingly, the first volatility stage results from the first half of the financial crisis and the second phase emerges from the Arab Spring event. Undoubtedly, volatility spillover is a salient fact during period of distress.

Even though the analysis of the time-movement of the total volatility spillover index is interesting, this index surrenders directional information contained in the 'contribution to others' and 'contribution from others'. Figure 7 plots the directional volatility spillover from each of the MENA indices to others, whereas Figure 8 illustrates the directional volatility spillover from each to other MENA indices.

From Figs. 7 and 8, the directional volatility spillovers from each index to others are more pronounced than directional volatility spillovers from others to each index. Figure 7 displays that directional volatility spillovers vary greatly over time. During the tranquil period, the spillovers from each market to others are below 4% and do not exceed 15%. However, they significantly increase during the distress period. For example, the directional volatility spillovers from Tunisian index to others (Fig. 7(a)) reach up to

[9] We calculate $\overline{\tilde{\theta}^g_{ij}}(H)$, which presents the basic spillover index using the method of column normalization. This method makes the sum of the variances in every column equal to one.

Table 4. The Empirical Results for the Direction and Degree of Volatility Spillovers Across Selected MENA Markets

	Tunisia	Jordon	Bahrain	Dubai	Egypt	Israel	Lebanon	Morocco	Oman	Abu Dhabi	Saudi Arabia	Contribution from Others
Tunisia	95.34	0.016	0.085	0.028	0.079	0.0013	0.010	2.376	1.63	0.187	0.013	4.66
Jordon	0.489	95.24	0.294	0.856	0.0003	0.092	1.947	0.178	0.566	0.044	0.276	4.75
Bahrain	3.000	0.181	87.904	1.743	2.827	0.677	0.068	0.243	0.307	0.702	2.335	12.09
Dubai	2.211	0.989	1.033	89.470	1.550	0.162	1.308	0.016	0.329	1.548	1.378	10.53
Egypt	21.853	1.248	0.091	7.796	60.329	3.958	0.419	0.006	0.866	0.989	2.439	39.67
Israel	1.365	0.052	0.353	59.103	3.287	31.519	0.911	0.313	2.052	0.256	0.789	68.48
Lebanon	1.249	2.369	0.065	0.783	0.232	0.661	90.895	0.016	0.553	1.979	0.598	9.105
Morocco	4.067	0.955	0.740	3.460	0.251	1.173	0.585	88.464	0.039	0.022	0.0335	11.53
Oman	0.011	2.412	0.989	45.511	2.418	0.519	0.117	0.101	45.274	0.362	1.118	54.72
Abu Dhabi	0.505	1.445	0.261	56.075	2.121	0.197	0.140	0.653	2.595	33.767	2.239	43.925
Saudi Arabia	0.001	0.154	0.496	46.194	2.948	4.652	0.823	0.050	7.428	4.586	32.664	67.335
Contribution to others	34.75	9.821	4.407	221.54	15.71	12.09	6.32	3.95	16.36	10.67	11.21	
Contribution including own	130.09	105.06	92.311	311.01	76.039	43.60	97.215	92.414	61.63	44.43	43.87	**Total Spillover index= (346.8/ 1097.7)= 31.6%**
Net spillovers	30.09	5.07	−7.68	211.01	−23.96	−56.3	−2.78	−7.58	−38.3	−33.25	−56.12	

Notes: In this table, we show a moderate cross-MENA markets volatility spillover. Also, the Saudi Arabia Stock Exchange and Israel Stock Exchange are greatly affected by the contribution of others. On average, the total volatility spillover equals to 31.6% across all the MENA indices. This implies that 31.6% of the volatility forecast error variance in all selected MENA markets comes from spillovers.

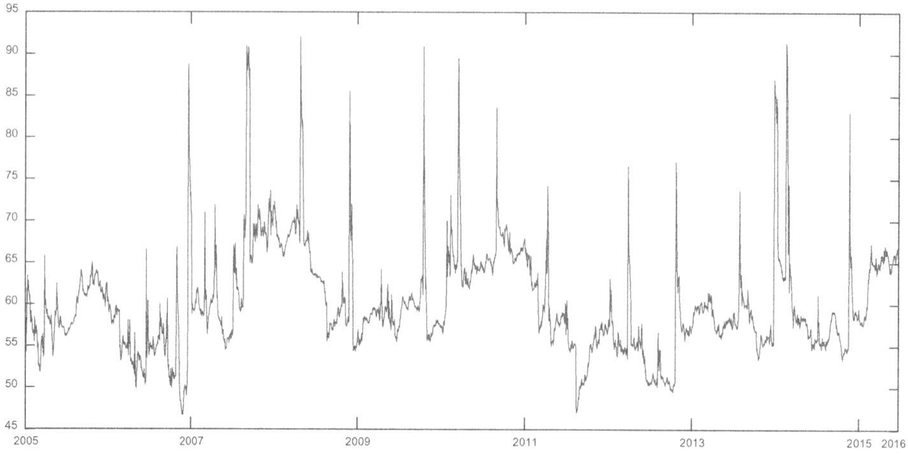

Figure 6. Total Volatility Spillovers Among Selected MENA Markets

Notes: The total volatility spillover among MENA markets is illustrated in this figure. Clearly, we can see a significant volatility spillover among MENA indices over the sample period.

80% at the end of 2010, although it did not exceed 10% before this year. This substantial volatility is linked to the 'Jasmine revolution' event. The second stage of excessive directional volatility spillovers, but not persistent, from the Tunisian market to others (40% level) is shown in 2013, which is characterized by the assassination of opposition leader Chokri Belaid in February.

The gross volatility spillovers from major GCC markets, belonging to our sample (Jordan (Fig. 7(b)), Oman (Fig. 7(i)), and Abu Dhabi (Fig. 7(j))) to others are generally greater than the spillovers from other markets.

Figure 8 illustrates the directional volatility spillovers from others to each of MENA indices. The plots (Figs. 8(a)–8(k)) reveal a relative variation pattern for all markets. Obviously, a relatively increase of the directional volatility spillovers is more pronounced during turbulent times.

Figures 9(a)–9(k) plot the net volatility spillovers which provide information about how much each index contributes to the volatility of other indices returns in net terms. A positive (negative) value of the index indicates a net volatility transmitter (receiver). The net volatility spillovers from the Tunisian market to other markets are positive throughout the two stages of the turbulence period. Egyptian and Lebanon markets are also net transmitters of volatility to other markets at the beginning of year 2011, which corresponds to January 25, 2011 political unrest in Egypt. Figure 9(k)

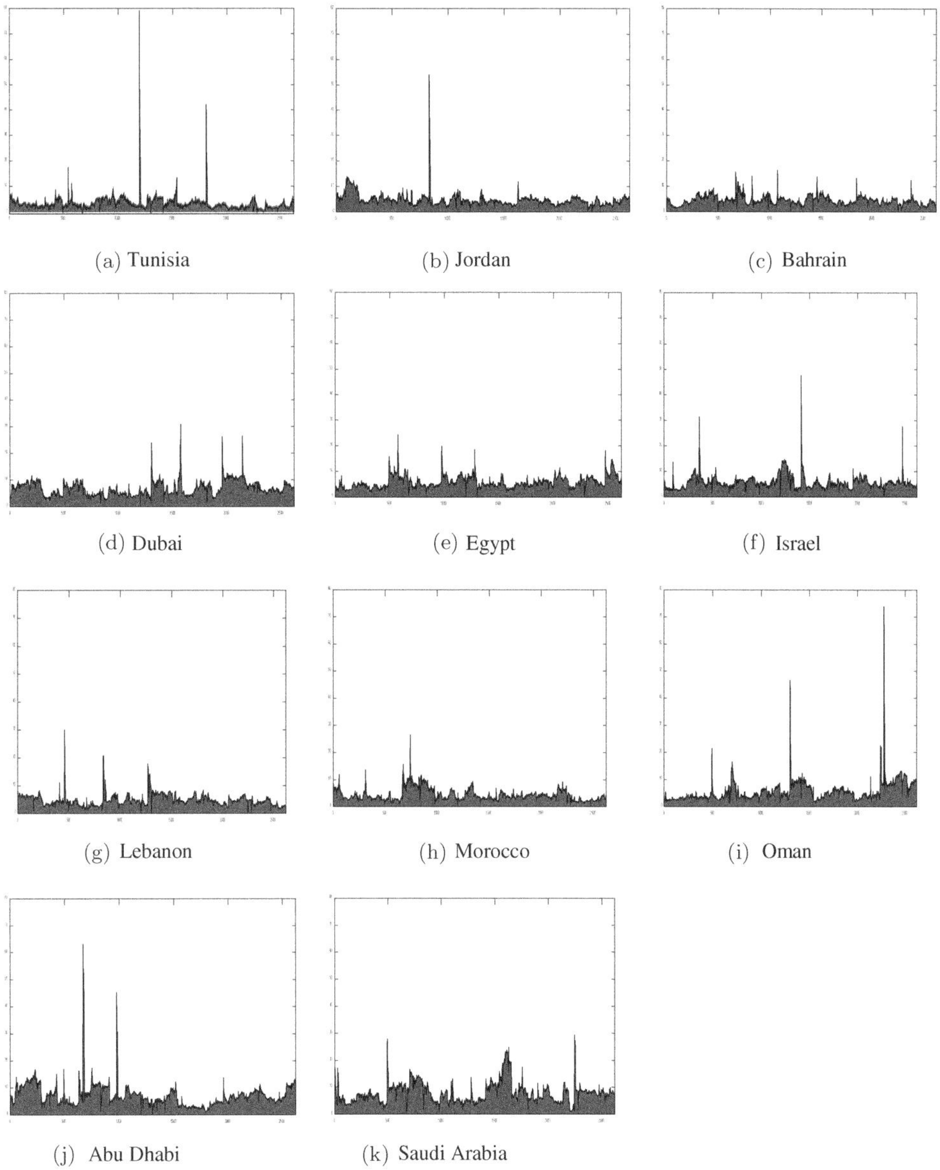

(a) Tunisia (b) Jordan (c) Bahrain

(d) Dubai (e) Egypt (f) Israel

(g) Lebanon (h) Morocco (i) Oman

(j) Abu Dhabi (k) Saudi Arabia

Figure 7. Directional Volatility Spillovers (From i to j)

Notes: This figure shows the direction of volatility spillovers between selected MENA markets. As shown in this figure, the directional volatility spillovers seem to change widely over time. Over the turbulent periods, the spillovers from one market to others tend to rise greatly, while they are below 4% during the calm periods.

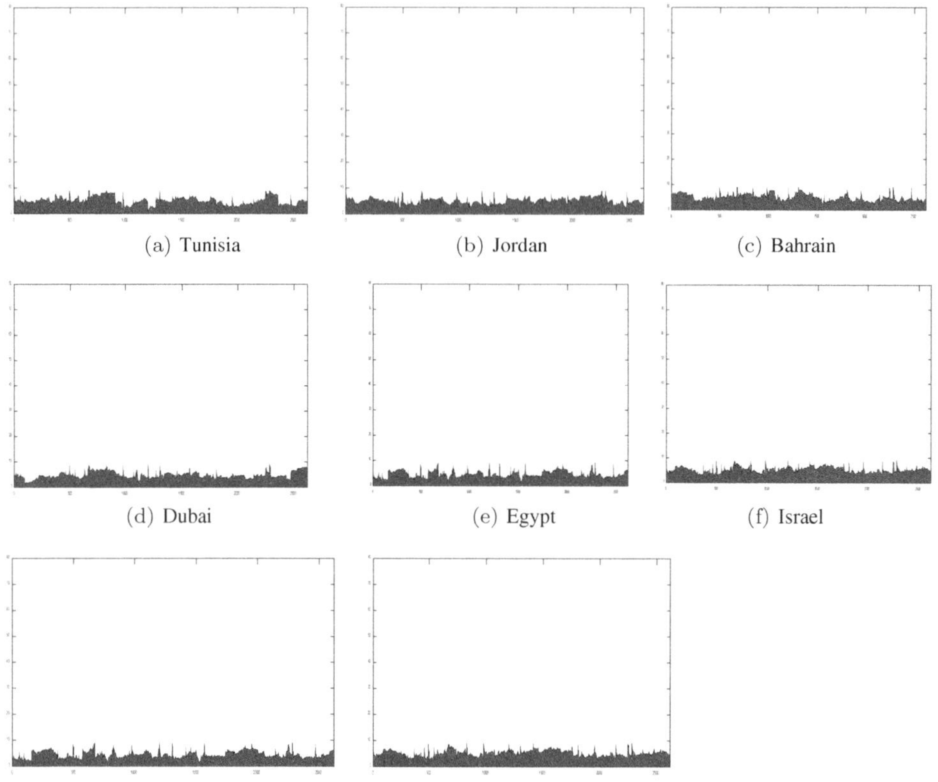

(a) Tunisia (b) Jordan (c) Bahrain

(d) Dubai (e) Egypt (f) Israel

(g) Lebanon (h) Morocco

Figure 8. The Directional Volatility Spillovers from Others to Each MENA Index

Note: Obviously, a relatively increase of the directional volatility spillovers is more pronounced during turbulent times.

displays that Saudi Stock Exchange (Fig. 9(k)) is the most important net volatility transmitter to others. This result shows that the Saudi Stock Exchange is a closed market and does not considerably affect other markets in terms of volatility.

At first sight, Tunisian index is a transmitter of high volatility spillovers to Egyptian market (Fig. 10(c)), Lebanon market (Fig. 10(e)), Oman market (Fig. 10(g)), and Abu Dhabi market (Fig. 10(h)) over the sample period. However, the volatility does not excess 5% during the first turbulence period (the end of year 2009).

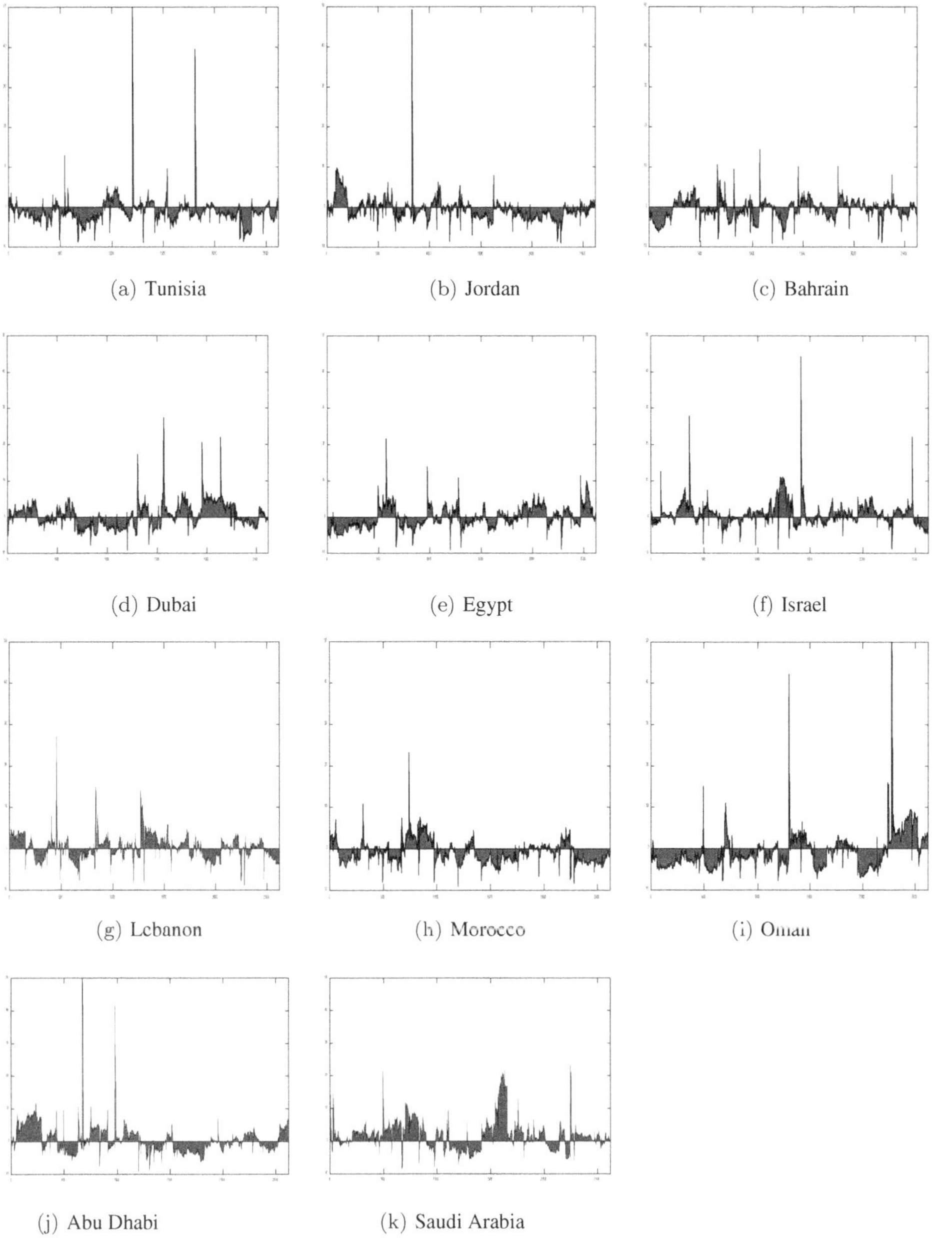

(a) Tunisia (b) Jordan (c) Bahrain

(d) Dubai (e) Egypt (f) Israel

(g) Lebanon (h) Morocco (i) Oman

(j) Abu Dhabi (k) Saudi Arabia

Figure 9. Net Volatility Spillover

Notes: This figure corresponds to the net volatility spillover of the selected MENA markets. A negative value of the index displays a net volatility receiver. However, a positive value of the index indicates a net volatility transmitter.

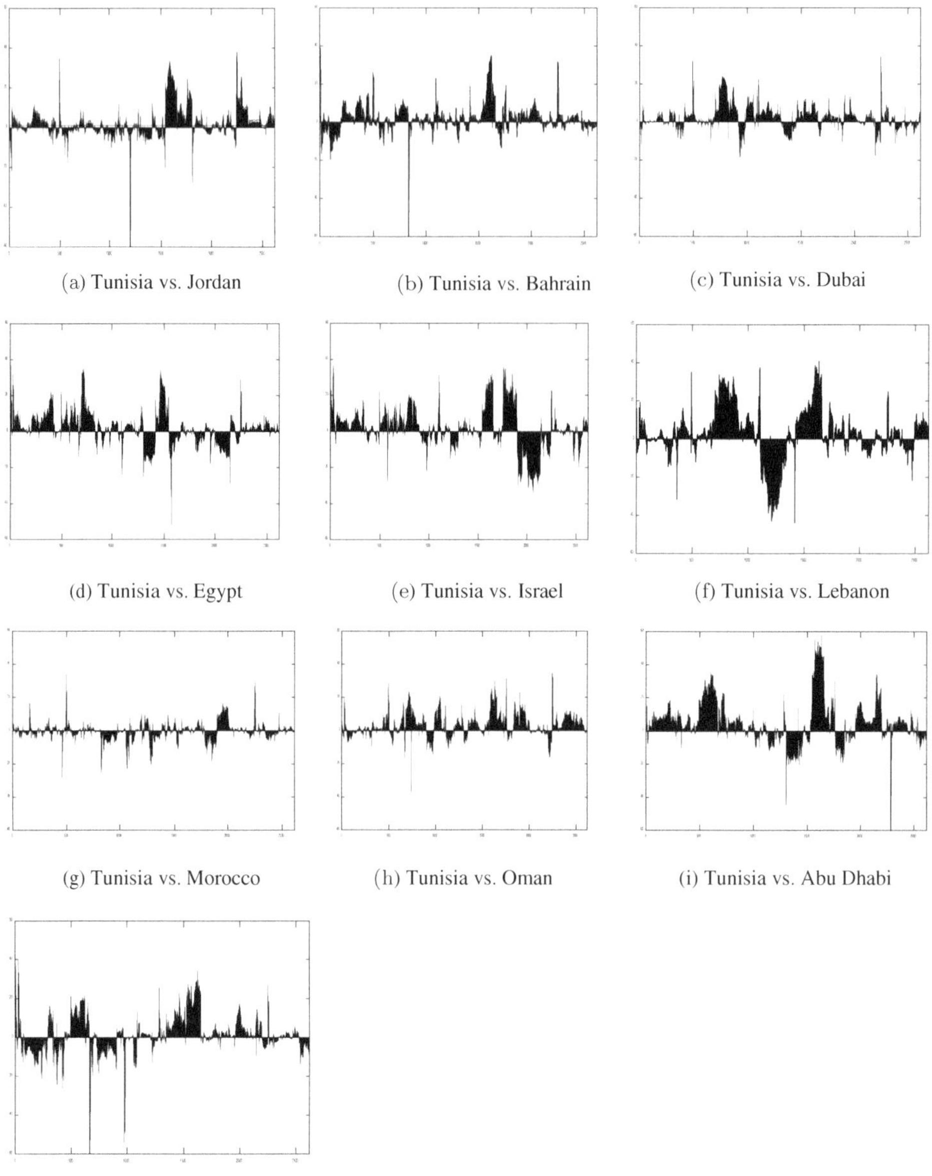

(a) Tunisia vs. Jordan
(b) Tunisia vs. Bahrain
(c) Tunisia vs. Dubai
(d) Tunisia vs. Egypt
(e) Tunisia vs. Israel
(f) Tunisia vs. Lebanon
(g) Tunisia vs. Morocco
(h) Tunisia vs. Oman
(i) Tunisia vs. Abu Dhabi
(j) Tunisia vs. Saudi Arabia

Figure 10. Pairwises Spillovers: Tunisia vs. MENA Region

Notes: This figure illustrates the volatility spillovers for Tunisia against the other selected MENA regions. As shown in this figure, Tunisian index was a transmitter of high volatility spillovers to Lebanon, Abu Dhabi, Egypt, and Oman during the sample period.

6. Robustness Checks

To assess the dependence and the lead–lag relationship for Tunisia market vs. Jordan market[10] pairwise, we use the Maximum Overlap Discrete Wavelet cross-correlation (MODWT) at all scales $\tau_j (j = 1, \ldots, 5)$. From Figs. 11(a)–11(e), the individual cross-correlation functions in wavelet scales are linked with changing of 2–4, 4–8, 8–16, 16–32, and 32–64 days.[11] The red lines bound refers to 95% confidence interval for wavelet cross-correlation.

Figure 11 clearly displays the leading/lagging effects of Tunisian market on the Jordanian market. At shorter scales (i.e., levels 1 and 2), the condensed peaks shown at the right side half of the figure reflect the instability of interactions between the two markets where the Jordanian market index is leading the Tunisian market index. The levels 3 and 4 are consistent with the aforementioned findings and reveal significant correlation between the two markets at medium scales. The cross-wavelet curve becomes smoother at scale 5, reflecting that the attraction powers are less impacted by unexpected changes after 32–64 days. These findings corroborate the previous wavelet coherency results.

7. Summary and Concluding Remarks

This chapter attempts to assess the co-movement and the volatility spillovers between 11 MENA stock markets (Tunisia, Egypt, Morocco, Saudi Arabia, Dubai, Abu Dhabi, Bahrain, Israel, Jordan, Oman, and Lebanon) for the period spanning from March 18, 2005 to March 18, 2016. To this end, we implement the wavelet coherence and the overlap wavelet cross-correlation approaches. The wavelet analysis allows us to detect the multi-horizon nature of comovements and lead–lag relationship between indices. We use the Diebold and Yilmaz (2012) method to assess the direction of volatility transmission between MENA markets.

---

[10] Given that we analyze 5 levels of lead–lag relationship between all of the selected MENA indices, about 200 figures are plotted. The results are available upon request.

[11] A common wavelet filter length of 8 is used in the MODWT transformation of indices' return series to study the linkages between financial time series. The maximum level of MODWT is 6 ($J_0 = 6$) to achieve an optima balance between sample size and the length of filter. For example, scale 1 or scale τ_1 (as $\tau_1 = 2^{1-1} = 1$) measures the dynamic of returns over 2 to 4 days. In other words, the MODWT coefficients are linked with oscillations in the period of 2^j *to* 2^{j+1}. For more details, see Gençay *et al.* (2002, 2003) and Dajčman (2013).

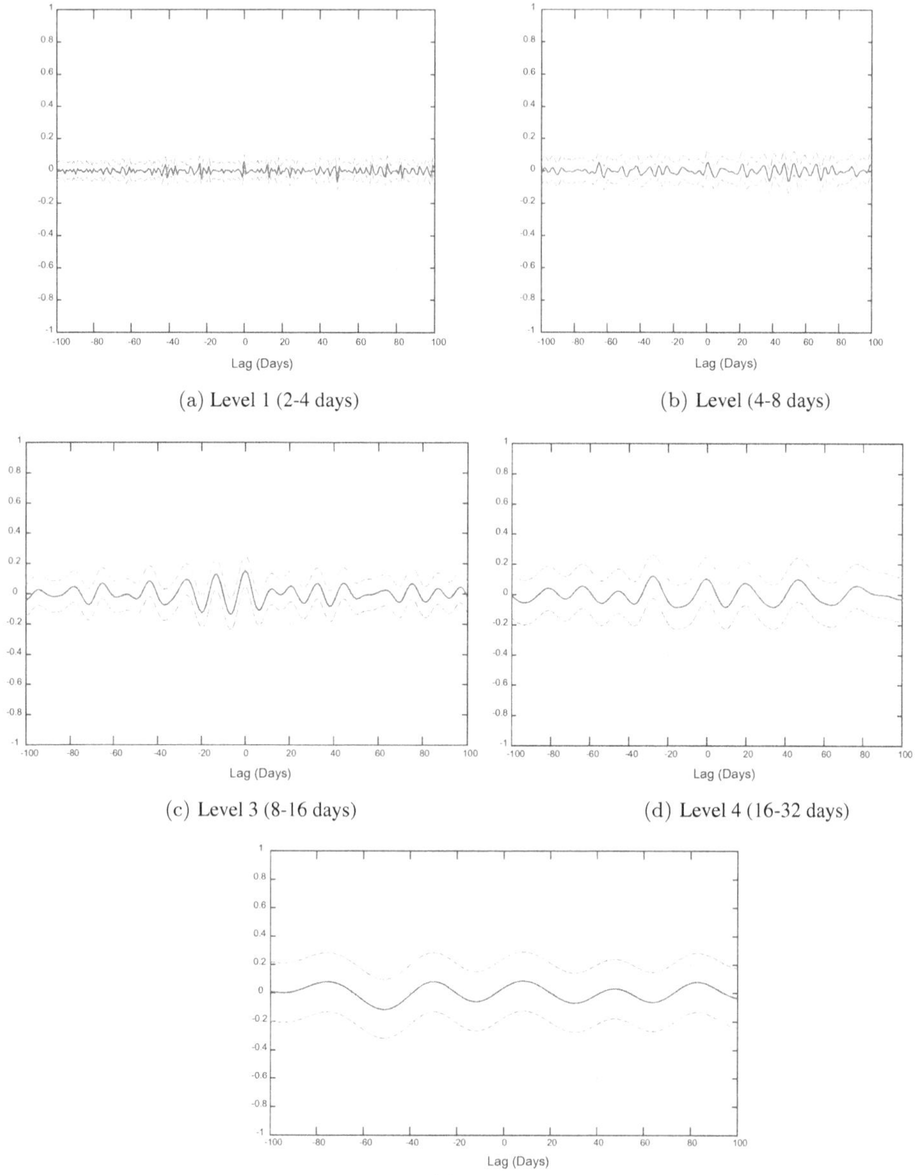

(a) Level 1 (2-4 days)

(b) Level (4-8 days)

(c) Level 3 (8-16 days)

(d) Level 4 (16-32 days)

(e) Level 5 (32-64 days)

Figure 11. The MODWT-Based Wavelet Cross-Correlation between the Tunisia and Jordan Indices

Notes: When the wavelet cross-correlation is skewed to the right (left) side of the graph, the second time series is leading (lagging) the first time series. If both the 95% confidence intervals are above (bellow) the horizontal axes, it means that there is a significant positive (negative) wavelet cross-correlation. The cross-correlation function is plotted for 100 time unit of leads/lags (where $\pi = -100, -99, \ldots, 0, 99, 100$).

From an empirical standpoint, the wavelet coherence analysis shows that comovements between selected MENA indices vary both at different frequencies and over time. Obviously, these results are due to political events. Moreover, the wavelet coherence analysis reveals frequent shifts in the pattern of the MENA markets behavior, especially over the period 2007–2011 at different horizons. For instance, at low frequencies, we see higher coherence for the couples (Dubai vs. Abu Dhabi; Israel vs. Oman; Israel vs. Bahrain; and Israel vs. Lebanon) over the period 2007–2013. These results indicate a long-term comovement, indicating the cointegration relationship between these couples of markets. At medium and low frequencies, the Egyptian market experiences an increased comovement of returns with Jordan, Israel, Bahrain, Abu Dhabi, and Lebanon markets. The same result is found between Jordan index and other MENA indices (except for Morocco index). Our results also show powerful comovement between Oman index and Jordan index, and Oman and Abu Dhabi indices. Also, our results highlight a greater comovement between the Morocco index and Bahrain index. At the high frequency, only the Tunisian index experiences a moderate co-movement of returns with other MENA indices over the sample period. This implies the short-run dynamic relationship between Tunisia and selected MENA indices. The cross-wavelet transformation mainly identifies the lead–lag relationship between the selected MENA markets.

The volatility spillovers across MENA markets are generally moderated over the sample period. Nonetheless, the volatility spillovers increase significantly over the period of both financial crisis (2007–2009) and 'Arab Spring' event (the 2010 year). This result is not surprising because periods of turmoil are considered as a signal of lack of investors' confidence and may cause waves of dissimilar interpretations. The directional volatility spillovers vary greatly over time. In particular, it increased significantly during the distress period. For example, the volatility spillovers from Tunisia index to others reached up 80% with the occurrence of 'Arab Spring' in 2010. The same phenomenon was observed in 2013 during the assassination of politician Chokri Belaid. Finally, Tunisian, Egyptian and Lebanon markets seem to be net transmitters of volatility to other markets at the beginning of 2011.

The use of MODWT as a robustness test allows us to confirm our previous findings and to show again the comovement behavior between the selected MENA markets which is mostly localized at medium scales. Furthermore, the attraction powers between indices are less impacted by unexpected changes in long-run horizon.

To sum up, we clearly document that spillover risks are spread far from evenly in the national markets, and the largest spillovers occur from the countries which experienced dramatic country-specific events. In other words, a few selected MENA stock markets tend to move with other markets which are characterized by a greater country-specific volatility. By and large, overwhelmingly, MENA stock markets are not entirely immune to spillovers emanating from the fallout of the political events. Consistent with previous results in the volatility spillover literature, the stock markets are exposed to market-wide shocks, affecting most of them simultaneously. Political events could have several implications beyond national boundaries for investors, business managers, and policymakers. Identifying the spillover mechanism offers information for investors to make more accurate portfolio decisions that must incorporate the impact of political events, enhance awareness of the behavior of stock returns during such events, and help deal with volatility of stock returns for more stable financial markets. For policymakers who are worried about the safety, soundness, and stability of the financial system, our results can help them to assess the vulnerabilities of the national markets to the ongoing adverse events. As a result, they can draw effective policies and regulation to ensure more stable stock markets in the face of international dramatic political events.

References

Abadie, A. and Gardeazabal, J. (2008). Terrorism and the world economy. *Eur. Econ. Rev.*, 52, pp. 1–27.

Adrangi, B., Chatrathb, A., and Raffieec, K. (2014). Volatility spillovers across major equity markets of Americas. *Inter. J. Bus.*, 19, pp. 1083–4346.

Aggarwal, R., Inclan, C., and Leal, R. (1999). Volatility in emerging stock markets. *J. Fin. Q. Analys*, 34, pp. 33–55.

Aguiar-Conraria, L., Azevedo, N., and Soares, M. J. (2008). Using wavelets to decompose the time-frequency effects of monetary policy. *Phys. A*, 387, pp. 2863–2878.

Ahmed, S. and Farooq, O. (2008). The effect of 9/11 on the stock market volatility dynamics: Empirical evidence from a front line state. *Inter. Res. J. Fin. Econ.*, 16, pp. 71–83.

Ait-Sahalia, J., Cacho-Diaz, J., and Laeven, R. J. A. (2010). Modeling financial contagion using mutually exciting jump processes, NBER Working Paper, 15850, p. 150.

Aloui, R., Aissa, M., and Nguyen, D. (2011). Global financial crisis, extreme interdependences, and contagion effects: The role of economic structure?. *J. Bank. Fin.*, 35, pp. 130–141.

Alsharairi, M. and Abubaker, W. (2016). Does Arab Spring have a spillover effect on Dubai financial market?, The Australia-Middle East Conf. on Bus. and Soc Sci. (in Dubai).

Apergis, E. and Apergis, N. (2016). The 11/13 Paris terrorist attacks and stock prices: The case of the international defense industry. *Fin. Res. Lett.*, pp. 1–18.

Arouri, M., Lahiani, A., and Nguyen, D. K. (2013). Equity market comovements and financial contagion: A study of Latin America and the United States. *Bank. Mark. and Inves.*, 126, pp. 17–29.

Aslam, F., Kang, H.-G., Mohti, W., Rafique, A., and Salman, A. (2016). The impact of terrorism on financial markets: Evidence from Asia. *The Sing. Econ. Rev.*, (forthcoming.)

Barth, J. R., Li, T., McCarthy, D., Phumiwasana, T., and Yago, G. (2006). Economic impacts of global terrorism: From Munich to Bali, Santa Monica, CA: Capit. Stud., Milken Institute.

Barunik, J., Vacha, L., and Krištoufek, L., (2011). Co-movement of Central European stock markets using wavelet coherence: Evidence from high-frequency data, IES Working Paper 22/2011, IESFSV, Charles University.

Ben Rejeb, A. and Boughrara, A. (2015). Financial integration in emerging market economies: Effects on volatility transmission and contagion. *Bors. Istanb. Rev.*, 15, pp. 161–179.

Bentes, S. R. (2016). Long memory volatility of gold price returns: How strong is the evidence from distinct economic cycles?. *Phys. A*, 443, pp. 149–160.

Bodart, V. and Candelon, B. (2009). Evidence of interdependence and contagion using a frequency domain framework. *Emerg. Mark. Rev.*, 10, pp. 140–150.

Boubaker, S., Jouini, J., and Lahiani, A. (2015). Financial contagion between the US and selected developed and emerging countries: The case of the subprime crisis. *Q. Rev. Econ. Fin.*, pp. 1–15.

Brounen, D. and Derwall, J. (2010). The Impact of terrorist attacks on international stock markets. *Europ. Fin. Manage.*, 16, pp. 585–598.

Calvo, S. and Reinhart, C. (1996). Capital flows to Latin America: Is the evidence of contagion effects?, In Private Capital flows to Emerging Markets After the Mexican Crisis, Washington, D.C. Inst. for Inter. Econ.

Chau, F., Deesomsak, R., and Wang, J. (2014). Political uncertainty and stock market volatility in the Middle East and North African (MENA) countries. *J. Inter. Fin. Mark, Inst. and Mon.*, 28, pp. 1–19.

Chen, A. H. and Siems, T. F. (2003). The effect of terrorism on global capital market. *Eur. J. Pol. Econ.*, 20, pp. 349–366.

Chesney, M., Karaman, M., and Reshetar, G. (2011). The impact of terrorism on financial markets: An empirical study. *J. Bank. Fin.*, 35, pp. 253–267.

Chiang, S. M., Chen, H. F., and Lin, C.T. (2013). The spillover effects of the sub-prime mortgage crisis and optimum asset allocation in the BRICV stock markets. *Glob. Fin. J.*, 18, pp. 147–159.

Dajčman, S. (2013). Interdependence between some major European stock markets-a wavelet lead/lag analysis. *Prague Econ. Pap.*, 1, 28–34.

Diamonte, R. L., Liew, J. M., and Stevens, R. L. (1996). Political risk in emerging and developed markets. *Fin. Analys. J.*, 52, pp. 71–76.

Diebold, F. X. and Yilmaz, K. (2009). Measuring financial asset return and volatility spillovers, with application to global equity markets. *Econ. J.*, 119, pp. 158–171.

Diebold, F. X. and Yilmaz, K. (2012). Better to give than to receive: Predictive directional measurement of volatility spillovers. *Int. J. Forecast.*, 28, pp. 57–66.

Drakos, K. (2010b). The determinants of terrorist shock's cross-market transmission. *The J. R. Fin.*, 11, pp. 147–163.

El-Chaarani, H. (2015). Volatility spillover between Lebanese political shocks and financial market returns. *Lebane, Sc. J.*, 16, pp. 95–111.

Essaddam, N. and Karagianis, J. M. (2014). Terrorism, country attributes, and the volatility of stock returns. *Res. Inter. Bus. and Financ.*, 31, pp. 87–100.

Forbes, K. J. and Rigobon, R. (2002). No contagion, only interdependence: Measuring stock market comovements. *J. Fin.*, 57, pp. 2223–2261.

Gallegati, M. (2008). Wavelet analysis of stock returns and aggregate economic activity. *Comput. Statist. Data. Anal.*, 52, pp. 3061–3074.

Gamba-Santamaria, S., Gomez-Gonzalez, J. E., Hurtado-Guarin, J. L., and Melo-Velandia, L. F. (2016). Stock market volatility spillovers. *Evidence Latin Am. Fin. Res. Lett.*, pp. 1–17.

Gençay, R., Selçuk, F., and Whitcher, B. (2001a). Scaling properties of foreign exchange. *Volatility. Phy. A*, 289, pp. 249–266.

Gençay, R., Selçuk, F., and Whitcher, B. (2002). *An Introduction to Wavelets and Other Filtering Methods in Finance and Economics*. London Academic Press.

Gençay, R., Selçuk, F., and Whitcher, B. (2003). Systematic risk and timescales. *Qu. Fin.*, 3, pp. 108–116.

Giovannetti, G. and Velucchi, M. (2013). A spillover analysis of shocks from US, UK and China on African financial markets. *Rev. Dev. Fin.*, 3, pp. 169–179.

Grinsted, A., Moore, J. C., and Jevrejeva, S. (2004). Application of the cross wavelet transform and wavelet coherence to geophysical time series. *Nonlinear Process, Geophys.*, 11, pp. 561–566.

Gul, T., Hussain, A., Bangash, S., and Khattak, S. W. (2010). Impact of terrorism on the financial markets of Pakistan. *Eur. J. Soc. Sc.*, 18, pp. 98–108.

Hamao, Y., Masulis, R. W., and Ng, V. (1990). Correlations in price changes and volatility across international stock markets. *Rev. Fin. Stud.*, 3, pp. 281–307.

Hammoudeh, S. and Li, H. (2008). Sudden changes in volatility in emerging markets: The case of Gulf Arab stock markets. *Intern. Rev. Fin. Analys.*, 17, pp. 47–63.

Hobbs, J., Schaupp, L. C., and Gingrich, J. (2016). Terrorism, militarism, and stock returns. *J. Fin. Crim.*, 23, pp. 70–86.

Hon, M., Strauss, J., and Yong, S-K. (2004). Contagion in financial markets after September 11: myth or reality?. *The J. Fin. Res.*, 27, pp. 95–114.

Hudgins, B., Parker, P., and Scott, R. N. (1993). A new strategy for multifunction myoelectric control. *IEEE Trans. Biomed. Eng.*, 40.

Jin, X. and An, X. (2016). Global financial crisis and emerging stock market contagion: A volatility impulsive response function approach. *Inter. Bus Fin.*, 36, pp. 179–195.

Johnston, R. B. and Nedelescu, O. M. (2006). The impact of terrorism on financial markets. *J. Fina. Crim.* 13, pp. 7–25.

Karanasos, M., Yfanti, S., and Karoglou, M. (2014). Multivariate FIAPARCH modelling of financial markets with dynamic correlations in times of crisis. *Int. Rev. Fina. Analys.*, pp. 1–16.

Karolyi, G. A. and Martell, R. (2010). Terrorism and the stock market. *Inter. Rev. App. Fin. Iss. Econ.*, 2, pp. 285–314.

Kolaric, S. and Schiereck, D. (2016). Are stock markets efficient in the face of fear? Evidence from the terrorist attacks in Paris and Brussels, *Fin. Res. Lett.*, (forthcoming).

Kollias, C., Papadamou, S., and Siriopoulos, C. (2012). Terrorism induced cross-market transmission of shocks: A case study using intraday data. Economics of Security, Working Paper, pp. 1–24.

Kollias, C., Papadamou, S., and Stagiannis, A. (2010). Armed conflicts and capital markets: The case of the Israeli military offensive in the Gaza strip. *Def. Peac. Econ.*, 21, pp. 357–365.

Kollias, C., Papadamou, S., and Stagiannis, A. (2011b). Terrorism and capital markets: The effects of the Madrid and London bomb attacks. *Int. Rev. Econ. Fina.*, 20, pp. 532–541.

Kumar, S. and Liu, J. (2013). Impact of terrorism on international stock markets. *J. App. Bus. Econ.*, 14, pp. 42–60.

Mensi, W., Hammoudeh, S., Nguyen, D. K., and Kang, S. H. (2015). Global financial crisis and spillover effects among the U.S. and BRICS stock markets. *Int. Rev. Econ. Fin.*, pp. 3–23.

Mnasri, A. and Nechi, S. (2016). Impact of terrorist attacks on stock market volatility in emerging markets. *Emerg. Mark. Rev.*, 28, pp. 184–202.

Mnif, A. (2017). Political uncertainty and behavior of Tunisian stock market cycles: Structural unobserved components time series models. *Res. Int. Bus. Fin.*, 39, pp. 206–214.

Mousavi, M. M. and Ouenniche, J. (2014). The impact of MENA conflicts (The Arab Spring) on global financial markets. *The J. Deve. Area*, 48, pp. 21–40.

Neaime, S. (2012). The global financial crisis, financial linkages and correlations in returns and volatilities in emerging MENA stock markets. *Emerg. Mark. Rev.*, 13, pp. 268–282.

Nguyen, A. P. and Enomoto, C. E. (2009). Acts of terrorism and their impacts on stock index returns and volatility: The cases of the Karachi and Tehran stock exchanges. *Int. Bus. Econ. Res. J.*, 8, pp. 75–86.

Panopoulou, E. and Pantelidis, T. (2009). Integration at a cost: Evidence from volatility impulse response functions. *App. Fin. Econ.*, 19, pp. 917–933.

Pritsker, M. (2001). The channels for financial contagion. In Claessens and Forbes (eds.), International Financial Contagion, Norwell, MA: Kluwer Academic Publishers.

Robbani, M. and Anantharaman, S. (2002). An econometric analysis of stock market reaction to political events in emerging markets. In *Second Annual ABIT Conf.* Pittsburgh, Pennsylvania.

Rua, A. and Nunes, L. (2009). International comovement of stock market returns: A wavelet analysis. *J. Emp. Fina.*, 16, pp. 632–639.

Saiti, B., Bacha, O., and Masih, M. (2015). Testing the conventional and Islamic financial market contagion: Evidence from wavelet analysis. *Emerg. Mark. Fina. Tr.*, 52, pp. 1832–1849.

Serroukh, A., Walden, A. T., and Percival, D. B. (2000). Statistical properties and uses of the wavelet variance estimator for the scale analysis of time series. *J. Am. Stat. Assoc.*, 95, pp. 184–196.

Suleman, M. T. (2012). Stock market reaction to good and bad political news. *Asia, J. Fin. Accout.* , 4, pp. 299–312.

Syriopoulos, T., Makramc, B., and Boubaker, A. (2015). Stock market volatility spillovers and portfolio hedging: BRICS and the financial crisis. *Inter. Rev. Fin. Anal.*, 39, pp. 7–18.

Theodossiou, P. and Lee, U. (1993). Mean and volatility spillovers across major national stock markets: Further empirical evidence. *The J. Fin. Res.*, 16, pp 337–350.

Torrence, C. and Compo, G. P. (1998). A practical guide to wavelet analysi. *Bull. Am Meteorol soc.*, 79, pp. 61–78.

Torrence, C. and Webster, P. J. (1999). Inter-decadal changes in the ENSO-monsoon system. *J. Clim.*, 12, pp. 2679–2690.

Vuchelen, J. (2003). Electroral systems and the effects of political events on the stock market: The Belgian case. *Econ. Pol.*, 15, pp. 85–102.

Wisniewski, T. P. (2016). Is there a link between politics and stock returns? A literature survey. *Inter. Rev. Fin. Analys.*, pp. 1–31.

Yarovaya, L. and Lau, C. K. (2016). Stock market comovements around the global financial crisis: Evidence from the UK, BRICS and MIST markets. *Res. Int. Bus. Fin.*, 37, pp. 605–619.

Yi, Y., Qi, W., and Wu, D. (2013). Are CIVETS the Next BRICs? A comparative analysis from scientometrics perspective. *Scientom.*, 94, pp. 615–628.

Chapter 6

Measuring the Contagion Effect in Emerging Markets

Igor Alexandre Clemente de Morais*, Guilherme Ribeiro de Macêdo†, Marcia Regina Godoy‡ and Leonardo Berteli Piveta*

*UNISINOS

†Universidade Federal do Rio Grande do Sul (UFRGS)

‡Universidade Federal do Rio Grande (FURG)

Abstract

This chapter investigates the existence of contagion in the stock market in emerging countries considering the impact of the subprime crisis in Latin America and Central and Eastern Europe. Eleven indices of stock exchanges using deterministic models GARCH and stochastic volatility, both univariate and multivariate are evaluated. The results indicated the presence of financial integration between countries and further suggest that the crisis intensified these relationships. In addition, several features common to financial series, such as the leverage effect, clustering volatility and persistence were identified.

1. Introduction

The period after 2000 was marked by the intensification of trade integration between countries; process resulting in greater mobility of capital with impact on financial integration and contagion effects of localized crises. In this scenario, emerging markets (EM) stood out, mainly through attracting funds in the capital market. This movement generated benefits to investors via portfolio and risk diversification. But, after a certain level, this already produces limited gains and result in greater exposure to international financial crises.

Since the seminal works of Markowitz (1952), Grubel (1968), and Solnik (1974), extensive literature about the benefits that investors can achieve in the performance of their portfolios by allocating into different classes of financial securities and industrial sectors, and international diversification is available. Stock markets of very different sizes, structures, and geographical locations can exhibit a high degree of comovement after a shock to one market, mainly in emergent markets. For Forbes and Rigobon (2002, pp. 22–27) a high degree of comovement suggests the existence of mechanisms through which domestic shocks are transmitted internationally.

For Dornbusch *et al.* (2000), Forbes and Rigobon (2001), and Rigobon (1999) contagion is defined as: (a) a significant increase in cross-market linkages after a shock to an individual country (or group of countries), as measured by the degree to which asset prices or financial flows move together across markets relative to this co movement in tranquil times; (b) the change in shock that spread among affected countries, may be more visible when a crisis occurs, but may still exist at any time when there is no occurrence of a crisis; (c) one crisis agreed upon that is when devastation occurs in a country, it would then create a speculative attack to another country. Thus, contagion can be characterized as transmission of volatility between one country to another.

As Rigobon (1999) and Dornbusch *et al.* (2000) state, the contagion can happen for several reasons, which can be divided into two main categories. The first category relates to the interdependence of markets. This interdependence means that shocks, whether of a global or local nature, can be transmitted across countries because of their real and financial linkages. The second category involves a financial crisis that is not linked to observed changes in macroeconomic or other fundamentals, but is solely the result of the behavior of investors or other financial agents.

The relationship between financial integration and contagion effect has been evidenced in literature, see Alba *et al.* (1998), Forbes and Rigobon (2002), Campello *et al.* (2010), Mun and Brooks (2012), and Bianconi *et al.* (2013). Moreover, after the crisis that hit the global financial system in 2007, several studies were carried out to investigate the negative effects of increased integration, particularly in emerging markets. At this point, Dooley and Hutchison (2009) evaluated the impact of the crisis in 14 countries, and Dufrénot *et al.* (2011) estimated the effects of the subprime crisis in the United States on Latin America stock market volatility. This integration, the effects of a crisis in other markets, especially through the volatility of assets, assists in the formulation of public policies and allows the investor to reduce the asymmetric information, improving the composition of degree occurring portfolio, minimizing risks, and increasing the chances of higher returns.

The present chapter studies the occurrence of financial contagion in EM and other stylized facts in financial time series like asymmetry, also known as leverage, persistence, clustering of volatility, and correlation. We use data from four Latin American countries, five Eastern European ones, and two Euro Zone ones. The methodology used is based on univariate and multivariate deterministic and stochastic models. This chapter contributes to the debate about the discussion of the impacts of integration of stock markets in EM, particularly in the second moment of returns in these selected countries.

The chapter is divided as follows. The Section 2 reviews the literature on investment in EM and the stylized facts highlighted in finance. The Section 3 analyzes data and main results. First, we estimate multivariate deterministic volatility VECH, CCC, and BEKK with normal distribution or t-student, GO-GARCH models and multivariate stochastic volatility models in order to investigate the extent of comovement within these various markets and the presence of the stylized facts within these various markets. Section 4 concludes.

2. Emerging Markets

From the 2000s, emerging markets have become more important for asset allocation, especially given the fast economic growth and the possibility of diversifying. However, integration has intensified and benefits of diversification for investors have decreased, that is, the differential returns among EM got smaller and the demand for countries with higher returns, too.

Empirical studies confirm the evidence of improved efficiency of returns of portfolios through diversification, as in Harvey (1995) and De Roon *et al.* (2001) who suggest that U.S. investors earned higher profits including EM stocks in its portfolio. Galagedera (2012) studied, from 2003 to 2010, the returns of 22 developed and 18 EMs, concluding that this one performed better at creating value with diversification opportunities for foreign long-term investors.

According to international finance literature, volatility of the stock market can change when there is economic and financial openness to foreign investors . In this case, investors share relevant information generating higher volatility, a characteristic that is enhanced in the presence of liquidity. In this sense, it is seen that the period before the liberalization process may show greater fluctuations in value, increasing volatility and intensifying reaction to shocks.

In this scenario, it is very important to consider the knowledge of risk, which can be estimated by the volatility of assets, and influence in the pricing of options, risk prediction, and selection of an optimal portfolio, for further details see Falkenstein (2009), Bekkers *et al.* (2009), Bekaert and Hoerova (2013), and Prokopczuk and Wese Simen (2013).

This evidence can be found from the results of two research groups on volatility. In the first group the models of deterministic volatility like GARCH and originally proposed by Engle (1982) and Bollerslev (1986). These have been widely used to measure univariate volatility in EM as in Bekaert and Harvey (1997), Herencia (1997) and Aggarwal *et al.* (1999), or in developed markets, as Awartani and Corradi (2005), and Morelli (2011). Apart from univariate formulations, it is possible to identify multivariate models, as in Lahrech and Sylwester (2011), who assessed the degree of integration of Argentina, Brazil, Chile, and Mexico stock markets with the U.S. between 1988 and 2004. In addition, several other studies have found evidence of comovement in volatility, as demonstrated by Chambet and Gibson (2008), Savva (2009), Saleem (2009), Butter and Hayo (2011), Walid *et al.* (2011), Gjika and Horváth (2013), and Ahmad *et al.* (2013).

The second group of volatility models is the stochastic, which is more flexible. They may also be univariate, as initially proposed by Taylor (1982, 1986) and used in Lee *et al.* (2011), or multivariate, as originally proposed by Harvey *et al.* (1994) and, subsequently, extended by Shepard (1996) and Jacquier *et al.* (1999). The multivariate models are widely used in the literature, as can be seen in Morais and Portugal (2001), Dao and Wolters (2008), Barrosi-Filho *et al.* (2010), Vo (2011), and Garnier *et al.* (2013).

A stylized fact is that different markets and instruments of financial markets and financial time series have become the focus of empirical study (Bekaert and Wu, 1997; Dao, 2008; Cont, 2001). The well-known stylized facts are: the 'leverage' effect (negative correlation between returns and future squared returns), the asymmetry volatility, asymmetry of distribution of returns, and persistence of volatility through the autocorrelation of squared returns.

The leverage effect was first discussed by Black (1976), who observed a negative correlation between past returns and future volatility in daily data from 1964 to 1975 in a sample of 30 stocks, mostly Dow Jones Industrial.

According to Bekaert and Wu (1997), the leverage effect is also synonymous with asymmetric volatility, because when there is a fall in value of an asset's financial, leverage increases impacting on stock volatility. The increase in expected volatility requires more return on capital, which implies an immediate drop in prices. The asymmetry is also characterized by stock returns, and volatility tends to increase following more a big price fall (bad news) than following a price increase, (good news) of the same magnitude (Black, 1976; Christie, 1982; Nelson, 1991).

One way to capture this asymmetry was proposed by Nelson (1991) with the EGARCH model and various applications, see Christofi and Pericli (1999), Ortiz and Arjona (2001), Brandt and Jones (2006), and Liu *et al.* (2012). In addition, there is the presence of persistence in financial series, which may represent the result of a tendency in the variance, or a structural change in the tendency of the variance.

A tool to assist interpretation of persistence is called half-life, which measures the period of time required for the effect of a shock decrease to half the conditional variance. This measure helps us to interpret how different markets react to uncertainty. Finally, the research literature on volatility documented that periods of large and low fluctuations in assets generate clusters, which is called volatility clustering.

3. Empirical Results

We used daily closing data of the stock exchanges in 11 EMs, beginning on January 07, 2002 and ending on May 31, 2013, totaling 2,082 observations. To implement the tests, the period is divided into non-crisis, crisis, and post-crisis samples.

The basic requirements for the daily returns based on the logarithmic difference tests indicated the presence of non-normality, time dependence, evidenced by the BDS test, and the presence of heteroscedasticity. This result was expected for financial series.

The first formulations of volatility applied use deterministic models with univariate normal distribution, GED, and t-student and also univariate stochastic volatility. In all indexes, it was possible to identify the presence of volatility clustering with $\alpha > 0$ in EGARCH model, with the largest being in Argentina. This leads us to the expectation that the presence of volatility at any given time is followed by more volatility.

All countries showed asymmetry in shocks, with the β coefficients, something to be expected as pointed out by Walid *et al.* (2011). As a complement to this research, formulation Beta-t-EGARCH signaled the presence of strong negative asymmetry in the residuals, confirming the existence of heavy tails (see Table 1).

Stochastic volatility for all countries shows similar behavior. This fact indicates the existence of a comovement in the second moment of returns, particularly in the period of subprime crisis, with extreme values and strong

Table 1. Beta-t-EGARCH Model — 1 and 2 Components — Asymmetry in Shocks

	Br	Arg	Mex	Chile	Estonia	Slov	Russia	Czech	Rom	Poland	Hung
1 component											
BIC	2.31	2.44	1.60	1,18	1.29	0.98	2.56	1.75	2.00	1.70	2.12
Skew	0.89	0.90	0.87	0.87	0.02	0.96	0.88	0.90	0.93	0.93	0.02
2 components											
BIC	2.29	2.44	1.60	1.18	1.29	0.98	2.55	1.76	2.00	1.69	2.12
Skew	0.89	0.90	0.88	0.87	0.97	0.96	0.88	0.91	0.92	0.95	0.96

persistence. In that case, the coefficient γ in EGARCH or $\alpha + \beta$ in GARCH capture this stylized fact, and they were always above 0.88.

The half-life persistence points out differences in the duration of a shock in volatility, ranging from 2.1 days for Russia to a maximum of 115 days for Estonia. Despite the goodness-of-fit of the univariate volatility, the international financial crisis produced changes in the price behavior of various assets with impacts on volatility.

To demonstrate this, we divided data into three periods and applied earlier models for each of them. In this case, the first period is the pre-crisis January 7, 2003 to January 31, 2007; the second one is the subprime crisis February 1, 2001 to January 30, 2009; and the last one, the post-crisis February 3, 2009 to May 13, 2013. The second investigation preserves the total data set and we used switching in volatility regime similar to Hamilton and Susmel is (1994) proposal (see Table 2).

The second period signals that volatility clustering is greater than others, as was expected in a stress market. The same can be said for the asymmetry, which was also higher during the years of crisis.

We applied univariate Hamilton and Susmel (1994) SWARCH (3.2) L with t-student distribution model to each markets. This formulation uses three possible volatility states and leverage effect to capture different volatility regimes. The results demonstrate relevance, confirming the presence of asymmetry in volatility, non-normal distribution, leverage effect, and ability to associate the crisis period to a regime of high volatility. The second set of charts shows the evolution of likelihood of high volatility regime and the estimated volatility for Russia. Note that the regime of high volatility was present only in the months of incidence of the international crisis. This feature was identified for Brazil, Argentina, and Hungary. In the other EMs, we identified that there are other periods of greater volatility.

Table 2. Stylized Facts in Three Selected Sub-periods — Univariate Deterministic Model

		Pre crisis			Crisis			Post crisis		
Country	**Index**	**Agglo**	**Skew**	**Persis**	**Agglo**	**Skew**	**Persis**	**Agglo**	**Skew**	**Persis**
Argentina	MERVAL	0.320	−0.192	0.810	0.219	−0.132	0.946	0.294	−0.083	0.909
Brazil	IBOV	0.046	−0.153	0.867	0.189	−0.232	0.931	0.145	−0.087	0.970
Chile	IPSA	0.197	−0.124	0.886	0.216	−0.169	0.931	0.200	−0.114	0.964
Slovakia[1]	SAX			0.992			0.759			0.775
Estonia	OMX	0.196	0.015	0.972	0.105	−0.052	0.985	0.176	−0.037	0.989
Hungary	BUX	0.146	−0.054	0.943	0.252	−0.093	0.959	0.111	−0.046	0.996
Mexico	IPC	0.176	−0.166	0.910	0.099	−0.315	0.949	0.158	−0.098	0.985
Poland	WIG	0.076	0.022	0.988	0.037	−0.194	0.915	0.141	−0.076	0.988
Czech Rep.	PX	0.289	−0.137	0.866	0.301	−0.244	0.938	0.172	−0.045	0.990
Romania	BET	0.064	0.021	0.995	0.206	−0.088	0.891	0.184	−0.051	0.992
Russia	RTS	0.420	−0.148	0.851	0.102	−0.171	0.973	0.221	−0.083	0.983

The univariate models capture important stylized facts. However, multivariate models contribute to see others like covariation, especially time-varying and infer on spill-over effects in volatility, namely contagion. Thus, we estimated multivariate deterministic volatility VECH, CCC, and BEKK with normal distribution or t-student, GO-GARCH models and multivariate stochastic volatility models.

To avoid an excessive number of parameters, which pose convergence problems, we created three groups: (i) Latin America with Argentina (MERVAL), Brazil (IBOV), Chile (IPSA), and Mexico (CPI); (ii) Euro Zone with Slovakia (SAX) and Estonia (OMX); (iii) Eastern Europe with Czech Republic (PX), Hungary (BUX), Poland (WIG), Romania (BET), and Russia (RTS).

The best results were identified in CCC formulation. The countries of the Euro Zone showed low correlation (0.021), and the largest one was seen in Latin America, especially Brazil and Mexico with 0.667. According to Gjika and Horváth (2013), correlation between 0.5 and 0.8 can be considered very high in an international perspective. A justification for low correlation can be the value of the total capital of the companies comprising the index. For example, in Latin America, the market value in 2013 was $1,121.47 billion, while the Euro Zone and Eastern Europe accounted for $6.904 and $259.167 billion, respectively, that is, a larger and more liquid market may offer more opportunities for investors to diversify risk, which results in higher correlation and smaller markets with low liquidity.

The presence of correlation between countries means that adverse shocks, which result in greater uncertainty in a specific stock market, have the power

Table 3. Constant Correlation Test for the Periods Analyzed — Tse (2000)

	Latin American	Euro Zone	Eastern Europe
Total	$\chi^2_{(10)} = 20.52[0.00]$	$\chi^2_{(10)} = 0.71[0.40]$	$\chi^2_{(10)} = 15.54[0.11]$
Pre-crisis	$\chi^2_{(10)} = 16.27[0.01]$	$\chi^2_{(10)} = 2.36[0.12]$	$\chi^2_{(10)} = 60.14[0.00]$
Crisis	$\chi^2_{(10)} = 7.04[0.32]$	$\chi^2_{(10)} = 2.15[0.14]$	$\chi^2_{(10)} = 59.54[0.00]$
Post-crisis	$\chi^2_{(10)} = 14.82[0.02]$	$\chi^2_{(10)} = 0.32[0.57]$	$\chi^2_{(10)} = 14.78[0.14]$

Table 4. Engle and Sheppard (2001) Test for the Periods Analyzed

	Latin American	Euro Zone	Eastern Europe
Total	1.399[0.496]	0.125[0.939]	3.290[0.192]
Pre-crisis	0.405[0.816]	0.843[0.655]	0.215[0.897]
Crisis	0.121[0.941]	0.040[0.980]	0.130[0.936]
Post-crisis	0.024[0.987]	0.018[0.990]	1.020[0.600]

to affect everyone in the same direction. But this is seen to be greater between Brazil and Mexico, an aspect also identified by Pereira (2009) and Morais and Portugal (2001), but using Par Bonds.

One aspect investigated in the literature is to test whether the correlation is constant over time or not. In this case, we used two proposals. The first was shown in Tse (2000), which compares the CCC model with an alternative specification, and it is used here for both the total sample and the subsamples.

As can be seen in Table 3, we rejected the null hypothesis of constant correlation in the Euro Zone for all periods. However, this does not seem constant to Eastern Europe before and during the crisis. In Latin America, the correlation is constant only for the crisis period, signaling that in a stress scenario the region suffers more from the contagion effect. In the total sample, Latin America and Eastern Europe support the existence of a variant correlation in time, as was seen in Gjika and Horváth (2013).

The second test used was proposed by Engle and Sheppard (2001). The authors test the correlation constant CCC model, but as a normal GARCH via Copula. The results show not to reject the null hypothesis of constant correlation in all sub-periods and regions (see Table 4).

As a way to supplement the evidence, we used Koutmos (1996) proposal, which estimates a VAR-EGARCH. The results confirm the existence of a temporal interdependence in volatility. In addition, the δ_j coefficient, which

Table 5. Estimated by Maximum Likelihood Between Markets — Full Sample – VAR-EGARCH

Group	Country	δ_j	α_j	$\|-1+\delta_j\|/(1+\delta_j)$
Euro Zone	Estonia	0.01	0.24	0.98
	Slovakia	−0.24	0.15	1.63
Latin American	Brazil	−0.61	0.10	4.13
	Mexico	−0.36	0.05	2.13
	Chile	−0.42	0.14	2.45
	Argentina	−0.01	0.12	1.02
Eastern Europe	Romania	−0.06	0.31	1.13
	Hungary	−0.53	0.07	3.26
	Czech Rep.	−0.32	0.08	1.94
	Russia	−0.35	0.14	2.08
	Poland	−0.15	0.10	1.35

measures the asymmetry, was significant for both Latin America and Eastern Europe considering Estonia in the Euro Zone. This supports the view that both the size and the sign of the volatility shocks are important to measure the contagion effect between these markets.

The coefficients that measures asymmetry, useful for leverage effect and the volatility in the markets, α_j obtained by VAR-EGARCH, are shown in Table 5. It was noted that in the case of Latin America, the negative values of δ_j combined with positive α_j show that negative shocks in one market have greater impact on volatility in another market than a positive one. This is a clear sign of the existence of asymmetry in the transmission of these shocks in the region. On the other hand, Estonia with $\delta_j > 0$ and $\alpha_j > 0$ signals positive shocks.

The leverage effect, given by $|-1+\delta_j|/(1+\delta_j)$, oscillates between a maximum of 4.1 for Brazil to a minimum of 0.98 in Estonia. We used the likelihood ratio test between the restricted model (Θ_2) and non-restricted model (Θ_1) to test the efficiency of markets. Rejecting null hypothesis of equality, we can infer that there is interdependence between countries in any of the sub-periods reviewed, as shown in Table 6. Thus, we can infer that news has a contagion effect on volatility between markets.

There are two other models used to confirm these results. The first is the GO-GARCH and the second is the DCC. Table 7 shows the independent factors for each region, and estimation of correlations reveals a smoothed one with low oscillation in every market, with the exception of the subprime crisis moment with strong positive correlation. Persistence is present in this model at parameters $\alpha_1 + \beta_1$, and it is high in all factors.

Table 6. LR Test for Model VAR-EGARCH

Group		Total	Pre-crisis	Crisis	Post-crisis
Euro Zone	LR	25.65	11.66	50.15	46.66
	$\chi^2_{(k)}$	0.00	0.02	0.00	0.00
Latin American	LR	124.51	110.53	251.06	106.97
	$\chi^2_{(k)}$	0.00	0.00	0.00	0.00
Eastern Europe	LR	135.42	262.55	312.46	161.68
	$\chi^2_{(k)}$	0.00	0.00	0.00	0.00

Table 7. Independent Factors — GO-GARCH (1,1)

	Latin American			Eastern Europe			Euro Zone		
Factors	Π	α_1	β_1	ϖ	α_1	β_1	ϖ	α_1	β_1
1	0.005	0.031	0.962	0.03	0.06	0.909	0.011	0.091	0.907
2	0.037	0.116	0.851	0.007	0.052	0.941	0.003	0.023	0.974
3	0.020	0.079	0.900	0.042	0.100	0.857	—	—	—
4	0.017	0.050	0.933	0.018	0.095	0.886	—	—	—
5	—	—	—	0.013	0.050	0.934	—	—	—

In graph 3, left picture, we see the correlation news–impact surface plot from GO-GARCH (1,1) for Chile and Brazil using factor 2 and 4. In the absence of shock, that is, factors around zero, the correlation is 0.55 and increase is independent if shock in both factors is in the same direction until a maximum of 0.7. This confirms the interdependence in these two markets. The same was obtained for 2×2 different countries at all regions.

We tried three different formulations for dynamic correlations, and the most efficient with lower information criterion was the aDCC, which is asymmetric for all 2×2 models in each region. Negative shocks in Brazil combined with positive ones in Chile produce negative correlation. But positive news in both countries produces a negative result. This result confirms that the two countries may offer opportunity for diversification, an interesting choice for building portfolio in Latin America.

In summary, investigation of Tse (2000) and Engle and Sheppard (2001) tests shows some differences but supports the existence of a constant correlation. However, this result should be viewed with caution. In Latin America, we noted that the correlation between markets is different before, during and after the crisis, getting bigger during the crisis, and despite a reduction in the volatility post 2009, it remains above the value found pre-crisis. This evidence must be confirmed with multivariate formulations that allow the capture of different shocks in each market.

In Eastern Europe, the results differ, with the correlation in the post-crisis period becoming higher than that observed before and during the crisis. Romania proved to be a country that has low correlation with other Eastern European countries before the crisis, but this has intensified the crisis, and the correlation has continued to increase afterwards, which may be related to its entry to European Union in 2007. In other countries, this increased correlation can be explained by problems in the financial system that hit the region.

These results confirm Forbes and Rigobon's (2002) evidence that relations between countries tend to intensify when one goes through a difficult period and there is existence of a pre-integration with another country. The Go-Ggarch and dynamic correlation models were used for all markets. At this point, the correlation is not constant in certain periods and there is some evidence of transmission of shocks across countries.

To complement this result, we investigated stochastic volatility models starting with univariate and then progressing to multivariate formulations. Furthermore, research is also made in subperiods, despite the variable model parameters. Wald test confirms that the hyperparameter $\phi_2 \neq 1$ in every country, that is, the h_t dynamic is not given by a random walk. Furthermore, the results confirm the evidences in the sub-periods, as identified by deterministic models.

The correlation can be found through multivariate stochastic volatility models, as proposed in Harvey *et al.* (1994) and applied by Dao and Wolters (2008) and Morais and Portugal (2001). Countries were divided into the same three groups.

In Latin America, the highest correlation was found between Brazil and Argentina, at 0.954, followed by Brazil and Mexico, 0,941. At the same time, countries that have shown a correlation between the lower groups were Argentina and Chile, with 0.735. On the whole, the results for Latin America indicate a high correlation between markets, thus confirming the contagion effect. Again, the stock market in Brazil has the greatest values, confirming the strong liquidity in this region.

One of the highest correlations in Eastern Europe was between the Czech Republic and Hungary, with 0.97, and the lowest was 0.93 between Poland and Russia. It is observed that this group is more correlated than Latina America and Euro Zone, perhaps due to the fact that many countries possess various trade agreements and they are part of the European Union.

4. Conclusions

The increased flow of information and market liberalization have helped investors to diversify their investments, thus seeking higher returns and protection against potential financial instability. The models studied in this chapter helped to identify some characteristics of the EM indexes and better understand the relations between markets.

Among these are the stylized facts such as the persistence of volatility, which was observed in all series and even close and very high values. It is noted that this persistence, when analyzed in sub-periods, deepened during the crisis. Similar to persistence, volatility clustering and leverage effect were present in all stock indexes. It is noteworthy that, from the value of persistence, we could estimate the half-life of the effects of a shock in the series. Estonia and Romania showed the highest values, indicating that these two countries have greater resilience to shocks than the others studied.

Another fact is the asymmetry, which was confirmed by all the models used. The asymmetry suggests that positive and negative news in the markets have different impacts. Through the VAR-EGARCH and EGARCH models, it can be stated that negative shocks have a greater impact on volatility than positive shocks.

As for estimating volatility, univariate deterministic models were less sensitive to shocks to volatility than stochastic models. However, when we compared the volatility estimates found by means of two models, the odds ratio showed that nine out of the eleven countries had values between 0.68 and 0.84, where Mexico can be highlighted for having had the two models generating very close estimates.

From this, the division of countries into three groups, and through the multivariate models, we tried to analyze the correlations among the indexes of each group. There was, then, a finding of the existence of transmission of volatility from one market to another. The three groups had, on average, a value very close to transmission, but the highest value was the Euro Zone. The multivariate deterministic and stochastic models showed a different correlation level between the studied markets, but it could be observed that for the full daily sample, the negative correlation was not found in any estimate, a clear signal to the markets of similar behavior in different countries.

The multivariate deterministic models indicated that the group with the highest level of integration was the Latin America, which may be explained by the size of the capital markets and the volume traded in these indexes. At the same time, the stochastic model leads us to a correlation at a higher level of volatility in all groups and, as a result, indicates that the correlation is higher in Eastern Europe, which can be explained not only by the geographic proximity of countries but also by the existence of bilateral agreements and the majority of this group of countries belonging to the European Union.

Finally, integration of markets studied was evident, and it is important to consider the sub-periods to seek correlation. However, during the sub-prime crisis, it was seen that integration intensifies and remains at higher levels than seen before the crisis and after the end of this instability. Therefore, it is possible that some markets, such as Chile and Brazil, show opportunity for investment diversification in Latin American portfolio.

A suggestion for future research that may complement this assessment is to identify the different results in the regions via portfolio and how these have changed in the post-crisis scenario.

References

Aggarwal, R., Inclan, C., and Leal, R. (1999). Volatility in emerging stock markets. *J. Fin. Quant. Anal.*, 34, pp. 33–55.

Ahmad, W., Sehgal, S., and Bhanumurthy, N. (2013). Eurozone crisis and BRIICKS stock markets: Contagion or market interdependence? *Econom. Modell.*, 33, pp. 209–225.

Alba, P., Bhattacharya, A., Claessens, S., Ghosh, S., and Hernandez, L. (1998). Volatility and Contagion in a Financially Integrated World: Lessons from East Asia's Recent Experience. Policy Research, Working Paper No 2008.

Awartani, B. and Corradi, V. (2005). Predicting the volatility of the S&P-500 stock index via GARCH models: The role of asymmetries. *Int. J. Forecasting*, 21, pp. 167–183.

Barossi-Filho, M., Achcar, J., and De Souza, R. (2010). Modelos de volatilidade estocástica em séries financeiras: Uma aplicação para o Ibovespa. *Economia Aplicada*, 14, pp. 25–40.

Bauwens, L., Laurent, S., and Rombouts, J. (2006). Multivariate GARCH models: A survey. *J. App. Economet.*, 21(1), pp. 79–109.

Bekaert, G. and Harvey, C. (1997). Emerging equity market volatility. *J. Fin. Econom.*, 43, pp. 29–78.

Bekaert, G. and Wu, G. (1997). Asymmetric volatility and risk in equity markets. National Bureau of Economic Research, Working Paper No 6022.

Bekaert, G. and Hoerova, M. (2013). The VIX, the Variance Premium and Stock Market Volatility. Columbia Business School Research, Paper, pp. 13–32.

Bekkers, N., Doeswijk, R., and E Lam, T. (2009). Strategic Asset Allocation: Determining the Optimal Portfolio with Ten Asset Classes. SSRN Working Paper No. 1368689.

Bianconi, M., Yoshino, J., and De Sousa, M. (2013). BRIC and the U.S. financial crisis: An empirical investigation of stock and bond markets. *Emerging Markets Rev.*, 14, pp. 76–109.

Billio, M., Caporin, M., and Gobbo, M. (2006). Flexible dynamic conditional correlation multivariate GARCH models for asset allocation. *App. Fin. Econom. Let.*, 2(02), pp. 123–130.

Black, F. (1976). Studies of stock price volatility changes. In *Proc. 1976 Meetings of the American Statistical Association*, Business and Statistics Section.

Bollerslev, T. (1986). Generalized autoregressive conditional heteroskedasticity. *J. Econometr.*, 31, pp. 307–327.
Bordo, M. and Murshid, A. (2000). Are financial crises becoming increasingly more contagious? What is the historical evidence on contagion? In *Proc. ADB/IMF/World Bank Conference on "International Financial Contagion,"* Washington D.C., February.
Boswijk, H. P. and Van Der Weide, R. (2006). Wake me up before you GO-GARCH, Tinbergen Institute Discussion Paper, TI 2006-079/4, University of Amsterdam and Tinbergen Institute.
Boswijk, H. P. and Van Der Weide, R. (2009). Method of Moments Estimation of GO-GARCH Models, Working Paper, University of Amsterdam, Tinbergen Institute and World Bank.
Brandt, M. and Jones C. (2006). Volatility forecasting with range-based EGARCH models. *J. Business Econom. Statist.*, 28, pp. 470–486.
Buttner, D. and Hayo, B. (2011). Determinants of European stock market integration. *Econom. Syst.*, 35, pp. 574–585.
Campello, M., Graham, J., and Harvey, C. (2010). The real effects of financial constraints: Evidence from a financial crisis. *J. Finan. Econo.*, 97, pp. 470–487.
Cappiello, L., Engle, R. F., and Sheppard, K. (2006). Asymmetric dynamics in the correlations of global equity and bond returns, *J. Fin. Econometr.*, 4, pp. 537–572.
Chambet, A. and Gibson, R. (2008). Financial integration, economic instability and trade structure in emerging markets. *J. Int. Money Fin.*, 27, pp. 654–675.
Christie, A. A. (1982). The stochastic behavior common stock variances: value, leverage and interest rate effects. *J. Fin. Econom.*, 10(4), pp. 407–432.
Christofi, A. and Pericli A. (1999). Correlation in price changes and volatility of major Latin American stock markets. *J. Multinational Fin. Manage.*, 9, pp. 79–99.
Cont, R. (2001). Empirical properties of asset returns: Stylized facts and statistical issues. *Quantit. Fin.*, 1, pp. 223–236.
Dao, Chi-Mai and Wolters, J. (2008). Common Stochastic Volatility trends in International Stock Returns. *Inte. Rev. Fin. Anal.*, 17(3), pp. 431–445.
Diamandis, P. (2008). Financial liberalization and changes in the dynamic behavior of emerging market volatility: Evidence from four Latin American equity markets. *Int. Business Fin.*, 22, pp. 362–377.
De Roon, F., Nijman T., and Werker, B. (2001). Testing for mean-variance spanning with short sales constraints and transaction costs: The case of emerging markets. *J. Fin.*, 56, pp. 721–742.
Dooley, M. and Hutchison, M. (2009). Transmission of the U.S. subprime crisis to emerging markets: Evidence on the decoupling–recoupling hypothesis. *J. Int. Money Fin.*, 28, pp. 1331–1349.
Dornbusch, R., Park, Y. C., and Claessens, S. (2000). Contagion: How it spreads and how it can be stopped?. World Bank Working Paper.
Dufrénot, G., Mignon, V., and Péguin-Feissolle, A. (2011). The effects of the subprime crisis on the Latin American financial markets: An empirical assessment. *Econom. Modell.*, 28, pp. 2342–2357.
Engle, R. (1982). Autoregressive Conditional Heteroskedasticity with Estimates of the variances of U.K. Inflation. *Econométrica*, 50, pp. 987–1008.
Engle, R. F, Kroner and K. F. (1995). Multivariate simultaneous GARCH, *Econometr. Theory*, 11, pp. 122–150.
Engle, R. F. and Sheppard, K. (2001). Theoretical and empirical properties of dynamic conditional correlation multivariate garch, NBER Working Paper.

Falkenstein, E. (2009). Risk and Return in General: Theory and Evidence. SSRN Working Paper no. 1420356.

Forbes, K. and Rigobon, R. (2002). No contagion, only interdependence: Measuring stock market co-movements. *J. Fin.*, 57, pp. 2223–2261.

Francq, C. and Zakoïan, J-M. (2010). *GARCH Models*. New York: Marcel Dekker.

Galagedera, D. U. A. (2012). Recent trends in relative performance of global equity markets, *J. Int. Fin. Markets, Institut. Money*, 22(4), pp. 834–854.

Garnier, C., Mertens, E., and Nelson, E. (2013). Trend inflation in advanced economies. FEDS Working Paper 2013–74.

Gjika, D. and Horváth, R. (2013). Stock market comovements in Central Europe: Evidence from the asymmetric DCC model. *Econom. Modell.*, 33, pp. 55–64.

Grubel, H. (1968). Internationaly diversified portfolios: Welfare gains and capital flows. *Am. Econom. Rev.* 58, pp. 1299–1314.

Hamilton, J. D. and Susmel, R. (1994). Autoregressive conditional heteroskesdasticity and changes in regime. *J. Econometr.*, 64, pp. 307–333.

Harvey, C. (1995). Predictable risk and returns in emerging markets. *Rev. Fin. Stu.*, 8, pp. 773–816.

Harvey, A. C. (2013). *Dynamic Models for Volatility and Heavy Tails*. New York: Cambridge University Press.

Harvey, A. C. and Chakravarty, T. (2008). Beta-t-(E)GARCH. Cambridge Working Paper in Economics 0840, Faculty of Economics, University of Cambridge.

Harvey, C., Ruiz, E., and Shephard, N. (1994). Multivariate stochastic variance models. *Rev. Econ. Stud.*, 61, pp. 247–264.

Herencia, M. (1997). Volatilidade nos Modelos ARCH e Variância Estocástica: Um estudo comparativo. Dissertação de Mestrado, Campinas, UNICAMP.

Yang, C. (1999). The impact of financial liberalization on stock price volatility in emerging markets. *J. Comparative Econom.*, 28, pp. 321–339.

Jacquier, E., Polson, N., and Rossi, P. (1999). Stochastic Volatility: Univariate and Multivariate Extensions. CIRANO Working Paper 99s-26.

Kaminsky, G. and Schmukler, S. (2003). Short-run pain, long-run gain: The effects of financial liberalization. NBER Working Paper 9787.

Koutmos, G. (1996). Modeling the dynamic interdependence of major European stock markets. *J. Business Fin. Account.*, 23(7), pp. 975–988.

Lahrech, A. and Sylwester, K. (2011). U. S. and Latin American stock market linkages. *J. Int. Money Fin.*, 30, pp. 1341–1357.

Lee, S., Kim, M., and Kim, S. (2011). Interest rates factor model. *Physical A*, 390, pp. 2531–2548.

Liu, H., Chiang, S., and Cheng, N. (2012). Forecasting the volatility of S&P depositary receipts using GARCH-type models under intraday range-based and return-based proxy measures. *Inte. Rev. Econom. Fin.*, 22, pp. 78–91.

Markowitz, H. (1952). Portfolio selection. *J. Fin.* 7, 77–91.

Morais, I. and Portugal, M. (2001). Uma investigação sobre os co-movimentos na volatilidade dos par bonds Latino Americanos. *Revista Brasileira de Economia*, 55, pp. 183–204.

Morelli, D. (2011). Joint conditionality in testing the beta-return relationship: Evidence based on the UK stock market. *J. Int. Fin. Markets, Institut. Money*, 21, pp. 1–13.

Mun, M. and Brooks, R. (2012). The roles of news and volatility in stock market correlations during the global financial crisis. *Emer. Markets Rev.*, 13, pp. 1–7.

Nelson, D. (1991). Conditional heteroskedasticity in asset returns: A new approach. *Econométrica*, 59, pp. 347–70.

Ortiz, E. and Arjona, E. (2001). Heterokedastic behavior of the Latin American emerging stock markets. *Int. Rev. Fin. Analy.*, 10, pp. 287–305.
Pereira, P. (2009). Testing the hypothesis of contagion using multivariate volatility models. Texto para discussão 174, Escola de Economia de São Paulo da Fundação Getulio Vargas FGV-EESP, São Paulo.
Prokopczuk, M. and Wese Simen, C. (2013). The importance of the volatility risk premium for volatility forecasting. SSRN Working Paper No. 2236370.
Saleem, K. (2009). International linkage of the Russian market and the Russian financial crisis: A multivariate GARCH analysis. *Res. Int. Business Fin.*, 23, pp. 243–256.
Savva, C. (2009). International stock markets interactions and conditional correlations. *J. Inte. Finan. Markets, Institut. Money*, 19, pp. 645–661.
Shephard, N. (1996). Statistical aspects of ARCH and stochastic volatility. In D. R. Cox, David V. Hinkley and Ole E. Barndorff-Neilsen (eds.), *Time Series Models in Econometrics, Finance and Other Fields*, London: Chapman & Hall, pp. 1–67.
Solnik, B. (1974). Why do not diversify internationally rather than domestically. *Fin. Anal. J.*, 30, pp. 48–54.
Sucarrat, G. (2013). Betategarch: Simulation, estimation an forecasting of beta-skew-t-EGARCH models, *The R J.* 5(2), pp. 137–147.
Taylor, S. (1982). Financial returns modelled by the product of two stochastic processes — A study of the daily sugar prices 1961–75. In O.D. Anderson (ed.), Time Series Analysis: Theory And Practice, Vol. 1, North-Holland, pp. 203–226.
Taylor, S. (1986). *Modelling Financial Time Series*. Chichester: Wiley.
Tse, Y. K. (2000). A test for constant correlations in a Multivariate GARCH model. *J. Econometr.*, 98, pp. 107–127.
Van Der Weide, R. (2002). GO-GARCH: A multivariate generalized orthogonal GARCH model. *J. App. Economet.*, 17(5), pp. 549–564.
Vo, M. (2011). Oil and stock market volatility: A multivariate stochastic volatility perspective. *Energy Econom.*, 33, pp. 956–965.
Walid, C., Chaker, A., Masood, O., and Fry, J. (2011). Stock market volatility and exchange rates in emerging countries: A Markov-state switching approach. *Emerging Markets Rev.*, 12, pp. 272–292.

Part II

Foreign Exchange Markets: Volatility, Integration and Spillovers

Chapter 7

Macroeconomic News and Exchange Rate Volatility: Evidence of Unstable Effect

Walid Ben Omrane[*,‡], Robert Welch[*,§] and Xinyao Zhou[†,¶]

[*] *Goodman School of Business, Brock University, ON, Canada*
[†] *Schulich School of Business, York University, Canada*
[‡] *wbenomrane@brocku.ca*
[$] *bwelch@brocku.ca*
[¶] *jozhou@yorku.ca*

Abstract

This chapter examines the effects of macroeconomic news on foreign exchange return and volatility across sequential regimes. Although the stable link between macroeconomic news announcements and exchange rates has been well documented in previous literature, this linkage could be unstable. Using a breakpoint regression model, a broad set of macroeconomic news announcements, and high-frequency Euro/Dollar foreign data from November 1, 2004 to March 31, 2014, we find macroeconomic news has unstable effects on Eurodollar returns and volatility across estimated regimes. Most news events exhibit variations in magnitude and/or switch signs between regimes. US news causes more instability than Euro news.

1. Introduction

Macroeconomic fundamental news and exchange rates linkage has been investigated in the literature by Andersen *et al.* (2003), Bauwens, *et al.* (2005), Dominguez and Panthaki (2006), among others. Recent literature tackled unstable effects of macro news using qualitative tools such as a survey of foreign exchange traders (Cheung and Chinn, 2001) or applying quantitative methods such as parameter instability tests made by Rossi (2006). Moreover, there is empirical evidence of unstable macroeconomic news effects on returns (Fatum *et al.*, 2012), on volatility (Laakkonen and Lanne, 2009), and evidence of sign switching effects (Ben Omrane and Savaser, 2016). Using high-frequency Euro/Dollar data and a new extensive and refined set of macroeconomic news involving the US and Europe, we extend the literature by analyzing the unstable effect of macroeconomic news on Eurodollar returns and volatility over a recent period (2004–2014) that includes a global crisis.

This study provides further information about the news categories that create instability as well as the dynamics of their effects on returns and volatility. The confusion raised by unstable news effects in foreign exchange markets makes understanding this instability critical because some scholars question the existence of this link. Bacchetta and Wincoop (2004, 2006, 2013) provide a possible theoretical explanation: they argue that the relationship between macroeconomic fundamentals and exchange rates is highly unstable due to rational "scapegoat" effects. Here, "scapegoat" means that news related to macroeconomic fundamentals are always blamed instead of the change in unobservable factors (Bacchetta and Wincoop, 2004), implying that news is disconnected from the exchange rate. However, we show that this link does exist under the assumption of multiple structural breaks.

Our empirical investigation involves breakpoint regressions developed by Bai and Perron (1998). This method is more efficient than the implementation of an exogenous dummy variable involving predetermined dates announced by The National Bureau of Economic Research (NBER) and Center for Economic Policy Research (CEPR). Our work contributes to the macroeconomic news stable effect literature (Andersen *et al.*, 2003; Bauwens *et al.*, 2005, amongst others) because we find empirical evidence of macroeconomic news instability over time by using a breakpoint regression model to define five regimes endogenously. Specifically, about 75% of US macroeconomic news affects returns and volatility, and these effects depend on the regime (economic state). US news has more impact than Euro news with more variable magnitudes and signs. Significant events tend to influence both return and volatility.

The remainder of the chapter is organized as follows. Section 2 provides a brief literature review. Section 3 explains the empirical model. Section 4 presents the analysis of the dataset. Section 5 displays the results and Sec. 6 concludes.

2. Literature Review

The intraday linkage between macroeconomic news and volatility has been investigated by several researchers since early 1990s. Andersen *et al.* (2003) use 5-min conditional return response of the major currency pairs such as Euro/Dollar, Pound/Dollar, and Yen/Dollar to US macroeconomic news. Bauwens *et al.* (2005) document the news impact on the Euro/Dollar volatility using scheduled and unscheduled news announcements and find that volatility increases in the 'pre-announcement periods', especially for scheduled news. Dominguez and Panthaki (2006) report that a fundamental news surprise can increase volatility immediately after the announcement in Euro/Dollar and Pound/Dollar. These studies assume the stability of news effects on both volatility and/or returns. Cheung and Chinn (2001) conduct a survey on US foreign exchange traders and find that the importance of a specific fundamental variable shifts over time. This time varying feature of parameters is also reported by Rossi (2006), who provides empirical evidence by running several kinds of tests on parameter instability.

While Andersen *et al.* (2007) find no significant asymmetrical news effects for different business cycles in foreign exchange markets, Faust *et al.* (2007) provide some limited evidence of asymmetry. Fatum *et al.* (2012) document a significant time varying response of the Yen/Dollar to Japanese macroeconomic news over different economic conditions. Laakkonen and Lanne (2009) study news impact on foreign exchange volatility over different economic states by including a broader set of macroeconomic news from US and Euro Zone countries. They show that the impact of good and bad news varies during expansion and recession periods. Ben Omrane and Savaser (2016) examine US macroeconomic news impact on three major currencies for two regimes (exogenously determined by NBER for the US subprime crisis) assuming constant coefficients within each regime for 2005–2012. They find news coefficients switch signs during the crisis and attribute this to different risk levels.

Some other features related to news could also play important roles with regard to return or volatility responses in the foreign exchange market. The timeliness (or the announcement timing) and news information content are important with regard to the news impact (Andersent *et al.*, 2003; Laakkonen and Lanne, 2013; Gilbert *et al.*, 2015). More specifically, early announcements have greater effect compared to later ones from the same news category. In addition, a larger difference between realized and forecasted figures has a larger impact because the information content increased.

One important feature of the foreign exchange intraday volatility is the intraday seasonality pattern. Neely (2011) reviews the debate between news announcement effects versus intraday periodicity patterns and daily volatility patterns. Several researchers have suggested different ways to control for the seasonal pattern as it is the volatility deterministic component. Ben Omrane and De Bodt (2007) show that seasonality itself has a dynamic component that should be captured by sophisticated methodologies based on neural networks. Seasonality should be controlled for or removed to avoid biased estimators.

Recent literature also documents significant findings in foreign exchange markets during the recent global crises. Fratzscher (2009) finds a stunning sign switch effect from US macroeconomic news surprises on the dollar against many other currencies in daily returns, especially for countries with weak current account positions. This sign switch effect is consistent with the findings of Ben Omrane and Savaser (2016) using intraday data. Melvin and Taylor (2009) show important events that happened during the US subprime crisis and suggest a financial stress index (FSI) to compare different crises over time.

3. Methodology

We consider the surprise component of macroeconomic news announcements and follow Balduzzi *et al.* (2001) who propose to measure the surprise element by first calculating the difference between the forecasted and the actual announced divided by the standard deviation of the difference. This method removes the potential problem caused by different measurement units. It is calculated by the formula: $S_{k,t} = \frac{A_{k,t}-F_{k,t}}{\hat{\sigma}_k}$, where $A_{k,t}$ denotes the actual figure of news k at time t, $F_{k,t}$ denotes the forecast figure for the same announcement, and $\hat{\sigma}_k$ is the sample standard deviation of the difference between actual and forecasts for news k through entire sample period.

We estimate first a baseline return–volatility model where we assume stability for macroeconomic news effects. The estimated coefficients in the baseline model will serve as benchmark estimators. Then we relax this stability assumption by considering instability through the implementation of a breakpoint regression.

Following Andersen *et al.* (2003), we model return response on the news surprise element

$$R_{t,n} = \theta_0 + \theta_i \sum_{i=1}^{I} R_{t,n-i} + \sum_{k=1}^{K} \beta_k \mathrm{S}_{k,t,n} + \tau_1 \mathrm{Unsch}_{t,n} + \tau_3 \mathrm{Speak}_{t,n} + \epsilon_{t,n}, \tag{1}$$

where $S_{k,t,n}$ is the surprise element for news k at date t and interval n. K is the total number of macroeconomic news announcements. I is the total lagged term of return. $I = 4$ based on the Schwarz and Akaike information criteria, $\epsilon_{t,n}$ is the residual term. In addition, $\mathrm{Unsch}_{t,n}$ and $\mathrm{Speak}_{t,n}$ are dummy variables controlling for two important events in the foreign exchange market. $\mathrm{Unsch}_{t,n}$ is the dummy variable capturing the unscheduled important news announcements, and $\mathrm{Speak}_{t,n}$ is a 2×1 vector of dummy variables with related speeches made in the US and Euro Zone countries by important government and central bank officials such as the US president, the Federal Reserve Chairman, and the President of the European Central Bank. These two important exogenous variables were documented in Dominguez and Panthaki (2006), Bauwens *et al.* (2005), and Beine *et al.*, (2007).

To analyze the volatility response to news surprise, we model the residual term of Eq. (1) as follows:

$$|\epsilon_{t,n}| = \omega_0 + \kappa_1 \frac{\hat{\sigma}_t}{\sqrt{N}} + \sum_{p=1}^{P} \left(\delta_{c,p} \cos\left(\frac{2\pi p}{N} n\right) + \delta_{s,p} \sin\left(\frac{2\pi p}{N} n\right)\right) + \sum_{d=1}^{3} \lambda'_d I_{d,t,n} + \sum_{k=1}^{k} \sum_{j'-1}^{J'} \vartheta_{k,j'} \left|\mathrm{S}_{k,t,n-j'}\right| + \tilde{\tau}_1 \mathrm{Unsch}_{t,n} + \tilde{\tau}_3 \mathrm{Speak}_{t,n} + \chi_{t,n}, \tag{2}$$

where $\frac{\hat{\sigma}_t}{\sqrt{N}}$ stands for the daily ARCH effects which capture the daily trend of volatility, $N = 288$ denotes the total number of 5-min intervals per day, I_d is the calendar effects such as the Japanese open, lunch, and the US late summer effect, and the sinusoids are the Fourier Flexible form for the intraday seasonality pattern. Based on the Schwarz and Akaike information criteria, $P = 4$. The value of J' denotes the length of volatility response to news announcements. We choose two hours to cover the volatility response for all the news according to recent literature (Laakkonen and Lanne,

2009), so $J^{'} = 24$. $\chi_{t,n}$ denotes the residual term. Note that there are 24 lags for $|S_{k,t,n-j'}|$ in Eq. (2), which is inefficient if we run the equation directly. Hence, we follow Andersen and Bollerslev (1998) and impose a third-order polynomial structure for each news event to avoid such problems (see Andersen and Bollerslev (1998) for the detailed characterization of the intraday seasonality pattern of the foreign exchange market).

Since the disturbance in Eq. (1) could be heteroskedastic, we apply the two-step weighted least-squares approach to estimate the coefficients: First, we run an ordinary least-square regression in Eq. (1) and obtain the residual terms to be used in volatility Equation (2). After estimating the news effect in the volatility equation, we run weighted least squares by imposing the fitted value of the absolute disturbance term on the left-hand side of Eq. (1) as the weight.

By relaxing the stability assumption, we follow Bai and Perron (1998) and model the breakpoint regression to allow for an unknown number of breaks without restricting the number of regimes in both the mean and volatility equations. Using this model, news coefficients become unstable outside the "structural breaks" but stable within each structural break sub-period. Once we estimate the unknown break dates, we can define the structural break sub-period accordingly and estimate the news coefficients within the corresponding sub-period using ordinary least-square method.

Hence, we model the mean and volatility equations as follows:

$$\begin{aligned} R_{t_b,n} &= \acute{\theta}_{0,b} + \acute{\theta}_{i,b} \sum_{i=1}^{I} R_{t_b-i} + \sum_{k=1}^{K} \acute{\beta}_{k,b} \mathrm{S}_{k,t_b,n} \\ &\quad + \tau_{1,b}\mathrm{Unsch}_{t_b} + \tau_{3,b}\mathrm{Speak}_{t_b} + \epsilon_{t_b,n} \end{aligned} \tag{3}$$

$$\begin{aligned} |\epsilon_{t_b,n}| &= \acute{\omega}_{0,b} + \acute{\kappa}_1 \frac{\hat{\sigma}_{t_b}}{\sqrt{N}} + \sum_{p=1}^{P} \left(\acute{\delta}_{c,p} \cos\left(\frac{2\pi p}{N} n\right) + \acute{\delta}_{s,p} \sin\left(\frac{2\pi p}{N} n\right) \right) \\ &\quad + \sum_{d=1}^{D} \acute{\lambda}_d' I_{d,t_b} + \sum_{k=1}^{k} \sum_{j'=1}^{J'} \acute{\vartheta}_{k,j',b} \left| \mathrm{S}_{k,t_b-j'} \right| \\ &\quad + \acute{\tau}_{1,b}\mathrm{Unsch}_{t_b} + \acute{\tau}_{3,b}\mathrm{Speak}_{t_b} + \chi_{t_b} \end{aligned} \tag{4}$$

with $(t_b = T_{b-1} + 1, \ldots, T_b), \quad b = 1, 2 \ldots m + 1.$

where b denotes the bth sub-period. $(T_1, \ldots, T_\mathrm{b} \ldots, T_m)$ are the unknown breakpoints corresponding to each sub-period. $T_0 = 0$ (by convention) and

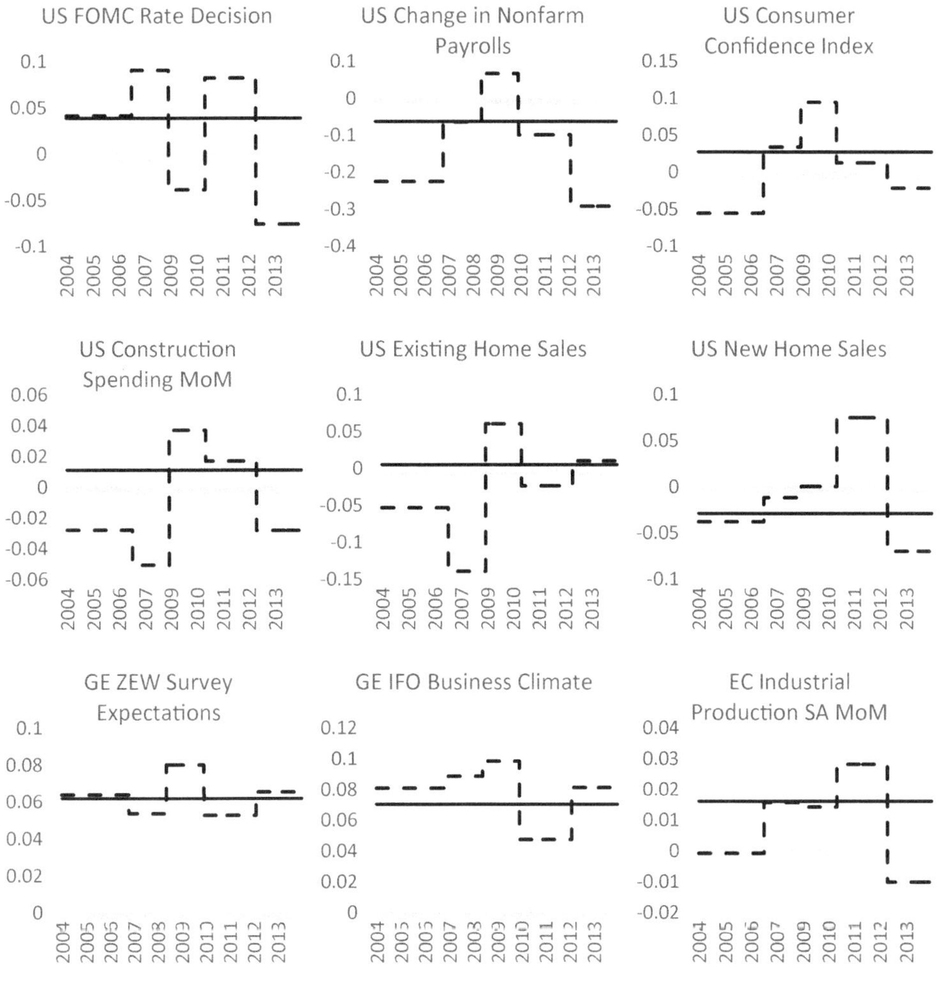

Figure 1. Change of News Coefficients on 5-min Return Over Time

Notes: The figure illustrates how the news coefficients in Eq. (3) change over time. News coefficients are assumed to be stable within each regime, but might be unstable between regimes. The solid line is the news coefficient assuming constant effects throughout the sample period. The dotted line is the step-wise line that represents the unstable news effects over regimes. The grey line is zero-value line.

$T_{m+1} = T$, where T equals the total number of 5-min intervals throughout the data set. t_b denotes the time frame starting after the previous breakpoint $(T_{b-1}+1)$ and ending at the current breakpoint (T_b) (See Fig. 3).

Equation (3) or (4) denotes a multiple linear regression system. If we use Δ_p to denote the vector of coefficients and X_t denotes the vector of

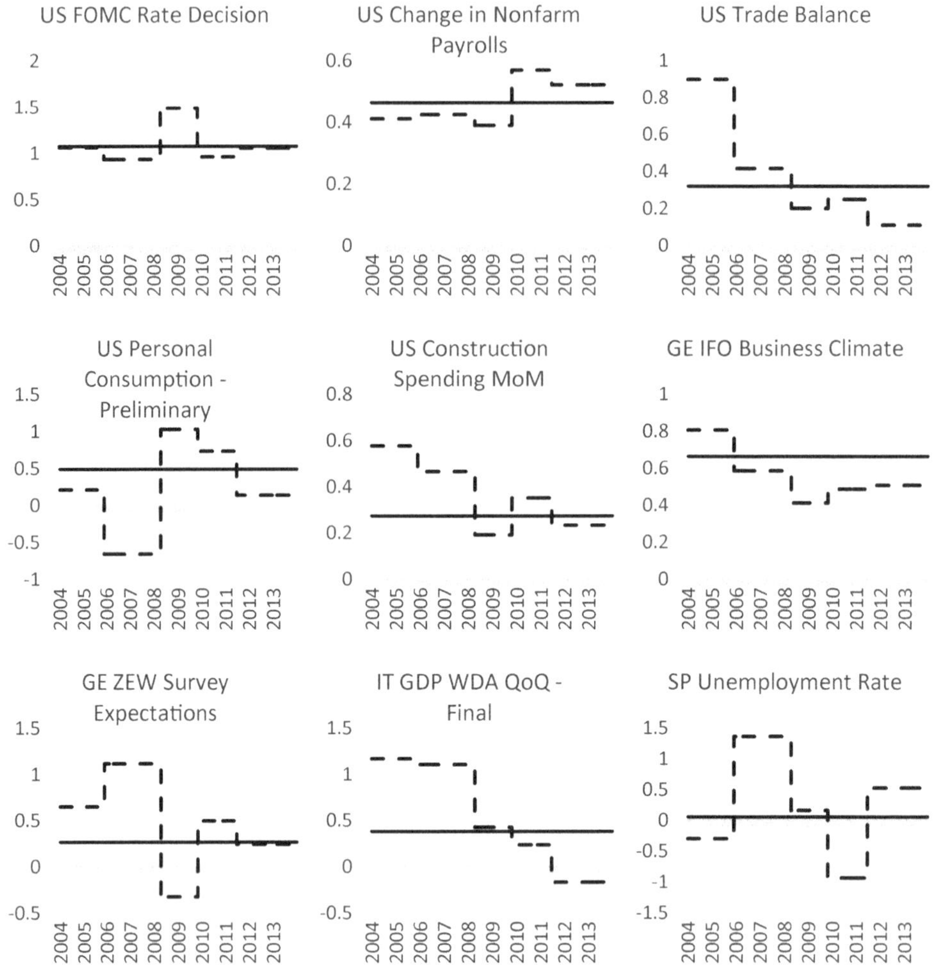

Figure 2. Change of News Coefficients on the Volatility of 5-min Return Over Time

Notes: The figure illustrates how the news coefficients in Eq. (4) change over time. News coefficients are assumed to be stable within each regime, but might be unstable between regimes. The solid line is the news coefficient assuming constant effects throughout the sample period. The dotted line is the step-wise line that represents the unstable news effects over regimes. The grey line is zero-value line.

all independent variables, we then estimate the unknown coefficients (Δ_p, $T_1, T_2, \ldots, T_m$), assuming $\Delta_p \neq \Delta_{p+1}(p \leq m)$. The estimation minimizes the sum of squared residuals: $\sum_{p=1}^{m+1} \sum_{t=T_{p-1}+1}^{T_p} [R_t - X'_t \Delta_p]^2$. Figures 1 and 2 illustrates polynomial structures corresponding to six US and three European news effects.

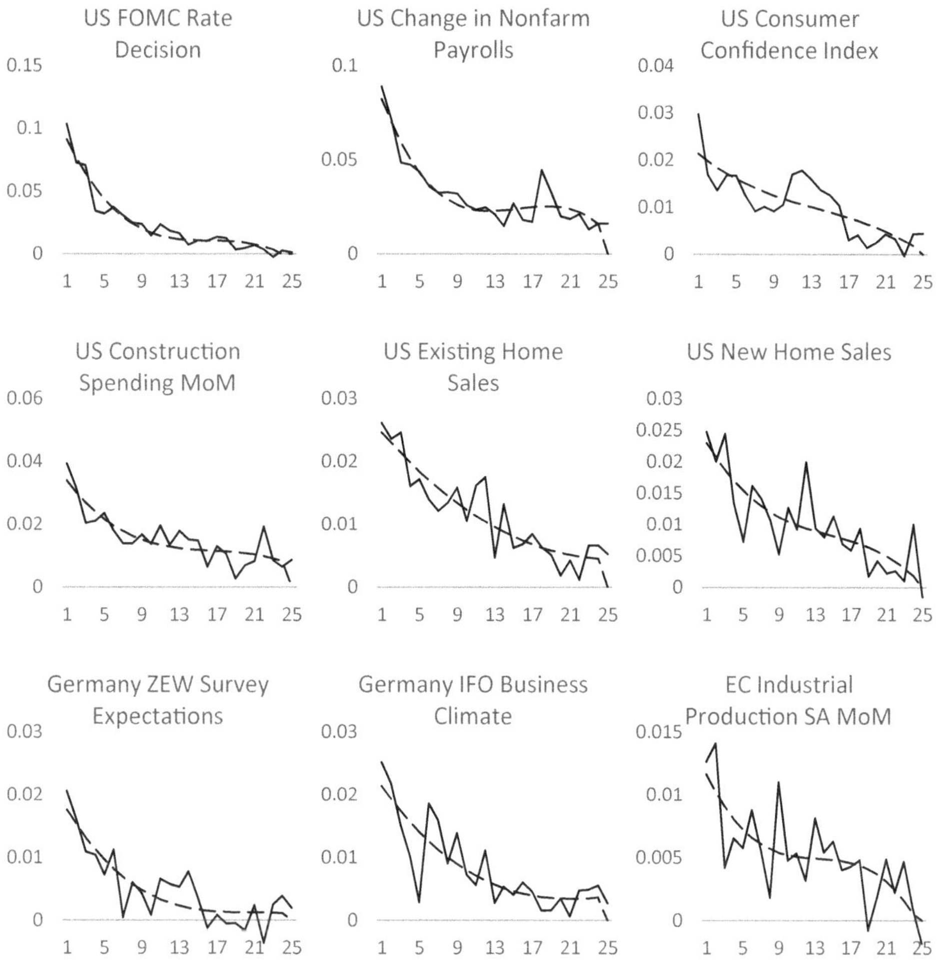

Figure 3. Polynomial Structure

Notes: The figure shows how the polynomial structure captures volatility response to nine news items within a two-hour post-announcement period. The X-axis includes 24 time intervals, which represent the 24 5-min intervals corresponding to the 2 h. The Y-axis indicates the difference between the total sample absolute returns and the post-announcements absolute return averages. The solid line is the post-announcement actual absolute average return. The dotted line represents the fitted value captured by the third-order polynomial structure.

If $\hat{\Delta}_p$ denotes the estimated coefficients, then

$$(\hat{T}_1, \hat{T}_2, \ldots, \hat{T}_m) = \operatorname{argmin}_{T_1, T_2, \ldots, T_m} \left(\sum_{p=1}^{m+1} \sum_{t=T_{p-1}+1}^{T_p} \left[R_t - X_t' \hat{\Delta}_p \right]^2 \right)$$

The breakpoint estimates are the results of the equation optimization, and the estimated coefficients are the corresponding estimates through all $m+1$ partitions $(T_1, T_2, \ldots, T_m)$.

4. Data

Our data set spans more than nine years from November 1, 2004 to March 31, 2014 and contains two kinds of data: (i) intraday Euro/Dollar 5-min spot exchange rate returns, and (ii) scheduled macroeconomic news announcements from the US and the Euro-zone. The sample period includes the US financial crisis from 2008 to mid-2009, while the European debt crisis lies in the 2010–2013 period. Several episodes of elevated risk and important economic uncertainty characterize the entire sample.

Our original high-frequency exchange rate data set, supported by Hotspot FXi, includes tick-by-tick tradable spot quotes. Each quote is time stamped to the millisecond. There are 288 5-min intervals during the 24-h foreign exchange market. We compute the mid-price for each interval by taking the average of each interval's last bid and ask $(\frac{(\text{Ask}+\text{Bid})}{2})$, then calculate the natural log difference of consecutive mid-prices multiplied by 100 to obtain percentage returns: $[\log(P_t) - \log(P_{t-1})] * 100$.

To minimize the disturbance generated from price outliers and anomalies, we implement some filtering procedures. We remove the quotes corresponding to the weekends, US statutory holidays,[1] and those after 21:00 on Friday due to lower quoting activity. We also exclude returns corresponding to the first interval for each day because it contains overnight effects, especially for Monday morning. This filtering procedure is consistent with Andersen and Bollerslev (1998) and Bauwens *et al.* (2005). We end up with 620,078 return observations. Table 1 presents some descriptive statistics for the filtered returns. We notice that the mean of 5-min return is almost zero, and there is relatively high kurtosis.

The news announcement data is collected from Bloomberg, which list all the economic news releases in its Economic Calendar (ECO) function with the date and time stamped to the minute. We incorporate the scheduled macroeconomic news from US and Euro-zone major countries including Germany, France, Italy, and Spain. Some news are announced quarterly such

[1]The 10 US statutory holidays deleted are: New Year's Day, Martin Luther King's Day, Presidents Day, Memorial Day, Independence Day, Labor Day, Columbus Day, Veterans Day, Thanksgiving Day, and Christmas Day.

Table 1. Descriptive Statistics for 5-min Returns

	EURUSD
Mean	0.000
Standard deviation	0.039
Skewness	0.095
Kurtosis	17.301
Num of observation	620,078
Num of zero return observation	18,424
Autocorrelation of order 1	-0.019^{***}
Autocorrelation of order 2	-0.005^{***}

Notes: The table presents main descriptive statistics corresponding to 5-min returns corresponding to the Euro/Dollar foreign exchange rate. 5-min returns are in percentage form. *** denotes the statistical significance of 1% level.

as GDP annualized QoQ Advance for US, but the majority are announced monthly like US Change in Nonfarm Payrolls, US Consumer Confidence Index (change from the previous month), and US New Home Sales. However, a minority of news is announced weekly such as US Initial Jobless Claims. The news announcement provides us with both actual figures and market forecasts, which is the median value of the survey conducted for predicting the scheduled news figures. Most of the news are monthly, and US figures are frequently announced at 8:30 am and 10:00 am, EST time. Euro News are primarily announced at 2:00 am and 5:00 am (see Tables 3 and 4, the first four columns).

Table 2 displays the observed largest return jumps occurring within 15 min just after the macroeconomic news announcement. We note that US news related to policy rates (Federal Open Market Committee Rate Decision — FOMC Rate Decision), unemployment (Unemployment Rate and Initial Jobless Claims), and payroll (Change in Nonfarm Payrolls) are frequently associated with larger returns.

Regarding the intraday seasonality, Fig. 4 shows the intraday pattern for the Euro/Dollar volatility. Starting from midnight EST, the volatility stays at a relatively low level because the most active markets in London and New York are closed, after 2:00 am EST, various European markets open gradually, which increases market activity to a maximum level between 8:00 am and 11:00 am EST when both the London and New York markets are open. After the European market is closed, volatility drops gradually to its lowest level after 17:00 EST.

Table 2. Largest Returns in Euro/Dollar

Return	Date	Country	News Announcement	Type
1.126	3/18/2009	US	FOMC Rate Decision	Scheduled
1.084	11/30/2011		Coordinated central bank action to address pressures in global money markets	Central Bank Intervention
1.020	3/25/2009	US	New Home Sales	Scheduled
0.852	11/13/2008	US	Restructuring of the Fed's Financial Support to AIG	Unscheduled
0.814	12/18/2008	UK	Stannard of BNP Paribas Speaks on Currency Markets	Speech
0.763	1/12/2005	US	Trade Balance	Scheduled
0.727	2/20/2009		Stocks Drop Around the World; Stoxx 600 Falls to 6-Year Low	Unscheduled News
0.712	12/16/2008	US	FOMC Rate Decision	Scheduled
−0.700	10/22/2008	US	Treasury's McCormick Speaks In Hong Kong	Speech
0.696	1/4/2008	US	Change in Nonfarm Payrolls	Scheduled
		US	Unemployment Rate	Scheduled
−0.669	5/5/2011	EC	Trichet Speaks at ECB Monthly News Conference	Speech
−0.669	5/5/2011	US	Initial Jobless Claims	Scheduled

Notes: The table shows largest Euro/Dollar returns realized within the 15-min post-announcement period. Returns are sorted using absolute values. Country column displays the country name corresponding to the news announcement: US — United States, UK — United Kingdoms, and EC — Euro Zone Aggregated. Type column contains the type of news, i.e. Scheduled News, Central Bank Intervention, Unscheduled News, or speech for senior officials.

Finally, we obtain major speech information from the Bloomberg Economic Calendar function (ECO) under speech sessions. The speeches are made by either country leaders like the US president or officers from central banks including Federal Reserve Bank and European Central Bank.

5. Empirical Results

Assuming stable news response coefficients (Eq. (1)), Table 3 presents the results for 36 US events of which 26 are significant (1% and 5% levels). Interestingly, only four of these are positive, which implies the US$ depreciates in response to a positive, news surprise (actual exceeds forecast). For example, the unemployment rate coefficient is 0.023 (significant at the

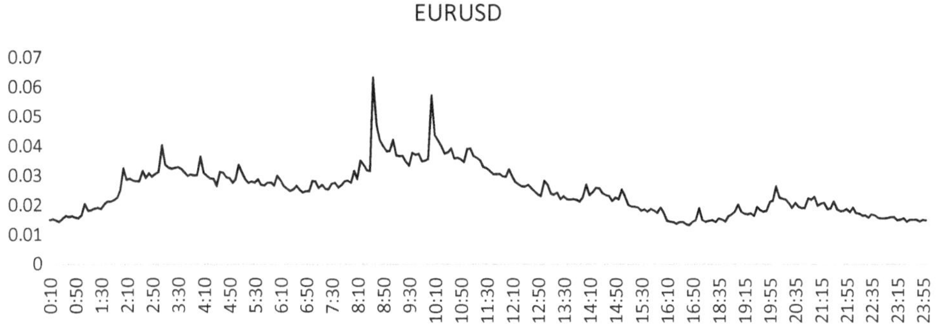

Figure 4. Intraday Volatility Seasonal Pattern

Notes: We calculate the average volatility for each 5-min interval by taking the average of absolute 5-min return through the entire sample for Euro/Dollar (EURUSD). In total, we have 288 intervals per day before removing the outliers with approximately 2,150 observations per interval from the sample period of 9 years and 5 months.

1% level) and indicates the US$ will depreciate by 23 basis points for a one standard deviation increase in positive news. The largest positive coefficient is 0.0386 of the FOMC rate decision. The 22 news events (61% of 36 events) with significant (1% and 5% level) negative coefficients signal US$ appreciation with respect to positive news. The largest of these are GDP Annualized QoQ Advance (−0.0675) and Change in Nonfarm Payrolls (−0.0631), which indicate that 'good' news (actual exceeds forecast) appreciates the US$, which is expected.

In comparison, Table 4 has 21 of 34 Euro News event coefficients significant at the 1% or 5% levels of which only 3 are negative — the opposite to the signs of US events in Table 3. Hence the majority of euro news appreciate the Euro for positive news — similar to the majority of US news which appreciate the dollar given positive news. We note that a negative surprise will depreciate both the Euro and the US$ for the majority of events. The three largest Euro events are positive and German — GDP SA QoQ preliminary (0.0792) IFO Business Climate (0.0703) and ZEW Survey Expectations (0.0619). The three negative euro coefficients are ECB announces interest rates (−0.0123), PPI MoM (−0.0096), and Exports QoQ (−0.0288). Hence, these three events will depreciate the euro with respect to positive news (actual exceeding expected) and it is not clear why exports would have this effect.[2] Lastly, important speeches in both the US and EC are

[2]This result stems from regime 3 in Table 9.

Table 3. News Stable Effect on Return: (US News)

Time	Country	Frequency	News Name	Coeff	Pvalue
8:30	US	37	GDP Annualized QoQ — Advance	−0.0675***	0.000
8:30	US	38	GDP Annualized QoQ — Preliminary	−0.007	−0.382
9:15	US	113	Industrial Production MoM	0.002	−0.500
8:30	US	38	Nonfarm Productivity — Final	−0.005	−0.214
10:00	US	113	Wholesale Inventories MoM	−0.0113***	−0.001
8:30	US	38	Nonfarm Productivity — Preliminary	−0.0328***	0.000
8:30	US	113	Retail Sales Ex Auto MoM	−0.0079**	−0.017
10:00	US	112	New Home Sales	−0.0286***	0.000
10:00	US	108	Pending Home Sales MoM	−0.001	−0.730
8:30	US	106	PCE Core MoM	−0.0249***	0.000
8:30	US	114	Personal Spending	0.004	−0.333
10:00	US	110	Existing Home Sales	0.005	−0.151
8:30	US	38	Personal Consumption — Preliminary	−0.0613***	0.000
10:00	US	113	Business Inventories	−0.0095***	−0.004
10:00	US	112	Construction Spending MoM	0.0111***	−0.001
10:00	US	112	Factory Orders	−0.0136***	0.000
8:30	US	113	Durables Ex Transportation	−0.0160***	0.000
8:30	US	113	CPI Ex Food and Energy MoM	−0.0311***	0.000
8:30	US	113	PPI Ex Food and Energy MoM	−0.0286***	0.000
8:30	US	111	PPI MoM	0.001	−0.866
8:30	US	112	Import Price Index MoM	−0.0215***	0.000
10:00	US	113	Consumer Confidence Index	0.0271***	0.000
8:30	US	111	Housing Starts	−0.0086*	−0.063
10:00	US	113	ISM Manufacturing	−0.0232***	0.000
9:45	US	113	Chicago Purchasing Manager	−0.0232***	0.000
8:30	US	113	Empire Manufacturing	−0.0335***	0.000
13:00	US	113	NAHB Housing Market Index	−0.0218***	0.000

(*Continued*)

Table 3. (***Continued***)

Time	Country	Frequency	News Name	Coeff	Pvalue
9:55	US	108	Univ. of Michigan Confidence — Preliminary	-0.0190^{***}	0.000
10:00	US	113	Philadelphia Fed Business Outlook	−0.004	−0.174
8:30	US	491	Initial Jobless Claims	-0.0141^{***}	0.000
8:30	US	113	Change in Nonfarm Payrolls	-0.0631^{***}	0.000
8:30	US	113	Unemployment Rate	0.0230^{***}	0.000
14:15	US	78	FOMC Rate Decision	0.0386^{***}	0.000
14:00	US	73	Minutes of FOMC Meeting	0.008	−0.157
8:30	US	113	Trade Balance	-0.0403^{***}	0.000
9:00	US	112	Net Long-term TIC Flows	-0.0167^{***}	0.000

Notes: The table presents the estimated coefficients for equation (1) using a two-step weighted least-square method. This table (B) present the US (Euro) news effects on returns. *, **, *** denote statistical significance of the coefficient at 10%, 5%, and 1%, respectively. Frequency and time provide the number and time for each announcement.

significantly negative, implying the Euro (US$) depreciates (appreciates). We note that about 62% (72%) of euro (US) events are significant, and Table 5 summarizes the number of significant US and Euro news coefficients and their signs for returns.

Tables 6, 7 provide the volatility coefficients (Eq. (2)) assuming stable effects over the whole sample. In Table 7, the US news affects currency volatility in 27 of 36 events (75%) with a significant (1% or 5%) coefficient and only one is negative (GDP Annualized QoQ Preliminary). Hence, nearly all US news increases volatility with the four largest coefficients being FOMC Rate Decision, Minutes of FOMC Meeting, Change in Nonfarm Payrolls, and Personal Consumption Preliminary.[3]

We note that a positive coefficient increases volatility for either positive or negative news. In addition, the larger return impact US news (Tables 3 and 4) typically has a high impact on volatility. Only 50% of the Euro News in Table 7 significantly impacts volatility (27 of 34 events), with only PPI MoM reducing volatility (negative coefficient). The four largest coefficients,

[3]Other high-impact events are Chicago Purchasing Manager, Trade Balance, Philadelphia Fed Business Outlook, Retail Sales Ex Auto MoM, GDP Annualized QoQ Advance, and Durables Ex Transportation.

Table 4. News Stable Effect on Return: (Euro News)

Time	Country	Frequency	News Name	Coeff	Pvalue
5:00	EC	113	Industrial Production SA MoM	0.0160***	−0.001
5:00	EC	113	Retail Sales MoM	0.0167***	−0.001
5:00	EC	37	Gross Fix Cap QoQ — Preliminary	0.0036	−0.703
5:00	EC	113	CPI Estimate YoY	0.0185***	0
5:00	EC	111	CPI Core YoY — Final	0.0022	−0.657
5:00	EC	112	Business Climate Indicator	0.0260***	0
5:00	EC	37	Household Cons QoQ — Preliminary	−0.0001	−0.989
7:45	EC	114	ECB Announces Interest Rates	−0.0123***	−0.003
5:00	EC	105	Trade Balance SA	0.0200***	0
5:00	EC	37	Govt Expend QoQ — Preliminary	0.0071	−0.447
2:45	FR	93	Own-Company Production Outlook	0.0039	−0.459
2:45	FR	105	PPI MoM	−0.0096***	−0.008
6:00	GE	113	Industrial Production SA MoM — Prelim	0.0081*	−0.092
2:00	GE	38	GDP SA QoQ — Preliminary	0.0792***	0
2:00	GE	112	Retail Sales MoM	0.0197***	0
5:00	GE	113	ZEW Survey Current Situation	0	−0.993
6:00	GE	112	Factory Orders WDA YoY — Preliminary	0.0124**	−0.012
2:00	GE	38	Private Consumption QoQ	0.0216*	−0.059
2:00	GE	38	Construction Investment QoQ	0.0198**	−0.043
2:00	GE	113	PPI MoM	−0.0065	−0.147
4:00	GE	113	IFO Business Climate	0.0703***	0
5:00	GE	113	ZEW Survey Expectations	0.0619***	0
3:55	GE	113	Unemployment Rate	−0.0025	−0.569
2:00	GE	38	Exports QoQ	−0.0288***	−0.001
4:00	IT	113	Industrial Production WDA YoY	0.0150***	−0.001
4:00	IT	35	GDP WDA QoQ — Preliminary	0.0272***	−0.001
4:00	IT	113	Retail Sales MoM	0.0123***	−0.004
5:00	IT	37	GDP WDA QoQ — Final	−0.012	−0.105
3:30	IT	113	Business Confidence	0.0207***	0

(Continued)

Table 4. (*Continued*)

Time	Country	Frequency	News Name	Coeff	Pvalue
4:00	IT	113	Trade Balance Total	−0.007	−0.258
3:00	SP	97	Retail Sales WDA YoY	0.0288***	0
3:00	SP	113	CPI MoM	0.0104**	−0.025
3:00	SP	110	CPI EU Harmonized YoY — Final	0.0092**	−0.034
3:00	SP	37	Unemployment Rate	−0.0082	−0.28
			EU speech	−0.0014**	−0.024
			US speech	−0.0014**	−0.021
			Unscheduled news	0	−0.825

Notes: The table presents the estimated coefficients for Eq. (1) using a two-step weighted least-square method. Table 3 A (B) present the US (Euro) news effects on returns. *, **, *** denote statistical significance of the coefficient at 10%, 5%, and 1%, respectively. Frequency and time provide the number and time for each announcement.

Table 5. Summary of Significant Event Coefficients for Tables 3, 4, 6 and 7 (Assume Constant Coefficients for Entire Sample 2004–2014)

	Returns		Volatility	
	Table 3 (US News)	Table 4 (Euro News)	Table 6 (US News)	Table 7 (Euro News)
Significant (−)	22	3	1	1
Coefficients (+)	4	18	26	16
Total	26	21	27	17
	(72%)	(62%)	(75%)	(50%)
Total number of news	36	34	36	34

Notes: This table summarizes the number of significant (1% and 5%) positive (+) and negative (−) news event coefficients in Tables 3, 4, 6 and 7.

all increasing volatility, are Industrial Production SA MoM, Trade Balance SA, IFO Business Climate, and ECB announces Interest Rates.[4] Similar to the US news, there is considerable overlap between the most influential euro news events on returns (Table 4) and volatility (Table 7). Lastly, US and Euro speeches as well as unscheduled news all increase volatility. Table 5 summarizes the number of significant volatility coefficients and their signs.

[4]Other important events are Business Climate Indicator, ZEW Survey Current Situation, GDP WDA QoQ Final, and Trade Balance Total.

Table 6. News Stable Effect on Volatility: (US News)

Time	Country	Frequency	News Name	Coeff	Pvalue
8:30	US	37	GDP Annualized QoQ — Advance	0.3050***	(0.000)
8:30	US	38	GDP Annualized QoQ — Preliminary	−0.1559**	(0.042)
9:15	US	113	Industrial Production MoM	0.0324	(0.412)
8:30	US	38	Nonfarm Productivity — Final	0.0872	(0.107)
10:00	US	113	Wholesale Inventories MoM	0.1784***	(0.000)
8:30	US	38	Nonfarm Productivity — Preliminary	−0.0162	(0.705)
8:30	US	113	Retail Sales Ex Auto MoM	0.3097***	(0.000)
10:00	US	112	New Home Sales	0.1445***	(0.001)
10:00	US	108	Pending Home Sales MoM	0.2369***	(0.000)
8:30	US	106	PCE Core MoM	0.1425***	(0.000)
8:30	US	114	Personal Spending	−0.0755*	(0.091)
10:00	US	110	Existing Home Sales	0.2079***	(0.000)
8:30	US	38	Personal Consumption — Preliminary	0.4914***	(0.000)
10:00	US	113	Business Inventories	0.0314	(0.456)
10:00	US	112	Construction Spending MoM	0.2751***	(0.000)
10:00	US	112	Factory Orders	0.2222***	(0.000)
8:30	US	113	Durables Ex Transportation	0.3008***	(0.000)
8:30	US	113	CPI Ex Food and Energy MoM	0.2780***	(0.000)
8:30	US	113	PPI Ex Food and Energy MoM	0.1493***	(0.001)
8:30	US	111	PPI MoM	−0.0255	(0.571)
8:30	US	112	Import Price Index MoM	0.0284	(0.368)
10:00	US	113	Consumer Confidence Index	0.2593***	(0.000)
8:30	US	111	Housing Starts	0.1789***	(0.000)
10:00	US	113	ISM Manufacturing	0.2930***	(0.000)
9:45	US	113	Chicago Purchasing Manager	0.3459***	(0.000)
8:30	US	113	Empire Manufacturing	0.1430***	(0.000)
13:00	US	113	NAHB Housing Market Index	−0.1405	(0.537)
9:55	US	108	Univ. of Michigan Confidence — Preliminary	0.2379***	(0.000)
10:00	US	113	Philadelphia Fed Business Outlook	0.3195***	(0.000)

(Continued)

Table 6. (*Continued*)

Time	Country	Frequency	News Name	Coeff	Pvalue
8:30	US	491	Initial Jobless Claims	0.1324***	(0.000)
8:30	US	113	Change in Nonfarm Payrolls	0.4638***	(0.000)
8:30	US	113	Unemployment Rate	0.2829***	(0.000)
14:15	US	78	FOMC Rate Decision	1.0752***	(0.000)
14:00	US	73	Minutes of FOMC Meeting	0.9954***	(0.000)
8:30	US	113	Trade Balance	0.3201***	(0.000)
9:00	US	112	Net Long-term TIC Flows	0.0378	(0.323)

Notes: The table presents the estimated coefficients for equation (2) using a two-step weighted least-square method. The table (B) present the US (Euro) news effects on volatility. *, **, *** denote statistical significance of the coefficient at 10%, 5%, and 1%, respectively. Frequency and time provide the number and time for each announcement.

To examine the stability assumption of Tables 3 and 4, the breakpoint regression (Eq. (3)) results are presented in Table 8(9) for US (Euro) news. Tables 8 and 9 have five regimes endogenously chosen from the data, with the first (November 2004 to June 2007) being the largest with 174,756 returns during an expansionary period, the second (June 2007 to December 2008) and third (December 2008 to June 2010) split the US crisis period, while the fourth (June 2010 to June 2012) and fifth (June 2012 to March 2014) cover the Euro crisis period. In Table 8 (US news), the Wald test shows significant differences (1% and 5% levels) between regimes for 32 of 36 (89%) news events, contradicting the constant parameter assumption of Table 3 and 4. In addition, there are 76 significant negative coefficients vs. 31 positive, which generally agrees with the preponderance of negative coefficients in Table 3, but there are relatively more positive coefficients than expected. We note that only regime 3 has more positive (11) coefficients than negative (7). The dominance of negative coefficients is strongest in regimes 1 (23 vs. 5) and 5 (16 vs. 4) compared to regimes 2 (18 vs. 5) and 4 (12 vs. 6).[5] However, there is significant variation of the coefficients between regimes for a given news event. For example, Change in Nonfarm Payroll (negative in Table 3) is significantly positive for regime 3 but negative in the other four regimes. The FOMC rate Decision (positive in Table 3) is significantly negative in regime 3 and positive in the other four regimes. In fact, almost all the negative US events in Table 3 have at least one significant positive coefficient in Table 7. This is not just

[5]Figures 3, shows positive regime coefficients for regime 3 in six of the nine diagrams.

Table 7. News Stable Effect on Volatility: (Euro News)

Time	Country	Frequency	News Name	Coeff	Pvalue
5:00	EC	113	Industrial Production SA MoM	0.7040***	(0.000)
5:00	EC	113	Retail Sales MoM	−0.5153	(0.342)
5:00	EC	37	Gross Fix Cap QoQ — Preliminary	0.5436	(0.262)
5:00	EC	113	CPI Estimate YoY	0.2831	(0.189)
5:00	EC	111	CPI Core YoY — Final	0.2420**	(0.037)
5:00	EC	112	Business Climate Indicator	0.5729***	(0.003)
5:00	EC	37	Household Cons QoQ — Preliminary	−0.4832	(0.172)
7:45	EC	114	ECB Announces Interest Rates	0.5932***	(0.000)
5:00	EC	105	Trade Balance SA	0.6388***	(0.000)
5:00	EC	37	Govt Expend QoQ — Preliminary	1.1910**	(0.039)
2:45	FR	93	Own-Company Production Outlook	0.1710**	(0.016)
2:45	FR	105	PPI MoM	−0.3000***	(0.002)
6:00	GE	113	Industrial Production SA MoM — Prelim	0.1418	(0.433)
2:00	GE	38	GDP SA QoQ — Preliminary	0.3010***	(0.002)
2:00	GE	112	Retail Sales MoM	0.2325***	(0.003)
5:00	GE	113	ZEW Survey Current Situation	0.5078***	(0.000)
6:00	GE	112	Factory Orders WDA YoY — Preliminary	0.1171	(0.341)
2:00	GE	38	Private Consumption QoQ	0.2231	(0.111)
2:00	GE	38	Construction Investment QoQ	0.0449	(0.690)
2:00	GE	113	PPI MoM	0.1649**	(0.019)
4:00	GE	113	IFO Business Climate	0.6643***	(0.000)
5:00	GE	113	ZEW Survey Expectations	0.2675***	(0.005)
3:55	GE	113	Unemployment Rate	0.2035**	(0.017)
2:00	GE	38	Exports QoQ	0.1370	(0.428)
4:00	IT	113	Industrial Production WDA YoY	0.0768	(0.534)
4:00	IT	35	GDP WDA QoQ — Preliminary	0.0582	(0.685)
4:00	IT	113	Retail Sales MoM	0.0732	(0.537)
5:00	IT	37	GDP WDA QoQ — Final	0.3813***	(0.003)
3:30	IT	113	Business Confidence	0.1352	(0.268)
4:00	IT	113	Trade Balance Total	0.3381*	(0.072)

(Continued)

Table 7. ***(Continued)***

Time	Country	Frequency	News Name	Coeff	Pvalue
3:00	SP	97	Retail Sales WDA YoY	−0.1249	(0.245)
3:00	SP	113	CPI MoM	0.1009	(0.186)
3:00	SP	110	CPI EU Harmonized YoY — Final	0.2035***	(0.000)
3:00	SP	37	Unemployment Rate	0.0536	(0.628)
			EU speech	0.0052***	(0.000)
			US speech	0.0109***	(0.000)
			Unscheduled news	0.0029***	(0.000)

Notes: The table presents the estimated coefficients for Eq. (2) using a two-step weighted least-square method. Table (B) present the US (Euro) news effects on volatility. *, **, *** denote statistical significance of the coefficient at 10%, 5%, and 1%, respectively. Frequency and time provide the number and time for each announcement.

occurring in regime 3 either, for example Nonfarm Productivity preliminary is positive in regimes 2 and 5 and negative in 3 and 4, which becomes an overall negative in Table 3. Clearly, there are more positive coefficients than expected from the predominantly negative US results of Table 3. Table 10 summarizes the number of positive and negative significant coefficients from Tables 8 and 9.

Table 9 has weaker results for the Euro because the Wald test shows significant differences for 21 of 34 (62%) news events, which is less than the 89% found in Table 8. In addition, all five regimes have more positive coefficients than negative. However, regime 1 (5) only has 3 (5) significant coefficients (1% and 5% levels), which is much smaller than the 16, 15, and 15 in regimes 2, 3, and 4, respectively. There are very few negative coefficients in any regime. In total, negative coefficients are about 20% the number of positive ones (9 vs. 45) — see Table 10 — and most (6) of these occur for the three negative news events of Table 4. However, two of these negative coefficient events (ECB announces interest rates and PPI MoM) have one significant positive regime. It is also clear that Euro news events vary in impact size between regimes, with many having only one or two significant regime coefficients. For example, EC Business Climate Indicator is only positive in regimes 3 and 4, while (GE) Retail sales MoM is only significantly positive in regime 2. Hence, there is substantial coefficient variability for half the news throughout the sample period.

We now examine Tables 11 and 12 for the volatility results of the five endogenously determined regimes, which are regime 1 (November 2004 to

Table 8. News Unstable Effects on Return Across Regimes: (US News)

CN	News Name	Regime 1	Regime 2	Regime 3	Regime 4	Regime 5	Wald
US	GDP Annualized QoQ — Advan	−0.169***	−0.237***	−0.003	−0.081**	−0.226***	***
US	GDP Annualized QoQ — Prelim	0.015	−0.025	−0.017	−0.012	−0.093***	***
US	Industrial Production MoM	−0.027***	−0.005	0.028***	0.013	−0.011	***
US	Nonfarm Productivity — Final	−0.036*	−0.025*	0.005	0.377***	−0.102***	***
US	Wholesale Inventories MoM	−0.018*	−0.016**	−0.010	−0.023***	0.025**	***
US	Nonfarm Productivity — Prelim	−0.019	0.073***	−0.015***	−0.250***	0.124***	***
US	Retail Sales Ex Auto MoM	−0.098***	−0.019**	0.016***	0.023**	−0.125***	***
US	New Home Sales	−0.038***	−0.012	0.001	0.075***	−0.070***	***
US	Pending Home Sales MoM	−0.045**	−0.031***	0.015**	−0.002	−0.013	**
US	PCE Core MoM	−0.030***	−0.081***	−0.046***	−0.022**	0.025**	***
US	Personal Spending	0.017	−0.027**	0.004	0.012	−0.026*	***
US	Existing Home Sales	−0.053***	−0.139***	0.060***	−0.023***	0.011	***
US	Personal Consumption — Prelim	−0.071**	−0.196***	0.005	−0.048***	0.032	***
US	Business Inventories	0.015**	−0.005	−0.030***	−0.017*	0.012	***
US	Construction Spending MoM	−0.028**	−0.051***	0.037***	0.017***	−0.028***	***
US	Factory Orders	−0.032***	0.000	−0.009*	−0.039***	−0.007	
US	Durables Ex Transportation	−0.085***	−0.084***	0.023***	0.002	−0.047***	***
US	CPI Ex Food and Energy MoM	−0.071***	−0.019**	−0.007	−0.045***	−0.014	***
US	PPI Ex Food and Energy MoM	−0.050***	−0.039***	−0.033**	0.009	−0.046*	***
US	PPI MoM	0.000	−0.011	0.018*	0.017	0.014	
US	Import Price Index MoM	−0.034***	−0.013*	0.014	0.001	0.036**	***
US	Consumer Confidence Index	−0.056***	0.034***	0.094***	0.013*	−0.021*	***
US	Housing Starts	−0.009	−0.034***	0.073***	−0.007	−0.086***	***
US	ISM Manufacturing	−0.064***	−0.013	0.009	−0.008	−0.071***	***

(*Continued*)

Table 8. *(Continued)*

CN	News Name	Regime 1	Regime 2	Regime 3	Regime 4	Regime 5	Wald
US	Chicago Purchasing Manager	−0.035***	−0.033***	−0.001	−0.014*	−0.011	
US	Empire Manufacturing	−0.076***	−0.038***	−0.008	−0.030***	−0.057***	***
US	NAHB Housing Market Index	−0.015	0.015	−0.014	−0.021**	−0.044***	
US	Univ. of Michigan Confi-Prelim	−0.026***	−0.012	−0.045***	−0.004	0.003	***
US	Phila. Fed Business Outlook	−0.059***	0.013**	0.059***	−0.008*	−0.059***	***
US	Initial Jobless Claims	0.030***	0.004	−0.044***	−0.016***	0.009	***
US	Change in Nonfarm Payrolls	−0.225***	−0.064***	0.068***	−0.099***	−0.291***	***
US	Unemployment Rate	0.151***	0.042***	0.016*	−0.006	0.001	***
US	FOMC Rate Decision	0.041***	0.091***	−0.039***	0.083***	−0.076***	***
US	Minutes of FOMC Meeting	0.067***	−0.014	0.056***	−0.021*	−0.056***	***
US	Trade Balance	−0.202***	−0.044***	−0.009	−0.005	−0.032***	***
US	Net Long-term TIC Flows	−0.149***	−0.025***	−0.002	0.022**	−0.008	***

Notes: The table displays macroeconomic news coefficients corresponding to five endogenously estimated regimes in Eq. (3). CN column provides the country name related to the news. Wald column provides probabilities triggered by the Wald test of equality, where the null hypothesis states equal coefficients. *, **, *** denote statistical significance at 10%, 5%, and 1%, respectively, within each regime. Panel A considers scheduled US news and Table 9 scheduled Euro News.

August 2006 with 120,726 returns), regime 2 (August 2006 to November 2008 with 141,232 returns), regime 3 (November 2008 to May 2010 with 95,143 returns), regime 4 (May 2010 to November 2011 with 104,947 returns), and the largest regime 5 (November 2011 to March 2014 with 158,030 returns).

First, the Wald test (Table 11) shows a significant difference (1% and 5%) for 25 of 36 US events (70%) with 92 (11) significant positive (negative) coefficients (see summary in Table 10). Hence, there is considerable variation across regimes which does not support the constant coefficient assumption of Table 6. We note that all five regimes only have a few negative coefficients (reducing volatility), so there is no unique regime as in Table 6 for US news impact on returns. An example of considerable variation across regimes for a given event is the FOMC Rate Decision coefficient of Tables 6 and 7

Table 9. News Unstable Effects on Return Across Regimes: (Euro News)

CN	News Name	Regime 1	Regime 2	Regime 3	Regime 4	Regime 5	Wald
EC	Industrial Production SA MoM	−0.001	0.016	0.014	0.028***	−0.010	**
EC	Retail Sales MoM	0.004	0.041***	0.011	0.013	0.013	**
EC	Gross Fix Cap QoQ — Prelim	−0.023	0.083**	0.027	−0.007	−0.009	*
EC	CPI Estimate YoY	0.010	0.008	0.039***	−0.018*	0.034***	***
EC	CPI Core YoY — Final	0.006	0.023*	0.001	−0.003	0.019	
EC	Business Climate Indicator	−0.002	0.016*	0.036***	0.029***	0.032*	**
EC	Household Cons QoQ — Prelim	0.005	0.004	−0.022	0.012	−0.006	
EC	ECB Announces Interest Rates	−0.026**	−0.065***	0.041***	−0.016**	−0.037***	***
EC	Trade Balance SA	0.000	−0.001	0.076***	0.010	0.025*	
EC	Govt Expend QoQ — Preliminary	0.023	0.040	0.029	0.021	0.005	
FR	Own-Company Production Outlook	0.000	0.036***	0.002	−0.057***	−0.112	**
FR	PPI MoM	−0.012	−0.011	−0.015***	0.037**	0.005	***
GE	Industrial Production SA MoM — Prelim	0.012	−0.015	0.018**	0.003	0.004	
GE	GDP SA QoQ — Preliminary	0.034	0.054***	0.110***	0.066***	0.179*	***
GE	Retail Sales MoM	0.009	0.042***	0.019	0.013	0.020	
GE	ZEW Survey Current Situation	−0.023	−0.042***	0.139***	0.019***	0.041*	***
GE	Factory Orders WDA YoY — Prelim	−0.005	0.003	0.011	0.030**	0.074**	***
GE	Private Consumption QoQ	−0.005	−0.039	0.129***	0.058	−0.028	***
GE	Construction Investment QoQ	−0.013	0.015	0.135***	0.047*	−0.006	***
GE	PPI MoM	−0.002	−0.009	−0.007	0.003	0.013	
GE	IFO Business Climate	0.081***	0.089***	0.099***	0.047***	0.081***	***
GE	ZEW Survey Expectations	0.064***	0.054***	0.080***	0.053***	0.066***	***
GE	Unemployment Rate	0.004	0.039***	−0.014*	−0.017	−0.037	**
GE	Exports QoQ	−0.006	−0.093*	−0.047***	0.032	−0.015	**

(Continued)

Table 9. (*Continued*)

CN	News Name	Regime 1	Regime 2	Regime 3	Regime 4	Regime 5	Wald
IT	Industrial Production WDA YoY	0.005	−0.007	0.014	0.039***	0.005	***
IT	GDP WDA QoQ — Preliminary	−0.015	0.042**	0.064***	0.036	0.033	***
IT	Retail Sales MoM	−0.009	0.049***	0.009	0.026***	−0.020*	***
IT	GDP WDA QoQ — Final	−0.010	−0.023	−0.017	−0.012	0.009	
IT	Business Confidence	0.000	0.056***	0.009*	0.041***	0.012	**
IT	Trade Balance Total	0.007	−0.052***	−0.005	−0.003	−0.001	
SP	Retail Sales WDA YoY	−0.027	0.190***	0.039***	0.040***	−0.008	***
SP	CPI MoM	−0.002	0.031***	0.016	0.024**	−0.011	*
SP	CPI EU Harmonized YoY — Final	0.011	0.011	0.016*	0.005	0.006	
SP	Unemployment Rate	−0.003	0.006	−0.022*	−0.012	0.019	

Notes: The table displays macroeconomic news coefficients corresponding to five endogenously estimated regimes in Eq. (3). CN column provides the country name related to the news. Wald column provides probabilities triggered by the Wald test of equality, where the null hypothesis states equal coefficients. *, **, *** denote statistical significance at 10%, 5%, and 1% respectively, within each regime. Table 8 considers scheduled US news and this table scheduled Euro News.

(1.0752), which comes from regime 4 (Table 11) having the only significant regime coefficient (0.542).

Similarly, the FOMC Meeting Minutes coefficient (0.9954 in Table 6) depends on regimes 1 (0.067) and 3 (0.056) which overwhelm regime 5 (−0.056) in Table 11. In contrast the Change in Nonfarm Payrolls is consistently positively significant[6] in all regimes of Table 11 and agrees with 0.4638 in Table 6. Another large coefficient in Table 6 is Personal Consumption Preliminary (0.4914), which depends on regimes 3 (0.292) and 5 (0.673) of Table 11. It appears that volatility coefficients are not stable over time. Table 10 summarizes the number of significant positive and negative volatility coefficients from Tables 11 and 12.

[6]Note that the Wald statistic is significant (1%), indicating that these positive regimes are distinctly different.

Table 10. Summary of Significant Event Coefficients for Tables 8, 9, 11 and 12

	Regime	Regime #	1	2	3	4	5	Subtotal
Tables 8 and 9(Returns)	Regime	End date	2007/6/22	2008/12/18	2010/6/4	2012/6/20	2014/3/31	
		Sample Size	174,756 (28.2%)	93,125 (15%)	96,090 (15.5%)	137,498 (22.2%)	118,609 (19.1%)	620,078 (100%)
	Panel A (US news)	–	23	18	7	12	16	76
		+	5	5	11	6	4	31
		Total	28	23	18	18	20	107
	Panel B (Euro news)	–	1	3	2	2	1	9
		+	2	13	13	13	4	45
		Total	3	16	15	15	5	54
		Regime #	1	2	3	4	5	Subtotal
Tables 11 and 12 (Volatility)	Regime	End date	2006/8/24	2008/11/17	2010/5/28	2011/11/18	2014/3/31	
		Sample Size	120,726 (19.5%)	141,232 (22.8%)	95,143 (15.3%)	104,947 (16.9%)	158,030 (25.5%)	620,078 (100%)
	Panel A (US news)	–	3	3	2	0	3	11
		+	21	18	20	15	18	92
		Total	24	21	22	15	21	103
	Panel B (Euro news)	–	2	2	1	2	0	7
		+	5	9	15	11	8	48
		Total	7	11	16	13	8	55

Note: This table summarizes the number of significant (1% and 5%) positive (+) and negative (–) news event coefficients in Table 8, 9, 11 and 12.

Table 11. News Unstable Effects on Volatility Across Regimes: (US News)

CN	News Name	Regime 1	Regime 2	Regime 3	Regime 4	Regime 5	Wald
US	GDP Annualized QoQ — Advance	−0.141	0.059	0.171**	−0.172	0.189	
US	GDP Annualized QoQ — Prelimi	0.094	−0.035	0.271***	0.174	0.215**	
US	Industrial Production MoM	−0.077	−0.014	−0.038	−0.079	1.010***	***
US	Nonfarm Productivity — Final	0.396***	0.279***	0.419***	−0.003	0.298***	***
US	Wholesale Inventories MoM	0.056	0.018	0.572***	0.227	0.590***	***
US	Nonfarm Productivity — Prelim	0.493*	0.413***	0.161*	0.164**	0.244**	
US	Retail Sales Ex Auto MoM	0.215**	0.105	0.128	0.151	0.196***	
US	New Home Sales	0.104	−0.070	−0.123	−0.078	−0.254***	
US	Pending Home Sales MoM	0.575***	0.604***	0.127*	0.063	0.062	***
US	PCE Core MoM	0.218	−0.661**	1.032***	0.734***	0.141	***
US	Personal Spending	−0.187**	0.119	−0.280***	0.647***	−0.024	***
US	Existing Home Sales	0.577***	0.467***	0.192**	0.353***	0.234***	**
US	Personal Consumption — Prelim	0.240*	0.090	0.292***	−0.110	0.673***	***
US	Business Inventories	0.532***	0.195***	0.531***	0.126	0.120	***
US	Construction Spending MoM	0.490***	0.331***	0.326***	0.473***	−0.099	***
US	Factory Orders	0.080	0.172**	0.437***	0.115	0.007	*
US	Durables Ex Transportation	0.217**	−0.106	−0.175*	−0.100	0.213	**
US	CPI Ex Food and Energy MoM	0.049	−0.048	−0.097	0.126	−0.107	
US	PPI Ex Food and Energy MoM	0.270**	0.020	0.299***	0.145	0.385***	*
US	PPI MoM	0.308***	0.256***	−0.217	−0.204	0.026	***
US	Import Price Index MoM	0.216***	0.423***	0.143	0.187**	0.203**	*
US	Consumer Confidence Index	0.232***	0.547***	0.391***	0.128	0.331***	***
US	Housing Starts	0.346***	0.211***	−0.225***	0.075	−0.009	***
US	ISM Manufacturing	−0.265	−0.321	−0.269	−1.248	0.522	
US	Chicago Purchasing Manager	0.507***	0.354***	0.067	−0.094	0.104	***

(*Continued*)

Table 11. (*Continued*)

CN	News Name	Regime 1	Regime 2	Regime 3	Regime 4	Regime 5	Wald
US	Empire Manufacturing	0.311**	0.173*	0.372**	0.432***	0.350***	
US	NAHB Housing Market Index	0.249***	0.201***	0.078**	0.183***	0.081**	***
US	Univ. of Michigan Confid. — Prelim	0.411***	0.425***	0.389***	0.570***	0.521***	***
US	Philadel. Fed Business Outlook	0.452***	0.342***	0.469***	0.117***	0.180***	***
US	Initial Jobless Claims	1.062***	0.934***	1.488***	0.961***	1.053***	***
US	Change in Nonfarm Payrolls	0.912***	0.892***	0.634***	0.725***	1.504***	***
US	Unemployment Rate	0.898***	0.415***	0.202***	0.251***	0.110**	***
US	FOMC Rate Decision	0.245	−0.080	0.128*	0.542***	−0.097	***
US	Minutes of FOMC Meeting	0.067***	−0.014	0.056***	−0.021*	−0.056***	***
US	Trade Balance	−0.202***	−0.044***	−0.009	−0.005	−0.032***	***
US	Net Long-term TIC Flows	−0.149***	−0.025***	−0.002	0.022**	−0.008	***

Notes: The table displays macroeconomic news coefficients corresponding to five endogenously estimated regimes in Eq. (4). CN column provides the country name related to the news. Wald column provides probabilities triggered by the Wald test of equality, where the null hypothesis states equal coefficients. *, **, *** denote statistical significance at 10%, 5%, and 1%, respectively, within each regime. Table 11 considers scheduled US news and Table 12 scheduled Euro News.

The Euro News of Table 12 has a significant Wald statistic (1% and 5%) for 19 of 34 events, indicating instability between the regimes. There are 48 (7) positive (negative) coefficients which generally supports the positive coefficients in Table 7. The four largest coefficients in Table 7 are Industrial Production SA MoM (0.704), (GE) IFO Business Climate (0.6643), Trade Balance SA (0.6388), and ECB Announces Interest Rates (0.5932). The first depends on regimes 1, 3, and 4; the second is equally supported by all five regimes (Wald test is not significant), the third depends on regimes 4 and 5, the fourth is supported unequally by all five regimes (Wald test is significant at 1%). In general, most significant Euro volatility coefficients in Table 7 depend on one or two regimes in Table 12 (for example, ZEW Survey Current Situation (GE) is typical as it depends on regimes 3 and 4), and we conclude that volatility reaction is unstable over time as it depends on the event, economic regime, and surprise.

Table 12. News Unstable Effects on Volatility Across Regimes: (Euro News)

CN	News Name	Regime 1	Regime 2	Regime 3	Regime 4	Regime 5	Wald
EC	Industrial Production SA MoM	0.918***	0.393*	0.834***	0.908***	0.147	***
EC	Retail Sales MoM	0.204	−1.718	0.525	−2.047*	0.383	
EC	Gross Fix Cap QoQ — Prelim	−0.259	−0.915	4.630***	1.203	0.618	*
EC	CPI Estimate YoY	−0.270	−0.586	0.136	0.683	0.239	
EC	CPI Core YoY — Final	0.058	0.168	−0.021	0.610**	0.561*	
EC	Business Climate Indicator	−0.204	0.869*	0.134	0.849**	1.500***	*
EC	Household Cons QoQ — Prelim	−0.397	−0.342	−3.238***	−0.547	2.205*	***
EC	ECB Announces Interest Rates	0.327***	0.445***	0.558***	0.733***	0.853***	***
EC	Trade Balance SA	0.805	0.174	0.082	1.714***	0.503**	***
EC	Govt Expend QoQ — Preliminary	1.812	−0.843	6.095***	0.476	−2.630	***
FR	Own-Company Production Outlook	0.284	−0.277**	0.434***	−0.139	3.265***	***
FR	PPI MoM	−0.553	−0.367	−0.213*	0.351	−0.040	
GE	Industrial Production SA MoM-Prelim	−0.703	−0.513	0.121	0.583	0.645	*
GE	GDP SA QoQ — Preliminary	0.434	0.309	0.201	0.085	−0.051	
GE	Retail Sales MoM	0.273	0.485***	0.632**	−0.189	0.420**	***
GE	ZEW Survey Current Situation	0.077	0.020	1.260**	0.507***	0.138	
GE	Factory Orders WDA YoY — Prelim	−0.657***	0.057	0.880***	1.143***	−0.589	***
GE	Private Consumption QoQ	−0.515**	1.686***	−0.831*	−0.705	−0.120	***
GE	Construction Investment QoQ	0.249	−0.515*	0.148	0.200	−0.228	
GE	PPI MoM	0.187	−0.206	0.272***	0.230	0.253	*
GE	IFO Business Climate	0.808***	0.586***	0.412***	0.488***	0.509***	
GE	ZEW Survey Expectations	0.649***	1.120***	−0.324	0.495	0.242	***
GE	Unemployment Rate	−0.045	0.303*	0.073	0.666***	0.933***	***
GE	Exports QoQ	0.207	−1.248**	0.188	0.191	0.450	

(Continued)

Table 12. (*Continued*)

CN	News Name	Regime 1	Regime 2	Regime 3	Regime 4	Regime 5	Wald
IT	Industrial Production WDA YoY	−0.254	−0.008	0.615**	1.398***	−0.163	***
IT	GDP WDA QoQ — Preliminary	−0.227	−0.472*	0.368	5.270***	0.504	***
IT	Retail Sales MoM	0.457*	−0.338	−0.171	0.458	0.164	
IT	GDP WDA QoQ — Final	1.171**	1.107***	0.428**	0.236	−0.168	**
IT	Business Confidence	−0.522	1.099***	0.102	−0.245	−0.629*	***
IT	Trade Balance Total	1.602*	1.146***	−0.014	−1.970*	0.336	**
SP	Retail Sales WDA YoY	−0.325	0.304	0.457**	−0.575**	−0.124	**
SP	CPI MoM	−0.061	−0.013	0.448**	−0.092	0.237	
SP	CPI EU Harmonised YoY — Final	−0.059	0.064	1.064***	−0.014	−0.127	***
SP	Unemployment Rate	−0.300	1.363***	0.160	−0.932***	0.531***	***

Notes: The table displays macroeconomic news coefficients corresponding to five endogenously estimated regimes in Eq. (4). CN column provides the country name related to the news. Wald column provides probabilities triggered by the Wald test of equality, where the null hypothesis states equal coefficients. *, **, *** denote statistical significance at 10%, 5%, and 1%, respectively, within each regime. Table 11 considers scheduled US news and Table 12 scheduled Euro News.

6. Conclusion

Throughout our ten year sample (2004–2014), we find that 72% (62%) of US (Euro) News announcements significantly affect Euro/US$ returns, most of which appreciate the currency given positive news (actual exceeds forecast). In the US, the opposite holds only for four events — the Unemployment Rate, FOMC Rate Decision, Consumer Confidence Index, and Construction Spending (4/36 news events is 11% of the US sub-sample). The counterintuitive result for the latter two appear to be caused by contrary results in sub-periods involved with the 2008 financial crisis. This becomes evident when the sample is endogenously split into five regimes by a breakpoint regression model. In fact, the middle (third) period (December 2008–June 2010) has the most sign changes compared to the other four regimes. In general, we observe more than twice as many contrary results in the regimes than observed for constant coefficients. This indicates that the news effects are not stable and vary with the event, regime, and surprise.

We also examine the volatility of an announcement effect during its following 2 hour period. Assuming a constant coefficient, we find that 75% (50%) of US (Euro) News is significant at the 1% or 5% level, with almost all causing an increase in Euro/US$ volatility (less than 3% of news events decreased volatility for US and Euro News). When the sample is endogenously split into five regimes, the difference between regime volatility for a given event is statistically significant for 70% (56%) of the US (Euro) sample, respectively. This is partly due to the increase in volatility reducing coefficients (11% for the five regimes compared to 3% for constant coefficients). Unlike returns, this result was fairly consistent across all regimes.

We conclude that volatility, like return, is unstable, being dependent on the news, its surprise, and the regime in which the announcement occurs. Either traders or policymakers would find our results useful when making decisions related to foreign exchange rates. Both FX traders and monetary policymakers need to be aware that macroeconomic news announcements have an unstable effect on exchange rates over time. This instability could be related to the business cycle itself. Consequently, some news effects could vary significantly over time depending on the economic state, implying that different announcements could lose their importance while others become significant.

References

Andersen, T. G. and Bollerslev, T. (1998). "Deutsche mark–dollar volatility: Intraday activity patterns, macroeconomic announcements, and long-run dependencies. *J. Fin.*, 53, pp. 219–265.

Andersen, T. G., Bollerslev, T., Diebold, F. X., and Vega, C. (2003). Micro effects of macro announcements: Real-time price discovery in foreign exchange. *Am. Econom. Rev.*, 93, pp. 38–62.

Andersen, T. G., Bollerslev, T., Diebold, F. X., and Vega, C. (2007). Real-time price discovery in stock, bond and foreign exchange markets. *J. Int. Econom.*, 73(2), pp. 251–277.

Bacchetta, P. and Wincoop E. V. (2004). A Scapegoat model of exchange rate fluctuation". *Ame. Econom. Rev., Papers Proce.*, 94, pp. 114–118.

Bacchetta, P. and Wincoop, E. V. (2006). Can information heterogeneity explain the exchange rate determination puzzle?. *Am. Econom. Rev.*, 96, pp. 552–576.

Bacchetta, P. and Wincoop, E. V. (2013). On the unstable relationship between exchange rates and macroeconomic fundamentals". *J. Int. Econom.*, 91(1), pp. 18–26.

Bai, J. and Perron, P. (1998). Estimating and testing linear models with multiple structural changes". *Econometrica*, 66, pp. 47–78.

Balduzzi, P., Elton, E. J., and Green, T. C. (2001). Economic news and bond prices: Evidence from the US Treasury market. *J. Fin. Quant. Anal.*, 49, pp. 523–543.

Bauwens, L., Ben Omrane, W., and Giot P. (2005). News announcements, market activity and volatility in the Euro/Dollar foreign exchange market. *J. Inter. Money Fin.*, 24, pp. 1108–1125.

Beine, M., Bos, C. S., and Laurent, S. (2007). The impact of central bank Fx interventions on currency components. *J. Fin. Econom.*, 5, pp. 154–183.

Ben Omrane, W. and Debodt, E. (2007). Using self-organizing maps to adjust for intra-day seasonality. *J. Banking Fin.*, 31(6), pp. 1817–1838.

Ben Omrane, W. and Savaser, T. (2016). The sign switch effect of macroeconomic news in foreign exchange markets. *J. Int. Fin. Markets, Institu. Money*, Forthcoming.

Cheung, Y. W. and Chinn, M. D. (2001). Currency traders and exchange rate dynamics: A survey of the US market. *J. Int. Money Fin.*, 20, pp. 439–471.

Dominguez, K. and Panthaki, F. (2006). What defines 'news' in foreign exchange markets?". *J. Int. Money Fin.*, 25, pp. 168–198.

Fatum, R., Hutchison, M., and Wu, T. (2012). Asymmetries and state dependence: The impact of macro surprises on intraday exchange rates. *J. Jap. Int. Econom.*, 26, pp. 542–560.

Faust, J., Rogers J. H., Wang S., and Wright J. H. (2007). The high-frequency response of exchange rates and interest rates to macroeconomic announcements. *J. Monetary Econom.*, 54, pp. 1051–1068.

Fratzscher, M. (2009). What explains global exchange rate movements during the financial crisis?. *J. Int. Money Fin.*, 28, pp. 1390–1407.

Gilbert, T., Scotti, C., Strasser, G., and Vega, C. (2015). "Is the intrinsic value of macroeconomic news announcements related to their asset price impact. Finance and Economics Discussion Series 2015–046. Board of Governors of the Federal Reserve System (U.S.).

Laakkonen H. and Lanne M. (2009). Asymmetric news effects on exchange rate volatility: Good vs. bad news in good vs. bad times". *Stud. Nonlin. Dynam. and Econometr.* 14, pp. 1–38.

Laakkonen H. and Lanne M. (2013). The relevance of accuracy for the impact of macroeconomic news on exchange rate volatility. *Int. J. Fin. Econom.*, 18, pp. 339–351.

Melvin, M. and Taylor, M. P. (2009). The crisis in the foreign exchange rate market. *J. Int. Money Fin.*, 28(8), pp. 1317–1330.

Neely, C. J. (2011). A survey of announcement effects on foreign exchange volatility and jumps. *Federal Reserve Bank of St. Louis Rev.*, 93, pp. 361–407.

Rossi, B. (2006). Are exchange rates really random walks? Some evidence robust to parameter instability. *Macroeconom. Dyn.*, 10, pp. 20–38.

Chapter 8

Currency Spillover Effects between the US Dollar and Some Major Currencies and Exchange Rate Forecasts Based on Neural Nets*

David E. Allen[*,†,‡], Petko Kalev[§], Shelton Peiris[*] and Abhay K. Singh[**]

[*] *School of Mathematics and Statistics, the University of Sydney, Australia*
[†] *Department of Finance, Asia University, Taiwan*
[‡] *School of Business and Law, Edith Cowan University, Joondalup, WA*
[§] *La Trobe Business School, La Trobe University, Melbourne, Victoria*
[**] *Department of Finance, Macquarie University, Sydney, Australia*

Abstract

This chapter features an analysis of major currency exchange rate return spillover effects in relation to the US dollar, as constituted in US dollar terms. The Euro (EUR/USD), British Pound (GBP/USD), Chinese Yuan (CHY/USD), and Japanese Yen (JPY/USD) are modeled using the Diebold and Yilmaz (2009, 2012) spillover index metric. A rolling window of 200 days is used to capture spillover effects between the different currency pair relationships over the ten year sample of daily exchange rate returns data, from August 2005 to November 2016. We then use a neural network regression model to forecast exchange rate movements and evaluate the results on the basis of error metrics for a twenty per cent hold-out sample forecast period. The spillover index analysis suggests that the greatest spillovers occur between the EUR/USD return series and the GBP/USD return series. The size and direction of spillovers changes across the sample period. This does not help for forecasting purposes, and the neural network regression models are relatively more successful in forecasting the CHY/USD relationship, possibly because of the managed nature of the Chinese currency.

*The analysis in the chapter was undertaken with Rats, and GMDHShell.

1. Introduction

The global financial crisis (GFC) had a major and sustained impact on the world's financial markets. This chapter examines whether the exchange rate behaviour of four major currencies, namely the Euro, British Pound, Chinese Yuan, and Japanese Yen, in the context of their paired relationships with the US Dollar, experienced spillover effects over the ten year sample of daily exchange rate returns data, from August 2005 to August 2015. The empirical analysis is based on the use of variance decompositions, generalized VAR analysis, in the context of a recently introduced spillover index measure, Diebold and Yilmaz (2009, 2012). The results of this analysis suggest significant comovements and volatility spillovers across two of the four exchange rate returns series. We also forecast the behavior of the four series using Neural Network regression models.

The modeling and forecasting of exchange rate behavior remains a difficult issue. Rogoff (1996) documented some of the difficulties, particularly in relation to purchasing power parity (PPP). This represents the simple empirical proposition that once converted to a single currency, national price levels should be equal. Rogoff mentions the paradoxical contrast between the extremely slow rate at which currencies appear to converge to long-run equilibrium and the enormous volatility of short-run real exchange rate movements.

The typical difficulties encountered in exchange rate modeling are discussed in Taylor and Sarno (2003), and more specifically nonlinear modeling dynamics are discussed in Taylor *et al.* (2001) and Sarno *et al.* (2004). Baillie and Bollerslev (1989), suggest that foreign currency rates are best characterized as pure unit-root (random walk or martingale) processes, which implies it is impossible to predict exchange rate movements. Engel and Hamilton (1990) applied a Markov switching model for exchange rate changes, while Diebold and Nason (1990) and Meese and Rose (1990) used variants of local regression. Morana and Beltratti (2004) examine long memory and structural breaks in the realized variance process for the DM/US$ and Yen/US$ exchange rates. Chang *et al.* (2013) have analyzed the hedging of major currencies using future contracts in a multivariate GARCH framework.

The use of neural networks to forecast exchange rate movements was stimulated in studies such as those by Kuan and Liu (1995), who used feedforward and recurrent artificial neural networks (ANNs) to produce conditional mean forecasts. In recent years, the argument in favor of the martingale hypothesis has been queried because of the possibility of long-memory (fractional) dynamic behavior in the foreign currency market. Other applications of the nonlinear time series models applied to this topic include Matias *et al.* (2012) and Reboredo *et al.* (2012), who model the behavior of high-frequency returns on the S&P500 index using intraday data. Gradojevic and Yang (2006) compare high-frequency US dollar–Canadian dollar exchange rate behavior and report that ANN models outperform linear time series models. The current chapter can be viewed as an extension of this modeling using nonlinear time series models to forecast currency pairs. It is a companion study to Allen *et al.* (2016). We confine ourselves to the use of ANNs for forecasting purposes and do not consider other types of machine learning techniques, such as support vector machines, in this chapter.

The results of the spillover index analysis suggest that the greatest spillovers occur between the EUR/USD return series and the GBP/USD return series, while the size and direction of spillovers change across the sample period. However, this does not help for forecasting purposes, and the neural network regression models are relatively more successful in forecasting the CHY/USD relationship, possibly because of the managed nature of the Chinese currency.

The chapter is divided into four sections: Section 2 follows the introduction and introduces the data set and econometric and data mining methods used, Section 3 presents the results, and Section 4 concludes.

2. Research Methods

2.1. *Data set and econometric models*

2.1.1. *Data sets*

The data set includes daily data for each currency, in US dollar terms, of the exchange rates paired with the euro, British pound, Chinese yuan, and Japanese yen, taken from an 11-year period drawn from August 29, 2005 to November 3, 2016 — 2804 observations in total. These daily US dollar-denominated exchange rate series are sourced from the FRED database (Federal Reserve Bank of St. Louis Economic Data). Unit root tests, based on KPSS tests, and fractional integration tests, indicated that the levels series of these exchange rates are non-stationary, as shown in Table 2. Therefore we chose to work with the logarithms of the first difference, that is, log differences, of our base series, for the purposes of the modeling of these

Table 1. Tests of Stationarity

	KPSS test	Probability	Fractional Integration (Whittle Estimator)	Z Statistic	Probability
Euro–US dollar exchange rate	8.97701	0.01*	1.0158	18.1711	0.0000
Chinese Yuan–US dollar exchange rate	22.4134	0.01*	1.0909	19.5146	0.0000
Japanese YEN–US dollar exchange rate	6.31481	0.01*	1.024	18.3179	0.0000
UK pound–US dollar exchange rate	15.3202	0.01*	0.9496	20.5254	0.0000

Note: The table features tests of stationarity KPSS tests and fractional integration tests.

Table 2. List of Countries and Exchange Rates

Country	Symbol	Abbreviations
Euro	EURET	Euro exchange rate return
China	CHRET	Chinese exchange rate return
Japan	JPRET	Japanese exchange rate return
UK	UKRET	UK exchange rate return

exchange rate movements and forecasts, as shown below

$$y_{it} = \ln(\mathrm{ER}_{it}) - \ln(\mathrm{ER}_{it-1}), \tag{1}$$

where ER_{it} indicates the US dollar-denominated exchange rate i, and t indexes the four series, on day t. We scaled the returns by 100 to make them easier to manage for the purposes of statistical analysis. Thus, the results are in percentage terms.

The data sets used are shown in Table 2. The tests of stationarity, featuring KPSS tests, with null hypothesis of stationarity, and tests of fractional integration, using a local Whittle approximation, are reported in Table 1. The KPSS tests strongly reject the null hypothesis of stationarity for the levels series of all four exchange rates, and the fractional integration tests all suggest values above 1 with the exception of the UK exchange rate. Hence, we use the logarithm of first differences of our base series.

A set of graphs of the base series is shown in Fig. 1.

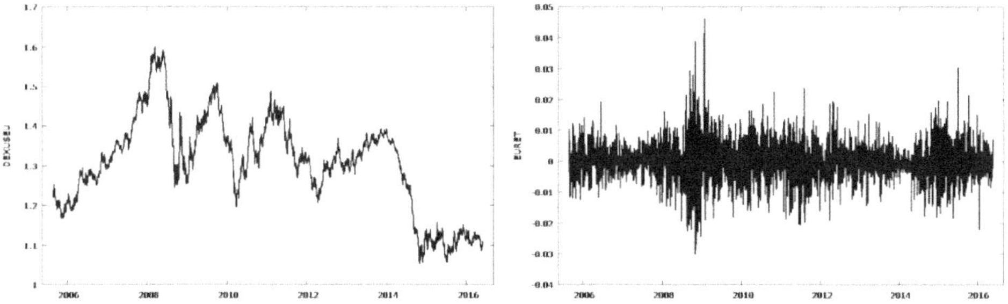

(a) US-EURO

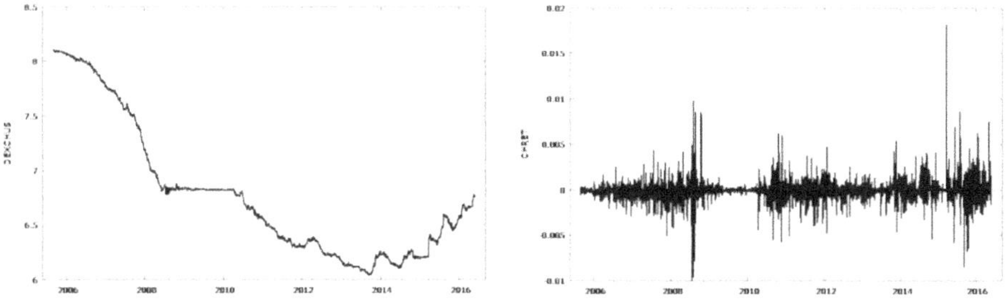

(a) US-CHINA

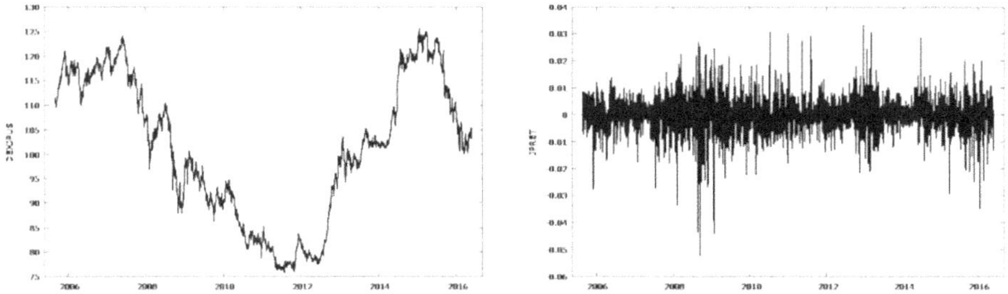

(a) US-JAPAN

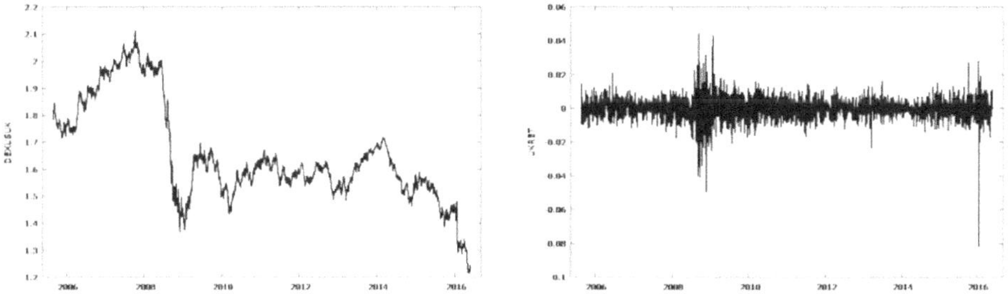

(b) US-UK

Figure 1. Series Plots

Table 3. Descriptive Statistics

Statistics	EURET	CHRET	JPRET	UKRET
Mean	−0.035	−0.0064	−0.0025	−0.0001
Median	0.000	0.000	0.00084	0.0008
Maximum	0.04621	0.018	0.033	0.044
Minimum	−0.03	−0.01	−0.052	−0.082
Skewness	0.209	1.304	−0.363	−0.964
Excess Kurtosis	3.047	25.16	4.824	14.02
Standard Deviation	0.0063	0.0013	0.0067	0.0065
Coefficient of Variation	19.97	19.99	272.8	49.16

2.2. *Data characteristics*

The characteristics of the basic index series used in our data set presented in Table 3 suggest substantial departures from normal distributions.

The summary statistics presented in Table 3 show that these exchange rate return series have means and medians that are either zero or close to it, and they are not particularly skewed. All series have excess kurtosis, which is very evident in the cases of China, and to a lesser degree in the other three.

The QQ plots, as shown in Fig. 2, show that all the exchange rate return series have too many extreme observations in their tails to conform to normal distributions.

2.3. *Econometric methods*

There are a variety of models that could be used to test for the existence of time-varying volatility, and for spillover effects in returns and volatility across markets. One approach is to use a time series vector autoregressive (VAR) framework. This was recently formalized by Diebold and Yilmaz (2009) and Diebold and Yilmaz (2012), who modelled spillovers using VAR models and variance decompositions. They constructed a spillover index based both on return spillovers and volatility spillovers. Their approach is initially attractive for our purposes, because it enables us to see which of the four currencies considered makes the largest contribution to the spillover of shocks to returns across pairs.

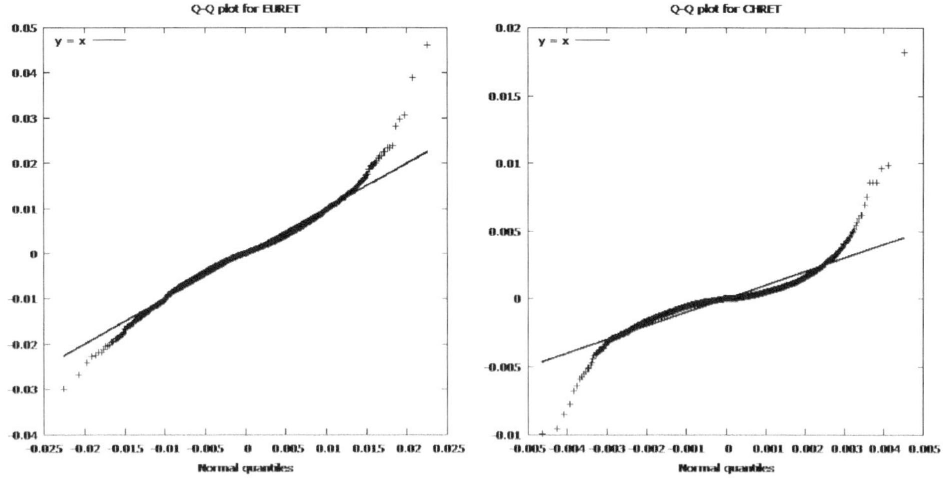

(a) EEU and China

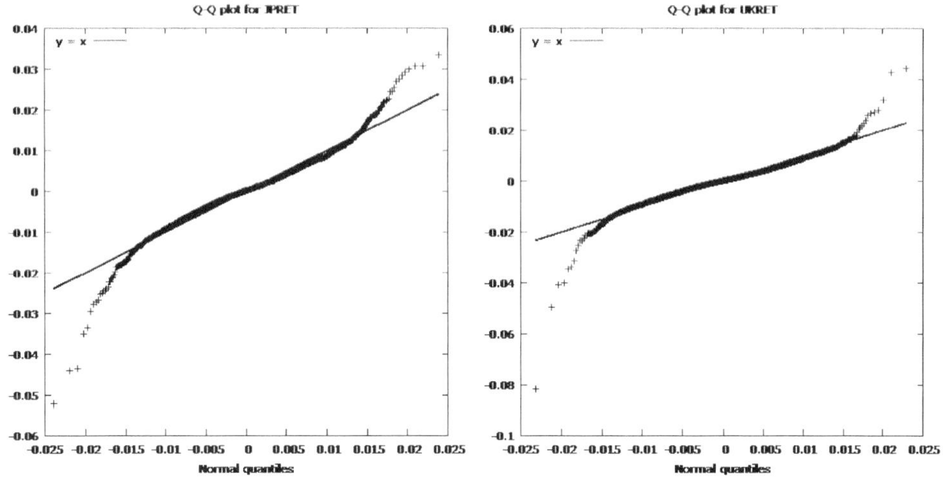

(b) Japan and UK

Figure 2. QQ Plots

2.4. *The Diebold and Yilmaz (2009, 2012) spillover index*

Diebold and Yilmaz (2009) suggest that the advantage of the adoption of a VAR framework and the use of variance decompositions is that they permit the aggregation of spillover effects across markets, distilling a wealth of information into a single spillover measure. This suits our current purposes and permits an examination of the relative contributions to spillovers made by the six markets in our sample. They proceed to develop their measure by taking each asset i, and adding the shares of its forecast error variance coming from shocks to asset j, for all $j \neq i$, all in the context of an n variable VAR. They then sum these error variances across all $i = 1, \ldots, N$. If we take the case of a covariance stationary, first-order, two-variable VAR, we have:

$$x_t = \Phi x_{t-1} + \varepsilon_t,$$

where $x_t = (x_{1t}, x_{2t})$ and Φ is a 2×2 parameter matrix. In the empirical analysis which follows, x will be either a vector of index returns or a vector of index volatilities. The moving average representation of the VAR can be written, given the existence of covariance stationarity, as:

$$x_t = \Theta(L)\varepsilon_t,$$

where $\Theta(L) = (1 - \Phi L)^{-1}$. The moving average representation can be conveniently written as:

$$x_t = A(L)u_t,$$

where $A(L) = \Theta(L)Q_t^{-1}, u_t = Q_t\varepsilon_t, E(u_t u_t') = I$, and Q_t^{-1} is the unique lower-triangular Choleski factor of the covariance matrix of ε_t.

Diebold and Yilmaz (2009) then proceed to consider the optimal one-step ahead forecast, given by

$$x_{t+1,t} = \Phi x_t,$$

with the corresponding one-step ahead error vector:

$$e_{t+1,t} = x_{t+1} - x_{t+1,t} = A_0 u_{t+1} = \begin{bmatrix} a_{0,11} & a_{0,12} \\ a_{0,21} & a_{0,22} \end{bmatrix} \begin{bmatrix} u_{1,t+1} \\ u_{2,t+1} \end{bmatrix}$$

which has the covariance matrix:

$$E(e_{t+1,t}e_{t+1,t}^{'}) = A_0 A_0'.$$

This suggests that the variance of a one-step ahead error in forecasting $x_{1,t}$ is $a_{0,11}^2 + a_{0,12}^2$ and the variance of the one-step ahead error in forecasting $x_{2,t}$ is $a_{0,21}^2 + a_{0,22}^2$. Diebold and Yalmiz (2009) demonstrate that it is possible to to split the forecast error variances of each variable into components attributable to the various system shocks. In this two-variable system, it is possible to distinguish between shocks to the variable itself, x_i and shocks to the other variable, x_j, for $i,\ j = 1, 2, i \neq j$.

Diebold and Yalmaz calculate a spillover index in the two variable case as:

$$S = \frac{a_{0,12}^2 + a_{2,1}^2}{\text{trace}(A_0 A_0')} \times 100. \tag{2}$$

They then generalize the measure to take into account multiple securities and multiple periods as shown below

$$S = \frac{\sum_{h=0}^{H-1} \sum_{\substack{i,j=1 \\ i \neq j}}^{N} a_{h,ij}^2}{\sum_{h=0}^{H-1} \text{trace}(A_h A_h')}. \tag{3}$$

Diebold and Yilmaz (2012) extend their approach to include a generalized vector autoregressive framework in which forecast-error variance decompositions are invariant to variable ordering. Diebold and Yilmaz (2012) define own variance shares as the fraction of the H-step-ahead error variances in forecasting x_i due to shocks to x_i, for $i = 1, 2, \ldots, N$, and cross-variance shares, or spillovers, as the fractions of the H-step-ahead variances in forecasting x_i, resulting from shocks to x_j, for $i,\ j = 1, 2, \ldots, N$, such that $i \neq j$.

Diebold and Yilmaz (2012) write the generalised H-step-ahead forecast error variance decompositions by $\theta_{i,j}^g(H)$, for $H = 1, 2, \ldots$, resulting in:

$$\theta_{i,j}^g(H) = \frac{\sigma_{ii}^{-1} \sum_{h=0}^{H-1} (e_i' A_h \sum e_j)^2}{\sum_{h=0}^{H-1} (e_i' A_h \sum A_h' e_i)}, \tag{4}$$

where $\sum$ is the variance matrix for the error vector ε and σ_{ii} is the standard deviation of the error term of the ith element and zero otherwise.

Given that they have used generalized impulse response functions, the sum of the elements of each row of the variance decomposition table is not equal to 1: $\sum_{j=1}^{N} \theta_{ij}^g(H) \neq 1$. They use the information available in the variance decomposition matrix for the construction of the spillover index by normalizing each entry of the variance decomposition matrix by the row sum as

$$\tilde{\theta}_{ij}^g(H) = \frac{\theta_{ij}^g(H)}{\sum_{j=1}^{N} \theta_{ij}^g(H)}. \tag{5}$$

Diebold and Yilmaz (2012) then proceed to construct a total volatility spillover index as

$$S^g(H) = \frac{\sum_{i,j=1,i\neq j}^{N} \tilde{\theta}_{ij}^g(H)}{\sum_{i,j=1}^{N} \tilde{\theta}_{ij}^g(H)}.100 = \frac{\sum_{i,j=1,i\neq j}^{N} \tilde{\theta}_{ij}^g(H)}{N}.100. \quad (6)$$

They further construct a directional spillover measure to illuminate how volatility spills across from different assets or asset classes. They do this by using the normalized elements of the generalized variance decomposition matrix. Their measure of directional volatility spillover received by market i from other markets j is given as

$$S_{i.}^g(H) = \frac{\sum_{j=1,i\neq j}^{N} \tilde{\theta}_{ij}^g(H)}{\sum_{j=1}^{N} \tilde{\theta}_{ij}^g(H)}.100. \quad (7)$$

By contrast, directional volatility spillovers transmitted by market i to all other markets j are computed as

$$S_{.i}^g(H) = \frac{\sum_{j=1,i\neq j}^{N} \tilde{\theta}_{ji}^g(H)}{\sum_{j=1}^{N} \tilde{\theta}_{ji}^g(H)}.100. \quad (8)$$

The net volatility spillover is the difference between gross volatility shocks transmitted to and gross volatility shocks received from all other markets. Diebold and Yilmaz (2012) compute net spillovers from market i to all other markets j as

$$S_i^g(H) = S_{.i}^g(H) - S_{i.}^g(H). \quad (9)$$

We use these measures in our subsequent analysis.

2.5. *Neural network analysis*

In the empirical analysis, we used a single approach for the empirical estimation of neural network models. The most straightforward linear approach, is available in the *R* package TsDyn (see Antonio *et al.*, 2009). A neural network model with linear input, D hidden units, and activation function g can be written as

$$x_{t+s} = \beta_0 + \sum_{j=1}^{D} \beta_j g\left(\gamma_{0j} + \sum_{i=1}^{m} \gamma_{ij} x_{t-(i-1)d}\right). \quad (10)$$

However, we decided to use a more general nonlinear neural net modelling approach, using the GMDH shell program (http:www.gmdhshell.com). This program is built around an approximation called the "Group Method of Data Handling". This approach is used in such fields as data mining, prediction, complex systems modeling, optimization, and pattern recognition. The algorithms feature an inductive procedure that performs a sifting and ordering of gradually complicated polynomial models and the selection of the best solution by external criterion.

A GMDH model with multiple inputs and one output is a subset of components of the base function

$$Y(xi_1, \ldots, x_n) = a_0 + \sum_{i=1}^{m} a_i f_i, \tag{11}$$

where f are elementary functions dependent on different inputs, a are unknown coefficients, and m is the number of base function components.

In general, the connection between input–output variables can be approximated by Volterra functional series, the discrete analog of which is the Kolmogorov–Gabor polynomial

$$y = a_0 + \sum_{i=1}^{m} a_i x_i + \sum_{i=1}^{m}\sum_{j=1}^{m} a_{ij} x_i x_j + \sum_{i=1}^{m}\sum_{j=1}^{m}\sum_{k=1}^{m} a_{ijk} x_i x_j x_k + \cdots, \tag{12}$$

where $x = (x_i, x_2, \ldots, x_m)$, the input variables vector, and $A = (a_0, a_1, a_2, \ldots, a_m)$ the vector of weights. The Kolmogorov–Gabor polynomial can approximate any stationary random sequence of observations and can be computed by either adaptive methods or a system of Gaussian normal equations. Ivakhnenko (1968) developed a new algorithm called 'The Group Method of Data Handling (GMDH)' by using a heuristic and perceptron type of approach. He demonstrated that a second-order polynomial (Ivakhnenko polynomial: $y = a_0 + a_1 x_i + a_2 x_j + a_3 x_i x_j + a_4 x_i^2 + a_5 x_j^2$) can reconstruct the entire Kolmorogorov–Gabor polynomial using an iterative perceptron-type procedure. This approach is featured in the second stage of the empirical analysis, as given below, which uses the GMDH shell software.

2.6. *Summary of econometric methods*

We have adopted a two-fold approach in this chapter. We commence our analysis with an application of the Diebold and Yilmaz (2009, 2012) spillover index metric. This is developed in a VAR framework and uses variance decompositions to aggregate and examine spillover effects across markets. The VAR analysis provides a preliminary insight into which of the currency markets considered influences the other markets in terms of the transmission of shocks, or whether they are immune from shocks to the other markets in the sample. The restriction of this approach is that only linear relationships are captured.

However, this preliminary analysis is followed by the application of nonlinear neural net modeling. Neural networks can, in principle, model nonlinearities automatically, and this is needed to explicitly model using transformations (splines, etc.) in linear regression. Artificial neural nets (ANNs) may be considered as a data processing technique that maps, or relates, some type of input stream of information to an output stream of processing. Variations of ANNs can be used to perform classification, pattern recognition, and predictive tasks. They can be calibrated on a training data sample and then tested using out-of-sample predictions. This is the approach adopted in this chapter. An advantage is that they are nonlinear. A potential disadvantage is that they may capture local optima in their iteration procedures rather than global maxima, though various techniques such as back-propagation can minimize this risk. ANNs are something of a black box and you cannot be sure that if you fit an ANN to a similar data set you will get the same results as with the original data set. This is related to the fact that ANNs have few, if any, probabilistic underpinnings, unlike their more statistical or Bayesian counterparts. The authors take the view that the proof of the pudding is in the eating and that out-of-sample predictions are a vital assessment tool.

3. Empirical Results

3.1. *Spillover index*

The results of the application of the spillover index to the return series and the various decomposition analyses are shown in Table 4. The table was constructed on the basis of VAR estimations using each of the series as the dependent variable in turn. Details of the VAR estimation, which used four lags, are omitted for the sake of brevity. All were significant at a 5% level or better and returned Durbin Watson statistics close to 2, which suggests that serial correlation is not an issue.

One of the main features of Table 4 is the degree of interdependence between the Euro/US dollar exchange rate rate of return and the UK/US dollar rate rate of return. The EURO returns series exerted a 29.20% influence on the variance of the UK exchange rate of return, while the UK, in return, contributed a similar 28.43% toward explaining the variance of the

Table 4. Spillover Index Variance Decomposition of Exchange Rate Returns

	EURET	CHRET	JPRET	UKRET	Contribution from others
EURET	67.63	0.57	3.38	28.43	32.4
CHRET	2.91	94.12	1.64	1.32	5.9
JPRET	4.53	0.40	94.60	0.46	5.40
UKRET	29.20	0.68	0.67	69.44	30.6
Contribution to others	36.6	1.7	5.7	30.2	74.2
Contribution including own	104.3	95.8	100.3	99.7	18.6%

Note: This table features the results of the application of Diebold and Yilmaz spillover index as described in Eqs. (3)–(9) inclusively.

EURO exchange rate rate of return. The UK does not participate in the use of the EURO but is the second largest economy in the EEC, as measured by gross domestic product in USD at market or official government exchange rates (nominal GDP) in 2016, as suggested by International Monetary Fund (IMF) data. Germany has the largest GDP in 2016 nominal terms, with a value of $3,467.8 billion, followed by the UK at $2,761.0, France at $2,467.8, and Italy at $1,848.7.

According to UK HM Revenue and Customs statistics, in September 2016, the proportion of total exports to the EU was 51%. Over the past 18 months, this proportion ranged from 38% to 51%. The proportion of total imports from the EU was 48% in September 2016. Over the same period, this ranged between 45% and 56%. Given this degree of economic interdependence, it is not surprising that there is a mutual influence on each others exchange rate behaviour. Furthermore, the single largest recipient of UK exports is the US, based on 2015 data from the same source. China ranked second in 2015 as a source of imports and fourth as a destination for exports. Japan has much less importance, and in 2015, on the basis of total trade, only ranked 17th as a UK trading partner. However, Japan and China are relatively more important to the EU in trade terms, Japan is the EU's second biggest trading partner in Asia after China. However, trading partnerships do not seem to explain directly the transmission of shocks shown in Table 4.

If we move across the first row in Table 4, we can see that EURET explains 67.63% of its own variance, while the influence of CHRET is a meager 0.57% and Japan contributes 3.38%. The big influence, as previously mentioned, is from UKRET at 28.43%. CHRET in the next row

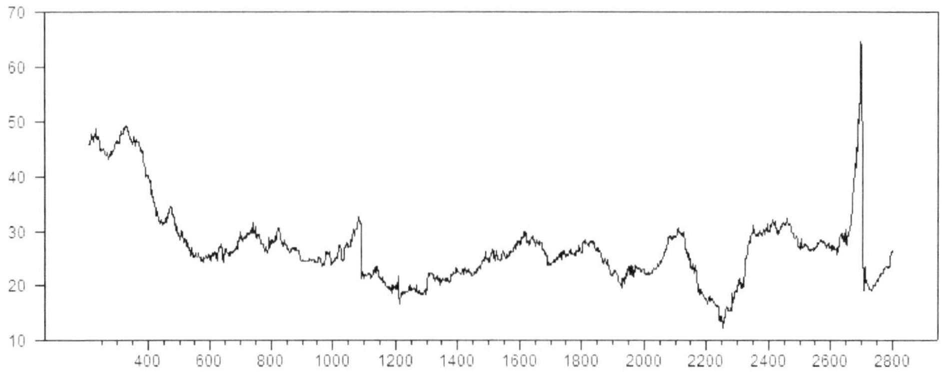

Figure 3. Total Volatility Spillovers Exchange Rate Return Series

is largely independent, explaining 94.12% of its own variance, while the total contribution from the other series toward explaining its variance is 5.9%, as shown in the right-hand column of Table 4. If we look at the end of the second row in Table 4 we an see that CHRET receives a total contribution from the other three markets of merely 5.9%, while its contribution to other markets, measured in the penultimate entry in column 2 of Table 4 is only 1.7%. Much the same can be said for JAPRET, which explains 94.6% of its own variance, while receiving 5.4% from other markets and contributing 5.7%. Finally, the spillover behavior of UKRET is very similar to that of EURET in that it determines 69.44% of its own variance, contributes 28.43% to EURET, and has a negligible impact on CHRET and JPRET. The analysis in Table 4 suggests that the behavior of CHRET and JPRET is largely independent of the other currencies considered in this analysis, while EURET and UKRET show a marked mutual influence in terms of spillovers.

Figure 3 provides a graph of the total volatility spillovers across the four exchange rate return series. It can be seen that there is considerable variation across the 11-year span, with the beginning of the sample in 2005–2006 and the end of the sample in 2016 revealed as times of relatively high spillovers.

We also applied the directional measures, mentioned in Sec. 2.4, and the results from this are shown in Fig. 4. It has to be borne in mind that the y axis in Fig. 4 has been scaled. The size of the spillovers to and from the Euro/USD and UK/USD exchange rates is relatively and absolutely larger.

The net volatility spillovers are shown in Fig. 5. Finally, the pairwise volatility spillovers are shown in Fig 6.

The volatility spillover analysis reveals that there is considerable variation in the size of the spillovers, between these four exchange rate series, in

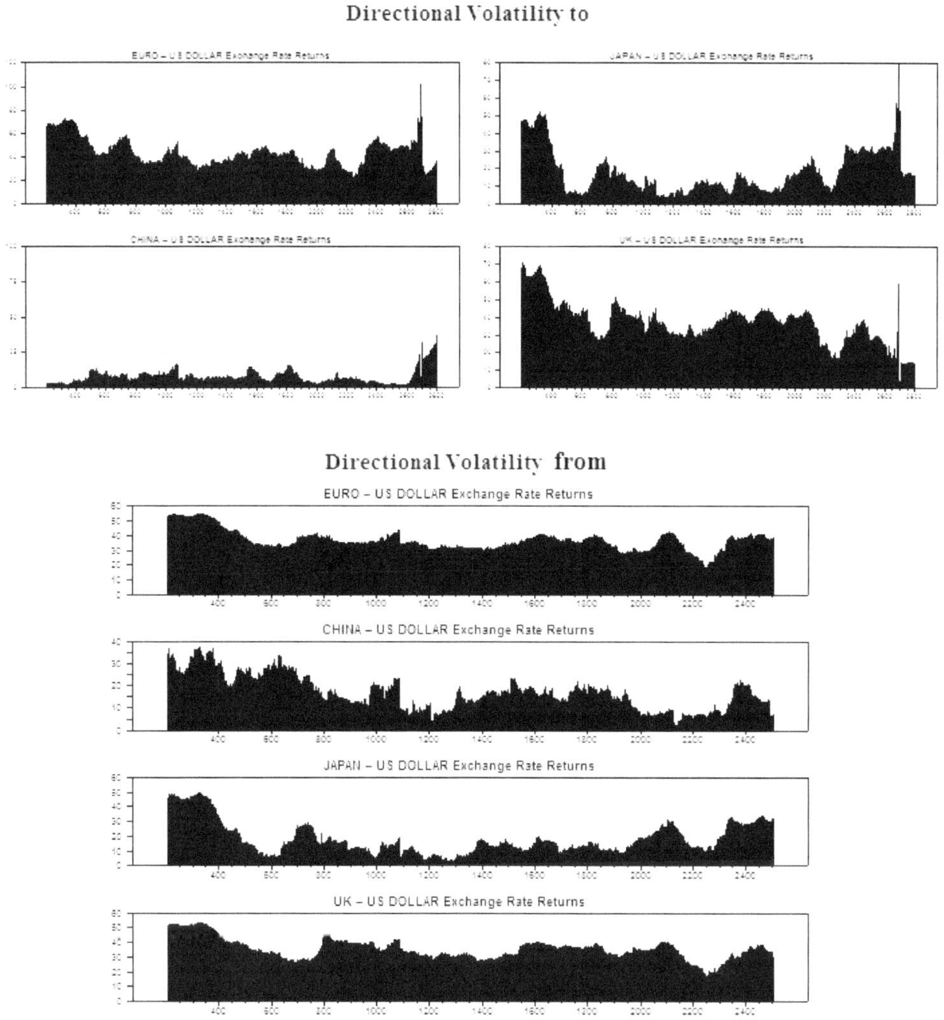

Figure 4. Directional Spillovers, To and From Exchange Rate Return Series

our sample period, and that the net direction of the spillovers between pairs of market does change between the markets. This is evident in Fig. 6.

3.2. *Neural network regressions and forecasts*

Regression analyses using higher-order polynomials produced the models shown in Table 5. In all cases where one individual currency exchange rate return was the dependent variable in the regression analysis, only lagged terms of the other exchange rates were used. The neural network analysis

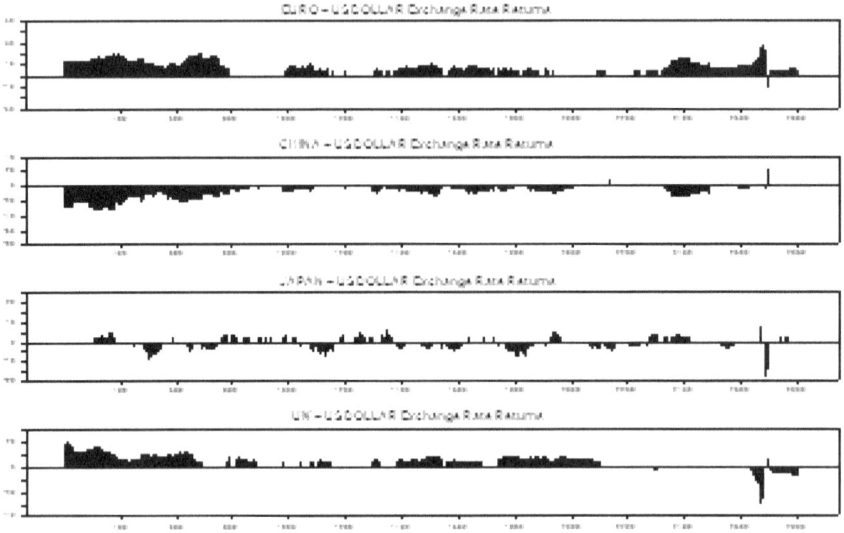

Figure 5. Net Volatility Spillovers.

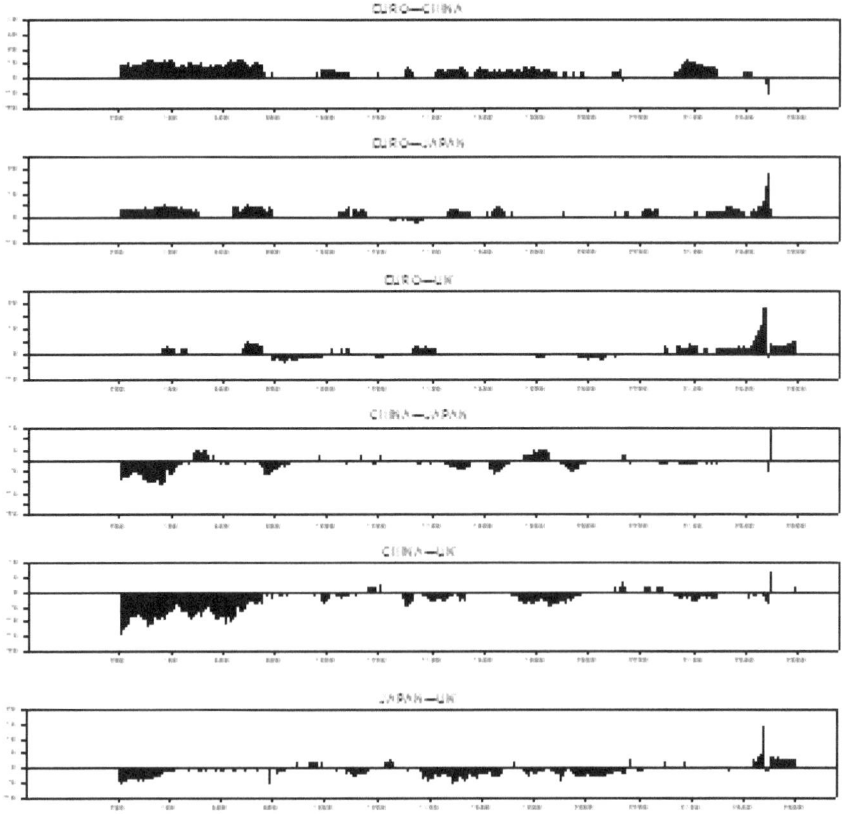

Figure 6. Net Pairwise Volatility Spillovers

Table 5. Neural Network Regression Analysis

Series	Neural Network Regression Models
EURET	$Y1 = -0.000259033 +''\text{ LCHRET, cubert}''{}^{*}0.00111622$
	$+''\text{LCHRET, cubert}''{}^{*}\text{N33}^{*}42.742 +''\text{ LCHRET, cubert}''{}^{\wedge}2^{*}0.0337701\text{N33}$
	$= -4.55972e - 05 - \text{LUKRET}^{*}''\text{LJPRET, cubert}''{}^{*}0.0712539$
CHRET	$\text{Y1} = -4.30992\text{e} - 05 + \text{N54}^{*}0.98186 + \text{N54}^{*}\text{N94}^{*}608.045\text{N94}$
	$= -6.02237\text{e} - 05 - \text{LEURET}^{*}0.0292883 + \text{LEURET}^{*}\text{LCHRET}^{*}16.6227\text{N54}$
	$= -5.73176\text{e} - 05 - \text{LCHRET}^{*}0.04878$
	$+\text{LCHRET}^{*}''\text{LEURET, cubert}''{}^{*}0.829085 - ''\text{LEURET, cubert}''{}^{*}0.00127342$
JPRET	$\text{Y1} = -3.07677\text{e} - 18 + \text{N3}^{*}1\text{N3} = -0.000128875 - ''\text{LCHRET, cubert}''{}^{*}0.000596838$
	$+''\text{LUKRET, cubert}''{}^{*}0.00051798$
UKRET	$\text{Y1} = -1.97037\text{e} - 05 - \text{N28}^{*}\text{N31}^{*}363.29 + \text{N31}^{*}0.538521\text{N31}$
	$= -0.000120826 - \text{LCHRET}^{*}0.142869 + \text{LJPRET}^{*}0.0518172\text{N28}$
	$= 5.95538\text{e} - 05 - \text{LCHRET}^{*}0.0857771 - \text{LUKRET}^{\wedge}2^{*}4.26471$

Note: This table features the results of the Neural Network Analysis as described in Eqs. (10)–(12) using the GMDH shell software trained on 80% of the sample.

produced quite complex models, with higher-order terms and new variables that were complex weights of existing variables. For example, in the CHRET model, the new variable N54 is a combination of lagged observations of the CHRET, cross-products of lagged CHRET, and the cube of the lagged EURET exchange rate return, in turn, multiplied by a coefficient minus another coefficient. This, as well, is also a function of cubed lagged EURET multiplied by another constant. The neural nets were trained on 80% of the available time series observations, and the forecasts were run on the remaining 20% of observations.

Plots of the predictions of the neural network regression models of the exchange rate return series are shown in Fig. 7. The hold-out forecast periods are the shaded segments at the right-hand- side of the plots.

Plots of the residuals are shown in Fig. 8. A noticeable feature of the four plots in Fig. 8 is the relatively reduced dispersion of the Chinese series CHRET when compared to those of the other three.

The error metrics from the neural net regressions are shown in Table 6. The most successful model is for China, which has the lowest mean absolute errors of 0.0067 and 0.0073 for model fit and predictions, respectively, and similarly root mean square errors of 0.0012 and 0.0014 for model fit and predictions. The coefficient of determination is 0.067 for model fit and 0.029 for predictions, respectively. The next best model is that for the UK, with

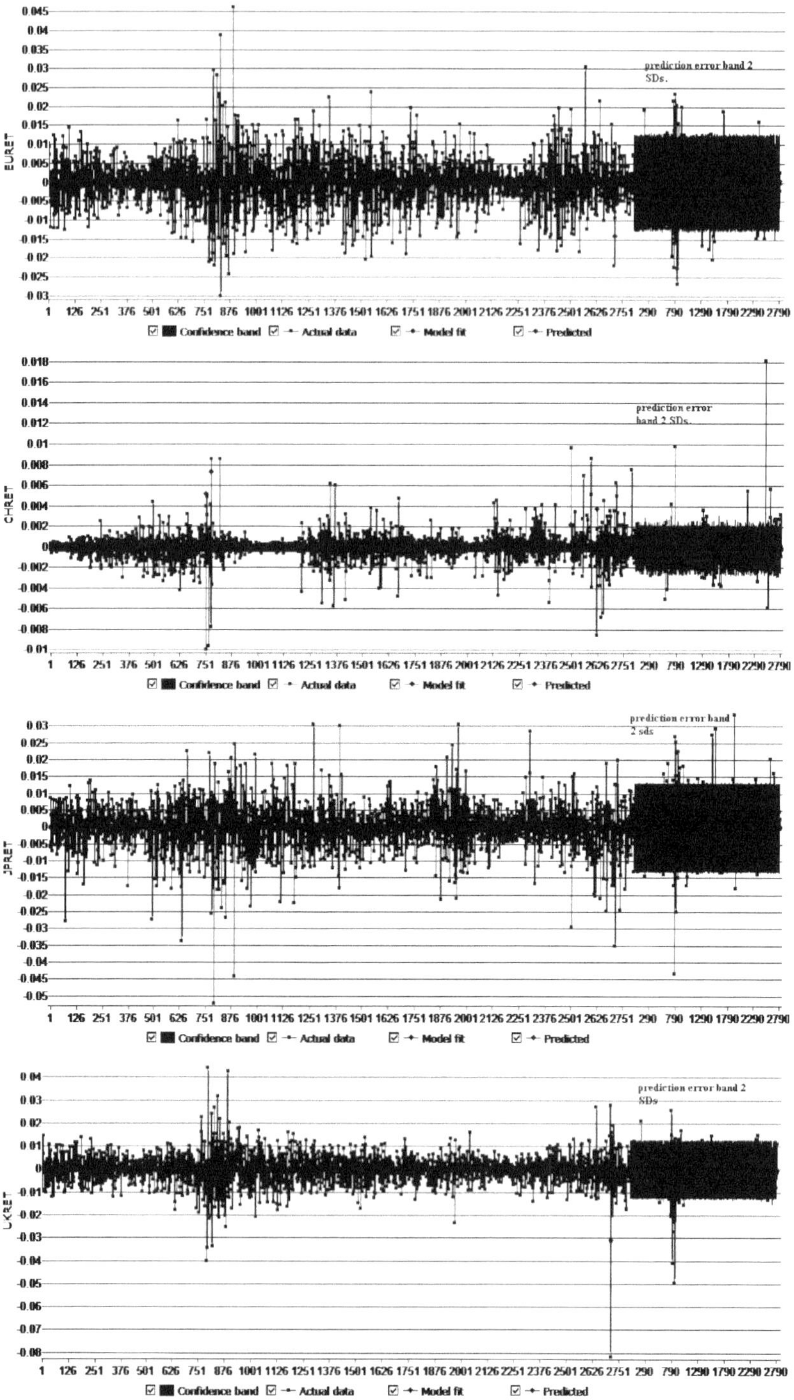

Figure 7. Neural Network Regression Model Predictions

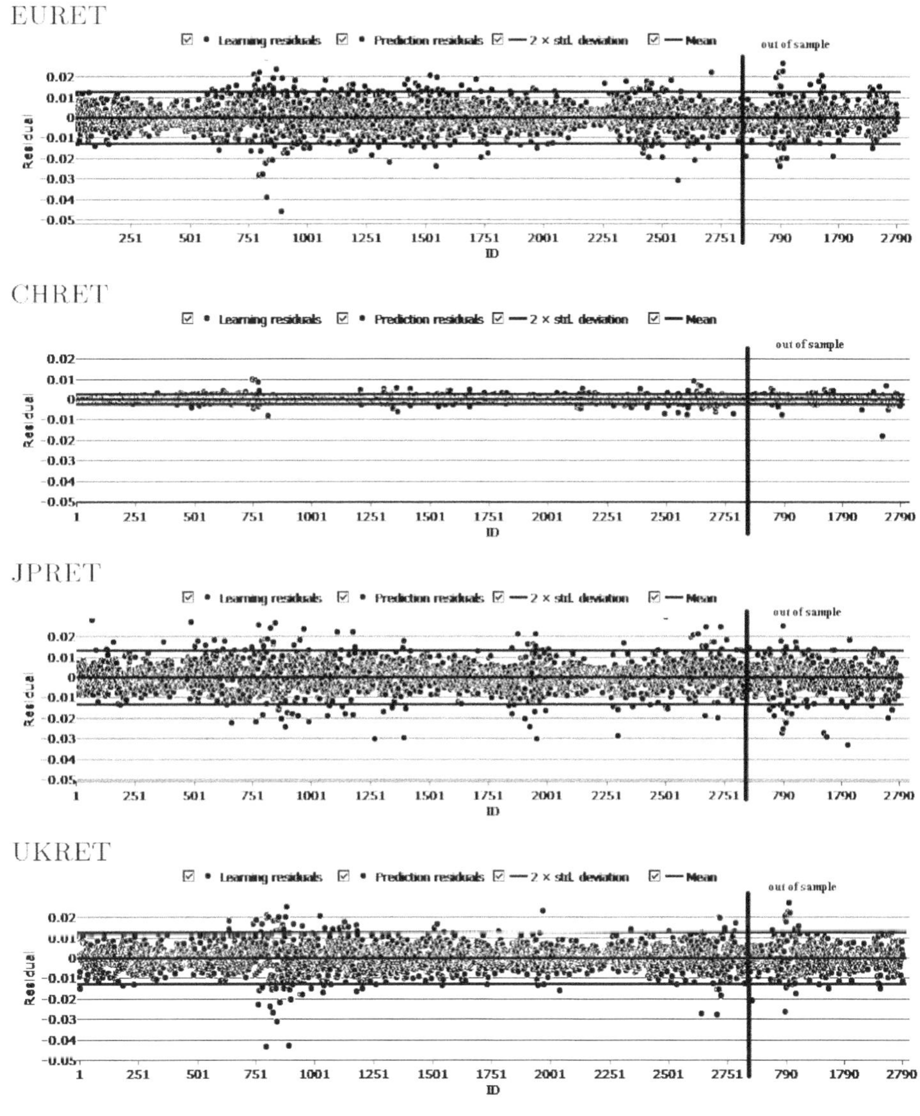

Figure 8. Plots of Neural Net Regression Model Residuals

a mean absolute error of 0.0046, a root mean square error of 0.0063, and a coefficient of determination of 0.0057 for model fit. Its errors are very slightly lower than those for the Euro, but its coefficient of determination for model fit is the same at 0.0057. Similarly, the metrics for the UK predictions are identical to those for the Euro. The metrics for Japan for both model fit and for predictions are slightly weaker. Clearly, the managed nature of the Chinese currency makes it much easier to forecast than the other three

Table 6. Neural Network Regression Error Metrics

Metrics	EURET	CHRET	JPRET	UKRET
Model fit	2243 observations	2243 observations	2243 observations	2243 observations
Mean absolute error	0.00462	0.00075	0.0048	0.0046
Root mean square error	0.0063	0.0012	0.0066	0.0063
Coefficient of Determination (R^2)	0.0057	0.067	0.00023	0.0057
Predictions	561 observations	561 observations	561 observations	561 observations
Mean absolute error	0.0045	0.00073	0.0050	0.0045
Root mean square error	0.0062	0.0014	0.0070	0.0062
Coefficient of Determination (R^2)	0.0025	0.029	−0.0055	0.0025

Note: This table features various error metrics derived from applying predictions from the Neural Network models developed to the 20% out of sample observations.

more freely floating currencies. It appears that the neural network regression techniques work best in the case of China.

4. Conclusion

In this chapter, we have applied the Diebold Yilmaz (2009, 2012) spillover index metric to capture spillovers between the rates of return on four major exchange rates indexed in US dollar terms, the EURO, the Chinese Yuan, the Japanese Yen, and the GB Pound. The spillover index variance decompositions showed that the largest net spillovers were between the EURET and the UKRET. The size of the spillovers was not constant over the sample time period taken from from August 29, 2005 to November 3, 2016. The net directional spillover between the paired series also changed over time.

We then attempted to forecast exchange rate return series using neural network-based regression analysis, after training the models on 80% of the sample observations and then forecasting the remaining 20% of the sample observations. The results were very weak, confirming those of a companion paper by Allen *et al.* (2016) which examines the relative effectiveness of nonlinear time series vs. neural network regression models, as forecasting methods for a sample of major currencies. This study confirms that it is very difficult to forecast exchange rate movements, given that all models had very low coefficients of determination. However, the Chinese yuan exchange rate return series appeared to be the most amenable to prediction, in that its coefficient of determination was higher and its error metrics slightly better than those of the other series considered. This is most probably related to the 'managed' nature of Chinese currency movements.

The fact that the largest spillovers occurred between the EURET series and the UKRET series did not appear to help for prediction purposes. A lagged UKRET term did appear in the EURET neural network regression model, but neither of the models for forecasting EURET or UKRET were particularly effective. Given that the prediction analysis is concerned with first moments rather than second moments, it might be instructive to further explore these relationships in a GARCH framework. In practical terms, the results confirm the difficulties experienced in any empirical attempts to forecast exchange rate movements but suggest that nonlinear machine learning approaches in general, and ANN approaches in particular, are worth further scrutiny.

Acknowledgements

For financial support, the first author acknowledges the Australian Research Council.

References

Allen, D. E., McAleer, M., Peiris, S. and Singh, A. K. (2016). Nonlinear time series and neural-network models of exchange rates between the US dollar and major currencies. *Risks*, 4(7), doi:10.3390/risks4010007.

Antonio, F. D., Narzo, J. L. A., and Stigler, M. (2009). tsDyn: Time series analysis based on dynamical systems theory, url = {http://stat.ethz.ch/CRAN/web/packages/tsDyn/vignettes/tsDyn.pdf}.

Baillie, R. T. and Bollerslev, T. (1989). Common stochastic trends in a system of exchange rates. *J. Fin.*, 44, pp. 167–181.

Chang, C., Gonzalez-Serrano, L., and Jimenez-Martin, J-A. (2013). Currency hedging strategies using dynamic multivariate GARCH. *Math. Comput. Simul.*, 94, pp. 164–182.

Diebold, F. and Nason, J. (1990). Nonparametric exchange rate prediction?. *J. Int. Eco.*, 28, pp. 315–332.

Diebold, F. X. and Yilmaz, K. (2009). Measuring financial asset return and volatility spillovers, with application to global equity markets. *The Econom. J.*, pp. 158–171.

Diebold, F. X. and Yilmaz, K. (2012). Better to give than to receive: Predictive directional measurement of volatility spillovers. *Int. J. Forecast.*, 28(1), pp. 57–66.

Engel, C. and Hamilton, J. D. (1990), Long swings in the dollar: Are they in the data and do markets know it?. *Amer. Econom. Rev.*, 80, 689–713.

Gradojevic, N. and Yang, J. (2006). Nonlinear, non-parametric, non-fundamental exchange rate forecasting. *J. Forecast.*, 25(4), pp. 227–245.

Ivakhnenko, A. G. (1968). The group method of data handling — A rival of the method of stochastic approximation. *Soviet Autom. Control c/c Avtomatika*, 1(3), pp. 43–55.

Kuan, C. M. and Liu, T. (1995). Forecasting exchange rates using feedforward and recurrent neural networks. *J. Appl. Econometr.*, 10, pp. 347–364.
Matias, J. M. and Reboredo, J. C. (2012). Forecasting performance of non-linear models for intra-day stock returns. *J. Forecast.*, 31, pp. 172–188.
Meese, R. A. and Rose, A. K. (1990). Nonlinear, nonparametric, nonessential exchange rate estimation. *Am. Econom. Rev. Papers Proc.*, 80, pp. 192–196.
Morana, C. and Beltratti, A. (2004). Structural change and long range dependence in volatility of exchange rates, either, neither or both?. *J. Empir. Fin.*, 11, pp. 629–658.
Reboredo, J. C, Matias, J. M., and Garcia-Rubio, R. (2012). Non-linearity in forecasting of high frequency stock returns. *Computat. Econom.*, 40(3), pp. 245–264.
Rogoff, K. (1996), The purchasing power parity puzzle. *J. Econom. Liter.*, 34, pp. 647–668.
Sarno, L., Taylor, M., and Chowdhury, L. (2004). Nonlinear dynamics in deviations from the law of one price: A broad-based empirical study. *J. Int. Money Fin.*, 23, pp. 1–25.
Taylor, M. P. and Sarno, L. (2003). *The Economics of Exchange Rates*. Cambridge U.K.: Cambridge University Press.
Taylor, M. P., Peel, D. A., and Sarno, L. (2001), Nonlinear mean-revision in real exchange rates: Towards a solution of the purchasing power parity puzzles. *Int. Econom. Rev.*, 42, pp. 1015–1042.

Chapter 9

Financial Integration of Foreign Exchange and Money Markets: Evidence from MENA

Somar Alomhamad* and Anil V. Mishra†

School of Business, Western Sydney University, Australia
**s.almohamad@westernsydney.edu.au,*
†a.mishra@westernsydney.edu.au

Abstract

Research in this chapter investigates the dynamic linkages among foreign exchange and money markets for MENA countries. The chapter also explores the impact of internal and external shocks, especially the global financial crisis, on these markets. The results in this chapter state that the financial markets in the MENA region are not isolated from global events. Furthermore, the financial markets in the MENA region are cointegrated at both regional and an international level, yet not fully bound to developed markets.

1. Introduction

The aim of this chapter is to investigate the financial integration among foreign exchange markets and money markets in the Middle East and North Africa (MENA) region, and between MENA and developed markets. The study of foreign exchange and money markets integration of MENA countries is mainly motivated by the fact that the majority of literature focuses on the financial integration of stock markets in the region with the rest of the world to assess the extent to which the financial system in MENA countries is integrated on both of regional and international levels.[1] There is very scare

[1]For instance, Darrat *et al.* (2000), Assaf (2003), Neaime (2005), Bley and Chen (2006), Legoarde-Segato and Lucey (2007), Alkulaib *et al.* (2009), Marashdeh and Shrestha (2010),

literature which examines dynamic linkages among foreign exchange and money markets in MENA countries, and in MENA and developed countries.

The contribution of this chapter to existing literature is twofold. First, previous studies including Addelaziz and Chortareas (2008), Samanta and Zadeh (2012), Paskelian *et al.* (2010), Ezzati (2011) and Nor (2012) use a relatively shorter time period between 1997 and 2008. Our study employs monthly data on foreign exchange and money markets in nine MENA countries, Bahrain, Egypt, Jordan, Kuwait, Morocco, Qatar, Saudi Arabia, Tunisia, and the UAE, over a longer time period, from 2000 to 2015. Second, the chapter explores the regional and global shocks that have led to structural changes in the performance of aforementioned markets throughout the last 15 years by applying Bai and Perron's (2003) test for multiple structural breaks. The empirical application of this test is based on two steps: the first is the double maximum test which explores the existence of at least one break, and the second step is to test for the maximum number of breaks, and this can be determined based on the sequential test of null hypothesis of ℓ break against the alternative hypothesis of $\ell + 1$ breaks.[2] The examination of the impact of global shocks, such as the global financial crisis (GFC) and Euro debt crisis, on financial markets in the MENA region might be an indication for financial amalgamation between MENA regional markets and developed markets. The empirical findings of this chapter have important implications for policymakers, as well as regional and international investors' trading strategies. The existence of long-run comovement among MENA and developed markets implies that the potential of investors in these markets for obtaining abnormal profit through portfolio diversification is limited in the long run. Moreover, the policymakers in the MENA region have to investigate and anticipate the major channels through which a future crisis (shocks) might affect their economies, and undertake further steps toward enforcement of more diversified economies and resilient financial systems.

The findings of this chapter suggest that, overall, global shocks such as the GFC and European debt crisis are found to have at least the same impact as local and regional events on foreign exchange and money markets in MENA countries. More specifically, the global financial crisis is the most significant structural change (destabilizer) in financial markets of the MENA

Genc *et al.* (2010), Chaudhry and Boldin (2012), Neaime (2012) and Goucha and Hamdi (2014) examine the interrelationship among stock markets in Middle East and North Africa (MENA) region, and in MENA and developed countries.

[2]We have also employed Zivot Andrews (1992) test for unit root hypothesis with presence of single/most significant structural break. Results are available from the authors.

region in the last 15 years. Research in this chapter also finds that the foreign exchange markets and money markets are bound in long-run cointegration relationships, and the foreign exchange markets in the MENA region are more cointegrated amongst each other as compared to money markets.

This chapter is organized as follows. Section 2 provides an overview of financial markets in the MENA region, and the impact of global financial crisis on these markets. Section 3 describes the literature review. Section 4 discusses data and descriptive statistics. Section 5 describes the empirical analysis and results of structural breaks and cointegration tests. Finally, Section 6 concludes the chapter and provides policy implications.

2. Overview of Foreign Exchange and Money Markets in the MENA Region

The financial system is the cornerstone of economic development. A well-developed financial system has positive effects on the whole economy because it enhances efficiency of resource allocation, improves efficiency in intermediation between borrowers, facilitates risk sharing, and reduces transaction costs (Levine, 2005). Historically, the financial system in the MENA region has been known for the dominance of banking finance because of the family-owned business structure and the underdevelopment of capital markets.

In the late 20th century, many countries in the region began developing their financial markets, mainly through improving their capital market laws and changing financial market regulation in order to encourage foreign investments. The following Secs. 2.1 and 2.2 provide an overview of the foreign exchange and money markets in the MENA region and highlight the major developments of these markets in the past 15 years and the impact of the global financial crisis on these markets.

2.1. *Foreign exchange markets*

Before World War I, countries in the MENA region and other parts of the world adopted a gold standard monetary system in which currencies could be freely exchanged for gold. In the MENA region, the first bank notes issued by the National Bank of Egypt were exchanged for gold until 1914. However, during World War I the gold standard monetary system in most countries was suspended. After the collapse of the gold standard system, most countries in the MENA region adopted a fixed adjustable exchange rate regime in the early 1970s.[3] In the period from 1990 to 1995, an estimated 51% of MENA countries used a fixed exchange rate regime in form of an adjustable peg. From 2000 to 2006, the number of countries adopting an adjustable peg increased to 67.5% (Ghanem and Bismut, 2009). This was due to the move by the Gulf Cooperation Council (GCC) member countries to peg their currencies against the US dollar as part of the effort towards monetary integration.

Another important change that occurred in the region's currency regimes was the move towards currency convertibility and the liberalization of foreign exchange transactions. Most countries in the region have now liberalized their currency regimes and few restrictions on convertibility exist. Morocco, for instance, has accepted the full convertibility of its dirham for current account transactions (Nsouli and Rached, 1998). Other countries in the region have also adopted convertibility measures. Countries in the MENA region have also experienced persistent currency inflation. MENA countries with floating exchange rates have been worst hit by inflationary pressures. Ghanem (2010) investigated the relationship between inflation and exchange rate regimes in MENA countries over the period 1980 to 2007. The results show a strong relationship between the two, with those with pegged regimes experiencing the lowest inflation rates. However, inflation among the MENA countries has fallen over the years. In addition to the liberalization of currency markets and persistent inflation, currency regimes in the region have moved towards monetary union, particularly in the GCC region. However, the development of a common currency in the region is yet to be realized.

2.2. *Money markets*

The modern money markets in the Middle East and North Africa began with the development of the banking industry in Egypt in the mid-19th century. The first bank to be opened in Egypt was the Bank of Egypt in 1858, and the Anglo-Egyptian Bank was opened in 1864. In 1866, the French Bank Credit Lyonnais began its operations in Egypt, followed by the Ottoman Bank in 1867. However, the first purely Egyptian bank was the Banque Misr, which opened in 1920. Previous banks had been owned by British, French, Italian, and Greek banks.

---

[3]The fixed adjustable exchange rate system was formulated under the Bretton Woods Agreement in which countries pegged their currencies against the US dollar and currencies were only allowed to float within a narrow range of 1%. This was motivated by the need to decrease inflationary pressures as well as promote macroeconomic stability.

Most of the other countries in the region followed a similar path of money market development. In these countries, the development of formal banking took place in the early to mid-20th century. Banking activities in Bahrain were introduced in 1920 when the Eastern Bank Limited was established, while Kuwait's first banking operations began in 1941 when the British Bank of the Middle East (BBME) was established. In Dubai, a bank operated in 1946, while the first bank in Abu Dhabi was established in 1958. Banking activities in Saudi Arabia began in 1927 when a foreign bank, the Netherlands Trading Society, opened a branch in Saudi Arabia. The first bank in Qatar was opened in 1965.

The money markets in the region trade in a variety of money market instruments. Government securities are among the major traded money markets instruments in the region. The popularity of government securities is attributable to high public debts among the MENA countries. For instance, Egypt and Jordan had debt to GDP levels of 73% and 65%, respectively, at the end of 2009, while Lebanon had debt to GDP levels of 160% during the same period (Garcia-Kilroy and Silva, 2011). Treasury bills and bonds are a common form of government securities in the region. For instance, treasury bonds accounted for 94% of debt in Lebanon while treasury bills accounted for 6%.

In addition to treasury bills, the MENA money markets trade in derivatives. In 2005, the Dubai Gold & Commodities Exchange (DGCX) was the first derivatives trading market in the region to offer trading in derivatives. Trading in derivatives had been conducted in other parts of the region, but these were not done in specialised derivatives trading markets. The most commonly traded derivatives in the region are futures, forwards, options, and swaps.

2.3. *Impact of Global Financial Crisis (GFC) on foreign exchange and money markets of MENA countries*

The major impact of the global financial crisis on foreign exchange markets in the MENA region was the devaluation of MENA currencies to crisis levels in some countries. The developed countries, including the US, were worst hit by the GFC as it led to a depreciation of the US dollar against other major currencies in the world. Since most MENA countries had pegged their currencies against the US dollar, its depreciation led to devaluation of currencies in the region. Kuwait was worst hit by the currency devaluation crisis and, in May 2007, Kuwait abandoned the US dollar peg and instead adopted a peg based on a portfolio of currencies of its major trading partners

(ESCWA, 2009). Although the MENA countries experienced currency volatility during the GFC, the scale was relatively low compared to other developing regions. The volatility of asset and currency markets continued in the MENA region until 2009. In addition, the region experienced a severe shortage in dollar liquidity, and central banks in the region had to react to maintain liquidity by direct deposits with local banks and the use of foreign exchange swaps (Al-Hamidy, 2010).

The money markets in the MENA region were significantly affected by the global financial crisis. The global financial crisis led to increased volatility of instruments traded in the foreign exchange markets in the region, including swaps, options, and other derivatives. The trading level of money market instruments reduced shortly after the financial crisis (Habibi, 2009). This was due to losses incurred by the banks as a result of non-performing loans; moreover, the fall in stock prices may have also led to low activity in the money markets in the MENA countries.

3. Literature Review

The literature review in this chapter concentrates on displaying previous studies aimed at investigating the financial integration among foreign exchange markets, and money markets in MENA region.

3.1. *Financial integration of foreign exchange markets in the MENA region*

Foreign exchange markets, like other financial markets, have achieved significant integration in various parts of the world. The integration of foreign exchange markets involves the establishment of interdependence between forex markets in different countries. An early study by Baillie and Bollerslev (1989) investigated the financial integration of foreign exchange rates in the UK, Germany, France, Italy, Switzerland, Japan, and Canada using daily spot and forward exchange rates. They found evidence of cointegration among the seven major currencies. Coleman (1990) investigated the financial integration of 18 foreign currencies using cointegration and causality approaches. The study found that no significant evidence of cointegration among the exchange rates under examination. Copeland (1991) measured the integration of foreign exchange markets in the UK, Germany, France, Switzerland, and Japan. He found an apparent lack of cointegration among the major exchange rates.

Tai (2007) investigated the level of integration and cointegration of foreign exchange markets from the emerging Asian economies of Korea, India, Philippines, Malaysia, Thailand, and Taiwan. The study found evidence of cointegration among these markets, and with developed markets. Kuhl (2007) investigated the comovement of a group of international currencies, including the Australian dollar, Canadian dollar, Swiss franc, British pound sterling, euro, Japanese yen, and Swedish krona. He employed the Johansen–Juselius cointegration approach and error correction model to detect the pairwise cointegration of these variables during the period covering the evolution of the European Union, from 1999 to 2006. He concluded that the null hypothesis of no cointegration cannot be rejected for almost all of the variables. Antonakakis (2012) investigated the cointegration of exchange markets in the UK, Japan, and the US, before and after the introduction of the euro. He found cointegration among the British pound, the US dollar, and the Japanese yen. Moreover, the study found cross-market volatility spillovers among these markets. Bohdalova and Gregus (2014) study the cointegration between foreign exchange rates of two Central European countries, Hungary and Poland, using daily observations for the period 2009–2014. They conclude that the foreign exchange rates of the two countries became integrated in August 2011.

In the MENA region, most countries have adopted a currency regime in which their currencies are pegged against the US dollar. Therefore, fluctuations in the US dollar cause similar changes in the foreign exchange markets in the region. Historically, the MENA countries have experienced comovements in their exchange rates to the US dollar. The Egyptian pound achieved huge devaluations in the period 1988–1991 when the currency lost 300% of its value against the dollar. During the same period, Jordan's currency experienced 200% devaluation against the dollar (Neaime, 2005). Between 1960 and 2002, countries in the GCC region exhibited near similar movements in the exchange rates to the dollar, and therefore the movements in the foreign exchange markets. The foreign exchange markets in the MENA region are strongly influenced by consumer prices, particularly the changes in oil prices. Tawadros (2007) tests the neutrality of the long-run money hypothesis for three MENA economies, Jordan, Egypt, and Morocco. The study involves the use of cointegration techniques to test the hypothesis using quarterly data for prices, money, and real incomes. The study concludes that there is cointegration among these markets and oil prices.

Abdelaziz and Chortareas (2008) examine the financial integration among stock prices and exchange rates in four MENA countries, Egypt,

Kuwait, Oman, and Saudi Arabia. They employ the Johansen–Juselius cointegration approach and the vector error correction technique to analyze monthly observations for the period 1992–2006. Their study does not detect evidence of cointegration between stock prices and real exchange rates in the four countries. Samanta and Zadeh (2012) investigate the linkages between gold, oil, and the US dollar and find significant correlations between the three. The MENA region is the world's largest producer of oil and, therefore, changes in oil, prices have important implications on foreign exchange markets.

3.2. *Financial integration of money markets in the MENA region*

Lin and Swanson (1997) examine the financial integration of money markets in the US, the UK, Singapore, and Hong Kong. They use the Granger causality approach as well as the multivariate cointegration approach. Their study finds evidence of cointegration among money market indices. Centeno and Mello (1999) employ the Engle and Granger (1987) cointegration approach to investigate the financial integration of six European money markets: Germany, the UK, France, Italy, Spain, and Portugal. The results find no evidence of cointegration among the aforementioned money markets. Santillan *et al.* (2000) measure the financial integration of European money markets. They find that the degree of financial integration slightly increased after the introduction of the European Union (EU). Kleimeier and Sander (2003) analyze the comovements of the European money markets pre- and post-introduction of the EU. They conclude that the financial integration of 15 EU money markets increased significantly after the introduction of the EU. In a similar study, Baele *et al.* (2004) find an increased comovement among EU money markets.

Studies on financial integration of money markets in the MENA region are scarce and lead to mixed results about whether or not cointegration exists. Some studies have found that money markets in the MENA move together in response to various economic and financial shocks. Neaime (2002) studied financial integration and liberalization in the region. Using the Johansen–Juselius cointegration tests, he found that the level of cointegration was lower in the GCC region compared to the rest of the MENA region, while cointegration was highest among Jordan, Egypt, and Morocco. In addition, the GCC markets have lower integration with other parts of the world compared to the rest of the MENA region. Lagoarde-Segot and Lucey (2007) investigate the integration of capital markets in the region. Their study indicates that the money markets in the region have started moving toward international integration. Soofi (2008) measures the integration among money markets in Egypt, Jordan, Lebanon, Tunisia, and Turkey on one hand, and the US and the UK on the other hand. Using the Johansen–Juselius cointegration approach and error correction model, he finds evidence of cointegration between money markets in Tunisia and the UK. Moreover, the results indicate an existence of causal relationships between money markets in Tunisia, the UK and the US.

Ezzati (2011) investigates financial market integration between Iran, Saudi Arabia, Kuwait, the US, Germany, and Japan. He analyses monthly observations of stock market indices, foreign exchange markets, and money markets between 1997 and 1999. The study utilizes the ARDL cointegration approach and finds that the foreign exchange and money markets in the MENA region are integrated with developed markets. However, financial integration of stock market indices in MENA and developed countries was rejected. Nor (2012) provides evidence of cointegration of the money markets in four MENA markets, Tunisia, Saudi Arabia, Egypt, and Oman for the period April 1999 to December 2008. Using the GARCH model, the study concludes that the region's financial markets had high financial integration levels but they were segmented globally. However, the money market in Saudi Arabia is found to be influenced by global markets to a larger extent compared to the regional markets. Paskelian *et al.* (2013) examine the behaviour and characteristics of the money market equity indices of MENA countries, as well as the cointegration of MENA money markets with each other and with the US. They find that the money markets in Jordan, Egypt, Kuwait, Qatar, Oman, Tunisia, and Saudi Arabia are cointegrated among themselves, and with the US market.

4. Data and Descriptive Statistics

The research in this chapter employs monthly data of foreign exchange and money markets indices of 10 countries including nine MENA countries (Bahrain, Egypt, Jordan, Kuwait, Morocco, Qatar, Saudi Arabia, Tunisia, and the UAE) and the UK[4] for the period between January 2000 and May 2015. For foreign exchange markets, we utilize the end-of-month observations of local nominal spot exchange rates as domestic currency per one US

[4]The UK market is included in the foreign exchange markets analysis instead of the US, since we use local nominal exchange rates per one US dollar.

Table 1. Descriptive Statistics of Financial Markets in the MENA Region

	Mean	Median	Maximum	Minimum	St Deviation	Skewness	Kurtosis
Panel A: Foreign Exchange Markets							
Bahrain	0.376	0.377	0.377	0.375	0.001	−3.007	7.308
Egypt	5.648	5.742	7.630	3.424	0.962	−0.549	3.206
Jordan	0.289	0.289	0.308	0.264	0.010	−0.090	2.365
Kuwait	0.708	0.708	0.711	0.704	0.001	−0.680	6.127
Morocco	9.018	8.648	11.956	7.276	1.120	0.973	3.027
Qatar	3.640	3.640	3.660	3.635	0.001	6.799	8.278
Saudi Arabia	3.750	3.750	3.757	3.723	0.002	−3.396	9.247
Tunisia	1.409	1.375	1.958	1.157	0.163	1.182	4.338
UAE	3.672	3.673	3.673	3.670	0.001	−4.105	5.279
UK	0.607	0.619	0.711	0.480	0.060	−0.365	2.152
Panel B: Money Markets							
Bahrain	−0.212	0.495	4.137	−3.577	2.304	−0.465	3.850
Egypt	−0.704	−0.196	5.157	−4.554	3.997	0.290	2.356
Jordan	−0.281	0.010	8.837	−13.043	4.154	0.434	3.995
Kuwait	0.362	0.004	13.750	−6.987	7.944	2.906	4.753
Morocco	−0.297	0.021	7.203	−7.725	5.369	−0.962	6.570
Qatar	0.555	0.395	11.578	−6.001	4.654	1.503	4.699
Saudi Arabia	0.224	0.023	12.345	−3.293	3.212	−0.894	3.187
Tunisia	0.024	0.011	8.454	−3.829	2.929	−1.115	4.481
UAE	−1.121	−0.259	9.240	−8.930	4.003	−0.911	5.231
US	0.189	0.024	7.002	−6.571	2.581	0.071	3.404

Note: This table illustrates the descriptive statistics of financial markets in the MENA region. Data on monthly foreign exchange markets and money market returns are from DataStream.

dollar. The money markets data are monthly observations of money market average interest rates as well as treasury bills rates[5] Monthly financial data is used because this type of data is less volatile than higher frequency data, and it avoids common biases arising from non-trading and non-synchronous trading. Furthermore, emerging markets, such as MENA markets, might be expected to react slowly to world events, hence the use of lower frequency data provides a clearer picture of the movement and reactions of the indices in response to global events.

Table 1 illustrates the descriptive statistics of foreign exchange and money market indices. Panel A demonstrates descriptive statistics of the local nominal exchange rates of MENA markets, and the UK, in terms of the US dollar. The results indicate that the Moroccan foreign exchange has the highest average return followed by Egypt and the Jordanian dinar

[5]The treasury bills rates are for Bahrain and Egypt.

has the lowest return. Results also reveal that the foreign exchange rates of GCC countries (Bahrain, Kuwait, Qatar, Saudi Arabia, and the UAE) have the lowest and negligible volatility compared to non-GCC countries (Egypt, Jordan, Morocco and Tunisia). This result is plausible since all GCC currencies are pegged to the US dollar, except for the Kuwaiti dinar, which moved from the US peg to peg to basket of foreign currencies in 2007. The exchange rates of Morocco and Jordan seem to be the most volatile. Panel B illustrates descriptive statistics of money market returns in MENA countries. The money market in Qatar exhibits the highest average return. Regarding volatility, the money market in Kuwait shows the highest standard deviation compared to money markets in other MENA countries. The skewness of money markets in Bahrain, Morocco, Saudi Arabia, Tunisia, and UAE is negative, and this indicates a greater probability of achieving lower returns. Most money markets in the region show an excess of kurtosis (greater than 3, except for the money market in Egypt), which indicates flat tails and sharp peaks.

5. Empirical Models and Results

Our methodology is divided into two main parts. First, we test the presence of multiple structural breaks in foreign exchange markets and money markets of MENA countries using Bai and Perron (2003) tests.[6] Second, we apply the Autoregressive Distributed Lag (ARDL) approach to investigate the cointegration among these markets, and between MENA and developed markets. We also estimate the long- and short-run causalities among these markets within the vector error correction model (VECM) and vector autoregressive (VAR) frameworks.

5.1. *Bai and Perron (2003) test for multiple structural breaks*

In this section, we aim to investigate whether the financial markets of MENA countries have been subject to multiple structural breaks. We employ the multiple structural breaks test introduced by Bai and Perron (2003) (BP). Their methodology pioneered the development of multiple structural change

[6] We have also employed Zivot Andrews (1992) test for unit root hypothesis in presence of single structural break. Results of Zivot Andrews (1992) test for single structural break indicate that the GFC is the most significant break in the variables. Results are available from the authors.

methods because it allows for the simultaneous estimation of multiple break dates.

The BP multiple structural breaks approach has been recognized as being preferable to other structural breaks tests as it enables the determination of both the number and location of structural changes with their autoregressive coefficients. Furthermore, it allows for the simultaneous forecast of breaks and reforecast of break points (Enders and Sandler, 2005). Additionally, the BP test allows for testing the alternative hypothesis of fewer structural changes against a large number of breaks. Prior to the introduction of the BP test, the Sup–Wald statistics has been utilized by other testing procedures in order to investigate the existence of break only against null hypothesis. Furthermore the BP method allows for heteroscedasticity and autocorrelation in error and enables us to investigate whether additional breaks lead to reducing the sum of forecasting residual squares (Antoshin *et al.*, 2008).

Bai and Perron (2003) suggest that the empirical application starts by applying the double maximum test in order to realise if at least one break is present, i.e., testing the null hypothesis of no structural break against the alternative hypothesis of an unknown number of breaks. Thereafter, the number of breaks can be determined based on the sequential test of null hypothesis of ℓ break against the alternative hypothesis of $\ell + 1$ breaks. Following Bai and Perron we base our empirical examination on the double maximum and sequential tests. We apply the sequential test $(\ell + 1|\ell)$ for variables exhibiting significant test statistics of $\mathrm{UD}_{\max}$ since this technique leads to the best results and is recommended for empirical application (Bai and Perron, 2003).

Table 2 illustrates results of the Bai and Perron test. Panel A illustrates multiple structural breaks for the foreign exchange markets in MENA countries. The results of the stability test are presented by $\mathrm{UD}_{\max}$ statistics that are significant at 5% level for MENA foreign exchange series, except Saudi Arabia. The results obtained from the sequential test indicate that the foreign exchange markets in Bahrain, Egypt, Jordan, and Morocco are subject to one break, while foreign exchange markets in Kuwait, Qatar, and the UAE have two breaks. The foreign exchange market in Tunisia exhibits three structural changes. In regard to markets with one structural break, the illustrated change in Bahrain could be attributed to the GFC. The estimated break point for the Egyptian exchange rate occurred in February 2003, which coincides with change in the exchange regime from the fixed peg to US dollar to the floating regime in 2003 (Selim, 2012). The structural change for Jordan

Table 2. Bai–Perron (2003) Test Results

Variable (1)	UD_{max} (2)	WD_{max} (3)	$F_T(2\|1)$ (4)	$F_T(3\|2)$ (5)	$F_T(4\|3)$ (6)	$F_T(5\|4)$ (7)	Optimal Number of Breaks (8)	Break Dates (9)
Panel A: Foreign Exchange Markets								
Bahrain	10.04**	13.88***	6.13	3.53	8.93	2.14	1	06/2009
Egypt	9.10**	19.97***	4.09	1.55	0.27	4.28	1	02/2003
Jordan	53.21***	53.21***	7.31	1.72	0.06	0.13	1	04/2002
Kuwait	23.81***	58.15***	18.56***	0.12	0.10	0.10	2	10/2003; 08/2007
Morocco	36.94***	57.84***	4.06	0.01	0.17	—	1	05/2003
Qatar	14.67***	19.27***	8.83*	1.40	1.40	—	2	10/2004, 12/2008
Saudi Arabia(2)	2.22	5.58	—	—	—	—	0	—
Tunisia	15.77***	31.84***	5.88	11.45**	0.51	0.24	3	01/2003; 11/2008; 06/2012
UAE	11.85**	19.73***	10.81**	1.06	1.06	—	2	04/2006, 07/2008
UK	14.78***	37.13***	6.94	2.59	0.65	—	1	01/2003
Panel B: Money Markets								
Bahrain	43.78***	98.30***	3.65	4.56	0.99	1.26	1	01/2009
Egypt	15.71***	15.84***	9.89*	0.65	1.50	—	2	06/2008; 04/2011
Jordan	25.67***	50.97***	8.12	1.13	0.23	—	1	04/2009
Kuwait	15.27***	32.80***	3.10	3.10	1.89	0.98	1	05/2009
Morocco	14.45***	33.81***	10.58**	7.48	3.12	2.21	1	03/2007
Qatar	10.59**	17.12***	10.04*	0.51	0.51	—	2	01/2006; 11/2007
Saudi Arabia	22.45***	56.21	2.57	1.98	2.57	—	1	01/2009
Tunisia	10.5**	18.22***	1.91	1.73	1.16	—	1	01/2009

(Continued)

Table 2. (*Continued*)

Variable (1)	UD_{max} (2)	WD_{max} (3)	$F_T(2\|1)$ (4)	$F_T(3\|2)$ (5)	$F_T(4\|3)$ (6)	$F_T(5\|4)$ (7)	Optimal Number of Breaks (8)	Break Dates (9)
Panel B: Money Markets								
UAE(3)	5.7	14.3***	—	—	—	—	0	—
US	13.22***	21.18***	11.73**	3.67	0.43	—	1	10/2008

Notes: This table illustrates Bai–Perron (2003) testing results. Column (2) presents UD_{max} test statistics of the null hypothesis of no breaks (zero number of breaks) against the alternative hypothesis of unknown number of breaks, critical values of UD_{max} equal 12.37, 8.88, and 7.46 at 1, 5, and 10% significance levels, respectively. Column (3) presents WD_{max} test statistics of the null hypothesis of no breaks against the alternative hypothesis of unknown number of breaks, critical values of WD_{max} equal 13.83, 9.91, and 8.20 at 1, 5, and 10% significance levels, respectively. Columns (4), (5), (5), and (7) present the sequential test of the null hypothesis of ℓ break against the alternative hypothesis of $\ell + 1$ breaks i.e., For $F_t(2|1), \ell = 1, \ldots, F_t(5|4), \ell = 4$; 1, 5, and 10% critical values are 13.98, 10.31, and 8.51 for $F_t(2|1)$, 14.80, 11.14 and 9.41 for $F_t(3|2)$, 15.28, 11.38, and 10.04 for $F_t(4|3)$, and 15.76, 12.25, and 10.58 for $F_t(5|4)$, respectively. Column (8) illustrates number of estimated breaks. Column (9) presents the break dates. *, **, *** denote rejection of null hypothesis at 1%, 5%, and 10% level, respectively. (1), (2), and (3) show that the test statistics of UD_{max} is lower than critical values, hence the sequential test is not applied as suggested by Bai and Perron (2003).

takes place in April 2002, which corresponds to the endorsement of bilateral Free Trade Agreement with the US. The date of break estimated for Morocco is May 2003. This may be due to the huge shift in the current account balance from a small deficit to sizeable surplus in 2003 as a result of the surge in expatriate remittances flowing from European and GCC countries (IMF, 2004). The two structural break points for the foreign exchange markets in Kuwait, Qatar, and the UAE are basically attributable to the GFC, followed by political instabilities in the region, such as the Iraq war and the Syrian crisis. Panel A also demonstrates that the foreign exchange market in Tunisia is subject to three structural changes. The main reasons for the breaks have already been mentioned; however, we believe that the last break date, in June 2012, is directly related to the reclassification of the Tunisian exchange rate regime to a crawling peg system, by the International Monetary Fund (Brixiova *et al.*, 2013).

Panel B demonstrates multiple structural breaks for MENA money markets. We notice that UD_{max} statistics are significant for all money markets, except the UAE. It is interesting that the single structural breaks for the money markets of Bahrain, Jordan, Kuwait, Morocco, Saudi Arabia, Tunisia, and the US all coincide with the GFC and the start of the Euro debt crisis, which has intensified in 2011. Panel B findings indicate that the money markets of Egypt and Qatar are subject to two structural breaks. The break points for Egypt are clearly attributable to the GFC in 2008 and the Arab Spring in 2011. The structural changes for the money market in Qatar in 2006 and 2007 are associated with the GCC stock market crash (bubble) in 2006 and the GFC, respectively.

5.2. *The autoregressive distributed lag (ARDL) cointegration approach*

The ARDL approach was developed by Pesaran and Shin (1995, 1998), Pesaran *et al.* (1996), Pesaran (1997), and Pesaran *et al.* (2001). This approach is considered to be a robust technique to test the cointegration among financial time series variables. It might be preferred over other approaches such as Engle and Granger (1987) and Gregory and Hansen (1996).

There are three reasons for using the ARDL approach in our study. First, it can be applied regardless of whether the underlying variables are $I(0)$ or $I(1)$, or mutually integrated. However, the conventional cointegration methodologies require the underlying regressors to be integrated in the same order.[7] The choice of the ARDL cointegration approach enables us to test the long-run relationships among these variables. Second, the ARDL approach is considered to be a statistically significant approach and more valid that other cointegration techniques for a small sample size. This study uses monthly observations from 2000 to 2015, and the number of data points for different variables ranges between 125 and 175: this is considered a small sample (Narayan *et al.*, 2004). Third, by using this approach, we can estimate the long- and short-run components of the model simultaneously. The dynamic error correction model (ECM), which combines short-run dynamics with long-run equilibrium, can be estimated from the ARDL via simple linear transformation (Marashdeh, 2006).

According to Pesaran and Pesaran (1997, 2009) and Pesaran *et al.* (2001), the augmented ARDL $(p, q_1, q_2, \ldots, q_k)$ is given in the following equation:

$$\alpha(L,p)y_t = a_0 + \sum_{i=1}^{k} \beta_i(L,q_i)x_{it} + \lambda' w_t + \varepsilon_t \quad \forall t = 1, \ldots, n \tag{1}$$

where $\alpha(L,p) = 1 - \alpha_1 L - \alpha_2 L^2 - \cdots - \alpha_p L^p$,

$$\beta_i(L,q_i) = \beta_{i0} + \beta_{i1}L + \beta_{i2}L^2 + \cdots + \beta_{iq_i}L^{q_i} \quad \forall_i = 1, 2, \ldots, k, \tag{2}$$

where y_t is dependent variable, L is lag operator, a_0 is a constant term and w_t is $s \times 1$ a vector of deterministic variables, such as intercept term, time trend, dummy variables, and other exogenous variables with fixed lags. The x_{it} represents i independent variables where $i = 1, 2, \ldots, k$.

The long-run coefficients for a response of dependent variable y_t to a unit change in independent variable x_{it} are estimated by

$$\phi_i = \frac{\hat{\beta}_i(1,\hat{q}_i)}{\alpha(1,\hat{p})} = \frac{\hat{\beta}_{i0} + \hat{\beta}_{i1} + \cdots + \hat{\beta}_{i\hat{q}}}{1 - \hat{\alpha}_1 - \hat{\alpha}_{2-\cdots-}\hat{\alpha}_{\hat{p}}} \quad \forall_i = 1, 2, \ldots, k, \tag{3}$$

where $\hat{p}$ and $\hat{q}_i, i = 1, 2, \ldots, k$ are estimated values of $\hat{p}$ and $\hat{q}_i, i = 1, 2, \ldots, k$.

The long-run coefficients associated with exogenous variables with fixed lags (i.e., the intercept term, time trend and dummy variables) are

[7] The results of the Zivot-Andrews (1992) unit root test indicate that the financial time series variables under examination are integrated for different orders.

estimated by

$$\pi = \frac{\hat{\lambda}(\hat{p}, \hat{q}_1, \hat{q}_2, \ldots, \hat{q}_k)}{1 - \hat{\alpha}_1 - \hat{\alpha}_{2-\ldots-}\hat{\alpha}_{\hat{p}}}, \tag{4}$$

where $\hat{\lambda}(\hat{p}, \hat{q}_1, \hat{q}_2, \ldots, \hat{q}_k)$ indicates the OLS estimates of λ in Eq. (1) for the selected ARDL model.

The error correction (ECM) representation of the ARDL $(\hat{p}, \hat{q}_1, \hat{q}_2, \ldots, \hat{q}_k)$ model is obtained by rewriting the Eq. (1) in terms of lagged values and first differences of $y_t, x_{1t}, x_{2t}, \ldots, x_{kt}$ and w_t

$$\Delta y_t = \Delta a_0 - \alpha(1, \hat{p})EC_{t-1} + \sum_{i=1}^{k} \beta_{i0} \Delta x_{it} + \lambda' w_t$$

$$- \sum_{j=1}^{\hat{p}-1} \alpha^* j \Delta y_{t-j} - \sum_{i=1}^{k} \sum_{j=0}^{\hat{q}_i - 1} \beta_{ij} \Delta x_{i,t-j} + \varepsilon_t \tag{5}$$

The error correction model ECM is defined as follows:

$$\mathrm{ECM}_t = y_t - \hat{a} - \sum_{i=1}^{k} \hat{\beta}_i x_{it} - \lambda' w_t, \tag{6}$$

where Δ is the first difference operator, α^*, β_{ij} and λ' are coefficients that are associated with short-run dynamics of the model convergence to equilibrium, and $\alpha(1, \hat{p})$ measures the speed of adjustment.

5.2.1. *Empirical results*

The ARDL cointegration approach requires a two-step procedure to investigate the long-run relationship among variables of interest. The first step is to investigate the existence of a cointegration relationship among variables. This can be done using the bound test approach to cointegration. The second step considers the estimation of long- and short-run coefficients using ECM to determine the short-run adjustment to long-run equilibrium.

The results of the F-statistics that indicate for cointegration among MENA markets are reported in Table 3. The order of the distributed lag on both dependent variables and regressors in the above equations is selected using the Schwarz Bayesian Criterion (SBC) since it is considered to be preferable to other lag selection criteria (Pesaran *et al.*, 1998). Panel A in Table 3 illustrates results of computed F-statistics for foreign exchange markets. It shows that the calculated F-statistics exceed the upper bounds critical values in Bahrain, Qatar, Saudi Arabia, and the UAE at 1%, Jordan

Table 3. *F*-Statistics of Testing for the Existence of Long-Run Relationships

	Equation	Calculated F-Statistics
Panel A: Foreign Exchange Markets		
Bahrain	F(Bf/Ef, Jf, Kf, Mf, Qf, Sf, Tf, Uf, UKf)	9.2832***
Egypt	F(Ef/Bf, Jf, Kf, Mf, Qf, Sf, Tf, Uf, UKf)	1.3631
Jordan	F(Jf/Bf, Ef, Kf, Mf, Qf, Sf, Tf, Uf, UKf)	3.8342**
Kuwait	F(Kf/Bf, Ef, Jf, Mf, Qf, Sf, Tf, Uf, UKf)	3.5559**
Morocco	F(Mf/Bf, Ef, Jf, Kf, Qf, Sf, Tf, Uf, UKf)	1.9241
Qatar	F(Qf/Bf, Ef, Jf, Kf, Mf, Sf, Tf, Uf, UKf)	7.6599***
Saudi Arabia	F(Sf/Bf, Ef, Jf, Kf, Mf, Qf, Tf, Uf, UKf)	7.2045***
Tunisia	F(Tf/Bf, Ef, Jf, Kf, Mf, Qf, Sf, Uf, UKf)	1.7051
UAE	F(Uf/Bf, Ef, Jf, Kf, Mf, Qf, Sf, Tf, UKf)	8.3256***
UK	F(UKf/Bf, Ef, Jf, Kf, Mf, Qf, Sf, Tf, Uf)	3.1831*
Panel B: Money Markets		
Bahrain	F(Bm/Em, Jm, Km, Mm, Qm, Sm, Tm, Um, USm)	6.1744***
Egypt	F(Em/Bm, Jm, Km, Mm, Qm, Sm, Tm, Um, USm)	2.5896
Jordan	F (Jm/Bm, Em, Km, Mm, Qm, Sm, Tm, Um,USm)	2.1582
Kuwait	F(Km/Bm, Em, Jm, Mm, Qm, Sm, Tm, Um, USm)	2.3599
Morocco	F(Mm/Bm, Em, Jm, Km, Qm, Sm, Tm, Um, USm)	4.4733***
Qatar	F(Qm/Bm, Em, Jm, Km, Mm, Sm, Tm, Um, USm)	2.3907
Saudi Arabia	F(Sm/Bm, Em, Jm, Km, Mm, Qm, Tm, Um, USm)	4.3401***
Tunisia	F(Tm/Bm, Em, Jm, Km, Mm, Qm, Sm, Um, USm)	1.8583
UAE	F(Um/Bm, Em, Jm, Km, Mm, Qm, Sm, Tm, USm)	4.9165***
US	F(USm/Bm, Em, Jm, Km, Mm, Qm, Sm, Tm, Um)	5.7939***

Notes: This table illustrates the results of *F*-statistics for the existance of long-term cointegration relationship among foreign exchange markets and money markets, in MENA region. Bf, Ef, Jf, Kf, Mf, Qf, Sf, Tf, Uf, and UKf represent the foreign exchange markets of Bahrain, Egypt, Jordan, Kuwait, Morocco, Qatar, Saudi Arabia, Tunisia, the UAE, and the UK, respectively. Bm, Em, Jm, Km, Mm, Qm, Sm, Tm, Um, and USm represent money market indices of Bahrain, Egypt, Jordan, Kuwait, Morocco, Qatar, Saudi Arabia, Tunisia, UAE, and US, respectively. The relevant critical value bounds are obtained from Pesaran and Shin (2001), table CI (V) (with unrestricted intercept and unrestricted trend). The critical values in the case of 9 regressors are 2.07–3.16 at a 10% significance level, 2.33–3.46 at a 5% significance level, and 2.84–4.10 at a 1% significance level. *, **, *** denote rejection of null hypothesis at 1%, 5%, and 10% level, respectively.

and Kuwait at 5%, and the UK at 10%. This implies that the foreign exchange markets of MENA countries are bound together in a long-run relationship when these markets are dependent variables. The results in Panel B of Table 3 illustrate the computed *F*-statistics for the money markets of MENA countries. The results indicate that we are able to reject the null hypothesis of no cointegration for Bahrain, Morocco, Saudi Arabia, the UAE, and the US at 1% level. The results are inconclusive for Egypt, Kuwait,

Qatar, and Jordan, as the F-statistics lie between upper and lower bounds. The computed F-statistics for Tunisia are below the lower bounds; hence, there is no cointegration among the variables.

In this study, the long-run coefficients of cointegration of MENA markets are calculated based on the significance of F-statistics. This implies that we investigate the long-run coefficients of the ARDL approach for the foreign exchange markets of Bahrain, Jordan, Kuwait, Qatar, Saudi Arabia, the UAE, and the UK, and for money market indices of Bahrain, Morocco, Saudi Arabia, the UAE, and the US.

(i) Long-run coefficients and error correction models (ECM) of MENA foreign exchange markets

Table 4 illustrates the long-run coefficients for foreign exchange markets in Bahrain, Jordan, Kuwait, Qatar, Saudi Arabia, the UAE, and the UK. Panel A displays the error correction version of the ARDL model for the foreign exchange market in Bahrain. The SBIC lag specification is ARDL (1,0,0,0,0,0,0,0,1,0). The results indicate that the foreign exchange markets in Morocco, Saudi Arabia, and Tunisia have significant long-run effects on the foreign exchange market in Bahrain. In the long run, there is a 0.17% increase in the Bahraini market following a 1% change in the Moroccan market. Similarly, an increase in the Saudi foreign exchange market by 1% leads to an increase in Bahraini market by 0.11%, whereas a change in Tunisian market has a negligible impact on its Bahraini counterpart. The dummy variable in panel A is statistically significant at 1% level, which indicates that the structural change has a long-run impact on the foreign exchange market index in Bahrain.

Panel B illustrates the estimation of long-run coefficients of cointegration among MENA foreign exchange markets when the Jordan foreign exchange market index is a dependent variable based on the SBC lag specification of ARDL (1,0,0,0,0,0,0,0,0,0). The results indicate that only the foreign exchange market in Egypt has a long-run impact on the Jordanian foreign exchange market. A 1% change in the foreign exchange market index of Egypt leads to a 0.27% decrease in the foreign exchange market index in Jordan. The results also display the absence of a dummy variable impact on the long-run movements of the Jordan foreign exchange market index.

Panel C depicts the estimation of foreign exchange market of Kuwait as a dependent variable. The SBIC lag specification is ARDL (1,0,0,0,0,0,0,1,0,0). The results indicate that the foreign exchange market indices in Egypt, Morocco, Tunisia and the UK exhibit long-run impact on Kuwait foreign exchange market. However, change in the stock market in Egypt seems

Table 4. Long-Run Coefficients of MENA Foreign Exchange Markets.

Regressors	Coefficients	T-Ratio
Panel A: ARDL (1,0,0,0,0,0,0,0,1,0) Model Selected Based on SBC		
Dependent Variable: Bahrain (Bf)		
Intercept	0.1449	0.5375
Ef	−0.1623	−0.4282
Jf	0.0153	0.8210
Kf	0.0060	1.3762
Mf	0.1701	1.9545*
Qf	−0.0011	−0.1152
Sf	0.1127	7.0850***
Tf	−0.0011	−1.9948**
Uf	−0.05416	−0.6540
UKf	−0.9097	−1.5967
T	0.5642	2.0323**
$D_{06/09}$	0.7565	2.9375***
Panel B: ARDL (1,0,0,0,0,0,0,0,0,0) Model Selected Based on SBIC		
Dependent Variable: Jordan (Jf)		
Intercept	1.2212	0.9202
Bf	0.1499	0.1660
Ef	−0.2670	−1.9050**
Kf	−0.0024	−0.0759
Mf	−0.4358	−0.7052
Qf	0.0523	0.7377
Sf	−0.0072	−0.1060
Tf	0.0027	0.7012
Uf	−0.1986	−0.5086
UKf	0.0015	0.4029
T	−0.1724	−0.8705
$D_{04/02}$	−0.2651	−0.1671
Panel C: ARDL (1,0,0,0,0,0,0,1,0,0) Model Selected Based on SBIC		
Dependent Variable: Kuwait (Kf)		
Intercept	14.1706	1.2767
Bf	4.5425	0.6308
Ef	0.0073	3.2389***
Jf	−0.9711	−0.8812
Mf	−0.1094	−2.2234**
Qf	0.3664	0.6307
Sf	0.1018	0.1803
Tf	0.0914	3.4104***
Uf	−4.5503	−1.3991
UKf	0.1191	3.2182***
T	−0.5697	−4.5150***
$D_{10/03}$	−0.0322	−2.1351**
$D_{08/07}$	−0.0309	−1.9460*

(*Continued*)

Table 4. *(Continued)*

Regressors	Coefficients	T-Ratio
Panel D: ARDL (0,0,0,0,0,1,0,1,0,0) Model Selected Based on SBIC Dependent Variable: Qatar (Qf)		
Intercept	2.2353	0.1681*
Bf	1.0334	1.9489**
Ef	0.5327	0.1983
Jf	0.1610	1.2226
Kf	0.0137	0.4150
Mf	0.3646	0.5858
Sf	0.0981	1.4596
Tf	−0.0021	−0.5364
Uf	0.1427	0.3668
UKf	0.0059	1.4703
T	0.1471	0.7222
$D_{10/04}$	0.3050	0.1972
$D_{12/08}$	0.0015	0.9425
Panel E: ARDL (1,1,0,0,0,0,0,0,1,0) Model Selected Based on SBIC Dependent Variable: Saudi Arabia (Sf)		
Intercept	−10.4876	−3.7131***
Bf	−0.5031	−0.3005
Ef	0.2048	0.5749
Jf	−0.0291	−0.1657
Kf	−0.0294	−0.6961
Mf	−0.0013	−1.7158*
Qf	0.2273	2.3341**
Tf	0.0096	1.8646*
Uf	3.7110	4.2606***
UKf	0.0017	0.3145
T	−0.4663	−1.8048*
Panel F: ARDL (0,1,0,0,0,0,0,1,0,0) Model Selected Based on SBIC Dependent Variable: UAE (Uf)		
Intercept	3.2348	4.9351***
Bf	1.4435	7.6708***
Ef	0.1022	2.1600**
Jf	−0.0232	−0.9746
Kf	−0.1187	−2.0627**
Mf	−0.8405	−0.7612
Qf	−0.7298	−0.0565
Sf	−0.0228	−1.399
Tf	0.5509	0.7704
UKf	0.0031	4.5298***
T	−0.4838	−1.3575
$D_{04/06}$	0.3768	1.3574
$D_{07/08}$	0.4086	1.4212

(Continued)

Table 4. (*Continued*)

Regressors	Coefficients	T-Ratio
Panel G: ARDL (1,0,0,0,1,1,0,0,0,0) Model Selected Based on SBIC Dependent Variable: UK (UKf)		
Intercept	−20.4796	−1.2627
Bf	−14.9038	−1.1839
Ef	−0.0439	−1.8522*
Jf	−2.7419	−0.1652
Kf	−7.9032	−1.1596
Mf	0.0589	−1.1596
Qf	−1.2259	−1.0797
Sf	9.6788	1.0601
Tf	0.1741	0.3287
Uf	7.4506	1.4456
T	−0.2477	−0.0965
$D_{01/13}$	0.0111	0.5767

Notes: This table illustrates the long-run coefficients of MENA foreign exchange markets. Refer to Table 3 note for Bf, Ef, Jf, Kf, Mf, Qf, Sf, Tf, Uf, and UKf. $D_{06/09}$ is a that dummy variable that takes value of 1 on 06/2009 and 0 otherwise. $D_{04/02}$ is a dummy variable that takes value of 1 on 04/2002 and 0 otherwise. $D_{10/03}$ is a dummy variable that takes value of 1 on 10/2003 and 0 otherwise. $D_{08/07}$ is a dummy variable that takes value of 1 on 08/2007 and 0 otherwise. $D_{10/04}$ is a dummy variable that takes value of 1 on 10/2004 and 0 otherwise. $D_{12/08}$ is a dummy variable that takes value of 1 on 12/2008 and 0 otherwise. $D_{04/06}$ is a dummy variable that takes value of 1 on 04/2006 and 0 otherwise. $D_{07/08}$ is a dummy variable that takes value of 1 on 07/2008 and 0 otherwise. $D_{01/13}$ is a dummy variable that takes value of 1 on 01/2013 and 0 otherwise. T is time trend. *, **, *** denote rejection of null hypothesis at 1%, 5%, and 10% level, respectively.

to have a negligible long-run impact on the Kuwaiti market compared to changes in the foreign exchange markets of Morocco, Tunisia, and the UK. A 1% change in these markets will lead to changes in the Kuwaiti market by −0.11%, 0.09% and 0.12%, respectively. Structural changes that occurred in 2003 and 2008 have significant negative impacts on this market in the long run.

Panel D shows the estimation of long-run coefficients of cointegration among MENA foreign exchange market indices when the Qatar foreign exchange market index is a dependent variable. The SBIC lag specification of ARDL is (0,0,0,0,0,1,0,1,0,0). Only the foreign exchange market in Bahrain has a long-run impact on the foreign exchange market in Qatar. The results indicate the absence of any long-run impact from other regressors on long-run movements of the foreign exchange market of Qatar.

Panel E displays the error correction version of ARDL model for foreign exchange market in Saudi Arabia. The SBC lag specification is ARDL (1,1,0,0,0,0,0,0,1,0). The foreign exchange markets in Morocco, Qatar, Tunisia, and the UAE have a long-run influence in the Saudi Arabian market. Obviously, the UAE market has the most significant influence on the Saudi Arabian market in the long -run, compared to other markets. For a 1% change in the UAE foreign exchange, the Saudi Arabian market will increase by 3.71%, while a 1% change in the foreign exchange markets of Morocco, Qatar, and Tunisia will lead to a change in the Saudi Arabian market of −0.0013%, 0.22%, and 0.009%, respectively.

Panel F shows the estimation of long-run coefficients of cointegration among MENA foreign exchange markets when the UAE is a dependent variable. The SBIC lag specification of ARDL is (0,1,0,0,0,0,0,1,0,0). In the long -run, the UAE market responds to changes in the foreign exchange markets of Bahrain, Egypt, Kuwait, and the UK by 1.44%, 0.10%, −0.11%, and 0.003%, respectively. There is no long-run impact from structural changes on the long-run movements of the foreign exchange market of the UAE.

Panel G illustrates the estimation of long-run coefficients of cointegration among the foreign exchange market in the UK and the MENA region. Only the foreign exchange market in Egypt has a long-run impact on the UK market. A 1% change in the foreign exchange market of Egypt leads to a −0.04% decrease in the foreign exchange market in the UK.

Table 5 illustrates long- and short-run causal relationships among foreign exchange markets in the MENA region. The error correction terms are estimated for markets in Bahrain, Jordan, Kuwait, Qatar, Saudi Arabia, the UAE, and the UK that exhibit significant F-statistics. The results indicate that the coefficient of ECT of ΔBf, ΔJf, ΔKf, ΔQf, ΔSf, and ΔUKf are negative and highly significant, and this affirms the existence of cointegration among foreign exchange markets in the region when these markets are dependent variables.

The proportions of short-run disturbances that are adjusted to long-run equilibrium are about 47% for Bahrain, 50% for Jordan, 13% for Kuwait, 21% for Qatar, 66% for Saudi Arabia, 51% for the UAE, and 6% for the UK. Table 5 illustrates short-run causalities for the markets under consideration. We notice five bidirectional causalities for Bahrain and

Table 5. ECT and Short-Run Causalities of Foreign Exchange Markets in MENA Region.

Dependent Variables	Independent Variables: T-Statistics										ECT_{t-1}	
	ΔBf	ΔEf	ΔJf	ΔKf	ΔMf	ΔQf	ΔSf	ΔTf	ΔUf	ΔUKf	Coefficients	*t*-statistics
(1)	(2)	(3)	(4)	(5)	(6)	(7)	(8)	(9)	(10)	(11)	(12)	(13)
ΔBf	—	−0.427	0.822	1.351	1.990**	−0.115	14.376***	−2.020**	3.027***	−1.586	−0.474	−9.235***
ΔEf	−0.083	—	0.973	−0.903	1.120	−0.588	0.096	0.728	0.901	0.667	—	—
ΔJf	0.165	−1.005	—	−0.075	−0.695	0.734	−0.105	0.690	−0.507	0.400	−0.498	−7.457***
ΔKf	0.618	3.426***	−0.896	—	−2.212**	0.631	0.182	9.287***	−1.431	3.718***	−0.126	−3.914***
ΔMf	−0.398	−2.909***	−0.467	0.759	—	1.655*	0.887	2.120**	1.387	−1.726*	—	—
ΔQf	1.148	0.198	1.222	0.415	5.999***	—	1.459	−6.034	0.366	1.470	−0.213	−5.412***
ΔSf	11.599***	0.573	−0.165	−0.692	−1.697*	2.434**	—	1.846*	2.885***	0.312	−0.656	−10.225***
ΔTf	−0.402	−1.903*	−0.058	−0.095	−1.306	1.696*	0.977	—	1.507	−1.238	—	—
ΔUf	2.627***	2.160**	−0.974	−2.062**	−0.761	−0.056	3.136***	0.770	—	4.529***	−0.512	−4.448***
ΔUKf	−1.347	−1.334	−0.167	1.374	7.120***	−1.387	1.153	0.353	1.556	—	−0.059	−1.973**

Notes: This table illustrates ECT and short-run causalities among foreign exchange markets in MENA region. Column 1 presents dependent variables Bf, Ef, Jf, Kf, Mf, Qf, Sf, Tf, Us, and UKf, see note in Table 3. Columns (2)–(11) presents in dependent variables. Columns (12) and (13) illustrate coefficients and t-statistics of ECT representing error correction model of selected ARDL procedure for foreign exchange markets in Bahrain, Jordan, Kuwait, Qatar, Saudi Arabia, UAE, and the UK. *, **, *** denote rejection of null hypothesis at 1%, 5%, and 10% level, respectively.

Saudi Arabia, Bahrain and the UAE, Morocco and Qatar, Morocco and the UK, and Saudi Arabia and the UAE.

The results also indicate that the foreign exchange markets in Egypt and Jordan are the most exogenous of the MENA markets, as they are not caused by other variables. The foreign exchange market in the UK also seems to be exogenous to short-term movements compared with its counterparts in the MENA region as it is only affected by short-run changes in the Moroccan foreign exchange.

(ii) Long-run coefficients and error correction models (ECM) of MENA money markets

The results of long-run coefficients of money markets in MENA region are illustrated in Table 6. Panel A shows the error correction version of the ARDL model for the money market in Bahrain. The SBIC lag specification is ARDL (1,0,0,0,0,0,0,0,1,0). The results indicate that the money market in Bahrain increases by about 0.29% following a 1% change in the money market in Qatar. In the long-run, a 1% change in the Saudi Arabian money market leads to about 0.47% increase in the money market in Bahrain. Furthermore, the change in developed markets as represented by the US money market has a significant long-term effect on the Bahraini market. For a 1% change in the US market, the Bahraini market responds by about 0.34%. The dummy variable that accounts for the structural change occurred in January 2009, which coincides with GFC, and has a negative long-run impact on the money market in Bahrain.

Panel B illustrates the estimation of long-run coefficients of cointegration among MENA money markets when Morocco is a dependent variable. The results indicate that in the long- run, the money market in Morocco responds to changes of 1% in the money markets of Egypt, Kuwait, and the US by decreases of 0.08%, 0.24%, and 0.23%, respectively, and it increases by 0.35% in accordance to 1% change in the UAE market.

Panel C displays the error correction version of the ARDL model for the money market in Saudi Arabia. The SBIC lag specification is ARDL (1,0,0,1,1,0,0,0,1,0). The results indicate that the money markets in Bahrain, Jordan, Tunisia, and the US have a long-run influence on the Saudi Arabian market. The Saudi Arabian market exhibits a positive reaction toward changes in these markets. Changes in the US money market seem to be very influential on the Saudi Arabian money market. In the long run, a 1% change in the US money market causes about 0.57% change on the Saudi Arabian money market.

Table 6. Long-Run Coefficients of MENA Money Markets

Regressors	Coefficients	T-Ratio
Panel A: ARDL (1,0,0,0,0,0,0,0,1,0) Model Selected Based on SBIC		
Dependent Variable: Bahrain (Bm)		
Intercept	0.9419	0.8037
Em	0.0607	1.3315
Jm	−0.0768	−0.9394
Km	−0.0027	−0.0269
Mm	0.1434	0.8987
Qm	0.2941	2.8080***
Sm	0.4722	3.1325***
Tm	−0.2299	−1.5752
Um	−0.1027	−0.6322
USm	0.3443	3.1000***
T	−0.0024	−0.7584
$D_{01/09}$	−2.9987	−2.9789***
Panel B: ARDL (1,0,0,0,0,0,0,0,0,0) Model Selected Based on SBIC		
Dependent Variable: Morocco (Mm)		
Intercept	3.9080	3.9832***
Bm	0.1002	0.4419
Em	−0.0821	−2.1243**
Jm	0.0958	1.2797
Km	−0.2443	−2.6810***
Qm	−0.0682	−1.0220
Sm	0.06795	0.4022
Tm	−0.2168	−1.4730
Um	0.3508	3.0501***
USm	−0.2334	−1.7799*
T	0.0043	1.7024*
$D_{03/07}$	0.6814	1.4219
Panel C: ARDL (1,0,0,1,1,0,0,0,1,0) Model Selected Based on SBIC		
Dependent Variable: Saudi Arabia (Sm)		
Intercept	−1.6009	−1.2335
Bm	0.5155	2.2634**
Em	0.0507	0.9823
Jm	0.2521	2.7617***
Km	−0.1750	−1.1955
Mm	0.1866	1.0212
Qm	0.0131	0.1425
Tm	0.3334	2.1310**
Um	−0.2433	−1.3204
USm	0.5683	2.7234***
T	−0.0092	−2.7878***
$D_{01/09}$	−1.1053	−1.5363

(*Continued*)

Table 6. (*Continued*)

Regressors	Coefficients	T-Ratio
Panel D: ARDL (1,0,0,0,0,0,0,1,0,0) Model Selected Based on SBIC		
Dependent Variable: UAE (Um)		
Intercept	−3.9565	−1.6890*
Bm	1.0783	2.5643**
Em	0.1526	1.6863*
Jm	−0.2793	−1.7690*
Km	0.3267	2.0653**
Mm	0.3505	1.5090
Qm	0.3946	3.0958***
Sm	0.6390	1.8995*
Tm	0.4903	1.6209
USm	−1.0855	−3.4687***
T	−0.0078	−1.8740*
Panel E: ARDL (1,0,0,0,1,0,0,0,0,1) Model Selected Based on SBIC		
Dependent Variable: US (USm)		
Intercept	8.6474	1.0642
Bm	2.8367	1.6509
Em	0.1448	0.4774
Jm	−0.0139	−0.0316
Km	−0.2765	−0.4344
Mm	−2.1571	−1.2499
Qm	2.2616	1.3144
Sm	−1.8416	−1.0185
Tm	0.2631	0.3074
Um	−1.9603	−1.9366*
T	−0.0395	−1.2671
$D_{10/08}$	−2.5256	−1.3230

Notes: This table illustrates the long-run coefficients of MENA money markets. Refer to Table 3 note for Bm, Em, Jm, Km, Mm, Qm, Sm, Tm, Um, and USm. $D_{01/09}$ is a dummy that variable takes value of 1 on 01/2009 and 0 otherwise. $D_{03/07}$ is a dummy variable that takes value of 1 on 03/2007 and 0 otherwise. $D_{10/08}$ is a dummy that variable takes value of 1 on 10/2008 and 0 otherwise. *, **, *** denote rejection of null hypothesis at 1%, 5%, and 10% level, respectively.

Panel D demonstrates the estimation of the cointegration of money markets in the region when the UAE is dependent variable. The results indicate that the money market of the UAE is more active than the above MENA money markets since it is more influenced by movements in other markets. The money markets of Bahrain, Egypt, Jordan, Kuwait, Qatar, Saudi Arabia, and the US all exhibit a long-run impact on the UAE market.

The 1% change in the US market is found to have the most significant response from the UAE market, about −1.10%, compared to other MENA markets.

Panel E illustrates the error correction version of the ARDL model for the money market in the US. We find that in the long run, the US money market is only influenced by changes in its UAE counterpart. A 1% change in the money market of the UAE leads to −1.96% decrease in the US market. We believe that this result is plausible since it implies that in the long- run the movements in the US money market are not predominantly caused by changes in the money markets of the MENA region.

Table 7 illustrates the long- and short-run causal relationships in the money markets in the MENA region. The error correction terms are estimated for the markets in Bahrain, Morocco, Saudi Arabia, the UAE, and the US that exhibit significant F-statistics, whereas the short-run causalities of money markets in Egypt, Jordan, Kuwait, Qatar, and Tunisia are estimated using the VAR approach. The results demonstrate that the coefficient of ECT of ΔBm, ΔMm, ΔSm, and ΔUm are significant. This implies that these markets adjust to correct the short-term disturbance from the long-run equilibrium. In Bahrain, 28% of the deviation is corrected after the first month, whereas a higher proportion of disturbance is corrected in Morocco (59%) during the same period. The money markets of Saudi Arabia and the UAE also adjust to correct about 25% and 17%, respectively, of short-term deviation.

However, the ECT coefficient pertinent to the US money market is insignificant. This implies that there is no long-run causal relationship running from money markets in the MENA region to the US market. The results of short-run causalities demonstrate the existence of bivariate causalities shared among the money markets of Bahrain and Saudi Arabia, Bahrain and the UAE, Bahrain and the US, Egypt and the UAE, Morocco and the US, Qatar and the UAE, Saudi Arabia and the UAE, and Saudi Arabia and the US. The money markets of Jordan and Tunisia are totally exogenous as they are not influenced by short-run movements of other markets. The money market in the UAE seems to be the most active in the region since it is influenced by six money markets: Bahrain, Egypt, Jordan, Kuwait, Qatar, and Saudi Arabia. Finally, while there are no long-run effects of the MENA money markets on the US market, in the short-run the US money market is influenced by changes in the money markets of Bahrain, Kuwait, Morocco, and the UAE.

Table 7. ECT and Short-Run Causalities of Money Markets in MENA Region

Dependent Variables	Independent Variables											
	T-Statistics										ECT_{t-1}	
	ΔBm	ΔEm	ΔJm	ΔKm	ΔMm	ΔQm	ΔSm	ΔTm	ΔUm	ΔUSm	Coefficients	*t*-statistics
(1)	(2)	(3)	(4)	(5)	(6)	(7)	(8)	(9)	(10)	(11)	(12)	(13)
ΔBm	—	1.372	−0.930	−0.026	0.944	4.031***	2.529**	−1.439	3.533***	2.446**	−0.284	−4.211***
ΔEm	−1.001	—	0.383	0.773	0.690	−0.387	1.671*	−2.176**	−2.109**	0.218	—	—
ΔJm	−0.160	0.588	—	−0.148	−0.043	−0.861	1.180	−1.297	−0.769	1.176	—	—
ΔKm	−1.013	0.872	−0.776	—	−1.525	2.595**	3.436***	−0.607	0.262	−0.131	—	—
ΔMm	0.446	−2.064**	1.276	−2.517**	—	−0.990	0.399	−1.415	2.639***	−1.793*	−0.593	−6.564***
ΔQm	1.234	1.934*	−0.618	0.287	−2.999***	—	1.527	−0.583	0.808	1.234	—	—
ΔSm	1.870*	0.988	−1.915*	1.512	1.049	0.144	—	1.818*	5.532***	3.525***	−0.247	−4.815***
ΔTm	−0.961	−0.470	0.767	−1.308	−0.767	1.491	1.232	—	−1.217	1.227	—	—
ΔUm	2.787***	2.058**	2.007**	1.878*	1.364	3.106***	5.410***	1.822	—	−4.816	−0.167	−4.536***
ΔUSm	2.388**	0.609	−0.031	1.914*	−2.703***	5.886	−1.875*	0.317	1.680*	—	−0.035	0.181

Notes: This table illustrates ECT and short-run causalities among money markets in MENA region.Column 1 presents dependent variables Bm, Em, Jm, Km, Mm, Qm, Sm, Tm, Um, and USm, see note in Table 3. Columns (2)–(11) presents in dependent variables. Columns (12) and (13) illustrate coefficients and t-statistics of ECT representing error correction model of selected ARDL procedure for foreign exchange markets in Bahrain, Jordan, Kuwait, Qatar, Saudi Arabia, UAE, and the UK. *, **, *** denote rejection of null hypothesis at 1%, 5%, and 10% level, respectively.

6. Conclusion and Policy Implications

In this chapter, we tested for the existence of structural breaks in financial markets — foreign exchange markets and money markets — in the MENA countries of Bahrain, Egypt, Jordan, Kuwait, Morocco, Qatar, Saudi Arabia, Tunisia, and the UAE, in addition to the US and the UK. We also tested for the existence of long-run cointegration among financial markets in these countries, as well as long- and short-term causal relationships.

We employed the Bai and Perron (2003) test for multiple structural changes. Results of the Bai–Perron (BP) test indicate that the foreign exchange markets in Kuwait and the UAE were subject to two structural changes, as were the money markets of Jordan and Qatar. The foreign exchange market in Tunisia is the only variable that was subject to three breaks. Most of these breaks can be attributed to the GFC in addition to financial liberalisation and political instabilities in the region.

The research in this chapter also tested the financial integration among MENA markets through the autoregressive distributed lag (ARDL) cointegration approach. The results of the bound test F-statistics show that foreign exchange markets in the MENA region exhibit a long-run co-movement when markets in Bahrain, Jordan, Kuwait, Qatar, Saudi Arabia, or the UAE are dependent variables. Furthermore, the money markets in the MENA region are bound together in a long-run equilibrium relationship when one of the markets of Bahrain, Morocco, Saudi Arabia, or the UAE is placed as a dependent variable.

The financial integration between MENA and developed markets is confirmed since the foreign exchange market in the UK, as well as the money market in the US, has significant F-statistics. The long-run coefficients of the ARDL model indicates that the financial markets in the region are bound by developed markets in long-run equilibrium relationships when the stock market in Jordan, foreign exchange markets in Kuwait and the UAE, and money markets in Bahrain, Morocco, and Saudi Arabia are dependent variables.

The results of long-run causalities of the error-corrected terms (ECT) indicate that all cointegrated variables exhibit significant t-ratio, except in the case of money market in the US. This implies that these variables adjust to clear the short-run deviation from the long-run equilibrium. In regard to short-run causal relationships, we find that the foreign exchange markets in Egypt and Jordan are the least affected by short-run movements in other MENA exchanges. The money market in the UAE seems to be most endogenous among MENA markets as it exhibits more response to short-term fluctuations in regional markets than others.

Overall, the results in this chapter illustrated that the financial markets in the MENA region are not isolated from global events. Moreover, global shocks such as the GFC and European debt crisis are found to have at least the same impact as local and regional events on the financial systems in MENA countries. This might be an indication for a noticeable increase in financial amalgamation between MENA regional markets and developed markets. Furthermore, the financial markets in the MENA region are cointegrated at an international level, yet not fully bound to developed markets. However, we believe that the opportunity of international portfolio diversification seems to be reduced since the MENA markets react swiftly and respond significantly to global shocks.

References

Abdelaziz, M. and Chortareas, G. (2008). Stock prices, exchange rates, and oil: Evidence from Middle East oil-exporting countries. Unpublished manuscript.

Al-Hamidy, A. (2010). The global financial crisis: Impact on Saudi Arabia. Bank International Settlement, WP. No. 54.

Alkulaib, Y. A., Najand, M., and Mashayekh, A. (2009). Dynamic linkages among equity markets in the Middle East and North African countries. *J. Multinational Fin. Manag.*, 6, pp. 43–53.

Antonakakis, N. (2012). Exchange return co-movements and volatility spillovers before and after the introduction of Euro. MPRA, WP. No. 37869.

Antoshin, S., Berg, A., and Souto, M. (2008). Testing for structural breaks in small samples. *International Monetary Fund*, WP. No. 08/75.

Baele, L., Ferrando, A., Hoerdal, P., Krylova, E., and Monnet, C. (2004). Measuring financial integration in the Euro area. European Central Bank, WP. No. 14.

Bai, J. and Perron, P. (2003). Critical values for multiple structural change tests. *Econometr. J.*, 6, pp. 72–78.

Baillie, R. T. and Bollerslev, T. (1989). Common stochastic trends in a system of exchange rates. *The J. Fin.*, XLV, pp. 167–181.

Bley, J. and Chen, K. H. (2006). Gulf cooperation council (GCC) stock markets: The dawn of new era. *Global Fin. J.*, 17, pp. 75–91.

Bohdalová, M. and Gregus, M. (2014). Cointegration analysis of the foreign exchange rate pairs, *CBU*. In Int. Conf. Innovation, Technology Transfer and Education, pp. 147–153 (in Czech Republic).

Brixiova, Z., Égert, B., and Essid, THA. (2013). The real exchange rate and external competitiveness in Egypt, Morocco and Tunisia. *Rev. Middle East Econom. Fin.*, 10. pp. 25–51.

Centeno, M. and Mello, A. S. (1999). How integrated are the money market and the bank loans market within the European Union? *J. Int. Money Fin.*, 18, pp. 75–106.

Chaudhry, M. and Boldin, R. J. (2012). GCC equity market indices integration. *Appl. Fin. Econom.*, 22, pp. 471–478.

Coleman, M. (1990). Cointegration-Based tests of daily foreign exchange market efficiency. *Econom. Lett.*, 32, pp. 53–59.

Copeland, L. S. (1991). Cointegration tests with daily exchange rates data. *Oxford Bullet. Econom. Statist.*, 53, pp. 185–197.
Darrat, A. F., Elkhal, K., and Hakim, S. R. (2000). On the integration of emerging stock markets in the Middle East. *J. Econom. Develop.*, 25, pp. 119–129.
Engle, R. F. and Granger, C. W. J. (1987). Co-integration and error correction: Representation, estimation and testing. *Econometrica*, 55, pp. 251–276.
Enders, W. and Sandler, T. (2005). After 9/11 is it all different now?. *J. Conflict Resolution*, 49, pp. 259–277.
ESCWA, (2009). The impact of the financial crisis on ESCWA member countries: Challenges and opportunities. *Economic and Social Commission for Western Asia*, WP. No. 3.
Ezzati, P. (2011). Financial markets integration of Iran within the Middle East and with the rest of the world. University of Western Australia, Discussion Paper. No. 12.24.
Garcia-Kilroy, C. and Silva, A. C. (2011). Reforming government debt markets in MENA, *The World Bank*, WP. No. 5611.
Genc, I. H., Jubain, A., and Al-Mutairi, A. (2010). Economic versus financial integration or decoupling between the US and the GCC. *Appl. Fin. Econom.*, 20, pp. 1577–1583.
Ghanem, D. (2010). Inflation and exchange rate regime: Evidence from MENA countries. In *Proc. 14th Ann. Conf. Macroeconomic Analysis and International Finance*, pp. 1–42 (in Montpellier).
Ghanem, D. and Bismut, C. (2009). The choice of exchange rate regimes in Middle Eastern and North African countries: An empirical analysis. University of Montpellier, WP. No. 1.
Goucha, N. B. S. and Hamdi, I. (2014). Financial integration before and after the crisis of 2008: Evidence from GCC and MENA stock market indices. In *Proc. 5th Asia-Pacific Business Research Conference*, pp. 23–52 (in Malaysia).
Gregory, A. W. and Hansen, B. E. (1996). Tests for cointegration in models with regime and trend shifts. *Oxford Bullet Econom. Statist.*, 58, pp. 555–560.
Habibi, N. (2009). The impact of global economic crisis on Arab countries: A year-end assessment. Brandeis University, WP. No. 40.
IMF (2004). Bahrain: Article IV consultation'. International Monetary Fund, WP. No. 04/96.
Kleimeier, S. and Sander, H. (2003). Towards a single European banking market? New evidence from Euroland on the role of the euro. CERC, WP. No. 4.
Kuhl, M. (2007). Cointegration in the foreign exchange market and market efficiency since the introduction of the euro: Evidence based on bivariate cointegration analysis. Georg-August-Universitat Gottingen, Discussion Paper.
Lagoarde-Segot, T. and Lucey, B. M. (2007). Capital market integration in the Middle East and North Africa. *Emerg. Markets Fin. Trade*, 43, pp. 34–57.
Levine, R. (2005). Finance and growth: Theory and evidence. *Handbook Econom. Growth*, 1, pp. 865–934.
Lin, A. and Swanson, P. E. (1997). The US dollar in global money markets: A multivariate cointegration analysis. *Quart. Rev. Econom. Fin.*, 37, pp. 139–150.
Marashdeh, H. A. (2006). Financial Integration of the MENA emerging stock markets, University of Wollongong, PhD Thesis.
Marashdeh, H. A. and Shrestha, M. B. (2010). Stock market integration in the GCC countries. *Int. Res. J. Fin. Econom.*, 37, pp. 102–114.
Narayan, P., Smith, R., and Nandha, M. (2004). Interdependence and dynamic linkages between the emerging stock markets of South Asia. *Account. Fin.*, 44, pp. 419–439.

Neaime, S. (2002). Liberalization and financial integration of MENA stock markets. In *Proc. 9th Annual Conference on Finance and Banking*, pp. 115–138 (in United Arab Emirates).

Neaime, S. (2005). Financial market integration and macroeconomic volatility in the MENA region: An empirical investigation. *Rev. Middle East Econom. Fin.*, 3, pp. 231–253.

Neaime, S. (2012). The global financial crisis, financial linkages and correlations in returns and volatilities in emerging MENA stock markets. *Emerg. Markets Rev.*, 13, pp. 268–282.

Nor, M. I. (2012). Financial market integration of Middle East and North Africa (MENA) countries. *Asian J. Manage. Sci. Edu.*, 1, pp. 63–72.

Nsouli, S. M. and Rached, M. (1998). Capital account liberalization in the Southern Mediterranean. International Monetary Fund, WP. No. 11/217.

Paskelian, O. G., Nguyen, C. V., and Jones, K. (2013). Did financial market integration really happened in MENA region?. *J. Econom. Coop. Develop.*, 34, pp. 111–134.

Pesaran, B. and Pesaran, M. H. (2009). *Time Series Econometrics using Microfit 5.0*, Oxford: Oxford University Press.

Pesaran, M. H. and Pesaran, B. (1997). *Microsoft 4.0: Interactive Econometric Analysis*, Oxford: Oxford University Press.

Pesaran, M. H. and Shin, Y. (1995). An autoregressive distributed lag modelling approach to cointegration analysis. University of Cambridge, DAE WP. No. 9514.

Pesaran, M. H. (1997). The role of economic theory in modelling the long run. *The Econom. J.*, 107, pp. 178–191.

Pesaran, M. H. and Shin, Y. (1998). An autoregressive distributed lag modelling approach to cointegration analysis. In *Econometrics and Economics Theory in the 20th Century, The Ragnar Frisch Centennial Symposium*. Cambridge University Press.

Pesaran, M. H., Shin, Y., and Smith, R. (1996). Testing for the existence of a long-run relationship, Department of Applied Economics. Cambridge University. DAE WP. No. 9622.

Pesaran, M. H. Shin, Y., and Smith, R. (2001). Bounds testing approaches to the analysis of level relationships. *J. Appl. Econometr.*, 16, pp. 289–326.

Samanta, S. K. and Zadeh, A. H. M. (2012). Co-movements of oil, gold, the U.S. dollar, and stocks. *Modern Econom.*, 3, pp. 111–117.

Santillan, J., Bayle, M., and Thygesen, C. (2000). The impact of the euro on money and bond markets. European Central Bank, WP. No. 1.

Selim, H. (2012). Has Egypt's exchange rate policy changed after the float? *Middle East Develop. J.*, 4, pp. 1–27.

Soofi, A. S. (2008). Global financial integration and the MENA countries: Evidence from equity and money markets. *Rev. Middle East Econom. Fin.*, 4, pp. 1–23.

Tai, C. (2007). Market integration and contagion: Evidence from Asian emerging stock and foreign exchange markets. *Emerg. Markets Rev.*, 8, pp. 264–283.

Tawadros, G. B. (2007). Testing the hypothesis of long-run money neutrality in the Middle East. *J. Econom. Stud.*, 34, pp. 13–28.

Zivot, E. and Andrews, D. W. K. (1992). Further evidence on the great crash, the oil-price shock, and the unit-root hypothesis. *J. Business Econom. Statist.*, 10, pp. 251–270.

Part III

Risk Assessment and Portfolio Management

Chapter 10

Coherent Asset Allocations with Liquidity-Adjusted Value-at-Risk Method: Review of Theoretical Algorithms and Applications

Mazin A. M. Al Janabi

Full Professor of Finance & Banking and Financial Engineering,
EGADE Business School, Tecnológico de Monterrey
Santa Fe Campus, Mexico City, Mexico
mazin.aljanabi@itesm.mx; mazinaljanabi@gmail.com

Abstract

This chapter reviews the method development aspects of Al Janabi (2012) theoretical foundations and optimization algorithms for the assessment of optimum and coherent (investable) portfolios. Specifically, the chapter reviews the implementation of a robust method for commodity portfolio selection and within a liquidity-adjusted value-at-risk (LVaR) framework. The proposed optimization algorithm demonstrates that better investable portfolios can be obtained than using the traditional Markowitz's (1952) technique. The commodity risk techniques and empirical findings are interesting in terms of theory as well as practical applications and have important implications for asset management, particularly in light of the aftermaths of the recent financial crisis. In a nutshell the advantages of the method include: (1) developed optimization algorithms can aid in advancing portfolio management in commodities and financial markets by testing for investable portfolios subject to meaningful financial and operational constraints; (2) investable commodity portfolios cannot be achieved via Markowitz's (1952) classical portfolio approach as the empirical results indicate that investable portfolios lie off the efficient frontier; (3) the proposed modeling technique can be used by portfolio managers for the assessment of appropriate asset allocations of different investable commodity portfolios under crisis market outlooks.

1. Introduction

The uncertainty of prices in commodity markets are commonly created by supply and demand inconsistencies that stem from: (1) the economical business cycle (e.g., energy products, metals, and agricultural crops); (2) political upheavals (energy products); or (3) unpredicted weather conditions (agricultural commodities). As such, Commodity prices have a tendency to fluctuate in the short term because of daily and recurring variations in supply and demand, but revert towards a long-term balance (Al Janabi, 2009).[1]

By and large, prices of energy commodities, for instance, have been more volatile than most other commodities. Accordingly, energy demand tends to fluctuate significantly from season to season, while energy supply tends to be comparatively steady. In this sense, energy products volatility tends to perform quite differently from most other commodity assets. For example, over the last decade, energy price volatility has become the most significant issue facing the oil industry and, as such, crude oil markets have all shown extreme price changes over the recent period. Also, abrupt changes and continued volatility of oil prices has added to a climate of uncertainty for investors, commodity fund managers, and energy corporations.

Recent years have witnessed the growing position of investment funds in most commodity markets (Satyanarayan and Varangis, 1994), with a particular emphasis on commodity-dependent countries. In the last two decades, commodity markets have played a crucial role as an alternative asset class for institutional investors, hence becoming an imperative risk diversification mechanism. Besides offering high expected rate of returns, commodity assets also offer important risk management advantages since commodity assets are typically negatively correlated with each other and with other assets classes (Satyanarayan and Varangis, 1994). However, commodities have recently show positive correlations to stock markets, and accordingly they are fundamentally used in active and passive portfolio management practices (Al Janabi, 2009).

On the other hand, commodity risk management has gained less devotion from researchers and that is why it is still in its early stages compared to

[1]The price risk of commodity assets is often more complicated and volatile than that related with interest rates, common stocks and currencies. In addition, commodity markets may well be less liquid than other financial markets, and thus fluctuations in supply and demand forces can have a remarkable influence on asset prices and volatility. As a result, the traits of these markets can make the application of price transparency and effective hedging of commodity risk much more challenging (Al Janabi, 2009).

the more established interest rates, stocks, and foreign exchange financial markets (Weron, 2000; Bartram, 2005). In fact, modeling market risk for commodity assets therefore poses an intrinsic complexity owing to the intense interaction among the trading of the commodity products and the supply and demand discrepancies that result from the conditions of the economy (Al Janabi, 2009; Giot and Laurent, 2003).[2] Therefore, the growth in tradability of commodities assets in emerging and developed markets demands a reassessment of existing commodity price risk management methods (Satyanarayan and Varangis, 1994), especially for commodity investment funds with large active trading portfolios — of both long and short-sales trading positions or merely long-only positions — and within short-to-medium horizons of rebalancing and risk reporting focuses.

In spite of the growing position of commodity markets, there is very little published research in this regard, and above all within the commodity trading risk management context. Given the general interest and acceptance of value-at-risk (VaR) method within the financial risk management community, VaR has the capability of being a useful risk measure for energy and agricultural risk management too. Therefore, it is necessary to gain an understanding of how traditional VaR estimation techniques operate in the context of commodity prices (Manfredo and Leuthold, 2001) and its practical implementation for commodity portfolios.

In commodity markets, the estimation of volatility and management of associated risks is a fairly new area of research, and only a few research papers deal with this particular topic (Bartram, 2005). For instance, applying VaR models to measuring crude oil price volatility and associated risks is a field that is only starting to draw the attention of researchers. Nonetheless, commodity price volatility and dynamics have been studied, among others, in works of Giot and Laurent (2003) and Manfredo and Leuthold (1999, 2001).

[2]Given that unexpected price changes are fundamentally determined by supply and demand imbalances, market participants in commodity markets basically place emphasis and focus on economic models that relate supply and demand forces to fundamental market variables. Together with the price deviations that stem from fundamental supply and demand discrepancies, commodity price volatility can initiate from the speculative activities of some market participants. As such, those traders many involve in short-term speculation operations, such as the short-selling of commodity futures contracts — if a bear market is anticipated in the very near future — or else building up stocks of commodities in expectation of a future rise in prices. Furthermore, commodity markets are strongly affected by: (1) storage limitations, (2) convenience yield, (3) physical substance, and (4) seasonality effects.

Against this backdrop and to deal with the above shortcomings, this chapter reviews and examines the use of a liquidity-adjusted value-at-risk (LVaR) technique (that was recently expanded by Al Janabi (2012)[3]) in the context of commodity assets under normal and adverse market settings.[4] As such, the overall goal of this chapter is to review and examine the risk characteristics of a large commodity portfolio, which contains quite a few crude oil and energy dataset along with other common commodities, in addition to exploring an optimization algorithm for the estimation of efficient and coherent commodity portfolios.[5] To this end, we review the implementation of a general trading risk model that accounts for the characteristics of the series of commodity price returns and effectively forecasts the market risk within a short-to-medium-term time horizon. As such, our focus on a short-to-medium-term time horizon is consistent with the application of a pure risk management process in which an economic model would be of little help in relation to short-to-medium-term risk estimations (Giot and Laurent, 2003). Likewise, it is possible to deal with the issue of non-normality for commodities assets with: (1) the ordinary implementation of a parametric LVaR process; (2) along with the incorporation of a sound stress-testing technique; (3) as well as improving the risk assessment process with a reasonable liquidity risk multiplier that takes into consideration real-world trading situations (Al Janabi, 2010, 2011).

[3]In his research paper, Al Janabi (2012) ("Optimal Commodity Asset Allocation with a Coherent Market Risk Modeling", *Review of Financial Economics*, Vol. 21, No. 3, pp. 131–140) has investigated and applied similar optimization algorithm for commodity markets. While his general optimization elements and parameters are adapted herein, this review chapter builds on Al Janabi's (2012) research paper and differs in the sense that it includes detailed methodological approach and research design that can be accessible to market practitioners, particularly commodity fund management services. This review chapter also includes in-depth analysis, discussion, and justification of the LVaR technique as well as further considerations and recommendation for possible practical applications.

[4]Some relatively recent literature examined the issue of liquidity risk and particularly the use of LVaR for the assessment of risk exposures in foreign exchange and stock markets portfolios. For the sake of presenting this chapter within a manageable size, these studies were not included within the literature review. However, for further details of previous approaches on asset liquidity risk and conventional LVaR methods, one can refer to Jarrow and Subramanian (1997), Almgren and Chriss (1999), Bangia *et al.* (1999), Berkowitz (2000), and Angelidis and Benos (2006).

[5]In this chapter, the concept of coherent (or investable) market portfolios refers to rational commodity portfolios that are subject to meaningful financial and operational constraints. In this sense, coherent market portfolios do not lie on the efficient frontiers as defined by Markowitz (1952), but instead have logical and well-structured long/short asset allocation proportions.

The remainder of the chapter proceeds as follows. Section 2 outlines the methodological approach, provides concise theoretical foundations of LVaR techniques, and highlights the required input parameters for quantitative risk analysis and optimization algorithms. Section 3 includes full discussion on the research design and method validation. This section also discusses and analyses the various parameters required for the optimization engine and the construction of efficient and coherent portfolios for two different case studies, that is long and short-sales positions and long-only portfolio positions. Section 4 includes concluding remarks along with possible practical applications of the posed technique.

2. Methodological Approach and Concise Theoretical Foundations[6]

In this review chapter, we discuss a model for optimizing portfolio risk-return with LVaR constraints using realistic operational and financial scenarios. Essentially, our proposed approach is a robust enhancement of the classic Markowitz (1952) mean-variance approach, where the original risk measure (variance) is replaced by LVaR algorithms. The task is accomplished here by minimizing LVaR, while demanding minimum expected returns subject to enforcing several financial and operational meaningful constraints under adverse market backgrounds. As a result, by allowing for different expected returns, we can generate an optimal LVaR frontier under adverse crisis outlooks. On the other hand, we can also maximize expected returns while not allowing for large exposure of risks.

Set against this background and to maximize its utility as a selective portfolio management method, we have constructed the tool such that the proposed risk-engine and robust scenario optimization algorithms proceed according to the following steps:

Methodological Step (1): In this first step, we attempt to outline a non-linear objective function (i.e., dynamic risk-function) of multivariable. For this purpose, the non-linear objective function can be defined as a vector of: (1) closeout periods or unwinding periods of each commodity asset class and the overall closeout periods of investable portfolios; (2) monetary investment in each commodity asset class; (3) overall trading volume of investible commodity portfolios; (4) downside risk constraints so

[6]Note: The methodological approach and related theoretical foundations are largely drawn from Al Janabi (2012, 2013, 2014) research papers.

that additional risk resulting from any non-normality and illiquid assets may be used to estimate the characteristics of investable commodity portfolios; (5) constrained commodity asset allocation proportions according to contemporary financial markets regulations and subject to the imposition of rational and meaningful operational and financial boundaries; (6) expected returns of investable commodity portfolios; (7) correlation coefficients among all commodity asset classes; (8) portfolio managers' choices of long-only commodity asset positions or a combination of long-short-sales trading asset positions; (9) confidence level of estimated parameters under different scenarios and market settings.

Against this backdrop, the objective risk function is outlined and clarified along these lines:

For multiple trading assets, the LVaR of a portfolio of commodity assets is a function of the individual risk of each asset, holding period (closeout or liquidation horizon), and the correlation factors[7] $[\rho_{i,j}]$ between the returns of the different commodities, as follows (Al Janabi, 2012, 2013, 2014):

$$\mathrm{LVaR}_{P_{adj}} = \sqrt{\sum_{i=1}^{n}\sum_{j=1}^{n} \mathrm{LVaR}_{i_{adj}}\,\mathrm{LVaR}_{j_{adj}}\,\rho_{i,j}} = \sqrt{[\mathrm{LVaR}_{adj}]^{T}[\rho][\mathrm{LVaR}_{adj}]}. \tag{1}$$

Indeed, Eq. (1) considers adverse price impact liquidity risk throughout the closeout period. As a result, the assumption of a given closeout horizon for orderly liquidation inevitably implies that commodity assets' liquidation occurs during the holding period. Accordingly, scaling the holding period to account for orderly liquidation can be justified if one allows the commodity assets to be liquidated throughout the closeout period. In order to perform the calculation of LVaR under accurate illiquid market circumstances, we

[7]Furthermore, three matrices of correlations can possibly be used for the assessment of LVaR, namely $\rho = 1$, 0, and empirical correlations. The objectives here are to establish the necessary quantitative infrastructures for advanced risk management analysis. Indeed, the assembled correlation matrices are essential parameters along with conditional volatility vectors for the calculations of LVaR, stress-testing, and LVaR of optimal and investable portfolios. As a result, these matrices and vectors can be integrated into the LVaR's engine to estimate optimal and investable portfolios under the notion of different unwinding horizon periods and for both long-only and/or a combination of varied long-short-sales assets trading positions (that is, by disallowing both pure long positions and borrowing constraints).

can define the following throughout the closeout period:

$$\mathrm{LVaR}_{i_{adj}} = \mathrm{VaR}_i \sqrt{\frac{(2t_i + 1)(t_i + 1)}{6t_i}} \tag{2}$$

where VaR_i is value-at-risk of commodity asset i under liquid market conditions; $\mathrm{LVaR}_{i\,adj}$ is value-at-risk of commodity asset i under illiquid market conditions; and t_i is number of trading days required for orderly liquidation of asset i. Moreover, the latter equation indicates that $\mathrm{LVaR}_{i\,adj} > \mathrm{VaR}_i$; however, when the required number of days to liquidate the entire commodity assets is one trading day, then we have a special case in which $\mathrm{LVaR}_{i\,adj} = \mathrm{VaR}_i$. Consequently, the difference between $\mathrm{LVaR}_{i\,adj} - \mathrm{VaR}_i$ should equal the residual market risk due to the illiquidity of commodity asset_i under adverse markets outlooks. Furthermore, it is imperative to note that Eq. (2) can be used for the assessment of LVaR for any time horizon subject to applying a bounding constraint on the total LVaR figure. In fact, the overall resultant LVaR figure should not exceed in any setting the nominal exposure, or in other words the total trading volume of the commodity portfolio.

In essence, the above liquidity scaling factor (or multiplier) is more realistic and less conservative than the conventional root-t multiplier and can aid commodity entities in allocating reasonable and liquidity market-driven regulatory and economic capital requirements. Furthermore, the above mathematical formulas can be applied for the calculation of LVaR for every commodity asset trading position and for the entire portfolio of commodity assets.

As a matter of fact, the number of liquidation days or closeout time (t_i) necessary to liquidate the entire position of asset i fully is related to the choice of the liquidity threshold; however, the size of this threshold is likely to change under severe markets conditions. Effectively, a linear liquidation procedure of assets is assumed in Eq. (2), i.e., selling equal parts of each commodity asset every day until the last trading day (t_i), where the entire asset is sold. The above model is more appropriate for daily trading circumstances where traders can unwind part of their positions on a daily basis.

Indeed, the choice of liquidation horizon can be estimated from the total trading position size and the daily trading volume of commodities that can be unwound into the market without significantly disrupting market prices, and in actual practice it is generally estimated as:

$$t_i = \text{Total trading position size of commodity asset}_i/\text{Average trading volume of commodity asset}_i \text{ during certain historical period.} \tag{3}$$

As such, the close out time (t_i) is the time required to bring the positions to a state where the commodity entity can make no further loss from the trading positions. It is either the time taken to sell the long commodity positions or alternatively the time required to buy commodities in case of short positions. In real practice, the daily trading volume of any trading commodity asset is estimated as the average volume over some period of time, generally a month of trading activities. In effect, the daily trading volume of commodity assets can be regarded as the average daily volume or the volume that can be unwound under severe crisis periods.[8] The trading volume in a crisis period can be roughly approximated as the average daily trading volume less a number of standard deviations. Although this alternative approach is quite simple, it is still relatively objective. Moreover, it is reasonably easy to gather the required data to perform the necessary liquidation scenarios.

Against this backdrop, we can now define VaR_i for single asset positions. By and large, the absolute value of VaR_i for any single commodity asset can be defined in monetary terms as

$$\text{VaR}_i = |(\mu_{\text{i}} - \alpha * \sigma_i)[\text{Asset}_i * Fx_i]| \approx |\alpha * \sigma_i[\text{Asset}_i * Fx_i]| \tag{4}$$

where μ_i is the expected return of asset_i, α is the confidence level (or in other words, the standard normal variant at confidence level α), and σ_i is the forecasted standard deviation (or conditional volatility[9]) of the returns of asset_i. While the term Asset_i denotes the mark-to-market monetary value, Fx_i indicates the unit foreign exchange rate of commodity asset_i.[10] Without a loss of generality, we can assume that the expected value of daily commodity returns μ_i is close to zero. As such, though equation (4) includes some simplifying assumptions, yet researchers and practitioners in financial

---

[8]Thus, if trading volume is low because of a "one-way market," in that most people are seeking to sell rather than to buy, then (t_i) can rise substantially (Saunders and Cornett, 2008).

[9]Indeed, the time-varying pattern of assets volatility has been widely recognized and modeled as a conditional variance within the GARCH framework, as originally developed by Engle (1982, 1995). Engle (1982) introduced a likelihood ratio test to ARCH effects and a maximum likelihood method to estimate the parameters in the ARCH model. This approach was generalized by Bollerslev (1986) and Engle and Kroner (1995). In fact, the generalized autoregressive conditional heteroskedasticity in mean, GARCH-M (1,1) model, is used in this empirical analysis for the estimation of expected return and conditional volatility for each of the time series variables.

[10]If the purpose of the risk analysis is to investigate diverse commodity dependences and related risk management measure, then $Asset_i$ should be the mark-to-market prices of the individual commodities.

and commodities markets routinely use it for the estimation of VaR for any single trading position.

Methodological Step (2): In the second stage, we define the corresponding robust scenario optimization algorithm that is based on quadratic programming techniques, subject to applying meaningful financial and operational constraints. Furthermore, in the development of portfolio investment policy there are many types of constraints that can be considered as an integral part of the optimization process. These constraints are drawn from rational financial investment considerations and can be used in various applications to bound percentiles of loss distributions, and it can include constraints on the asset classes that are allowable and concentration limits on investments. Moreover, in making the asset allocation decision, consideration must be given to any risk-based capital requirements. For this objective, the scenario optimization algorithms can be defined as a minimization algorithmic process of the dynamic objective risk function. The optimization process is achieved through rigorous algorithms according to the following steps:

(1) The minimization process is attained here by minimizing the objective risk function while requiring minimum expected returns subject to enforcing several rational and meaningful financial and operational constraints;
(2) As a minimum, the bounding limits may include the following: (a) total volume of the investable commodity portfolio; (b) the target investable commodity portfolio's expected returns; (c) portfolio managers' choices of long-only commodity positions or a combination of long-short-sales trading positions; (d) monetary asset allocation of each commodity asset class; (e) closeout or unwinding liquidity horizons of each commodity asset class.

For the objective of this study, the optimization problem is formulated as follows:

From Eq. (2), we can define liquidation horizon factor (LHF_i) for each commodity asset as

$$\text{LHF}_i = \sqrt{\frac{(2t_i + 1)(t_i + 1)}{6t_i}} \geq 1.0;\ \forall_i \quad i = 1, 2, \ldots, n. \tag{5}$$

After substituting Eq. (5) into Eq. (1), we can now compute the minimum portfolio downside risk by solving the following nonlinear quadratic algorithm (objective function) under adverse and illiquid market outlooks

$$\begin{aligned}\text{Minimize}: \mathrm{LVaR}_{P_{adj}} &= \sqrt{\sum_{i=1}^{n}\sum_{j=1}^{n} \mathrm{LVaR}_{i_{adj}}\,\mathrm{LVaR}_{j_{adj}}\,\rho_{i,j}} \\ &= \sqrt{[\mathrm{LVaR}_{adj}]^T[\rho][\mathrm{LVaR}_{adj}]}. \end{aligned} \tag{6}$$

The above objective function can be minimized conditional on satisfying the following operational and financial budget constraints as specified by the commodity portfolio manager:

$$\sum_{i=1}^{n} R_i x_i = R_P;\ l_i \le x_i \le u_i \quad i = 1, 2, \ldots, n, \tag{7}$$

$$\sum_{i=1}^{n} x_i = 1.0;\ l_i \le x_i \le u_i \quad i = 1, 2, \ldots, n, \tag{8}$$

$$\sum_{i=1}^{n} V_i = V_P \quad i = 1, 2, \ldots, n. \tag{9}$$

$$|LHF| \ge 1.0;\ \forall_i \quad i = 1, 2, \ldots, n \tag{10}$$

Here, R_P and V_P denote the target portfolio mean expected return and total commodity portfolio volume, respectively, and x_i indicates the weight or percentage asset allocation for each commodity asset. The values l_i and $u_i, i = 1, 2, \ldots, n$, denote the lower and upper constraints for the commodity portfolio weights x_i. If we choose $l_i = 0, i = 1, 2, \ldots, n$, then we have the situation where no short-sales are allowed. Moreover, |LHF| indicates an $(n \times 1)$ liquidity risk factor vector for all $i = 1, 2, \ldots, n$.

Now the commodity portfolio manager can specify different liquidity horizon and correlation factors and calculate the necessary LVaR to sustain the trading operation of the commodity entity without subjecting the entity to insolvency matters. The rationality behind imposing the above constraints is to comply with current regulations (e.g., Basel III capital accord) which enforce capital requirements on investment companies, proportional to their LVaR and economic capital, besides other operational limits (for instance, volume trading limits).

Methodological Step (3): In this final phase, we validate and compare the output results of investable commodity portfolios obtained in Step (2) with the optimal commodity portfolios defined in Step (1). To this end, we attempt to rerun the optimization engine until a new convergence to meaningful investable commodity portfolios is attained. At this stage, new investable portfolios with coherent commodity asset allocation structures that satisfy the boundary conditions defined in Step (2) are accomplished accordingly.

The below graphical flowchart illustrates a summarized view of the three methodological steps and their interrelationships.

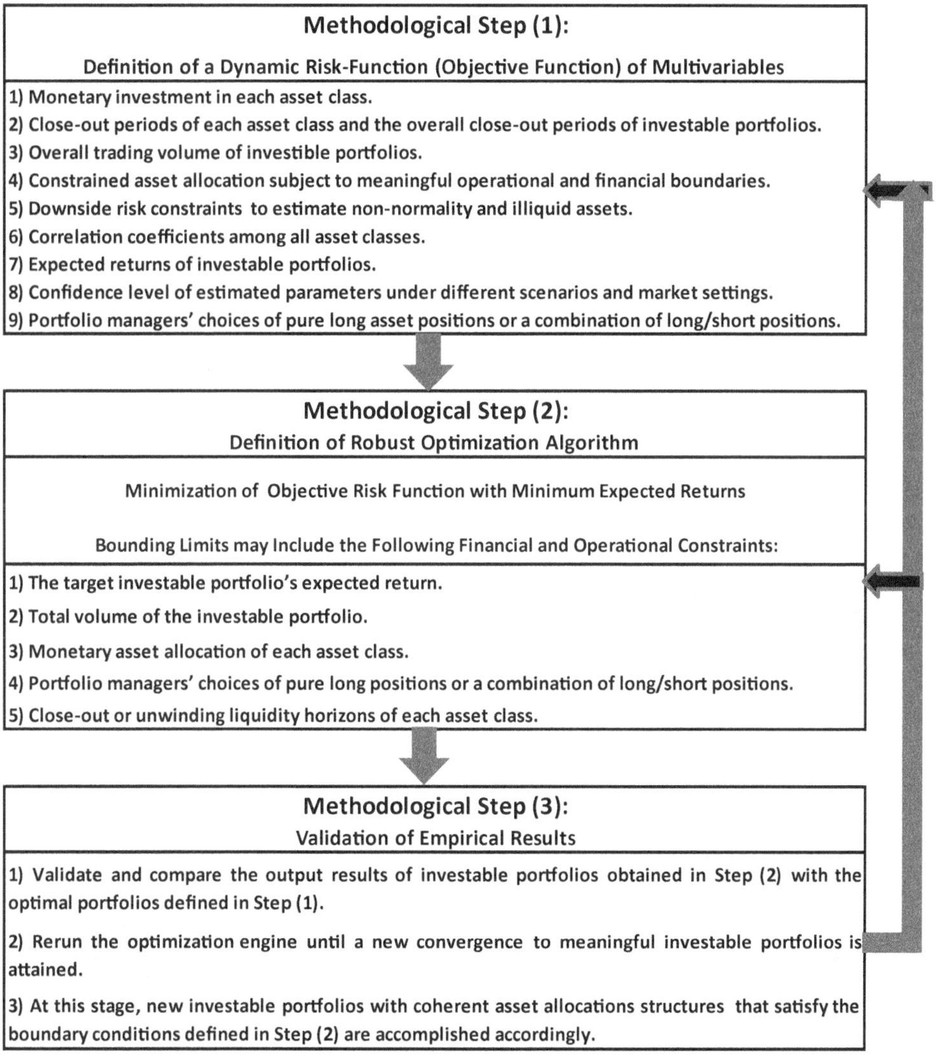

3. Research Design and Method Validation

3.1. *Optimization of efficient and investable (coherent) commodity portfolios–case study of long and short-sales positions*

Against this backdrop, one example where the application of the method development aspect of LVaR is useful is in its implementation for commodity portfolios and asset management services at large. As such, the above developed methodology is applied to a diverse portfolio of 25 commodities, including:

(1) Energy (Petroleum: average crude price, Dubai, West Texas Intermediate, and UK Brent; gasoline; natural gas; coal),
(2) metals (gold, silver, copper, zinc, lead, aluminum, nickel, iron ore, phosphate rock),
(3) agriculture (wheat, cotton, sugar, maize, tobacco, coffee, tea), and
(4) other miscellaneous commodities (rubber, wool).[11]

As such, Figures 1 and 2 provide evidence of the empirical LVaR efficient frontier (under normal and severe market settings) defined using a 97.5% confidence level. In this case, the optimal portfolio selection is performed by relaxing the short-sale constraint for the different commodity assets. On the other hand, efficient portfolios cannot always be attained (e.g., short sales without realistic lower boundaries on x_i) in the day-to-day real-world portfolio management operations, and hence portfolio managers should establish proactive "coherent investable portfolios" under more realistic and restricted budget constraints.[12]

[11]For further details on the applied time series dataset (of 20 years of monthly time series) and empirical testing, refer Al Janabi's [2012] research paper. Furthermore, all figures presented in this section and quantitative analyses of empirical results are drawn from Al Janabi's [2012] paper.

[12]In fact, there is no readily available time series database on the liquidity of different commodity markets. However, as indicated in Eq. (3) this can be estimated from the specific daily (or monthly) trading volume of any commodity on a certain date and the historical average trading volume of that commodity for a certain period of time (for instance, the average daily/monthly trading volume for the last six months). In the real world of financial/commodity markets, the number of days/months required to unwind a trading position can be assessed intuitively by individual traders, based on their daily experience of how much volume of each commodity asset they can liquidate (closeout) into the market without disturbing market prices. For our purpose of introducing a robust portfolio management methodology to a diverse portfolio of 25 commodities, the monthly liquidation horizon for each commodity are included in parenthesis as follows:

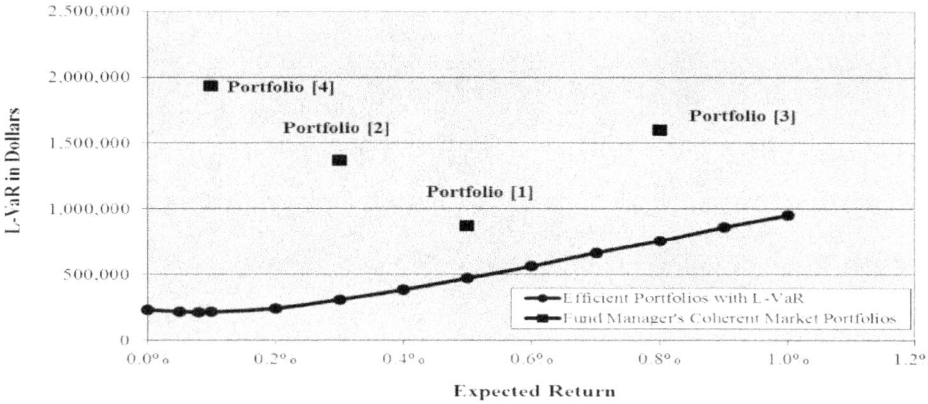

Figure 1. Efficient and Coherent Portfolios Under Normal Market Conditions (Case of Long and Short Trading Positions)

Notes: This figure Demonstrates the empirical LVaR efficient frontier and "coherent investable portfolios" under normal market scenarios by relaxing short-sale constraints. As indicated, the four-benchmark coherent investable portfolios [1], [2], [3], and [4]) are not located near the efficient frontier because real-world realities make it less likely that a structured portfolio behaves accurately as theory expects. This figure is designed by the author.

Source: Al Janabi (2012) research paper.

In this first case study, the weights are allowed to take negative or positive values; however, since arbitrarily high or low percentages have no financial sense, we determined the introduction of lower and upper boundaries for the weights in accordance with reasonable trading practices. Accordingly, it is interesting to note here that the four benchmark portfolios (investable (coherent) portfolios [1], [2], [3] and [4]) are not positioned near the efficient

---

(1) energy (Petroleum: average crude price [1.2], Dubai [1.2], West Texas Intermediate [1.2], and UK Brent [1.2]; Gasoline [1.3]; Natural Gas [1.4]; Coal [1.5]),

(2) metals (gold [1.2], silver [1.5], copper [1.7], zinc [2.0], lead [2.5], aluminum [1.5], nickel [2.5], iron ore [1.8], phosphate rock [3.0]),

(3) agriculture (wheat [1.5], cotton [1.8], sugar [1.7], maize [2.0], tobacco [3.0], coffee [1.6], tea [1.7]), and

(4) other miscellaneous commodities (rubber [3.0], wool [2.0]).

Furthermore, it is possible to run the optimization engine in such a way to determine the optimal number of days/months for liquidation (threshold) by building a portfolio where one can specify the required asset allocations for each asset, expected return of the portfolio, risk parameters for each asset, and any other operational and financial constraints the portfolio manager would like to enforce on the portfolio and then solve for the optimal liquidation thresholds that can minimize the objective function with all its boundaries.

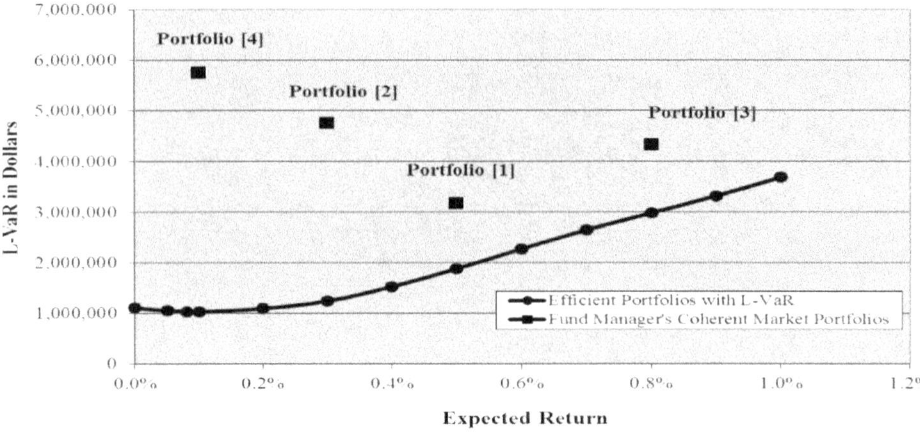

Figure 2. Efficient and Coherent Portfolios Under Severe Market Conditions (Case of Long and Short Trading Positions)

Notes: This figure shows the empirical LVaR efficient frontier and "coherent investable portfolios" under severe market scenarios by relaxing short-sale constraints. As indicated, the four-benchmark coherent investable portfolios [1], [2], [3], and [4]) are not located near the efficient frontier because real-world realities make it less likely that a structured portfolio behaves accurately as theory expects. This figure is designed by the author.

Source: Al Janabi (2012) research paper.

frontier as indicated in Figures 1 and 2, respectively. This is because real-world considerations make it unlikely that a trading portfolio will behave exactly as theory predicts. Imperfections such as restriction on the asset allocation of long and short trading positions, total trading volume, and liquidation closeout (or unwinding) horizons make it unlikely to create an efficient trading portfolio. Thus, this analysis and the implemented LVaR algorithm permit one to determine the asymmetric aspect of risk, and, as such, it is a substantial improvement on the classical Markowitz's (1952) mean–variance approach (Al Janabi, 2012).

3.2. *Optimization of efficient and investable (coherent) commodity portfolios — case study of long-only positions*

For the sake of comparison of the first empirical optimization procedure with another real-world operational constraint, a second optimization process is carried out; however, this time it is done by considering long-only trading positions and by imposing a restriction on short-sales of commodities. Similarly, in this second study, the optimization process is based on the definition of LVaR as the minimum possible loss over a specified time horizon within a given confidence level. The optimization technique solves

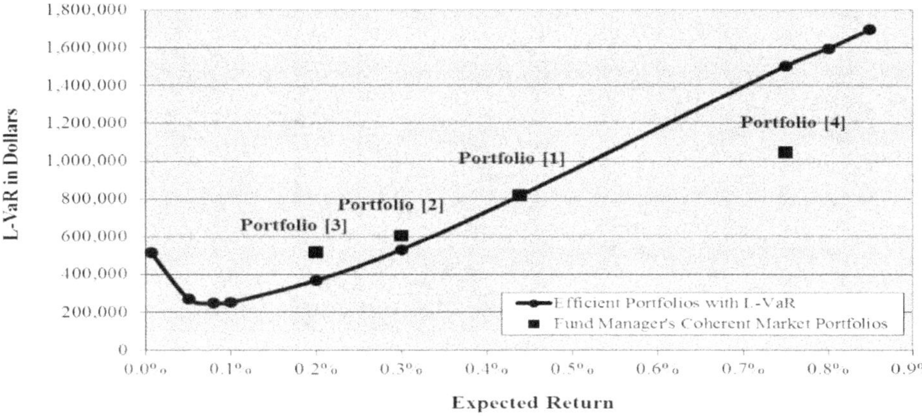

Figure 3. Efficient and Coherent Portfolios Under Normal Market Conditions (Case of Long Trading Positions)

Notes: This figure displays the empirical LVaR efficient frontier and "coherent investable portfolios" under normal market scenarios by enforcing a short-sales excluding constraint (i.e., long-only trading positions). As indicated, the four-benchmark coherent investable portfolios [1], [2], [3], and [4]) are located near the efficient frontier. It seems that for long-only commodity positions, it is likely that the performance of efficient and coherent investable portfolios are close to each other, while this was not the case for long and short positions as indicated in this figure. This figure is designed by the author.

Source: Al Janabi (2012) research paper.

the problem by finding the market long-only trading commodity positions that minimize the loss, subject to the fact that all constraints are satisfied within their boundary values. As such, Figures 3 and 4 provide evidence of the empirical LVaR efficient frontier (under normal and severe market settings) defined using a 97.5% confidence level. As indicated above, the optimal portfolio selection is performed by enforcing a short-sales prohibition constraint, for the different commodity assets.

In this particular case study, the weights are allowed to take only positive values; however, since arbitrarily high or low positive weights could have no financial investment sense, we determined the introduction of lower and upper boundaries for the weights and in accordance with reasonable trading practices. As a result, it is interesting to note here that the four-benchmark portfolios (coherent investable portfolios [1], [2], [3], and [4]) are located near the efficient frontier as indicated in Figures 3 and 4, respectively. As discussed above, it seems that this optimization phenomenon could not be attained for a combination of long- and short trading positions because real-world considerations make it unlikely that a trading portfolio will behave exactly as theory predicts; however, for long-only commodity trading

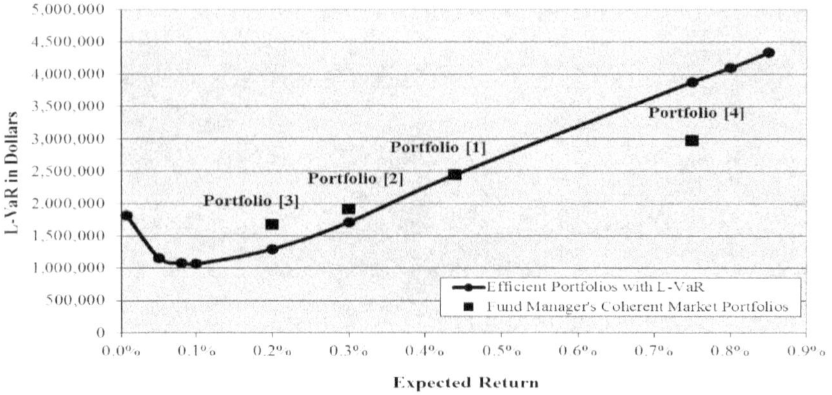

Figure 4. Efficient and Coherent Portfolios Under Severe Market Conditions (Case of Long Trading Positions)

Notes: This figure depicts the empirical LVaR efficient frontier and "coherent investable portfolios" under severe market scenarios by enforcing a short-sales excluding constraint (i.e., long-only trading positions). As indicated, the four-benchmark coherent investable portfolios [1], [2], [3], and [4]) are located near the efficient frontier. It seems that for long-only commodity positions, it is likely that the performance of efficient and coherent investable portfolios are close to each other, while this was not the case for long and short positions as indicated in this figure. This figure is designed by the author.

Source: Al Janabi (2012) research paper.

positions, it seems that it is possible to match more closely the performance of efficiences with coherent investable portfolios. Moreover, it is important to note here that incorporating the above realistic and restricted budget constraints into the portfolio manager's operational process has caused that coherent portfolio [4] to be more coherent (or super-efficient) than other efficient portfolios allocated on the efficient frontier. Thus, it seems that by incorporating the liquidity holding periods and other operational constraints into the constrained optimization function, commodity portfolio managers could apply active trading strategies in order to earn excess returns that could be, one way or another, beyond what the classical mean-variance efficient-frontier indicates (Al Janabi, 2012).

4. Concluding Remarks and Possible Practical Applications

This review chapter fills a fundamental gap in assets price risk management and optimal portfolio selection literatures by contributing a thorough reflection on trading risk modeling with a dynamic asset allocation process and under the supposition of illiquid and adverse market settings. Moreover, in this chapter, the author develops a portfolio selection model and an optimization algorithm that allocates commodity assets by minimizing the LVaR subject to applying credible operational and financial constraints based on fundamental asset management considerations. The proposed optimization algorithm demonstrates that better investable portfolios can be obtained than using the traditional Markowitz (1952) portfolio theory. The results show that the obtained investable portfolios lie off the efficient frontier, but that long-only portfolios appear to lie much closer to the frontier than portfolios including both long- and short-sales positions. The empirical optimization results indicate that this alternate LVaR technique can be regarded as a robust portfolio management tool and can have many uses and applications in real-world asset management practices and predominantly for fund managers with large commodity portfolios.

The presented methodology and empirical results of this review chapter can have important practical uses and applications for commodity trading entities, financial institutions, risk managers, portfolio managers, regulators, and policymakers operating in both developed and emerging markets, particularly in the wake of the most recent financial crisis. For instance, risk managers and portfolio managers for the assessment of appropriate asset allocations of different structured investable commodity portfolios can use the proposed modeling technique and simulation algorithms. In fact, the proposed optimization algorithm has the potential of producing realistic risk return profiles and may improve real-world understanding of embedded risks and asymmetric microstructure patterns and could potentially create better investable portfolios for commodity portfolio managers. Finally, the modeling framework can be constructive as well for financial service industries in developed and emerging economies, particularly in reinforcing rational economic capital allocation in light of the aftermath of the sub-prime financial crisis.

References

Al Janabi, M. A. M. (2012). Optimal commodity asset allocation with a coherent market risk modeling. *Rev. Finan. Econom.*, 21, pp. 131–140.

Al Janabi, M. A. M. (2013). Optimal and coherent economic-capital structures: Evidence from long and short-sales trading positions under illiquid market perspectives. *Ann. Oper. Res.*, 205, pp. 109–139.

Al Janabi, M. A. M. (2014). Optimal and investable portfolios: An empirical analysis with scenario optimization algorithms under crisis market prospects. *Econom. Modell.*, 40, pp. 369–381.

Bartram, S. (2005). The impact of commodity price risk on firm value an empirical analysis of corporate commodity price exposures. *Multinat. Fin. J.*, 9, pp. 161–187.

Bollerslev, T. (1986). Generalized autoregressive conditional heteroskedasticity. *J. Econometr.*, 31, pp. 307–327.

Engle, R. F. (1995) *ARCH Selected Readings, Advanced Texts in Econometrics.* (Oxford: Oxford University Press).

Engle, R. F. and Kroner K. (1995). Multivariate simultaneous generalized ARCH. *Econometr. Theory,* 11, pp. 122–150.

Engle, R. F. (1982). Autoregressive conditional heteroskedasticity. *Econometrica*, 50, pp. 987–1008.

Giot, P. and Laurent, S. (2003). Market risk in commodity markets: A VaR approach. *Energy Econom.*, 25, pp. 435–457.

Manfredo, M. and Leuthold, R. (2001). Market risk and the cattle feeding margin: An application of value-at-risk. *Agribusiness: An Int. J.*, 17, pp. 333–353.

Manfredo, M. and Leuthold, R. (1999). Value-at-risk analysis: A review and the potential for agricultural applications. *Rev. Agricul. Econom.*, 21, pp. 99–111.

Markowitz, H. (1952). Portfolio selection. *J. Fin.*, 7, pp. 77–91.

Satyanarayan, S. and Varangis, P. (1994). An efficient frontier for international portfolios with commodity assets, Policy Research Working Paper, WPS 1266, The World Bank, International Economics Department, International Trade Division, Washington, DC.

Saunders, A. and Cornett, M. (2008). *Financial Institutions Management*, 6th edn. Singapore: McGraw Hill International Edition.

Weron, R. (2000). Energy price risk management. *Physica A*, 285, pp. 127–134.

Chapter 11

Low Carbon Indexing and Correlation Indices: Implications for Portfolio Management

Julien Chevallier

Université Paris 8 (LED), 2 avenue de la Liberté,
93526 Saint-Denis cedex, France
IPAG Business School (IPAG Lab),
184 boulevard Saint-Germain,
75006 Paris, France
julien.chevallier@ipag.fr

Abstract

This chapter deals with the construction of a tracker of low carbon index (such as the MSCI low carbon) and its performance in a portfolio management application. The tracker is built from raw data with PCA, factor detection, and DCC models techniques. The portfolio application is a standard Markowitz application with and without the desired low carbon index. The data is composed of financial data in addition to commodities. Another related topic is discussed in the chapter, i.e., the performance of correlation indices (constructed similarly to the low carbon index but in a DCC framework) with respect to financial stress on the market (proxied by the St Louis Fed Stress Index). The "horse race" concerns the correlation index built from our methodology versus its main competitor the VIX correlation index. Key results include that the PCA–DCC technique is easily reproducible and efficient to construct a tracker of the targeted index at the least cost for the financial advisor (e.g., no subscription fee).

1. Introduction

Climate change has wide-ranging impacts on human lives throughout the world. According to a World Bank report by Fay *et al.* (2015), global warming may trap into poverty up to 100 million people by 2030. The transition to a low-carbon economy has become a cornerstone of new environmental and development policies. A low-carbon economy is characterized by reduced electricity consumption, controlled emissions of pollutants, and especially a low carbon intensity of human-related production activities. This societal shift calls for changes of paradigms as well as tremendous energy innovations. The Stern Review (2007) has documented that the costs of inaction with regard to climate change could add up to 20% of the world's GDP, compared with only 1% if decisive action is enacted. The Nobel prize winner IPCC (2007) has underlined as well the GDP losses that could occur due to global warming, ranging from 4% in 2030 to 12% in 2100.

Against this background, the financial industry attempts to develop new low-carbon indexes that select only a subset of companies with a reduced environmental impact (i.e., reduced energy consumption or explicit reduction in greenhouse gases emissions) to reduce long-term risks. To name a few, Merrill Lynch has launched in 2008 the MLCX Global CO_2 Emissions Index in 2008. Meanwhile, S&P has proposed in 2009 the S&P US Carbon Efficient Index that measures the performance of a large sample of US companies with a low carbon footprint. WilderHill has created a pure-play Clean Energy Index by including stocks based on their significance for clean energy, technological influence, and relevance to pollution prevention. However, the construction of such indexes appears as a 'black box', once the user has read the abbreviated white papers available for public use.

This chapter is devoted to the analysis of Low Carbon indexes with practical applications to portfolio management. To cope with the 'black-box' drawback of existing indexes, the empirical study is based on the replication of the MSCI low carbon index, by means of principal component analysis (PCA) and factor modelling. Therefore, the construction of the low carbon tracker index is entirely transparent and data-driven. Then, its performance is assessed by comparing the performance of Markowitz mean–variance portfolios with and without the low carbon tracker index. To further assess its robustness, the portfolio with low carbon asset is tested in a cointegration framework.

International stock markets being highly integrated (Chan *et al.*, 1997; Bracker *et al.*, 1999), another area of research in this chapter is related to correlation dynamics. Indeed, the growth process entails an increase in correlation between stock markets. For portfolio managers, inter-sectoral correlations are less prevalent, and therefore greater diversification can be achieved by relying on sectoral indices.

Correlation indices have gained momentum in the financial industry thanks to option prices (Driessen *et al.*, 2009). Moreover, the Chicago Board of Exchange (CBOE) has developed correlation indicators as part of its broad array of financial data available to the public, based on implied correlation on the S&P 500, known as CBOE Implied Correlation Indexes (ICI). However, their use shall not be restricted to the sphere of derivatives, as several scholars have extended the concept of correlation risk to optimal portfolio choice (Krishnan *et al.*, 2009; Buraschi *et al.*, 2010).

In this chapter, we thoroughly check the correlation between low-carbon assets and traditional assets (equities, bonds, FX). Besides, we compare the performance of a cross-market correlation index (including explicitly low carbon assets) with that of the CBOE's ICI in predicting a broad measure of financial stress constructed by the St. Louis Fed.

This work relates to another strand of literature dedicated to future markets, where researchers typically aim at evaluating the diversification benefits of correlation indices by resorting to time-varying correlations and stress events studies (see, e.g., Lien and Yang, 2006; Park and Jei, 2010). More precisely, the correlation index literature is drawn from the options literature, as published by Skintzi and Refenes (2005). Only a few scholars have attempted to build correlation indices with standard closing prices for equities, bonds, FX, and commodities, i.e. from a cross-market perspective.

This chapter mixes several methodological tools (PCA and factor models) to construct a correlation index based on dynamic conditional correlations (including low carbon assets) to predict financial stress, very close in the spirit to the paper by Jobst *et al.* (2015). Last but not least, a 'horse race' is conducted between the new correlation index and that of the CBOE Implied Correlation index (from the S&P 500 options literature) in order to gauge their respective predictive power. Each empirical section has been approved by applying the necessary robustness checks.

Key results feature the usefulness of the proposed approach to construct trackers of the targeted index for each practitioner, instead of subscribing to costly 'black-box' index tracking methodologies. With respect to correlation indices, the VIX correlation cannot be easily outperformed, and so it is a serious contender for building dispersion trading strategies (Marshall, 2009) based on correlations.

The remainder of the chapter is structured as follows. Section 2 presents the methodology and dataset. Section 3 contains the empirical results. Section 4 concludes.

2. Methodology and Data

The motivation to build a tracker on the MSCI Low Carbon Index is to provide a transparent methodology to retrieve the weights of the index constituents (in percentage), absent experts' additions and being entirely data-driven. By following this methodology, the practitioner can then tailor a low carbon index suited to her/his own needs and activities.

2.1. *Dataset*

Data with a daily frequency has been extracted from Bloomberg during the period ranging from November 30, 2010 to January 1, 2015, i.e., totalling 1068 observations. The data is composed of 330 companies that are listed on the main stock exchanges (DJIA, CAC40, DAX, TSX, HSE, NIKKEI, MIB, and FTSE).

The companies were selected to match the sector and industry coverage of the MSCI Low Carbon index, as indicated in its methodology white paper [MSCI, 2014]. For instance, in our setting, the total health care sector represents 12.23% of the subset of companies. The financial sector captures 22.33% of the index, with 73 companies. Only 38 companies are selected from the industrial sector (11.67%), due to a selection of those industries with low-carbon activities only. These characteristics match those of the MSCI Low Carbon index. Further details are provided in Fig. 1.

2.2. *Methodology*

The econometric methodology to build the tracker unfolds in several steps as detailed below. Initially, we detail the successful replication of the MSCI low carbon index. Then, we explain how to construct correlation indices based on pairwise DCC estimates.

2.2.1. *Automatic choice detection for the number of factors*

The Alessi–Barigozzi–Capasso (ABC) criterion by Alessi *et al.* (2010) is implemented to determine the appropriate number of factors needed to extract principal components from the full database of 330 companies.

The result is displayed in Fig. 2.

Visually, we observe that at least five factors are needed to accurately model the dynamics of the underlying data. This number is rounded upward; therefore, six factors are selected during the course of the principal components extraction.

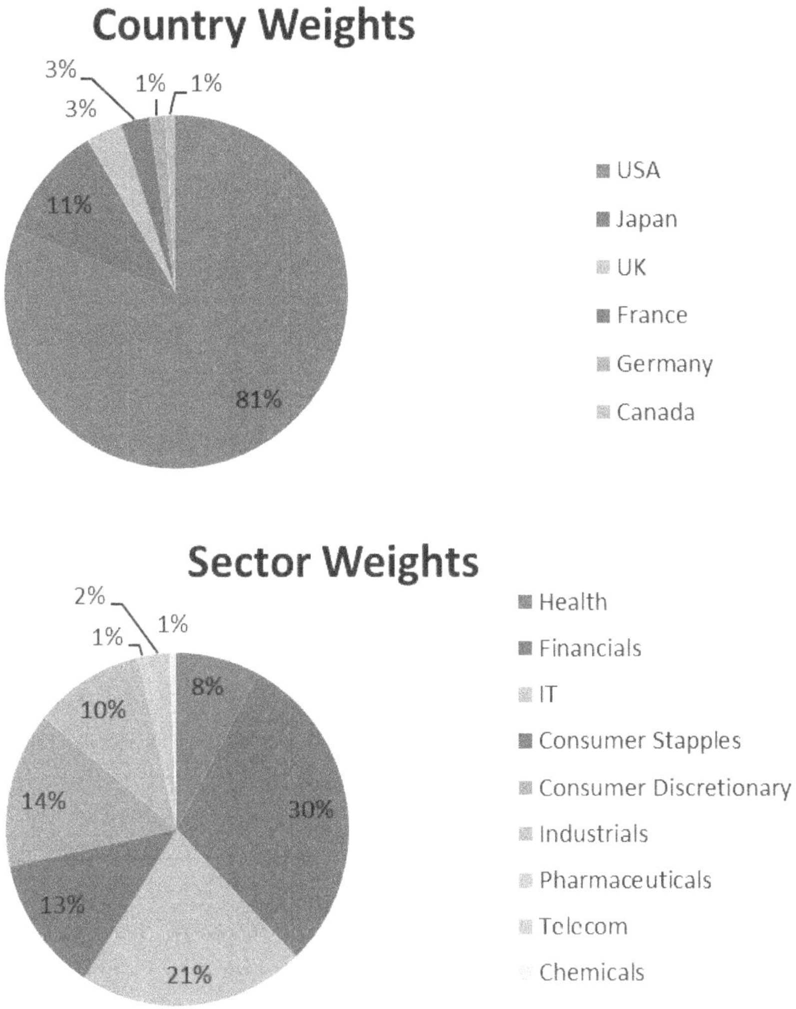

Figure 1. Country and Sector Weights of the MSCI Low Carbon Index Tracker

2.2.2. *Principal components analysis, factor modeling, and tracker construction*

PCA is run on the 330 companies with a choice of 6 factors. This computational procedure returns the weight of each company for each of the six factors (for a review, see Stock and Watson, (2002a, 2002b).

The contribution of a selected company to the tracker is computed based on its average weight across the six factors. In other words, we do not favor one factor over another (based on purely statistical grounds) and set their

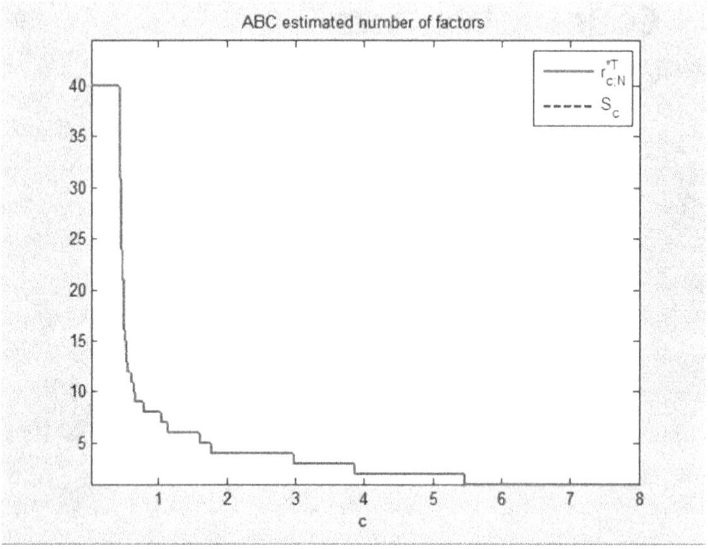

Figure 2. ABC Criterion Results for the Low Carbon Tracker Dataset

influence to be equal to construct the index tracker. The composition of the MSCI low carbon tracker index (in percentage terms) is reproduced in the appendix.

In Fig. 3, we represent the performance of the tracker against the MSCI Low Carbon as well as the leading international equity indexes S&P 500 and EuroStoxx 600.

Visually, these graphs reveal that our methodology has been able to successfully replicate the targeted MSCI Low Carbon index, since both series (the tracker and its MSCI counterpart) vary closely together. From November 30, 2010 to July 31, 2011, the tracker seems to under-represent the variations of the index. From 2012 until November 30, 2014, the tracker seems to slightly overshoot the behavior of the underlying index.

Interestingly, the tracker appears to also be moving closely in sync with the S&P 500, since we only notice one episode where the tracker moves away from it during November 2013. The comments are broadly similar with respect to the Eurostoxx 600: the two series move closely together, with the tracker being above the European equity index from September 30, 2011 to November 30, 2014.

Following these descriptive comments, we compute model validation statistics known as the excess returns (ER) and tracking errors (TE) in order to assess statistically the performance of the index replication exercise.

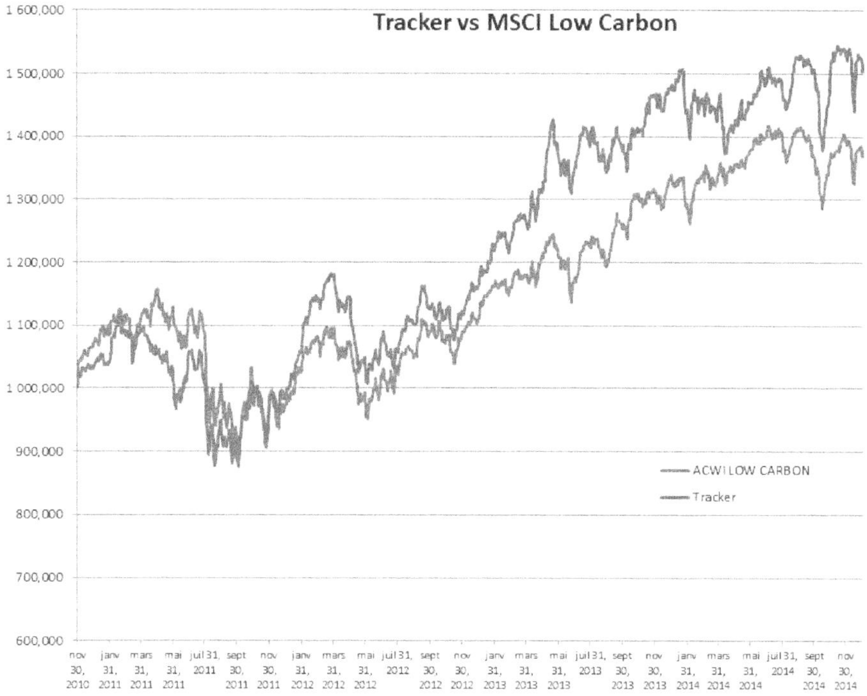

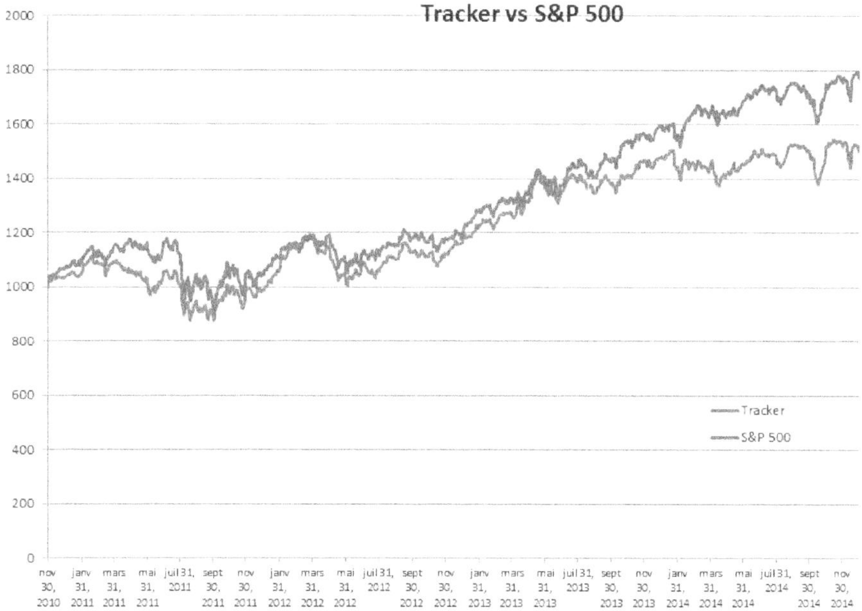

Figure 3. Tracker Represented versus the MSCI Low Carbon Index, as well as S&P500 and Eurostoxx 600 Equity Indexes

Figure 3. (*Continued*)

Formally, the TE is defined as the root mean squared error between the tracker index return noted, $r_{t,tracker}$, and the MSCI Low Carbon index return noted, $r_{t,MSCI}$. T is the terminal period.

$$\mathrm{TE} = \sqrt{\frac{1}{T}\sum_{t-1}^{T}(r_{\mathrm{t,tracker}} - r_{\mathrm{t,MSCI}})^2} \tag{1}$$

Next, ER is the average difference between the tracker index return and the MSCI Low Carbon index return:

$$\mathrm{ER} = \frac{1}{T}\sum_{t-1}^{T}(r_{\mathrm{t,tracker}} - r_{\mathrm{t,MSCI}}) \tag{2}$$

For a review of these performance metrics in the index tracking literature, see Beasley *et al.* (2003), Dose and Cincotti (2005), and Chen and Kwon (2012).

Table 1 provides the TE and ER for each comparison between the tracker and the MSCI Low Carbon, S&P 500, and Eurostoxx 600 indexes.

Table 1. Index Tracking Performance Metrics

Series	ER	TE
Tracker vs. MSCI Low Carbon	0,055787797	1,860898
Tracker vs. S&P 500	0,097714473	2,186142
Tracker vs. Eurostoxx 600	0,097713511	2,185076

Note: TE stands for tracking error. ER stands for excess returns.

Model validation tests confirm the remarkable performance of our methodology to track the underlying MSCI Low Carbon and equity markets indices. Indeed, the TE and ER scores are very low, on average around zero with two decimals. We have therefore demonstrated the ability of our methodology to construct an efficient tracker of the benchmark portfolio.

2.2.3. *Building correlation indices*

This section builds on the notations by Koch (2014). Consider n time series of returns under the hypothesis of absence of serial auto-correlation. Define a white noise vector of mean zero $\varepsilon_t = r_t - \mu$, with r_t the $n \times 1$ vector of returns, and μ the vector of anticipated returns.

Returns exhibit a contemporaneous correlation under the form

$$\sum_t := E_t - 1[(r_t - \mu)(r_t - \mu)']. \tag{3}$$

Besides, this contemporaneous variance can vary through time, depending on past information.

The GARCH-DCC model unfolds in two steps. The first step takes into account the conditional heteroskedasticity. It consists in estimating, for each of the n series of returns r_{it}, the conditional volatility σ_{it} from a GARCH(p, q) model. Let D_t be a diagonal matrix with these conditional volatilities, i.e., $D_{i,it} = \sigma_{it}$ and, for all $i \neq j$, $D_{i,jt} = 0$. Standardized residuals are written as:

$$\nu_t = D_t^{-1}(r_t - \mu). \tag{4}$$

Standardized residuals have a unitary conditional volatility. The matrix that corresponds to the Constant Conditional Correlation (CCC) model by Bollerslev (1990) is defined as

$$\overline{R} = \frac{1}{T}\sum_{t=1}^{T} \quad v_t v_t'. \tag{5}$$

The second step consists in generalizing Bollerslev's CCC model in order to capture correlation dynamics, hence the name *Dynamic Conditional Correlation* was coined by Engle (2002). DCC correlations are written as

$$Q_t = \overline{R} + \propto (v_{t-1}v'_{t-1} - \overline{R}) + \beta(Q_{t-1} - \overline{R}) \quad (6)$$

with $Q_{\mathrm{i,jt}}$ being the correlation between r_{it} and r_{jt} at time t.

Based on a subset of 16 series selected from the full dataset,[1] we have launched a loop to compute the corresponding $[n*(n-1)]/2$ pairs, i.e., 120 iterations of the DCC model.

Once the dynamic conditional correlations have been stored, we can investigate briefly the most significant ones, as reproduced in Table 2.

The main information that can be gleaned from Table 2 can be summarized as follows. First, in case of negative correlations, greater bond yields tend to decrease market uncertainty as proxied by the VIX. Commodity prices (such as for aluminum) seems counter-cyclical with respect to market uncertainty. Second, in the case of positively correlated series, we notice that the MSCI Low Carbon and the S&P 500 go hand-in-hand.

Table 2. Top 10 DCC Correlations (Positive on the Left-Hand Side and Negative on the Right-Hand Side)

Natural Gas NBP UK & VSTOXX	−1.29%	MSCI Low Carbon & SP500	0.69%
Crude Oil WTI & VSTOXX	−0.58%	Aluminum & US 10y T-Bill	1.96%
EUR-USD & CBOE VIX	−1.13%	Crude oil WTI & US 10y T-Bill	1.40%
Nikkei 225 & CBOE VIX	−1.62%	MSCI Low Carbon & EUROSTOXX 600	0.70%
CBOEVIX & Aluminum	−2.17%	SP500 & EUROSTOXX 600	0.60%
Crude Oil WTI & CBOE VIX	−4.34%	USD-JPY & US 10y T-Bill	0.49%
CBOEVIX & US 10y T-Bill	−7.93%	Nikkei 225& US 10y T-Bill	0.50%
Gold & US 10y T-Bill	−0.37%	CBOE VIX & VSTOXX	0.55%
USD-JPY & CBOE VIX	−0.86%	Natural gas NBP UK & CBOEVIX	0.96%
VSTOXX & Corn	−0.48%	Crude oil WTI & Aluminum	0.66%

[1]The MSCI Low Carbon, the S&P 500, the Crude Oil Brent, the Natural Gas NBP UK, the Nikkei 225, the Nasdaq, the CBOE VIX, the VSTOXX, the Crude Oil WTI, the 10-Year US T-Bill, the USD-EUR/USD-JPY/USD-GBP exchange rates, Gold, Aluminium, and Corn futures from a cross-asset management perspective.

The correlation index is built from the 120 time-varying correlations by resorting to automatic factor detection (six factors were also needed), PCA, and factor modelling, similar to the methodology described in Sec. 2.2. For each series, index weight is obtained by averaging the influence of each factor (i.e., we do not favour one factor over another based on purely statistical grounds). Once the correlation index has been created, we can evaluate its performance in a horse race versus the CBOE ICI, including as low carbon asset either the MSCI Low Carbon original index or its tracker.

3. Empirical Results

3.1. *Mean–variance portfolio optimization with and without low carbon indexes*

Consider the mean–variance approach (Markowitz, 1952)

$$\max_{\omega} U = \omega' \mu - \frac{\delta}{2} \omega' \Sigma \omega, \tag{7}$$

with U the investor's utility, ω the vector of portfolio weights, $\sum$ the covariance matrix, μ the vector of return estimates, and δ the risk aversion coefficient. Upper volatility bounds are added as a constraint in the optimization strategy

$$\sqrt{\omega' \Sigma \omega} \leq \hat{\sigma}. \tag{8}$$

Two investor types are distinguished

(i) A *Conservative* investor with a maximum desired volatility of 5% p.a. (e.g., risk aversion coefficient equal to 10). Typically, the investor holds 80% bonds, 15% stocks, and 5% commodities.
(ii) An *Aggressive* investor with a maximum desired volatility of 15% p.a. (e.g., risk aversion coefficient equal to 2). Typically, the investor holds 60% stocks, 20% bonds, and 20% commodities.

Strategic weights are indicators typically used in the industry by asset managers and practitioners. They are to be followed as a rough guide for portfolio allocation and set as flexible upper/lower bounds in the optimization problem.

From a cross-market perspective, we construct the following portfolios:

(1) The *benchmark portfolio* composed of equities (S&P 500, Nasdaq, CBOE VIX, Eurostoxx 600, Nikkei 225), bonds (US 10-year T-Bill), and

Table 3. Mean-variance Portfolio Optimization Results

Investor Type	Risk	Return
Conservative		
Benchmark Portfolio	4.50%	3.23%
Extended Portfolio with MSCI Low Carbon	2%	3.71%
Extended Portfolio with Tracker	2.75%	3.80%
Aggressive		
Benchmark Portfolio	11.30%	8.45%
Extended Portfolio with MSCI Low Carbon	6.40%	5.08%
Extended Portfolio with Tracker	8.34%	6.84%

commodities (Gold, Crude Oil WTI Crude Oil Brent, Natural Gas NBP UK, Natural Gas Henry Hub).

(2) The *extended portfolios* include either the original MSCI Low Carbon index or its tracker.

Table 3 reports the portfolio gains for each portfolio depending on the investor type.

Several comments arise. First, the extended portfolio with tracker dominates the conservative strategy, with a higher return and only slightly higher risk than the extended portfolio with the original MSCI index. The benchmark portfolio underperforms in this setting.

Second, the benchmark portfolio dominates the aggressive strategy, delivering much higher returns than alternative portfolios with low carbon series. On the downside, the investor must accept a significantly higher level of risk to achieve this performance.

Regarding portfolio weights, in the aggressive investor type, the benchmark portfolio is composed of 64.85% of equities, 31.70% of bonds, and only 3.45% of commodities. For Low Carbon extended portfolios, in the conservative investor type, commodities (including either the MSCI or its tracker) rise up to 6% (relaxing the upper bound for the 5% portfolio weight constraint invested into commodities) whereas the bulk of this portfolio is still invested in US T-Bill (80%).

Another look at the performance of the *extended* portfolio (with Low Carbon asset) can be obtained from the estimation of a vector error-correction model (VECM, Johansen, 1991) with one lag.

Table 4 provides the results for a reduced form of the extended portfolio with the MSCI Low Carbon index. Error-correction terms are mostly

Table 4. VECM Error-Correction Mechanism for a Reduced Form of the Extended Portfolio with MSCI Low Carbon Asset

	D(EUROSTOXX600)	D(OAT_10Y)	D(EUR_USD)	D(BRENT)	D(MSCI)
Error Correction	0.016370 [1.16532]	−2.80E-07 [−0.10445]	−0.000104 [−2.46711]	−0.015903 [−1.98980]	0.171638 [3.59687]

Note: D(.) refers to the first-differenced series. Coefficient estimates are reproduced, with t-statistics in brackets.

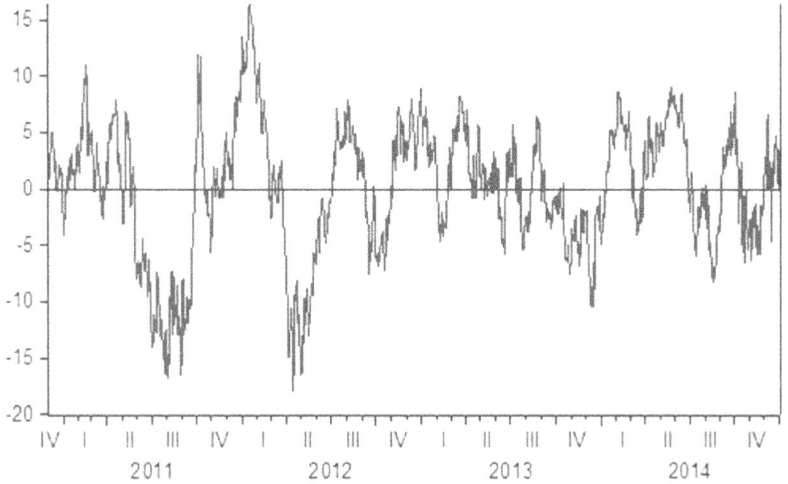

Figure 4. Cointegration Relationship for a Reduced Form of the Extended Portfolio with MSCI Low Carbon Asset

significant, with a negative sign registered for the exchange rate and the Crude Oil Brent series, indicating their predominant role in the adjustment toward the long-run equilibrium.

As depicted in Fig. 4, the cointegration relationship appears stationary. As a robustness check, we have therefore demonstrated that the market practitioner could successfully implement a VECM model with his/her own Low Carbon tracker in order to capture long-run trends in the portfolio under management.

3.2. *Predicting financial stress based on correlation indices*

In the remainder of the empirical application, we are interested in gauging the explanatory power of correlation indices with respect to the stress level on financial markets.

A widely accepted measure of financial stress in the literature can be found at the St. Louis Federal Reserve, under the form of a stress index composed of interest rates, returns spreads, and other forward-looking indicators. The St. Louis Fed Financial Stress Index is shown in Fig. 5.

Compared to the benchmark level of stress being zero (the solid black line), we remark that there was little stress on financial markets between 1994 and 2003 (except the dot-com bubble burst of the years 2001–2002). Relative to this 'tranquil' period, the years 2007–2010 have been characterized by a surge in financial stress in the aftermath of the 2008 sub-primes crisis in the USA, before resuming quiet territories amid Central Banks non-conventional monetary policies.

In what follows, we set up an original regression model in order to predict the financial stress based on correlation indices

$$\Delta \text{Stress}_t = \alpha + \beta 1 \ \Delta \text{Correlation\_Index}_t + \beta 2 \ \Delta \text{CBOE\_ICI}_t + \varepsilon_t \qquad (9)$$

with ΔStress_t the first-differenced value of the St. Louis Fed Financial Stress Index at time t, α_{i} the constant term, $\beta 1$ and $\beta 2$ the estimated coefficients for, respectively, $\text{Correlation\_Index}_t$ the correlation index built from the cross-market dataset and low carbon tracker used in this chapter, and CBOE_ICI_t the S&P 500 options counterpart built by the CBOE. ε_t is the error term.

Ordinary least-squares regression results are reproduced in Table 5. They indicate, by and large, that financial stress can be significantly explained by the CBOE ICI (at the 5% level), whereas the correlation index (including low carbon) fails to do so. Financial stress therefore seems weakly impacted by a broad cross-market correlation index.

To further ascertain this result, we conduct a sensitivity analysis based on rolling regressions (with a window of 200 observations) for the coefficient estimates β_1 and β_2. Detailed computer outputs have been stored and are not reproduced for brevity. Fig. 6 displays this picture.

The sensitivity analysis reveals that the influence of the CBOE ICI coefficient (aka, β_2) on financial stress is not stable through time; therefore, it also cannot be claimed as the winner of the horse-race. The main implication for portfolio managers would be that, essentially, broad cross-market correlation indices (including stocks, bonds, and commodities such as low carbon) would be *less* impacted during crises periods than the S&P 500.

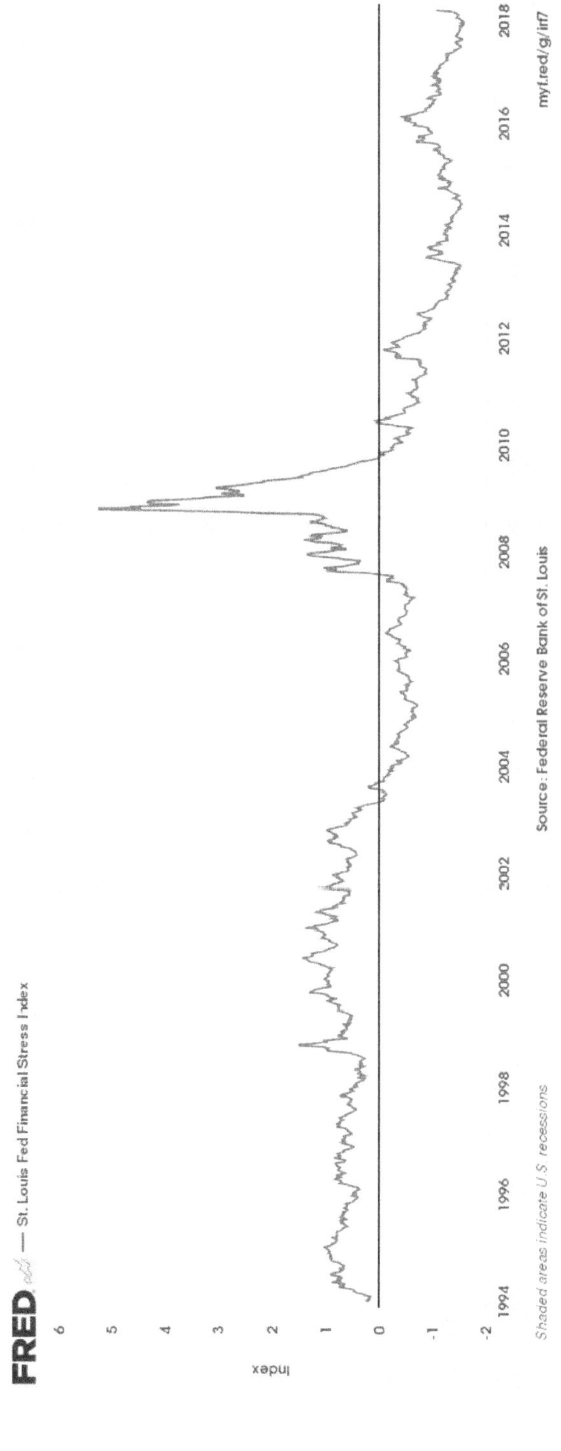

Figure 5. St. Louis Fed Financial Stress Index

Table 5. Predicting Financial Stress Based on Correlation Indices: A Horse-Race between the CBOE ICI and Broad Cross-Market Correlation Indices (Including Low Carbon)

Dependent Variable: $\Delta\mathbf{STRESS_t}$
Method: Least Squares
Included observations: 1066 after adjustments

Variable	Coefficient	Std. Error	*t*-Statistic	Prob.
α	0.897554	0.835586	1.074162	0.2830
ΔCorrelation_Index$_t$	0.004062	0.006211	0.653948	0.5133
ΔCBOE_ICI$_t$	−0.044176	0.020313	−2.174721	0.0299
R-squared:	0.6187			

Note: Ljung–Box–Pierce test confirms residuals are not autocorrelated (available upon request).

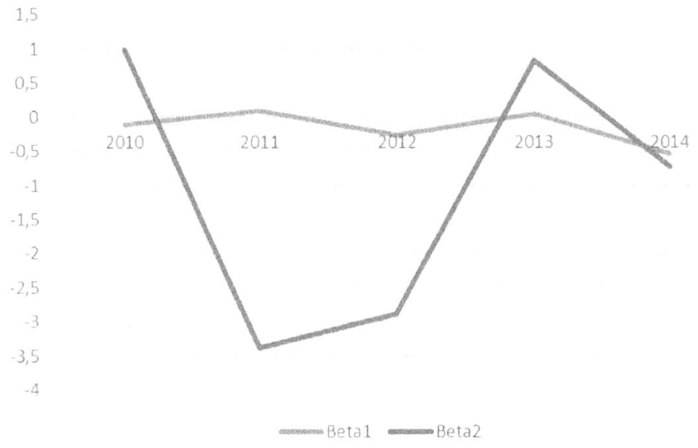

Figure 6. Rolling Regression Results for the Influence of β_1 and β_2

4. Conclusion

This chapter details step-by-step an innovative methodology to construct a tracker of a Low Carbon index, e.g., the MSCI. Several uses of such an index tracker are advanced, one of them being part of broad cross-market correlation indices.

In the portfolio optimization exercise, the inclusion of a Low Carbon index (either the original MSCI or its tracker) is profitable for the conservative-type of investor, where it dominates the benchmark portfolio. Only a small percentage of the portfolio weights (below 6%) invested into commodities (including low carbon) allows this conclusion to be reached, which has interesting implications from a cross-asset management perspective. However, an aggressive-type investor would dominate a portfolio composed of Low Carbon indexes, at the expense of a much higher risk profile. As robustness check, a cross-market vector error-cointegration with low carbon asset can be formulated to long-run trends, with a predominant role played by the oil price.

In the correlation index application (extending the present factor modelling exercise to the DCC framework), we reach the main result that — during periods of high financial stress — broad cross-market indices (including low carbon assets or trackers) are less impacted than any S&P 500-based (implied) correlation index. Hence, we reclaim the main interest in building tailored version of our (low carbon and correlation) indexes in order to achieve greater diversification benefits.

Practical implications for the practitioners include a step-by-step PCA–DCC methodology that is easily reproducible in order to track a targeted index. This contribution allows the practitioners to avoid 'black box' subscription fees with index tracking companies. Regarding the correlation indexes, our main conclusion gears toward using the VIX parent index (that outperforms our correlation index) for use in dispersion trading.

References

Alessi, L., Barigozzi, M., and Capasso, M. (2010). Improved penalization for determining the number of factors in approximate factor models. *Statist. Probab. Lett.*, 80, pp. 1806–1813.

Beasley, J. E., Meade, N., and Chang, T. J. (2003). An evolutionary heuristic for the index tracking problem. *Eur. J. Oper. Res.*, 148(3), pp. 621–643.

Bollerslev, T. (1990). Modelling the coherence in short-run nominal exchange rates: A multivariate generalized ARCH model. *Rev. Econom. Statis.*, 72(3), pp. 498–505.

Bracker, K., Docking, D. S., and Koch, P. D. (1999). Economic determinants of evolution in international stock market integration. *J. Empir. Fin.*, 6(1), pp. 1–27.

Buraschi, A., Porchia, P., and Trojani, F. (2010). Correlation risk and optimal portfolio choice. *J. Fin.*, 65(1), pp. 393–420.

Chan, K. C., Gup, B. E., and Pan, M. S. (1997). International stock market efficiency and integration: A study of eighteen nations. *J. Business Fin. Account.*, 24(6), pp. 803–813.

Chen, C. and Kwon, R. H. (2012). Robust portfolio selection for index tracking. *Comput. Oper. Res.*, 39(4), pp. 829–837.

Dose, C. and Cincotti, S. (2005). Clustering of financial time series with application to index and enhanced index tracking portfolio. *Physica A: Statist. Mech. Appl.*, 355(1), pp. 145–151.

Driessen, J., Maenhout, P. J., and Vilkov, G. (2009). The price of correlation risk: Evidence from equity options. *J. Fin.*, 64(3), pp. 1377–1406.

Engle, R. (2002). Dynamic conditional correlation: A simple class of multivariate generalized autoregressive conditional heteroskedasticity models. *J. Business Econom. Statist.*, 20(3), pp. 339–350.

Fay, M., Hallegatte, S., Bangalore, M., Kane, T., Rozenberg, J., Vogt-Schilb, A., and Treguer, D. (2015). *Shock Waves: Managing the Impacts of Climate Change on Poverty.* Washington, DC, USA: World Bank Publications.

IPCC. (2007). *The scientific basis. Contribution of Working Group I to the Fourth Assessment Report of the Intergovernmental Panel on Climate Change.* United Nations, New-York, USA.

Jobst, R., Rösch, D., Scheule, H., and Schmelzle, M. (2015). A simple econometric approach for modeling stress event intensities. *J. Futures Markets*, 35(4), pp. 300–320.

Johansen, S. (1991). Estimation and hypothesis testing of cointegration vectors in Gaussian vector autoregressive models. *Econometrica*, 59(6), pp. 1551–1580.

Koch, N. (2014). Dynamic linkages among carbon, energy and financial markets: A smooth transition approach. *Appl. Econom.*, 46:7, pp. 715–729.

Krishnan, C. N. V., Petkova, R., and Ritchken, P. (2009). Correlation risk. *J. Empir. Fin.*, 16(3), pp. 353–367.

Lien, D. and Yang, L. (2006). Spot-futures spread, time-varying correlation, and hedging with currency futures. *J. Futures Markets*, 26(10), pp. 1019–1038.

Markowitz, H. (1952). Portfolio selection. *J. Fin.*, 7(1), pp. 77–91.

Marshall, C. M. (2009). Dispersion trading: Empirical evidence from US options markets. *Global Fin. J.*, 20(3), pp. 289–301.

MSCI. (2014) MSCI Global Low Carbon Target Indexes Metholology. *Working Paper*, MSCI, New York, NY, USA. Available at: https://www.msci.com/eqb/methodology/meth_docs/MSCI_Low_Carbon_Target_Indexes_Methodology.pdf.

Park, S. Y. and Jei, S. Y. (2010). Estimation and hedging effectiveness of time-varying hedge ratio: Flexible bivariate garch approaches. *J. Futures Markets*, 30(1), pp. 71–99.

Skintzi, V. D. and Refenes, A. P. N. (2005). Implied correlation index: A new measure of diversification. *J. Futures Markets*, 25(2), pp. 171–197.

Stern, N. H. (2007). *The Economics of Climate Change: The Stern Review.* Cambridge, UK: Cambridge University press.

Stock, J. W. (2002a). Forecasting using principal components from a large number of predictor. *J. Am. Statist. Associ.*, 97, pp. 1167–1179.

Stock, J. W. (2002b). Macroeconomic forecasting using diffusion indexes. *J. Business Econom. Statist.*, 20, pp. 147–162.

Appendix: Basket Weights of the MSCI Low Carbon Tracker (in %)

Company	Tracker Weight	Company	Tracker Weight	Company	Tracker Weight
APPLE	1.76%	Western Digital	0.43%	Bank of America Corp	0.51%
MICROSOFT	1.05%	Western Union Co	0.24%	The Bank of New York Mellon Corp.	0.51%
GENERAL ELECTRIC	0.80%	Xerox Corp.	0.36%	BB&T Corporation	0.22%

(*Continued*)

Company	Tracker Weight	Company	Tracker Weight	Company	Tracker Weight
JOHNSON & JOHNSON	0.75%	Xilinx Inc	0.29%	Berkshire Hathaway	0.21%
WELLS FARGO & CO	0.71%	Yahoo Inc.	0.20%	BlackRock	0.17%
AMAZON.COM	0.64%	Altria Group Inc	0.28%	Block H&R	0.13%
JP MORGAN CHASE & CO.	0.64%	Archer-Daniels-Midland Co	0.13%	Boston Properties	0.18%
PROCTER & GAMBLE	0.58%	Brown-Forman Corporation	0.16%	Capital One Financial	0.17%
GOOGLE 'A'	0.56%	Campbell Soup	0.25%	CBRE Group	0.25%
Bed Bath & Beyond	0.30%	The Clorox Company	0.28%	Charles Schwab Corporation	0.19%
BorgWarner	0.19%	The Coca Cola Company	0.24%	Chubb Corp.	0.18%
Darden Restaurants	0.27%	Coca-Cola Enterprises	0.17%	Cincinnati Financial	0.15%
Dollar Tree	0.70%	Colgate-Palmolive	0.24%	Citigroup Inc.	0.44%
Ford Motor	0.31%	ConAgra Foods Inc.	0.27%	CME Group Inc.	0.15%
Genuine Parts	0.16%	Constellation Brands	0.20%	Comerica Inc.	0.24%
Harley-Davidson	0.13%	Costco Co.	0.27%	Crown Castle International Corp.	0.22%
Home Depot	0.15%	CVS Caremark Corp.	0.19%	Discover Financial Services	0.11%
Interpublic Group	0.48%	Dr Pepper Snapple Group	0.25%	E*Trade	0.30%
Johnson Controls	0.14%	Estee Lauder Cos.	0.21%	Equifax Inc.	0.17%
Mohawk Industries	0.14%	General Mills	0.28%	Essex Property Trust Inc	0.16%
Nordstrom	0.13%	Kellogg Co.	0.31%	Fifth Third Bancorp	0.21%
Omnicom Group	0.14%	Keurig Green Mountain	3.11%	Franklin Resources	0.16%
PVH Corp.	0.18%	Kimberly-Clark	0.28%	General Growth Properties Inc.	0.15%
Ross Stores	0.21%	Kroger Co.	0.20%	Genworth Financial Inc.	0.70%
Stanley Black & Decker	0.11%	McCormick & Co.	0.24%	Goldman Sachs Group	0.25%
TJX Companies Inc.	0.19%	Molson Coors Brewing Company	0.15%	Hartford Financial Svc.Gp.	0.37%
Urban Outfitters	0.11%	Mondelez International	0.27%	HCP Inc.	0.16%
Wyndham Worldwide	0.14%	Monster Beverage	0.23%	Host Hotels & Resorts	0.18%
AUTONATION	0.57%	PepsiCo Inc.	0.25%	Huntington Bancshares	0.22%
AUTOZONE	0.38%	Philip Morris International	0.21%	Intercontinental Exchange	0.17%
BEST BUY	0.46%	Reynolds American Inc.	0.27%	Invesco Ltd.	0.24%
CABLEVISION SYS.	0.50%	Smucker (J.M.)	0.28%	JPMorgan Chase & Co.	0.24%

(*Continued*)

Company	Tracker Weight	Company	Tracker Weight	Company	Tracker Weight
CARMAX	0.45%	Sysco Corp.	0.25%	KeyCorp	0.20%
CARNIVAL	0.47%	The Hershey Company	0.25%	Kimco Realty	0.16%
CBS 'B'	0.72%	Tyson Foods	0.17%	Legg Mason	0.21%
CHIPOTLE MEXN.GRILL	0.43%	Wal-Mart Stores	0.24%	Leucadia National Corp.	0.21%
COACH	0.73%	Walgreens Boots Alliance	0.13%	Lincoln National	0.37%
COMCAST 'A'	0.52%	Whole Foods Market	0.18%	Loews Corp.	0.19%
D R HORTON	0.76%	3M Company	0.20%	M&T Bank Corp.	0.16%
DISCOVERY COMMS.'A'	0.44%	Ametek	0.16%	Macerich	0.15%
EXPEDIA	0.55%	Amphenol Corp A	0.14%	Marsh & McLennan	0.15%
FOSSIL GROUP	0.65%	Boeing Company	0.14%	McGraw Hill Financial	0.12%
GAMESTOP 'A'	0.57%	C. H. Robinson Worldwide	0.10%	MetLife Inc.	0.34%
GAP	0.45%	Caterpillar Inc.	0.12%	Moody's Corp	0.13%
GARMIN	0.44%	Cintas Corporation	0.16%	Morgan Stanley	0.54%
GOODYEAR TIRE & RUB.	0.89%	Corning Inc.	0.12%	NASDAQ OMX Group	0.11%
HARMAN INTL.INDS.	0.57%	CSX Corp.	0.12%	Northern Trust Corp.	0.21%
HASBRO	0.32%	Cummins Inc.	0.24%	People's United Financial	0.17%
KOHL'S	0.45%	Danaher Corp.	0.17%	Plum Creek Timber Co.	0.16%
L BRANDS	0.46%	Deere & Co.	0.16%	PNC Financial Services	0.22%
L'OREAL	0.15%	Delta Air Lines	0.23%	Principal Financial Group	0.18%
LVMH	0.11%	Dover Corp.	0.14%	Progressive Corp.	0.15%
ACCOR	0.19%	Dun & Bradstreet	0.16%	Prologis	0.17%
BRITISH AMERICAN TOBACCO	0,10%	Eaton Corporation	0.13%	Prudential Financial	0.19%
ROLLS-ROYCE HOLDINGS	0.20%	Emerson Electric Company	0.15%	Public Storage	0.19%
KDDI	0.32%	Expeditors Int'l	0.15%	Regions Financial Corp.	0.45%
Accenture plc	0.26%	Fastenal Co	0.14%	Simon Property Group Inc	0.17%
Adobe Systems Inc	0.25%	FedEx Corporation	0.13%	State Street Corp.	0.24%
Akamai Technologies Inc	0.48%	FLIR Systems	0.14%	SunTrust Banks	0.32%
Alliance Data Systems	0.24%	Flowserve Corporation	0.12%	T. Rowe Price Group	0.19%

(Continued)

Company	Tracker Weight	Company	Tracker Weight	Company	Tracker Weight
Alphabet Inc Class A	0.22%	Fluor Corp.	0.20%	The Travelers Companies Inc.	0.16%
Altera Corp	0.39%	General Dynamics	0.17%	Torchmark Corp.	0.17%
Analog Devices, Inc.	0.29%	Grainger (W.W.) Inc.	0.13%	U.S. Bancorp	0.21%
Applied Materials Inc	0.33%	Honeywell Int'l Inc.	0.16%	Unum Group	0.15%
Autodesk Inc	0.42%	Ingersoll-Rand PLC	0.15%	Ventas Inc	0.14%
Automatic Data Processing	0.30%	Iron Mountain Incorporated	0.20%	Vornado Realty Trust	0.15%
Broadcom Corporation	0.32%	Jacobs Engineering Group	0.10%	Wells Fargo	0.20%
CA, Inc.	0.26%	AT&T Inc	0.22%	Weyerhaeuser Corp.	0.11%
Cisco Systems	0.34%	CenturyLink Inc	0.20%	Zions Bancorp	0.28%
Citrix Systems	0.43%	Frontier Communications	0.18%	STANDARD CHARTERED	0.13%
Cognizant Technology Solutions	0.27%	Level 3 Communications	0.27%	BARCLAYS	0.46%
Computer Sciences Corp.	0.31%	Verizon Communications	0.24%	ROYAL BANK OF SCTL.GP.	0.43%
eBay Inc.	0.31%	MS&AD INSURANCE GP.HDG.	0.49%	AVIVA	0.19%
Electronic Arts	0.34%	DAIWA SECURITIES GROUP	0.17%	PRUDENTIAL	0.14%
EMC Corp.	0.28%	CHIBA BANK	0.41%	AXA	0.41%
F5 Networks	0.55%	BANK OF YOKOHAMA	0.43%	CAP GEMINI	0.17%
Fidelity National Information Services	0.23%	NOMURA HDG.	0.64%	SAP	0.13%
First Solar Inc	0.86%	SHIZUOKA BANK	0.42%	CARREFOUR	0.19%
Fiserv Inc	0.30%	FUKUOKA FINANCIAL GP.	0.45%	DANONE	0.17%
Harris Corporation	0.27%	RESONA HOLDINGS	0.40%	ALCATEL-LUCENT	0.47%
Hewlett Packard Enterprise	0.28%	CREDIT SAISON	0.57%	SANOFI	0.11%
Intel Corp.	0.25%	SUMITOMO MITSUI FINL.GP.	0.38%	BASF	0.11%
International Bus. Machines	0.27%	SONY	0.63%	K + S	0.11%
Intuit Inc.	0.28%	HITACHI CON.MCH.	0.43%	BAYER	0.13%
Juniper Networks	0.53%	CASIO COMPUTER	0.46%	FRESENIUS MED.CARE	0.18%
KLA-Tencor Corp.	0.35%	FUJITSU	0.45%	MERCK KGAA	0.14%

(Continued)

Company	Tracker Weight	Company	Tracker Weight	Company	Tracker Weight
Lam Research	0.33%	TOSHIBA	0.53%	3M	0.20%
Linear Technology Corp.	0.32%	SHARP	0.83%	JOHNSON & JOHNSON	0.25%
Mastercard Inc.	0.28%	TOYOBO	0.35%	MERCK & COMPANY	0.20%
Microchip Technology	0.29%	KIKKOMAN	0.37%	PFIZER	0.22%
Micron Technology	0.68%	TAKARA HDG.	0.55%	UNITEDHEALTH GROUP	0.14%
Microsoft Corp.	0.24%	UNITIKA	0.56%	GLAXOSMITHKLINE	0.21%
Motorola Solutions Inc.	0.27%	TORAY INDS.	0.43%	ASTRAZENECA	0.19%
NetApp	0.34%	HONDA MOTOR	0.32%	SHIRE	0.14%
Netflix Inc.	0.80%	TOYOTA TSUSHO	0.49%	Gilead Sciences Inc	0.09%
Nvidia Corporation	0.42%	KAWASAKI HEAVY INDUSTRY	0.57%	Allergan	0.12%
Oracle Corp.	0.27%	PIONEER	0.80%	Amgen Inc	0.14%
Paychex Inc.	0.28%	ISUZU MOTORS	0.58%	Bristol-Myers Squibb	0.24%
QUALCOMM Inc.	0.30%	ACE Limited	0.16%	Medtronic	0.15%
Red Hat Inc.	0.39%	AFLAC Inc	0.22%	ASTELLAS PHARMA	0.29%
Salesforce.com	0.44%	Affiliated Managers Group Inc	0.21%	CHUGAI PHARM.	0.42%
SanDisk Corporation	0.46%	Allstate Corp	0.18%	DAIICHI SANKYO	0.28%
Seagate Technology	0.54%	American Express Co	0.14%	SUMITOMO DAINIPPON PHA.	0.43%
Symantec Corp.	0.33%	American International Group, Inc.	0.25%	Eisai	0.31%
Teradata Corp.	0.36%	American Tower Corp A	0.18%	KYOWA HAKKO KIRIN	0.38%
Texas Instruments	0.30%	Ameriprise Financial	0.21%	SHIONOGI	0.39%
Total System Services	0.28%	Apartment Investment & Mgmt	0.11%	TAKEDA PHARMACEUTICAL	0.31%
Verisign Inc.	0.23%	Assurant Inc	0.14%	CATAMARAN	0.18%
Visa Inc.	0.21%	AvalonBay Community	0.14%	EXTENDICARE	0.27%

Chapter 12

Alternative Approach to Risk Mitigation

Guldem Gokcek

Management School, University of Liverpool, UK
Division of Graduate Business Program
New York University, USA
ggokcek01@gmail.com

Abstract

The issue of shadow banking system became a global phenomenon originating from the USA due to financial crisis. It is believed by many researchers that interest rates were kept too low for too long by the Federal Reserve Bank in the early year 2000. This, of course, has caused credit boom in the economy. Thereby, this situation led to the post-2007 financial and economic crisis. However, low interest rates during boom period of early 2000s were not the only reason for the financial crisis. In fact, many academicians and policymakers raised an argument that the crisis was result of the interaction of micro- and macrofactors. It is true that shadow banking system bears the same risk as banks. As stated by Financial Stability Board (2011), shadow banking system raises concern about systemic risk and concerns about regulatory arbitrage. After FSB 2010, 2011, and 2012 reports, FSB published final policy documents on Strengthening Oversight and Regulation of Shadow Banking in August 2013 to mitigate potential systemic risks associated with shadow banking. Therefore, the aim of this research is to search for alternative approach to risk mitigation to address potential systemic risk associated with shadow banking.

1. Introduction

Shadow banking system consists of financial institutions that are either unregulated or less regulated. It is considered as an intermediary to connect consumer and commercial borrowers indirectly to investors in capital markets. In a way, this system can be described as a financial network of financial institutions and instruments, and it is a result of the occurrences of financial activities outside the regulated banking sector.

Lawyers, policymakers, academicians, and financiers have been discussing the issues related to the shadow banking system since 2007. The real focus on shadow banking system through discussions, studies, and research by academicians and policymakers began in 2008. There is an evolving literature for understanding the operation of shadow banking since then.

The aim of this chapter is to provide an alternative approach for risk mitigation to address potential systemic risk associated with shadow banking. It was established through financial crisis that shadow banking system raises concern about systemic risk. Kaufman and Scott (2003, pp. 1–2) defined the systemic risk as 'the risk or probability of breakdowns in an entire system, as opposed to breakdowns in individual parts or components'. Boran (2010) addressed the core of the problem of systemic risk to provide a solution to financial crisis in his study. Martin et al. (2011) took the empirical facts of the Bear Stearns and Lehman crises as a starting point in their study to provide a model for run in repo markets. In fact, most of shadow banking funding comes from repo market. This market has been considered as a major source of short-term secured funding for financial institutions (Cullen, 2017). The focus of this model by Martin *et al.* (2011) was on the differences between the tri-party repo market and the bilateral repo market. Adrian *et al.* (2013) provided a very good overview of both markets in their research. The run in the tri-party repo market was presented as a simple withdrawal of funding (Copeland *et al.*, 2011). Runs in the ABCP market were also characterized by a withdrawal of funding in the study by Covitz *et al.* (2012). The reason for decline in the credit supply during the financial crisis was related to the decline of short-term shadow bank funding. Gallin (2013) provided a framework to justify the reason by providing the flow of the amount of short-term funding from the shadow banking system to the real economy. Bengtsson (2016) also emphasized the role of investment funds in the credit intermediation process of shadow banking in his study. This study empirically demonstrated how systemic risk was raised due to the activities of shadow banking system. Some conclusion on the policy challenges for regulating shadow banking system was also drawn. Capital requirement is one of the policy challenges because increasing cost of capital requirement pushes banks into shadow banking sector, thereby allowing for regulatory arbitrage. Plantin (2015) explained this aspect of cost and tradeoff very well in his study.

This chapter, first, contributes to the ongoing policy debate on the shadow banking and systemic risk by providing risk mitigation framework. Second, it identifies the areas for data analytics, policymakers, supervision, and financial regulation by addressing potential systemic risk associated with shadow banking. Finally, this chapter contributes to the literature with its findings that it is necessary to incorporate the shadow banking system into regulatory framework. Researchers have tried to use different approaches to understand the relationship between shadow banking system and systemic risk. However, their understanding of this relationship was lacking the sources of systemic risk related to the activities of shadow banking sector. Nabilou and Pacces (2017) fill the literature gap with their study on the systemic risk and regulation of shadow banking system by discussing the issues from the perspectives of law and economics of shadow banking. This chapter aligns with Nabilou and Pacces (2017) but differs from their study mainly compared with what different aspects of shadow banking system in that it includes they included in their study.

This chapter focuses on 10 specific areas as key findings in which policies may be needed to mitigate the potential systemic risks associated with shadow banking system. Risk-mitigating framework is rather based on conceptual approach, so the link between systemic risk and activities of shadow banking system is clearly established. The main findings of this chapter build on ten specific recommendations. First, securitization market should be redesigned to mitigate risk. Second, the connection between shadow banking system and traditional commercial banks should be supervised and its interconnectedness should be within the regulatory framework. Third, micro- and macroprudential policies should include regulation and supervision of shadow banking system. Fourth, new policies should be established to monitor the regulatory arbitrage by shadow banking system activities. Fifth, there should be applicable system-wide shadow banking policies for spillover effect. Sixth, a global framework should be established to mitigate risk because foreign shadow banking system can also create spillover effect. Seventh, shadow banking can lead to large information gaps. There should be new types of reform to control the information gaps. Eight, connection between credit hedge fund activity and entities of shadow banking system should be carefully examined and supervised to prevent the occurrences of systemic risk. Ninth, the reliance on credit rating agencies should be reviewed and necessary rules should be established. Finally, the problems of governance and supervision should be minimized. Overall, the findings of this chapter help academics, practitioners, and policymakers to have better understanding of the determinants of risk-mitigating framework in the case of shadow banking.

The remainder of the chapter is organized as follows. Section 2 introduces the shadow banking system. It focuses on the definition of shadow banking system and defines roles of shadow banking system. Section 3 discusses the sources of systemic risk which help to establish the risk-mitigation framework. Each source of systemic risk is discussed in detail. This section highlights several key findings to establish the clear link between systemic risk and activities of shadow banking system. The last section concludes, addresses key findings and makes recommendations for policies.

2. What is Shadow Banking System?

Shadow banking system was defined by the Financial Stability Board (2011) as the system of credit intermediation. This system involves the entities and activities outside traditional banking system. Most activities of shadow banking system usually take place outside the commercial banking system except some activities. Functions of shadow banking are transferring credit risk and transformation of maturity and liquidity outside of commercial banks without access to central bank liquidity.

What does shadow banking system include? Pozsar *et al.* (2010, revised 2012) included the examples of shadow banking system as nonbank finance companies, asset-backed commercial paper (ABCP) conduits, structured investment vehicles (SIVs), credit hedge funds, money market mutual funds, securities lenders, limited-purpose finance companies (LPFCs), and the government-sponsored enterprises (GSEs). Nonbank finance companies are involved in loan originating process. Loans and leases are the two examples of loan origination process among others. Asset-backed commercial paper (ABCP) conduits' job is to fund loan warehousing. Limited-purpose finance companies (LPFCs), structured investment vehicles (SIVs), and credit hedge funds are involved in asset-backed securities (ABS) intermediation. Pooling and structuring loans into ABS is done by broker-dealers' ABS syndicate desks. Broker-dealers' ABS also conduct pooling and structuring of asset-backed securities into collateralized-debt obligations (CDOs). All these activities take place in wholesale funding markets and are performed by securities lenders (Pozsar *et al.*, 2013).

Shadow banking system is specialized in providing a chain of wholesale-funded, securitization-based lending by transforming risky long-term loans into credit risk-free short-term money-like instruments. This process of credit intermediation takes place within a single institution — this is shadow banking system. This system delegates chains of nonbank financial intermediaries to perform the credit intermediation process. However, shadow banking system has uninsured liabilities because it does not have full access to government-provided liquidity. Therefore, its credit intermediation is without guaranteed liabilities, but shadow banking system has a way solving this problem. That is via a commercial bank. Credit lines of commercial banks can provide indirect access to government backstop for some shadow banking uninsured liabilities. This way, shadow banking institutions benefits from government backstop for the pricing of their uninsured liabilities through commercial banks. Another role of shadow banking is to create money. Gorton and Metrick (2011, 2012) discussed this money creation role in their studies. Basically, central banks can only create money. However, the authors stated that shadow bank liabilities in the form of money creation complement traditional forms of money creation. Shadow bank money creation is funded by money market funds and short-term investment funds. Commercial paper and repo markets are the markets where shadow bank money creation occurs. Studies by Sunderam (2015), and Moreira and Savov (2012) also analyzed the role of shadow bank liabilities on the money supply and demand, and the impact of shadow bank money creation on macroeconomic fluctuations, respectively. Securitization and higher capital requirements allow for regulatory arbitrage. Regulatory arbitrage refers to the restructuring of financial activity. It does not change the risk of the activity but reduces the cost of regulation. This is also one of the activities of shadow banking system, particularly in the case of capital requirement. For example, a rapid expansion of asset-backed commercial papers since 2004 was partially due to regulatory arbitrage caused by change in capital rules. A very good example of regulatory arbitrage was provided in the study by Acharya *et al.* (2013).

3. Sources for Systemic Risk

The issue of shadow banking system became a global phenomenon originating from the USA due to financial crisis. It is believed by many researchers that interest rates were kept too low for too long by the Federal Reserve Bank in the early year 2000. This, of course, has caused credit boom in the economy. Thereby, this situation led to the post-2007 financial and economic crisis. Verona *et al.* (2013) attempted to assess the role of a *too low for too long* interest rate policy in the development of a boom and bust in their study. However, low interest rates during the boom period of early 2000s were not the only reason for the financial crisis. In fact, many academicians and policymakers raised an argument that the crisis was result of the interaction of micro- and macrofactors (development of Shadow Banking system, the boom of securitization, and the difficulty in measuring and locating financial risk as micro-factors; and loose policy, financial globalization, and global imbalances as macro-factors were at the beginning of the list of factors). Borio (2008), Blanchard (2009), Trichet (2009), Bean *et al.* (2010), and Bernanke (2010) were among the believers of this argument as academics and policymakers. Most of the empirical research in the literature was based on justifying the link between shadow banking system and global financial crisis related to risk. It is now certain that shadow banking can contribute to systemic risk (FSB, 2013).

The Bank for International Settlements (BIS) defined systemic risk as *the risk that the failure of a participant to meet its contractual obligations may in turn cause other participants to default with a chain reaction leading to broader financial difficulties* (BIS, 1994, p. 177). There have been many definitions of systemic risk. The most commonly used definition is jointly developed by the International Monetary Fund, the Financial Stability Board (FSB), and Bank for International Settlements. This definition included three indicators of systemic risk assessment of financial institution namely complexity, size, and interconnectedness. However, these indicators focus on the effect on markets (Georg, 2014).

According to a study by Gennaioli *et al.* (2013), shadow banking system works well under the rational expectation and improves welfare as well as insurance opportunities. They also demonstrated in this study that how financial fragility in terms of insurance was created when the tail risk is neglected. This is another role of shadow banking activity. This banking system accumulates assets which are sensitive to tail risk. It is true that shadow banking system bears the same risk as banks. As stated by Financial Stability Board (2013), shadow banking system raises concern about systemic risk. So then, what is the reason for using shadow banking system? The reason depends on the activities of shadow banking system.

The sub-sections below discuss the activities of shadow banking system and highlight several key findings related to systemic risk.

3.1. *Securitization and funding*

Another component of the shadow banking sector is related to *securitization.* The process of creating a new financial instrument by combining other financial assets is called securitization. The securitization process consists of maturity transformation, financing of longer-term assets through money market, and packaging up of loans and other assets into tradable securities. Traders and investors use secured financing transactions (SFTs) technique to structure these activities. Repos (repurchase agreements) are the most widely used STFs. They are the source of money market liquidity. Gorton and Metrick (2011) emphasized in their study that the rapid growth of repurchase agreements due to the changing regulatory and legal structure was an advantage for shadow banking system. This also proves that the reason for the switch in bank business models form asset to liability balance sheet management was related to shadow bank credit intermediation (Claessens *et al.*, 2012). The fundamental reason of securitization is to allocate credit risk between traditional banks and non-banking financial institutions (Knight, 2007). For example, loan pools that are transferred to the shadow banking system are securitized in the form of ABCP (asset-backed commercial paper). As Pozsar *et al.* (2010) pointed out in their study, "resecuritization process" takes place within the system because maturity mismatch is not an issue of the ABS (asset-backed security) structure, and they can be purchased by other entities and funded through ABCP.

Factors such as global imbalances (Bernanke, 2011) and inadequate regulation (Levine, 2010) have been considered as contributing factors to the financial crisis. In addition to these factors, shadow banking system has also been considered as one of the reasons for the financial crisis due to its bank-like activities such as maturity transformation, liquidity transformation, and credit intermediation. These activities have contributed to the credit bubble. Financial companies started to grant loans, and these loans were sold to the asset-back security issuers through securitization. These loans were no longer included in the balance sheet of financial companies, and there was no incentive to monitor the borrowers any more. Thereby, subprime market was expanded. These loans were repackaged with the development of structured products. However, risk was underestimated, and it was a mistake to completely rely on credit rating agencies for assessing these developed products. In the end, the US housing market collapsed, borrowers were not able to repay their loans, and shadow banking system faced huge problems, thereby leading to the financial crisis. Therefore, it is believed that shadow banking system raises risk, and it is one of the causative factor of financial crisis. Academics such as Adrian and Shin (2009), Brunnermeier (2009), Gorton (2009), and Adrian and Shin (2010) were among the believers of this result. Money market funds were also contributors of the financial crisis even though they carried low risk. These funds were the key players in the securitization chains.

Funding is one important component of shadow banking. Most of its funding comes from short-term instruments such as commercial paper and re-purchase agreement (repo). However, there is a maturity mismatch because its assets are of longer maturity, but it is worth mentioning that money market funds are not subject to maturity mismatch because these funds are short-term liabilities and short-term assets. Shadow banking performs bank-like activities and is a useful source of funding for traditional banking for providing commercial paper and repo as a funding source. According to the Financial Stability Board, entities of shadow banking system are good for providing additional sources of funding as well as providing investors with alternatives to bank deposits. For example, money market funds invest in commercial paper and provide additional funding source for financial and non-financial institutions which are in need of funding for short-term debt. Securities lenders also provides additional source of capital and allow borrowers to have securities at below-market rates. By doing so, these entities of shadow banking system enhance market liquidity. Therefore, regulators were sometimes in favor of the expansion of shadow banking system.

Securitization and funding process was really behind the fast growth of shadow banking system. If the securitization activity of shadow banking system is the source of risk, then what should be done to minimize or mitigate this risk? The answer is the re-designing the securitization market so that risk would be minimized. First, key functions of securitization market should be identified. Second, benefits of securitization to the economy should be identified. In this the regard, the Bank of England and European Central Bank suggested that four functions of securitization market should be used to mitigate the risk. These are related to investment function, funding tool, market-based financing to transfer risk, and generation of collateral. Particularly, repo market was the biggest problem to the funding markets during 2007–2008 financial crisis. Since then, the concepts of repo and the use of collateral have become the top discussion topics in the economics, law, and finance fields.

3.2. *Regulatory arbitrage*

Regulatory arbitrage includes legal structuring and occurs when firm switches from a regulated activity to another that is subject to less regulation and lower legal costs. Legal structuring is done by the lawyers for financial firms to escape or loosen regulations. It was observed that there was a huge increase in the transactions of asset-backed securities, credit derivatives, and asset-backed commercial papers in the market after the year 2000. These were all the instruments of shadow banking system. These instruments enabled arbitrage of bank capital regulation.

Banking regulations exist to prevent excessive risk and protect investors and depositors. Capital requirement is one of these regulations. Since the 2008 banking crisis, imposition of capital requirements on traditional banking system has heightened. The reason for imposing higher capital and liquidity requirements is to prevent the severity of banking crises. Shadow banking system can address the liquidity and solvency risks faced by banks by transforming illiquid loans into liquid securities which are sold to investors in capital markets.

It was noted in many studies that higher level of capital requirements encourages regulatory arbitrage. This encourages the development of shadow banking system. One of the appealing functions of shadow credit intermediation is related to tax and regulatory arbitrage (Acharya *et al.*, 2013). Regulation means putting more pressure and constraints on the institutions. Therefore, institutions behave in ways to avoid paying taxes or disclosing additional information to investors or holding more capital against financial exposure. Regulatory arbitrage can be thought of simply as avoiding legal restrictions. However, regulatory arbitrage can be limited by regulating the shadow banking system.

Capital regulation can depend on bank's securitization (Stein, 2010). One of the components of shadow banking is securitization. The process of creating a new financial instrument by combining other financial assets is called securitization. The fundamental reason of securitization is to allocate credit risk between traditional banks and non-banking financial institutions. For example, loan pools that are transferred to the shadow banking system are securitized in the form of ABCP (asset-backed commercial paper) (Acharya *et al.*, 2013). In this case, regulatory arbitrage has been viewed as a way of evading capital requirement regulation to engage in securitization. The reason for engaging in securitization is to lower capital charges, and to comply with Basel rules.

Banks can meet higher capital requirements either by raising money by issuing extra shares or by reducing the size of their balance sheets or by reducing the riskiness of their loans. Of course, higher bank capital requirements have several benefits. For example, having higher capital requirements can reduce bank failure and provide better risk management. However, there is the cost side of higher capital requirements that must be considered. Higher capital requirements can reduce credit supply and decrease credit demand by raising lending rates (Ordonez and Piguillem, 2015). Thereby, this may slow down economic growth. Higher capital requirements can also drive banking activities into the institutions that have not had strong regulations such as shadow banks. This leads to increase in systemic risk. This is also true for Europe because financial markets in Europe have raised concerns due to the changes in market activity through either financial innovation, changing market preferences, or regulatory arbitrage. Therefore, European regulators have become concerned about a shift toward shadow banking. Thus, shadow banking could be source of systemic risk in Europe too.

3.3. *Hedge funds*

Hedge funds played an important role in shadow banking system. These funds are unregulated; at least, they were until Dodd–Frank Act. The vital role of hedge funds in the shadow banking system is related to buying some of the riskiest instruments in the system, which banks and other regulated entities are not allowed to buy due to the preclusion of the law. This situation allowed hedge funds to earn profit and to inject liquidity into the shadow banking system.

There has been a debate on whether to include the hedge funds as a part of the shadow banking system or not. I think hedge funds should be included in the shadow banking system since they are part of a chain of activities of shadow banking system. They can be part of the system by performing credit intermediation activities such as credit hedge funds as a shadow bank entity and hedging as part of shadow banking activities (Pozsar *et al.*, 2010). Credit hedge funds use credit product investment strategies and are financed by repos. During the 2007 and 2008 financial crisis, hedge funds played an important role in securitization as investors. Bear Stearns' hedge funds activity in the securitization market can be given as a good example for the link between hedge funds and shadow banking system. They invested in subprime, and this investment was financed through repo. The link between securitization and repo market was also observed during the financial crisis (Gorton, 2011). This is the proof that hedge funds were part of the securitization activity and had maturity mismatch through repo. Especially, if we consider the use of shadow banking system for the funding of residential mortgage-backed securities (RMBS), then we must think that the risk in these securities being hedged in various swap markets such as credit default swaps, interest rate swaps, and foreign exchange swaps. Another proof of the link between hedge funds and shadow banking comes from the activity of securities lending. Hedge funds' short selling is an important factor for the securities lender in borrowing. There is also a link between collateral and hedge funds' short-selling activity. Hedge funds provides cash collateral to the securities lender. This cash collateral can be reinvested in money market funds by the securities lenders. This means that the link between hedge funds activity and credit intermediation within shadow banking system is established when reinvestment of cash collateral happens. Another reason for including hedge funds in shadow banking is related to rehypothecation. Rehypothecation is a practice that allows hedge funds to pledge collateral to their prime brokers. This pledged collateral is used by the brokers for their own funding. Singh and Aitken (2010) emphasized in their study that rehypothecation was an important source of non-bank funding for US banks.

Interconnectedness of hedge funds with shadow banking activities can raise systemic risk. This claim was studied by Billio *et al.* (2011). Their findings suggested that relationship among hedge funds, banks, insurance companies, and brokers causes systemic risk. Shadow banking system is a non-bank institution which consists of insurance companies, hedge funds, money market funds, and pension funds. Therefore, the connection between credit hedge funds activity and entities of shadow banking system should be carefully examined and supervised to prevent the occurrences of systemic risk because they contribute to credit transformation within shadow banking system (Johns, 2015).

3.4. *Foreign shadow banking*

The issue of shadow banking is a global phenomenon, and foreign shadow banking system can create spillover effects in the global financial system. This also raises concern for systemic risk. However, activities and components of the shadow banking system vary from one country to another (Ricks, 2010). For example, the shadow banking system in China consists of commercial banks which are the dominating power in the system, insurance companies, and trusts. Components of shadow banking systems in China are non-bank financial products, products issued by trust companies and financial leasing companies, credit creation products produced by small loan companies, investment companies, credit guarantee companies, insurance brokerage firms, pawn shops, private equity investment funds, and venture capital funds (Li and Hsu, 2013). China's shadow banking system has been growing. The size and the growth of shadow banking system in China captured the attention of Financial Stability Board (2014) because of its rapid growth. Despite this growth, Mohd-Farid (2012) pointed out that the shadow banking system in Asia is of a less complex nature. Activities of shadow banking in this region usually include traditional provision of finance, while lending was done to certain segments of the economy. The shadow banking system in emerging countries does not look like the systems in developed countries. For example, micro- and macroprudential policies in emerging countries may not be the same as those in developed countries (Acharya *et al.*, 2013). Changes in policies and regulations for the shadow banking system may have positive or negative effects on the global financial systems due to varying results of these policies in different regions of the world. The information gaps also varies from country to country around the world. A wealth of information resides in these gaps, and there is a possibility that large information gaps can grow through shadow banking system. Thus, this raises the concern for systemic risk.

As I mentioned before, shadow banking is a global issue. China can be given as a good example for the growth of money market mutual funds and finance companies. Substantial growth of non-bank activities has also been seen among certain emerging economies. I think this is a clear indication that shadow banking is a global issue. Therefore, challenges of shadow banking, solutions for problems of shadow banking, and regulations of shadow banking should be analyzed globally.

3.5. *Spillover effect*

Failures of the relationship between regulated banking sector and shadow banking system create spillover effect. For example, shadow banking system was working efficiently in the US before the 2007/2008 financial crisis. Therefore, it was not considered to be systematically important and it was not necessary to apply the same degree of regulation on shadow banking system as it was on the regulated banking sector. There was no monitoring system for the build-up risk and potential spillover effect on the stability of the financial system. However, this system suffered a sudden crash during the 2007–2008 financial crisis. There was a negative spillover effect in the system. This happened due to each bank's securitization decision. Thereby, idiosyncratic risks were converted to systemic risk within the financial system. The Financial Stability Board has suggested 'Securitized Banking' model so that the systemic instability of shadow banking system would be mitigated. This means distributing originating loans to the entities which are not in the regulated banking system. These entities would be able to contribute to increasing leverage at the systemic level because they are not subject to capital or liquidity regulation (Meeks *et al.*, 2014).

The shadow banking system does not have access to government backstop. Therefore, they are generally vulnerable. These vulnerabilities of shadow banking activities can create externalities for parts of the financial system. Due to the systemic nature of shadow banking activities, instability or distress within the shadow banking system can create spillover effect on the other part of the financial system, which in turn, affects real economy (Claessens *et al.*, 2012).

3.6. *Governance problem*

Bank capital is the focus of many regulations. Capital regulation can strengthen market incentives for bank shareholders and managers to resolve governance problems. Considering the growth of shadow banking system in the financial system and its interconnectedness with the banking sector, there is a strong case for strengthening the governance framework to protect the financial stability in the economy. However, there is lack of corporate governance in the traditional banking and shadow banking systems. A systemic failure of corporate governance has led to the failure of regulatory and internal governance, and contributed to the financial crisis. Regulatory governance is one of the segments of corporate governance system and refers to the control exercised by regulators over firms through policies and regulations.

Governance regulation is also considered as one of the primary reasons for regulatory arbitrage because institutions prefer to shift the regulatory regime and go to a less regulated or loosely regulated market. Effective regulation improves corporate governance, and objectives of regulation can be met through effective corporate governance. However, there is a difference between the traditional banking and shadow banking related to regulation. Contrary to traditional banking, shadow banking is a less-regulated market.

4. Conclusion

It was proven that shadow banking system raises concern about the systemic risk. The 2007/2008 global financial crisis made regulators around the world take a tougher approach to regulate and supervise the shadow banking system. In the beginning, current regulations were applied to banking, insurance companies, and the pensions sector, but many countries extended their regulatory scope to include commodity futures, credit rating agencies, money market funds, and hedge funds. This was due to the fact that shadow banking system can pose a systemic risk to the financial system if it is not regulated or supervised.

This study examined the sources of systemic risk in the case of shadow banking to provide a risk-mitigation framework. There are several key findings in this study for mitigating risk, and policies may be needed to mitigate the potential systemic risk associated with the shadow banking system. The First finding is related to securitization and funding. The securitization market should be redesigned to mitigate risk. Therefore, key functions of securitization market should be identified, and then the benefits of securitization to the economy should be identified. Second, shadow banking system does not have access to government backstop, but its relationship with commercial banks helps it is funding. The focus of regulating shadow banking system should be on the connection between the shadow banking and traditional banking system because bank-holding companies or insurance companies or even banks themselves are involved in some activities of shadow banking such as housing money market funds or activities related to the securitization. Large commercial banks in the US are part of bank-holding companies. However, bank-holding companies or broker dealers do not have access to discount window and deposit insurance, but commercial bank subsidiaries do have access to deposit insurance and discount window (Adrian, 2014). It is worth noting that commercial banks are separate legal entities and are regulated. However, it was established by the global financial crisis that the shadow banking system raises concern about the systemic risk. This concern was not just related to the its activities outside regulated banks, it was also related to the its interaction and interconnectedness with commercial banks. Therefore, the connection between shadow banking system and traditional commercial banks should be supervised, and its interconnectedness should be within the regulatory framework. Third, there is a difference between the regulation of the shadow banking system and traditional banking. In the case of traditional banking system, prudential regulatory standards and supervisory oversight are applied. In the case of shadow banking credit intermediation, these standards either are not applied or are applied to a lesser degree. In other words, the majority of the credit intermediation activities of shadow banking are regulated in some way but this regulation does not include the prudential supervision (Moreira and Savov, 2014). The Fourth finding is related to regulatory arbitrage. There are a number of shadow banking activities that involve regulatory arbitrage to minimize the capital requirement of the regulated institutions. Capital requirements should be changed in such a way that the regulatory arbitrage can be prevented. In fact, Basel III capital regulations has closed the gaps in preventing the regulatory capital arbitrage. However, there is still a possibility that new regulatory capital arbitrage would emerge in the future. Fifth, spillover effect is another source for systemic risk. Systemic risk is created through transaction spillover into the shadow banking system and between shadow banking and regulated institutions. Therefore, there should be system-wide shadow banking policies applicable. Sixth, foreign shadow banking system can also create a spillover effect. Shadow banking is a global issue. Regulations and activities of shadow banking vary from country to country. Therefore, challenges of shadow banking, solutions for problems of shadow banking, and regulations of shadow banking should be analyzed globally. A global framework should be established to mitigate risk. Seventh, there is strong reliance on credit rating agencies in credit intermediation process. Credit rating agencies should publish additional information to provide transparency of credit ratings. This would improve the investors' understanding about the varied risk of securitization. Therefore, new regulatory standards should be established for credit ratings. Eight, shadow banking operates in the capital markets and fulfills many of the economic functions. However, shadow banking can lead to large information gaps. These gaps can cause fragility in the system. Therefore, it is necessary to recognize and understand the importance of information gaps to prevent systemic risk arising from shadow banking system. Perhaps, it would be much better to require new types of reform to control the information gaps. Ninth, interconnectedness of hedge funds with shadow banking activities can raise systemic risk. Shadow banking system is a non-bank institution that consists of insurance companies, hedge funds, money market funds, and pension funds. Therefore, the connection between credit hedge funds activity and entities of shadow banking system should be carefully examined and supervised to prevent the occurrences of systemic risk because they contribute to credit transformation within the shadow banking system. In addition, reliance on credit rating agencies should be reviewed and necessary rules should be established. Finally, the 10th finding is related to the need for governance regulation. Governance regulation is also considered as one of the primary reasons for regulatory arbitrage because institutions prefer to shift the regulatory regime and go to a less-regulated or loosely regulated market.

In conclusion, the financial crisis indicated the urgent need for improving transparency and monitoring activities of shadow banking system to minimize systemic risk. Efforts and actions for the matters abovementioned were done on an international and coordinated by G20 and Financial Stability Board (FSB). Since then, monitoring the size, trends, and adaptation of global banking system have become the first priority of the Financial Stability Board. However, policies aiming to mitigate systemic risk from shadow banking system should start with an analysis of the economics that motivates the activities of the shadow banking system. A major challenge for financial stability policies for shadow banking is related to the regulatory system. Policies for the shadow banking system should be system-wide and have a macroprudential view because of the interconnections and potentially powerful spillovers among shadow banking entities, and between shadow banks and core regulated financial institutions.

References

Acharya, V. V., Schnabl, P., and Suarez, G. (2013). Securitization without risk transfer. *J. Fin. Econom.*, 107(3), pp. 515–536.

Acharya, V., Khandwala, H., and Öncü, T. S. (2013). The growth of a shadow banking system in emerging markets: Evidence from India. *J. Int. Money Fin.*, 39, pp. 207–230.

Adrian, T., Hyun Song and Shin, H. S. (2009). The shadow banking system: Implications for financial regulation. NY Fed Staff report No 382, July.

Adrian, T. and Shin, H. S. (2010). The changing nature of financial intermediation and the financial Crisis of 2007–09. NY Fed Staff report No 439, March.

Adrian, T. (2014). Financial stability policies for shadow banking. NY Fed Staff report No 664, February.

Adrian, T., Begalle, B., Copeland, A., and Martin, A. (2013). Repo and securities lending. In Haubrich, J. G. and Lo, A. W. (eds.), *Quantifying Systemic Risk Measurement: NBER Research Conference Report Series*, University of Chicago Press.

Bank for International Settlements (1994). Annual Report, 1993–1994. Basle, Switzerland, June.

Bean, C., Paustian, M., Penalver, A., and Taylor, T. (2010). Monetary Policy after the Fall, paper presented at the *2010 Jackson Hole Symposium on Macroeconomic Challenges: The Decade Ahead*, Jackson Hole, Wyoming.

Bengtsson, E. (2016). Investment funds, shadow banking and systemic risk. *J. Fin. Regul. Compl.*, 24(1), pp. 60–73.

Bernanke, B. S. (2010). Causes of the recent financial and economic crisis. Testimony before the Financial Crisis Inquiry Commission, Washington, D.C., September 2.

Bernanke, B. (2011). Global imbalances: Links to economic and financial stability. Speech at the Banque de France, 18 February.

Billio, M., Getmansky, M., Lo, A. W., and Pelizzon, L. (2012). Econometric Measures of Systemic Risk in the Finance and Insurance sectors. *J. Fin. Econom.*, 104(3), pp. 535–559.

Blanchard, O. (2009). The crisis: Basic mechanisms, and appropriate policies. IMF Working Paper 09/80: International Monetary Fund.

Boran, M. (2010). Market dynamics & systemic risk. Paper presented at *23rd Australasian Finance and Banking Conference*. Cambridge: Harvard University.

Borio, C. (2008). The financial turmoil of 2007-?: A preliminary assessment and some policy considerations. BIS Working Papers 251: Bank for International Settlements.

Brunnermeier, Markus. (2009). Deciphering the Liquidity and Credit Crunch 2007–2008. *J. Econom. Persp.*, 23(1).

Claessens, S., Pozsar, Z., Ratnovski, L., and Singh, M. (2012). Shadow banking: economics and policy. IMF Staff Discussion Note 12/12: Washington, D.C.

Copeland, A., Martin, A., and Walker, M. (2011). Repo runs: Evidence from the tri-party repo market. Federal Reserve Bank of New York Staff Report 506.

Covitz, D., Liang, N., and Suarez, G. (2012). The evolution of a financial crisis: Panic in the asset-backed commercial paper market. *J. Fin.*, 68(3).

Cullen, J. (2017). The Repo market: Collateral and systemic risk, In Iris H. Chiu and Iain MacNeil (eds.), *Research Handbook on Shadow Banking: Legal and Regulatory Aspects*. Edward Elgar.

Financial Stability Board. (2011). Shadow banking: Strengthening oversight and regulation.

Financial Stability Board. (2012). Strengthening oversight and regulation of shadow banking, Consultative Document.

Financial Stability Board. (2013). Strengthening oversight and regulation of shadow banking: Policy framework for addressing shadow banking risks in securities lending and repos, 29 August.

Financial Stability Board. (2014). Strengthening oversight and regulation of shadow banking: Regulatory framework for haircuts on non-centrally cleared securities financing transactions, October.

Gallin, J. (2013). Shadow banking and the funding of the nonfinancial sector, Federal Reserve Board Finance and Economics Discussion Series 2013–50.

Gennaioli, N., Shleifer, A., and Vishny, R. (2013). A model of shadow banking. *J. Fin.*, 68(4), pp. 1331–1363.

Georg, C. P. (2014). Bail-out of African Bank risks future problems, *Business Day*.

Gorton, G. (2009). Slapped in the face by the invisible hand: Banking and the panic of 2007+, Paper presented at *the 2009 Financial Markets Conference: Financial Innovation and Crisis*. Federal Reserve Bank of Atlanta.

Gorton, G. and Metrick, A. (2011). Regulating the shadow banking system. Brookings Paper on Economic Activity, pp. 261–312.

Gorton, G. and Metrick, A. (2012). Securitized banking and the run on repo. *J. Fin. Econom.*, 104, pp. 425–451.

Johns, Andrews. (2015). Regulating hedge funds for systemic stability: The EU's approach. *Eur. Law J.*, 21(6).

Kaufman, G. G. and Scott, K. E. (2003). What is systemic risk and do bank regulators retard or contribute to it? *The Independent Rev.* VII(3), pp. 371–390.

Knight, M. D. (2007). Financial risks: A view from the BIS, Speech at the Central Bank of Argentina 2007 Money and Banking Conference, Buenos Aires, 4–5 June. Available at http://www.bis.org/speeches/sp070606a.htm.

Levine, R. (2010). An Autopsy of the U.S. financial system. *J. Fin. Econom. Policy*, 2(3), pp. 196–213.

Li, J. and Hsu, S. (2013). Shadow banking in China: Institutional risks. Working Paper series no 334: 1–17. Political Economic Research Institute of the University of Massachusetts.

Martin, A., Skeie, D., and Thadden von E. (2011). Repo runs. Federal Reserve Bank of New York Staff Report 444.

Meeks, R., Nelson, B., and Alessandri, P. (2014). Shadow banks and macroeconomic instability. Bank of England Working Paper No.487, p. ii.

Mohd-Farid, M. A. (2012). Monitoring shadow banking and its challenges: The Malaysian experience. Available at: http://www.bis.org/ifc/events/6ifcconf/mohdfarid.pdf.

Moreira, A. and Savov, A. (2013). The macroeconomics of shadow banking. Yale University Working Paper. Available at: http://faculty.som.yale.edu/alanmoreira/Papers/ShadowMacro.pdf.
Moreira, A. and Savov, A. (2014). The macroeconomics of shadow banking. Working Paper 20335, NBER.
Nabilou, H. and Pacces, A. (2017). The law and Economics of Shadow Banking, In Iris H. Chiu and Iain MacNeil (eds.), *Research Handbook on Shadow Banking: Legal and Regulatory Aspects*. Edward Elgar.
Ordonez, G. and Piguillem, F. (2015). Retirement in the shadow (Banking), mimeo, University of Pennsylvania and Einaudi Institute for Economics and Finance.
Plantin, G. (2015). Shadow banking and bank capital regulation. *Rev. Fin. Stud.*, 28(1), pp. 146–175.
Pozsar, Z., Adrian, T., Ashcraft, A., and Boesky, H. (2010 revised 2012). Shadow banking. New York Fed Staff Report No 458.
Pozsar, Z., Adrian, T., Ashcraft, A.B., and Boesky, H. (2013). Shadow banking. Federal Reserve Bank of New York Economic Policy Review 19(2), pp. 1–16.
Ricks, M. (2010). Shadow banking and financial regulation. Columbia Law and Economics Working Paper 370. Vanderbilt University: Nashville.
Singh, M. and Aitken, J. (2010), The (sizeable) role of rehypothecation in the shadow banking system. IMF working paper No 172, July.
Stein, J. (2010). Securitization, shadow banking, and financial fragility. *Daedalus*, 139(4), pp. 41–51.
Sunderam, A. (2015). Money creation and the shadow banking system. *Rev. Fin. Stud.*, 28(4), pp. 939–977.
Trichet, J. C. (2009). The global dimension of the crisis. Speech delivered at the Foreign Correspondents' Club of Japan, Tokyo, April 18.
Verona, F., Martins, M. F., and Drumond, I. (2013). (Un)anticipated monetary policy in a DSGE model with a shadow banking system. Bank of Finland Research Discussion Papers 4: Bank for Finland.

Chapter 13

The Impact of News Sentiment on Financial Risk: An Extreme Value Approach

Peter Julian Cayton*,† and Kin-Yip Ho‡

*School of Statistics, University of the Philippines Diliman
†Research School of Finance, Actuarial Studies, and Statistics, The Australian National University, Australia

Abstract

Methods of estimating and analysing the impact of news sentiment on the behaviour of prices of financial instruments are proposed, based on the block maxima approach. The methods assume that news sentiment affects the maximum and minimum returns of an instrument through their generalised extreme value distributions. By applying these methods to the stock return data of the S&P500 firms, the predictive ability and accuracy of our methods are assessed from a risk-management perspective. To quantify the impact of news sentiment, we make use of the various sentiment measures from the comprehensive and unique RavenPack® database, which captures more than 1200 types of firm-specific and macroeconomic-specific events. The empirical results suggest that news sentiment has the potential of enhancing the predictive ability of our methods.

1. Motivation and Background

News about a company such as press releases, business news shows, and company reports is one of the main sources of information about the company for investment decisions. As new information is being processed, market participants trade their company's shares based on perceived profitability or risk of transactions.

News sentiments affect stock price movements and return levels. In the cross-sectional analysis done by Baker and Wurgler (2006) between stock returns and investor sentiment, they conclude that investor sentiment at the beginning of the period has larger effects on securities that are difficult to arbitrage and with highly subjective valuations. High-sentiment episodes make stocks more attractive to optimists and speculators, yet not for arbitrage traders; such is reversed in low sentiment states.

In an event analysis by Berkman, *et al.* (2009), high differences in opinions among investors about a specific stock will have significantly lower returns around earnings announcements than stocks with low differences of opinions between investors. Such a phenomenon of high-difference-of-opinions stocks is exacerbated for a subsample of stocks which are difficult to sell short. In addition, their analysis concludes that these high-difference-of-opinions and short-sales-constrained stocks will have price run-ups before earnings announcements but will have larger drops after the event.

With the Dow Jones Industrials stock index, the time span of the impact of Reuters news sentiments does not only lasts for days as previously discussed but can be measured over months with negative news sentiments being more persistent than positive news sentiment (Uhl, 2011).

News sentiments also affect the correlations between the futures and underlying stock markets, especially as matching quotes of individual stocks is adopted by algorithmic traders. Ho *et al.* (2012) conclude that sufficiently large news uncertainty can break down quote return correlations, which leads futures traders to switch from automating quote matching to manually analysing and updating quotes, and such a breakdown phenomenon is more prominently observed in larger stocks but this firm size effect falls during high volatility periods.

With regards to news topics, Ho *et al.* (2013) find that firm-specific news sentiments tend to have a larger impact than macroeconomic news sentiments with respect to the volatility of price. Their work also concludes that news sentiments account for a larger proportion in more volatile periods than in calmer periods of price movements.

Different investors and market participants have different ways of reading news, fitting their strategies and kind of financial transaction. Key results from Liebmann *et al.* (2016) on their analysis of Reuters news sentiments among traders show that: (1) there is difference in focus by equity and credit default swaps (CDS) traders for the same news content, (2) there is disagreement among traders concerning news about debt, especially on mergers and acquisitions, and (3) there is the impact of the Great Recession on debt news and its altering of the inverse relationship between the two trading markets on news days.

News sentiments influence the price movements and returns on stocks as investors absorb the news. These effects may be instantaneous, in terms of days such as press release events, or may persistent longer, in terms of months. Investors may change their behaviours, especially in terms of whether to use automated quoting technology or manually monitor, or depending on the kind of investor they are with respect to the financial contracts they are trading. News sentiments also introduces more uncertainty in the markets, as in sentiments explain a larger amount of volatility. However, no published research has been found on analysing the impact of news sentiments on extreme stock price fluctuations and on providing a risk-management perspective on such analysis, which this chapter takes as an open research opportunity.

The chapter presents novel research in analysing the impact of news sentiments on extreme stock price fluctuations through time series analysis and extreme value theory with a perspective on financial risk estimation and management. In this respect, the chapter uses the gathered wisdom of previous work and suggests new methodologies to look at using news sentiments in a risk-management approach as price movements contribute to volatility.

In our application of the methodology to the Johnson and Johnson (JNJ) and JPMorgan (JPM) stock prices from the years 2004 to 2014, we found that previous-day's news sentiments can increase volatility overall, with extremely negative returns becoming likely for the JPM stock than the positive extreme returns. For the JNJ, negative news sentiments on the previous day would open for higher positive extreme returns on the current day. When these results were applied to risk estimation, the chapter shows that with news sentiments, risk is adequately measured through lower instances of price movement exceedances, and if exceedances were observed, they would be smaller compared to when news was not accounted in the measurement.

The rest of the chapter is presented as follows. News sentiments data from the RavenPack News Analytics Database and the weighing scheme to aggregate the news sentiments scores into a daily statistic is discussed in the second section. Statistical methodologies, namely autoregressive moving average model, conditional heteroscedasticity model, extreme value theory methods, value-at-risk, and loss function statistics, are discussed in the third section. The fourth section discusses the features of the stock price data used for the chapter, and the fifth section presents the statistical results and their discussion. Conclusions and future directions of the research are contained in the sixth section.

2. Data on News Sentiments

As a variable for news sentiments, the RavenPack News Analytics database is used (RavenPack News Analytics, 2013). It is a news sentiments and events database that tracks and monitors news that can potentially impact the financial market, the news concerning locations such as countries, corporations, organizations such as the World Bank, currencies, and commodities such as rice or wheat. For each news article or release that comes into their stream, metadata such as time stamp, entity identification, and kind of news are gathered as data. From the data, two systems of scoring are computed. One is a relevance scoring (REL) from 0 to 100 which is based on whether the entity in a news story is the main topic or title or identifying at which part of the body of the news article it is present. A REL of 100 means the entity is the main subject of the news, any number less than 100 indicates positioning in the article. Another score is the composite sentiments scores (CSS) that range from 0 to 100 based on a proprietary algorithm. The CSS represents a combination of various sentiment analysis techniques with respect to generating a score for a given news story. CSS values below 50 imply negative sentiment on the entity concerned, while those above 50 imply positive sentiments.

For the chapter, a weighted score of news sentiment was used. Suppose that within a time period $(t-1, t]$, there are k news articles coming into the database about firm f, each happening in times $\{t_1, t_2, \ldots, t_k\}$. For each news article, the scoring scheme generates a pair of scores $(\mathrm{REL}_{f,t_j}, \mathrm{CSS}_{f,t_j})$. The weighted news sentiment (WNS) score at time t for firm f is

$$\mathrm{WNS}_{f,t} = \sum_{j=1}^{k} \left[\left(\mathrm{CSS}_{f,t_j} - 50\right) \frac{\mathrm{REL}_{f,t_j}}{100} \right]. \tag{1}$$

This adjusts for positive and negative sentiments accumulated between time $t-1$ and t based on the relevance of the news. Positive WNS firm scores mean that over the period, the firm has an accumulated a net positive news sentiment for the period, while negative WNS means that negative news sentiment dominated the period.

The WNS score is an important variable for news sentiment and will be used for our analysis. As the chapter focuses on how news sentiments affect extreme price movements, the WNS score will be used on extreme value methodology as a covariate.

3. Methodology

In analysing extreme price fluctuations, the methodology is a system of statistical techniques that describe volatility and extreme fluctuation behaviour in hourly data. The specifications are as follows: (1) an autoregressive moving average (ARMA) of order (1,1) model to describe the mean return levels, (2) the multiplicative component generalised autoregressive conditional heteroscedasticity (MCGARCH) for intra-daily volatility, and (3) the block maxima method using the generalised extreme value distribution for the maximum and minimum return levels. The risk measure called value-at-risk is also discussed as a means of evaluating the methodology. Comparison statistics facilitate the evaluation by comparing the method with different model specifications. In the chapter, the return level is defined as the log-difference of stock prices at a period between time $v-1$ and v, or $r_v = 100 \times (\ln P_v - \ln P_{v-1})$.

3.1. *The ARMA(1,1) model*

The specification of the ARMA(1,1) model (Box *et al.*, 1994) for a return series r_t with index t is as follows:

$$r_t = \phi_0 + \phi_1 r_{t-1} + \theta_1 \epsilon_{t-1} + \epsilon_t. \tag{2}$$

The parameters ϕ_0, ϕ_1, and θ_1 are the intercept, autoregressive, and moving average parameters, respectively. For the model to produce stable results, its parameters should follow the constraints $|\phi_1| \leq 1$ and $|\theta_1| \leq 1$. The series ϵ_t is a residual series with zero mean and no autocorrelation, i.e., $E[\epsilon_t] = 0$ and $Cov(\epsilon_{t-k}\epsilon_t) = 0$ for any positive integer k.

The model describes the serial correlation behaviours of the mean return levels. As will be shown later, there are some intra-daily stock returns with serial correlation among hours. However, the mean model cannot describe inherent volatility even in intra-daily data, so a GARCH model is considered.

3.2. *The MCGARCH model*

The multiplicative component generalised autoregressive conditional heteroscedasticity (MCGARCH) model is an intra-daily conditional volatility model proposed by Engle and Sokalska (2012) and breaks down the conditional volatility of intra-daily returns as follows:

$$r_{t,i} = \mu_{t,i} + \epsilon_{t,i}, \tag{3}$$

$$\epsilon_{t,i} = \sqrt{q_{t,i} h_t s_i} z_{t,i}. \tag{4}$$

Equation (3) is the mean specification, where $r_{t,i}$ is the return series for day $t = 1, 2, \ldots, T$ at hour $i = 1, 2, \ldots, N$ and $\mu_{t,i}$ is the predefined mean structure of the intra-daily data, such as an ARMA model or any structural specification. The error structure is described in Eq. (4) and shows how the error series $\epsilon_{t,i}$ can be broken into 4 components: (1) the standardised series of uncorrelated terms $z_{t,i}$ with common mean $E[z_{t,i}] = 0$ and $[z_{t,i}] = 1$, (2) the stochastic volatility term $q_{t,i}$, (3) the volatility of the daily returns h_t, and (4) the intra-daily seasonal volatility term s_i.

To estimate h_t, a GARCH(p,q) model (Bollerslev, 1986) on the daily return series r_t is fit first, and the estimated volatility is extracted. The estimation specification to conduct this is specified below

$$r_t = \mu_t + \epsilon_t, \quad \epsilon_t = \sqrt{h_t} z_t, \tag{5}$$

$$h_t = \alpha_0 + \sum_{i=1}^{p} \alpha_p \epsilon_{t-p}^2 + \sum_{i=1}^{q} \beta_q h_{t-q}. \tag{6}$$

Other GARCH specifications can be used for estimating h_t but for the purpose of the chapter, the GARCH(1,1) model is used as convergence was achievable by this specification.

The next step is to estimate the seasonal intra-daily volatility term s_i, which is done by the following formula below:

$$\tilde{s}_i = \frac{1}{T} \sum_{t=1}^{T} \frac{\tilde{\epsilon}_{t,i}^2}{\tilde{h}_t} \tag{7}$$

The term $\tilde{\epsilon}_{t,i}^2$ is the square of the residual series after generating the estimated mean series $\tilde{\mu}_{t,i}$ such that $\tilde{\epsilon}_{t,i} = r_{t,i} - \tilde{\mu}_{t,i}$ and $\tilde{h}_t$ is based on the estimates of equation 6.

From the $\tilde{s}_i$ estimates, adjusted intra-daily residuals $\bar{\epsilon}_{t,i} = \tilde{\epsilon}_{t,i}/\sqrt{h_t s_i}$ can be extracted and used to estimate $q_{t,i}$ with a GARCH(1,1) model

$$\bar{\epsilon}_{t,i} = \sqrt{q_{t,i}} z_{t,i}, \tag{8}$$

$$q_{t,i} = \alpha_0^* + \alpha_1^* \bar{\epsilon}_{t,i-1} + \beta_1^* q_{t,i-1}. \tag{9}$$

In the case when $i = 1, \bar{\epsilon}_{t,i-1} = \bar{\epsilon}_{t-1,N}$ and $q_{t,i-1} = q_{t-1,N}$. By this result, the standardised residual series $\tilde{z}_{t,i}$ can be generated and will be used to estimate for the generalised extreme value distributions for analysis and financial risk estimation.

3.3. *Block maxima approach*

From the $\tilde{z}_{t,i}$ series, the daily maximum series $\tilde{z}_{t,\max} = \max\{\tilde{z}_{t,1}, \ldots, \tilde{z}_{t,N}\}$ and daily minimum series $\tilde{z}_{t,\min} = \min\{\tilde{z}_{t,1}, \ldots, \tilde{z}_{t,N}\}$ are generated. These two series are fitted to the generalised extreme value distribution (GEVD) (Fisher and Tippett, 1928; Coles, 2001) described below:

$$\Pr[Z_t \leq z_t] = \exp\left\{-\left[1 + \xi_{\mathrm{EV}}\left(\frac{z_t - \mu_{\mathrm{EV},t}}{\sigma_{\mathrm{EV}}}\right)\right]^{-1/\xi_{\mathrm{EV}}}\right\}. \tag{10}$$

The range for z where the GEVD works is $1+\xi_{\mathrm{EV}}(z_t-\mu_{\mathrm{EV}})\ \sigma_{\mathrm{EV}} \geq 0$. The $\mu_{\mathrm{EV},t}$ is the location parameter of the GEVD and can be any real number. It is with $\mu_{\mathrm{EV},t}$ that linear modelling will be done with the WNS score as the covariate with specification

$$\mu_{\mathrm{EV},t} = \beta_{\mathrm{EV},0} + \beta_{\mathrm{EV},1}\mathrm{WNS}_{t-1}. \tag{11}$$

The specification assumes that traders will react to the accumulative news sentiment of the previous day, and such a phenomenon affects the magnitude of the extreme fluctuations.

The parameters σ_{EV} and ξ_{EV} are the scale and shape parameters of the GEVD, respectively, with $\sigma_{\mathrm{EV}} > 0$ and ξ_{EV} being any real number. In the case when $\xi_{\mathrm{EV}} = 0$, the GEVD reduces to the Gumbel distribution (Gumbel, 1941; Coles, 2001) specified below, for any value of z_t

$$\Pr[Z_t \leq z_t] = \exp\left\{-\exp\left[-\left(\frac{z_t - \mu_{\mathrm{EV},t}}{\sigma_{\mathrm{EV}}}\right)\right]\right\}. \tag{12}$$

By inverting Eqs. (10) and (12), the $(100\tau)\%$ percentile at time $t, \omega_{\tau,t}$, for the GEVD are derived as follows:

$$\omega_{\tau,t} = \mu_{\mathrm{EV},t} + \frac{\sigma_{\mathrm{EV}}}{\xi_{\mathrm{EV}}}\left[(-\ln\tau)^{-\xi_{\mathrm{EV}}} - 1\right], \quad \xi_{\mathrm{EV}} \neq 0, \tag{13}$$

$$\omega_{\tau,t} = \mu_{\mathrm{EV},t} + \sigma_{\mathrm{EV}}\ln(-\ln\tau), \quad \xi_{\mathrm{EV}} = 0. \tag{14}$$

These GEVD percentiles are important in generating financial risk measures called value-at-risk as a means of evaluating the proposed methodology.

The GEVD distribution is the asymptotic distribution of the sample maximum of the data (Fisher and Tippett, 1928; Coles, 2001; De Haan and Ferreira, 2006). In modelling minima, the negative of the minimum is fitted to the GEVD as it is like modelling the maximum in that perspective. The GEVD has stability conditions that data should fulfil for the approximation purposes. These conditions are weak such that financial data fulfil these conditions and the data have been modelled using the distribution, such as Embrechts *et al.* (1999), McNeil *et al.* (2005) and Tsay (2010). In their discussion of the distribution, they generate risk measures for financial data as a tool for assessing risk and allocating risk capital for financial institutions.

3.4. *Risk measurement: Value-at-risk*

Value-at-Risk (VaR) with $100(1-\tau)\%$ coverage probability at time t, $VaR_t(\tau)$, is a risk measure defined as the return level in which there is a $100(1-\tau)\%$ chance that it will not be exceeded (Jorion, 2006). Depending on the kind of transaction, the VaR can be defined as the $(100\tau)\%$ percentile of the return distribution for a long position or the $100(1-\tau)\%$ percentile for the short position.

In a typical set-up on time t given that a mean estimate $\hat{\delta}_t$, a variance estimate $\hat{\sigma}_t^2$, and a $(100\tau)\%$ residual distribution percentile $\hat{d}_\tau$ is generated, then the VaR for the long position is

$$\mathrm{VaR}_t(\tau) = \hat{\delta}_t + \hat{\sigma}_t \hat{d}_\tau. \tag{15}$$

To derive the VaR for the short position, change $\hat{d}_\tau$ to $\hat{d}_{1-\tau}$, or for symmetric distributions, to $-\hat{d}_\tau$.

For the purpose of the chapter, VaRs have been derived in the following specifications: (1) ARMA(1,1)-MCGARCH with normal or Gaussian distribution assumption on errors and without news sentiments, (2) ARMA(1,1)-MCGARCH with GEVD assumption on the distributions of the maximum and minimum but without news sentiments, and (3) ARMA(1,1)-MCGARCH with GEVD assumption on the distributions of the maximum and minimum with news sentiments as covariates in the GEVD location parameter. The corresponding formulas for the one-hour-ahead long position VaRs are

$$\mathrm{VaR}_{t,\mathrm{Gaussian}}(\tau) = \tilde{\mu}_{t,i+1} - \sqrt{\tilde{q}_{t,i+1}\tilde{h}_t\tilde{s}_{i+1}} \times \Phi^{-1}(\tau), \tag{16}$$

$$\mathrm{VaR}_{t,\mathrm{EV}(no\ \mathrm{WNS})}(\tau) = \tilde{\mu}_{t,i+1} - \sqrt{\tilde{q}_{t,i+1}\tilde{h}_t\tilde{s}_{i+1}} \times \omega_{1-\tau}, \tag{17}$$

$$\mathrm{VaR}_{t,\mathrm{EV}(\mathrm{WNS})}(\tau) = \tilde{\mu}_{t,i+1} - \sqrt{\tilde{q}_{t,i+1}\tilde{h}_t\tilde{s}_{i+1}} \times \omega_{1-\tau,t}. \tag{18}$$

The term $\Phi^{-1}(\tau)$ means the $(100\tau)\%$ percentile of the standard normal or Z distribution. The terms $\omega_{1-\tau}$ and $\omega_{1-\tau,t}$ are based on Eq. (13), but ω_τ has $\mu_{\mathrm{EV},t} = \mu_{\mathrm{EV}} = \beta_{\mathrm{EV},0}$ since the WNS score is not used in modelling. To solve for long position VaR for GEVD, the negative of the minimum is modelled. For the short position, the VaR equations become

$$\mathrm{VaR}_{t,\mathrm{Gaussian}}(\tau) = \tilde{\mu}_{t+1,i} + \sqrt{\tilde{q}_{t,i+1}\tilde{h}_t\tilde{s}_{i+1}} \times \Phi^{-1}(\tau), \tag{19}$$

$$\mathrm{VaR}_{t,\mathrm{EV}(no\ \mathrm{WNS})}(\tau) = \tilde{\mu}_{t,i+1} + \sqrt{\tilde{q}_{t,i+1}\tilde{h}_t\tilde{s}_{i+1}} \times \omega_\tau, \tag{20}$$

$$\mathrm{VaR}_{t,\mathrm{EV(WNS)}}(\tau) = \tilde{\mu}_{t,i+1} + \sqrt{\tilde{q}_{t,i+1}\tilde{h}_t\tilde{s}_{i+1}} \times \omega_{\tau,t}. \tag{21}$$

The result of these three using selected S&P500 stocks will be facilitated by comparison statistics that are evaluated with in-sample and out-of-sample perspectives.

3.5. *Comparison statistics*

In evaluating multiple VaR models, the comparison statistics are based on a family of loss functions introduced by Lopez (1998). These loss functions tend to have this general form for the long-position VaR for a model m at time $t+1$:

$$L_{m,t+1} = \begin{cases} f, & \text{if } r_{t+1} < \mathrm{VaR}_{t,m}(\tau) \\ g, & \text{if } r_{t+1} \geq \mathrm{VaR}_{t,m}(\tau) \end{cases}. \tag{22}$$

The relationship is switched when dealing with the short-position VaRs. Two loss functions are used as they have pragmatic implications, and they are the (1) the binary loss function $L^{\mathrm{Bin}}_{m,t+1}$ and (2) the linear loss function $L^{\mathrm{Lin}}_{m,t+1}$. Their corresponding specifications for the long position are:

$$L^{\mathrm{Bin}}_{m,t+1} = \begin{cases} 1, & \text{if } r_{t+1} < \mathrm{VaR}_{t,m}(\tau) \\ 0, & \text{if } r_{t+1} \geq \mathrm{VaR}_{t,m}(\tau) \end{cases}. \tag{23}$$

$$L^{\mathrm{Lin}}_{m,t+1} = \begin{cases} |r_{t+1} - \mathrm{VaR}_{t,m}(\tau)|, & \text{if } r_{t+1} < \mathrm{VaR}_{t,m}(\tau) \\ 0, & \text{if } r_{t+1} \geq \mathrm{VaR}_{t,m}(\tau) \end{cases}. \tag{24}$$

The short-position loss functions would simply be a switch of the direction of the inequalities. Low levels of loss function values are desired for purposes of comparison.

The binary loss function counts on how many instances the data exceeded the estimated VaR model and how many times the linear loss function would be hourly exceeding from the VaR value.

In the chapter, the hourly average loss function values for each model in both in-sample and out-of-sample periods will be analyzed for comparison.

4. Application to Real Data

The methodology is applied to two widely traded stocks in the S&P 500: the JPMorgan Chase (JPM) and the Johnson & Johnson (JNJ) hourly stocks data from 9:00 h to 16:00 h Eastern Standard Time covering the dates from January 5, 2004 to August 29, 2014 for the JPM data making up 20952 hourly observations and January 4, 2011 to July 31, 2014 for the JNJ data for 7144 hourly observations. The out-of-sample period for the data is the most recent 2000 observations, making an approximate 250 days for 8 hourly observations per day with the rest of each stock dataset as in-sample periods. End-of-day stock prices corresponding with the spans for each firm are used to estimate the daily volatility which is necessary for the MCGARCH model. The hourly tick data and the end-of-day stock price data are downloaded from the Thomson Reuters Tick History database (https://tickhistory.thomsonreuters.com/).

With the dataset, the return series $r_{t,i} = 100 \times (\ln P_{t,i} - \ln P_{t,i-1})$ is derived for the hourly tick data, with the first hourly tick of the day having returns based on subtracting the previous day's last hourly tick. The ARMA-MCGARCH procedure is estimated using the rugarch package in *R* (Ghalanos, 2015). With the Gaussian model assumption, the GEVD estimation is skipped. For the other two models, to facilitate the estimation of the GEVD parameters, the daily maximum return and daily negative minimum return levels are derived from the hourly data. The collection of daily maximum series and daily negative minimum series of returns are used to estimate the GEVD parameters for each series. The fgev function of the evd package (Stephenson, 2002) in *R* estimates the distribution parameters. As covariate to facilitate solving VaR in Eq. (18), the WNS score as defined in Eq. (1) and derived from the RavenPack® database are solved for daily time points. After estimating the corresponding ARMA-MCGARCH and GEVD parameters, the behaviour of extreme fluctuations is analysed with respect to news sentiment score levels.

To assess the ability of describing extreme fluctuations, the 99% one-hour-ahead VaR and the 95% 1-h-ahead VaR measures for both the long and the short positions using Eqs. (16)–(21) are derived. The loss functions described in Eqs. (23) and (24) are used as measures of accuracy in terms of accounting price fluctuations not exceeding the VaR.

5. Results and Discussion

5.1. *Descriptive analysis*

Figure 1 below shows the time plot for the JPM hourly stock tick data set. Noticeable troughs correspond to the years 2008 and 2012, which are years of financial crises such as the 2007–2008 Great Recession (Temin, 2010) and the European debt crisis of 2011–2012 (Stracca, 2013).

With respect to the hourly stock price of the JNJ as seen in Fig 2, the trend is relatively more stable and on incline, as the period of 2011 to 2014 did not introduce any major shock to the firm.

With respect to hourly return levels, Fig. 3 shows that there is volatility clustering in the JPM stock in the years between 2007 to 2009, and in a weaker scale for 2011. The JNJ stock had minor volatility clustering during the latter part of 2011–2012 but spikes in two directions occurred during the latter part of 2013 and on the first few days of 2014.

The daily WNS were plotted in Fig. 4 below and showed that for JPM there were certain days when the firm was getting negative news sentiment in 2012 but had two sets of days in 2013 with very high positive sentiment. For JNJ, the years of 2011 and 2012 brought some uncertainty with respect to their news sentiments as scores varied in a wide range of values, but there was a bias toward negative sentiments. Years 2013 and 2014 were calmer years for news sentiments for JNJ.

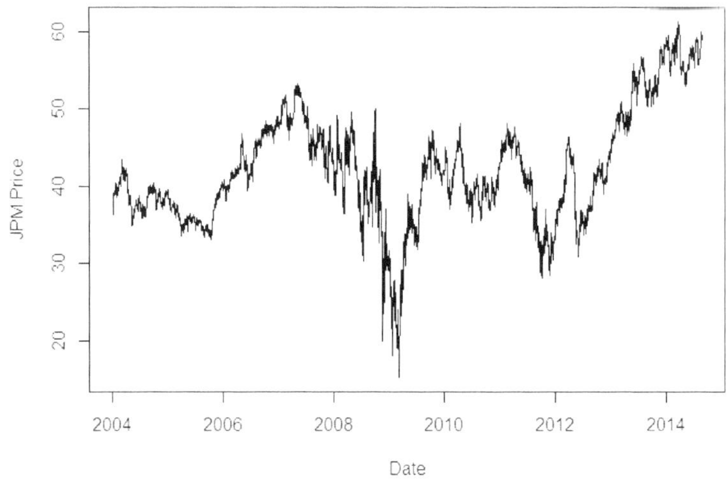

Figure 1. Time Plot of the JPM Hourly Tick Stock Price

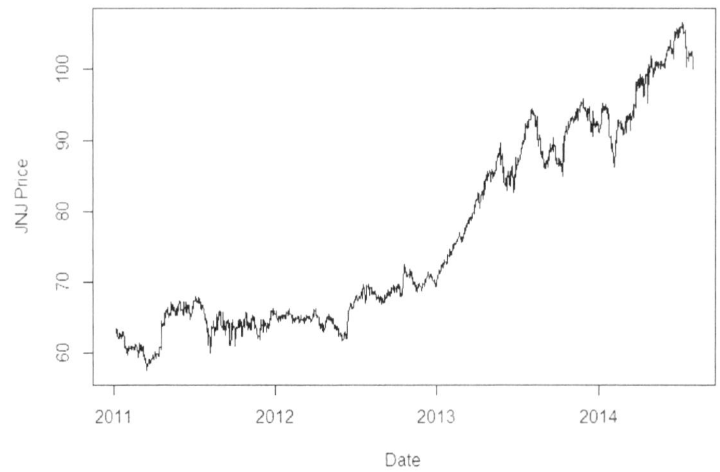

Figure 2. Time Plot of the JNJ Hourly Tick Stock Price

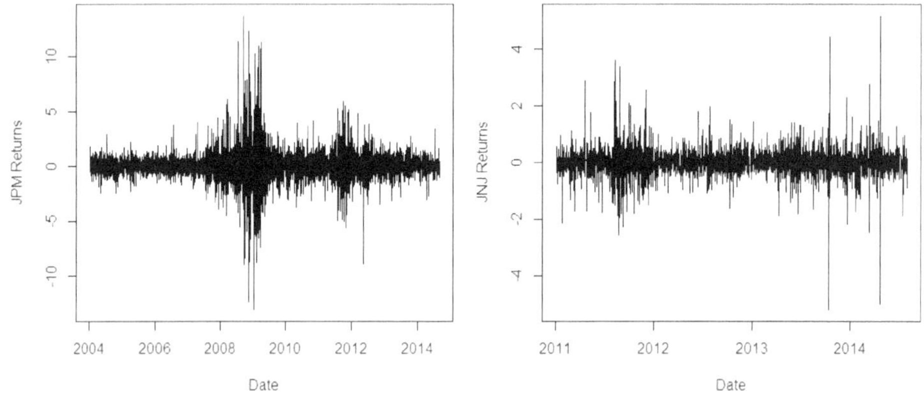

Figure 3. Return Plot of the JPM and JNJ Hourly Tick Data

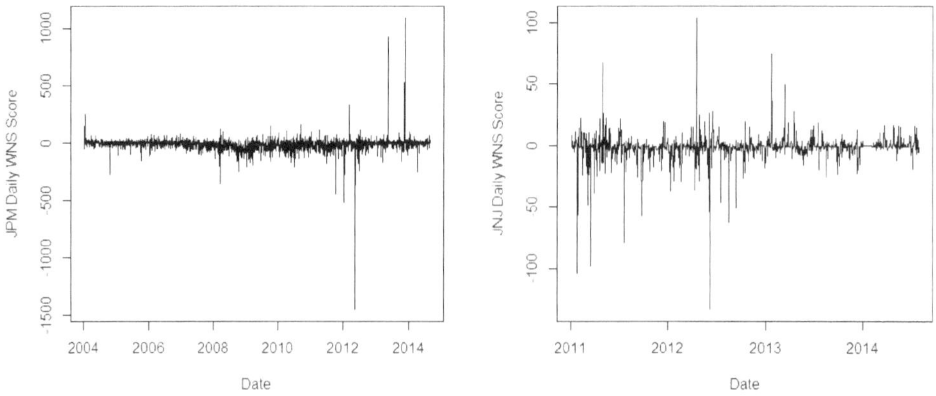

Figure 4. Daily WNS Scores for JPM and JNJ

Table 1. Summary Statistics for JPM and JNJ Variables

	JPM		JNJ	
	Returns	**WNS**	**Returns**	**WNS**
Mean	0.0035	−16.370	0.0069	−1.688
Minimum	13.0900	−1453.000	−5.1620	−133.100
First Quartile	−0.2412	−31.360	−0.1329	−3.400
Median	0.0000	−8.750	0.0015	−0.960
Third Quartile	0.2426	6.605	0.1458	0.530
Maximum	13.6600	1087.00	5.1510	103.70
Standard Deviation	0.8498	61.559	0.3549	11.856
Skewness	0.5163	−3.227	0.2416	−2.332
Excess Kurtosis	35.5164	192.217	30.671	40.979

Note: Nonzero skewness and high excess kurtosis indicate poor fit of the normal distribution to describe returns.

The summary statistics for the hourly returns and the daily WNS scores are displayed below in Table 1. All variables exhibit non-normal distribution features such as skewness being non-zero and excess kurtosis being higher than zero, and special notice should be given to returns not being Gaussian as it is an assumption in the first VaR model, Eqs. (16) and (19).

5.2. *Covariate GEVD analysis*

The estimates for the ARMA-MCGARCH model and the GEVD model without covariates will be left in the appendix. The estimates for the covariate GEVD model will be displayed in Table 2.

On the JPM results, the coefficient of the news sentiments score, $\beta_{\mathrm{EV},1}$, is significant for the negative minimum but not for the maximum. With the negative minimum, there is a small but statistically significant positive relationship. This means that if the previous day there was more optimism in terms of growing positive news sentiment for JPM, then the range of returns for the current day will expand from the minimum while the maximum might be flat, given that stochastic, diurnal, and daily volatility have been accounted. This means that negative returns become more possible in days when previously there was positive news sentiment for the firm. In terms of range volatility, an interpretation is that for JPM, optimism in terms of positive news sentiment on the previous day, the current day will have increases in volatility with negative returns being more likely than positive returns.

Table 2. Model Estimates for the Covariate GEVD Model for JPM and JNJ

	JPM Results			JNJ Results		
	Estimate	Standard Error	Asymp. p-Value	Estimate	Standard Error	Asymp. p-Value
GEVD for maximum						
$\beta_{\text{EV},0}$	0.96814	0.01459	0.00000	0.95837	0.02272	0.00000
$\beta_{\text{EV},1}$	0.00000	0.00012	1.00000	−0.00339	0.00171	0.04772
σ_{EV}	0.67294	0.01412	0.00000	0.58128	0.01618	0.00000
ξ_{EV}	0.00000	0.01113	1.00000	0.04589	0.01902	0.01586
GEVD for negative minimum						
$\beta_{\text{EV},0}$	0.98554	0.01375	0.00000	0.86908	0.02366	0.00000
$\beta_{\text{EV},1}$	0.00023	0.00007	0.00074	0.00006	0.00157	0.96865
σ_{EV}	0.60863	0.01023	0.00000	0.60274	0.01749	0.00000
ξ_{EV}	0.09479	0.01369	0.00000	0.10894	0.02029	0.00000

Note: High p-values indicate that the null hypothesis that a GEVD parameter equals zero is not rejected.

For the JNJ results, $\beta_{\text{EV},1}$ for the maximum is statistically significant but in the negative direction. The $\beta_{\text{EV},1}$ for the negative minimum is not significant and negligible. This means that if there was an observed increase in news sentiment in the previous day, the maximum tends to decline while the minimum may not change, given that volatility factors and expected mean return movements have been accounted. It also implies that if there was a developing level of pessimism in terms of news sentiment in the previous day, then the maximum tends to be higher while the minimum might stay unchanged. In terms of range volatility, optimism in the previous day in terms of increasingly positive news sentiment on JNJ would imply smaller volatilities in the current day. On the other hand, if previous day sentiment was more pessimistic with declining sentiment scores, volatility would increase for the current day with higher returns being more likely.

In both cases, the results tend to support a contrarian approach. This phenomenon is typically observable in big news events such as earning announcements (Kaniel *et al.*, 2012) where overreaction and underreaction pre-earnings announcement can bring abnormal returns in either long or short positions. These occurrences tend to agree with the idea of overconfidence (Daniel and Hirschleifer, 2015) with respect to the treatment of news sentiments.

Table 3. In-Sample Loss Function Statistics

	In-Sample			
	Maximum		Negative Minimum	
	Binary	Linear	Binary	Linear
99% VaR Model Results for JPM				
ARMA-MCGARCH	0.01287	7,127.235	0.01639	6,566.422
ARMA-MCGARCH-GEVD	0.00136	1,364.895	0.00164	1,112.253
ARMA-MCGARCH-GEVD-WNS	0.00147	1,393.101	0.00164	1,115.665
Model Results for JNJ				
ARMA-MCGARCH	0.02551	4,233.131	0.03125	4,903.569
ARMA-MCGARCH-GEVD	0.00230	587.423	0.00207	543.456
ARMA-MCGARCH-GEVD-WNS	0.00207	578.087	0.00207	543.529
95% VaR Model Results for JPM				
ARMA-MCGARCH	0.03743	18,234.160	0.04271	18,260.020
ARMA-MCGARCH-GEVD	0.00550	3,556.140	0.00596	2,802.544
ARMA-MCGARCH-GEVD-WNS	0.00147	1,393.101	0.00164	1,115.665
Model Results for JNJ				
ARMA-MCGARCH	0.06824	11,557.710	0.07123	12,487.830
ARMA-MCGARCH-GEVD	0.01356	2,183.251	0.01264	2,257.700
ARMA-MCGARCH-GEVD-WNS	0.01379	2,192.716	0.01264	2,257.817

Note: Lower loss statistics means better performance in risk estimation within sample used for estimating the model parameters.

5.3. *Value-at-risk evaluation*

As the chapter makes inferences on extreme fluctuations and their relationship with news sentiments, a VaR approach is used to evaluate the methodology.

The three models are compared in-sample in Table 3 and out-of-sample in Table 4. A multiplication of 1,000,000 was done for both in-sample and out-sample linear loss values to effectively show the differences between models.

In the in-sample table, the ARMA-MCGARCH model without GEVD performs the poorest of the three models, while the two GEVD methodologies perform fairly similarly in the 99% VaR for both stocks, while in the 95% VaR for JPM, the ARMA-MCGARCH-GEVD-WNS dominates the other two models. For the JNJ, the two GEVD models have similar values.

With out-of-sample results, the ARMA-MCGARCH is the poorest of the three models in the 99% VaR and 95% VaR. The ARMA-MCGARCH-GEVD-WNS was the best performing model for the 95% VaR in JPM,

Table 4. Out-of-Sample Loss Function Statistics

	Out-of-Sample			
	Maximum		Negative Minimum	
	Binary	Linear	Binary	Linear
99% VaR Model Results for JPM				
ARMA-MCGARCH	0.00950	3,249.223	0.00800	2,696.517
ARMA-MCGARCH-EVT	0.00150	868.694	0.00100	47.763
ARMA-MCGARCH-EVT-WNS	0.00150	889.947	0.00100	46.701
Model Results for JNJ				
ARMA-MCGARCH	0.01400	3,575.711	0.01750	7,831.638
ARMA-MCGARCH-EVT	0.00150	1,115.371	0.00150	4,372.371
ARMA-MCGARCH-EVT-WNS	0.00700	2,138.148	0.00650	5,533.473
95% VaR Model Results for JPM				
ARMA-MCGARCH	0.02800	7,881.376	0.03150	7,311.500
ARMA-MCGARCH-EVT	0.00300	1,844.894	0.00350	1,121.035
ARMA-MCGARCH-EVT-WNS	0.00150	889.947	0.00100	46.701
Model Results for JNJ				
ARMA-MCGARCH	0.03700	8,291.222	0.04950	14,136.270
ARMA-MCGARCH-EVT	0.00700	2,121.462	0.00650	5,533.811
ARMA-MCGARCH-EVT-WNS	0.00700	2,138.148	0.00650	5,533.473

Note: Lower loss statistics means better performance in risk estimation outside the sample, which assesses risk forecasting ability.

similar to the in-sample. For the JNJ, the ARMA-MCGARCH-GEVD was better in the 99% VaR while in the 95% VaR, ARMA-MCGARCH-GEVD-WNS were comparably similar.

6. Conclusions and Further Directions

News sentiments have an impact on stock price movements as investors and speculators perceive on the profitability of holding and trading the stock. However, it has been an open problem on how news sentiments affect extreme stock price fluctuations and thus the risk of holding or trading the stock. Our research poses a methodology that takes account of news sentiments and analyses its impact on extreme price movements within a day, thus bringing it to the risk management point of view. The methodology accounts intra-daily factors of volatility and the effect of news sentiments in the direction of extreme fluctuations. In our analysis of extreme stock price movements of the

JNJ and JPM stocks, we gathered insight on the impact of news sentiments of the previous day. Positive news in the previous days increases volatility and makes negative price fluctuations more possible for the JPM, while negative news sentiments from the JNJ would increase volatility but in the direction of positive price fluctuations. In both these results, a contrarian approach to trading was inferred. The results show that it can work in accounting for behaviours of extreme fluctuations by VaR model evaluation. We show that with using news sentiments, exceedances from measured risk were lower in frequency, and if exceedances are observed, the gap is lower when news sentiments are accounted. Future work on the methodology is to use it on a wider set of stocks and to refine the model to integrate other sources of investor sentiments.

A. Appendices

Table A.1. ARMA-MCGARCH and GEVD Results for JPM

	Estimate	Std. Error	t Value	Pr($>|t|$)
Daily				
mu	0.04927	0.02237	2.20220	0.02765
ar1	0.83695	0.25142	3.32890	0.00087
ma1	−0.86146	0.23352	−3.68900	0.00023
alpha0	0.01420	0.00537	2.64610	0.00814
alpha1	0.06676	0.00925	7.21920	0.00000
beta1	0.93191	0.00898	103.73220	0.00000
Hourly				
9	0.47337			
10	0.16973			
11	0.10655			
12	0.07123			
13	0.07364			
14	0.10127			
15	0.13314			
16	0.00410			
Stochastic				
mu	0.00668	0.00604	1.10650	0.26852
ar1	0.42503	0.24625	1.72600	0.08434

(Continued)

Table A.1. (*Continued*)

	Estimate	Std. Error	t Value	Pr(> |t|)
ma1	−0.44091	0.24414	−1.80600	0.07092
alpha0	0.01568	0.00174	9.00400	0.00000
alpha1	0.04661	0.00362	12.87580	0.00000
beta1	0.93816	0.00564	166.25800	0.00000
GEVD without WNS for Maximum				
mu	0.98428	0.01301	75.64983	0.00000
sigma	0.58376	0.00951	61.39026	0.00000
xi	0.06289	0.01238	5.08038	0.00000
GEVD without WNS for Negative Minimum				
mu	0.98147	0.01369	71.69248	0.00000
sigma	0.60916	0.01024	59.48828	0.00000
xi	0.09419	0.01365	6.90037	0.00000

Table A.2. ARMA-MCGARCH and GEVD Results for JNJ

	Estimate	Std. Error	t Value	Pr(> |t|)
Daily				
mu	0.05631	0.02392	2.35420	0.01856
ar1	−0.88838	0.11237	−7.90570	0.00000
ma1	0.87441	0.11895	7.35100	0.00000
alpha0	0.08416	0.02559	3.28840	0.00101
alpha1	0.22466	0.04821	4.66010	0.00000
beta1	0.67325	0.06537	10.29880	0.00000
Hourly				
9	0.78631			
10	0.20743			
11	0.12289			
12	0.11269			
13	0.08164			
14	0.08137			
15	0.15876			
16	0.10289			

(*Continued*)

Table A.2. (*Continued*)

	Estimate	**Std. Error**	***t* Value**	**Pr(> |*t*|)**
Stochastic				
mu	0.00537	0.00725	0.74057	0.45895
ar1	0.63474	0.04439	14.30015	0.00000
ma1	−0.76845	0.03565	−21.55408	0.00000
alpha0	0.08303	0.00933	8.90200	0.00000
alpha1	0.13130	0.01407	9.33564	0.00000
beta1	0.80728	0.01724	46.82049	0.00000
GEVD without WNS for Maximum				
mu	0.96380	0.02262	42.60831	0.00000
sigma	0.58370	0.01621	36.00864	0.00000
xi	0.04370	0.01887	2.31585	0.02057
GEVD without WNS for Negative Minimum				
mu	0.86900	0.02349	36.99447	0.00000
sigma	0.60280	0.01749	34.46541	0.00000
xi	0.10890	0.02028	5.36982	0.00000

References

Baker, M. and Wurgler, J. (2006). Investor sentiment and the cross section of stock returns. In *The J. Fin.*, 61(4), pp. 1645–1680.

Berkman, H., Dimitrov, V., Jain, P. C., Koch, P. D., and Tice, S. (2009). Sell on the news: Differences of opinions, short-sales constraints, and returns around earnings announcements. In *J. Fin. Econom.*, 92, pp. 376–399.

Bollerslev, T. (1986). Generalized autoregressive conditional heteroskedasticity. *J. Econometr.*, 31(3), pp. 307–327.

Box, G., Jenkins, G. M. and Reinsel, G. C. (1994). *Time Series Analysis: Forecasting and Control, 3rd edn.* Prentice-Hall.

Coles, S. (2001). *An Introduction to Statistical Modeling of Extreme* Values. London: Springer-Verlag.

Daniel, K. and Hirschleifer, D. (2015). Overconfident investors, predictable returns, and excessive trading. *The J. Econom. Perspe.*, 29(4), pp. 61–87.

De Haan, L. and Ferreira, A. (2006). *Extreme Value Theory — An Introduction.* Springer.

Embrechts, P., Resnick, S. I. and Samorodintsky, G. (1999). Extreme value theory as a risk management tool. *North Am. Actu. J.*, 3(2), pp. 30–41.

Engle, R. F. and Sokalska, M. E. (2012). Forecasting intraday volatility in the US equity market. Multiplicative component GARCH. *J. Fin. Econometr.*, 10(1), pp. 54–83.

Fisher, R. A. and Tippett, L. H. C. (1928). Limiting forms of the frequency distribution of the largest or smallest member of a sample. *Math. Proc. Cambridge Philosoph. Soc.*, 24, pp 180–190.

Ghalanos, A. (2015). Rugarch: Univariate GARCH models. R package version 1.3-6.

Gumbel, E. J. (1941). The return period of flood flows. *The Ann. Math. Statist.*, 12, pp. 163–190.

Ho, K. Y., Liu, W. M. and Yu, J. (2012). Public news arrival and cross-asset correlation breakdown: Implications for algorithmic trading. Available at SSRN: http://ssrn.com/abstract=2023079 or http://dx.doi.org/10.2139/ssrn.2023079

Ho, K. Y., Shi, Y. and Zhang, Z. (2013). How does news sentiment impact asset volatility? Evidence from long memory and regime-switching approaches. *North Ame. J. Econom. Fin.*, 26, pp 436–456.

Jorion, P. (2006). *Value at Risk: The New Benchmark for Managing Financial Risk, 3rd edn.* McGraw-Hill.

Kaniel, R., Liu, S., Saar, G. and Titman, S. (2012). Individual investor trading and return patterns around earnings announcements. *The J. Fin.*, 67(2), pp. 639–680.

Liebmann, M., Orlov, A. G. and Neumann, D. (2016). The tone of financial news and the perceptions of stock and CDS traders. *Int. Rev. Fin. Anal.*, 46, pp. 159–175.

Lopez, J. A. (1998). Methods for evaluating value-at-risk estimates. *Federal Reserve Bank of New York Econom. Policy Rev.*, 4(3), pp. 119–124.

McNeil, A. J., Frey, R. and Embrechts, P. (2005). *Quantitative Risk Management.* Princeton, New Jersey: Princeton University Press.

RavenPack News Analytics (2013), User's Guide to Sample Data and Service Overview.

Stephenson, A. G. (2002) evd: Extreme Value Distributions. *R News*, 2(2):31–32. URL: http://CRAN.R-project.org/doc/Rnews/.'

Stracca, L. (2013) The global effects of the euro debt crisis. European Central Bank Working Paper Series, No. 1573.

Temin, P. (2010). The great recession & the great depression. *Daedalus*, 139(4), pp. 115–124.

Tsay, R. (2010). *Analysis of Financial Time Series, 3rd edn.* Wiley.

Uhl, M. W. (2011). Measuring media sentiment — essays on its impact on the economy and financial markets. ETH Zurich KOF Dissertation Series No. 12.

Chapter 14

Do Commodity Prices Cause Financial Instability in the United States? A Time-Varying Perspective through Rolling Window Bootstrap Approach

Muhammad Shahbaz[*,§] and Syed Jawad Hussain Shahzad[*,¶]

[*]*Energy and Sustainable Development (ESD)*
Montpelier Business School, France
[§]*shahbazmohd@live.com*
[¶]*jawad.kazmi5@gmail.com*

Sandrine Kablan[†,||] and Shawkat Hammoudeh[‡,**]

[†]*ERUDITE, Université de Paris Est Créteil, France*
[||]*sandrine.kablan@u-pec.fr*
[‡]*Lebow College of Business, Drexel University*
United States Energy and Sustainable Development (ESD)
Montpelier Business School, France
[**]*hammousm@drexel.edu*

Abstract

This chapter examines the casual links between financial instability and commodity prices for the US economy. The monthly data of six commodity indices and US financial instability is used from January 1991 to September 2015. Using the bootstrap full-sample Granger causality test, the results show that causality runs from commodities to financial instability; however, the short-run parameters are unstable. To overcome the limitations of the full sample tests and to accommodate possible regime shifts, we apply dynamic Granger causality using bootstrap and rolling window techniques. Analogous to the parameter stability test results, the results show varying levels of the causal nexuses between commodity prices and financial instability. Over most of the sample period, increase in commodity prices cause financial instability. However, a reinforcing effect is observed during the turmoil market conditions of the global financial crisis in 2007–2008.

1. Introduction

The linkages between commodities price fluctuations and stock market instability is of interest for the policymakers because the movements in the stock markets strongly influence macroeconomic variables (Coronado *et al.*, 2015). Changes in commodity prices and financial stability, or lack thereof, are linked through several channels including terms of trade, exchange rates and domestic credit growth. Rajan and Ramcharan (2015) argue that credit profusion during the commodity price boom in the 1920s was associated with a greater number of bank failures. On the other hand, Kinda *et al.* (2016) show that negative shocks to commodity prices are associated with a deterioration in the banks prudential ratios which leads to banking crises. This outcome occurs especially in countries with poor governance and weak macroprudential policies. Particularly, Kinda *et al.* (2016) identify increases of non-performing loans and banking crises during commodity price downturns and empirically show that there is an impact from commodity price shocks on the financial sector's fragility. To sum up, the studies quoted above advocate that causality runs from commodity shocks to financial instability.

On the other hand, speculation and the price channel explain the reverse causality that runs from financial instability towards commodity price fluctuations. Speculation occurs when economic agents buy commodities in physical form or in the form of derivatives with the expectation of making profits, particularly in an abnormal situation. During the global financial crisis of 2007–2009, many investors bought commodities or commodity derivatives (futures or options) to hedge and diversify their risks, and these investments provided an effective hedge against the financial downturn (Gelos and Ustyugova, 2012). Thus, one of the explanations of the boom in commodity prices in 2008 is the fact that speculators invested in commodities derivatives rather than financial assets, which in turn impacted commodity prices.

Concerning the price channel, some authors (Blot *et al.*, 2015) argue that the relationship between commodity price fluctuations and financial instability is a source of overall market instability. Commodity price fluctuations are related to inflation and economic uncertainty, which eventually leads to financial instability (Schwartz, 1995). The commodities as goods enter the production process, and therefore their prices are an important component of the general inflation rate. Therefore, commodity price fluctuations impact inflation, which then translates into financial instability. Indeed, the literature shows that price instability may lead to financial instability directly by influencing financial variables i.e. yields and interest rates, national debt, etc. or indirectly through the business cycle. Fisher (1932, 1933) defends the idea that the movement in price levels is a major cause of business cycles through its effect on the real cost of debt. Bernanke and Gertler (1989, 1999) show that commodity price fluctuations may influence business cycles through information asymmetries and other frictions in the credit market. High prices encourage more investments and stock market speculations. Particularly, when debts are financed through deposits and credits, this increases money supply and the general price level. The increases of money supply and the price level fuel optimism that feeds speculative bubbles and creates euphoria (Fisher, 1932, 1933). Therefore, price fluctuations, especially commodity price fluctuations, may translate into financial instability.

All these considerations lead us to raise the following question: does commodity prices pass through into financial instability or the reverse? From the theoretical point of view, the causality between commodity prices and financial instability may run in the two directions. Therefore, our study is the first attempt to assess the causality between commodity prices and financial instability in the U.S. using the VIX as a proxy for financial stability. Therefore, if the causality runs from commodity to stock markets, changes in stock markets could be monitored by observing changes in the returns of commodities. However, if the causality is reversed that is from the stock market to commodity, it could also be interesting to know it, as the impact of commodity price fluctuations on the world economy has increased (Choi and Hammoudeh, 2010; Arouri and Rault, 2011; Awartani and Maghyereh, 2013; Chen, 2009; Elder and Serletis, 2010; Masish *et al.*, 2011).

As indicated earlier, we focus on the U.S economy because of its size, the size of its financial markets, and its interrelations with the other financial markets worldwide. It is also one of the largest exporters and importers of commodities. Further, the subprime crisis and resulting financial instability may have been transmitted from the US domestic financial markets to the commodity market. The research question is also relevant because of acute volatility of commodities during recent years.

On the methodology side, the full-sample time series data may experience structural changes (Balcilar *et al.*, 2010) and the financial instability and commodity prices must have gone through some structural breaks due to the global financial crises of 2007–2009. The causal nexuses are expected not to be stable over the sample period (Coronado *et al.*, 2015). Therefore, estimates based on full-sample and with the assumption that the relationship will be stable over time may lead to inappropriate conclusions. Furthermore, structural changes result in unstable dynamic links across different subsamples (Balcilar *et al.*, 2010). Interestingly, the studies on the commodity prices–financial instability link do not consider the structural changes in the parameter estimates. We find that increase in commodity prices cause financial instability. However, a reinforcing effect is observed during the turmoil market conditions of the global financial crisis in 2007–2008.

Our study is organized as follows. Section 2 describes the methodology used to investigate the causality between commodity prices and financial instability. Section 3 describes the data employed in the analysis and discusses the findings. Finally, Section 4 makes some concluding remarks.

2. Methodology

Granger (1969) explains that variable A is said to Granger-cause variable B if variable A will improve the forecast of variable B. Existing applied economics literature provides a variety of causality tests such as the Wald, likelihood ratio (LR), and Langrage Multiplier (LM) which are not free from nonstandard asymptotic properties problem if the variables have cointegration. Park and Phillips (1989) and Toda and Yamamotoo (1993, 1994) pointed out the problems relating to the level estimations while applying VAR models. In such situation, Toda-Yamamatoo (1995) and Dolado and Lutkepohl (1996) recommend applying the Wald test as the variables are found to be integrated of I(1), using the lag-augmented (LA-VAR) process as the Wald statistic based on the LA-VAR follows a standard chi-squared distribution (Toda and Yamamoto, 1995).

To improve the standard asymptotic distribution properties of the Wald test, Shukur and Mantalos (1997a) followed Dolado and Lutkepohl (1996) simplified the Granger causality approaches in the case of integrated–cointegrated VAR systems. Dolado and Lutkepohl (1996) using Monte Carlo simulations found that the Wald test did not exhibit correct size in small or even in medium-sized samples. To cover the mentioned deficiencies, Shukur and Mantalos (1997b) suggest applying the residual-based (RB) bootstrap approach that improves the critical values. Mantalos and Shukur (1998) apply the RB bootstrap approach containing the cointegration of VAR models and find that the RB approach provides consistent critical values.

The Granger (1969), Toda and Yamamatoo (1995), and Hatemi and uddin (2012) causality techniques are not free of criticism. For instance,

Shukur and Mantalos (1997a) assert that the Toda and Yamamatoo (1995) causality test has low explanatory and power properties and may lead to misleading causality results for small sample as well as for the medium sample size. Furthermore, Tang (2013) pointed out that the Toda and Yamamatoo (1995) and Hatemi and uddin (2012) causality techniques are unable to capture the time-varying causality features. The reason is that both causality techniques are based on full samples. In order to examine the causality between commodity prices and financial instability, we apply bootstrapping rolling causality covering all raised issues, following Balcilar *et al.* (2010) and Tang *et al.* (2015). Tang *et al.* (2015) suggest that the bootstrap LR Granger causality test is flexible in capturing the time-varying causality features. Zapata and Rambaldi (1997) note that the LR test is more convenient and provides efficient results not only for the larger samples but also for the small sample even the medium-sized sample due to its size and explanatory power. Furthermore, Mantalos (2000) proves that the bootstrap test exhibits the highest accuracy in all estimates, regardless of the cointegration properties. These pioneering findings motivate us to choose the bootstrap LR Granger causality test which relies on the following the bivariate VAR(p) specification:

$$y_t = \Phi_0 + \Phi_1 y_{t-1} + \cdots + \Phi_p y_{t-p} + \varepsilon_t. \tag{1}$$

The ε_t is error term assumed to normally distributed and containing a non-singular covariance matrix. p indicates the process of order which is determined. The lag length is determined following the Akaike information criterion (AIC). We have partitioned y_t into two sub-vectors, namely financial instability (VIX_t) and commodity price (Commodity_t). Equation 3 can be modified as follows:

$$\begin{pmatrix} \text{VIX}_t \\ \text{Commodity}_t \end{pmatrix} = \begin{pmatrix} a_1 \\ a_2 \end{pmatrix} + \begin{bmatrix} \phi(L)11 & \phi(L)12 \\ \phi(L)21 & \phi(L)22 \end{bmatrix} \begin{pmatrix} \text{VIX}_t \\ \text{Commodity}_t \end{pmatrix} + \begin{pmatrix} \varepsilon_{1t} \\ \varepsilon_{2t} \end{pmatrix} \tag{2}$$

VIX_t and Commodity_t are natural-log of financial instability and commodity price respectively. The error terms are denoted by ε_{1t} and ε_{2t}. $\phi(L)_{ij} = \sum_{k=1}^{p} \phi_{ij,k} L^k, I, j = 1, 2$ and L shows lag operator according to definition of the bivariate framework. Various tests are available in applied economics literature in order to examine the causal relationship between the variable. Efron (1979) developed the bootstrap causality test. Later, Horowitz (1994), Mantalos and Shukur (1998), and Mantalos (2000) empirically proved that critical values produced by bootstrap causality test are consistent and robust. This leads us to apply the version of Toda and Yamamatoo (1995) that contains various empirical advantages. This test of causality is applicable whether variables have cointegration or not but are integrated at I(1). Shukur and Mantalos (2000) further define the bootstrap LR Granger causality test as follows:

$$
\begin{array}{ll}
Y_t = (y_1,\ y_2, \ldots y_T) & (2 \times T) \text{ matrix} \\
B = (\Phi_0,\ \Phi_1, \ldots \Phi_T) & (2 \times (2p+1) \text{ matrix} \\
Z_t = (1,\ y_{t-1}, \ldots y_{t-p}+) & ((2p+1)\ \times 1) \text{ matrix} \\
Z = (Z_0,\ Z_t, \ldots Z_{t-1}) & (2p+1)\ \times T) \text{ matrix} \\
\eta = (\varepsilon_1,\ \varepsilon_2, \ldots \varepsilon_T) & (2 \times T) \text{ matrix.}
\end{array}
$$

These notations can be summarized in the VAR(p) model for $t = 1, 2, \ldots, T$ containing intercept term Φ_0 capacity as:

$$Y = BZ + \eta. \tag{3}$$

The unrestricted regression (2) is used to estimate the residuals which are denoted by η_u. The restricted residual, i.e., η_r, is used to estimate the equivalent matrix of residuals under the null hypothesis of no causal association. For instance, the matrix of cross-products of these residuals can be denoted by $S_u = \eta_u^{'}\eta_u$ and $S_r = \eta_r^{'}\eta_r$, respectively. The modified LR statistic containing null hypothesis that financial instability does Granger-cause commodity prices or commodity prices do not Granger-cause financial instability can be written as follows:

$$\text{LR} = (T-k)\ln\left(\frac{\det S_r}{\det S_u}\right) \tag{4}$$

T shows number of observation and $k = 2 \times (2p+1) + p$ denotes the small sample correction term and lag order in VAR model is shown by p. The determinant of respective matrix is denoted by det and ln is for natural-log. The bootstrap LR Granger causality test has χ^2 distribution containing degrees of freedom equivalent to the number of restrictions to be examined, that is equal to$p$ containing null hypothesis that financial instability does Granger-cause commodity prices or commodity prices do not Granger-cause financial instability.

It is argued by Granger (1996) that due to structural instability, researchers may face a problem of ambiguous and biased empirical results. To overcome the issue of structural instability, we employ rolling-window Granger causality approach to examine the impact of structural changes. These structural changes may be cause a shift in parameters that seem to change the direction of causal association between the variables. In the presence of structural changes and non-constancy of parameters, bootstrap causality test is suitable for rolling-window sub-samples. For instance, $t = T-l+1,\ \tau-l\ldots,\tau,\tau=l,\ l+1,\ldots,\ T$, where rolling window size is shown by l.

3. Data and Findings

We use monthly data from January 1991 to September 2015 for six US commodity indices (i.e., food prices, beverage prices, agricultural raw materials, metals prices, fuel (energy) prices, and crude oil (petroleum) price) and the financial instability proxies by the VIX index. This index is the Chicago Board Options Exchange (CBOE) Volatility index and measures the implied volatility of the S&P 500 index options over the next 30 days. The VIX, which is also called the fear index, is often interpreted as a global measure of risk aversion. Higher values of VIX indicate greater uncertainty in equity markets and vice versa. The data for the commodities prices indices are obtained from http://www.bloomberg.com/markets/commodities and for the for VIX index from http://www.bloomberg.com/quote/VIX.

To gain insights into the data, Fig. 1 depicts the evolution of the VIX index, which is a proxy for financial instability. We see in the graph the two main periods of financial instability: the dot-com crisis in 2000 which was followed by a recession in 2003, and the 2007 subprime crisis followed by the 2008–2009 Great recession and the 2010–2012 European sovereign debt crisis. We notice that the peaks of those periods are generally preceded by peaks of commodity prices, particularly the peaks during 2008 and 2012.

Table 1 reports the descriptive statistics of the variables. The average price index is the highest for beverage prices and the lowest for crude oil prices. However, the highest variability (maximum, minimum, and standard deviations) is observed for crude oil prices. On average, financial instability is zero (-0.130), suggesting that normal financial conditions are stable in the U.S. over the sample period.

The unit root properties of the variables are examined by using the ADF and PP tests. Notably, the Toda and Yamamoto (1995) Granger non-causality test can be applied irrespective of the integration properties of the variables. However, none of the variable should be integrated of order two i.e. $I(2)$. Table 2 reports the results of the unit root analysis. All the six commodities prices indices have unit root problem in the levels and they become stationary when first difference is used. The financial instability

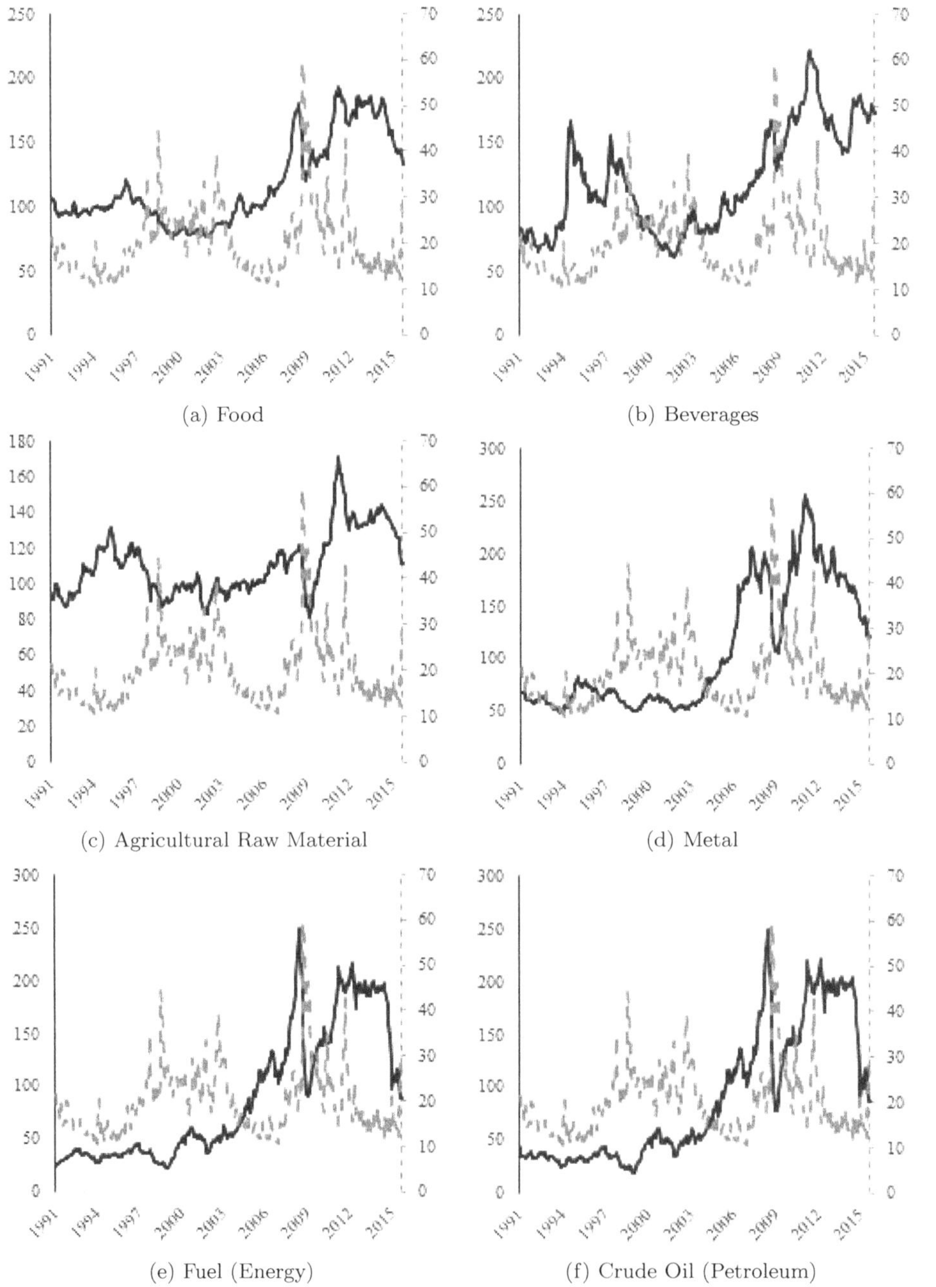

Figure 1. Time Trend of Commodity Price Indices (on Left Axis) and VIX (on Right Axis)

Note: These figures show the trend of commodities (on left axis) and the financial stability index (on right axis) for the sample period.

Table 1. Descriptive Statistics of Commodity Price Indices and Financial Instability

Variables	Mean	Std. Dev.	Skew.	Kurt.
Food	117.1	33.68	0.810	2.296
Beverage	119.7	40.22	0.469	2.135
Agricultural raw materials	110.5	17.75	0.829	3.268
Metals	108.6	58.88	0.711	2.019
Fuel (energy)	89.65	61.92	0.728	2.109
Crude oil (petroleum)	89.51	63.54	0.746	2.123
Financial instability (VIX)	−0.130	0.720	1.754	9.058

Note: Std. Dev., Skew., and Kurt., stand for standard deviations. Skewness, and kurtosis.

Table 2. Unit Root Tests Results

	Level		First Difference	
Variable	ADF	PP	ADF	PP
Food	−1.570	−1.187	−10.60***	−10.987***
Beverage	−1.574	−1.395	−12.98***	−12.790***
Agricultural raw materials	−2.349	−2.348	−12.38***	−13.022***
Metals	−1.358	−1.109	−12.56***	−12.405***
Fuel (energy)	−1.845	−1.553	−10.47***	−12.642***
Crude oil (petroleum)	−1.930	−1.149	−10.80***	−13.394***
Financial instability	−4.748***	−4.314***	−15.82***	−25.140***

Note: ADF and PP are the empirical statistics of the Augmented Dickey–Fuller (1979), and the Phillips–Perron (1988) unit root tests, respectively. *** indicates rejection of null hypothesis of unit root at the 1% level of significance.

series is stationary in the level. Due to this mixed order of integration, the traditional tests of Granger causality may not be appropriate and since none of the series is $I(2)$, we proceed with the causality analysis.

To ascertain the Granger causality between commodity prices and financial instability, we use the residual-based modified-LR tests (see e.g., Mantalos, 2000). The optimal lag length is determined with the VAR model by using the AIC. The optimal lag order for each commodity-financial instability pair is shown in the second column of Table 3. The null hypothesis that financial instability does not Granger-cause commodity prices or vice versa is tested using full sample bootstrap LR statistics, and their respective bootstrap p-values are shown in the adjacent columns.

Columns (3)–(6) of Table 3 show the full sample bootstrap LR statistics and their bootstrap p-values for both hypotheses. The null hypothesis of

Table 3. Full Sample Granger Causality Analysis

Variable	k	LR-Statistics	Bootstrap p-Values
Panel A: H_0: VIX -/-> Commodity			
Food	4	0.3143	[0.8400]
Beverage	7	0.9004	[0.6599]
Agricultural raw materials	2	3.7892	[0.2100]
Metals	4	3.1915	[0.2500]
Fuel (energy)	6	0.5061	[0.8000]
Crude oil (petroleum)	5	0.3149	[0.8200]
Panel B: H_0: Commodity -/-> VIX			
Food	4	4.7538	[0.3143]
Beverage	7	1.2456	[0.5100]
Agricultural raw materials	2	5.7405	[0.1100]
Metals	4	23.993***	[0.0000]
Fuel (energy)	6	6.6715*	[0.0600]
Crude oil (petroleum)	5	6.1413*	[0.0999]

Note: *** and * indicate the rejection of the null hypothesis at the 1% and 10% levels, respectively. The optimal lag order (k) is determined by AIC. The p-values are based on 2000 bootstrap repetitions.

financial instability does not Granger-cause commodity prices is not rejected for all cases. The results reported in Columns (5) and (6) of Table 5 display as true the null hypothesis that commodity prices do not Granger-cause financial instability. Metal prices Granger-cause financial instability at the 1% level of significance, while fuel and crude oil prices also Granger-cause financial stability at the 5% level of significance. The overall results using the full-sample bootstrap Granger causality tests indicate that commodity prices cause financial instability in the US. Indeed, the causality runs from commodity price to financial instability because commodities as assets are a transmission channel for monetary policy. Therefore, the monetary policy used by central banks to mitigate undesirable effects of economic fluctuations has an impact on commodity prices. This happens because following a drop in interest rates, economic agents supersede liquidity in financial assets. These effects are observed during the expansionary monetary policies in 1933, 1970, 2001–2004, and most recently 2008 (Frankel, 2008; Browne and Gronin, 2010; Ciccarelli and Mojon, 2010). This process has been reinforced with the financialization of commodity markets and the strengthened connection with the foreign exchange rates, which are the fastest moving financial asset.

The causality from commodity price to financial instability is observed more specifically for the metals and energy indices, due to the specificities of these two types of commodities. Metals and energy (and oil) are special commodity types in the sense that they are closely linked to economic activity in the case of energy (and oil) and industrial activity in the case of metals (IMF, WEO, 2012). Thus, more than other types of commodities, metal and energy indices are highly sensitive to fluctuations in the US business cycle, especially since the US economy is heavily industrialized. Indeed, these two types of commodities are very important in industrialization and infrastructure construction. Therefore, their prices are more correlated with the global business cycle than the prices of other types of commodities (IMF, WEO, 2012). In addition, according to the thesis of the link between price instability and financial instability, fluctuations in business cycles cause commodity price fluctuations. The fluctuation of commodities prices is more pronounced for metals and energy because of their close link with the economic and industrial activity (IMF, WEO, 2012). Thus, this instability of energy and metal prices affects financial instability.

However, as the literature shows mixed evidence on the causality flow between commodities and financial instability, we deepen our analysis by doing some tests. Indeed, the findings of full-sample Granger non-causality tests depend on the sample period and model specifications and are sensitive to regime shifts. For instance, Andrews (1993) and Andrews and Ploberger (1994) provide various tests to examine the temporal stability of the VAR models. These empirical tests designed for investigating stability are suitable due to their strong size and explanatory power. The null hypothesis of the Sup-LR, Mean-LR, and Exp-LR tests is that parameters are stable but the alternate hypothesis is that parameters contain structural instability. This empirically is tested based on the sequence of Lagrange multiplier statistics. The data are trimmed from both ends of the sample which is a prerequisite of short-run parameter stability tests. These stability tests use a fraction of the data [0.15, 0.85] with the 15% trimming suggested by Andrews (1993) and later by Balcilar *et al.* (2010). Following Balcilar *et al.* (2010), we use the Monte Carlo simulation with 2000 samples generated using the VAR model to generate critical and parametric bootstrap p-values for the stability tests. These bootstrapped p-values avoid the problem of non-standard asymptotic distributions.

Table 4 reports the results of the short-run parametric stability test estimates and their associated p-values. We report the results of the sequential Sup-LR, Mean-LR, and Exp-LR tests for both the commodities

Table 4. The Short-Run Parameter Stability Analysis

	VIX Equation		Commodity Equation	
	Stats	*p*-Values	Stats	*p*-Values
(1) Food Price Index				
Sup-LR	5.226**	[0.021]	5.614**	[0.035]
Exp-LR	0.703	[0.349]	1.606**	[0.013]
Mean-LR	1.133	[0.492]	2.609**	[0.027]
(2) Beverage Price Index				
Sup-LR	4.851**	[0.035]	2.001	[0.874]
Exp-LR	0.641	[0.417]	0.494	[0.786]
Mean-LR	0.976	[0.617]	0.935	[0.773]
(3) Agricultural Raw Materials Index				
Sup-LR	6.347***	[0.003]	6.085**	[0.015]
Exp-LR	0.870	[0.156]	1.131*	[0.072]
Mean-LR	1.202	[0.412]	1.766	[0.132]
(4) Metals Price Index				
Sup-LR	4.996**	[0.016]	4.620	[0.126]
Exp-LR	0.625	[0.437]	1.391**	[0.046]
Mean-LR	0.988	[0.605]	2.471*	[0.056]
(5) Fuel (Energy) Index				
Sup-LR	5.226**	[0.021]	5.614**	[0.035]
Exp-LR	0.703	[0.349]	1.606**	[0.013]
Mean-LR	1.133	[0.492]	2.609**	[0.027]
(6) Crude Oil (petroleum), Price index				
Sup-LR	5.104**	[0.033]	4.078	[0.201]
Exp-LR	0.871	[0.168]	1.197*	[0.090]
Mean-LR	1.542	[0.204]	2.281	[0.072]

Notes: ***, ** and * indicate significance at the 1%, 5%, and 10% levels, respectively.
The *p*-values are calculated using 2000 bootstrap repetitions. The Sup-LR test statistics are appropriate for examining a swift regime shift, while the Mean-LR and the Exp-LR tests are the optimal tests to examine whether the model captures a stable relationship over time.

and financial instability VAR specifications. The Sup-LR test statistics are appropriate to examine a swift regime shift, while the Mean-LR and the Exp-LR tests are the optimal tests to examine whether the model captures a stable relationship over time. The results indicate that there is significant evidence of short-run parameter instability in both equations for almost all the commodities and financial instability pairs. The results show that financial instability and commodity markets undergo structural and regime changes over the sample period. Therefore, the overall evidence based on the parameter stability tests indicates that the VAR models' parameters are not constant over time, and thus the statistical inference based on the stable parameter assumption is invalid. Further, the inference drawn using the Granger causality test based on the full-sample VAR model estimates may not be reliable. Indeed, commodity prices evolve with cycles. Jacks and Stuermer (2015) use a structural VAR to assess the long-run drivers of the real commodity prices. They find two drivers which are the global demand shocks and the inventory shock, especially for commodities such as agricultural raw material and beverages. However, their findings also stress that the contribution of global demand shocks to real commodity price varies across different types of commodities. Besides, Frankel (2014) emphasize that the fluctuations of commodity prices since 2000 have various explanations such as global growth, speculation, and easy monetary policy. Because the fluctuation sources are different, we do not necessarily have the same impact on financial instability. This may explain those regimes change over the sample period as well as the short-run parameter instability in the equations.

It is argued by Balcilar *et al.* (2010) and Tang *et al.* (2015) that the empirical investigation process of rolling-window Granger causality is conditioned with the window size and the number of estimation windows. This condition reveals that an increase in window size lowers the number of estimation windows and vice versa, i.e., the use of large window size provides less precise results. As a result, it provides less window estimates, and on the other hand, smaller window size use may provide large variance of estimates. Pesaran and Timmermann (2005) focus on two conflicting points in choosing the optimal window size. For obtaining correct parameter estimation, the degree of freedom contains a large (small) in the presence of the potential of multiple structural breaks. The selection of the window size depends on the frequency of the sample data. Following these flexibilities and having strong precision of rolling estimates of the small windows, we apply the bootstrap approach for robust causality results.

We test the Granger non-causality from commodity prices to financial instability and/or vice versa through the residual-based p-values of the LR statistic (VAR model). The magnitude of the impact of commodity prices on financial instability and financial instability on commodity prices is also obtained through the bootstrap rolling VAR models. The impact of commodity prices on financial instability is calculated as the mean of all bootstrap estimates, which are $N_b^{-1}\sum_{k=1}^{p}\hat{\phi}_{21,k}^{*}\cdot$ and $N_b^{-1}\sum_{k=1}^{p}\hat{\phi}_{12,k}^{*}\cdot$, respectively, where, $\hat{\phi}_{21,k}^{*}$ and $\hat{\phi}_{12,k}^{*}$ are the bootstrap least squares estimates.

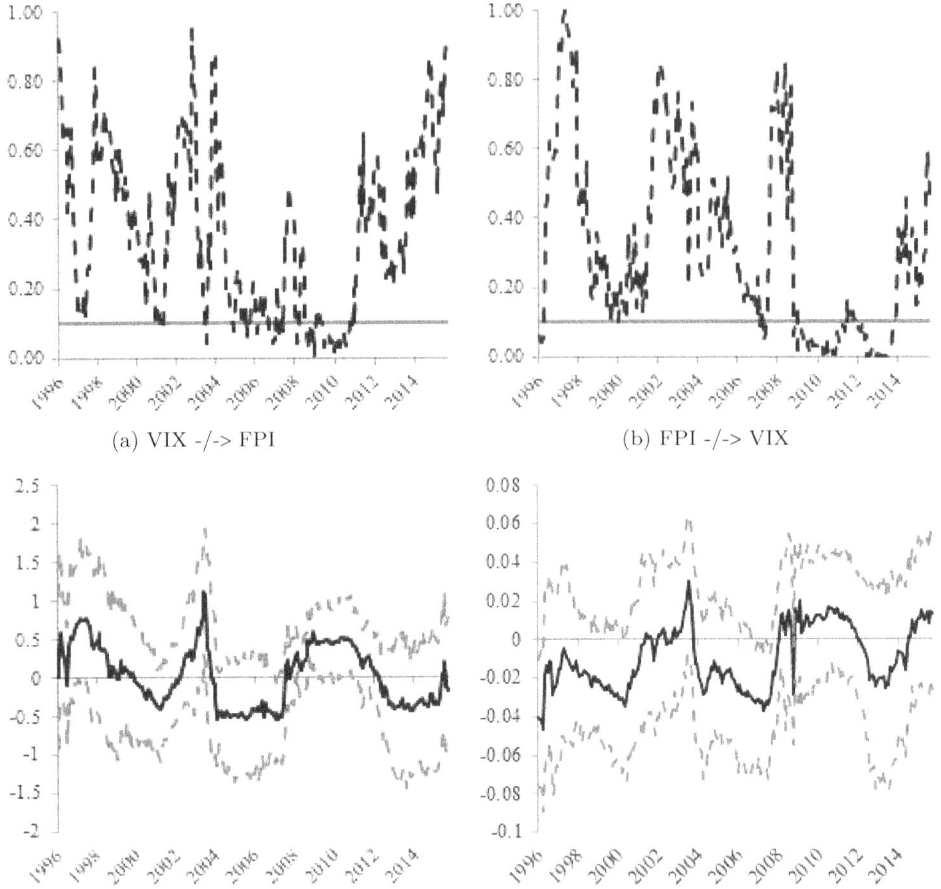

(a) VIX -/-> FPI

(b) FPI -/-> VIX

(c) Impact of VLX on FPI

(d) Impact of FPI on VIX

Figure 2. Rolling Window Estimates for Food Price Index (FPI)

Note: In this figure, (a) and (b) show the rolling window bootstrap p-values for the Granger causality tests. The straight line indicates 10% significance level. Both (c) and (d) show the rolling window impact of one variables on the other. The dashed lines indicate 95% confidence bands.

The 95% confidence intervals, i.e., the lower and upper limits, are calculated as the 2.5th and 97.5th quantiles of each of $\hat{\phi}^*_{21,k}$ and $\hat{\phi}^*_{12,k}$, respectively.

The bootstrap p-values and the magnitude of the effect for financial instability and commodity price pairs are shown in Figs. 2–7. The time period starting from the first rolling window to the end is shown on horizontal axes. Panels A and C (B and D) in each of these figures show the bootstrap p-values of the rolling test statistics testing the null hypothesis that financial

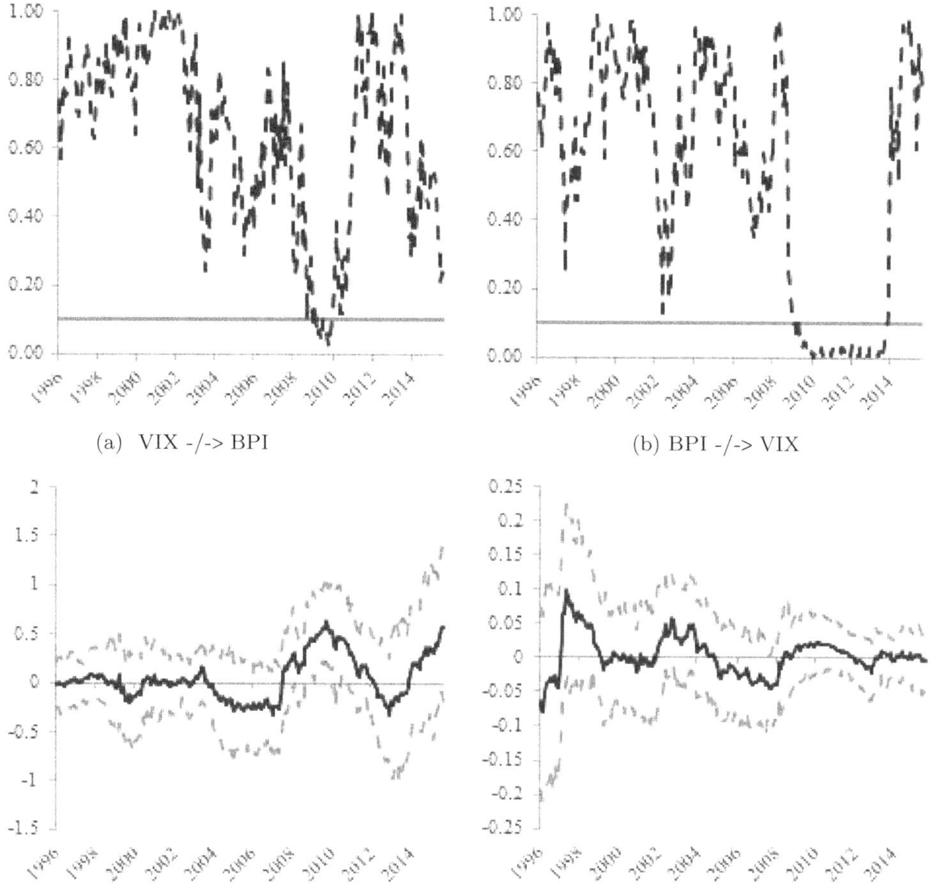

(a) VIX -/-> BPI

(b) BPI -/-> VIX

(c) Impact of VIX on BPI

(d) Impact of BPI on VIX

Figure 3. Rolling Window Estimates for Beverage Price Index (BPI)
Note: See notes to Fig. 2.

instability does not Granger-cause commodity prices and the opposite case (the impact of financial instability on commodity prices and vice versa), respectively.

The results of the food price index and financial instability are shown in Fig. 2. The null hypothesis that financial instability does not Granger-cause food prices is rejected at the 10% significance level during the sub-period 2005–2011. The food prices cause financial instability during the sub-period 2008–2013. During the period for which financial instability causes food prices and vice versa, both variables have a positive impact on each other. It

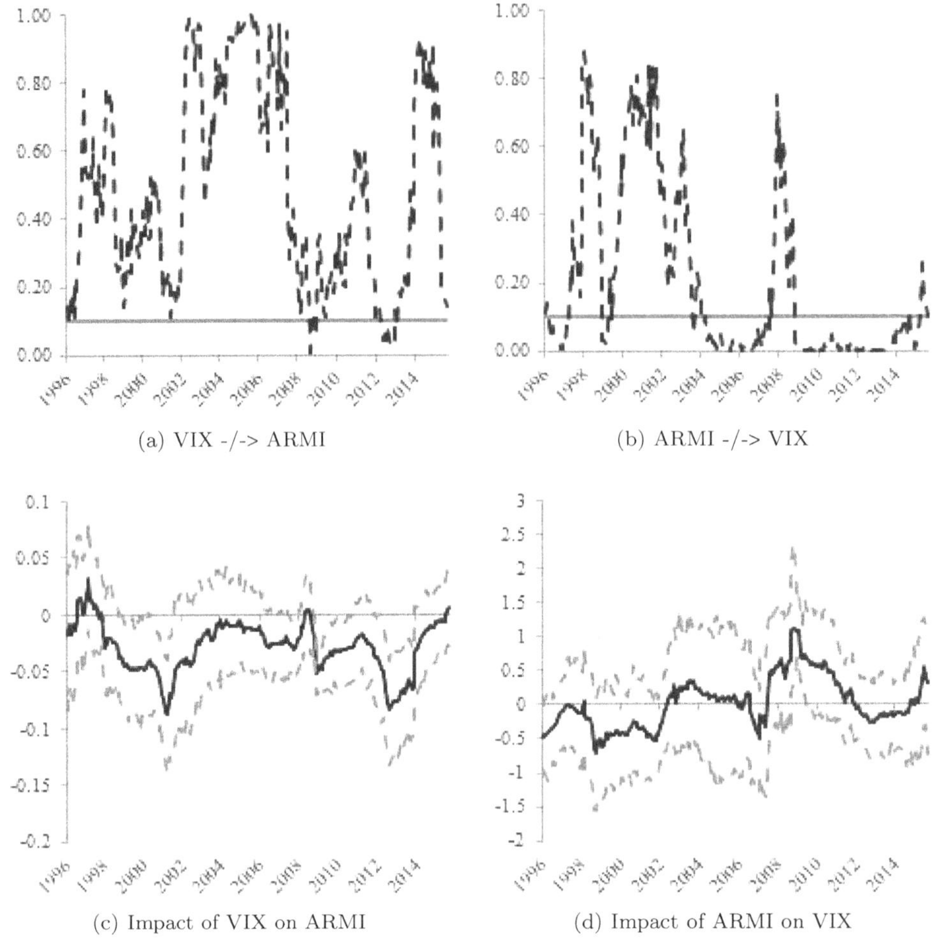

(a) VIX -/-> ARMI (b) ARMI -/-> VIX

(c) Impact of VIX on ARMI (d) Impact of ARMI on VIX

Figure 4. Rolling Window Estimates for Agricultural Raw Materials Index (ARMI)

Note: See notes to Fig. 2.

can be inferred that financial instability results in an increase in food prices during the period 2005–2011, and there exists a feedback effect thereafter. Indeed, after the subprime crisis, economic agents invest in commodity derivatives (for commodities such as maize, wheat, etc.) to hedge against the collapse of financial asset prices. This practice increases commodity prices in general, and food in particular. This has even caused riots in some developing countries whose populations were no longer able to afford bread. Thus, the prices of commodities have risen sharply, due to a strong demand from speculators and other economic agents who have used them to hedge. Again, the reverse causality estimated in our article may be

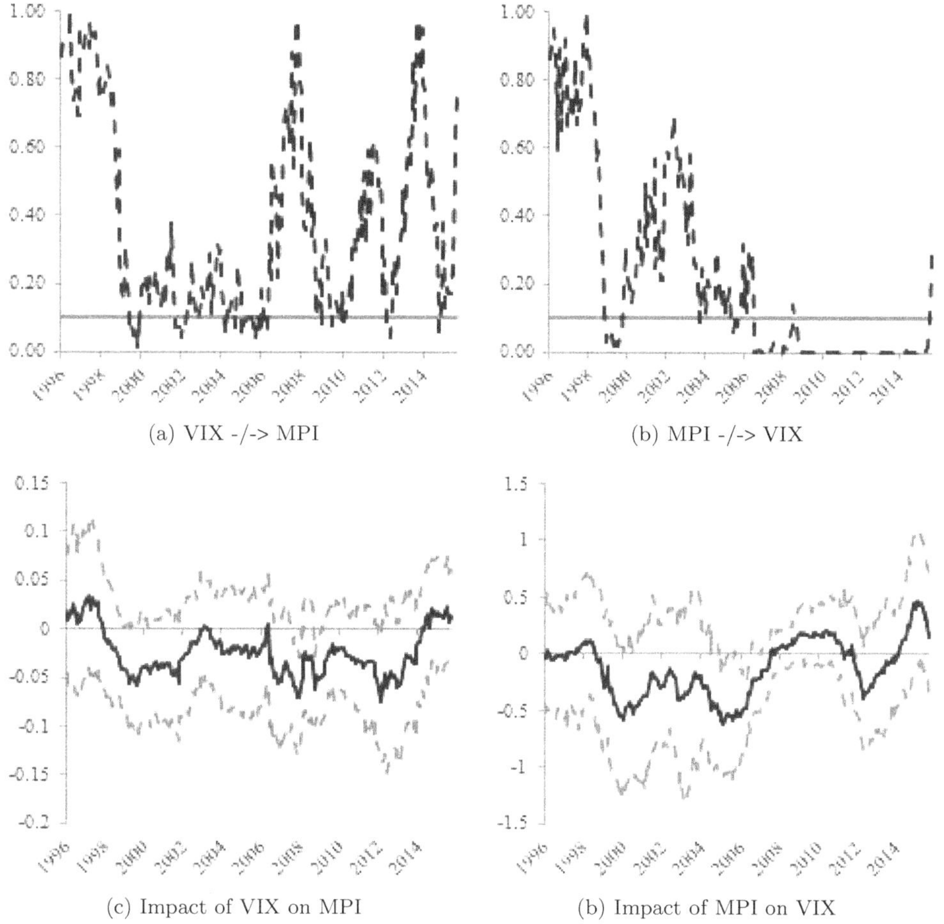

Figure 5. Rolling Window Estimates for Metals Price Index (MPI)
Note: See notes to Fig. 2.

explained by the expansionary monetary policy that feeds the purchase of commodities rather than other financial assets. Indeed, as we note in the introduction, commodities are financial assets and when the central bank sets an expansionary monetary policy, economic agents supersede liquidity by commodities. Thus, commodity prices influence financial stability.

This phenomenon was also observed for beverages. Financial instability Granger-causes beverage prices (Fig. 3(a)) from 2009 till 2014, with a strong positive impact (Fig. 3(c)), especially during the start of the causality period, but decreases towards the end of the period (i.e., 2014). On the other hand, the beverage price index Granger-causes financial instability (Fig. 3(b)), with a slight positive impact (Fig. 3(d)).

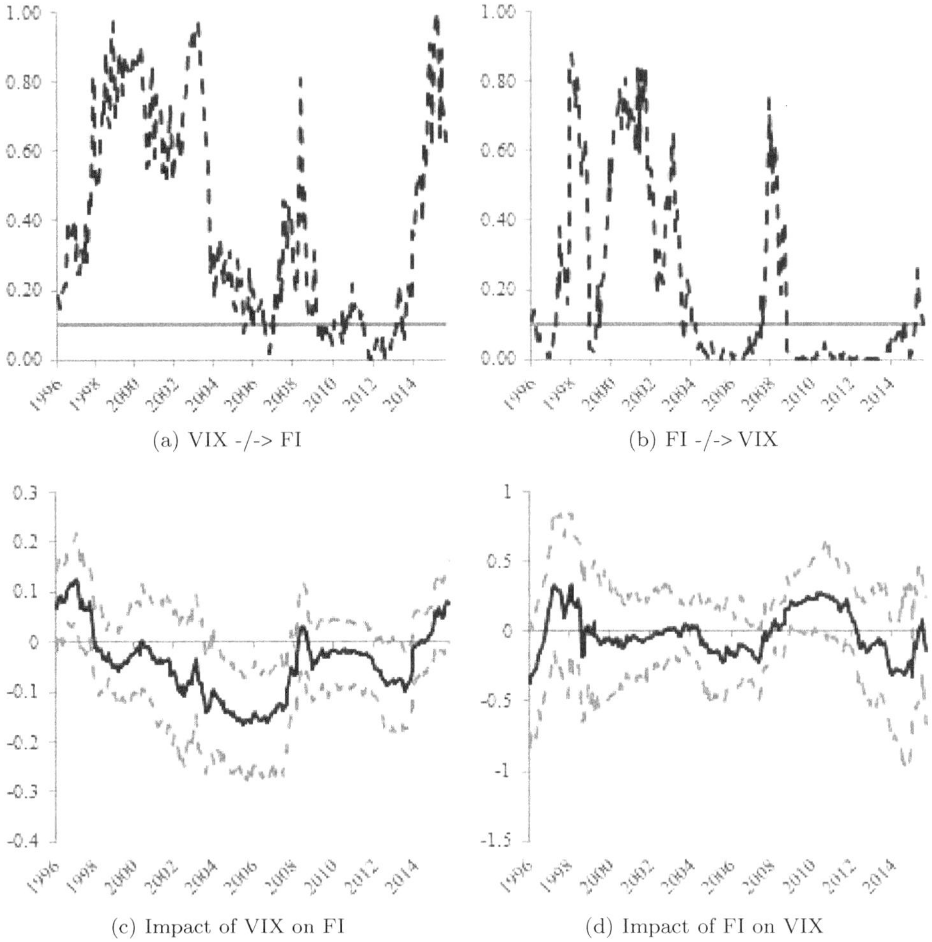

Figure 6. Rolling Window Estimates for the Fuel (Energy) Index (FI)
Note: See notes to Fig. 2.

Figures 4(a)–4(d) show the results of the casual nexuses between agricultural raw materials index and financial instability. The causality mainly runs from agricultural raw material prices to financial stability (Fig. 4(b)) during the sub-period 1999–2002, 2008 and 2011–2014. During the initial period (i.e., 1999–2001), the impact of agricultural raw material prices on financial instability (Fig. 4(d)) is negative; however, during the 2008 casual period, the increase in agricultural raw material prices increase financial instability. Regarding the agricultural raw materials, the 1999–2002, 2008, and 2011–2014 sub-periods, respectively, mark economic slowdown, crisis, and recovery. This implies that fluctuations due to business cycle

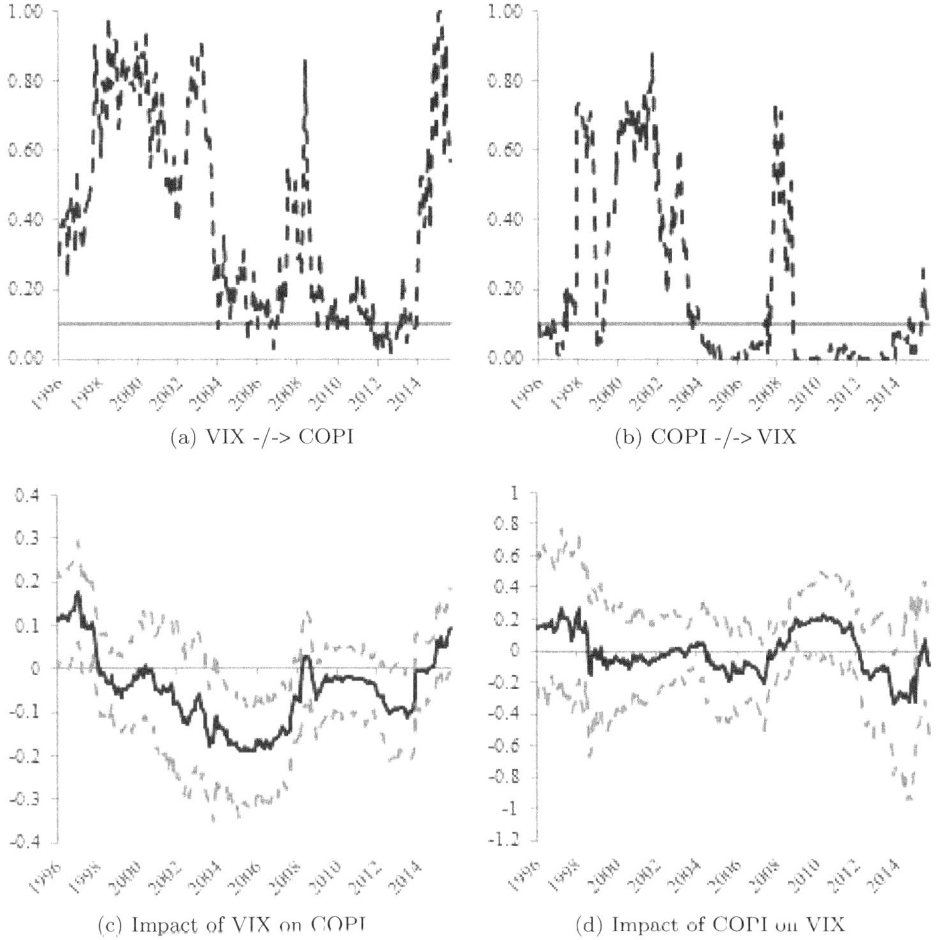

(a) VIX -/-> COPI

(b) COPI -/-> VIX

(c) Impact of VIX on COPI

(d) Impact of COPI on VIX

Figure 7. Rolling Window Estimates for the Crude Oil (Petroleum) Price Index (COPI)

Note: See notes to Fig. 2.

have affected the price of agricultural raw materials used in manufacturing industries.

Similarly, there is a significant casual flow from metal prices to financial stability (Fig. 5(b)) from 2008 until the end of the sample period, which is also associated with a positive impact (Fig. 5(d)). Similarly, because the metals are heavily used in industry, fluctuations in metal prices significantly influence financial instability. Indeed, after the subprime crisis, emerging countries had shown resilience and exhibited strong demand for metals for the use in their industrial sector. This causes a pressure that led to arise in metal prices. Again, the relationship between commodity price stability and financial stability explains this causality from the metal price fluctuations towards financial instability.

Figures 6 and 7 present the results of the casual links of fuel (energy) price index, and the crude oil (petroleum) price index with financial stability, respectively. Interestingly, overall energy prices and crude oil prices cause financial instability from 2005 onward until the end of the sample period with a positive impact. However, there is a feedback effect during 2007 and then from 2010 to 2013. Notably, the full sample Granger causality analysis shows a unidirectional casual flow from metal- and energy-related prices to financial stability. However, the findings of the rolling window procedure indicate a bidirectional casual flow, particularly during turmoil financial conditions (i.e., the global financial crises of 2007–2008). This conclusion could not have been possible with the traditional causality test that mainly relies on the full-sample estimates, especially when the short-term parameters are unstable due to structural changes. Oil and energy are commodities that are heavily used in the economy; this explains why the fluctuations of oil prices and energy impact financial instability, which happen through the business cycle. However, the feedback is explained by the fact that speculators have used oil derivatives after the 2007–2008 subprime crisis to cover losses on the financial markets. This has subsequently led to an oil bubble.

4. Conclusion and Policy Implications

This chapter examines the casual nexuses between commodity prices and financial instability, using monthly data from January 1991 to September 2015. The bootstrap full-sample Granger causality test shows that commodity prices Granger-cause financial instability; however, the short-run parameters are unstable. To overcome the limitations of the full-sample tests and to accommodate the possible regime shifts, we utilize the rolling-window approach and bootstrap techniques for Granger causality estimates. The rolling-window causality results, analogous to parameter stability estimates, show varying levels of casual nexuses between commodity prices and financial instability. Metal and energy prices Granger-cause financial instability during majority of the time period, and a reinforcing effect exists between these commodity prices and financial instability during the turmoil market conditions (i.e., financial crisis 2007–2008).

Given the size of the US economy, it plays a key role in driving the fluctuations of the global economy. As several authors such as Frankel (2014) and Jacks and Stuermer (2015) state, the fluctuations in the prices of commodities can come from fluctuations in the American demand, as well as from other sources such as the American easy monetary policy, or speculation. This can then affect financial instability through the commodity price channel, as we explained in our analysis. That is, monetary policy implemented by the Federal Reserve may translate into commodity price fluctuations, then financial instability. This means that monetary policy of the Federal Reserve may also be used to dampen commodity prices fluctuations and prevent financial instability. This policy recommendation is important in the sense that fluctuations in commodity prices affect both commodity-consuming countries and commodity-producing countries. However, even though this decision is at the discretion of the Federal Reserve, recent commodity price turmoil as well as financial instability point out the importance of such a decision for the global economy.

References

Andrews, D. W. K. (1993). Tests for parameter instability and structural change with unknown change point. *Econometrica*, 61, pp. 821–856.

Andrews, D. W. K. and Ploberger, W. (1994). Optimal tests when a Nuisance parameter is present only under the alternative. *Econometrica*, 62, pp. 1383–1414.

Arouri, M. E. H. and Rault, C. (2011). Oil prices and stock markets in GCC countries: Empirical evidence from panel analysis. *Int. J. Fin. Econom.*, 17(3), pp. 242–253.

Awartani, B. and Maghyereh, A. I. (2013). Dynamic spillovers between oil and stock markets in the Gulf Cooperation Council Countries. *Energy Econom.*, 36, pp. 28–42.

Balcilar, M., Ozdemir, Z, A., and Arslanktur, Y. (2010). Economic growth and energy consumption causal nexus viewed through a bootstrap rolling window. *Energy Econom.*, pp. 1398–1410.

Bernanke, B. and Gertler, M. (1989). Agency costs, net worth, and business fluctuations. *The Am. Econom. Rev.*, 791, pp. 14–31.

Bernanke, B. and Gertler, M. (1999). Monetary policy and asset price volatility in new challenges for monetary policy. In *Proceedings of the Federal Reserve Bank of Kansas Economic Symposium*, Jackson Hole, pp. 77–128.

Blot, C., Creel, J., Hubert, P., Labondance, F., and Saraceno, F. (2015). Assessing the link between price and financial stability. *J. Fina. Stabi.*, 16, pp. 71–88.

Browne, F. and Cronin, D. (2010). Commodity prices, money and inflation. *J. Econom. Business*, 62(4), pp. 331–345.

Chen, S. S. (2009). Do higher oil prices push the stock market into bear territory? *Energy Econom.*, 32, pp. 490–495.

Choi, K. and Hammoudeh, S. (2010). Volatility behavior of oil, industrial commodity and stock markets in a regime-switching environment. *Energy Policy*, 38, pp. 4388–4399.

Ciccarelli, M. and Mojon, B. (2010). Global inflation. *The Rev. Econom. Statist.*, 92(3), pp. 524–535.

Coronado, S., Jiménez-Rodriguez, R., and Rojas, O. (2015). An empirical analysis of the relationship between crude oil, gold and stock markets. Download November, 2016 at https://arxiv.org/pdf/1510.07599v2.pdf

Dolado, J. J. and Lütkepohl, H. (1996). Making Wald tests work for cointegrated VAR system. *Econometr. Rev.*, 15, pp. 369–386.

Efron, B. (1979). Bootstrap methods: Another look at the jackknife. *Ann. Statis.* 7, pp. 1–26.

Elder, J. and Serletis, A. (2010). Oil price uncertainty. *J. Money, Credit and Banking*, 42, pp. 1137–1159.

Fisher, I. (1932). *Booms and Depressions.* New York: Adelphi.

Fisher, I. (1933). The debt-deflation theory of great depressions. *Econometrica*, 14, pp. 337–357.

Frankel, J. (2008). Snake-oil tax cuts. Working Paper Series rwp08-056, Harvard University, John F. Kennedy School of Government. Boston, Mass.

Frankel, J. (2014). Estimated effects of speculation and interest rates in a carry trade model of commodity prices. *J. Int. Money Fin.*, 42, pp. 88–112.

Gelos G. and Ustyugova, Y. (2012). When commodity price surges. *Fin. Develop.*, 49(4).

Granger, C. W. J. (1969). Investigating causal relations by econometric models and cross spectral methods. *Econometrica*, 37, pp. 424–438.

Hatemi-J, A. and Uddin, G. S. (2012). Is the causal nexus of energy utilization and economic growth asymmetric in the US? *Econom. Syst.*, 36, pp. 461–469.

Jacks, D. and Stuermer, M. (2015). What drives commodity in the long run? Working paper Banque du Canada, Accessed in December 2015.

Kinda, T., Montfort, M. and Ouedraogo, R. (2016). Commodity price shocks and financial sector fragility, IMF Working paper 16/12. Washington DC.

Mantalos, P. (2000). A graphical investigation of the size and power of the granger causality tests in integrated-cointegrated VAR systems. *Stud. Nonlin. Dynam. Econometr.*, 4, pp. 17–33.

Mantalos, P. and Shukur, G. (1998). Size and power of the error correction model (ECM) of cointegration tests. A bootstrap approach. *Oxford Bullet. Economi. Statist.*, 60, pp. 249–255.

Masish, R., Peters, S., and Mello, L. D. (2011). Oil price volatility and stock price fluctuations in an emerging market: Evidence from South Korea. *Energy Econom.*, 33, pp. 975–986.

Park, J. and Phillips, P. C. B. (1989). Statistical inference in regressions with integrated processes: Part 2. *Econometr. Theory*, 5, pp. 95–131.

Rajan, R. and Ramcharan, R. (2015). The anatomy of a credit crisis: The boom and bust in farm land prices in the United States in the 1920s. *The Am. Econom. Rev.*, 105, pp. 1439–1477.

Pesaran, M. H. and Timmermann, A. (2005). Small sample properties of forecasts from autoregressive models under structural breaks. *J. Econometr.*, 129, pp. 183–217.

Schwartz, A. J. (1995). Why financial stability depends on price stability. *Econ. Affairs* 154, pp. 21–25 [reproduced in *Money, Price and the Real Economy*, G. Wood ed. Cheltenham: Edward Elgar].

Shukur, G. and Mantalos, P. (1997b). Tests for Granger causality in integrated-cointegrated VAR systems. Working paper 1998:1, Department of Statistics, University of Lund, Sweden.

Shukur, G. and Mantalos, P. (1997a). Size and power of the RESET test as applied to systems of equations: A bootstrap approach. Working paper No. 3/1997. Department of Statistics, University of Lund, Sweden.

Tang, C. F., Lai, Y. W., and Ozturk, I. (2015). How stable is the export-led growth hypothesis? Evidence from Asia's Four Little Dragons. *Econom. Model.*, 44, pp. 229–235.

Tang, C. F. (2013). A revisitation of the export-led growth hypothesis in Malaysia using the leveraged bootstrap simulation and rolling causality techniques. *J. Appl. Statist.*, 40(11), pp. 2332–2340.

Toda, H. Y. and Phillips, P. C. (1994). Vector autoregression and causality: A theoretical overview and simulation study. *Econometr. Revi.*, 13, pp. 259–285.

Toda, H. Y. and Phillips, P. C. B. (1993). Vector autoregressions and causality. *Econometrica*, 61, pp. 1367–1393.

Toda, H. Y. and Yamamoto, T. (1995). Statistical inference in Vector Autoregressions with possibly integrated processes. *J. Econometrics*, 66, pp. 225–250.

Zapata, H. O. and Rambaldi, A. N. (1997). Monte Carlo evidence on cointegrating and causation. *Oxford Bullet. Econom. Statist.*, 59, pp. 285–298.

Part IV

European Sovereign Debt Markets: Yields, Risk and QE Effectiveness

Chapter 15

Measuring and Analyzing Liquidity and Volatility Dynamics in the Euro-Area Government Bond Market

Conall O' Sullivan* and Vassilios G. Papavassiliou†

University College Dublin, UCD Michael Smurfit Graduate Business School Carysfort Avenue, Blackrock, Co Dublin, Ireland

*conall.osullivan@ucd.ie

†vassilios.papavassiliou@ucd.ie

Abstract

This chapter examines the impact the European sovereign debt market crisis had on liquidity and volatility dynamics and their interdependencies in the eurozone government bond market. In particular, we examine the impact across different countries and across different maturity buckets within individual countries. A comprehensive high-frequency dataset from MTS, Europe's premier electronic fixed-income trading market, is employed to construct a variety of microstructure liquidity and volatility measures. We analyze important trends in these measures over both tranquil and crisis periods. Additionally, we study time-varying correlations as well as the intertemporal interactions of liquidity proxies with volatility and returns. Our findings provide useful insights to regulators and policymakers on the relative strengths and weaknesses of domestic and global financial systems.

1. Introduction

There is a significant amount of interest in the empirical work on the microstructure of financial markets. Given the large market capitalization and trading volume in sovereign bond markets relative to equity markets, as well as the obvious importance of sovereign markets to their economies, these markets have received an increasing amount of attention from a microstructure perspective. The recent availability of high-frequency data on bond markets has significantly improved our understanding of bond market liquidity and trading. High-frequency data is the original form of market prices, also called tick-by-tick data, and not regularly spaced artifacts derived from the original market prices (Dacorogna *et al.*, 2001). Thus, high-frequency data provide a much clearer picture of variation in trading as well as access to constructing more efficient volatility and liquidity indicators.

In this chapter, we study high-frequency volatility and liquidity measures from the eurozone government bond market using a rich, comprehensive, and unique dataset provided by MTS (Mercato dei Titoli di Stato), Europe's premier electronic fixed-income trading market for euro-denominated government bonds. The European sovereign debt crisis offers a unique opportunity to study the behavior of bond market volatility and liquidity as the market moves from the pre-crisis period to full blown crisis mode. Within each particular local market, we point out subsets of bonds that suffer the least as the crisis deteriorates. We also investigate whether the results for the PIIGS countries are more pronounced in terms of liquidity and volatility interdependence.[1]

Our study contributes to the literature in a number of ways. First, we strive to analyze important trends in volatility and liquidity in the eurozone bond markets over both tranquil and crisis periods. Subsequently, we address the following questions: Has liquidity deteriorated across countries during the crisis? How does liquidity vary across countries and different maturity buckets? Has bond volatility intensified between calm and turbulent periods? Second, we analyze both static and time-varying correlations among various liquidity and volatility measures across countries. Whether or not liquidity and volatility shocks are significantly correlated with each other could be an indication of the systemic nature of those shocks and can also provide evidence on the existence of contagion effects across countries.

Third, the intertemporal interactions of liquidity proxies with returns and volatility across countries and asset classes have not been examined extensively, and we aim at filling this gap by drawing attention to the joint dynamics of liquidity, returns, and volatility. Specifically, we study causality and volatility-liquidity spillovers across countries by employing VAR-type econometric techniques. Our findings are of great significance as they offer useful insights on the workings of bond markets during periods of stress and

[1]PIIGS is an acronym which refers to the economies of Portugal, Ireland, Greece, Italy, and Spain that were unable to refinance their government debt or to rescue their problematic banking sector, and the term was popularized during the European sovereign debt crisis of the late 2000s.

on the future of the global economy where it seems inevitable for similar crises to happen again.

Finally, we employ the Forbes and Rigobon (2002) cross-market correlation coefficient, which adjusts the correlation estimate for heteroscedasticity, in order to test for financial contagion between (and within) PIIGS and non-PIIGS bond returns across different maturity segments. Our results document a deterioration of liquidity during the crisis period as transaction costs rise and quoted depth declines — with the exception of the 30-year benchmark. Flight-to-liquidity effects are present in our sample period, as investors move into shorter-term and more liquid bonds. Additionally, flight-to-quality episodes are documented, as trading for benchmarks of higher credit ratings intensified during the crisis period.

Volatility intensified during the crisis for PIIGS countries, whereas it declined for non-PIIGS across all maturities. Shorter maturity bonds are more adversely affected than their longer-term counterparts by aggregate liquidity shortages and increases in volatility during the crisis period. Our VAR results suggest contemporaneous commonalities are driving daily volatility and returns, volatility and spreads, volatility and depth, as well as spread and depth liquidity measures, in both pre-crisis and crisis periods within and across PIIGS and non-PIIGS countries. We find strong evidence for a decoupling among European sovereign debt markets during the crisis, where shocks to PIIGS country volatility result in less PIIGS trading for benchmark securities but more non-PIIGS trading. We also provide strong evidence for a decoupling within the PIIGS countries, whereas results are mixed within the non-PIIGS countries, as there are contagion effects among Germany, Netherlands, and Finland and also between Finland and Austria.

The remainder of this chapter is organized as follows. Section 2 provides a selective literature review on the microstructure of the European bond markets. Section 3 discusses the MTS market structure, while Section 4 describes the data handling procedures and the construction of liquidity and volatility measures. Section 5 describes the econometric methodology. Section 6 presents the empirical results. Finally, Section 7 provides some concluding remarks.

2. A Selective Literature Review

The existing literature on the microstructure of the European sovereign bond markets is fairly limited and mainly refers to periods prior to the financial crisis. Also, there is only a handful of papers that have employed high-frequency data from the MTS platform. Cheung *et al.* (2005) study the intraday price-order flow relation in the Euro bond market using data from the MTS platform. They find a larger impact of order flow during announcement days and a higher price impact of trading after a longer period of inactivity. Dunne *et al.* (2007) provide a formal theoretical argument on the meaning of 'benchmark' bond and consider its role in pricing when there is concentration of liquidity and price discovery. Benchmarks in the European bond market are identified with the use of high-frequency transaction data from the EuroMTS platform.

Coluzzi *et al.* (2008) provide a description of the liquidity of the Italian wholesale secondary market using data from the corresponding MTS domestic platform. They find no sharp differences in terms of liquidity of the order book between on-the-run and off-the-run securities. They also show that modifications of issuance policies help securities in gaining their benchmark status. Girardi (2008) employs daily transaction prices from eleven European countries and finds that EuroMTS market's contribution to price discovery is about twenty percent and that price discovery turns out to be strongly related to trading activity and price volatility, even after controlling for institutional factors. Beber *et al.* (2009) use intraday European bond quotes and transactions from the MTS interdealer markets spanning the period from April 2003 to December 2004. Their evidence suggests that the bulk of sovereign yield spreads are explained by differences in credit quality, though liquidity plays a nontrivial role, especially for low credit risk markets and during times of heightened market uncertainty.

Favero *et al.* (2010) explore the determinants of observed yield differentials between eurozone sovereign bonds. Results indicate strong comovement in yield differentials of benchmark bonds, being explained by just the first principal component. Their econometric analysis reveals that the aggregate market risk factor is consistently priced and that the interaction of liquidity differentials with the risk factor is always negative when significant. Dufour and Nguyen (2012) analyze four years of transaction data for euro-area sovereign bonds traded on the MTS platform and find strong evidence of information asymmetry as well as evidence of demand for higher yields for bonds with larger permanent trading impacts.

Bai *et al.* (2012) investigate how variations in bond yields are affected by credit risk and liquidity risk in the euro area sovereign bond markets in order to shed light on the underlying causes of the European sovereign debt crisis. Using bond transaction data from MTS and CDS and interest rate swap spread data, they dispute the notion that the European sovereign bond crisis mainly propagates through the fundamental credit risk channel. Pelizzon *et al.* (2013) study market microstructure and liquidity in the Italian sovereign bond market using tick-by-tick data from MTS for the period June 2011 to November 2012. They conclude that credit risk resulted in unprecedented levels of illiquidity during the sovereign debt crisis. In particular, dealers reduced their liquidity position, which led to a drop in prices and a spike in bond yields, causing deep losses in investors' portfolios. ECB's intervention has been successful as it improved market liquidity and substantially lowered credit risk, at least in the near term.

Darbha and Dufour (2013a, 2013b) studied the relationship between bond illiquidity and bond characteristics before and after the onset of the liquidity crisis in August 2007 and showed that government bonds were not immune to the liquidity crisis. After controlling for standard risk factors, they conclude that liquidity does not provide a significant incremental explanatory contribution to yield dynamics before the crisis, but becomes an important explanatory factor during the crisis period.

3. The MTS Market

The MTS market is the largest quote-driven interdealer electronic fixed-income market for euro-denominated government bonds. A smaller percentage of quasi-government and structured bonds (asset-backed securities and covered bonds) are also listed and traded on MTS platforms. It was launched in 1988 by the Italian Treasury and the Bank of Italy in an effort to enhance liquidity and transparency of the Italian secondary government bond market (Darbha and Dufour, 2013a). The electronic platform was expanded in later years to include all major European countries and domestic MTS markets were subsequently developed.[2] According to Persaud (2006), excluding HDAT — the second largest electronic platform in Europe — the Bank of Greece's proprietary system for secondary trading in Greek government bonds (representing around 5% of outstanding Euro government bonds), the market share of MTS stands at 88.7%.

Apart from the domestic MTS markets for secondary trading, a platform for trading benchmark fixed-income securities, EuroMTS has also been

[2]Cheung *et al.* (2005) argue that the structure of the MTS trading platforms is similar to the EBS and D2002 electronic trading system for the foreign exchange market, but different from the quote screen-based US Treasury bond trading system.

established since 1999. Euro benchmark bonds are those bonds with an outstanding value of at least €5 billion. Bonds are allowed to trade on both domestic MTS and the EuroMTS platforms, therefore, liquidity is fragmented between the benchmark and the domestic markets. Despite the apparent fragmentation of trading between the two platforms, markets are closely connected in terms of liquidity as Cheung *et al.* (2005) demonstrate. The domestic MTS markets typically offer slightly better quoted and effective spreads, however, differences are infinitesimal if they exist. Dunne *et al.* (2006) argue that EuroMTS has been adopted by many of the smaller European issuers as their preferred location for the monitoring of the trading obligations of their primary dealers. As a consequence, the pre- and post-trade transparency in trading of the smaller issues has increased and has allowed smaller issuers to issue debt at more favorable rates.

Since October 2007, MTS is majority owned by the London Stock Exchange Group plc. In 2013, MTS expanded into US bond markets allowing for global coverage and increased harmonization and consistency in regulated electronic fixed-income trading. It currently facilitates fixed-income trading with over 500 global counterparties and average daily turnover exceeding €100 billion. MTS services are currently offered in more than 30 communities with enhanced market-making on interdealer and B2C markets. Specifically, MTS trades bonds of the following countries: Austria, Belgium, Bulgaria, Croatia, Czech Republic, Cyprus, Denmark, Finland, France, Germany, Greece, Hungary, Ireland, Israel, Italy, Latvia, Lithuania, Luxembourg, the Netherlands, Norway, Poland, Portugal, Romania, Slovenia, Spain, Sweden, Turkey, Ukraine, United Kingdom, and United States.

MTS trading platforms support pre-trade, trade execution, and post-trade capabilities across cash and repo markets and provide benchmark market data and comprehensive fixed-income indices. Participants are split into two categories, *primary dealers* and *dealers*. Primary dealers are obligated to continuously quote bid and ask proposals on a given number of bonds they have been assigned to, enhancing markets' liquidity (price makers-takers). On the other hand, dealers act as price takers and can only issue orders for proposals formulated by primary dealers (Dufour and Skinner, 2004).

The MTS system, effectively, works as a limit order book. Trading is anonymous and the identity of the counterparty is only revealed after a trade is executed. Market makers' quotations are aggregated according to price and side of the market, and order execution takes place based on the principle of price-time priority. The MTS system is highly transparent as quotes and trades data are instantly available to all market participants (at a cost) through data vendors such as Bloomberg and Reuters.

4. MTS Data

4.1. *Data handling procedures*

Our dataset is by far the most complete representation of the eurozone sovereign bond market available and covers the period from January 2008 to December 2010, thereby it includes both tranquil and crisis periods. The euro sovereign debt crisis finds its origin in Greece. Toward the end of October 2009, bond yields rose significantly and benchmark bond prices fell, following the country's sovereign debt downgrade by Fitch (Papavassiliou, 2014). A second development in November 2009 that disrupted the tranquility of European financial markets and led to increased risk aversion was when Dubai World conglomerate asked creditors for a six-month standstill on its debt obligations (Dellas and Tavlas, 2013). A sharp increase in bond yields and a decline in prices intensified during November 2009, resulting in the yield curve to flatten considerably. Thus, we consider November 2009 as the period when the European debt crisis actually started.

Our high-frequency dataset consists of the following 11 countries: Austria, Belgium, Finland, France, Germany, Greece, Ireland, Italy, the Netherlands, Portugal, and Spain. It contains the three best bid and ask quotations (three levels of depth) throughout the trading day, time-stamped to the nearest second (*Best Proposals file*). We have selected to work with benchmark fixed coupon-bearing government bonds from both the EuroMTS and the domestic MTS markets. We consider bonds within four time-to-maturity groups: 2, 5, 10, and 30 year. For each country and each maturity category, we select the most heavily traded benchmark security. The dataset has been filtered as follows: (a) we only consider quotes recorded during the regular trading hours from 8:15 am until 5:30 pm CET. Thus, we exclude pre-sessional and end-of-day quotations in order to mitigate microstructure effects (b) we discard quotes with zero and negative bid–ask spreads and (c) we exclude observations with relative quoted spread higher than 100 basis points.

4.2. *Liquidity measures*

Liquidity is an elusive concept and many different liquidity proxies have been proposed. Following the earlier literature (Bollen and Whaley, 1998;

Hasbrouck and Seppi, 2001; Chordia *et al.*, 2005; Coluzzi *et al.*, 2008; Darbha and Dufour, 2013b; Pelizzon *et al.*, 2013) we have estimated a wide variety of spread and depth liquidity measures, as well as measures combining a number of liquidity dimensions, as follows:

- **Best bid–ask spread:** defined as the difference between the best ask quote and the best bid quote (best spread = best ask price − best bid price)$A_{it} - B_{it}$, where A_{it} is the posted best ask price for security i at time t, and B_{it} is the best posted bid price for security i at time t
- **Quoted spread:** defined as the difference between the simple average of the three best ask prices and bid prices
- **Relative or proportional spread:** defined as the best bid–ask spread divided by the midpoint of the bid and ask quotes, i.e. $100(A_{it} - B_{it})/M_{it}$, where the midpoint is estimated as: $(A_{it} + B_{it})/2$.
- **Best log spread**: defined as the logarithmic ratio of best ask over best bid $-\log(A_{it}/B_{it})$
- **Quoted depth:** defined as best bid size + best ask size (quantity of securities bid or offered for sale at the posted bid and offer prices)
- **Log quoted depth:** defined as log (best bid size) + log (best ask size)
- **Quote slope:** defined as (best bid–ask spread/log quoted depth)
- **Log Quote slope:** defined as best log spread/log quoted depth = $\log(A_{it}/B_{it})/$ log quoted depth
- **Euro depth:** defined as the sum of the euro value of the bonds bid and offered at the best quotes
- **Market quality index:** defined as (1/2) quoted depth/relative spread[3]
- **Steepness:** defined as the absolute difference between the best and the worst quote, scaled on the mid-point between the two, i.e. steepness = (bid steepness + ask steepness)/2, where bid (ask) steepness equals: best bid (ask) price − worst bid (ask) price × 100/best bid (ask) price + worst bid (ask) price/2.

The corresponding daily average liquidity measures, derived from the aforementioned high-frequency liquidity measures, have also been constructed per country and maturity bucket.

[3]The market quality index has been proposed by Bollen and Whaley (1998) in order to measure the effect on overall market liquidity following a regime change in financial markets. It is designed to capture the trade-off between quoted bid–ask spread and market depth.

4.3. *Bond returns and volatility*

We employ midpoints of bid–ask quotes as price measures which are generally less noisy measures of the efficient price than are transaction prices, as they do not suffer from bid–ask bounce effects (Bandi and Russell, 2006). An intraday return has the same definition as a daily return defined as the change in the logarithm of the price during a time interval. When using quotation data, returns are calculated from midpoint prices as follows:

$$r_{it} = \log\left(\frac{m_{i,t}}{m_{i,t-1}}\right) \tag{1}$$

where $m_{i,t}$ represents the midpoint of the bid–ask spread for security i prevailing at the end of interval t. Intraday prices (tick-by-tick) are generally only available at unevenly spaced time points, so the calculation of evenly spaced high-frequency returns inevitably relies on interpolation techniques applied around the endpoints of the desired sampling intervals. We artificially construct 5-min returns from the linearly interpolated logarithmic midpoint of the continuously recorded bid and ask quotes. The selection of 5-min returns as the optimal sampling frequency is probably the most popular choice and has been used extensively in the realized volatility literature (Andersen and Bollerslev, 1997; Andersen *et al.*, 2001). We also estimate daily bond returns as the summation of the 5-min intraday returns for each security.

The emerging theory on volatility emphasizes the advantages of the realized volatility estimator. Andersen and Bollerslev (1998) show that realized volatility computed from high-frequency intraday returns is effectively an error-free volatility measure as the sampling frequency of the returns approaches infinity. Along these lines, we construct daily realized variance measures by the summation of squared 5-min intraday returns, while daily realized volatility is obtained using the square-root of the variance series. Formally, for $N = 1, 2, 3, \ldots$ the realized variance for day t is defined as

$$\hat{\sigma}^2_{t,N} = \sum_{j=1}^{N} r^2_{t,j,N} \tag{2}$$

and the realized volatility is defined as $\hat{\sigma}_{t,N}$.

5. Econometric Methodology

The extant literature has examined the dynamic interaction of liquidity and returns in stock markets (Hasbrouck, 1991), time-varying liquidity in Treasury bond markets (Krishnamurthy, 2002), and the joint dynamics of liquidity, trading activity, returns, and volatility in stock and US Treasury bond markets (Chordia *et al.*, 2005). However, the intertemporal interactions of liquidity proxies with returns and volatility across the eurozone countries have not been examined extensively. We aim at filling this gap by drawing attention to the joint dynamics of liquidity, returns and volatility over both tranquil and crisis periods.

Univariate relationships between liquidity and returns have been discussed in Amihud and Mendelson (1986), among others, while volatility and liquidity univariate interactions have been addressed in Benston and Hagerman (1974) and Subrahmanyam (1994). The main findings have demonstrated (a) a bidirectional causality between liquidity and returns, mainly exemplified through future trading behaviour and a premium for greater trading costs, (b) a bidirectional causality between liquidity and volatility, the idea being that increased volatility leads to higher bid–ask spreads as inventory risks increase, and decreased liquidity leads to increased price fluctuations. Given that cross-market effects and bidirectional causalities may be significant, especially during periods of stress, we follow Chordia *et al.* (2005) and adopt a p-th order multivariate vector autoregression model VAR(p) of the following form:

$$X_t = \sum_{j=1}^{K} a_{1j} X_{t-j} + \sum_{j=1}^{K} b_{1j} Y_{t-j} + u_t, \tag{3}$$

$$Y_t = \sum_{j=1}^{K} a_{2j} X_{t-j} + \sum_{j=1}^{K} b_{2j} Y_{t-j} + v_t, \tag{4}$$

where X is the vector containing volatility, returns, relative spread, and quoted depth measures in the (domestic MTS or EuroMTS) non-PIIGS market, and where Y is the vector containing the corresponding variables in the (domestic MTS or EuroMTS) PIIGS market.

The VAR(p) process is the basic multivariate model that is used to represent a set of dynamically dependent stationary time series. VAR models have several advantages compared with univariate time series models or simultaneous equations structural models, as (a) there is no need to specify which variables are endogenous or exogenous — all are endogenous, and

(b) VAR models allow the value of a variable to depend on more than just its own lags or combinations of white noise terms, thus they provide more flexibility than univariate AR models and are able to capture more features of the data (Brooks, 2014). Our VAR methodology also deals with Granger causality testing and impulse responses. Granger causality enables the proper identification of the direction of causality and the characterization of a set of variables either as exogenous or independent. Impulse responses trace out the responsiveness of the dependent variables in the VAR to shocks to each of the variables. For calculating impulse responses, the ordering of the variables is important (based on the Cholesky factor), especially when there is strong contemporaneous correlation between the shocks (Lütkepohl, 1991).

In a second step, we strive to investigate for the presence of contagion by analyzing the correlation degree between PIIGS and non-PIIGS countries, across all four maturity buckets. As Claessens and Forbes (2001) note, contagion incorporates many different ideas and concepts. Not only is contagion a disease, but it also refers to the transmission of a disease among different markets and countries. The most popular definition of contagion is the one proposed by Forbes and Rigobon (2002). They define contagion as a significant increase in cross-market linkages after a shock to one country. Even if two markets continue to be highly correlated after a shock to one market, this does not necessarily constitute contagion. Only if cross-market linkages increase significantly after a shock, this suggests that the transmission mechanism between the two markets strengthened after the shock and contagion occurred. Insignificant increases in cross-market relationships are characterized as *interdependence.*

Cross-market correlation coefficients are conditional on market volatility. The higher the volatility, the more upward biased the estimates of correlation coefficients are. Forbes and Rigobon (2002) propose an adjusted unconditional correlation coefficient that adjusts for this bias, and this is the approach we take in the following section. Specifically, assuming there are no omitted variables or endogeneity between markets, the conditional correlation is written as

$$\rho^* = \rho\sqrt{\frac{1+\delta}{1+\delta\rho^2}}, \tag{5}$$

where ρ^* is the conditional correlation coefficient, ρ is the unconditional correlation coefficient, and δ is the relative increase in the variance of market x

$$\delta \equiv \frac{\sigma_{xx}^h}{\sigma_{xx}^l} - 1, \tag{6}$$

where l and h denote the tranquil period and the period of market turmoil, respectively. Manipulating Eqs. (5) and (6) to solve for the unconditional correlation coefficient, adjusted for heteroskedasticity, yields

$$\rho = \frac{\rho^*}{\sqrt{1 + \delta[1 - (\rho^*)^2]}} \tag{7}$$

Our empirical analysis is complemented by a Dynamic Conditional Correlation (DCC) approach proposed by Engle (2002), which is a generalization of the Bollerslev (1990) constant conditional correlation (CCC) estimator. Define the variance–covariance matrix, H_t, as

$$H_t = D_t R_t D_t, \tag{8}$$

where D_t is a diagonal matrix containing the conditional standard deviations on the leading diagonal and R_t is the conditional correlation matrix. Engle advocates a two-step estimation procedure where each variable in the system is first modeled separately as a univariate GARCH process. In the second stage, the conditional likelihood is maximized with respect to any unknown parameters in the correlation matrix. The log-likelihood function of the second stage takes the form:

$$l(\theta_2|\theta_1) = \sum_{t=1}^{T} (\log|R_t| + u_t' R_t^{-1} u_t), \tag{9}$$

where θ_1 denotes all the unknown parameters that were estimated in the first stage and θ_2 denotes all those to be estimated in the second stage. The DCC model allows for not only heteroskedasticity in time-series returns but also time-varying correlation processes.

6. Empirical Results

6.1. *Descriptive statistics*

We present descriptive statistics on liquidity and volatility measures across the 2-, 5-, 10-, and 30-year maturity category in Table 1. The table shows the mean, standard deviation, as well as the minimum and maximum values of spread-based liquidity proxies which capture the tightness dimension of

Table 1. Summary Statistics of Tightness Liquidity Measures Over the Pre-Crisis and Crisis Periods

		Mean		SD		Min.		Max.	
LM	Maturity	Pre-Crisis	Crisis	Pre-crisis	Crisis	Pre-crisis	Crisis	Pre-crisis	Crisis
Best spread	02-year	0.1221	0.2972	0.1107	0.3700	0.0089	0.0085	1.3969	2.0000
	05-year	0.1943	0.3467	0.1835	0.3614	0.0126	0.0073	1.6000	1.9083
	10-year	0.3148	0.4316	0.3081	0.4061	0.0119	0.0087	1.9948	1.9908
	30-year	0.6529	0.6010	0.3976	0.3194	0.1000	0.1728	2.2904	1.9900
Quoted spread	02-year	0.1706	0.4531	0.2143	0.6653	0.0116	0.0113	3.8374	6.7428
	05-year	0.2506	0.4762	0.2720	0.6928	0.0165	0.0102	6.9857	22.1599
	10-year	0.3964	0.5523	0.4212	0.6416	0.0163	0.0122	8.9447	15.3984
	30-year	0.8088	0.7461	0.5402	0.5848	0.1000	0.1988	7.6783	15.9233
Relative spread (bps)	02-year	11.96	29.29	10.83	36.65	0.84	0.82	136.16	198.88
	05-year	18.91	34.67	18.16	37.81	1.22	0.70	166.08	199.69
	10-year	30.79	43.32	30.29	43.73	1.13	0.83	194.19	199.99
	30-year	64.77	61.09	38.83	42.51	9.26	13.99	197.39	199.96

Note: The Mean, Standard Deviation, Minimum, and Maximum values are shown for Best, Quoted, and Relative spreads across the 2, 5, 10, and 30 year maturity segments.

liquidity of the pan-European government bond market.[4] At a first glance, best spreads, quoted spreads, and relative spreads widen for bonds with longer maturities. This observation holds for both the pre-crisis and the crisis period and is consistent with findings from earlier literature — bonds with lower maturities are more desirable and have greater liquidity (Pasquariello and Vega, 2009). Also, volatility, as measured by the standard deviation, increases as we move from shorter to longer maturity buckets, and this result is more pronounced during the pre-crisis period.

Transitioning from the calm period to the turbulent, there is a sharp increase in all tightness measures for the 2-, 5-, and 10-year benchmark securities. This is an indication that liquidity has worsened during the crisis period as transaction costs have risen significantly.

An interesting observation for the 30-year bonds is that their liquidity does not deteriorate during the crisis period, instead it is slightly improved. More specifically, the mean value of the best spread for the 30-year instrument declines from 0.6529 to 0.6010 after November 2009.

[4]Market liquidity has several dimensions. Tightness refers to the difference between buy and sell prices. Depth relates to the size of the transactions that can be absorbed without affecting prices. Immediacy denotes the speed with which orders can be executed, and resiliency denotes the ease with which prices return to "normal" after temporary order imbalances. A discussion is provided in Borio (2000).

Table 2. Summary Statistics of Depth Liquidity Measures Over the Pre-Crisis and Crisis Periods

		Mean		SD		Min.		Max.	
LM	Maturity	Pre-Crisis	Crisis	Pre-crisis	Crisis	Pre-crisis	Crisis	Pre-crisis	Crisis
Quoted depth (in millions)	02-year	25.11	21.67	10.42	8.48	5.00	2.00	82.53	57.22
	05-year	28.67	23.20	14.99	8.78	5.00	2.06	148.11	70.26
	10-year	27.16	22.58	12.25	8.14	5.39	2.02	108.78	60.34
	30-year	10.85	10.35	2.56	2.96	5.00	1.70	25.79	29.64
Log quoted depth	02-year	32.34	31.97	0.73	1.19	29.46	27.63	34.49	34.04
	05-year	32.53	32.12	0.77	1.07	29.46	28.04	35.61	34.31
	10-year	32.44	32.05	0.73	1.06	29.57	28.01	34.96	34.01
	30-year	30.82	30.65	0.47	0.68	29.46	27.13	32.48	32.15
Euro depth (in billions)	02-year	2.53	2.20	1.04	0.87	0.50	0.18	8.36	5.88
	05-year	2.89	2.39	1.48	0.92	0.49	0.15	15.13	7.28
	10-year	2.75	2.36	1.24	0.89	0.48	0.13	11.43	6.33
	30-year	1.08	1.11	0.27	0.36	0.40	0.11	2.63	3.73

Note: The Mean, Standard Deviation, Minimum, and Maximum values are shown for Quoted, Log Quoted, and Euro depth across the 2, 5, 10, and 30 year maturity segments.

The same observation holds for the quoted and relative spreads whose mean values decline by approximately 8% and 6%, respectively. This result could indicate that, for bonds with very long maturities (so called "buy-and-hold" bonds), the selling pressure was not as high as for bonds with shorter maturities resulting in lower spreads. Friewald *et al.* (2012) found similar results using data from the US corporate bond market during the subprime crisis. Obviously, the shorter maturity benchmark bonds have been more vulnerable to liquidity disturbances during the crisis than the longer maturity bonds. Standard deviation values increase from the pre-crisis to the crisis period, indicating higher volatility in liquidity across all maturity buckets.

Table 2 shows summary statistics for the depth liquidity measures. The average quoted depth of the 5-year bonds which amounts to 28.67 million euros turns out to be the largest across the four maturity segments. The 30-year bonds exhibit a much lower quoted depth than the medium and shorter term bonds. This finding reconfirms the inverse relationship between spreads and depth — lower quoted spreads are associated with larger depth. Furthermore, the variability of the 30-year bond quoted depth is very small, as shown by its standard deviation of around 3 million euros. In contrast, dispersion around the mean value of quoted depth for shorter maturities is

Table 3. Summary Statistics of Breadth and Other Multidimensional Liquidity Measures Over the Pre-Crisis and Crisis Periods

		Mean		SD		Min.		Max.	
LM	Maturity	Pre-Crisis	Crisis	Pre-crisis	Crisis	Pre-crisis	Crisis	Pre-crisis	Crisis
Steepness	02-year	0.0570	0.2056	0.2152	0.5979	0.0026	0.0023	5.0546	8.1022
	05-year	0.0646	0.1528	0.1678	0.5839	0.0029	0.0027	7.1863	22.4294
	10-year	0.0941	0.1425	0.2420	0.4701	0.0031	0.0028	8.7858	15.9938
	30-year	0.1912	0.1966	0.8487	0.7129	0.0210	0.0195	50.0730	27.2430
Quote slope	02-year	0.0038	0.0093	0.0035	0.0116	0.0003	0.0003	0.0434	0.0648
	05-year	0.0059	0.0109	0.0057	0.0116	0.0004	0.0002	0.0519	0.0596
	10-year	0.0096	0.0135	0.0095	0.0130	0.0004	0.0003	0.0617	0.0637
	30-year	0.0210	0.0195	0.0129	0.0106	0.0036	0.0054	0.0765	0.0675
Log quote slope ($\times 10^5$)	02-year	3.73	9.42	3.43	12.00	0.26	0.25	42.28	68.31
	05-year	5.85	11.03	5.69	12.34	0.38	0.21	53.84	64.73
	10-year	9.53	13.77	9.42	14.29	0.35	0.26	60.88	68.82
	30-year	21.06	20.10	12.71	14.38	3.89	4.53	64.99	71.48
Market quality index (in billions)	02-year	26.04	19.57	28.02	24.43	0.73	0.08	210.30	225.78
	05-year	22.21	13.61	29.91	18.69	0.25	0.06	218.40	219.99
	10-year	14.41	7.34	20.41	8.56	0.17	0.05	135.84	195.10
	30-year	1.37	1.35	1.13	0.88	0.16	0.05	7.05	5.12

Note: The Mean, Standard Deviation, Minimum, and Maximum values are shown for Steepness, Quote slope, Log quote slope, and Market Quality Index measures across the 2, 5, 10, and 30 year maturity segments.

much larger. The average quoted depth for the 2-year benchmark declines by 14 percent during the crisis period, indicating a deterioration in liquidity. Liquidity drops of similar magnitude are also observed for the 5- and 10-year benchmark between the tranquil and the crisis period. However, the decline in quoted depth for the 30-year instrument is less pronounced than the corresponding decline in shorter maturities depth — about only 4%.

Similar to the quoted depth, both the log quoted depth and the euro depth have declined during the crisis period. Shrinking liquidity exposes markets to crunches in response to shocks stemming from financial instabilities in global markets. Table 3 describes the features of breadth and multidimensional liquidity measures. In terms of steepness, the shorter maturity bonds exhibit lower values, which indicates increased liquidity. For example, the average distance between the best and the worst quote of 2-year bonds amounts to 5.7%, followed by the 5- and 10-year benchmarks. The 30-year instrument has clearly the highest average steepness of all, exceeding 19%. Despite the fact that steepness is sometimes not consistent with other measures of liquidity, it behaves correctly in this case; that is, it is lower

Table 4. Summary Statistics of 5-minute Returns and Realized Volatility

		Mean		SD	
Measures	Maturity	Pre-crisis	Crisis	Pre-crisis	Crisis
5-min returns	02-year	0.0119	−0.0107	0.1278	0.2663
	05-year	0.0196	−0.0144	0.2139	0.3154
	10-year	0.0289	−0.0196	0.3659	0.4757
	30-year	0.0640	0.0327	0.8388	0.6429
Realized volatility (%)	02-year	0.1240	0.1846	0.0938	0.2320
	05-year	0.2121	0.2416	0.1395	0.2193
	10-year	0.3625	0.3750	0.1768	0.2463
	30-year	0.7672	0.6232	0.2962	0.2266

Note: The Mean and Standard Deviation values are shown over the pre-crisis and crisis periods across the 2, 5, 10, and 30 year maturity segments.

for more liquid securities. However, during the crisis period the picture is reversed, as the 2-year bond takes on the highest value of all. A rise in steepness between the two episodes implies that the government securities face less liquidity during the crisis period.

As a more transparent indicator of liquidity, quote slope (as well as log quote slope) confirms the higher liquidity for shorter maturities. Goyenko *et al.* (2011) provide evidence of a steeper liquidity term structure during periods of stress, indicating a flight to liquidity effect, as investors rebalance their portfolios by moving into shorter-term and more liquid bonds. Clearly, liquidity has deteriorated during the crisis period, as the mean value of quote slope has risen across all maturities, with the exception of the 30-year instrument. Standard deviation values are higher during the crisis period showing that the volatility of liquidity has intensified. The market quality index takes on higher values for shorter maturities. In agreement with other proxies, it shows that the longer a bond's maturity the more illiquid the bond is. As shown in Table 3, the mean value of the market quality index declined between the pre-crisis and crisis period.

This result suggests that the decrease in liquidity due to smaller depths and wider spreads leads to a deterioration in market quality. Table 4 describes the daily average bond returns, derived from the 5-minute returns set, along with the daily realized volatility estimator of the pan-European market.

At a quick glance daily returns are higher for longer maturity bonds, which makes perfect sense as investors incur additional risks by holding longer-term instruments. The average daily return for the 30-year bond is

0.064 prior to the crisis and plummets to roughly one-half this level during the crisis period. Furthermore, the average daily returns for 2-, 5-, and 10-year maturity buckets become negative in the midst of the eurozone debt crisis. Similar to daily returns, daily realized volatility is higher for longer maturity benchmarks.

During the crisis, volatility intensified as shown in the table for the 2-, 5-, and 10-year instrument. However, the 30-year benchmark follows an autonomous path, as its volatility and the dispersion around it dropped moderately. This is an indication of a decline in investors' appetite towards longer-term bonds, as they prefer to trade on their most liquid assets in search of liquidity. To sum up, with the exclusion of the 30-year instrument, shorter maturity bonds are more adversely affected than longer maturity bonds by liquidity dry ups and an intensification of volatility during the debt crisis period.

Figure 1 provides an interesting visual illustration of realized volatility and cumulative daily returns for both PIIGS and non-PIIGS countries, across the 5- and 10-year benchmarks. A significant decline in returns for the PIIGS countries during the crisis period is apparent in both graphs. Table 5 presents descriptive statistics of liquidity and volatility measures across the PIIGS and non-PIIGS countries. Overall, the sovereign bond markets of non-PIIGS countries are far more liquid than the PIIGS bond markets, as evidenced by lower transaction costs, higher depth and an enhanced market quality index. These results hold in both pre-crisis and crisis periods. Obviously, the PIIGS countries are more adversely affected than their non-PIIGS counterparts during the crisis. Figures for the PIIGS countries rise up to eight times as much as that for non-PIIGS nations.

Although volatility has strengthened for the PIIGS countries during the crisis, the opposite result has been observed for the non-PIIGS countries, as documented by smaller realized volatility indicators across all maturity buckets.

This result is due to the fact that trading intensity for non-PIIGS government bonds lowered during the crisis, which is also evidenced by the smaller quoted depths for non-PIIGS bonds across all maturity buckets. It can also be partly attributed to the role played by hedge funds and derivatives markets that helped reduce volatility. Results for the non-PIIGS countries are mixed between the tranquil and the crisis periods in terms of liquidity. With the exception of the 5-year instrument, realized spreads have narrowed during the crisis period. This result implies that trading for benchmarks of higher credit ratings has intensified during the crisis, as

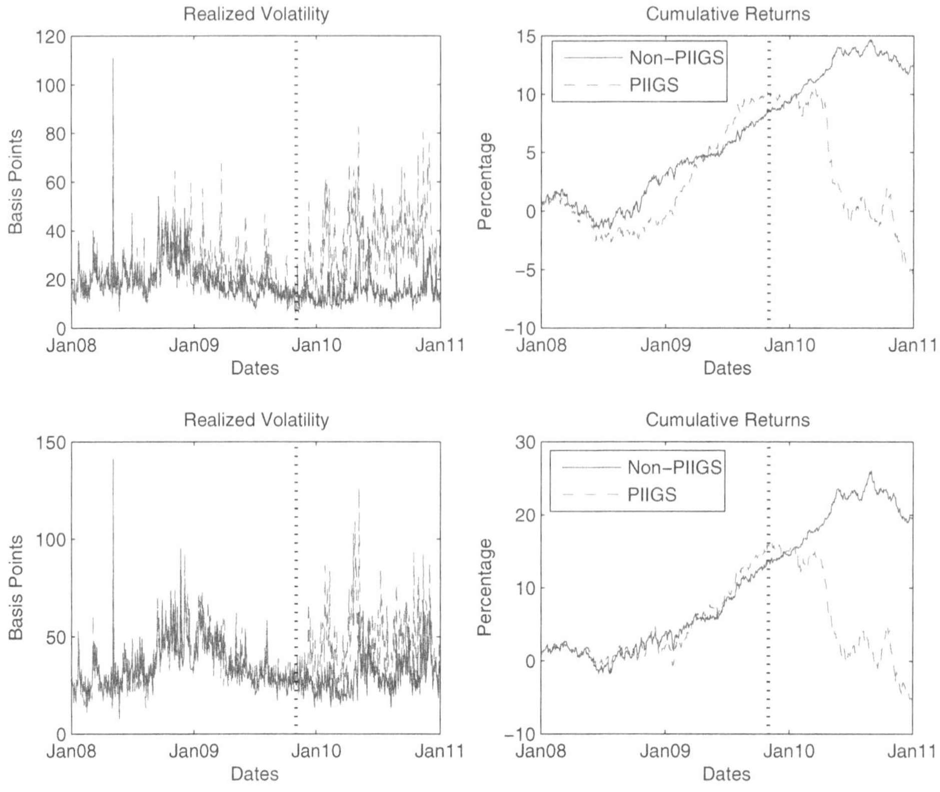

Figure 1. Top panel refers to realized volatility and cumulative returns for 5-year bonds and bottom panel refers to the corresponding measures for the 10-year benchmark for both PIIGS and non-PIIGS countries

investors try to rebalance their portfolios by getting rid of lower quality instruments.

Mixed results are also documented for the quote slope and the market quality index. Although the market quality index declines from its pre-crisis levels across the 5- and 10-year maturity category, it increases for the shortest and longest maturity benchmarks.

Figure 2 provides a visual illustration of PIIGS vs. non-PIIGS 10-year relative spread and quoted depth and highlights the trends revealed by descriptive statistics. A noticeable variation in spreads and depth can be observed around September 2008 when Lehman Brothers collapsed. Lehman's demise, which contributed to the erosion of roughly $10 trillion in market capitalization from global equity markets, also affected the European government bond market.

Table 5. Comparisons between PIIGS — Non-PIIGS Countries Over the Pre-Crisis and Crisis Periods

		Mean				SD			
		Pre-crisis		Crisis		Pre-crisis		Crisis	
Measures	Maturity	Non-PIIGS	PIIGS	Non-PIIGS	PIIGS	Non-PIIGS	PIIGS	Non-PIIGS	PIIGS
Relative spread (bps)	02-year	9.17	14.49	7.81	46.05	5.80	8.56	4.30	25.25
	05-year	14.91	23.18	17.39	57.17	9.32	16.60	6.64	28.44
	10-year	27.76	34.63	22.42	69.72	20.26	25.32	9.07	31.23
	30-year	61.71	68.71	44.68	87.05	29.77	35.13	13.29	25.38
Quote depth (in millions)	02-year	27.31	23.16	25.97	18.39	5.66	6.95	3.14	3.50
	05-year	29.98	27.34	26.52	18.98	10.73	11.13	3.12	3.45
	10-year	28.64	25.36	25.70	18.67	10.32	8.29	3.01	3.39
	30-year	11.09	10.52	10.73	9.70	1.67	1.64	1.05	1.81
Quote slope	02-year	0.0029	0.0046	0.0024	0.0146	0.0018	0.0028	0.0014	0.0079
	05-year	0.0047	0.0073	0.0056	0.0177	0.0029	0.0052	0.0022	0.0087
	10-year	0.0087	0.0108	0.0074	0.0212	0.0064	0.0079	0.0030	0.0093
	30-year	0.0211	0.0210	0.0166	0.0243	0.0108	0.0109	0.0052	0.0068
Market quality index (in billions)	02-year	28.17	24.01	31.40	10.52	19.85	22.69	12.60	12.46
	05-year	23.87	20.53	17.41	8.68	25.81	25.24	5.78	12.59
	10-year	16.91	11.37	10.07	3.92	19.75	14.80	4.03	4.85
	30-year	1.45	1.26	1.61	0.93	1.10	0.98	0.51	0.40
Realized volatility (%)	02-year	0.1117	0.1354	0.0704	0.2749	0.0591	0.0584	0.0512	0.1642
	05-year	0.2033	0.2214	0.1570	0.3497	0.0870	0.0896	0.0511	0.1468
	10-year	0.3594	0.3658	0.3015	0.4675	0.1328	0.1384	0.0964	0.1628
	30-year	0.7474	0.7891	0.6281	0.6272	0.2595	0.2790	0.1688	0.1729

Note: The Mean and Standard Deviation values are shown for the Relative spread, Quoted depth, Quote slope, Market Quality Index, and Realized Volatility measures across the 2, 5, 10, and 30 year maturity segments.

Table 6 compares liquidity and volatility of the individual PIIGS members with the corresponding measures of the eurozone as a whole during the crisis period. For brevity, we provide comparisons across the 5- and 10-year benchmarks only.

Clearly, Greece experienced the most turbulent financial conditions, followed by Ireland and Portugal. The relative spreads in these markets are more than double of the European average. Similar patterns are detected in the slope and volatility measures.

An interesting observation is that Italy and Spain, although severely affected by the crisis, are in a less dramatic situation than Greece, Ireland and Portugal. Their relative spreads and slopes are lower than the European average, especially for Italy, confirming Italy's position as the largest and most liquid bond market in Europe. Volatility levels in Italy are lower than

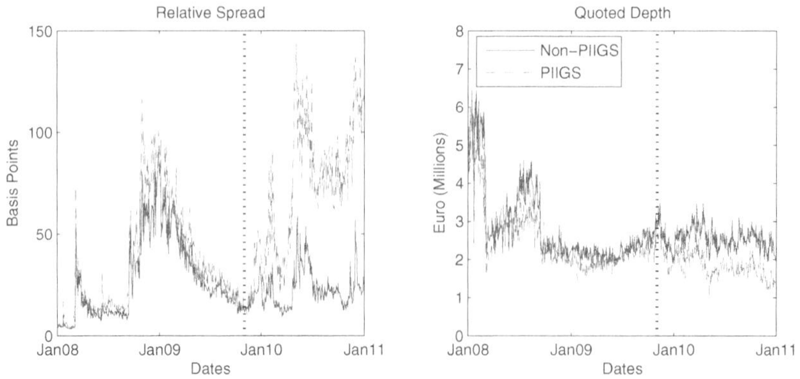

Figure 2. Relative spread and quoted depth for PIIGS and non-PIIGS 10-year benchmark bonds

Table 6. Comparisons between PIIGS Countries vs. the Pan-European Bond Market

		Relative Spread (bps)		Slope		Realized Volatility	
Countries	**Maturity**	**Domestic**	**EU**	**Domestic**	**EU**	**Domestic**	**EU**
Greece	05-year	86.74	34.67	0.0264	0.0116	0.5722	0.2416
	10-year	99.55	43.32	0.0282	0.0130	0.7165	0.3750
Ireland	05-year	74.77	34.67	0.0234	0.0116	0.3583	0.2416
	10-year	94.08	43.32	0.0294	0.0130	0.4370	0.3750
Italy	05-year	19.56	34.67	0.0063	0.0116	0.2089	0.2416
	10-year	25.30	43.32	0.0082	0.0130	0.3345	0.3750
Portugal	05-year	68.63	34.67	0.0212	0.0116	0.3415	0.2416
	10-year	88.64	43.32	0.0272	0.0130	0.4731	0.3750
Spain	05-year	34.35	34.67	0.0107	0.0116	0.2732	0.2416
	10-year	40.50	43.32	0.0126	0.0130	0.3723	0.3750

Note: Mean values are shown for the Relative spread, Slope, and Realized Volatility measures across the 5 and 10 year maturity segments.

the corresponding European volatility averages, whereas results are mixed for Spain, displaying higher sensitivity for the 5-year instrument. Table 7 shows pairwise static correlations across liquidity and volatility proxies. Not surprisingly, the best spread and relative spread are strongly correlated. Yet, the quoted spread exhibits a weaker correlation with the other two spread proxies. The positive correlation coefficient between spreads and volatility indicates that the increase in volatility coincides with wider spreads. On the contrary, quoted depth shows a weak and negative correlation with volatility. Similar results have been documented in Darbha and Dufour (2013a) where spreads are small for bonds with low volatility and large depth.

Table 7. Pairwise Correlations Across Liquidity and Volatility Measures

	Best Spread	Quoted Spread	Relative Spread	Quoted Depth	Quote Slope	Euro Depth	MQI	Steepness	RV
Best spread	1								
Quoted spread	0.825	1							
Relative spread	0.989	0.831	1						
Quoted depth	−0.397	−0.368	−0.409	1					
Quote slope	0.997	0.829	0.995	−0.409	1				
Euro depth	−0.410	−0.382	−0.427	0.994	−0.422	1			
MQI	−0.452	−0.374	−0.440	0.761	−0.448	0.761	1		
Steepness	0.276	0.759	0.305	−0.195	0.287	−0.206	−0.126	1	
RV	0.497	0.472	0.512	−0.293	0.499	−0.320	−0.302	0.264	1

Note: The measures considered are the Best spread, Quoted spread, Relative spread, Quoted depth, Quote slope, Euro depth, Market Quality Index (MQI), Steepness, and Realized Volatility.

Inferentially, when the variation in price changes increases, the size quoted by market makers shrinks.

Tightness and depth liquidity measures exhibit a negative correlation. It is evident that when the market becomes more liquid, depth proxies become larger and the spread dwindles. In terms of steepness, its correlation with the quoted spread is much stronger than its correlation with the best spread (a value of 0.7589 vs. 0.2764). It is also worth noting that the comovement produced by volatility and steepness is quite weak. The evidence from the correlation analysis confirms the expected behavior of the slope measure. A decrease in quote slope leads to tighter spreads and at the same time to increased market depth and volatility. As a hybrid liquidity measure, market quality index shows reasonable correlations with depth and tightness proxies — the two liquidity dimensions it is comprised of.

Furthermore, market quality index and volatility exhibit an inverse relationship with each other.

Table 8 depicts a correlation analysis between volatility and all proxies of liquidity with respect to different periods and across various maturity segments. In brief, the degree of correlations is magnified during the crisis period regardless of the sign of the correlation.[5] The 30-year benchmark is the only exception in which the correlation between volatility and liquidity

[5]The link between liquidity and volatility is shared by the models of Stoll (1978) and Grossman and Miller (1988), among others.

Table 8. PairWise Correlations between Liquidity and Volatility Over the Pre-Crisis and Crisis Periods

	2-year		5-year		10-year		30-year	
	Pre-crisis	Crisis	Pre-crisis	Crisis	Pre-crisis	Crisis	Pre-crisis	Crisis
Best spread	0.505	0.610	0.481	0.582	0.524	0.451	0.420	0.215
Quoted depth	−0.016	−0.421	−0.124	−0.371	−0.287	−0.349	−0.214	−0.100
Quote slope	0.496	0.615	0.484	0.588	0.539	0.455	0.416	0.205
Euro depth	−0.021	−0.431	−0.124	−0.396	−0.305	−0.379	−0.235	−0.104
MQI	−0.240	−0.395	−0.264	−0.420	−0.346	−0.353	−0.375	−0.265
Steepness	0.036	0.450	0.229	0.271	0.289	0.252	0.056	−0.024

Note: The measures considered are the Best spread, Quoted depth, Quote slope, Euro depth, Market Quality Index (MQI), and Steepness across the 2, 5, 10, and 30 year maturity segments.

becomes weaker in the turbulent period. This implies that higher volatility will not necessarily cause liquidity to worsen.

6.2. *Vector autoregression*

The goal in this section is to study the cross-market intertemporal associations in volatility, returns, and liquidity between PIIGS and non-PIIGS bond markets in the pre-crisis period (January 1, 2008–October 30, 2009) and during the European sovereign bond market crisis period (November 1, 2009–December 31, 2010). For this, we use the daily volatility, returns, liquidity spread, and liquidity depth measures, constructed for PIIGS and non-PIIGS countries using intra-day data, as the VAR endogenous variables. For the sake of space, we focus on the 10-year benchmarks that are the most liquid across all maturities. We denote the volatility measures as VOL-NP and VOL-P, the returns measures as RETS-NP and RETS-P, the spread measures as SPD-NP and SPD-P, and the depth measures as DPT-NP and DPT-P, where NP denotes non-PIIGS measures and P denotes PIIGS measures.

There is reason to expect that cross-market effects across non-PIIGS and PIIGS markets may be significant and that these effects may change from the pre-crisis to the crisis period. In the pre-crisis period, we expect non-PIIGS and PIIGS returns to be related with causation flowing from the larger non-PIIGS returns to the peripheral economy's PIIGS returns. However, in the European sovereign debt crisis the relationship may reverse in sign and causal flows from PIIGS returns to non-PIIGS returns may increase.

Furthermore it will be interesting to discover the bidirectional causalities between volatility, returns, and liquidity both within non-PIIGS and PIIGS measures and across markets e.g., how PIIGS liquidity affects non-PIIGS liquidity and vice versa. Finally, we will use the VAR results to describe how these bidirectional causalities change from the pre-crisis period to the European sovereign debt crisis period.

We adopt an eight-equation variable autoregression that uses the following variables: VOL-NP, VOL-P, RETS-NP, RETS-P, SPD-NP, SPD-P, DPT-NP, and DPT-P. These consist of four variables from each market (non-PIIGS and PIIGS) which are realized volatility, returns, and two dimensions of liquidity: relative spread and quoted depth. Hence, we use a system of interlinked equations as shown in (3) and (4). Note that depth is multiplied by 1×10^{-8} so that it is comparable to the other measures in terms of scale.

We estimate these VAR equations in both the pre-crisis and crisis periods using domestic MTS data only and EuroMTS data only.[6] In the pre-crisis period we have 466 days of data, whereas there are 297 days of data in the crisis period. We use the log likelihood ratio test with Sims (1980) correction to test K lags versus $K-1$ lags and find that the model does not deteriorate in a statistically significant manner if we choose K to be 5 lags. Specifically, the chi-squared distributed test statistic which has degrees of freedom equation to the number of restrictions imposed is:

$$\text{LR} = (T - c)\left(\log|\textstyle\sum r| - \log|\textstyle\sum u|\right), \tag{10}$$

where T is the number of observations, c is a degrees of freedom correction factor proposed by Sims (1980), and $|\sum r|$, $|\sum u|$ denote the determinant of the error covariance matrices from the restricted and unrestricted models respectively. The correction factor, c, recommended by Sims is the number of variables in each unrestricted equation of the VAR model.

Table 9 presents the LR test statistic and the corresponding p-values using data from the domestic MTS market during the crisis period. We elect to choose 5 lags in the interests of parsimony. The results on the EuroMTS market and in the pre-crisis period are qualitatively very similar so we also choose to use 5 lags for the cases considered in the chapter (domestic MTS pre-crisis, domestic MTS crisis, EuroMTS pre-crisis and EuroMTS crisis).

[6]The domestic and Euro MTS market data are highly correlated so we elect not to group these data into a 16 equation VAR system to keep the model more parsimonious and the interpretations less complex.

Table 9. Log Likelihood Test Ratios and *p*-Values Used to Choose the Lag Length in the VARs

nlag-u	nlag-r	LR stat	*p*-value
12	11	67.34	0.363
11	10	84.98**	0.041
10	9	72.80	0.211
9	8	65.42	0.427
8	7	75.78	0.149
7	6	91.40	0.014
6	5	55.95	0.753
5	4	82.80*	0.057
4	3	80.49*	0.080
3	2	97.59***	0.004
2	1	107.34***	0.001

Note: nlag-u and nlag-r denote the lag length from the unrestricted and restricted models, respectively.

6.2.1. *Unfiltered correlations*

Before presenting results from the VAR estimation we present correlations of the unfiltered variables in the pre-crisis period and in the crisis period using both domestic MTS and EuroMTS data.

The pre-crisis correlation coefficients are reported in Table 10 for the domestic MTS market and Table 11 for the EuroMTS market. The correlation coefficients and their statistical significance are very similar across both markets, so the following analysis applies to both the domestic and EuroMTS markets.

There are strong positive cross-market correlations between non-PIIGS (NP) and PIIGS (P) volatility (0.86), NP and P returns (0.82), NP and P spreads (0.95), and NP and P depth measures (0.91).[7] The correlation between returns and volatility is negative as expected across the two markets, with the exception of RET-NP which is not statistically significantly negatively correlated with VOL-P. The correlation between relative spread and volatility is strongly positive both within NP/P markets and across NP to P (or P to NP) markets. The correlation between quoted depth and volatility is strongly negative both within and across markets. Finally, the

[7]The correlation coefficients reported in brackets are those estimated using domestic MTS market data in the pre-crisis period and are very similar to the correlations estimated using EuroMTS market data in the same period.

Table 10. Pre-Crisis Correlations of Unfiltered Domestic MTS Variables

	VOL-NP	VOL-P	RET-NP	RET-P	SPD-NP	SPD-P	DPT-NP	DPT-P
VOL-NP	1.00							
VOL-P	0.86***	1.00						
RET-NP	−0.13***	−0.07	1.00					
RET-P	−0.10**	−0.09*	0.82***	1.00				
SPD-NP	0.64***	0.69***	−0.02	−0.03	1.00			
SPD-P	0.64***	0.72***	−0.05	−0.06	0.95***	1.00		
DPT-NP	−0.37***	−0.44***	0.02	0.01	−0.61***	−0.59***	1.00	
DPT-P	−0.41***	−0.47***	0.03	0.04	−0.63***	−0.61***	0.91***	1.00

Note: VOL (volatility), RET (returns), SPD (spread), DPT (depth), P (PIIGS), NP (non-PIIGS).

Table 11. Pre-Crisis Correlations of Unfiltered EuroMTS Variables

	VOL-NP	VOL-P	RET-NP	RET-P	SPD-NP	SPD-P	DPT-NP	DPT-P
VOL-NP	1.00							
VOL-P	0.81***	1.00						
RET-NP	−0.15***	−0.07	1.00					
RET-P	−0.11**	−0.12**	0.83***	1.00				
SPD-NP	0.62***	0.68***	−0.03	−0.06	1.00			
SPD-P	0.62***	0.71***	−0.05	−0.07	0.94***	1.00		
DPT-NP	−0.37***	−0.47***	0.02	0.03	−0.62***	−0.60***	1.00	
DPT-P	−0.38***	−0.49***	0.02	0.04	−0.62***	−0.61***	0.92***	1.00

Note: VOL (volatility), RET (returns), SPD (spread), DPT (depth), P (PIIGS), NP (non-PIIGS).

correlation between spread and depth is strongly negative both within and across markets.

The crisis period correlation coefficients are reported in Table 12 for the domestic MTS markets and Table 13 for the EuroMTS market. As with the pre-crisis period the correlation coefficients and their statistical significance are very similar across both markets, so the following analysis applies to both the domestic and Euro MTS markets. There are still statistically significant positive cross-market correlations, but they drop considerably from their pre-crisis levels to 0.47 for NP and P volatility, 0.16 for NP and P returns, 0.64 for NP and P spreads, and 0.57 for NP and P depth measures.

The negative correlations between returns and volatility within the NP and P markets are slightly more negative than their pre-crisis levels (−0.21 for crisis vs. −0.11 for pre-crisis) but there are no longer negative cross-market correlations between returns in one market and the volatility in the other market e.g., between RET-NP and VOL-P or between RET-P and VOL-NP.

Table 12. Crisis Correlations of Unfiltered Domestic MTS Variables

	VOL-NP	VOL-P	RET-NP	RET-P	SPD-NP	SPD-P	DPT-NP	DPT-P
VOL-NP	1.00							
VOL-P	0.47***	1.00						
RET-NP	−0.21***	−0.09	1.00					
RET-P	−0.04	−0.20***	0.16***	1.00				
SPD-NP	0.59***	0.34***	−0.04	0.04	1.00			
SPD-P	0.53***	0.40***	−0.03	−0.08	0.64***	1.00		
DPT-NP	−0.28***	−0.19***	0.04	−0.06	−0.44***	−0.44***	1.00	
DPT-P	−0.44***	−0.41***	0.05	0.08	−0.55***	−0.77***	0.57***	1.00

Note: VOL (volatility), RET (returns), SPD (spread), DPT (depth), P (PIIGS), NP (non-PIIGS).

Table 13. Crisis Correlations of Unfiltered EuroMTS Variables

	VOL-NP	VOL-P	RET-NP	RET-P	SPD-NP	SPD-P	DPT-NP	DPT-P
VOL-NP	1.00							
VOL-P	0.48***	1.00						
RET-NP	−0.21***	−0.04	1.00					
RET-P	−0.08	−0.21***	0.18***	1.00				
SPD-NP	0.59***	0.32***	−0.04	0.02	1.00			
SPD-P	0.54***	0.38***	−0.03	−0.10*	0.64***	1.00		
DPT-NP	−0.35***	−0.26***	0.05	−0.01	−0.49***	−0.53***	1.00	
DPT-P	−0.43***	−0.36***	0.06	0.07	−0.57***	−0.76***	0.59***	1.00

Note: VOL (volatility), RET (returns), SPD (spread), DPT (depth), P (PIIGS), NP (non-PIIGS).

The correlation between relative spread (quoted depth) and volatility is strongly positive (negative) both within and across markets and similar to pre-crisis levels. The correlations, within and across markets, between spread and depth, weaken slightly from pre-crisis levels of approximately −0.60 to crisis levels of approximately −0.44.

6.2.2. *VAR estimation results*

This section presents and interprets the VAR estimation results. Tables 14 and 15 report correlations of the VAR innovations using the domestic MTS data in the pre-crisis period and crisis period, respectively. We decide not to report the innovation correlations for the EuroMTS market in both the pre-crisis and crisis periods because results are qualitatively similar to the domestic market results as was shown to be the case in the unfiltered correlations.

Volatility is still negatively associated with returns within and across markets. However, volatility is positively (negatively) associated with

Table 14. Pre-Crisis Period Correlations of VAR Innovations in the Domestic MTS Variables

	VOL-NP	VOL-P	RET-NP	RET-P	SPD-NP	SPD-P	DPT-NP	DPT-P
VOL-NP	1.00							
VOL-P	0.72***	1.00						
RET-NP	−0.15***	−0.08*	1.00					
RET-P	−0.10**	−0.11**	0.83***	1.00				
SPD-NP	0.20***	0.20***	0.01	−0.06	1.00			
SPD-P	0.19***	0.34***	−0.09*	−0.19***	0.42***	1.00		
DPT-NP	−0.15***	−0.17***	0.08*	0.07	−0.12***	−0.19***	1.00	
DPT-P	−0.19***	−0.21***	0.08*	0.13***	−0.19***	−0.21***	0.50***	1.00

Note: VOL (volatility), RET (returns), SPD (spread), DPT (depth), P (PIIGS), NP (non-PIIGS).

Table 15. Crisis Period Correlations of VAR Innovations in the Domestic MTS Variables

	VOL-NP	VOL-P	RET-NP	RET-P	SPD-NP	SPD-P	DPT-NP	DPT-P
VOL-NP	1.00							
VOL-P	0.40***	1.00						
RET-NP	−0.14**	−0.13**	1.00					
RET-P	−0.10*	−0.21***	0.22***	1.00				
SPD-NP	0.47***	0.29***	−0.06	−0.08	1.00			
SPD-P	0.15***	0.19***	0.06	−0.12**	0.16***	1.00		
DPT-NP	−0.13**	−0.14**	0.03	−0.04	−0.28***	−0.16***	1.00	
DPT-P	−0.21***	−0.24***	0.04	0.07	−0.24***	−0.14**	0.31***	1.00

Note: VOL (volatility), RET (returns), SPD (spread), DPT (depth), P (PIIGS), NP (non-PIIGS).

spreads (depths) within and across markets. Furthermore, return innovations in both NP and P markets are negatively associated with spreads in the PIIGS markets, but there is no association with spreads in the non-PIIGS markets. Similarly, return innovations in both NP and P markets are positively associated with depth in the PIIGS markets, but the association with depth in the non-PIIGS markets is much weaker. As with the correlation results in the unfiltered data, innovations in spread and depth are negatively correlated both within and across markets.

Volatility innovations are still negatively associated with returns innovations within and across markets in the crisis period, and are positively (negatively) associated with spreads (depths) within and across markets. These results are comparable to the pre-crisis results. However, return innovations in non-PIIGS markets are not associated with spread innovations or depth innovations in non-PIIGS or PIIGS markets although there is a negative association between return and spread innovations in the PIIGS markets.

Table 16. Pre-Crisis Period Granger Causality *p*-Values Where the Variable Along the Row Does (Or Not) Cause the Variable Along the Column

	VOL-NP	VOL-P	RET-NP	RET-P	SPD-NP	SPD-P	DPT-NP	DPT-P
VOL-NP	0.03**	0.53	0.37	0.64	0.55	0.10	0.55	0.62
VOL-P	0.31	0.04**	0.54	0.84	0.13	0.04	0.24	0.88
RET-NP	0.43	0.45	0.02**	0.09*	0.96	0.97	0.27	0.88
RET-P	0.79	0.67	0.00***	0.00***	0.61	0.39	0.90	0.70
SPD-NP	0.47	0.11	0.00***	0.05**	0.00***	0.00***	0.32	0.89
SPD-P	0.25	0.23	0.00***	0.00***	0.03**	0.00***	0.97	0.33
DPT-NP	1.00	0.74	0.94	0.95	0.93	0.72	0.00***	0.07*
DPT-P	0.37	0.94	1.00	0.58	0.30	0.70	0.00***	0.00***

Note: Tests were run using the domestic MTS data. VOL (volatility), RET (returns), SPD (spread), DPT (depth), P (PIIGS), NP (non-PIIGS).

Table 17. Crisis Period Granger Causality *p*-Values Where the Variable Along the Row Does (Or Not) Cause the Variable Along the Column

	VOL-NP	VOL-P	RET-NP	RET-P	SPD-NP	SPD-P	DPT-NP	DPT-P
VOL-NP	0.00***	0.82	0.22	0.11	0.02**	0.01***	0.71	0.03**
VOL-P	0.11	0.00***	0.24	0.02**	0.36	0.18	0.22	0.04**
RET-NP	0.01***	0.59	0.67	0.59	0.58	0.48	0.88	0.56
RET-P	0.83	0.42	0.12	0.00***	0.01***	0.90	0.28	0.13
SPD-NP	0.92	0.89	0.28	0.01***	0.00***	0.22	0.46	0.16
SPD-P	0.29	0.46	0.85	0.00***	0.36	0.00***	0.81	0.04**
DPT-NP	0.39	0.13	0.58	0.34	0.56	0.45	0.00***	0.45
DPT-P	0.59	0.77	0.94	0.36	0.20	0.00***	0.11	0.00***

Note: Tests were run using the domestic MTS data. VOL (volatility), RET (returns), SPD (spread), DPT (depth), P (PIIGS), NP (non-PIIGS).

Spread and depth innovations are still strongly negatively associated within and across markets in the crisis period at similar levels to the pre-crisis period levels. These results suggest contemporaneous commonalities are driving volatility and returns, volatility and spreads, volatility and depths, spreads and depths in both pre-crisis and crisis periods both within non-PIIGS and PIIGS markets and across non-PIIGS and PIIGS markets.

Furthermore in pre-crisis periods there are contemporaneous commonalities driving returns and liquidity measures (spread and depth) that weaken considerably in the crisis period.

Tables 16 and 17 present pairwise Granger causality tests between the endogenous variables in the VAR separately for pre-crisis and crisis periods. The results are only reported for domestic MTS data as they are qualitatively very similar if the domestic MTS data is replaced by EuroMTS data. Table 16 illustrates that causation in volatility does not operate across markets but only within markets in the pre-crisis period i.e., VOL-NP(P) causes VOL-NP(P) but there is no causality from NP(P) to P(NP).

There is bidirectional causality in returns across markets although the causality from NP to P returns is significant at the 1% level, whereas the reverse causality is only significant at the 10% level. This is to be expected given the NP market is the more important market. There is also bidirectional causality in spreads (and in depths) across markets. There is strong bidirectional causality between returns and spreads both within and across markets but not between returns and depth.

Table 17 illustrates that the causal directions in the volatility variables do not change from their pre-crisis directions. There is no cross-market causation for volatility and only causation within markets for volatility i.e., VOL-NP(P) causes VOL-NP(P) but there is no causality from VOL-NP(P) to VOL-P(NP). Unlike for the pre-crisis case, there is no longer bidirectional causality in returns across markets with causality in returns only running from P to P itself in the crisis period. Furthermore in the crisis period, the cross-market bidirectional causality in spreads (and in depths) breaks down, with causality only running within markets i.e., SPD-NP(P) causes SPD-NP(P) but there is no causality from SPD-NP(P) to SPD-P(NP).

Returns in PIIGS cause spreads in both PIIGS and non-PIIGS markets in the crisis period, but this is not the case for the returns in non-PIIGS. This is a direct result of the increasing importance of the PIIGS returns during the crisis. Before the crisis, there was bidirectional causality with the non-PIIGS returns being the more important variable. There are strong causal links between PIIGS liquidity measures (SPD and DPT) and non-PIIGS volatility that were not present in the pre-crisis period. This demonstrates that liquidity effects are more important during the crisis with PIIGS liquidity impacting non-PIIGS volatility. Furthermore, there are feedback effects in PIIGS liquidity measures during the crisis period that were not present in the pre-crisis period. This is demonstrated by the bidirectional causality between SPD-P causing DPT-P.

6.2.3. *VAR impulse response functions*

To investigate these findings further, we present impulse response functions from the VAR estimated using pre-crisis data in Fig. 3 and crisis data in Fig. 4. Impulse responses use the orthogonalized VAR residual covariance matrix to estimate the effect a one-unit standard deviation shock to one of the variables has on current and future values of the shocked variable and the other variables.

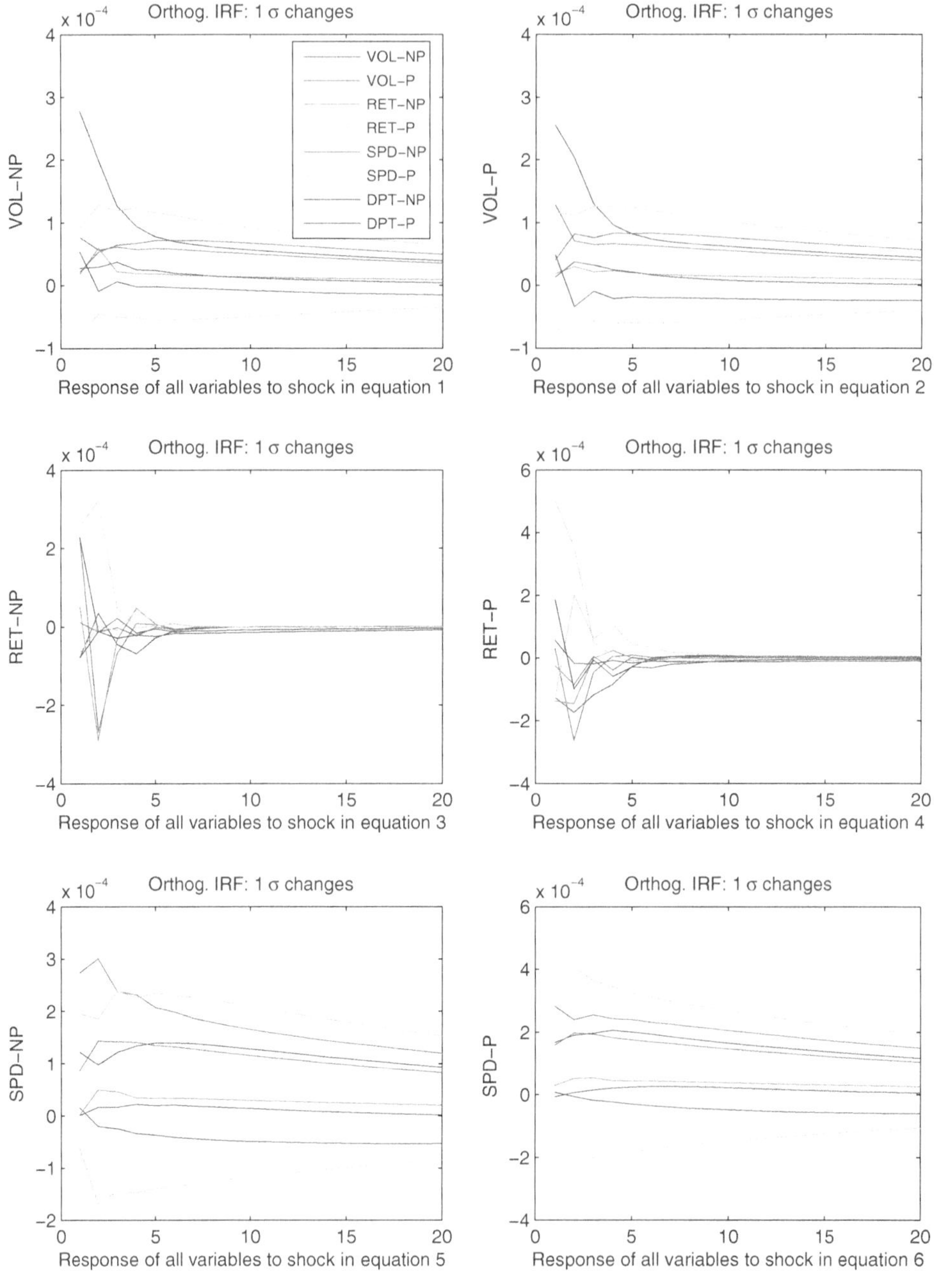
Orthog. IRF: 1 σ changes
x 10^-4
VOL-NP
VOL-P
RET-NP
RET-P
SPD-NP
SPD-P
DPT-NP
DPT-P
Response of all variables to shock in equation 1
Response of all variables to shock in equation 2
Response of all variables to shock in equation 3
Response of all variables to shock in equation 4
Response of all variables to shock in equation 5
Response of all variables to shock in equation 6

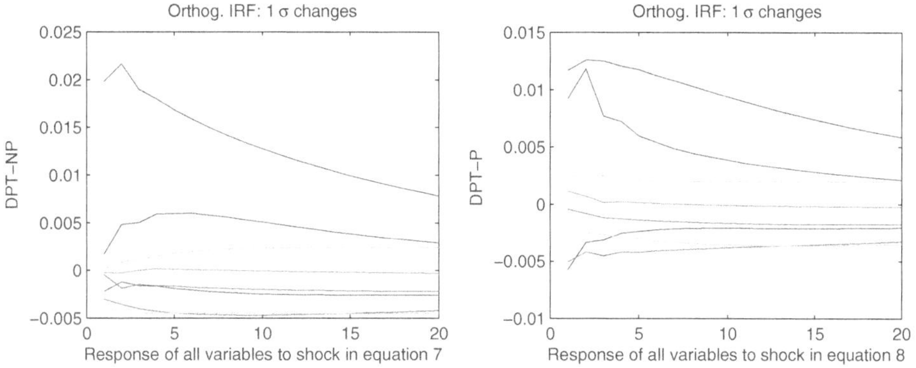

Figure 3. Pre-crisis Impulse Response Functions

For example the top left panel of Fig. 3 depicts the response of all eight variables to a one standard deviation shock to the first variable VOL-NP. VOL-NP is the variable most affected by a shock to itself, with the shock decaying to halve its magnitude within two days, but it displays strong persistence with the initial shock of 2.75×10^{-4} taking 20 days to decay to just under 0.5×10^{-4}. The VOL-NP shock strongly affects the returns (RET-P) and liquidity (SPD-P) of the peripheral economies demonstrating strong cross-market dynamics from non-peripheral volatility to peripheral returns and liquidity in the pre-crisis period. Similar cross market dynamics can be observed in the top right panel in Fig 3. A one standard deviation shock to VOL-P has an even larger effect on VOL-NP although this cross-market effect decays much faster than the effect VOL-P has on itself. The shock to VOL-P also increases the spreads in the non-peripheral countries (SPD-NP).

The shocks to both RET-NP and RET-P also display cross-market dynamics, but these effects decay much faster than volatility shocks. Shocks to spreads in one market increase spreads in the other market, and increase volatility and decrease depth in both markets (both NP and P). Furthermore shocks to spreads in both markets decrease returns in the peripheral market. Finally, shocks to depth in either markets increase depth and reduce spreads in both markets.

Fig. 4 presents impulse responses from the VAR estimated during the crisis period. The top left panel of Fig. 4 depicts the response of all eight variables to a one standard deviation shock to the first variable VOL-NP. As with the tranquil period, VOL-NP is the variable most strongly affected by a shock to itself. The shock decays to halve its magnitude within two days, but

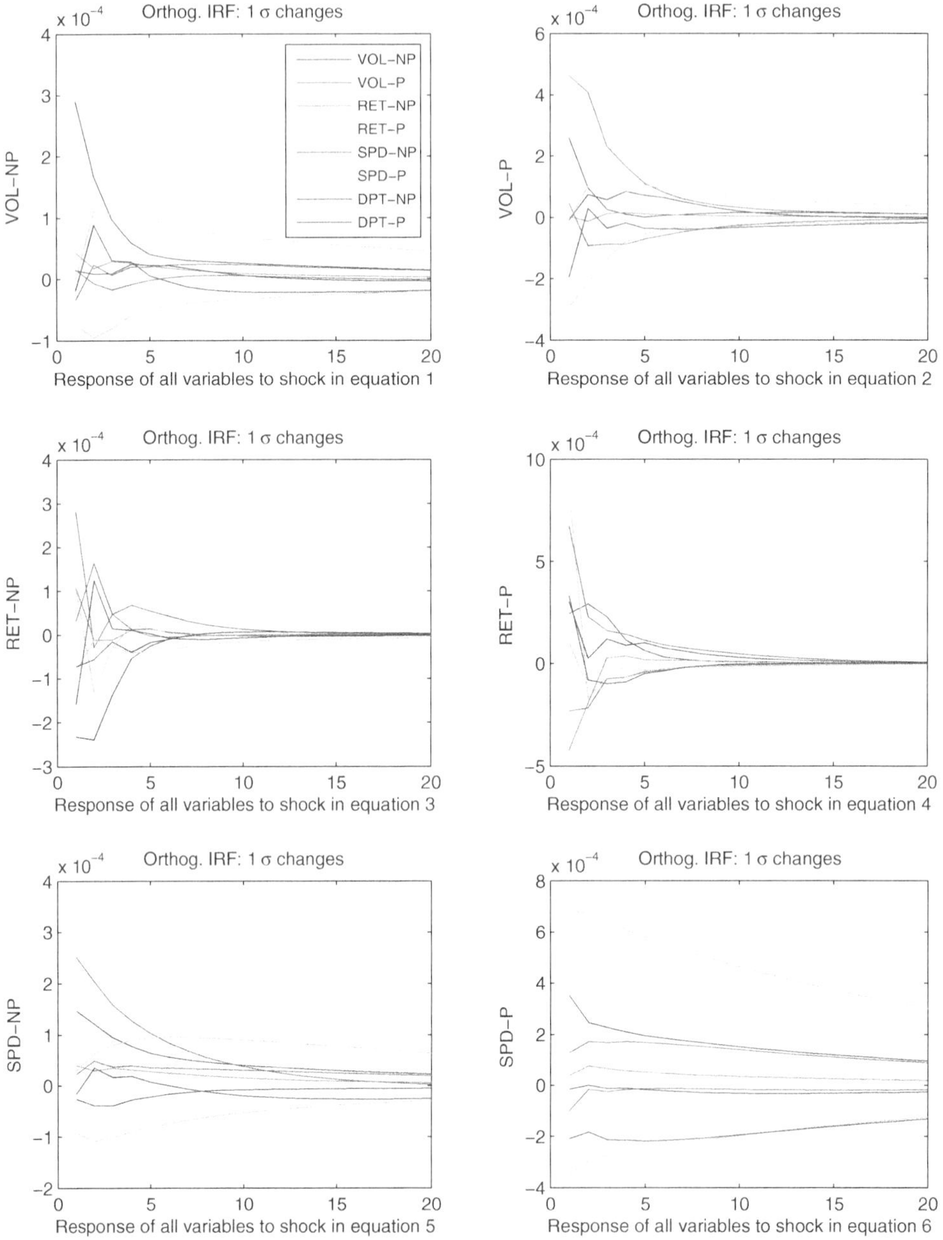
x 10⁻⁴
Orthog. IRF: 1 σ changes
VOL–NP
VOL–P
RET–NP
RET–P
SPD–NP
SPD–P
DPT–NP
DPT–P
Response of all variables to shock in equation 1
Response of all variables to shock in equation 2
Response of all variables to shock in equation 3
Response of all variables to shock in equation 4
Response of all variables to shock in equation 5
Response of all variables to shock in equation 6

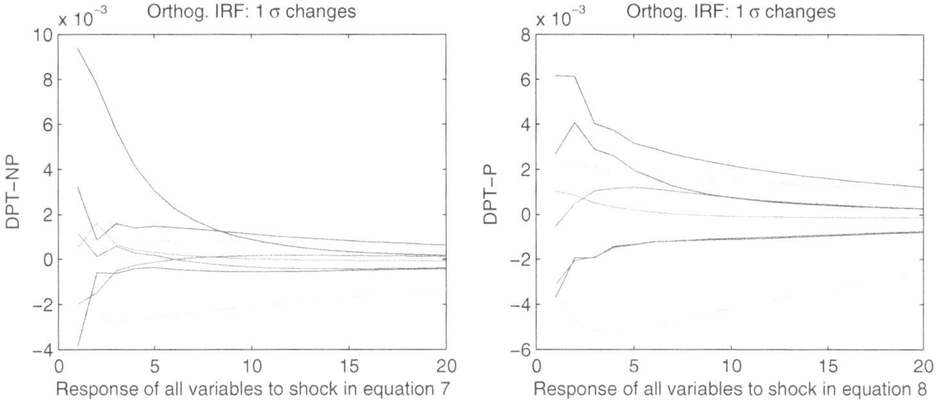

Figure 4. Crisis Impulse Response Functions

displays strong persistence with a slow decay thereafter. Shocks to VOL-NP barely affect VOL-P which is a change from the tranquil period however, VOL-NP shocks do strongly increase SPD-P and reduce RET-P. Shocks to VOL-P increase VOL-NP by approximately half the magnitude of the shock. In the crisis period, shocks to VOL-P strongly reduce RET-P. Interestingly, shocks to VOL-P increase SPD-P but decrease SPD-NP in an almost mirror image, indicating that shocks to PIIGS volatility decrease PIIGS liquidity but increase non-PIIGS liquidity. This is evidence of a market decoupling where shocks to PIIGS country volatility result in less PIIGS trading but more non-PIIGS trading.

The returns impulse responses in Fig. 4 also demonstrate this market decoupling. Shocks to RET-NP are associated with decreases in VOL-NP as expected but large increases in VOL-P. Shocks to RET-P are associated with decreases in RET-NP. Shocks to liquidity (measured either by SPD or DPT) are more persistent than shocks to returns or even volatility. The crisis period liquidity impulse responses in PIIGS countries generally remain within the PIIGS countries with a lower degree of cross-market dynamics when compared to the pre-crisis period liquidity impulse response functions.

6.3. *Forbes and Rigobon test for contagion*

As described in the methodology section, we test for changes in equivalent maturity correlations for non-PIIGS and PIIGS bond returns between the tranquil and crisis period using the Forbes and Rigobon unconditional correlation measure adjusted for heteroscedasticity. We do this using both unfiltered raw returns series (RET-UF) and filtered return residuals (RET-F)

Table 18. Heteroskedasticity-Adjusted Correlation Values for Tranquil, Crisis, and the Full Data Periods Run on Both Unfiltered Returns (RET-UF) and VAR Filtered Return Residuals (RET-F) between Non-PIIGS and PIIGS and Across the 2, 5, 10, and 30 Year Maturity Segments

Heteroskedasticity adjusted correlation values					
	Tranquil	Crisis	Full	t-stat	Decoupling
2Y RET-UF	0.90	0.04	0.49	19.52	Y
2Y RET-F	0.90	0.05	0.49	20.01	Y
5Y RET-UF	0.89	0.13	0.59	17.38	Y
5Y RET-F	0.89	0.14	0.59	16.82	Y
10Y RET-UF	0.84	0.24	0.58	12.94	Y
10Y RET-F	0.85	0.18	0.58	14.12	Y
30Y RET-UF	0.91	0.39	0.81	15.03	Y
30Y RET-F	0.92	0.41	0.81	15.41	Y

Note: Also reported are t-statistics computing statistical differences and whether or not we detect a significant drop in correlation (decoupling).

from the previous VAR estimation for all four benchmark maturities but where the VAR is estimated over the full period. The use of the filtered returns, allows us to strip out the within and cross-market effects that volatility and liquidity have on returns thereby isolating filtered returns, that are orthogonalized to these volatility and liquidity effects. Results are presented in Table 18 for both unfiltered and VAR filtered return residuals.

The results reported in Table 18 clearly illustrate large and statistical significant drops in correlations between non-PIIGS and PIIGS bond returns of the same maturity. The largest drop is the correlation between 2 year bonds, which drops from 0.90 in the tranquil period to 0.04 in the crisis period. Furthermore as the maturity of the bonds rises, the drop in correlations from tranquil to crisis period reduces, although still remaining statistically significant. These results are in agreement with Jotikasthira *et al.* (2015) who show that while the monetary policy channel often causes short-term international yields to diverge, the risk compensation channel results in longer term international bond yields diverging by much less than their shorter term counterparts.

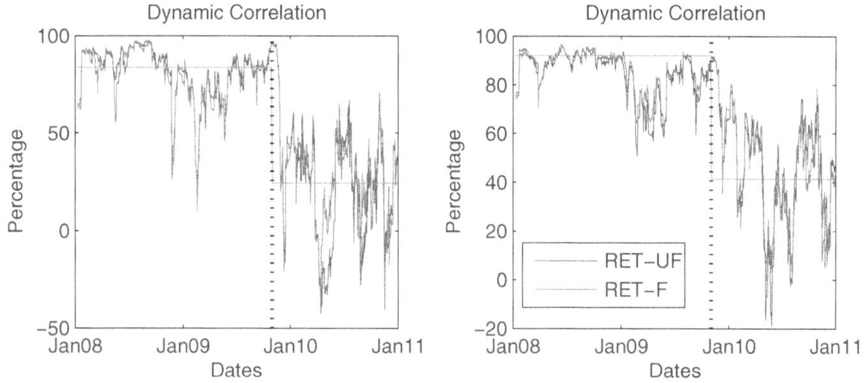

Figure 5. LHS panel refers to 10-year bond DCC dynamic correlations, and the RHS panel refers to 30-year bond DCC dynamic correlations between non-PIIGS and PIIGS countries. RET-UF (unfiltered returns), RET-F (filtered returns)

These results show that there is no evidence of contagion between non-PIIGS and PIIGS bond returns of the same maturity. In fact, we find strong evidence for a decoupling between non-PIIGS and PIIGS sovereign debt markets during the crisis, with changes in a country's debt being transmitted to neighboring countries much less intensively during the debt crisis period than the pre-crisis period.[8] These results are in line with those of Beirne and Fratzscher (2013) who analyzed the drivers of sovereign risk for 31 advanced and emerging economies during the European sovereign debt crisis.

Figure 5 depicts the DCC time-varying correlation coefficients between non-PIIGS and PIIGS countries using both unfiltered and filtered 10-year and 30-year bond returns. The drop in correlations during the crisis period for the 30-year benchmark, although statistically significant, is not as dramatic as the corresponding drop in correlations for the 10-year benchmark security. It is apparent from Fig. 5. that the relation between non-PIIGS and PIIGS returns has been rather unstable over time. The estimates of the correlations illustrate a significant fluctuation from high positive levels in the pre-crisis period to large negative levels in the crisis period.

The correlation levels of the 30-year benchmark reach their minimum in May 2010 with negative values for both filtered and unfiltered returns

[8]Decoupling implies a break in a relationship that was previously more coupled and closely linked. For a discussion see Pesce (2015).

Table 19. Heteroskedasticity-Adjusted Correlation Values for Tranquil, Crisis, and the Full Data Periods Calculated Using 10-Year Returns within Non-PIIGS and PIIGS Countries

Heteroskedasticity adjusted correlation values					
	Tranquil	Crisis	Full Period	t-Stat	C/D/N
GER-AUS	0.67	0.70	0.68	−0.76	N
GER-BEL	0.78	0.54	0.70	6.08	D
GER-FIN	0.84	0.92	0.86	−4.69	C
GER-FRA	0.89	0.84	0.88	2.83	D
GER-NLD	0.85	0.92	0.87	−4.48	C
FRA-AUS	0.75	0.77	0.75	−0.84	N
FRA-BEL	0.85	0.73	0.81	4.19	D
FRA-FIN	0.87	0.90	0.87	−1.75	N
FRA-NDL	0.90	0.89	0.89	0.29	N
NDL-AUS	0.67	0.70	0.68	−0.76	N
NDL-BEL	0.78	0.54	0.70	6.08	D
NDL-FIN	0.84	0.92	0.86	−4.69	C
FIN-AUS	0.67	0.79	0.70	−3.59	C
FIN-BEL	0.79	0.68	0.75	3.20	D
AUS-BEL	0.88	0.75	0.84	5.51	D
GRE-SPN	0.46	0.14	0.23	4.76	D
GRE-IRE	0.45	0.25	0.30	3.00	D
GRE-ITY	0.58	0.14	0.26	7.08	D
GRE-PTG	0.55	0.24	0.32	5.00	D
IRE-SPN	0.62	0.34	0.48	5.00	D
IRE-ITY	0.60	0.31	0.47	4.93	D
IRE-PTG	0.63	0.51	0.55	2.47	D
PTG-SPN	0.70	0.32	0.46	7.11	D
PTG-ITY	0.73	0.29	0.46	8.60	D
SPN-ITY	0.73	0.66	0.69	2.04	D

Note: Also reported are t-statistics computing statistical differences and whether or not we detect a significant increase (contagion: C), drop (decoupling: D) or no change (N) in correlation.

and their maximum level in June 2008. Results for the 10-year benchmark show that correlation levels reach their minimum in April 2010 for unfiltered returns and in November 2010 for filtered returns, whereas their maximum values are reached in September 2008 and July 2008, respectively.

Table 19 depicts the adjusted-for-heteroskedasticity correlation values for tranquil, crisis, and the full data periods calculated using 10-year returns within non-PIIGS and PIIGS countries. The results shown in the lower panel of the table are striking and provide strong evidence for a decoupling among all PIIGS countries, as correlation coefficients take on much lower and statistically significant values during the crisis period. The results for non-PIIGS countries, however, are mixed as shown in the upper panel of Table 19. There is evidence of contagion among Germany, Netherlands, and Finland as well as between Finland and Austria. This contagion effect can be possibly explained by income shocks that are transferred from one country to the other due to trade and economic linkages. There is also evidence of decoupling among Germany, France, and Belgium and between Belgium and Netherlands — Austria — Finland.

7. Conclusions

This study measures and analyzes liquidity and volatility dynamics in the eurozone government bond market from a microstructure perspective, during both the pre-crisis and crisis periods. It employs a unique and comprehensive high-frequency dataset obtained from MTS, the world's largest trading platform for euro-denominated government bonds. Our dataset is comprised of benchmark fixed coupon-bearing government bonds of various maturities from both the EuroMTS and the domestic MTS markets.

We document wider spreads for benchmarks with longer maturities during both pre-crisis and crisis periods, as well as heightened volatility and returns for longer maturity benchmarks, especially amidst the crisis. Liquidity deteriorates and volatility intensifies during the crisis period as spreads rise and quoted depth declines, with the exception of the 30-year instrument.

Evidence of a flight-to-liquidity effect is provided, as investors rebalance their portfolios by moving into shorter-term and more liquid government securities. However, shorter maturity bonds are more vulnerable than their longer-term counterparts to liquidity episodes in which market liquidity disappears rapidly.

Volatility strengthened for PIIGS, whereas it declined for non-PIIGS countries during the crisis across all maturities. Trading for benchmarks of a higher credit quality increased during the crisis period, providing evidence of flight-to-quality episodes that have taken place, as investors move their capital away from riskier investments to the safest possible investment vehicles.

We provide a more thorough understanding of liquidity and volatility dynamics by analyzing the intertemporal interactions of liquidity proxies with returns and volatility across countries and maturity segments. Volatility shocks are found to be negatively associated with returns within and across markets and positively and significantly associated with spreads (negatively associated with depth) across the PIIGS and non-PIIGS countries, indicating that liquidity and volatility shocks can be systemic in nature and can cause market-wide effects.

Interestingly, our results find no evidence of contagion between non-PIIGS and PIIGS returns, as the correlation coefficients drop significantly during the crisis period. Instead, we show that returns between non-PIIGS and PIIGS markets actually decouple and many of the bidirectional causalities from one market to the other break down as we move from pre-crisis to crisis mode. From an investor's perspective, a lower level of correlation implies that the benefits from portfolio diversification are amplified during the crisis relative to the pre-crisis period. Strong evidence of decoupling within the PIIGS countries is also documented, whereas we provide mixed results within the non-PIIGS countries, where contagion effects are exhibited among Germany, Netherlands, Finland, and Austria.

We hope that our study has undertaken a systematic rethink of the functioning of eurozone's sovereign bond markets and will provide useful insights to policymakers and regulators. Knowing the mechanisms via which financial shocks are transmitted would be beneficial to those who design fiscal and monetary policies and would enable them to establish policy measures that could mitigate the adverse effects of financial crises.

Acknowledgements

We thank Thao Thi Phuong Nguyen for excellent research assistance. Papavassiliou thanks University College Dublin for financial assistance under grant number SF1258.

References

Amihud, Y. and Mendelson, H. (1986). Asset pricing and the bid–ask spread. *J. Fin. Econ.*, 17, pp. 223–249.

Andersen, T. G. and Bollerslev, T. (1997). Intraday periodicity and volatility persistence in financial markets. *J. Empir. Fin.*, 4, pp. 115–158.

Andersen, T. G. and Bollerslev, T. (1998). Answering the skeptics: yes, standard volatility models do provide accurate forecasts. *Int. Econ. Rev.*, 39, pp. 885–905.

Andersen, T. G., Bollerslev, T., Diebold, F. X., and Ebens, H. (2001). The distribution of realized stock return volatility. *J. Fin. Econ.*, 61, pp. 43–76.

Bai, J., Julliard, C., and Yuan, K. (2012). Eurozone sovereign bond crisis: liquidity or fundamental contagion, Working Paper, London School of Economics.

Bandi, F. M. and Russell, J. R. (2006). Separating microstructure noise from volatility. *J. Fin. Econ.*, 79, pp. 655–692.

Beber, A., Brandt, M. W., and Kavajecz, K. A. (2009). Flight-to-quality or flight-to-liquidity? evidence from the Euro-area bond market. *Rev. Fin. Stud.*, 22, pp. 925–957.

Beirne, J. and Fratzscher, M. (2013). The pricing of sovereign risk and contagion during the European sovereign debt crisis. *J. Int. Money. Fin.*, 34, pp. 60–82.

Benston, G. and R. Hagerman.(1974). Determinants of bid–asked spreads in the over-the-counter market. *J. Fin. Econ.*, 1, pp. 353–364.

Bollen, N. P. B. and Whaley, R. E. (1998). Are "teenies" better?. *J.Portfolio. Manage.*, 25, pp. 10–24.

Bollerslev, T. (1990). Modeling the coherence in short-run nominal exchange rates: A multivariate generalized ARCH model. *Rev. Econ. Stat.*, 72, pp. 498–505.

Borio, C. (2000). Market liquidity and stress: selected issues and policy implications. *BIS Quart. Rev.*, November, pp. 38–48.

Brooks, C. (2014) *Introductory Econometrics for Finance*, 3rd edn, Cambridge University Press.

Cheung, Y. C., de Jong, F., and Rindi, B. (2005). Trading European sovereign bonds: the microstructure of the MTS trading platforms, ECB Working Paper No. 432.

Chordia, T., Sarkar, A., and Subrahmanyam, A. (2005). An empirical analysis of stock and bond market liquidity. *Rev. Fin. Stud.*, 18, pp. 85–129.

Claessens, S. and Forbes, K. (2001). International financial contagion: An overview, In Stijn Claessens and Kristin Forbes (eds.), *International Financial Contagion*. Kluwer Academic Publishers, pp. 3–17.

Coluzzi, C., Ginebri, S., and Turco, M. (2008). Measuring and analyzing the liquidity of the Italian treasury security wholesale secondary market, Economics & Statistics Discussion Paper No. 44/08, University of Molise.

Dacorogna, M. M., Gençay, R., Müller, U., Olsen, R. B., and Pictet, O. V. (2001). *An Introduction to High-Frequency Finance*. San Diego, CA: Academic Press.

Darbha, M. and Dufour, A. (2013a). Microstructure of the Euro-Area government bond market. In (eds.), *Market Microstructure in Emerging and Developed Markets: Price Discovery, Information Flows, and Transaction Costs*, Baker, H. K., Kiymaz, H., The Robert W. Kolb Series in Finance. John Wiley & Sons, Inc.

Darbha, M. and Dufour, A. (2013b). Measuring Euro area government bond market liquidity and its asset pricing implications, Working Paper, ICMA Centre, Henley Business School, University of Reading, UK.

Dellas, H. and Tavlas, G. S. (2013). The gold standard, the Euro, and the origins of the Greek sovereign debt crisis. *Cato. J.*, 33, pp. 491–520.

Dufour, A. and Nguyen, M. (2012). Permanent trading impacts and bond yields. *Eur. J. Fin.*, 18, pp. 841–864.

Dufour, A. and Skinner, F. (2004). MTS time series: Market and data description for the European bond and repo database, Discussion Paper 07, ISMA Centre, University of Reading.

Dunne, P., Moore, M., and Portes, R. (2006). European government bond markets: transparency, liquidity, efficiency, Research Report, Centre for Economic Policy Research (CEPR), City of London.

Dunne, P., Moore, M., and Portes, R. (2007). Benchmark status in fixed-income asset markets. *J. Bus. Fin. Account.*, 34, pp. 1615–1634.

Engle, R. (2002). Dynamic conditional correlation: a simple class of multivariate generalized autoregressive conditional heteroskedasticity models. *J. Bus. Econ. Stat.*, 20, pp. 339–350.

Favero, C., Pagano, M., and von Thadden, E-L. (2010). How does liquidity affect government bond yields?. *J. Fin. Quant. Anal.*, 45, pp. 107–134.
Forbes, K. and Rigobon, R. (2002). No contagion, only interdependence: measuring stock markets comovements. *J. Fin.*, 57, pp. 2223–2261.
Friewald, N., Jankowitsch, R., and Subrahmanyam, M.G. (2012). Illiquidity or credit deterioration: A study of liquidity in the US corporate bond market during financial crises. *J. Fin. Econ.*, 105, pp. 18–36.
Girardi, A. (2008). The informational content of trades on the EuroMTS platform, Working Paper No.97, University of Rome "Tor Vergata".
Goyenko, R., Subrahmanyam, A., and Ukhov, A. (2011). The term structure of bond market liquidity and its implications for expected bond returns. *J. Fin. Quant. Anal.*, 46, pp. 111–139.
Grossman, S. J. and Miller, M. H. (1988). Liquidity and market structure. *J. Fin.*, 43, pp. 617–633.
Hasbrouck, J. (1991). Measuring the information content of stock trades. *J. Fin.*, 56, pp. 179–207.
Hasbrouck, J. and Seppi, D. J. (2001). Common factors in prices, order flows, and liquidity. *J. Fin. Econ.*, 59, pp. 383–411.
Jotikasthira, P., Le, A., and Lundblad, C. T. (2015). Why do term structures in different currencies comove?. *J. Fin. Econ.*, 115, pp. 58–83.
Krishnamurthy, A. (2002). The bond/old-bond spread. *J. Fin. Econ.*, 66, pp. 463–506.
Lütkepohl, H. (1991). *Introduction to Multiple Time Series Analysis.* New York: Springer-Verlag.
Papavassiliou, V. G. (2014). Cross-asset contagion in times of stress. *J. Econ. Bus.*, 76, pp. 133–139.
Pasquariello, P. and Vega, C. (2009). The on-the-run liquidity phenomenon, *J. Fin. Econ.*, 92, pp. 1–24.
Pelizzon, L., Subrahmanyam, M. G., Tomio, D., and Uno, J. (2013). The microstructure of the European sovereign bond market: A study of the Euro-zone crisis, Working Paper, Ca' Foscari University of Venice.
Persaud, A. D. (2006). Improving efficiency in the European government bond market, Research Report, ICAP plc.
Pesce, A. (2015). The decoupling of emerging economies, a long-debated issue but still an open question: A survey, In *Economic Cycles in Emerging and Advanced Countries, Contributions to Economics.* Springer International Publishing.
Sims. S. A. (1980). Macroeconomics and reality. *Econometrica*, 48, pp. 1–48.
Stoll, H. R. (1978). The supply of dealer services in securities markets. *J. Fin.*, 33, pp. 1133–1151.
Subrahmanyam, A. (1994). Circuit breakers and market volatility: A theoretical perspective. *J. Fin.*, 49, pp. 237–254.

Chapter 16

Bank Dividend Policy and the European Debt Crisis: Is Sovereign Credit Risk of Relevance?

Tobias Basse[*,‡], Thomas Bürkle[*], Frederik Kunze[*] and Christoph Wegener[†]

[*]*NORD/LB Berlin Friedrichswall 10 30159 Hannover, Germany*

[‡]*tobias.basse@nordlb.de*

[†]*IPAG Business School 184 bd Saint Germain 75006 Paris, France*

Abstract

This chapter examines the dividend policy of European banks. The empirical evidence presented here suggests that financial institutions in the Eurozone react to stress in international financial markets by reducing or omitting dividend payouts to strengthen their capital position. Additionally, a negative reaction of dividend payouts of European banks to an increase of the yield differential between German and Spanish bonds seems to exist. However, this response of dividends to sovereign credit risk in the Eurozone is not statistically significant. The financial crisis starting in 2007 does not seem to materially change the relationships among the variables examined here.

1. Introduction

Due to the financial crisis, bank dividend policy issues have recently attracted strong attention in academic literature (see, for example, Basse *et al.*, 2014; Ashraf *et al.*, 2016). There is a similar discussion regarding the insurance industry (see Reddemann *et al.*, 2010; Basse *et al.*, 2011). While economic theory has some problems justifying the existence of dividend payments in general (see, for example, Black, 1976; Basse and Reddemann, 2011), it meanwhile seems to be generally accepted among financial economists that banks can reduce or omit dividend payments in a financial crisis to strengthen their capital position.

This empirical study tries to improve the understanding of the reaction of bank dividends to variables that can act as proxies for risk factors caused by financial crises. Given the current sovereign debt crisis, the paper focuses on financial institutions in the Eurozone. Relative to other segments of the stock market European banks were in general more or less consistently paying quite high dividends before the crisis. In fact, many investors back then seem to have invested in bank stocks because of attractive dividend payments. During the crisis, dividends have been adjusted. The volume of dividends paid by the financial institutions that are part of the bank sub-sector of the Euro Stoxx equity index dropped by more than 60% from 2008 to 2009, and in 2016 still it is below the mark of 30% compared to the level of payouts in the year 2008.

This chapter is structured as follows. Section 2 provides a brief literature overview focusing on the relationships between banks and sovereigns and bank dividend policy issues in financial crises. Section 3 subsequently discusses the research question, introduces the data examined and provides some thoughts about methodological issues. Section 4 discusses and evaluates the results of the empirical model estimated, before Sec. 5 finally concludes. Summarizing the results of this chapter, banks seem to react to financial stress by reducing their dividend payouts. This empirical finding probably is no major surprise, as a reaction to stress in financial markets European banks seem to have tried to strengthen their capital base by reducing or omitting dividend payments. The empirical evidence reported here does suggest that this behavior is quite robust and does not materially change in the crisis years. Banks simply have responded to stress in financial markets. Moreover, sovereign credit risk does seem to be less important for the dividend policy of European banks.

2. Literature Review

The global financial turbulences and the European sovereign debt crisis have recently highlighted again the importance of the interrelationships between sovereign credit risk and the financial services industry (see Ang and Longstaff, 2013 as well as Kräussl *et al.*, 2016). In this context, it is important to note that there is a historical dimension to the problem. In fact, Reinhart and Rogoff (2011) have taken a long-term view and argued convincingly that turbulences in the banking sector of countries often precede or accompany sovereign debt crises. Meanwhile, this perspective seems to be generally accepted in the field of financial economics, and hence is also relevant for bank stocks. For example, Correa *et al.* (2014) have empirically investigated the relationship between sovereign credit risk, government support for financial institutions, and bank stock returns. Furthermore, Acharya *et al.* (2014) have investigated EMU sovereign CDS data and empirically shown that a two-way feedback exists between sovereign credit risk measured by CDS premia and the banking sector. The authors showed that the announcements of state support for banks in the euro area caused an immediate widening of sovereign CDS premia, whereas bank CDS premia narrowed. However, in the post-bailout era that a significant comovement between bank CDS and sovereign CDS premia has been observable. Ejsing and Lemke (2011) presented similar results, testing for structural breaks and finding empirical evidence of structural shifts in the long-term relationship between bank and sovereign CDS premia after the announcements of the rescue measures for European banks. The work of Ang and Longstaff (2013) holds strong relevance in this context, since the authors also reported that financial market variables and sovereign credit risk are highly correlated.

Furthermore, in the context of the global financial crisis, the dividend policy of financial institutions has been discussed intensively (see for example Theis and Dutta, 2009; Goodhart, *et al.*, 2010; Acharya *et al.*, 2011; Kanas, 2013; Onali, 2014; Floyd *et al.*, 2015, as well as more recently Achary *et al.*, 2017; Ashraf *et al.*, 2016). In fact, financial institutions can reduce or omit dividend payments to strengthen their capital position (see for example Basse *et al.*, 2014). However, theories of dividend smoothing or signaling have to be considered in this context. These ideas have been *inter alia* discussed and empirically analyzed by Goodard *et al.* (2006) in general, as well as — for example — by Mayne (1980), Akhigbe *et al.* (1993), Boldin (1995), Bessler and Nohel (1996), Eriotis *et al.* (2007), Reddemann *et al.* (2010), and Basse *et al.* (2014) for financial institutions. In theory, investors might assume that dividend cutting or omitting dividend payments are clear signs for severe future challenges for the banking sector. However, Basse *et al.* (2014) have convincingly argued that European banks facing financial difficulties should considered changes to their payout policy by cutting or omitting dividends in order to strengthen their financial position, given that they found no empirical evidence verifying that the theories of dividend smoothing or signaling are economic phenomena of relevance in this context. This discussion about bank dividend policy issues meanwhile is of central importance in financial economics (see, for example, Ashraf *et al.*,

2019). Dividend reductions and omissions can, in fact, be an elegant way to strengthen the capital base of financial firms in a banking crisis and therefore might help to increase financial stability.

3. Research Question, Data, and Methodological Issues

This empirical study examines the reaction of bank dividends in the Eurozone to relevant risk factors. More specifically, two different proxies for financial risk are used. The VIX index is the proxy for global financial market volatility (see Ang and Longstaff, 2013). This time series reflects the market estimate of future volatility of US blue chip stocks and is also known as the "fear index" in financial markets (see, for example, Bekaert and Hoerova, 2014; Esqueda *et al.*, 2015). The spread between 10-year government bond yields in Germany and Spain is the proxy variable for sovereign credit risk in the Eurozone (see Ang and Longstaff, 2013 and Sibbertsen*et al.*, 2014). The dividend payout time series of the bank sub-sector of the Euro Stoxx index is the third variable examined. Managerial decisions concerning dividend policy issues are obviously firm-specific. However, it is appropriate to focus on specific sectors of the stock market, analyzing the dividend policy of firms because companies often tend to imitate the behavior of their rivals (see van Caneghem and Aerts, 2011). Given the strong seasonal pattern found in the dividend payouts, we examine the seasonally-adjusted time series. This variable is generated using the Census X12 procedure. All data is taken from Bloomberg. Owing to the inclusion of dividends in the model, we analyze quarterly data.

The econometric technique of vector autoregression (VAR) — suggested by Sims (1980) — has become a very popular analytic tool in the field of applied time series analysis. This approach is appropriate to describe feedback relationships among a set of relevant variables that are included in an empirical model. Each of the n variables in a VAR is explained by past values of itself and the past values of the remaining $n-1$ variables in the model. More formally, Y_t in Eq. (1) is a vector of $(n \times 1)$ endogenous variables, A_i are $(n \times n)$ coefficient matrices, while ε_t and c are $(n \times 1)$ vectors of error terms respectively constants:

$$Y_t = c + A_1 Y_{t-1} + A_2 Y_{t-2} + \cdots + A_p Y_{t-p} + \varepsilon_t. \quad (1)$$

Given that there might by a dynamic relationship among the yield spread and the VIX, it definitely makes sense to estimate a VAR model analyzing the variables examined here.

Table 1. Results Unit Root Test

Phillips Perron Test MacKinnon (1996) One-Sided *p*-Values			
Indicator	**adj. *t*-Stat**	**5% c.v.**	***p*-value**
DIV_SA	−2.996612	−2.904198	0.0401
SPREAD	−1.481501	−2.904198	0.5371
D(SPREAD)	−7.237469	−2.904848	0.0000
VIX	−4.019264	−2.904198	0.0023

Two of the three time series analyzed here — namely, the dividend payouts and the volatility index — seem to be stationary variables (see Table 1.). There are some problems with the VIX, as is well documented in the literature (most importantly, see Mencía and Sentana, 2013). In fact, the exact results searching for a unit root in volatility indices seem to depend on the time period examined. Therefore, we simply follow the results of the unit root tests for the period analyzed here and assume that the VIX is stationary. Given that two of the three variables analyzed are stationary, time series cointegration cannot be a phenomenon of relevance here. Consequently, a VAR model with the three variables of bank dividend payouts (DIV_SA), VIX and the spread between 10-year government bond yields in Spain and Germany (SPREAD) is estimated. Given that the yield differential seems to be integrated of order one, this variable is included in first differences. The two other time series are considered in levels. Subsequently, the technique of impulse response analysis is employed to examine lead/lag relationships and Granger causality among the variables included in the model. In order to avoid problems with structural change due to the introduction of the Euro, the sample analyzed is 1999 I to 2016 II. Thus, there are a sufficient number of data points available to estimate the VAR model. Based on the AIC criterion, three time lags are considered.

4. Results

In order to avoid the well-documented problems with the Cholesky decomposition (see Peseran and Shin, 1998; Basse and Reddemann, 2010), the impulse response functions are generated using the technique of generalized impulses. The empirical results reported in Fig. 1 indicate that a lagged and statistically significant negative reaction of bank dividends to a positive shock to the VIX exists. Thus, Granger causality running from US equity

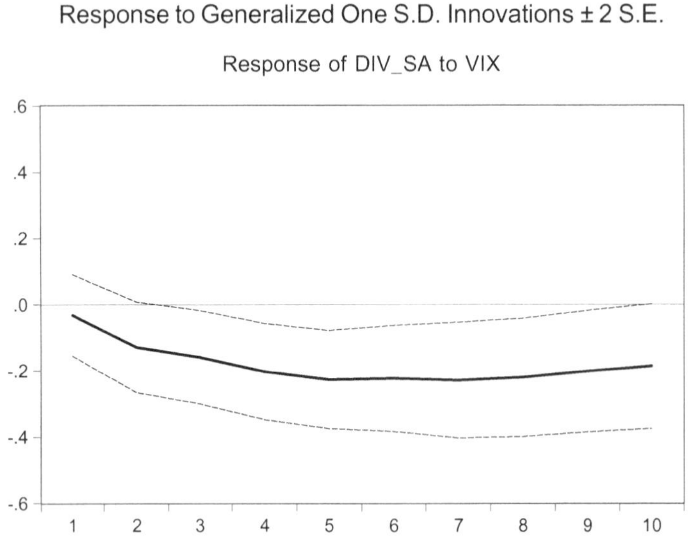

Figure 1. The reaction of Bank Dividends to Shocks to the VIX: A Shock to the VIX has Statistically Significant Negative Effects on Future Dividends

market volatility to dividend payments of the banking industry in Europe is a relevant phenomenon. Phrased somewhat differently, European banks seem to react to higher volatility in the US stock market by cutting dividends. Given that an increase to the VIX is a signal of more financial stress, this result is not a major surprise. In fact, banks seem to react to stress in international financial markets by making changes to their dividend policy. There also is a negative reaction of dividend payments to a shock to the spread between German and Spanish bond yields (see Fig. 2). Again, this finding is intuitively understandable because an increase to the spread is a sign of higher sovereign credit risk and consequently more financial stress (see Gruppe and Lange, 2014; Sibbertsen *et al.*, 2014). However, this response is not statistically significant.

In order to avoid possible problems with structural change due to the financial crisis, we have also estimated a VAR model examining the sample 2007 I to 2016 II. Phrased somewhat differently, we have excluded the pre-crisis data points from our empirical investigation. This does not affect the results (although probably not too much weight should be given to these results, given the limited number of available data points). In sum, our empirical investigations quite clearly suggest that bank dividends in the Eurozone mainly seem to react to global financial risk and that sovereign credit risk of member countries of the monetary union in Europe tends to play a less important role.

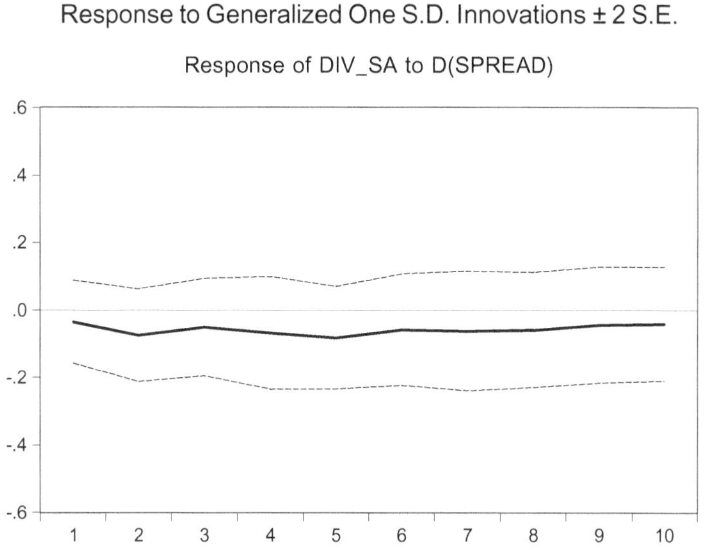

Figure 2. Reaction of Bank Dividends to Shocks to Sovereign Credit Risk in the Eurozone: A Shock to the Spread Between German and Spanish Bond Yields does not have Significant Effects on Future Dividend Payments

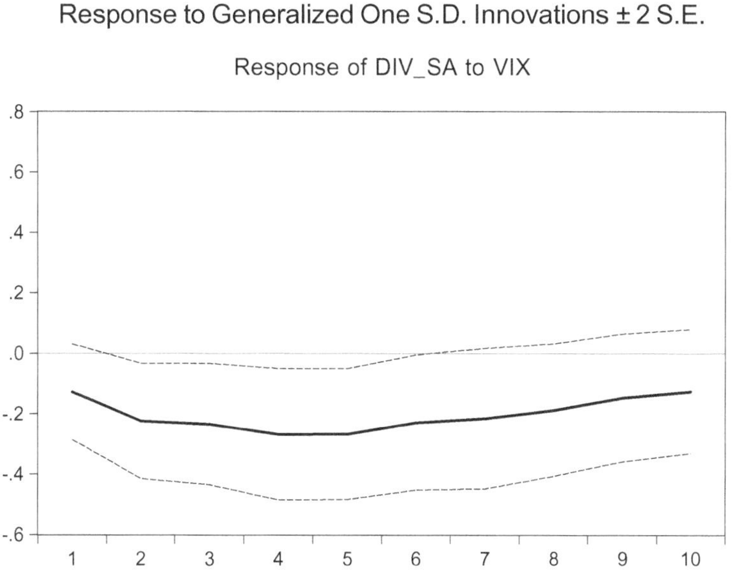

Figure 3. Reaction of Bank Dividends to Shocks to the VIX (Post-Crisis): A Shock to the VIX has Statistically Significant Negative Effects on Future Dividends

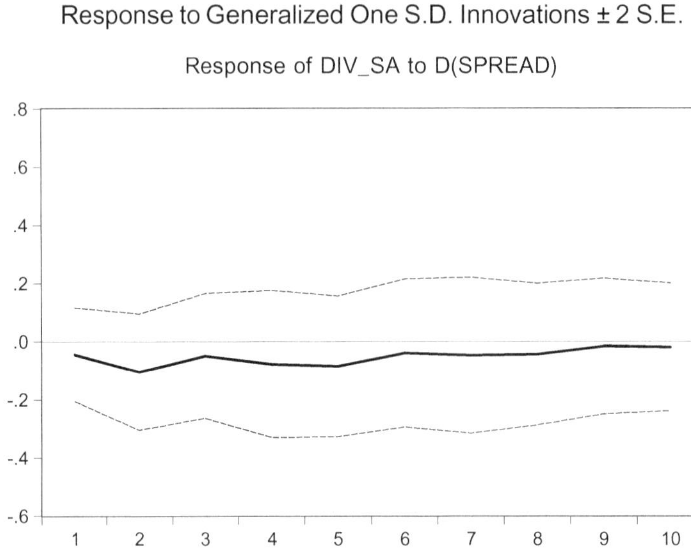

Figure 4. Reaction of Bank Dividends to Shocks to Sovereign Credit Risk in the Eurozone (Post-Crisis): A Shock to the Spread Between German and Spanish Bond Yields Still Does not have Significant Effects on Future Dividend Payments

5. Conclusion

This Chapter uses techniques of time series analysis to improve the understanding of the reaction of bank dividends in Europe to variables that can be used as proxies for risk factors caused by financial crisis. The empirical results reported indicate that a lagged and statistically significant negative reaction of bank dividends to a positive shock to the VIX exists. Therefore, European banks seem to react to higher volatility in the US stock market by cutting dividends. Given that the VIX is a kind of "fear index" in global financial markets, this empirical finding is no major surprise. European banks seem to react to stress in international financial markets by trying to strengthen their capital position. Additionally, a negative reaction of dividend payouts of European banks to an increase of the yield differential between German and Spanish bonds seems to exist, although this relationship is not statistically significant. Interestingly, our empirical findings are quite robust. Most importantly, the crisis starting in 2007 does not seem to materially change the relationships among the variables examined here. Summing up, bank dividends in the Eurozone react to global financial risk. Adjustments to the dividend policy of banks might, in fact, be helpful to promote financial stability. The sovereign credit risk of member countries of the monetary union in Europe seems to be less important for the dividend policy of European banks.

References

Acharya, V. V., Gujral, I., Kulkarni, N., and Shin, H. S. (2011). Dividends and bank capital in the financial crisis of 2007–2009 (No. w16896). National Bureau of Economic Research.

Acharya, V., Drechsler, I., and Schnabl, P. (2014). A pyrrhic victory? Bank bailouts and sovereign credit risk. *The J. Fin.*, 69(6), pp. 2689–2739.

Acharya, V. V., Le, H., and Shin, H. S. (2017). Bank capital and dividend externalities. *Rev. Fin. Stud.*, 30(3), pp. 988–1018.

Akhigbe, A., Borde, S. F., and Madura, J. (1993). Dividend policy and signaling by insurance companies. *J. Risk Insurance*, pp. 413–428.

Ang, A. and Longstaff, F. A. (2013). Systemic sovereign credit risk: Lessons from the US and Europe. *J. Monetary Econom.*, 60, pp. 493–510.

Ashraf, B. N., Bibi, B., and Zheng, C. (2016). How to regulate bank dividends? Is capital regulation an answer?. *Econom. Model.*, 57, pp. 281–293.

Basse, T. and Reddemann, S. (2010). Variable-ordering induced problems of impulse-response analysis and other difficulties: The dividend policy of Austrian firms. *Int. J. Comput. Econom. Econometr.*, 1, pp. 278–293.

Basse, T. and Reddemann, S. (2011). Inflation and the dividend policy of US firms. *Managerial Fin.*, 37, pp. 34–46.

Basse, T., Reddemann, S., Riegler, J. J., and von der Schulenburg, J. M. G. (2011). Dividend policy and the global financial crisis: Empirical evidence from the Italian insurance industry. *Zeitschrift für die gesamte Versicherungswissenschaft*, 100, pp. 131–140.

Basse, T., Reddemann, S., Riegler, J. J., and von der Schulenburg, J. M. G. (2014). Bank dividend policy and the global financial crisis: Empirical evidence from Europe. *Eur. J. Polit. Economy*, 34, pp. S25–S31.

Bekaert, G., and Hoerova, M. (2014). The VIX, the variance premium and stock market volatility. *J. Economet.*, 183, pp. 181–192.

Bessler, W. and Nohel, T. (1996). The stock-market reaction to dividend cuts and omissions by commercial banks. *J. Banking and Fin.*, 20(9), pp. 1485–1508.

Black, F. (1976). The dividend puzzle. Journal of Portfolio Management, 2, pp. 5–8.

Correa, Ricardo, Kuan-Hui, Lee, Horacio, Sapriza, Suarez, Gustavo (2014) Sovereign credit risk, banks' government support, and bank stock returns around the world. *J. Money, Credit Bank.*, 46(1), pp. S93–S121.

Esqueda, O. A., Luo, Y., and Jackson, D. O. (2015). The linkage between the US "fear index" and ADR premiums under non-frictionless stock markets. *J. Econom. Fin.*, 39, pp. 541–556.

Floyd, E., Nan L., and Douglas J. S. (2015). Payout policy through the financial crisis: The growth of repurchases and the resilience of dividends. *J. Fin. Econom.*, 118.2, pp. 299–316.

Gruppe, M. and Lange, C. (2014). Spain and the European sovereign debt crisis. *European J. Polit. Economy*, 34, pp. S3–S8.

Goddard, J., McMillan, D. G., and Wilson, J. O. (2006). Dividend smoothing vs dividend signalling: evidence from UK firms. *Managerial Fin.*, 32(6), pp. 493–504.

Goodhart, C. A., Peiris, M. U., Tsomocos, D. P., and Vardoulakis, A. P. (2010). On dividend restrictions and the collapse of the interbank market. *Ann. Fin.*, 6(4), pp. 455–473.

Kanas, A. (2013). Bank dividends, risk, and regulatory regimes. *J. Bank. Fin.*, 37(1), pp. 1–10.

MacKinnon, J. G. (1996). Numerical distribution functions for unit root and cointegration tests. *Journal of Applied Econometrics*, 11, pp. 601–618.

Mayne, L. S. (1980). Bank dividend policy and holding company affiliation. *J. Fin. Quantit. Anal.*, 15(2), pp. 469–80.

Mencía, J. and Sentana, E. (2013). Valuation of VIX derivatives. *J. Fin. Econom.*, 108(2), pp. 367–391.

Onali, E. (2014). Moral hazard, dividends, and risk in banks. *J. Business Fin. Account.*, 41(1–2), pp. 128–155.

Pesaran, H. H. and Shin, Y. (1998). Generalized impulse response analysis in linear multivariate models. *Econom. Lett.*, 58, pp. 17–29.

Reddemann, S., Basse, T., and Von der Schulenburg, J. M. G. (2010). On the impact of the financial crisis on the dividend policy of the European insurance industry. *The Geneva Papers Risk Insurance Issues Practice*, 35, pp. 53–62.

Sibbertsen, P., Wegener, C., and Basse, T. (2014). Testing for a break in the persistence in yield spreads of EMU government bonds. *J. Bank. Fin.*, 41, pp. 109–118.

Sims, C. A. (1980). Macroeconomics and reality. *Econometrica*, 48, pp. 1–48.

Theis, J. and Dutta, A. S. (2009). Explanatory factors of bank dividend policy: Revisited. *Managerial Fin.*, 35(6), pp. 501–508.

Van Caneghem, T. and Aerts, W. (2011). Intra-industry conformity in dividend policy. *Managerial Fin.*, 37, pp. 492–516.

Chapter 17

Impact of QE on European Sovereign Bond Market Equilibrium

Franck Martin and Jiangxingyun Zhang

University of Rennes 1 and CREM-CNRS

Abstract

This chapter evaluates the impact of the European Central Bank's (ECB's) quantitative easing (QE) programmes on bond market equilibrium. Therefore, we develop an original theoretical model to understand the formation of long-term sovereign rates in the euro zone. More specifically, it is a two-country international bond portfolio choice model that generalizes the traditional results of the term structure interest rates theory. In particular, in addition to traditional properties, long-term equilibrium rates depend on future bond yields' anticipated variances and covariances, which are considered as a component of a volatility risk premium. Using CDS as a variable to control for default risks, we test the model empirically for the period January 2006 to September 2016. We conclude that the ECB's QE programme, which began in March 2015, has accelerated the 'defragmentation process' of the European bond markets that began with the Outright Monetary Transactions programme. However, the results of a Forbes and Rigobon test do not show that the QE programme has led to a significant increase in the conditional correlations between bond markets. In a supplementary empirical test, we show that QE has significantly reduced the sensitivities of bond yield spreads to the premiums paid on sovereign CDS.

1. Introduction

The European Central Bank's (ECB's) quantitative easing (QE) programme, launched in March 2015, has proved an essential, but paradoxical experience. It is essential because it is the first such experiment conducted in the euro zone, while the United States, Japan, and the United Kingdom already have

The authors thank the Research Chair of Rennes 1 Foundation "Nouveaux défis de la banque" for its support.

some experience with this type of unconventional monetary policy. In the euro zone, the QE1 programme (from March 2015) and QE2 programme (from March 2016) are the only available economic policies to fight deflation risks in a context in which fiscal policies are restrictive and focused on reducing public deficits and debts following the implementation of the new European fiscal compact on January 1, 2013.

The QE experience in the euro zone is also paradoxical, because brokers seem to be convinced that the large-scale government bond purchase programme allows the ECB effective control of long-term sovereign rates. Therefore, we have switched to a fixed-rate regime, guided by short-term rates via the REFI rate, and by long-term rates through ECB bond purchases. When fears of 'tapering' are stronger, the occasional increases in long-term interest rates show that market operators are also convinced of the ECB's capacity to maintain sovereign bond yields close to zero. The paradox comes precisely from the fact that the academic literature is much more nuanced than brokers' opinions on the effectiveness of QE programmes. This includes the first transmission mechanism, where the effective control of long-term interest rates determines the financial costs of sovereign states.

De Santis (2016) points out that studies on the US bond market estimate that bond purchases from the Federal Reserve (FED) between December 2008 and March 2010 have contributed to decreasing long-term government rates by about 90 basis points.[1] Comparable purchases by the BoE in the United Kingdom have reduced long-term rates by 50 basis points between March 2009 and January 2010.[2] While evaluating the impact of monetary policy announcements of by the ECB, relayed by Bloomberg between September 2014 and February 2015, before the implementation of the APP, showing, De Santis (2016) considers that the monetary policies of the ECB have reduced the GDP-weighted European long-term rate by 63 basis points, with more pronounced effects on the most vulnerable countries. These are the *ex ante* effects related to the APP announcement. Valiante (2016) considers that *ex ante* effects are as important as *ex post* effects, once

[1]Most of the empirical literature on asset purchases by the Federal Reserve (FED) and Bank of England (BoE) has focused on their effects on government bond markets. Studies focusing on the US government bond yields include Doh (2010), Gagnon *et al.* (2011), Krishnamurthy and Vissing-Jorgensen (2011), Meaning and Zhu (2011), D'Amico and King (2013),d'Amico *et al.* (2012), and Li and Wei (2012).

[2]Studies focusing on the UK government bond yields includeare Meier (2009), Joyce *et al.* (2011), Joyce and Tong (2012), Meaning and Zhu (2011), Breedon *et al.* (2012), Christensen and Rudebusch (2012), and McLaren *et al.* (2014).

asset purchases are conducted. Using the double difference method (DDIF) on a market panel that has undergone solely QE treatment, he estimates that the contribution of the APP to the decrease in euro zone bond rate is about 1%.

Overall, whether in the USA, the UK, or the Euro Zone, we find that the contribution of QE to the decline in sovereign rates is not highly significant, and even more modest for the euro zone between the announcement of QE in September 2014 and September 2016 (see Figs. 1 and 2). This might suggest that other mechanisms have played a role in this process, such as the effects of deflation risks on nominal rates (Fisher effect), the significant improvement of sovereign issuers, and so on.

Our contribution to the debate on the impact of QE on the bond market equilibrium is summarized as follows. First, we use an original theoretical model developed by Martin and Zhang (2017) to identify the normal mechanisms of bond markets and the potential effects of asset purchases by the ECB. This is an international bond portfolio choice model with two countries: one country with few default risks (core countries in the zone), and a more vulnerable country (periphery countries). The optimal bond demand is not only met by the supply of bonds, based on the evolution of public deficit and debt, but also by the ECB's purchases, which effectively reduce the net supply of bonds in circulation. The properties of the equilibrium model thus generalize the traditional term structure of interest rates theory (Mankiw *et al.* (1986); Shiller and McCulloch (1987); Walsh (1985); Jones and Roley (1983); Artus (1987)). Long-term equilibrium rates depend crucially on the variances and anticipated covariances of the bond yields of the two countries. Therefore, the expression of a volatility risk premium is enriched by a covariance effect, that is, the joint risks between markets. Thus, from a theoretical point of view, we note that purchases by the ECB affect the long-term equilibrium rates, which depend on the sign of the covariances anticipated by investors.

Second, the model is estimated econometrically over the period January 2006 to September 2016 using daily data. The anticipated variances and covariances of the bond yields are simulated using a bivariate DCC-GARCH model, with a 500-day rolling window. Risk forecasts are given by the one-step-ahead forecasts of variances and covariances. The default risk is controlled by introducing the premium of sovereign credit default swaps (CDS). A global uncertainty variable, the Vstoxx index, and short-term rates in the euro zone rated AAA complete the set of explanatory variables of sovereign bond rates. We estimate 21 pairs of European countries in

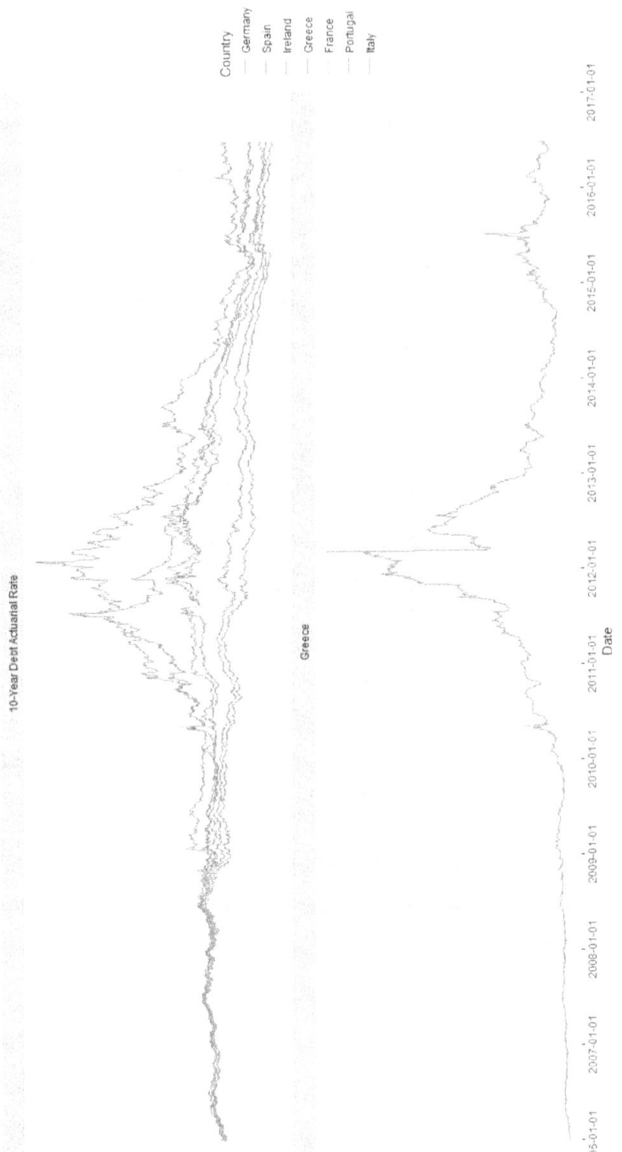

Figure 1. 10-Year Bond Rates

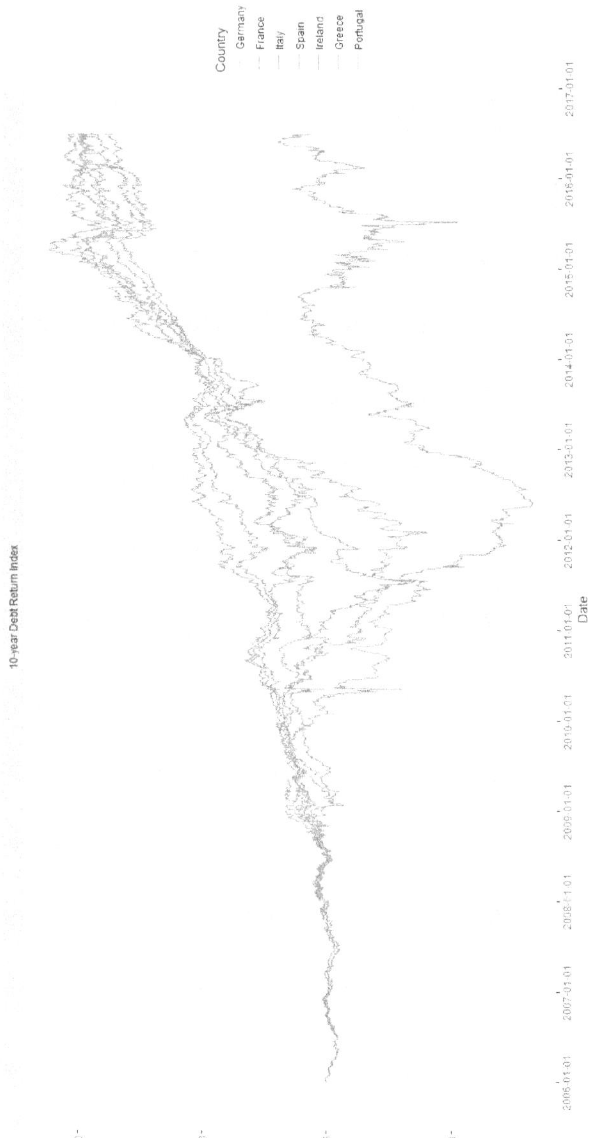

Figure 2. 10-Year Debt Return Index

a framework of conditional heteroscedasticity with a VECH specification matrix of the variance–covariance for innovations. Estimations are performed over several periods, plus a series of estimations with 500-day rolling windows in order to evaluate possible deformation of the market mechanisms over the post-crisis period with the implementation of the OMT and APP by the ECB.

Finally, by applying the test of Forbes and Rigobon (2002) and Pesaran and Pick (2007), we examine whether the implementation of the APP has led to a significant increase in the correlations between non-fundamental or residual components of interest rates. From our point of view, this tests an indirect way of identifying whether QE led to a significant decrease in sovereign bond yields. We further propose a complementary test, centered on the impact of QE on credit risk premiums, to evaluate possible deformations since the implementation of QE of the sensitivity of credit spreads to the premiums paid on the sovereign bonds.

The results of this chapter can be summarized as follows. First, if we look at the significance of variances and covariances anticipated by investors, it seems that the mechanism of optimal portfolio allocation among the Euro Zone bond markets disappeared during the sovereign debt crisis and reappeared closely after the implementation of the OMT in September 2012. From this point of view, the ECB's QE from March 2015 had only prolonged the defragmentation process, which is initiated by the OMT, in the bond markets. Second, the formal test à la Forbes and Rigobon shows the QE has led to a clear rebound in the correlation between non-fundamental determinants of long term rates. However, since the correlation levels were already high on average before the implementation of the QE, it would be inaccurate to conclude that the QE had led to a significant and general increase in the correlations between markets. It would be improper to say that the QE had played a determining role over this falling rate period. Finally, the regressions of interest rate spreads on sovereign CDSs show that QE had significantly crushed the credit risk premiums of long-term rates. With the exception of Portugal, the sensitivity of interest rate spreads to CDSs had decreased by about half since the implementation of the QE in March 2015.

The remainder of the chapter is organized as follows. Section 2 presents the practical terms of the QE programmes. Section 3 shows the main assumptions and the results of the theoretical model of bond yields. Section 4 presents the different econometric methods and the construction of the correlation structural break test. Section 5 presents both the econometric and test results. Lastly, Section 6 gives a general conclusion.

2. Asset Purchase Programme (APP) and Public Sector Purchase Programme (PSPP) in Practice

The ECB's QE programmes mainly correspond to the Public Sector Purchase Programme (PSPP) launched on March 9, 2015. It is part of a broader framework of the ECB's Assets Purchase Programmes (APP) initiated internally with the Securities Markets Programme (SMP, Table 1). Purchases made in the framework of the PSPP mainly concern sovereign bonds (government bonds), but marginally on those of agencies and supranational organizations. Since June 2016, the QE programmes began focusing on investment-grade corporate bonds (Table 1).

The ECB has set several constraints on these purchasing programs: (1) purchases are for securities with a maturity between 2 and 30 years; (2) purchases may not relate to securities whose returns are below the deposit rates of the ECB (–0.2% by 03/2015, and –0.4% by 03/2016); and (3) the ECB may not hold more than 25% of securities from the same issue, and no more than 33 of the same issuer.[3]

The proposed purchase amounts were 60 billion euros per month in March 2015. This was raised to 80 billion in March 2016, and then to 70 billion in December 2016. The distribution of purchases between countries is based on the weight of each country in terms of the capital of the ECB (Tables 2 and 3). The important issues here are to evaluate the effect of these purchases on the equilibrium of the bond markets and to be able to compare the amounts purchased with the available quantity of securities in each market. These quantities are given by a country's debt stock at market value. They evolve with new issues and the amortization of capital. Claeys *et al.* (2015) shows that these purchases are, for most countries, quite significant in terms of available securities. They show, for example, that the cumulative purchases by the ECB would saturate the constraints of 25% by May 2017 for Germany and by January 2017 for Portugal. The constraint will already be saturated for Livia (May 2015), Cyprus (June 2015), and

[3]In March 2015, the ECB's assets in Greece were, as a result of the aid program, in excess of the national debt limit of 33%. This is why Greece was excluded since the beginning of ECB's purchase program.

Table 1. Asset Purchase Programmes in Practice

		Monthly Net, Purchases at Book Value				Quarter-End, Amortization Adjustment				Holdings			
		Asset-Backed Securities Purchase Programme	Covered Bond Purchase Programme 3	Corporate Sector Purchase Programme	Public Sector Purchase Programme	Asset-Backed Securities Purchase Programme	Covered Bond Purchase Programme 3	Corporate Sector Purchase Programme	Public Sector Purchase Programme	Asset-Backed Securities Purchase Programme	Covered Bond Purchase Programme 3	Corporate Sector Purchase Programme	Public Sector Purchase Programme
2014	October	0	4.768	0	0	0	0	0	0	0	4.768	0	0
	November	368	13.033	0	0	0	0	0	0	368	17.801	0	0
	December	1.376	11.885	0	0	0	−54	0	0	1.744	29.632	0	0
2015	January	582	10.623	0	0	0	0	0	0	2.326	40.255	0	0
	February	1.137	10.953	0	0	0	0	0	0	3.463	51.209	0	0
	March	1.158	12.587	0	47.383	0	−190	0	−27	4.622	63.606	0	47.356
	April	1.163	11.464	0	47.701	0	0	0	0	5.785	75.07	0	95.057
	May	1.42	10.039	0	51.622	0	0	0	0	7.205	85.108	0	146.679
	June	1.59	10.215	0	51.442	1	−326	0	−592	8.796	94.997	0	197.53
	July	943	9.006	0	51.359	0	0	0	0	9.739	104.003	0	248.889
	August	1.348	7.459	0	42.826	0	0	0	0	11.087	111.462	0	291.715
	September	1.928	10.11	0	51.008	0	−422	0	−1.261	13.015	121.151	0	341.462
	October	1.563	9.993	0	52.175	0	0	0	0	14.577	131.144	0	393.637
	November	601	6.869	0	55.105	0	0	0	0	15.178	138.013	0	448.742
	December	145	5.803	0	44.309	−1	−476	0	−1.836	15.322	143.34	0	491.215
2016	January	2.26	7.197	0	52.956	0	0	0	0	17.582	150.537	0	544.171
	February	989	7.784	0	53.358	0	0	0	0	18.571	158.321	0	597.529
	March	418	7.819	0	53.059	1	−503	0	−2.565	18.991	165.638	0	648.022
	April	−16	6.615	0	78.499	0	0	0	0	18.975	172.253	0	726.521
	May	84	5.556	0	79.673	0	0	0	0	19.059	177.809	0	806.194
	June	526	6.098	6.401	72.072	0	−530	−3	−3.064	19.585	183.377	6.398	875.201
	July	783	3.258	6.816	69.65	0	0	0	0	20.368	186.634	13.214	944.852
	August	−226	3.504	6.707	50.513	0	0	0	0	20.142	190.139	19.921	995.364
	September	530	4.731	9.872	69.972	0	−566	−72	−4.093	20.672	194.304	29.722	1.061.244
	October	589	3.437	8.422	72.974	0	0	0	0	21.261	197.741	38.144	1.134.218
	November	1.253	4.993	9.036	70.145	0	0	0	0	22.514	202.734	47.18	1.204.362
	December	317	1.369	4.042	55.032	−1	−588	−152	−4760	22.83	203.516	51.069	1.254.635

Note: History of cumulative purchases under the APP. End of month, in euro millions. Holdings are end-of-month book value at amortised cost.
Source: European Central Bank.

Table 2. Part 1 of Breakdown of Debt Securities Under the Public Sector Purchase Programme: Monthly Net Purchases and WAM of PSPP Portfolio Holdings

	31/03/2015	30/04/2015	31/05/2015	30/06/2015	31/07/2015	31/08/2015	30/09/2015	30/10/2015	30/11/2015	31/12/2015	31/01/2016	29/02/2016
Monthly net purchases												
Austria	1.216	1.205	1.314	1.31	1.363	1.064	1.279	1.324	1.411	1.155	1.348	1.359
Belgium	1.528	1.53	1.656	1.657	1.642	1.362	1.633	1.678	1.764	1.446	1.709	1.707
Cyprus	0	0	0	0	98	0	0	90	97	0	0	0
Germany	11.07	11.148	12.144	11.97	11.975	9.926	11.851	12.195	12.903	10.443	12.347	12.44
Estonia	0	0	0	5	15	10	8	3	7	0	6	7
Spain	5.447	5.471	5.909	5.915	5.891	4.882	5.789	6.042	6.334	5.137	6.107	6.125
Finland	774	786	841	836	850	687	825	844	909	734	865	879
France	8.757	8.624	9.485	9.426	9.465	8.087	9.485	9.95	10.221	8.267	9.969	9.989
Ireland	722	735	775	784	771	639	824	809	840	684	782	803
Italy	7.609	7.585	8.228	8.164	8.248	6.719	8.234	8.365	8.876	7.181	8.559	8.499
Lithuania	39	83	123	133	126	143	125	114	117	104	109	109
Luxembourg	183	205	84	261	80	86	138	6	30	42	169	110
Latvia	75	177	205	46	22	23	19	63	31	23	41	30
Malta	5	53	85	66	24	11	18	11	2	7	60	21
the Netherlands	2.487	2.527	2.667	2.663	2.657	2.213	2.603	2.721	2.883	2.191	2.84	2.794
Portugal	1.074	1.084	1.174	1.164	1.16	966	1.148	1.184	1.248	1.018	1.197	1.214
Slovenia	209	219	231	228	232	192	227	245	248	197	252	280
Slovakia	506	522	529	546	442	423	467	377	533	277	575	554
Supranationals	5.682	5.748	6.173	6.267	6.3	5.393	6.335	6.153	6.65	5.403	6.021	6.437
Total	47.383	47.701	51.622	51.442	51.359	42.826	51.008	52.175	55.105	44.309	52.956	53.358
WAM of PSPP portfolio holdings												
Austria	7.79	7.99	7.84	7.74	7.92	8.03	8.01	8.11	8.25	8.52	8.37	8.43
Belgium	8.8	9.1	9.13	9.09	8.84	8.8	9	9.21	9.62	9.51	9.53	9.59
Cyprus					5.41	5.32	5.24	5.43	5.91	5.82	5.74	5.66
Germany	8.12	7.9	7.11	6.87	6.91	7.09	6.96	6.98	7.02	7	7	6.96
Estonia				3.05	2.96	2.87	2.78	2.71	2.63	2.54	2.46	2.38
Spain	11.66	9.73	9.71	9.82	9.66	9.68	9.68	9.66	9.74	9.7	9.77	9.75
Finland	7.26	7.15	7.16	7.24	7.25	7.33	7.39	7.51	7.61	7.59	7.6	7.72
France	8.22	7.84	7.83	7.83	7.93	7.87	7.84	7.83	7.81	7.73	7.69	7.69
Ireland	9.43	9.14	9.61	9.55	9.77	9.66	9.1	8.98	9.34	9.4	9.48	9.49
Italy	9.07	8.41	8.68	8.83	9.03	9.12	9.27	9.29	9.28	9.27	9.33	9.34
Lithuania	6.46	5.22	6.11	5.9	5.69	5.55	5.4	5.36	5.64	6.01	6.24	6.47
Luxembourg	7.01	6.88	6.71	6.41	6.29	6.26	6.29	6.15	6.13	6.07	6.08	6.1
Latvia	6.43	5.93	6.3	6.23	6.13	6.07	5.96	6	5.88	5.85	5.7	5.58
Malta	10.37	8.47	11.05	12.01	11.03	10.49	9.99	9.7	9.6	9.62	9.58	9.53
the Netherlands	6.71	6.97	6.85	6.82	6.72	6.64	6.6	6.56	6.59	6.51	6.51	6.7
Portugal	10.96	10.77	10.84	10.61	10.59	10.77	10.86	10.64	10.57	10.36	10.22	10.12
Slovenia	6.33	7.92	7.5	7.57	7.21	7.73	8.04	8.05	8.13	7.97	7.74	7.57
Slovakia	9.49	9.26	9.29	9.21	8.85	8.66	8.66	8.47	8.54	8.58	8.41	8.33
Supranationals	7.26	8.05	7.8	7.43	7.19	7.05	6.88	6.9	7.05	6.97	6.91	7.03
Total	8.56	8.25	8.07	8	8	8.03	7.99	8	8.06	8.02	8.02	8.03

Table 3. Part 2 of Breakdown of Debt Securities Under the Public Sector Purchase Programme: Monthly Net Purchases and WAM of PSPP Portfolio Holdings

	31/03/2016	30/04/2016	31/05/2016	30/06/2016	31/07/2016	31/08/2016	30/09/2016	30/10/2016	30/11/2016	31/12/2016	31/01/2017	28/02/2017	31/03/2017
Monthly net purchases													
Austria	1.353	2.06	2.14	1.849	1.878	1.354	1.884	1.959	1.88	1.495	1.97	1.888	1.958
Belgium	1.71	2.612	2.695	2.341	2.368	1.704	2.377	2.477	2.372	1.867	2.489	2.37	2.398
Cyprus	−16	0	0	0	0	0	−21	0	0	0	0	0	0
Germany	12.411	18.985	19.573	16.888	17.247	12.368	17.188	18.016	17.29	13.568	17.713	16.96	16.977
Estonia	0	5	0	0	0	0	0	0	0	0	0	0	0
Spain	6.111	9.318	9.619	9.238	8.453	6.112	8.487	8.827	8.461	6.656	8.789	8.367	8.459
Finland	871	1.324	1.366	1.224	1.197	871	1.205	1.258	1.206	939	777	726	730
France	9.852	14.933	15.398	13.683	13.569	9.769	13.609	14.16	13.48	10.689	14.24	13.558	13.707
Ireland	808	1.078	1.112	1.085	986	697	982	1.022	979	648	547	557	565
Italy	8.53	12.998	13.442	12.772	11.867	8.476	11.808	12.323	11.707	9.417	12.302	11.785	11.89
Lithuania	125	104	113	105	72	48	73	125	99	75	70	65	75
Luxembourg	144	35	16	26	6	0	10	3	75	34	10	74	67
Latvia	44	76	58	90	27	72	45	90	39	16	39	56	65
Malta	60	60	66	37	12	11	7	37	99	55	29	49	30
the Netherlands	2.759	4.224	4.355	3.781	3.834	2.915	3.842	3.996	3.831	3.041	4.021	3.825	3.869
Portugal	1.213	1.405	1.451	1.438	958	722	1.022	1.021	1.023	726	688	656	663
Slovenia	237	236	242	254	223	153	219	225	216	168	160	152	150
Slovakia	433	329	323	233	221	123	133	164	230	216	334	301	294
Supranationals	6.413	8.717	7.706	7.028	6.732	5.117	7.102	7.271	7.157	5.425	7.185	6.818	6.919
Total	53.059	78.499	79.673	72.072	69.65	50.513	69.972	72.974	70.145	55.032	71.362	68.208	68.814
WAM of PSPP portfolio holdings													
Austria	8.51	8.71	8.7	8.92	9.11	9.23	9.32	9.38	9.32	9.26	9.26	9.31	9.31
Belgium	9.74	9.79	9.78	9.65	9.79	9.92	10	10.07	9.98	10.04	10.11	10.03	10.14
Cyprus	5.52	5.44	5.36	5.27	5.19	5.1	5.09	5.01	4.92	4.86	4.76	4.67	4.59
Germany	7.05	7.18	7.31	7.44	7.6	7.69	7.88	8	8.06	8.16	8.15	7.88	7.65
Estonia	2.28	2.2	2.13	2.04	1.96	1.87	1.78	1.71	1.62	1.56	1.46	1.37	1.29
Spain	9.68	9.61	9.66	9.73	9.71	9.64	9.57	9.47	9.37	9.27	9.13	8.94	8.82
Finland	7.67	7.6	7.58	7.53	7.55	7.56	7.61	7.65	7.44	7.38	7.39	7.29	7.26
France	7.67	7.68	7.68	7.65	7.71	7.7	7.75	7.8	7.73	7.71	7.68	7.66	7.64
Ireland	9.42	9.47	9.38	9.38	9.31	9.25	9.38	9.35	9.19	9.19	9.07	9.03	8.92
Italy	9.35	9.36	9.31	9.29	9.24	9.2	9.15	9.07	8.95	8.92	8.85	8.79	8.72
Lithuania	6.7	6.61	6.57	6.62	6.5	6.42	6.41	6.6	6.61	6.59	6.69	6.69	6.79
Luxembourg	6.16	6.09	6.01	5.98	5.9	5.81	5.74	5.66	5.52	5.47	5.39	5.52	5.54
Latvia	5.45	5.37	5.66	6.62	6.56	6.59	6.57	7.32	7.29	7.26	7.51	7.53	7.66
Malta	10.4	10.15	10.57	10.87	10.89	10.75	10.81	11.12	11.54	11.57	11.52	11.36	11.3
the Netherlands	6.86	7.15	7.4	7.57	7.71	7.76	7.9	8.01	8.01	8.02	7.99	7.93	7.83
Portugal	10.18	10.17	10.21	10.14	10.07	9.91	9.84	9.8	9.68	9.53	9.37	9.28	9.19
Slovenia	7.74	8.09	8.32	8.27	8.23	8.25	8.41	8.56	8.71	8.9	8.89	8.93	9.2
Slovakia	8.24	8.24	8.11	8.02	7.92	7.85	7.86	7.83	7.79	7.9	7.93	8.04	8.09
Supranationals	6.92	6.79	6.83	6.86	7.06	7.12	7.27	7.33	7.25	7.31	7.32	7.36	7.36
Total	8.05	8.08	8.13	8.18	8.26	8.28	8.35	8.38	8.33	8.33	8.3	8.2	8.11

Ireland (November 2016). There would be more margin for Austria, Belgium, Ireland, France, Italy, and Spain.

3. Theoretical Background: An International Portfolio Model

In order to understand the formation of bond yields, we use the theoretical model proposed by Martin and Zhang (2017).

3.1. *Hypothesis*

The model is a three-asset bond portfolio choice model: a risk-free monetary asset at rate r and two zero-coupon bonds ($i = 1, 2$) of the same maturity, including mainly interest rate risks. The sensitivity of the bond is denoted by S. The optimal demand of bonds, following Markowitz, can be written as follows:

$$\alpha_1^* = \frac{(\mu_1 - r)}{r_a[\sigma_1^2 - (\frac{\sigma_{12}}{\sigma_2})^2]} - \frac{\sigma_{12}(\mu_2 - r)}{r_a\sigma_2^2[\sigma_1^2 - (\frac{\sigma_{12}}{\sigma_2})^2]}, \tag{1}$$

$$\alpha_2^* = \frac{(\mu_2 - r)}{r_a[\sigma_2^2 - (\frac{\sigma_{12}}{\sigma_1})^2]} - \frac{\sigma_{12}(\mu_1 - r)}{r_a\sigma_1^2[\sigma_2^2 - (\frac{\sigma_{12}}{\sigma_1})^2]}, \tag{2}$$

where μ_1, μ_2, σ_1, σ_2, and σ_{12} represent the first and second order moments of bond yields over one period.

The supply–demand equilibrium conditions in each market are given by

$$\alpha_{1,t}^*[\mu_1(R_{1,t}), \mu_2(R_{2,t})]W_t = \varepsilon_{1,t}^S W_t, \tag{3}$$

$$\alpha_{2,t}^*[\mu_1(R_{1,t}), \mu_2(R_{2,t})]W_t = \varepsilon_{2,t}^S W_t, \tag{4}$$

where $\varepsilon_{i,t}^S$ is the supply of bonds (in percentage of total wealth W_t), considered as a random process and a primary source of risk in the model. If we introduce a random ECB demand ($\varepsilon_{i,t}^{\text{ECB}}$) to take into account the purchases of bonds through unconventional monetary policy, the net supply of bonds is given by

$$\sum_{1,t} = \varepsilon_{1,t}^S - \varepsilon_{1,t}^{\text{ECB}}, \tag{5}$$

$$\sum_{2,t} = \varepsilon_{2,t}^S - \varepsilon_{2,t}^{\text{ECB}}. \tag{6}$$

The bond demand of ECB decreases the net bond supply.

3.2. *Equilibrium properties*

The market equilibrium conditions give a 2-2 system, with respect to μ_1 and μ_2. Solving the system, we find the equilibrium expected return (rational expectations) of each obligation. The solutions are given by

$$\mu_1^* = r + \sigma_1^2 r_a \left(\sum_{1,t} + \frac{\sigma_{12}}{\sigma_1^2} \sum_{2,t} \right), \tag{7}$$

$$\mu_2^* = r + \sigma_2^2 r_a \left(\sum_{2,t} + \frac{\sigma_{12}}{\sigma_2^2} \sum_{1,t} \right). \tag{8}$$

The expected equilibrium returns are expressed as the risk-free rate plus a risk premium, which depends crucially on the total bond supply, which, in turn, measures the quantity of risk in the portfolio. The bond supply of country 2 has an impact on μ_1^*, depending on the covariance on variance $(\frac{\sigma_{12}}{\sigma_1^2})$, which plays the role of a beta factor.

Using the definition of expected returns ($\mu_i = E_t(H_{i,t}) \simeq (1+S)R_{i,t} - SE_t(R_{i,t+1})$ with $H_{i,t} = \frac{P_{i,t+1} - P_{i,t}}{P_{i,t}}$), the solutions are obtained in the form of an actuarial rate of return on bonds, which are the true endogenous variables of the model.

$$R_{1,t}^* = \frac{1}{1+S} \Bigg[r_t + SE_t(R_{1,t+1}) + S^2 V_t(R_{1,t+1}) r_a \left(\sum_{1,t} + \frac{\mathrm{Cov}_t(R_{1,t+1}, R_{2,t+1})}{V_t(R_{1,t+1})} \sum_{2,t} \right) \Bigg], \tag{9}$$

$$R_{2,t}^* = \frac{1}{1+S} \Bigg[r_t + SE_t(R_{2,t+1}) + S^2 V_t(R_{2,t+1}) r_a \left(\sum_{2,t} + \frac{\mathrm{Cov}_t(R_{1,t+1}, R_{2,t+1})}{V_t(R_{2,t+1})} \sum_{1,t} \right) \Bigg] \tag{10}$$

The third term in bond rates appears as a one-period risk premium with (net) supply effects depending on covariance regime. If $\mathrm{Cov}_t(R_{1,t+1}, R_{2,t+1}) = 0$, we have

$$R_{i,t}^* = \frac{1}{1+S} \left[r_t + SE_t(R_{i,t+1}) + S^2 V_t(R_{i,t+1}) r_a \left(\sum_{i,t} \right) \right]. \tag{11}$$

That is the standard Euler's equation of long-term rate in a domestic term structure model. By resolving Euler's equation with respect to $R^*_{i,t}$, by forward substitutions on $R_{i,t+1}$, and by supposing S is constant in time, we find

$$R^*_{1,t} = \frac{r_t}{1+S} + \frac{1}{1+S}\left[\sum_{i=1}^{\infty}\left(\frac{S}{1+S}\right)^i E_t(r_{t+i})\right] + \frac{1}{1+S}\left[\sum_{i=0}^{\infty}\left(\frac{S}{1+S}\right)^i E_t\left[S^2 V_{t+i}(R_{1,t+i+1}) \times r_a\left(\sum_{1,t+i} + \frac{\mathrm{Cov}_{t+i}(R_{1,t+i+1}, R_{2,t+i+1})}{V_{t+i}(R_{1,t+i+1})}\sum_{2,t+i}\right)\right]\right], \tag{12}$$

$$R^*_{2,t} = \frac{r_t}{1+S} + \frac{1}{1+S}\left[\sum_{i=1}^{\infty}\left(\frac{S}{1+S}\right)^i E_t(r_{t+i})\right] + \frac{1}{1+S}\left[\sum_{i=0}^{\infty}\left(\frac{S}{1+S}\right)^i E_t\left[S^2 V_{t+i}(R_{2,t+i+1}) \times r_a\left(\sum_{2,t+i} + \frac{\mathrm{Cov}_{t+i}(R_{1,t+i+1}, R_{2,t+i+1})}{V_{t+i}(R_{2,t+i+1})}\sum_{1,t+i}\right)\right]\right]. \tag{13}$$

The equilibrium rates of rational expectations include forecasts of all future equilibrium of the two bond markets. Covariance forecasts play an essential role.

Compared to the traditional properties of term structure of interest rates theory, additional properties of our model are given by the presence of the term

$$\frac{\mathrm{Cov}_{t+i}(R_{1,t+i+1}, R_{2,t+i+1})}{V_{t+i}(R_{1,t+i+1})}\sum_{2,t+i}$$

in Eq. (12) and its equivalent in Eq. (13). Based on this, we can find the following three results.

Additional property 1: Impacts of anticipated covariance

Higher anticipated covariance leads to higher interest rates in both two countries; bond demands are lower, because the hedging opportunities are lower as well. This means, in particular, that a contagion scenario between

Table 4. Impacts of Covariance Regime on Long-term Rates

Covariance Regime	Anticipated Evolution of Rates	
$\mathrm{Cov}(R_1,R_2)\nearrow$	$R_1\nearrow,R_2\nearrow$	$R_1\searrow,R_2\searrow$
Contagion or End of crisis	Contagion is amplified	End of crisis is reduced
$\mathrm{Cov}(R_1,R_2)\searrow$	$R_1\rightarrow$ or $\searrow$, $R_2\nearrow$	$R_1\nearrow$, $R_2\rightarrow$ or $\nearrow$
FTQ	Amplified in the country which benefits from FTQ	

the two markets, defined as an increase in raising of both the correlation and the covariance between rates, and with a scenario of future increases in long-term rates, is amplified. A 'belief' that long-term rates will increase in both countries leads immediately (as soon as the portfolios are reoptimized) to higher present current rates.

We use the term 'amplified' to describe the fact that the results of a contagion on interest rates, found in this mechanism of optimal portfolio choice, is to enhances the existing contagion. Conversely, rather than being amplified, the scenario of the end of the crisis, with lower long-term rates in the country ($i = 1, 2$) and a decreasing covariance between markets, is not amplified but on the contrary reduced. The scenario with higher future covariance in the future reduces the possibilities of hedging, limits the bond demand, and leads to rising rates in both countries.

We can also evaluate the nature of 'amplified' in a scenario where covariance declines decreases between two markets. In this case, a flight-to-quality (FTQ) will favor one of the two markets. This scenario brings down rates in both two countries. Therefore, it is amplified only in the market which is supposed to benefit from the flight-to-quality mechanism. These results are summarized in Table 4.

Additional property 2: Impacts of news on public finance

Present and future conditions on bond supply (i.e., bond issue and debt amount) of each country have an impact on the bond market equilibrium of the other country. This impact fundamentally depends on the covariance regime anticipated by investors. For example, bad news about deficits and debt in Greece ($i = 2$) lead to higher interest rates in Greece ($i = 2$) but lower in Germany ($i = 1$) if the covariances are assumed as negative. This mechanism becomes a component of the flight-to-quality process.

The opposite case occurs in a regime of positive covariance, the bad news about Greece's public finances lead long-term rates to rise in both countries. The scenario of contagion here is again amplified.

Additional property 3: Impacts of ECB's QE

The model also throws some light on the impact of unconventional monetary policy on long-term rates in different countries. For example, in a regime of positive covariance, when the ECB buys (QE) or announces that it will buy (OMT and QE) Greek bonds ($i = 2$),[4] this leads to a decline of interest rates in both Greece and Germany ($i = 1$). On the contrary, this leads to higher rates in Germany if the covariances are supposed as negative. In either case, this leads to a lower rate in Greece.

The willingness of the ECB, which aims to drive down long-term rates in the countries in difficulty, may therefore be reduced by the beliefs of investors. Remember that the variances here are exogenous, but the ambition of the ECB with the QE will trigger a joint process of falling rates. To achieve this, it would be right to make balanced purchases of bonds, which means not only in country 2 but also in country 1, in reality, on all the bond markets. For investors, the fact of knowing that purchases are joined and strongly correlated will clearly to increase the level of anticipated covariance, and thus enhance the efficiency of QE.

Finally, note that bond purchases by the ECB have an impact on the volatility premium and equilibrium long-term rates, which could be considered as a partial debt cancellation with an explicit modeling of the credit risk premium. The fact that the ECB puts on its balance sheet a portion of the debt of countries in difficulty means, for investors, a disappearance of the bonds purchased by the ECB, and therefore a lower potential volatility in portfolios. The impact on rates is analogous to a partial debt cancellation along with a disappearance of certain quantity of credit risks.

4. Empirical Modeling

4.1. *Data*

The daily time series used in this paper are from January 2006 to September 2016 (*Source*: DataStream). As in many related literature, we use the Return Yield ($R_{i,t}$) of 10-year government bonds[5] of seven major countries in

[4]We consider Greece as an emblematic case of the countries in difficulty, even if since March 2015 this country is not eligible for purchases from the ECB (Sec. 2)

[5]Most of the recent papers (Ehrmann and Fratzscher (2017), Silvapulle *et al.* (2016), Costantini *et al.* (2014), Gómez-Puig and Sosvilla-Rivero (2016)) use 10-year sovereign bond yields as benchmark. However, De Santis and Stein (2016) propose to use 5-year

the European Monetary Union including France, Germany, Italy, Portugal, Spain, Ireland, and Greece; Vstoxx index (global factor); 3-month AAA Bond Rate (who represents the risk-free rate); as well as 5-year Credit Default Swaps (indicator of default risks).[6]

In the dynamics of interest rates, there exists obviously different phases. By applying the unit root test proposed by Lee and Strazicich (2003) on the daily Return Index of Greece, we are able to separate the time series into three sub-periods: pre-crisis (2006/01/01 to 2009/12/01), crisis (2009/12/01 to 2012/08/06), and post-OMT (2012/08/06 to 2016/09/09). We should notice that the two break dates 2009/12/01 and 2012/08/06 are very close to respectively the Downgrading of Greece sovereign bond and the Implementation of Outright Monetary Transaction.[7]

4.2. *Modeling choice*

We pay attention to Eqs. (7) and (8) of the theoretical model. It describes expected market equilibrium returns. By introducing a time index on the risk-free rates and both variances and covariances of yields, the equilibrium relation for country i is written as

$$\mu^*_{i,t} = r_t + \sigma^2_{i,t} r_a \left(\sum_{i,t} + \frac{\sigma_{ij,t}}{\sigma^2_{i,t}} \sum_{j,t} \right), \tag{14}$$

with

$$\mu_{i,t} = \frac{E_t(P_{i,t+1}) - P_{i,t}}{P_{i,t}}. \tag{15}$$

This relation assumes that the bond price $P_{i,t}$, or the associated yield $R_{i,t}$, is daily adjusted so that the expected return $\mu_{i,t}$ given the anticipated future price $E_t(P_{i,t+1})$ is consistent with the risk-free rate and the equilibrium risk premium. Since the absolute risk aversion coefficient (r_a) and the net bond supply ($\Sigma_{i,t}$, $\Sigma_{j,t}$) are not directly observable, the equilibrium relation can be considered as a linear relation between the expected yield ($\mu_{i,t}$),

sovereign bond yield as a benchmark for the reason that aggregate demand is typically affected by long-term interest rates, and therefore the correlation between long-term sovereign yields and the risk-free rate is a key economically relevant question.

[6]The market for CDS spreads used to measure the price of the credit risk is more liquid at 5-year maturity (De Santis and Stein (2016)).

[7]In a previous version of this paper, by using the Zivot and Andrews (2002) test, twice we have obtained very similar results.

the risk-free rate (r_t), the variance ($\sigma^2_{i,t}$), and covariance ($\sigma^2_{ij,t}$) anticipated one-step-ahead.

To estimate this equilibrium relation from Eqs. (7) and (8), it is necessary to do it, as for the estimation of CAPM models by replacing the expected returns by the observed daily returns in the sample. If the anticipations of investors especially on tomorrow's prices are rational, the difference between the two series should be a white noise. If these anticipations are not rational, there exists some inconvenience.

We use rather actuarial yields $R_{i,t}$, which also reflects the necessary adjustment on prices $P_{i,t}$ in order to respect the equilibrium relation. Due to the non-stationarity of actuarial rate series, finally the first-differenced actuarial rates are explained by the first-differenced risk-free rate, first-differenced variances and covariance, and two first-differenced control variables presented before, Vstoxx and CDS.

The second concern for this modelling is the definitions and estimations of variables and covariances anticipated by investors. A simple solution consists in estimating and evaluating the impact of the second-order moments on the yield with a single step in the framework of a bivariate GARCH-in-mean model. We prefer to perform the estimations in two steps rather than a bivariate GARCH-in-mean model, because this auxiliary model is more manipulable and it provides actual out-of-sample risk predictions.

4.3. *Model and estimation*

In this empirical approach, we try to verify the results found in the theoretical model by applying two different methods: a two-step bivariate GARCH model and a two-step[8] rolling linear regression model.

4.3.1. *Two-step GARCH model*

In this two-step GARCH model, the first step aims to forecast conditional variances and covariances which can be described as investors' anticipations of second-order moments in our theoretical model. In the second step, estimations will be performed by using the forecast values of both variances

[8]As has already been discussed in many literature, especially by Murphy and Topel (2002), this two-step procedure fails to account for the fact that imputed repressors are measured with sampling error, so hypothesis tests based on the estimated covariance matrix of the second-step estimator are biased, even in large sample. However, we consider in our case that this sampling error is under control with a limited bias.

and covariances from the first step, in order to understand the role of portfolio effects in the formation of sovereign bond yields.

Step 1: Investors' anticipations are simulated by using rolling window of classic bivariate DCC(1,1)-GARCH(1,1) model proposed by Engle (2002) and widely applied by for example Jones and Olson (2013) and Celık (2012).

$$H_t = D_t R_t D_t, \quad \text{where} \quad D_t = \text{Diag}(\sqrt{h_{i,t}}), \tag{16}$$

where R_t is a 2×2 matrix of time-varying correlations. D_t is a 2×2 diagonal matrix of time-varying standard deviations of residual returns. The variances are obtained with univariate GARCH(1,1) processes. Specifically,

$$h_t = c + a\varepsilon_{t-1}^2 + bh_{t-1}. \tag{17}$$

One single sample of 500 days will give us a one-step-ahead prediction of conditional variance and covariance.[9] By using a rolling window of 500 days, we obtain some of one-step-ahead forecast values which can be considered as investors' anticipations of conditional variances and covariances.

Step 2: In this step, we try to determine the role of portfolio effects in the formation of sovereign bond yields by applying a bivariate GARCH Model. We have two countries in each estimation.[10] For $i = 1$ and 2, the mean equations are presented as follows:

$$\begin{aligned} \Delta R_{i,t} = \beta_{0,i} + \beta_{1,i}\Delta E_t(V_{i,t+1}) + \beta_{2,i}\Delta E_t(\text{Cov}_{ij,t+1}) \\ + \beta_{3,i}\Delta V\text{stoxx}_t + \beta_{4,i}\Delta r_t + \beta_{5,i}\Delta\text{CDS}_{i,t} + \varepsilon_{i,t}. \end{aligned} \tag{18}$$

with $R_{i,t}$ actuarial rate (Yield to maturity) of each bond, $E_t(V_{i,t+1})$ anticipated variance, $E_t(\text{Cov}_{ij,t+1})$ anticipated covariance,[11] $V\text{stoxx}_t$ Vstoxx Index, r_t 3-month AAA Government Bond Rate. In accordance with the canonical contagion approach of Pesaran and Pick (2007), Eq. (16) tries to explain bond yields with global and specific factors. $V\text{stoxx}_t$ denotes the implied volatility risks and also a global factor as discussed by Afonso *et al.* (2012), Arghyrou and Kontonikas (2012), and Metiu (2012). The specific factors are the credit default swaps, $\text{CDS}_{i,t}$ which denotes credit

[9]For example, a sample from t to $t + 500$ will be able to give a forecasting for $t + 501$.

[10]In order to avoid the non-stationary problem of the series, all the variables used in this model are first differenced. It is also the same case for the first step.

[11]Both anticipated variance and covariance simulate the investors' expectations as described in our theoretical model. We use a DCC-GARCH model with a rolling window of 500 daily data to forecast these two terms using one-step-ahead method.

default risks, and both anticipated variances $E_t(V_{i,t+1})$ and anticipated covariances $E_t(\mathrm{Cov}_{ij,t+1})$ denote portfolio effects described in our theoretical model.

Under the hypothesis of conditional normal distribution of disturbances, the parameters of the model are estimated by the method of maximum likelihood. The log likelihood function which should be optimized is given as follows:

$$L_T(\theta) = -\frac{1}{2}\sum_{t=1}^{T}[\ln[\det(H_t(\theta))] + \varepsilon_t(\theta)' H_t(\theta)^{-1}\varepsilon_t(\theta)], \tag{19}$$

with

$$H_t = V(\epsilon_t/I_{t-1}) = \begin{bmatrix} h_{11,t} & h_{12,t} \\ h_{21,t} & h_{22,t} \end{bmatrix} \quad \text{and} \quad \varepsilon_t = \begin{bmatrix} \varepsilon_{1,t} \\ \varepsilon_{2,t} \end{bmatrix}.$$

The matrix of variance–covariance is based on a diagonal VECH specification. Therefore, the conditional variance and covariance are expressed by

$$h_{ii,t} = c_{ii} + a_{ii}\varepsilon_{i,t-1}^2 + b_{ii}h_{ii,t-1}, \tag{20}$$

$$h_{ij,t} = c_{ij} + a_{ij}\varepsilon_{i,t-1}\varepsilon_{j,t-1} + b_{ij}h_{ij,t-1}, \tag{21}$$

where c_{ij}, a_{ij}, and b_{ij} are parameters and ε_{t-1} is the vector of errors from the previous period. This specification supposes that the current conditional variances and covariances are determined by their own past and past shocks. Precisely, with algorithm Simplex and some guessing values, we stop the calculation at the fifteenth iteration. Next, with the values obtained from this pre calculation, we use the method BHHH to estimate the GARCH model.

4.3.2. *Two-step rolling linear regression*

In this part, in order to estimate the evolution of amplifying factor discussed in section above, we perform a rolling linear regression model.

Step 1: It is exactly the same method here to generate a set of forecast conditional variances and covariances as performed in Step 1 in Sec. 4.3.1. Therefore, we obtain a set of one-step-ahead forecast conditional variances and covariances which can be considered as investors' anticipations of these second-order moments.

Step 2: The linear model is same as the mean equation (18) presented above in the GARCH framework. For easy reading, we rewrite it here:

$$\Delta R_{i,t} = \beta_{0,i} + \beta_{1,i}\Delta E_t(V_{i,t+1}) + \beta_{2,i}\Delta E_t(\mathrm{Cov}_{ij,t+1}) + \beta_{3,i}\Delta V\mathrm{stoxx}_t + \beta_{4,i}\Delta r_t + \beta_{5,i}\Delta \mathrm{CDS}_{i,t} + \varepsilon_{i,t}.$$

To be more specific, in accordance with the forecasting of conditional variance and covariance with DCC-GARCH model, the rolling window here is also 500 days. Each estimation of this linear model gives us several fitted coefficients, thus, the rolling window generates the dynamics of fitted coefficients, which can be presented as sensibilities to the return yields.

4.4. *Principals of correlation test*

In this section, we test the hypotheses of structural changes of correlation coefficients across the pre-QE and post-QE periods. As pointed out by Forbes and Rigobon (2002), the estimation of the correlation coefficient is biased because of the existence of heteroscedasticity in the return of bond. More specifically, compared to the estimation over a stable period, the correlation coefficients are overestimated over a turmoil period. In our study, we consider the pre-QE period as the turmoil period and post-QE as the stable period. Because the correlations are conditional and dynamic in our model, we need to modify the adjustment formula of correlation coefficient proposed by Forbes and Rigobon into the following formula:

$$\rho^*_{ij,p} = \frac{\rho_{ij,p}}{\sqrt{1 + \delta(1 - \rho^2_{ij,p})}}, \tag{22}$$

where $\delta = \frac{h^{pre}}{g^{post}} - 1$ is the relative increase in the variance of the source country across pre-QE period and post-QE period. $\rho_{i,p}$ is the average of dynamic conditional correlations over period p, where $p =$ (pre, post), while *pre* and *post* indicate the pre-QE period and post-QE period. With the adjusted correlation coefficients, we apply the test proposed by Collins and Biekpe (2003) to detect the existence of structural breaks across pre-QE period and post-QE period.

The Student test is:

$$\begin{cases} H_0: \rho^*_{\mathrm{post}} = \rho^*_{\mathrm{pre}} \\ H_1: \rho^*_{\mathrm{post}} > \rho^*_{\mathrm{pre}} \end{cases},$$

where ρ^*_{post} is the adjusted correlation coefficient over post-QE period and ρ^*_{pre} is the adjusted correlation coefficient over pre-QE period. The statistic of the Student test applied by Collins and Biekpe is

$$t = (\rho^*_{\text{post}} - \rho^*_{\text{pre}})\sqrt{\frac{n_{\text{post}} + n_{\text{pre}} - 4}{1 - (\rho^*_{\text{post}} - \rho^*_{\text{pre}})^2}}, \tag{23}$$

where $t \sim T_{n_{\text{post}}+n_{\text{pre}}-4}$.

If we accept H_1, it means that the correlation coefficient across two periods has increased significantly over the post-QE period, which is evidence of the impact of QE.

Finally, note that the test proposed here refers to residues, in other words, the non-fundamental components of an explanatory model. In accordance with the recommendations of Pesaran and Pick (2007), we have global variables that explain both countries' (Vstoxx, r, covariance) and country-specific variables for each bond market (variance, CDS).

4.5. *Sensitivity of spread to CDS*

It is logical to expect that the ECB's massive purchases of sovereign bonds will, *ceteris paribus*, raise the prices of bonds and, thus, reduce the credit risk premiums on bond yields and the spreads of bond yields. Under this assumption, interest rate spreads for Germany should be less sensitive to changes in premiums paid on sovereign CDSs. This represents market appreciation on credit risks. We test this hypothesis by estimating the following model over different sub-periods:

$$\text{Spread}_{i,t} = \beta_{0,i} + \beta_{1,i} CDS_{i,t} + \epsilon_{i,t}, \tag{24}$$

with spread$_{i,t}$: spread of country i compared to Germany; CDS$_{i,t}$ premiums paid on CDS.[12] The model will be estimated over a pre-QE period and a post-QE period.

[12]The CDS premium is purged of the effects related to the overall uncertainty variable Vstoxx as in De Santis and Stein (2016).

5. Empirical Results

5.1. *Dynamics of price and yields and patterns of anticipated variances and covariances*

The patterns of variance and covariance evolutions anticipated by investors (Appendices B and C) are inextricably related to the dynamics of sovereign bond prices and the associated actuarial rates (Figs. 1 and 2). Recall that the important phases of the market dynamics have implications in terms of covariances and volatility.

The first bond price collapse took place on October 16, 2009, accompanying the beginning of the fiscal crisis in Greece. Only the Greek obligations are affected (Figs. 1 and 2). The downgrade of Greece's debt by Moody's on December 8, 2009, amplified the collapse of the Greek bond market. The first effects of the contagion occurred in March 2010 in the Irish, Spanish, and Portuguese markets. In contrast, the German and French markets kept improving. According to our estimations, the first increase in anticipated volatility occurred in March 2010, which affected all seven bond markets analyzed.

The contagion reached a historical level at the end of 2010, where, for the first time, the bond markets of seven countries began suffering significantly, and showed simultaneous downward movements (Fig. 1). The short-term downward trend for the German and French markets began to increase again from March 2011 in a low volatility context. In fact, in addition to a decrease in anticipated volatility in these two markets, our estimations show a pronounced decrease in the covariances between the German, French, and other markets. Clearly, the beginning of the flight-to-quality phenomenon favors the two countries considered to be the healthiest, because they represent a lower credit risk. This phase is the first nodal point in the bond market trajectory during the sovereign debt crisis. The second nodal point appears in 2011, on December 8, when the ECB announced the implementation of an exceptional three-year refinancing programme for Euro Zone banks (LTRO), and Mario Draghi implied that the ECB would not make massive purchases of sovereign bonds. Then, December 8, 2011, represents a peak of anticipated volatility for the German and French markets. Since this date, Italy, Spain, and Ireland have joined Germany and France in a stable phase in terms of obligation yields. For the former three countries, the anticipated covariances with Germany and France step out of their lowest level, and gradually rebound. This signified the end of the crisis. Then, Portugal joined this group in early 2012. It was not until July 26, 2012, when Mario Draghi gave the "whatever it takes speech" and announced the implementation of the OMT in the Euro Zone, that Greece stepped into the new post-crisis phase.

The anticipated variances of the 10-year bond yield variations show strong disparities in the observed average levels, ranging from 0.04 for Germany to 2.5 for Greece. The evolution patterns over time present more similarities. In all seven markets, the volatility anticipated by the investors began to rise from the beginning of 2010. However, the profiles are different in the peripheral countries of the Euro Zone, where the volatility rose significantly from early 2010, reaching a peak at the end of 2011. The date of this volatility peak is December 8, 2011, and is associated with the decision by the ECB to grant 3-year special financing to banks in the Euro Zone (LTRO). This event, which is favorable for the resolution of the sovereign debt crisis, was counterbalanced by Mario Draghi claiming that the ECB did not intend to carry out massive purchases of sovereign bonds. Therefore, December 8, 2011, is a break point in the history of the interest rate trajectory in the Euro Zone.

5.2. *Two-step GARCH results*

The results of 21 bivariate model estimations are shown in Tables D.1–D.7. With regard to the one-step-ahead forecasts of variances and covariances, the results quite clearly show that covariances are playing a more significant and systematic role in the dynamics of sovereign rates. Most of the estimated parameters have the expected positive signs. In general, the effects are more present in the German and French markets than they are in the Euro Zone peripheral markets. The parameters associated with the covariance often show a U-shape pattern, with lower values over the crisis period. For example, we observe the following sequence. The impacts of the Germany–Portugal covariance on German yields are 1.62 (pre-crisis), 0.48 (crisis), and 1.86 (post-OMT), and 0.90 (crisis) and 4.84 (post-OMT) for the impacts of the France–Ireland covariance on French yields. In general, we find that in terms of covariance impacts on the evolution of sovereign bond yields, the French yields are twice as sensitive as the German yields. The impacts of the one-step-ahead forecasts of variances are higher at the end of the sample (i.e., over the post-OMT period), particularly in the German and French markets. The sensitivity of the first-differenced yield to variance variation is 2.97 for Germany (Germany–France in Table D.1) and 1.82 for France (France–Italy in Table D.3). Note that the same coefficients may vary widely from one estimation to another, depending on the selected pairs and, therefore, depend on the covariances included in the regression model.

The variable Vstoxx reflects an overall uncertainty that should impact the yields of risky assets in general, as well as sovereign bonds. This mechanism has been well supported by our estimates, with generally positive coefficients for this variable. The obtained coefficients are again higher for Germany (0.013), France (0.021), and Ireland (0.014). The risk-free rate also shows the expected positive sign. Throughout the overall period, the estimated coefficients range from 0.12 to 0.20 for Germany, France, and Greece. This coefficient is never significant for Ireland. In terms of the influence of the CDS (cleaned by Vstoxx), we obtain similar results to those obtained for the covariances. The fitted coefficients are higher and more significant for Germany and France, with slightly higher values over post-OMT period. The coefficients of the CDS are also higher in the Ireland bond market, according to the regression results. Finally, we note that the parameters of the variance–covariance H_t of the VECH model are almost always significant at the 5% level, with the usual positive signs.

5.3. *Two-step rolling regression results*

Next, we examine the patterns of coefficient evolutions associated with variances and covariances obtained from the 500-day rolling window regressions. The results are given in Appendix E. For each country, the curve shows the estimated coefficient ($\hat{\beta}_{1,i}$) associated with changes in the variances described in equation (18), which explains the first-differenced yields. There are as many coefficients as estimated pairs, that is, six for each country. As emphasized above, the estimated coefficients ($\hat{\beta}_{1,i}$) may be affected by the selected pairs and, therefore, by the selected covariances in Eq. (18). For each country, the graphic also shows rolling estimates of the coefficients ($\hat{\beta}_{2,i}$) associated with different variations of covariances. Again, there are as many coefficients as there are pairs of covariances. Note that all coefficient estimates ($\hat{\beta}_{1,i}$ and $\hat{\beta}_{2,i}$) are modulated by considering the uncertainty of the estimates (i.e., the estimated standard deviation ($\hat{\sigma}_{\hat{\beta}_i}$)). Each graphic reports the central value of the estimate, a lower bond ($\hat{\beta}_i - 1.96\hat{\sigma}_{\hat{\beta}_i}$), and an upper bond ($\hat{\beta}_i + 1.96\hat{\sigma}_{\hat{\beta}_i}$) for the estimate. A coefficient β_i is considered significant at the 5% level if neither the lower nor the higher bonds of the estimate cross zero ($\hat{\beta}_i = 0$).

In order to qualify the different phases of our sample between pre-crisis, crisis, and post-OMT periods, we adopt the following principle. A coefficient $\hat{\beta}_i$ is considered specific to a particular phase if the majority of dates included in the estimations (i.e., more than 250 days) are within this range. Using this principle, the phases associated with the coefficients $\hat{\beta}$ correspond to the historical ranges with a lag of 251 days, which, in practice, corresponds to a lag of 11 months. Thus, from the point of view of the coefficients $\hat{\beta}$ associated with the covariances and variances anticipated by investors, the crisis period begins on November 1, 2010 and the post-OMT period begins on August 4, 2013.

More specifically, with regard to coefficients $\hat{\beta}_2$ associated with the covariances, these rolling windows make it possible to give a much more precise pattern of estimates than in the case of the sub-period estimations (Tables D.1–D.7), where a U-shape emerged, especially for Germany and France.

We highlight the following results. The pattern of coefficients $\hat{\beta}_2$ with a U-shape is confirmed globally for Germany and France. To a lesser extent, this is also true of Portugal (covariances with Italy, France, and Spain) and Spain (covariances with Germany, Ireland, and France). In some cases, the U-shape curve during the crisis period is accompanied by the non-significance of the coefficient β, which is sometimes even negative. Italy, Ireland, and Greece show atypical profiles, where bond yields become sensitive to covariances from the beginning of the post-OMT period only: the covariances of Italy with Germany, Ireland, and France; the covariances of Ireland with Italy, Spain, and France; and the covariance of Greece with Ireland. Again, the negative impacts of the covariances on the long-term rates need to be highlighted: the covariance between Italy and Portugal on Italian rates, and the covariance between Greece and Germany on the Greek rates.

Overall, these results show that bond portfolio mechanisms have played a clear role between Germany, France, Portugal, and Spain during the pre-crisis period, before becoming less important, or disappearing during the crisis, and reappearing in the post-OMT period. For the second group of countries, Italy, Ireland, and to a lesser extent, Greece, the portfolio mechanisms only appear in the post-OMT phase.

Furthermore, it is possible to quantify the effects of the first-differenced anticipated covariance on the formation of interest rates. For illustrative purposes, we evaluate the contribution of the decrease in bond yield covariances between Germany and France and other European countries on

Table 5. Example of Covariance Effects on German Market

Pair with	Cumulative ΔCov	$\hat{\beta}_2$ Mean	Cumulative Effects (%)
Italy	−0.05	7	−0.35
Portugal	−0.06	2.5	−0.15
Spain	−0.06	7	−0.42
Ireland	−0.06	2.5	−0.15
Greece	−0.12	2	−0.24
			Total effects: −1.31 (%)

Table 6. Example of Covariance Effects on French Market

Pair with	Cumulative ΔCov	$\hat{\beta}_2$ Mean	Cumulative Effects (%)
Italy	−0.06	15	−0.90
Portugal	−0.06	10	−0.60
Spain	−0.06	13	−0.78
Ireland	−0.08	5	−0.40
Greece	−0.07	7	−0.49
			Total effects: −2.81 (%)

the trajectory of German and French rates during the period of the sovereign debt crisis. Tables 5 and 6 below summarize the cumulative effects on the German and French rates, as shown in the graphics in Appendix F, with the means of the coefficients $\hat{\beta}_2$ used in the first phase of the estimations.

The cumulative declines in the covariance between the German and French yields with those of the other five countries are very similar. On the other hand, the sensitivity of the yields to covariances is significantly higher in the French market, where the coefficients vary between 5 (covariance with Ireland) and 15 (covariance with Italy), with most being twice as big as the coefficients $\hat{\beta}_2$ associated with the German yields.

Overall, being aware of the transitory nature of the covariance effects on the yields due to the estimation of the model in variation, we estimate that the decrease in covariances at the beginning of the crisis period (beginning of 2011) potentially contributed to the decreases in French and German yields of 131 and 281 bps, respectively. Finally, we find some evidence supporting the mechanism of an amplified flight-to-quality process, led by anticipated covariances and portfolio effects, as presented in Table 4.

We emphasize that, in contrast to the post-OMT period, the phase beginning November 3, 2015 with the implementation of the QE by the

Table 7. Results of Correlation Structural Break Tests *à la* Forbes and Rigobon

Country Pair	*t*-stat	Sig.	Country Pair	*t*-stat	Sig.
Germany–France	−1.250	0.211	France–Germany	−1.207	0.227
Germany–Italy	0.089	0.928	Italy–Germany	0.118	0.905
Germany–Portugal	0.028	0.977	Portugal–Germany	0.028	0.977
Germany–Spain	−0.889	0.373	Spain–Germany	−0.923	0.355
Germany–Ireland	0.004	0.996	Ireland–Germany	0.008	0.993
Germany–Greece	−0.083	0.933	Greece–Germany	0.168	0.866
France–Italy	−0.325	0.744	Italy–France	−0.505	0.613
France–Portugal	**−2.003**	**0.045**	Portugal–France	**−2.005**	**0.045**
France–Spain	−1.126	0.260	Spain–France	−1.266	0.205
France–Ireland	0.406	0.684	Ireland–France	0.814	0.415
France–Greece	−0.136	0.891	Greece–France	−0.202	0.839
Italy–Portugal	−0.589	0.555	Portugal–Italy	−0.451	0.651
Italy–Spain	**−1.777**	**0.075**	Spain–Italy	−1.434	0.151
Italy–Ireland	0.054	0.956	Ireland–Italy	0.073	0.941
Italy–Greece	1.425	0.154	Greece–Italy	1.421	0.155
Portugal–Spain	−0.375	0.707	Spain–Portugal	−0.393	0.694
Portugal–Ireland	0.028	0.977	Ireland–Portugal	0.058	0.953
Portugal–Greece	**−1.902**	**0.057**	Greece–Portugal	**−2.308**	**0.021**
Spain–Ireland	0.595	0.551	Ireland–Spain	1.095	0.273
Spain–Greece	−0.857	0.391	Greece–Spain	−0.977	0.328
Ireland–Greece	0.272	0.785	Greece–Ireland	0.186	0.852

ECB is associated with a sensitive increase in the German and French yields and those of the other five countries. In the same period, the sensitivity of bond yields to the covariances rises as well. We deduce that the portfolio effects reduce the process of decreases in German and French bond yields. This time, we illustrate a process of decreasing yields and exiting the crisis, reducing the covariance and portfolio effects, as presented in Table 4.

Finally, we examine the effects of anticipated variances on the yield variations, because they are provided by the two-step rolling linear regression estimations. With the exception of France and Greece, it is always possible to identify at least a sub-period where the coefficient $\hat{\beta}_1$ is significantly different from zero and positive. Unlike the results obtained on the covariances, the periods with significant coefficients generally do not cover the three phases of pre-crisis, crisis, and post-OMT. In fact, the $\hat{\beta}_1$ coefficients can only be significant in an occasional way over a short period.

As in the case of Germany, several estimations agree on a coefficient $\hat{\beta}_1$ being close to 5 over a short period of one year, beginning from mid-2015. A similar result is obtained for Ireland with a coefficient close to 8. For Italy

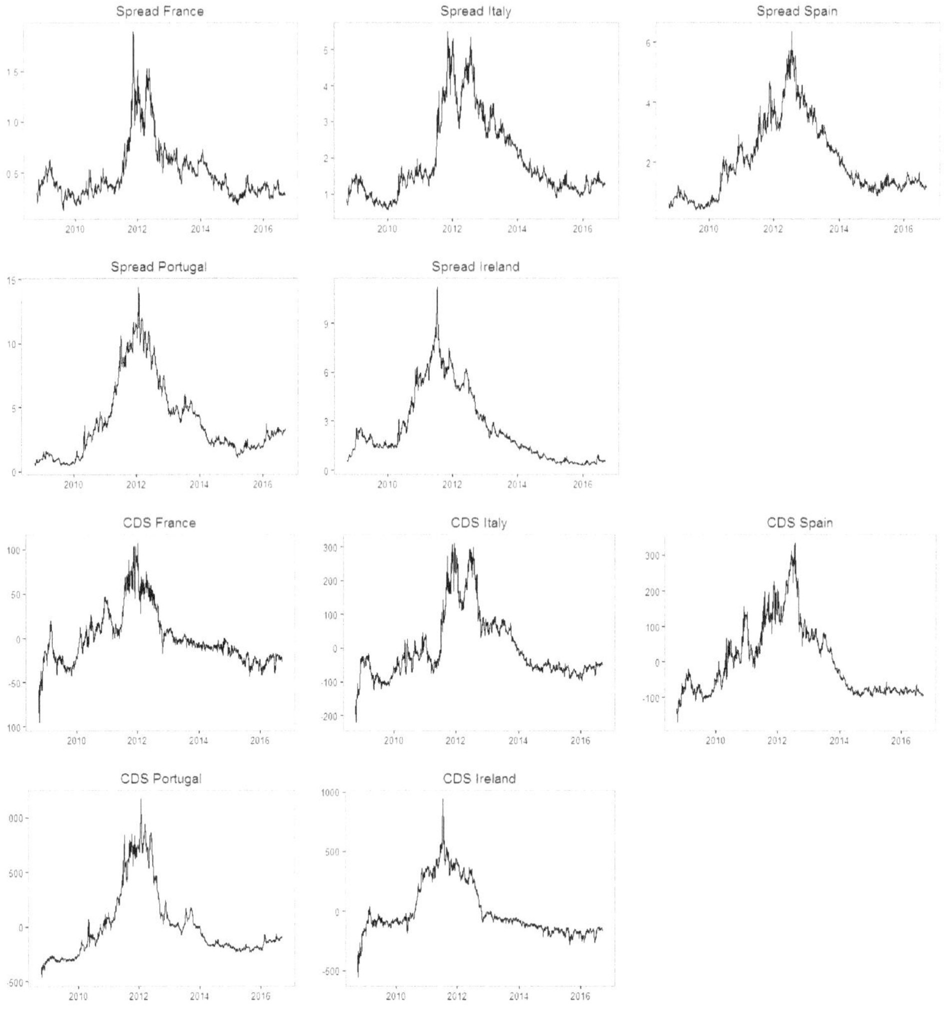

Figure 3. CDSs and Spreads

and Portugal, the coefficients are also significant from mid-2015, with some values close to 1 and 0.5, respectively. Finally, for Spain, there is a U-shape pattern for the coefficient $\hat{\beta}_1$, with the following values: close to 3 till 2012, 0 till mid-2015, and 1 afterward.

5.4. *Higher correlations between yields since APP?*

The correlations between the residuals of the first-differenced bond yields are reported in Appendix F. These clearly show that, beginning in March 2015, there is a very strong rebound in dynamic conditional correlations estimated

Table 8. Sensitivities of Spreads to CDSs Over Different Periods

Regression model[a]: $\text{Spread}_{i,t} = \beta_{0,i} + \beta_{1,i}\text{CDS}_{i,t} + \epsilon_{i,t}$

Country	Period	$\bar{R}^2$	β_1	t-stat	Sig.
France	Full sample	0.6112	0.0071	57.0186	0.0000
	Before QE	0.5882	0.0073	48.9736	0.0000
	During QE	0.3471	−0.0049	−14.4181	0.0000
Italy	Full sample	0.9237	0.0109	158.2638	0.0000
	Before QE	0.9186	0.0109	137.6247	0.0000
	During QE	0.2588	0.0059	11.6981	0.0000
Spain	Full sample	0.8528	0.0115	109.4617	0.0000
	Before QE	0.8490	0.0120	97.1619	0.0000
	During QE	0.0842	0.0067	6.0651	0.0000
Portugal	Full sample	0.9560	0.0093	212.1261	0.0000
	Before QE	0.9543	0.0093	187.3026	0.0000
	During QE	0.8682	0.0133	50.6342	0.0000
Ireland	Full sample	0.9439	0.0096	186.6597	0.0000
	Before QE	0.9441	0.0093	168.3740	0.0000
	During QE	0.0101	−0.0004	−2.2300	0.0263

Note: [a]Spreads are calculated by the difference between the 10-year government bond yield of the country studied and that of Germany. Variable CDS_t takes residual values ($\hat{u}_{i,t}$) from following auxiliary regression: $\text{CDS}_{i,t} = \beta_{0,i} + \beta_{1,i}V\text{stoxx} + u_{i,t}$

by the bivariate GARCH model. Therefore, this is where the 'visible hand' of the APP appears. However, Table 7, which reports the statistics of the T-test, *à la* Forbes and Rigobon, shows that it is not possible to conclude that all correlations are higher after the APP, as a general result. This is mainly because, on average, the correlations were already high before the implementation of QE.

5.5. *Lower sensitivity of spread to CDS since APP?*

Figure 3 reproduce the sovereign bond spreads with Germany and the CDSs for the period 2008–2016, suggesting a strong correlation between spreads and CDSs. Table 8 shows the results of bond spread regressions on the CDSs. They clearly show that the implementation of QE in March 2015 greatly reduced the spread sensitivity to the CDS, and thus artificially crushed the credit risk premiums weighing on bond yields.

The spread sensitivity to the CDS decreases by half in Italy and Spain, and becomes negative for France, and almost null for Ireland. Only Portugal, where there is no change in the sensitivity to credit risk, is an exception to the rule.

6. Conclusion

This study analyzes the impact of the ECB's APP on the European bond market equilibrium and, particularly, on its contribution to the decline in sovereign rates. Therefore, we use a conceptual framework to understand the formation of long-term interest rates over the pre-crisis and post-crisis periods with the implementation of the ECB's QE. We adopt the portfolio theory framework to examine the specific role of short-term risks, as perceived by investors, in the formation of sovereign bond yields. Our study is different to most existing works, which focus on the impact of credit risk on changes in CDS premiums, the formation of interest rates, the measurement of the contagion, and the flight-to-quality between bond markets (De Santis and Stein (2016); Metiu (2012); Afonso *et al.* (2012); Arghyrou and Kontonikas (2012); Pesaran and Pick (2007); Krishnamurthy and Vissing-Jorgensen (2011); Silvapulle *et al.* (2016)).

The theoretical model proposes a portfolio framework with three assets: a risk-free monetary rate and two sovereign bonds, including default risks and volatility risks, when the holding period is less than the maturity of the bond. The market equilibrium of each country results from the global demand for obligations and the supply of bonds (i.e., the available bond stock). Demand is given by the optimal portfolio choices and the purchase programmes by the ECB in the context of QE. Bond purchases by the ECB actually reduce the net bond supply, and limit the volatility of risks in the international monetary and bond portfolios. The anticipated variances and covariances play a key role in the future trajectories of long-term equilibrium sovereign bond rates.

In particular, the anticipated covariances constitute a channel that is likely able to amplify the mechanisms of contagion and the flight-to-quality between markets. A downgrade of public finance in a country leading to new bond issues not only raises rates in this country but also in neighboring countries if the anticipated covariances are positive (amplified contagion). In contrast, bad news on public finances decreases the rates in neighboring countries if the anticipated covariances are negative (amplified flight-to-quality). Our theoretical model also suggests that the bond purchase programmes of the ECB in the QE framework should not be targeted to a single market, but should rather target several diversified markets in order to trigger a joint decreasing rate process.

The empirical approach is based on daily data for the period January 2006 to September 2016 and is integrated in the first step of a bivariate DCC-GARCH model. Then, to generate the series, we estimate it using 500-day rolling windows in order to simulate the variances and covariances anticipated by investors. In the second step, bivariate GARCH models with a VECH specification for the variance–covariance matrix are proposed and estimations are performed on 21 country pairs over both the whole period October 2008 to September 2016, and three sub-periods qualified as pre-crisis, crisis, and post-OMT. All variables used in the models are first-differenced variables. The mean equation explains the bond yields by the variances and covariances anticipated by investors, the short-term interest rate of Euro Zone issuers rated AAA, the VSTOXX index, and the premium paid on CDS as an essential determinant of the default risk premium required on sovereign bonds. In the third step, a linear version of this model, without ARCH effects, is estimated using 500-day rolling windows to analyze and identify possible dynamics of the coefficients by taking into account the matrix of variance–covariance anticipated by investors.

The estimates over the whole period, sub-periods, and, more importantly, those using rolling windows show that bond markets do not evolve solely as a result of changes in default risks and CDS premiums. The bond yields of the seven European countries are also sensitive to the volatility risks of covariances implied in bond portfolios. All the results can be summarized as follows:

(i) German and French bond yields are more sensitive to the volatility risks of covariances than those of peripheral countries.
(ii) The covariance effects are stronger than those of variances that are often present in an occasional way.
(iii) The decrease in covariance between the German and French markets at the beginning of the crisis period significantly reduced the risk premiums required by investors and contributed to the decrease in yields by 131 bps for Germany and 281 bps for France.
(iv) Overall, the short-term risk premium intensity on portfolios and bond yields declines sharply during the crisis, and reappear later over the post-OMT and post-QE periods. Everything happens as if the mechanism of international bond portfolio allocation ceased during the sovereign debt crisis and then reappeared.

These results are consistent with those of other recent studies (De Santis and Stein (2016), Ehrmann and Fratzscher (2017)), highlighting the hypothesis of possible fragmentation on the European bond markets during the crisis.

Note too that the implementation of the ECB's QE on actual purchases from March 2015 contributed to a process of returning to normal or defragmenting the bond markets. According to our evaluations, this defragmentation was initiated before the implementation of the QE, before being strengthened by the APP. Finally, according to the test of *à la* Forbes and Rigobon (2002), it seems difficult to affirm that QE programmes have had a significant increase on correlations between bond markets, simply because the correlations were already high before the implementation of QE. The complementary tests of the regression of the CDS on spreads show that the QE significantly reduced their sensitivity to credit risk premiums.

By construction, our dynamic econometric model, estimated in first difference, does not allow us to propose an absolute quantification of the QE's impact on the bond rates of each country. However, the combination of results obtained from econometric estimates, particularly the rolling model, the conditional correlation test (*à la* Forbes and Rigobon), and the CDS spread sensitivity tests, suggest that the impact of QE on bond market equilibrium is not as strong as expected. Therefore, the cessation of QE from 2019 would not, from this point of view, lead to a significant increase in interest rates.

References

Afonso, A., Arghyrou, M., and Kontonikas, A. (2012). The determinants of sovereign bond yield spreads in the emu. ISEG Economics Working Paper.

Arghyrou, M. G. and Kontonikas, A. (2012). The emu sovereign-debt crisis: Fundamentals, expectations and contagion. *J. Inte. Fin. Markets, Institut. Money*, 22(4), pp. 658–677.

Artus, P. (1987). Structure par terme des taux d'intérêt: Théorie et estimation dans le cas français. *Cahiers économiques et monétaires*, 27, pp. 5–47.

Breedon, F., Chadha, J. S., and Waters, A. (2012). The financial market impact of UK quantitative easing. *Oxford Rev. Econom. Policy*, 28(4), pp. 702–728.

Celık, S. (2012). The more contagion effect on emerging markets: The evidence of dcc-garch model. *Econom. Modell.*, 29(5), pp. 1946–1959.

Christensen, J. H. and Rudebusch, G. D. (2012). The response of interest rates to US and UK quantitative easing. *The Econom. J.*, 122(564), pp. F385–F414.

Claeys, G., Leandro, Á., Mandra, A. *et al.* (2015). European central bank quantitative easing: The detailed manual. *Bruegel Policy Contribution*, 2.

Collins, D. and Biekpe, N. (2003). Contagion: A fear for african equity markets? *J. Econom. Business*, 55(3), pp. 285–297.

Costantini, M., Fragetta, M., and Melina, G. (2014). Determinants of sovereign bond yield spreads in the emu: An optimal currency area perspective. *Eur. Econom. Rev.*, 70, pp. 337–349.

De Santis, R. and Stein, M. (2016). Correlation changes between the risk-free rate and sovereign yields of euro area countries. Technical report.

De Santis, R. A. (2016). Impact of the asset purchase programme on euro area government bond yields using market news.

Doh, T. (2010). The efficacy of large-scale asset purchases at the zero lower bound. *Econom. Rev. — Federal Reserve Bank of Kansas City*, 95(2), p. 5.

d'Amico, S., English, W., López-Salido, D., and Nelson, E. (2012). The federal reserve's large-scale asset purchase programmes: Rationale and effects. *The Econom. J.*, 122(564), pp. F415–F446.

D'Amico, S. and King, T. B. (2013). Flow and stock effects of large-scale treasury purchases: Evidence on the importance of local supply. *J. Fin. Econom.*, 108(2), pp. 425–448.

Ehrmann, M. and Fratzscher, M. (2017). Euro area government bonds–fragmentation and contagion during the sovereign debt crisis. *J. Inte. Money Fin.*, 70, pp. 26–44.

Engle, R. (2002). Dynamic conditional correlation: A simple class of multivariate generalized autoregressive conditional heteroskedasticity models. *J. Business Econom. Statist.*, 20(3), pp. 339–350.

Forbes, K. J. and Rigobon, R. (2002). No contagion, only interdependence: Measuring stock market comovements. *The J. Fin.*, 57(5), pp. 2223–2261.

Gagnon, J., Raskin, M., Remache, J., Sack, B. *et al.* (2011). The financial market effects of the federal reserve's large-scale asset purchases. *Int. J. Central Bank.*, 7(1), pp. 3–43.

Gómez-Puig, M. and Sosvilla-Rivero, S. (2016). Causes and hazards of the euro area sovereign debt crisis: Pure and fundamentals-based contagion. *Econom. Modell.*, 56, pp. 133–147.

Jones, D. S. and Roley, V. V. (1983). Rational expectations and the expectations model of the term structure: A test using weekly data. *J. Monetary Econom.*, 12(3), pp. 453–465.

Jones, P. M. and Olson, E. (2013). The time-varying correlation between uncertainty, output, and inflation: Evidence from a dcc-garch model. *Econom. Lett.*, 118(1), pp. 33–37.

Joyce, M., Lasaosa, A., Stevens, I., Tong, M. *et al.* (2011). The financial market impact of quantitative easing in the united kingdom. *Int. J. Central Bank*, 7(3), pp. 113–161.

Joyce, M. A. and Tong, M. (2012). Qe and the gilt market: A disaggregated analysis. *The Econom. J.*, 122(564), pp. F348–F384.

Krishnamurthy, A. and Vissing-Jorgensen, A. (2011). The effects of quantitative easing on interest rates: channels and implications for policy. Technical report, National Bureau of Economic Research.

Lee, J. and Strazicich, M. C. (2003). Minimum lagrange multiplier unit root test with two structural breaks. *Rev. Econom. Statist.*, 85(4), pp. 1082–1089.

Li, C. and Wei, M. (2012). Term structure modelling with supply factors and the federal reserve's large scale asset purchase programs. Available at SSRN 2082112.

Mankiw, N. G., Goldfeld, S. M., and Shiller, R. J. (1986). The term structure of interest rates revisited. *Brookings Papers Econom. Activity*, 1986(1), pp. 61–110.

Martin, F. and Zhang, J. (2017). Modelling european sovereign bond yields with international portfolio effects. *Econom. Modell.*, 64, pp. 178–200.

McLaren, N., Banerjee, R. N., and Latto, D. (2014). Using changes in auction maturity sectors to help identify the impact of qe on gilt yields. *The Econom. J.*, 124(576), pp. 453–479.

Meaning, J. and Zhu, F. (2011). The impact of recent central bank asset purchase programmes. *BIS Quart. Rev.*, December.

Meier, A. (2009). Panacea, curse, or nonevent? Unconventional monetary policy in the United Kingdom. Number 9–163. International Monetary Fund.

Metiu, N. (2012). Sovereign risk contagion in the eurozone. *Econom. Lett.*, 117(1), pp. 35–38.

Murphy, K. M. and Topel, R. H. (2002). Estimation and inference in two-step econometric models. *J. Business Econom. Statist.*, 20(1), pp. 88–97.

Pesaran, M. H. and Pick, A. (2007). Econometric issues in the analysis of contagion. *J. Econom. Dynam. Control*, 31(4), pp. 1245–1277.

Shiller, R. J. and McCulloch, J. H. (1987). The term structure of interest rates.

Silvapulle, P., Fenech, J. P., Thomas, A., and Brooks, R. (2016). Determinants of sovereign bond yield spreads and contagion in the peripheral EU countries. *Econom. Modell.*, 58, pp. 83–92.

Valiante, D. (2016). The 'visible hand' of the ecb's first quantitative easing. *Int. Econom. Econom. Policy*, pp. 1–24.

Walsh, C. E. (1985). Rational expectations model of term premia with some implications for empirical asset demand equations. *The J. Fin.*, 40(1), pp. 63–83.

Zivot, E. and Andrews, D. W. K. (2002). Further evidence on the great crash, the oil-price shock, and the unit-root hypothesis. *J. Business Econom. Statist.*, 20(1), pp. 25–44.

Appendix A: Descriptive Statistics

Statistic	N	Mean	SD	Min	Max
German	2,070	1.826	1.078	−0.187	4.117
Spain	2,070	3.858	1.529	0.983	7.590
Ireland	2,070	4.408	2.779	0.338	13.895
Greece	2,070	11.645	7.564	4.393	48.602
France	2,070	2.323	1.105	0.100	4.346
Portugal	2,070	5.752	3.110	1.368	16.211
Italy	2,070	3.772	1.434	1.049	7.288
AAA	2,070	0.230	0.573	−0.682	3.637
CDSES	2,070	155.339	100.322	45.420	492.070
CDSFR	2,070	49.722	32.422	14.006	171.560
CDSIR	2,070	228.386	226.935	29.280	1,191.158
CDSDE	2,070	25.017	16.671	6.640	92.500
CDSGR	2,070	9,209.199	6,805.436	66.500	14,911.740
CDSIT	2,070	163.326	99.781	48.000	498.660
CDSPT	2,070	346.660	314.960	37.000	1,521.450
Vstoxx	2,070	26.048	9.553	12.713	87.513

Appendix B: One-step-ahead Variance Forecasts

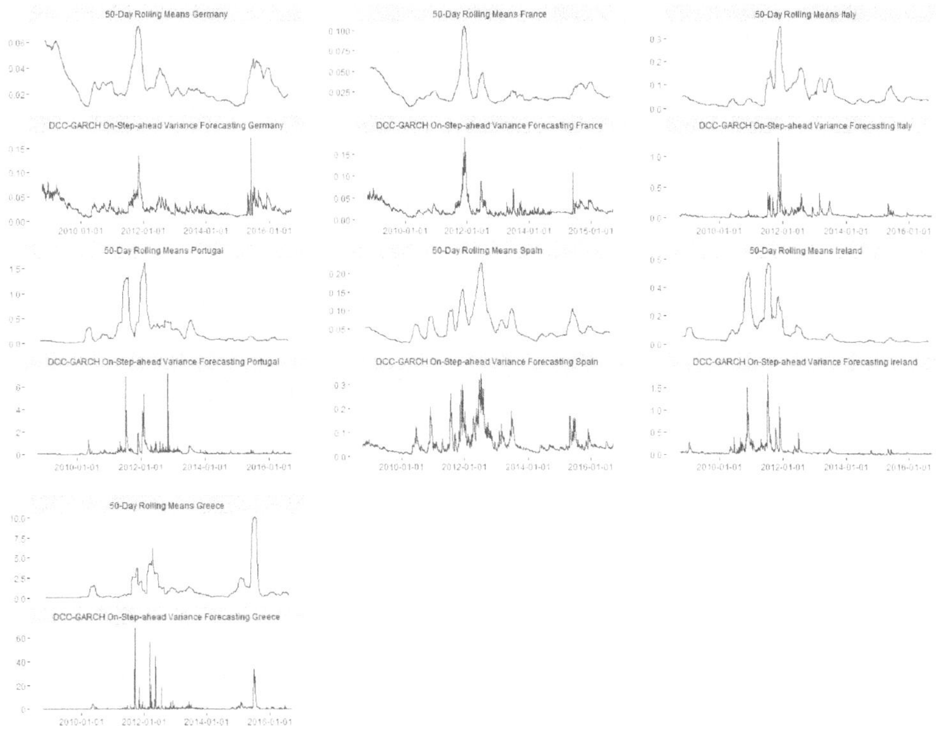

Appendix C: One-step-ahead Covariance Forecasts

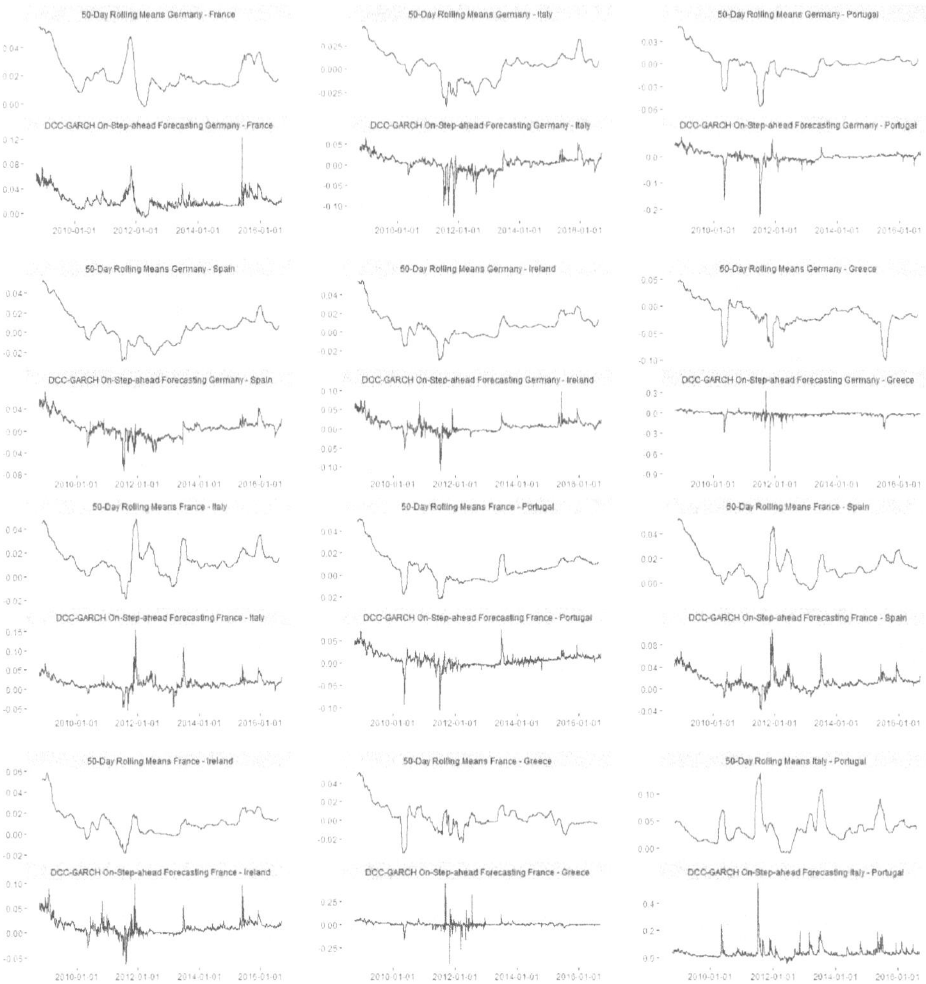

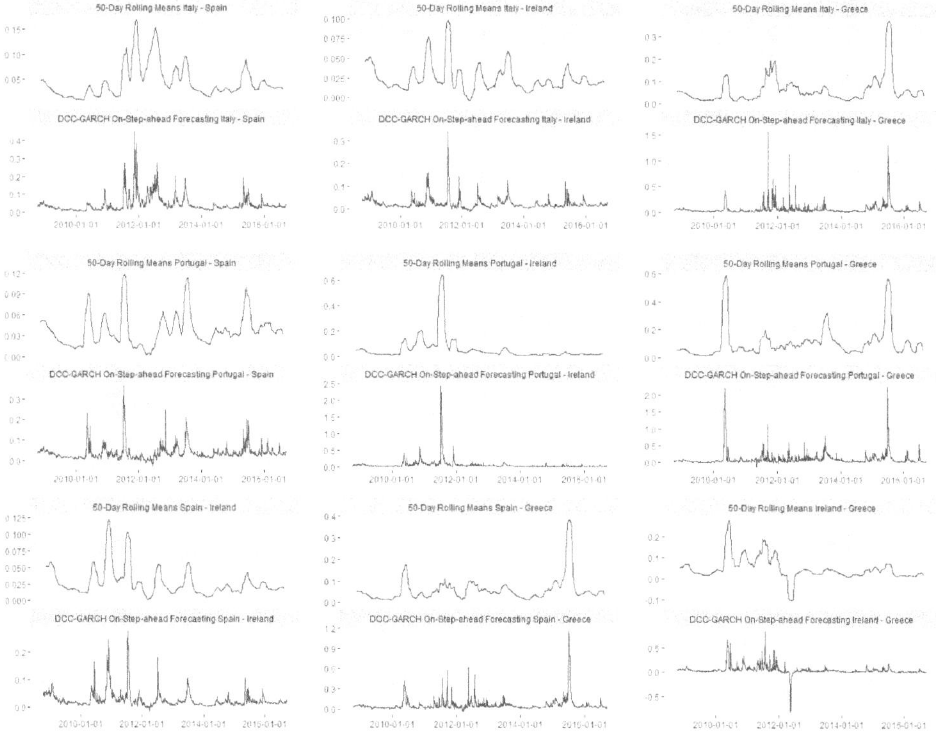
50-Day Rolling Means Italy - Spain
DCC-GARCH On-Step-ahead Forecasting Italy - Spain
50-Day Rolling Means Italy - Ireland
DCC-GARCH On-Step-ahead Forecasting Italy - Ireland
50-Day Rolling Means Italy - Greece
DCC-GARCH On-Step-ahead Forecasting Italy - Greece
50-Day Rolling Means Portugal - Spain
DCC-GARCH On-Step-ahead Forecasting Portugal - Spain
50-Day Rolling Means Portugal - Ireland
DCC-GARCH On-Step-ahead Forecasting Portugal - Ireland
50-Day Rolling Means Portugal - Greece
DCC-GARCH On-Step-ahead Forecasting Portugal - Greece
50-Day Rolling Means Spain - Ireland
DCC-GARCH On-Step-ahead Forecasting Spain - Ireland
50-Day Rolling Means Spain - Greece
DCC-GARCH On-Step-ahead Forecasting Spain - Greece
50-Day Rolling Means Ireland - Greece
DCC-GARCH On-Step-ahead Forecasting Ireland - Greece
2010-01-01
2012-01-01
2014-01-01
2016-01-01

Appendix D: Two-step GARCH Models

Table D.1. Parameter Estimates of the GARCH Models

	Germany–France				Germany–Italy				Germany–Portugal			
Coefficient	Full Sample	Pre-crisis	Crisis	Post-OMT	Full Sample	Pre-crisis	Crisis	Post-OMT	Full Sample	Pre-crisis	Crisis	Post-OMT
β_{01}	**–0.003**		**0.008**	**–0.005**	**–0.003**		**0.006**	**–0.006**	**–0.003**	**–0.003**	**0.003**	**–0.005**
	(0.015)		**(0.000)**	**(0.002)**	**(0.006)**		**(0.012)**	**(0.000)**	**(0.006)**	**(0.375)**	**(0.282)**	**(0.001)**
β_{02}	–0.001		**0.051**	**–0.010**	**–0.007**		**–0.006**	**–0.008**	**–0.007**	–0.006	0.002	**–0.010**
	(0.775)		**(0.000)**	**(0.001)**	**(0.000)**		**(0.005)**	**(0.000)**	**(0.000)**	(0.112)	(0.403)	**(0.000)**
β_{11}	0.584		**–2.332**	**2.976**	0.010		**–2.637**	0.413	0.116	**–2.837**	**–2.203**	**0.496**
	(0.121)		**(0.020)**	**(0.000)**	(0.953)		**(0.003)**	(0.128)	(0.491)	**(0.005)**	**(0.000)**	**(0.005)**
β_{12}	**–2.669**		–0.220	–0.696	0.035		0.065	**0.210**	0.006	0.715	0.000	0.010
	(0.000)		(0.913)	(0.484)	(0.328)		(0.222)	**(0.011)**	(0.456)	(0.479)	(1.00)	(0.189)
β_{21}	0.139		0.274	–0.975	**0.266**		**–2.191**	**1.868**	**0.704**	**1.629**	**0.487**	**1.879**
	(0.795)		(0.842)	(0.111)	**(0.039)**		**(0.000)**	**(0.000)**	**(0.000)**	**(0.044)**	**(0.000)**	**(0.000)**
β_{22}	**3.464**		**–4.812**	**3.609**	**1.197**		0.346	**2.28**	**0.430**	–0.270	0.021	**1.319**
	(0.000)		**(0.096)**	**(0.004)**	**(0.000)**		(0.206)	**(0.000)**	**(0.092)**	(0.774)	(0.96)	**(0.012)**
β_{31}	**0.005**		**0.011**	**0.013**	**0.008**		**0.013**	**0.016**	**0.005**	**–0.005**	**0.008**	**0.013**
	(0.000)		**(0.000)**	**(0.000)**	**(0.000)**		**(0.000)**	**(0.000)**	**(0.000)**	**(0.001)**	**(0.000)**	**(0.000)**
β_{32}	**0.004**		**0.006**	**0.021**	**–0.010**		**–0.010**	**–0.011**	**0.003**	–0.001	**0.003**	**0.008**
	(0.000)		**(0.017)**	**(0.000)**	**(0.000)**		**(0.000)**	**(0.000)**	**(0.000)**	(0.800)	**(0.026)**	**(0.000)**
β_{41}	**0.122**		**–0.148**	0.054	0.070		**–0.119**	–0.072	**0.106**	**0.161**	–0.089	(0.55)
	(0.005)		**(0.003)**	(0.595)	(0.122)		**(0.067)**	(0.488)	**(0.025)**	**(0.021)**	(0.248)	(0.620)
β_{42}	**0.201**		–0.178	–0.139	**0.188**		0.078	–0.135	**0.125**	**0.159**	–0.089	0.098
	(0.023)		(0.329)	(0.453)	**(0.000)**		(0.332)	(0.105)	**(0.012)**	**(0.086)**	(0.371)	(0.424)
β_{51}	**0.004**		**0.005**	**0.006**	**0.006**		**0.006**	**0.007**	**0.003**	–0.001	**0.003**	**0.006**
	(0.000)		**(0.000)**	**(0.003)**	**(0.000)**		**(0.000)**	**(0.000)**	**(0.000)**	(0.540)	**(0.000)**	**(0.001)**
β_{52}	**0.002**		**0.002**	**0.010**	**–0.003**		**–0.002**	**–0.004**	**0.000**	0,000	**0.000**	**0.001**
	(0.000)		**(0.029)**	**(0.000)**	**(0.000)**		**(0.000)**	**(0.000)**	**(0.006)**	(0.612)	**(0.078)**	**(0.000)**

c_{11}	**0.000**		**0.000**	**0.000**	**0.000**		**0.000**	**0.000**	**0.000**	**0.005**	**0.000**	**0.000**
	(0.000)		**(0.000)**	**(0.000)**	**(0.000)**		**(0.000)**	**(0.000)**	**(0.000)**	**(0.000)**	**(0.001)**	**(0.000)**
c_{22}	**0.003**		**0.004**	**0.004**	**0.000**		**0.001**	**0.001**	**0.001**	**0.002**	**0.001**	**0.003**
	(0.000)		**(0.000)**	**(0.000)**	**(0.000)**		**(0.000)**	**(0.000)**	**(0.000)**	**(0.000)**	**(0.000)**	**(0.000)**
c_{12}	**0.005**		**0.001**	**0,000**	**0.000**		0.000	**0.002**	**0.000**	**0.004**	**0.000**	**0.000**
	(0.000)		**(0.039)**	**(0.066)**	**(0.002)**		(0.117)	**(0.000)**	**(0.000)**	**(0.000)**	**(0.000)**	**(0.002)**
b_{11}	**0.905**		**0.697**	**0.916**	**0.895**		**0.634**	**0.942**	**0.879**	**−0.927**	**0.833**	**0.840**
	(0.000)		**(0.000)**	**(0.000)**	**(0.000)**		**(0.000)**	**(0.000)**	**(0.000)**	**(0.000)**	**(0.000)**	**(0.000)**
b_{22}	**0.457**		**0.398**	**0.195**	**0.692**		**0.532**	**0.220**	**0.478**	**0.271**	**0.626**	**0.236**
	(0.000)		**(0.000)**	**(0.000)**	**(0.000)**		**(0.000)**	**(0.004)**	**(0.000)**	**(0.001)**	**(0.000)**	**(0.000)**
b_{12}	**−0.992**		**0.557**	**0.895**	**0.935**		0.084	**−0.977**	**0.783**	**−0.938**	**0.771**	**0.870**
	(0.000)		**(0.005)**	**(0.000)**	**(0.000)**		(0.867)	**(0.000)**	**(0.000)**	**(0.000)**	**(0.000)**	**(0.000)**
a_{11}	**0.072**		**0.333**	**0.060**	**0.094**		**0.380**	**0.041**	**0.077**	0.022	**0.165**	**0.077**
	(0.000)		**(0.000)**	**(0.000)**	**(0.000)**		**(0.000)**	**(0.000)**	**(0.000)**	(0.121)	**(0.000)**	**(0.000)**
a_{22}	**0.568**		**0.855**	**0.678**	**0.202**		**0.238**	**0.347**	**0.379**	**0.446**	**0.400**	**0.366**
	(0.000)		**(0.000)**	**(0.000)**	**(0.000)**		**(0.000)**	**(0.000)**	**(0.000)**	**(0.000)**	**(0.000)**	**(0.000)**
a_{12}	0.002		**0.147**	**0.027**	**0.029**		**0.110**	−0.005	**0.080**	**0.019**	**0.188**	**0.024**
	(0.127)		**(0.031)**	**(0.056)**	**(0.002)**		**(0.082)**	(0.473)	**(0.000)**	**(0.028)**	**(0.000)**	**(0.038)**

Notes: Mean equation: $\Delta R_{i,t} = \beta_{0,i} + \beta_{1,i}\Delta E_t(V_{i\ t+1}) + \beta_{2,i}\Delta E_t(\text{Cov}_{ij,t+1}) + \beta_{3,i}\Delta \text{Vstoxx}_t + \beta_{4,i}\Delta r_t + \beta_{5,i}\Delta \text{CDS}_{i,t} + \varepsilon_{i,t}$
Columns without estimates represent the periods during which estimations have not converged.

Table D.2. Parameter Estimates of the GARCH Models

	Germany–Spain				Germany–Ireland				Germany–Greece			
Coefficient	Full Sample	Pre-crisis	Crisis	Post-OMT	Full Sample	Pre-crisis	Crisis	Post-OMT	Full Sample	Pre-crisis	Crisis	Post-OMT
β_{01}	**–0.004**		0.002	**–0.005**	**–0.003**		**0.004**	**–0.006**	**–0.002**	–0.003	**0.005**	
	(0.000)		(0.285)	**(0.001)**	**(0.012)**		**(0.061)**	**(0.001)**	**(0.044)**	(0.358)	**(0.032)**	
β_{02}	**–0.011**		-0.003	**–0.010**	0.004		**0.016**	–0.006	**–0.005**	–0.005	–0.003	
	(0.000)		(0.550)	**(0.000)**	(0.300)		**(0.010)**	(0.442)	**(0.000)**	(0.286)	(0.219)	
β_{11}	0.067		**–2.073**	**0.640**	–0.028		**–1.923**	0.353	–0.006	–1.476	**–1.918**	
	(0.704)		**(0.007)**	**(0.014)**	(0.890)		**(0.009)**	(0.321)	(0.974)	(0.218)	**(0.034)**	
β_{12}	**–0.775**		**–1.170**	0.000	0.080		0.079	**3.531**	–0.001	**1.410**	0.000	
	(0.000)		**(0.000)**	(1.00)	(0.344)		(0.435)	**(0.027)**	(0.195)	**(0.066)**	(0.496)	
β_{21}	0.080		**–1.250**	**2.190**	**2.241**		**1.126**	**4.311**	–0.010	–0.635	0.010	
	(0.683)		**(0.001)**	**(0.000)**	**(0.000)**		**(0.000)**	**(0.000)**	(0.797)	(0.325)	(0.911)	
β_{22}	**2.207**		**2.335**	**1.847**	–0.359		–0.759	-3.634	0.032	**–1.251**	0.093	
	(0.000)		**(0.009)**	**(0.000)**	(0.658)		(0.485)	(0.317)	(0.519)	**(0.073)**	(0.233)	
β_{31}	**0.005**		**0.011**	**0.011**	**0.006**		**0.011**	**0.016**	**0.009**	**–0.004**	**0.014**	
	(0.000)		**(0.000)**	**(0.000)**	**(0.000)**		**(0.000)**	**(0.000)**	**(0.000)**	**(0.014)**	**(0.000)**	
β_{32}	–0.001		0.004	–0.001	**0.016**		**0.010**	**0.108**	**–0.005**	**0.580**	–0.006	
	(0.196)		(0.171)	(0.246)	**(0.000)**		**(0.008)**	**(0.000)**	**(0.036)**	**(0.002)**	(0.134)	
β_{41}	0.070		**–0.177**	0.020	**0.079**		**–0.213**	–0.004	0.048	**0.117**	**–0.199**	
	(0.135)		**(0.002)**	(0.857)	**(0.095)**		**(0.000)**	(0.970)	(0.260)	**(0.064)**	**(0.000)**	
β_{42}	0.094		**–0.491**	–0.048	0.161		–0.262	0.326	**0.203**	**0.216**	**0.210**	
	(0.146)		**(0.022)**	(0.616)	(0.320)		(0.359)	(0.595)	**(0.000)**	**(0.043)**	**(0.004)**	
β_{51}	**0.003**		**0.004**	**0.004**	**0.004**		**0.005**	**0.007**	**0.006**	0.001	**0.007**	
	(0.000)		**(0.000)**	**(0.076)**	**(0.000)**		**(0.000)**	**(0.001)**	**(0.000)**	(0.704)	**(0.000)**	
β_{52}	**0.001**		**0.002**	0.000	**0.002**		**0.002**	**0.014**	0.000	**–0.002**	0.000	
	(0.000)		**(0.000)**	(0.389)	**(0.000)**		**(0.000)**	**(0.000)**	(0.924)	**(0.002)**	(0.859)	

c_{11}	**0.000**	**0.000**	**0.000**	**0.000**	**0.000**	**0.000**	**0.000**	0.000	**0.000**
	(0.000)	**(0.018)**	**(0.000)**	**(0.000)**	**(0.039)**	**(0.000)**	**(0.000)**	(0.711)	**(0.054)**
c_{22}	**0.001**	**0.003**	**0.001**	**0.003**	**0.009**	**0.004**	**0.001**	**0.003**	**0.000**
	(0.000)	**(0.000)**	**(0.000)**	**(0.000)**	**(0.000)**	**(0.000)**	**(0.000)**	**(0.001)**	**(0.005)**
c_{12}	**0.000**	**0.000**	**0.000**	**0.000**	**0.001**	0.003	**0.000**	**0.002**	0.000
	(0.000)	**(0.011)**	**(0.027)**	**(0.000)**	**(0.000)**	(0.111)	**(0.001)**	**(0.035)**	(0.173)
b_{11}	**0.899**	**0.792**	**0.918**	**0.908**	**0.779**	**0.899**	**0.889**	**0.982**	**0.779**
	(0.000)	**(0.000)**	**(0.000)**	**(0.000)**	**(0.000)**	**(0.000)**	**(0.000)**	**(0.000)**	**(0.000)**
b_{22}	**0.653**	**0.560**	**0.240**	**0.547**	**0.294**	**0.713**	**0.620**	0.147	**0.869**
	(0.000)	**(0.000)**	**(0.000)**	**(0.000)**	**(0.000)**	**(0.000)**	**(0.000)**	(0.429)	**(0.000)**
b_{12}	**0.876**	**0.815**	**0.943**	**0.787**	**0.545**	–0.346	**0.930**	–0.022	**0.929**
	(0.000)	**(0.000)**	**(0.000)**	**(0.000)**	**(0.000)**	(0.656)	**(0.000)**	(0.965)	**(0.000)**
a_{11}	**0.090**	**0.238**	**0.057**	**0.084**	**0.265**	**0.074**	**0.102**	0.013	**0.266**
	(0.000)	**(0.000)**	**(0.000)**	**(0.000)**	**(0.000)**	**(0.000)**	**(0.000)**	(0.125)	**(0.000)**
a_{22}	**0.358**	**0.438**	**0.564**	**0.672**	**1.345**	**0.308**	**0.221**	**0.188**	**0.102**
	(0.000)	**(0.000)**	**(0.000)**	**(0.000)**	**(0.000)**	**(0.000)**	**(0.000)**	**(0.017)**	**(0.000)**
a_{12}	**0.066**	**0.100**	**0.024**	**0.072**	**0.181**	**–0.043**	**0.030**	**–0.083**	**0.047**
	(0.000)	**(0.009)**	**(0.006)**	**(0.000)**	**(0.020)**	**(0.095)**	**(0.000)**	**(0.048)**	**(0.021)**

Notes: Mean equation: $\Delta R_{i,t} = \beta_{0,i} + \beta_{1,i}\Delta E_t(V_{i,t+1}) + \beta_{2,i}\Delta E_t(\mathrm{Cov}_{ij,t+1}) + \beta_{3,i}\Delta V\mathrm{stoxx}_t + \beta_{4,i}\Delta r_t + \beta_{5,i}\Delta \mathrm{CDS}_{i,t} + \varepsilon_{i,t}$
Columns without estimates represent the periods during which estimations have not converged.

Table D.3. Parameter Estimates of the GARCH Models

	France–Italy				France–Portugal				France–Spain			
Coefficient	Full Sample	Pre-crisis	Crisis	Post-OMT	Full Sample	Pre-crisis	Crisis	Post-OMT	Full Sample	Pre-crisis	Crisis	Post-OMT
β_{01}	–0.002		**0.014**	**–0.007**	–0.002		**0.014**	**–0.008**	**–0.004**		**0.013**	**–0.007**
	(0.156)		**(0.000)**	**(0.005)**	(0.120)		**(0.000)**	**(0.001)**	**(0.010)**		**(0.000)**	**(0.004)**
β_{02}	**–0.007**		**–0.006**	**–0.009**	**–0.008**		0,000	**–0.011**	**–0.011**		0.008	**–0.011**
	(0.000)		**(0.003)**	**(0.000)**	**(0.000)**		(0.911)	**(0.000)**	**(0.000)**		(0.137)	**(0.000)**
β_{11}	0.495		**–1.976**	**1.828**	**0.905**		**–2.967**	0.212	**–1.378**		**–3.983**	–0.380
	(0.308)		**(0.028)**	**(0.005)**	**(0.023)**		**(0.000)**	(0.745)	**(0.015)**		**(0.000)**	(0.626)
β_{12}	**0.063**		0.049	**0.148**	–0.001		–0.020	0.005	–0.235		**–0.565**	0.062
	(0.013)		(0.211)	**(0.051)**	(0.879)		(0.112)	(0.483)	(0.103)		**(0.057)**	(0.619)
β_{21}	0.375		–0.798	–0.204	0.003		**–1.209**	**2.379**	**3.468**		0.260	**5.231**
	(0.208)		(0.205)	(0.567)	(0.982)		**(0.000)**	**(0.000)**	**(0.000)**		(0.767)	**(0.000)**
β_{22}	**0.747**		0.023	**1.562**	**0.987**		0.386	**2.192**	**2.747**		0.764	**1.444**
	(0.000)		(0.937)	**(0.000)**	**(0.000)**		(0.472)	**(0.000)**	**(0.000)**		(0.486)	**(0.000)**
β_{31}	**0.009**		**0.004**	**0.024**	**0.007**		0.003	**0.017**	**0.005**		0.002	**0.021**
	(0.000)		**(0.025)**	**(0.000)**	**(0.000)**		(0.174)	**(0.000)**	**(0.000)**		(0.369)	**(0.000)**
β_{32}	**–0.010**		**–0.011**	**–0.011**	**0.003**		0.001	**0.009**	**–0.002**		–0.001	–0.001
	(0.000)		**(0.000)**	**(0.000)**	**(0.000)**		(0.351)	**(0.000)**	**(0.008)**		(0.534)	(0.167)
β_{41}	**0.160**		–0.040	–0.099	**0.155**		–0.010	–0.192	0.095		–0.056	–0.236
	(0.066)		(0.743)	(0.497)	**(0.035)**		(0.942)	(0.175)	(0.254)		(0.716)	(0.105)
β_{42}	**0.161**		**0.170**	–0.018	**0.142**		0.128	0.032	**0.138**		–0.190	0.021
	(0.000)		**(0.028)**	(0.808)	**(0.005)**		(0.179)	(0.806)	**(0.034)**		(0.347)	(0.803)
β_{51}	**0.006**		**0.006**	**0.008**	**0.003**		**0.005**	0.002	**0.003**		**0.003**	**0.006**
	(0.000)		**(0.000)**	**(0.000)**	**(0.000)**		**(0.000)**	(0.202)	**(0.000)**		**(0.000)**	**(0.000)**
β_{52}	**–0.003**		**–0.002**	**–0.004**	**0.001**		**0.001**	**0.001**	**0.001**		**0.001**	0.000
	(0.000)		**(0.000)**	**(0.000)**	**(0.000)**		**(0.000)**	**(0.000)**	**(0.000)**		**(0.014)**	(0.323)

c_{11}	**0.000**		0.000	**0.000**	**0,000**		**0.000**	**0.000**	**0.000**		**0.001**	**0.000**
	(0.000)		(0.597)	**(0.000)**	**(0.000)**		**(0.035)**	**(0.000)**	**(0.000)**		**(0.000)**	**(0.000)**
c_{22}	**0.001**		**0.001**	**0.001**	**0.001**		**0.000**	**0.002**	**0.000**		**0.010**	**0.001**
	(0.000)		**(0.000)**	**(0.000)**	**(0.000)**		**(0.001)**	**(0.000)**	**(0.000)**		**(0.000)**	**(0.000)**
c_{12}	**0.001**		0.001	**0.001**	**0,000**		**0.001**	**0.001**	**0.000**		**0.003**	**0.001**
	(0.000)		(0.103)	**(0.032)**	**(0.000)**		**(0.014)**	**(0.031)**	**(0.000)**		**(0.000)**	**(0.001)**
b_{11}	**0.856**		**0.696**	**0.824**	**0.847**		**0.681**	**0.856**	**0.859**		**0.674**	**0.821**
	(0.000)		**(0.000)**	**(0.000)**	**(0.000)**		**(0.000)**	**(0.000)**	**(0.000)**		**(0.000)**	**(0.000)**
b_{22}	**0.564**		**0.557**	**0.280**	**0.670**		**0.625**	**0.363**	**0.702**		**0.113**	**0.232**
	(0.000)		**(0.000)**	**(0.000)**	**(0.000)**		**(0.000)**	**(0.000)**	**(0.000)**		**(0.009)**	**(0.000)**
b_{12}	**−0.746**		**−0.890**	−0.391	**0.830**		−0.197	**0.714**	**0.847**		**0.496**	0.156
	(0.000)		**(0.000)**	(0.539)	**(0.000)**		(0.660)	**(0.000)**	**(0.000)**		**(0.000)**	(0.486)
a_{11}	**0.167**		**0.565**	**0.132**	**0.171**		**0.574**	**0.095**	**0.162**		**0.522**	**0.125**
	(0.000)		**(0.000)**	**(0.000)**	**(0.000)**		**(0.000)**	**(0.000)**	**(0.000)**		**(0.000)**	**(0.000)**
a_{22}	**0.259**		**0.240**	**0.350**	**0.308**		**0.464**	**0.359**	**0.301**		**0.768**	**0.565**
	(0.000)		**(0.000)**	**(0.000)**	**(0.000)**		**(0.000)**	**(0.000)**	**(0.000)**		**(0.000)**	**(0.000)**
a_{12}	**0.060**		0.048	0.048	**0.102**		**0.206**	**0.049**	**0.090**		**0.297**	**0.144**
	(0.004)		(0.176)	(0.165)	**(0.000)**		**(0.020)**	**(0.017)**	**(0.000)**		**(0.000)**	**(0.000)**

Notes: Mean equation: $\Delta R_{i,t} = \beta_{0,i} + \beta_{1,i}\Delta E_t(V_{:,t+1}) + \beta_{2,i}\Delta E_t(\text{Cov}_{ij,t+1}) + \beta_{3,i}\Delta V\text{stoxx}_t + \beta_{4,i}\Delta r_t + \beta_{5,i}\Delta\text{CDS}_{i,t} + \varepsilon_{i,t}$
Columns without estimates represent the periods during which estimations have not converged.

Table D.4. Parameter Estimates of the GARCH Models

	France–Ireland				France–Greece				Italy–Portugal			
Coefficient	Full Sample	Pre-crisis	Crisis	Post-OMT	Full Sample	Pre-crisis	Crisis	Post-OMT	Full Sample	Pre-crisis	Crisis	Post-OMT
β_{01}	–0.003		**0.015**	**–0.007**	0.000		**0.011**		**–0.003**		**–0.003**	**–0.003**
	(0.109)		**(0.000)**	**(0.004)**	(0.200)		**(0.000)**		**(0.000)**		**(0.042)**	**(0.008)**
β_{02}	0.002		**0.018**	–0.011	**–0.010**		0.000		**–0.008**		**–0.001**	**–0.010**
	(0.668)		**(0.009)**	(0.188)	**(0.000)**		(0.111)		**(0.000)**		**(0.042)**	**(0.000)**
β_{11}	–0.484		**–2.066**	–0.481	0.380		–1.130		–0.007		–0.023	**0.213**
	(0.243)		**(0.017)**	(0.545)	(0.390)		(0.322)		(0.776)		(0.354)	**(0.000)**
β_{12}	0.048		0.070	0.956	0.000		0.000		**–0.020**		**–0.033**	–0.011
	(0.621)		(0.539)	(0.608)	(0.130)		(0.717)		**(0.001)**		**(0.075)**	(0.116)
β_{21}	**1.738**		**0.906**	**4.848**	**0.330**		**0.341**		**0.117**		0.028	0.104
	(0.000)		**(0.006)**	**(0.000)**	**(0.000)**		**(0.000)**		**(0.002)**		(0.699)	(0.142)
β_{22}	–0.590		–1.008	2.715	0.050		0.021		**0.957**		**1.263**	**0.760**
	(0.346)		(0.283)	(0.458)	(0.150)		(0.734)		**(0.000)**		**(0.000)**	**(0.000)**
β_{31}	**0.005**		0.002	**0.021**	**0.010**		**0.000**		**–0.010**		**–0.011**	**–0.010**
	(0.000)		(0.322)	**(0.000)**	**(0.000)**		**(0.015)**		**(0.000)**		**(0.000)**	**(0.000)**
β_{32}	**0.014**		**0.010**	**0.076**	**–0.010**		**–0.012**		**0.005**		0.002	**0.011**
	(0.000)		**(0.021)**	**(0.000)**	**(0.040)**		**(0.072)**		**(0.000)**		(0.111)	**(0.000)**
β_{41}	0.124		–0.069	–0.158	**0.140**		–0.101		**0.137**		**0.102**	0.037
	(0.108)		(0.638)	(0.302)	**(0.080)**		(0.423)		**(0.000)**		**(0.011)**	(0.483)
β_{42}	0.092		–0.138	0.104	**0.200**		**0.247**		**0.135**		**0.234**	0.050
	(0.603)		(0.684)	(0.858)	**(0.000)**		**(0.000)**		**(0.015)**		**(0.008)**	(0.687)
β_{51}	**0.003**		**0.004**	**0.006**	**0.010**		**0.018**		**–0.002**		**–0.002**	**–0.003**
	(0.000)		**(0.000)**	**(0.000)**	**(0.000)**		**(0.000)**		**(0.000)**		**(0.000)**	**(0.000)**
β_{52}	**0.002**		**0.002**	**0.009**	0.000		0.000		**0.001**		**0.001**	**0.003**
	(0.000)		**(0.000)**	**(0.002)**	(0.940)		(0.971)		**(0.000)**		**(0.000)**	**(0.000)**

c_{11}	**0.000**	**0.000**	**0.000**	**0.000**	0.000	**0.000**	**0.000**	**0.000**
	(0.000)	**(0.021)**	**(0.000)**	**(0.000)**	(0.493)	**(0.000)**	**(0.049)**	**(0.001)**
c_{22}	**0.003**	**0.011**	**0.005**	**0.000**	**0.000**	**0.000**	**0.000**	**0.001**
	(0.000)	**(0.000)**	**(0.000)**	**(0.000)**	**(0.012)**	**(0.000)**	**(0.000)**	**(0.000)**
c_{12}	**0.001**	**0.006**	**0.001**	**0.000**	**0.000**	**0.000**	**0.000**	**0.000**
	(0.000)	**(0.000)**	**(0.049)**	**(0.000)**	**(0.053)**	**(0.000)**	**(0.046)**	**(0.003)**
b_{11}	**0.842**	**0.674**	**0.815**	**0.840**	**0.711**	**0.943**	**0.907**	**0.692**
	(0.000)	**(0.000)**	**(0.000)**	**(0.000)**	**(0.000)**	**(0.000)**	**(0.000)**	**(0.000)**
b_{22}	**0.565**	**0.294**	**0.714**	**0.500**	**0.863**	**0.692**	**0.563**	**0.497**
	(0.000)	**(0.000)**	**(0.000)**	**(0.000)**	**(0.000)**	**(0.000)**	**(0.000)**	**(0.000)**
b_{12}	**0.724**	–0.427	**0.813**	**0.750**	**–0.636**	**0.892**	**0.462**	**0.715**
	(0.000)	(0.111)	**(0.000)**	**(0.000)**	**(0.023)**	**(0.000)**	**(0.040)**	**(0.000)**
a_{11}	**0.176**	**0.569**	**0.130**	**0.200**	**0.560**	**0.037**	**0.052**	**0.107**
	(0.000)	**(0.000)**	**(0.000)**	**(0.000)**	**(0.000)**	**(0.000)**	**(0.002)**	**(0.000)**
a_{22}	**0.618**	**1.266**	**0.293**	**0.300**	**0.126**	**0.296**	**0.530**	**0.325**
	(0.000)	**(0.000)**	**(0.000)**	**(0.000)**	**(0.000)**	**(0.000)**	**(0.000)**	**(0.000)**
a_{12}	**0.146**	**0.265**	**0.053**	**0.090**	**0.144**	**0.049**	**0.118**	**0.067**
	(0.000)	**(0.012)**	**(0.029)**	**(0.000)**	**(0.057)**	**(0.000)**	**(0.002)**	**(0.008)**

Notes: Mean equation: $\Delta R_{i,t} = \beta_{0,i} + \beta_{1,i}\Delta E_t(V_{i,t+1}) + \beta_{2,i}\Delta E_t(\mathrm{Cov}_{ij,t+1}) + \beta_{3,i}\Delta V\mathrm{stoxx}_t + \beta_{4,i}\Delta r_t + \beta_{5,i}\Delta \mathrm{CDS}_{i,t} + \varepsilon_{i,t}$
Columns without estimates represent the periods during which estimations have not converged.

Table D.5. Parameter Estimates of the GARCH Models

	Italy–Spain				Italy–Ireland				Italy–Greece			
Coefficient	Full Sample	Pre-crisis	Crisis	Post-OMT	Full Sample	Pre-crisis	Crisis	Post-OMT	Full Sample	Pre-crisis	Crisis	Post-OMT
β_{01}	**–0.003**		**–0.003**	**–0.003**	**–0.002**		**–0.002**	**–0.003**	**–0.002**	–0.002	–0.002	
	(0.001)		**(0.050)**	**(0.003)**	**(0.003)**		**(0.073)**	**(0.003)**	**(0.034)**	(0.581)	(0.201)	
β_{02}	**–0.010**		–0.003	**–0.012**	0.003		**0.017**	–0.007	**–0.004**	–0.004	–0.003	
	(0.000)		(0.609)	**(0.000)**	(0.456)		**(0.015)**	(0.408)	**(0.000)**	(0.380)	(0.243)	
β_{11}	**–0.088**		**–0.082**	–0.033	–0.049		**–0.056**	**–0.253**	–0.024	–1.035	–0.041	
	(0.011)		**(0.041)**	(0.686)	(0.456)		**(0.002)**	**(0.001)**	(0.204)	(0.455)	(0.108)	
β_{12}	–0.169		0.071	–0.210	0.131		**0.232**	3.531	0.000	0.694	0.000	
	(0.259)		(0.876)	(0.447)	(0.228)		**(0.068)**	(0.154)	(0.472)	(0.319)	(0.798)	
β_{21}	**(0.401)**		0.177	**0.691**	**0.710**		**0.324**	**2.806**	–0.018	**1.337**	–0.014	
	(0.000)		(0.120)	**(0.000)**	**(0.000)**		**(0.000)**	**(0.000)**	(0.160)	**(0.096)**	(0.466)	
β_{22}	**0.506**		–0.719	**0.613**	0.281		**–1.638**	0.157	–0.024	0.236	–0.018	
	(0.000)		(0.117)	**(0.012)**	(0.407)		**(0.015)**	(0.946)	(0.349)	(0.819)	(0.703)	
β_{31}	**–0.010**		**–0.011**	**–0.010**	**–0.010**		**–0.011**	**–0.009**	**–0.009**	**–0.008**	**–0.011**	
	(0.000)		**(0.000)**	**(0.000)**	**(0.000)**		**(0.000)**	**(0.000)**	**(0.000)**	**(0.000)**	**(0.000)**	
β_{32}	**–0.001**		0.000	**–0.002**	**0.018**		**0.012**	**0.146**	**–0.005**	0.179	**–0.009**	
	(0.025)		(0.931)	**(0.004)**	**(0.000)**		**(0.005)**	**(0.000)**	**(0.000)**	(0.345)	**(0.013)**	
β_{41}	**0.135**		**0.108**	0.057	**0.165**		**0.140**	**0.075**	**0.147**	**0.180**	**0.099**	
	(0.000)		**(0.005)**	(0.267)	**(0.000)**		**(0.000)**	**(0.097)**	**(0.000)**	**(0.016)**	**(0.011)**	
β_{42}	**0.184**		**–0.355**	0.070	0.128		–0.264	0.328	**0.218**	0.232	**0.222**	
	(0.004)		**(0.096)**	(0.417)	(0.436)		(0.467)	(0.569)	**(0.000)**	(0.025)	**(0.003)**	
β_{51}	**–0.002**		**–0.002**	**–0.002**	**–0.002**		**–0.001**	**–0.002**	**–0.001**	**–0.001**	**–0.001**	
	(0.000)		**(0.000)**	**(0.000)**	**(0.000)**		**(0.000)**	**(0.000)**	**(0.000)**	**(0.021)**	**(0.000)**	
β_{52}	**0.003**		**0.003**	**0.001**	**0.003**		**0.002**	**0.020**	0.000	–0.001	0.000	
	(0.000)		**(0.000)**	**(0.000)**	**(0.000)**		**(0.000)**	**(0.000)**	(0.327)	(0.334)	(0.688)	

c_{11}	**0.000**		**0.000**	**0.000**	**0.000**		**0.000**	**0.000**	**0.000**	0.000	**0.000**
	(0.000)		**(0.053)**	**(0.000)**	**(0.000)**		**(0.056)**	**(0.000)**	**(0.000)**	(0.207)	**(0.034)**
c_{22}	**0.000**		**0.002**	**0.001**	**0.002**		**0.009**	**0.003**	**0.001**	**0.003**	**0.000**
	(0.000)		**(0.000)**	**(0.000)**	**(0.000)**		**(0.000)**	**(0.000)**	**(0.000)**	**(0.000)**	**(0.002)**
c_{12}	**0.000**		0.001	**0.000**	**0.000**		0.000	0.000	**0.002**	**0.003**	**0.000**
	(0.000)		(0.213)	**(0.000)**	**(0.043)**		(0.241)	(0.527)	**(0.000)**	**(0.052)**	**(0.044)**
b_{11}	**0.946**		**0.890**	**0.637**	**0.948**		**0.879**	**0.723**	**0.839**	**0.891**	**0.902**
	(0.000)		**(0.000)**	**(0.000)**	**(0.000)**		**(0.000)**	**(0.000)**	**(0.000)**	**(0.000)**	**(0.000)**
b_{22}	**0.718**		**0.616**	**0.318**	**0.556**		**0.291**	**0.735**	**0.339**	0.146	**0.876**
	(0.000)		**(0.000)**	**(0.000)**	**(0.000)**		**(0.000)**	**(0.000)**	**(0.000)**	(0.403)	**(0.000)**
b_{12}	**0.905**		0.249	**0.770**	**0.777**		0.403	**−0.973**	−0.379	−0.116	**0.926**
	(0.000)		(0.659)	**(0.000)**	**(0.000)**		(0.131)	**(0.000)**	(0.237)	(0.843)	**(0.000)**
a_{11}	**0.036**		**0.054**	**0.124**	**0.036**		**0.063**	**0.124**	**0.048**	0.031	**0.049**
	(0.000)		**(0.008)**	**(0.000)**	**(0.000)**		**(0.005)**	**(0.000)**	**(0.000)**	(0.232)	**(0.002)**
a_{22}	**0.316**		**0.388**	**0.568**	**0.682**		**1.353**	**0.284**	**0.294**	**0.201**	**0.102**
	(0.000)		**(0.000)**	**(0.000)**	**(0.000)**		**(0.000)**	**(0.000)**	**(0.000)**	**(0.005)**	**(0.000)**
a_{12}	**0.047**		**0.106**	**0.060**	**0.054**		**0.174**	**0.014**	**−0.033**	**−0.057**	**0.034**
	(0.000)		**(0.019)**	**(0.010)**	**(0.006)**		**(0.018)**	**(0.023)**	**(0.007)**	**(0.074)**	**(0.000)**

Notes: Mean equation: $\Delta R_{i,t} = \beta_{0,i} + \beta_{1,i}\Delta E_t(V_{i,t+1}) + \beta_{2,i}\Delta E_t(\text{Cov}_{ij,t+1}) + \beta_{3,i}\Delta V\text{stoxx}_t + \beta_{4,i}\Delta r_t + \beta_{5,i}\Delta \text{CDS}_{i,t} + \varepsilon_{i,t}$
Columns without estimates represent the periods during which estimations have not converged.

Table D.6. Parameter Estimates of the GARCH Models

Coefficient	Portugal–Spain				Portugal–Ireland				Portugal–Greece			
	Full Sample	Pre-crisis	Crisis	Post-OMT	Full Sample	Pre-crisis	Crisis	Post-OMT	Full Sample	Pre-crisis	Crisis	Post-OMT
β_{01}	**–0.004**		0.000	**–0.005**	**–0.003**		0.001	**–0.005**	**–0.003**	–0.004	0.000	
	(0.000)		(0.794)	**(0.001)**	**(0.002)**		(0.420)	**(0.003)**	**(0.002)**	(0.154)	(0.807)	
β_{02}	**–0.010**		–0.003	**–0.009**	0.002		**0.017**	–0.006	**–0.005**	–0.004	–0.003	
	(0.000)		(0.635)	**(0.000)**	(0.540)		**(0.011)**	(0.439)	**(0.000)**	(0.410)	(0.162)	
β_{11}	**–0.055**		**–0.029**	**–0.053**	–0.007		0.005	**–0.037**	–0.002	–1.992	**0.017**	
	(0.000)		**(0.006)**	**(0.000)**	(0.250)		(0.639)	**(0.000)**	(0.407)	(0.128)	**(0.000)**	
β_{12}	**0.351**		**–1.159**	0.188	0.143		0.078	1.850	–0.001	0.451	(0.000)	
	(0.000)		**(0.000)**	(0.236)	(0.391)		(0.589)	(0.256)	(0.253)	(0.569)	(0.670)	
β_{21}	**1.671**		**1.138**	**1.732**	**0.087**		**0.058**	**2.166**	**0.107**	**2.814**	**0.097**	
	(0.000)		**(0.000)**	**(0.000)**	**(0.000)**		**(0.035)**	**(0.000)**	**(0.000)**	**(0.004)**	**(0.000)**	
β_{22}	**0.163**		**0.525**	**0.312**	–0.047		0.021	1.366	0.021	0.853	0.000	
	0.091		**0.000**	**(0.021)**	(0.853)		(0.941)	(0.234)	(0.301)	(0.388)	(0.994)	
β_{31}	**0.005**		**0.005**	**0.009**	**0.005**		**0.005**	**0.011**	**0.006**	0.000	**0.005**	
	(0.000)		**(0.000)**	**(0.000)**	**(0.000)**		**(0.000)**	**(0.000)**	**(0.000)**	(0.951)	**(0.000)**	
β_{32}	**–0.001**		0.000	**–0.001**	**0.018**		**0.012**	**0.128**	**–0.004**	**0.799**	**–0.008**	
	(0.032)		(0.986)	**(0.047)**	**(0.000)**		**(0.004)**	**(0.000)**	**(0.063)**	**(0.000)**	**(0.053)**	
β_{41}	**0.132**		0.031	**0.139**	**0.111**		–0.022	**0.177**	**0.106**	0.074	–0.015	
	(0.001)		(0.496)	**(0.083)**	**(0.002)**		(0.656)	**(0.032)**	**(0.003)**	(0.311)	(0.746)	
β_{42}	**0.135**		–0.333	0.082	0.116		–0.203	0.318	**0.203**	**0.261**	**0.221**	
	(0.029)		(0.129)	(0.303)	(0.466)		(0.531)	(0.591)	**(0.000)**	**(0.016)**	**(0.002)**	
β_{51}	**0.001**		**0.001**	**0.001**	**0.001**		**0.001**	**0.002**	**0.001**	0.001	**0.001**	
	(0.000)		**(0.000)**	**(0.000)**	**(0.000)**		**(0.000)**	**(0.000)**	**(0.000)**	(0.165)	**(0.000)**	
β_{52}	**0.001**		**0.003**	0.000	**0.002**		**0.002**	**0.017**	0.000	**–0.002**	0.000	
	(0.000)		**(0.000)**	(0.638)	**(0.000)**		**(0.000)**	**(0.000)**	(0.743)	**(0.000)**	(0.965)	

c_{11}	**0.000**		**0.000**	**0.000**	**0.000**		**0.000**	**0.000**	**0.000**	**0.000**	**0.000**
	(0.000)		**(0.000)**	**(0.000)**	**(0.000)**		**(0.001)**	**(0.001)**	**(0.000)**	**(0.096)**	**(0.001)**
c_{22}	**0.000**		**0.003**	**0.001**	**0.002**		**0.010**	**0.004**	**0.001**	**0.003**	**0.000**
	(0.000)		**(0.000)**	**(0.000)**	**(0.000)**		**(0.000)**	**(0.000)**	**(0.000)**	**(0.001)**	**(0.003)**
c_{12}	0.002		0.001	**0.002**	**0.000**		**0.002**	0.001	**0.000**	**0.003**	0.000
	(0.626)		(0.230)	**(0.000)**	**(0.029)**		**(0.036)**	(0.274)	**(0.000)**	**(0.000)**	(0.144)
b_{11}	**0.885**		**0.630**	**0.890**	**0.898**		**0.589**	**0.907**	**0.901**	**0.967**	**0.658**
	(0.000)		**(0.000)**	**(0.000)**	**(0.000)**		**(0.000)**	**(0.000)**	**(0.000)**	**(0.000)**	**(0.000)**
b_{22}	**0.668**		**0.545**	**0.169**	**0.550**		**0.282**	**0.710**	**0.489**	0.136	**0.847**
	(0.000)		**(0.000)**	**(0.000)**	**(0.000)**		**(0.000)**	**(0.000)**	**(0.000)**	(0.496)	**(0.000)**
b_{12}	−0.736		0.404	**−0.733**	**0.809**		−0.199	−0.287	**0.926**	−0.452	**0.940**
	(0.836)		(0.397)	**(0.000)**	**(0.000)**		(0.653)	(0.781)	**(0.000)**	(0.234)	**(0.000)**
a_{11}	**0.100**		**0.477**	**0.059**	**0.094**		**0.564**	**0.065**	**0.091**	**0.022**	**0.450**
	(0.000)		**(0.000)**	**(0.000)**	**(0.000)**		**(0.000)**	**(0.000)**	**(0.000)**	**(0.015)**	**(0.000)**
a_{22}	**0.358**		**0.450**	**0.608**	**0.687**		**1.365**	**0.316**	**0.282**	**0.194**	**0.117**
	(0.000)		**(0.000)**	**(0.000)**	**(0.000)**		**(0.000)**	**(0.000)**	**(0.000)**	**(0.018)**	**(0.000)**
a_{12}	−0.001		0.101	**−0.043**	**0.046**		0.138	−0.040	**0.028**	**−0.064**	**0.033**
	(0.947)		(0.242)	**(0.068)**	**(0.018)**		(0.161)	(0.292)	**(0.000)**	**(0.012)**	**(0.051)**

Notes: Mean equation: $\Delta R_{i,t} = \beta_{0,i} + \beta_{1,i}\Delta E_t(V_{i,t+1}) + \beta_{2,i}\Delta E_t(\text{Cov}_{ij,t+1}) + \beta_{3,i}\Delta V\text{stoxx}_t + \beta_{4,i}\Delta r_t + \beta_{5,i}\Delta\text{CDS}_{i,t} + \varepsilon_{i,t}$
Columns without estimates represent the periods during which estimations have not converged.

Table D.7. Parameter Estimates of the GARCH Models

	Spain–Ireland				Spain–Greece				Ireland–Greece			
Coefficient	Full Sample	Pre-crisis	Crisis	Post-OMT	Full Sample	Pre-crisis	Crisis	Post-OMT	Full Sample	Pre-crisis	Crisis	Post-OMT
β_{01}	**−0.003**		−0.002	**−0.005**	**−0.003**	−0.004	0.000		0.001	−0.002	0.006	
	(0.013)		(0.566)	**(0.001)**	**(0.007)**	**(0.183)**	**(0.908)**		**(0.787)**	**(0.631)**	**(0.187)**	
β_{02}	0.004		**0.012**	−0.008	**−0.006**	−0.006	−0.004		**−0.005**	−0.003	**−0.004**	
	(0.248)		**(0.069)**	**(0.367)**	**(0.000)**	**(0.188)**	**(0.118)**		**(0.000)**	**(0.475)**	**(0.093)**	
β_{11}	**0.778**		**−0.547**	0.336	**0.735**	1.247	**−0.472**		0.013	−0.291	0.068	
	(0.000)		**(0.017)**	(0.111)	**(0.000)**	(0.382)	**(0.034)**		(0.878)	(0.678)	(0.545)	
β_{12}	**0.137**		0.037	1.742	−0.001	**1.683**	0.000		0.000	**−1.796**	0.000	
	(0.073)		(0.806)	(0.553)	(0.183)	**(0.023)**	(0.575)		(0.605)	**(0.071)**	(0.839)	
β_{21}	**0.855**		**0.376**	**2.435**	−0.018	**2.108**	**−0.117**		**0.975**	**3.961**	**0.966**	
	(0.000)		**(0.009)**	**(0.000)**	(0.683)	**(0.014)**	**(0.098)**		**(0.000)**	**(0.000)**	**(0.000)**	
β_{22}	**−0.558**		−0.486	2.465	0.046	0.356	0.030		**0.076**	**4.197**	0.045	
	(0.046)		(0.248)	(0.477)	(0.213)	(0.630)	(0.636)		**(0.010)**	**(0.000)**	(0.245)	
β_{31}	0.000		−0.002	**0.002**	0.000	−0.001	−0.001		**0.014**	**0.007**	**0.004**	
	(0.850)		(0.470)	**(0.006)**	(0.509)	(0.156)	(0.706)		**(0.000)**	**(0.006)**	**(0.059)**	
β_{32}	**0.014**		**0.008**	**0.122**	**−0.005**	**0.858**	**−0.008**		**−0.005**	**0.961**	**−0.007**	
	(0.000)		**(0.052)**	**(0.000)**	**(0.032)**	**(0.000)**	**(0.049)**		**(0.046)**	**(0.000)**	**(0.079)**	
β_{41}	0.064		−0.310	0.046	0.077	**0.118**	−0.304		0.175	0.016	**0.567**	
	(0.284)		(0.110)	(0.637)	(0.207)	**(0.098)**	(0.102)		(0.053)	(0.877)	**(0.000)**	
β_{42}	0.122		−0.412	0.419	**0.189**	**0.192**	**0.246**		**0.238**	**0.242**	**0.264**	
	(0.451)		(0.143)	(0.471)	**(0.000)**	**(0.068)**	**(0.000)**		**(0.000)**	**(0.032)**	**(0.000)**	
β_{51}	**0.003**		**0.003**	**0.002**	**0.003**	**0.002**	**0.004**		**0.002**	**0.002**	**0.002**	
	(0.000)		**(0.000)**	**(0.000)**	**(0.000)**	**(0.000)**	**(0.000)**		**(0.000)**	**(0.000)**	**(0.000)**	
β_{52}	**0.002**		**0.002**	**0.016**	0.000	**−0.002**	0.000		0.000	**−0.003**	0.000	
	(0.000)		**(0.000)**	**(0.000)**	(0.917)	**(0.000)**	(0.921)		(0.864)	**(0.000)**	(0.925)	

c_{11}	**0.000**	**0.001**	**0.001**	**0.000**	**0.002**	**0.001**	**0.000**	**0.000**	**0.002**
	(0.000)	**(0.000)**	**(0.000)**	**(0.000)**	**(0.000)**	**(0.004)**	**(0.001)**	**(0.090)**	**(0.000)**
c_{22}	**0.002**	**0.009**	**0.004**	**0.001**	**0.003**	**0.000**	**0.001**	**0.003**	**0.000**
	(0.000)	**(0.000)**	**(0.000)**	**(0.000)**	**(0.001)**	**(0.004)**	**(0.000)**	**(0.001)**	**(0.002)**
c_{12}	**0.003**	**0.003**	0.000	**0.000**	**0.002**	0.000	**0.000**	0.001	0.001
	(0.000)	**(0.005)**	(0.104)	**(0.000)**	**(0.005)**	(0.805)	**(0.001)**	(0.177)	(0.103)
b_{11}	**0.876**	**0.718**	**0.472**	**0.892**	−0.046	**0.788**	**0.696**	**0.937**	**0.448**
	(0.000)	**(0.000)**	**(0.000)**	**(0.000)**	(0.535)	**(0.000)**	**(0.000)**	**(0.000)**	**(0.000)**
b_{22}	**0.549**	**0.296**	**0.707**	**0.471**	0.224	**0.845**	**0.558**	0.182	**0.816**
	(0.000)	**(0.000)**	**(0.000)**	**(0.000)**	(0.160)	**(0.000)**	**(0.000)**	(0.296)	**(0.000)**
b_{12}	**−0.658**	**0.524**	**0.680**	**0.899**	−0.187	−0.407	**0.489**	**0.555**	0.071
	(0.000)	**(0.000)**	**(0.000)**	**(0.000)**	(0.552)	(0.279)	**(0.000)**	**(0.063)**	(0.848)
a_{11}	**0.121**	**0.240**	**0.151**	**0.110**	**0.480**	**0.191**	**0.539**	**0.058**	**1.322**
	(0.000)	**(0.000)**	**(0.000)**	**(0.000)**	**(0.000)**	**(0.000)**	**(0.000)**	**(0.002)**	**(0.000)**
a_{22}	**0.691**	**1.307**	**0.324**	**0.294**	**0.280**	**0.125**	**0.271**	**0.271**	**0.144**
	(0.000)	**(0.000)**	**(0.000)**	**(0.000)**	**(0.003)**	**(0.000)**	**(0.000)**	**(0.001)**	**(0.000)**
a_{12}	**0.139**	**0.263**	**0.095**	**0.053**	**0.135**	**0.116**	**0.171**	**0.083**	**0.200**
	(0.000)	**(0.000)**	**(0.005)**	**(0.000)**	**(0.062)**	**(0.044)**	**(0.000)**	**(0.052)**	**(0.036)**

Notes: Mean equation: $\Delta R_{i,t} = \beta_{0,i} + \beta_{1,i}\Delta E_t(V_{i,t+1}) + \beta_{2,i}\Delta E_t(\mathrm{Cov}_{ij,t+1}) + \beta_{3,i}\Delta V\mathrm{stoxx}_t + \beta_{4,i}\Delta r_t + \beta_{5,i}\Delta \mathrm{CDS}_{i,t} + \varepsilon_{i,t}$
Columns without estimates represent the periods during which estimations have not converged.

Appendix E: Two-step Rolling Linear Regression Estimates

dvar represents the sensitivity of interest rates to conditional variances. *dcov* represents the sensitivity of interest rates to conditional covariances.

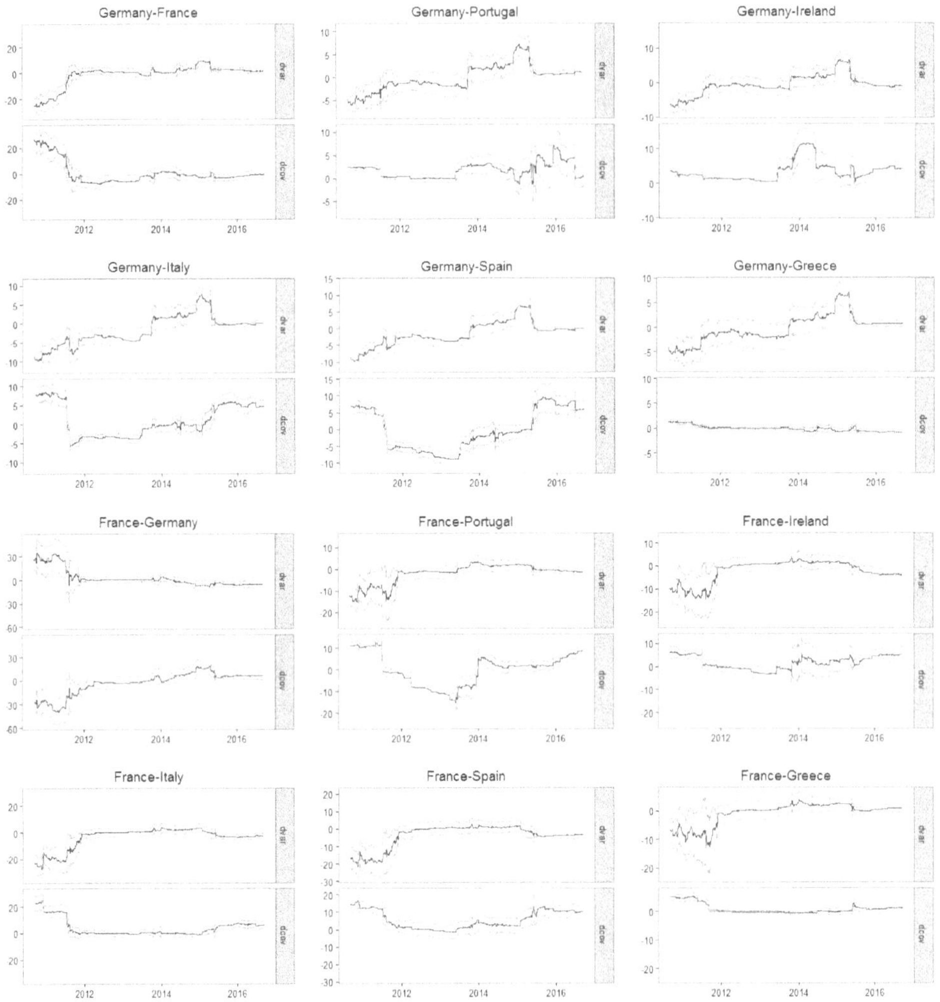

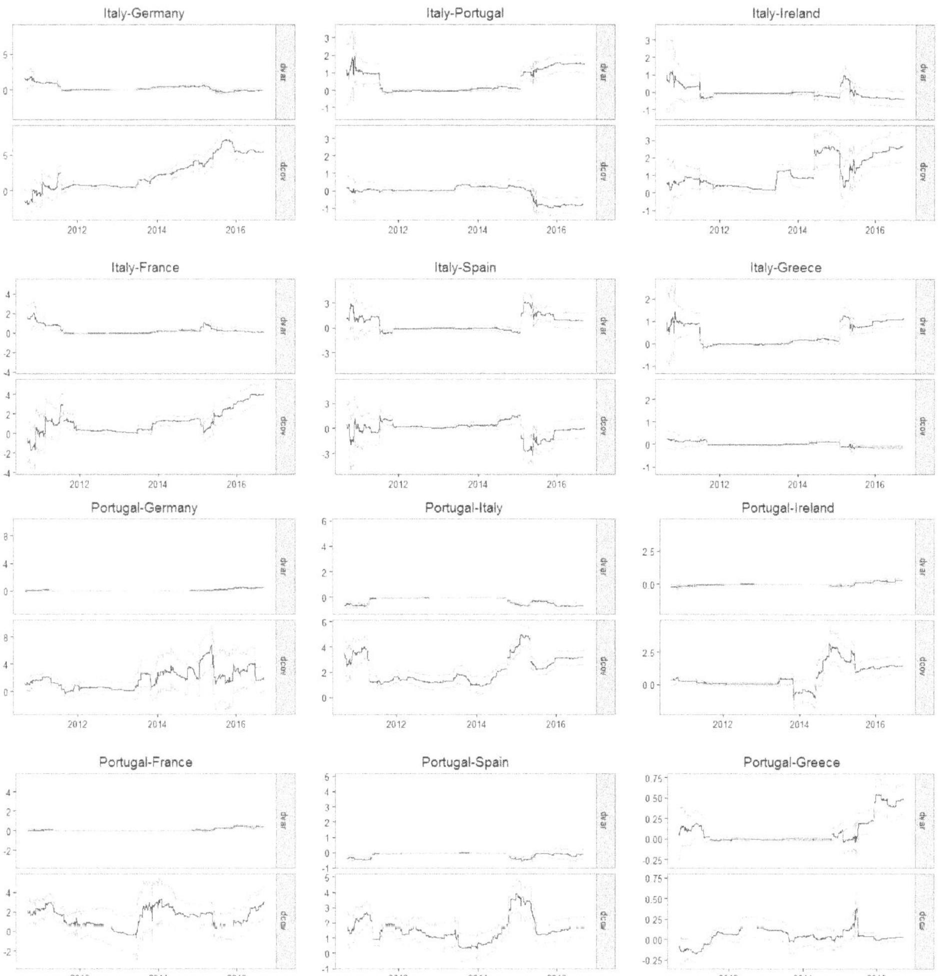
Italy-Germany
Italy-Portugal
Italy-Ireland
Italy-France
Italy-Spain
Italy-Greece
Portugal-Germany
Portugal-Italy
Portugal-Ireland
Portugal-France
Portugal-Spain
Portugal-Greece
dvar
dcov
2012
2014
2016

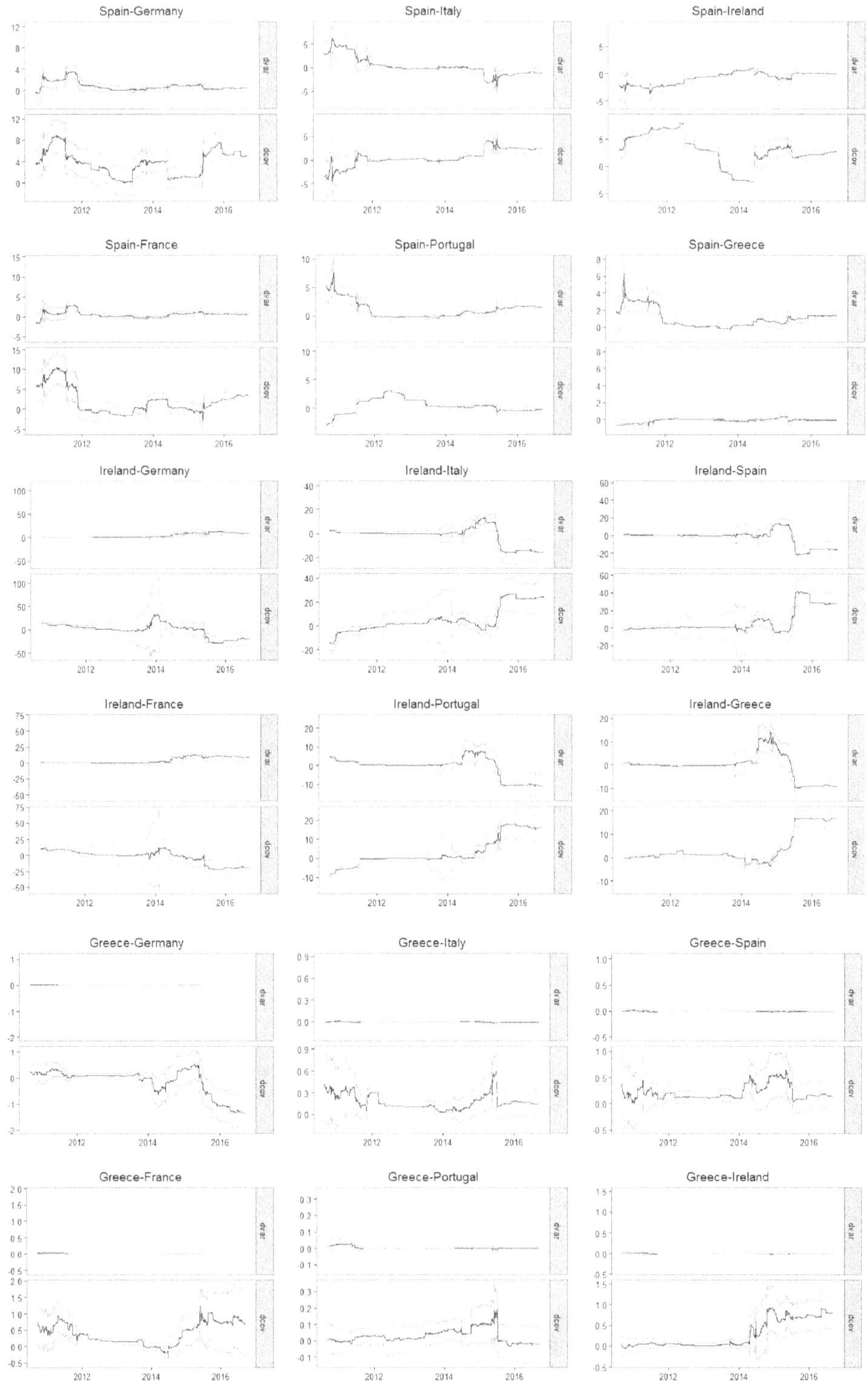
Spain-Germany
Spain-Italy
Spain-Ireland
Spain-France
Spain-Portugal
Spain-Greece
Ireland-Germany
Ireland-Italy
Ireland-Spain
Ireland-France
Ireland-Portugal
Ireland-Greece
Greece-Germany
Greece-Italy
Greece-Spain
Greece-France
Greece-Portugal
Greece-Ireland
dvar
dcov
2012
2014
2016

Appendix F: Conditional Correlation Dynamics

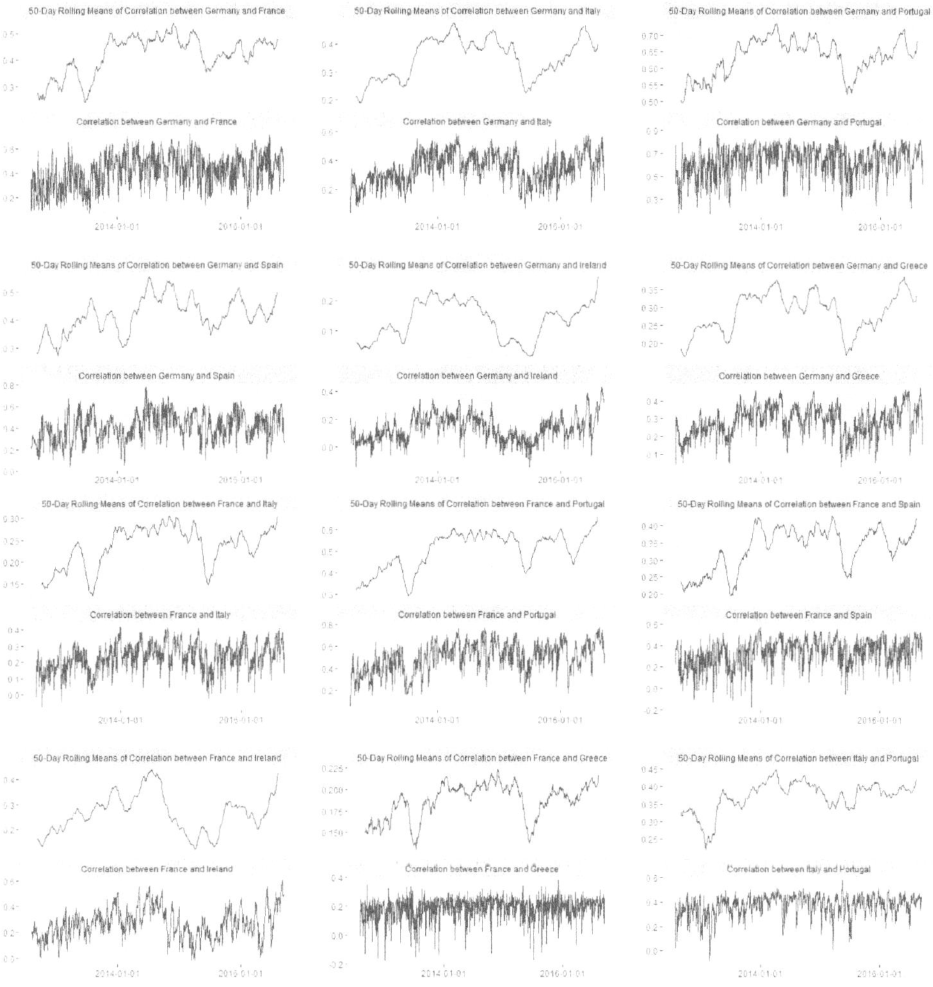

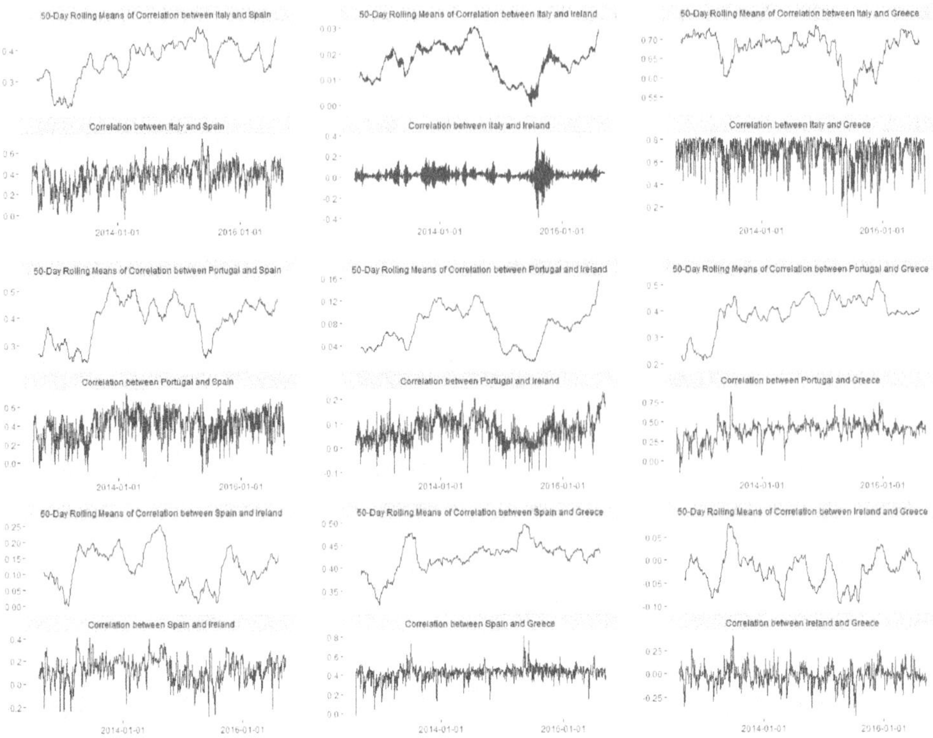
50-Day Rolling Means of Correlation between Italy and Spain
Correlation between Italy and Spain
50-Day Rolling Means of Correlation between Italy and Ireland
Correlation between Italy and Ireland
50-Day Rolling Means of Correlation between Italy and Greece
Correlation between Italy and Greece
50-Day Rolling Means of Correlation between Portugal and Spain
Correlation between Portugal and Spain
50-Day Rolling Means of Correlation between Portugal and Ireland
Correlation between Portugal and Ireland
50-Day Rolling Means of Correlation between Portugal and Greece
Correlation between Portugal and Greece
50-Day Rolling Means of Correlation between Spain and Ireland
Correlation between Spain and Ireland
50-Day Rolling Means of Correlation between Spain and Greece
Correlation between Spain and Greece
50-Day Rolling Means of Correlation between Ireland and Greece
Correlation between Ireland and Greece
2014-01-01
2016-01-01

Chapter 18

Repurchase Agreements and the European Sovereign Debt Crises: The Role of European Clearinghouses

Angela Armakolla*, Raphael Douady† and Jean-Paul Laurent‡

** Université Paris 1 Panthéon-Sorbonne*
PRISM Sorbonne and Labex ReFi, France
† Stony Brook University, USA, and Labex ReFi, France
‡ Université Paris 1 Panthéon-Sorbonne
PRISM Sorbonne and Labex ReFi, France

Abstract

This chapter investigates the European repo market and its role as an amplifier of tensions in the sovereign debt markets. We focus on the centrally cleared segment, representing the majority of European repos. A novel data set on repo and margin haircuts applied to sovereign bonds by central clearing counterparties (CCPs) is gathered, allowing us to assess the haircut methodologies used by the major European CCPs. We document that following increases in sovereign risk, haircuts set by major CCPs on peripheral sovereign bonds increased significantly. The procyclicality of haircuts and the concentration of bilateral repos raise concerns about the CCP-intermediated repo market as a source of systemic risk in the euro area. This is however mitigated by the countercyclical monetary policy of the European Central Bank (ECB).

1. Introduction

Post-crisis interbank transactions in the Euro Zone occur mainly via the secured market, where repurchase agreements (repos)[1] account for an increasing share of liquidity in European financial institutions (CGFS, 2013). This change in the financing patterns of European banks was caused by increased awareness of counterparty credit risk and the expansion of the liquidity operations of the European Central Bank (ECB).

Our work complements the existing literature by providing a broader view of the various European repo market segments. We focus on haircuts and margin haircuts[2] for General Collateral Pooling (GCP)[3] and classical repos by major central clearing counterparties (CCPs).[4] During the crisis, most CCPs raised their repo and margin haircuts on (peripheral) sovereign bonds of countries in financial distress. This empirical evidence raises concerns about the European repo market as a potential transmission channel of systemic risk and as an amplifier of tensions in the sovereign debt markets.

Some of our concerns are similar to those expressed when studying the US market. While the market structures in the EU and the US are strikingly different (Hördahl and King, 2008), repos largely financed the US shadow banking system and were targeted as a possible source of financial instability related to the procyclicality of leverage (Adrian and Shin, 2009, 2010), the maturity mismatch in investment banks' balance sheets (Brunnermeier, 2009), and the negative consequences of rises in haircuts on banking liquidity (Gorton and Metrick, 2010, 2012). Krishnamurthy *et al.* (2014) and Copeland *et al.* (2014) analyze, respectively, repo transactions of money market funds and security lenders and the tri-party repo[5] market in the US, finding results contradicting the "repo run" explanation for the liquidity crisis in 2007–2009. The latter reports that in the tri-party market, haircuts and the amount of funding were stable between 2008 and 2010, while the former argues that the collapse in the asset-backed commercial paper (ABCP) market

[1]A repurchase agreement is an agreement between two parties on the sale and subsequent repurchase of securities at an agreed price.

[2]Margin haircuts refer to the haircuts applied to the collateral securities that a clearing member can provide as margin to the CCP (margin collateral).

[3]GCP repos are collateralized by a large basket of high-quality and liquid securities that can be equivalently pledged to the ECB.

[4]A CCP is a financial intermediary that provides post-trade services such as clearing and settlement. The CCP guarantees trade delivery if either party to the trade defaults.

[5]Tri-party repos involve a third party, usually a custodian bank, acting as an intermediary.

was the primary cause of the shadow banking system's breakdown. Martin *et al.* (2014) document that haircuts in the bilateral markets increased dramatically, whereas haircuts in the tri-party market barely changed. They argue that the tri-party repo market is much more vulnerable to runs due to its microstructure, as runs take place, when margins do not increase sufficiently to reassure the investor. They identify the early settlement of repos (unwind) as a destabilizing feature of this market. Blundell-Wignall *et al.* (2014) show the raise in the gross credit exposure of derivatives and collateral demanded in the US market during 2007–2008, illustrating the pressure on the liquidity of banks in respect to margin calls related to derivatives and repo positions.

Ebner *et al.* (2016), Mancini *et al.* (2016), and Boissel *et al.* (2016) investigated repos transacted on the principal European anonymous electronic trading platforms (ETPs). Mancini *et al.* (2016), considering GCP repos from Eurex Repo, found that volumes, rates, and haircuts of this market segment were resilient during the crisis. On the contrary, Boissel *et al.* (2016), focusing on overnight repos collateralized by sovereign debt, find that this market became stressed in terms of rates and haircuts in the periphery of the Euro Zone in 2011. Molteni (2015) shows that raises in haircuts on peripheral bonds have intensified tensions in the European sovereign debt market, tightening the link between sovereign weakness and banking fragility. Also, as outlined by Acharya and Steffen (2015), Coimbra (2014), Claeys (2014), and Drechsler *et al.* (2016), the ECB's monetary policy had a significant impact on the European sovereign debt markets and stakeholder strategies. As the ECB's haircut policy is key to understanding the behavior of sovereign debt in the Euro Zone in troubled times, we consider the ECB's collateral policy and its impact on the European sovereign debt crisis.

Our main contribution to the emerging literature on centrally cleared repos is the creation of a novel dataset on haircuts applied by the main European CCPs on sovereign bonds. As the haircuts set by these major CCPs may significantly affect the value of the security, we analyze CCP haircut policies during the sovereign debt crisis in the Euro Zone for the period 2011–2012, emphasizing the role of CCPs with regard to procyclicality and systemic risk in the sovereign debt market.

Our empirical analysis yields the following findings:

- Following an increasing trend since 2009, the majority of European repos is centrally cleared.
- The repo market is concentrated in few market participants, CCPs, and underlying collateral assets.

- CCP haircuts and margin haircuts have been highly procyclical, while ECB haircuts have dampened procyclical effects.

The remainder of this chapter is organized as follows. Section 2 explains the different types of repos and introduces technical terminology. Section 3 describes the European repo market. Section 4 focuses on haircut methodologies and haircuts during the crisis. Finally, Section 5 concludes.

2. Repurchase Agreements for European Sovereign Bonds

2.1. *Concepts and definitions*

A repurchase agreement is an agreement between two parties on the sale and subsequent repurchase of securities at an agreed price. The original seller is called cash borrower. The sell side are securities dealers, commercial banks, and leveraged investors such as hedge funds, using their securities as collateral for a secured cash loan at a fixed interest rate (repo rate), which is the difference between the repurchase price and the original sale price. The original buyer is the cash lender, typically central banks, commercial banks, investment funds, and money market funds. Central banks use repo to implement monetary policy operations, involving the provision of liquidity against a predefined range of collateral (ECB, 2015).

The seller registers the transaction as a liability on its balance sheet and the buyer as an asset (reverse repo). We define repo transactions between two private financial institutions (i.e., interbank liquidity) as *private repo* and transactions conducted with the ECB (i.e., central bank liquidity) as *public repo*.

Unlike a secured loan, legal title to the securities passes from the seller to the buyer, who may "reuse" the respective asset in another transaction with a third party. Due to differing title transfer arrangements and impending stricter regulatory rules for collateral reuse, collateral-chains will shorten (Singh, 2011, 2012).

The purpose of the collateral is to protect a lender against the risk of a borrower's default. The difference between the cash and the value of the collateral is called *haircut* or *initial margin*.

According to settlement type, repos can be divided into two categories (Adrian *et al.*, 2014; Choudhry, 2010):

- *Bilateral agreements* are concluded between two counterparties on a "delivery vs. payment" basis, meaning that the transfer of the collateral to the cash lender occurs simultaneously with the transfer of the cash to the collateral provider. Bilateral agreements can be conducted on the private market or via a CCP.

- *Tri-party repo agreements* are based on the initial bilateral agreement, and involve a third party, usually a custodian bank, acting as an intermediary. Tri-party providers offer the necessary back-office services to their clients, such as collateral management, risk management, settlement service, etc.

Repos occur with different maturities, but the majority of repos are short term, overnight, or weekly (ECB, 2012). Repos can be categorized as *overnight repo*, referring to a one-day maturity transaction, *short-date repo*, with a term of one month or shorter, and *term repo*, with a term of one year or longer. Other categories are *forward repo*, starting one or more months in the future, and *open repo*, which does not have a fixed maturity and can be terminated at any future date by either party.

Repos can also be distinguished by the underlying collateral asset: *General Collateral (GC) repos* are collateralized by a large basket of high-quality and liquid securities that can be equivalently pledged to the ECB, characterized by very similar repo rates. *Special repos* focus on a specific asset demanded as collateral. GC repos are cash driven and motivated by the liquidity needs of the cash lender, while special repos are security driven and may be part of short-selling strategies. Special repo rates are lower than GC repo rates. *Credit repo* is a repo using underlying collateral other than high-quality securities, such as bonds issued by central governments in emerging markets.

There are several analogies between repo contracts in the "securitized" banking system and deposits in the traditional banking system, as highlighted by Gorton and Metrick (2012). Both provide liquidity to credit intermediaries and are funding sources for long-term activities. The haircut forces banks to keep a fraction of their assets in reserve when borrowing through repos, similar to a reserve requirement for traditional banks. Repo rates remunerate cash lenders similar to the deposit rate for depositors. Finally, as the maturity transformation makes traditional banks subject to the risk of bank runs (Diamond and Dybvig, 1983), analogously the securitized banking system faces the risk of repo runs. Increases in haircuts reduce the amount of liquidity available to banks like a massive withdrawal of deposits, causing liquidity shortages which may force asset fire-sales.

2.2. *Cleared repo*

In a cleared repo, a CCP interposes itself between the cash lender and the cash borrower. The CCP guarantees that the trade will be delivered to both parties and assumes the counterparty risk (Gregory, 2014). To protect the CCP against participant default, each participant has to provide margin and contribute to the default fund. In contrast to bilateral repos, a CCP demands margin from both the cash lender and cash borrower (CPSS, 2010). We can distinguish between the security that the borrower provides to the lender in the repo (underlying security) and securities that the borrower and the lender can provide as margin to the CCP (margin collateral). Margin requirements can be met in cash or by posting securities. If the margin requirement is provided in securities, the CCP will again apply a haircut (margin haircut).

The exact composition of the overall margin depends on the CCP, but generally comprises:

- variation margin (VM) to cover daily portfolio variations;
- initial margin (IM) to cover potential losses (between the last VM payment and the final close-out of the defaulter's position) the CCP may face in case a member defaults. IM models have to meet established regulatory confidence levels;
- additional margin (add-on) demanded on portfolio level
  - when a concentration limit for a deposited security is breached or in case of wrong-way risk (negative correlation between issuer and provider of a security);
  - to cover currency risk, if the trading currency and the margin currency are not identical;
  - when participants have a lower credit standing or capital resources.

The IM amount is obtained from the haircut set by the CCP (see Eurex Clearing, 2012). Contrary to the bilateral haircut, IM is a percentage premium that is added to the market value of the asset (CPSS, 2010).

2.3. *Regulatory incentives*

International repo markets are subject to a wide range of new regulatory measures and incentives, possibly resulting in fundamental changes in the use of repos and repo market structures.

At European level, a Financial Transaction Tax (FTT) is foreseen for financial transactions, including certain types of repos (EC, 2013a, 2013b). Besides the fact that the FTT would only be applied by 11 member states

(Gabor, 2016), the expected negative impacts for the repo markets include overall volume decline, vanishing of overnight repos, and decrease of available liquidity (Comotto, 2013).

The Basel III Liquidity Coverage Ratio (LCR), which aims at promoting short-term resilience, has a direct impact on repos (BCBS, 2013a, 2014). If the market participant faces potential maturity mismatches in his cash flows for security financing transactions (SFTs), such as repos, with a maturity of less than thirty days, he must cover this possible liquidity risk by holding high-quality liquid assets (HQLAs). The LCR addresses cash in- and outflows over a period of 30 days with a roll off of repo transactions determined by asset quality. For short-term transactions, this may incentivize banks to use lower quality assets for central bank operations and HQLAs for private repos (Schmitz, 2013). Under the LCR, government bonds, which do not

> "have a proven record as a reliable source of liquidity [...] during stressed market conditions"

(BCBS, 2013a, p. 13), are not considered as HQLAs. When the creditworthiness of a government erodes and haircuts on such debt increases, banks sell off these securities. This is not only to avoid a cut of leverage and funding, but also to meet the new regulatory requirements, reinforcing flight-to-liquidity towards the bonds of the core and debt market fragmentation.

As for the Basel III Leverage Ratio (LR), the June 2013 proposal of Basel III (BCBS, 2013b) did not allow for netting of SFTs, whereas the revised Basel III LR framework (BCBS, 2014) allows for limited netting of repos with the same counterparty. In contrast, CCP-cleared contracts can even be netted across different asset classes. If SFTs cannot be netted, the LR would constrain banks' leverage, which may lead to an increase in cleared repos. Altogether, the Basel III requirements may increase costs for repo trading and funding, besides resulting in an increase of HQL demand and possibly amplifying the feedback loop between the raise in haircuts and the fall in the value of the security collateral described by Brunnermeier and Pedersen (2009).

The Financial Stability Board (FSB) has focused on the implementation of policies associated with shadow banking (FSB, 2012, 2013, 2014a), issuing recommendations regarding repos: collection of detailed data on repo exposures, implementation of rules to improve rehypothecation, adaption of minimum regulatory standards for collateral evaluation, possible move of repos to CCPs, and the introduction of minimum regulatory haircuts to address the procyclicality of haircuts associated with repos (FSB, 2012, 2013,

2014a, 2014b; EP, 2013). The first Quantitative Impact Study (QIS) on the procyclicality of haircuts (FSB, 2014b) shows that haircuts for non-centrally cleared repos increased for all underlying securities during the crisis, except for government bonds. Consequently, regulators will implement minimum standards for non-centrally cleared repos with non-government collateral (FSB, 2014a). This will increase funding costs for non-banks for all collateral, possibly leading to a reduction in trading activity in the private markets.

The systemic importance of CCPs, clearing banks, and dealer banks must be considered in case such an institution fails and needs to be resolved or recovered. Except for the UK, current regulation does not cover the resolution of CCPs (Armakolla and Laurent, 2017). Thus, regulators must carefully consider the consequences of a possible boost in repo clearing.

3. The European Repo Market

Due to the lack of comprehensive and standardized information, we rely on the following public data sources:

- **Bankscope:** Database on banks' balance sheets at yearly and quarterly frequency.
- **European Repo Market Survey (ERMS):** Semi-annual survey conducted by the International Capital Market Association (ICMA) since 2001.
- **Euro Money Market Survey (EMMS):** Yearly survey published by the ECB since 2002.

The significant expansion of the European repo market is documented in Fig. 1, showing the amount of repos in the balance sheet liabilities of European banks.

Repo volumes tripled between June 2001 and December 2007 from €0.92 trillion to €3.44 trillion. In December 2009, volumes contracted to €2.79 trillion in December 2009, recovering rapidly in June 2010, reaching €3.70 trillion. This estimate is close to the about €4 trillion of the outstanding repo business of the US primary dealers in 2009 (Acharya and Öncü, 2013).

Repos have become a key source of liquidity for European financial institutions, as shown in Table 1.

Repo data reported by Bankscope includes repos transacted with the ECB, thus we analyze the data in 2010 before the two large-scale LTROs in December 2011 and February 2012. As shown in Table 1, European G-SIB banks hold a considerable high fraction of repos in their balance

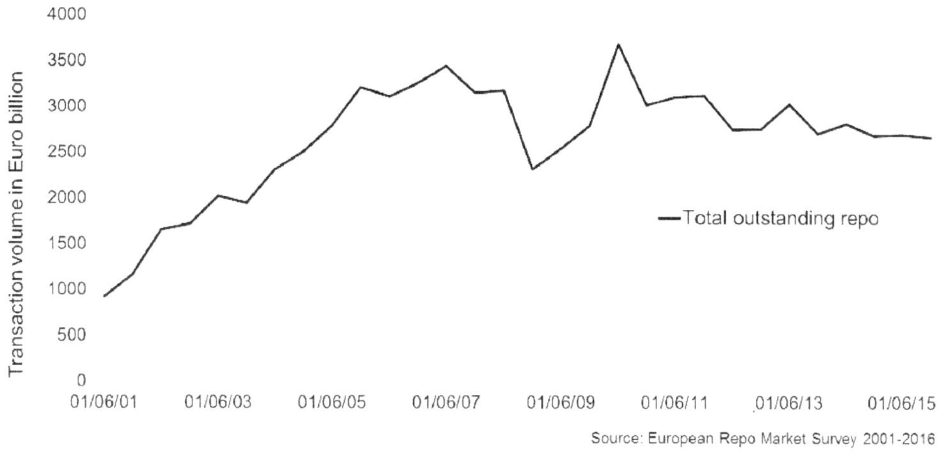

Figure 1. The European Repo Market

Note: The figure based on Molteni (2017) plots the amount of repos in the balance sheet liabilities of European banks, pointing out the rapid expansion of the European repo market.

Table 1. Funding Structure of European G-SIB Banks in 2010 (in Percentage of Total Liabilities)

Bank	Customer Deposits	Bonds	Repos	Interbank Deposits
BNP Paribas	26.62	6.19	10.48	7.07
Barclays Bank	23.41	9.89	13.26	5.89
Banco Santander	45.04	16.92	9.60	4.69
Société Générale	24.47	8.74	9.58	7.62
UBS AG	24.13	10.04	12.52	2.13

Source: Bankscope and based on Molteni (2017).

Note: This table shows bank balance sheet data from Bankscope in 2010. We can see that European G-SIB banks hold a considerable fraction of repos on their balance sheets.

sheet (approximatively 10% or more of their liabilities), and for most of the European banks, secured funding accounts for a larger share than unsecured funding.

The EMMS (ECB, 2012) reports that the unsecured market contracted steadily from 2008 to 2012, as shown in Fig. 2. This resulted in a switch from unsecured to secured lending. The diverging evolution of the two markets follows the decoupling of interest rates between the unsecured and the secured markets during the crisis (Heider and Hoerova, 2009). The EMMS

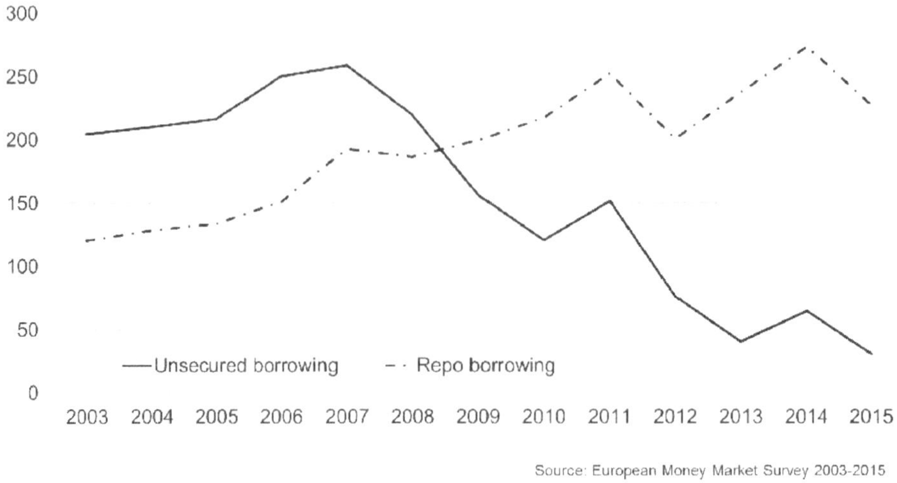

Figure 2. Cumulative Quarterly Turnover in Unsecured Cash Lending and Repo Borrowing (Index: Cash Lending Volume in 2003 = 100)

Note: Figure adapted from Molteni (2017) plots the quarterly turnover in unsecured and repo borrowing, showing a switch from unsecured to secured lending after the financial crisis.

also reports that the largest five banks accounted for 40% and the top ten banks for 62% of the total turnover for repo transactions, respectively, suggesting that European repos are highly concentrated between few financial institutions.

Approximatively 70% of European bilateral repos are cleared by CCPs, following an increasing trend since 2009 (see Fig. 3). Trilateral repos account for approximatively 10%, contrasting the approximately 70% of repos managed by a tri-party provider in the US (Copeland *et al.*, 2012).

A further structural characteristic of the European repo market to consider is the type of collateral used by market participants as repo underlying. Government bonds are the main type of repo underlying collateral used in the European market, representing approximatively between 76% and 84% for the period 2007–2015. The proportion of government bonds fell below 80% following the onset of the worldwide crisis, its further evolution then dampened by the European sovereign debt crisis. The percentage of government bonds within the pool of all EU-originated collateral as reported in the ERMS from 2007 to 2015 is shown in Fig. 4. The values are in percentage of total repo activity, according to collateral issues in the relevant country.

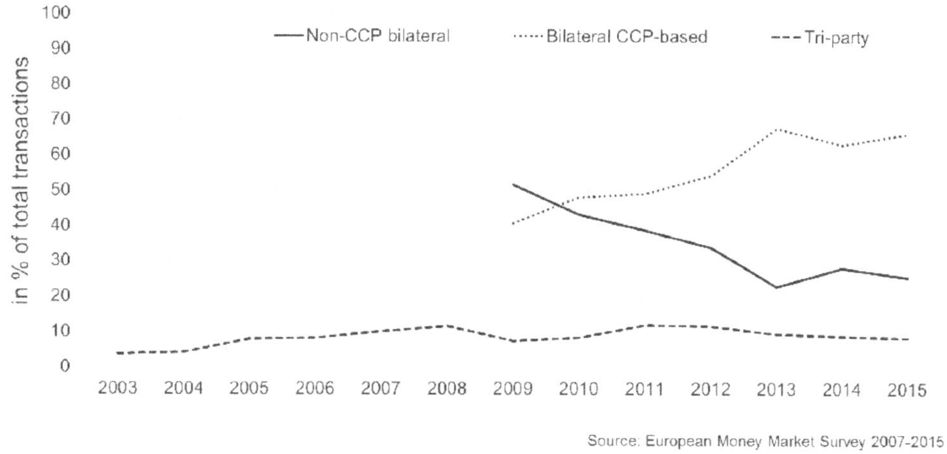

Figure 3. Composition of the European Repo Market

Note: This figure based on Molteni (2017) plots the composition of transaction types on the European repo market. Following an increasing trend since 2009, the majority of European repos is centrally cleared.

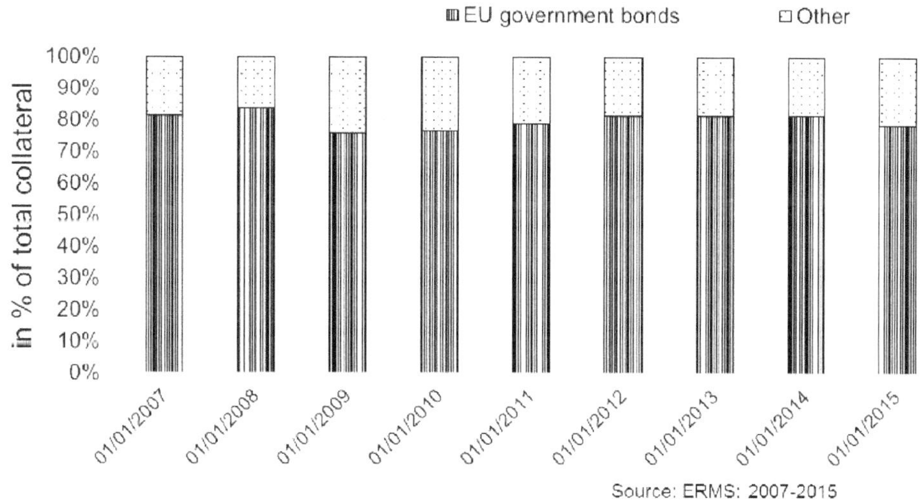

Figure 4. Percentage of EU Government Bond Collateral from 2007 to 2015

Note: This figure based on Molteni (2017) plots the type of collateral used by market participants as repo underlying. The main type of repo underlying are government bonds.

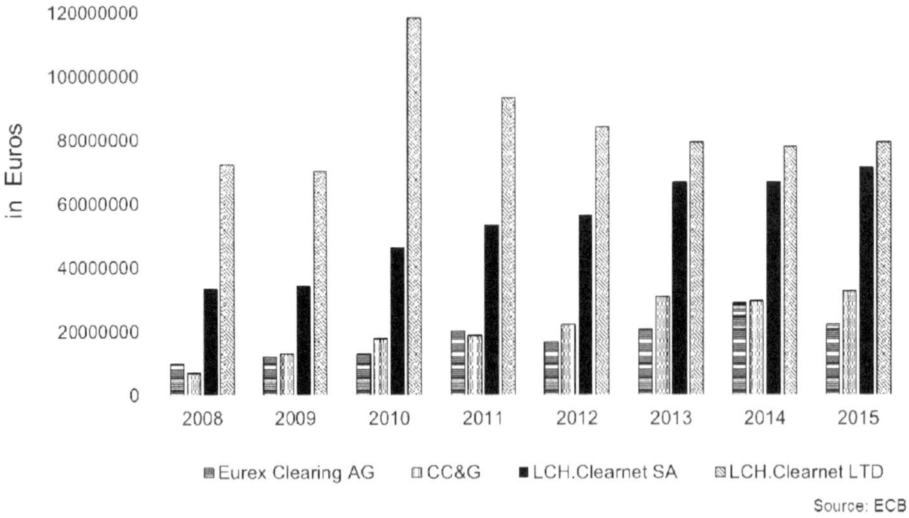

Figure 5. Volume of Cleared Repos per CCP from 2008 to 2015

Note: This figure plots the volume of repo transactions cleared by the four major European CCPs. The increase in cleared volumes mirrors the increase in cleared repos since 2009.

Interestingly, the use of government securities as collateral in the European private repo market seems to reflect their credit risk and liquidity. For instance, according to the ERMS, the share of Italian government bonds within the pool of collateral fell from 11.8% to 6.4% between December 2008 and December 2001, respectively, recovering to 9.2% in December 2013, when tensions in the Italian debt market alleviated and both the yields and the haircuts on Italian bonds reduced.

Finally, the Euro Zone repo market is concentrated in only a few clearing houses: LCH.Clearnet SA (Paris), LCH.Clearnet LTD (London), Eurex Clearing AG (Frankfurt), and Cassa di Compensazione e Garanzia SpA (CC&G) (Rome). Figure 5 shows the volume of cleared repos for these main CCPs.

To sum up, we observe a rapid expansion of European repos in the last decade, as well as a radical transformation of the interbank market during the crisis associated with an increase of repos cleared via CCPs.

Our work complements the FSB's study (FSB, 2014b) regarding non-centrally cleared SFTs, according to which the contraction in the repo market during the crisis was substantial in both absolute and relative terms, especially for non-banks. The decline in the share of non-CCP-based repos in the European repo market, see Fig. 3, seems to confirm these findings for the European jurisdiction. FSB (2014b) finds that haircut levels and dispersion increased dramatically for all collateral types except government securities, while in the next Section we show that haircuts on government bonds issued by the peripheral EU countries sharply augmented during the crisis.

4. CCPs and Repo Haircuts

4.1. *Eligibility criteria and repo haircut methodologies*

Haircut calculation methodologies are based on VaR and liquidity measures, the credit rating of the collateral or the issuer, credit spreads, the maturity of the collateral, and benchmark haircuts set by central banks (EP, 2013; CGFS, 2010). To be compliant with EMIR, CCP haircuts should be established taking into account criteria related to the quality of the asset (asset type, credit risk level, maturity, historical and hypothetical future price volatility, market liquidity, and FX risk), wrong way risk, and limit procyclicality (ECB, 2013).

Eurex Repo offers trading, clearing, and settlement services within the GC and special repo segment. Post-trade services, such as margining, are performed by Eurex Clearing AG. We study haircuts applied to sovereign debt instruments in the GC Pooling (GCP) ECB basket, which are based on the ECB's haircuts (see Table 2). The collateral framework of the GCP ECB basket is based on the collateral framework of the ECB's open-market operations.

In 2012, the basket comprised around 7500 securities from the following eligible issuer countries: Austria, Belgium, Finland, France, Germany, Luxembourg, Netherlands, Slovakia, and Slovenia.

Given the rare revision of ECB haircuts and the independence of daily or even monthly changes in market conditions (Nyborg, 2017), Eurex Clearing

Table 2. ECB Haircuts for 10-Year Government Bonds

01/02/2009	01/01/2011	01/10/2013	Rating
4%	4%	3%	AAA to A−
4%	9%	11.5%	BBB+ to BB−

Source: (ECB).

Note: This table shows the haircuts applied by the ECB to 10-year government bonds according to credit rating. These haircuts are used as benchmark haircuts for GCP baskets.

AG conducts its own risk assessment, often resulting in higher haircuts than those of the ECB (Eurex Repo, 2012).

Securities that do not have at least a credit rating of 'A-' from Standard and Poor's\Fitch Ratings or an 'A3' from Moody's are excluded from the basket. On January 27, 2012, Italian government bonds were excluded from the GCP ECB basket as Italy was downgraded (Eurex Repo, 2012). The cash provider can reuse the received collateral for refinancing within the ECB framework, the Eurex GCP market, and as margin.

The London Stock Exchange Group (LSEG) comprises LCH.Clearnet LTD, LCH.Clearnet SA, and CC&G. We rely on general documentation and information from the risk notices on the website of the LCH.Clearnet Group. LCH.Clearnet SA and CC&G use the same methodology for setting repo haircuts.

For LCH.Clearnet LTD's RepoClear classical repos, the following government bonds are eligible: Austrian, Belgian, Dutch, German, Irish, Finnish, Portuguese, Slovakian, Slovenian, Spanish, and United Kingdom. For a government bond, a spread of 450 basis points over a 10-year 'AAA' benchmark (e.g., German government bond) serves as an indicative level at which haircuts may be reviewed (LCH.Clearnet Group LTD, 2014). If the spread exceeds 450 basis points, a haircut of 15% is applied (LCH.Clearnet Group LTD, 2010). CDS prices and market-implied rating data are used to assess whether additional margin is required (LCH.Clearnet Group LTD, 2014).

LCH.Clearnet SA accepts French, Italian, and Spanish government debt for classical repos, whereas CC&G only clears Italian government debt. CC&G and LCH.Clearnet SA monitor sovereign risk via a market data-based model including several indicators for sovereign risk: CDS spreads, sovereign bond spreads, default probabilities, and credit ratings (CC&G, 2012).

4.2. *Haircut levels during the crisis*

Now we assess the evolution of CCP haircuts applied to government bonds with 10-year maturity during the European sovereign debt crises. Government bonds are categorized according to their haircut level during the crisis: bonds issued by European core countries (France and Germany) with rather stable haircuts, Italian and Spanish bonds with considerable haircut increases, and Irish and Portuguese bonds with extremely high levels of haircuts.

Haircuts on Italian debt were increased several times by LCH.Clearnet SA and CC&G. Figure 6 shows the jump of the haircut applied by both CCPs from 6.65% to 11.65% on November 9, 2011 during the most acute

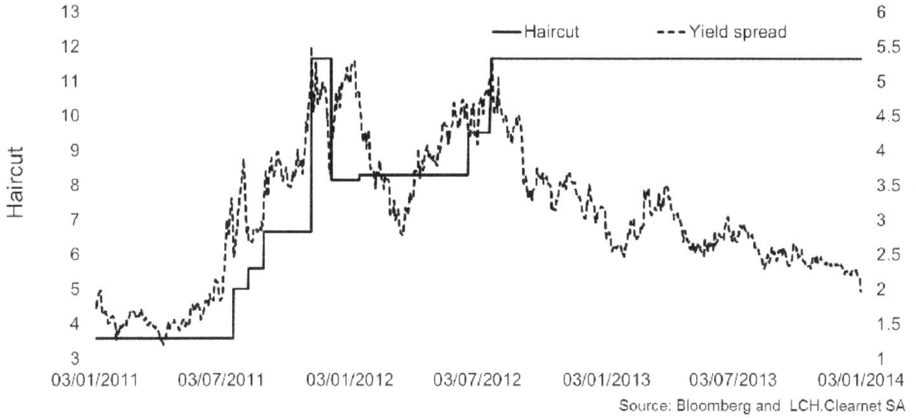

Figure 6. Haircut and Yield Spread of 10-year-Italian on 10-Year-German Sovereign Bond

Note: This figure plots the haircut applied by LCH.Clearnet SA to a 10-year Italian sovereign bond together with the yield spread of a 10-year Italian sovereign bond on a 10-year German sovereign bond.

phase on the Italian debt market. Following the reduction in the bond yields, the haircut decreased to 8.3% between January and June 2012, rising again to 11.65% on July 23, 2012.

The volume of Italian government repos intermediated by the two CCPs via the inter-operability agreement highly increased throughout 2012 and 2013 (Banca d'Italia, 2013b). This may also explain why the haircut on Italian government bonds was maintained at such a high level (Banca d'Italia, 2013a). As Italian debt was downgraded to 'BBB+' on January 13, Italian bonds were excluded from the Eurex GCP ECB basket (Eurex Repo, 2012). A collateral framework that is based on central bank haircuts does not function in the same way as a collateral framework in which haircuts are increased or decreased if necessary. If central bank haircuts are used, the range of eligible assets is narrowed down by the CCP, when the rating of a bond falls below a certain threshold.

As shown in Fig. 7, LCH.Clearnet SA also increased the haircut on Spanish government bonds in 2012 from 8.53% in January to 12.2% in July, and went down to 8.5% in August 2014.

A more striking sequence of haircuts increases was observed for Irish bonds as shown in Fig. 8. For the Irish government bonds, the dynamic of the haircut tracks that of the bond spreads closely. The haircut on Irish bonds increased from 15% to 80% between November 2010 and June 2011, falling back to 15% in February 2012. On April 1, 2011, LCH.Clearnet LTD

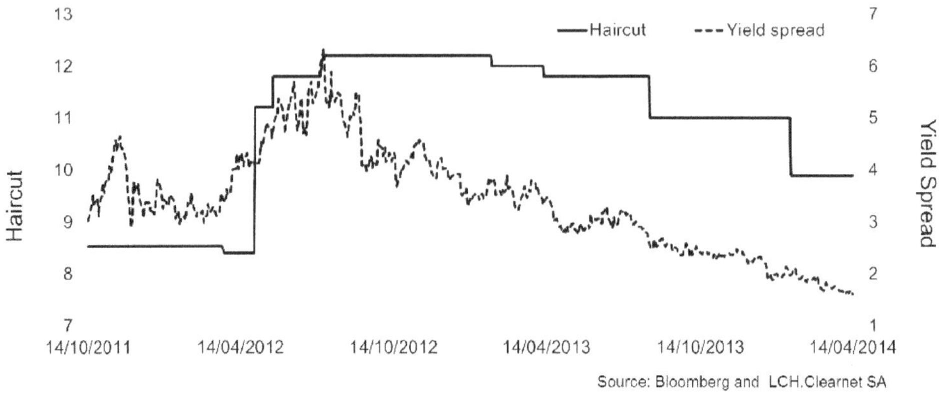

Figure 7. Haircut and Yield Spread of 10-Year-Spanish on 10-Year-German Sovereign Bond

Note: This figure plots the haircut applied by LCH.Clearnet SA to a 10-year Spanish sovereign bond together with the yield spread of a 10-year Spanish sovereign bond on a 10-year German sovereign bond.

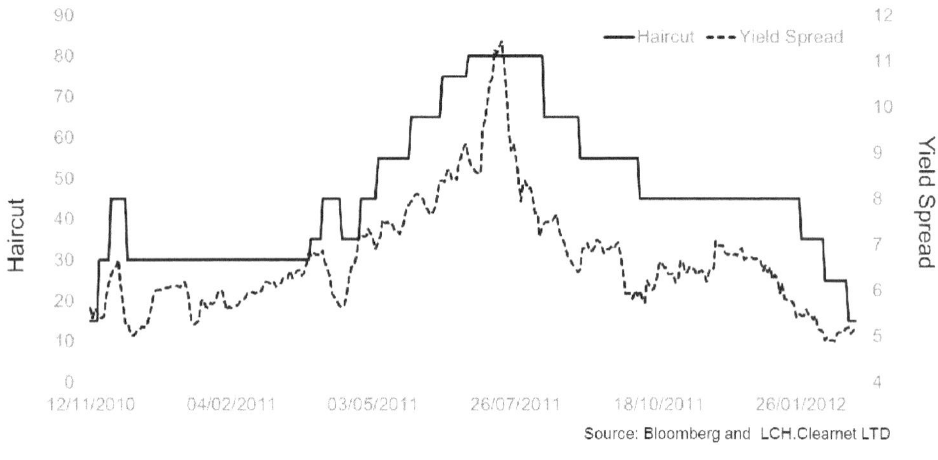

Figure 8. Haircut and Yield Spread of 10-Year-Irish on 10-Year-German Sovereign Bond

Note: This figure adapted from Molteni (2017) plots the haircut applied by LCH.Clearnet LTD to a 10-year Irish sovereign bond together with the yield spread of a 10-year Irish sovereign bond on a 10-year German sovereign bond.

increased the haircut to 45% from an initial 35% and decreased it again to 35% on April 13, 2011, suggesting that the haircut was set as a function of the spread. As stated in the member notices, LCH.Clearnet LTD, in each case, increased the haircut as a response to the yield spread of the 10-year Irish bond on an 'AAA'-rated benchmark.

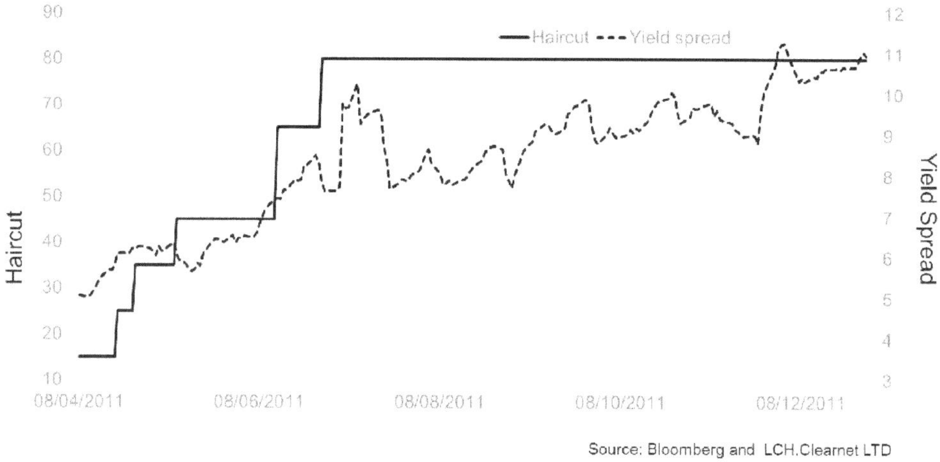

Figure 9. Haircut and Yield Spread of 10-Year-Portuguese on 10-Year-German Sovereign Bond

Note: This figure adapted from Molteni (2017) plots the haircut applied by LCH.Clearnet LTD to a 10-year Portuguese sovereign bond together with the yield spread of a 10-year Irish sovereign bond on a 10-year German sovereign bond.

In Fig. 9, a similar evolution can be observed for the haircuts on Portuguese bonds, which steadily augmented between April 2011 and June 2011, passing from 15% to 80%. These increases were associated with a widening of the yield spread, while the double downgrade in March 2011 from an initial 'A-' to 'BBB-' did not have an impact. Eurex Repo excluded Portuguese bonds from all its repo markets in January 2012 (Eurex Repo, 2012), corresponding to a haircut of 100%. The increase of CCP haircuts on Irish and Portuguese government bonds in 2010 and especially in 2011 caused CCP repo activity to almost cease for both securities in 2011 (Boissel *et al.*, 2016; Morgan Stanley Research, 2011).

The haircut increases on peripheral bonds have two important economic consequences. First, they shrink the amount of funding that financial institutions can obtain. For instance, if before the crisis a bank could borrow €85 by pledging a portfolio of Irish and Portuguese bonds which was worth €100, in the midst of the crisis with the same value of collateral securities they could borrow only €20. Second, the haircut increases cut the maximum leverage of financial institutions.

As banks fund their bond purchases mainly via repos, the haircut also determines the maximum possible leverage: before the crisis in order to purchase Irish and Portuguese bonds which were worth €100, banks could borrow up to €85 by pledging these securities in repos cleared by LCH.Clearnet LTD with a haircut of 15%; thus, the leverage was 100/15 = 6.6. When the haircuts spiked to 80%, the leverage fell to only 1.25.

The prolonged pre-crisis periods of low yields and risk premia on peripheral bonds along with the low levels of haircuts encouraged banks to expand their leverage, by pledging these securities in the repo market. The surge of sovereign risk led to an increase in yields and haircuts, exacerbating deleveraging incentives during the crisis. The procyclicality of haircuts in the private markets[6] reinforces the procyclicality of leverage and consequently of the asset prices (Adrian and Shin, 2009).

Structural characteristics of the European repo market, such as the required provision of margin by both the cash lender and the cash borrower for CCP-based repos, reinforce the "margin spiral" mechanism (Brunnermeier and Pedersen, 2009). A raise in the margin haircut makes the posted security less liquid and increases funding costs for the margin requirement for both parties.

Figure 10 shows the minimum haircuts applied by Eurex Clearing AG to government bonds posted as margin collateral. Until the beginning of 2010, Irish, Italian, Portuguese, and Spanish government bonds were regarded as high-quality collateral and received low margin haircuts (approximatively 3%). Throughout 2010 and 2011, the haircuts on these securities were notably increased.

In analogy to the rises in repo haircuts, the margin haircuts for Italian and Spanish government bonds rose considerably, whereas the margin haircuts for Portuguese and Irish bonds reached extremely high levels. In November 2011, Eurex Clearing AG's margin haircuts reached their peak with at least 22% for Italian government bonds, and in October 2012 the Spanish government bonds were subject to a margin haircut of 22.3%. From late September 2011 to late February 2012, Eurex Clearing AG applied a margin haircut of 59.5% to Irish and Portuguese government bonds. In contrast, the margin haircut for high-quality government bonds, such as French and German, remained rather stable at approximatively 3% throughout the crisis.

As shown in Fig. 11, the margin haircuts applied by CC&G to Italian government bonds with a 10-year maturity never fell below 16% between

[6]As shown by Koulischer and Struyven (2014), the ability of a central bank to alleviate such procyclical effects in the private markets by relaxing its collateral policy is crucial to avoid credit crunches, transferring additional credit risk, and possibly imposing costs to the central bank.

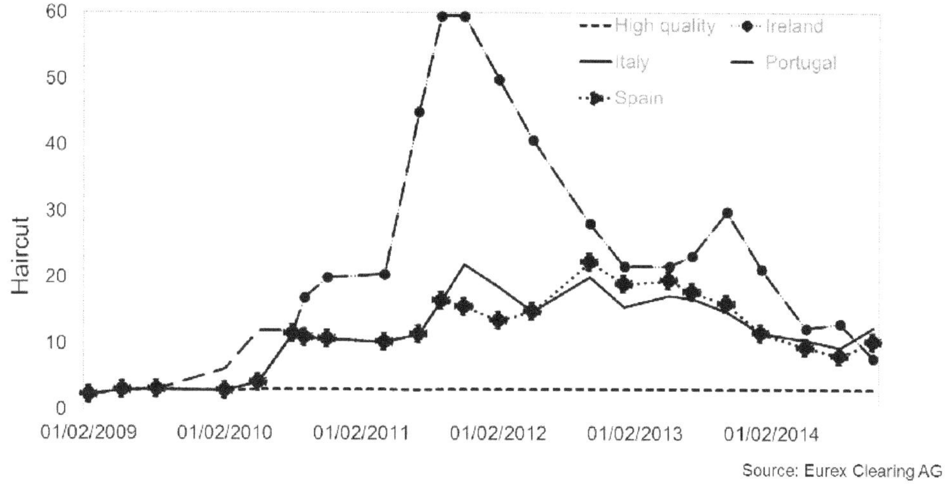

Figure 10. Minimum Haircuts for Margin Collateral by Eurex Clearing AG

Note: This figure plots the minimum haircuts applied by Eurex Clearing AG to government bonds posted as margin collateral. Throughout 2010 and 2011, Irish, Italian, Portuguese, and Spanish government bonds received increasingly high margin haircuts.

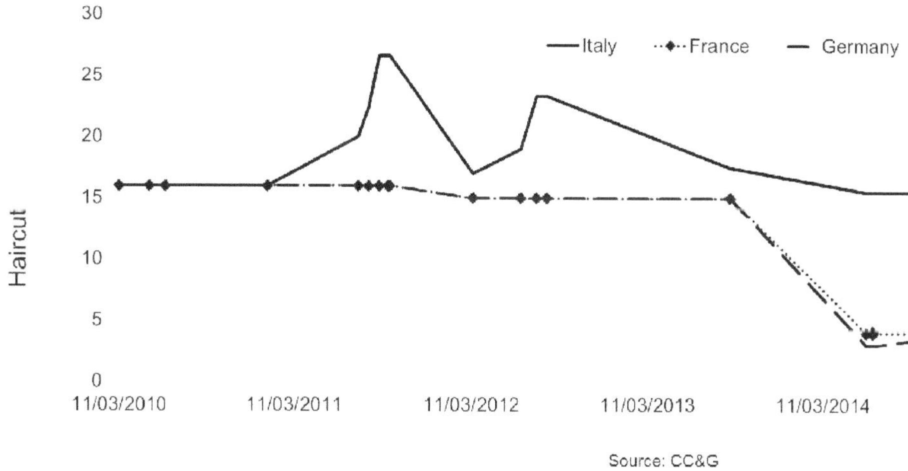

Figure 11. Haircuts for Margin Collateral for 10-Year Government Bonds by CC&G

Note: This figure plots the margin haircuts applied by CC&G to 10-year Italian, French, and German government bonds. CC&G margin haircuts on French and German were higher than those applied by Eurex Clearing AG throughout the crisis.

March 2010 to August 2013, reaching its peak in September 2011 at 26.6%. In contrast to Eurex Clearing AG, the margin haircuts for French and German bonds remained rather high at around 15% throughout the crisis.

Similar to developments in haircut increases for repos and collateral securities, margin haircuts may be a further factor contributing to the magnification of downward margin spirals.

As government debt is principally used by the largest European banks to obtain more funding through repos cleared by few CCPs and possibly to cover margin requirements, the possibility of synchronized actions must be considered as clearing members are informed in advance of upcoming haircut changes either via internal messages or circulars. When a CCP raises the repo haircut and margin haircut on sovereign debt, banks will tend to react synchronically with a stronger impact on the price of the bond.

5. Conclusion

Policymakers and regulators are aware of the implications of the different repo market segments for systemic risk (ESMA, 2016; Constâncio, 2016). The ECB recognizes that

> "risk concentration within CCPs will grow, both nationally and internationally. CCPs are increasingly turning into institutions of unprecedented systemic importance"

(Coeuré, 2014). The European Parliament (EP) worries about the procyclical effects caused by changes in haircuts and proposes the introduction of minimum standards for the calculation of haircuts, in order to stabilize them across the cycle (EP, 2013). FSB (2014a) recommends imposing a numerical haircut floor applied to non-centrally cleared SFTs, excluding transactions backed by government securities and centrally cleared SFTs and financing provided to banks and broker–dealers subject to adequate capital and liquidity regulation on a consolidated basis.

Our analysis has highlighted new findings on the cleared repo market, which have several repercussions for financial stability deserving the attention of policymakers. Secured transactions are concentrated in few CCPs, which play a determinant role in the functioning of the interbank markets. Also, in the EU, the size of the CCP-cleared repo market has become much larger than that of unsecured and non-CCP cleared repo markets. However, little information is available on how CCPs set haircuts and how they acted in time of crisis. This is a key challenge for macroprudential authorities and financial regulators.

As illustrated by the Euro zone debt crisis, sovereign bonds are not immune to asset price shocks and liquidity shocks. The main European CCPs increased the haircuts on peripheral bonds in response to the surge of perceived sovereign risk. Due to the extensive use of sovereign bonds as collateral, stress in the European repo market jeopardizes financial stability, because it creates an additional channel which ties the bank–sovereign nexus as discussed and reviewed in Armakolla *et al.* (2017).

Peripheral banks augmented their exposure on domestic sovereign bonds (Gennaioli *et al.*, 2014) after the onset of the global financial crisis and increasingly pledged these assets in the interbank market, since the unsecured market shrank. However, the raises in CCP haircuts on government bonds reduced the funding liquidity of banks (Miglietta *et al.*, 2015). Ashcraft *et al.* (2010), CGFS (2015), Corradin and Rodriguez-Moreno (2014)) suggest that might overall have led to a substitution effect.

This was, in part, offset by the unconventional policy of the ECB, which lent at lower haircuts than those applied by the CCPs, but at a higher rate and with differentiated haircuts for safe and risky bonds: it increased the haircuts on sovereign bonds that were downgraded from 'A−' to 'BBB+' as a measure of risk management (see Table 2). ECB also expanded the range of eligible collateral and suspended the minimum rating threshold for Greek, Irish, and Portuguese bonds.

When analyzing the effects of CCP haircut policies on the financial markets, it should be considered that CCP haircuts and margin requirements serve to protect the CCP. Although CCPs have public utility-like functions, they remain private sector entities. Thus, central bankers, regulatory authorities, CCPs, and other involved stakeholders should consider the introduction of approaches that allow to maintain CCP haircuts at predictable levels, limit procyclicality, and create a safe haven for government bonds, preserving the function of repo haircuts and margins to protect the CCP from price changes in collateral assets and member defaults. Nevertheless, the documented increases in haircuts create negative externalities and destabilizing effects that regulators should take into account.

Reducing the procyclicality of repo haircuts would certainly disconnect this link between sovereign weakness and banks' fragility. In particular, the crisis has shown the lack not only of a *safe* asset (see Corsetti *et al.*, 2015) — but also of a *liquid* asset that can be generally used by banks as collateral in the repo market greasing the functioning of the interbank market, especially in times of crisis avoiding the frictions emerged because of the increases in haircuts, the fragmentation of the interbank market, and the flight-to-liquidity towards core bonds.

During a crisis, the stabilizing effect of CCPs on repo markets depends on the smooth functioning of the link to monetary policy (Boissel *et al.*, 2016). In the context of cleared repos and the effects of CCP haircut and margin policies on financial stability, there are two considerations to be taken into account: first, it should be considered that haircuts and margins serve to protect CCPs. Second, from a systemic point of view, the effects of sharp increases in haircuts and margins may lead to tensions in other parts of the financial system. In this spirit, a number of regulatory and supervision-related issues should be investigated:

- *Creation of countercyclical capital standards*: in analogy to the countercyclical capital buffers of the Basel III framework, CCPs may consider introducing countercyclical capital standards as part of their risk management framework to avoid haircut increases above a certain threshold. This would however increase costs to users during calm periods.
- *Systemwide monitoring*: policymakers and supervisory authorities at European and national level might assess the systemic impact of simultaneous increases in haircuts and margins on systemwide procyclicality and funding capacities of clearing members in a CCP stress-testing framework.
- *Monitoring of margin add-ons*: CCP margins consist of several add-ons that are "added" to the margin on portfolio level. In times of volatile markets, besides increasing haircuts and margins, CCPs may also need to increase the margin add-ons, possibly exacerbating procyclicality.
- *Collateral swap with the ECB:* in case of high volatility in the sovereign debt market, CCPs could exchange risky bonds against safe bonds with the ECB paying a fee (collateral swap).
- *Insurance-like* mechanisms: market participants and CCPs might use insurance-like mechanisms to protect themselves from increases in haircuts in times of stressed markets.

Acknowledgements

This work was achieved through the Laboratory of Excellence on Financial Regulation (Labex ReFi) supported by PRES heSam under the reference ANR-10-LABX-0095. It benefited from a French government support managed by the National Research Agency (ANR) within the project Investissements d'Avenir Paris Nouveaux Mondes (investments for the future

Paris-New Worlds) under the reference ANR-11-IDEX-0006-02. The authors would like to thank Fabien Defrance, Teo Floor, Francesco Molteni, Martin Ockler, Jens Seiler, Rodolphe Teychene, Pietro Villano and Manuel Wiegand for their helpful and very detailed comments.

References

Armakolla, A., Douady, R., Laurent, J.-P. and Molteni, F. (2017). Repurchase agreements and systemic risk in the European sovereign debt crises: the role of European clearing houses, Working Paper.

Armakolla, A. and Laurent, J.-P. (2017). CCP resilience and clearing membership, Working Paper.

Acharya, V. V. and Öncü, T. S. (2013). A proposal for the resolution of systemically important assets and liabilities: The case of the repo market. *Int. J. Cent. Bank.*, 9(S1), pp. 291–349.

Acharya, V. V. and Steffen, S. (2015). The "greatest" carry trade ever? Understanding Eurozone bank risks. *J. Finan. Econ.*, 115(2), pp. 215–236.

Adrian, T., Begalle, B., Copeland, A., and Martin, A. (2014). Repo and securities lending. In Brunnermeier, M. K. and Krishnamurthy, A., (eds.), *Risk Topography: Systemic Risk and Macro Modeling*, (University of Chicago Press), pp. 131–148.

Adrian, T. and Shin, H. S. (2009). Money, liquidity, and monetary policy. *Amer. Econ. Rev.*, 99(2), pp. 600–605.

Adrian, T. and Shin, H. S. (2010). Liquidity and leverage. *J. Finan. Intermediation*, 19(3), pp. 418–437.

Ashcraft, A., Garleanu, N., and Pedersen, L. H. (2010). Two monetary tools: Interest rates and haircuts. *NBER Macroecon. Annu.*, 25(1), pp. 143–180.

Bagehot, W. (1873). *Lombard Street: A Description of the Money Market.* London: H. S. King.

Banca d'Italia (2013a). Financial stability report, 5.

Banca d'Italia (2013b). Financial stability report, 6.

Basel Committee on Banking Supervision (2013a). Basel III: The liquidity coverage ratio and liquidity risk monitoring tools.

Basel Committee on Banking Supervision (2013b). Revised Basel III leverage ratio framework and disclosure requirements.

Basel Committee on Banking Supervision (2014). Basel III leverage ratio framework and disclosure requirements.

Blundell-Wignall, A., Atkinson, P., and Roulet, C. (2014). Bank business models and the Basel system. *OECD J.: Fin. Market Trends*, 2013(2), pp. 43–68.

Boissel, C., Derrien, F., Örs, E., and Thesmar, D. (2016). Systemic risk in clearing houses: Evidence from the European repo market, *J. Financ. Econ.* (Forthcoming).

Brunnermeier, M. K. (2009). Deciphering the liquidity and credit crunch 2007–2008. *J. Econ. Perspect.*, 23(1), pp. 77–100.

Brunnermeier, M. K. and Pedersen, L. H. (2009). Market liquidity and funding liquidity. *Rev. Finan. Stud.*, 22(6), pp. 2201–2238.

Cassola, N., Hortaçsu, A., and Kast, J. (2013). The 2007 subprime market crisis through the lens of European Central Bank auction for short-term funds. *Econometrica*, 81, pp. 1309–1345.

Cassola, N. and Koulischer, F. (2014). The collateral channel of monetary policy: evidence from the European Central Bank, Working Paper.

CC&G (2012). CC&G's sovereign risk framework: a summary for participants.

Cheun, S., von Köppen-Mertes, I., and Weller, B. (2009). The collateral frameworks of the Eurosystem, the Federal Reserve System and the Bank of England and the financial market turmoil, ECB Occasional Paper Series, 107.

Choudhry, M. (2010). *The Repo Handbook*. United Kingdom: Butterworth-Heinemann.

Claeys, G. (2014). The (not so) unconventional monetary policy of the European Central Bank since 2008, Bruegel Working Paper.

Coeuré, B. (2014). Panel speech at the policy panel during the conference "Mapping and Monitoring the Financial System: Liquidity, Funding, and Plumbing" organized by Office of Financial Research and Financial Stability Oversight Council, Washington D.C.

Coimbra, N. (2014). Sovereigns at Risk: A dynamic model of sovereign debt and banking leverage, Working Paper.

Committee on the Global Financial System (2010). The role of margin requirements and haircuts in procyclicality, CGFS Papers, 36.

Committee on the Global Financial System (2013). Asset encumbrance, financial reform and the demand for collateral assets, CGFS Papers, 49.

Committee on the Global Financial System (2015). Central bank operating frameworks and collateral markets, CGFS Papers, 53.

Committee on Payment and Settlement Systems (2010). Strengthening repo clearing and settlement arrangements.

Comotto, R. (2013). Collateral damage: The impact of the Financial Transactions Tax on the European repo market and its consequences for the financial markets and the real economy, International Capital Market Association Report.

Constâncio, V. (2016). Margins and haircuts as a macroprudential tool. Remarks at the ESRB Conference on Macroprudential Margins and Haircuts, Frankfurt.

Copeland A., Davis, I., LeSueur, E., and Martin, A. (2012). Mapping and sizing the U.S. repo market, libertystreeteconomics.newyorkfed.org, June 25.

Copeland, A., Martin, A., and Walker, M. (2014). Repo runs: Evidence from the tri-party repo market. *J. Fin.*, 69(6), pp. 2343–2380.

Corradin, S. and Rodriguez-Moreno, M. (2014). Limits to arbitrage: Empirical evidence from Euro area sovereign bond markets, Working Paper.

Corsetti, G., Feld, L. P., Lane, P. R., Reichlin, L., Rey, H., Vayanos, D., and Weder di Mauro, B. (2015). A new start for the Eurozone: dealing with debt/ monitoring the Eurozone 1. CEPR Press.

Darracq Pariès, M. and De Santis, R. A. (2015). A non-standard monetary policy shock: The ECB's 3-year LTROs and the shift in credit supply. *J. Int. Money Fin.*, 54, pp. 1–34.

Diamond, D. W. and Dybvig, P. H. (1983). Bank runs, deposit insurance, and liquidity. *J. Polit. Economy*, 91(3), pp. 401–419.

Drechsler, I., Drechsel, T., Marques-Ibanez, D., and Schnabl, P. (2016). Who borrows from the lender of last resort?, *J. Fin.*, 71(5), pp. 1933–1974.

Ebner, A., Fecht, F., and Schulz, A. (2016). How central is central counterparty clearing? A deep dive into a European repo market during the crisis, Deutsche Bundesbank Discussion Papers, 14/2016.

European Securities and Markets Authority (2016). Report on securities financing transactions and leverage in the EU. Report prepared under the mandate in Article 29(3) SFTR.

Eurex Clearing (2012). GC Pooling — margining concept.
Eurex Repo (2012). Monthly News. Euro & GC Pooling news. February 7.
European Central Bank (2010). Monthly Bulletin: July.
European Central Bank (2012). Euro Money Market Study.
European Central Bank (2013). Collateral eligibility requirements. A comparative study across specific frameworks.
European Central Bank (2015). The financial risk management of the Eurosystem's monetary policy operations.
European Commission (2013a). Proposal for a Council Directive implementing enhanced cooperation in the area of Financial Transaction Tax.
European Commission (2013b). How the FTT works in specific cases and other questions and answers.
European Parliament (2013). Directorate General for Internal Policies. Policy Department A: Economic and Scientific Policy. Shadow banking — minimum haircuts on collateral, *Note*.
Financial Stability Board (2012), Securities Lending and Repos: Market Overview and Financial Stability Issues, Interim Report of the FSB Workstream on Securities Lending and Repos.
Financial Stability Board (2013). Strengthening Oversight and Regulation of Shadow Banking: Policy Framework for Addressing Shadow Banking Risks in Securities Lending and Repos.
Financial Stability Board (2014a). Strengthening Oversight and Regulation: Regulatory framework for haircuts on non-centrally cleared securities financing transactions.
Financial Stability Board (2014b). Background document. Regulatory framework for haircuts on non-centrally cleared securities financing transactions. Procyclicality of haircuts: evidence from the QIS1.
Gabor, D. (2016). A step too far? The European financial transactions tax and shadow banking. *J. Euro. Public Policy*, 23(6), pp. 925–945.
Gennaioli, N., Martin, A., and Rossi, S. (2014). Banks, government bonds, and default: What do the data say?, CEPR Discussion Papers, 10044.
Gorton, G. and Metrick, A. (2010). Haircuts, *Fed. Reserve Bank St. Louis Rev.*, 92(6), pp. 507–519.
Gorton, G. and Metrick, A. (2012). Securitized banking and the run on repo. *J. Finan. Econ.*, 104(3), pp. 425–451.
Gregory, J. (2014). *Central counterparties. Mandatory Clearing and Bilateral Margin Requirements for OTC Derivatives*. United Kingdom: John Wilcy & Sons.
Heider, F. and Hoerova, M. (2009). Interbank lending, credit-risk premia, and collateral. *Int. J.Cent. Bank.*, 5(4), pp. 5–43.
Hördahl, P. and King, M. (2008). Developments in repo markets during the financial turmoil. *BIS Quarterly Review*, December 2008, pp. 37–53.
Koulischer, F. and Struyven, D. (2014). Central bank liquidity provision and collateral quality. *J. Bank Fin.*, 49, pp. 113–130.
Krishnamurthy, A., Nagel, S., and Orlov, D. (2014). Sizing up Repo, *J. Fin.*, 69(6), pp. 2381–2417.
LCH.Clearnet Group LTD (2010). LCH.Clearnet Ltd Circular No 2692. Management of Sovereign Credit Risk for RepoClear Service.
LCH.Clearnet Group LTD (2014). Frequently asked questions on the sovereign risk framework.
Lenza, M., Pill, H., and Reichlin, L. (2010). Monetary policy in exceptional times, *Econom. Policy*, 25(62), pp. 295–339.

Mancini, L., Ranaldo, A., and Wrampelmeyer, J. (2016). The Euro interbank repo market. *Rev. Fin. Stud.*, 29(7), pp. 1747–1779.

Martin, A., Skeie, D., and Von Thadden, E. L. (2014). Repo runs. *Rev. Finan. Stud.*, 27(4), pp. 957–989.

Mayordomo, S., Abascal, M., Alonso, T., and Rodriguez-Moreno, M. (2015). Fragmentation in the European interbank market: Measures, determinants, and policy solutions. *J. Fin. Stab.*, 16, pp. 1–12.

Miglietta, A., Picillo, C., and Pietrunti, M. (2015). The Impact of CCPs' margin policies on repo markets, BIS Working Paper, 515.

Molteni, F. (2017). Liquidity, government bonds and sovereign debt crises, ADEMU Working paper 72.

Morgan Stanley Research (2011). European interest rate strategy. BTPs: An adverse development.

Nyborg, K. G. (2017). Central bank collateral frameworks, *J. Bank. Fin.*, 76, pp. 198–214.

Schmitz, S. W. (2013). The impact of the liquidity coverage ratio (LCR) on the implementation of monetary policy, *Econ. Notes*, 42(2), pp. 135–170.

Singh, M. (2011). Velocity of pledged collateral: analysis and implications. IMF Working Papers, 11/256.

Singh, M. (2012). The (other) Deleveraging, IMF Working Papers, 12/179.

Part V

Finance-Growth Nexus and Macroeconomic Effects on Financial Markets

Chapter 19

The Environmental Kuznets Curve: Is There a Financial Analogue?

Imad A. Moosa

School of Economics, Finance and Marketing, RMIT, Australia
imad.moosa@rmit.edu.au

Abstract

The objective of this chapter is to introduce the concept of the financial Kuznets curve (FKC) as an analogue to the already well-established notion of the environmental Kuznets curve (EKC). It is envisaged that the FKC can be introduced on the grounds that too much of a good thing is not good and that countries with large financial sectors are more susceptible to financial crises. The empirical results, based on a variety of econometric techniques, show that the adverse effect of financialization on growth materializes only at high levels of financialization as measured by the ratio of credit to GDP. This is why the FKC, which symbolizes the "finance curse" resulting from over-dependence on the financial sector, can be observed only in the case of high-income OECD countries, which have high levels of financialization.

1. Introduction

The objective of this chapter is to introduce the concept of the financial Kuznets curve (FKC) as an analogue to the already well-established notion of the environmental Kuznets curve (EKC). The basic idea behind the EKC is that as a country becomes more affluent (in terms of income per capita) the level of environmental degradation (measured, for example, by pollutants or emissions of various kinds on a per capita basis) rises at first, then starts to decline. The FKC, on the other hand, can be introduced on the grounds that too much of a good thing is not good. While finance is important for capital formation and economic growth, excessive financialization can be detrimental to economic growth because an abnormally large financial sector competes with the productive sectors of the economy for a limited amount of resources (particularly human resources). It has been observed that countries with large financial sectors are more susceptible to financial crises — this is the "finance curse", the financial counterpart of the "resource curse".

The presence of the FKC depends on whether the relation between economic growth and the degree of financialization looks monotonic or more like an inverted U-shaped curve that resembles the EKC. In this chapter, some evidence is presented on the relation between growth and financialization by using as a measure of financialization, the value of credit granted by financial institutions as a percentage of GDP. Some justifications for the choice of this measure of financialization will be presented based on the proposition that the macroeconomic effects of financialization are transmitted through debt accumulation.

While an extensive amount of work has been conducted on the EKC, the FKC is a new concept that appeared for the first time in Moosa (2016). The results presented in this chapter corroborate the results of Moosa (2016) in that evidence for the FKC is found in the case of high-income OECD countries and countries with a high level of financialization. Furthermore, the evidence presented in this chapter shows that the adverse effect of financialization on growth materializes only at high levels of financilization. This is why the FKC, which symbolizes the "finance curse" resulting from over-dependence on the financial sector, can be observed only in high-income OECD countries, which have high levels of financialization.

The rest of this chapter is organized as follows. We start with the theory of and empirical evidence on the EKC; then we move on to a consideration of the hazard of excessive financialization and why it may have adverse effects on economic growth and other economic indicators. Model specification and the methodology used to estimate and test the FKC are then presented, followed by a presentation of the data and empirical results. The last section contains some concluding remarks.

2. The Environmental Kuznets Curve: Theory and Evidence

The EKC is a graphical representation of the relation between measures of environmental degradation (such as the level of pollution) and income per capita. The underlying idea is that at low-income levels, growth causes environmental degradation but beyond a certain point, growth leads to environmental improvement. The implication of this changing pattern is that the relation between the two variables takes the form of an inverted U-shaped curve. The inversion is explained in terms of the proposition that higher levels of income per capita are associated with a gradual shift towards less polluting activities such as information-intensive industries and services. Furthermore, it is plausible to suggest that higher income levels are associated with increased environmental awareness, enforcement of environmental regulation, better technology, and a higher level of environmental expenditure to curb pollution. These factors lead to a levelling off followed by a gradual decline of environmental degradation — in the process forming the inverted U-shaped curve.

The EKC is explained by the interaction of the time and scale effects. The scale effect results from growth in the scale of the economy, which is expected to produce a proportional growth in pollution and other environmental impacts. In the absence of changes in the structure of the economy or technology, the scale effect on its own produces a proportional relation between economic growth and environmental degradation. The time effect means that environmental degradation decelerates with the passage of time as a result of structural, institutional, and policy factors. Stern (2014) describes the time effect as implying the decline of pollution over time in the absence of economic growth. However, even under moderate growth, pollution and environmental degradation decline as a result of structural shifts (moving away from heavy industry), institutional awareness of the hazard of pollution, and the pursuit of active anti-pollution policies.

A number of theoretical and intuitive explanations can be put forward as to why the impact of growth on the environment becomes less severe (even positive) as income rises. The first explanation is that environmental quality can be considered to be a normal good, the demand for which rises as income rises (Beckerman, 1992; World Bank, 1992). Barrett and Graddy (2000) argue that as income rises, people demand improvement in environmental quality, which is delivered by the political system. The second possible explanation is that as the level of income rises, a tendency appears to use less pollution-intensive technology (Grossman and Krueger, 1995). Another explanation is that the share of pollution-intensive sectors in total output goes down as the share of service sectors goes up, which is associated with rising income (for example, Jänicke *et al.*, 1997). Yet another explanation is that the tendency of people to breed declines as they become richer, thus alleviating pressure on the environment. These explanations are not perfect but they are plausible.

The empirical evidence on the EKC is mixed as the results are sensitive to variations in model specification, variable measurement, and other factors. For example, Harbaugh *et al.* (2002) contend that the locations of the turning points for various pollutants (and their existence) are sensitive to variations in data and model specification. Stern and Common (2001) show that estimates of the EKC for sulfur emissions are very sensitive to the selected sample. More recent literature produces mixed results while attention is paid to the problem of specification search and the consequent sensitivity of the results to model variation. Aufhammer and Steinhauser (2012) test the performance of existing models and a large set of potential reduced-form models. They find the best existing models to be inferior to the best model chosen on the basis of the out-of-sample loss measure as applied to aggregate emissions. Yang *et al.* (2015) contend that the EKC hypothesis cannot be considered valid for any of the seven emission indicators they use. Farhani *et al.* (2014) emphasize human development and show that there is an inverted U-shaped relation between environmental degradation and income. Robalino-Lopez *et al.* (2015) examine the relation between economic growth and CO_2 emissions in Venezuela and conclude that while there is no evidence for the EKC, environmental stabilization can be accomplished by combining economic growth with increasing use of renewable energy as well as appropriate changes in the energy mix.

Moosa (2017) considers four econometric issues associated with the estimation and testing of the EKC with reference to Australian CO_2 emissions. The four issues are: (i) model specification with respect to the order of the polynomial, (ii) model specification with respect to the use of log–log specifications, (iii) integration and cointegration considerations, and (iv) missing variables and time trends. The empirical results show that the quadratic specification fits best and that turning points are observed for CO_2 emissions albeit at much higher levels of income per capita than for other, more localized pollutants. The intuitive arguments for using log–log specifications are not as strong as the argument that the choice should be an empirical issue. Non-nested model selection tests produce evidence against the log–log specification for all measures of CO_2 emissions and income per capita. It is suggested that cointegration considerations are often exaggerated and that the application of the conventional residual-based test of cointegration can produce misleading results because the critical values of the test statistics are not valid for a quadratic specification. It is also suggested that while it is legitimate to include additional variables in the EKC model, it is rather difficult to pinpoint those variables, some of which are not easily quantifiable. A possible way out is to use the unobserved components model to account for missing variables and stochastic trends. This issue in particular is relevant to the FKC.

3. The Hazard of Excessive Financialization

Financialization is a term that describes the dominance of the financial sector over other sectors of the economy, including manufacturing industry and agriculture. Komlik (2015) describes financialization simply as "the ascendancy of finance", suggesting that it represents "the capturing impact of financial markets, institutions, actors, instruments and logics on the real economy, households and daily life". Black (2011) lists the ways in which the financial sector harms the real economy, arguing that it causes misallocation of capital in ways that harm the real economy. On the other hand, a modern economy cannot function properly without a financial sector, as economic activity requires the availability of credit and means of payment, which are provided by the financial sector. But just like everything else in life, too much of a good thing is not good, and finance is no exception. Excessive levels of financialization have been found to exert adverse effects on the economy in more than one way. This is why it is envisaged that the relation between financialization and economic growth is likely to look like an inverted U-shaped curve, which resembles the original Kuznets curve and the subsequent environmental Kuznets curve. If the relation between growth and financialization assumes an inverted U-shaped curve, it is legitimate to call it the "financial Kuznets curve".

The adverse effects of financialization have been widely recognized as being mostly related to the accumulation of debt. As the level of debt rises, the corporate and household sectors divert increasing portions of their financial resources to debt service, which in turn become profit for the financial sector. The problem is that the financial sector's receipts are not turned into fixed capital formation to boost output, but rather they are used to create new claims on aggregate output and income. Increasingly, firms become unable to invest in new physical capital equipment or buildings because they are obliged to use their operating revenue to pay creditors. In a financialized economy, those running the show do not aim at producing physical capital because they are in the business of generating interest income, fees, and commissions from mergers and acquisitions and other parasitic activities that do not involve the creation of new wealth.

Tomaskovic-Devey (2015) points out that "the concentration of wealth and power in the financial service industry has led to lower living standards and weaker state investment in citizens and infrastructure", which means that the financialization of non-finance sectors leads to a lower level of production. He actually sees financialization as the move of non-financial firms in more speculative directions, into stock, credit, currency, and even derivative markets — this move has been detrimental to value-added. His estimates show that "Main Street stripped the US economy of at least 3.9% of aggregate growth, or about three years of lost growth in GNP", compared with the great recession that produced aggregate negative growth of 2.9%. The adverse effects of financialization, he argues, include lower employment, lower capital investment, lower wages, and lower tax revenue. The tendency of non-financial firms to channel a big portion of profits to the acquisition of financial assets has been observed by Krippner (2005), Epstein and Jayadev (2005), Lin and Tomaskovic-Devey (2013), Orhangazi (2008), Lin (2013), and Davis (2014).

Financialization has adverse macroeconomic consequences because it makes the financial sector weaker and more vulnerable by boosting leverage, opacity, complexity, and spillover effects within and outside financial institutions and by accelerating debt deflation (Sinapi, 2014). Furthermore, the dominance of finance fuels capital asset price inflation as suggested by Bellofiore (2013). Financialization is believed to have a depressive effect on productive investment, consumption, and aggregate demand. For example, Lavoie (2012) suggests that financialization is associated with the development of a consumption-led accumulation regime fuelled by increasing household debt as households strive to compensate for stagnating purchasing power. Given that financial crises cause subsequent recessions and that financialization leads to a bigger and more unstable financial sector, the link between financialization and output becomes conspicuous. According to the IMF (2009), recessions associated with financial crises last on average 18 months longer than other recessions and take almost three years to go back to pre-recession output levels.

Cecchetti and Kharroubi (2015) examine the real effects of financial sector growth and conclude that it is a drag on productivity growth — that is, rapid growth in the financial sector reduces productivity growth because the financial sector competes for resources with the rest of the economy. In another paper, Cecchetti and Kharroubi (2012) conclude that financial sector size has an inverted U-shaped effect on productivity growth — that is, there comes a point where further enlargement of the financial sector can retard real growth. This is the FKC, for which cross-sectional evidence has been provided by Moosa (2016) who measures financialization in terms of the ratio of publicly traded shares to GDP.

4. Model Specification and Methodology

The FKC can be represented by the quadratic function

$$g_t = \gamma_0 + \gamma_1 f_t + \gamma_2 f_t^2 + \varepsilon_t, \tag{1}$$

where g is GDP growth rate and f is the level of financialization. The inverted U-shaped FKC is indicated by the coefficient restrictions $\gamma_2 < 0$ and $\gamma_1 > 0$. The turning point, at which the relation between GDP growth and financialization changes from positive to negative, can be determined by differentiating Eq. (1) with respect to f and equating the derivative to 0. Thus,

$$\frac{dg}{df} = \gamma_1 + 2\gamma_2 f = 0 \tag{2}$$

which gives

$$f = -\frac{\gamma_1}{2\gamma_2}. \tag{3}$$

If the relation between growth and finacialization is negative and monotonic, it can be represented by the equation

$$g_t = \alpha_0 + \alpha_1 f_t + \varepsilon_t \tag{4}$$

such that $\alpha_1 < 0$. The choice between the quadratic and linear functions may be determined by conducting variable deletion tests. By imposing the restriction $\gamma_1 = 0$, a significant test statistic implies that the linear term is important (hence it should not be deleted). Likewise, by imposing the restriction $\gamma_2 = 0$, a significant test statistic implies that the quadratic term is important. Since a valid inverted U-shaped representation requires both terms to be important, the null hypotheses $\gamma_1 = 0$ and $\gamma_2 = 0$ must be rejected to establish evidence for the FKC.

Two of the econometric issues considered by Moosa (2017) with respect to the EKC are worthy of investigating in the case of FKC: the order of polynomial and omitted variables. As far as the first issue is concerned, Shafik and Bandyopadhyay (1992) estimated the relation between degradation and income per capita using three different functional forms: linear, quadratic, and cubic. They concluded that some environmental indicators improve with rising incomes, other indicators worsen then improve (the envisaged EKC), and others worsen steadily (what Perman and Stern (2003) describe as "monotonic"). Van Alistine and Neumayer (2010) justify the use of a cubic function on the grounds that a second turning point may be observed. Canas *et al.* (2003) use both quadratic and cubic specifications, obtaining results of robust support for both of them. While they find evidence for an inverted U-shaped curve (with the trend being mostly on the rising part of the curve), they suggest that statistical support for the cubic specification means that their results need to be viewed with caution. Studies detecting two turning points include De Bruyn and Opschoor (1997) and Binder and Neumayer (2005). Zhang (2012) argues that the inverted U-shaped curve may be "an artefact of restrictive functional forms in the sense that the 'true' relationship could be N-shaped or an even more flexible shape". Yang *et al.* (2015) consider linear, quadratic, and cubic specifications without suggesting *a priori* which specification is more plausible.

To consider the possibility that a better representation of the FKC is a higher order polynomial in the fiancialization variable, the following two equations are considered:

$$g_t = \gamma_0 + \gamma_1 f_t + \gamma_2 f_t^2 + \gamma_3 f_t^3 + \varepsilon_t, \tag{5}$$

$$g_t = \gamma_0 + \gamma_1 f_t + \gamma_2 f_t^2 + \gamma_3 f_t^3 + \gamma_4 f_t^4 + \varepsilon_t, \tag{6}$$

The issue of omitted variables is dealt with by Stern (2003), who suggests that a time trend is added to the EKC equation to account for time-varying omitted variables and stochastic shocks. Stern and Common (2001) contend that the EKC is an incomplete model that suffers from significant omitted variables bias. Stern (1998) argues that testing different variables individually is subject to the problem of potential omitted variables bias and that, given the poor statistical properties of most EKC models, it is hard to come to any conclusions about the roles of other additional variables such as trade. These arguments are also valid for the FKC, since it is implausible to assume that growth is determined by financialization on its own.

One way to account for missing variables (without identifying them explicitly) while introducing a stochastic time trend is to use an unobserved components model, which is specified as

$$g_t = \mu_t + \delta_1 f_t + \delta_2 f_t^2 + \varepsilon_t, \tag{7}$$

where μ_t is the trend and ε_t is the random component. The trend, which represents the long-term movement of the dependent variable, is specified as

$$\mu_t = \mu_{t-1} + \beta_{t-1} + \eta_t, \tag{8}$$

$$\beta_t = \beta_{t-1} + \zeta_t, \tag{9}$$

where $\eta_t \sim \text{NID}(0, \sigma_\eta^2)$, and $\zeta_t \sim \text{NID}(0, \sigma_\zeta^2)$. As in Eq. (1), evidence for the FKC requires the coefficient restrictions $\delta_2 < 0$ and $\delta_1 > 0$. The significance of the trend implies that factors other than financialization affect growth. Equation (7) is estimated by maximum likelihood and the Kalman filter to update the state vector (Harvey, 1989; Koopman *et al.*, 2006). Allowance is made for a stochastic trend to avoid imposing the restriction of a deterministic trend when this restriction is not valid. If the trend is deterministic, the results will show that.

5. Data and Empirical Results

The notion of the EKC is extrapolated from the original Kuznets curve, when Kuznets (1955) suggested that income inequality rose with growth at low levels of income per capita, then declined beyond a certain point (beyond a certain level of income). In this chapter, extrapolation is taken a step further by moving from the EKC to its financial counterpart, the FKC. Before extrapolation is made possible, supportive evidence for the FKC must be found.

In this exercise, the variable used to represent and measure financialization is the ratio of credit given by financial institutions to GDP. This choice can be justified on the grounds that financialization is closely associated with debt in both the corporate and household sectors. In fact, the macroeconomic effects of financialization are explained in terms of debt accumulation. Firms have been increasingly substituting debt for equity (by resorting to stock buy-backs). Stockhammer (2012) argues that financialization has allowed more access of households to credit, which has led to consumption and asset price booms (and busts), and that financialization has encouraged households to take on more debt, which has fuelled consumption or was necessary to buy property in the face of soaring house prices. Because debt has to be serviced out of current income, debt service means either reduction in spending or default.

Cecchetti and Kharroubi (2012) also consider the effect of financialization on productivity growth in terms of private sector debt, using as a measure of financialization the ratio of private debt to GDP. The OECD (2015) emphasizes the role of debt, arguing that credit is a stronger drag on growth when it goes to households rather than businesses (hence the emphasis is on household debt) and that bank loans are more effective than bonds in impeding economic growth.

Annual data on domestic credit provided by financial sector as a percentage of GDP were obtained from the World Bank database covering the period 2001–2014 and 111 countries. This variable is defined to include the credit granted to various sectors on a gross basis by the financial sector, which encompasses the monetary authorities as well as depository and non-depository financial institutions. Corresponding data on the growth rates of real GDP were obtained from the same database. The countries are classified according to per capita income into five country groups: (i) high income (non-OECD), (ii) high income (OECD), (iii) low income, (iv) low/middle income, and (v) upper middle income.

Figure 1 shows how the observations fit into a quadratic function for country groups and the overall sample. We can see two cases of inverted U-shaped curves for high-income OECD countries and to a lesser extent for upper middle-income countries. The fit is far away from being perfect, but this is not physics and the FKC is not Boyle's law. As a matter of fact, the quadratic fit for high-income OECD countries is remarkable, given that tens of other factors affect growth. For all country groups, the relation looks negative, but there is no evidence for an inverted U-shaped FKC. However, when a polynomial of order 4 is fitted to the observations on all country groups (without the negative growth rates), we can readily observe an inverted U-shaped curve for countries with high levels of financialization (Fig. 2). When the sample is split into two groups of low and high financialization, we can see some evidence for the FKC for countries with a high degree of fiancialization. In Fig. 3, we can see that higher order polynomials (3 and 4) do not improve the fit dramatically for high-income OECD countries. As a matter of fact, the curve still looks like an inverted U.

In Table 1, we observe the goodness of fit as measured by R^2. It is typically higher for the quadratic than the linear function. The highest value of R^2 is that for high-income OECD countries. Table 2 presents the results of estimating the FKC (quadratic function) by the Phillips–Hansen (1990) fully modified ordinary least squares (FMOLS). In only two cases are the restrictions $\gamma_2 < 0$ and $\gamma_1 > 0$ satisfied, thus providing evidence for the FKC: high-income OECD and high-financialization countries. These country groups overlap, in the sense that the same countries appear in the two groups. For these two groups, the turning points occur at 126.2 for high-income OECD countries and 143.7 for high-financialization countries. The ratio of

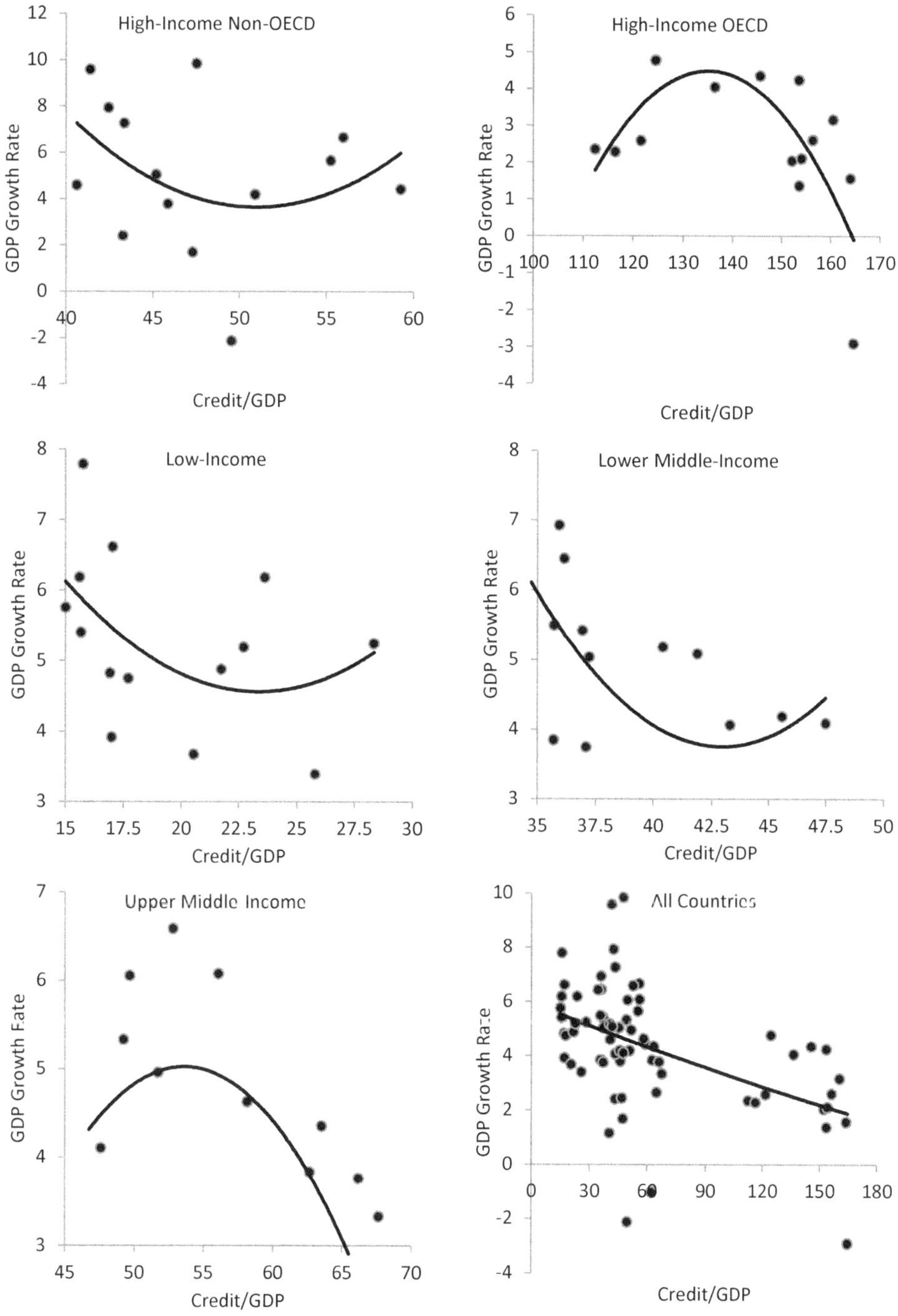

Figure 1. The Financialization–Growth Nexus (by Income)

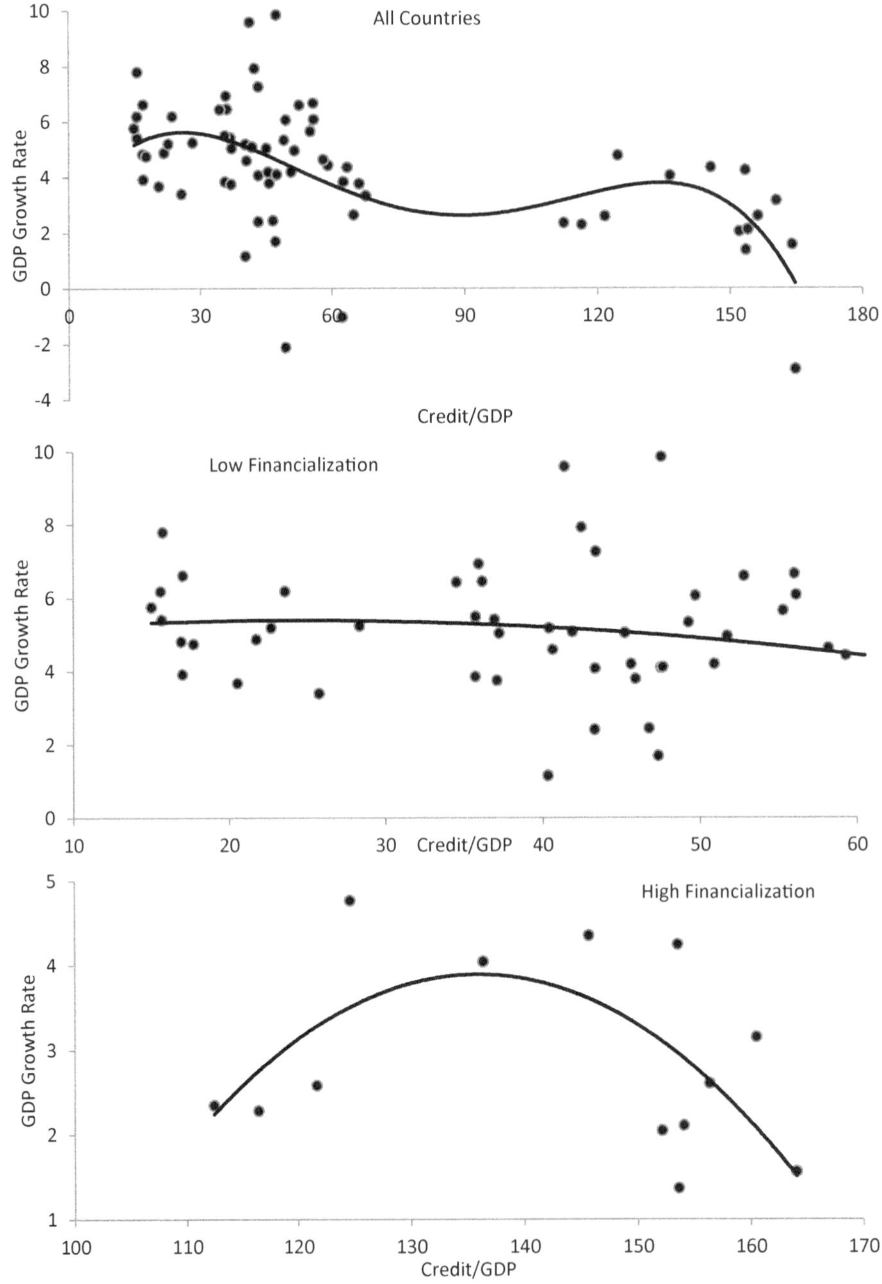

Figure 2. The Financialization–Growth Nexus (by Level of Financialization)

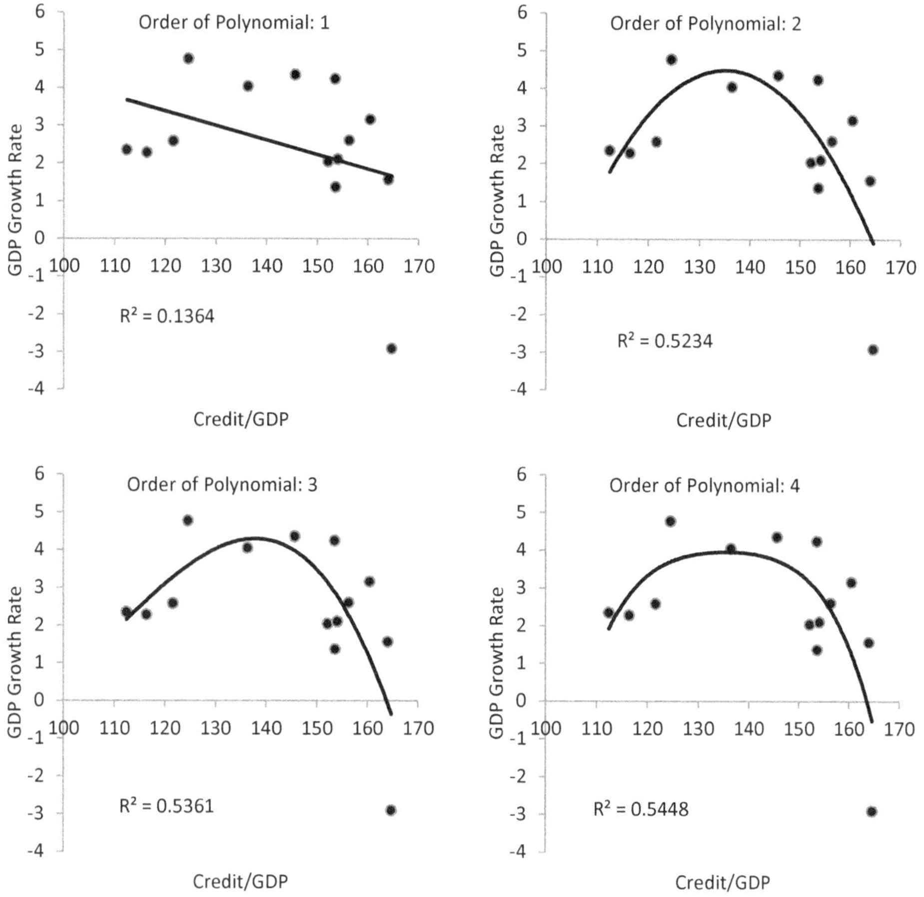

Figure 3. The Financialization–Growth Nexus for High-Income OECD Countries

credit to GDP must be greater than 100% before financialization starts to exert a negative effect on growth. Since these high values are only observed in high-income OECD countries and (by definition) high-financialization countries, evidence for the FKC is found for these two country groups only.

Table 3 reports the results of three variable deletion tests as applied to Eq. (1). The tests are based on the Lagrange multiplier (LM) and the likelihood ratio (LR), both of which have $\chi^2(1)$ distribution, as well as the F-test for coefficient restriction. Evidence for the FKC requires the rejection of the restrictions, which means that both the linear and quadratic terms are important. As implied by the p-values, which are reported in square brackets, the restrictions are rejected in two cases only: high-income OECD countries

Table 1. Goodness of Fit (R-Squared) of Linear and Quadratic Functions

Country Group	Linear	Quadratic
High income (non-OECD)	0.03	0.13
High income (OECD)	0.14	0.52
Low income	0.14	0.22
Low/middle income	0.19	0.30
Upper middle income	0.15	0.28
All countries	0.23	0.23
Low financialization	0.04	0.04
High financialization	0.03	0.34

Table 2. Phillips–Hansen FMOLS Estimates of the FKC

Country Group	γ_0	γ_1	γ_2	R^2
High income (non-OECD)	198.111	−7.885	0.079	0.13
	(4.71)	(−4.60)	(4.58)	
High income (OECD)	−44.676	0.757	−0.003	0.52
	(−2.74)	(3.23)	(−3.54)	
Low income	12.092	−0.497	0.008	0.22
	(4.16)	(−1.73)	(1.12)	
Low/middle income	84.055	−3.478	0.044	0.30
	(5.98)	(−5.39)	(5.13)	
Upper middle income	−8.271	0.577	−0.006	0.23
	(−0.44)	(0.86)	(−1.04)	
All countries	6.092	−0.027	−0.0001	0.24
	(7.12)	(−1.05)	(−0.09)	
Low financialization	5.143	0.032	−0.008	0.26
	(4.16)	(0.48)	(−0.92)	
High financialization	−55.269	0.862	−0.003	0.34
	(−4.79)	(5.11)	(−5.21)	

and countries with a high level of financialization. These results support the results presented in Table 2.

Table 4 displays the estimates of the unobserved components model for various country groups. The reported results include the estimated final state vector (and the t statistics in parentheses) as well as the modified coefficient of determination R_d^2 and the diagnostics for serial correlation (Q) and heteroscedasticity (H). R_d^2, which is calculated on the basis of first differences, is more appropriate for trended data (Harvey, 1989). Q is the Ljung–Box statistic, which has a χ^2 distribution, and H is a test

Table 3. Variable Deletion Tests

	$H_0: \gamma_1 = 0$			$H_0: \gamma_2 = 0$		
Country Group	***LM***	***LR***	***F***	***LM***	***LR***	***F***
High income (non-OECD)	1.52	1.61	1.34	1.46	1.53	1.27
	[0.22]	[0.20]	[0.27]	[0.22]	[0.21]	[0.28]
High income (OECD)	6.08	7.98	8.45	5.27	8.32	8.93
	[0.01]	[0.01]	[0.01]	[0.01]	[0.01]	[0.01]
Low income	1.56	1.66	1.38	1.30	1.37	1.13
	[0.21]	[0.19]	[0.26]	[0.25]	[0.24]	[0.31]
Low/middle income	2.03	2.19	1.87	1.85	1.98	1.68
	[0.15]	[0.19]	[0.20]	[0.17]	[0.16]	[0.22]
Upper middle income	1.16	1.22	1.01	1.31	1.37	1.13
	[0.28]	[0.27]	[0.34]	[0.25]	[0.24]	[0.31]
All countries	1.13	1.14	1.09	0.03	0.03	0.03
	[0.29]	[0.28]	[0.29]	[0.87]	[0.87]	[0.88]
Low financialization	0.22	0.22	0.21	0.58	0.59	0.56
	[0.64]	[0.64]	[0.65]	[0.44]	[0.49]	[0.46]
High financialization	4.07	4.87	4.55	4.15	5.02	4.69
	[0.04]	[0.03]	[0.04]	[0.04]	[0.03]	[0.05]

Notes: LM and LR are the Lagrange multiplier and likelihood ratio test statistics, both with $\chi^2(1)$ distribution. F is the F statistic for the corresponding null hypothesis. p-Values are given in square brackets.

Table 4. Estimation Results of the Unobserved Components Model

	μ_t	β_t	γ_1	γ_2	R_d^2	Q	HS
High income (non-OECD)	−8.63	−0.72	0.76	−0.01	0.38	1.72	0.30
	(−2.14)	(−1.95)	(0.32)	(−0.97)			
High income (OECD)	−110.40	−0.19	1.64	−0.01	0.54	4.07	0.79
	(−2.91)	(−1.05)	(3.09)	(−3.18)			
Low income	19.36	0.14	−1.12	0.28	0.14	0.30	1.19
	(2.56)	(0.43)	(−0.96)	(0.78)			
Low/middle income	78.09	0.72	−2.60	0.02	0.15	3.23	0.34
	(2.22)	(1.25)	(−0.79)	(0.53)			
Upper middle income	31.15	1.83	0.62	0.02	0.53	4.27	0.36
	(2.17)	(3.42)	(0.52)	(−1.52)			
All countries	5.41	−0.04	−0.04	0.01	0.22	4.12	0.48
	(2.92)	(−0.05)	(−0.58)	(0.22)			
Low financialization	7.34	−0.01	0.71	−0.01	0.12	4.15	0.26
	(2.37)	(−1.11)	(1.27)	(−1.72)			
High financialization	−55.44	0.14	0.91	−0.03	0.31	1.23	1.01
	(−2.83)	(0.35)	(2.75)	(−3.70)			

Notes: t-Statistics are in parentheses. The Q statistic follows a $\chi^2(2)$ distribution. The H statistic follows an F(3,3) distribution.

statistic for heteroscedasticity with an F distribution. The results show that the model has a reasonable explanatory power and passes the diagnostics for serial correlation and heteroscedasticity. As in the case of the FMOLS estimates, the coefficient restrictions $\delta_2 < 0$ and $\delta_1 > 0$ are satisfied only for high-income OECD countries and high-financialization countries. In all cases, however, the level of the trend, μ, is statistically significant, implying (as expected) that variables other than financialization affect growth. The results therefore provide strong evidence for the FKC in high-income OECD countries, which typically have greater ratios of credit to GDP than other country groups.

6. Conclusion

The results presented in this chapter provide cross-sectional evidence on what may be called the financial Kuznets curve (FKC). The FKC is a representation of the proposition that the financial sector plays a useful and growth-conducive role in the economy up to a certain point, then any further expansion in its size relative to the economy will have adverse effects on growth. The evidence shows that the adverse effect of financialization on growth materializes only at high levels of financialization as measured by the ratio of credit to GDP. This is why the FKC, which symbolizes the "finance curse" resulting from over-dependence on the financial sector, can only observed in high-income OECD countries, which have high levels of financialization.

References

Auffhammer, M. and Steinhauser, R. (2012). Forecasting the path of U.S. CO_2 emissions using state-level information. *Rev. Econom. Statist.*, 94, pp. 172–185.

Barrett, S. and Graddy, K. (2000). Freedom, growth and the environment. *Environment and Development Economics*, 5, pp. 433–456.

Beckerman, W. (1992). Economic growth and the environment: Whose growth? Whose environment? *World Develop.*, 20, pp. 481–496.

Bellofiore, R. (2013). Two or three things I know about her: Europe in the global crisis and heterodox economics. *Cambridge J. Econom.*, 37, pp. 497–512.

Binder, S. and Neumayer, E. (2005). Environmental pressure group strength and air pollution: An empirical analysis. *Ecol. Econom.*, 55, pp. 527–538.

Black, W. (2011). How the servant became a predator: Finance's five fatal flaws, 25 May. http://www.huffingtonpost.com/william-k-black/how-the-servant-became-a_b_318010.html.

Canas, A., Ferrao, P., and Conceicao, P. (2003). A new environmental Kuznets curve? Relationship between direct material input and income per capita: Evidence from industrialised countries. *Ecol. Econom.*, 46, pp. 217–229.

Cecchetti, S. G. and Kharroubi, E. (2012). Reassessing the impact of finance on growth. BIS Working Papers, No. 381.

Cecchetti, S. G. and Kharroubi, E. (2015). Why does financial sector growth crowd out real economic growth?. BIS Working Papers, No. 490.

Davis, L. E. (2014). The Financialization of the nonfinancial corporation in the post-1970 U.S. economy. Ph.D. Dissertation, University of Massachusetts, Amherst.

De Bruyn, S. M. and Opschoor, J. B. (1997). Developments in the throughput-income relationship: Theoretical and empirical observations. *Ecol. Econom.*, 20, pp. 255–268.

Epstein, G. A. and Jayadev, A. (2005). The rise of rentier incomes in OECD countries: Financialization, Central Bank policy and labor solidarity. In Epstein, G.A. (ed.), *Financialization and the World Economy*. Northampton (MA): Elgar.

Farhani, S., Mrizak, S., Chaibi, A., and Rault, C. (2014). An environmental Kuznets curve and sustainability: A panel data analysis. *Energy Policy*, 71, pp. 189–198.

Grossman, G. M. and Krueger, A. B. (1995). Economic growth and the environment. *Quart. J. Econom.*, 110, pp. 353–377.

Harbaugh, W., Levinson, A., and Wilson, D. (2002). Re-examining the empirical evidence for an environmental Kuznets curve. *Rev. Econom. Statist.*, 84, pp. 541–551.

Harvey, A. C. (1989). *Forecasting, Structural Time Series Models and the Kalman Filter*. Cambridge: Cambridge University Press.

IMF (2009). *World Economic Outlook*. Washington DC: International Monetary Fund.

Jänicke, M., Binder, M., and Mönch, H. (1997). Dirty industries: Patterns of change in industrial countries. *Environ. Res. Econom.*, 9, pp. 467–491.

Komlik, O. (2015). What is financialization? Marxism, post-keynesianism and economic sociology's complementary theorizing. *Econom. Sociol. Polit. Economy*, 31 January. http://economicsociology.org/2015/01/31/what-is-financialization-marxism- post-keynesianism-and-economic-sociologys-complementary-theorizing/.

Koopman, S. J., Harvey, A. C., Doornik, J. A., and Shephard, N. (2006). *Structural Time Series Analyser, Modeller and Predictor*. London: Timberlake Consultants Ltd.

Krippner, G. (2005). The financialization of the American economy, *Socio-Econom. Rev.*, 3, pp. 173–208.

Kuznets, S. (1955). Economic growth and income inequality. *Am. Econom. Rev.*, 49, pp. 1–28.

Lavoie, M. (2012). Financialization, neo-liberalism, and securitization. *J. Post Keynesian Econom.*, 35, pp. 215–233.

Lin, K. H. (2013). The rise of finance and firm employment dynamics. 1982–2005. SSRN: http://dx.doi.org/10.2139/ssrn.2284507.

Lin, K. H and Tomaskovic-Devey, D. (2013). Financialization and US income inequality, 1970–2008. *Am. J. Sociol.*, 118, pp. 1284–1329.

Moosa, I. A. (2016). International evidence on the financial Kuznets curve. *Economia Internazionale*, 69, pp. 361–374.

Moosa, I. A. (2017). The econometrics of the environmental Kuznets curve: An illustration using Australian CO_2 emissions. *Appl. Econom.* (published on-line).

OECD (2015). How to restore a healthy financial sector that supports long-lasting, inclusive growth? OECD Economics Department Policy Notes, No. 27.

Orhangazi, Ö. (2008). Financialization and capital accumulation in the non-financial corporate sector. *Cambridge J. Econom.*, 32(6), pp. 863–886.

Perman, R. and Stern, D. I. (2003). Evidence from panel unit root and cointegration tests that the environmental Kuznets curve does not exist. *Austr. J. Agri. Res. Econom.*, 47, pp. 325–347.

Phillips, P. C. B. and Hansen, B. E. (1990). Statistical inference in instrumental variables regression with I(1) processes. *Rev. Econom. Stud.*, 57, pp. 99–125.

Robalino-López, A., Mena-Nieto, A., García-Ramos, J., and Golpe, A. (2015). Studying the relationship between economic growth, CO_2 emissions, and the environmental Kuznets curve in Venezuela (1980–2025). *Renewable Sustainable Energy Rev.*, 41, pp. 602–614.

Shafik, N. and Bandyopadhyay, S. (1992). Economic growth and environmental quality: Time series and cross-country evidence, background paper for the World Development Report 1992. Washington DC: The World Bank.

Sinapi, C. (2014). The role of financialization in financial instability: A post-Keynesian institutionalist perspective. Working Paper, Burgundy School of Business. Geopoliticki Casopis (special issue on world economic and social crisis, pp. 207–232.

Stern, D. I. (1998). Progress on the environmental Kuznets curve? *Environ. Develop. Econom.*, 3, pp. 173–196.

Stern, D. I. (2003). The environmental Kuznets curve. *Online Encyclo. Ecol. Econom.*, International Society for Ecological Economics, http://isecoeco.org/pdf/stern.pdf.

Stern, D. I. (2014). The environmental Kuznets curve: A primer, Crawford School of Public Policy, Australian National University, Working Paper 1404.

Stern, D. I. and Common, M. S. (2001). Is there an environmental Kuznets curve for sulfur? *J. Environ. Econom. Manage.*, 41, pp. 162–178.

Stockhammer, E. (2012). Financialization, income distribution and the crisis. *Investigacion Economica*, 71, pp. 39–70.

Tomaskovic-Devey, D. (2015). The rise of financialization has led to lower living standrads and reduced growth in the U.S. Institute for New Economic Thinking, 12 June. http://ineteconomics.org/ideas-papers/blog/the-rise-of-financialization-has-led-to-lower-living-standards-and-reduced-growth-in-the-u-s.

Van Alistine, J. and Neumayer, E. (2010). The environmental Kuznets curve, In Gallagher, K.P. (ed.), *Handbook on Trade and the Environment.* Cheltenham: Edward Elgar.

World Bank (1992). *World Development Report 1992: Development and the Environment.* New York: Oxford University Press.

Yang, H., He, J., and Chen, S. (2015). The fragility of the environmental Kuznets curve: Revisiting the hypothesis with China data via an "Extreme Bound Analysis". *Ecol. Econom.*, 109, pp. 41–58.

Zhang, J. (2012). Delivering Environmentally Sustainable Economic Growth: The Case of China, Working Paper, Asia Society, September.

Chapter 20

The Interaction of Real and Financial Markets in the Global Economy: What Role Does China Play?

Sumru Altug[*,†], Cem Çakmaklı[*] and Rüveyda Nur Gözen[‡]

[*] *American University of Beirut, Lebanon*
[†] *CEPR, United Kingdom*
[‡] *University of Illinois, United States*

Abstract

This chapter examines the role that China plays in the global economy for the propagation of financial uncertainty and volatility. For this purpose, it seeks to measure the interdependence of real and financial markets for a key set of developed markets — the US, the UK, Germany, and Japan — in relation to China. We employ vector auto-regressions (VARs) and make use of generalized impulse responses and variance decompositions to explore the interconnections among these countries. Among other results, we find that the US, Japan, UK, and Germany are highly integrated and form a cluster in terms of financial market volatility and industrial production growth. Surprisingly, we find that financial market volatility in developed countries is strongly affected by volatility shocks emanating from the Hong Kong Stock Exchange, attesting to the growing importance of Asian financial markets and real activity in the global economy. By contrast, China has a different story. Chinese financial and production markets are decoupled, and Chinese industrial production growth is mainly determined by its own shocks to domestic conditions.

1. Introduction

Developed and emerging economies tend to experience similar and synchronized fluctuations, and macroeconomic aggregates such as output, consumption, and investment within countries and across regions exhibit strong contemporaneous correlations.[1] The existence of such synchronization across disparate economies suggests a potential role for a global level shock or the spillover effects of country- and sector-specific shocks. The development of financial markets globally has created a further impetus for understanding the propagation of financial shocks and their impact on real sectors of the economy. Given the extent of trade and financial linkages among different economies, when one country faces a negative shock in one sector, there is a strong chance for contagious behavior in other countries. Therefore, allowing for the interactions between real and financial markets seems key in understanding dynamic interrelationships in the global economy. The stock market has a crucial role to play in this regard as it channels funds to the real economy and enables the valuation of real activity through claims on productive firms. Hence, movements in stock prices may be expected to reflect the changes in the fundamental value of real economic activity within a given economy. Production decisions in one economy are also affected by the dynamics of other economies through trade and financing decisions, the existence of value-added chains, and similar linkages. Changes in financial activity, such as increases in global financial volatility, may also have important effects on a country's production decisions and financial activity by altering the nature and availability of finance or by affecting trade flows.

While much attention has been devoted to understanding common movements in real and financial variables among developed and emerging economies or different regions around the globe, the unavailability of data, and/or its insufficient quality, has typically precluded a consideration of the role of China, which now ranks as the second-largest economy in the world. Hence, an investigation of the role of China's financial system and its industrial production growth in other economies that drive real and financial activity globally appears to be crucial. In this chapter, we consider the interdependence of real and financial markets for a set of countries that represent a dominant part of developed economies, namely, the US, the UK, Germany, and Japan, together with China. To understand the propagation of financial shocks for the Chinese economy, we also consider the roles of two stock exchange markets, namely, the Shanghai Stock Exchange and Hong Kong Stock Exchange, separately.

[1]See, for example, Kose *et al.* (2003), who provides evidence regarding the synchronization in economic fluctuations across countries and regions by studying the existence of a world business cycle, and examining global, regional, and country-specific factors.

As is well known, China does not practice full capital account liberalization, and investment by foreign entities in onshore financial markets occurs through various quota systems, whereby the Chinese government sets a quota for all foreign institutions investing in stocks, bonds, and other securities. The Hong Kong–Shanghai and the newly launched Hong Kong–Shenzhen Stock Exchange Connect schemes allow investors in each market to trade shares in the other market using their local brokers and clearinghouses through Qualified Foreign Institutional Investor (QFII) programs. In contrast to the stock exchanges in China such as the Shanghai or Shenzhen Stock Exchanges, however, the Hong Kong Stock Exchange market is a fully integrated and open market in global financial markets. Hong Kong's transparent and stable exchange rate system (pegged to the US dollar), its practice of free capital mobility, and its deep bond, loan, and equity markets make the Hong Kong Stock Exchange a thriving financial center. He *et al.* (2014) find that Hong Kong's business cycle, when compared to China, is more synchronized with the US in the short run whereas, in the long run, it is more correlated with mainland China, reflecting its role as the re-export and re-import hub for the Chinese economy. Therefore, to account for the peculiar institutional arrangements in China, we use observations from both the Hong Kong and Shanghai Stock Markets. Our choice is further justified by noting the lack of perfect dependence between the two markets.[2]

Our empirical analysis uses the realized volatility of stock prices and the growth rates of industrial production to capture the interrelated dynamics of financial markets and the real economy, respectively. Our main goal is to analyze whether there is a co-movement between China and developed markets in terms of industrial production growth and stock market volatility. Employing a vector auto-regression (VAR) approach, we make use of generalized impulse responses and variance decompositions to explore the interconnections among these countries, and conduct a structural analysis by using a structural VAR (SVAR). SVARs have the advantage of allowing a structural analysis while remaining tractable at the computational level; see Sims (1981, 1986), Bernanke (1986), Shapiro and Watson (1988), Blanchard (1989) for details. Not surprisingly, SVAR models have become a workhorse for empirical studies of macroeconomics and finance.

Specifically, we obtain (partial) identification of structural shocks using sign restrictions; see Faust (1998), Canova and De Nicolo (2002), and

[2]Specifically, the correlation between the stock indices on the Shanghai Stock Exchange and Hong Kong Stock Exchange is found to be 0.30, ruling out the incidence of perfect dependence.

Uhlig (2005). This type of modeling requires that each identified shock is associated with a unique sign pattern; see Lutkepohl (2010) for further details. We first make static restrictions as we restrict the sign of the contemporaneous effects of different structural shocks. We also investigate dynamic sign restrictions where we impose restrictions for longer horizons. The financial integration among countries and spillover effects resulting from the actions of agents in the markets may lead to an increase in volatility in financially integrated countries. Moreover, volatility may create a ripple effect within financial markets due to various behavioral biases, i.e., risk-aversion on the part of investors or institutional constraints. As a consequence, lending activities may decrease in an uncertain economic environment, leading to a macroeconomic slowdown and creating negative spillovers in other markets. These considerations motivate the choices for our sign restrictions. First, we hypothesize that stock price volatility in one market may cause a decline in industrial production growth in both domestic and foreign markets. Second, we surmise that a volatility shock in one market leads to an increase in realized volatility in another market. In both cases, we consider contemporaneous as well as dynamic restrictions.

Using this methodology, we investigate the channels through which shocks in volatility and industrial production growth in China affect financial markets in other developed economies and to what extent Chinese industrial production growth is affected by shocks in other countries. Furthermore, we suppose that Chinese industrial production growth is not affected by volatility shocks from its own stock markets due to the immature connection between its real and financial markets. However, we surmise that there is an indirect impact on Chinese industrial production performance via the volatility channel. In this case, a volatility shock to the Hong Kong and Shanghai Stock Exchanges, which would cause an increase in financial volatility in foreign markets, is hypothesized to lead to a decline in China's industrial production growth through an induced decline in demand in developed economies.

Our empirical findings reveal some interesting conclusions. First, we uncover a set of findings regarding the dynamic interrelationships between the developed countries. In this respect, we find that the US, Japan, the UK, and Germany are highly integrated and form a cluster in terms of financial market volatility and industrial production growth. This reflects the convergence of business cycle fluctuations exhibited among industrialized economies, as demonstrated by Kose *et al.* (2012). Second, financial market volatility in developed countries is strongly affected by volatility shocks emanating from the Hong Kong Stock Exchange, but much less so from volatility from the Shanghai Stock Exchange. We interpret this finding as attesting to the growing importance of Asian financial markets and real activity in the global economy. Given the increasing share of Chinese companies listed on the Hong Kong Stock Exchange, we also interpret this as an indirect effect of changes in Chinese economic conditions on developed economies. We also uncover a "Chinese story." First, Chinese financial and production markets appear essentially decoupled, i.e., a shock to Chinese financial markets has little impact on its own industrial production growth performance. Second, volatility shocks emanating from developed countries, aside from the US, have a negligible effect on Chinese industrial production, while those from the US show some negative impact. Thus, in the absence of any other significant impact from real shocks in the remaining developed economies, Chinese industrial production growth appears essentially driven by shocks to its own domestic production conditions.

The remainder of this chapter is as follows: Section 2 presents a literature review; Section 3 describes the data; Section 4 explains our methodology; and Section 5 contains the results. Here, we first discuss the findings based on the nature of the VAR coefficients. We also examine the validity of sign restrictions based on how often they hold in repeated trials, as well as implied impulse response functions and variance decompositions. Then, Section 6 discusses the findings for China, and a conclusion is made in Section 7.

2. Literature Review

Many recent studies show that there are business cycle similarities and international co-movement among countries in terms of the contemporaneous correlations in output, consumption, investment and trade. At the same time, there is evidence of the decoupling or divergence of economic activity between emerging market economies and developed market economies. For instance, Backus *et al.* (1993) reveals that synchronization exists among developed economies. Similarly, Baxter (1995) finds that there is a definite tendency for business cycle synchronization in major industrialized economies. In a recent study, Kose *et al.* (2012) show that there is a convergence of cyclical fluctuations within industrialized economies and emerging markets, but that there is a decoupling between these two groups of countries. Specifically, using a dynamic factor structure that allows for global, group- and country-specific factors, they find evidence for decoupling in the cyclical dynamics of developed countries and emerging markets beginning in the 1980s. They show that the relative importance of global factors has diminished as one of the main drivers of key macroeconomic aggregates such as real output, consumption and investment, whereas the increase in the importance of group-specific factors has become more clearly discernible. They further find that country-specific factors have become more important in accounting for the co-movement of output, consumption, and investment for emerging economies but less so for developed ones, suggesting that the role of policies that rely on domestic savings rather than foreign capital boost investment in the former group. Benczur and Ratfai (2014) examine the characteristics of 62 countries to uncover the sources of fluctuations in industrialized and emerging market economies. Altug and Bildirici (2012) examine the cyclical experiences of 27 developed and emerging countries using a regime-switching approach. They find that business cycles in emerging economies show greater heterogeneity relative to developed countries and relative to each other even in well-defined geographical groupings.

Several studies investigate the connection between industrial production and stock market volatility as a proxy for real production and finance in developed and emerging market economies. Errunza and Hogan (1998) find that European stock return volatility is explained to some extent by industrial production in several European countries. Goswami and Jung (1997) reveal a similar conclusion in the sense that stock market movements and GDP, Industrial Production, oil prices, and interest rates have a positive relationship in the S. Korean market. Lastly, Wongbangpo and Sharma (2002) observe that in ASEAN-5 countries, namely, Thailand, Indonesia, Malaysia, Singapore, and the Philippines, stock markets dynamically interact with macroeconomic aggregates both in the long and short run.

It has often been argued that when markets are financially integrated, an unexpected event in one market may influence not only returns but also variances in other related markets; see Joshi and Pandya (2012). Strohsal and Weber (2015) state that if higher volatility in one market leads to an increase in volatility of another market, then the changes in volatility tend to reflect the operation of the information hypothesis initially proposed by Epps and Epps (1976) and elaborated further by Ross (1989) and Fleming (1998). This hypothesis states that high volatility in the target market is associated with high spillover power to other financial markets.

Recently, the aftermath of the Brexit vote that took place on June 24, 2016, was observed to influence the volatility of stock markets in a variety of countries. The volatility of stock prices on the German Stock Index (DAX), Tokyo Stock Index (Nikkei 225), New York Stock Exchange (NYSE), Hong Kong Stock Exchange (HSI), and Shanghai Stock Exchange (SHCOMP) significantly increased due to the effects from this event.

In a different vein, Sheicher (2001) identifies regional and global shocks in terms of financial integration and argues that innovations to volatility have primarily a regional character. The IMF Report from 2015 states that financial development and stability stimulate a country's economic growth by promoting information sharing, resource allocation, and management of risk. In addition, the report states that stock market volatility is successful at capturing the trends in economic growth at a six-month and one-year period. For instance, Fornari and Mele (2009) find that stock market volatility explains future real economic growth up to 55% at the one- and two-year horizons. The authors state that during the "Great Moderation" period beginning in the early 1980s, the predictive power of stock market volatility increased significantly. Papadopoulos *et al.* (2011) investigate the relationship among several macroeconomic and financial indicators in 12 European countries and find a negative relationship between stock market prices and industrial production.

3. Data

We use two key variables representing the financial and real sectors of the countries we focus on. First, we use (seasonally adjusted) industrial production (IP) indices on a monthly frequency. We opt for a higher frequency by using industrial production rather than GDP to circumvent data availability problems. This also enables us to capture the dynamic links between financial and real markets much more precisely. We transform the data into growth rates prior to analysis to obtain a stationary system.[3] We use IP growth as a proxy for economic activity, which reflects the real side of the relevant economies.

Second, we construct a monthly series of average realized volatility for each country by using daily end-of-day price quotes on the stock exchanges. Our set of market indices consists of the London Stock Exchange (FTSE100), Shanghai Stock Exchange (SHCOMP), Tokyo Stock Exchange (Nikkei 225), New York Stock Exchange (NYSE), Frankfurt Stock Exchange (DAX), and

[3]Industrial Production data are obtained from OECD database.

the Hong Kong Stock Exchange (HSI).[4,5] We first obtain end-of-day prices for the relevant stock indices from the Bloomberg Database for each stock market, then compute monthly (log) realized volatility by using the daily returns that correspond to the given months. It can be seen that (log) realized volatility, computed in this way, is a good proxy for real volatility in general conditions; see Andersen *et al.* (2010).

We use a sample that starts in February 1999 and lasts until May 2014. The reason this sample period was chosen stems from the fact that Chinese Industrial Production existed only from 1999 onward. In summary, we have 185 observations for all variables in the system, and it covers 15 years. An important point is that the Shanghai Stock Exchange Market and Hong-Kong Stock Exchange Market are jointly included in our system in order to analyze the degree to which the Chinese financial system integrated into the world financial system.

4. Methodology

We employ a VAR model and make use of generalized impulse responses and variance decompositions to explore the interconnections among these countries. We proceed by using a SVAR that exploits restrictions motivated by the theory.

4.1. *Vector auto-regressive model*

Following the pioneering work of Sims (1980), VAR models have acquired a coherent and credible place in the toolkit of macroeconomists for data description, forecasting, structural inference, and conducting policy experiments. VAR models are generally used to capture empirical evidence about the rich dynamics of multiple time series. Let K be the number of countries, p be the number of lags, and T be the sample size. The VAR *(p)* model can

---

[4]Among these stocks exchanges, NYSE is the largest by market capitalization of its listed companies at US\$19.3 trillion as of June 2016. Likewise, the Tokyo Stock Exchange is the fourth-largest stock exchange in the world by aggregate market capitalization of its listed companies, and the largest in East Asia and Asia. Finally, the Stock Exchange of Hong Kong Limited (SEHK) is East Asia's and Asia's third-largest stock exchange in terms of market capitalization behind the Tokyo Stock Exchange and the Shanghai Stock Exchange.

[5]For future reference, we note that the Hang Seng Index (HSI) is used to record and monitor daily changes of the largest companies of the Hong Kong Stock Exchange and is the main indicator of overall market performance in Hong Kong. These 50 constituent companies represent about 58% of market capitalization in the Hong Kong Stock Exchange.

be expressed as follows:

$$y_t = \vartheta + A_1 y_{t-1} + \cdots A_p y_{t-p} + u_t, \quad t = 1, 2, \ldots, T, \tag{1}$$

where $y_t = (y_{1t}, \ldots y_{Kt})'$ is a $K \times 1$ random vector. The A_i matrices are the coefficient matrices with $K \times K$ dimension and the intercept is a $K \times 1$ vector such that $\vartheta = (\vartheta_1, \ldots, \vartheta_K)'$. Also, the residuals are assumed to be vector white noise, with zero expectations and constant contemporaneous covariance matrix.

We take the lag length as 4. This assumption captures the notion that a shock to volatility is transmitted to industrial production usually within a couple of months. On the other hand, a larger number of lagged coefficients may easily lead to over-parameterization as the number of parameters increase substantially with an increasing number of lags. Therefore, embracing a 4-lag VAR model provides coherent information for understanding the dynamic interrelationship between financial volatility and economic activity among selected countries. Finally, we go through a battery of stationarity tests, including Augmented Dickey Fuller (ADF) tests; based on these tests, we conclude that all of the series are stationary. All characteristic roots of the system lie outside the unit circle, confirming our findings.[6] Next, we focus on estimating the SVAR model and examine the sign restrictions with which we perform our analysis.

4.2. *Structural VAR: Sign restrictions*

Under the VAR model, impulse response functions are crucial in terms of analyzing the relations between the variables. Impulse responses can be defined as the response of the system over time to a unit shock (impulse) in a specific variable. This can be obtained using the Wold decomposition of y_t, i.e.,

$$y_t = \sum_{i=0}^{\infty} \Phi_i u_t, \tag{2}$$

where u_t are the innovations from the reduced-form model and, hence, potentially cross-correlated. Here, we suppress any deterministic component for notational convenience. One fundamental problem of the reduced-form VARs, such as ours, is that the independent structural shocks required for a proper impulse response analysis are unidentified, as the observed shocks

[6] All results are available upon request.

are cross-correlated. Hence, any impulse response analysis without further restrictions is misleading. To demonstrate this, let ε_t be the (unobserved) structural shocks that are independent. Note that in the observed reduced-form, shocks are simply linear combinations of these underlying structural shocks (normalized to have unit variance) as follows:

$$u_t = B\varepsilon_t, \quad \varepsilon_t \sim N(0, I_K). \tag{3}$$

The ith column of the B matrix describes the immediate impact on all variables of an innovation in the ith structural variable, see Uhlig (2005) for an alternative exposition. Using this transformation matrix, we can construct the covariance matrix of the reduced-form shocks as

$$\sum_u = B \sum_\varepsilon B^{'} \tag{4}$$

which implies that

$$\sum_u = BB^{'} \tag{5}$$

since the covariance matrix of ε_t is the $(K \times K)$ identity matrix.

As the covariance matrix is full, the matrix B defines the observed correlations between the reduced-form shocks. In this case, we can write the impulse responses as

$$y_t = \sum_{i=0}^{\infty} \Psi_i \varepsilon_t, \tag{6}$$

where $\varepsilon_t = B^{-1}u_t$ and $\Psi_{\mathrm{i}} = \Phi_i B$. The identification problem inherent in the impulse response analysis stems from the fact that the B matrices are not uniquely identified. An analytical solution to this problem is replacing B with the Cholesky decomposition, P, of the covariance matrix where $\sum_u = PP'$, where P is a lower triangular matrix. This implies that $B \equiv P$. However, in this case, the lower triangular structure of B imposes a recursive ordering scheme on the system, in the sense that the first variable affects all other variables in the system, but it is not affected by other variables. In this case, the ordering of the variables in the system affects structural relations; see, for example, Lutkepohl (2010) for a textbook exposition.

Another option is to use those B matrices that obey certain sign restrictions dictated by the theory. By doing so, the structural shocks are set-identified, i.e., certain impulse responses that obey those sign restrictions can be extracted. Structural VARs that are partially identified through the use of sign restrictions were pioneered by Faust (1998), Canova and De Nicolo

(2002) and Uhlig (2005) in the context of VAR models of monetary policy. For instance, Uhlig (2005) showed that sign-identified models may produce substantially different results from conventional structural VAR models. Sign-identified VAR models have become increasingly popular in other areas as well and are now part of the mainstream of empirical macroeconomics, see Casson (2013).

Specifically, let D be an orthogonal matrix such that $DD' = I$. Unlike P, PD does not, in general, impose any recursive scheme. We can examine a wide range of possible solutions B by repeatedly drawing at random from the set of orthogonal matrices D. In order to obtain the desired system with sign restrictions, we first draw K^2 random draws from a standard normal distribution and construct a $K \times K$ matrix L using these draws. Then we employ a QR decomposition such that $L = QR$ and $QQ' = I$. By setting $D = Q'$, we compute impulse responses using the transformation matrix $B = PD$. If the impulse response functions satisfy the identifying restrictions, we retain D. We repeat these two steps 10,000 times to obtain further information about whether the sign restrictions hold in the population.

We use two sets of sign restrictions. The first set of sign restrictions is as follows:

Assumption 1. A realized volatility impulse vector is an impulse vector such that the impulse responses to a realized volatility shock have a negative impact on industrial production growth and the impulse responses are negative, for all countries $N = 1, \ldots, 5$ and at $t, t+1, t+2, t+3$, and $t+4$.

In Table 1, we display the sign restrictions regarding the effects of realized volatility on industrial production growth, which are assumed to be negative as described by Assumption 1. An important point here is that we assume a non-negative impact by Chinese financial markets on Chinese industrial production growth. The colored (N) in Table 1 indicates this non-negativity assumption. The basic reason behind this assumption is that a volatility increase in Chinese financial markets does not have a negative impact on the production side due to the limited connection between financial and real markets in China.

The next assumption pertains to the volatility-to-volatility sign restrictions in the structural VAR.

Assumption 2. A realized volatility impulse vector is an impulse vector such that the impulse responses to realized volatility shock has positive impact on volatility and the impulse responses are positive, for all countries $N = 1, \ldots, 5$ and at $t, t+1, t+2, t+3$, and $t+4$.

Table 1. Volatility-to-Industrial Production Growth Sign Restrictions

$$\begin{pmatrix} u_t^1 \\ u_t^2 \\ u_t^3 \\ u_t^4 \\ u_t^5 \\ u_t^6 \\ u_t^7 \\ u_t^8 \\ u_t^9 \\ u_t^{10} \\ u_t^{11} \end{pmatrix} = \begin{bmatrix} X & X & X & X & X & - & - & - & - & - & - \\ X & X & X & X & X & - & N & - & - & - & N \\ X & X & X & X & X & - & - & - & - & - & - \\ X & X & X & X & X & - & - & - & - & - & - \\ X & X & X & X & X & - & - & - & - & - & - \\ X & X & X & X & X & X & X & X & X & X & X \\ X & X & X & X & X & X & X & X & X & X & X \\ X & X & X & X & X & X & X & X & X & X & X \\ X & X & X & X & X & X & X & X & X & X & X \\ X & X & X & X & X & X & X & X & X & X & X \\ X & X & X & X & X & X & X & X & X & X & X \end{bmatrix} + \begin{pmatrix} \varepsilon_t^1 \\ \varepsilon_t^2 \\ \varepsilon_t^3 \\ \varepsilon_t^4 \\ \varepsilon_t^5 \\ \varepsilon_t^6 \\ \varepsilon_t^7 \\ \varepsilon_t^8 \\ \varepsilon_t^9 \\ \varepsilon_t^{10} \\ \varepsilon_t^{11} \end{pmatrix}$$

Note: This table shows the sign restrictions from volatility-to-industrial production growth where "–" and "+" below denote the postulated sign of the impact response and "×" denotes no restriction. Here, the first 5 columns (rows) represent IP growth in the UK, China, Japan, the US, and Germany, respectively, while the remaining 6 columns (rows) represent realized volatility on the stock exchanges of the UK, Shanghai, Japan, the US, Germany, and Hong Kong.

We impose the negativity and positivity sign restrictions, displayed in Tables 1 and 2, separately. Our model is partially identified by the responses of industrial production growth and realized volatility to a volatility increase. We first place identifying restrictions at time zero, a static analysis. Then, we look at lagged relationships between realized volatility and industrial production growth. This is motivated by the fact that a shock in financial markets might have a delayed effect on industrial production growth. Therefore, by placing restrictions on upcoming months we sharpen our inferences considerably. A similar study was also done by Inoue and Kilian (2013), who find that sudden monetary policy tightening leads to a decline in real GDP six months later.

5. Empirical Findings

5.1. *Results for VAR coefficients*

Since we make assumptions for sign restrictions in the following sections, it is important to check the significance of the coefficients from the VAR

Table 2. Volatility-to-Volatility Sign Restrictions

$$\begin{pmatrix} u_t^1 \\ u_t^2 \\ u_t^3 \\ u_t^4 \\ u_t^5 \\ u_t^6 \\ u_t^7 \\ u_t^8 \\ u_t^9 \\ u_t^{10} \\ u_t^{11} \end{pmatrix} = \begin{bmatrix} X & X & X & X & X & X & X & X & X & X & X \\ X & X & X & X & X & X & X & X & X & X & X \\ X & X & X & X & X & X & X & X & X & X & X \\ X & X & X & X & X & X & X & X & X & X & X \\ X & X & X & X & X & X & X & X & X & X & X \\ X & X & X & X & X & + & + & + & + & + & + \\ X & X & X & X & X & + & + & + & + & + & + \\ X & X & X & X & X & + & + & + & + & + & + \\ X & X & X & X & X & + & + & + & + & + & + \\ X & X & X & X & X & + & + & + & + & + & + \\ X & X & X & X & X & + & + & + & + & + & + \end{bmatrix} * \begin{pmatrix} \varepsilon_t^1 \\ \varepsilon_t^2 \\ \varepsilon_t^3 \\ \varepsilon_t^4 \\ \varepsilon_t^5 \\ \varepsilon_t^6 \\ \varepsilon_t^7 \\ \varepsilon_t^8 \\ \varepsilon_t^9 \\ \varepsilon_t^{10} \\ \varepsilon_t^{11} \end{pmatrix}$$

Note: This table shows the sign restrictions from volatility-to-realized volatility; "+" below denotes the postulated sign of the impact response and "×" denotes no restriction. Here, the first 5 columns (rows) represent IP growth in the UK, China, Japan, the US, and Germany, respectively, while the remaining 6 columns (rows) represent realized volatility on the stock exchanges in the UK, Shanghai, Japan, the US, Germany, and Hong Kong.

results. We divide the significance test results into three subsections. First, we investigate the industrial production growth coefficients by looking at cross-relations with other countries' industrial production growth variables. In the second subsection, we consider coefficients resulting from the lags of realized volatility on IP growth in each country. In the last subsection, we consider coefficients resulting from the lags of realized volatility on volatility in each country. The full results of the VAR coefficients are available upon request. Here, we provide a heuristic description of the results.

5.1.1. *Industrial production coefficients*

Our first result regarding the VAR coefficients suggests that the link between realized volatility and industrial production growth is rather low compared to the link between industrial production growth for different countries. That is, there exists a cluster of countries where their real activity indicators affect each other but are relatively less affected by realized volatility. Mostly, we find a positive relationship among all countries with several exceptions. First, we see a positive effect of IP growth in the US on real activity in the UK, Germany, and Japan, as well as positive effects, in turn, of each of these countries on IP growth in the three remaining developed countries.[7] This co-movement in industrial production among developed markets was also found by Kose *et al.* (2003) in terms of the synchronization of output, investment, and consumption.

The case of China slightly differs from other results, in that only US production growth seems to have a significant impact on Chinese production growth, the coefficient being (−0.73) with a t-statistic of [−2.073]. Interestingly, there is an asymmetrical effect of Chinese industrial production growth on US IP growth, which is positive by (0.04) with a t-statistic of [1.892]. In addition, we observe that Chinese industrial production growth is mainly affected from within, and is only slightly influenced by IP growth in other countries.

5.1.2. *Volatility-to-industrial production growth coefficients*

In the next part of our analysis, we also examine the significance of coefficients of volatility on industrial production growth. The first important finding is that realized volatility in Japan affects industrial production growth in the remaining countries both negatively and significantly in the short run, although we observe relatively low and insignificant effects on UK production growth.[8] More interestingly, Japan seems to be the most connected, and most vulnerable, industrial market to changes in both industrial production performance and in stock market volatilities in other countries. This may have to do with Japan's being an export-oriented economy with a large manufacturing sector. Its IP growth is negatively and significantly affected by an increase in volatility in the UK, US, and Hong Kong stock

[7]That is, an increase in IP growth in the US gives rise to IP growth in the UK, Japan, and Germany with coefficients of (0.31), (1.02), and (0.59) and the corresponding t-statistics of [2.914], [3.262], and [3.467], respectively, in the short run. Similarly, an increase in IP growth in the UK stimulates IP growth in Japan, the US, and Germany significantly, with coefficients being (0.57), (0.13), and (0.37) and corresponding t-statistics of [2.803], [2.149], and [2.621], respectively, in the short run. The same pattern is also observed for: Germany, in that it gives rise to IP growth in the UK with the coefficient of (0.077) and t-statistics [1.688]; Japan, with the coefficient of (0.26) and t-statistic of [2.133]; and US with the coefficient of (0.058) and t-statistic of [1.707]. Likewise, Japanese IP growth also has a positive effect on IP growth in the US, UK, and Germany, with coefficients of (0.08), (0.07), and (0.21) and t-statistics of [1.848], [3.249], and [3.391], respectively.

[8]For instance, IP growth in China is affected negatively by stock market volatility in Japan, where the coefficient is (−0.42) with a t-statistic of [−1.759]. Also, IP growth in the US is affected negatively by stock market volatility in Japan by (−0.11) with a t-statistic of [−2.043], while German IP growth is affected by Japan with a coefficient of (−0.27) with a t-statistic of [−1.960].

markets, with the coefficients being (−0.82), (−0.62), and (−0.48) with t-statistics of [−2.722], [−2.008], and [−1.971], respectively. Apart from the vulnerability of Japanese IP growth to outside volatility shocks, in addition to its own volatility, our results mostly show insignificant effects of volatility on industrial production growth. In our results, the successful number of sign restrictions in 10,000 trials, defined in Assumption 1, is lower compared to those for Assumption 2, which we discuss below.

5.1.3. *Volatility-to-volatility coefficients*

In this section, we examine the coefficients of realized volatility and find several significant results. One of the most noteworthy findings is that volatility on the Hong Kong Stock Exchange affects the volatility of other stock markets in a significant and positive manner.[9] Also, for most variables, we observe that a country's own lagged volatility effects are highly significant and positive, i.e., each market's volatility is significantly affected by their own volatility spillover compared to volatility spillovers from other countries. For instance, in the UK, the impact sustained from its own lagged variable is significant in that the coefficient is (0.24) with a t-statistic of [2.001]. Another example is Japan, whose lagged volatility variable has a significant and positive impact on its own volatility, the coefficient being (0.22) with a t-statistic of [2.545]. This phenomenon is also mentioned in several other papers. Worthington and Higgs [2004] find that stock market volatility spillovers felt within one country are generally higher than cross-volatility spillovers for all markets. Moreover, Kose *et al.* (2003, p. 1228) state that, in Asia, "the country factors again play the dominant role in explaining the volatilities of growth in output (...)" and "Country factors explain about 70% of output variation (...)". However, the authors do not examine the role of stock market volatility on output dynamics or stock market volatility directly, as we do.

5.2. *The results for sign restrictions*

In this section, we examine the significance of the sign restrictions imposed under Assumptions 1 and 2. We examine the number of successful sign restrictions and employ generalized impulse response functions and variance decompositions to further understand the impact of the sign restrictions.

[9] As examples, it increases the volatilities of the UK, Shanghai, Japan, and the US stock markets positively, coefficients being (0.14), (0.23), (0.25), and (0.187) with t-statistics [1.7], [1.937], [2.31], and [1.92].

The impulse responses and variance decompositions for selected countries are displayed in the text, while a comprehensive set of results is provided in the Appendix.

5.2.1. *Volatility-to-industrial production growth sign restrictions*

We now relate the results of the significance of the different sets of VAR coefficients to the sign restrictions that we postulated earlier. Under the first set of sign restrictions, i.e., the negative response of industrial production growth to volatility shocks, we observe from Fig. 1 a similar pattern in all markets. First, we observe a significant increase in the number of satisfied sign restrictions in the third month, denoted as horizon $t+3$, regarding the impact of volatility shock on industrial production growth. The success of these trials is the largest for the impact of the US, with a success rate of nearly 14%. That is, a financial volatility shock in the US has the largest negative effect on industrial production growth in all countries. This result attests to the importance of US financial markets and the news content of any changes that occur in them on real activity in a global context. The impact of a shock from the US stock market is followed by the impact of shocks to volatility from the stock markets in Hong Kong and Germany, which have the second- and third-highest negative effects on IP growth in the remaining countries at rates of 11.8% and 11.1%, respectively. Hence, we conclude that our first restriction holds for these countries, whereas for stock markets in Japan, the UK, and Shanghai, we find a fewer number of significant and satisfied sign restrictions.

In all markets, we also observe a delayed effect of volatility on industrial production growth, in that there are a significant number of sign restrictions satisfied in the fourth month, which is denoted as $t+4$. These results suggest that including four lags of each variable in the VAR system makes sense in terms of analyzing the relationship between the financial and real sides of the economy.

This delayed effect of the volatility shock on industrial production growth is also evident in the selected impulse response functions reported in Fig. 2. Here, we observe the major effect of a volatility shock occurring in Month 3 and Month 4, which causes a fall in industrial production growth in the selected countries. To have a better understanding of the impact of volatility changes on IP growth, we also provide a comprehensive set of impulse responses of IP growth in all countries that result from a volatility shock

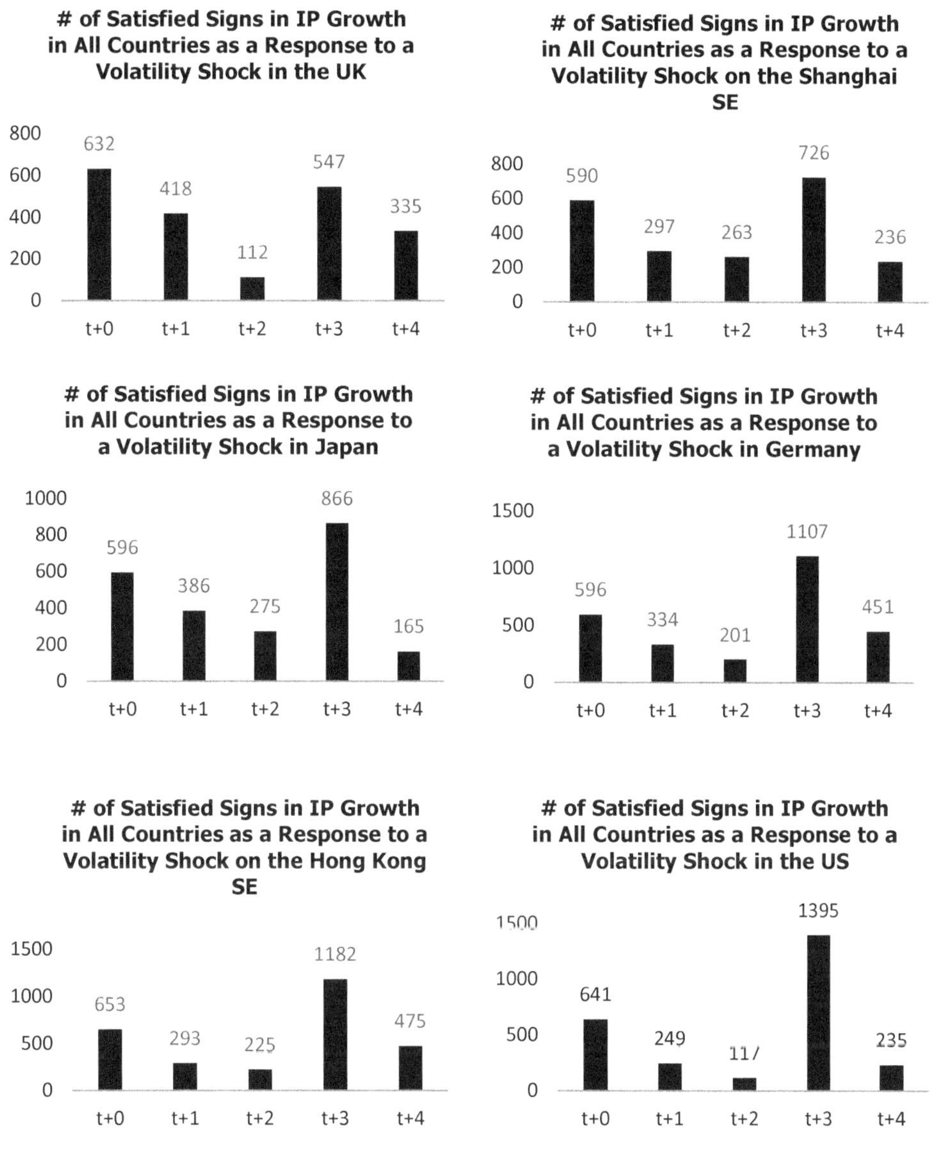

Figure 1. Successful Sign Restrictions of Volatility Shock-to-IP Growth

Note: This table shows the number of satisfied sign restrictions imposed under Assumption 1 regarding the behavior of IP growth at time interval t to $t+4$ out of 10,000 trials. The table indicates the total number of negative responses of industrial production growth in the UK, China, Japan, the US, and Germany to a positive volatility shock in the respective financial market.

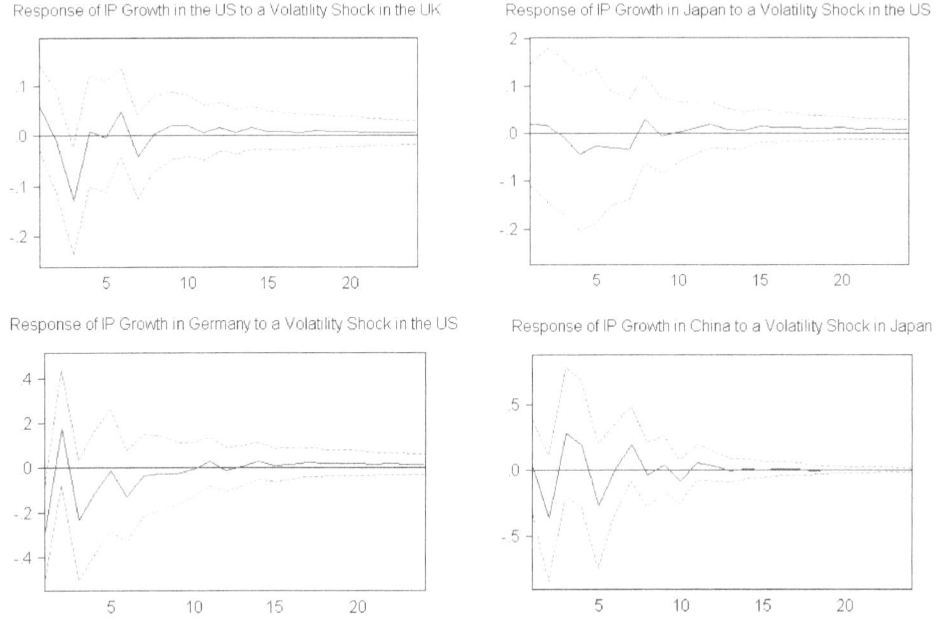

Figure 2. Response of IP Growth to Volatility Shocks in Selected Countries
Note: See Fig. A.1 in the Appendix for the full set of results on the response of IP growth in each country to a volatility shock from other all countries.

emanating from each country in Fig. A.1 in the Appendix. These results also show the same pattern as the selected impulse responses displayed in Fig. 2.

5.2.2. *The results of volatility-to-volatility restrictions*

Turning to our second assumption regarding volatility-to-volatility effects, Fig. 3 shows that it holds more significantly in terms of the number of satisfied sign restrictions, impulse responses, and variance decompositions compared to the volatility-to-IP growth effects. Overall, we observe that, at $t + 2$, there is a significant jump in the successful number of positive sign restrictions. In other words, when a positive volatility shock occurs in one market, the positive effect in another market becomes evident at $t+2$, except for a shock coming from the US. In the case of the US, a financial shock quickly spreads to other markets at $t + 1$, where the number of successful sign restrictions increases from 6.11% to 16.52% from t to $t + 1$. This reflects the size and depth of the US' financial markets and their interconnections with the rest of the world. In general, the sign restrictions hold by an average of 15% at $t + 2$ for all markets, suggesting a delayed response in

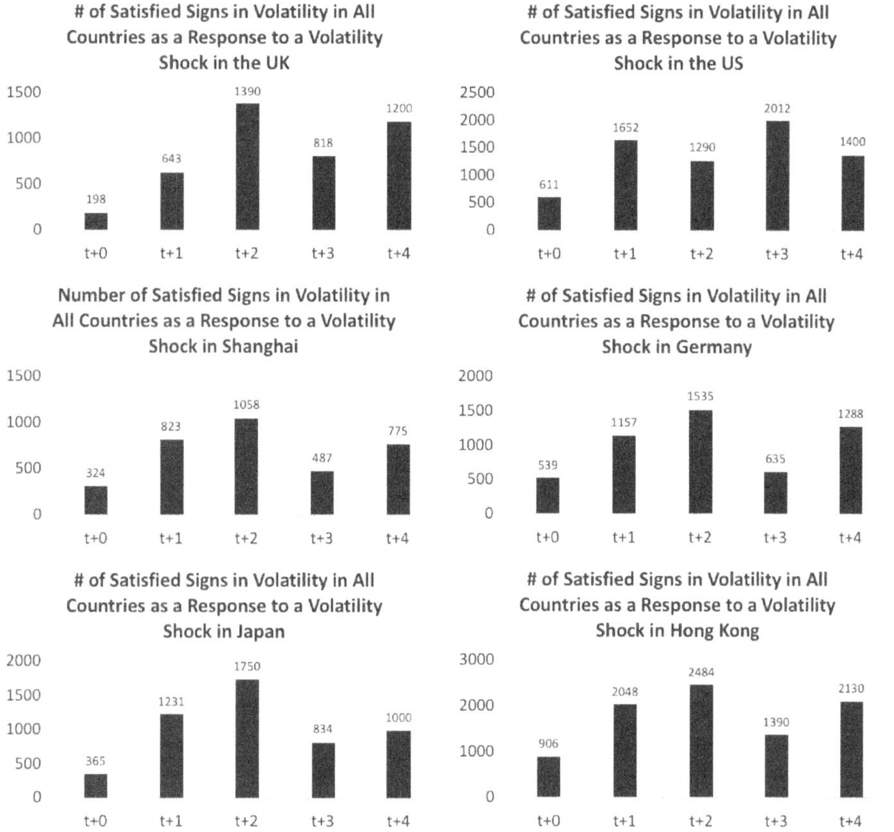

Figure 3. Successful Sign Restrictions of Volatility Shock-to-Realized Volatility

Notes: This table shows the number of satisfied sign restrictions imposed under Assumption 2 regarding the behavior of realized volatility at time interval t to $t+4$ out of 10,000 trials. The table indicates the total number of positive responses of realized volatility in the UK, China, Japan, the US, and Germany to a positive volatility shock in the respective financial market.

global financial activity from volatility shocks that emanate from individual financial markets.

One particularly interesting finding from our study pertains to the influence of the Hong Kong stock market. We find that an increase in the financial volatility of the Hong Kong Stock Exchange overwhelmingly increases volatility in other financial markets at horizons $t, t+1$, and $t+2$. The number of successful trials holds at 20.4% for $t+1$ and 24.8% for $t+2$, which is the highest overall ranking. Given Hong Kong's role as a conduit of trade and finance between mainland China and the rest of the world, as

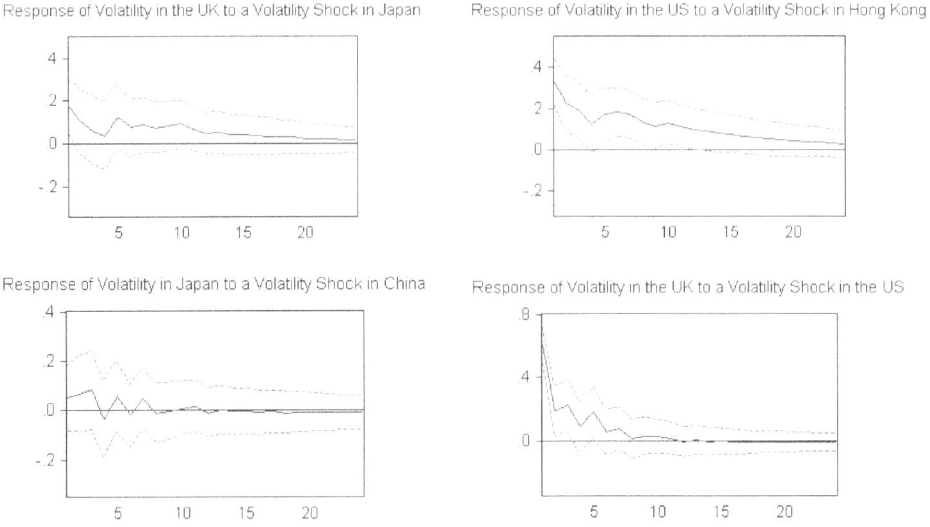

Figure 4. Response of Own Volatilities to Volatility Shocks in Selected Countries

Note: See Fig. A.2 in the Appendix for the full set of results on the response of realized volatility in each country to volatility shocks from all countries.

well as its being the third-largest stock exchange in Asia, these results point to the importance of financial flows emanating to and from Asia in terms of global financial conditions.

Figure 4 further shows the response of realized volatility in selected countries to a volatility shock arising from other countries.[10] We observe that, besides shocks from the Hong Kong Stock Exchange, volatility shocks from the stock exchanges in the US, the UK, and Japan tend to have significantly positive effects on the realized volatility of other developed economies, but those from the Shanghai Stock Exchange do not. This suggests that the channel for the diffusion of financial shocks from China itself is still relatively underdeveloped, whereas financial shocks arising from the developed financial markets in Hong Kong have strong effects globally.

6. An Investigation into the Importance of the Chinese Economy

As we discussed earlier, one of the main objectives of our analysis is to understand the impact of China on global financial markets and real activity.

[10]A full set of impulse responses of realized volatility in each country, and its reaction to its own volatility shocks, as well as from all other countries, is shown in Fig. A.2.

Hence, in this section, we focus on the interaction of Chinese industrial production growth and financial volatility, in terms of its effects on both the domestic and global economy.

6.1. *The impact of Chinese financial shock on Chinese IP growth*

We begin by examining the degree of synchronization between the Chinese financial sector and the real sector. Despite the rapid growth of the stock market in China, it is well known that a limited connection exists between its growing financial markets and the real sectors of the Chinese economy. Allen *et al.* (2005) state that financial markets in China have not been effective in allocating resources to the economy, are highly speculative, and driven by insider trading. Therefore, we hypothesize that there is no significant effect on Chinese industrial production growth resulting from volatility in its own stock markets. However, we also hypothesize that there is an indirect impact on Chinese industrial production performance via the volatility channel. According to this hypothesis, the shock felt by foreign markets from either the Hong Kong or Shanghai Stock Exchanges causes an increase in global volatility, which negatively affects industrial production growth of China through a fall in global demand. On June 12, 2015, stock market turbulence in China led to a dramatic drop in the value of A-shares (shares of Chinese companies traded on the Shanghai and Shenzhen Stock Exchanges), corresponding to a decline of more than 30% of the value on both stock exchanges. However, the direct effects from such turbulence on real production were observed to be quite limited. Nevertheless, Arslanap *et al.* (2016) argues that financial spillovers from China are on the rise for regional markets, and are primarily due to trade linkages, but also are due to an increase in direct financial linkages. They argue that, if shocks to Chinese markets are combined with increases in global risk premia, as was the case in August 2015 and January 2016, these effects could be considerably larger. These observations lend credence to our hypotheses regarding the potential indirect effects of Chinese volatility shocks on regional and global demand and real activity.

To investigate these hypotheses, we examine the sign restrictions, generalized variance decompositions, and impulse response functions. For the sign restrictions, we impose the non-negative impact of volatility on Chinese financial markets to Chinese IP growth as explained in Assumption 1. The non-negativity restriction is observed to be valid, because the successful number of non-negative sign restrictions hold for an average of about 25% in 10,000 trials (shown in Fig. 5).

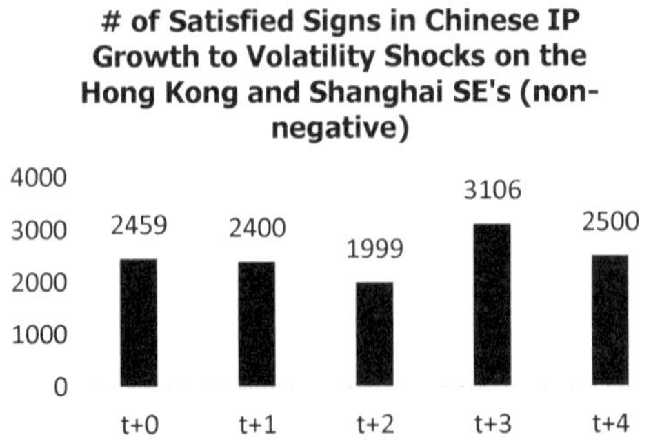

Figure 5. Successful Chinese Volatility-to-Chinese IP Growth Sign Restrictions

Note: This table shows the number of satisfied sign restrictions imposed under Assumption 1 regarding the behavior of Chinese IP growth at time interval t to $t + 4$ out of 10,000 trials. The table indicates the total number of non-negative responses of industrial production growth in China to a positive volatility shock on the Shanghai Stock Exchange and the Hong Kong Stock Exchange.

Turning to the generalized variance decompositions for $t + 2$ and $t + 4$ provided in Tables A.1 and A.2 in the Appendix, we note that a shock to the Shanghai Stock Exchange affects IP growth in China by only 0.19%, while a shock to the Hong Kong Stock Exchange affects it by 0.50%, see Table A.1. The biggest impact on Chinese IP growth comes from its own industrial production growth. That is, a shock to Chinese IP growth is responsible for a variation of about 95% in this variable. Moreover, this result changes slightly under $t+4$ variance decomposition results, as can be seen in Table A.2. Aside from the impact of own shocks to IP growth, a shock to US IP growth at $t + 2(t + 4)$ explains 2.2% (2.5%) variation in Chinese IP growth. We thus conclude that Chinese production growth is mainly affected by itself. The much smaller fraction of variation in Chinese IP growth explained by changes in US IP growth most likely reflects the inter-linkages in trade between China and the US, implying that a decline in US real activity is also manifested by a decline in Chinese IP growth. As Fig. 6 shows, the negative response to a shock from US IP growth occurs on impact and dies out after period $t + 4$.

6.2. *The impact of a Chinese financial shock on realized volatility in other markets*

There are two main stock exchanges in China: the Shanghai Stock Exchange and the Shenzhen Stock Exchange. As stated by Elliott and Yan (2013), another major stock exchange in China is the Hong Kong Stock Exchange, which traditionally focuses on the equities of locally based firms, but has

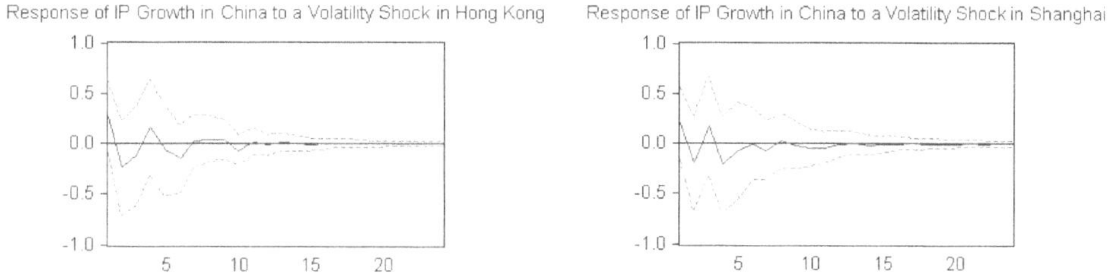

Figure 6. Response of Chinese IP Growth to Volatility Shocks on the Hong Kong and Shanghai Stock Exchanges

Note: See Fig. A.1 in the Appendix for the full set of results on the response of Chinese IP growth to volatility shocks emanating from all other countries.

expanded to trade a considerable volume of H-shares (shares of companies located in Chinese territories traded on the Hong Kong Stock Exchange). Bearing in mind that China has three important stock exchange markets, the question thus emerges: "How influential is the Chinese financial system on foreign markets?"

First, as we showed in Table 4, volatility shocks from the Hong Kong Stock Exchange have the highest success rate at $t + 1$ of 20.84%, followed by a success rate of 16.52% for volatility shocks from the US stock market. Likewise, at $t + 2$, almost 25% of the sign restrictions hold for Hong Kong, whereas, on average, this fraction remains at less than 15% in other markets. Figure 7 provides a direct comparison of the impact of volatility shocks from the Hong Kong versus the Shanghai stock markets. From this table, we observe that the success rate of sign restrictions for shocks from the Shanghai Stock Exchange is lower compared to that of the Hong Kong Stock Exchange, and never exceeds 10% for any of the horizons.

Likewise, the selected generalized variance decompositions for $t + 2$, displayed in Fig. 8, shows that the variation in the Hong Kong Stock Exchange is observed to have the greatest influence on variation in foreign stock markets, much more so than the Shanghai Stock Exchange.[11] The generalized variance decomposition tells us how much the variation on the Hong Kong Stock Exchange is responsible for the variation in other markets at $t+2$. For example, at $t+2$, the volatility of the Hong Kong Stock Exchange is responsible for 10.59% of the volatility in US markets, 11.85% in Germany, 9.62% in the UK, 5.89% in Japan, and lastly, 4.81% in the Shanghai Stock Exchange. By contrast, the variation in the Shanghai Stock Exchange is

[11]For the full set of variance decompositions, see Table A.1 in the Appendix.

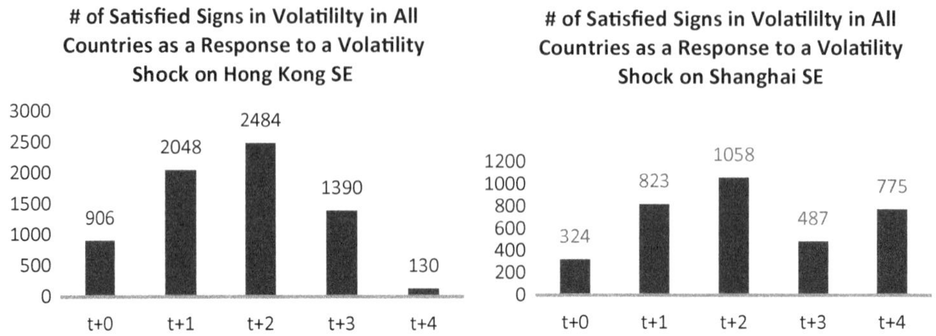

Figure 7. Successful Sign Restrictions for Other Countries' Volatility to a Financial Shock on the Hong Kong and Shanghai SE

Note: This table shows the number of satisfied sign restrictions imposed under Assumption 2 regarding the behavior of realized volatility at time interval t to $t+4$ out of 10,000 trials. This table shows the response in the UK, the US, Japanese, and German financial markets to a positive shock on the Hong Kong Stock Exchange and the Shanghai Stock Exchange.

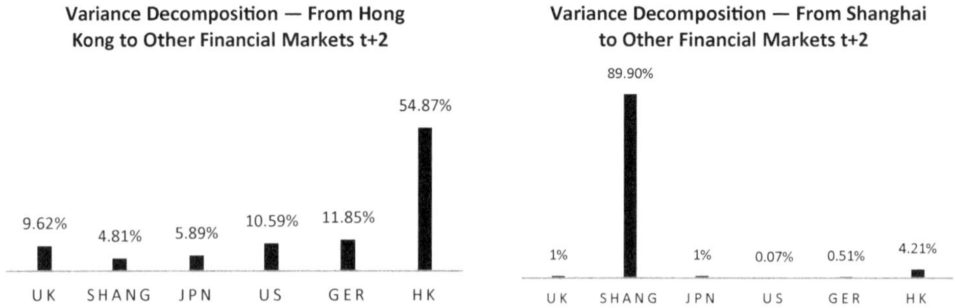

Figure 8. Generalized Variance Decomposition from Hong Kong and Shanghai Stock Markets to Realized Volatility of All Other Markets at t+2

Note: This table shows the fraction of variation explained by the Hong Kong and Shanghai Stock Exchanges in the realized volatility of the remaining stock markets. See Table A.1 in the Appendix for results on the variance decompositions at $t+2$ and $t+4$.

responsible for considerably lower variation in foreign stock markets: 0.07% of volatility in US markets; 0.51% of volatility in German markets; 1% of volatility in UK markets; 1% of volatility in Japanese markets; and 4.21% of volatility in Hong Kong markets.

As further evidence, the impulse responses in Fig. 9 show the response of realized volatility of the Japanese and US stock markets to a volatility shock from the Hong Kong Stock Exchange and the Shanghai Stock Exchange, respectively. We observe that the shocks to these markets are initially accompanied by an increase in the volatility in both the Japanese and the US

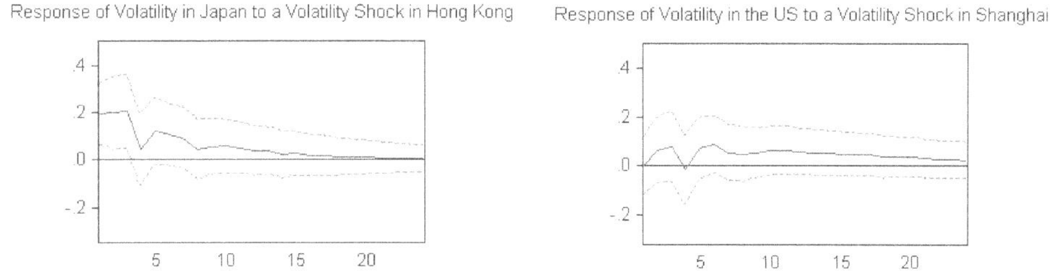

Figure 9. Response of Realized Volatility in Japan and the US to Chinese Financial Shocks

Note: See Fig. A.2 in the Appendix for the full set of results on the response of realized volatility in each country to volatility shocks emanating from all other countries.

financial markets. Also, this figure shows that a volatility shock emanating from the Hong Kong Stock Exchange has a small but persistent effect on the Japanese stock market. Likewise, the response to a volatility shock from the Shanghai Stock Exchange, which imposes the sign restrictions, has a similar hump-shaped response in the US stock market. We also observe that shocks continue for a prolonged period of time, indicating that there is still some impact after $t + 4$.

6.3. *The effects of foreign shocks on industrial production growth in China*

In this section, we study the impact of financial and real shocks arising from foreign markets on industrial production growth in China. We begin by considering the impact of foreign financial volatility shock on IP growth in China. We surmise that an increase in volatility in foreign financial markets might result in a deterioration in global demand, suggesting a fall in consumption and, hence, a decline in trade prospects for China. Therefore, a shock in foreign developed markets might cause Chinese production growth to slow down. The results from generalized variance decompositions and impulse responses provide some evidence about this channel, namely, the negative impact on Chinese production growth due to financial volatility in foreign markets. As Fig. 10 shows, the sign restrictions regarding the impact of foreign financial shocks on Chinese IP growth exceed 8% out of 10,000 trials, suggesting some role for the foreign financial volatility channel.

However, as we discussed in relation to Fig. 5 regarding the impact of volatility shocks on Chinese IP growth, the generalized variance decomposition results reported show that the largest fraction of variance

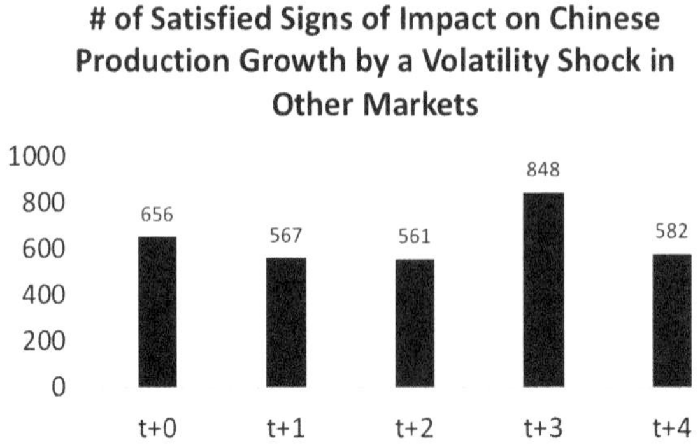

Figure 10. Successful Sign Restrictions of Other Countries' Volatility-to-Chinese IP Growth

Note: This table shows the number of satisfied sign restrictions imposed under Assumption 1 regarding the behavior of IP growth in China at time interval t to $t+4$ out of 10,000 trials. The table indicates the response of Chinese industrial production growth to a volatility shock on other countries' financial markets.

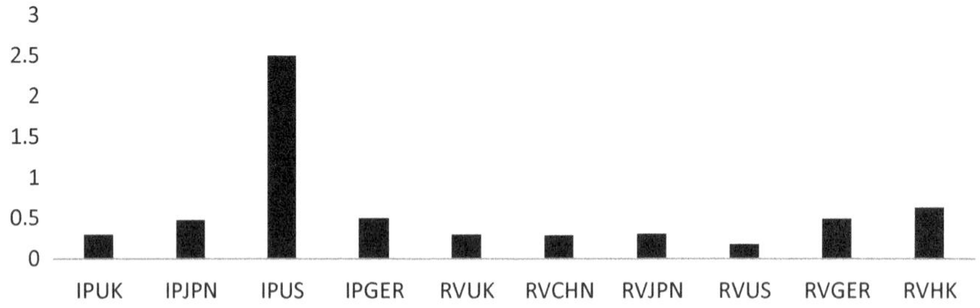

Figure 11. Generalized Variance Decomposition from All Other Variables to Chinese IP Growth at t+4

Note: This table shows the variation explained in Chinese industrial production growth by the respective country's industrial production and realized volatility shocks. See Tables A.1 and A.2 in the Appendix for the full set of results on the variance decompositions for the dates $t+2$ and $t+4$.

explained in Chinese IP growth for horizons of $t + 2$ and $t + 4$ is due to own shocks; see Tables A.1 and A.2. Overall, our results suggest that Chinese industrial production growth is hardly affected by own or foreign financial shocks. Outside of own shocks to IP growth, the largest contribution to Chinese IP growth derives from the behavior of US IP growth with a contribution of (2.2%) 2.5% at horizon $t + 2$ ($t + 4$), as shown in Fig. 11. Hence, we conclude that Chinese IP growth is essentially driven by domestic dynamics.

One way to account for these results is that we have omitted the role of local credit markets and the monetary policy channel of financial shock impact on real activity in China. As Prasad (2016)[12] and others have emphasized, the Chinese financial system remains bank-dominated, with state banks comprising an important source of lending. Furthermore, local government authority lending, for better or worse, is also an important source of funds for spurring real activity at the local level; see Lu and Sun (2013). Recently, Fernald *et al.* (2014) examine the effectiveness of monetary policy in China. However, they do not link changes in domestic monetary policy to foreign economic conditions or to foreign financial shocks. One way to extend our results would be to include indicators of domestic monetary and credit conditions in China to further study the links between Chinese and foreign financial markets and real activity.

While Fig. 11 shows that Chinese IP growth shows little response to either financial or real shocks in other industrialized countries such as Japan or the UK, nevertheless, in the impulse responses reported in Fig. A.4 in the Appendix, we observe a fall in the growth rate of Chinese industrial production at $t + 1$, and especially at $t + 4$, to financial shocks that arise in these countries. When taken together, these findings suggest that, while the impact from turmoil in foreign financial markets on Chinese production growth is relatively small, nevertheless there is still some evidence in favor of our restriction.

7. Sensitivity Analysis

In this section, we seek to account for the impact of the outstanding Chinese economic growth during the period which our study encompasses. Specifically, we seek to examine the hypothesis that higher Chinese IP growth, relative to other countries' performance, leads to insignificant results of the effect of other countries' IP growth on China. For this purpose, we control for the impact of Chinese IP growth by giving weights to each year's industrial production growth for each country. We couple the modified IP growth variables together with the same realized volatility variables. This modification does not lead to a significant change in the impulse responses, as we continue to find that Chinese industrial production growth is still

[12]For example, see his report to the US–China Economic and Security Review Commission at the Brookings Institution.

primarily affected by itself and the relationships between realized volatility and industrial production growth do not change considerably.

8. Conclusion

Our analysis reveals some interesting regularities. First, our results suggest that there is a very close relationship between developed countries in terms of both industrial production growth and realized volatility when sign restrictions, generalized impulse responses, and variance decompositions are considered. This reflects the strong trade, investment, and financial flows among these countries and provides indirect evidence about the existence of a global business cycle. Second, while financial shocks emanating from local stock exchanges such as the Shanghai Stock Exchange have only minor effects on realized volatility or IP growth in other developed markets, we observe that shocks to the Hong Kong Stock Exchange have a significant impact on global financial markets. Turning to the findings for the Chinese economy, we find that financial and product markets in China are essentially "decoupled," i.e., a shock in Chinese stock markets has little impact on its industrial production growth. Second, we find that financial or real shocks in foreign developed markets do not have a large impact on Chinese industrial production growth.

Our findings pose many intriguing questions. Despite becoming the second-largest economy globally, the Chinese economy appears to be driven primarily by domestic conditions. This might reflect choices made by Chinese policymakers in their creation of domestic monetary and fiscal policy. As an example, the Chinese authorities implemented a $586 billion stimulus package in response to the 2008 global financial crisis, which enabled the Chinese economy to avert the worst effects of this crisis. However, it is well known that this stimulus package also led to an increase in the net indebtedness for both local governments and the corporate sector in China. Consequently, any future extensions of this initiative would involve accounting for the role of credit conditions in the Chinese domestic economy.

In this chapter, we have only considered the dynamic interrelationships between China and a small set of industrialized economies. Yet the existence of value-added chains among various Asian economies, including Japan, S. Korea, Taiwan, Vietnam, etc., imply that it is important to increase the number of emerging and developed countries in future analyses to account for the transmission of real and financial shocks between China and other markets. Relatedly, it is widely known that trade is still the major channel through which the Chinese economy interacts with other global economies. Hence, it appears important to account for the trade channel, which would allow an examination of the impact of Chinese exports and imports on global trade and growth. The Trump administration's recent calls to reduce the US trade deficit with China through the imposition of border taxes, and further prohibitions on trade barriers or currency manipulation, suggests that understanding the role of the trade channel in the propagation of real and financial shocks will be of utmost importance in future policy debates.

A final area in which our results could prove useful is in terms of understanding the process toward the liberalization and deepening of financial markets in China itself. While domestic stock markets in China appear to be essentially de-coupled from the real sector of the economy, and have a limited impact on global financial markets, we find strong evidence of the importance of the Hong Kong Stock Exchange in the transmission of financial shocks that emanate from China and Asia and that propagate to the rest of the world. Given their relatively developed status, this suggests an important role for financial markets in Hong Kong for guiding the process of financial liberalization and capital account convertibility, a medium-term goal of Chinese policymakers. One key requirement for the eventual internationalization of the *renminbi* and its acceptance as a global reserve currency is the availability of offshore *renminbi* trading centers, with Hong Kong currently serving as a main trading hub (see Chan, 2014). Evaluating different strategies for achieving this goal, together with an analysis of Hong Kong's role as a testing ground for further financial reforms in China, appears to be an important new area for future research.

References

Allen, F., Qian, J., and Qian, M. (2007). China's financial system: Past, present, and future. In T. Rawski and L. Brandt (eds.), *China's Great Economic Transformation.* New York: Cambridge University Press, pp. 506–568.

Altug, S. and Bildirici, M. (2012). Business cycles in developed and emerging economies: Evidence based on a univariate Markov switching approach. *Emerging Markets Finance and Trade* 48(6), pp. 73–106.

Andersen, T., Bollerslev, T., and Diebold, F. (2010). Parametric and nonparametric measurements of volatility. In Y. Ait-Sahalia and L. Hansen (eds.), *Handbook of Financial Econometrics, Volume 1: Tools and Techniques*, Amsterdam: Elsevier, pp. 67–137.

Arslanalp, A., Liao, W., Piao, S., and Seneviratne, D. (2016). China's growing influence on Asian financial markets. IMF WP 16/173.

Baxter, M. (1995). International trade and business cycles. *Handbook Int. Econom.*, 3, pp. 1801–1864.

Benczúr, P. and Rátfai, A. (2014). Business cycles around the globe: Some key facts. *Emerg. Markets Fin. Trade*, 50(2), pp. 102–109.

Bernanke, B. S. (1986). Alternative explanations of the money-income correlation. In *Carnegie-Rochester Conference Series on Public Policy*, Vol. 25. North-Holland, pp. 49–99.

Blanchard, O. J. (1989). A traditional interpretation of macroeconomic fluctuations. *Am. Econom. Rev.*, 79(5), pp. 1146–1164.

Canova, F. and De Nicolo, G. (2002). Monetary disturbances matter for business fluctuations in the G-7. *J. Monetary Econom.*, 49(6), pp. 1131–1159.

Casson, M. (Ed.). (2013). *The Growth of International Business*. Routledge: RLE International Business.

Chan, N. (2014). Reform and liberalisation in China: The positioning and future of Hong Kong, Speech at the Hong Kong Economic Summit 2015, Hong Kong Monetary Authority.

D'Agostino, A., Gambetti, L., and Giannone, D. (2013). Macroeconomic forecasting and structural change. *J. Appl. Economet.*, 28(1), pp. 82–101.

Elliott, D. J. and Yan, K. (2013). *The Chinese Financial System: An Introduction and Overview*. Brookings Institution.

Epps, T. W. and Epps, M. L. (1976). The stochastic dependence of security price changes and transaction volumes: Implications for the mixture-of-distributions hypothesis. *Econometrica*, pp. 305–321.

Errunza, V. and Hogan, K. (1998). Macroeconomic determinants of European stock market volatility. *Euro. Fin. Manage.*, 4(3), pp. 361–377.

Faust, J. (1998). The robustness of identified VAR conclusions about money. In *Carnegie-Rochester Conference Series on Public Policy* Vol. 49, Amsterdam: North-Holland, pp. 207–244.

Fernald, J., Spiegel, M., and Swanson, E. (2014). Monetary policy effectiveness in China: Evidence from a FAVAR Model. *J. Int. Money Fin.*, 49, pp. 83–103.

Fleming, J. (1998). The quality of market volatility forecasts implied by S&P 100 index option prices. *J. Empir. Fin.*, 5(4), pp. 317–345.

Fornari, F. and Mele, A. (2013). Financial volatility and economic activity. *J. Fin. Manage. Markets Instit.*, 1(2), pp. 155–198.

Giannellis, N. and Papadopoulos, A. P. (2011). What causes exchange rate volatility? Evidence from selected EMU members and candidates for EMU membership countries. *J. Int. Money Fin.*, 30(1), pp. 39–61.

Goswami, G. and Jung, S. (1997). Stock market and economic forces: Evidence from Korea. *J. Fin.*, 56, pp. 500–757.

He, D., Liao, W., and Wu, T. (2015). Hong Kong's growth synchronization with China and the US: A trend and cycle analysis. *J. Asian Econom.*, 40, pp. 10–28.

Inoue, A. and Kilian, L. (2013). Inference on impulse response functions in structural VAR models. *J. Econometr.*, 177(1), pp. 1–13.

Joshi, P. and Pandya, K. (2012). Volatility in stock markets of India and Canada. *J. Appl. Econom.*, 11(4), pp. 72–79.

Kose, M. A., Otrok, C., and Whiteman, C. H. (2003). International business cycles: World, region, and country-specific factors. *Am. Econom. Rev.*, 93(4), pp. 1216–1239.

Kose, M. A., Otrok, C., and Prasad, E. S. (2012). Global business cycles: Convergence or decoupling? *Int. Econom. Rev.*, 53(2), pp. 511–538.

Lu, Y. and Sun, T. (2013). Local government financing platforms in China: Fortune or misfortune. IMF WP No. 13/243.

Lütkepohl, H. (2005). *New Introduction to Multiple Time Series Analysis*. Berlin: Springer.

Prasad, E. (2016). China's Economy and Financial Risks. Statement to the US-China Economic and Security Review Commission, Hearing on "China's 13th Five-Year Plan", April 27.

Ross, S. A. (1989). Information and volatility: The no-arbitrage martingale approach to timing and resolution irrelevancy. *J. Fin.*, 44(1), pp. 1–17.

Scheicher, M. (2001). The co-movements of stock markets in Hungary, Poland and the Czech Republic. *Int. J. Fin. Econom.*, 6(1), pp. 27–39.

Shapiro, M. and Watson, M. (1988). Sources of business cycles fluctuations. In *NBER Macroeconomics Annual 1988*, Vol. 3. Boston: MIT Press, pp. 111–156.

Sims, C. A. (1981). An autoregressive index model for the US 1948–1975. In J. Kmenta and J. B. Ramsey (eds.), *Large-Scale Macro-Econometric Models*. Amsterdam: North-Holland, pp. 283–327.

Sims, C. A. (1986). Are forecasting models usable for policy analysis? Federal Reserve Bank of Minneapolis. *Quart. Rev.*, 10(1), pp. 2–16.

Strohsal, T. and Weber, E. (2015). Time-varying international stock market interaction and the identification of volatility signals. *J. Banking Fin.*, 56, pp. 28–36.

Uhlig, H. (2005). What are the effects of monetary policy on output? Results from an agnostic identification procedure. *J. Monetary Econom.*, 52(2), pp. 381–419.

Wongbangpo, P. and Sharma, S. C. (2002). Stock market and macroeconomic fundamental dynamic interactions: ASEAN-5 countries. *J. Asian Econom.*, 13(1), pp. 27–51.

Worthington, A. and Higgs, H. (2004). Transmission of equity returns and volatility in Asian developed and emerging markets: A multivariate GARCH analysis. *Int. J. Fin. Econom.*, 9(1), pp. 71–80.

Appendix

Table A.1. Generalized Variance Decompositions for $(t + 2)$

	IPUK	IPCHN	IPJPN	IPUS	IPGER	RVUK	RVCHN	RVJPN	RVUS	RVGER	RVHK
IPUK	90.76	0.14	4.32	1.51	3.02	0.06	0.02	0.00	0.04	0.09	0.04
IPCHN	0.10	95.13	0.42	2.21	0.56	0.19	0.19	0.24	0.08	0.38	0.51
IPJPN	5.52	0.45	85.19	1.49	3.90	0.27	1.60	1.43	0.04	0.08	0.03
IPUS	0.97	1.99	9.44	83.57	2.47	0.47	0.18	0.31	0.44	0.08	0.07
IPGER	3.53	0.49	7.02	2.50	77.06	0.40	0.18	0.43	3.38	1.90	3.11
RVUK	0.01	0.04	0.16	0.24	0.25	47.91	0.98	3.39	24.08	13.31	9.63
RVCHN	0.00	0.13	1.69	0.03	0.11	1.02	89.95	1.25	0.02	0.99	4.82
RVJPN	0.01	0.05	1.58	0.03	0.43	4.95	1.01	74.87	6.12	5.05	5.89
RVUS	0.02	0.05	0.01	0.14	1.85	23.70	0.08	3.80	44.32	15.44	10.60
RVGER	0.06	0.13	0.18	0.03	1.17	15.91	0.52	3.50	17.70	48.95	11.86
RVHK	0.17	0.21	0.00	0.01	2.11	9.65	4.22	4.30	11.38	13.07	54.87

Table A.2. Generalized Variance Decompositions for $(t + 4)$

	IPUK	IPCHN	IPJPN	IPUS	IPGER	RVUK	RVCHN	RVJPN	RVUS	RVGER	RVHK
IPUK	89.81	0.22	4.55	1.75	3.03	0.15	0.03	0.10	0.14	0.14	0.08
IPCHN	0.22	94.45	0.51	2.61	0.55	0.19	0.20	0.29	0.08	0.39	0.51
IPJPN	5.48	0.47	83.72	2.33	3.98	0.37	1.59	1.51	0.15	0.19	0.21
IPUS	2.09	1.73	8.28	71.31	2.99	3.01	0.87	3.30	2.86	2.00	1.55
IPGER	3.97	0.59	6.92	3.22	73.07	0.73	0.26	1.46	3.71	2.65	3.42
RVUK	0.01	0.07	0.17	0.33	0.27	46.16	1.19	3.48	24.10	13.48	10.24
RVCHN	0.00	0.14	1.66	0.03	0.10	1.13	89.09	1.31	0.06	1.12	5.36
RVJPN	0.02	0.10	1.62	0.04	0.44	4.96	1.01	74.65	6.13	5.06	5.96
RVUS	0.03	0.05	0.02	0.19	1.80	23.57	0.24	3.84	42.62	16.43	11.22
RVGER	0.07	0.12	0.17	0.07	1.18	16.45	0.61	3.56	17.93	47.57	12.26
RVHK	0.15	0.21	0.09	0.04	2.03	10.08	5.05	4.31	11.51	13.04	53.48

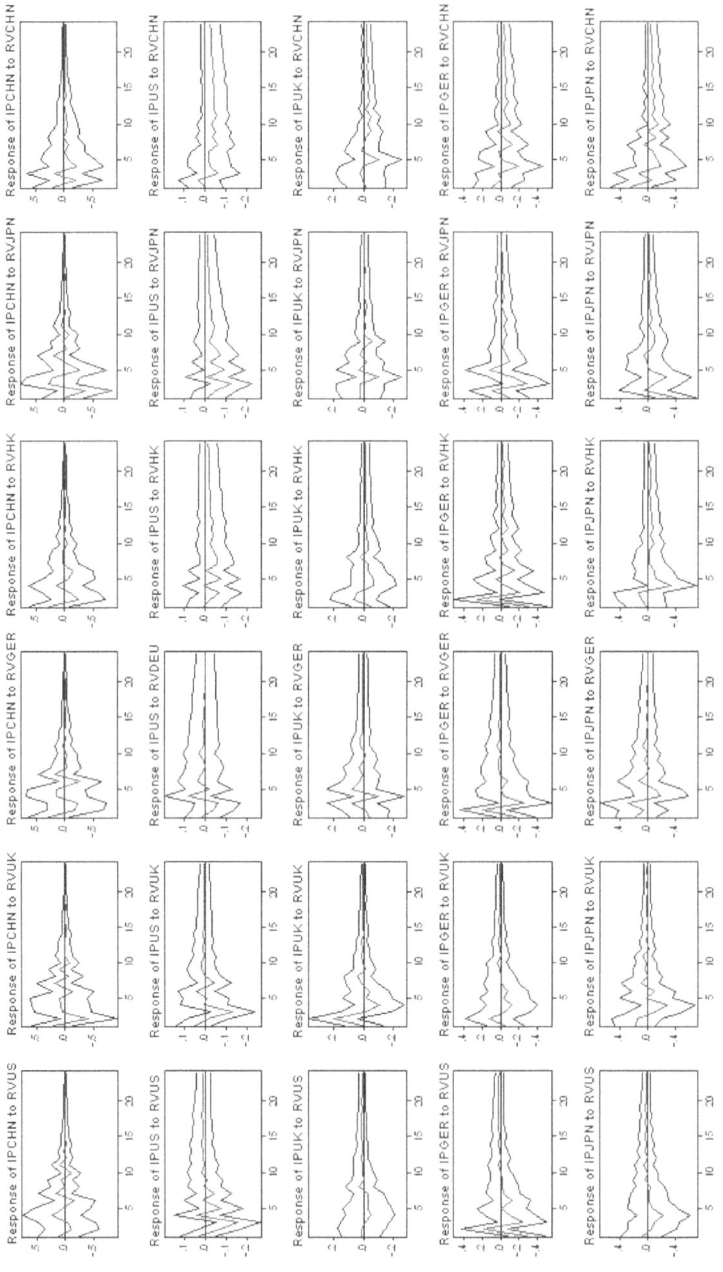

Figure A.1. Impulse Responses of IP Growth in All Countries to Volatility Shock in Other Markets

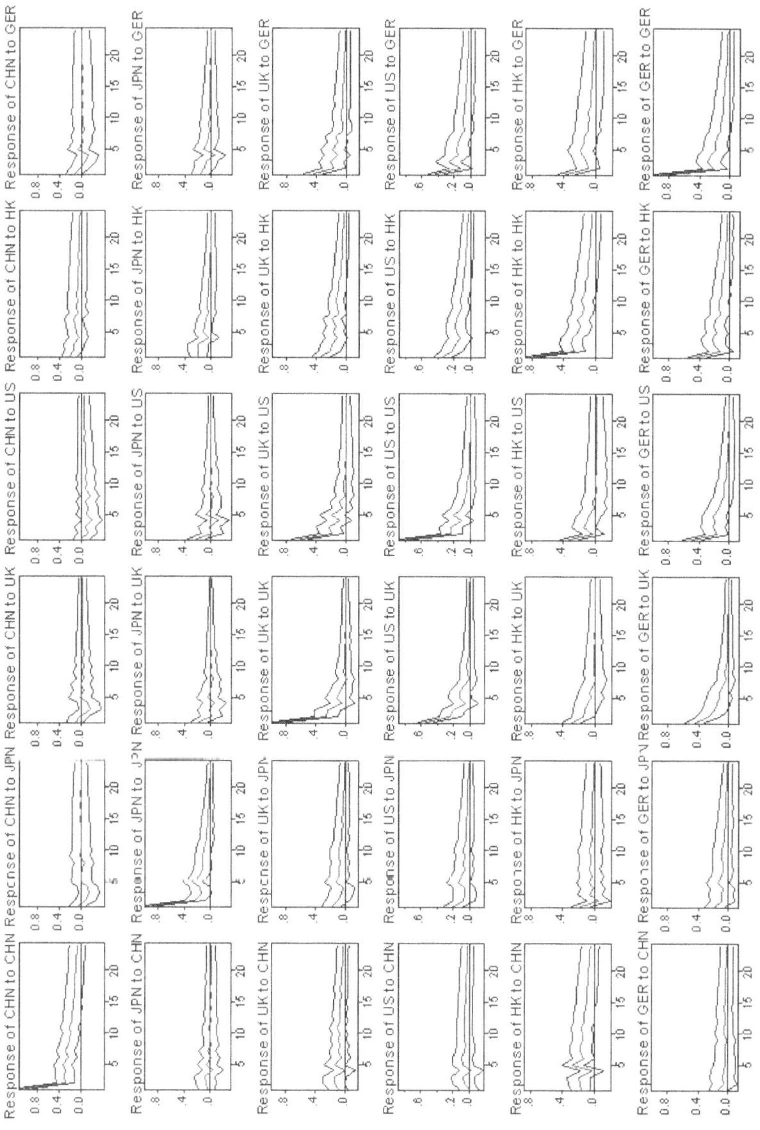

Figure A.2. Impulse Responses of Volatility in All Countries to Volatility Shocks

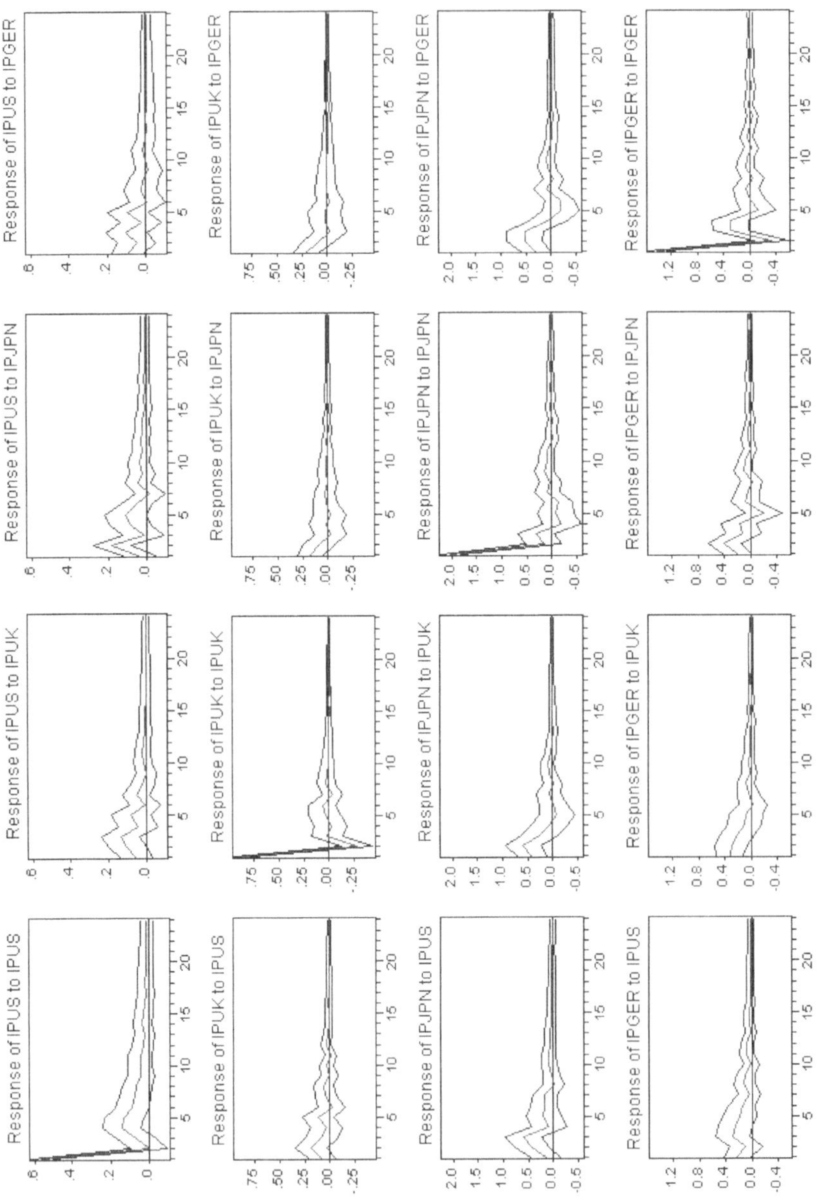

Figure A.3. Impulse Responses of IP Growth in All Countries to IP Shocks

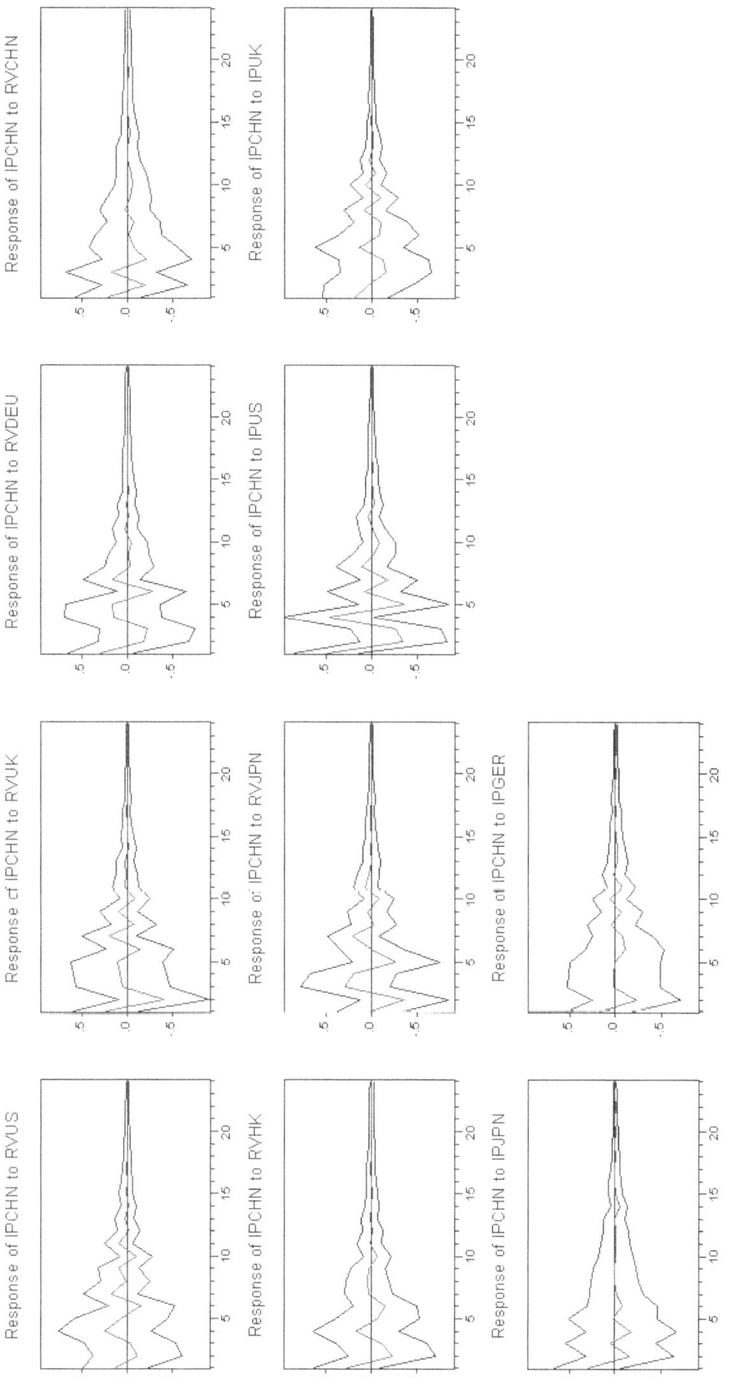

Figure A.4. Impulse Response of IP Growth in China to Shocks in Realized Volatility and IP Growth in Other Countries

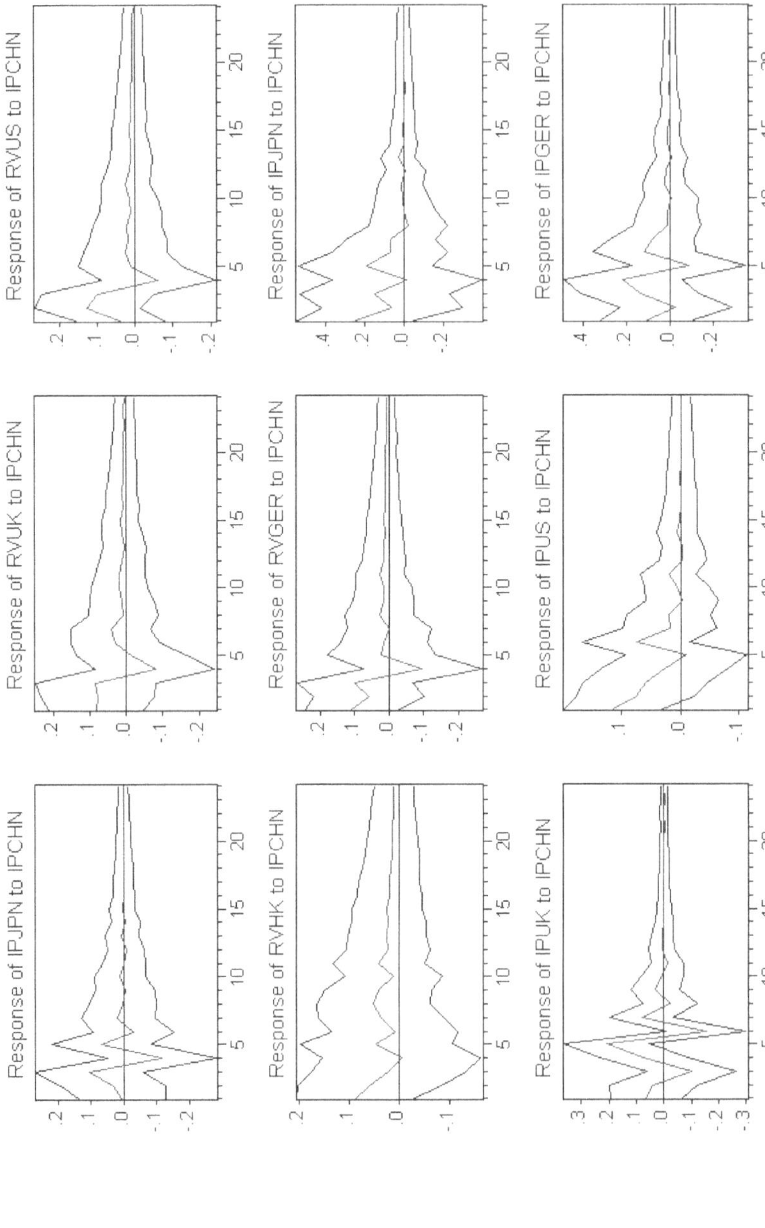

Figure A.5. Impulse Responses of Realized Volatility and IP Growth in Others to IP Growth Shocks in China

Chapter 21

The Impact of Technology on the Financial Services Industry

Arindam Bandopadhyaya* and Jinglin Yang

Department of Accounting and Finance
University of Massachusetts Boston
100 Morrissey Boulevard Boston MA 02125
**arindam.bandopadhyaya@umb.edu*

Abstract

Technological changes have had an impact on every traditional industry, including financial services. Brick and mortar banks are no longer the face of this industry. New technological inventions, such as bitcoin-inspired distributed system, Open Application Program Interface (API), and crowd-sourced identity schemes have shaped the industry into something faster, safer, and cost-efficient. In this chapter, we explore the influence of technology on the financial service industry. We first investigate the impact of technology on existing market elements like retail investors, commercial banking, traditional exchanges, and the emergence of exchange traded funds. We examine high-frequency trading and the link between technology flash crashes. We also investigate how technology has influenced the profession of equity research. We then document new inventions like Open APIs and Blockchains and discuss how such innovations have and are likely to change the business landscape in the financial services industry.

Any sufficiently advanced technology is equivalent to magic

Arthur Clarke

1. Introduction

All segments of the financial service industry have been deeply affected by myriad technical innovations. In this chapter, we provide an overview of how technology has shaped different components of the financial services industry. We examine the impact of technology on the existing market elements. We discuss the effect technology has had on retail investors and commercial banks. We document the advent and growth of passive management instruments and explore the changes in trading practices and their impact on trading exchanges. We survey the consequences of algorithm trading and how technology has affected the way in which investment research is conducted. We also examine some new innovations in the industry and how these have affected the business arena. The chapter covers multiple topics to give a synopsis of how technology has affected the financial services industry, rather than focusing on one particular aspect of the changes. The overview utilizes data and factual information from various sources, and then each section relates the discussion to the one that prevails in the extant academic literature.

The key observations of this chapter include:

(1) Technology enables the smoother flow of information, shortening the time to access information which accelerates decision-making.
(2) Discount brokerage, which is accessible at a low cost, is rapidly replacing the traditional brokerage.
(3) Brick-and-mortar commercial banks, which have generally been relatively slow to update their technology, have decreased steadily over time. Large digital lenders have seen tremendous growth in their loan origination business.
(4) Exchange traded funds (ETFs) have emerged as a popular investment vehicle. ETFs and index mutual funds have steadily diverted capital inflows from actively managed mutual funds.
(5) Technology has greatly altered the way in which securities and other assets are traded. As a result, traditional exchanges like the New York Stock Exchange have been greatly downsized greatly. Such trends make certain tasks less pertinent, which threatens jobs in some segments in the industry.
(6) With the advance of technology, investment research is undergoing fundamental changes. Readily available, reliable financial data has facilitated the spotting of new investment themes.
(7) Algorithm trading, which is based on supreme computer capability, while often cited as culprit in market problems like flash crashes, improves market liquidity.
(8) Innovations like open Application Programming Interface (API) and Blockchain have changed the way in which information is are shared, resulting in more operational efficiencies.

The remainder of this chapter is organized as follows. Section 2 is divided in to five subsections. In Secs. (2.1) and (2.2) we discuss the impact of technology on retail investors and commercial banking, respectively. Section (2.3) documents the emergence of exchange traded funds as a popular investment vehicle. The impact of technology on traditional exchanges is presented in Sec. (2.4). We also briefly touch upon the role of technology on academic research in this section in Sec. (2.5). New inventions driven by technology — API and Blockchain — are the focus of the discussion in Sec. 3. Concluding thoughts and reflections are provided in Sec. 4.

2. The Impact of Technology on Existing Market Elements

2.1. *Retail investors*

For retail investors, technological boom in the form of fast internet has played an important role in how they are able to conduct business. Internet, which serves as an embodiment of changing technology, allows different financial stakeholders to browse economic data, news or any relevant reports in a timely manner. More importantly, the physical boundaries of information flow have been essentially eliminated. This enables financial institutions in the US to access data or news stories in other countries with one click of a mouse. Communications, even ones that are face to face, do not necessarily mean physical travel any more. With the improvement of web cameras and advanced instant messaging technology, applications provide conference call functionality in different geographic locations so that retail clients can effectively communicate with brokers and advisors in an instant.

The proliferation of discount brokers and the associated cost efficiency is another aspect of the change in the technological landscape that has affected retail investors. The increase of online brokers is due to their transparency, accessibility, and efficiency, which are a direct product of internet advancement. Brokerage accounts used to be a privilege enjoyed by moneyed capitalists or at least the rich middle class several decades ago. To open a traditional brokerage account, one must meet the minimum capital requirement, often beyond an average working family's annual salary. While charging annual fees of 2% for wealth management, some shops have minimum commitment requirements of $250,000 (Table 1). Now, those traditional accounts supervised by financial advisors are not the only mainstream tools. Discount brokerage, which is accessible at a low cost, is rapidly replacing the traditional brokerage (Fig. 1). In 2013, retail investors used discount brokerages almost as much as wirehouses. Cost

Table 1. Major Wirehouses Wealth Management Fee Structure

Wirehouse	Minimum Commitment	Annual Fee[a]
Bank of America Merrill Lynch	$250,000	2%
UBS	$100,000	2%
Morgan Stanley	$100,000	2%
Weils Fargo	$100,000	2%

[a]Fees depend on assets under management.

Notes: For traditional brokerage accounts, one must meet the minimum capital requirement while paying annual fees of 2% for asset under management. Annual fees and minimum commitments of some house are shown in this exhibit.

Source: Website of Bank of America, UBS, Morgan Stanley, and Wells Fargo.

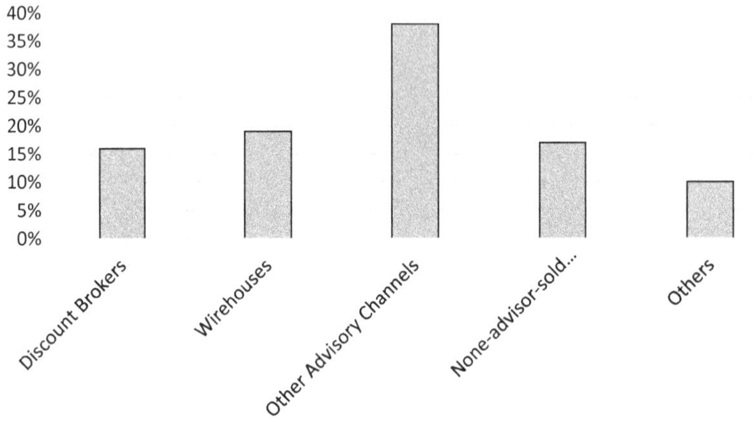

Figure 1. US Retail Investor Investment Channels (2013)

Notes: This exhibit shows major channels through which investors choose to participate in the financial market. The role of discount brokers has increased over time. As of 2013, the market share of discount brokers was over 15%.

Source: InvestmentNews.com.

per trade conducted in those brokerages is usually below $10 per trade and is sometimes as low as $4 (Table 2). From the perspective of a long-term investor, instead of being charged at 2% of the entire assets under management annually, constructing a portfolio and trading in a discount brokerage can save him or her significant amount money.

Observers (e.g., Barber and Odean, 2001) are in near unanimity in suggesting that internet makes financial service more accessible to retail investors in a faster and cheaper way. However, many argue that when

Table 2. Discount Brokers Trading Fee Comparison

Discount Brokers	Minimum Commitment	Per Trade Cost
TD Ameritrade	None	\$9.99
Merrill Edge	None	\$6.95
Charles Schwab	\$1,000	\$8.95
OptionHouse	None	\$4.95
TradeKing	\$500	\$4.95
Capital One Investing	None	\$4.00
Scottrade	\$2,500	\$7.00

Notes: Trading costs at discount brokerages are typically lower as compared to other institutions. This exhibit summarizes how much mainstream discount brokers charge for each trade and minimum commitment to open an account.

Source: Website of TD Ameritrade, Merrill Edge, Charles Schwab, OptionHouse, TradeKing, Capital One Investing, Scottrade.

given more information on which a forecast is based, investors gain much more confidence in the accuracy of their forecasts than the accuracy of the forecasts themselves. In addition, a greater volume of information gives retail investors an illusion of knowledge. They consider themselves an expert in stock picking, but they only search information that confirms their original opinions and ignore other contradictory evidence. Those biased behaviors gives investors an exaggerated sense of control, which leads to excessive trading, ignoring the risk of trading on margins and investing in stocks that are hard to value.

While retail investors can obtain financial data at low cost and a timely fashion, they face challenges of collecting all relevant information and analyzing it objectively when making a forecast. Transparency of the internet and accessibility of information have raised the bar for all retail investors, as the real test is to see who can pick the most useful information and remain unbiased throughout the whole process.

2.2. *Commercial banking*

When talking about the influence of technological innovations on the finance industry, it is natural to think of commercial banks, since they are the backbone of the economy. Advances in information technology threaten the existence of traditional commercial banks through three channels. First, technology has changed the efficient size of a bank (Jordan and Katz, 1999). Some banking products, such as payments processing, are more technological intensive, which is more efficient on a large scale. This has led

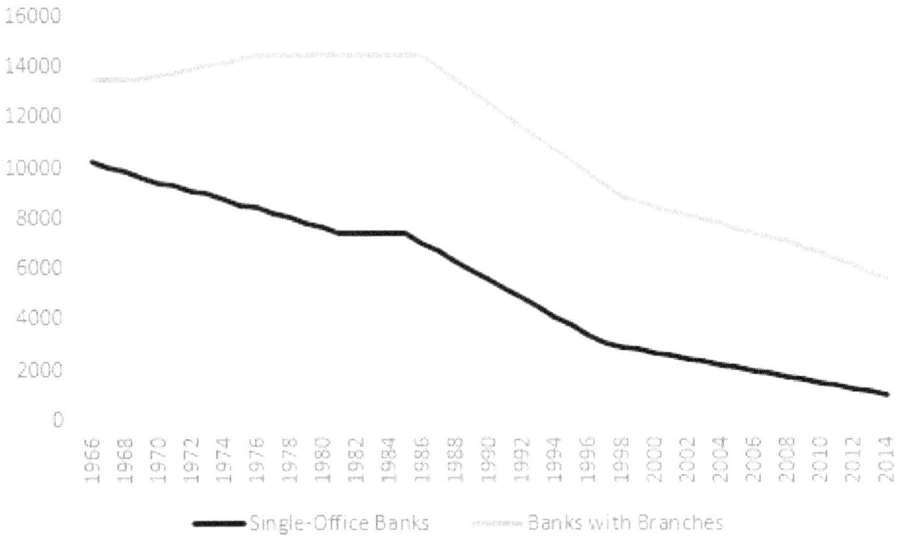

Figure 2. Number of Commercial Banks in the US

Notes: Number of brick and mortar banks, including single-office banks and banks with branches, declined gradually. Single-office banks have steadily declined in number since the middle of the 1960s to less than 2000 in 2014. Banks with branches peaked in number to more than 14,000 in the 1970–1980 period, but have been on a steady decline to less than 6000 in 2014.

Source: Institute for Self-Reliance.

to mergers and acquisitions in the banking industry. Second, marketplace players with strong technological platforms increase the competition among existing banks. For example, Lending Club and Prosper, the two leading US marketplace lenders, saw their total originations of consumer credit in the US grow from \$871 million in 2012 to \$2.4 billion in 2013 (McWaters, 2015). Their main strategy is to prove that the industry can function with discipline without the need for additional government intervention. By distinguishing themselves from businesses like payday lenders whose predatory tactics have drawn regulatory fire, online lenders hope to avoid a similar crackdown (Finkle, 2016). Brick-and-mortar commercial banks, which have been relatively slow to update their technology, bear the brunt of both phenomena described above. Thus, the number of commercial banks has decreased steadily (Fig. 2). Single-office banks have steadily declined in number since the middle of the 1960s to less than 2000 in 2014. Banks with branches peaked in number to more than 14,000 in the 1970–1980 period, but have been on a steady decline to less than 6000 in 2014. Third, technology firms themselves have tapped into the loan origination business

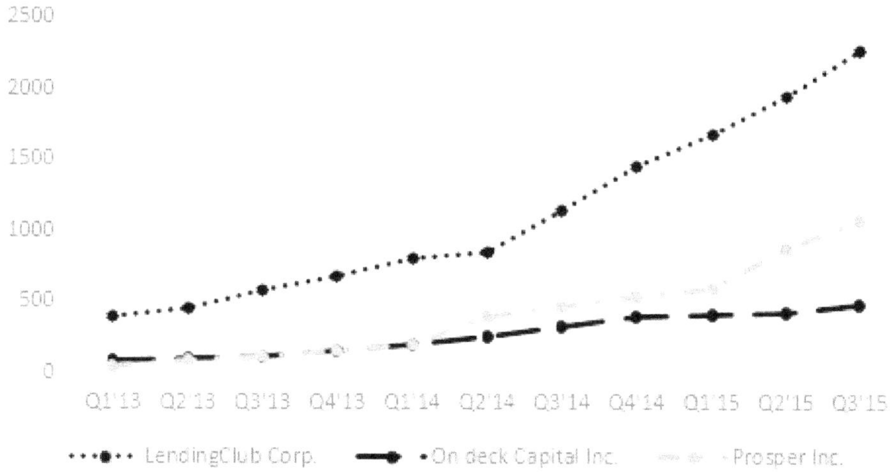

Figure 3. Loans Originated by Selected Digital Lenders (in Millions of US Dollars)

Notes: Historically, small businesses have struggled to obtain loans from traditional banks. Now, there are firms that help consumers or small businesses get small loans quickly online. Some of the biggest digital lenders have seen tremendous growth in their loan origination business. LendingClub Corp has led the way originating almost 2,400 loans per quarter in 2015.

Source: Bankingexhange.com.

to rival with traditional competitors. Historically, small businesses struggled to obtain loans from traditional banks because of complicated, redundant paperwork and considerable time required for the approval process. Now, firms such as LendUp help consumers or small businesses get small loans quickly online. Some of the biggest digital lenders have seen tremendous growth in their loan origination business (Fig. 3). LendingClub Corp has led the way originating almost 2,400 loans per quarter in 2015. The digital lenders have seen significant growth over the years — LendingClub Corp had 92% year-over-year growth in consumer lending in the third quarter of 2015, and OnDeck Capital Inc. posted a 54% growth rate in the same period (Fox, 2015).

The impact of technology on commercial banking has been a widely discussed topic in academic literature. Casolaro (2007) showed that costs and profits of a bank are strongly correlated with accumulation of information technology (IT) capital. In other words, the more money a bank spends on updating technology, the more efficiently a bank operates. This view corroborates the first point made in the previous paragraph. Also, Oliveira *et al.* (2014) suggested that users are competing against conventional commercial banks as well. To be specific, they showed that 85% of mobile banking-related innovations come from developing countries and users are the pioneers for more than half of the innovations. Users are the ones that are most clear about what they need. Instead of letting the commercial banks spend money and time to study consumer behavior to know the needs of the customer and to create apps to market themselves, customers seem to know their own habits and needs better and they can come up with solutions more promptly to target their needs given they have adequate knowledge in the respective area. This shows that the competing force against the conventional commercial banks are in fact more than just the three listed in the last paragraph, as users themselves are also very powerful. In general, conventional commercial banks have challenges. Whether they can survive or even thrive in the competition depends on how fast they can adopt new user-friendly technologies and how loyal their customers are. Recently, several established financial institutions and some financial start-ups announced a new tool known as "chatbots" that will allow customers to ask questions about their financial accounts, initiate transactions and get financial advice via text messages or services (Popper, 2016). The banking industry is likely to see many such user-friendly innovations in the future as companies compete for customers and customer loyalty.

2.3. *Exchange traded funds*

The growth of ETFs has been striking. During the second quarter of 2015, the total assets in ETFs reached almost $3 trillion and surpassed those in hedge funds (Rennison, 2015), (Fig. 4). Also, ETF's growth has dimmed the prospect of actively mutual funds. Increasingly, funds from actively managed mutual funds have been diverted to index mutual funds and ETFs (Fig. 5). The trend toward passive investing is accelerating. ETFs have emerged as a convenient investment vehicle which has turned out to be better performing than most actively managed mutual funds (Rubino, 2016). As a result, they have become the favorite vehicle for financial planners who as fiduciaries are required to prioritize such qualities.

ETFs started to appear as an investment instrument in the early 1990s, which is about the same time that internet usage took off. This has led many authors to investigate if the growth of ETFs is related to the popularity of the internet. According to Birdthistle (2008), ETFs are designed to imitate mutual funds but at the same time to avoid the moral hazard associated with the mutual fund industry. Specifically, in 2003 the mutual fund industry

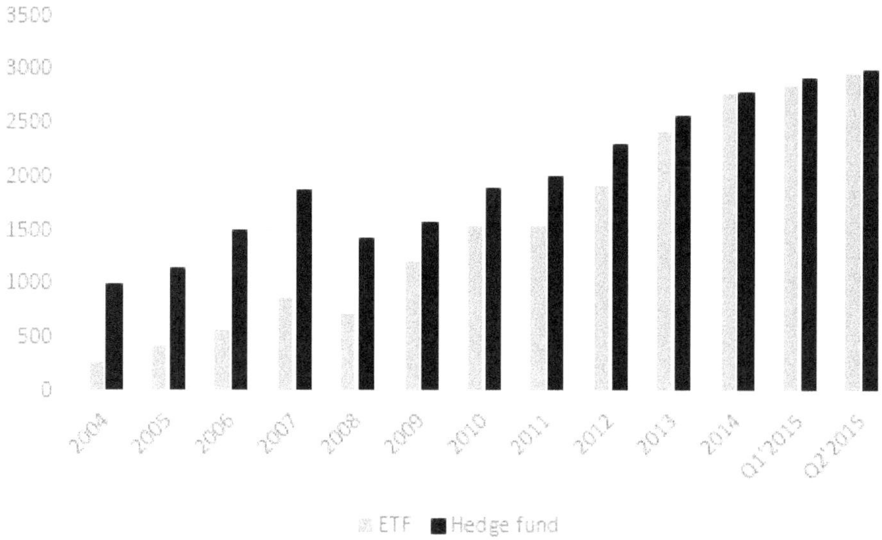

Figure 4. Exchange Traded Funds vs. Hedge Fund Assets (in Billions of US Dollars)

Notes: The growth of ETFs has been remarkable. During the second quarter of 2015, the total assets in ETF reached almost $3 trillion, surpassing assets under management in hedge funds.

Source: Financial Times.

witnessed a series of scandals of its own, such as late trading, front running, and unfair valuation. One can conjecture that ETFs became popular to preserve mutual funds' performance while improving its integrity. Another driver of the growth of ETFs is the endorsement by many famous economists. For example, both Burton Malkiel, author of *A Random Walk down Wall Street*, and Robert Shiller, author of *Irrational Exuberance*, are enthusiasts of ETFs. Although internet did not directly drive the formation of ETFs, it did provide a platform for the public to learn about the mutual funds scandals and the economists' point of views. In a way, the internet may have indirectly accelerated the development of ETFs through efficient dissemination of information.

Another important question that scholars pose is whether mutual funds will be completely replaced by ETFs. Agapova (2011) argued that conventional mutual funds and ETFs are substitutes, but they are not perfect substitutes for each other. These two vehicles focus on different niche markets. ETFs are beneficial to investors sensitive to changes in tax rates while conventional mutual funds fit people who are more insensitive to tax rate and are inclined to receive services from fund companies. Nonetheless,

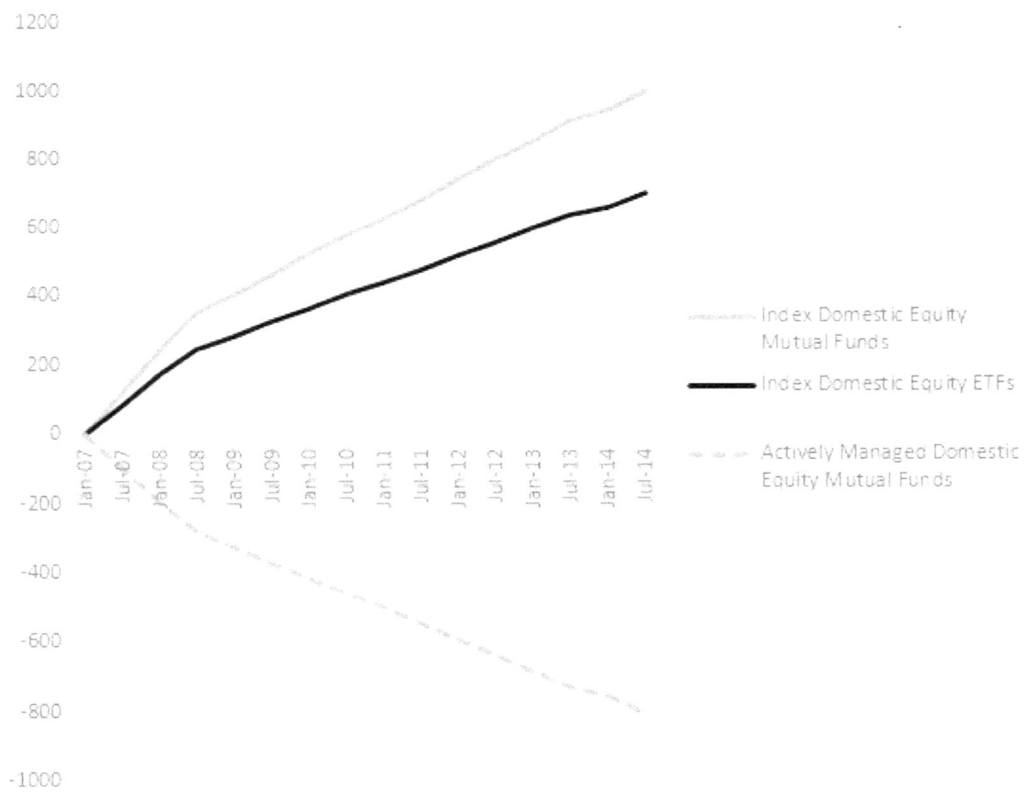

Figure 5. Flows in to Mutual Funds vs. Exchange Traded Funds

Notes: ETFs have emerged as a popular alternative to actively managed mutual funds. The trend toward passive investing is accelerating. Increasingly, funds from actively managed mutual funds have been diverted to index mutual funds and ETFs.
Source: Investment Company Institute.

the popularity of ETFs is rapidly rising while the demand for conventional funds is declining. The future fate of both vehicles depends on specific market needs in terms of cost, trading speed and transparency.

2.4. *Trading and traditional exchanges*

Trading is a significant part of the overall finance arena, since it is the actual process of executing on investment ideas. Basic trading process is supposedly to be straight-forward. When an investor decides to buy or sell a stock, he or she will contact a broker. The broker then will route the order to an exchange, and the trade is executed when the bids and offers are matched. In the 1970–1980s, it was for traders to shout across the trading floor to search for the other side of the trade. With the advancement of technology and proliferation of algorithms, the whole process is much more complicated. For example, a broker or dealer can use algorithms to route various portions of a trade to different venues to minimize the information leakage and market impact (PwC, 2015).

Trading is mostly done through major exchanges, which are going through dramatic changes because of technology. Let us take New York Stock Exchange (NYSE) and NASDAQ's history as example. In the 1970s and 1980s, NYSE and NASDAQ dominated the stock trading. After the Securities and Exchange Commission enacted a series of regulations to fuel competition and put downward pressure on the commission costs for retail investors, NYSE and NASDAQ responded by posting orders electronically with an emphasis on immediate execution (Bowley, 2011). The regulatory changes fostered growth of start-up operations that were faster and cheaper, but market share of NYSE and NASDAQ remained remarkably high. Fearing that this duopoly would charge them heavily for the right to trade, brokerage firms created their own exchanges, two prominent of which are Direct Edge and BATS Exchange.

In 2005, NYSE accounted for 70% of the trading of stocks which are listed on the NYSE. By 2010, NYSE was only responsible for 36% of those by itself. The rest was divided among other public exchanges, electronic trading platforms, and unlit markets (Fig. 6). Also, according to CME Group, the pit trading volume as a percentage of total trading volume is decreasing while the total trading volume is generally increasing since 2008 (Fig. 7).

With the growth of electronic trading and the increasing use of algorithms in trades, a unique form of the algorithm trading — high-frequency trading (HFT) — has attracted special attention. HFT refers to utilization of computer power to transact large number of orders in a short amount

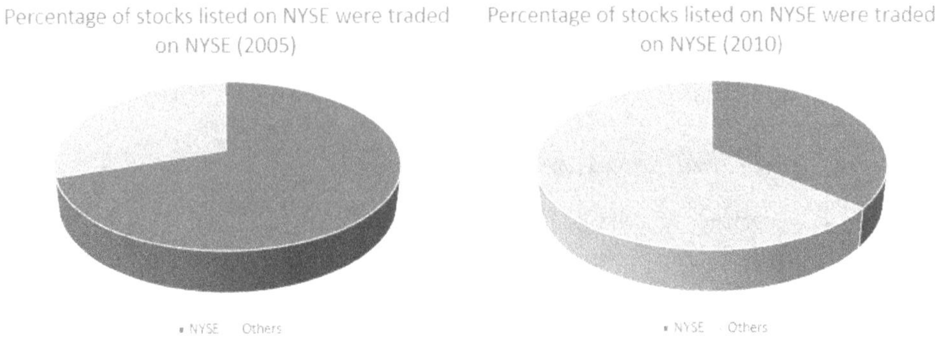

Figure 6. Percentage of Stocks Traded on NYSE

Notes: Traditional exchanges are being challenged by alternatives. The percentage of stocks listed on NYSE and traded on NYSE has been decreased. In 2005, NYSE accounted for 70% of the trading of stocks which are listed on the NYSE. By 2010, NYSE was only responsible for 36% of those by itself. The rest was divided among other public exchanges, electronic trading platforms and unlit markets.
Source: *New York Times*.

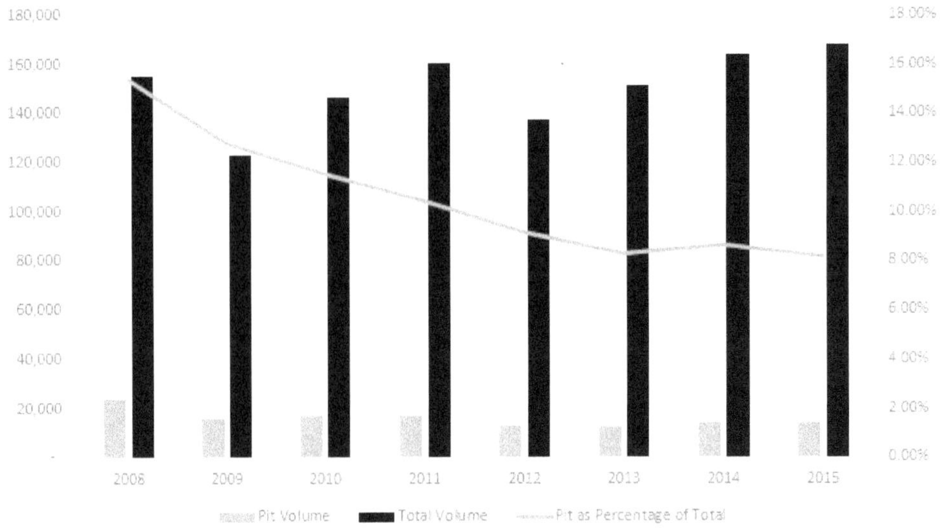

Figure 7. Pit Trading Volume as a Percentage of Total Trading Volume at CME

Notes: Even as the total trading volume has been generally increasing, pit trading volume as a percentage of total trading volume at CME has been decreasing gradually.
Source: Data from CME Group.

of time. This is mainly done by hedge fund, investment banks, or other institutional investors. The perception of HFT by observers of the financial services industry is mixed. On one hand, HFT is found to have a positive effect in price efficiency "by trading in the direction of permanent price changes and in the opposite direction of transitory pricing errors on average days and the highest volatility days" (Hendershott and Riordan, 2011). On the other hand, HFT has also been increasingly associated with flash crashes. On May 6, 2010, Dow Jones Industrial Average plunged 998 points and recovered most of it in less than an hour (Whitman, 2010). A survey done by ishares/Blackrock showed that 46% of investors believed that HFT is the biggest cause of the crash (Subrahmanyam, 2013). Later, Kirilenko *et al.* (2016)) showed that HFT traders' inventories remained rather small throughout the flash crash, suggesting HFT may not have been the main perpetrators of the crash.

In trying to investigate the "real culprits" of the flash crash Golub *et al.* (2012) mentioned that quote stuffing and delays in data feeds formed a feedback loop that triggered the crash. At the same time, in a paper in *Foresight* (2012), the author suggested that culprits of the crash were self-reinforcing feedback loops and a psychological process called "normalization of deviance". Feedback loop and normalization of deviance belong to the realm of psychology. There are different types of feedback loops. One type of feedback loops is volume feedback loop. Simply put, in this loop, when some investors start to sell first, price of a security will fall and this increases the inventory level of the HFT funds. To balance the inventory levels, these HFT funds need to dump the share at a lower price quickly, which increases volume. The soaring sell volume triggers the original algorithms to sell even more. The steps described above constitute a reinforcing loop. Under a calm market condition when there are no major events during trading hours, the feedback loops are short-lived, because the liquidity will be provided by traders possessing information. Under a choppy market condition, as presented on May 6, 2010, when the market was already roiled by Europe's debt crisis, the accelerating price movements due to the high-frequency trading activity will result in a directional price move.

"Normalization of deviance" is defined as risky events that are thought to be normal and nothing is in place to prevent the possible disasters until a catastrophic failure strikes. To put this definition in the context of flash crash of 2010, investors had observed increased price volatility due to various trading instruments before the flash crash. The US market had even seen the UK exchanges implementing circus breaker rules, requiring suspension of trading if a security moves more than a certain percentage within a short period. In other words, market participants had predicted the possibility of a speedy crash before it happened. However, they started to think that maybe that level of volatility was normal, because nothing yet had occurred. This normalization led to the inaction of regulatory agencies. If circuit breaker rules had been in place, the flash cash on May 6, 2010 would have been avoided.

To summarize the relationship between HFT and flash crashes, we can conclude that HFT did not initiate the sell, but it did magnify the selling volume once unrelated concerning events pressured the market, such as Europe's debt crisis. Joseph Stiglitz, a Nobel prize-winning economist, cited in Salmon (2014) pointed out three points worth contemplating. First, HFT rewards the "wrong people" who do not discover engage in discovery but hijack the trade from others (Salmon, 2014). Second, he claimed that HFT discourages people from finding important information when they know HFT will font-run them anyways. Third, the flood of non-transparent information infused by HFT, which can only be seen by dark pools, can potentially frustrate the market by encouraging investors to analyze on inaccessible data. In a grey area where a trading methodology has the potential to cause massive damage to financial markets, tightening regulations to ensure the perceived fairness may become a necessity in the future.

2.5. *The impact of technology on research on investment analysis*

Another critical component of the financial service industry is investment research professionals. With the advance of technology, the way to conduct investment research by professionals is undergoing fundamental changes due to market data availability, data reliability, and ease of spotting new investment themes.

First, market data is no longer the privilege enjoyed by big investment firms. Bloomberg and Reuters, two high-priced market data providers, had dominated the market for years before the era of open access via API. Now, well-financed FinTech players with leverage of API platforms provide data to consumers with the pay-as-you-go flexibility. Not only the data itself are more available, but also compatible analytical tools are more abundant. Under these circumstances, quality research no longer needs tremendous resources (Bouland, 2015). Second, the trustworthiness of published company fundamentals has improved. Nowadays, data collection does not rely on manual readings of a company's annual report. There are algorithms allowing cross-checking official financial statements and standardizing them among periods or companies. Third, it has become exceedingly easy for the analyst to sense the market pulse. For example, some new systems enable delivery of relevant theme to the attention of the analysts. This will shorten the analysts' time spent on theme discovery process, which leaves them more time to analyze the trend and connection among the market events.

Due to the changes above, competitions among investment analysts have become fierce. Analysts not only have to produce investment themes that make sense, but also need to organize the themes into a coherent story to present to investors. Also, analysts with a unique angle often attract the public's attention. Therefore, the key emphasis of the new era is both content and creativity. Undoubtedly, traditional research professionals need to equip themselves with more skills to satisfy new customers' needs.

3. New Inventions — Open Application Programming Interface and Blockchain

Technological influence on existing components of the financial service industry is an important part of the discussion in this topic. However, there are finance-related innovations that are worth exploring.

One of the most mentioned technologies in recent literature is Open API, which allows for two different softwares to interface with each other. The popularity of this concept is due to banking industry's increasing integration with third parties and the open bank project. A few decades ago, it was difficult to imagine that banks would share their proprietary knowledge or resources with one another. They tended to safeguard those as carefully as possible. Currently, such practices would be considered archaic and would deter efficient business operations. The emphasis nowadays in the banking industry is integration with third parties through APIs and open source to promote industry growth and attract more talented professionals with different skillsets (Montoro, 2015). This trend is called "open banking", an idea inherited from computer industry which witnessed the process of open systems surpassing closed solutions. In the past, banks' applications were limited by their developer's imagination, experience, and also hindered by bureaucracy within the large organization. By welcoming external developers, the big banks are more likely to come up with appealing solutions in a time-efficient manner. BBVA, a digital bank, is a pioneer in building an open ecosystem by engaging entrepreneurs, developers, students, customers, and employees through open innovation framework (Jimenez, 2014). An annual contest hosted by BBVA is geared towards finding interesting ideas and applications from massive data sets representing a whole year's credit card activity of a major city in the world. The feedback regarding the contest has been extremely positive, corroborating the value of exposing transaction data and allowing collective effort.

Another often-mentioned invention is Blockchain — a general ledger recording details of transactions without disclosing confidential information regarding the parties involved. This new distribution channel is closely related to the Bitcoin, which was developed after the 2008 financial crisis to serve as an alternative to traditional currency (Deloitte, 2015). Bitcoin is a digital peer-to-peer payment system allowing transaction execution between end users without engaging third parties. Blockchain was initially a means to create Bitcoins, but it can be a stand-alone software protocol today, and it is widely used in such applications as virtual wallet, process payment, settlement solutions, and developing cryptocurrency-denominated products. The usage goes even beyond what was originally envisioned; its use is now in areas like the storage and management of assets and the storage of personal data, money transfers, and trading shares (Deloitte, 2015).

Many observers believe that the new Blockchain technology is going to change the current security model, which ensures that the information is only accessible to a few key people. However, the Blockchain welcomes as many people to view the general ledger as possible so that the validation is done by the public. This trust-based technology has six prominent advantages. First, it reduces inflation risk since the digital currency is detached from any country. Second, it improves the operational efficiency by asset digitalization. Third, it decreases settlement and accounting fraud risk. Fourth, the data are open to everyone. Fifth, the transaction reconciliation is speedy. Sixth, it lowers supervising and back-office costs tremendously (Deloitte, 2015). According to a report from the World Economic Forum, the majority of the experts attending the forum agreed that governments would collect tax using the Blockchain and the value of 10% of the global GDP is going to be stored on a Blockchain. The current value stored in a Blockchain is only 0.025% of the global GDP.

Although this form of technology is promising, it does not mean it grows without any hurdles. Two biggest challenges are security concerns and government. With regard to the security risk, the decentralized consensus needs a large network. If there are not many participants in the network, the security will be weaker due to the existence of fewer Blockchain copies. Regarding the government, the Blockchain will weaken the power of monetary policies, which diminishes the role of the policymakers. Since the market share of Blockchain remains small, the effect on governments is close to zero. However, if the market grows as the economic forum has predicted in ten years, the technology will exert substantial influence on controlling inflation, which is one of the main tasks for the Federal Reserve Banks. The key question is whether governments will implement new policies to limit the applications of the Blockchain or will they allow this distribution method to grow without harness.

Another note regarding this technology is that it might involve a third party in some form when the market share of Blockchain is sizable. For example, when half of the population on the planet participates in a Blockchain, the maintenance cost of the backstage computing system will be far beyond anyone's imagination. Thus, the Blockchain companies need to find a viable business model to survive, which might involve charging end users or joining forces with banks to support the whole system. Whichever of the two models those companies choose, the essence is the same — they themselves will become a third party in a transaction. If a technology cannot provide what it claims it can, then the popularity of this technology will gradually diminish. In the end, it will not be big enough to provide the benefit of decentralized consensus.

The academic literature has mixed views towards Blockchain technology. Zyskind *et al.* (2015) argued that Blockchain can be used to protect personal data by using a decentralized personal data management system that controls their own data. Since nowadays online banking and cloud services are more prevalent, data security has become increasingly important. If Blockchain can tackle data security issue, it is undoubtfully a boon for the public. However, Ammous (2016) does not seem to be so confident toward the new technology. He claimed that the only advantage of the Blockchain technology is removing third-party intermediation to allow for the digital cash creation. Further, he pointed out that Blockchain technology will not solve any economic problems due to its costly redundancies, scaling problems, and barriers to comply with regulations. The hard evidence to support his view is the fact that no commercial applications came out during the eight years since the technology was invented.

It is still too soon to tell the exact effect of those new technologies on the financial service industry. New inventions for the most part bring the public excitement and concerns at the same time when they are first introduced, and the Blockchain technology is no exception.

4. Concluding Thoughts and Reelections

Advances in technology have changed the way in which we live our daily lives and how firms conduct their business. For the financial services sector, technology has meant easier and less expensive access to information, making investment opportunities a reality for retail investors. Technology has enabled discount brokers to compete with established houses, which has lowered trading costs. Trading through traditional exchanges has declined, and with the advent of exchange traded funds, investors are moving away from actively traded mutual funds. Traditional commercial banks, especially ones that are not keeping abreast with technological changes, have been declining over time. Large digital lenders are moving quickly to capture the loan origination business. Technological advances have made readily available reliable financial data, which has simplified recognizing new research ideas. Algorithm trading has improved market liquidity and innovations like Open API and Blockchain, allowing for more operational efficiencies.

Technology is eventually a powerful tool, and it has shaped financial service industry into something we hardly recognize. Before feeling exhilarated about how far the technology has taken us in terms of acquiring financial information and executing on investment ideas, we should really ask ourselves, "What finance was like before the advent of computer and internet? What has really changed?" We will soon realize that the core of finance stays the same. What has changed is the format, which will keep changing until the end of time. One analogy will help to explain the impact of technology on financial service industry. Technology is a ladder on the ground. Before the advent of it, all investors stand on the ground; after it appears, some investors who know how to climb the ladder use it to reach to a higher level while the rest still stay on the ground. With the help of more ladders, some people will continue to climb and ultimately rise to the top and there might be others still remaining on the ground. The distance between the top and bottom represents exactly the inequality impossible to amend.

Joseph Stiglitz (cited in Salmon, 2014) suggests one critical theme — technology, no matter how advanced it might be is a tool, the usefulness of it is determined by people's needs and wants. Simply put, it can do social good or harm. What the financial sector does with technology is to quickly understand a new product, tailor it according to its own needs, and finally utilize it to its gain advantage. With respect to new practices like HFT, the end goal of those funds is to earn profits using automated programs, so the fund employees will have to use technology in a way to exploit monetary gains. Compared to searching for a brilliant idea regarding the underlying economy, hijacking someone else's is much more cost-efficient and this soon leads to creation of "dark pools" and HFTs. Depending on how big the HFT market is with respect to the entire market, it might magnify the market inequalities at an exponential pace.

While the rise of technology is celebrated in general, there is one imminent question to be addressed by regulators — how to minimize the inequality in the market while the powerful tool, technology, seems to be in hand of the very people who want to gain unfair advantage by widening the inequality? Implementing a strategy to stop this vicious trend is critical because the trend will accelerate if it is not interrupted now, and then playing catch up by regulators can be exceedingly difficult. The reality seems indeed gruesome. However, regulators have already started to address the inequality in the financial service space, especially in the field of HFT. For example, Keller (2013) revealed that SEC has adopted the "Large Trader Reporting" rule, which impose "record keeping, reporting, and limited monitoring requirements on certain registered broker-dealers through whom large traders execute their transactions". By doing so, regulators hope to improve transparency of the market. This monitoring tactic is a good start, although there are many more steps to be taken in the future. As long as the distance between investors who know how to utilize technology and the ones who do not decreases little by little, the market is still perceived to the equal and fair. After all, equality and fairness matter to everyone who participates in the broad financial market.

Acknowledgements

The authors thank Zaur Rzakhanov for valuable comments and suggestions.

References

Agapova, A. (2011). Conventional mutual index funds versus exchange-traded funds. *J. Fin. Markets*, 14, pp. 323–343.

Ammous, S. (2016). Blockchain technology: What is it good for? Available at SSRN: https://ssrn.com/abstract=2832751.

Barber, B. and Terrance, O. (2001). The internet and the investor. *J. Econom. Perspect.*, 15, pp. 41–54.

Birdthistle, W. (2008). The fortunes and foibles of exchange-traded funds: A positive market response to the problems of mutual funds. *Delaware J. Corporate Law*, 33, pp. 71–109.

Bouland, F. (2015). The new financial analyst: How technology is revolutionizing equity research. *Equity Research Observer*. https://blog.alphametry.com/the-new-financial-analyst-how-technology-is-revolutionizing-equity-research/.

Bowley, G. (2011). The new speed of money, reshaping markets. *New York Times.* http://www.nytimes.com/2011/01/02/business/02speed.html?_r=1.

Casolaro, L. (2007). Information technology and productivity changes in the banking industry. *Econom. Notes Banca Monte dei Paschi di Siena Spa*, 36(1), pp. 43–76.

Deloitte, (2015). Blockchain disrupting the financial services industry? October, 2015. https://www2.deloitte.com/content/dam/Deloitte/ie/Documents/FinancialServices/IE_ Cons_Blockchain_1015.pdf.

Finkle, V. (2016). Online lenders seek to shape industry before regulators do. *New York Times.*

Foresight (2012). The future of computer trading in financial markets. *Final Project Report.* The Government Office for Science, London.

Fox, Z. (2015). Fintech and banks shaking hands. *SNL Financial.* http://www.bankingexchange.com/news-feed/item/5995-fintech-and-banks-shaking-hands.

Golub, K., John K., and Ser-Huang, P. (2012). High frequency trading and mini flash crashes. Available at: SSRN: https://ssrn.com/abstract=2182097 or http://dx.doi.org/10.2139/ssrn.2182097.

Hendershott, T. and Ryan, R. (2013). High frequency trading and price discovery. Working Paper, No. 1602. European Central Bank.

Jimenez, A. (2014). Open APIs hold the key to the future of banking. ProgrammableWeb. http://www.programmableweb.com/news/open-apis-hold-key-to-future-banking/sponsored-content/2014/12/18.

Jordan, J. and Jane, K. (1999). Banking in the age of information technology. *Boston Federal Reserve.* https://www.bostonfed.org/economic/nerr/rr1999/q4/katz99_4.htm.

Kirilenko, A., Albert K., Mehrdad S., and Tugkan, T. (2016). The flash crash: High frequency trading in an electronic market. *The J. Fin.*, forthcoming.

McWaters, J. (2015). 5 ways technology is transforming finance. *Weforum.* https://www.weforum.org/agenda/2015/06/5-ways-technology-transforming-finance/.

Montoro, A. (2015). APIs for the banking industry: Prediction for 2015. *BBVAopen4u.com.* http://www.bbvaopen4u.com/en/actualidad/apis-banking-industry-predictions-2015.

Oliveira, P., Van der Boor, P., and Francisco, V. (2014). Users as innovators in developing countries: The global sources of innovation and diffusion in mobile banking services. *Res. Policy*, 43(9), pp. 1594–1607.

Popper, N. (2016). Banks bet on next big thing: Financial chatbots. *New York Times.*

PwC (2015). An objective look at high-frequency trading and dark pools. www.pwc.com/us/InvestorResourceInstitute

Rennison, J. (2015). Exchange traded funds grow bigger than hedge funds. *Financial Times.*

Rubino, J. (2016). My favorite robot. *CFA Institute Magazine*, pp. 42–46.

Salmon, F. (2014). The problems of HFT, Joe Stiglitz edition. *Reuters.* http://blogs.reuters.com/felix-salmon/2014/04/15/the-problems-of-hft-joe-stiglitz-edition/

Subrahmanyam, A. (2013). Algorithmic trading, the flash crash, and coordinated circuit breakers. *Borsa Istanbul Rev.*, 13, pp. 4–9.

Whitman, J. (2010). The markets' wild ride. *Montreal Gazette.* http://www.montrealgazette.com/business/fp/markets+wild+ride/2994890/story.html

Zyskind, G., Oz N., and Alex 'Sandy', P. (2015). Decentralizing privacy: using blockchain to protect personal data. *Security and Privacy Workshops*, IEEE.

Keller, A. (2013). Robocops: Regulating high frequency trading after the flash crash of 2010. *Ohio State Law J.*, 73, 1477–1478.

Chapter 22

Assessment of the Economic Impact of Stock Market Development: An African Perspective

Shashi Jeevita Matadeen and Boopen Seetanah

Faculty of Law and Management
University of Mauritius, Mauritius

Abstract

With the ever-growing importance of stock markets, an overwhelming number of studies have been carried out worldwide to investigate the link which exists between stock market development and economic growth. However, studies analyzing this link are scant in the African region. As such, this chapter uses a dynamic panel vector error correction model (PVECM) to analyze the relationship among stock market development, banking development, and economic growth in a unified framework for the period 1988–2011. The results suggest that stock market development plays an important role in generating gains in terms of economic growth both in the short run and in the long-run within the sample of African countries under consideration.

1. Introduction

One of the most enticing and long-lasting debates in economics revolves around the relationship between financial development and economic growth. Its root can be traced back to as early as Schumpeter (1912), who vehemently argues that financial services are of paramount importance for enhancing economic growth. The financial sector can in fact be roughly split into two systems: the bank-based system and the market-based system. Historically, however, research has been confined solely to the role of banking sector on economic growth. Bagehot (1873) and Schumpeter (1912) lay emphasis on the importance of the banking system in promoting economic growth.

Empirically, many studies (King and Levine, 1993, 1994; Rousseau and Wachtel, 1998; Levine and Zervos, 1998; Arestis, Demetriades, and Luintel, 2001; Beck and Levine, 2002) also demonstrate that financial systems do accelerate the long-run economic growth.

In the recent past, however, with the phenomenal growth of equity markets, a burgeoning number of policymakers and researchers began to query about the possible impact that equity market development might have on economic growth. This has duly shifted the focus towards the link between stock market development and economic development. Although research about the specific contributions of stock markets to economic development has increased extensively, arguments and evidence, both theoretical and empirical, have been diverse.

Researches revolve around two interesting questions: is there any relationship between equity market development and economic expansion? And if there is one, then what are the nature and the direction of this relationship? Analysts share different views regarding these questions. On one hand, some believe that stock market development is highly positively correlated to economic growth (Atje and Jovanovich, 1993; Demirgüç-Kunt and Levine, 1996; Levine and Zervos, 1998, Rousseau and Wachel, 2000; Beck and Levine, 2004), while on the other hand, some claim that stock market development affects the economy adversely (Stiglitz, 1985; Bencivenga and Smith, 1991; Naceur and Ghazouani, 2007; Devereux and Smith, 1994).

This chapter departs from but also contributes to the existing literature in several ways. First, the chapter will examine the link in the African region as opposed to most studies, which mainly focused on investigating the link in developing countries. Stock markets in the African region are expected to have a somewhat different impact on growth as they are relatively new and have to face some serious challenges. Indeed, the African stock exchanges are smaller, usually highly illiquid, and have a low market capitalization, with only a few firms accounting for a high proportion of that total market capitalization. As such, it is important to determine whether the effect of development of such stock exchanges will be the same on growth, as in developing countries.

Second, to add on to existing literature, a dynamic panel vector error correction model (PVECM) is used intensively to determine the relationship between stock market development and economic growth while simultaneously allowing the identification of any bi-directional and/or unidirectional causality between the variables of interest. Possible determinants of stock market development and the effect of stock market development on the control variables can also be analyzed through the PVAR model. Additionally, the chapter analyses stock market development, economic growth, as well as banking development in a unified framework, thus simultaneously allowing the complementary or substitutability element of banks and stock markets to be determined.

The study finds that equity markets in the African region do contribute to economic growth, both in the long-run and the short-run. However, banking development is not seen to have any significant impact on economic growth in the long-run. On the other hand, the short-run results reveal that stock market development complements banking development in the region.

The rest of this chapter is organized as follows: Section 2 paints a picture of the state of stock markets in the African region under consideration. As for Sec. 3, it provides a brief overview of the existing literature. Next, Sec. 4 describes the variables and models which will be used in this study. Section 5 eventually constructs the PVECM for the purpose of the study and provides a detailed interpretation of the results. Finally, based on the results obtained, some conclusions and policy implications are provided in the last section.

2. Overview of Stock Markets in the African Region

Traditionally, most African countries depended solely on the banking system. However, in the last decade, Africa, particularly sub-Saharan Africa, has witnessed a remarkable growth in the number of financial markets as well as a boom in stock market capitalization. Indeed, the number of capital markets in the African region has sky-rocketed from a mere 5 in 1989 to over 25 exchanges in 2015. About 24 of those exchanges are full members of the African Securities Exchanges Association (ASEA). Furthermore, necessary steps are being taken to fill the gap in countries where stock exchanges have not yet been set up.

Despite their small size and low liquidity, they have consistently been ranked among the best performing exchanges in the world. In 2004, six African countries were among the world's 10 best-performing stock markets. Indeed, the Ghana Stock Exchange was nominated the world's best-performing market at the end of 2004. Compared to 30% return by Morgan Stanley Capital International Global Index, the Ghana Stock Exchange experienced a year return of 144% in US dollar terms (Databank Group, 2004). Moreover, according to a list of top 20 emerging markets compiled by Bloomberg Markets in 2013, Namibia ranks 13th, Zambia 14th, South Africa

15th, and Morocco 19th. Stock exchanges in Africa have also received several awards. The Stock Exchange of Mauritius has won the "Most innovative African Stock Exchange of the year award" at the Institutional Investment Capital Market Awards 2015 organized by Africa investor (Ai). In the same year, the Nigerian Stock Exchange won the "Best Corporate Social Responsibility Award" at the 2015 African Business Awards. Investors are thus shifting their interest to Africa as the next frontier. Indeed, in a paper entitled "Africa's Future and the World Bank's Role in it", the World Bank says that Africa "could be on the brink of an economic take-off, much like China was 30 years ago, and India 20 years ago."

However, Yartey and Adjasi (2007) caution that the rapid development of stock markets in the African region is not tantamount to their maturity. While there is ample evidence that African stock exchanges can perform well, the recognition that they have to face some serious challenges also persists. One is that the market capitalization in African stock exchanges is relatively low. Still relatively smaller than other emerging stock markets, African stock markets are usually dominated by a few firms that account for a high proportion of the total market capitalization. The stock exchange in South Africa dominates the region in terms of market capitalization. In 2012, it had a market capitalization ratio of about 159% and was closely followed by the stock markets in Zimbabwe and Jordan, whose market capitalization ratios add up to 109% and 86%, respectively. However, during the same year, Swaziland, Tanzania, and Ghana accounted for the lowest market capitalization ratio in the region, with each of them having a market capitalization ratio of 2.5%, 6.4%, and 8.5%, respectively.

Andrianaivo and Yartey (2009) also highlight other plights of the African stock exchanges. First, they argue that exchanges fail to be used in an effective and efficient manner because institutional investors and governments with minority stockholdings are not active traders in secondary markets. Another common setback of most African stock markets is that shares are rarely traded and there are huge gaps between buy and sell orders, causing the markets to be thin and illiquid. Yartey and Adjasi (2007) clarified that trading is usually limited to only a select handful of stocks. This implies that the larger listings often affect the performance of exchanges disproportionately. Indeed, most African markets are described as "frontier markets" owing to their relatively small capitalization and liquidity levels. Low liquidity implies more difficulty in supporting a local market with its own trading systems, market analysis, and brokers because business volume is too low (Andrianaivo and Yartey, 2009). Moreover, serious informational and disclosure deficiencies occur for less actively traded stocks. Within the sample under investigation. South Africa and Egypt stock markets record the highest turnover ratios in 2012 at 55% and 38%, respectively. On the other hand, Swaziland, Uganda, and Malawi registered the lowest turnover ratios.

The small size of African stock markets coupled with the lack of liquidity are often cited by foreign investors as the major impediments to investing in the region. Many remain skeptical that African countries can indeed host efficiently performing stock markets. Singh (1999) warned that stock markets might not develop efficiently given the high costs and poor financial structures within African countries.

Yet another problem faced by African stock markets is infrastructural bottlenecks. The blame lies mostly on technological constraints as manual systems are still widely used within the African region despite it being slow and unreliable. Senbet (2008) maintains that the execution of a single transaction can take months since most exchanges have manually operated systems and slow trading, clearing, and settlement systems. Moreover, most markets do not have central depository systems, while some even restrict foreign participation. This induces a domino effect which not only slows the production of information but also thwarts activity and turnover, thus rendering financial integration difficult (Andrianaivo and Yartey, 2009). Yartey and Adjasi (2007) argue that such bottlenecks induce inactivity. Furthermore, as pointed out by Nkontchou (2010), the development of African financial markets is also hindered by a lack of timely and accurate data, which prevents both governments and development institutions from implementing adequate policies.

Unfortunately, most direct investors, private equity firms, and, sometimes, local entrepreneurs often fail to view African equity markets as a source of capital. In the African Stock Exchanges Handbook, published by the United Nations Development Program (UNDP) in 2003, it is stated that even in South Africa, which is one of the largest emerging markets in the world, many large companies seek listing on international exchanges presumably to gain access to a larger pool of capital and to reduce the cost of capital. Nevertheless during the past few years, capital-raising has been buoyant even though deal sizes were small.

Given the rapid growth and numerous challenges faced by African stock markets, it is crucial to investigate whether these markets also help in generating gains in terms of economic growth, as is the case in other developed and developing countries.

3. Literature Review

The importance of financial development on growth has been stressed for a very long time (Goldsmith, 1969; Shaw, 1973; McKinnon, 1973). Theoretical literature highlights various channels through which stock market development positively influences economic growth. Indeed, with enhanced liquidity (Levine, 2004), better risk diversification (Hargis, 2000; Levine, 2004), improved savings mobilization (Sirri and Tufano 1995; Levine, 2004), better information aggregation and dissemination (Dow and Gorton 1997; Demirgüç-Kunt and Maksimovic, 1998), and superior corporate control (Stein, 1988; Shleifer and Vishny, 1997), stock market development helps stimulate economic growth.

The role of stock markets in boosting economic growth is however still questionable. It is often feared that economic growth might be hindered because of free-rider problems, information asymmetry (Stiglitz, 1985), impaired corporate control (Shleifer and Vishny, 1997), and poor resource allocation (Morck *et al.*, 1990) that are occasionally associated to stock markets.

The relationship between financial development and growth has also been extensively investigated empirically. The brief literature review below focuses mostly on studies investigating the link between stock market development and economic growth within the African region.

Mohtadi and Agarwal (2004) resort to a random-effects model to examine the relationship between stock market development and economic growth using sample data from 21 emerging markets (including a few markets from the African region) over 21 years. They find that turnover ratio directly influences economic growth, while market capitalization ratio indirectly influences growth. On the other hand, Adjasi and Biekpe (2006) use a GMM approach to study the effect of stock market development on economic growth in 14 African countries. The results indicate a positive relationship between stock market development (as measured by total value of shares traded) and economic growth in the group of African countries. Naceur and Ghazouani (2007) make use of an unbalanced, dynamic panel model with GMM estimators across 11 Middle East North Africa region countries. Empirical results suggest that there is no significant relationship between banking and stock market development and economic growth. As far as the West African Monetary Union is concerned, the impact of equity market development on growth in the region over the period 1995–2006 is investigated by Tachiwou (2010). The results of a two-step procedure of Engle and Granger indicate that both measures of stock market development have a positive and significant impact on growth, with liquidity playing a more important role than stock market size.

Anyamele (2010) also analyzes the impact of stock market development on economic growth in 11 countries of sub-Saharan Africa during the period 1992–2002 using a fixed effect regression model. Results show that both stock market capitalization and bank development have a positive and significant link with per capita output in the selected sub-Saharan African countries. However, stock market turnover is not found to significantly influence economic growth. Moreover, the dynamic causal relationship between stock market development, banking development, and economic growth in South Africa during 1980–2009 is also investigated by Odhiambo (2011) using a trivariate Granger causality model. The empirical results indicate a bi-directional causal relationship between the two proxies of financial sector development (bank sector development and stock market development), both in the short run and the long run. He concludes that the development of the financial sector in South Africa is largely driven by the stock market activities.

In addition, Rioja and Valve (2014) demonstrate that while in low-income countries stock markets do not contribute to productivity growth, in high-income countries stock markets do have sizable positive effects on both productivity. Another study carried out by Naik and Padhi (2015) indicate that stock market development significantly contributes to economic growth in a set of emerging market economies. They resort to a GMM approach over a time frame of 1995–2012 and show that there is a unidirectional causality running from stock market development to economic growth. On the other hand, Nyasha and Odhiambo (2016) use an ARDL approach during 1980–2012 to investigate the link between market-based and bank-based financial development on economic growth in Kenya. They find that market-based financial development positively influences economic growth but bank-based financial development does not influence economic growth in the country. However, Pradhan, Arvin, and Bahmani (2015), who used a PVAR model over the period of 1960–2012, find that stock market development does not spur economic growth in the long run within a sample of 34 OECD countries.

4. Methodology and Data Analysis

To analyze the relationship between stock market development and economic growth in the set of African countries (Egypt, Arab Rep., Iran, Islamic Rep., Jordan, Lebanon, Morocco, Tunisia, West Bank and Gaza, Botswana, Cote d'Ivoire, Ghana, Kenya, Malawi, Mauritius, Namibia, South Africa,

Swaziland, Nigeria, Tanzania, Uganda, Zimbabwe, and Zambia), panel data spanning over a period of 24 years (1988–2011) is considered. This section describes the model adopted and the empirical indicators of stock market development, banking development, and, other control variables used in the model.

The basic specification of the model is based on the principles of growth models developed by earlier studies carried out by King and Levine (1993), Levine and Zervos (1998), Levine, Loayza, and Beck (2000), Bekaert *et al.* (2001), and Tang (2006) and takes the following functional form:

$$Y = f(\text{MCR, TR, TVTSR, DCTPS, GFCF, FDI, OPNS, SER}) \quad (1)$$

The dependent variable Y is proxied by gross domestic product growth (GDPG). Drawing from Pagano (1993), Demirgüç-Kunt, and Levine (1996), Levine and Zervos (1998), Rousseau and Wachtel (2000), Mazur and Alexander (2001), and Mohtadi and Agarwal (2004), three different stock market development indicators are used: The first one is market capitalization ratio (MCR), which is the value of listed shares in the stock exchange divided by GDP. It measures the stock market size relative to the country's economy. A country with a well-developed stock market tends to have a larger stock market relative to the size of its economy (Tang, 2006). MCR also captures the extent to which the stock market allocates capital to investment projects, as well as the opportunities for risk diversification that investors have (Demirgüç-Kunt and Levine, 1996); Next, turnover ratio (TR) and total value traded share ratio, (TVTSR) are two measures which are used to capture stock market liquidity. TR, which is the value of total traded shares expressed as a percentage of total market capitalization, is used as an indicator of transactions costs (Levine and Zervos, 1998). Finally, TVTSR, which is the total value of shares traded on a country's stock exchanges expressed as a percentage of GDP, measures the investors' ability to trade economically significant positions on a stock market. It complements the market capitalization ratio as even if a market is large, there might be little trading. Although each of these indicators has its limitations, the use of a variety of measures provides a broader view of the links between stock market development and economic growth than if only a single indicator was used (Levine and Zervos, 1998). Indeed, there is no single measurement that can capture all the aspects of stock market development. Several measures of stock market development maximize the use of information extracted from data and provide a more comprehensive picture of stock market development as opposed to information provided by only one indicator.

To measure banking development, we follow, Levine and Zervos (1998), Rousseau and Wachtel (2000), Mazur and Alexander (2001), and, Beck and Levine (2002) and use domestic credit to private sector (DCTPS), which is the value of credits by financial intermediaries to the private sector divided by GDP, since it improves on other measures of banking sector size. Another control variable used in the model is trade openness (OPNS). It is measured as the sum of exports and imports divided by GDP (Dollar, 1992; Edwards, 1993; Barro and Sala-i-Martin, 1995; Sachs and Warner, 1995; Frankel and Romer, 1999. We also follow Tang (2006) and Naceur and Ghazouani (2007) and include two measures of investment: GFCF, which is the country's gross fixed capital formation divided by its GDP (investment ratio), FDI, which is the foreign direct investment expressed as the percentage of GDP. Lastly, drawing from Seetanah, Ramessur, and Rojid (2009), the secondary enrolment ratio (SER), a human capital measure, is also added as a control variable in the model to account for the quality of labor.

The time series data has been extracted from the World Development Indicator database from the World Bank.

The specification used in this model is a linear–log one. Taking logs on the right-hand side of Eq. (1) results in the following:

$$\begin{aligned} Y_{it} = \beta_0 + \beta_1 \text{mcr}_{it} + \beta_2 \text{tr}_{it} + \beta_3 \text{tvtsr}_{it} + \beta_4 \text{dctps}_{it} + \beta_5 \text{gfcf}_{it} \\ + \beta_6 \text{fdi}_{it} + \beta_7 \text{opns}_{it} + \beta_8 \text{ser}_{it} + \varepsilon_{it}, \end{aligned} \tag{2}$$

where i denotes the different countries in the sample and t denotes the time dimension. (From here onwards, the small letters denote the natural logarithm of the variables.)

It is expected that the proxies of stock market development (mcr, tr, and tvrsr) will have a positive impact on the economic growth of the region (Levine and Zervos, 1998; Rousseau and Wachel, 2000; Beck and Levine, 2004; Tang, 2006; Wong and Zhou, 2011). Moreover, banking development is also expected to trigger economic growth in the region (Beck and Levine, 2002; Liang and Reichert, 2007). As for the other control variables (proxies of investment, trade openness, and human capital), they are also expected to stimulate economic growth.

4.1. *Panel unit root tests*

Before proceeding with the estimation of the model to investigate the statistical relationship between stock market development and economic growth, it is important to determine whether the time series are stationary or not. To this end, we make use of panel unit root tests to find the order of integration of the various variables under consideration. Levine, Lin, and Chu panel unit root tests are applied on our time series in levels. Overall, the results of all the different unit root tests reject stationarity in favor of a unit root for all the variables. This implies that the variables are integrated of order one, that is, they are non-stationary in levels but achieve stationarity after being differenced once. The results are also confirmed by the ADF — Fisher, PP — Fisher, and Levin at the 5% significance level for each variable.

4.2. *Panel cointegration test*

Since the variables are all integrated of order 1, the next step involves investigating whether there is a long-run relationship among the variables. For this, panel cointegration tests are used. Both Johansen Fisher Panel Cointegration Test and Kao Residual Cointegration Test are used, and the results indicate the presence of a cointegrating relationship among the variables. Thus, having established the presence of a long-run relationship, the study opts for a panel vector error correction model and proceeds with its estimation.

5. Estimation and Analysis

5.1. *Panel vector error correction model, PVECM*

The PVECM is an econometric model that caters for the dynamic nature of the panel data under consideration. It can be viewed as a hybrid of the traditional VAR/VECM approach and panel data approach. As such, in addition to treating all the variables as endogenous and accommodating for the non-stationary features of the data to offer a convenient way to parameterize and specify any co-integration present, it also allows for unobserved heterogeneity. This framework, through which the dynamics of feedbacks are captured, also permits the detection of any indirect effects which might be present among the variables. Interestingly, the PVECM specification forces the long-run behavior of the endogenous variables to converge to their cointegrated relationships, while simultaneously accommodating for the short-run dynamics as well. Moreover, given the possibility of endogeneity and causality issues, the PVECM also proves to be particularly helpful in scrutinizing the link between stock market development and economic growth. The pth order PVECM is specified as follows:

$$\Delta y_{it} = \Pi_i y_{i,t-1} + \Gamma_{i1}\Delta y_{i,t-1} + \cdots + \Gamma_{i,p-1}\Delta y_{i,t\text{-}p+1} + u_{it}, \tag{3}$$

Table 1. The Long-Run Equation of the PVECM

Variables	**Coefficient**
Economic growth (GDPG)	1
Market capitalization ratio (mcr)	−0.15
	[−0.639]
Turnover ratio (tr)	**0.47****
	[2.072]
Total value traded share ratio (tvtsr)	**−0.06***
	[−2.583]
Banking development (dctps)	−0.23
	[−0.647]
Foreign direct investment (fdi)	**0.89*****
	[6.830]
Gross fixed capital formation (gfcf)	**5.18*****
	[9.468]
Openness (opns)	**−1.16****
	[−1.942]
Human capital (ser)	0.03
	[0.059]

Notes: *Indicates significance at 1% level, **at 5%, and ***at 10%, respectively. The small letters denotes variables in natural logarithmic, and *t*-statistics are in parentheses.

where y_{it} is a vector comprising of eight variables used in the model as defined above (GDPG, mcr, tr, tvtsr, dctps, opns, invs, fdi, ser), i denotes the different countries in the sample, t denotes the time dimension, and u_{it} is a standard white noise process. In this study, an optimal lag length of 1 is chosen based on the Akaike Information Criterion (AIC), Schwarz Information Criterion (SC), and Hannan–Quinn Information Criterion (HIC). The PVECM is then estimated. The results of the model are reported in Table 1.

5.2. *The long-run equation of the PVECM*

The long-run equation (as illustrated in Table 1) yields very interesting results. All variables except banking development and human capital have a significant impact on economic growth within this set of African countries. Regrettably though, total value traded share ratio and trade openness seem to hamper long-run growth rather than boosting it, as indicated by their negative coefficients.

Of prime importance to this study, we first focus on the impact of stock market development indicators on economic growth. Out of the three stock market development proxies, only turnover ratio and total value traded share ratio have a significant impact on economic growth in the long run. While turnover ratio brings a significantly positive impact on economic development (as indicated by its positive and significant coefficient of 0.47), total value traded share ratio's brings a negative and significant impact on growth (as revealed by the negative and significant coefficient of −0.06). Taken as a whole, however, the total influence of stock market development on economic growth in the long run is argued to be positive and significant. Indeed, the negative influence of total value traded share ratio is negligible as opposed to the positive boost brought about by turnover ratio. The specification being a linear–log one implies that a 1% increase in turnover ratio generates (0.01×0.47) unit increase in economic growth and a 1% increase in total value traded share ratio causes a (0.01×0.06) unit decrease in growth. Coupled together, they account for 0.0041 unit increase in economic development $[(0.01 \times 0.47) + (0.01 \times -0.061)]$. This positive impact is in line with previous studies such as that of Levine and Zervos (1998), Rousseau and Wachel (2000), Beck and Levine (2004), Tang (2006), and Wong and Zhou (2011).

Shifting our focus on the banking development indicator domestic credit to private sector, we interestingly see that it has no significant impact on economic growth in the long run. The failure to find a link between banking development and economic growth contrasts with much of the theory that insists that such a relationship does exist. The result is contrary to that of Rousseau and Wachtel (2000), Arestis *et al.* (2001), Beck and Levine (2002), and Liang and Reichert (2007), who all find that banking development plays an important role on economic growth. One of the possible reasons that could explain this phenomenon is that banks tend to monitor more carefully when lending in an environment with poor creditor protection, thus causing it to become far too conservative (but nevertheless further research is required to better understand this issue). This lack of relationship can also be linked either to underdeveloped financial systems or to the unstable growth rates in the region that affect the quality of the association between finance and growth as pointed out by Naceur and Ghazoani (2007), who obtained similar results. The root of the negative relationship can also be the banking and currency crises in some of the countries under consideration. Indeed, poor regulation, inadequate supervision and bad practice are not foreign to certain African countries. Nonetheless, similar results are obtained by Mazur and Alexander (2001), who put the blame mostly on bank crises. On the other hand, some studies even detected a negatively significant relationship between banking development and economic growth. For instance, Kassimatis and Spyrou (2001) detect a negative link between these two variables in Chile and Mexico. Additionally, Shen and Lee (2006) also obtain empirical results that suggest an unfavorable impact of banking development on growth. On the other hand, Naceur and Ghazoani (2007), who also find negative and significant links between banking development and growth, argue that it might be directly linked to the overwhelming public sector in credit allocation. They suggest that these countries must improve the credit allocation process by privatizing national banks, strengthening credit regulation, and reinforcing competition in the banking sector.

Moving on to the investment proxies, we find evidence that both the gross fixed capital formation proxy as well as the foreign direct investment proxy have highly significant and positive roles to play in generating gains in terms of economic growth. This can be clearly seen from the highly significant and positive coefficients of both variables in the long-run equation. Indeed, while foreign direct investment has a positive and significant coefficient of 0.89, gross fixed capital formation has a much higher positive and significant coefficient of 5.18. In other words, investment accounts for a total of $[(0.01 \times 0.89) + (0.01 \times 5.18)]$ unit increase in economic development. More specifically, a 1% increase in foreign direct investment causes a (0.01×0.89) unit increase in growth, and a 1% increase in gross fixed capital formation causes (0.01×5.18) unit increase in economic growth. This suggests that gross fixed capital formation has a much bigger impact on long-run economic growth within this particular set of African countries than foreign direct investment.

Zooming in on the trade openness proxy, rather disappointing results are obtained. Indeed, trade openness is seen to have a significant but negative influence on long run economic growth, as indicated by the significant coefficient -1.17. Rather similar results are also detected by Naceur and Ghazoani (2007), who find that trade openness in the MENA region hampers growth. Although this might seem counterintuitive, it is possible to unearth some of its causes. Interestingly, the impact of trade openness on economic growth might depend on the countries and regions under consideration. Indeed, Kim and Lin (2009) show that the effect of trade openness on long-run growth is dependent on the level of economic growth. On the other hand, North (1990) and Dollar and Kraay (2002) argue that institutional arrangements (quality of governance, rent seeking, corruption, and policies), market institutions (bureaucracy and competition), and social norms also dictate the degree to which trade openness influences growth. Even more recently, studies by Foster (2008) and Dufrenot *et al.* (2009)

blamed structural characteristics (geography, demographic issues, ecology diseases, and cultural factors) as the causes. Additionally, it is also possible that political factors (ethnic fractionalization, lack of democracy, quality of governance, and high incidences of conflict) are reflected in this negative link. Indeed, such factors are a crucial influence on the impact of trade, especially in the African region. Moreover, the finger of blame can also be pointed to the high dependence on primary commodities, poor infrastructure, unskilled labor, and dire transport facilities. These cause a substantial rise in the trade costs, especially in African countries which rely heavily on the export of their natural resources, thus limiting the impact of trade. Indeed, volatile prices and declining terms of trade for raw or semi-processed goods prove to be detrimental to growth in the region.

5.3. *The short-run equation of the PVECM*

The Panel VECM model also estimates the short-run relationships which exist among the variables.[1] An examination of the short-run estimates of the equation having GDPG as the dependent variable indicates that only stock market development proxies influence growth in the short term. In fact, both market capitalization ratio (mcr) and turnover ratio (tr) induce economic growth in the short run, as indicated by their statistically significant coefficients of 2.33 and 2.13, respectively. This implies that a 1% increase in mcr generates a (0.01×2.33) unit increase in economic development, while a 1% rise in tr causes a (0.01×2.13) unit increase long-run growth. This is in line with several studies including that of Levine and Zervos (1998), Rousseau and Wachel (2000), Beck and Levine (2004), Tang (2006), and Wong and Zhou (2011). On the other hand, the other stock market development proxy, total value traded share ratio (tvtsr), appears to significantly but negatively influence long-run economic growth. Indeed, it has a significant coefficient of −2.43. A likely explanation for the negative impact of tvtsr on GDPG is that the series tvtsr and GDPG are diverging, which implies that while GDPG is an increasing function, tvtsr fluctuates a lot periodically. Thus, tvtsr may not be an effective measure of stock market liquidity as pointed out by Levine and Zervos (1998) and Rousseau and Wachtel (2000). Indeed, countries in the African region, being developing countries, have a highly volatile stock market which makes tvtsr a misleading indicator of liquidity (This is in line with Mohtadi and Agarwal (2004)).

[1]Results are available upon request. Only the main results are discussed in this section.

Interestingly, results also indicate some potential determinants of stock market in the short run. Investment is seen to foster stock market development in the short run. Indeed, the foreign direct investment (fdi) proxy generates highly significant and positive impacts on each of the three stock market development proxies, namely market capitalization ratio (mcr), turnover ratio (tr), and total value traded share ratio (tvtsr). This is evident from the positive and significant coefficients of fdi in the equations having mcr, tr, and tvtsr as the dependent variables. In fact, a 1% increase in fdi generates a (0.01×0.03) unit increase in mcr, a 1% increase in fdi generates a (0.01×0.06) unit increase in tr, and a 1% increase in fdi generates a (0.01×0.09) unit increase in tvtsr.

The PVECM also enables us to analyze the impact of stock market development on other variables in the short run. Market capitalization ratio (mcr), a proxy of stock market development, appears to enhance banking development (dctps) and investment in the short run. Indeed, mcr has a positive and significant coefficient of 0.07 when banking development as the dependent variable, thus implying that a 1% increase in mcr generates a (0.01×0.07) unit increase in dctps. This suggests that, initially, stock market development does not substitute banking development within the set of countries under consideration, but, on the contrary, the former tends to complement the latter. Similarly, mcr seems to foster investment through its gross fixed capital formation proxy (gfcf) in the short run as indicated by its positive and significant coefficient of 0.07. As such, a 1% increase in mcr can be translated into a (0.01×0.07) unit increase in gfcf. On the other hand, turnover ratio (tr), another proxy of stock market development, helps in promoting investment as well, but unlike mcr this occurs through the foreign direct investment (fdi) indicator of investment. As a matter of fact, tr has a significantly positive coefficient of 0.33 when fdi is considered as the dependent variable. Again, this can be interpreted as a (0.01×0.33) unit increase in fdi if tr is increased by 1%.

6. Conclusion and Policy Recommendations

Based on the PVECM method, this empirical study investigates whether any link exists between stock market development and economic growth in a selected group of African countries during the years 1989–2011. The study simultaneously takes into account banking development along with stock market development in a unified framework. The African equity market is found to be a contributor of economic growth, as depicted by the presence of significant positive links between the two, both in the long run and the short run. Interestingly, banking development has no impact on economic growth in the long run in the African region taken under consideration. This can be explained by the high degree of corruption or banking crises in the region. A close scrutiny also reveals that in the short run, stock market development does not substitute but, on the contrary, complements banking development.

The study also unleashes interesting ideas to promote equity growth in the region. First, the positive, but nonetheless small, impact of stock market liquidity on growth detected in the African region suggests that measures have to be taken for the markets in the African region to become more liquid. Unfortunately, African stock markets are notoriously known for having a low market liquidity compared to international norms. There are several avenues that can be explored to spark off the much-needed liquidity. It is believed that the introduction of a wider range of products in the different market segments should be encouraged. Moreover, most foreign investors have been reluctant to invest in the region for fear of the operational risk that relates to the lack of standardization. It is as such important to standardize products and contract documentation. Its impact will be twofold: first, it will mirror international standards and, second, it will help eliminate counterparty and settlement risk. Additionally, the restrictive limits on short selling, which is poorly regarded in Africa, should be eliminated. Indeed, such a step can promote liquidity if it is properly managed and effectively conducted. More retail investors must also be attracted into the market. It is additionally recommended that the number of counters in the exchanges be increased. Unfortunately, most counters in Africa are now dominated by listings of brewery, banks, and telecom, as opposed to the much sought after platinum, copper, oil, and gas. Furthermore, the benefits of listing privately held companies should be more aggressively marketed. Other propositions for the development of stock markets in Africa include an increase in automation, demutualization, and regional integration of exchanges as well as educational programs.

On the other hand, foreign direct investment and gross capital formation are also seen to encourage growth in the African region under consideration. Even though FDI in Africa is relatively higher and more diverse than before, it is still important to maintain the efforts to increase FDI. This can be achieved through several routes: First, the image of the region must be improved by reducing the inherent political risk, enhancing macroeconomic stability, and protecting property rights and rule of law. It is also crucial to support existing investors so as to increase their investments, reduce capital flight, and, at the same time, attract new investors. Moreover, investment opportunities should also be marketed. Existing investors and the internet are the best tools for that. It would also be wise to have a targeted investment promotion strategy in areas where Africa has comparative and competitive advantages.

References

Adjasi, C. K. D. and Biekpe, N. B. (2006). Stock market development and economic growth: the case of selected African countries. *African Development Review*, 18(1), pp. 144–161.

"Africa's Future and the World Bank's Role in it" [Online]. World Bank. Available at:http://siteresources.worldbank.org/INTAFRICA/Resources/Africa_s_Future_and_the_World_Bank_s_Role_in_it.pdf [Assessed on August 2015].

African Stock Exchanges Handbook (2003). UNDP. Available at: http://emerging-africa.com/files/UNDPafricanstockmarkets.pdf

Agarwal, S. and Mohtadi, H. (2004). Financial markets and the financing choice of firms: evidence from developing countries. *Global Finance Journal*, 15(1), pp. 57–70.

Andrianaivo, M. and Yartey, C. A. (2009). Understanding the growth of African financial markets. IMF Working Papers, pp. 1–40.

Anyamele, O. D. (2010). The role of stock market in sub-Saharan African economies. *Int. J. Business, Account. Fin.*, 4(2), pp. 129–143.

Arestis, P., Demetriades, P. O., and Luintel, K. B. (2001). Financial development and economic growth: The role of stock markets. *J. Money, Credit Bank.*, 33(1), pp. 16–41.

Atje, R. and Jovanovic, B. (1993). Stock markets and development. *Europ. Econo. Rev.*, 37, pp. 632–40.

Bagehot, W. (1873). Lombard Street. Homewood IL, Irwin. 319.

Barro, R. J. and Sala-i-Martin, X. (1995). Technological diffusion, convergence, and growth. NBER Working Papers 5151, National Bureau of Economic Research, Inc.

Beck, T. and Levine, R. (2002). Industry growth and capital allocation: Does having a market- or bank-based system matter? *J. Fin. Econom.*, 64(2), pp. 147–180.

Beck, T. and Levine, R. (2008). Legal institutions and financial development. In *Handbook of New Institutional Economics* Springer Berlin Heidelberg, pp. 251–278.

Bekaert, G., Harvey, C., and Lundblad, C. (2001). Does financial liberalization spur growth?. *J. Fin. Econom.*, 77(1), pp. 3–55.

Bencivenga, R. and Smith, D. (1991). Financial intermediation and endogenous growth. *Rev. Econom. Stud.*, 58, pp. 195–209.

Demirgüç-Kunt, A. and Levine, R. (1996). Stock market development and financial intermediaries: Stylized facts. *The World Bank Econom. Rev.*, 10, pp. 291–321.

Demirgüç-Kunt, A. and Maksimovic, V. (1998). Law, finance and firm growth. *J. Fin.*, 53, pp. 2107–2137.

Devereux, B. and Smith, W. (1994). International risk sharing and economic growth. *Int. Econom. Rev.*, 35, pp. 535–50.

Dollar, D. and Kraay, A. (2002). Growth is good for the poor. *J. Econom. Growth*, 7, pp. 195–225.

Dollar, D. (1992). Outward-oriented developing economies really do grow more rapidly: Evidence from 95 LDCs, 1976–1985. *Econom. Develop. Cultural Change*, 40(3), pp. 523–544.

Dow, J. and Gorton, G. (1997). Stock market efficiency and economic efficiency: Is there a connection? *J. Fin.*, 52, pp. 1087–1129.

Dufrenot, G., Mignon, V., and Tsangarides, C. (2010). The trade-growth nexus in the developing countries: A quantile regression approach. *Rev. World Econom.*, 146(4), pp. 731–761.

Edwards, S. (1993). Openness, trade liberalization, and growth in developing countries. *J. Economic Literature, Am. Econom. Assoc.*, 31(3), pp. 1358–1393.

Foster, N. (2008). The impact of trade liberalization on economic growth: Evidence from a quantile regression analysis, *Kyklos*, 61, pp. 543–567.

Frankel, J. A. and Romer, D. (1999). Does trade cause growth? *Am. Econom. Rev.*, 89(3), pp. 379–399.

Goldsmith, R. (1969). *Financial Structure and Development*. New York: Yale University Press.

Hargis, K. (2000). International cross-listing and stock market development in emerging economies. *Int. Rev. Econom. Fin.*, 9, pp. 101–122.

Kassimatis, K. and Spyrou, S. (2001). Stock and credit market expansion and economic development in emerging markets: Further evidence utilizing cointegration analysis. *Appl. Econom.*, 33(8), pp. 1057–1064.

Kim, D-H. and Lin, S-C. (2009). Trade and growth at different stages of economic development. *J. Develop. Stud.*, 45, pp. 1211–1224.

King, G. and Levine, R. (1993). Finance, entrepreneurship, and growth: Theory and evidence. *J. Monetary Econom.*, 32, pp. 513–542.

Levine, R. and Zervos A. (1998). Stock markets, banks and economic growth. *Am. Econom. Rev.*, 88(3), pp. 537–558.

Levine, R. (2005). Finance and growth: Theory and evidence. *Handbook Econom. Growth*, 1, pp. 865–934.

Levine, R., Loayza, N., and Beck, T. (2000). Financial intermediation and growth: Causality and causes. *J. Monetary Econom.*, 46, pp. 31–77.

Liang, H. and Reichert, A. (2007). Economic growth and financial sector development. *Int. J. Business Fin. Res.* (IJBFR), 1(1), pp. 68–78.

Mazur. E. A. and Alexander, R. J. (2001). Financial sector development and economic growth in New Zealand. *Appl. Econom. Lett.*, 8(8), pp. 545–549.

McKinnon, J. G. (1998). Numerical distribution functions for unit root and cointegration tests. *J. Appl. Econometr.*, 11, pp. 601—618.

Morck, R., Shleifer, A., and Vishny, W. (1990). Do managerial objectives drive bad acquisitions? *J. Fin.*, 45, pp. 31–38.

Naceur, S., Ghazouani, S., and Omran, M. (2007). The determinants of stock market development in the Middle-Eastern and North African region. *Managerial Fin.*, 33(7), pp. 477–489.

Naik, P. K. and Padhi, P. (2015). On the linkage between stock market development and economic growth in emerging market economies: Dynamic panel evidence. *Rev. Account. Fin.*, 14(4), pp. 363–381.

Nkontchou, C. (2010). Recent evolution of the African financial markets. *Private Sector Develop Proparco's Magaz.*, 5, pp. 3–5.

North, D. (1990). *Institutions, Institutional Change and Economic Performance.* Cambridge University Press.

Nyasha, S. and Odhiambo, N. M. (2017). Banks, stock market development and economic growth in Kenya: An empirical investigation. *J. African Business*, 18(1), pp. 1–23.

Odhiambo, N. M. (2011). Financial intermediaries versus financial markets: A South African experience. *Int. Business Econom. Res. J.*, 10(2), pp. 77–84.

Pagano, M. (1993). Financial markets and growth: An overview. *Eur. Econom. Rev.*, 37, pp. 613–22.

Pradhan, R. P., Arvin, M. B., and Bahmani, S. (2015). Causal nexus between economic growth, inflation, and stock market development: The case of OECD countries. *Global Fin. J.*, 27, pp. 98–111.

Rioja, F. and Valev, N. (2014). Stock markets, banks and the sources of economic growth in low and high income countries. *J. Econom. Fin.*, 38(2), pp. 302–320.

Rousseau, L. and Wachtel, P. (1998). Financial intermediation and economic performance: Historical evidence from five industrial countries. *J. Money, Credit Bank.*, 30, pp. 657–678.

Rousseau, L. and Wachtel, P. (2000). Equity market and growth: Cross-country evidence on timing and outcomes, 1980–1995. *J. Bank. Fin.*, 24, pp. 1933–57.

Sachs, J. D. and Warner, A. (1995). Economic reform and the process of global integration. brookings papers on economic activity, economic studies program, The Brookings Institution, 26 (1), pp. 1–118.

Schumpeter, R. (1912). Theorie der Wirtschaftlichen Entwicklung, Liepzig, Dunker and Humblot In (*The Theory of Economic Development*). Harvard University Press.

Seetanah, B., Ramessur, S., and Rojid, S. (2009). Financial development and economic growth: New evidence from a sample of island economies. *J. Econom. Stud.*, 36(2), pp. 124–134.

Senbet, L. (2008). African stock markets. In *African Finance for the 21st Century*. High-level Seminar organized by the IMF Institute in collaboration with the Joint Africa Institute Tunis Tunisia, March 4–5, 2008.

Shaw, E. S. (1973). *Financial Deepening in Economic Development*. New York: Oxford University Press.

Shen, C. and Lee, C. (2006). Same financial development, yet different economic growth — why? *J. Money, Credit Bank.* 38(7), pp. 1907–1944.

Shleifer, A. and Vishny, R. W. (1997). A survey of corporate governance. *The J. Fin.*, 52(2), pp. 737–783.

Singh, A. (1999). Should Africa promote stock market capitalism? *J. Int. Develop.*, 11, pp. 343–65.

Sirri, R. and Tufano, P. (1995). The economic of pooling. In Dwight, B. (ed.), *The Global Financial System: A Functional Perspective*. Boston: Harvard Business School Press.

Stein, C. (1988). Takeover threats and managerial myopia. *J. Polit. Economy*, 96, pp. 61–80.

Stiglitz, J. (1985). Credit markets and control of capital. *J. Money, Credit, Bank.*, 17, pp. 133–152.

Tachiwou, A. M. (2010). Stock market development and economic growth: The case of West African monetary union. *Int. J. Econom. Fin.*, 2(3), pp. 97–103.

Tang, D. (2006). The effect of financial development on economic growth: Evidence from the APEC countries, 1981–2000. *Appl. Econom.*, 38, pp. 1889–1904.

"The top 20 Emerging Markets [Online]. Bloomberg. Available at: http://www.bloomberg.com/slideshow/2013-01-30/the-top-20-emerging-markets.html [Assessed on February 2014]".

Adjasi, C. K. and Yartey, C. A. (2007). Stock market development in sub-Saharan Africa: Critical issues and challenges (No. 7–209). International Monetary Fund.

Chapter 23

Optimal Financial Structure and Economic Growth in Emerging Markets

İlkay Şendeniz-Yüncü*, Levent Akdeniz† and Kürşat Aydoğan†

*Middle East Technical University, Department of Business Administration, Ankara, Turkey

†Bilkent University, Faculty of Business Administration, Ankara, Turkey

Abstract

This study endeavors to determine the optimal bank–market mixtures of different countries and their effects on economic activity. We particularly examine emerging markets, following the view that optimal financial structures differ according to different levels of economic development. Our findings show that development in economic activity has a negative impact on financial structure ratio. As economies grow, the financial structure ratio decreases, i.e., the financial system becomes more market based. We also document a negative relationship between countries' economic growth and the financial structure gap, which suggests that deviation of a country's actual financial structure from the estimated optimal financial structure leads to lower levels of economic output. We believe that our findings will have policy implications for developing countries that are seeking to improve their financial systems.

1. Introduction

Research on the relationship of financial development and economic growth has existed in the literature for decades. Goldsmith (1969) is one of the leading proponents of the view that financial intermediation contributes to economic growth, stating that there is a positive correlation between the size of the financial system and the supply and quality of financial services. Among many others, King and Levine (1993), Beck *et al.* (2000b), and

Levine *et al.* (2000) examine the relationship between financial intermediary development, namely, banking sector development and economic growth. Jeong *et al.* (2003), Berger *et al.* (2004), Şendeniz-Yüncü *et al.* (2008), and Cheng and Degryse (2010) are among the researchers who analyze the impact of the banking sector on economic growth, while Atje and Jovanovic (1993), Demirgüç-Kunt and Levine (1996a, 1996b), Harris (1997), Levine and Zervos (1998), Rousseau and Wachtel (1998), and Arestis *et al.* (2001) study the relationship between stock market development and economic growth. Beck and Levine (2004) investigate the impact of both stock markets and banks on economic growth, applying generalized method of moments (GMM) techniques developed for dynamic panels. Şendeniz-Yüncü *et al.* (2018) analyze the relationship between stock index futures market development and economic growth for 32 developed and developing countries.

There also exists a huge literature on the investigation of the effects of different financial structures on economic growth. Recent studies refer to the fact that the financial structure of each country is different and it is important to understand the differences between such structures and their different effects on economic growth. These studies investigate the existence of an optimal financial structure for each economy and the variation in the financial structures of different economies in accordance with their level of economic growth. A theoretical hypothesis has been developed by Lin *et al.* (2009) to clarify the relationship between financial system and economic growth, suggesting that the optimal financial structure in an economy depends on the level of economic development of that country and that there is an optimal financial structure that is determined endogenously for each level of the economic development. The authors note that the current literature does not adequately consider the characteristics of the real sector in an economy and therefore does not adequately assess the efficiency of countries' alternative financial structures at different levels of development, and thus is not able to determine what type of financial structure is most beneficial to economic development. The authors add that when the characteristics of the financial structure match those of the structure in the economy, the financial system can more efficiently perform its functions and contribute to economic growth. This chapter provides empirical support to the theoretical literature that has developed in the wake of Lin *et al.* (2009) referenced above, stating that optimal financial structure in an economy depends on the level of economic development of that country and that there is an optimal financial structure that is determined endogenously for each level of the economic development.

There exist in the literature a number of studies based on the assumption that OECD countries have optimal financial structures; there are also other studies that investigate highly developed countries with perfectly functioning financial systems. Demirgüç-Kunt *et al.* (2011) select benchmark countries that arguably have few impediments to their financial systems achieving an optimal financial structure. They use the OECD countries from 1980 to 2008, with the assumption that these countries have optimal financial structures, after taking into account key national characteristics. This approach is similar to that employed by Rajan and Zingales (1998), who use the United States (along with other highly developed countries such as Canada) as a benchmark for a perfectly functioning financial system. Following the view that optimal financial structure differs according to the level of economic development, we examine emerging markets in particular in our study; we endeavor to determine the optimal bank–market mixture for a number of emerging countries and assess the effect of this on economic activity. We also agree with the notion that linking financial structure to economic growth can help to improve policy practices in developing countries that are seeking to improve their financial systems.

In this study, we estimate the optimal financial structure ratios for the emerging markets in our sample and calculate the financial structure gap: in other words, the difference between the realized structure values and the estimated optimal financial structures for those countries. Our findings show that as economies grow, the financial structure ratio decreases; i.e., the financial system becomes more market based. We also show that the financial structure gap has a significantly negative effect on economic activity in the presence of different combinations of control variables in emerging markets. This finding supports the view that deviation of the existing financial structure from the predicted optimal financial structure causes a decline in the level of economic activity, and is in line with the existing literature. Our results further show that while stock market development, foreign direct investment, and trade openness have statistically significant positive effects on economic activity, banking sector development has a statistically significant negative effect, which may be due to the negative effects of high amounts of debt and non-performing loans in the economies of some of the countries studied.

The rest of the chapter proceeds as follows: Section 2 reviews the literature on financial structure, optimal financial structure, and the relationship of financial structure to economic growth; Sec. 3 introduces our data, summary statistics, and correlations; Sec. 4 presents the calculations of optimal financial structure and financial structure gap, and discusses the effect of the financial structure gap on economic activity; and Sec. 5 summarizes the findings, discusses policy implications, and presents conclusions.

2. Review of the Literature on Financial Structure, Optimal Financial Structure, and the Relationship of Financial Structure to Economic Growth

Many studies have suggested that developments in the financial system positively affect economic growth. However, as Song and Thakor (2010) point out in their work, it is not clear whether this effect comes from developments in the banking sector or from developments in the financial markets. The main theoretical finding of the current literature is that bank-oriented financial systems and market-oriented financial systems exhibit different behaviors, and the two systems have different advantages. As Song and Thakor (2010) argue, competition between banks and markets has strong policy implications; however, the empirical evidence is insufficient. They investigated how banks and markets affect each other and found that interaction between banks and markets takes place in three different forms: competition, complementarity, and coevolution.

Financial structure is defined as the mixture of financial institutions and markets functioning in an economy and their relative importance for that economy. An accepted view regarding the relative importance of banks and financial markets for economic growth states that in countries with high per capita income, financial markets are more active than banks (Goldsmith, 1969; Demirgüç-Kunt and Levine, 2001; Lin *et al.*, 2009). Demirgüç-Kunt and Levine (2001) have developed indices for financial structure organization in many countries and have measured the importance of bank- or market-based financial structures relative to each other in terms of transaction volume and productivity. They investigate the relationship between financial structure and long-term economic growth and examine the nature of different bank- or market-based financial structures in different countries. They show that the banking sectors and financial markets of developed countries are larger, more active, and more efficient than those of developing countries, concluding that the growth of banks and markets is directly proportional to the growth of economies and that stock markets are growing faster than the banking sector. According to their findings, financial systems become more market based in the process of economic development, with the systems of underdeveloped or developing countries having more of a bank-based structure. Demirgüç-Kunt *et al.* (2011) also refer to the above study and note that it has not yet been shown that countries at different economic development levels need a single type of bank–market mix in order to maintain productivity; they suggest that economic development remains at a lower level as countries move away from the optimal financial structure for their level.

Some studies examine the causal relationship between financial structures and economic growth and attempt to determine whether market-oriented financial structures or bank-oriented financial structures are better for such growth. As Lin *et al.* (2009) also note in their study, Levine (2005) summarizes the relevant arguments in four categories. First, on one hand, proponents of bank-based financial structures point out that banks and other financial intermediary institutions have advantages over financial markets in terms of gathering and processing information and monitoring borrowers (Grossman and Hart, 1980; Stiglitz, 1985; Bhide, 1993). On the other hand, proponents of market-based financial structures focus on the problems created by strong banks and note that bank-based structures include intermediaries with enormous influence on firms that may harm economic growth (Rajan, 1992). A third view is offered by economists who reject the bipartite categorization of financial systems as market-based or bank-based and argue that markets and banks complement each other (Merton, 1995; Merton and Bodie, 1995). Demirgüç-Kunt and Levine (1996a, 1996b) demonstrate that stock markets are associated with the development of the banking sector, the insurance sector, and other financial institutions, and are a significant influence on economic growth. They show that financial intermediaries are highly developed in countries with highly developed equity markets and that there is no difference between bank-based and market-based financial structures. Finally, the fourth view focuses on the legal system *vis-à-vis* financial development and financial structure, arguing that the effects of the legal system are more important than whether an economy is bank-based or market-based (La Porta *et al.*, 1997, 1998). Empirical studies by Beck and Levine (2002), Demirgüç-Kunt, and Maksimovic (2002), and Levine (2002), have basically supported the latter two views, arguing that financial structures are not of primary significance for economic growth. In another study examining the relationship between financial structure and economic growth, Beck *et al.* (2000a) investigate whether economic growth rates are related to an economy being bank-based or market-based. Findings of this study suggest that the two different financial structures do not have different impacts on economic growth. The authors conclude that it is only the level of financial development that affects economic growth and that external finance-oriented economies grow faster.

Boyd and Smith (1998) suggest that banks are more important at low levels of development, while markets become more important as income rises. Allen and Gale (2000) investigate the relationships of financial structure and economic growth in Germany, Japan, the United Kingdom, and the United States. The authors state that banks and markets provide different financial services, that economies at different levels of economic development need different mixes of financial services, and that different bank–market mixture ratios are needed as an economy develops. They also argue that unless an optimal financial structure is provided, economic activity will be adversely affected. Demirgüç-Kunt and Huizinga (2000) examine the impact of financial development and financial structure on bank performance. They discuss the effects of different financial structures on long-term economic development and show that each country depends on the banking sector or the market system to a different degree. For example, Germany and Japan have bank-based financial structures, while the US and the UK are more likely to have market-based financial structures. In his study of financial structure in relation to the real economy, Tadesse (2002) shows that market-based financial structures perform better than bank-based structures in countries with well-developed financial sectors, while bank-based structures perform better than market-oriented structures in countries that have less developed financial sectors.

Recently, Demirgüç-Kunt *et al.* (2011) examined the increasing importance of the banking sector and the financial markets in the process of economic growth as well as the relationship between financial structure and economic growth. In particular, they investigated the question of whether each level of economic development is associated with an optimal financial structure, such that deviations from this optimum are associated with lower levels of economic activity. Their study indicates that as economies evolve, the services provided by the financial markets also increase in importance. The authors conclude that insofar as a difference exists between the actual financial structure of a country and its predicted optimal financial structure, a decline in the level of economic activity is seen, and therefore financial structure is important. Lin and Xu (2012) review the relevant literature and state that findings there have important implications. They note that the optimal financial structure changes, becoming more market-oriented, as economies develop, with new evidence suggesting that different financial structures may be better at promoting economic activity at different stages of a country's economic development. The authors contend that these findings point to financial structure as being an independent financial policy consideration. They also note that politics, legal origins, and the beliefs of government leaders may cause the actual financial structure in a country to deviate from what is optimal, resulting in a loss of efficiency and well-being in the economy.

Lin (2012) proposes a new structural economics that focuses attention on the endowment structure and level of development of each country, and suggests a path toward country-based research that is rigorous, innovative, and relevant to development policy. This framework stresses the need to better understand the implications of structural differences at various levels of a country's development — especially in terms of determining the appropriate institutions and policies, and examining the constraints on and incentives for the private sector during the process of structural change. Lin (2013) also advances a new structural economics hypothesis concerning financial structure. This study proposes that the appropriate financial structure in an economy depends on the latter's industrial structure, which is determined in turn by its endowment structure. The author concludes that a financial structure is appropriate for an economy at a particular level of economic development only when the characteristics of that financial structure are in accord with the characteristics of the industrial structure determined by the endowments in the economy. Thus, the appropriate financial structure varies across countries at different levels of economic development; the appropriate financial structure for an economy is also dynamic over time. As an economy develops and its endowment structure is updated, the appropriate financial structure for the economy evolves correspondingly. The author additionally states that the policy implications of this are that the government should be restrained from inappropriate interventions in the financial sector. The appropriate financial structure for a developing country is systemically different than that for developed economies. Thus, imitating the financial model of developed economies will not lead to improved efficiency of the financial system, nor will it generate better economic performance in developing countries.

3. Data, Summary Statistics, and Correlations

In this study, analyses have been conducted for 21 emerging markets. The countries in our data set are listed in Table 1 in three groups: (1) the Americas, (2) Europe, the Middle East, and Africa, and (3) Asia. These

Table 1. Countries in Our Dataset

Americas	Europe, Middle East & Africa	Asia
Brazil	Czech Republic	China
Chile	Egypt, Arab Rep. of	India
Colombia	Hungary	Indonesia
Mexico	Morocco	Korea, Rep. of
Peru	Poland	Malaysia
	Qatar	Philippines
	Russian Federation	Thailand
	South Africa	
	Turkey	

Note: Analyses were conducted for 21 emerging markets. The countries in our dataset are grouped in three categories by region: (1) the Americas, (2) Europe, the Middle East, and Africa, and (3) Asia. These countries are considered to be among the world's emerging markets by the Morgan Stanley Capital International (MSCI) Emerging Markets Index.

countries are considered to be among the world's emerging markets by the Morgan Stanley Capital International (MSCI) Emerging Markets Index.

We use the following variables in our study. First, banking sector activity is used as an indicator of banking sector development. Banking sector activity (hereafter BAN) is defined as the value of deposit money bank credits to the private sector divided by GDP. This measure isolates bank credit to the private sector and excludes loans made to governments, government agencies, and the public sector by development banks. It also excludes credits issued by central banks. Second, as an indicator of stock market development, value-traded ratio (hereafter STO) is used, following Levine and Zervos (1998). The value-traded ratio is calculated by dividing the total value of domestic equities traded on domestic exchanges by GDP. The total value traded is the product of market price and the number of shares traded. The source of the BAN and STO data is the World Bank Financial Structure Database. Third, to measure the mixture of banks and markets operating in an economy, we use the financial structure ratio (STR), which is calculated as private credit divided by total value traded. Finally, as an indicator of economic activity, the logarithm of annual real GDP per capita (RGDPC) is used. This item is obtained from the World Bank World Development Indicators (WDI) online database.

In order to assess the strength of the independent link between financial structure and economic growth, control for other potential determinants of economic activity is needed in the analyses. We use the following control variables, which are commonly used in the literature: inflation (INF), foreign direct investment as a percentage of GDP (FDI), openness to trade, i.e., total share of exports and imports as a percentage of GDP (OPE), and unemployment (UNEMP). The WDI online database is also the source for the data for the control variables.

Following Demirgüç-Kunt *et al.* (2011), we construct a measure of optimal financial structure (OPT), which is estimated by the panel least squares method. A detailed explanation regarding the estimation of OPT is provided in the next section. We also construct a measure of financial structure gap (SGAP), which is equal to the natural logarithm of the absolute value of the difference between the actual financial structure ratio and the estimated optimal financial structure ratio. SGAP becomes larger as a country's financial structure ratio deviates from the estimated optimal structure. The ratio of actual financial structure to optimal financial structure is also calculated (STROPT). In our regressions, we include variables that may have effects on financial structure, such as distance to the equator (LAT), population (POP), and legal origin dummies for British, French, German, and socialist legal origins (LEGUK, LEGFR, LEGGR, and LEGSOC, respectively). Names, abbreviations, descriptions, and data sources for the variables are presented in Table A.1.

Descriptive statistics and the correlation matrix for the variables are presented in Tables 2 and 3, respectively. In Table 3, we observe that banking sector development and stock market development are positively correlated with economic activity. Banking sector development and stock market development are also positively correlated with each other. Financial structure gap is negatively correlated with economic activity, banking sector development, and stock market development.

Our data period is 1980–2014, which is the widest possible range that we were able to obtain. The data period for some countries in our sample is shorter than this; therefore, we use unbalanced panel data in order to avoid loss of data.

4. Optimal Financial Structure and Financial Structure Gap

We aim to determine the optimal financial structure ratios for the countries studied and also to see whether deviation of a country's actual financial structure from the estimated optimal structure affects economic output.

Table 2. Descriptive Statistics

	RGDPC	BAN	STO	STR	OPT	SGAP	STROPT	INF	FDI	OPE	UNEMP	POP	LAT
Mean	8.45	43.86	19.58	11.45	11.45	1.71	0.03	48.95	2.37	62.68	7.57	17.71	0.31
Median	8.63	35.72	9.55	3.54	11.18	1.87	0.14	6.62	1.70	53.62	7.00	17.67	0.32
Max.	11.22	165.86	160.45	273.83	27.87	5.53	4.14	7481.66	50.78	220.41	27.20	21.03	0.62
Min.	5.84	2.96	0.07	0.34	−5.51	−3.87	−18.26	−4.86	−16.09	12.01	0.30	12.32	0.04
Std.Dev.	0.97	29.54	25.78	27.65	8.37	1.29	0.96	355.91	3.45	37.81	5.03	1.58	0.17
Obs.	675	673	593	589	589	589	589	700	686	681	566	735	735

Note: This table presents the descriptive statistics for the variables.

Table 3. Correlation Matrix

	RGDPC	BAN	STO	SGAP	STROPT	INF	FDI	OPE	UNEMP	POP	LAT
RGDPC	1.00										
BAN	0.09	1.00									
STO	0.30	0.57	1.00								
SGAP	−0.28	−0.29	−0.35	1.00							
STROPT	−0.07	−0.05	−0.16	0.25	1.00						
INF	−0.02	−0.11	−0.08	0.06	0.07	1.00					
FDI	0.21	0.13	0.02	0.06	0.01	−0.07	1.00				
OPE	0.27	0.55	0.25	−0.06	0.04	−0.12	0.26	1.00			
UNEMP	−0.07	−0.25	−0.14	0.09	−0.06	−0.02	−0.05	−0.23	1.00		
POP	−0.48	0.07	0.19	−0.20	−0.10	0.00	0.20	−0.41	−0.14	1.00	
LAT	0.40	−0.12	0.11	0.06	0.01	−0.06	0.12	−0.01	0.19	−0.14	1.00

Note: This table presents the correlation matrix for the variables.

We first estimate optimal structure ratios for these countries. Optimal financial structure is estimated by regressing financial structure on real GDP per capita and other country-specific variables that may have an influence on optimal financial structure. Following La Porta *et al.* (1998) and Demirgüç-Kunt *et al.* (2011), we include dummy variables for the legal origins of the country (British, French, and socialist, with German being the omitted category). Our regression model is as follows:

$$\mathrm{STR}_{i,t} = \alpha + \beta_1 \mathrm{RGDPC}_{i,t} + \beta_2 \mathrm{LEGUK}_i + \beta_3 \mathrm{LEGFR}_i + \beta_4 \mathrm{LEGSOC}_i + \beta_5 \mathrm{LAT}_i + \beta_6 \mathrm{POP}_{i,t} + \varepsilon_{i,t}, \quad (1)$$

where ε is the error term, and i and t represent the country and time, respectively.

In the above model, the dependent variable is the financial structure ratio, i.e., the ratio of private credit to stock market total value, while the estimated structure values in the LS regression are considered to be the countries' optimal financial structures. Regression results are presented in Table 4.[1]

A finding of the regression is that economic activity has a negative impact on financial structure ratio. As economies grow, the financial structure ratio decreases; i.e., the financial system becomes more market based. This finding supports the view that as economies grow, the need for services provided by

[1]The EViews program was used for the analysis.

Table 4. Financial Structure Ratio Regression

	Dep. Var.: STR
RGDPC	−10.19***
	(1.70)
LEGUK	−8.46
	(5.69)
LEGFR	1.03
	(5.19)
LEGSOC	8.81*
	(5.26)
LAT	−7.82
	(9.66)
POP	−6.26***
	(1.05)
Constant	212.25***
	(31.22)
Number of Observations	589
R-squared	0.09
Adjusted R-squared	0.08

Note: The estimates in this table come from panel LS model. The dependent variable is the financial structure ratio. The estimated coefficient is given on the first line for each item, with the standard error reported in parantheses on the second line; the corresponding significance level appears on the first line adjacent to the estimated coefficient. *** Significant at 1%; ** significant at 5%; * significant at 10%.

securities markets increases as compared with the need for those provided by the banking sector.[2]

Next, we calculate the financial structure gap. The difference between the actual structure values and the estimated structure is the residual value obtained from the above LS regression. The financial structure gap is defined as the log of the absolute value of this difference and shows the deviation of the actual financial structure from the estimated optimal structure for a given country.

$$\text{SGAP} = \ln(|\text{STR} - \text{OPT}|). \tag{2}$$

[2]See Boyd and Smith (1998), Allen and Gale, (2000), Demirgüç-Kunt *et al.* (2011), and Cull *et al.*, (2013) for further discussions.

Table 5. Effect of Financial Structure Gap on Economic Activity

Dep. Var.: RGDPC				
Models	(1)	(2)	(3)	(4)
SGAP	-0.167^{***}	-0.143^{***}	-0.124^{***}	-0.117^{***}
	(0.025)	(0.027)	(0.028)	(0.028)
BAN	-1.023^{***}	-0.897^{***}	-0.326^{***}	-0.315^{**}
	(0.144)	(0.151)	(0.137)	(0.136)
STO	1.040^{***}	0.839^{***}	0.781^{***}	0.768^{***}
	(0.146)	(0.153)	(0.160)	(0.160)
INF	0.006	0.010	0.005	
	(0.008)	(0.008)	(0.009)	
FDI	3.930^{***}	3.875^{***}	5.490^{***}	5.391^{***}
	(0.851)	(0.918)	(0.933)	(0.932)
OPE	0.707^{***}	0.773^{***}		
	(0.099)	(0.104)		
UNEMP	-0.083			
	(0.634)			
Constant	8.560^{***}	8.431^{***}	8.611^{***}	8.608^{***}
	(0.107)	(0.088)	(0.088)	(0.088)
Number of Observations	528	587	587	589
R-squared	0.268	0.210	0.134	0.129
Adjusted R-squared	0.259	0.202	0.127	0.123

Notes: This table presents the relationship between financial structure gap and economic growth, derived using the panel LS method. The dependent variable is RGDPC. The independent variables that appear as percentages (BAN, STO, INF, FDI, OPE, and UNEMP) were predivided by 100 to obtain informative coefficients. The estimated coefficient is given on the first line for each item, with the standard error reported in parantheses on the second line; the corresponding significance level appears on the first line adjacent to the estimated coefficient. *** Significant at 1%; ** significant at 5%; * significant at 10%.

4.1. *Effect of financial structure gap on economic activity*

We examine the relationship between financial structure gap and economic growth with the panel LS method. In order to do so, we use control variables that are frequently used in the literature. Our regression model is as follows:

$$\begin{aligned}\text{RGDPC}_{i,t} = \alpha + \beta_1\text{SGAP}_{i,t} + \beta_2\text{BAN}_{i,t} + \beta_3\text{STO}_{i,t} + \beta_4\text{INF}_{i,t} \\ + \beta_5\text{FDI}_{i,t} + \beta_6\text{OPE}_{i,t} + \beta_7\text{UNEMP}_{i,t} + \varepsilon_{i,t}.\end{aligned} \quad (3)$$

Regression results are presented in Table 5.

The results in Table 5 show that financial structure gap has a significantly negative effect on economic activity in the presence of different combinations of control variables.[3] This finding supports the view that deviation of the existing financial structure of a country from the predicted optimal financial structure causes a decline in the level of economic activity. Our finding is in line with the existing literature.

Our results further show that while stock market development, foreign direct investment, and trade openness have statistically significant positive effects on economic activity, banking sector development has a statistically significant negative effect, which may be due to the negative effects of high amounts of debt and non-performing loans in the economies of some of the countries studied. In the literature, there exist studies documenting an insignificant or negative effect of the banking sector on the real economy. Arestis *et al.* (2001) state that the relationship between bank development and growth may not be so robust. Similarly, Beck and Levine (2004) report that the effect of banking sector development becomes statistically insignificant when the regression is controlled for inflation and trade openness. In their study, Shen and Lee (2006) investigate the relationship between financial development and real GDP per capita growth in 48 countries and document that only stock market development has a positive effect on growth while banking development has an effect that at best does not favor growth and may be negative. Zhang (2003) also documents a significant negative relationship between banking development and economic growth in East Asia during the 1960–1999 period.

5. Conclusion

This chapter provides empirical support to the theoretical literature, which states that the optimal financial structure for an economy depends on the level of economic development of that country, and that there is an optimal financial structure that is determined endogenously for each level of development. We aimed to determine the optimal financial structure ratios for emerging economies and also to see whether deviation of a country's actual financial structure from its estimated optimal structure affects economic output.

We first estimated the optimal financial structure ratios for the emerging economies in our sample. Our findings show that as economies grow, the

[3]We performed a Hausman test for endogeneity, and confirmed that our LS estimates are consistent and not biased. Using the likelihood ratio omitted variables test, we also checked for possible endogeneity due to an omitted variables problem and confirmed that we do not have such a problem.

financial structure ratio decreases; i.e., the financial system becomes more market based. This finding supports the view that as economies grow, the need for services provided by securities markets increases in comparison with the need for those provided by the banking sector. We then calculate the financial structure gap — in other words, the difference between the actual structure value and the estimated optimal financial structure for the countries studied. Our results show that financial structure gap has a significantly negative effect on economic activity in the presence of different combinations of control variables in emerging markets. This finding supports the view that deviation of the existing financial structure of a country from the predicted optimal financial structure causes a decline in the level of economic activity.

Our results further show that while stock market development, foreign direct investment, and trade openness have statistically significant positive effects on economic activity, banking sector development has a statistically significant negative effect, which may be due to the negative effects of high amounts of debt and nonperforming loans in the economies of some of the countries studied.

We believe that our findings have policy implications for developing countries that are seeking to improve their financial systems. We agree with the view that policymakers need to consider the development level of their country when developing strategies with regard to the country's financial structure. The financial structure that best suits an emerging market will differ from that of a developed market. Therefore, we recommend fashioning financial structure strategies that are tailor-made for individual emerging economies, rather than following the strategies of developed economies, in order to achieve higher levels of economic development.

Acknowledgements

We thank the TÜBİTAK-BİDEB 2232-Research Grant Program for support of the earliest version of this chapter.

References

Allen, F. and Gale, D. (2000). *Comparing Financial Systems*. Cambridge, MA: MIT Press.

Arestis, P., Demetriades, P. O., and Luintel, K. B. (2001). Financial development and economic growth: the role of stock markets. *J. Money Credit Bank*, 33(1), pp. 16–41.

Atje, R. and Jovanovic, B. (1993). Stock markets and development. *Eur. Econ. Rev.*, 37, pp. 632–640.

Beck, T., Demirgüç–Kunt, A., Levine, R., and Maksimovic, V. (2000a). Financial structure and economic development: Firm, industry and country evidence, In Demirgüç–Kunt, A. and Levine, R. (eds.), *Financial Structure and Economic Growth, A Cross–Country Comparison of Banks, Markets, and Development*. Cambridge, MA: MIT Press, pp. 189–241.
Beck, T. and Levine, R. (2002). Industry growth and capital accumulation: Does having a market- or bank-based system matter? *J. Financ. Econ.*, 64, pp. 147–180.
Beck, T. and Levine, R. (2004). Stock markets, banks, and growth: Panel evidence. *J. Bank Fin.*, 28, pp. 423–442.
Beck, T., Levine, R., and Loayza, N. (2000b). Finance and the sources of growth. *J. Fin. Econ.*, 58(1), pp. 261–300.
Berger, A. N., Hasan, I., and Klapper, L. F. (2004). Further evidence on the link between finance and growth: An international analysis of community banking and economic performance. *J. Fin. Serv. Res.*, 25, pp. 169–202.
Bhide, A. (1993). The hidden costs of stock market liquidity. *J. Fin. Econ.*, 34, pp. 1–51.
Boyd, J. H. and Smith, B. D. (1998). The evolution of debt and equity markets in economic development. *Econ. Theor.*, 12, pp. 519–560.
Cheng, X., and Degryse, H. (2010). The impact of bank and non-bank financial institutions on local economic growth in China. *J. Fin. Serv. Res.*, 37, pp. 179–199.
Cull, R., Demirgüç-Kunt, A., and Lin, J. Y. (2013). Financial structure and economic development: A reassessment. *World Bank Econ. Rev.*, 27(3), pp. 470–475.
Demirgüç-Kunt, A., Feyen, E., and Levine, R. (2011). Optimal financial structures and development: The evolving importance of banks and markets. Policy Research Working Paper Series 5805, The World Bank.
Demirgüç-Kunt, A. and Huizinga, H. (2000). Financial structure and bank profitability. In Demirgüç–Kunt, A. and Levine, R. (eds.), *Financial Structure and Economic Growth, A Cross–Country Comparison of Banks, Markets, and Development*. Cambridge, MA: MIT Press, pp. 243–261.
Demirgüç-Kunt, A. and Levine, R. (1996a). Stock markets corporate finance and economic growth. *World Bank Econ. Rev.*, 10(2), pp. 223–240.
Demirgüç-Kunt, A. and Levine, R. (1996b). Stock market development and financial intermediaries: stylized facts. *World Bank Econ. Rev.*, 10(2), pp. 291–322.
Demirgüç-Kunt, A. and Levine, R. (2001). *Financial Structures and Economic Growth: A Cross-Country Comparison of Banks, Markets, and Development*. Cambridge, MA: MIT Press.
Demirgüç-Kunt, A. and Maksimovic, V. (2002). Funding growth in bank-based and market-based financial systems: Evidence from firm level data. *J. Fin. Econ.*, 65, pp. 337–363.
Goldsmith, R. W. (1969). *Financial Structure and Development*. New Haven, CT: Yale University Press.
Grossman, S. J. and Hart, O. (1980). Takeover bids, the free-rider problem, and the theory of the corporation. *Bell J. Econ.*, 11, pp. 42–64.
Hall, R. E. and Jones, C. I. (1999). Why do some countries produce so much more output per worker than others. *Q. J. Econ.*, 114(1), pp. 83–116.
Harris, R. D. F. (1997). Stock markets and development: A re-assessment, *Eur. Econ. Rev.*, 41, pp. 139–146.
Jeong, W., Kymn, K. O., and Kymn, C. J. (2003). The long-run interdependence of bank-health, investment-oriented bank loans, and economic performance: A time-series analysis. *Q. Rev. Econ. Fin.*, 43, pp. 11–30.
King, R. G. and Levine, R. (1993). Finance and growth: Schumpeter might be right. *Q. J. Econ.*, 108, pp. 717–38.

La Porta, R., Lopez-de-Silanes, F., Shleifer, A., and Vishny, R. (1997). Legal determinants of external finance. *J. Fin.*, 52, pp. 1131–1150.

La Porta, R., Lopez-de-Silanes, F., Shleifer, A., and Vishny, R. (1998). Law and finance. *J. Polit. Econ.*, 106, pp. 1113–1155.

Levine, R. (2002). Bank-based or market-based financial systems: Which is better? *J. Fin. Int.*, 11, pp. 398–428.

Levine, R. (2005). Finance and growth: Theory and evidence. In Philippe Aghion and Steven Durlauf (eds.), *Handbook of Economic Growth*. The Netherlands: Elsevier Science, pp. 865–934.

Levine, R., Loayza, N., and Beck, T. (2000). Financial intermediation and growth: Causality and causes. *J. Monetary Econ.*, 46, pp. 31–77.

Levine, R. and Zervos, S. (1998). Stock markets, banks, and economic growth. *Am. Econ. Rev.*, 88(3), pp. 537–558.

Lin, J. Y. (2012). *New Structural Economics: A Framework for Rethinking Development and Policy*. Washington, D.C: The World Bank.

Lin, J. Y. (2013). Endowment, industrial structure, and appropriate financial structure: A new structural economics perspective. *J. Econ. Policy Reform.*, 16(2), pp. 109–122.

Lin, J. Y., Sun, X., and Jiang, Y. (2009). Toward a theory of optimal financial structure, Policy Research Working Paper Series 5038, The World Bank.

Lin, J. Y. and Xu, L. C. (2012). Financial structure and economic development. In Lin, J. Y. (eds.), *New Structural Economics: A Framework for Rethinking Development and Policy*. Washington, D.C.: The World Bank, pp 259–283.

Merton, R. C. (1995). A functional perspective of financial intermediation. *Fin. Manage*, 24, pp. 23–41.

Merton, R. C. and Bodie, Z. (1995). A conceptual framework for analyzing the financial environment, In (eds.), D. Crane, B. *et al.*, *The Global Financial System: A Functional Perspective*, Boston, MA: Harvard Business School Press, pp. 3–31.

Rajan, R. G. (1992). Insiders and outsiders: The choice between informed and arms length debt. *J. Fin.*, 47, pp. 1367–1400.

Rajan, R. G. and Zingales, L. (1998). Financial dependence and growth. *Am. Econ. Rev.*, 88(3), pp. 559–586.

Rousseau, P. L. and Wachtel, P. (1998). Financial intermediation and economic performance: Historical evidence from five industrial countries. *J. Money Credit Bank*, 30, pp. 657–678.

Shen C. and Lee, C. (2006). Same financial development yet different economic growth–Why? *J. Money Credit Bank*, 38, pp. 1907–1944.

Şendeniz-Yüncü, İ., Akdeniz, L., and Aydoğan, K. (2008). Interdependence of the banking sector and the real sector: Evidence from OECD countries. *Appl. Econ.*, 40, pp. 749–764.

Şendeniz-Yüncü, İ., Akdeniz, L., and Aydoğan, K. (2018). Do stock index futures affect economic growth? Evidence from 32 countries. *Emerg. Mark. Fin. Tr*, 54, pp. 410-429.

Song, F. and Thakor, A. V. (2010). Financial system architecture and the co-evolution of banks and capital markets. *Econ. J.*, 120, pp. 1021–1055.

Stiglitz, J. E. (1985). Credit markets and the control of capital. *J. Money Credit Bank*, 17, pp. 133–152.

Tadesse, S. (2002). Financial architecture and economic performance: International evidence. *J. Fin. Intermed*, 11, pp. 429–454.

Zhang K. H. (2003). Does financial development promote economic growth in the East Asia? *China J. Fin.*, 1(2), pp. 1–10.

Appendix

Table A.1. Names and Descriptions of the Variables and Data Sources

Variable Name	Abbreviation	Description	Data Source
Real GDP per capita	RGDPC	Log real GDP per capita (constant 2010 USD)	World Bank World Development Indicators
Banking sector activity	BAN	Volume of deposit money bank credit extended to the private sector as % of GDP	World Bank Financial Development and Structure dataset
Value-traded ratio	STO	Stock market total value traded as % of GDP	World Bank Financial Development and Structure dataset
Financial structure ratio	STR	Mixture of banks and markets operating in an economy; private credit to stock market total value traded ratio	Authors' calculations
Optimal financial structure ratio	OPT	Estimated optimal financial structure ratio in an economy	Authors' calculations
Financial structure gap	SGAP	Natural logarithm of the absolute value of the difference between the actual financial structure ratio and the estimated optimal financial structure ratio	Authors' calculations
Financial structure ratio/optimal financial structure ratio	STROPT	Actual financial structure ratio/expected optimal financial structure ratio	Authors' calculations
Inflation	INF	% annual	World Bank World Development Indicators

(Continued)

Table A.1. (*Continued*)

Variable Name	Abbreviation	Description	Data Source
Foreign direct investment	FDI	Foreign direct investment net inflows, % of GDP	World Bank World Development Indicators
Openness to trade	OPE	Total of exports and imports, % of GDP	World Bank World Development Indicators
Unemployment	UNEMP	Total unemployment, % of total labor force	World Bank World Development Indicators
Population	POP	Log population	World Bank World Development Indicators
Distance from the equator	LAT	Abs(latitude)/90 as distance from the equator	Hall, R. E. and Jones, C.I. [1999]
British legal origin	LEGUK	Dummy variable referring to British legal origin	Global Development Network Growth Database
French legal origin	LEGFR	Dummy variable referring to French legal origin	Global Development Network Growth Database
German legal origin	LEGGR	Dummy variable referring to German legal origin	Global Development Network Growth Database
Socialist legal origin	LEGSOC	Dummy variable referring to socialist legal origin	Global Development Network Growth Database

Note: This table provides the names, abbreviations, descriptions, and data sources for the variables used in the empirical analyses.

Chapter 24

Crowdf(o)unding, in Context

Maria Lucia Passador

Bocconi University, Italy

Abstract

In such a rapidly developing world, crowdfunding is gaining in popularity. The present chapter provides the reader with an overview of the topic in different geographical contexts, bearing in mind the financial markets' perspective and zooming in on one of its main forms: equity crowdfunding. First, it outlines a comprehensive picture on platforms' characteristics, then, after a comparative analysis on its functioning, the chapter focuses on a groundbreaking experience: in fact, Italian law represents the very first (at least European) nation in which a specific regulation on that topic was implemented. Lastly, comments, suggestions for policymakers and ideas for further research are developed.

The future is always beginning now.
– Mark Strand

1. Introduction

Crowdfunding is a fast-growing phenomenon, consisting of a strong link between investors and entrepreneurs sharing the common purpose of developing businesses in a way that is radically changing the entire world of finance.[1] This open internet call, widely considered as a subset of crowdsourcing,

[1]On FinTech *see* Chishti, S., Barberis, J. (2016). *The FinTech Book: The Financial Technology Handbook for Investors, Entrepreneurs and Visionaries*, Hoboken, NJ; Alt, R., Puschmann, T. (2016). *Digitalisierung der Finanzindustrie: Grundlagen der Fintech-Evolution*, Berlin-Heidelberg; Giancarlo, J.C. (2016). *The Digitization of Financial Markets. The Harvard Law School Forum on Corporate Governance and Financial Regulation*, available at *blogs.law.harvard.edu*; Bschor, B. (2015). EBF calls for Fairer Fintech Regulations, *Int'l Financial Law Rev.*; Lee, A. (2015). Why Regulators must adapt to Fintech, *Int'l Financial Law Rev.*

encompasses financial support and provides funds to entities that may not have access to the traditional financial system (banks, venture capital (VC) funds, business angels,[2] etc.), also sharing some similarities with microfinance.[3] In order to pursue the abovementioned goals,[4] technologically qualified funders (even if dispersed)[5] increase capital in return for diverse types of benefits. There is not just one method available: the incredibly dynamic spirit of the technique under analysis[6] — which lies "at the crossroad of microfinance and social networking" (Cordova, Dolci, Gianfrate, 2015).[7] — can be shaped according to the specific needs of each investment.[8] Thus, it can be classified in donation-based (backers donate money for a certain cause, without getting anything in return),[9] reward-based (backers

[2]If the relationship of crowdfunding with venture capitalists is clear, since they are interested in larger deals and are more structured companies, the relationship with business angels is both competitive and complementary. The latter invest a minor but still consistent stake of target companies while crowdfunders may invest obtaining minimal equity percentages, an also possess financial and specialized expertise. Moreover, equity crowdfunding represents an intermediate level of reward-risk between bank loans and VC/business angel investments, in a potential and theoretical position, since not enough deals of this kind have been closed in order to determine well-defined information about its yields and risks. See Collins, L., Pierrakis, Y. (2012). *The Venture Crowd: Crowdfunding Equity Investment into Business*, available at *www.nesta.org.uk*.

[3]On the one hand, crowdfunding addresses to start-ups without warranties and a confirmed debt repayment track record; on the other hand, microfinance addresses to low-income and unemployed individuals. *See*, Otero, M. (1999). *Bringing development back into microfinance*. Latin America: ACCION International.

[4]Among them, the solution of the potential antithesis "*web 2.0* vs mercato finanziario": *see* Mazzarella, M. (2014). *Speech, 40th Anniversary of Consob*, Rome; Troisi, A. (2014). Crowdfunding e mercato creditizio: profili regolamentari, *Contr. impr.*, II, p. 519, § 3 and fn. 11; Mosco, G.D. (2013). La nuova regolamentazione dell'*equity crowdfunding*, available at *www.crowdfundingitalia.com*, p. 9 s.

[5]Armour, J., Enriques, L. (2015).*Financial Disruption*, available at *www.iast.fr*, p. 5.

[6]Mollick, E.R. (2014). The Dynamics of Crowdfunding: An Exploratory Study. *J. Business Venturing*, vol. 29, n. 1, pp. 1–16, available at *ssrn.com*.

[7]See also Hazen, T.L. (2012). Crowdfunding or Fraudfunding? Social Networks and the Securities Laws — Why the specially Tailored Exemption must be Conditioned on Meaningful Disclosure, *North Carolina Law Rev.*, vol. 90, n. 5, pp. 1735–1770, at pp. 1765–1768.

[8]See also Gerber, S. (2012). The Jobs Act Signing: a Giant Step for Entrepreneurship in America, *Time*, also quoted by Capelli, I. (2014). L'*equity based crowdfunding* e i diritti del socio, *Orizzonti del diritto commerciale*, note 1.

[9]Crowdfunding efforts, such as art or humanitarian projects, follow a patronage model, placing funders in the position of philanthropists expecting no direct return for their donation. Donations are typical in contexts in which companies are structured as a non-for-profit organization (Glaeser, E.L., Shleifer, A. (2001). Not For Profit Entrepreneurs. *J. Public Economics*, vol. 81, n. 1, 99–115). Such model is the mere evolution of on-line

receive a reward, such as a pre-purchase of the product or service, in exchange for a pledge),[10] credit-based (backers loan the money in exchange for an interest rate), and equity-based crowdfunding (the most complicated and relevant one for studying entrepreneurial signaling).[11] Such categorization is based on what investors receive for their contributions and on the legal capacity and degree of information asymmetry.

In a contractual perspective, equity-based crowdfunding proposes a third method of financial contracting. *Inter alia*, the German situation is unique in many respects, thus, it is particularly relevant: German crowd investors usually obtain subordinated profit-participating loans resembling aspects of equity shares on a contractual basis (Klöhn *et al.*, 2016). Contracts are standardized (no modification or specific bargaining allowed), since there is no face-to-face debate. Such method also offers a less effective mechanism of protection, when compared to structured contracts of venture capitalists[12] and experienced business angels.

---

donation collections that charitable organizations used to practice before the current models appeared (Feedman, D.M., Nutting, M.R. (2015). *A Brief History of Crowdfunding Including Rewards, Donation, Debt, and Equity Platforms in the USA*, available at *www.freedman-chicago.com*).

[10]Funds are exchanged for rewards, which are not directly linked to financial results, but may be proportional to the sum granted by investors. Such rewards — normally symbolic compensations or discounts on the sale prices or pre-purchases of the product the fundraising is developing — are usually less worthy than the contribution itself, in order to allow a convenient financing. (Cumming D.J., Leboeuf G., Schwienbacher A. (2015). *Crowdfunding models: Keep-it-all vs. all-or-nothing*, available at *leeds-faculty.colorado.edu*).

[11]Schwartz, A.A. (2015). The Nonfinancial Returns of Crowdfunding. *Rev. Banking and Fin. Law*, vol. 34, n. 2, pp. 565–580; Rossi, M. (2014). The New Ways to Raise Capital: an Exploratory Study of Crowdfunding, *Int'l J. Fin. Research*, vol. 5, n. 2, pp. 8–18, at p. 13 and Cordova, A., Dolci, J., Gianfrate, G. (2015). *Crowdfunding: Towards the Democratization of Innovation Financing*. Archibugi, D., Filippetti, A., *Handbook of Global science, Technology and Innovation*, p. 249 ff. and Ahlers, G. K., Cumming, D., Guenther C., Schweizer, D. (2012). *Signaling in Equity Crowdfunding*, available at *papers.ssrn.com*. In the French literature, see Poissonnier, A., Bévan, Q. (2016). *Crowdfunding et solidarité, Réalités Industrielles*, pp. 29–32.

[12]To be honest, crowdfunding differs from VC in many aspects: VC strongly relies on a network of offices located in many centers in order to identify and support start-ups, it is typically run by a few people with a strong expertise in a given business, and it is not necessarily rewarded anyhow. Still, it is arguable that in the entrepreneurial finance environment, crowdfunding represents a meaningful substitute of traditional VC activity as a means to raising seed capital for entrepreneurs at the very beginning of their initiative. By selecting start-ups, venture capitalists implicitly prevent the other agents in the institutional network of innovation from collaborating with the new ventures that do not get VC funding, and sometimes potential valuable innovations do not reach

This chapter provides the reader with an overview of the topic in different geographical contexts, where crowdfunding is gaining popularity, keeping financial markets' perspective in mind.

It aims to offer a comprehensive picture of platform characteristics and it is articulated as follows: after an overview on how crowdfunding works in a comparative perspective as in October 2015 (*see* Section 2), it will focus on the Italian context, as it is the very first (at least European) country in which a specific regulation on that topic was implemented. Comments, suggestions for policymakers and ideas for further research are provided in Section 3.

2. Equity Crowdfunding: General Remarks

Equity crowdfunding, in other words, is the offering of securities, enabling anyone to acquire shares in a privately held business, "*i.e.* those that have yet to float on the stock exchange, by allowing a business to offer a certain proportion of its equity for a set amount of capital it is aiming to raise" [Pierrakis, Collins, 2012].

Such an alternative model for financing projects and new businesses[13] comes in the form of donation[14] or in exchange for some form of reward and/or voting rights to support initiatives,[15] involving active cooperation

customers simply because they did not get VC financing to get connected to the network. Moreover, through VC, entrepreneurs are not likely to maintain control over the project. Legitimately, concerns have been raised about the quality of entrepreneurial projects and the viability of the new VC firms that have strong expertise and business background (Bogost, 2012). However, according to some authors, venture capitalists used such methods to select portfolio companies, also used by crowdfunders, so that good projects get financed while lower-quality projects receive little to not backers (Mollick, 2014, pp. 1–16). Thus, it is our contention that crowdfunding — which now plays as a respectable competitor of VC in the provision of seed capital — might evolve as a main actor in the field.

[13]Anglicism of the year 2012, it describes an "*evolving alternative financing method, putting a new twist on a relatively old practice of raising money*" (Danmayr, 2014).

[14]Schäfer, M.S., Metag, J., Feustle, J., Herzog, L. (2016). Selling science 2.0: What scientific projects receive crowdfunding online? *Public Understanding of Science.*

[15]Lambert, T., Schwienbacher, A. (2010). *An Empirical Analysis of Crowdfunding, Crowdsourcing*, available at *www.crowdsourcing.org*; Belleflamme, P., Lambert, T., Schwienbacher, A. (2011). *Crowdfunding: Tapping the Right Crowd*, Center for Operations Research and Econometrics, Louvain-la-Nouve, Belgium. Platforms can be divided in "all or nothing" or "take it all" (respectively when a target goal must be achieved in a given period of time is set and when transactions are completed even if the target set was not reached, *see* Cumming, D.J., Leboeuf, G., Schwienbacher, A. (2014). Crowdfunding Models: Keep-it-All vs. All-or-Nothing, *Finance Meeting Eurofidai — Affi Paper*, available at *ssrn.com* and An, J., Quercia, D., Crowdcroft, J. (2014). *Recommending Investors for*

among participants.[16] One of the possible early trallblazers of the business model that crowdfunding platforms adopt could be identified in the notion of collective fundraising that was used during the 17th century to sponsor publications: hence, the cooperative movements of the 19th and 20th centuries allowed collective groups of people to pool funds to develop new concepts in the interest of the community in the rural areas of Europe and in the northern part of America. Even if the word itself is quite recent, the idea of crowdfunding is surely rooted in the past and "inspired",[17] *inter alia*, the processing of many projects, such as crowdsourcing, that permitted the completion of the *Oxford English Dictionary* in the 19th century. Nevertheless, something new really exists in this case: the digital revolution undeniably has a prime role in this context,[18] by allowing each party to obtain information on investments related to the interests of each party and intending to rapidly transfer them,[19] and to be remunerated in terms of shares (Moritz *et al.*, 2016).

After all, the recognized "granddaddy of crowdfunding" (Kappel, 2009) is the Sellaband platform, established in 2006, in Amsterdam, which worked as follows: music artists created their profile on that platform, where they could include demo songs, so that investors could get to know them and their music. The success of the model brought the website to establish a partnership with the well-known music site of Soundcloud giving artists the chance to import their playlists creating vast network effects.

Crowdfunding Projects, World wide web: Proceedings of the 23rd international conference (WWW '14), pp. 261–270.

[16]The idea of social *community* and *social lending* platforms is illustrated in Manzi, V. (2013). *Il fenomeno del crowdfunding e del* social lending: *caratteristiche operative e profili contrattuali*, F. Capriglione (ed.), *I contratti dei risparmiatori* (Giuffrè, Milan) p. 394 ff. and in Piattelli, U. (2013). *Il* Crowdfunding *in Italia. Una regolamentazione all'avanguardia o un'occasione mancata?* (Giappichelli, Turin).

[17]Securities crowdfunding literally builds off the earlier concept of crowdsourcing (Brabham, D.C. (2013). *Crowdsourcing* (MIT Press, Cambridge, MA) and Schwartz, A.A. (2013). Crowdfunding Securities, *Notre Dame Law Rev.*, vol. 88, n. 3, pp. 1457–1477).

[18]De Martin, J.C. (2013). *Crowdfunding*, le "collette" per il rilancio, *La Stampa* (italics added). See also Brabham, D.C. (2013). *Crowdsourcing* (MIT Press, Cambridge, MA) and Kozinets, R., Hemetsberger, A., Schau, H.J. (2008). The Wisdom of Consumer Crowds: Collective Innovation in the Age of Networked Marketing, *J. Macromarketing*, vol. 28, p. 339 ff.

[19]"*Crowdfunding itself is not new.* [...] *Issuers and intermediaries relying on Regulation Crowdfunding expect to further democratize investing in start-ups, because any investor, whether or not accredited, may invest in these securities*", [Norked, 2014].

2.1. *Advantages and disadvantages*

An inherent problem faced by entrepreneurs from the outset is to attract outside capital, given the lack of collateral and sufficient cash flows and the presence of significant information asymmetry with investors.[20] In response to this need, equity crowdfunding certainly presents some strengths, which are not immune to downsides.

Among its advantages, it is noteworthy to focus on the validation and promotion of the business idea (launching it on an equity crowdfunding platform is a mode of quick validation because it gives a projection of the target market); on the control they allow (entrepreneurs do not lose the right to decide on the company, while venture capitalists and business angels, providing a huge amount of funds, gain significant control over the decisions within the corporations and also force entrepreneurs to establish precise time and objectives); on their ability to reach the majority of entrepreneurs,[21] on the low transaction costs (which permit to invest small amounts of money in many different projects), and on the absence of geographical constraints (allowing a synchronous search and investment process among entrepreneurs, investors, and platforms without being in the same place).[22]

Among its drawbacks, it cannot be avoided to recall the waste expense of time and effort required, its limited capacity to raise money (due to the heavier regulatory set and the legal and procedural burdens often imposed), the excessive standardization of contracts (whereas business angels and venture capitalists tend to customize contracts with covenants such as anti-dilution provisions and liquidation preferences, which secure priority in the distribution of value); the total absence of both advisors (that make it difficult for unsophisticated investors to decide which intermediary and business can be trusted),[23] and valuation of the company (which proved its effectiveness, as confirmed by experiences in the VC field),[24] the administrative and accounting challenges it offers and the loss of

---

[20]Cosh, A., Cumming, D.J., Huges, A. (2009). Outside Entrepreneurial Capital, *The Economic J.*, vol. 119, n. 40, pp. 1494–1533.

[21]Bechter, C., Jentzsch, S., Frey, M. (2011). From Wisdom of the Crowd to Crowdfunding. *J. Communication and Computer*, vol. 8, pp. 951–957.

[22]Vass, T. (2013). *Adding a geographical component to an equity crowdfunding project (paper III)*, available at *crowdsourcing.org*.

[23]Valanciene, L., Jegelviciute, S. (2013). Valuation of crowdfunding: benefits and drawbacks, *Economics and Management*, vol. 18, n. 1, pp. 39–48.

[24]Furthermore, venture capitalists can benefit from crowdfunding as it can help to identify promising corporations easily and, simultaneously, gather public reviews giving a long-term picture of any business future (Manchanda, K., Muralidharan, P. (2014).

confidentiality (since the idea is shared with many others and there is a risk that it is stolen and implemented before the pioneer does). The asymmetry information problem raises even higher problems and risks related to the investment in start-ups, more precisely, the risk of dilution, investment and illiquidity.

2.2. *The US experience*

On April 5, 2012, President Obama signed the *Jumpstart Our Business Startups Act*, whose main purpose is to provide a stimulus to the national economy, facilitating access to new capital for start-ups and small- and medium-sized enterprises that tended to remain excluded from the traditional supply channels.

The Google search volume for the single word, crowdfunding,[25] makes the upward trend self-evident, conditioned by the different events involving crowdfunding, and the *Jobs Act* signature peak demonstrated how this act played a crucial role overseas, where, interestingly enough, the highest interest on the topic is shown in Utah, whereas the New York State, California, and Massachusetts are ranked, respectively, in the 5th, 8th, and 11th place only.[26]

The Securities and Exchange Commission (SEC) approved a regulation on crowdfunding on October 30, 2015, and it was fully operative starting from May 16, 2016.[27] During this period, some States filled the regulatory gap by approving the *Blue Sky Laws*,[28] which regulated the topic: for example, Kansas legalized the use of the technique in 2011, making interstate

Crowdfunding: a New Paradigm in Startup Financing, *Global Conference on Business and Finance Proceedings*, vol. 9, n. 1, pp. 369–374).

[25] *See*, in particular, the search results available at *https://www.google.com/trends/explore?date=all&q=crowdfunding.*

[26] *See*, in particular, the search results available at *https://www.google.com/trends/explore?date=all&geo=US&q=crowdfunding.*

[27] The Regulation Crowdfunding adopting release is available at http://www.sec.gov/rules/final/2015/33-9974.pdf. The March 31th, 2017 release adopting inflation adjustments to the dollar amount thresholds in Regulation Crowdfunding is available at https://www.sec.gov/rules/final/2017/33-10332.pdf.

[28] This is a purchase and sale of securities in order to protect the investing public against the risk of fraud set of laws enacted by individual states to regulate. But the phrase has originated in times far from recent: in the twentieth century a judge of the supreme court declared its will to protect savers from investments of dubious reliability, whose proponents, just to make a profit, they would also "sell building lots in the sky blue in fee sample" [Macey, Miller, 1991].

operations extremely complex.[29] This choice, however, limited the impact of the new rules and slowed down the progress of the SEC activity.

To analyze the phenomenon in the United States,[30] it is appropriate to point out that the intervention tended, at the same time, to allow the most complete investor protection in the financial investments and the most detailed regulatory complex, that results from three fundamental elements, applicable to intermediaries and issuers: *(i)* the authorization for brokers to operate through the supervisory authority and the consequent insertion in a special register; *(ii)* the preparation, for each operation, of a *prospectus* relating to the transaction itself and to the proponent; and *(iii)* the periodic information by the issuers.

Compliance with these standards implies that these are hardly achievable for small companies, especially in the drafting of the *prospectus*, so, the legislation mentions a *series* of exclusions that allow easier access to capital: a method used by the *Jobs Act* also for regulating crowdfunding. The document provides that any offer has to be made through an intermediary, registered as a broker or a funding portal, which can enjoy certain exemptions in relation to the number of investors to whom it is addressed.

According to *Rule 506*, should such offer be restricted to less than 35 non-accredited investors, as well as to an unlimited number of accredited investors, no registration is due: it is, in other words, a "safe harbour". "Do-it-yourself" operations are prohibited and platforms have to abide by the rule to encourage people to invest in securities, to remunerate employees or agents, not to advise clients on investments, to manage funds and securities owned by investors. The SEC also has the power to increase this list of charges.

The funding platform registered with the SEC must, at the same time, be registered with a national securities association, such as the *Financial Industry Regulatory Authority*, or FINRA. It is a not-for-profit organization authorized by Congress, acting independently to protect the US investors by making sure that the securities industry operates fairly and honestly.

Companies running portals must comply with a *series* of informative obligations to investors in order to reduce information asymmetries and the risk of fraud.

---

[29]Wiens, J. (2014). State Equity Crowdfunding Policies Hold Promise, *Forbes*, available at *www.forbes.com*.

[30]Laroppe, J.-C., Le financement participatif aux États-Unis: une réglementation récente sur un phénomène de société déjà ancien, *Revue Int. Serv. Fin. / Int'l J. Financial Services (RISF)*, n. 4, pp. 67–73.

Platforms must also inform the audience of investors about the applicant and the offers of securities at least 21 days before the operation, and they have to ensure themselves about the truthfulness and correctness of the information.

Portals are not allowed to collect personal information regarding investors (and to compensate third parties for this purpose), as it is forbidden to members and administrators to have any economic interest in the companies that have access to the crowdfunding service.

Jobs Act also regulates the status of the proponent, and requires it to be a US resident corporation: such barrier confirms that the purpose of the law is to promote the economic growth of the nation and not to create a world market for IPOs of start-ups and SMEs.

Unlike what has been decided elsewhere, such as in Italy, the Northern American legislator did not want to impose any limit on the category of issuers. In fact, there are no limits, neither to the sector in which the company operates, nor to the type of activity performed or to the types of names of the company. Access is denied to financial intermediaries only, to companies listed on regulated markets and issuers who recently started public offers with a mandatory *prospectus*. The reason for such an exclusion is clear: to shape this instrument in the most suitable way to meet the financial needs of small companies and to prevent larger companies to receive significant benefits in terms of lower costs. Companies wishing to engage in equity crowdfunding operations are allowed to raise upto $1 million yearly, even through several campaigns. There is no maximum amount to be assigned to institutional investors, but the proponent has, indeed, the obligation to attach and to make accessible to potential investors a range of essential information. The issuer must also specify how it intends to use the funds collected and must disclose a list of those who hold at least 20% of the issuer's stakes.

The company must provide a documentation of increasing importance, when the required resources do not reach the threshold of $100,000, whereas it is sufficient to declare the income of the proposing party if the applications do not exceed the threshold of $500,000, and it is necessary to present a financial statement audited by independent accountant, under professional standards, if they do not exceed the threshold of $1 million, for which it is required to submit the financial statements of the certified proponent (audited financial statements). The *Jobs Act* also regulates the resources that an individual can invest, setting a maximum amount that depends on the annual income of investors: it corresponds to the 10% of the income if the total annual income is greater than $100,000, whereas it corresponds to the highest value of $2,000 and 5% of income if the total annual income is under $100,000.

TheCrowdCafe, a website providing news and research about the industry of crowdfunding allows us to know this world in depth, monitoring the typology of business models, the development of their activity, the size of platforms in terms of fund-raising, revenues, financed companies, and number of investors. Its data, as of June 2015, reported that the majority of platforms are located in the United States and the recent update of the US regulation, in October 2015, allowing non-accredited investors to participate in equity crowdfunding, even enlarged the number of platforms based overseas, in connection with a greater demand for investment. The total amount of money provided to companies until September 2015 was approximately €1,867 billion and each platform raised an average of €1,326 million per month. The average operating lifespan of platforms, between 4 years and 4 months, may be compatible with that of their regular customers, start-ups. The services offered by platforms are grouped into two major clusters: information services, on the one hand, and support services, on the other hand. As to the former, we may recall the analysis of campaign timing (Marelli, 2016) and the availability of information on previously funded projects, while, as to the latter, we may promotional ideas, the tech and media support, as well as the legal and banking one. Investors are also offered services including meetings, updates regarding the status of the companies, and diagnostic information about investments and supported by leading platforms such as the British *Crowdcube* or its American version, called *CircleUp*, offering "circles", *i.e.*, separately managed funds that invest in platform's companies, to investors.

Like the recent software developed by the e-commerce giant *Amazon*, *MTurk* (Buhrmester *et al.* 2011), it can be found out that the potential economic impact of crowdfunding to eliminate gender bias frictions is substantial[31]: if start-ups led by women are disadvantaged in their ability

[31]Nowadays, a growing number of studies examine how women business-owners use various sources of financing available in the market for an early-stage business idea (see, *inter alia*, Marom, D., Robb, A., Sade, O. (2016). *Gender Dynamics in Crowdfunding (Kickstarter): Evidence on Entrepreneurs, Investors, Deals and Taste-Based Discrimination*, available at *ssrn.com*; Brooks, A.W., Huang, L., Kearney, S.W., Murray F. (2014). Investors Prefer Entrepreneurial Ventures Pitched by Attractive Men, *Proceedings of the National Academy of Sciences of the United States of America*, vol. 111, n. 12, pp. 4427–4431, available at *hbs.edu*; Fairlie, R., Marion, J. (2012). Affirmative Action Programs and Business Ownership among Minorities and Women, *Small Business Economics*, vol. 39, n. 2,

to collect funds in the stock market, this could truly affect the feasibility and financial condition of their companies, their ability to grow and expand throughout the entire market. It is worth mentioning that, according to a study, there is a positive correlation between the gender of the entrepreneur and the percentage of the same gender investors (Marom *et al.*, 2016). Furthermore, even though women have lower capital goals, they enjoy higher rate of success compared to men. Once successful in their first round of financing through crowdfunding, companies will surely be well equipped to take a further step. Some of its interesting key results are the following: (i) the female gender is proven to be successful at the same rate as male entrepreneurs when collecting funds; (ii) diverse geographic areas and industrial environments provide opportunities for female enterpreneurs, eliminating geographic constraints allowing women to enter men-led businesses, thus, democratizing the private equity market by serving as a system to women investors and entrepreneurs to participate deeply in the field; and (iii) experience is confirmed to be crucial at the basis of financing decisions, as in other early stages of financing start-ups, notwithstanding the fact that we could expect the project attribute to weight more in the value assessment of business ideas. Not surprisingly, there was recently a development of many marketing agencies that specialize in helping entrepreneurs to raise money with crowdfunding platforms, supporting founders in the right to sustain entrepreneurs throughout the campaign and confirming how the space for future guidance in this field is particularly interesting to be filled with future research.

---

pp. 319–339; Carter, S., Shaw, E., Lam, W., Wilson, F. (2007). Gender, Entrepreneurship, and Bank Lending: The Criteria and Processes Used by Bank Loan Officers in Assessing Applications, *Entrepreneurship Theory and Practice*, vol. 31, n. 3, pp. 427–444; Brush, C., Carter, N.M., Gatewood, E.J., Greene, P.G., Hart, M. (2011). *The Diana Project: Women Business Owners and Equity Capital: The Myths Dispelled. Babson College Center for Entrepreneurship Research Paper No. 2009–2011*, available at *ssrn.com;* Kourilsky, M.L., Walstad, W.B. (1998). Entrepreneurship and female youth: knowledge, attitudes, gender differences, and educational practices, *J. Business Venturing,* vol. 13, n. 1, pp. 77–88). However, in the acquisition of capital phase, research showed that women tend to have difficulties in collecting the adequate amount of funds they need compared to men. "Overall, the weight of research evidence considering gender, entrepreneurship, and bank lending, suggests that while the bank financing profiles of men and female entrepreneurs are distinctly different, much, but not all, is attributable to structural dissimilarities" (Carter, *et al.*, 2007). The real perceived recognition of the important market that women as entrepreneurs are creating and research evidences that the criteria used to assess loan application do not vary by the loan applicant gender.

Thus, these considerations trigger an attempt at a new classification of equity crowdfunding platforms, according to their approach towards funders and fundraisers (Gierczak, 2016), thus segmenting equity crowdfunding platforms among investor-oriented, company-oriented, and balanced approach platforms. Investor-oriented ones are normally addressed to funders only, while company-oriented ones are oriented to fundraises and if they provide services to both or none of the counterparties, they are defined as balanced, since they represent a pure and symmetrical intermediary between the offering services to both and that do not offer them any specific support counterparties.

In recent literature, an in-depth analysis of crowdfunding investment contracts was carried out, in light of the fact that, during the five months in which this type of investment has become legal, two new contractual vehicles were elaborated: SAFE, *Simple Agreement(s) for Future Equity*, and KISS, *Keep It Simple Security*, which typically negotiate when investing in start-ups with high-growth potential that may continue to be acquired or to attract subsequent rounds of investment.[32]

2.3. *The French experience*

After many years, even France provided its investors with an *ad hoc* crowdfunding discipline, approved on May 30, 2014 and entered into force in the following October, at the end of a long consultation period that led to the formation of two figures[33]: *conseillers en investissements partecipatifs* (CIP) and *intermediaires en financement partecipatif* (IFP), reserved to platforms that respectively offer services and equity lending-based crowdfunding.

The companies running these platforms are required to operate exclusively online, through web sites that allow investors, even before accessing the services, to be aware of the risks assumed.

According to the rules, the *prospectus* requirement might be disaggregated when no case of public offer can occur, or when the amounts claimed within the previous 12 months are less than €1 million, the platform and the proponent provide potential investors with simple and balanced information regarding the characteristics of the project, the costs, and the risks of the

[32]For further references, see Wroldsen, J. (2017). Crowdfunding Investment Contracts, *Virginia Law and Business Rev.*, vol. 11, available at *ssrn.com*.

[33]Before the introduction of recent legislation, platforms operated under a *status* which still remains and which is allowed to operate in crowdfunding, as *prestataire de services d'investissement*.

offer. The offer was made through a progressive-access website, so that the investor gives her consent to assume certain risks in view of a possible economic return at a later registration and, then (even before actually investing money), answers a questionnaire about her financial and family situation,[34] her experience in the field of investments and her objectives, risk appetite, and skills.

The French legislation, it is worth emphasizing, does not envisage any restrictions for applicants: all companies can have access to this source of funding, without quantitative limits.

2.4. *The German and Spanish experiences*

In April 2015, both the *Kleinanlegerschultzgesetz* and *Disposición 4067* affirmed the role of this noteworthy topic in Europe, in particular in Germany and Spain.

On the one hand, in Germany, the law sets an annual total investment of €1,000 limit for retail investors (which can be increased up to 10 times, proving the ability to withstand a certain loss); poses an authorization requirement for platforms, while it does not limit an investment for professional investors and corporations (or *Kapitalgesellschaftern*) and it also exempts companies that collect less than €2,5 million from the realization of the *prospectus*.[35]

On the other hand, in Spain,[36] the provisions distinguish accredited investors (institutional investors, corporations, and individuals with

[34]Entrepreneurial finance research papers always refer to the role that family, fool and friends [Guerzoni *et al.*, 2016] plays as the most decisive source of capital for start-up and early stage of financing. Literary pieces suggest that crowdfunding platforms eliminate most distant related economic frictions; however, they do not eliminate asymmetrics associated with the type of information about the entrepreneur that is more likely to be held by personally connected individuals. Such investors are decisive for bootstrapping a business and interpersonal relations play a pivotal role in early stages of financing.

[35]Deckert, K., Le *crowdfunding* en droit allemand, *Revue Int. Serv. Fin./Int'l J. Financial Services (RISF)*, n. 4, pp. 53–58; Kloehn, L., Hornuf, L., Shilling, T. (2015). The Regulation of Crowdfunding in the German Small Investor Protection Act Content, Consequences, Critique, Suggestions, *European Crowdfunding Network*; Kelly, E. (2015). *Germany to Introduce Crowdfunding Restrictions*, available at *www.sciencebusiness.net*.

[36]Simon-Moreno, H. (2016). The legal framework on crowdfunding in Spain, *Revue Int. Serv. Fin./Int'l J. Financial Services (RISF)*, n. 4, pp. 13–27; Alois, J. (2015). *Scan Updates. Crowdfunding Regulations, Crowdcube Spain Shares Perspective*, available at *www.crowdfundinsider.com* and Allegreni, F. (2015). *Anche la Spagna ha il suo regolamento sul* crowdfunding. *Molto più flessibile del nostro*, consultabile all'indirizzo *crowdfundingbuzz.it*.

substantial income and assets), who can make investments without limitation, and not accredited investors, who can spend a maximum amount of €10,000 per year, even if divided in a series of operations, each of which individually may not be worth more than €3,000. Moreover, these rules rely on the supervisory role of the *Comisión Nacional del Mercado de Valores* (CNMV), limit the raising capital to €2 million (or €5 million, if the offer is intended only for professional investors or accredited) and set capital requirements, capitalization, and obligation to take out adequate insurance for platforms in order to obtain permission from the aforementioned Authority.

2.4.1. *The UK experience*

Finally, in November 2015, after a period of transition and adaptation to the new rules by existing market operators, issued by the *Financial Conduct Authority* (FCA) (FCA, 2014), crowdfunding became fully effective at the end of the consultation period, which lasted several years. Prior to this act, the platform's activities were similar to the ones of other operators in the context of soliciting investments and, thus, subject to specific exceptions, the promoter requires an *ad hoc* authorization by the FCA in order to operate.

The brand new rules are only addressed to the investment-based and the loan-based crowdfunding, while deliberately ignoring the donation-based and reward-based ones. The resulting regulation expressly provides that platforms offering equity crowdfunding services must obtain a specific authorization from the FCA, then, a significant economic amount of economic resources (about \$15,000, reduced to £3,000 for companies that already have a license), and time (about six months are required to carry out the practices, indeed).

Of course, once authorized (and, thus, when the sketched business plan showed the sustainability and adequacy of the project, demonstrated the financial viability of the same, and was made available via the website of the corporation, complying with the requirements of the authorization) (Robinson, 2015), the platforms can perform tasks related to equity crowdfunding that were not permitted before.

In other words, the new regulation limits promotion and undertakes platforms to create a new figure: the "compliance director". The FCA also requires the preparation of a specific brochure, which is compulsory only if there is a public offer of securities, to be approved by the Authority and made public prior to the offer of securities. However, most of the transactions are (relatively) quantitatively small, and fall under the exemption regime: in fact, the *prospectus* is not required when the offer is addressed to less than 150 non-accredited investors and a vast number of qualified investors, and funds required in the previous year are lower than €5 million.

The implemented rules increased the number of potential investors and the rules for their protection, limiting the right to promote offers from the public and offer advices.

Such legislation intends to regulate the way in which information and promotion reaches customers and to improve their awareness of the risks they take, by extending the definition of investors beyond the duality between qualified investors and customers as regards their assets.

A company cannot directly perform communication or promote a non-readily realizable security among retail investors, unless the client is a certified restricted investor, who spent less than a tenth of her assets on non-readily available securities in the last 12 months; or certified sophisticated investor, authorized by the FCA, assessed over the previous 36 months as an individual who can effectively assess the risks of investing; between certified high-net-worth investors, whose annual income is not inferior (with the exception of their legal residence) to £250,000 and the investor requested to receive communications about advices related to the crowdfunding platform or any other authorized intermediary before the promotion was implemented.

2.5. *Comparative overview*

Despite the similarities in the approaches taken by the legislators, the regulations led to numerous differences, especially in the treatment of investors and in the limits to fundraising, due to the different attention given to the various participants in the crowdfunding process. In hindsight, regulatory interventions produced a rather uneven situation and, in Italy, where the regulation was developed at the very beginning of the legal phenomenon, it revealed the need for further action, in order to broaden and strengthen the scope of the laws, as well as to overcome the problems that emerged in practice, rendering the 2016 amendment essential.

While, on the one hand, the US and the UK turned their attention especially to public investors, both countries imposed a cap on the investment of the individuals in terms of income and wealth. The UK also expanded investment opportunities for individual investors, creating a limited category of qualified investors, while France did not limit investment opportunities through this technique. As to platforms, all the regulations taken into account mention the requirement of obtaining authorization from the competent authority to operate in the market. France was the only one that opted for adding a burden in relation to the companies involved in the management of the portals to be adequately insured. As to the amount of resources that proposing companies can accept without the specific need to publish the *prospectus*, US, British, and French laws appear to be aligned, while American law only requires an annual audit of financial statements, consequently increasing the accounts of companies using such a system.

The geographic horizons mentioned up to now could be (and will be) even widened (Keeper, 2016), taking into account several examples.[37] In Australia, the *Securities Investment Commission* (ASIC) published a document highlighting the main risks related to the capital gathering through equity crowdfunding and the *Corporations Amendment (Crowd-sourced Funding) Bill* was delayed due to federal elections, but is going to be reintroduced shortly, as the Turnbull Government returned to power; while in Canada the issue is dealt with by Authorities of the single countries, as evidenced by the *consultation paper* released by the *Ontario Securities Commission* (OSC) (Tchotourian, 2016). In April 2011, *Demohour*, the Chinese *Kickstarter*, started raising funds and, a few months later other platforms were also launched, thus, equity crowdfunding became "the" approach to raising investments for projects in exchange for equity for investors in the resulting business, as if it was an "internet-based private equity funding". It is essential to highlight that the rapid economic growth led a large number of high-net-worth individuals to the stage, but investment channels for wealth management in China are still very limited (Ramos, 2016). Besides, the financial capability of entrepreneurs in the country needs

[37]Funk, A.S. (2016). *Institutions Influencing the Evolution of Crowdfunding in China a Review of the World Bank Report on Crowdfunding's Potential for the Developing World*, Brüntje, D., Gajda, O. (eds.), *Crowdfunding in Europe: State of the Art in Theory and Practice* (Springer, Berlin) pp. 125–131; Hu, Y. (2015). *Crowdfunding in China - Crowdfunding in China*, 今日中国：英文版 — China Today, n. 5, pp. 31–33; Sibin, W., Bin, W., Yuanqing, L. (2015). How to Attract the Crowd in Crowdfunding?, *Int. J. of Entrepreneurship and Small Business*, vol. 24, n. 3, pp. 322–334; Hu, T., Yang, D. (2014). The People's Funding of China: Legal Developments of Equity Crowdfunding — Progress, Proposals, and Prospects. (Crowdfunding Regulations and Their Implications), *University of Cincinnati Law Rev.*, vol. 83, n. 2, pp. 445–476; Zheng, H.; Li, D.; Wu, J.; Xu, Y. (2014). The role of multidimensional social capital in Crowdfunding: A Comparative Study in China and US, *Information and Management*, vol. 51, n. 4, pp. 488–496; Sibin, W., Bin, W., Yuanqing, L. (2015). How to Attract the Crowd in Crowdfunding? *Int. J. Entrepreneurship and Small Business*, vol. 24, n. 3, pp. 322–334.

to be cultivated and a large amount of the potentialities crowdfunding offers are still taking a wait-and-see attitude.

Many well-funded projects had encountered difficulties in achieving their obligations, and there have been many reported cases of fraud on the projects, which is always the major concern in the industry. Many potential backers are hesitating to invest due to distrust. Project initiators and platforms are also afraid to cross the bottom line with illegal fundraising, as a clear regulation has not been published yet. To avoid the problem, the first reward-based platform in China turned into a pure pre-sales website — no longer calling itself a crowdfunding site. Unfortunately, projects on such platforms currently tend to lack innovation, also in light of the strong plagiarism issue and weak IP protection, which rendered the platforms mentioned above a sort of pre-sales sites rather than platforms encouraging and promoting innovations (Nasrabadi, 2016).

2.6. *The Italian experience*

"Crowdfunding is the outcome of the open mind which represents the foundation of crowdfunding itself, shaped by collaborative dynamics and aimed, of course, to sharing and participation, within a context activated and helped by 2.0 technologies; validation comes from the bottom, democratization gets new meanings: everyone has a voice, everyone has an opportunity" (Piattelli, 2013). In Italy, even in the absence of explicit legislative recognition, platforms were active[38] and operating according to mechanisms agreed with the supervisory authorities. Then, the resulting system[39] allowed us to consider the Italian equity crowdfunding, which is subject to a dual regulatory regime and, precisely, one related to innovative start-ups and other related to the remaining companies. Interestingly, the Italian legislator

[38]Castrataro, D., Wright, T. (2014). *Crowdfunding. Come finanziarsi online* (Green Books Editore, Milan) e Castrataro, D., Pais, I. (2014). *Analisi delle piattaforme italiane di crowdfunding, Italian Crowdfunding Network* and Ordanini, A., Miceli, L., Pizzetti, M., Parasuraman, A. (2011). Crowdfunding: Transforming Customers into Investors through Innovative Service Platforms, *J. Service Management*, vol. 22, n. 4, pp. 443–470, available at *didattica.unibocconi.it.* As to archetypical, stereotypical and prototypical crowdfunding platforms, see Danmayr, F. (2014). *Archetypes of Crowdfunding Platforms. A Multidimensional Comparison* (Springer, Berlin) p. 48.

[39]*See* Annunziata, F. (2015). *La disciplina del mercato mobiliare* (Giappichelli, Turin) and De Mari, M. (ed.) (2009). *La nuova disciplina degli intermediari dopo le direttive MiFID: prime valutazioni e tendenze applicative*, a (Cedam, Padua). In a comparative perspective, see Busuioc, M. (2013). Rule-Making by the European Financial Supervisory Authorities: Walking a Tight Rope. *European Law J.*, vol. 19, n. 1, p. 111 ff., available at *astrid.eu.*

understood the spirit even before any other European State, being one of the first countries to promptly intervene in the regulation of the phenomenon, balancing the essential rigidity of financial markets, on the one hand, and the extremely flexible web 2.0, on the other hand.[40]

Such regulation, according to the mechanisms agreed with national authorities, with the technological ideas and the determinants of these platforms,[41] will be addressed in a more detailed perspective in the upcoming paragraphs, also considering their implications with regard to the rules of conduct.

Furthermore, the Belpaese Regulation is also specifically devoted to non-listed innovative start-ups and SMEs (Miglietta *et al.*, 2013, §3). Moreover, the norms are constantly updated:[42] Law 221/2012, issued on December 17th (also known as Decree Crescita-*bis*, Crescita 2.0 or Sviluppo-*bis*, already Decree 179/2012, issued on October 18th)[43] is followed by the Consob Regulation n. 18592/2013,[44] issued by the Italian Securities

[40]Cordova, A., Dolci, J., Gianfrate, G. (2013). *The Bearable Lightness of Crowdfunding. Evidence from Technology Projects. 4thEuropean Conference on Corporate R&D and Innovation* and Harms, M. (2007). *What Drives Motivation to Participate Financially in a Crowdfunding Community?*, available at *ssrn.com*.

[41]Castrataro, D., Pais, I. (2014). Analisi delle piattaforme italiane di *crowdfunding*, *Italian Crowdfunding Network* and Ordanini, A. *et al.* (2011) *Crowdfunding*: Transforming Customers into Investors through Innovative Service Platforms, *J. Service Man.*, vol. 22, n. 4, pp. 443–470, available at *didattica.unibocconi.it*.

[42]For an updated overview of the regulation — whose most recent amendments are visually perceivable thanks to the version of the document (*Regolamento sulla raccolta di capitali di rischio tramite portali on-line. (Adottato con delibera n. 18592 del 26 giugno 2013. Aggiornato con le modifiche apportate dalla delibera n. 19520 del 24 febbraio 2016)*, March 2016, available at *www.consob.it*) — *see* Laroppe, J.-C., Le financement participatif en Italie: une réglementation, première en date, récemment modifiée, *Revue Int. Serv. Fin. / Int'l J. Financial Services (RISF)*, n. 4, pp. 31–36; Passador, M.L. (2016). The Need for Suitability and Appropriateness in Crowdfunding Regulation, *Revue Int. Serv. Fin. / Int'l J. Financial Services (RISF)*, n. 4, pp. 37–52; Passador, M.L. (2015). *Crowdfunding:* tra profili di adeguatezza ed appropriatezza e profili di applicabilità all'aumento di capitale, *Banca, impresa e società*, p. 287 ff.; Di Lorenzo, L. (2016). *Crowdfunding* e *start up* innovative: tecnica redazionale, *Notariato*, p. 437 ff. and Marabini, F. (2016). Analisi dei possibili profile anticoncorrenziali della normativa italiana in tema di*crowdfunding*, *Contratto e impresa*, p. 552 ff., where the Author aims at comprehending the potential implications of such regulation in the area of competition law.

[43]Assonime (2013). Commento alla Circolare n. 11/2013. *Riv. soc.*, p. 776 ff.

[44]These amendments modify also the Legislative Decree No. 58/1998, Consolidated Law on Finance, as stated in Capelli, I. (2014) *Brevissime considerazioni sull'*equity based crowdfunding, available at *www.dirittobancario.it*, §3 and Crucil, A. (2014). La disciplina dell'*equity crowdfunding* in Italia: emanato il regolamento Consob sulla raccolta di capitali di rischio da parte di *start-up* innovative, *Riv. soc.*, p. 1058 ff.

and Exchange Commission, and, once, by the Consob Regulation 19520/2016.[45]

The above-mentioned rules are in line with the essence of overseas provisions, even though the US regulation differs as to its recipients (institutional investors, not retail ones)[46] and the Italian discipline incentivizes the simplification of processes, promoting crowdfunding.[47]

In fact, even though the Markets in Financial Instruments Directive only required an exemption in favor of a specific target group of operators (see Art. 3, §1), the Italian legislator opted for a different approach, earmarking the activity of public offerings through platforms to equity crowdfunding only and applying the regulation of this activity also to offers whose objects are exclusively financial products, that should normally not fall under the European discipline (Enriques, 2013, p. 72 ff.; Castrataro, 2013).

The technique permits to collect investments up to a certain amount, as well as to obtain relevant tax incentives.

The offer document is functional to the necessary understanding of the key information by investors, to the indication of the risks (concerning the subscribed shares, software development, or start-up) and to the comparison among different offers. It is surely peculiar, if compared to the

[45]The document is the product of a consultation period (December 3, 2015–January 11, 2016), whose results and detailed comments are available at *www.consob.it.*

[46]"On May 16, 2016, the much-anticipated era of retail crowdfunding officially began [also] in the United States". While it is far too early to pass judgment on the long-term prospects of the project, this element certainly brings new issues on the topic, as proved by the extremely recent article by Green, J.M., Coyle, J.F. (2016). *Crowdfunding and the Not-So-Safe SAFE*, available at *ssrn.com.* The difference is mainly pointed out by Pinto, M. (2015). L'equity based crowdfunding in Italia al di fuori delle fattispecie regolate dal "Decreto Crescita", *Società*, p. 818 ff., fn. 10–23.

[47]For a comparative analysis of the American and Italian regulation, *see* Hanks, S., Romeno, G., Tonelli, E. (2014). Madness of Crowds or Regulatory Preconception?: The Weak Foundation of Financial Crowdfunding Regulation in the US and Italy, *Eur. Company Law*, vol. 11, n. 5, pp. 237–252; Lynn, J., De Buysere, K. (2014). *Crowdfunding Laws Based on Global Jurisdiction*, Dresner, S. (ed.) *Crowdfunding. A Guide to Raising Capital on the Internet* (John Wiley & Sons, Hoboken, New Jersey) p. 203 f. and p. 209; Bowman, B. (2015). A Comparative Analysis of Crowdfunding Regulation in the United States and Italy, *Wisconsin Int'l Law J.*, vol. 33, p. 318 ff. and Passador, M.L. (2015). *Crowdfunding:* tra profili di adeguatezza ed appropriatezza e profili di applicabilità all'aumento di capitale. *Banca, impresa e società*, p. 287 ff.

The study of a sample of financial return crowdfunding platforms active in Europe confirms that, notwithstanding being a largely unregulated activity, its role is now undeniable (Borello, G., De Crescenzo, V., Pichler, F. (2015). The Funding Gap and the Role of Financial Return Crowdfunding: Some Evidence from European Platforms. *J. Internet Banking and Comm.*, vol. 20, n. 1, pp. 1–20).

prospectus — which is the offer document characterizing the IPOs and, in general, the world of equity — since it is *not* linked to the Consob greenlight.

Once the operation is concluded, best practices should be implemented, documents should be periodically available, members should be informed of the rights within which they can exercise their rights, shedding some light on pricing and creating an alternative market (Pais *et al.*, 2014, p. 22).

Due to the need to rearrange the entire financial regulation, the 2013 Consob Regulation was also amended. Some cornerstones remain unchanged: the Register, available through the Consob website, is still divided into an "ordinary" section, where operators duly authorized by Consob are indicated, after verification of the fulfillment of the requirements; and a "special" section, where banks and investment firms duly authorized to provide the relevant services already communicated to Consob are registered (Art. 5 of the Italian Crowdfunding Regulation, as amended in 2016). Some features were changed, specifying the new offerors and simplifying the most burdensome aspects of previous regulations: the subscription by professional investors and the procedures for orders' execution. As to the former, a reduction in transaction costs was *de facto* possible to facilitate the online costs, in case portal managers intend to carry out the checks necessary for evaluating the appropriateness of the transaction directly (Art. 13, paragraphs 5-*bis* and 5-*ter*). Thus, in accordance with the Advice of the supervisory Authority,[48] banks are almost substituted for all offers concluded through companies. From an organizational point of view, opt-in involves a number of economical charges and structural impacts for the managers of portals, only partially offset by investment certainty and by the speed with which individual transactions are concluded, without any duplication of activities.

In case managers do not intend to provide this service, banks and investment firms will continue to verify the appropriateness in charge of order execution, even though by canceling any overlap between the Markets in Financial Instruments Directive (hereinafter, MiFID regulation) and the

---

[48]ESMA considered possible for platforms to operate within the scope of the exemption, but that the requirement to transmit orders only to authorized firms, which is a precondition under Art. 3 "is likely to mean involving an additional party for which the business model would not otherwise have a need, while the requirement introduced by national law in one jurisdiction to provide advice makes it mandatory to provide a service that is otherwise often not part of platforms' business models. We understand that the intention behind this is to ensure investor protection. However, this could also raise costs for platforms and hence potentially investors" [European Securities and Markets Authority, 2014. *Advice*, at pp. 19–20].

questionnaire that clients are invited to complete. As to the latter, the chance to extend the use of such a tool to professional investors "on demand", classified according to the MiFID, by the intermediaries of whom they are clients, and to professional investors "in supporting innovation", identified by the supervisory authority on the basis of objective criteria, has been positively evaluated (Article 24, paragraph 2 and 2-*bis*).

All in all, besides clarifying the definitions of "offeror" and "professional investors" (Art. 2),[49] detailing the authorization procedure for registration (Art. 7), strengthening the supervisory activities on the managers operating in MiFID exemption (Art. 8),[50] specifying the evaluation carried out by the managers of the platform (Art. 13, paragraphs 5-*bis* and 5-*ter*), the information concerning their activity (Arts. 14-15-16) and the quantitative limits (Art. 17, paragraph 3), the 2016 version of the Regulation spoke out strongly on the key elements outlined above.

Both the June 2015 and the December 2015 consultation phase discussed the effectiveness of the provision of a compulsory subscription by competent and experienced investors. In light of the difficulty of identifying who is in a position to advise the market about the fact that the offer is attractive at least to a person who acquired the necessary experience to support innovative companies, notwithstanding the high risk, the Commission further investigated the issue, by analyzing data on business angels. Given that Consob is only allowed to dictate standards aimed to ensure "the subscription by professional investors or special categories of investors identified by the same", the above-mentioned further category is created, calibrated on the specific nature of operations to be carried out. This is the major reason related to the amendment of Article 24, paragraph 2, which also covers the category of "supporting innovation investors", who possess the necessary requirements of integrity that normally members who control managers and administrators possess, characterized by a value of the portfolio of financial instruments, including cash deposits, of the amount (at least) of €500,000 (identical to one of the three requirements needed for professional investors "on request"). The ability to bear losses will be accompanied by requirements

[49]Such changes represent a mere adaptation of the secondary regulations to the ones introduced in the primary legislation.

[50]This exemption regime and the separation between the portal and the entity that manages the organs adopted in the primary legislation will also be assessed in the light of the ESMA's Guidelines and of the European Commission's decisions on regulatory developments, in order to prevent the creation of a competitive disadvantage for Italian portals if compared to their European competitors.

proving the experience and expertise in the field.[51] As a result of discussions carried out, two major profiles shall be considered: "financial institutions", in case they are investing VC or shareholder loans, and "keepers", if they participate as administrators, thanks to their skilled experience and strong network. Since these figures may also represent a tradeoff, it is suggested to link the "financial capacity" to one of the following requirements: (i) at least three investments, in the last two years, in share capital or shareholder loans in innovative start-ups or SMEs for an amount of €15,000 or even more each; (ii) at least 12 months of cooperation in corporate positions as executive director in an innovative start-up or SME (excluding the offeror). In order to assess the quality of "supporting innovation" investors, the interested party shall submit to the manager the documents confirming the possession of the requirements. The financial capacity of the investor can be proved demonstrated by one or more statements from banks or investment companies, required to show that the value of the portfolio of financial instruments, including cash deposits, of the investor/client is larger than €500.000. In addition, to demonstrate their skills, a document derived from the Companies' House database will show that the individual held that position for a minimum period of a year. Alternatively, should the experience not be linked to the performance of social roles, but to its financing, the investor will have to certify each investment made in the last two years by the innovative start-up or SME. The documents should be made freely available to allow anyone the right to exercise such power, with particular regard to pricing, and on the content of the declarations confirming the *status* of "professional client", received pursuant to Art. 24, paragraph 2-*bis*.

Furthermore, the reduction of the number of shares to be mandated at 2.5% does not appear feasible, since it diminishes the amount excessively and, thus, denies any potential benefits. In the same sense, the previous subscriptions by the same offerors appear to be in conflict with the law, requiring the "signing of a share of the available tools".

Lastly, a new principle (Art. 11-*bis*) is introduced, in light of the fact that in the Italian market only a minority of portals (if compared to the number of authorizations granted) seem to be fully operational. Thus, it provides that

[51] Kim, K. (2013). *The Experts in the Crowd: the Role of Reputable Investors in a Crowdfunding Market*, College Park, MD, available at *ftp.zew.de* and Kim, K., Viswanathan, S. (2016). *The 'Experts' in the Crowd: The Role of 'Expert' Investors in a Crowdfunding Market, TPRC 41: The 41st Research Conference on Communication, Information and Internet Policy,* available at *ssrn.com*.

managers shall begin the performance of the asset within six months after the date of the relevant authorization and those who stopped the activities should resume them within six months or, alternatively, they will be obliged to ask for another authorization. Nevertheless, there is no definition of the "interruption" that requires to repeat the authorization process. In fact, it is self-evident that the lack of offers may neither necessarily result in an interruption nor be regarded as if no commencement date occurred. In fact, offer pipelines, scouting activities, and offer evaluations might require a timing which is not fully in line with Art. 11-*bis*. As a consequence, in a (hopefully not-too-distant) future revision of the document, the beginning or the interruption of the activities shall be approved by directors or, in the case of inaction, by the supervisory Authority.

3. Conclusion and Future Perspectives

Despite its growing importance since the first project was successfully funded in 2009, and a large-scale action by the US Congress to encourage such source of capital for new ventures, very little is known about this new fundraising method and it has arguably received less attention than necessary. It is still uncertain if crowdfunding may be an alternative or a complementary source of funding to traditional VC or angel investments, or, alternatively, if they will be swept away by crowdfunding.[52] Some elements showed that crowdfunding loosens geographical constraints among funders, but the effect of geography on project funders is less clear.[53] Other authors document the concentration of crowdfunding in the same main centers as VC activities or in different areas.[54] There is no doubt that crowdfunding tends to present geographical drivers as VC investments — that acted as a key player in the institutional environment of technology entrepreneurship, also as alternative fundraising sources — and to be concentrated in the same areas, making the

[52]Cf. Mollick, E.R. (2013). *Swept Away by the Crowd? Crowdfunding, Venture Capital, and the Selection of Entrepreneurs*, available at *ssrn.com* and Id. (2014). The Dynamics of Crowdfunding: An Exploratory Study. *J. Business Venturing*, vol. 29, n. 1, pp. 1–16.
[53]See Agrawal, A., Catalini, C., Goldfarb, A. (2011). *Friends, Family, and the Flat World: The Geography of Crowdfunding*, available at *www.law.northwestern.edu*
[54]Cf. Mollick, E.R. (2013). *Swept Away by the Crowd? Crowdfunding, Venture Capital, and the Selection of Entrepreneurs*, available at *ssrn.com* and Id. (2014). The Dynamics of Crowdfunding: An Exploratory Study. *J. Business Venturing*, vol. 29, n. 1, pp. 1–16.

provision of capital for any location through the internet easier, but not mitigating the effects of geography on project founders.[55]

A study about factors affecting the success of crowdfunding campaigns was edited by Millick in 2014, taking into account multiple variables linked to the goals and categories of projects, funding amounts, number of funders, communication strategies, and presence of the company on social networks. Nevertheless, there is a link between the success of crowdfunding and the quality of the project, large social network community, cultural and geographical affinity between funders and fundraisers.

That link helped the crowdfunding phenomenon, whose main peculiarity is the broad geographic dispersion of investors that finance projects all over the world, to gather in recent years, a considerable amount of attention in the business arena and platforms tremendously raised their power and collected a huge amount of money. Online platforms helped investors overcome offline frictions, by gathering information, monitoring financing phases, and providing the right inputs which are really important for investors to be involved in early stage ventures, reducing the costs of all activities that appear to be particularly sensitive to distance.[56]

Although, in general, it can be pointed out that the phenomenon does not (and will not)[57] fall within the harmonized disciplines, this chapter addressed the principles governing the entire system; secondly, then, it focused on the rules of conduct requiring an *ad hoc* test of adequacy and appropriateness and it investigated their reflection on equity crowdfunding, by expressing a clear opinion in favor of the application of rules also by banks and investment companies with regard to financial instruments issued via online platforms by innovative start-ups.

---

[55]Gompers, P., Kovner, A., Lerner, J. (2009). Specialization and Success: Evidence from Venture Capital, *J. Economics and Management Strategy*, vol. 18, n. 3, pp. 817–844. For the purposes of the present work, it would be impossible to delve into the details of all the empirical investigations related to crowdfunding, but the figures presented in the cited literature show how crowdfunding functions evolved in these years, and especially the change of size occurred in the past five years, thus giving readers some sense of the importance of this new funding model.

[56]The study presented by Agrawal, A., Catalini, C., Goldfarb, A. (2011). *Friends, Family, and the Flat World: The Geography of Crowdfunding*, available at *www.law.northwestern.edu* emphasizes how the average distance between artists, entrepreneurs, and investors is about 5.000 km, suggesting a reduced role for spatial proximity even though local investors, that who appear to be less responsive to decisions, provide the majority of the funds in the early stages of financing.

[57]*Report on Crowdfunding in the EU Capital Market Union*, available at *europa.eu*.

This approach is perfectly consistent with the provisions contained in the original MiFID, as well as with its amended version. Needless to say, technological developments in the trading of financial instruments present both opportunities and challenges. Although the effects are generally perceived as positive for market liquidity and surely improved market efficiency, specific regulatory and supervisory measures — which are necessary to adequately address the possible threats to the orderly functioning of markets — have been identified. This is why the upcoming version of the Directive, MiFID II,[58] maintains the optional exemption from the legislature, which amended the requirements for Member States to carry out their activities, strengthening those concerning entities making use of this exemption.

In spite of the recent introduction of art. 32, Law Decree n. 179/2012, Consob, the Ministry of Economic Development, Istat, and several Universities actively integrated their skills and prepared an annual report on the ecosystem of innovative start-ups, related to the implementation of individual measures and to the achievement of the objectives underpinning the Decree. With the aim of assessing the impact of policies adopted in terms of growth, employment, new business culture, innovation, and internationalization, these organizations focus their attention on the suitability of equity crowdfunding platforms, based on the responses to questionnaires, in order to act as alternative channels for the financing and development of innovative start-ups through the offer of additional services for start-ups and investors, such as: (i) the publication of regular information on milestones achieved or periodic reports on the progress of society; (ii) the provision of mechanisms to facilitate the flow of information between the innovative start-ups and

[58]The daily application of MiFID led to its further implementation, to primarily increase factors such as transparency and control of markets; then, to raise awareness as to the quality of the choices made by customers; to refine its elements, in particular, with regard to the category of services provided to investors, as well as to the mechanism of protection and efficient competitiveness of trading platforms. With reference to the choices, see also European Commission (2011). *Commission Staff Working Paper. Impact Assessment, Accompanying the document: Proposal for a Directive of the European Parliament and of the Council on Markets in Financial Instruments [Recast] and the Proposal for a Regulation of the European Parliament and of the council on Markets in Financial Instruments*, available at *ec.europa.eu*.

The prime importance of the provision of advisory services in investments also reverbs in the process of revision of MiFID, which calls for the completion of a working model that is even more focused on the obligations of disclosure and ongoing information, especially if the consultancy operates "on an independent basis", forcing intermediaries to envisage the customer a wide range of financial products among which she can wittingly choose.

investors or between investors and their participation in companies; (iii) the possibility of adopting mechanisms which are relevant to esteem the financial instruments purchased through the portal or to fix the prices for each transaction.

Among the most recent evolutions of the discipline, there are two horizons on which to focus: a national and a European one.

First of all, the issue must be considered in light of the Law Decree n. 3/2015, applied to innovative start-ups, preferring a renewed definition of them, including companies which are resident in a Member State of the European Union or States that signed the European Economic Area, provided that they have their headquarters or branches in Italy.

It must necessarily focus on innovative SMEs as well. Indeed, the Decree presents an introduction specifically linked to bonds and securities by non-listed companies; then, in June 2013, the Consob Regulation specifically adopted rules designed to compare the level of investor protection with the risks associated to the offers of risk capital through online platforms. Thus, Italy is the first country to adopt an organic framework regarding equity crowdfunding, albeit non-exhaustive, an opportunity for SMEs to create and develop high-tech, a starting point for the current economic and social crisis. The Investment Compact Decree, then Law 33/2015, n. 3, also introduced a new type of SME in its Art. 4, the so-called innovative SMEs. The companies to which crowdfunding is applicable are not listed in regulated markets or multilateral trading facilities, do not operate for more than 7 years, benefit from simplification and reduction of initial burdens, rules for alternative forms of remuneration, such as stock options, and are mentioned in a specific section of the Company Register, pursuant to Art. 2188 of the Italian Civil Code. The one and only requirement is the possession of at least two requirements among: the ownership of a patent or software filed with the SIAE biotechnological or industrial investment in research; the development and innovation investment of at least 3% of the difference between selling and production costs; the employment of highly qualified people (*i.e.* PhD students, postdocs, and researchers) at least equal to 20% of the workforce. Inevitably, such an additional category should be taken into account (in particular Articles 5-*undecies*, 50-*quinquies*, and 100-*ter* of the Italian Consolidated Law on Finance).

In the meantime, relevant assessments in the broader European context cannot be ignored: the European Commission and ESMA, in fact, addressed that issue with constant perseverance from its very beginning, mainly through public consultations, studies, and focus groups among experts, regulators, or stakeholders. Among them, the growing interest of the market in the rise and impact of new technologies is underlined by the Communication "Unleashing the Potential of Crowdfunding in the European Union", COM (2014) 172 final, dated March 27th, 2014.

The recent *Opinion*, published by ESMA in December 2014, addressed the applicable European norms in the field of crowdfunding to the competent National Authorities (§3), and its *Advice* — primarily directed to the Commission, Parliament, and Council — highlighted the first issues of regulatory convergence and supervision in Europe, show — once again — the considerable potentialities of the instrument. Steven Maijoor, Chairman of the Supervisory Authority, clearly states that "ESMA's aim is to enable crowdfunding to reach its potential as a source of finance, while ensuring that risks to users of crowdfunding platforms are identified and addressed in a proportionate and convergent way across the EU. We believe that there are benefits both for investors as well as for platforms by operating inside rather than outside the regulated space".

In light of recent Directives, such as AIFMD (§§63–78), and Regulations, such as the ones connected to funds for venture capital (EuVECA), and social entrepreneurship (EuSEF) (namely, n. 345/2013 and n. 346/2013) (§§ 8, 79–83), the European Authority focused on investment-based crowdfunding (§§ 5, 14, 15), both analyzing the evolution of business models, platforms, and risks associated with each activity.

The European Commission is nowadays investigating the potential and the risks of this almost new and growing form of finance, as well as the national legal structure applicable to it, in order to identify whether there is a value added in European level policy action in this domain. A series of ever-changing norms, increasingly involving the European Commission and the Authorities, both in the interests of uniform rules with respect to a composite patchwork and of a strong supervision over the conduct of States were also considered by the EBA. In February 2015, legislators were recommended to clearly define the applicability of the existing regulations on the model of lending-based crowdfunding, thus, ensuring the required level of confidence to market participants. The EBA opinion identified a number of risks and possible regulatory approaches in order to avoid regulatory arbitrage, which might be raised by the fact that crowdfunding platforms do not fall under the definition of credit institutions. Indeed, in doing so, it clearly protected competition within the boundaries of European market and created a genuine convergence of rules and supervision of such activities (EBA, 2015).

Policy makers have been convinced of the potential of crowdfunding to help small businesses and entrepreneurs with creative ideas and started to develop specific rules to tackle such phenomenon, on the one hand, by stimulating it through simple rules and procedures, as well as with shortened period of time and tax incentives; on the other hand, by preserving investor protection against fraud and illegal actions to which unaccredited investors may be exposed (Hooghiemstra, 2016).

Both the findings and the considerations expressed on the phenomenon surely show additional, promising roads for its future, and some interesting outcomes are open to further discussions.

In the future, the above-described situation will surely be modified (i) from an empirical, economic point of view, through an active debate with the operators and the use of both private and public financings, which would also benefit from the growing number of observations since the limited data collected might be scarce to draw a tough conclusion; (ii) from a regulatory and supervisory point of view, through the use of insights, guidelines, or interpretations agreed upon with the supervisory Authority, as well as with European norms. Therefore, further analysis is needed to catch market developments and the latest updates as to the legal regulation on the topic.

Equity crowdfunding is still at its early stage, so data available are few and not homogeneous [Hagedorn, 2016]. Each platform, in fact, has different formats and some information is missing. Despite these limits, this study could be useful for both entrepreneurs and platforms, in order to focus the attention on the elements of pitches, related to the underlying quality of the projects, that result to be more attractive. For further researches, it would also be interesting to analyze if the same attractive variables affect the long-term success of the company and if an effective harmonization of rules in the EU would be also legally positive.[59] In fact, without imposing excessive burdens on companies, such harmonization — towards which the latest documents published by the European Commission seem to move, developing specific rules that are autonomous from the general ones in the

[59]Torris, T. (2015). *It's a Long Way to European Equity Crowdfunding Regulation, in Crowdfundinsider*, available at *www.crowdfundinsider.com*. A focus on how each country is doing things differently from the U.S. and the rest of Europe is really interesting: the study of comparative regimes turns to be extremely helpful since each one offers a lesson for the others in taking different approaches. See, CrowdfundingHub (2016). *Current State of Crowdfunding in Europe. An Overview of the Crowdfunding Industry in more than 25 Countries: Trends, Volumes and Regulations*, available at *www.sbs.ox.ac.uk*.

field of investment services — would at least partially eliminate the strict barriers as for as cross-border business are concerned.

References

Agrawal, A., Catalini, C., and Goldfarb, A. (2011). *Friends, Family, and the Flat World: The Geography of Crowdfunding*, available at *www.law.northwestern.edu.*

Ahlers, G. K., Cumming, D., Guenther C., and Schweizer, D. (2012). *Signaling in Equity Crowdfunding*, available at *papers.ssrn.com.*

Allegreni, F. (2015). *Anche la Spagna ha il suo regolamento sul* crowdfunding. *Molto più flessibile del nostro*, consultabile all'indirizzo *crowdfundingbuzz.it.*

Alois, J. (2015). *Scan Updates. Crowdfunding Regulations, Crowdcube Spain Shares Perspective*, available at *www.crowdfundinsider.com.*

Alt, R. and Puschmann, T. (2016). *Digitalisierung der Finanzindustrie: Grundlagen der Fintech-Evolution.* Berlin-Heidelberg.

Alvisi, P. (2014). *Equity Crowdfunding*: uno sguardo comparatistico. *Rivista di diritto bancario.*

An, J., Quercia, D., and Crowdcroft, J. (2014). *Recommending Investors for Crowdfunding Projects*, World Wide Web: Proceedings of the 23rd international conference (WWW '14), pp. 261–270.

Armour, J. and Enriques, L. (2015). *Financial Disruption*, available at *www.iast.fr*, p. 5.

Assonime (2013). Commento alla Circolare n. 11/2013, *Riv. soc.*, p. 776 ff.

Bechter, C., Jentzsch, S., and Frey, M. (2011). From wisdom of the crowd to crowdfunding. *J. Commun. Comput.*, 8, pp. 951–957.

Belleflamme, P., Lambert, T., and Schwienbacher, A. (2011). *Crowdfunding: Tapping the Right Crowd*, Center for Operations Research and Econometrics, Louvain-la-Nouve, Belgium.

Bogost, I. (2012), *Kickstarter: Crowdfunding Platform Or Reality Show?*, available at *bogost.com.*

Borello, G., De Crescenzo, V., and Pichler, F. (2015). The funding gap and the role of financial return crowdfunding: Some evidence from European platforms. *J. Internet Banking and Comm.*, 20(1), pp. 1–20.

Bowman, B. (2015). A comparative analysis of crowdfunding regulation in the United States and Italy. *Wisconsin Int'l Law J.*, 33, p. 318 ff.

Brabham, D. C. (2013). *Crowdsourcing.* Cambridge, MA: MIT Press.

Brooks, A. W., Huang, L., Kearney, S. W., and Murray F. (2014). Investors prefer entrepreneurial ventures pitched by attractive men. *Proceedings of the National Academy of Sciences of the United States of America*, vol. 111, n. 12, pp. 4427–4431, available at *hbs.edu.*

Brush, C., Carter, N. M., Gatewood, E. J., Greene, P. G., and Hart, M. (2011). *The Diana Project: Women Business Owners and Equity Capital: The Myths Dispelled. Babson College Center for Entrepreneurship Research Paper No. 2009-11*, available at *ssrn.com.*

Brydon, J. *et al.* (2012). *Private equity crowdfunding*, 6 ff., available at *academia.edu.*

Bschor, B. (2015). EBF calls for Fairer Fintech Regulations, *Int'l Financial Law Rev.*

Buhrmester, M., Kwang, T., and Gosling, S. D. (2011). Amazon's mechanical turk. A new source of inexpensive, yet high-quality, data?, *Perspect. Psychol. Sci.*, 6(1), pp. 3–5.

Busuioc, M. (2013). Rule-Making by the European Financial Supervisory Authorities: Walking a Tight Rope. *Eur. Law J.*, 19(1), p. 111 ff., available at *astrid.eu.*

Capelli, I. (2014) *Brevissime considerazioni sull'*equity based crowdfunding, available at *www.dirittobancario.it.*

Capelli, I. (2014). L'*equity based crowdfunding* e i diritti del socio. *Orizzonti del diritto commerciale.*

Capriglione, F. (2016). Prime riflessioni sulla MiFID II (Tra aspettative degli investitori e realtà normativa). In V. Troiano, R. Motroni (eds.), *La MiFID II. Rapporti con la clientela — regole di* governance *— mercati.* Padua: Cedam.

Carter, S., Shaw, E., Lam, W., and Wilson, F. (2007). Gender, entrepreneurship, and bank lending: The criteria and processes used by bank loan officers in assessing applications. *Entrepreneurship Theory Practice*, 31(3), pp. 427–444.

Castrataro, D. (2013). *Il Crowdfunding in Italia Open hearing "Indagine conoscitiva sul Crowdfunding.* Rome: Consob.

Castrataro, D. and Pais, I. (2014). *Analisi delle piattaforme italiane di crowdfunding, Italian Crowdfunding Network.*

Castrataro, D. and Wright, T. (2014). *Crowdfunding. Come finanziarsi online.* Milan: Green Books Editore.

Chishti, S. and Barberis, J. (2016). *The FinTech Book: The Financial Technology Handbook for Investors, Entrepreneurs and Visionaries.* NJ: Hoboken.

Collins, L. and Pierrakis, Y. (2012). *The Venture Crowd: Crowdfunding Equity Investment into Business*, available at *www.nesta.org.uk.*

Consob (2012). *Communication n. 12084516*, available at *www.consob.it.*

Consob (2014). *Practical Guide to test suitability and appropriateness*, available at *www.assosim.it.*

Cordova, A., Dolci, J., and Gianfrate, G. (2013). The bearable lightness of crowdfunding. Evidence from technology projects. In 4th *European Conference on Corporate R&D and Innovation.*

Cordova, A., Dolci, J., and Gianfrate, G. (2015). Crowdfunding: Towards the democratization of innovation financing. Archibugi, D., and Filippetti, A. (eds.), *Handbook of Global science, Technology and Innovation*, p. 249 ff.

Cordova, A., Dolci, J., and Gianfrate, G. (2015). The determinants of crowdfunding success: Evidence from technology projects. *Procedia. Social Behavioural Sci.*, 181, pp. 115–124.

Cosh, A., Cumming, D. J., and Huges, A. (2009). Outside entrepreneurial capital. *The Econom. J.*, 119(40), pp. 1494–1533.

CrowdfundingHub (2016). *Current State of Crowdfunding in Europe. An Overview of the Crowdfunding Industry in more than 25 Countries: Trends, Volumes and Regulations*, available at *www.sbs.ox.ac.uk.*

Crucil, A. (2014). La disciplina dell'*equity crowdfunding* in Italia: Emanato il regolamento Consob sulla raccolta di capitali di rischio da parte di *start-up* innovative, *Riv. soc.*, p. 1058 ff.

Cumming, D. J., Leboeuf G., and Schwienbacher A. (2015). *Crowdfunding models: Keep-it-all vs. all-or-nothing*, available at *leeds-faculty.colorado.edu.*

Cumming, D. J., Leboeuf, G., and Schwienbacher, A. (2014). Crowdfunding Models: Keep-it-All vs. All-or-Nothing, *Finance Meeting Eurofidai — Affi Paper*, available at *ssrn.com.*

Danmayr, F. (2014). *Archetypes of Crowdfunding Platforms. A Multidimensional Comparison.* Berlin: Springer.

De Mari, M. (2010). *I "nuovi" poteri della Consob e la vigilanza sull'attività di intermediazione mobiliare,* D'Apice, R., *L'attuazione della MiFID in Italia.* Bologna: Il Mulino, p. 653 ff.

De Mari, M. (2015). *Product governance* e *product intervention* nella MiFID II: dalle regole di comportamento al controllo sui prodotti finanziari? *Riv. dir. impr.*

De Martin, J. C. (2013). *Crowdfunding*, le "collette" per il rilancio, *La Stampa.*

Di Lorenzo, L. (2016). *Crowdfunding* e *start up* innovative: tecnica redazionale, *Notariato*, p. 437 ff.

Di Majo, A. (1993). La correttezza nell'attività di intermediazione mobiliare, *Banca, borsa e tit. cred.*, I, p. 290.

Di Nella, L. (2016). Le regole comportamentali nella distribuzione di prodotti finanziari complessi. In Troiano, R. Motroni (eds.), *La MiFID II. Rapporti con la clientela — regole di* governance *— mercati*. Padua: Cedam, pp. 139–147.

EBA (2015). *Opinion on Lending-Based Crowdfunding*, n. 3.

Enriques, L. (2013). *La disciplina italiana uccide il* crowdfunding *nella culla?*, available at *www.crowdfundingitalia.com*, p. 72 ff.

ESMA (2012). *Orientamenti su alcuni aspetti dei requisiti di adeguatezza della direttiva MiFID*, available at *www.esma.europa.eu.*

ESMA (2014). *Advice. Investment-based Crowdfunding*, n. 1560, at pp. 19–20, available at *www.esma.europa.eu.*

ESMA (2014). *Final Report. Technical Advice to the Commission on MiFID II and MiFIR*, available at *www.esma.europa.eu.*

ESMA (2015). *Final Report. Guidelines on complex debt instruments and structured deposits*, n. 1783, available at *www.esma.europa.eu.*

European Commission (2011). *Commission Staff Working Paper. Impact Assessment, Accompanying the document: Proposal for a Directive of the European Parliament and of the Council on Markets in Financial Instruments [Recast] and the Proposal for a Regulation of the European Parliament and of the council on Markets in Financial Instruments*, available at *ec.europa.eu.*

European Commission (2016). *Commission Staff Working Document. Crowdfunding in the EU Capital Markets Union*, available at *ec.europa.eu.*

Fairlie, R. and Marion, J. (2012). Affirmative action programs and business ownership among minorities and women. *Small Business Econom.*, 39(2), pp. 319–339.

FCA (2014). *Policy Statement 14/4: The FCA's regulatory approach to crowdfunding over the internet, and the promotion of non-readily realisable securities by other media*, available at *www.fca.org.uk.*

Feedman, D. M. and Nutting, M. R. (2015). *A Brief History of Crowdfunding Including Rewards, Donation, Debt, and Equity Platforms in the USA*, available at *www.freedman-chicago.com.*

Fioruzzi, P. and Saccone, F. (2016). *Revisione del regolamento sulla raccolta di capitali di rischio da parte di* startup *innovative tramite portali* on line, available at *www.consob.it.*

Funk, A. S. (2016). Institutions influencing the evolution of crowdfunding in China a review of the world bank report on crowdfunding's potential for the developing world. In Brüntje, D., Gajda, O. (eds.), *Crowdfunding in Europe: State of the Art in Theory and Practice.* Berlin: Springer, p. 125 ff.

Gerber, S. (2012). The Jobs Act Signing: A Giant Step for Entrepreneurship in America, *Time.*

Giancarlo, J. C. (2016). *The Digitization of Financial Markets. The Harvard Law School Forum on Corporate Governance and Financial Regulation*, available at *blogs.law.harvard.edu.*

Gierczak, M. M. (2016). Crowdfunding Outlining the new era of fundraising. In Brüntje, D., Gajda, O. (eds.), *Crowdfunding in Europe: State of the Art in Theory and Practice.* Berlin: Springer, p. 7 ff.

Giudici, P. (2008). *La responsabilità civile nel diritto dei mercati finanziari.* Milan: Giuffrè.

Glaeser. E. L. and Shleifer, A. (2001). Not for profit entrepreneurs. *J. Public Econom.*, 81(1), pp. 99–115.

Gompers, P., Kovner, A., and Lerner, J. (2009). Specialization and success: Evidence from Venture capital. *J. Econom. Manage. Strategy*, 18(3), pp. 817–844.

Green, J. M. and Coyle, J. F. (2016). *Crowdfunding and the Not-So-Safe SAFE*, available at *ssrn.com.*

Guerzoni, M. *et al.* (2016). The emerging crowdfunding market in Italy: Are "the crowd" friends of mine?. In Brüntje, D., and Gajda, O. (eds.), *Crowdfunding in Europe: State of the Art in Theory and Practice* Berlin: Springer, p. 87 ff.

Hagedorn, A. *et al.* (2016). The financing process of equity-based crowdfunding: An empirical analysis. In Brüntje, D., Gajda, O. (eds.), *Crowdfunding in Europe: State of the Art in Theory and Practice.* Berlin: Springer, p. 71 ff.

Hanks, S., Romeno, G., and Tonelli, E. (2014). Madness of crowds or regulatory preconception?: The weak foundation of financial crowdfunding regulation in the US and Italy, *Eur. Company Law*, 11(5), pp. 237–252.

Harms, M. (2007). *What Drives Motivation to Participate Financially in a Crowdfunding Community?*, available at *ssrn.com.*

Hazen, T. L. (2012). Crowdfunding or Fraudfunding? Social networks and the securities laws — Why the specially tailored exemption must be conditioned on meaningful disclosure. *North Carolina Law Rev.*, 90(5), pp. 1735–1770.

Heminway, J. (2016). *Securities Crowdfunding and Investor Protection, DICE Report*, Summer 2016, vol. 14, n. 2, pp. 11–15.

Herbst, J. (ed.) (2015). *A Practitioner's Guide to MiFID II.* London: Sweet & Maxwell.

Hooghiemstra, S. N. (2016). The perfect regulation of crowdfunding: What should the European regulator Do?. In Brüntje, D., and Gajda, O. (eds.), *Crowdfunding in Europe: State of the Art in Theory and Practice.* Berlin: Springer, p. 135 ff.

Kappel, T. (2009). Ex ante crowdfunding and the recording industry: A model for the U.S.? (The Grammy Foundation Entertainment Law Initiative 2009 Writing Competition). *Loyola of Los Angeles Entertainment Law Rev.*, 29(3), pp. 375–385.

Keeper, T. (2016). *Equity Crowdfunding in New Zealand: A Progressive Experiment. Victoria University of Wellington, Centre for Accounting, Governance and Taxation Research School of Accounting and Commercial Law Working Paper No. 103*, available at *ssrn.com.*

Kelly, E. (2015). *Germany to Introduce Crowdfunding Restrictions*, available at *www.sciencebusiness.net.*

Kim, K. (2013). *The Experts in the Crowd: The Role of Reputable Investors in a Crowdfunding Market*, College Park, MD, available at *ftp.zew.de.*

Kim, K. and Viswanathan, S. (2016). *The 'Experts' in the Crowd: The Role of 'Expert' Investors in a Crowdfunding Market, TPRC 41: The 41st Research Conference on Communication, Information and Internet Policy,* available at *ssrn.com.*

Klöhn, L., Hornuf, L., and Schilling, T. (2016). *Financial Contracting in Crowdinvesting: Lessons from the German Market*, available at *ssrn.com/abstract=2839041.*

Kourilsky, M. L. and Walstad, W. B., (1998). Entrepreneurship and female youth: Knowledge, attitudes, gender differences, and educational practices. *J. Business Venturing,* 13(1), pp. 77–88.

Kozinets, R., Hemetsberger, A., and Schau, H. J. (2008). The wisdom of consumer crowds: Collective innovation in the age of networked marketing. *J. Macromarket.*, 28, p. 339 ff.

Lambert, T. and Schwienbacher, A. (2010). *An Empirical Analysis of Crowdfunding, Crowdsourcing*, available at *www.crowdsourcing.org*.

Laroppe, J.-C., Le financement participatif aux États-Unis: une réglementation récente sur un phénomène de société déjà ancien. *Revue Int. Serv. Fin./Int'l J. Financial Services (RISF),* 4, pp. 67–73.

Laroppe, J.-C., Le financement participatif en Italie: une réglementation, première en date, récemment modifiée, *Revue Int. Serv. Fin. / Int'l J. Fina. Services (RISF),* 4, pp. 31–36.

Lee, A. (2015). Why Regulators must adapt to Fintech, *Int'l Financial Law Rev.*

Lener, R. (2014). *Crisi dei mercati finanziari e* corporate governance: *poteri dei soci e tutela del risparmio*, Rome: Minerva Bancaria.

Lener, R. and Lucantoni, P. (2012). Regole di condotta nella negoziazione degli strumenti finanziari complessi: *disclosure* in merito agli elementi strutturali o sterilizzazione, sul piano funzionale, del rischio come elemento tipologico e/o normativo?. *Banca, borsa e tit. cred.*, I, p. 369 ff.

Lucantoni, P. (2011). Le regole di condotta. In Lener, R. (ed.), *Diritto del mercato finanziario.* Turin: Utet, p. 117 ff.

Lynn, J. and De Buysere, K. (2014). Crowdfunding laws based on global jurisdiction. In Dresner, S. (ed.) *Crowdfunding. A Guide to Raising Capital on the Internet.* Hoboken, New Jersey: John Wiley & Sons, p. 203 ff.

Macey, J. R. and Miller, G. P. (1991). Origin of the blue sky laws. *Texas Law Rev.*, 70(2), p. 347 ss.

Manchanda, K. and Muralidharan, P. (2014). Crowdfunding: A new paradigm in startup financing, *Global Conf. Business Fin. Proce.*, 9(1), pp. 369–374.

Manzi, V. (2013). Il fenomeno del crowdfunding e del social lending: Caratteristiche operative e profili contrattuali. In F. Capriglione (ed.), *I contratti dei risparmiatori.* Milan: Giuffrè, p. 394 ff.

Marabini, F. (2016). Analisi dei possibili profili anticoncorrenziali della normativa italiana in tema di *crowdfunding, Contratto e impresa*, p. 552 ff.

Marelli A. (2016). What makes crowdfunding projects successful 'before' and 'during' the campaign?. In Brüntje, D., Gajda, O. (eds.), *Crowdfunding in Europe: State of the Art in Theory and Practice.* Berlin: Springer, p. 175 ff.

Marom, D., Robb, A., and Sade, O. (2016). *Gender Dynamics in Crowdfunding (Kickstarter): Evidence on Entrepreneurs, Investors, Deals and Taste-Based Discrimination*, available at *ssrn.com*

Mazzarella, M. (2014). *Speech, 40th Anniversary of Consob*, Rome.

Miglietta, A., Parisi, E., Pessione, M., and Servato, F. (2013). Gli strumenti finanziari a supporto delle *start-up* innovative: Le opportunità offerte dal *crowdfunding, Sinergie Italian J. Manage.*, p. 494 ff.

Mollick, E. R. (2013). *Swept Away by the Crowd? Crowdfunding, Venture Capital, and the Selection of Entrepreneurs*, available at *ssrn.com.*

Mollick, E. R. (2014). The Dynamics of crowdfunding: An exploratory study. *J. Business Venturing*, 29(1), pp. 1–16, available at *ssrn.com.*

Moritz, A. *et al.* (2016). *Crowdfunding: A Literature Review and Research Directions*, Brüntje, D., Gajda, O. (eds.), *Crowdfunding in Europe: State of the Art in Theory and Practice.* Berlin: Springer, p. 25 ff.

Mosco, G. D. (2013). La nuova regolamentazione dell'*equity crowdfunding*, available at *www.crowdfundingitalia.com*, p. 9 s.

Nasrabadi, A. G. (2016). *Equity Crowdfunding: Beyond Financial Innovation* Brüntje, D., Gajda, O. (eds.), *Crowdfunding in Europe: State of the Art in Theory and Practice* (Springer, Berlin), p. 201 ff.

Ordanini, A. *et al.* (2011), Crowdfunding: Transforming customers into investors through innovative service platforms. *J. Service Man.*, 22(4), pp. 443–470, available at *didattica.unibocconi.it.*

Ordanini, A., Miceli, L., Pizzetti, M., and Parasuraman, A. (2011). Crowdfunding: Transforming customers into investors through innovative service platforms. *J. Service Manage.*, 22(4), pp. 443–470, available at *didattica.unibocconi.it.*

Otero, M. (1999). *Bringing development back into microfinance.* Latin America: ACCION International.

Pais, I., Perelli, P., and Spinelli, C. (2014). *Crowdfunding, La via collaborativa all'imprenditorialità* (Egea, Milan) p. 22.

Passador, M. L. (2015). *Crowdfunding:* tra profili di adeguatezza ed appropriatezza e profili di applicabilità all'aumento di capitale, *Banca, impresa e società*, p. 287 ff.

Passador, M. L. (2016). The Need for Suitability and Appropriateness in Crowdfunding Regulation, *Revue Int. Serv. Fin. / Int'l J. Financial Services (RISF),* 4, p. 37 ff.

Piattelli, U. (2013). *Il* Crowdfunding *in Italia. Una regolamentazione all'avanguardia o un'occasione mancata?* Turin: Giappichelli.

Pinto, M. (2015). L'equity based crowdfunding in Italia al di fuori delle fattispecie regolate dal "Decreto Crescita", *Società*, p. 818 ff.

Poissonnier, A. and Bévan, Q. (2016). *Crowdfunding et solidarité, Réalités Industrielles*, pp. 29–32.

Ramos, J. (2016). Crowdfunding and employment: An analysis of the employment effects of crowdfunding in Spain. In Brüntje, D., Gajda, O. (eds.), *Crowdfunding in Europe: State of the Art in Theory and Practice.* Berlin: Springer, p. 97 ff.

Robinson, S. (2015). *FCA Reviews: Crowdfunding Regulation Regime*, available at *www.nabarro.com.*

Rossi, M. (2014). The new ways to raise capital: An exploratory study of crowdfunding. *Int'l J. Fin. Research*, 5(2), pp. 8–18.

Schäfer, M. S., Metag, J., Feustle, J., and Herzog, L. (2016). Selling science 2.0: What scientific projects receive crowdfunding online? *Public Understanding of Science.*

Schwartz, A. A. (2013). Crowdfunding securities. *Notre Dame Law Rev.*, 88(3), pp. 1457–1477.

Schwartz, A. A. (2015). The nonfinancial returns of crowdfunding. *Rev. Banking and Fin. Law*, 34(2), pp. 565–580.

Sepe, M. (2016). *La MiFID II e i Mercati.* V. Troiano, R. Motroni (eds.), *La MiFID II. Rapporti con la clientela — regole di* governance — mercati. Padua: Cedam.

Sfameni, P. and Giannelli, A. (2015). *Diritto degli intermediari e dei mercati finanziari.* Milan: Egea.

Tchotourian, I. (2016). Le financement participatif au Canada: Légalisation récente du financement en capital. *Revue Int. Serv. Fin./Int'l J. Fin. Services (RISF)*, 4, p. 74 ss.

Torris, T. (2015). *It's a Long Way to European Equity Crowdfunding Regulation, in Crowdfundinsider*, available at *www.crowdfundinsider.com.*

Troisi, A. (2014). Crowdfunding e mercato creditizio: Profili regolamentari. *Contr. impr.*, II, p. 519 ff.

Valanciene, L. and Jegelviciute, S. (2013). Valuation of crowdfunding: Benefits and drawbacks. *Economics Managem.*, 18(1), pp. 39–48.

Vass, T. (2013). *Adding a Geographical Component to an Equity Crowdfunding Project (paper III)*, available at *crowdsourcing.org*.
Wiens, J. (2014). State Equity Crowdfunding Policies Hold Promise, *Forbes*, available at *www.forbes.com*.
Wroldsen, J. (2017). Crowdfunding investment contracts. *Virginia Law Business Rev.*, 11, available at *ssrn.com*.

Chapter 25

Terrorism and Resilience: How Family Businesses Respond to Terrorist Activity

Luis Alfonso Dau

Northeastern University 309 Hayden Hall,
Boston MA 02115 1-803-381-6204
L.Dau@northeastern.edu

Elizabeth M Moore

Northeastern University
918 Renaissance Park, Boston MA 02115
1-508-369-4034
e.moore@northeastern.edu

Katharine Petrich

Northeastern University
928 Renaissance Park, Boston MA 02115
1-206-714-7646
petrich.k@husky.neu.edu

Max Abrahms

Northeastern University
215F Renaissance Park, Boston MA 02115
1-617-373-2796
m.abrahms@northeastern.edu

Abstract

The purpose of this chapter is to explain the impact of global security threats on the performance of family firms. A large body of theoretical and empirical research analyzes the impact of terrorism on governments, but it is also important to understand the effects on other types of actors. This is among the first analyses of terrorism's effects on family business. We argue that family businesses tend to be more resilient to terrorist activity due to superior social capital stemming from the strength of their social ties and motivation to persevere. Further, we propose that family firm performance in the aftermath of terrorist activity is positively moderated by institutional quality, which can both mitigate contextual complications and provide stability. A case study analysis of Indian family firms is developed to substantiate these arguments.

1. Introduction

There is growing scholarly interest in understanding the outcomes of various global security threats (Abadie and Gardeazabal, 2008). Terrorist attacks have been the focal point since the September 11, 2001 attacks (Abrahms, 2006). Although a definitional consensus continues to elude resolution, a terrorist attack is generally defined as the "premeditated use, or threat of use, of extra-normal violence to obtain a political objective through intimidation or fear directed at a large audience" (Sandler and Enders, 2002). Observers do not have direct access into the minds of terrorists, so their motives are often unclear. It is widely assumed, however, that at a minimum terrorist groups seek to inflict severe psychological damage to disrupt normalcy for citizens (Anderton and Carter, 2004). To date, the scholarly literature has tended to focus on the impacts of terrorism on governments, largely ignoring the effects on firms. This study is the first serious examination of how terrorist activity impacts firms, a unit fundamental to economies and societies more generally throughout the world. Our theory suggests that family firms are unusually resilient to terrorism, conditional on certain institutional factors.

This analysis extends our understanding of several related research programs. Political scientists have conducted numerous studies on how terrorism affects our polities. Although the theoretical literature emphasizes the rationality of terrorism for non-state actors given their constraints (Kydd and Walter, 2006; Pape, 2003), the main empirical finding contends that governments are actually surprisingly resilient, seldom acceding to the perpetrators' political demands (Abrahms 2011; Cronin 2002; Getmansky and Sinmazdemir 2012). Research on the consequences of terrorism has paid short shrift, however, to the economic outcome, including to firms. This chapter also contributes to the conversation centered around family firms and their specific toolkits and advantages relative to non-family firms (Lin *et al.*, 2007). Additionally, our analysis expands the burgeoning research program on the subject of resilience (Aldrich, 2012). Finally, this chapter broadens current understandings about the benefits of institutions for international stability (Keohane, 2005). Specifically, we consider the impact of institutional quality on firm performance, when stable institutions are perhaps most needed yet disrupted. Finally, this chapter offers important insights for policy makers and managers on how different firms respond to the terrorism threat.

The results of our case study indicate that family businesses are more resilient to terrorist activity than non-family businesses. Family businesses possess unique toolkits and have social capital from their social ties and underlying motivations. This allows these businesses to persevere amidst a terrorist attack. Moreover, the research yields that this relationship is moderated by the institutional context that the firms exist in. We suggest that institutional quality lessens the difficulties and challenges presented by terrorist activity, and provides family firms with the stability and order to maintain financial resilience.

Structurally, the chapter will unfold with an overview of how terrorism affects the global economy, especially as this relates to strategies available to family firms to maximize their safety and chances of survival. A theoretical examination of the logic behind our propositions, including corresponding logic models, will follow. Case-study evidence and descriptive statistics from India will be provided to examine our main arguments, as a form of plausibility probe (Levy, 2008). The chapter concludes by discussing the implications of the research for both policy makers and managers.

2. Family Business Ventures and Security Threats in a Globalizing World

2.1. *Family business ventures*

Family firms are arguably the oldest form of economic organization in history (Dyer, 2006). A family firm is defined as a firm where blood, or marriage lines, influence decision-making strategies (Baker *et al.*, 2014). To be a family firm, the bloodline must be multigenerational for the family influence to become well established. For publicly listed firms, the bloodline must account for at least 32% of the voting rights. For privately held firms, 50% of the voting rights must be held by the bloodline (Center for Family Business, 2016). Family businesses account for over 30% of the registered companies across the globe and range from small corner stores to large multinational publicly listed organizations; and in light of globalization and the ease of moving across borders, this number is on the rise (Aguilera *et al.*, 2008).

The three-circles business model dominates family business research (Mandelman and Zlate, 2012). The three circles are family, business, and ownership, and each represents an important subsystem within a family firm (Sharma *et al.*, 1997). Family incorporates all members of the family and can either be members of the family involved in the business, involved in ownership, or neither. Business refers to participants actively involved in the business. These members are either family or non-family. Ownership included both familial and external owners. As these firms operate, all three circles intersect and show the dynamics of family firms, and highlight the seven different positions an individual can be in within the model based on the amalgamations listed above (Banalieva and Eddleston, 2011). It is important to highlight that individuals within the family can belong to each of the three different circles and can oscillate between them. However, this moving between circles, and the interconnected relationships, present both obstacles and toolkits that are unique to family firms (Chrisman *et al.*, 2010, 2012). Additionally, it is critical to note that non-family members can oscillate within the business and ownership circles and cannot avoid working with the family circle.

Unlike other firms, family businesses face a unique set of problems stemming from conflicts in values, goals, and actions among family members (Gedajlovic and Carney, 2010). Unlike in non-family firms, personality clashes and personal sentiments can oftentimes arise. In other words, the social relationships and dynamics in the family often translate directly into business activity. If this social network is not kept organized and clearly delineated, it can threaten the family business (Zellwege *et al.*, 2012). This can emerge through family rifts or disagreements. If a controversy runs deep enough, it can have lasting impacts on the business structure and the three circles (Villalonga and Amit, 2006; Zellwege *et al.*, 2012).

Family firms not only have unique obstacles, however, they also have unique assets and toolkits that separate them from non-family firms (Yan and Sorenson, 2006). Family position typically establishes leadership, resulting in longevity and higher levels of organizational stability than in non-family firms (Villalonga and Amit, 2009). Commitment and an increased personal stake in the success of the firm are additional benefits of family firms. Families that operate in a business together are typically more accountable to the organization and have an increased stake in the success of the firm (La Porta *et al.*, 1999; Sirmon *et al.*, 2008). This is not to say that other firms do not have high levels of commitment, but rather that due to the familial ties, accountability and relationship strength is higher within family firms (Jiang and Peng, 2011). Finally, family firms benefit from a long-term outlook and flexibility. Family firms are rooted in multigenerational traditions and are often a large source of income for the family as a whole (Lim *et al.*, 2010; Miller *et al.*, 2010). As a result, family firms have long-term goals to ensure family economic stability for current and future generations and are more willing to adapt to different environments to ensure the success of the business over time (Schulze *et al.*, 2001; Werner *et al.*, 2005). In other words, if the business is an extension of your family, you are more likely to maintain the business and work for its success at all costs.

As family firms continue to rise and diffuse across the globe, it is critical to understand the advantages and disadvantages that family firms face. In light of globalization, scholars must examine how different institutional environments and changing global norms impact different business governance structures.

2.2. *Security threats and terrorist activity*

Terrorism is not a new phenomenon. Rather, it has been a common asymmetric form of conflict for centuries (Boot, 2013). There are many operationalized definitions attached to terrorism, but for the purpose of this study, terrorist activity must fulfill each of the three criteria developed by the Global Terrorism Database, the most comprehensive source on terrorist activity globally. The three criteria are: (1) seek to attain a political, economic, religious, or social goal, (2) intend to coerce, intimidate, or convey a message to an audience beyond the immediate victims, and/or (3) occur outside the context of legitimate warfare activities (LaFree and Dugan, 2009; National Consortium for the Study of Terrorism and Responses to Terrorism (START), 2015). All three criteria must be realized before an act will constitute a terrorist act.

Over the past few decades the world has experienced many changes as a result of globalization, including evolution of global norms, increases in international organizations and institutions, and spikes in security threats and terrorism (Alexandroff and Cooper, 2010; Vezirgiannidou, 2013). Terrorism is driven by globalization, in part because it increases the number and accessibility of both targets and weapons, but also because driving ideologies can be easily communicated transnationally (Cronin, 2003). Economic and organizational resiliency from a firm perspective merits academic conversation and attention in light of globalization and the rise of terrorist activity (Frey, 2009).

It is critical to note that terrorism happens in both developed and developing countries, and like other features of globalization, can either be national or transnational (Wilkinson, 1996, 2001). Further, historical trends suggest that terrorist activity increases in times of major international paradigmatic or ideological shifts (Cronin, 2002). Based on this pattern, the recent rise in terrorist activity follows logically as the world is currently undergoing a change in the global normative structure. Although this broader discussion is outside the scope of this chapter, it is important to emphasize that globalization is forcing states to realize that sovereignty is perhaps giving way to interconnectedness and global networks across nations.

This chapter pertains to both international and domestic terrorism, which are increasingly difficult to distinguish in our interconnected world (Abrahms, 2007). Terrorist organizations often target "illegitimate" targets, such as civilian populations, nonmilitary infrastructures, businesses, and public spaces (Kydd and Walter, 2006). Further, traditional conventional force structures are afflicted by common structural limitations and are thus inefficient reaction tools to mitigate the consequences of terrorist activity in the modern strategic environment, leaving domestic actors such as businesses exposed (Finlan, 2003). Due to the reality that terrorism occurs outside of the scope of traditional conflict space, commonly referred to as a 'war zone,' nonmilitary responses and coping mechanisms (forms of resiliency) are of critical importance (Coaffee and Rogers, 2008). Resiliency and coping mechanisms represent the way that different microlevel actors respond to terrorist activity and attempt to survive (Carp, 2010).

Although a multitude of coping mechanisms exist ranging from psychological to material mechanisms, it is critical to point out the impact that the domestic environment can have on these mechanisms. Institutions are the rules and guidelines that help shape the way different actors operate within a society (North, 1990). Different contexts and markets have different levels of institutional quality based on enforcement, stability of the government, effectiveness and functionality of policies, trust in the government, etc. (Dau, 2016; Khoury *et al.*, 2014). Institutional level plays a large role in behavior of micro-actors within a country. Higher institutional quality levels reduce cheating and encourage that rules are followed (Swank, 2002). Conversely, lower levels of institutional quality result in lack of enforcement mechanisms to mitigate cheating and breaking the rules (Tiberghien, 2014). Additionally, however, institutional quality impacts the level of resiliency and efficiency in dealing with crises scenarios and rebounding from damage (Berke and Campanella, 2006). Higher institutional quality results in stable and clear policies for rebuilding infrastructure postconflict. Further, it encourages governments to have structures in place to provide economic and physical security measures for all actors within in (Busenitz *et al.*, 2000). Lower levels of institutional quality lack these features. The results can be seen through the different speeds and manners in which countries responded after the global market crash of 2008. Countries with higher levels of institutional quality suffered but rebounded economically within an average of 15–18 months (Lambert, 2011; Nabli and Bank, 2011). Many countries with lower institutional quality levels are still in the process of economic recovery (Chowdhury, 2013). Institutions and levels of institutional quality, then, have an impact on resiliency.

3. Family Business Resiliency Amidst Global Security Risks

As a result of decades of globalization, the economic and political distances between countries have shrunk (Bhagwati, 2004). Further, nations are forced to deal with the increased flow of people, products, and capital across borders, as well as the subsequent pressures that each of these imposes on different actors (Crane, 2008; Dau *et al.*, 2016a, 2016b). These increased cross-border flows have both negative and positive consequences (Dau *et al.*, 2016c). One such negative consequence is that it often facilitates global security threats. In today's world, terrorist organizations and other non-state actors have proven to be serious obstacles for nation states and the actors within them, such as businesses (Cronin, 2002). From a scholarly perspective, it is critical to examine the impacts of these global security threats in an effort to better understand ways that both governments and individual actors can combat their adverse effects. For the purpose of this chapter, family businesses will be posited as one type of domestic level actor that is seriously impacted by terrorist, and other violent non-state actor, activity. The purpose of this chapter is to understand the unique toolkit that family businesses have that makes them more resilient to terrorist activity in different institutional contexts. The following will serve as a theoretical exploration of the connection between global security risks and family business resiliency in a globalizing world.

3.1. *Family firm's increased resiliency*

As previously mentioned, terrorist activity, both domestically and internationally, is on the rise (National Consortium for the Study of Terrorism and Responses to Terrorism (START), 2015; Shelley, 2013). Likely due to a multitude of factors, globalization is promoting increased acts of non-state violence as normative environments remain in flux and uncertain (Haque, 2002; Nathan and Scobell, 2013). Further, as global norms continue to change, trends indicate that the potential for terrorist activity is heightened, and thus, this pattern is likely to continue. As a result, it is critical to understand the different outcomes of terrorist activity.

From an organizational perspective, terrorists aim to cause chaos and wreak havoc (Herzenstein *et al.*, 2015). A primary goal of terrorism is confusion and disruption in normalcy. Terrorists inflict added costs on governments to maintain stability and exert pressures on policy makers to be responsive and protective of their constituents (Kydd and Walter, 2006). In the aftermath of a terrorist attack, government personnel must reallocate both tangible and non-tangible assets to preserve order to maintain a semblance of stability (Blomberg *et al.*, 2011; Wilkinson, 2001). Money must be put into restructuring and rebuilding cities and inflicted areas, as well as to emergency relief projects (Stoddard, 2002). Increased military and police personnel must be deployed in order to provide protection to civilians (Davis, 2014). Finally, increased time and effort must be spent into resiliency planning in order to secure the conflict zone for the future (Berke and Campanella, 2006; Blackhurst *et al.*, 2011).

It is not only communities and infrastructure that suffers from a terrorist attack. Economic growth also suffers as a result of violent extremist activity (Prabha, 2016; Turk, 2004). Organizational needs and added infrastructural costs spill over to negatively impact economic activity (Levy, 2008). Money that would have been placed into economic programs and stimulus often has to be reallocated for community rebuilding post terrorist attack (Savun and Phillips, 2009). Additionally, violence and conflicts tend to produce a lack of trust that decreases spending from the host community (Blomberg *et al.*, 2011; Sending and Neumann, 2006). Simultaneously, it is important to highlight that not only do terrorist activities impact economic growth in terms of spending, but also in terms of cost for businesses. For example, if a terrorist successfully utilizes a bomb to destroy several local businesses, it is the responsibility of the owners to find the funds to rebuild storefronts, warehouses, machinery, and any lost products. Although governments may rally behind the businesses, and communities may support them, the cost burden falls largely on the owners (Kogut, 1985). As a result, local businesses suffer and take profit losses.

Are there corporate governance structures, however, that are better equipped to adapt to the chaos of terrorist activities? As previously outlined, family businesses have both unique advantages and disadvantages (Aguilera and Crespi-Cladera, 2012). Among the key advantages that family firms have in their toolkit are increased stability in leadership due to longevity, shared long-term goals, a greater stake in the firm, and increased flexibility as a result of familial ties (Benavides-Velasco *et al.*, 2013). Each of these advantages aids family firms in building increased resiliency to terrorist activity and allows them to maintain levels of profitability and stability in a post-terrorist host environment.

Stability in leadership can be conceptualized in a similar way as dictatorship is abstracted in the political science literature. Although a dictator, or head of a family firm, may not always make decisions that the entire family agrees with, there is certainty in the leadership and power structure that promotes stability in the overall organization (Boix and Svolik, 2013). Typically, family firms are organized around a central individual who is usually well respected within the family, or holds the most power (Brenes *et al.*, 2011). As a result, even if values conflict and clashes occur, outright dissent is less likely than in a flatter organizational model (Benavides-Velasco *et al.*, 2013; Ward, 1997). Further, this corporate governance structure promotes a solid foundation that is established and reinforced over many generations (Zachary, 2011).

In the context of terrorist activity, this highly stable corporate governance structure is desirable. Terrorists attempt to disrupt day-to-day activity and instill fear in civilians, businesses, and other actors (LaFree and Dugan, 2009; Crenshaw, 2009). In order to remain resilient to terrorist disorder, an organization must have strong leadership and authority from the top-down to mitigate the damaging effects of the attack (Berke and Campanella, 2006). Family businesses are thus well equipped to remain stable despite terrorist activity because of their strong leadership and longevity.

Long-term goals and increased stake in the business organization is a second facet of a family business that prepares the firm to remain resilient post-terrorist activity (Anderson and Reeb, 2003; Eddleston and Kellermanns, 2007). Unlike non-family firms, the goal of a family firm is to remain in operation indefinitely and provide many generations to come with an income flow (Yan and Sorenson, 2006). The longer the family business is in operation, the more generations it encompasses. Although this may seem obvious, it has an important influence on stakes in the business. The longer something has lasted, the more attached individuals become to it. This sentimentality is only increased when it relates to familial ties (Carney, 2005; Villalonga and Amit, 2006). Over time, entities and organizations become important solely because they have been in the family for generations, regardless of what the business is or how successful it is — they become part of the family narrative and identity (Sirmon and Hitt, 2003; von Schlippe and Frank, 2013). A pivotal component of legacy and memory is time (Neisser and Winograd, 1988). As a result, stakes are higher for family firms that have been around for more generations and have incorporated more family members. In short, family firms have more to lose because their personal histories and narratives increasingly become intertwined with the business (Carp, 2010; Fletcher *et al.*, 2012).

This facet of family business is a distinct advantage in post-terrorist climates. Terrorist attacks instill fear and threaten the very building blocks of humanity (Weinberg *et al.*, 2004). In a post-terrorist society, individuals are forced to face questions of mortality and must discern what is important to them and what is not (Schmid, 2004). A critical component of resiliency is maintaining personal narratives and not letting a terrorist organization strip those intimate details (Hartman and Winsler, 2006). Using this strain of logic in concert with the logic of increased stake and long-term goals from family business corporate structure, family businesses are thus typically better able to sustain themselves amidst terrorist activity because the business transcends merely a source of profit or even purpose, but rather represents a family narrative that individuals within the family will seek to preserve.

Further, the flexibility family firms possess also gives them an advantage of coping with terrorist activity and promoting organizational resiliency (Morck and Yeung, 2003). As previously established, family firms, unlike non-family firms, are significantly more flexible — meaning that individuals within the organization are willing to go above and beyond normal calls of duty because their family's livelihood and legacy is at stake (Royer *et al.*, 2008). Using similar familial logic, flexibility suggests that family members tend to put in extra hours of work, expose themselves to greater risks, and take on added costs for the sake of the overall well-being of the firm because the success of the firm represents both a source of income and identity for the entire family (Zachary, 2011). Flexibility represents the final unique tool that family firms have at their disposal that allows them to adapt and survive in a post-terrorist environment. In the aftermath of a terrorist act, family firms and the members that make up these firms will be more willing to put in added effort, resources, and time to remain resilient because business success represents personal family resiliency and well-being.

The preceding logic leads to the following proposition:

Proposition 1. *Family firms are better equipped to experience economic resiliency in a post-terrorist attack climate than non-family firms.*

3.2. *Resiliency in divergent institutional contexts*

Terrorist groups are rational actors that engage in classic cost-benefit analysis before they carry out acts of terrors or engage in violence (Crenshaw, 1981). Terrorist organizations recognize power vacuums left by gaps in governance and seek to fill those gaps in a variety of ways (Shelley, 2013). These organizations aim to accomplish one or more long-term goals through political violence (Meierrieks and Gries, 2013). Goals include, but are not limited to: regime change, resource absorption, social control, policy change, or status quo maintenance (Kydd and Walter, 2006). As a result, terrorist groups often have increased success in areas with lower institutional quality (Blackhurst *et al.*, 2011). As noted previously, institutional quality refers to the strength and effectiveness of government-level policies. This is not to suggest that terrorist activity does not have detrimental consequences in areas with high institutional quality, but rather that these consequences can be minimized and dealt within a more efficient timeline than in areas with lower institutional quality.

Further, it is important to reiterate that terrorist groups seek legitimacy and loyalty among certain populations, and gain this legitimacy by carefully selecting targets (Cronin, 2002). Common targets for violence and extortion are entrepreneurs and corporations, particularly through assassinations, robberies, and kidnappings, as these targets offer valuable assets in the form of capital, products, and infrastructure that terrorists can use to further their missions (Abrahms, 2012). As a result of increased targeting of businesses and entrepreneurs, terrorism negatively influences economic growth and stability of the state attacked, supporting their mission of demonstrating government illegitimacy (Blomberg *et al.*, 2011; Gaibulloev and Sandler, 2009). Literature and empirical research suggests that economic growth is inhibited by 1.5% annually for each attack per million people in an inflicted location (Herzenstein *et al.*, 2015).

As a result of the inverse relationship between terrorist activity and economic growth and stability, and propensity for terrorists to target corporations and entrepreneurs, levels of institutional quality have an impact on the economic resiliency at the firm level. Institutions are defined as the rules of the game and scholarship points out the benefits of strong institutional quality as it relates to rebounding from economic or conditional crises (Dau, 2011, 2012, 2013, 2016; North, 1990). As seen with the Great Recession of 2008, countries with higher institutional profiles were able to rebound from collapse in an average of 15–18 months, whereas countries with low institutional quality took significantly longer, as seen by the reality that some developing countries are still recovering (Beckworth, 2012).

From an economic standpoint, terrorist activity can be seen as another driver of economic collapse. In the time frame during and after the attack, the economy suffers. As a result, the businesses within those areas with higher institutional quality are more likely to rebound and remain economically resilient to terrorist attacks than those businesses in areas with lower institutional quality. We propose that the aforementioned relationship is thus moderated by the institutional quality of the country.

The preceding logic leads to the following proposition:

Proposition 2. *The relationship between family firm economic resiliency and terrorist activity is positively moderated by institutional quality.*

4. Contextual Evidence of the Resiliency of Family Firms Amidst Terrorist Activity in a Globalized World: An Examination of India

India represents an attractive, yet challenging, business environment. The third largest economy in the world according to the World Bank, it is also ranked 130th in the group's "Ease of Doing Business" annual report (ET Bureau, 2014; World Bank Group, 2017). In addition to a range of opaque and unclear rules and regulations, according to the Global Terrorism database, India has experienced an extremely high rate of terrorist activity since 1977. The country has had 9,940 discrete attacks from 270 different extremist actors (National Consortium for the Study of Terrorism and Responses to Terrorism (START), 2015).

Terrorism causes significant uncertainties that may be off-putting for international companies considering investment in India, allowing a window of opportunity for domestic Indian firms to respond to internal market demands (Jain, 2011). For example, despite experiencing 1305 instances of terrorism in 2012–2013, 74% of Indian family businesses expanded aggressively during 2013 fiscal year (PwC India, 2013). Like many developing states, India has a very high rate of family-owned businesses, accounting for roughly 80% of all Indian companies, producing approximately two-thirds of India's GDP, and employing 50% of the country's workforce (Helmuth *et al.*, 2011). According to the Family Business Index, 24 of the largest 500 family firms in the world are Indian, showing that family based firms are not only ubiquitous in India, they are also successful on the global scale (Center for Family Business, 2016).

Family businesses in India exhibit a high rate of social responsibility, both internally and externally. In part, this is due to an emphasis on "family values", such as teamwork, tenacity, and durability (Helmuth *et al.*, 2011; Tata Group, 2016). One of the primary reasons Indian family businesses have been so successful in the face of significant violent disruption is their emphasis on diversification across sectors, backed by resources to finance new ventures (Helmuth *et al.*, 2011). Because of the generational nature of a family run company, these firms tend to have a longer-term outlook, allowing for greater adaptability to fluctuations in the business environment (Helmuth *et al.*, 2011; Jain, 2011). As such, they are particularly successful in overcoming the disruption created by terrorist attacks.

To understand this particular resiliency of family firms, consider the Tata Group. The Tata Group spans over one hundred businesses in diverse sectors ranging from manufacturing to financial services (Helmuth *et al.*, 2011; Tata Group, 2016). Founded in 1868 by Jamsetji Nusserwanji Tata as a trading company, the Tata Group quickly diversified into a variety of industries. Over the twentieth century, the Group continued to expand, entering new sectors ranging from insurance to philanthropic education (Tata Group, 2016). Today, the Tata Group publicly emphasizes its pride in being a family company with ethical business practices and a commitment to the wider community (Tata Group, 2016).

In 2008, India experienced a historic high of terrorist attacks, jumping from 149 incidents in 2007 to 516 attacks in 2008 (National Consortium for the Study of Terrorism and Responses to Terrorism (START), 2015). This spike included the three-day assault on Mumbai in November, where 172 people were killed in multiple, coordinated attacks perpetrated by Lashkar-e-Taiba (BBC News, 2008). The Tata Group headquarters is located in Mumbai and owns one of the primary targets of the November attack — the Taj Mahal Palace and Towers (BBC News, 2008; India, 2015). The Group was thus directly impacted by the chaos surrounding the dramatic increase in instability. Nevertheless, they reported a record high of $70.8 billion in revenue for the year (Tata Group, 2016).

One of the major factors in this success is the Tata Group's commitment to their employees; for example, following the Mumbai terror attack, the Group implemented both short- and long-term response programs (Deshpande and Raina, 2011). They established grief and trauma counseling centers for the hotel's employees and guests within 24 hours, and later extended psychological counseling and social services to the wider Mumbai community (Rodrigues, 2010). Further, the Group committed to paying the salaries of employees killed during the attack to their families for the rest of the beneficiary's life (Dey, 2009; India, 2015). They have increased this financial commitment in several ways: by establishing a trust to provide immediate financial relief to the families of anyone killed in the attacks, regardless of their affiliation with the Tata Group, committing to financially support the education of the 62 children and dependents of those employees killed in the attack, and pledging to cover all medical expenses for employees and their families for the rest of their lives (Rodrigues, 2010).

Ratan Tata, chairman of the Tata Group at the time of the attacks, has been publicly lauded for his commitment to Tata employees and Mumbai in the wake of November 26, 2008, in part because of the company's financial assistance, but also because of his commitment to personally visiting all of his employees and their families who were hurt or killed during the strike (Dey, 2009; India, 2015). This "people centric" response was broadly seen as evidence of broad Indian values of loyalty, family, and resiliency, and helped the Tata Group consolidate domestic brand loyalty that lead to a profitable year, despite the significant disruption caused by terrorism (Deshpande and Raina, 2011; Rodrigues, 2010).

Demonstrating community commitment and social responsibility, beyond the immediate response to an attack, appears to be central to the Tata Group. Supported programs range from disaster relief to educational grants, to broader sustainable development initiatives, both domestically within India as well as internationally in the other states where the group has holdings (Tata Group, 2016). Examples of Tata Group community projects include disaster relief following the 2010 Chilean earthquake, educational and literacy programs in the United States, and 2004 tsunami relief in the Maldives (Deshpande and Raina, 2011). Each of the companies held under the Tata Group umbrella have institutionalized corporate social responsibility policies and recognize these initiatives as central to the success of the company (Deshpande and Raina, 2011).

Additionally, the Tata Group has been extremely active in creating and maintaining institutions within India, endowing a range of projects like the Indian Institute of Science, Tata Memorial Hospital, and the National Centre for the Performing Arts. Recognizing government absence or inability in certain sectors, the Tata Group has actively sought to fill these institutional vacuums. For example, following the Mumbai attacks in November 2008, the Tata Group established a variety of financial support and other resources for those impacted, regardless of their connection to any of the Tata Group companies (Dey, 2009; India, 2015; Rodrigues, 2010). They initially focused their programs on low income, underprivileged sectors, implementing projects ranging from welfare payments to microfinance to vocational training, with the goal of mitigating both the psychological trauma and deleterious economic effects on the wider Mumbai community (Rodrigues, 2010).

5. Discussion and Conclusion

The purpose of this chapter has been to understand the interplay between terrorist threats, institutional quality, and family firm economic resiliency in a globalized world. This chapter focuses on family businesses across different institutional environments and adds to the growing discussion on family businesses and their unique toolkits. By using firm performance and institutional stability in a globalizing world as focal points, this chapter teases out the advantages and divergent toolkits of family firms. This conversation is particularly relevant given the wave of anti-globalization sentiments spreading across borders, and the rising profile of the developing world. With no sign of slowing down, scholars and practitioners must examine the outcomes of globalization, both negative and positive.

Through the analysis of these dynamics and environments, this chapter provides several critical theoretical contributions that may serve as focal points for cross-disciplinary dialogue. The political science literature has examined the effects of terrorist activity on economic growth and development and suggested that terrorism has adverse effects for growth, especially in areas of low institutional quality (Gaibulloev and Sandler, 2009; Meierrieks and Gries, 2013). Further, these scholars have assessed resiliency mechanisms and explored factors that make communities and governments more or less resilient and able to survive and cope during and after a terrorist attack (Abadie and Gardeazabal, 2008). Limited attention, however, has been devoted towards understanding firm level resiliency and sustainability in the face of global security threats. Through an analysis of the relationship between family businesses, terrorist activity, and institutional stability, this chapter fosters a dialogue between corporate governance structure and resiliency-building post-terrorist attacks (Benavides-Velasco *et al.*, 2013; Hoffman, 2006). By combining these two sets of literatures in the context of economic resiliency and global sustainability, this chapter contends that family firms are better equipped to maintain firm performance than other firm types. This knowledge is imperative for both managers and policy-makers. From a practitioners' standpoint, cognitive, regulatory, and normative elements of the host community must be considered (Dau *et al.*, 2015). From a policy standpoint, resiliency mechanisms of all domestic actors need to be accounted for (Davis, 2014). This chapter provides a space to engage in both of these conversations.

Additionally, amidst the current political and security climate that the world is facing, projects which interweave global sustainability, resiliency, and institutional stability merit academic scholarship. As terrorist activity continues to rise simultaneously with anti-globalization sentiments, family business corporate governance structures may be able to mitigate the detrimental consequences of global security threats.

Despite the limitations of single-case study contextual evidence, this chapter propels further theoretical and empirical analyses on the arguments and propositions put forth. It may be intellectually beneficial to examine other regions that have more or less family-business activity such as Peru or México. Additionally, it may be fruitful to look at areas that host more terrorist activity such as Pakistan or Afghanistan. By examining areas that have varying amounts of family businesses and terrorist activity, other patterns of family business resiliency and institutional stability could help to further ease out and bridge the interdisciplinary gap between political science and international business. Another alternative route for examination would be to explore other firm types and their economic resilience to terrorist activity across different institutional contexts. This chapter argues that family businesses have unique toolkits that equip them for survival post-terrorist attack. Other types, however, may have divergent toolkits that merit academic and practitioner-based conversations. As political science and international business scholars continue to focus on questions of global sustainability and resiliency, it is imperative to examine the impacts of terrorist activity beyond the national security context.

Table 1. Summary of Main Findings

Findings	Argument
Family firms are better equipped to experience economic resiliency in a post-terrorist attack climate than non-family firms.	Because family firms have stability in leadership, long-term goals, and flexibility in operations they are better equipped to cope and ultimately survive in an environment that has experienced a terrorist attack.
The relationship between family firm economic resiliency and terrorist activity is positively moderated by institutional quality.	Because stronger regulatory quality provides clear and stable rules, they help lessen the negative impacts of a terrorist attack on firms. As such, they positively moderate the tools and capabilities already exhibited by family firms in the time of a terrorist attack.

References

Abadie, A. and Gardeazabal, J. (2008). Terrorism and the world economy. *Euro. Econom. Rev.*, 52(1), pp. 1–27.

Abrahms, M. (2006). Why terrorism does not work. *Int. Secur.*, 31(2), pp. 42–78.

Abrahms, M. (2007). Why democracies make superior counterterrorists. *Secur. Stud.*, 16(2), pp. 223–253.

Abrahms, M. (2011). Does terrorism really work? Evolution in the conventional wisdom since 9/11. *Defence Peace Econom.*, 22(6), pp. 583–594.

Abrahms, M. (2012). The political effectiveness of terrorism revisited. *Compar. Polit. Stud.*, 45(3), pp. 366–393.

Aguilera, R., Filatotchev, I., Gospel, H., and Jackson, G. (2008). An organizational approach to comparative governance in family firms. *Organiz. Sci.*, 19(3), pp. 475–492.

Aguilera, R. and R., C.-C. (2012). Firm family firms: Current debates of corporate governance in family firms. *J. Family Business Strategy*, 3(2), pp. 66–69.

Aldrich, D. P. (2012). *Building Resilience: Social Capital in Post-Disaster Recovery*. USA: University of Chicago Press.

Alexandroff, A. S. and Cooper, A. F. (2010). *Rising States, Rising Institutions: Challenges for Global Governance*. Washington, D.C.: Brookings Institution Press.

Anderson, R. C. and Reeb, D. M. (2003). Founding-family ownership, corporate diversification, and firm leverage. *J. Law Econom.*, 46, pp. 653–680.

Anderton, C. and Carter, J. R. (2004). *Applying Intermediate Microeconomics to Terrorism* Vol. 4, 1&. 12.

Baker, T., Gedajlovic, E., and Lubatkin, M. (2014). *Nations Across*, 36(5), pp. 492–504.

Banalieva, E. R. and Eddleston, K. (2011). Home-region focus and performance of family firms: the role of family vs non-family leaders. *J. Int. Business Stud.*, 42(8), pp. 1060–1072.

BBC News. (2008, November). How the Mumbai attacks unfolded. *BBC News*. Mumbai.

Beckworth, D. M. (2012). *Boom and Bust Banking The Causes and Cures of the Great Recession*. CA: Independent Institute.

Benavides-Velasco, C. A., Quintana-García, C., and Guzmán-Parra, V. F. (2013). Trends in family business research. *Small Business Econom.*, 40(1), pp. 41–57.
Berke, P. R. and Campanella, T. J. (2006). Planning for postdisaster resiliency. *The ANNALS Am. Acad. Polit. Soc. Sci.*, 604(1), pp. 192–207.
Bhagwati, J. (2004). *In Defense of Globalization.* New York: Oxford University Press.
Blackhurst, J., Dunn, K. S., and Craighead, C. W. (2011). An empirically derived framework of global supply resiliency. *J. Business Logis.*, 32(4), pp. 374–391.
Blomberg, S. B., Hess, G. D., and Tan, D. Y. (2011). Terrorism and the economics of trust. *J. Peace Res.*, 48(3), pp. 383–398.
Boix, C. and Svolik, M. W. (2013). The foundations of limited authoritarian government: Institutions, commitment, and power-sharing in dictatorships. *The J. Polit.*, 75(2), pp. 300–316.
Boot, M. (2013). *Invisible Armies: An Epic History of Guerrilla Warfare from Ancient Times to the Present.* New York: Liveright Publishing Corporation.
Brenes, E. R., Madrigal, K., and Requena, B. (2011). Corporate governance and family business performance. *J. Business Res.*, 64(3), pp. 280–285.
Busenitz, L. W., Gómez, C., and Spencer, J. W. (2000). Country institutional profiles: Unlocking entrepreneurial phenomena. *Acad. Manage. J.*, 43(5), pp. 994–1003.
Carney, M. (2005). Corporate governance and competitive advantage in family-controlled firms. *Entrepreneurship: Theory Practice*, 29(3), pp. 249–265.
Carp, J. M. (2010). Resiliency: The essence of survival in chaos. *Families Soc. The J. Contemporary Soc. Ser.*, 91, pp. 266–271.
Center for Family Business. (2016). *Global Family Business Index.* Database, St. Gallen: University of St. Gallen.
Chowdhury, A. (2013). The Great Recession, jobs and social crises: Policies matter. *Int. J. Soc. Econom.*, 40(3), pp. 220–245.
Chrisman, J., Chua, J., Pearson, A., and Barnett, T. (2012). Family involvement, family influence, and family-centered non-economic goals in small firms. *Entrepreneurship: Theory Practice*, 36(2), pp. 267–293.
Chrisman, J., Kellermanns, F. W., Chan, K. C., and Liano, K. (2010). Intellectual foundations of current research in family business: An identification and review of 25 influential articles. *Family Business Rev.*, 23(1), pp. 9–26.
Coaffee, J. and Rogers, P. (2008). Reputational risk and resiliency: The branding of security in place-making. *Place Branding Public Diplomacy*, 4(3), pp. 205–217.
Crane, D. (2008). Globalization and Cultural Flows/Networks. In *The SAGE Handbook of Cultural Analysis*. SAGE, pp. 774–778.
Crenshaw, M. (1981). The causes of terrorism. *Comparative Poli.*, 13(4), pp. 379–399.
Cronin, A. K. (2002). Rethinking sovereignty: American strategy in the age of terrorism. *Survival*, 44(2), pp. 119–139.
Dau, L. A. (2011). Reforms, multinationalization, and profitability. In L. Toombs (ed.), *AOMBest Paper Proceedings.*
Dau, L. A. (2012). Pro-market reforms and developing country multinational corporations. *Global Strategy J.*, 2(3), pp. 262–276.
Dau, L. A. (2013). Learning across geographic space: Pro-market reforms, multinationalization strategy, and profitability. *J. Int. Business Stud.*, 44(3), pp. 235–262.
Dau, L. A. (2016). Knowledge will set you free: Enhancing the firm's responsiveness to institutional change. *Int. J. Emerging Markets*, 11(2), pp. 121–147.
Dau, L. A., Moore, E. M., and Bradley, C. (2015). Institutions and international entrepreneurship. *Int. Business: Res., Teaching Practice*, 9(1), pp. 1–20.

Dau, L. A., Moore, E. M., and Soto, M. (2016a). Informal transnational political actors and emerging markets: Understanding entrepreneurship in a changing normative atmosphere. In *Entrepreneurship and Firm Performance*. New York: NOVA Publishers pp. 19–42.

Dau, L. A., Moore, E. M., and Soto, M. (2016b). The great recession and emerging market firms: Unpacking the divide between global and national level sustainability expectations. In *Lessons from the Great Recession: At the Crossroads of Sustainability and Recovery*. Emerald Group Publishing Limited, pp. 165–187.

Dau, L. A., Moore, E. M., Soto, M., and LeBlanc, C. (2016c). How globalization sparked entrepreneurship in the developing world: The impact of formal economic and political linkages. In B. Christiansen (ed.), *Corporate Espionage, Geopolitics, and Diplomacy Issues in International Business*, 1st ed. Hershey, PA: IGI Global, pp. 72–91.

Davis, L. E. (2014). Have we gone too far with resiliency? *Social Work Res.*, 38(1), pp. 5–6.

Deshpande, R. and Raina, A. (2011). The ordinary heroes of the Taj. *Harvard Business Rev.*

Deutch, J. (1997). Terrorism. *Foreign Policy*, 108, 10.

Dey, A. (2009). What Tatas did post 26/11. Asian Correspondent.

Dyer, W. G. (2006). Examining the “family effect” on firm performance. *Family Business Rev.*, 19(4), pp. 253–273.

Eddleston, K. and Kellermanns, F. W. (2007). Destructive and productive family relationship: A stewardship theory perspective. *J. Business Ventur.*, 22(4), pp. 545–565.

ET Bureau. (2014, April). India displaces Japan to become third-largest world economy in terms of PPP: World Bank. *The Econom. Times*. New Delhi.

Finlan, A. (2003). Warfare by other means: Special forces, terrorism and grand strategy. *Small Wars Insurgencies*, 14(1), pp. 92–108.

Fletcher, D., Melin, L., and Gimeno, A. (2012). Culture and values in family business-A review and suggestions for future research. *J. Family Business Strat.*, 3(3), pp. 127–131.

Frey, B. S. (2009). How can business cope with terrorism? *J. Policy Model.*

Gaibulloev, K., and Sandler, T. (2009). The impact of terrorism and conflicts on growth in Asia. *Econom. Polit.*, 21(3), pp. 359–383.

Gedajlovic, E. and Carney, M. (2010). Markets, hierarchies, and families: Toward a transaction cost theory of the family firm. *Entrepreneurship: Theory Practice*, 34(6), pp. 1145–1172.

Haque, M. S. (2002). The changing balance of power between the government and NGOS in Bangladesh. *Int. Polit. Sci. Rev.*, 23(4), pp. 411–435.

Hartman, S. and Winsler, A. (2006). *Resiliency. Encyclopedia of Human Development*, Vol. 3.

Helmuth, J., Angur, M., and Singh, A. (2011). An assessment of business failures: A comparative study between India and American family businesses, England Cambridge, pp. 1–11.

Herzenstein, M., Horsky, S., and Posavac, S. S. (2015). Living with terrorism or withdrawing in terror: Perceived control and consumer avoidance. *J. Consumer Behav.*, 14(4), pp. 228–236.

Hoffman, B. (2006). Inside Terrorism. *Polit. Sci. Quart.*, 114, 432.

India, T. of. (2015, December). 26/11 attack a life-changing moment for me: Ratan Tata. *The Times of India*. Vadodara.

Jain, V. (2011). Indian Entrepeneurship and Challenges to Growth. *Ivery Business J.*

Jiang, Y. and Peng, M. (2011). Are family ownership and control in large firms good, bad, or irrelevant? *Asia Pacific J. Manage.*, 28(1), pp. 15–39.

Keohane, R. O. (2005). *After hegemony: Cooperation and Discord in the World Political Economy*. USA: Princeton Press.

Kogut, B. (1985). Designing global strategies: Profiting from operation flexibility. *Sloan Manage. Rev.*, 27(1), pp. 27–38.

Kydd, A. H. and Walter, B. F. (2006). The Strategies of Terrorism. *Int. Security*, 31(1), pp. 49–80.

La Porta, R., Lopez-de-Silanes, F., and Shleifer, A. (1999). Corporate ownership around the world. *J. Fin.*, 54(1), pp. 471–517.

LaFree, G. and Dugan, L. (2009). Research on terrorism and countering terrorism. *Crime Justice*, 38(1), pp. 413–477.

Lambert, T. E. (2011). Falling income and debt: Comparing views of a major cause of the great recession. *World Rev. Polit. Economy*, 2(2), pp. 249–261.

Levy, Jack S. (2008). Case studies: Types, designs, and logics of inference. *Conflict Manage. Peace Sci.*, 25(1), pp. 1–18.

Levy, S. (2008). *Good Intentions, Bad Outcomes, Social Policy, Informality, and Economic Growth in Mexico*. Washington, D.C.: Brookings Institution Press.

Lim, E. N., Lubatkin, M., and Wiseman, R. M. (2010). A family firm variant of the behavioral agency theory. *Strategic Entrepreneurship J.*, 4(3), pp. 197–211.

Lin, C. H., Liou, D. Y., and Wu, K. W. (2007). Opportunities and challenges created by terrorism. *Technol. Forecast. Soc. Change*, 74(2), pp. 148–164.

Mandelman, F. and Zlate, A. (2012). Immigration, remittances and business cycles. *J. Monetary Econom.*, 59(2), pp. 196–213.

Meierrieks, D. and Gries, T. (2013). Causality between terrorism and economic growth. *J. Peace Res.*, 50(1), pp. 91–104.

Miller, D., Le Breton-Miller, I., and Lester, R. (2010). Family ownership and acquisition behavior in publicly traded companies. *Strat. Manage. J.*, 31, pp. 201–223.

Morck, R. and Yeung, B. (2003). Agency problems in large family business groups. *Entrepreneurship Theory Practice*, 27(4), pp. 367–382.

Nabli, M. K. and Bank, W. (2011). *The Great Recession and Developing Countries: Economic Impact and Growth Prospects*. Washington, D.C.: World Bank.

Nathan, A. J. and Scobell, A. (2013). Globalization as a security strategy: Power and vulnerability in the China model. *Polit. Sci. Quart.*

National Consortium for the Study of Terrorism and Responses to Terrorism (START). (2015). GTD Global Terrorism Database. In *START*, p. 63.

Neisser, U. and Winograd, E. (1988). *Remembering Reconsidered: Ecological and Traditional Approaches to the Study of Memory*. Cambridge, UK: Cambridge University Press.

North, D. C. (1990). *Institutions, Institutional Change and Economic Performance*. Cambridge: Cambridge University Press.

Pape, R. A. (2003). The strategic logic of suicide terrorism. *Am. polit. Sci. Rev.*, 97(03), pp. 343–361.

Prabha, K. (2016). Defining Terrorism. *Strat. Anal.*, XXIV(1), pp. 125–135.

Presented, A. D. and Basole, A. (2012). Knowledge, Gender, and Production Relations in India's Informal Economy, (February).

PwC India. (2013). *Family firm: The India Perspective*.

Rodrigues, C. (2010, February). Taj Public Service Welfare Trust. Tata Group.

Royer, S., Simons, R., Boyd, B., and Rafferty, A. (2008). Promoting family: A contingency model of family business succession. *Family Business Rev.*, 21(1), pp. 15–30.

Sandler, T. and Enders, W. (2002). *An Economic Perspective on Transnational Terrorism*, Vol. 4 No. 2. Tuscaloosa.

Savun, B. and Phillips, B. J. (2009). Democracy, Foreign Policy, and Terrorism. *The J. Conflict Resol.*, 53(6), pp. 878–904.

Schmid, A. P. (2004). Frameworks for Conceptualising Terrorism. *Teerorism Poli. Violence*, 16(2), pp. 197–221.

Schulze, W. S., Lubatkin, M., Dino, R., and Buscholtz, A. (2001). Agency relationships in family firms: Theory and evidence. *Organiz. Sci.*, 12(2), pp. 99–116.

Sending, O. J., and Neumann, I. B. (2006). Governance to governmentality: Analyzing NGOs, states, and power. *Int. Stud. Quart.*, 50(3), pp. 651–672.

Sharma, P., Chrisman, J. J., and Chua, J. H. (1997). Strategic management of the family business: Past research and future challenges. *Family Business Rev.*, 10(1), p. 35.

Shelley, L. I. (2013). *Dirty Entanglements: Corruption, Crime, and Terrorism.* (USA).

Sirmon, D., Arregle, J. L., Hitt, M., and Webb, J. (2008). The role of family influence in firms' strategic responses to threat of imitation. *Entrepreneurship: Theory Practice*, 32, pp. 979–998.

Sirmon, D. and Hitt, M. A. (2003). Managing resources: Linking unique resources, management and wealth creation in family firms. *Entrepreneurship: Theory Practice*, 27(4), pp. 339–35.

Stoddard, A. (2002). Humanitarian NGO's: Challenges and Trends. *Humanitarian Action and the "Global War on Terror"?: A Review of Trends and Issues*, pp. 25–36.

Swank, D. (2002). *Global Capital, Political Institutions, and Policy Change in Developed Welfare States.* New York: Cambridge University Press.

Tata Group. (2016). Tata Group — About Us.

Tiberghien, Y. (2014). An uncertain world: Rising powers, systemic risk and the role of institutions and entrepreneurship: A response to brantly Womack's "China's future in a multinodal world order." *Pacific Affairs*, 87(2), pp. 285–301.

Turk, A. T. (2004). Sociology of Terrorism. *Annual Review of Sociology*, 30(2004), pp. 271–286.

Villalonga, B. and Amit, R. (2006). How do family ownership, control and management affect firm value? *J. Fin. Econom.*, 80(2), pp. 385–417.

Villalonga, B. and Amit, R. (2009). How are U.S. family firms controlled? *Rev. Fin. Stud.*, 22(8), pp. 3046–3091.

von Schlippe, A. and Frank, H. (2013). The theory of social systems as a framework for understanding family businesses. *Family Relations*, 62(3), pp. 384–398.

Ward, J. L. (1997). Growing the family business: Special challengs and practices. *Family Business Rev.*, 10(4), pp. 323–338.

Weinberg, L., Pedahzur, A., and Hirsch-Hoefler, S. (2004). The Challenges of Conceptualizing Terrorism. *Terrorism Polit. Violence*, 16(4), pp. 777–794.

Werner, S., Tosi, H., and Gomez-Mejia, L. R. (2005). Organizational governance and employee pay: How ownership structure affects the firm's compensation strategy. *Strat. Manage. J.*, 26, pp. 377–384.

Wilkinson, P. (1996). How to combat the reign of terror. *New Statesman*, 9(414), pp. 12–14.

Wilkinson, P. (2001). Current and future trends in domestic and international terrorism: Implications for democratic government and the international community Paul Wilkinson. *Strat. Rev. Southern Africa*, 23(2), pp. 106–121.

World Bank Group. (2017). *Doing Business 2017: Equal Opportunity for All*. Washington D.C.

Yan, J. and Sorenson, R. (2006). The effect of Confucian values on succession in family business. *Family Business Rev.*, 19, pp. 235–250.

Zachary, R. K. (2011). The importance of the family system in family business. *J. Family Business Manage.*, 1(1), pp. 26–36.

Zellwege, T., Kellermanns, F. W., Chrisman, J., and Chua, J. (2012). Family control and family firm valuation by family CEOs: The importance of intentions for transgenerational control. *Organiz. Sci.*, 23(3), pp. 851–868.

Part VI

Stylized Facts and Asset Pricing

Chapter 26

Asset Pricing of Individual Stocks in Periods of Crisis

Marc Desban and Souad Lajili Jarjir

University Paris-Est, IRG (EA2354)

Abstract

The financial crisis of the last decade reopens the question of asset pricing for researchers and practitioners. In this study, we analyze common variation of stock returns during the financial crisis in the French market. We focus on the empirical disparities between the Capital Asset Pricing Model (1964) and the Fama-French three-factor model (1993) for individual stocks (336 firms). We show that market premium, size and value factors provide a better description of single stock returns in a specific period of high uncertainty. This new finding underlines the usefulness of *ad hoc* models for asset managers. Furthermore, small stocks underperform the market and, surprisingly, are less volatile than large capitalizations. Conversely, stocks with high book-to-market ratios outperform the market, making the existence of additional risk factors consistent. Nevertheless, both models have difficulty explaining the returns on small stocks. Finally, in line with Roll (1977), the choice of market proxy is essential.

1. Introduction

The existence of a positive and linear relation between risk and the expected rate of return on securities is one of the most basic assumptions made by financial academics over the past six decades. In terms of market efficiency, rational investors seek to optimize their investment by both maximizing return and minimizing risk (Markowitz, 1952). Academics and practitioners in the asset management industry try to predict or at least understand the determinants of assets' past variations. Finding relevant explanatory factors would enable time-series variables to be properly modeled, thus allowing market players to define and implement successful investment strategies.

Following the pioneering work of Markowitz (1952), finance has undergone considerable development since the early Asset Pricing Models of Sharpe (1964), Lintner (1965), Mossin (1966), and Black (1972). The financial community has responded positively to this innovation, which is highly relevant without being too complex to use. Its relative ease of use has no doubt contributed to its development and implementation worldwide. The Capital Asset Pricing Model (CAPM) seeks to compute the sensitivity of an asset relative to its risk, as measured by its beta to the market portfolio. The central feature of the model involves displaying the positive and linear relation between the expected rate of return and the systematic risk of an asset. A large body of research criticizes beta as unsatisfactory for explaining past returns from securities, as it relies on an unobservable market portfolio that includes every single existing asset. Roll (1977) argues that former methodologies used to empirically test the CAPM are basically incorrect. The only way to properly assess the model involves using real market portfolios. Secondly, the validity of the CAPM assumes that the market portfolio is constantly mean-variance efficient with respect to all investment opportunities. Subsequently, empirical studies underlined several unexpected results in the CAPM framework, and the assumption of an additional risk factor became relevant.

Ross (1976) presents Arbitrage Pricing Theory (APT), a multi-factor model using several explanatory variables to replicate past returns (in respect of the no-arbitrage condition). Merton (1973) offers an alternative to the CAPM, namely the Inter-temporal Capital Asset Pricing Model (ICAPM), a consumption-based asset-pricing model, which takes into account how investors act in the market. Despite its international success, the Sharpe–Lintner–Black model is still confronted by a (growing) number of empirical contradictions.

Nicholson (1960) reports that US stocks with a high earnings-to-price ratio have higher returns than the US market. Basu [1977], Stattman (1980), and Rosenberg *et al.* (1985) observe the same phenomenon with the book-to-market ratio. From those empirical observations, researchers anticipate what later is named the value effect. The remaining problem is still the selection of an appropriate criterion to proxy this effect. Chan *et al.* (1991) and Fama and French (1992) use the book value of common equity-to-market ratio as the proxy and thus as an explanatory variable of stock returns. Banz (1981), Chan and Chen (1991) report the existence of a negative relationship between the size of a firm and its return. Banz terms this the size effect and concludes that the capitalization of a stock may be a proxy for one or more true unknown factors correlated with size. If firms with poor outlooks have both low stock prices and a high book-to-market ratio, they would thus be penalized by a higher cost of capital due to higher expected returns from investors. Fama and French (1993) present a three-factor model integrating two parameters to proxy the value and size effects. They argue that stock returns can be empirically explained by three explanatory variables: market, book-to-market ratio, and size. The financial literature has produced a number of economic justifications for explaining size and value effects.

More recently, Fama and French (2012) explore size, value, and momentum anomalies in a sample of international stock returns by comparing global and local models. They reject global models in explaining regional returns and find that local models give acceptable descriptions of local average returns. Asness *et al.* (2014) document strong and consistent abnormal returns to quality. They propose a quality-minus-junk (QMJ) factor that goes long on high-quality stocks and shorts low-quality stocks. This QMJ factor earns significant risk-adjusted returns in the US and globally across 24 countries. Furthermore, Fama and French (2015a, 2015b, 2015c) suggest a five-factor asset pricing model that captures size, value, profitability, and investment patterns for average US stock returns. They find that the list of anomalies shrinks in the five-factor model, partly because anomalous returns become less anomalous and partly because the returns associated with different anomaly variables share factor exposures that suggest they are largely the same phenomenon.

Our paper contributes another piece to the puzzle bringing new hindsight on the French market. Our objective is to study the empirical disparities between the Sharpe–Lintner–Black CAPM and the Fama-French three-factor model for individual stocks over financial crisis and to determine whether one of them might be more accurate for the French market. Given the above, we raise the question of whether the three variables together (market, size, and value) provide a better description of individual stock returns in a crisis period. Testing models with individual stocks is the contribution of this study reinforced by the analysis of the French market during a specific period that is challenging for all pricing models.

The chapter gives updated results on the French market and yields unexpected conclusions, namely that big stocks are more volatile and pricing models are more accurate in periods of crisis. During a period of 324 weeks (October 2008 to October 2014) for 336 single French stocks based on weekly returns, the three-factor model can be considered as a better tool than the CAPM to describe time series variation of returns.

The paper proceeds as follows. Section 1 gives the theoretical background to the Sharpe–Lintner–Black and the Fama–French three-factor models. Section 2 introduces the data sets and applied methodology used. Section 3 summarizes the results of empirical tests and Section 4 presents main conclusions.

2. Literature Review

The CAPM underlines the positive and linear relation of a stock between its expected return and its systematic risk. Originally, the CAPM followed the mean–variance optimization framework first proposed by Markowitz (1952). The large body of empirical work on CAPM is generally inconclusive and fails to account for the anomalies unexplained by the vanilla CAPM (there are various CAPMs). Of the various criticisms, the most well-known was developed by Fama and French who, in a series of papers, proposed the existence of additional risk factors as a pertinent hypothesis. Basu (1977) analyzes several portfolios based on book-to-market ratio (and controlled for market betas) and observes significant abnormal returns. Similar results are also reported by Rosenberg *et al.* (1985) and DeBondt and Thaler (1987).

Chan *et al.* (1991) observe the phenomenon in the Japanese market. Basu (1977) concludes that it is reasonable to expect that the ratio might explain excess returns as compensation for additional risk, omitted in the original CAPM. At a theoretical level, Basu tacitly accepts as consistent the hypothesis of the existence of an additional risk factor. For Ball (1978), the ratio could be a catch-all proxy for unnamed factors in expected returns. He warns that the tests made on market efficiency must be implemented with due precautions. These anomalies could be attributable either to lack of market efficiency or to a misspecification of the asset pricing model. The value effect still appears easily detectable empirically, but remains difficult to measure with a well-defined criterion. For instance, Novy-Marx (2013) reports that the profitability ratio (measured by gross profits to assets) produces approximately the same results as book-to-market in predicting the cross-sectional difference of average stock returns. Even though there is great uncertainty as to which indicators to use, book-to-market ratio is still the principal proxy used in the literature. Several studies report that the beta of the original single-factor model bears little relation to small stock returns (Reinganum, 1981; Breeden *et al.*, 1989; Fama and French, 1992). Banz (1981) suggests that small (big) companies have higher (lower) returns than the market, terming this the size effect. On the US market, Reinganum (1981) finds that the smallest firms corresponding to the lowest 10% percentile outperform the highest 10% by +19.20% per annum. Brennan *et al.* (1998), Amihud (2002), Pastor and Stambaugh (2003), Hou and Moskowitz (2005), Acharya and Pedersen (2005), Sadka (2006), and Ibbotson *et al.* (2013) report that the size effect could be an indirect proxy of a hidden liquidity effect. Small firms are less liquid and therefore (must) provide a higher return to offset their transaction costs. Chan *et al.* (1985) acknowledge that small stocks may over-react in response to changes in the economic environment. Their study shows that small companies are generally marginal firms which have lost a significant part of their market value due to poor past performance and mostly are highly leveraged with debt. Chan *et al.* (1985) suggest that the risk factors such as debt leverage or default risk would be better if they were economically verified, rather than simply using market capitalization to proxy the effect. This said, there are indications that the size effect identified in 1981 by Banz tends to disappear. Dichev (1998) analyzes Chan and Chen's assumption, in which the effect might be a dependent variable of financial distress. He specifies that the distress factor is related to the probability of bankruptcy. Dichev studies US market from 1981 to 1995 and concludes that bankruptcy risk is not related to higher returns, implying that the size effect is not economically explained. Campbell *et al.* (2008) state that value and size effects are proxies for a distress premium. It is important to underline that even if the size effect was first detected in the US market, it has been confirmed in a number of studies using different data sets. Eleswarapu and Reinganum (1993) and Amihud (2002) detect no additional risk premium regarding size over the periods 1980–1990 and 1980–1997 in the US market. Horowitz *et al.* (2000) even note that big stocks on average outperformed small companies between 1979 and 1995. Dimson and Marsh (1999) report an anomaly in the returns related to size, where micro caps outperformed bigger ones by +4.1% per annum between 1955 and 1983. However, microcaps underperformed big stocks by −2.4% between 1983 and 1997. Reinganum (1999) generalizes the phenomenon in noting that big stocks outperform smaller ones during economic contractions. More recently, the robustness of the size effect does not appear strong enough to resolve the data-mining issue. *Is the size effect dead*? becomes a relevant question which will be debated (van Dijk, 2011; Israel and Moskowitz, 2013; Chordia *et al.*, 2014; McLean and Pontiff, 2016). However, a reversal of the size effect during economic contractions does not mean that small individual stocks do not generate higher returns than their respective beta suggests, which is a specific problem linked to the capacity of a model to compute risk and return. We demonstrate in this study that big-beta assets mainly concern big stocks, consistently with Frazzini and Pedersen (2014). Small stock returns are not necessarily higher than those of big stocks, but they are very often higher than expected by the CAPM. Might the size effect ultimately be a reliable new risk factor? The answer to this question could have major implications for both practitioners and academics. It would be an empirical and direct demonstration that (1) the CAPM is not an accurate asset pricing model and (2) small firms do not correctly compute their cost of equity capital. If these higher returns are induced by an additional underlying risk factor, investors take more risks than they imagine. The size effect would then not only modify the academic perception as to the validity of current asset pricing models, but would overturn the established research methodologies.

Fama and French (1993) provide an innovative asset pricing model designed from a purely theoretical model but extended from empirical observations, that remains irrelevant for most academics. They present their model by demonstrating empirically that market, size, and value proxies capture a significant proportion of the time-series variation in the returns between 1963 and 1991 in the US market. Their model still lacks economic support and the used methodology remains criticized (Michou *et al.*, 2014; Stambaugh and Yuan, 2017). For some academics and practitioners, the three-factor model becomes an equilibrium pricing model. The Sharpe–Lintner–Black and the three-factor models are the two main tools for market operators, and we wonder if one or other of them should be used for single stocks during economic contractions.

More recently, Fama and French (2012) explore size, value, and momentum anomalies in a sample of international stock returns by comparing global and local models. They reject global models in explaining regional returns and find that local models give acceptable descriptions of local average returns. These findings are consistent with the study of Griffin (2002) on portfolio and individual stocks. Furthermore, Fama and French (2015a, 2015b, 2015c) suggest a five-factor asset pricing model that captures size, value, profitability, and investment patterns for average US stock returns. They find that the list of anomalies shrinks in the five-factor model.

For the French market, Lajili Jarjir (2007) compares Fama and French (1993) and Daniel and Titman (1997) models. Time series regressions results are consistent with the factor pricing model and inconsistent with the characteristic-based pricing model. Furthermore, Lajili Jarjir (2006) explores the coskewnes and cokurtosis explanatory power. The results are consistent with the Fama and French conclusions. Moreover, co-skewness seems to be more significant in explaining stock returns of big capitalizations and cokurtosis is more related to small capitalizations in the French case. Using 25 size/book to market and 25 size/momentum portfolios over the 1981–2013 period, Nasreddine and Lajili Jarjir (2017) find that the four-factor model with momentum accounts better for common variation in stock returns, but it adds little compared to the three-factor one.

3. Data and Variables

3.1. *Database*

In this study, we analyze single stocks' returns with the two most frequently used asset pricing models. We study the empirical disparities between the Sharpe–Lintner–Black CAPM (1964) and the Fama–French three-factor model (1993). Our objective is to determine whether one of them could be more accurately used during financial crisis (October 2008 to October 2014, 324 weeks) for single French stocks. The period studied is characterized by negative returns for stocks associated with high volatilities. Our sample comprises 336 French stocks, for which we compute historical returns on a weekly basis. We focus on individual stocks for at least two reasons. (i) To reduce data-snooping biases induced in portfolio-based approaches (Lo and MacKinlay, 1990). Our methodology allows us to significantly reduce the loss of information. Aggregated results from stocks mixed into portfolios are in fact very often diluted (Litzenberger and Ramaswamy, 1979). (ii) Because the great majority of empirical tests were implemented in the US market and especially on portfolios as dependent variables. Testing models with individual stocks is an innovative project reinforced by the analysis of the French market during a specific period that is challenging for all pricing models. We use both Bloomberg and Reuters to extract and construct our database. The 10-year French government bond (rated AA+) is used as the risk-free rate. The highly diversified CAC All Shares index (PAX.PA) portfolio constitutes the market proxy.

We compose six different portfolios. Stocks are assigned to three groups depending on their book-to-market ratio. Breakpoints are the 30th and the 70th percentiles, corresponding to the groups characterized by low (L), medium (M), and high (H) book-to-market. Stocks are subsequently distributed between two size groups (Big and Small, based on the median breakpoint). Six portfolios are generated from the intersections of size and value [3×2]. Portfolios are then labeled SL, SM, SH, BL, BM, and BH. In line with Fama and French, three independent variables are used in the time-series regressions: VWMkt (for value-weighted market), HML for the value effect, and SMB for the size effect. HML portfolio corresponds to the difference between the average weekly stock returns of the two portfolios of high book-to-market ratio (SH and BH) and the average weekly stock returns of the two portfolios of low book-to-market ratio (SL and BL): HML = [(SH + BH) − (SL + BL)]/2. SMB portfolio corresponds to the difference between the average weekly stock returns of the three portfolios of small capitalizations (SL, SM, and SH) and the average weekly stock returns of the three portfolios of high capitalizations (BL, BM, and BH): SMB = [(SL + SM + SH) − (BL + BM + BH)]/3. For the dependent variables, we consider past returns of single stocks on (i) weekly-excess returns from the market portfolio

$$R_{i,t} - R_{f,t} = \alpha_i + \beta_i \left(R_{M,t} - R_{f,t}\right) + \epsilon_{i,t}, \tag{1}$$

and (ii) weekly returns from the three variables: VWMkt, HML, and SMB according to the following regression:

$$R_{i,t} - R_{f,t} = \alpha_i + \beta_i (R_{M,t} - R_{f,t}) + s_i(\mathrm{SMB}_t) + h_i(\mathrm{HML}_t) + \epsilon_{i,t}. \tag{2}$$

3.2. *Summary statistics*

As shown in Table 1, the six Fama and French portfolios show high levels of correlation over the period studied. The average correlation among big stocks is 93.20% and 85.6% for small stocks. The SMB portfolio is negatively correlated with the other portfolios (except with HML) and particularly with the market (−0.54). Unsurprisingly, SMB increases its negative correlation with big stocks strongly correlated with the market (0.64). Small portfolios are value-weighted. Even if they comprise small stocks in relation to the sample's median capitalization, the largest small stocks tend to be overrepresented, which is the reason why the average correlation between portfolios comprising big and small stocks is 0.80. HML is negatively correlated with five of the six Fama and French portfolios (exception for SH). It has a correlation of 0.39 with SMB, which is unsurprising. Most of high book-to-market firms are also small stocks.

Table 2 gives summary statistics of explanatory variables and the six size/book to market portfolios. It is not surprising to find mean weekly returns about zero because of the financial crisis.

Figure 1 shows a replication of the six Fama–French portfolios over the period from October 2008 to October 2014. By considering an index of 100

Table 1. Correlation Matrix of the Three Explanatory Variables and the Six Fama–French Portfolios

	BL	BM	BH	SL	SM	SH	SMB	HML
BL								
BM	0.939							
BH	0.913	0.944						
SL	0.837	0.861	0.827					
SM	0.813	0.839	0.803	0.916				
SH	0.726	0.765	0.743	0.83	0.821			
SMB	−0.655	−0.62	−0.646	−0.239	−0.201	−0.086		
HML	−0.509	−0.355	−0.233	−0.417	−0.328	0.033	0.388	
VWMkt	0.624	0.633	0.651	0.487	0.463	0.432	−0.539	−0.202

Notes: Stocks are assigned to three book-to-market groups (low L, medium M, and high H) and two size groups (Big and Small). Six portfolios are generated. Three independent variables are considered: VWMkt (for value-weighted market), HML for the value effect, and SMB for the size effect. HML portfolio corresponds HML = [(SH + BH) − (SL + BL)]/2. SMB portfolio corresponds to: SMB = [(SL + SM + SH) − (BL + BM + BH)]/3. Returns are calculated from October 2008 to October 2014 on weekly basis.

Table 2. Summary Statistics of Explanatory Variables and the Six Fama and French Portfolios

	VWMkt	SMB	HML	BL	BM	BH	SL	SM	SH
Mean	0.00	0.00	0.01	0.00	0.00	0.00	0.00	0.00	0.00
St. Dev.	0.03	0.05	0.02	0.04	0.03	0.03	0.02	0.02	0.03
Min.	−0.14	−0.23	−0.08	−0.21	−0.20	−0.19	−0.18	−0.16	−0.13
Max.	0.14	0.14	0.08	0.11	0.08	0.07	0.06	0.07	0.08
Kurtosis	2.74	2.12	0.84	4.57	7.43	7.84	10.45	7.82	3.84
Skewness	−0.25	−0.32	−0.07	−1.04	−1.61	−1.53	−1.93	−1.41	−1.04

Notes: Stocks are assigned to three book-to-market groups (low L, medium M, and high H) and two size groups (Big and Small). Six portfolios are generated. Three independent variables are considered: VWMkt (for value-weighted market), HML for the value effect, and SMB for the size effect. HML portfolio corresponds HML = [(SH + BH) − (SL + BL)]/2. SMB portfolio corresponds to: SMB = [(SL + SM + SH) − (BL + BM + BH)]/3. Returns are calculated from October 2008 to October 2014 on weekly basis.

on October 2008, we can see that low and medium book-to-market portfolios are less profitable than high book-to-markets ones, whatever the size is.

The security market line in Fig. 2 shows the expected rate of return of an asset i according to its non-diversifiable risk. The figure summarizes the 336 stocks of the sample.

Figure 1. Replication of the Six Fama–French Portfolios over October 2008 to October 2014 Period on Weekly Basis by Investing 100 Units in $t = 0$ (October 2008)

Are there homogeneous characteristics among the six Fama–French portfolios? We split the SML into six sub-SMLs, corresponding to the six Fama–French portfolios in Fig. 3.

We observe that big stocks have betas homogeneously distributed on the SML, while most of the small companies have betas concentrated in a restricted range (0–0.5). This concentration represents a first difficulty for the CAPM in explaining (through the market parameter) past returns from small stocks. Reinganum (1981), Breeden *et al.* (1989), and Fama and French (1992) note that the systematic risk of a small stock is lower than for a big one, a finding in line with these observations. Small firms are assumed to be riskier because of their greater idiosyncratic risk. The literature is unanimous that all the models encounter difficulties, particularly when they try to explain past returns from small stocks. One of the main messages here and in Fama and French (1993, 2012) is that the problems of asset pricing models are largely found in small stocks. The three-factor model has added value regarding small caps compared to the CAPM, but is still unsatisfactory. Their low beta levels may be easily explained by their lower

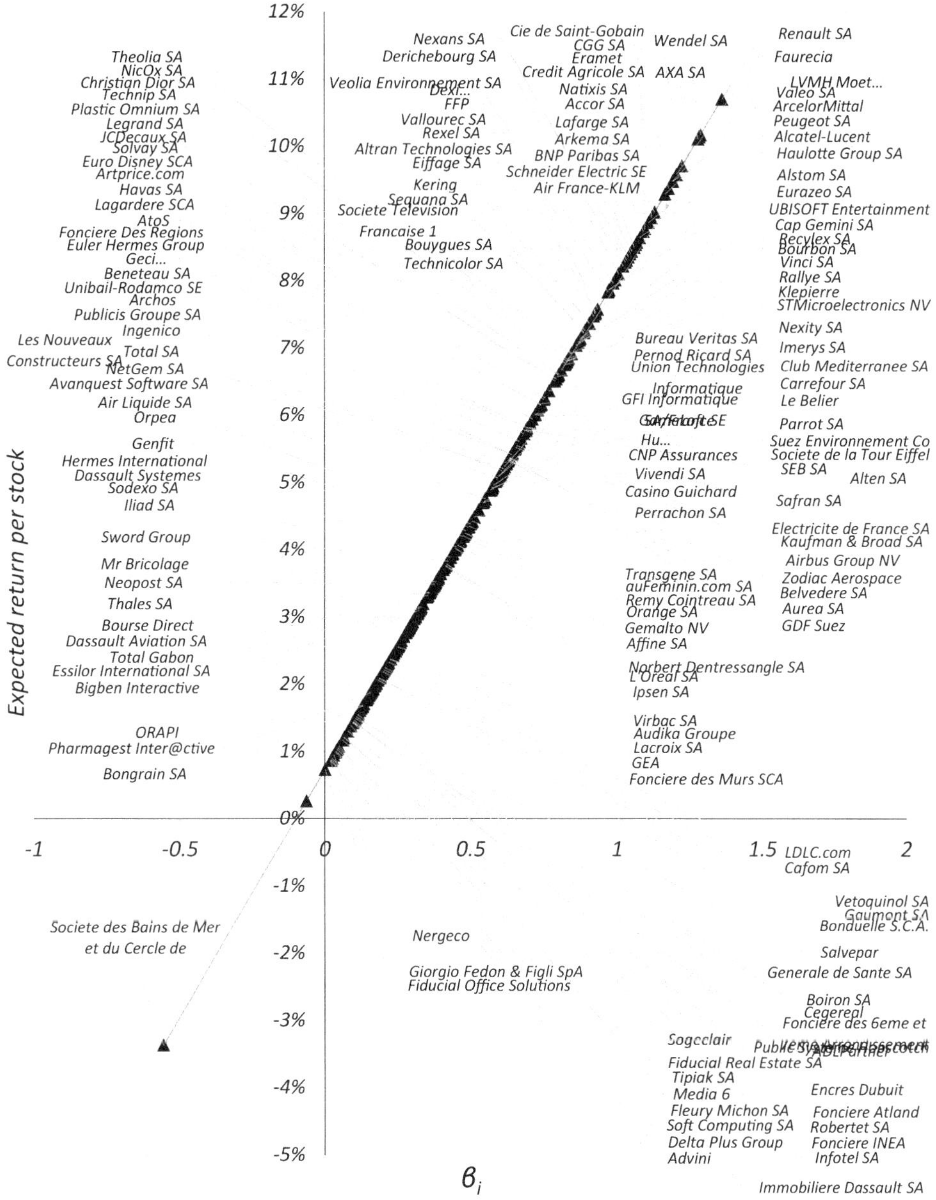

Figure 2. The French Security Market Line with an Expected Market return of 8% and a Risk-Free Rate of 0.6% per Annum

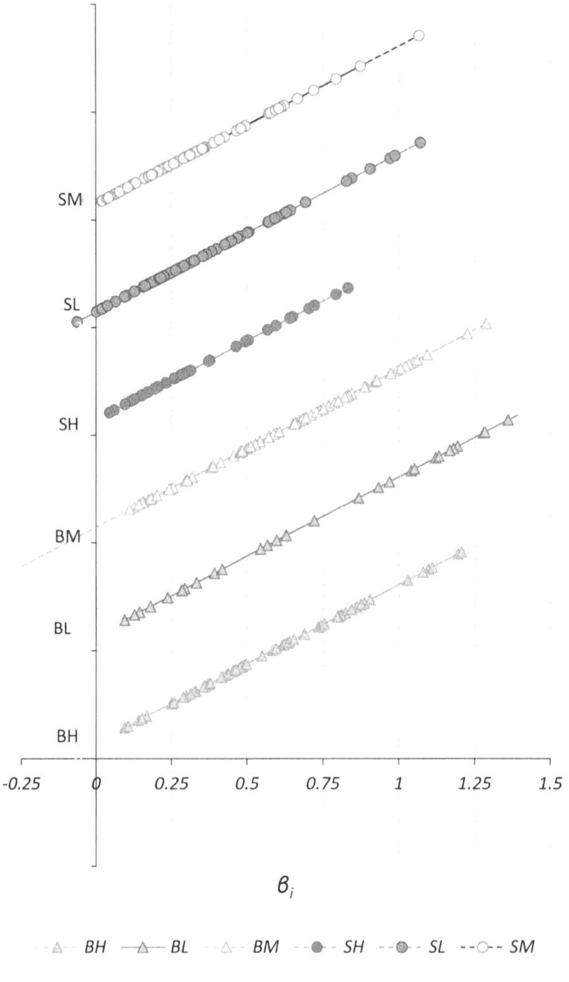

Figure 3. The French Security Market Line Decomposition in Function of Portfolios

comovement with the market index. We formulate three hypotheses: (1) the choice of the proxy for the market portfolio is not good enough, (2) the existence of additional risk factors related to the size becomes consistent, and (3) both are true.

The following graph in Fig. 4 corresponds to the level of the adjusted R^2 for both models per stock depending on the model used. Every line corresponds to the adjusted r-squared level of a firm resulting from the regression with the three-factor model in the right hand and the CAPM in the left hand. To provide a deeper analysis, we order the firms into their

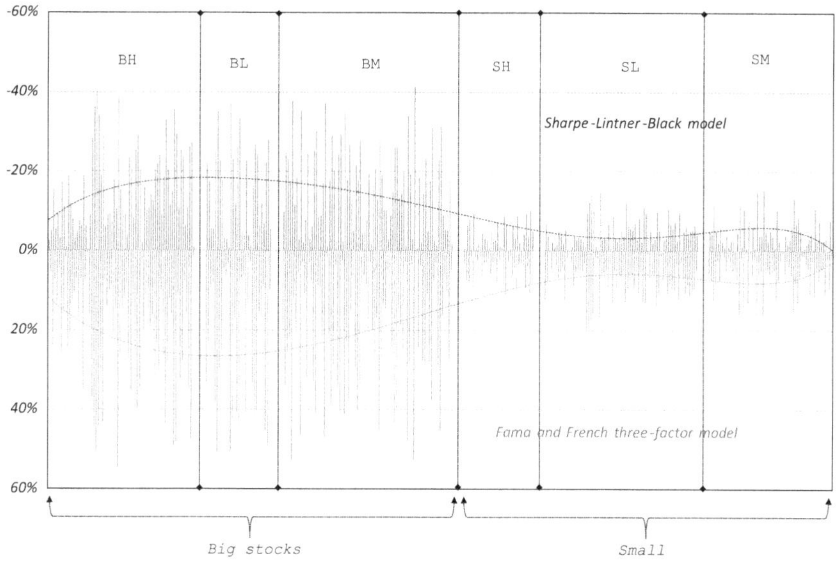

Figure 4. Adjusted R^2 from the Regressions of Each Stock Return per Model

respective portfolios. The horizontal axis should be viewed as an absolute value for the adjusted R^2 of the CAPM.

Two observations can be made. The three-factor model has an adjusted r-square higher for every single stock (from 0.50% to 54.64% vs. 0.00% to 41.36% for the CAPM). Adjusted r-squares of big stocks are far higher than adjusted r-squares of small ones, independently of the model used. Time-series regressions related to big caps have a higher quality. Their comovement with the market index is higher than for small stocks. Despite its marked diversification, the index remains highly correlated with the CAC 40 index, inducing a favorable bias for large caps. This correlation between the two indices reached almost 99% during the period studied and is explained by their value-weighted characteristic. Big stocks have capitalizations far bigger than small stocks, and are overrepresented. The average correlation between the market and big stocks is 63.6%, as against 46.07% for small stocks. The observed higher levels of adjusted R^2 for portfolios comprising big stocks is thus unsurprising. It accounts for why past returns from small stocks are harder to explain during an economic crisis and, secondly, it reinforces the importance of choosing a reliable proxy of the market portfolio, in view of Roll's criticism (1977).

Based on 324 observations for each stock we test both the models using the Durbin Watson statistic, with a 99.00% confidence level for alpha.

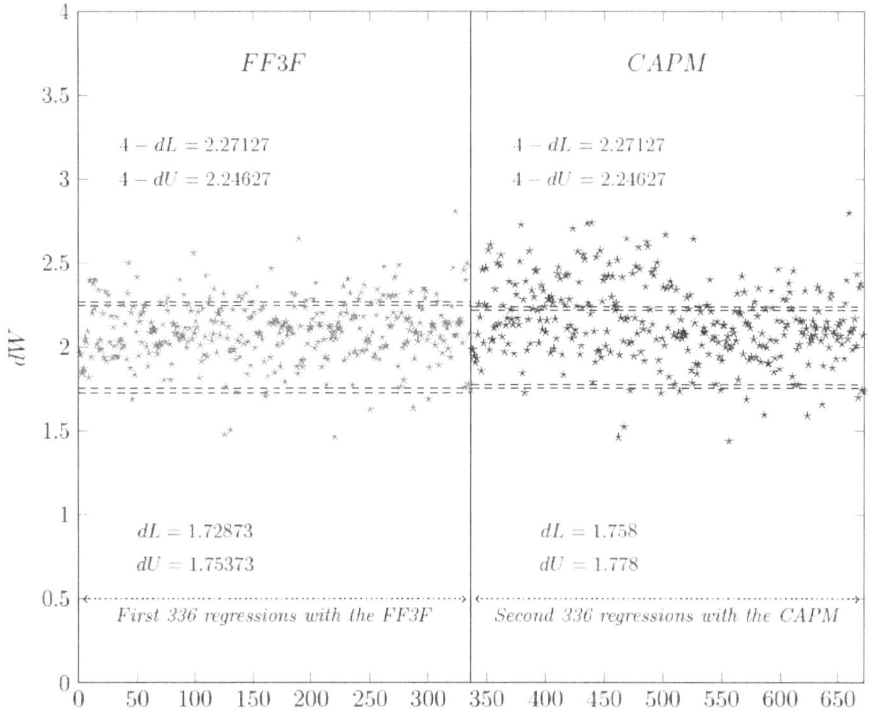

Figure 5. Scatter Plot of the Durbin Watson Coefficients for Each Stock per Model

On the basis of the CAPM, 60.12% of the sample show no evidence of autocorrelation. The test remains however inconclusive for 3.27% of the stocks. A significant portion (32.14%) of the regressions show negative autocorrelations and only 4.46% of the stocks are positively autocorrelated. The results for the three-factor model are far better: 77.08% of the sample show no evidence of autocorrelation, an improvement of 16.96%. The test is inconclusive for 4.17%. The proportion of negatively autocorrelated regressions is halved (16.37% vs. 32.14%). The proportion of positive autocorrelation is 2.38% vs. 4.46%. The three-factor model does a better job than the CAPM. The presence of a positive or negative autocorrelation underlines the omission of a significant factor in a model. Our results are in line with Fama and French and strengthen the consistency of additional risk factors. The multidimensional risk hypothesis is partially verified for single stocks. Figure 5 below shows the dispersion of the Durbin Watson statistics for each firm per model.

4. Contributions and Conclusion

Empirical studies, both old and recent, show that the Capital Asset Pricing Model developed by Sharpe (1964), Lintner (1965), Mossin (1966), and Black (1972) never had any empirical success. Despite its weaknesses, it is still used to calculate cost of equity and remains the main model utilized in the financial community. Regarding the two market anomalies — size and value effects — we challenge the CAPM with the three-factor model for the period of the financial crisis in the French market for single stocks. We detect no evidence of a size effect, as described by Banz (1981). The small-minus-big factor, however, remains statistically significant and increases the quality of the time-series regressions. Firms with a high book-to-market ratio strongly outperformed the market over the period studied. The existence of an additional risk factor related to the value effect appeared naturally consistent and is (as expected) also significant. The Fama–French three-factor model does a better job than the Sharpe–Lintner–Black CAPM. Market, size, and value factors provide better description of single stock returns. Moreover, the two additional parameters related to the size and the value effects are more significant when stock markets are febrile. Nevertheless, both models have difficulty explaining the historical returns from small firms. We conclude that the low comovement with the market proxy is a relevant explanation. We investigate on the choice of the market proxy in view of Roll's (1977) criticism. The selection of a proxy has a major impact on the time series regressions, but we see that the correlations between the indices tend to increase in periods of economic crisis. This global correlation among market indices reduces the impacts related to the choice of market portfolio and explains why pricing models give better results during periods of crisis. We then hypothesized that this particular financial crisis systematically had a negative impact on firms with high beta, in other words, on big stocks. This reasoning would explain why big stocks are more volatile.

The paper gives updated results on the French market and yields unexpected conclusions, namely that big stocks are more volatile and pricing models are more accurate in periods of crisis. Behavioral finance may provide some significant insights, especially with regard to the predictive character of the value effect.

Our observations show that small capitalizations underperformed the market. This finding is in line with previous studies by Eleswarapu and Reinganum (1993), Dimson and Marsh (1999), Dichev (1998), Amihud

(2002), and Horowitz *et al.* (2000). Small stocks do not have adequate access to capital or credit, accounted for by the credit crunch that prevents them being flexible. This situation suggests why they underperformed the market. The flight to quality occurred when investors sold what they perceived to be riskier and bought safer assets (government bonds, for instance). During the period covered, bond yields were low and, despite the growing uncertainty in the market, some investors preferred to buy big stocks, betting on "too big to fail". The flight to quality has thus also been a flight to liquidity. Investors sold their small stocks, perceived as illiquid, and bought big stocks. The final question is why were small stocks less volatile? Their free float proportions are smaller and they are not immediately impacted by the crisis due to their weak market exposure.

Overall, we conclude that during the financial crisis for single stocks the Fama–French three-factor model is more satisfactory on an empirical basis than the Sharpe–Lintner–Black CAPM. This methodology, initially oriented toward single stocks, reduces the data-snooping biases usually induced in portfolio-based approaches (Lo and MacKinlay, 1990). The existence of new risk factors additional to the three existing ones seems relevant, but we rejected the idea of replacing one of them by a new one. Some researchers see additional evidence of market inefficiency in anomalies, while others perceived misspecification of the existing models. Carhart (1997) introduces a fourth factor into the Fama-French model. The momentum factor is defined as the empirical tendency for rising stocks to rise further, and falling ones to keep falling. This factor is much debated among academics. Fama and French (2015) have extended the CAPM to a new five-factor model comprising market, size, value, operating profitability, and investment parameters. In view of this study, it would be interesting to test these models over a long period with a view to confirming our findings in several crises. For future research issues, some questions remain, challenging researchers and practitioners, as: Which would be the most accurate asset pricing model for single stocks? How can we distinguish anomalies from risk factors? Is there any relation between expected returns and extra-financial ratings?

References

Acharya, V. and Pedersen, L. (2005). Asset pricing with liquidity risk. *J. Fin. Econom.*, 77, pp. 375–410.

Asness, C., Frazzini, A., and Pedersen, L. (2014). Quality minus junk. Available at https://ssrn.com/abstract=2312432.

Amihud, Y. (2002). Illiquidity and stock returns: Cross-section and time series effects. *J. Fin. Markets*, 5, pp. 31–56.
Ball, R. (1978). Anomalies in relationships between securities' yields and yield-surrogates. *J. Fin. Economi.*, 6, pp. 103–126.
Banz, R. (1981). The relationship between return and market value of common stocks. *J. Fin. Econom.*, 9, pp. 3–18.
Basu, S. (1977). Investment performance of common stocks in relation to their price-earnings ratios: A test of the efficient market hypothesis, *The J. Fin.*, 32, pp. 663–682.
Black, F. (1972). Capital market equilibrium with restricted borrowing. *J. Business*, 45, pp. 444–455.
Bondt, W. and Thaler, R. (1987). Further evidence on investor overreaction and stock market seasonality. *The J. Fin.*, 42, pp. 557–581.
Breeden, D. T., Gibbons, M. R., and Litzenberger, R. H. (1989). Empirical tests of the consumption-oriented CAPM. *The J. Fin.*, 44, pp. 231–262.
Brennan, M. J., Chordia, T., and Subrahmanyam, A. (1998). Alternative factor specifications, security characteristics and the cross-section of expected stock returns. *J. Fin. Econom.*, 49, pp. 345–373.
Campbell, J. Y., Hilscher, J., and Szilagyi, J. (2008). In search of distress risk. *The J. Fin.*, 63, pp. 2899–2939.
Carhart, M. (1997). On persistence in mutual fund performance. *The J. Fin.*, 52, pp. 57–82.
Chan, K. and Chen, N. (1991). Structural and return characteristics of small and large firms. *The J. Fin.*, 46, pp. 1467–1484.
Chan, K., Chen, N., and Hsieh, D. A. (1985). An exploratory investigation of the firm size effect. *The J. Fin.*, 14, pp. 451–471.
Chan, L., Hamao, Y., and Lakonishok, J. (1991). Fundamentals and stock returns in japan. *The J. Fin.*, 46, pp. 1739–1764.
Dichev, I. D. (1998). Is the risk of bankruptcy a systematic risk? *The J. Fin.*, 53, pp. 1131–1147.
Dimson, E. and Marsh, P. (1999). Murphy's law and market anomalies. *J. Portfolio Manage.*, 25, pp. 53–69.
Eleswarapu, V. R. and Reinganum, M. R. (1993). The seasonal behavior of the liquidity premium in asset pricing. *J. Fin. Econom.*, 34, pp. 373–386.
Fama, E. and French, K. (1992). The cross section of expected stock returns. *The J. Fin.*, 47, pp. 427–65.
Fama, E. and French, K. (1993). Common risk factors in the returns on stocks and bonds. *J. Fin. Econom.*, 33, pp. 3–56.
Fama E. and French, K. (2012), Size, value, and momentum in international stock returns. *J. Fin. Econom.*, 105, pp. 457–472.
Fama, E. and French, K. (2015a). International tests of a five-factor asset pricing model. *J. Fin. Econom.*, 123, pp. 441–463.
Fama, E. and French, K. (2015b). A five-factor asset pricing model. *J. Fin. Econom.*, 116, pp. 1–22.
Fama E. and French, K. (2015c), Dissecting anomalies with a five-factor model. *Rev. Fin. Stud.*, 29, pp. 69–103.
Frazzini, A. and Pedersen, L. (2014). Betting against beta. *J. Fin. Econom.*, 111, pp. 1–25.
Griffin, J. M. 2002. Are the Fama and French Factors global or country specific? *The Rev. Fin. Stud.*, 15, pp. 783–803.
Horowitz, L., Loughran, T., and Savin, N. (2000). Three analyses of the firm size premium. *J. Empiri. Fin.*, 7, pp. 143–153.

Hou, K. and Moskowitz, T. (2005). Market frictions, price delay, and the cross-section of expected returns. *The Rev. Fin. Stud.*, 18, pp. 981–1020.

Ibbotson, R., Chen, Y., Kim, D., and Hu, W. (2013). Liquidity as an investment style. *Fin. Analys. J.*, 69, pp. 1–15.

Israel, R. and Moskowitz, T. (2013). The role of shorting, firm size, and time on market anomalies. *J. Fin. Econom.*, 108, pp. 1–27.

Lajili Jarjir, S. (2006). Les modèles d'évaluation des actifs financiers et les co-moments d'ordre trois et quatre. *Banque & Marchés*, 81, pp. 39–50.

Lajili Jarjir, S. (2007). Explaining the cross-section of stock returns in France: Characteristics or risk factors? *The Euro. J. Fin.*, 13, pp. 145–158.

Lintner, J. (1965). The valuation of risk assets and the selection of risky investments in stock portfolios and capital budgets. *Rev. Econom. Statist.*, 47, pp. 13–37.

Litzenberger, R. and K., R. (1979). The effect of personal taxes and dividends on capital asset prices: Theory and empirical evidence. *J. Fin. Econom.*, pp. 163–195.

Lo, A. and MacKinlay, A. (1990). Data-snooping biases in tests of financial asset pricing models. *Rev. Fin. Stud.*, 3, pp. 431–467.

Markowitz, H. (1952). Portfolio selection. *The J. Fin.*, pp. 77–91.

McLean, D. and Pontiff, J. (2016). Does academic research destroy stock return predictability? *The J. Fin.*, 71, pp. 5–32.

Merton, R. (1973). An intertemporal capital asset pricing model. *Econometrica*, 41, pp. 867–887.

Mossin, J. (1966). Equilibrium in a capital asset market. *Econometrica*, 34, pp. 768–783.

Michou, M., Mouselli, S., and Stark, A. (2014). On the differences in measuring SMB and HML in the UK — Do they matter? *The Brit. Account. Rev.*, 46, pp. 281–294.

Nasreddine, A. and Lajili Jarjir, S. (2017). Scrutinizing portfolio strategies and asset pricing models: The French case. *Bankers, Markets & Investors*, 146, pp. 38–48.

Nicholson, S. (1960). Price-earnings ratios. *Fin. Analyst. J.*, 16, pp. 43–45.

Novy-Marx, R. (2013). The other side of value: The gross profitability premium. *J. Fin. Econom.*, 108, pp. 1–28.

Pastor, L. and Stambaugh, R. (2003). Liquidity risk and expected stock returns. *The J. Politi. Economy*, pp. 642–685.

Reinganum, M. (1981). Misspecification of capital asset pricing: Empirical anomalies based on earnings' yields and market values. *J. Fin. Economi.*, pp. 19–46.

Reinganum, M. (1999). The significance of market capitalization in portfolio management over time. *The J. Portfolio Manage.*, 25, pp. 39–50.

Roll, R. (1977). A critique of the asset pricing theory's tests. *J. Fin. Econom.*, pp. 129–76.

Rosenberg, B., Reid, K., and Lanstein, R. (1985). Persuasive evidence of market inefficiency. *J. Portfolio Manage.*, 11, pp. 9–16.

Ross, S. (1976). The arbitrage theory of capital asset pricing. *J. Econom. Theory*, pp. 341–360.

Sadka, R. (2006). Momentum and post-earnings-announcement drift anomalies: The role of liquidity risk. *J. Fin. Econom.*, 80, pp. 309–349.

Sharpe, W. (1964). Capital asset prices: A theory of market equilibrium under conditions of risk. *The J. Fin.*, 19, pp. 425–442.

Stambaugh, R. and Yuan, Y. (2017). Mispricing factors. *Rev. Fin. Stud.*, 30, pp. 1270–1315.

Stattman, D. (1980). Book values and expected stock returns. The Chicago MBA, *A. J. Selected Papers*, pp. 25–45.

van Dijk, M. (2011). Is size dead? A review of the size effect in equity returns. *J. Bank. Fin.*, pp. 3263–3274.

Chapter 27

Higher-Order Tail Moments in Asset-Pricing Theory

Juan C. Arismendi Zambrano

ICMA Centre, Henley Business School, University of Reading, Whiteknights, Reading RG6 6BA, UK

j.arismendi@icmacentre.ac.uk

Abstract

In this chapter, we review the literature about the use of third- and fourth-order moments in finance, the main papers on asset pricing theory with higher-order moments, and the definitions of skewness and kurtosis in the statistical literature. Contagion, skewness and kurtosis investor preferences, and tail regimes are some of the topics discussed in this chapter. We derive theoretical results about the higher-order moments of the bivariate truncated normal distribution, and analyze the implications of the results for previous empirical tests. We provide these results as a tool to be used in the empirical testing of asymmetries and heavy-tailedness of assets returns.

1. Introduction

The need for new advanced models to properly measure the risk of financial institutions such as investment banks, mutual funds, hedge funds or insurance companies has driven academia in the search for new mathematical, statistical, and econometric methodologies and results to fill the gap. We focus our research on the third- and fourth-order moments of lower truncated distributions, principally because the first- and second-order moments have been developed well enough, and moments beyond the fifth usually have less impact on applications. The third- and fourth-order moments are essential to calculate skewness and kurtosis. These measures are used in applications to assess the deviation of distributions from the normal distribution; nowadays, they are also used to measure risk in financial applications.

Previously, Arismendi (2013), and Arismendi and Broda (2017), have derived higher-order moments of different distributions. In this Chapter we use a simpler approach to calculate the higher-order moments of a bivariate standard normal distribution (BVSN).

The major contributions in this chapter are the closed-form formulae to calculate the truncated moments of a BVSN distribution. We also reproduce empirical examples of the tail correlations in four different markets: equities, currencies, interest rates, and commodities, for two extremes: lower-lower tail (both assets with negative returns) and upper-upper tail (both assets with positive returns).

In the latter part of the section, we construct a time-varying VaR valuation methodology based on the tail moments of the distribution. This *tail normal* VaR is constructed with the correlation and the volatilities of the lower-lower returns. A first parametric example shows that the VaR could be overestimated or underestimated, depending on the unconditional correlation (the correlation of the whole distribution). An additional empirical example of *tail* VaR is constructed with the stock prices of Bank of America (BAC) and Citigroup (C). For an equally-weighted portfolio of these two assets, a Cornish–Fisher VaR is estimated, one with unconditional moments, and another with the tail moments: tail variance, tail skewness and tail kurtosis. The unconditional normal VaR underestimates the value reported by the Cornish–Fisher; unconditional normal VaR was almost one-third of the Cornish–Fisher VaR during the peak of the 2008 crisis. The Cornish–Fisher tail VaR is contrasted with a normal tail VaR. The example exposed that VaR value is underestimated when the normal tail VaR is used; the Cornish–Fisher tail VaR was approximately twice the value reported by normal tail VaR during the 2008 crisis.

The structure of this chapter is as follows: In Sec. 2, we review the main papers on asset pricing theory with higher-order moments, and the definitions of skewness and kurtosis in the statistical literature. Section 3 presents a literature review about the associated higher-moments topics: tail correlation, contagion, and extreme value theory in finance. Section 4 presents empirical examples of the tail correlation in four different markets: equities, currencies, commodities, and interest rates. Section 5 examines the use of tail moments in asset pricing theory and presents an example of the tail-beta of a stock. Section 6 shows an example where the tails of the distribution of the asset prices will have implications for the pricing of options. Section 7 presents some notation and recalls the results on truncated moments on the bivariate standard normal (BVSN) distribution.

Section 8 shows an example of the implications of tail moments in risk measurement. Section 9 presents the first results of the thesis on bivariate truncated moments, and Sec. 10 describes an example where the bivariate truncated moments are inadequate for a multivariate setting. Section 11 presents concluding remarks.

2. Economic Importance of Higher-Order Moments: Skewness and Kurtosis in Asset Pricing Models

Since the work of Markowitz (1952) in the early 1950s to mid 1970s, all the literature related to asset pricing models has focused exclusively on the first two moments of the assets' return distribution. However, Kraus and Litzenberger (1976) started to assess the importance of skewness on investor preferences. They constructed a new Capital Asset Pricing Model (CAPM) with skewness preferences. Two leading papers, Blume and Friend (1973) and Fama and MacBeth (1973), arose after criticisms of the original model. They found empirical results inconsistent with the Sharpe–Lintner model (Sharpe, 1964; Lintner, 1965). In their research, they enhanced the CAPM to include skewness preferences in the valuations of assets. For this purpose, they modeled the expected utility with a three-moment Taylor's expansion of non-polynomial functions, such as logarithmic, power and negative exponential functions. This function can be expressed as

$$E(U(\tilde{W})) = U(\bar{W}) + [U''(\bar{W})/2!]\sigma_W^2 + [U'''(\bar{W})/3!]m_W^3 + \text{higher-order terms}, \quad (1)$$

where $U(\tilde{W})$ is utility of the final wealth $\tilde{W}$, $\bar{W} = E(\tilde{W})$, $\sigma_W^2 = E[(W - \bar{W})^2]$, and $m_W^3 = E[(\tilde{W} - \bar{W})^3]$. A cubic polynomial will determine the preference of the first three moments in an exact way. Nevertheless, this assumption is unsuitable for a risk averse function (see Arrow, 1971 for more details). With this Taylor expansion of the expected utility function, they develop a new CAPM, with the relationship between market returns and assets returns as

$$\bar{R}_i - R_F = a_1\beta_i + a_2\gamma_i, \quad (2)$$

where $\beta_i = \sigma_{iM}/\sigma_M^2$ is the market beta or variance sensitivity of the i-th asset return, σ_{iM} is the covariance of the asset with the market, $\gamma_i = m_{iMM}/m_M^3$ is the market gamma or skewness sensitivity of the i-th asset return, $a_1 = (d\bar{W}/d\sigma_W)\sigma_M$, $a_2 = (d\bar{W}/dm_W)m_M$, and σ_M, m_M are the standard deviation and skewness of the market returns. The empirical results support this new model, and they find a positive skewness preference, and risk aversion to variance, consistent with a rational investor preference model. The conclusions finally suggest that the earlier findings of Blume and Friend (1973) and Fama and MacBeth (1973) are the result of the omission of systematic (non-diversified) skewness. They confirm the validity of the model including the third-order moment inside investor preferences.

Harvey and Siddique (2000) extend the work of Kraus and Litzenberger (1976), driving a cross-sectional analysis of the CAPM with factors based on size, book-to-market, and price-to-earnings ratio. They test portfolios with the three-factor model of Fama and MacBeth (1973). This research arises as a natural extension to verify the three-moment CAPM on the cross-sectional test of Fama and French. The conditional model is defined as

$$E_t[R_{i,t+1}] = V_{1,t}E_t[R_{M,t+1}] + V_{2,t}E_t[R^2_{M,t+1}], \tag{3}$$

where $R_{i,t}$ is the excess return of the asset i over the market $(\bar{R}_i - R_M)$, $V_{1,t}$ and $V_{2,t}$ are functions of market variance, skewness, covariance, and coskewness. This model is conditional on the information known at time t. The empirical tests of this cross-sectional study prove that it is possible to explain the failure of one-factor asset pricing models that do not account for skewness. The risk premium can be 360 basis points per year in some cases. However, the tests can have limitations for the out-of-sample measure of skewness.

Jondeau and Rockinger (2003) develop a more statistical analysis, that searches for the existence of skewness and kurtosis on asset returns. They use a GARCH model, initially proposed by Hansen (1982), where the residual errors are modeled using a generalized t distribution. This distribution is skewed and heavy-tailed for certain parameters, and the moments of the generalized t student distribution will change over time t. They calibrate the GARCH model over five stock indices returns and six different foreign-exchange currency rates. The empirical results reveal that all foreign-exchange series have a similar behavior in the changing sign of the asymmetry (skewness) parameter of the distribution, with the interpretation of being time dependent. Meanwhile, the kurtosis of the distribution is constant. In the case of stock indices' returns, the behavior of the kurtosis is complex, and the behavior of the skewness is straightforward. They finally found there existed covariability in moments over the second (variance) concluding that extreme realizations could appear on different markets.

A study from Patton (2004) analyzed the out-of-sample significance of two different asymmetries in the market: one was the skewness on the returns of stocks, and the other is the asymmetry on the correlation of two stocks. Previous studies such as Longin and Solnik (2001), Ang and Bekaert (2002), and Ang and Chen (2002),[1] show that there exists asymmetric dependence on equity market states. An interesting proposal by Arrow (1971) is that utility functions must have a decreasing risk aversion factor, and this implies that we need to consider a third-order moment on utility functions as mentioned before in the work of Kraus and Litzenberger (1976). These results lead this study to test three hypotheses: (1) to verify that asymmetries exist, (2) to prove that we are able to capture these asymmetries out-of-sample, (3) to confirm if portfolio decisions based on models that capture these asymmetries provide better decisions. Patton tries to compare models that consider up to the fourth-order moment of asset returns' distribution, and models with time-varying dependence to distinguish between bull market and bear market states. The utility function used is a constant relative risk aversion (CRRA) function, defined as

$$U(\gamma) = \begin{cases} (1-\gamma)^{-1} \cdot (W_0 \cdot (1 + \omega_X R_{X_t} + \omega_Y R_{Y_t}))^{1-\gamma} & \text{if } \gamma \neq 1, \\ \log(W_0 \cdot (1 + \omega_X R_{X_t} + \omega_Y R_{Y_t})) & \text{if } \gamma = 1, \end{cases} \tag{4}$$

where R_{X_t}, R_{Y_t} are the continuously compounded excess return of the two assets (two equities) over the risk-free asset at time t, W_0 is the initial wealth, and $\omega_X, \omega_y = 1 - \omega_X$ is the percentage held on every asset. To capture moments of third- and higher-order, Patton uses copula theory.[2] With skewed distributions generated using copulas like Gumbel, Clayton, and Joe-Clayton, he modeled the asset returns. They test the performance of 11 different portfolio strategies. Three strategies of buy and hold an index, or a mixture of two indices, four strategies that optimize portfolios with empirical, Gaussian, Gaussian copula, and Gumbel copula distributions, and four strategies as before subject to a short-sales constraint. The final results demonstrate that there exists economic evidence that, considering models with skewness and asymmetric dependence for portfolio decisions, gives up to 27 basis points per annum of reward.

There also exist publications that highlight the importance of using a four-moment CAPM in a cross-sectional analysis with a portfolio of international assets. Guidolin and Timmermann (2008) discovered that the bias to invest at home by US investors can be explained by skewness' and kurtosis' preferences. They use a modified version of intertemporal capital

[1] Publications on the asymmetry of correlation will be described in more depth in Sec. 4.
[2] See Nelsen (2006) for a detailed reference on copula theory.

asset pricing model (ICAPM), with a four-moment expansion as in Harvey and Siddique (2000), adding dependence on a regime-switching variable. The empirical results prove that regime-switching and inclusion of the four moments in the asset pricing model is relevant to clarify the home bias of US investors. While with the CAPM the US investors should allocate only 30% of their wealth to home stocks, with this four-moment regime-switching version the optimal allocation increases to 70%, much closer to the actual allocation of 86% (Thomas *et al.*, 2006).

The use of higher-order moments helped researchers in developing certain important puzzles in finance, and they were even used as a solution. Martin (2012) uses a four-order moment expansion of a consumption asset pricing model (CCAPM). Guidolin and Timmermann (2008) explain the US vs. international investment bias using a Taylor expansion of the CAPM, and Barroso and Santa-Clara (2015) find that the momentum puzzle is even more baffling when controlling the higher-order moments of the portfolio that are one-day out-of-sample predictable. An interesting hypothesis is whether in a dynamic setting the higher-order cumulants are subsumed in the variance: Feunou *et al.* (2013) found that the risk factors of the term structure of variance extracted from option prices can reveal predictors of the equity-, bond-, and variance-premium, and that higher-order term structures can reveal risk factors that are already explained by the variance.

3. Multivariate Tail Correlation, Skewness and Kurtosis

The correlation of financial markets is of central importance for portfolio optimization and risk management, and for this reason it has been actively researched. This section presents some classical papers on extreme correlations in a parametric setting. We begin by describing extreme correlation in a parametric multivariate normal (MVN) framework. Then we discuss the theory of extreme correlation in an extreme value theory (EVT) setting. These are the only two approaches to extreme correlation that have been used until now. The EVT approach is based on the assumption that the tail of the returns' distribution is unknown, but it can be estimated with information in the boundary of the observed samples, which is generally regarded as being more appropriate to measure extreme risk in financial markets than using the MVN framework. We also describe papers that consider regime-switching (R-S) models for tail correlation asymmetry, which differ in a bull and bear market, and its implications for portfolio diversification. Finally, we describe empirical work that uses extreme correlation to explore market contagion during a financial crisis.

3.1. *Tail correlation in the MVN framework*

The Longin and Solnik (2001) methodology consists of finding the optimal threshold for defining the tail of a distribution, and modeling the tails of the marginals and the dependence structure. They use this methodology to test the tail correlations of stock returns against the tail correlations of a bivariate normal (BVN) distribution. They ensure that there is no small sample bias in the measure of tail correlation for large movements (because they use the correlation of an asymptotic tail distribution). Their final model has seven parameters in this bivariate setting: the tail probabilities, the variance parameters, and the tail indices for both variables, and the dependence parameter. They fit it to monthly equity returns in five countries: the US, UK, France, Germany, and Japan. The data are extracted from the MSCI index from 1959 to 1996. They test portfolios consisting of US and other-country index pairs. The main finding is that the correlations between downside returns are larger than ordinary correlations, but the correlations between upside returns are smaller.

Ang and Chen (2002) begin by establishing some empirical facts about the nature of correlations in the US equity market. They also provide a theoretical example which highlights the importance of modeling asymmetric correlation in investment decisions, and derive a statistical test for the difference between two asymmetric correlations. Finally, they test which of the following four models best fits the asymmetric correlations that are observed in US stocks returns: GARCH-M, Poisson jump diffusion, R-S normal, and R-S GARCH.

Let $\tilde{X}, \tilde{Y}$ be the market returns of two equity assets. Longin and Solnik (2001) use the following definition of empirical exceedance correlation:

$$\begin{aligned} \tilde{\rho}(\varsigma) &= \operatorname{corr}(\tilde{X}, \tilde{Y} | \tilde{X} > \varsigma, \tilde{Y} > \varsigma), \quad \text{if } \varsigma \geq 0, \\ &= \operatorname{corr}(\tilde{X}, \tilde{Y} | \tilde{X} < \varsigma, \tilde{Y} < \varsigma), \quad \text{if } \varsigma < 0, \end{aligned} \tag{5}$$

where ς is the predefined exceedance threshold. Define as $\hat{\rho}(\varsigma, \phi)$ the exceedance correlation associated with the BVN distribution. With these definitions they measure the exceedance correlation of a BVN distribution when the exceedance parameter increases, showing that it decreases when the threshold parameter increases in the case of the BVN.

Then they develop a parametric measure of *asymmetric correlation* called the H statistic, which is based on the difference between the observed exceedance correlation and the correlation of a BVN distribution:

$$H = \left[\sum_{i=1}^{N} \omega(\varsigma_i)(\hat{\rho}(\varsigma_i, \phi) - \tilde{\rho}_i(\varsigma_i))^2\right]^{1/2}.$$

With this H statistic, Ang and Chen (2002) perform some empirical research based on a variety of value-weighted industry portfolios. The industries analyzed are petroleum, finance, durables, basic industries, food and tobacco, construction, capital goods, transportation, utilities, textile and trade, service, leisure, and miscellaneous. Within each month, for each portfolio, they calculate the daily returns of a buy-and-hold strategy. At the beginning of every month, each portfolio is rebalanced and reformed according to the strategy. The returns are aggregated into a weekly frequency by calculating the total buy-and-hold return of each strategy from the end of every Wednesday to the end of the following Wednesday. This yields 1,852 weekly returns' observations. The other three types of portfolios have 1,852 weekly returns, calculated using value-weighted indices, but now the stocks are sorted by size (or value or momentum) rather than industry. Ang and Chen use market capitalization to represent size, book-to-market ratio to represent value, and past returns to represent momentum. In each case, they sort the stocks according to the chosen characteristic, and then take the top 20% into the size 1 (or BM 1 or Mom 1) portfolio, the next 20% into the size 2 (or BM 2 or Mom 2) portfolio, and so on. Then the downside and upside market correlations are calculated, i.e., the asymmetric correlations between the portfolio and the market returns.

The results show that, far from being symmetric, the downside correlations are always greater than the upside correlations. Second, instead of going to zero, the downside correlations are flat or tend to increase as the threshold ς becomes more negative. The upside correlations are more variable than the negative ones, but there is evidence that, as ς increases, these correlations taper off to zero for some portfolios. Finally they found that, between the four models tested to model correlation asymmetry, in most cases the R-S GARCH fits the empirical exceedance correlations best.

A parallel research of Ang and Bekaert (2002) establishes that international asset allocation does contribute to diversification, despite the increasing correlation in downside markets. They use a very elaborate methodology that reproduces the asymmetric correlation found in the equities' market. They use a two-state R-S to model stocks returns. Their analysis is made on the "home bias puzzle" problem, asserting that US investors tend to invest more in US equities than they need to. Guidolin and Timmermann (2008) mention that the actual proportion invested in the US markets by the US investors is about 85%, while on international equities' markets it is only 15%. The market capitalization of US equities' markets is only 50%, thus suggesting that the proportion invested in international equities must increase. But previous studies such as Longin and Solnik (2001) and Ang and Chen (2002) demonstrate that the correlation in stock markets increases during *bear* markets, precisely when the need for diversification is most important. They test this new hypothesis about the reason US investors tend to invest more in home equities based on the supposition that international assets do not offer diversification when markets fall. They formulate an asset allocation model similar to Ang and Chen's (2002) model, which tests the economic significance of ignoring the increasing correlation in *bear* markets.

Ang and Bekaert (2002) propose a discrete setting where the investor has to allocate his wealth to N assets over a T-month horizon. The investor can change the asset allocation every month. The objective of the investor is to optimize the expected final utility

$$\max_{\alpha_0,\ldots,\alpha_{T-1}} E_0[U(W_T)], \tag{6}$$

where α_i, $i = 0, \ldots, T-1$ are the portfolio weights for every period, W_T is the final wealth, subject to portfolio constraint $\alpha\mathbf{1} = 1$. Ang and Bekaert use the CRRA utility function

$$U(W_T) = \frac{W_T^{1-\gamma}}{1-\gamma},$$

similar to Eq. (4), and they find that portfolio weights after using dynamic programming are

$$\alpha_t^* = \arg\max_{\alpha_t} E_t[Q_{t+1,T} W_{t+1}^{1-\gamma}], \tag{7}$$

where

$$Q_{t+1,T} = E_{t+1}[(R_T(\alpha_{T-1}^*) \cdots R_{t+2}(\alpha_{t+1}^*))^{1-\gamma}], \tag{8}$$

and $Q_{T,T} = 1$. To complement the model they introduce regimes. Suppose there exist K regimes. Then y_{t+1} has a distribution selected from the different K regimes. Samuelson (1969) demonstrates that in case of returns drawn from i.i.d. random variables the optimal solution is the same "myopic" solution for each period. In the other case, Merton (1971) demonstrates the existence of an optimal solution drawn from a myopic solution and a hedging component. With this setting, they find an optimal numerical solution to the optimal dynamic portfolio allocation problem. The markets used are US, Germany, and UK equities market and the US cash market. They perform a sensitivity analysis to check the robustness of the solution. Finally, they check the economic significance in cost of cents per dollar between the two strategies. The first strategy does not diversify internationally. The second strategy applies international diversification and does not take into consideration the high correlation during *bear* market times. The main conclusion of the article is that they cannot reject the benefits of international diversification, despite the existence of high volatility and high correlation regimes, although they cannot reject the optimality of home biased portfolios. The economic cost of not being diversified between a system of US, Germany, and UK market is approximately 0.94% and 3.40% per dollar annually. They also test the impact on the results of having conditional risk-free asset, and they found that the presence of this asset affects the results on being aware of the R-S. In the absence of a conditional risk-free asset, the cost of ignoring the R-S is about 0.21% and 0.38%, but in the presence of this asset the cost of ignoring the R-S rises to 2.70% per year. Finally, they found that there is little economic significance in solving the hedging problem for the optimal solution of a long investment horizon, against the optimal myopic solution of one time period.

The research of Longin and Solnik (2001) was the first to address the issue of measuring extreme correlations, i.e., correlations in the tails of a bivariate distribution, in stock markets. In common with Ang and Chen (2002), Longin and Solnik found that the correlations are higher between large returns than they are between small returns. The authors establish that this conclusion could be misleading, because the conditional correlation depends on the returns' magnitude. Then the correlation of large returns will be higher than the correlations of smaller returns, *ceteris paribus*. It is important to specify a suitable null hypothesis and the statistics used to test correlations. An initial idea used by Longin and Solnik (2001) is to take a BVN distribution as a benchmark against which they can test the correlations. This is useful for establishing differences between the real behavior of stock markets and a well-known distribution that has closed formulae for extreme correlations Rosenbaum (1961). It also allows us to compare differences between correlations of large upside moves with correlations of large downside moves, a concept that Ang and Chen defined as "asymmetric correlation". However, it is well known that financial returns do not behave according to a normal distribution. For this reason, we expand the main results of the EVT.

Denote by $F_R(x)$ the distribution function of returns R. Define an exceedance threshold level θ. Denote by $F_R^\theta(x)$ the distribution of θ exceedance, or the distribution of the returns greater than θ. This distribution is equal to

$$F_R^\theta(x) = (F_R(x) - F_R(\theta))/(1 - F_R(\theta)), \qquad \text{for } x > \theta. \tag{9}$$

For practical purposes, it is important to study the asymptotic behavior of this distribution. EVT explores if there exists an extreme distribution to which Eq. (9) converges when we take the limit $\theta \to \infty$. But there is a problem because, for most distributions, the exceedance distribution is a degenerate one, i.e., a distribution with only two possible values, 0 and 1. For that reason we apply a transformation, after which we obtain one of the most important results of the univariate EVT. Pickands (1975) shows that the exceedance of any distribution converges to the following distribution:

$$G_R^\theta(x) = 1 - ((1 + \varepsilon(x - \theta)/\sigma)^+)^{1/\varepsilon}, \tag{10}$$

where σ is a dispersion parameter that depends on θ and F_R, and ε is called the tail index, a value related to the distribution F_R that has the following practical interpretations: Distributions with a finite tail have a value of $\varepsilon < 0$; distributions with an exponentially declining tail (normal distribution) have $\varepsilon = 0$; and distributions with a heavy tail have $\varepsilon > 0$. The distribution in Eq. (9) is called the generalized pareto distribution (GPD).

Longin and Solnik (2001) show that there does not exist a theorem for the convergence of the exceedance distribution to a unique distribution in the multivariate case. However, there are general theorems for the forms of the marginals and the dependence function (This is a special function which defines the relation between the marginals.) This dependence function maps from $\mathbb{R}^N$ into $\mathbb{R}$, and satisfies

$$G_R^\theta(x_1, \ldots, x_q) = \exp\left(-D_{G_R}\left(\frac{-1}{\log G_{R_1}^{\theta_1}(x_1)}, \ldots, \frac{-1}{\log G_{R_q}^{\theta_q}(x_q)}\right)\right).$$

In the case where the variables are independent, the dependence function D_{G_R} is characterized by

$$D_{G_R}(y_1, \ldots, y_q) = \left(\frac{1}{y_1} + \cdots + \frac{1}{y_q}\right),$$

where $y_i = -1/G_{R_i}^{\theta_i}$. For a large number of known distributions it is possible to obtain asymptotic independence of the marginals, and for the case of the normal distribution it is possible to obtain asymptotic independence even with dependent marginals. The most important fact for future research is that modeling the dependence function is not unique for the multivariate case, as it is for the univariate case. Again, the use of the normal distribution in a bivariate setting lets the authors establish important results, but empirical research into other forms of dependence functions is extremely important, to extend the results to a wider range of distributions.

Another work using EVT is made by Poon *et al.* (2004). They describe four kinds of extreme dependence structures in multivariate distributions: independent, perfect dependence, asymptotic dependence, and asymptotic independence. They define an asymptotic dependence measure

$$\chi = \lim_{s \to \infty} P(T > s | S > s),$$

where T and S are the marginals of the bivariate returns distribution (R_1, R_2) transformed to a Fréchet distribution as $S = -1/\log F_{R_1(R_1)}$, and in the same way for R_2. They also mention an asymptotic dependence measure for variables asymptotically independent ($\chi = 0$) defined by Coles *et al.* (1999), defined as

$$\overline{\chi} = \lim_{s \to \infty} \frac{2 \log \Pr(S > s)}{\log \Pr(S > s, T > s)},$$

where $-1 < \overline{\chi} \leq 1$. They make a non-parametric estimation of these measures and an empirical study with international equity indices from the US, UK, Germany, France, and Japan for estimating χ and $\overline{\chi}$. They form portfolios with a pair of these indices. The data are of daily frequency and from 1968 to 2001. The results show when $\overline{\chi}$ is estimated that the null hypothesis of the returns of the markets being not asymptotically independent is rejected in almost all cases. One of the first conclusions is that to use the Pearson correlation measure ρ in the tails of a distribution is not correct, and could give misleading results. The empirical study shows the estimation of asymptotic dependence χ for the pair of portfolios. They find that in the European pairs there exist high-fitted values for χ that represent the asymptotic dependency. As this behavior is only for 13 of 84 sub-periods, the authors conclude that the assumption of asymptotic dependence is not correct for most of the cases. The main implication in this work is that χ can be used as a systemic risk measure for extreme events. As the authors conclude, the results show that the pair *US–Germany* is not asymptotically dependent and can be used for diversification purposes, against the pair *US–UK* that is not asymptotically dependent. This bivariate study is of great importance for the measure of asymmetric correlation using EVT because it expands the Longin and Solnik work on how the dependence structures in the tails for more general distributions can be defined.

3.2. *Contagion in financial markets and limits on the use of the unconditional correlation measure in multiple regimes' markets*

The financial markets behave in a particular way, sometimes irrationally for some classical economists. Generally, macroeconomic and global events are the triggers of this behavior. One example of such behavior is the "contagion" effect, that is a market behavior related to the spread of the financial crisis in some particular country or region to another. This event is of particular interest in our research because of its intrinsic relation to extreme correlation. For a formal definition of contagion there exists a comprehensive literature, and the definition is not universal. One of the reasons that contagion behavior is of such interest for researchers is the economic importance of such an event. However, authors have historically used a formal definition of contagion as a significant increase in cross-market linkages.

The research of Forbes and Rigobon (2002) is one of the classical papers in the literature. In their research, they find that on three of the most recent financial crises, there existed no contagion, but an interdependence effect based on the unconditional correlation of the countries and regions. They use the change in unconditional correlation as the measure for the increase in the cross-market linkage. This result is contrary to the results of earlier literature. They revealed the existence of an heteroskedastic bias in the measure of extreme correlation, and they conclude this bias could have mislead the earlier results. The crises studied by the authors are the 1987 US market crash, the 1994 Mexican devaluation, and the 1997 Asian crisis. The authors search for a linear regression model with no endogeneity that shows that the exceedance correlation or conditional correlation on the extremes will be biased. Let Y_t, X_t be two stochastic variables representing the market returns of two different countries or regions. The linear model used is

$$Y_t = \alpha + \beta X_t + \epsilon_t. \quad (11)$$

Forbes and Rigobon (2002) propose this measure for conditional correlation to correct for any heteroskedastic bias

$$\rho^* = \rho\sqrt{\frac{1+\delta}{1+\delta\rho^2}}, \tag{12}$$

where ρ is the unconditional correlation, and δ is defined as

$$\delta = \frac{\sigma_X^h}{\sigma_X^l} - 1, \tag{13}$$

where σ_X^l is the variance of market returns X in normal conditions or low volatility, and σ_X^h is the variance of market returns X in crisis conditions or high volatility. This unconditional correlation measure is important for our research because it does not assume any distribution for the market returns. The restrictions are on the hypothesis of the linear relation of market returns and in the absence of endogeneity ($E[X_t \epsilon_t]] = 0$). In the empirical research Forbes and Rigobon (2002) use a linear model to test the unconditional correlation over 28 countries between East Asia, Latin America, Organization for Economic Cooperation and Development (OECD), and other emerging markets such as China, India, and Russia. Then they measure the traditional unconditional correlation in two sets: one defined as a low-volatility scenario in a pre-crisis and post-crisis time. And the other as a high-volatility scenario during the crisis. They also measure the unbiased unconditional correlation in both sets and investigate if there exist any significant changes in both sets. They found that the tests rejected the null hypothesis using the traditional unconditional correlation. The measure is made between the country that originates the crisis and the other countries. The test hypothesis is

$$H_0 : \rho > \rho_t^h, \tag{14}$$

$$H_1 : \rho \leq \rho_t^h. \tag{15}$$

The conclusion with this assumption is that there exists contagion. But when they used the unbiased unconditional correlation measure for the same test, they found that the test failed to reject the null hypothesis, with the conclusion of "no contagion". This chapter explores the hypothesis that the correct measure of extreme correlation is of importance for economic theories.

Some other important results in the contagion literature are in Bae *et al.* (2003). This chapter expands the results of Forbes and Rigobon (2002), exploring a new way to measure the contagion effect.

3.3. *Bivariate truncated moments*

The previous results of Ang and Bekaert (2002); Ang and Chen (2002), and Forbes and Rigobon (2002) suggest the existence of regimes. These regimes could be broadly classified as two: a *normal market* regime where unconditional moments prevail, and an *extreme market* regime where market shocks affect the behavior of the returns and distort the long-term returns' unconditional distribution. It is not the intention of our research to explore this hypothesis and the previous theoretical results over the market data. Such research would imply an immense load of data processing and empirical work that we propose to tackle in future extensions to our research.

4. Empirical Examples

With the purpose of clarifying the previous definitions of tail correlations and tail moments, we produce some examples. Consider a pair of *standardized returns* $(\tilde{X}, \tilde{Y}) \sim \text{BVN}(\mathbf{0}, \mathbf{\Sigma})$ where $\mathbf{\Sigma}$ has unit variances and unconditional correlation ρ. Define the tail central moments of $(\tilde{X}, \tilde{Y})$ as

$$m_{ij} = E[\tilde{X}^i \tilde{Y}^j | h < \tilde{X}, k < \tilde{Y}],$$

define the tail covariance between $\tilde{X}$ and $\tilde{Y}$ as

$$\text{cov}(h, k) = m_{11} - m_{10} m_{01},$$

and define the tail variance of $\tilde{x}$ and $\tilde{y}$ as

$$v(x) = m_{20} - m_{10}^2,$$
$$v(y) = m_{02} - m_{01}^2.$$

The *tail covariance* matrix is defined as

$$\Sigma = \begin{pmatrix} v(X) & \text{cov}(h, k) \\ \text{cov}(h, k) & v(Y) \end{pmatrix}.$$

We shall consider a special case of the previous definitions, where $k = h = \varsigma$. Longin and Solnik (2001) define the *conditional exceedance correlation* as in Eq. (5).

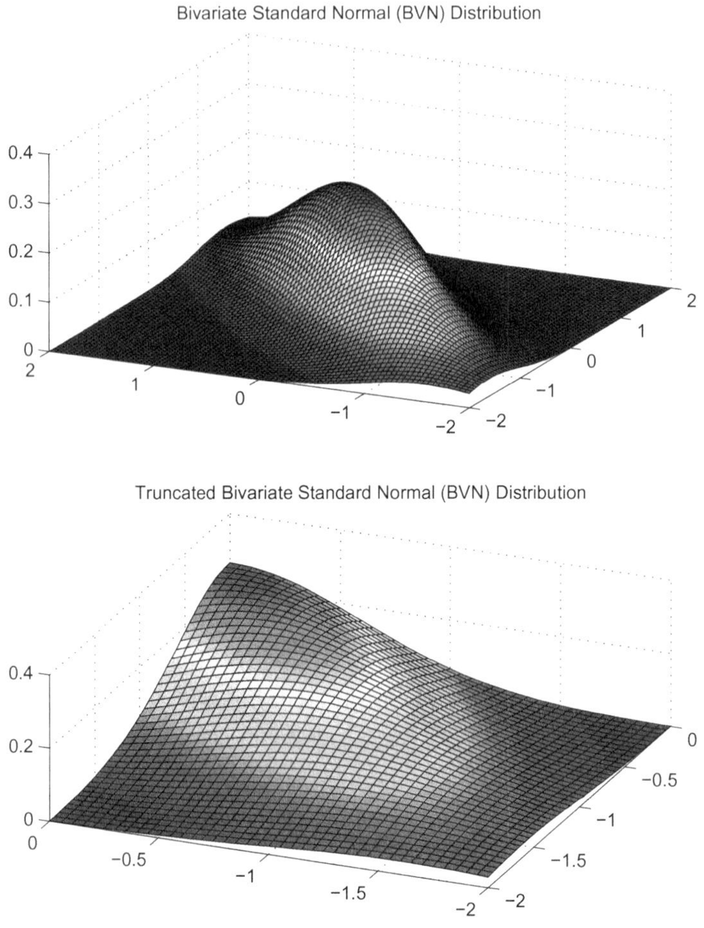

Figure 1. Density Function of a Standard BVN Distribution with $\rho = 0.8$, and the Lower-Lower Tail Distribution for the Threshold $\varsigma < 0$

In Fig. 1, we plot a standard BVN distribution with correlation $\rho = 0.8$, that will represent the joint returns of the two assets. We extract and plot the section of the distribution whose bivariate returns are negative. We need to divide this sliced section by a scalar factor, the integral of the sliced area; and it will become a density function. This new tail distribution could be considered the distribution of the *extreme market* regime, and will be defined as the extreme (tail) distribution. The extreme distribution does not necessarily need to be exactly similar to the sliced section with the same threshold parameters of the unconditional distribution. What Longin and Solnik (2001) and Ang and Chen (2002) demonstrate is that they differ.

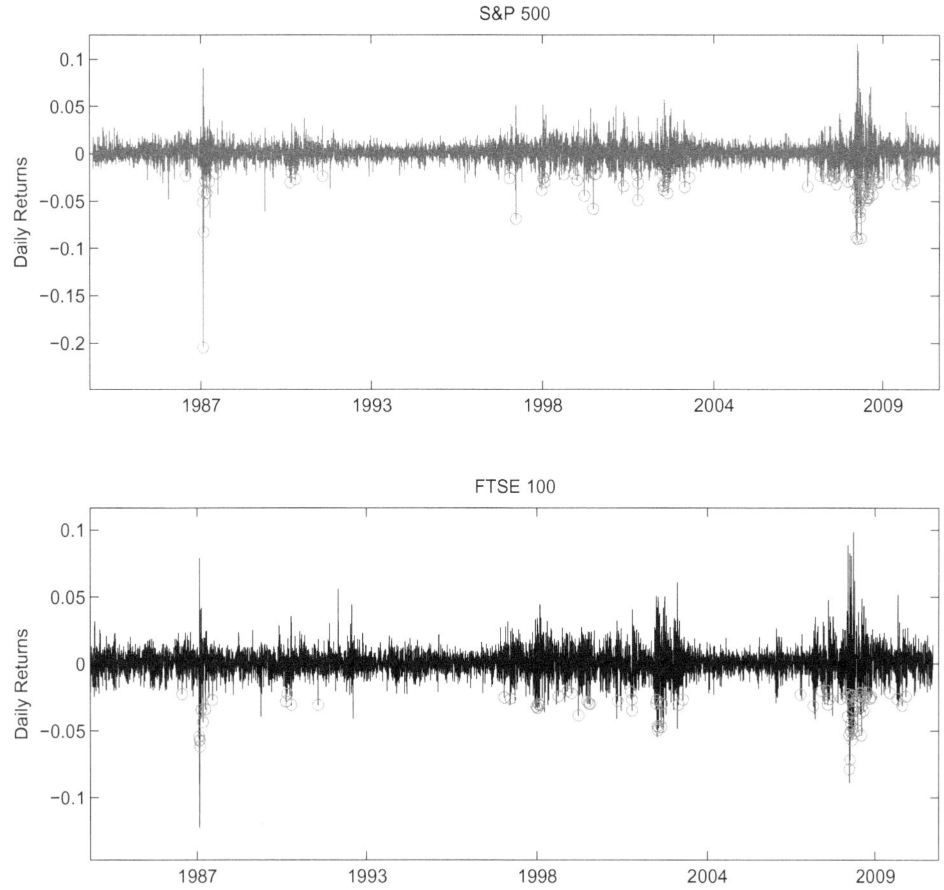

Figure 2. Daily Returns of the S&P500 and FTSE100 Indices from 1984 Until Late 2009, with the Days of -2% or Lower Returns in Red Dots

In Fig. 2 we plot the daily returns of the S&P500 and FTSE100 indices. Then we plot a red dot each time the returns of both indices are less than -2%. This extreme distribution will be sub-classified into a lower-lower extreme distribution and an upper-upper extreme distribution. The set of red dots will constitute the sliced area of Fig. 1, the tail distribution.

We review the bivariate extreme distribution in four different markets.

Example 1. The first is the equity market. We select the daily closing prices of the Microsoft (MSFT) stock and the S&P500 index, from August 31, 2001 until November 17, 2009. The days where there are no data reported from any of the two equities are dismissed. Then the returns are calculated and standardized. Figure 3(a) displays the joint returns. It can be seen that the

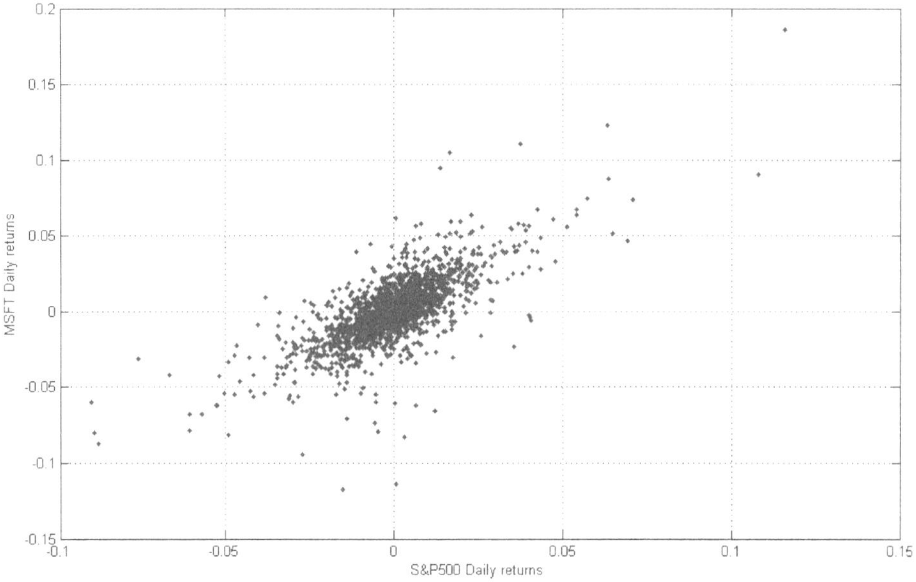

(a) Scatter plot of returns of the pair MSFT stock price and S&P500 index

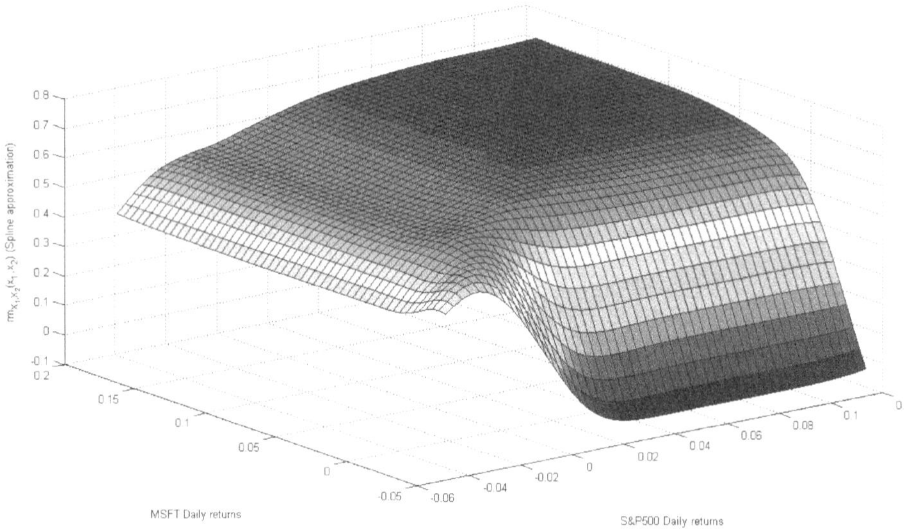

(b) Lower-lower tail correlation of the pair MSFT stock price and S&P500 index.

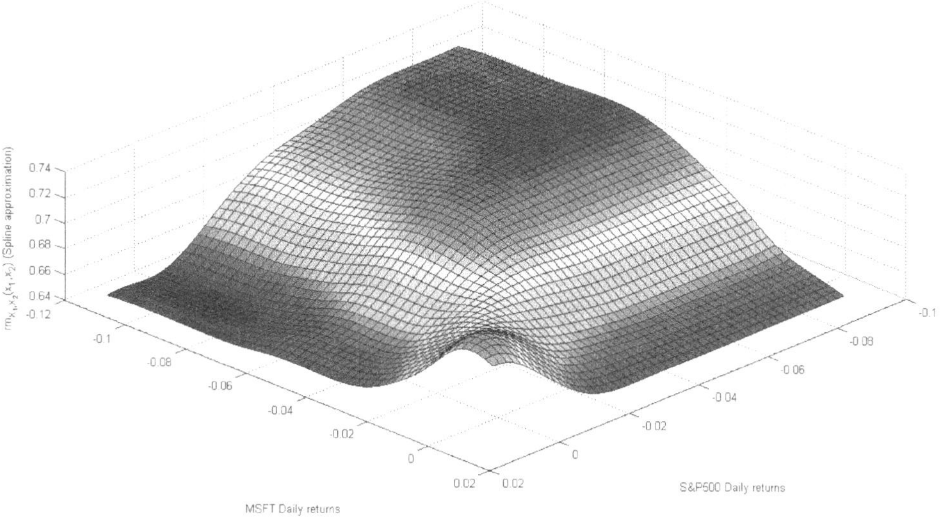

(c) Upper-upper tail correlation of the pair MSFT stock price and S&P500 index

Figure 3. Tail Correlation of MSFT Stock and S&P500 Index Prices from 31/08/2001 until 17/11/2009

linear correlation of the CAPM, given that the beta of MSFT is similar to the market beta, $\beta = 1$. An important question with a not unique answer is under which exceedance threshold values the sliced distribution becomes extreme. When measuring value-at-risk (VaR), the industry selects a distribution percentile threshold for extreme returns between 95%, 97.5%, 99%, and more recently 99.5%; however, to transform the percentile into an absolute return number will depend on the asset's distribution. We select $\varsigma = -5\%$ for the lower-lower tail and $\varsigma = 2\%$ for the upper-upper tail, and then we measure the empirical threshold from the exceedance correlation defined in Eq. (5) for increasing values of ς. A spline algorithm is applied over the final extracted threshold correlation to plot the lower-lower extreme correlation in Fig. 3(b), and the upper-upper extreme correlation in Fig. 3(c). The flat form of the empirical lower-lower tail correlation indicates a high correlation, and the steepest form of the upper-upper tail correlation corroborates the asymmetry of tails tested in Ang and Chen (2002). The difference in the correlation in the boundaries, for the MSFT stock returns of -5%, demonstrate the non-systematic risk of the stock. There is a second mode in the extreme boundary (2% on both assets) of the upper-upper tail correlation, the result of the leverage effect on the bull markets on all stocks by systemic events.

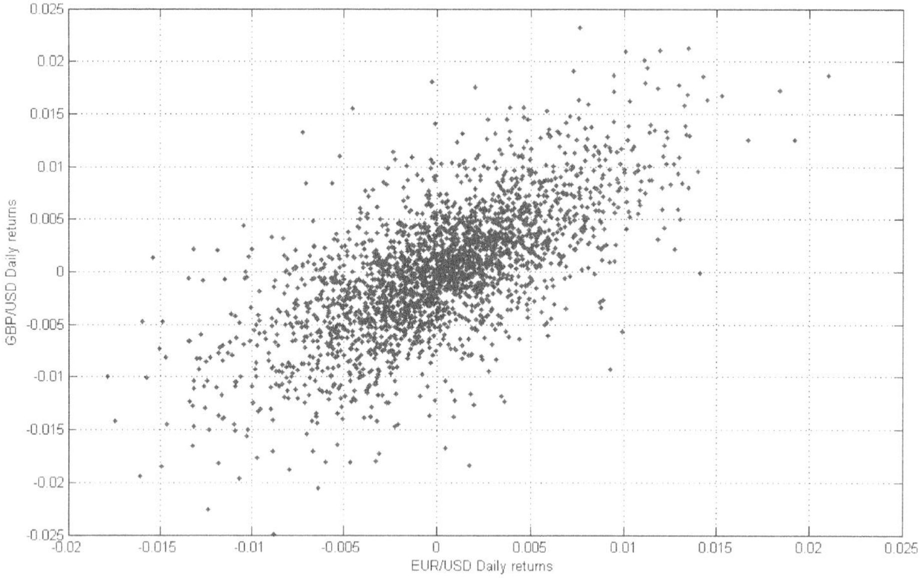

(a) Scatter plot of returns of the pair EUR/USD and GBP/USD currency prices.

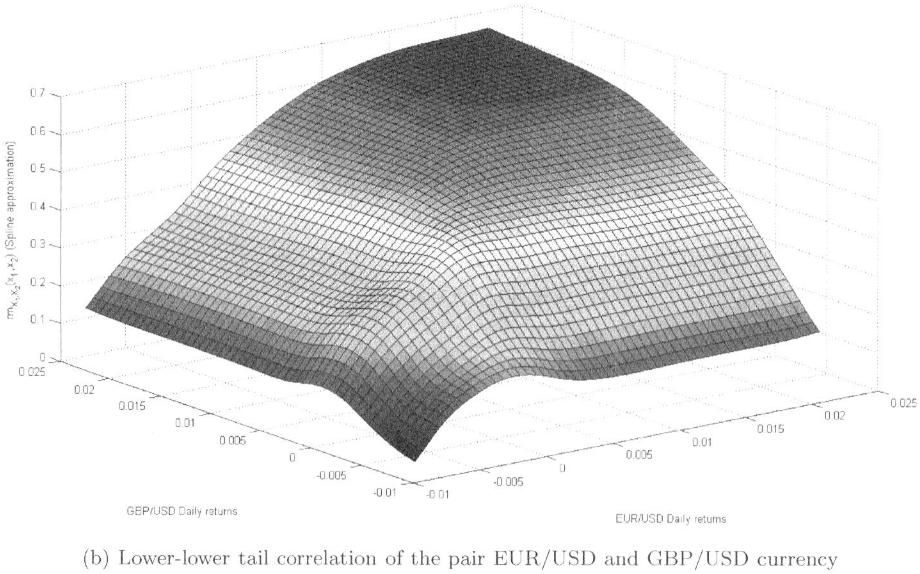

(b) Lower-lower tail correlation of the pair EUR/USD and GBP/USD currency prices.

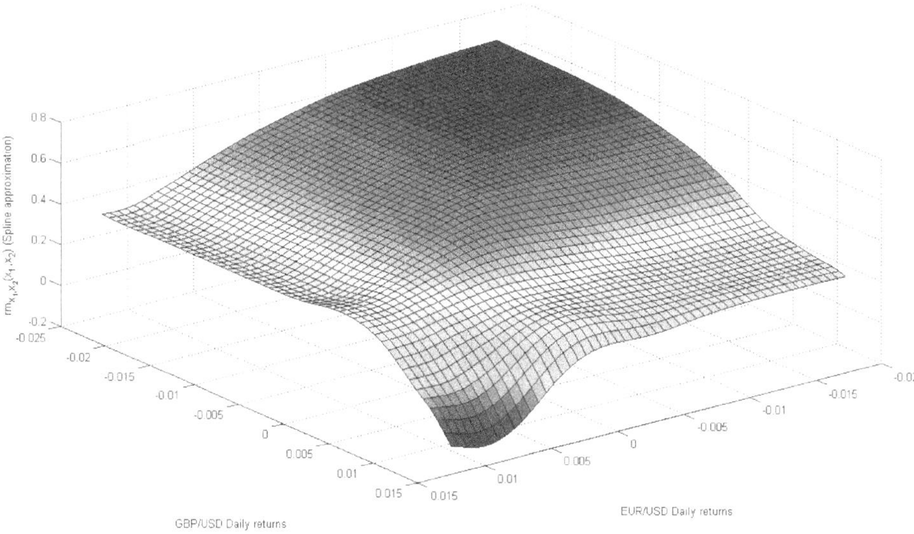

(c) Upper-upper tail correlation of the pair EUR/USD and GBP/USD currency prices.

Figure 4. Tail Correlation of Pairs EUR/USD and GBP/USD Currency Exchange Rates from 01/01/1999 up to 10/03/2008

The second market under review is the currency market. The data are from the daily exchange rates of the pair EUR/USD and GBP/USD settled at 5:00 pm, Eastern time, from January 1, 1999 up to March 10, 2008. The filtering process of eliminating non-common trading days is applied and returns are calculated. In this example and for subsequent market examples, the returns are not standardized to explore the effect of the volatility. Figure 3(a) shows the joint returns. There exists a linear relationship as result of the arbitrage pricing theory (APT) by triangular arbitrage. The threshold is fixed at $\varsigma = -1\%$ for the lower-lower tail correlation and $\varsigma = 1.25\%$ for the upper-upper tail, and they are plotted in Figs. 4(b) and 4(c), respectively. The currency market is less regulated and of higher transaction volume than the equity market, and because there is no trend in the long term of a currency pair, unless there is a devaluation policy in one of the currencies, it seems possible that there will be no asymmetry between the lower-lower tail and the upper-upper tail. The difference in the slope of Figs. 4(b) and 4(c) seems to indicate the contrary and it seems that the correlation is higher in bear markets. This could be the result of the carry trades that have driven the currency market in the last decade.

The third market under review is the commodity market. The data are from daily closing prices settled by the electronic clearinghouse and run from

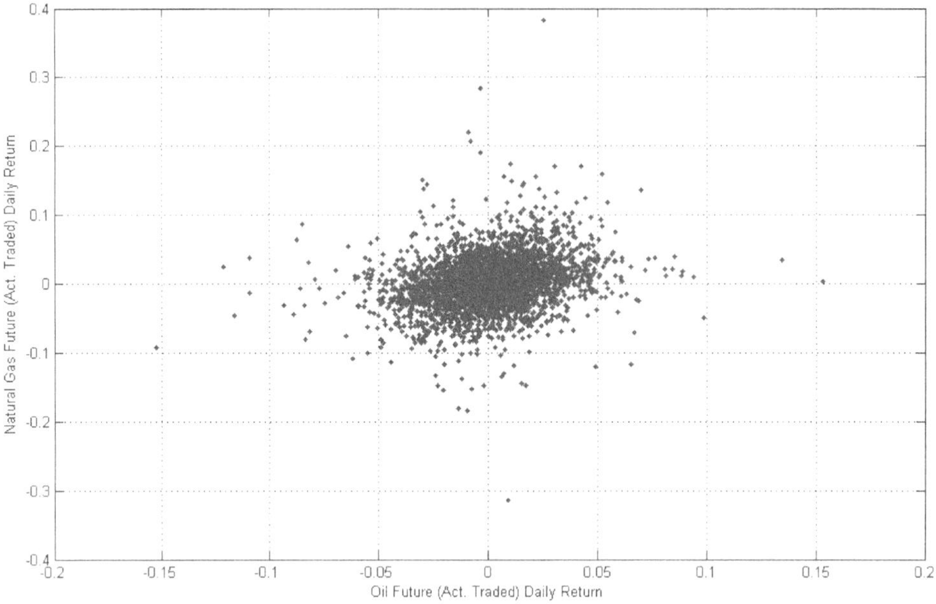

(a) Scatter plot of returns of the pair CL (crude oil) and NG (natural gas) futures'prices.

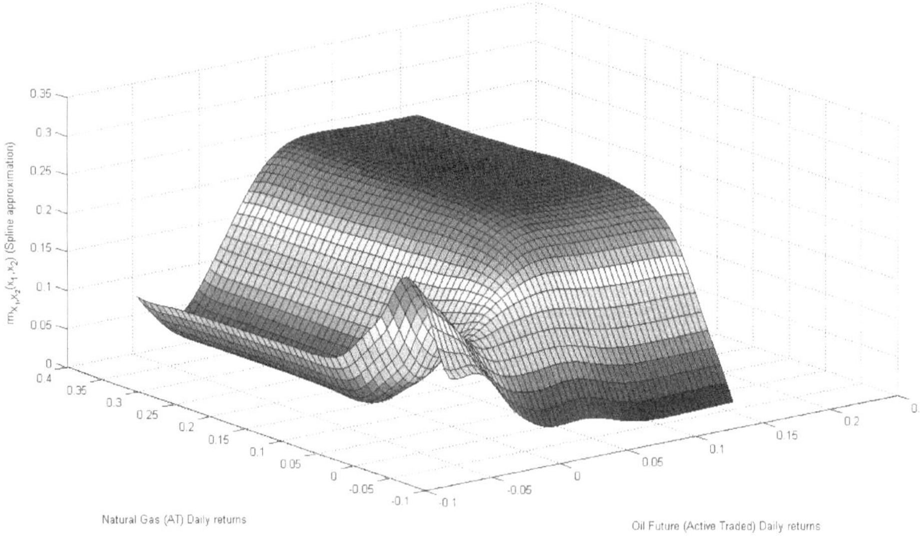

(b) Lower-lower tail correlation of the pair CL (crude oil) and NG (natural gas) futures' prices.

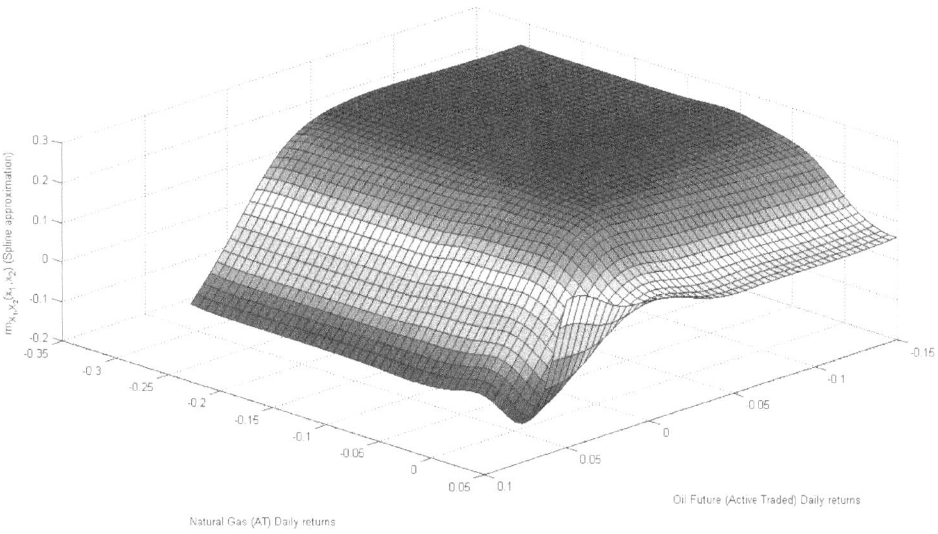

(c) Upper-upper tail correlation of the pair CL (crude oil) and NG (natural gas) futures' prices.

Figure 5. Tail Correlation of Crude Oil (CL) and Natural Gas (NG) Daily Future Prices from 29/06/1994 until 05/03/2008

June 29, 1994 until March 5, 2008. Figure 3(a) plots the joint returns with the threshold fixed at $\varsigma = -6\%$ for the lower-lower tail and $\varsigma = 5\%$ for the upper-upper tail. Figures 5(b) and 5(c) show the resulting tail correlations. The linear relationship in the daily returns is lower than in previous markets, and the lower-lower and upper-upper empirical tail correlations seem to corroborate this result. A possible explanation is that daily returns are noisy in commodities' market when compared with monthly or annual returns. However, the second mode in the boundary of the lower-lower empirical tail correlation indicates a high correlation in bear markets, and this empirical result suggests that it would be interesting to research the contagion effect of Forbes and Rigobon (2002) between equities and commodity markets. The tails appear to be asymmetric, and the similarity in the boundaries of the upper-upper tail correlations to the equity lower-lower tail systemic effect can be evidence of the spillover effect of the prices of natural gas over crude oil in bull markets.

The fourth and final market under review is the interest rate market. The daily rates are from UK LIBOR and USD 3-month Treasury Bills quoted at the US stock market closing time, from the January 2, 1987 up to September

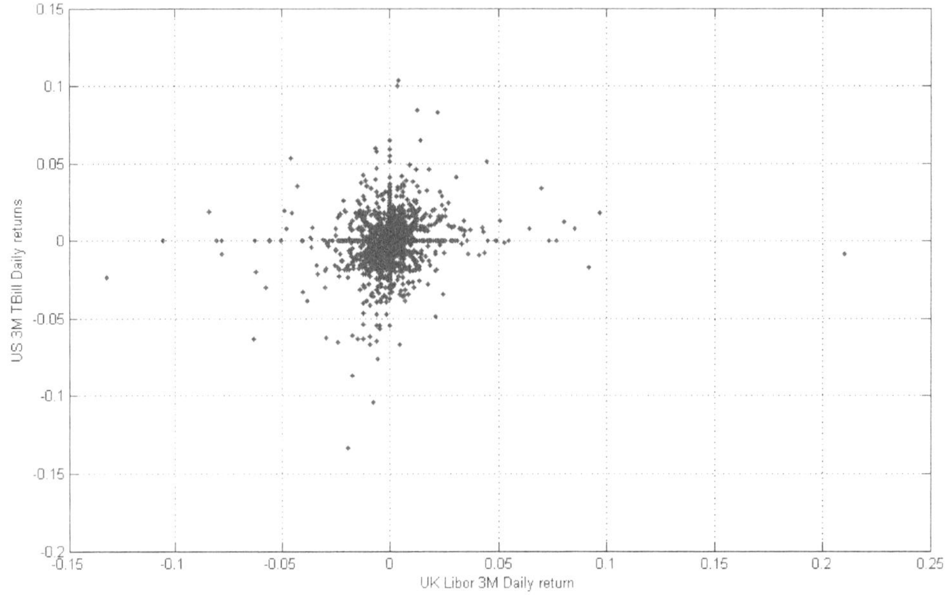

(a) Scatter plot of returns of the pair UK LIBOR and the USD 3-month Treasury bills' interest rates.

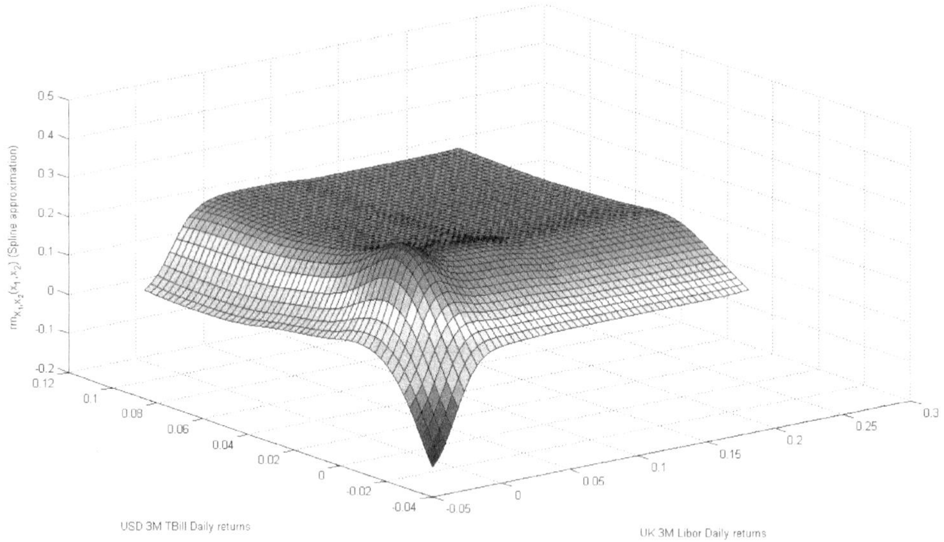

(b) Lower-lower tail correlation of the pair UK LIBOR and the USD 3-month Treasury bills' interest rates.

Figure 6.

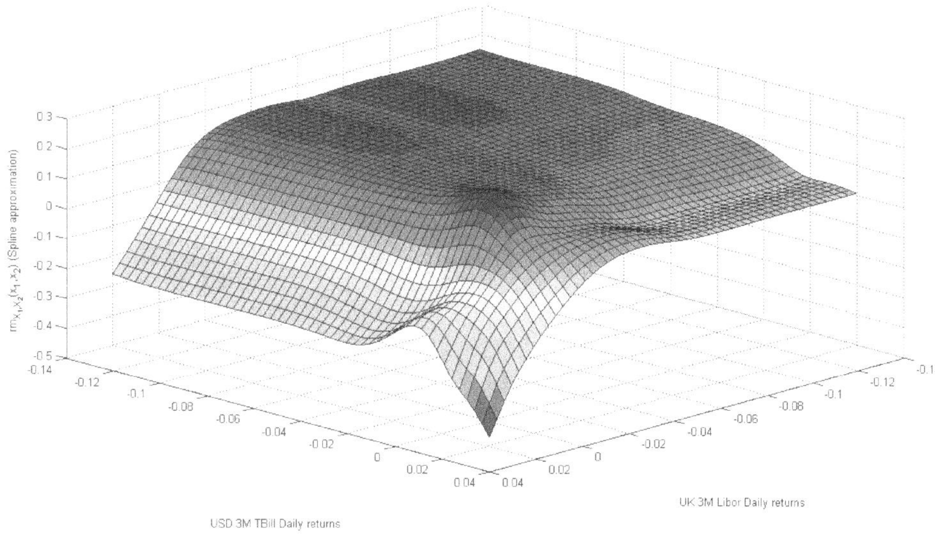

(c) Upper-upper tail correlation of the pair UK LIBOR and the USD 3-month Treasury bills' interest rates.

Figure 6. Tail Correlation of UK LIBOR and USD 3-Month Treasury Bills' Interest Rates from 02/01/1987 Until 26/09/2008

26, 2008. The threshold is fixed at −2.5% for the lower-lower tail and 3% for the upper-upper tail. The results are in Figs. 6(a)–6(c). The interest rate market is mean-reverting, which is in line with the non-linear relationship in the plots. From the four markets under review, it appears to be the most symmetric. The the black Monday of 1987 in the US, and black Wednesday of 1992 in the UK and their following days are represented by the extreme dots that account for a heavy-tailed distribution.

The empirical plots suggest that there could exist asymmetry in the tail correlations in other markets than equities, with important consequences in the asset pricing theory and risk management of those markets.

5. Tail Moments and Asset Pricing Theory

The anomalies in the empirical observations of the traditional CAPM (Sharpe, 1964) motivated the development of enhancements to the classical model. The conditional CAPM has been a proposed solution, and it has been an active topic of research. Jagannathan and Wang (1996) and

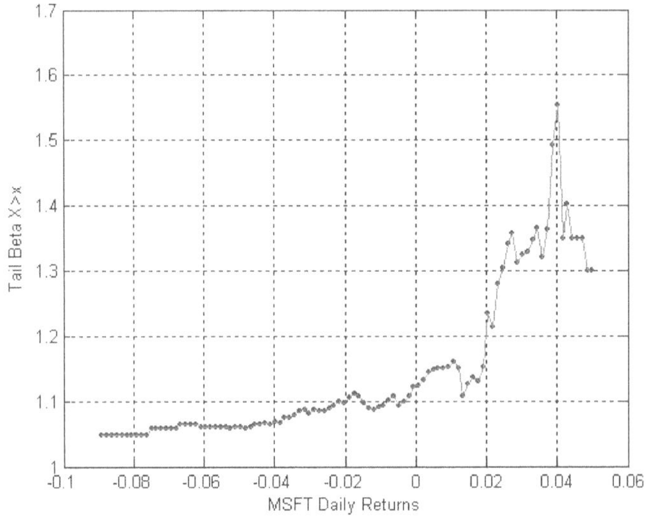

(a) Upper-tail beta of MSFT stock.

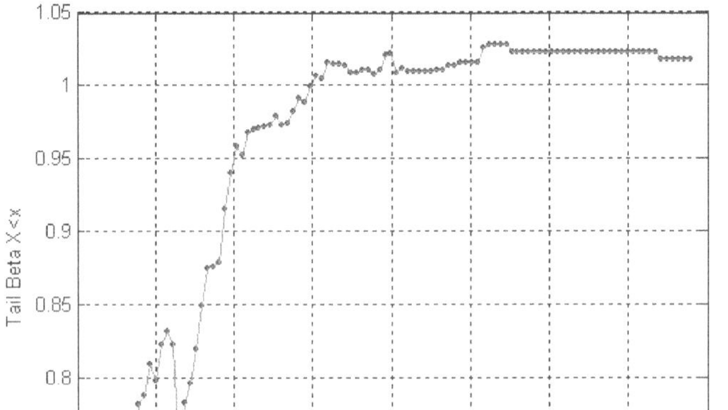

(b) Lower-tail beta of MSFT stock.

Figure 7. The Empirical Tail Beta of MSFT Estimated from Daily Close Prices 31/08/2001 Until 17/11/2009.

Lettau and Ludvigson (2001) are two of the publications that tested the conditional CAPM and successfully verified the improvement over the traditional model in a cross-sectional study. Lewellen and Nagel (2006) criticized the performance of the conditional CAPM with a time-varying research; however, academia continued the analysis of this theory, as the work of Stefan and Singleton (2011) provides a more complex statistical test to assess the fitness of the conditional CAPM. New findings of tail moments' theory could be applied for this purpose. For example, the research of Koenker and Basset (1978) about *quantile regression* is used by Barnes and Hughes (2001) to assess a cross-section of the equity market. The more recent paper of Engle (2012) proposed a *dynamic conditional beta* model, and it could be used to enhance the CAPM.

Define the tail beta of an asset as the beta conditional to the tail of the distribution. Using the daily data of the MSFT stock closing prices of the previous section, Figures 7(a) and 7(b) reproduce the upper-upper incremental beta and the lower-lower incremental beta. The empirical example is constructed by selecting the days where the stock and the S&P500 index are jointly negative and less than a threshold of -3% for the lower-lower beta and 5% for the upper-upper beta, and the threshold is increased/decreased until the tail corresponds to the unconditional distribution. The plot shows how both converge to a number barely above the market beta. An interesting question is how the tail beta behaves for a cross-section of different stocks. In Figs. 7 and 7(b) we observe a difference in the overshot of bull markets where the increase of the beta is near 0.4, against a reduction of 0.2 when the bear markets beta is measured. This effect could be related to the second mode in the upper-upper tail correlation of Fig. 3(c). Further investigation must address these questions, and we will provide statistical tools for such a task.

6. Higher-Order Bivariate Tail Moments and Option Pricing

Tail moments play an important role in options pricing. The asset pricing theory established that the price of an option is the expected value of the option contract under the risk-neutral measure. Recently, Neumann and Skiadopoulos (2013) found that there is economic value in predicting the risk-neutral higher-order moments (skewness) in a portfolio of S&P options.

Many contracts in options take the form of basket options

$$\Pi(\mathbf{x}) = [f(\mathbf{x}) - K]^+,$$

where K is a positive or negative scalar value, and $f(\mathbf{x})$ is a function of the asset prices $\mathbf{x}$. The value of these contracts is calculated as the first truncated moment at a plane threshold of a multivariate density.

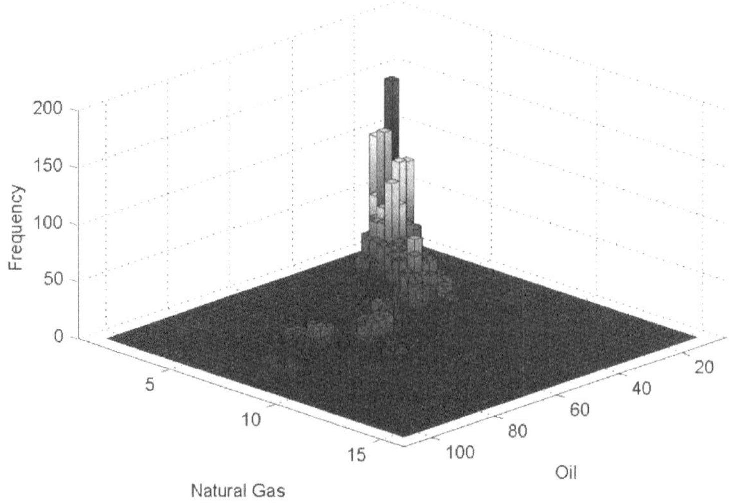

Figure 8. Histogram of the Crude Oil and Natural Gas Futures Prices (29/06/1994–05/03/2008)

Similarly, an important area currently under development is the design of new multi-asset option pricing methodologies, where the features of the multivariate distributions are accounted for in the formula. Traditional multi-asset option pricing considers approximations of the multivariate densities of the assets into a univariate density: for example, the sum of lognormal' distributions is *de facto* standard density used to price options under a multivariate GBM process.

Example 2. In Fig. 8, an histogram of the bivariate prices of the crude oil futures and the natural gas futures' contracts is plotted. Under the classical theory, to use a multivariate geometric Brownian motion (GBM) to price options over these assets, the returns must be bivariate lognormal distributed. The histogram shows the sectors where the distribution is highly skewed and the sectors where the skewness direction changes from one asset to the other. The second derivatives of the multivariate lognormal density function indicate that it is a monotonic function, suggesting that it will be a poor fit to the bivariate sample of these future prices.

The use of truncated moments could be utilized to price the anomalies in actual financial theories. In Preis *et al.* (2007) the distribution of price changes is modeled through a truncated Levy distribution. During market shocks, the regulators will force a market shutdown to avoid collapse (as in September 2001). These mechanisms derive into an implicit truncated distribution of the trading order book.

7. First and Second Bivariate Standard Normal Tail Moments

The results on truncated moments over the bivariate standard normal (BVSN) case were developed after the multivariate case, and thus it could be inferred that Birnbaum and Meyer's (1953) results were not fully spread throughout the literature. Rosenbaum (1961) calculated explicit formulae for the first and second moments of a lower truncated BVSN. Rao *et al.* (1968) calculated the sampling correlation of a bivariate normal (BVN) case, with lower truncation of only one variable. He also derived moments up to the fifth-order when only one variable is truncated. Ang and Chen (2002) extended Rosenbaum's results for the doubly truncated BVSN case, and used these formulae to test for asymmetries of correlation in different financial market regimes. Arnold *et al.* (1993) calculated the marginal of a BVN distribution with double truncation over one variable as in Rao *et al.* (1968).

We introduce some notation to calculate the bivariate higher-order moments:

Define (X_1, X_2) to be a bivariate random variable with absolutely continuous distribution function $F_{X_1,X_2}(h, k)$. We assume that F is differentiable and the joint density function $f_{X_1,X_2}(h, k)$ exists. We assume also that $E(X_1X_2)$, $E(X_1)$, and $E(X_2)$ are finite. The product upper-upper moment tail function of (X_1, X_2) is define by

$$m_{\alpha\beta}(h, k) = E[(X_1 - h)^\alpha (X_2 - k)^\beta | h < X_1, k < X_2],$$

where $\alpha, \beta \in \mathbb{I}$ and $h, k \in \mathbb{R}$ are truncation points. These moments can be computed with the integral

$$m_{\alpha\beta}(h, k) = \int_h^\infty \int_k^\infty \frac{(z_1 - h)^\alpha (z_2 - k)^\beta f_{X_1,X_2(z_1,z_2)}}{F_{X_1,X_2}(h, k)} dz_1 dz_2.$$

Similar functions can be defined changing the tail over which the moment is defined, like lower-lower $X_1 < h, X_2 < k$, upper-lower $X_1 > h, X_2 < k$, and lower-upper $X_1 < h, X_2 > k$. However, we develop results only for the upper-upper moment function as other moment tail definitions in the case of symmetric tail distributions can be calculated using these results. We refer to this upper-upper tail moment just as the tail moment. There also exist definitions of tail moments for double truncation $h_1 < X_1 < h_2, k_1 < X_2 < k_2$, but calculations for these definitions are extensions to our results.

Let (X_1, X_2) be BVSN random variable, with correlation ρ, truncated on $h < X_1, k < X_2$. The probability density function ϕ is defined as

$$\phi(x_1, x_2; \rho) = \begin{cases} \frac{1}{2\pi\sqrt{1-\rho^2}} e^{-\frac{1}{2}\left(x_1^2 - 2\rho x_1 x_2 + x_2^2\right)/(1-\rho^2)}, & h < X_1, k < X_2; \\ 0, & \text{otherwise.} \end{cases}$$

The total probability $L(h, k; \rho)$ under this truncated density function will be defined as

$$L(h, k; \rho) = \int_k^\infty \int_h^\infty \phi(x, y; \rho) dx dy.$$

BVN tail moments $m_{\alpha\beta}$ are defined as

$$\begin{aligned} m_{\alpha\beta}(x_1, x_2) &= E[x^\alpha y^\beta | h < x, k < y], \\ &= \frac{1}{2\pi\sqrt{1-\rho^2} L(h, k; \rho)} \int_k^\infty \int_h^\infty x^\alpha y^\beta e^{-\frac{1}{2}\left(x^2 - 2\rho x y + y^2\right)/(1-\rho^2)}. \end{aligned}$$

We use the following notation for the cross-moments of higher-order: A cross moment $m_{\alpha\beta}$ is of order i if $\alpha, \beta \geq 1$ and $\alpha + \beta = i$.

Using a change of variable, Birnbaum and Meyer (1953) and Rosenbaum (1961) find the first and second moments as follows:

$$m_{10} = L(h, k; \rho)^{-1} \left(\phi(h)(1 - \Phi(k_\rho)) + \rho\phi(k)(1 - \Phi(h_\rho))\right), \tag{16}$$

$$\begin{aligned} m_{20} = 1 + L(h, k; \rho)^{-1} \Bigg(& h\phi(h)(1 - \Phi(k_\rho)) + \rho^2 k\phi(k)(1 - \Phi(h_\rho)) \\ & + \frac{\rho\sqrt{1-\rho^2}}{\sqrt{2\pi}} \phi\left(\sqrt{h_\rho^2 + k^2}\right) \Bigg), \end{aligned} \tag{17}$$

$$\begin{aligned} m_{11} = \rho + L(h, k; \rho)^{-1} \Bigg(& \rho h\phi(h)(1 - \Phi(k_\rho)) + \rho k\phi(k)(1 - \Phi(h_\rho)) \\ & + \frac{\sqrt{1-\rho^2}}{\sqrt{2\pi}} \phi\left(\sqrt{h_\rho^2 + k^2}\right) \Bigg), \end{aligned} \tag{18}$$

where $k_\rho = (k - \rho h)/\sqrt{1-\rho^2}$ and $h_\rho = (h - \rho k)/\sqrt{1-\rho^2}$. The moments m_{01} and m_{02} follow by symmetry. An empirical version of the truncated moments will be used in the next section to assess VaR.

8. Normal Value-at-Risk (VaR): Unconditional Variance vs. Tail Variance

The theory about the tails of the distributions is fundamental for risk management. The standard measure of risk of the industry, the VaR, is considered the essential instrument for hedging unwanted loses. Banks' capital adequacy regulations, enumerated in Basels II and III, use VaR to measure the acceptable levels of risk an institution can tolerate. Several academics and companies have developed software and methodologies to calculate the VaR, but recent findings on asymmetrical correlations challenge the principles of such methodologies. For example, Bernard *et al.* (2015) found an improvement of the VaR of credit portfolios using a rearrengement algorithm (Embrechts *et al.*, 2013) with higher-order cumulants.

Let $\omega = (\omega_1, \ldots, \omega_n)$ be the weights in a portfolio of N assets. Let $\mathbf{r} = (R_1, \ldots, R_n)$ be the asset returns. Define $\mathbf{V}$ as the asset returns' covariance matrix. When stated as a percentage of the portfolio value, the $\alpha\%$ h-day VaR is minus the α percentile of the h-day returns' distribution.

The normal VaR_α of the portfolio is defined as

$$\text{VaR}_\alpha(\omega) = z_\alpha \sqrt{\omega' \mathbf{V} \omega}, \tag{19}$$

where z_α is the standard normal percentile at level α.

To calculate $\mathbf{V}$, both academia and industry use the covariance matrix of the whole distribution. But Rosenbaum (1961) proves that the covariance matrix is different in the tail of the distributions, and we have seen in Longin and Solnik (2001) and Ang and Chen (2002) that the tail correlation differs between bear and bull regimes in equity markets. To have a proper definition of normal VaR, a covariance matrix of the tail of the distribution is then required.

Define $\omega = (\omega, 1 - \omega)$ as the weights on a two-asset portfolio. Let x, y be the asset returns, normally distributed with annual standard deviation of 25% each (5% 10-day). Consider $\omega = 0.5$, $\rho = 0.5$, the unconditional correlation between x, y in the first case and $\rho = -0.5$ in the second. Now, we calculate the 1% 10-day normal VaR using the unconditional variance matrix, and the tail variance matrix:

VaR with unconditional variance $z_\alpha \sqrt{\omega' \mathbf{V} \omega}$:

$$\text{VaR}_\alpha(\omega; \rho = 0.5) = 10.07\%,$$
$$\text{VaR}_\alpha(\omega; \rho = -0.5) = 5.82\%.$$

VaR with tail variance $z_\alpha\sqrt{\omega'\Sigma\omega}$:

$$\text{VaR}_\alpha(\omega;\rho = 0.5) = 9.22\%,$$
$$\text{VaR}_\alpha(\omega;\rho = -0.5) = 7.71\%.$$

The VaR is lower when the calculation is made with the tail moments, for the unconditional positive correlation case ($\rho = 0.5$). This is counter-intuitive, but it is in line with the results of Ang and Chen (2002), as the exceedance correlation is a decreasing function on the tail, and it is always lower than the unconditional correlation (Fig. 12). When the unconditional correlation is negative ($\rho = -0.5$) the VaR calculated with the exceedance moments is higher; this result is new and is in line with the increasing function of truncated moments (Fig. 12(b)).

The conditional autoregressive VaR model of Engle and Manganelli (2000) (CAViAR) could be a solution to the problem of measuring the VaR with a time-varying volatility. We explore the benefits of a conditional VaR in the next example.

It is a well-known fact that stock return distributions are negative skewed and heavy-tailed (Kim and White, 2004). To calculate the VaR for non-normal distributions we could use a percentile approximation.

Let $f(x)$ be the unknown univariate probability density function of the returns of a portfolio, and $\phi(x)$ the standard normal distribution. Our next application is to calculate the *VaR* using a $f(x)$ approximation like *Gram–Charlier A series*. Let $\tilde{k}_3$ be the skewness, $\tilde{k}_4$ the kurtosis, and $\phi(x)$ the density of a normal standard; the Gram–Charlier A series expansion up to the fourth-order of $f(x)$ is

$$f(x) = \left(1 + \frac{\tilde{k}_3}{3!}H_3\left(\frac{x-\mu}{\sigma}\right) + \frac{\tilde{k}_4}{4!}H_4\left(\frac{x-\mu}{\sigma}\right) + \frac{\tilde{k}_3^2}{5!}H_5\left(\frac{x-\mu}{\sigma}\right)\right)\phi(x), \tag{20}$$

where $H_3 = (x^3 - 3x)$, $H_4 = (x^4 - 6x + 3)$, and $H_5 = (x^6 - 15x^4 + 45x^2 - 15)$ correspond to the Hermite polynomials. To calculate the semi-parametric non-normal VaR, we would need this approximation to estimate the percentiles of the distribution by its moments, known as the *Cornish–Fisher* VaR.

The publication of Harvey and Siddique (2000) offer some insights about using time-varying skewness and kurtosis, and they find the market accounts premium for investor preferences on these higher-order moments. We

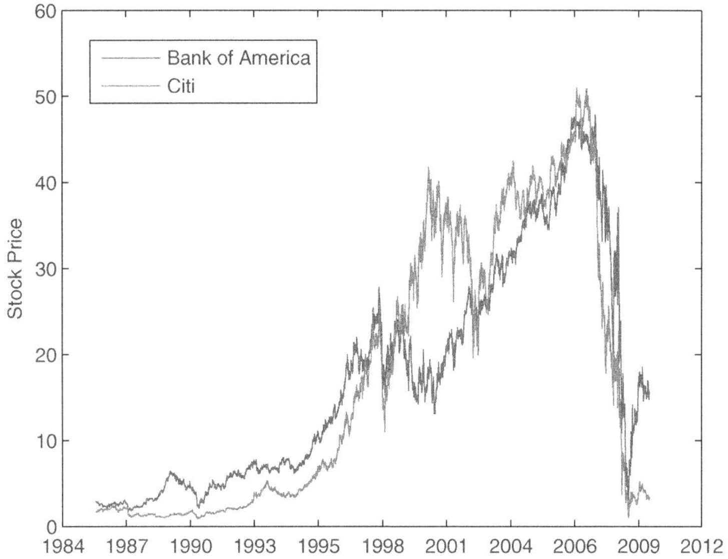

Figure 9. Stock Prices of Citigroup (C) and Bank of America (BAC) from 29/05/1986 to 03/02/2010

reproduce an example of the VaR calculation with time-varying correlations, skewness, and kurtosis, using equity data:

Example 3. In this exercise, daily stock prices of Citigroup (C) and Bank of America (BAC) from May 29, 1986 until February 3, 2010 are used to estimate an empirical returns' distribution. The filtering process includes the elimination of non-common trading days. An equal weights' portfolio $\omega = (0.5, 0.5)$ is defined. In Fig. 9, we plot the stock prices, where the slump of the financial crisis in 2008 is evident. The moving window for the calculation of time-varying moments is set to $1,000$ days (≈ 4 years). An exponentially moving weighted factor is applied to the returns, with the lag parameter of $\lambda = 0.999$, giving an adjusting factor of 0.61. With these exponentially weighted returns, the tail conditional portfolio correlation, volatility, skewness, and kurtosis are calculated. The conditional moments are calculated for the lower-lower tail and the upper-upper tail returns. The threshold parameter for both tails is established at the 20th percentile and 80th percentile of the returns, respectively. The moments calculated over the returns of the whole window are defined as *unconditional* moments, and the moments calculated over the set restricted to the tails will be defined as *lower-lower* (LL) and *upper-upper* (UU) moments. The three sets of moments are conditional on time.

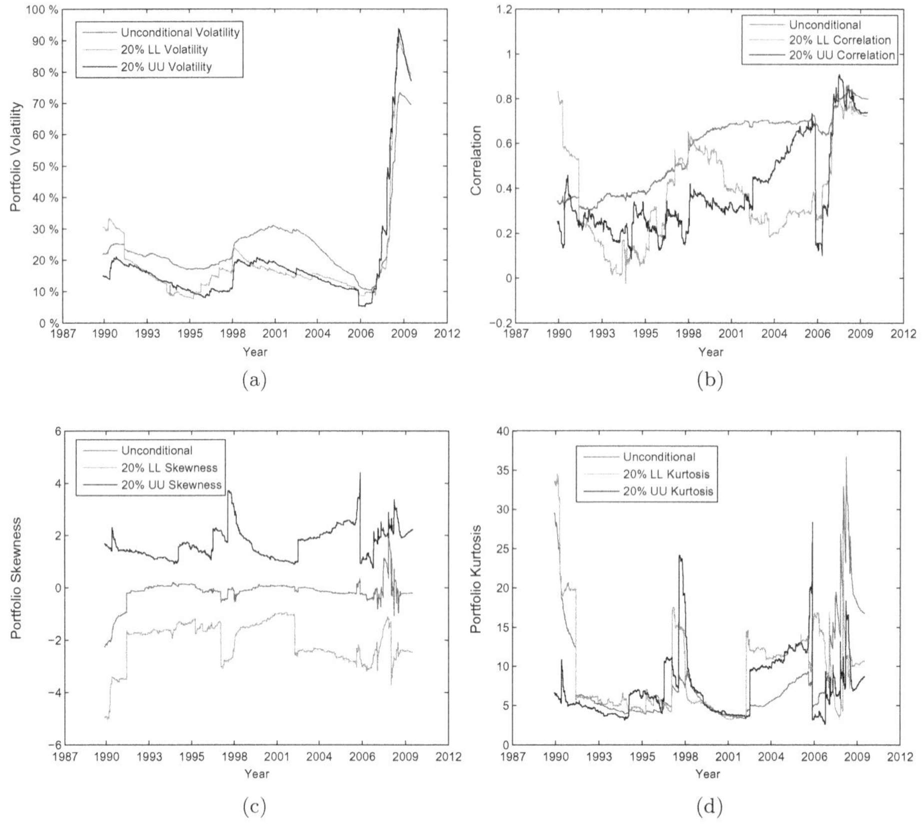

Figure 10. Unconditional and conditional tail moments of pair Citigroup (C) and Bank of America (BAC). (a) Unconditional, and conditional tail volatility with the lower-lower tail volatility calculated at the 20-th percentile and upper-upper tail at the 80-th percentile. (b) Unconditional, and conditional tail correlation with the lower-lower tail correlation calculated at the 20-th percentile and upper-upper tail at the 80-th percentile. (c) Unconditional, and conditional tail skewness with the lower-lower tail skewness calculated at the 20-th percentile and upper-upper tail at the 80-th percentile. (d) Unconditional, and conditional tail kurtosis with the lower-lower tail kurtosis calculated at the 20-th percentile and upper-upper tail at the 80-th percentile.

Then, the 1-day normal VaR at the 99% confidence level is calculated applying Eq. (19). Using Eq. (20), a 1-day *Cornish–Fisher VaR* at the 99% confidence level is calculated. Figs. 10(a)–10(d) are the plots of the tail moments. The tail moments will be noisier than the unconditional by definition, but they expose the financial crisis events in a better way: the increase in volatility is higher in tail moments, and a similar effect is seen in

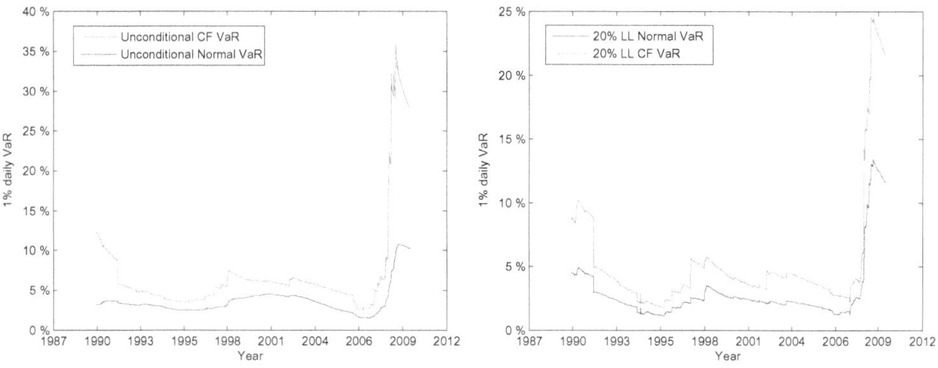

Figure 11. Unconditional and Tail Moment *VaR*. (a) Unconditional 1-day *VaR* at the 99%-th percentile. (b) Cornish-Fisher four moment 1-day *VaR* at the 99%-th percentile.

the correlation. For skewness, the upper-upper tail version seems to sound a first alarm during the year 1998 during the emerging market bond crisis, and in 2006 when the real estate crash started.

For kurtosis the unconditional detects the crisis in an early stage for the 2009 crisis, while it appears not capable of uncovering the crisis of 1998. In Fig. 11(a) the unconditional normal VaR and the unconditional *Cornish–Fisher VaR* are plotted. Including the moments in the VaR calculation reveals the effects and the dimension of the 2008 crisis. In Fig. 11(b), the chart of the lower-lower tail normal VaR and lower-lower tail *Cornish-Fisher VaR* are given. Again, the graph shows that conditioning on the tail of the distribution unmasks the magnitude of the crisis.

The bivariate tail higher-order moments results of Propositions 1 and 2 could be used in conjunction with *Cornish-Fisher VaR* to develop new methods and new statistical tests for risk management.

9. Third- and Fourth-Order Moments of a BVN Distribution

In the previous section, an example with the limitations of classical normal VaR methodology was demonstrated. The use of truncated moments is of central importance in risk assessment when using parametric distributions like the BVN. In this section, we provide new results on the truncated higher-order moments of a BVSN distribution. We calculate third- and fourth-order moments applying a double integral with a change of variable methodology as in Rosenbaum (1961):

Proposition 1. *Let (X, Y) be bivariate normal standard random variable, with correlation ρ, truncated on $h < X, k < Y$. The third-order moment and cross moments are as follows:*

$$\begin{aligned} m_{30} &= L(h,k;\rho)^{-1}(((4-h^2)\rho^6 + h^2 + 2)\phi(h)(1-\Phi(k_\rho)) \\ &\quad + \frac{(1-\rho^2)^{1/2}}{(2\pi)^{1/2}}(\rho h + \rho^3 h - \rho^2(1-\rho^2)^{1/2})\phi(\sqrt{h_\rho^2 + k^2}) \\ &\quad \times (3\rho - \rho^3 + \rho^3 k^2)\phi(k)(1-\Phi(h_\rho))), \\ m_{21} &= L(h,k;\rho)^{-1}\big((\rho h^2 + 2\rho)\phi(h)(1-\Phi(k_\rho)) \\ &\quad + (1/(2\pi)^{1/2})(1-\rho^2)^{1/2}(h + \rho k)\phi(\sqrt{h_\rho^2 + k^2}) \\ &\quad \times (1 + \rho^2 + \rho^2 k^2)\phi(k)(1-\Phi(h_\rho))\big), \end{aligned}$$

where $k_\rho = (k - \rho h)/\sqrt{1-\rho^2}$ and $h_\rho = (h - \rho k)/\sqrt{1-\rho^2}$. The moments m_{03} and m_{12} follow by symmetry.

Proof. The extreme third-order moment m_{30} is defined as

$$\begin{aligned} m_{30} &= E[X^3 | h < X < \infty, k < Y < \infty] \\ &= \frac{1}{2\pi\sqrt{1-\rho^2}L(h,k;\rho)} \int_k^\infty \int_h^\infty x^3 e^{-\frac{1}{2}(x^2 - 2\rho xy + y^2)/(1-\rho^2)} dx dy. \end{aligned}$$

To solve this double integral, we use the transformation $x - \rho y = z\sqrt{1-\rho^2}$. This leads us to change one of the integrand extremes to: $u = (h - \rho y)/\sqrt{1-\rho^2}$, so that

$$m_{30} = \frac{1}{2\pi\sqrt{1-\rho^2}L(h,k;\rho)} \int_k^\infty \int_u^\infty \left(z\sqrt{1-\rho^2} + \rho y\right)^3 e^{-\frac{1}{2}(y^2+z^2)} dz dy.$$

The cubic term inside the integral expands to four terms and the integral becomes

$$\begin{aligned} &\int_k^\infty \int_u^\infty (z^3(1-\rho^2)^{3/2} + 3z^2(1-\rho^2)\rho y + 3z(1-\rho^2)^{1/2}\rho^2 y^2 + \rho^3 y^3) \\ &\quad \times e^{-\frac{1}{2}(y^2+z^2)} dz dy. \qquad (21) \end{aligned}$$

Now, we integrate each of these four terms. Define

$$f_n(y,z;c) = \int_c^\infty y^n e^{-\frac{1}{2}(y^2+z^2)}dy.$$

The first term is, after applying integration by parts,

$$\begin{aligned}(1-\rho^2)^{3/2}\int_k^\infty\int_u^\infty z^3 dz dy &= (1-\rho^2)^{3/2}\int_k^\infty f_3(z,y;u)dy\\ &= (1-\rho^2)^{3/2}\int_k^\infty (u^2 e^{-\frac{1}{2}(y^2+u^2)} + 2f_1(z,y;u))dy.\end{aligned} \quad (22)$$

The first term of Eq. (22) expands into three terms. Then we apply the change of variable:

$$\begin{aligned} w &= (y-\rho h)/\sqrt{1-\rho^2}, \\ dw\sqrt{1-\rho^2} &= dy.\end{aligned} \quad (23)$$

After applying integration by parts recursively we obtain:

$$\begin{aligned}&(1-\rho^2)^{3/2}\int_k^\infty\int_u^\infty z^3 e^{-\frac{1}{2}(y^2+z^2)}dzdy\\ &= (1-\rho^2)^{3/2}\Big(h^2(1-\rho^2)^{3/2}f_0(w,h;v) - 2h\rho(1-\rho^2)e^{-\frac{1}{2}(k^2+n^2)}\\ &\quad +\rho^2(1-\rho^2)^{1/2}\Big(e^{-\frac{1}{2}(k^2+n^2)}m + f_0(w,h;v)\Big) + 2f_0(y,u;k)\Big),\end{aligned} \quad (24)$$

where $m = (k-\rho h)/\sqrt{1-\rho^2}$ and $n = (h-\rho k)/\sqrt{1-\rho^2}$.

To calculate the second term of Eq. (21), we apply integration by parts recursively

$$\begin{aligned}&3(1-\rho^2)\rho\int_k^\infty\int_u^\infty z^2 y e^{-\frac{1}{2}(y^2+z^2)}dzdy\\ &= 3(1-\rho^2)\rho\int_k^\infty y f_2(z,y;u)dy\\ &= 3(1-\rho^2)\rho(f_2(z,k;u) - f_2(u,y;k))\\ &= 3(1-\rho^2)\rho(ne^{-\frac{1}{2}(n^2+k^2)} + f_0(z,k;u) - f_2(u,y;k)).\end{aligned} \quad (25)$$

For the last term of Eq. (25) we apply change of variable w by y (Eq. (23)) and finally, we have:

$$
\begin{aligned}
&3(1-\rho^2)\rho\int_k^{\infty}\int_u^{\infty} z^2 y e^{-\frac{1}{2}(y^2+z^2)}dzdy\\
&\quad = 3(1-\rho^2)\rho\big(ne^{-\frac{1}{2}(n^2+k^2)} + f_0(z,k;u)\\
&\quad\quad + \frac{\rho}{\sqrt{1-\rho^2}}(h^2(1-\rho^2)^{3/2} f_0(w,h;m) - 2\rho(1-\rho^2)he^{-\frac{1}{2}(k^2+n^2)}\\
&\quad\quad + \rho^2\sqrt{1-\rho^2}(me^{-\frac{1}{2}(k^2+n^2)} + f_0(w,h;m)))\big). \qquad (26)
\end{aligned}
$$

Now, we calculate the third term of Equation (21):

$$
\begin{aligned}
&3(1-\rho^2)^{1/2}\rho^2\int_k^{\infty}\int_u^{\infty} zy^2 e^{-\frac{1}{2}(y^2+z^2)}dzdy\\
&\quad = 3\rho^2\sqrt{1-\rho^2}\int_k^{\infty} y^2 f_1(z,y;u)dy\\
&\quad = 3\rho^2\sqrt{1-\rho^2}\left(kf_1(z,k;n) + \int_k^{\infty} f_1(z,y;u)dy\right.\\
&\quad\quad \left. + \frac{\rho}{\sqrt{1-\rho^2}}\int_k^{\infty} yue^{-\frac{1}{2}(y^2+u^2)}\right) \qquad (27)\\
&\quad = 3\rho^2\sqrt{1-\rho^2}\left(ke^{-\frac{1}{2}(k^2+n^2)} + f_0(y,u;k)\right.\\
&\quad\quad \left. + \frac{\rho}{\sqrt{1-\rho^2}}\int_k^{\infty} yue^{-\frac{1}{2}(y^2+u^2)}dy\right). \qquad (28)
\end{aligned}
$$

Substitute u and make the change of variable of Eq. (23) into Eq. (28). Developing, we found the final value

$$
\begin{aligned}
&3(1-\rho^2)^{1/2}\rho^2\int_k^{\infty}\int_u^{\infty} zy^2 e^{-\frac{1}{2}(y^2+z^2)}dzdy\\
&\quad = 3\rho^2\sqrt{1-\rho^2}\left(ke^{-\frac{1}{2}(k^2+n^2)} + f_0(y,u;k) + \frac{\rho}{\sqrt{1-\rho^2}}\right.
\end{aligned}
$$

$$\times\,(h^2\rho(1-\rho^2)f_0(y,h;m)+h(1-2\rho^2)(1-\rho^2)^{1/2}e^{-\frac{1}{2}(m^2+h^2)}$$

$$-\,m\rho(1-\rho^2)e^{-\frac{1}{2}(m^2+h^2)}-\rho(1-\rho^2)f_0(y,h;m))\Big). \quad (29)$$

Finally, the value of the last term of Eq. (21) is found:

$$\rho^3\int_k^\infty\int_u^\infty y^3e^{-\frac{1}{2}(y^2+z^2)}dzdy=\rho^3\int_k^\infty y^3f_0(z,y;u)dy$$

$$=\rho^3\left(k^2f_0(z,k;n)+\int_k^\infty 2yf_0(z,y;u)dy+\frac{\rho}{\sqrt{1-\rho^2}}f_2(y,u;k)\right)$$

$$=\rho^3\Bigg(k^2f_0(z,k;n)+2f_0(z,k;n)+2\frac{\rho}{\sqrt{1-\rho^2}}(2f_0(y,u;k)$$

$$+f_2(y,u;k))\Bigg). \quad (30)$$

For the last term of Eq. (30), the change of variable of Eq. (23) is applied to obtain

$$\rho^3\int_k^\infty\int_u^\infty y^3e^{-\frac{1}{2}(y^2+z^2)}dzdy$$

$$=\rho^3\Bigg(f_0(z,k;n)(k^2+2)+2\frac{\rho}{\sqrt{1-\rho^2}}f_0(y,u;k)$$

$$+\rho((1-\rho^2)me^{-\frac{1}{2}(k^2+n^2)}+(1-\rho^2)f_0(w,h;m)$$

$$+2\rho\sqrt{1-\rho^2}he^{-\frac{1}{2}(k^2+n^2)}+\rho^2h^2f_0(w,h;m))\Bigg). \quad (31)$$

With no loss of generality, $f_i(w,h;c)=f_i(y,h;c)$. Into the integral terms of Eqs. (24), (26), (29), and (31) appear different forms of the *pdf* and the *cdf* of univariate standard normal

$$f_0(y,h;m)=\phi(h)(1-\Phi(m))),$$

$$e^{-\frac{1}{2}(k^2+n^2)}=e^{-\frac{1}{2}(h^2+m^2)}=\phi(\sqrt{n^2+k^2}),$$

$$f_0(y,u;k)=(1-\rho^2)^{1/2}\phi(h)(1-\Phi(n))),$$

$$f_0(z,k;n)=\phi(k)(1-\Phi(n))),$$

where $n = (h - \rho k)/\sqrt{1-\rho^2}$. On noting this, the formula for m_{30} may be written

$$m_{30} = L(h,k;\rho)^{-1}(((4-h^2)\rho^6 + h^2 + 2)\phi(h)(1-\Phi(m))$$
$$+\frac{(1-\rho^2)^{1/2}}{(2\pi)^{1/2}}(\rho h + \rho^3 h - \rho^2(1-\rho^2)^{1/2})\phi(\sqrt{n^2+k^2})$$
$$\times (3\rho - \rho^3 + \rho^3 k^2)\phi(k)(1-\Phi(n))).$$

The formula for m_{03} follows by symmetry.

The extreme cross-moment m_{21} is defined as

$$m_{21} = E[X^2Y|h < X < \infty, k < Y < \infty]$$
$$= \frac{1}{2\pi\sqrt{1-\rho^2}L(h,k;\rho)}\int_k^\infty\int_h^\infty x^2 y e^{-\frac{1}{2}(x^2-2\rho xy+y^2)/(1-\rho^2)}.$$

After applying the change of variable over x, the quadratic term inside the integral expands into three terms and the integral becomes

$$\int_k^\infty\int_u^\infty (z^2(1-\rho^2)y + 2z(1-\rho^2)^{1/2}\rho y^2 + \rho^2 y^3)$$
$$\times e^{-\frac{1}{2}(y^2+z^2)/(1-\rho^2)}dzdy. \tag{32}$$

Now we integrate each of these three terms:

The first term of Eq. (32) is

$$(1-\rho^2)\int_k^\infty\int_u^\infty z^2 y e^{-\frac{1}{2}(y^2+z^2)/(1-\rho^2)}dzdy$$
$$= (1-\rho^2)\Big(ne^{-\frac{1}{2}(k^2+n^2)} + f_0(z,k;n)$$
$$+\frac{\rho}{\sqrt{1-\rho^2}}(h^2(1-\rho^2)^{3/2}f_0(y,h;m) - 2\rho(1-\rho^2)he^{-\frac{1}{2}(k^2+n^2)}$$
$$+\rho^2\sqrt{1-\rho^2}(me^{-\frac{1}{2}(k^2+n^2)} + f_0(y,h;m)))\Big). \tag{33}$$

The second term integral is

$$\begin{aligned}
&2(1-\rho^2)^{1/2}\rho\int_k^\infty\int_u^\infty zy^2e^{-\frac{1}{2}(y^2+z^2)/(1-\rho^2)}dzdy\\
&\quad = 2\rho\sqrt{1-\rho^2}(ke^{-\frac{1}{2}(k^2+n^2)} + f_0(y,u;k)\\
&\qquad + \frac{\rho}{\sqrt{1-\rho^2}}(h^2\rho(1-\rho^2)f_0(y,h;m) + h(1-2\rho^2)(1-\rho^2)^{1/2}\\
&\qquad \times e^{-\frac{1}{2}(m^2+h^2)} - m\rho(1-\rho^2)e^{-\frac{1}{2}(m^2+h^2)} - \rho(1-\rho^2)f_0(y,h;m))). \qquad (34)
\end{aligned}$$

The third term integral is

$$\begin{aligned}
&\rho^2\int_k^\infty\int_u^\infty y^3e^{-\frac{1}{2}(y^2+z^2)/(1-\rho^2)}dzdy\\
&\quad = \rho^2(f_0(z,k;n)(k^2+2) + 2\frac{\rho}{\sqrt{1-\rho^2}}f_0(y,u;k)\\
&\qquad + \rho((1-\rho^2)me^{-\frac{1}{2}(k^2+n^2)} + (1-\rho^2)f_0(y,h;m)\\
&\qquad + 2\rho\sqrt{1-\rho^2}he^{-\frac{1}{2}(k^2+n^2)} + \rho^2h^2f_0(y,h;m))). \qquad (35)
\end{aligned}$$

The three integral equations (33)–(35) are factorized in common terms. After some calculations, the formula for m_{21} becomes

$$\begin{aligned}
m_{21} &= L(h,k;\rho)^{-1}((\rho h^2+2\rho)\phi(h)(1-\Phi(m))\\
&\quad + (1/(2\pi)^{1/2})(1-\rho^2)^{1/2}(h+\rho k)\phi(\sqrt{n^2+k^2})\\
&\quad \times (1+\rho^2+\rho^2k^2)\phi(k)(1-\Phi(n))).
\end{aligned}$$

The formula for m_{12} follows by symmetry.

In general, we define m_{ij} as

$$\begin{aligned}
m_{ij} &= E[X^iY^j|h<X,k<Y]\\
&= \frac{1}{2\pi\sqrt{1-\rho^2}L}\int_k^\infty\int_h^\infty x^iy^je^{-\frac{1}{2}(x^2-2\rho xy+y^2)/(1-\rho^2)}.
\end{aligned}$$

A numerical integration algorithm in *MATLAB* is used to verify all the formulae $(m_{30}, m_{21}, m_{40}, m_{31}, m_{22})$. The algorithm is based on the triple quadrature method for double integrals, with a tolerance level for convergence purposes. □

Proposition 2. *Let (X,Y) be the bivariate normal standard random variable, with correlation ρ, truncated on $h < X, k < Y$. The fourth-order moment and cross-moments of fourth-order are as follows:*

$$
\begin{aligned}
m_{40} = L(h,k;\rho)^{-1}\Big\{ & (3h+h^3)\phi(h)(1-\Phi(k_\rho)) \\
& + \frac{\rho(1-\rho^2)^{1/2}}{(2\pi)^{1/2}}(3hk\rho-\rho^2k^2-6\rho^2+4\rho h+h^2+5)\phi(\sqrt{h_\rho^2+k^2}) \\
& - 2\rho^2(6+\rho^2)\phi(k)(1-\Phi(h_\rho))+3L(h,k;\rho)\Big\},
\end{aligned}
$$

$$
\begin{aligned}
m_{31} = L(h,k;\rho)^{-1}\Big\{ & \rho(3h+h^3)\phi(h)(1-\Phi(k_\rho)) \\
& + \frac{(1-\rho^2)^{1/2}}{(2\pi)^{1/2}}(h^2+\rho^2+k^2\rho^2+hk\rho+2)\phi(\sqrt{h_\rho^2+k^2}) \\
& + 3\rho(k+k^3)\phi(k)(1-\Phi(h_\rho))+3\rho L(h,k;\rho)\Big\},
\end{aligned}
$$

$$
\begin{aligned}
m_{22} = L(h,k;\rho)^{-1}\Big\{ & ((2h+h^3)\rho^2+h)\phi(h)(1-\Phi(k_\rho)) \\
& + (1/(2\pi)^{1/2})(1-\rho^2)^{1/2}(3\rho+h^2\rho+kh+k^2\rho)\phi(\sqrt{h_\rho^2+k^2}) \\
& + ((2k+k^3)\rho^2+k)\phi(k)(1-\Phi(h_\rho))+(1+2\rho^2)L(h,k;\rho)\Big\},
\end{aligned}
$$

where $k_\rho = (k-\rho h)/\sqrt{1-\rho^2}$ and $h_\rho = (h-\rho k)/\sqrt{1-\rho^2}$. The moments m_{04} and m_{13} follows by symmetry.

Proof. To calculate fourth-order extreme moments, m_{40}, m_{31}, m_{22}, a similar approach of direct integration with change of variable of the third-order moments is made. To calculate m_{04}, m_{13} we swap k by h, and also swap x by y, and the result follows by symmetry. □

These new results on bivariate truncated moments could be used to measure differences in the skewness and kurtosis of the tails of the markets' return distribution, an effect we would define as asymmetry of the tail moments. For example, we could define a statistic H similar to that in (Ang and Chen, 2002) to measure the differences of the tail moments in different markets. Let $\tilde{m}_{\alpha\beta}$ represent the empirical moments; the H statistic of the asymmetry of the tail moments is:

$$H = \left[\sum_{i=1}^{N} \omega(\varsigma_i)(m_{\alpha\beta} - \tilde{m}_{\alpha\beta})\right]^{1/2}, \tag{36}$$

for N samples of the distribution, where ω are the weights that sum to 1, and $\alpha + \beta = 3$ for third-order moments' asymmetry, and $\alpha + \beta = 4$ for fourth-order moments' asymmetry.

10. Limitations in the Use of Bivariate Truncated Moments

The results on correlation asymmetry in equity markets depend on the positiveness of the correlations of the assets. The following example will reveal an important insight about BVSN tail correlations.

Example 4. Define a BVSN distribution, and calculate the exceedance correlation using Eq. (5) and the truncated moments with Eq. (18), with different unconditional positive correlations, $\rho = 0.8, 0.7, 0.6, 0.5$ and positive unconditional correlations, $\rho = -0.8, -0.7, -0.6, -0.5$. Figs. 12(a) and 12(b) show the exceedance correlation for the positive and negative unconditional correlations.

In the BVN normal case, the exceedance correlation decreases with the increase in absolute value of the threshold. This is the case when the unconditional correlation is positive (Fig. 12(a)). But in the case of

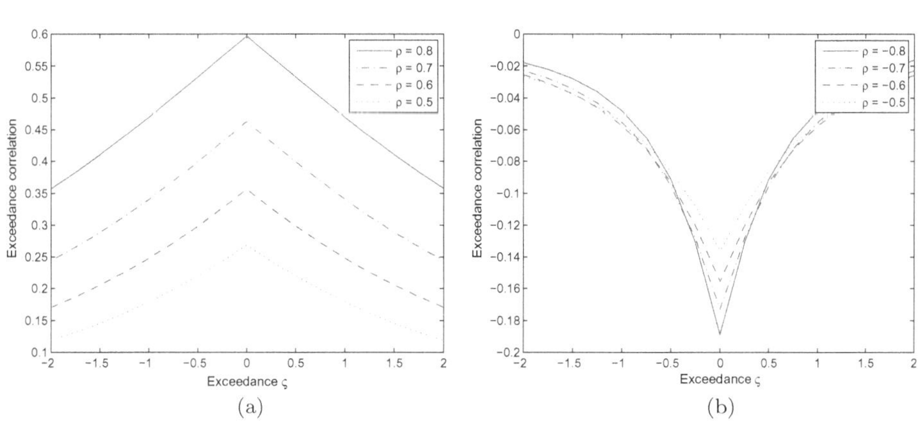

Figure 12. Tail exceedance correlations of a BVN distribution. (a) Plot of BVN exceedance correlation with $\rho > 0$. (b) Plot of BVN exceedance correlation with $\rho < 0$.

a negative unconditional correlation, the exceedance correlation increases (Fig. 12(b)).

This fact is very important when the extreme moments are calculated. The unconditional correlation is a parameter of the density function. To calculate the tail correlation of assets with negative unconditional correlation like some assets existing in the commodity or currency markets, we will need *Multivariate Truncated Moments.*

Example 5. Suppose we have $X = (X_1, X_2, X_3)$ a trivariate normal random vector, with mean vector $\mu = (0, 0, 0)$ and covariance matrix

$$\Sigma = \begin{pmatrix} 1 & 0.1 & -0.7 \\ 0.1 & 1 & 0.4 \\ -0.7 & 0.4 & 1 \end{pmatrix}.$$

The unconditional correlation between X_1 and X_2 is positive. Then its extreme correlation must decrease in the tail (increasing the threshold). If we calculate the extreme correlation between (X_1, X_2) using the bivariate central moments definition, we have:

$$\begin{aligned}\tilde{\rho}(\varsigma) &= \frac{\operatorname{cov}(X_1, X_2 | X_1, X_2 \in \mathcal{I})}{v(X_1|X_1, X_2 \in \mathcal{I})^{1/2} v(X_2|X_1, X_2 \in \mathcal{I})^{1/2}}, \\ &= \frac{m_{11} - m_{10}m_{01}}{(m_{20} - m_{10}^2)^{1/2}(m_{02} - {}_{01}^2)^{1/2}},\end{aligned}$$

with $\mathcal{I}$ the interval defined by the threshold ς, $\mathcal{I} = (\varsigma, \infty)$ if $\varsigma >= 0$, or $\mathcal{I} = (-\infty, \varsigma)$ if $\varsigma < 0$. The value of $\tilde{\rho}(\varsigma) = 0.012953$.

But this definition is useless in a trivariate normal setting.

Define the product upper-upper third-order moment tail function of $X = (X_1, X_2, X_3)$ as

$$\begin{aligned}&m_{\alpha\beta}(h_1, h_2, h_3) \\ &\quad = E[(X_1 - h_1)^{\alpha_1}(X_2 - h_2)^{\alpha_2}(X_3 - h_3)^{\alpha_3} | h_1 < X_1, h_2 < X_2, h_3 < X_3],\end{aligned}$$

where h_1, h_2, h_3 are truncation points. These moments can be computed with the integral:

$$\begin{aligned}&m_{\alpha_1\alpha_2\alpha_3}(h_1, h_2, h_3) \\ &\quad = \int_{h_1}^{\infty}\int_{h_2}^{\infty}\int_{h_3}^{\infty} \frac{(z_1 - h_1)(z_2 - h_2)(z_3 - h_3) f_{X_1,X_2,X_3(z_1,z_2,z_3)}}{F_{X_1,X_2,X_3}(h_1, h_2, h_3)} dz_1 dz_2 dz_3.\end{aligned}$$

The definition of the exceedance correlation is

$$\begin{aligned}\tilde{\rho}(\varsigma) &= \frac{\operatorname{cov}(X_1, X_2|X_1, X_2, X_3 \in \mathcal{I})}{v(X_1|X_1, X_2, X_3 \in \mathcal{I})^{1/2} v(y|X_1, X_2, X_3 \in \mathcal{I})^{1/2}},\\ &= \frac{m_{110} - m_{100}m_{001}}{(m_{200} - m_{100}^2)^{1/2}(m_{002} - m_{001}^2)^{1/2}}.\end{aligned}$$

For this integral we do not have a closed form formula as in Proposition 1 and 2. Instead, we use a Monte Carlo method to estimate the value of the integral. When the exceedance correlation of (x_1, x_2) is calculated with this new definition, we find that the exceedance correlation increases. The new value of $\tilde{\rho}(\varsigma) = 0.114832$. This value is even greater than the unconditional correlation between x_1 and x_2, $\rho_{x_1,x_2} = 0.1$.

Example 6. A multi-dimensional example is produced, with a vector of dimension $n = 10$. For this example we produce two sets of data. Let $X = (X_1, X_2)$ be a BVN random vector, and $Y = (Y_1, \ldots, Y_{10})$ a MVN random vector with dimension 10. Daily data of the first 10 stocks of the Dow Jones industrial index (DJI) is used for the example.

The first set is constructed with the stock prices of “MMM” and “AA”. We calculate the returns, the vector of mean returns, and the covariance matrix. A BVN is adjusted with these values. We calculate the exceedance correlation of the left tail $\tilde{\rho}(\varsigma)$ with $\varsigma = (\varsigma_{X_1}, \varsigma_{X_2}) = (-2\sigma_{X_1}, -2\sigma_{X_2})$. In this case, we take different thresholds for each component of the vector:

$$\tilde{\rho}(\varsigma) = \frac{m_{11} - m_{10}m_{01}}{((m_{20} - m_{10}^2)(m_{02} - m_{01}^2))^{1/2}}.$$

The value found is approximately $\tilde{\rho}(\varsigma) = 0.15404$.

The second set is constructed with the stock prices of “MMM”, “AA”, “MO”, “AXP”, “AIG”, “T”, “BA”, “CAT”, “C” and “KO” (The first ten components of the DJI). Then we calculate the returns, the vector of mean returns, and the covariance matrix, and we adjust a MVN of dimension 10 with these values. Finally, we calculate the exceedance correlation of “MMM” and “AA” as:

$$\tilde{\rho}(\varsigma) = \frac{m_{1100000000} - m_{1000000000}m_{0100000000}}{((m_{2000000000} - m_{1000000000}^2)(m_{0200000000} - m_{0100000000}^2))^{1/2}}.$$

The value found is approximately $\tilde{\rho}(\varsigma) = 0.2146$.

These results suggest that we need multivariate truncated moments for calculating the statistical tests of asymmetry over assets with negative unconditional correlations.

11. Conclusions

In this chapter, we introduced the concept of truncated moments. We presented empirical examples where the threshold correlation, defined as a truncated moment of second order were calculated in equities, currencies, commodities, and interest rates markets. Empirical examples of the tail beta in equity markets and the price distribution in commodity markets were presented as a motivation for including higher-moments in asset pricing and option pricing theories. As a major contribution of this chapter, we developed new formulae for calculating the truncated moments of a bivariate standard normal (BVSN) distribution. The last section presents a counter-example where the results of Ang and Chen (2002) could not be applied, motivating the development of the multivariate truncated moments theory.

Appendix A

A.1 Univariate measures of skewness and kurtosis

The study of Ferreira and Steel (2006) has a review of univariate measures of skewness. Let F and G denote two distributions, and let X be a random variable with distribution F. Recalling Oja (1983), a measure of skewness b should satisfy the following:

(1) For any symmetric F, $b = 0$.
(2) Let $a_1 \in \mathbb{R}^+$, $a_2 \in \mathbb{R}$ and $a_1X + a_2$ with distribution G, then $b(G) = b(F)$.
(3) For any F, if $-X$ is distributed like G then $b(G) = -b(F)$.
(4) If G^{-1} is convex then $b(F) \leq b(G)$.

The most popular measures of univariate skewness are as follows:

(1) $b(X) = E[(X - \mu)^3]/\sigma^3$ (Edgeworth, 1904; Charlier, 1906), where μ is the mean,
(2) $b(X) = (Q_3 + Q_1 - 2\mu^+)/(Q_3 - Q_1)$ (Bowley, 1920), where μ^+ is the median, and Q_1, Q_3 are the first and third percentile of F,
(3) $b(X) = 1 - 2F(\mu^*)$ (Arnold and Groeneveld, 1995), where μ^* is the mode.

These definitions of skewness measure the asymmetry of a distribution or a sample against the normal distribution. The *Charlier–Edgeworth* measure is the standard used in statistics. The *Bowley* measure is robust because it is insensitive to outliers. The *Arnold–Groeneveld* measure is also robust against outliers. The importance of univariate skewness measures in a multivariate setting is they are the foundation of some multivariate skewness' definitions. In a multivariate random sample, the skewness of marginals can be measured with a univariate function.

A.2 Multivariate measures of skewness and kurtosis

While the concept of univariate skewness seems to be straightforward and intuitive, the multivariate is much more complex. Moments of a distribution are mathematical objects called tensors. Statisticians have done a lot of research to try to simplify the third- and fourth-order moment concepts into simpler measures like scalars. The multivariate measures of skewness and kurtosis developed by Mardia (1970) are the standard measures in the academic literature. Fields like finance use these measures. In other fields like physical sciences, they are also the standard measures. The multivariate statistical analysis represents the actual framework to measure deviations from normality. This is the concept that Mardia and other statisticians used to develop different multivariate skewness measures to determine the normality of a sample, or deviations from normality.

Skewness and Kurtosis Definitions: (Mardia, 1970). Let $X = (X_1, X_2, \ldots, X_p)$ be a multivariate random vector. Let $\mu = (\mu_1, \ldots, \mu_p)$ denote the mean vector of X and $\mathbf{V}$ the covariance matrix. Denote by $Y = (X-\mu)\mathbf{V}^{-1/2}$ the standardized vector. Let Z be a random vector with the same distribution of Y, but independent of Y. Mardia's skewness measure of X is

$$\beta_1 = E[(YZ)]^3. \tag{A.1}$$

A fundamental property of this skewness measure is that it is invariant under non-singular transformations. Mardia's kurtosis measure is:

$$\beta_2 = E[(Y'Y)]^4. \tag{A.2}$$

The sample skewness and kurtosis are defined as:

Sample Skewness and Kurtosis Definition: (Mardia, 1970). Let $\mathbf{x}_i = (x_{1,i}, \ldots, x_{p,i})$, $i = \{1, \ldots, n\}$ be a random sample of size n, from a multivariate population of dimension p. Let $\bar{\mathbf{x}} = (\bar{x}_1, \ldots, \bar{x}_p)$ and $\bar{\mathbf{V}} = \{\bar{V}_{ij}\}$ denote the sample mean and the sample covariance. The definition for this sample multivariate skewness measure is

$$\bar{b}_1 = \sum_{r,s,t} \sum_{r',s',t'} \{\bar{V}^{-1}\}^{rr'} \{\bar{V}^{-1}\}^{ss'} \{\bar{V}^{-1}\}^{tt'} M_{111}^{rst} M_{111}^{r's't'}, \tag{A.3}$$

where $\{\bar{V}^{-1}\}^{rr'}_{\{r=1\dots,p\}} = \bar{\mathbf{V}}^{-1}$ are components of the inverse sample covariance matrix with the tensor notation and $M^{rst}_{111} = \frac{1}{n}\sum_{i=1}^{n}(x_{r,i} - \bar{x}_r)(x_{s,i} - \bar{x}_s)(x_{t,i} - \bar{x}_t)$. A fundamental characteristic common in skewness measures is to be invariant under non-singular transformations. The sample kurtosis measure is

$$\bar{b}_2 = \sum_{r,s}\sum_{r',s'}\{\bar{V}^{-1}\}^{rr',2}\{\bar{V}^{-1}\}^{ss',2}M^{rs,2}_{1111}M^{r's',2}_{1111}, \tag{A.4}$$

where $\{\bar{V}^{-1}\}^{rr',2}_{\{s=1,\dots,p\}} = \bar{\mathbf{V}}^{-1}\odot\bar{\mathbf{V}}^{-1}$, $M^{rs,2}_{1111} = \frac{1}{n}\sum_{i=1}^{n}\{(x_{r,i}-\bar{x}_r)(x_{s,i}-\bar{x}_s)\}^2$, with $\odot$ the element-wise product. The kurtosis measure is also invariant under non-singular transformations. Mardia (1970) shows an application where he tested the normality from two artificially generated samples: one generated from a symmetric distribution and the other from a skewed one, and the results confirm the applicability of these measures to recognize the deviations from the normal distribution in a sample. However, Mardia's measures have the problem that they report zero values for distributions of different shapes like the class of elliptical symmetric distributions.

Besides being the standard measure for multivariate skewness and kurtosis, Mardia's measures have the problem that they report the same numeric value for distributions of different shapes. (Morí *et al.*, 1993) developed a new skewness measure to fix this problem:

Skewness Definition: (Morí *et al.*, 1993). Let Y, Z be random vectors defined as in (Mardia, 1970). The skewness is the random vector:

$$\mathbf{b} = \|E(Y\|Y\|^2)\|^2 = E[(Y'Z)(Y'Y)(Z'Z)], \tag{A.5}$$

where $\|\cdot\|$ is the Euclidean norm.

Sample Skewness Definition: (Morí *et al.*, 1993). Let $\mathbf{z}_i = (z_{1,j},\dots, z_{p,i})' = \bar{\mathbf{V}}^{-1/2}(\mathbf{x}_i - \bar{\mathbf{X}})$, $i = \{1,\dots,n\}$ denote the sample standardized, the (Morí *et al.*, 1993) definition of sample skewness is a vector:

$$\bar{\mathbf{b}} = \frac{1}{n^2}\sum_{i=1}^{n}\sum_{j=1}^{n} z_i' z_j\|z_i\|^2\|z_j\|^2. \tag{A.6}$$

Klar (2002) developed a robust measure of skewness using some properties of the skewness measures of Mardia (1970) and Morí *et al.* (1993). He proposed a new measure of multivariate skewness and kurtosis whose limit laws are asymptotically distribution-free under elliptical symmetry. This will be an essential characteristic to consider for the simulation of skewness of the extremes of a distribution.

The study of Ferreira and Steel (2006) makes a compelling review of all the different definitions of multivariate skewness, then redefines the concept on what they call *directional skewness*. In addition to the Mardia (1970) and Morí *et al.* (1993) definitions, Malkovich and Afifi (1973) made a definition of multivariate skewness based on projections of the random variable into a line. Then the algorithm selects the square of the value that maximizes the univariate skewness in the projection. They indicate that Oja (1983) created a definition based on the volume of simplexes. Unfortunately, Malkovich and Afifi's (1973) measure has the same problem as Mardia's measure, as Baringhaus and Henze (1991) remark. All these measures are scalar values, have zero values for symmetric distributions, are invariant to non-singular transformations, are informative about deviations from symmetry, like elliptical distributions, but are weak to for characterizing and describing the skewness for a multivariate distribution.

Skewness Definition: (Ferreira and Steel, 2006). Let X denote a random vector of dimension p, with uni-modal distribution F and mode μ^*. Let b be an univariate measure of skewness, like Mardia's measure, $d \in \mathbb{R}^p$ denote a direction, and O^d be an orthogonal matrix with the first column equal to d. Let $Y = (y_1, \ldots, y_p) = (O^d)(X - \mu^*)$ be a standard transformation of X with distribution G. The directional skewness along d is

$$b(F, d) = b(G_{y_1|y_{(-1)}=0}) = b(F_d), \tag{A.7}$$

where $y_{(-1)}$ denotes the last $p - 1$ components of Y. This technique of adding a directional vector to the traditional definitions allows a better characterization of skewness. However, it is a complex definition. After checking some properties of this new definition, they use the directional skewness to characterize classes of distributions like the skew-normal of Azzalini and Dalla (1996) and Ferreira and Steel (2006). Finally, they use this concept in a Bayesian regression setting, where the errors have skew-normal distributions.

Another approach to overcome the problems found with scalar measures of multivariate skewness and kurtosis is the Kollo (2008) vector definition, similar to the Morí *et al.* (1993) approach. We follow his notation:

Let $\mathbf{A}$ be an $m \times n$ matrix with elements $a_{i,j}$, and $\mathbf{B}$ an $mr \times ns$ partitioned matrix with blocks $\mathbf{B}_{i,j}$ of $m \times n$. The star product of $\mathbf{A}, \mathbf{B}$ is an $r \times s$ matrix:

$$\mathbf{A} \star \mathbf{B} = \sum_{i=1}^{m} \sum_{j=1}^{n} a_{i,j} \mathbf{B}_{i,j}. \tag{A.8}$$

Skewness and Kurtosis Definition: (Kollo, 2008). Let X, Y be multivariate random vectors defined as in Mardia's definition of skewness. The tensor skewness is defined as the p-vector:

$$\mathbf{b}(X) = \mathbf{1}_{p \times p} \star E(Y \otimes Y' \otimes Y), \tag{A.9}$$

where $\otimes$ is the Kronecker product of two matrices. $E(Y \otimes Y' \otimes Y)$ is the third-order moment of Y in matrix notation. The kurtosis is defined as the $p \times p$ matrix

$$\mathbf{B}(X) = \mathbf{1}_{p \times p} \star E(Y \otimes Y' \otimes Y \otimes Y'). \tag{A.10}$$

Sample Skewness and Kurtosis Definition: (Kollo, 2008). Let $\mathbf{x}_i$ be a random vector of n samples of dimension p, $i \in \{1, \ldots, n\}$, with sample covariance matrix $\bar{\mathbf{V}}$ and mean vector $\bar{\mathbf{x}}$. Define $\mathbf{y}_i = \bar{\mathbf{V}}^{-1/2}(\mathbf{x}_i - \bar{\mathbf{x}})$. The sample skewness is defined like the p-vector

$$\bar{\mathbf{b}}(\mathbf{X}) = \frac{1}{n}\mathbf{1}_{p \times p} \star \sum_{i=1}^{n}(\mathbf{y}_i\mathbf{y}_i' \otimes \mathbf{y}_i), \tag{A.11}$$

where $\otimes$ is the Kronecker product of two matrices. The sample kurtosis is defined like the $p \times p$ matrix

$$\bar{\mathbf{B}}(\mathbf{X}) = \frac{1}{n}\mathbf{1}_{p \times p} \star \sum_{i=1}^{n}(\mathbf{y}_i\mathbf{y}_i' \otimes \mathbf{y}_i\mathbf{y}_i'). \tag{A.12}$$

The basic properties and characteristics of these measures were analyzed and contrasted against the measures of Mardia (1970) and Morí *et al.* (1993). Finally, Kollo applies the $p \times p$ matrix measure of kurtosis to solve a problem of independent component analysis (ICA), where the eigenvalues of the matrix determine the transformation. These measures have the advantage that they are a more descriptive measures of the asymmetry and heavy-tailedness of distributions.

References

Ang, A. and Bekaert, G. (2002). International asset allocation with regime shifts. *Rev. Fin. Stud.*, 15(4), pp. 1137–1187.

Ang, A. and Chen, J. (2002). Asymmetric correlations of equity portfolios. *J. Fin. Econom.*, 63(3), pp. 443–494.

Arismendi, J. C. (2013). Multivariate truncated moments. *J. Multivariate Anal.*, 117, pp. 41–75.

Arismendi, J. C. and Broda, S. (2017). Multivariate elliptical truncated moments. *J. Multivariate Anal.*, 157, pp. 29–44.

Arnold, B., Beaver, R., Groeneveld, R., and Meeker, W. (1993). The nontruncated marginal of a truncated bivariate normal distribution. *Psycometrika*, 58(3), pp. 471–488.

Arnold, B. C. and Groeneveld, R. A. (1995). Measuring skewness with respect to the mode. *Am. Statist.*, 49, pp. 34–38.

Arrow, K. (1971). *Essays in the Theory of Risk-Bearing.* Markham Publishing Co.

Azzalini, A. and Dalla, A. (1996). The multivariate skew-normal distribution. *Biometrika*, 83(4), pp. 715–726.

Bae, K.-H., Karolyi, G. A., and Stulz, R. M. (2003). A new approach to measuring financial contagion. *The Rev. Fin. Stud.*, 16(3), pp. 717–763.

Baringhaus, L. and Henze, N. (1991). A class of consistent tests for exponentiality based on the empirical Laplace transform. *Ann. Instit. Statist. Mathe.*, 43, pp. 551–564.

Barnes, M. and Hughes, A. W. (2001). A quantile regression analysis of the cross section of stock market returns. Technical Report 02-2, Federal Reserve of Boston.

Barroso, P. and Santa-Clara, P. (2015). Momentum has its moments. *J. Financial Economics*, 116(1), pp. 111–120.

Bernard, C., Rschendorf, L., Vanduffel, S., and Yao, J. (2015). How robust is the value-at-risk of credit risk portfolios? *The Euro. J. Fin.*, 23(6), pp. 507–534.

Birnbaum, Z. and Meyer, P. L. (1953). On the effect of truncation in some or all co-ordinates of a multi-normal population. *J. Ind. Soc. Agri. Statist.*, 5, pp. 17–28.

Blume, M. E. and Friend, I. (1973). A new look at the capital asset pricing model. *The J. Fin.*, 28(1), pp. 19–33.

Bowley, A. L. (1920). *Elements of Statistics.* King, P. S. 4th edn.

Charlier, C. V. L. (1906). Über das Fehlergesetz. *Arkiv fór Matematik, Astronomi och Fysik*, 2(20), pp. 1–35.

Coles, S., Heffernan, J., and Tawn, J. (1999). Dependence measures for extreme value analyses. *Extremes*, 2(4), pp. 339–365.

Edgeworth, F. Y. (1904). The law of error. *Trans. Cambridge Philosoph. Soc.*, 20, pp. 26–65 and 113–114.

Embrechts, P., Puccetti, G., and Rschendorf, L. (2013). Model uncertainty and VaR aggregation. *J. Bank. Fin.*, 37(8), pp. 2750–2764.

Engle, R. (2012). Dynamic conditional beta. *National Bureau of Economic Research (NBER); New York University (NYU) — Department of Finance.* New York University, Leonard N. Stern School of Business, Department of Economics.

Engle, R. and Manganelli, S. (2000). 'CAViaR: Conditional autoregressive Value at Risk by regression quantiles'. In *Econometric Society World Congress*, No. 0841.

Fama, E. F. and MacBeth, J. D. (1973). Risk, return, and equilibrium: Empirical tests. *J. Polit. Economy*, 81(3), pp. 607–636.

Ferreira, J. T. A. S. and Steel, M. F. J. (2006). On describing multivariate skewed distributions: A directional approach. *Canad. J. Statist.*, 34(3), pp. 441–429.

Feunou, B., Fontaine, J.-S., Taamouti, A., and Tedongap, R. (2013). Risk premium, variance premium, and the maturity structure of uncertainty. *Rev. Fin.*, 18(1), pp. 219–269.

Forbes, K. J. and Rigobon, R. (2002). No contagion, only interdependence: Measuring stock market comovements. *The J. Fin.*, 57(5), pp. 2223–2261.

Guidolin, M. and Timmermann, A. (2008). International asset allocation under regime switching, skew, and kurtosis preferences. *Rev. Fin. Stud.*, 21(2), pp. 889–935.

Hansen, B. E. (1982). Autoregressive conditional density estimation. *Int. Econom. Rev.*, 35(3), pp. 705–730.

Harvey, C. R. and Siddique, A. (2000). Conditional skewness in asset pricing tests. *The J. Fin.*, 55(3), pp. 1263–1295.

Jagannathan, R. and Wang, Z. (1996). The conditional CAPM and the cross-section of expected returns. *The J. Fin.*, 51(1), pp. 3–53.
Jondeau, E. and Rockinger, M. (2003). Conditional volatility, skewness, and kurtosis: Existence, persistence, and comovements. *J. Econom. Dynam. Control*, 27(10), pp. 1699–1737.
Kim, T. and White, H. (2004). On more robust estimation of skewness and kurtosis. *Fin. Res. Lett.*, 1(1), pp. 56 – 73.
Klar, B. (2002). A treatment of multivariate skewness, kurtosis, and related statistics. *J. Multivariate Anal.*, 83(1), pp. 141–165.
Koenker, R. and Basset, G. (1978). Regression quantiles. *Econometrica*, 46(1), pp. 33–50.
Kollo, T. (2008). Multivariate skewness and kurtosis measures with an application in ICA. *J. Multivariate Anal.*, 99(10), pp. 2328–2338.
Kraus, A. and Litzenberger, R. H. (1976). Skewness preference and the valuation of risk assets. *The J. Fin.*, 31(4), pp. 1085–1100.
Lettau, M. and Ludvigson, S. (2001). Resurrecting the CAPM: A cross-sectional test when risk premia are timevarying. *J. Polit. Economy*, 109(6), pp. 1238–1287.
Lewellen, J. and Nagel, S. (2006). The conditional CAPM does not explain asset-pricing anomalies. *J. Fin. Econom.*, 82, pp. 289–314.
Lintner, J. (1965). The valuation of risk assets and the selection of risky investments in stock portfolios and capital budgets. *Rev. Econom. Statist.*, 47(1), pp. 13–37.
Longin, F. and Solnik, B. (2001). Extreme correlation of international equity markets. *The J. Fin.*, 56(2), pp. 649–676.
Malkovich, J. F. and Afifi, A. A. (1973). On tests for multivariate normality. *J. Am. Statist. Assoc.*, 68(341), pp. 176–179.
Mardia, K. V. (1970). Measures of multivariate skewness and kurtosis with applications. *Biometrika*, 57(3), pp. 519–530.
Markowitz, H. (1952). Portfolio selection. *The J. Fin.*, 7(1), pp. 77–91.
Martin, I. W. R. (2012). Consumption-based asset pricing with higher cumulants. *The Rev. Econom. Stud.*, 80(2), pp. 745–773.
Merton, R. (1971). Optimum consumption and portfolio rules in a continuous-time model. *J. Econom. Theory*, 3(4), pp. 373–413.
Morí, T. F., Rotaghi, V. K., and Szekely, G. J. (1993). On multivariate skewness and kurtosis. *Theory Probab. Appl.*, 38, pp. 547–551.
Nelsen, R. (2006). *An Introduction to Copulas*. Springer Verlag.
Neumann, M. and Skiadopoulos, G. (2013). Predictable dynamics in higher-order risk-neutral moments: Evidence from the s&p 500 options. *J. Fin. Quantit. Anal.*, 48(03), pp. 947–977.
Oja, H. (1983). Descriptive statistics for multivariate distributions. *Statist. Probab. Lett.*, 1(6), pp. 327–332.
Patton, A. J. (2004). The out-of-sample importance of skewness and asymmetric dependence for asset allocation. *J. Fin. Econometr.*, 2(1), pp. 130–168.
Pickands, J. (1975). Statistical inference using extreme order statistics. *Ann. Statist.*, 3(1), pp. 119–131.
Poon, S.-H., Rockinger, M., and Tawn, J. (2004). Extreme value dependence in financial markets: Diagnostics, models, and financial implications. *The Rev. Fin. Stud.*, 17(2), pp. 581–610.
Preis, T., Golke, S., Paul, W., and Schneider, J. (2007). Statistical analysis of financial returns for a multiagent order book model of asset trading. *Phys. Rev. E*, 76(1).
Rao, B. R., Garg, M. L., and Li, C. C. (1968). Correlation between the sample variances in a singly truncated bivariate normal distribution. *Biometrika*, 55(2), pp. 433–436.

Rosenbaum, S. (1961). Moments of a truncated bivariate normal distribution. *J. Roy. Statist. Soc. Ser. B (Methodol.)*, 23(2), pp. 405–408.

Samuelson, P. (1969). Lifetime portfolio selection by dynamic stochastic programming. *Rev. Econom. Statist.*, 51, pp. 239–246.

Sharpe, W. F. (1964). Capital asset prices: A theory of market equilibrium under conditions of risk. *The J. Fin.*, 19(3), pp. 425–442.

Stefan, N. and Singleton, K. (2011). Estimation and evaluation of conditional asset pricing models. *The J. Fin.*, 66(3), pp. 873–909.

Thomas, C., Warnock, F., and Wongswan, J. (2006). The performance of international equity portfolios. Technical report, National Bureau of Economic Research.

Chapter 28

What Do We Know About Local Bias of Individual Investors? A Literature Review

Evren Arik* and Ömür Süer[†,‡]

*Galatasaray University and Borsa Istanbul, Turkey
†Department of Business Administration, Galatasaray University, Istanbul, Turkey
‡osuer@gsu.edu.tr

Abstract

This study reviews the limited academic literature on the local bias of individual investors. Local bias can be defined as the tendency of investors to invest in geographically proximate firms' stocks, despite several advantages of diversification. Several researchers have documented the extent to which the portfolios of investors are concentrated in the local equities. Most of this research has focused on individual investors in developed countries. The research so far has put forward mainly two competing potential causes: informational advantage and familiarity.

1. Introduction

The idiom *"Don't put all your eggs in one basket!"* sums up the "diversification" process in the terminology of finance. This process is carried out by investors, in order to reduce the level of investment risk, through distribution of wealth among a variety of assets. Though the idea of diversification dates back centuries, the modern viewpoint was first expressed by Nobel prize winner Harry Markowitz (1952), and his approach to diversification can be considered as a breakthrough. Markowitz's contribution is the recognition that a real diversification consists of a group of assets having low covariance in their rates of return. In other words, Markowitz recognized that the appropriate risk facing an investor, who holds a portfolio of assets, should be measured not only by the variances of the assets but also by their covariances. According to Markowitz's "Modern Portfolio Theory", a rational investor's objective is to maximize returns for a given level of risk, or alternatively, to reduce risk for a given level of return. This theory led to the development of "Capital Asset Pricing Model (CAPM)" by Sharpe (1964), Lintner (1965), and Mossin (1966). CAPM classifies the risk as either diversifiable or non-diversifiable. Diversification is a crucial factor to consider for risk-averse investors, who are assumed to be rational, and aim to maximize returns while minimizing risk. Since the pioneering study of Markowitz, the benefits of diversification have been examined extensively in the finance literature. Diversification can be applied to both domestic and international assets. Alongside the documented benefits of domestic diversification, Levy and Sarnat (1970) have shown that international diversification may induce further benefits. Many studies have reported low correlations among international assets' returns (e.g., Granger and Morgenstern, 1970; Speidell and Sappenfield, 1992) and indicated that greater profits can be made by diversifying internationally.

Contrary to these empirical findings, in practice, investors do not diversify their portfolios sufficiently, and domestically diversified portfolios are much more common than internationally diversified portfolios. One explanation is that investors may be more likely to weigh the assets in their own territories. This phenomenon is called *home bias*, and can be defined as the tendency of investors to favor their own country's assets. Home-biased investors have a tendency to overweight domestic equities and underweight international equities in investment portfolios (Pompian, 2006). This tendency against diversification seems to be the result of investor choices rather than institutional constraints (French and Poterba, 1991). Similarly, Coval and Moskowitz (1999) have shown that the preference for investing close to home also applies to portfolios of domestic stocks. More specifically, the study of Coval and Moskowitz (1999) on US investment managers suggests that asymmetric information between local and non-local investors may drive the preference for geographically proximate investments. Many studies support the argument of asymmetric information. According to this argument, investors earn greater returns from their local investments due to their greater information on these equities as a result of their geographical proximity, e.g., Coval and Moscowitz (2001), Ivkovic and Weisbenner (2005), and Massa and Simonov (2006). In contrast, another group of studies argue that local bias does not generate excessive returns, and the reason for the existence of local bias is mostly behavioral, e.g., familiarity (Zhu, 2002; Pirinsky and Wang, 2006; Seasholes and Zhu, 2010).

In this context, *local bias* may be regarded as an intra-country version of home bias, which is a cross-border phenomenon. Within the context of local bias, we also use terms *local investors* and *local stocks* throughout the text. *Local investor* refers to individuals investing in firms which are geographically close to his/her hometown and *local stock* to stocks issued by the firms which are geographically close to the hometown of the investor.

Within this framework, the objective of this study is to review the relatively scarce literature on local bias. To the best of our knowledge, this study is the first comprehensive review of the existing literature in this area and thus contributes to an understanding of the local bias phenomenon in stock markets. The contents of this study include various contributions to the relevant literature: First, being a relatively recent and ambiguous concept, it attempts to illuminate "local bias" by providing various discussions and findings on the definitions, measurement types, as well as constituents of this concept, including familiarity and informational advantage. Second, it contains a comparative and contrasting analysis of the former arguments and findings on this concept. Thus, this study strives to shed light for potential researchers by providing a brief yet clarifying review on growing local bias literature.

Firstly, we assimilate and organize the knowledge obtained to date on local bias and then critically discuss existing evidence on the reasons for investors tending to have a local bias. As mentioned previously, research so far has led to the conclusion that local bias is potentially the consequence of either informational advantage or familiarity.

The chapter is organized as follows. In Sec. 2, we comprehensively define the concepts of *local investment* and *local bias* and their measurement. Section 3 reviews the empirical evidence on the local bias of individual investors in both developed and developing countries. Section 4 discusses potential explanations of local bias. Finally, Sec. 5 concludes.

2. Definition of Local Bias and its Measurement

This section is devoted to define comprehensively the concepts of *local investment* and *local bias*, and their measurement.

2.1. *Definition of local bias*

In spite of the well-documented gains of international diversification, there is still a clear investor preference for domestic equities in international markets.

Since 1970s, finance researchers have been noticing that the share of foreign assets in the portfolios of domestic investors is much lower than predicted by the modern portfolio theory (e.g., Levy and Sarnat, 1970; French and Poterba, 1991; Tesar and Werner, 1995). In the finance literature, this tendency of investors towards domestic assets, despite many benefits of international diversification, is called *home bias puzzle.* Investor bias in favor of geographically close firms has been documented not only at international level but also at domestic level. Coval and Moskowitz (1999) refer to this type of *local bias* as *home bias at home.* Some of the definitions of *local bias* proposed so far are as follows:

> "... *local bias*, that is, disproportionate preference for local stocks..." [Ivković and Weisbenner, 2005]
> "The phenomenon of investor preference for nearby domestic companies has become known as *local bias.* Its commonly accepted interpretation is that people prefer to invest in the familiar." [Bodnaruk , 2009]
> "... investors tend to tilt their domestic portfolios towards local stocks-investment anomaly which has been dubbed *local bias* in the literature." [Baltzer, Stolper and Walter, 2013]

2.2. *Measurement of local investment and local bias*

Following a comprehensive literature review, we observe that the measurement of *local bias* is, first of all, related to the definition of *local investment* adopted by different researchers. These different *local investment* definitions can be categorized in three groups: (1) defined as a prespecified distance, (2) defined as a computed distance, and (3) defined as a specific city or region (Table 1). In the literature, the measurement of *local bias* first requires a definition of *local investment.*

2.2.1. *Local investment defined as a prespecified distance and measurement of local bias*

In some studies, in order to denominate an investment as *local investment*, prespecified distances are used, e.g., (100 Km, 250 miles, etc.). For instance, in their pioneering study in this field, Coval and Moskowitz (2001) classify any stock within 100 Km of the fund headquarters as a local stock, and in order to measure the degree to which a manager invests locally, they compute the fraction of fund assets invested in these local stocks. However, since funds differ in terms of the density of available investments within

Table 1. Measurement of Local Investment

Pre-specified Distance Based Measure	
Coval and Moskowitz (2001)	100 km
Hau (2001)	100 km
Ivkovic and Weisbenner (2005)	250 miles
Gaspar and Massa (2007)	100 km
Ivković, Sialm Weisbenner (2008)	50 miles
Goetzmann and Kumar (2008)	250 miles
Seasholes and Zhu (2010)	250 miles
Chhaochharia, Kumar and Niessen-Ruenzi (2012)	250 miles
Baltzer, Stolper and Walter (2015)	100 km
City or region based measure	
Grinblatt and Keloharju (2001)	Municipalities of Finland
Loughran and Schultz (2004)	US cities
Pirinsky and Wang (2006)	US MSAs
Feng and Seasholes (2008)	Chinese cities
Kedia and Zhou (2011)	US MSAs
Das (2011)	US MSAs
Nofsinger and Varma (2012)	US states
Jacobs and Weber (2012)	German cities
Computed distance based measure	
Coval and Moskowitz (1999)	
Zhu (2002)	
Dorn and Huberman (2005)	
Massa and Simonov (2006)	
Dorn, Huberman and Sengmueller (2008)	
Bodnaruk (2009)	
Cumming and Dai (2010)	

their local area, they compare this fraction to the fraction of the market of available investments within 100 Km of the fund. The difference between these two fractions is their local bias measure, representing the degree to which managers invest locally in excess of the level of local investments that would be held in the market portfolio.

Following Coval and Moskowitz (2001), Gaspar and Massa (2007) define a mutual fund as local with respect to a firm if the mutual fund manager is located within a 100 Km radius of the firm's headquarters. In another study on the equity trades of professional traders from different countries, Hau (2001) uses different locational dummy variables, one of which concerns traders located within a 100 Km of the corporate headquarters, in the case that the corporation is headquartered outside Frankfurt.

In a more recent study, Baltzer *et al.* (2015) also use a distance-based measure of local bias and categorize each stock issued by a company headquartered within 100 km of a given representative portfolio i as local; shares beyond this radius are referred to as remote. They compute the fraction of locally available float-adjusted market capitalization for each of the representative portfolios and subtract it from their actual local investments in order to obtain their local bias measure.

In other studies, 250 miles is used for discriminating the local from the non-local. For instance, Ivkovic and Weisbenner (2005) compute a household's local bias by subtracting the fraction of the market portfolio headquartered within 250 miles from the fraction of household's portfolio headquartered within this distance. Similarly, the local bias measure for Goetzmann and Kumar (2008) is the proportion of a portfolio that is invested in stocks of firms located within a 250-mile radius from investor's location (zip code). For robustness tests, the same method is used by Chhaochharia *et al.* (2012) in order to determine local institutional investors. Stocks whose headquarters are within a 250-mile radius of the investor location are considered local by Seasholes and Zhu (2010).

On the other hand, Ivković *et al.* [2008] favor a limit of 50 miles between the corporate headquarters and the investor's household.

2.2.2. *Local investment defined as a specific city or region and measurement of local bias*

For an investment to be considered local, some researchers accept a city- or region-based measure. In their study on localized trading behavior in NASDAQ, Loughran and Schultz (2004) incorporate companies located in the city's metropolitan area, and not just the city itself, into their sample. Local investors are considered as those located in the same city as a NASDAQ firm's headquarters.

Following Loughran and Schultz (2004), Pirinsky and Wang (2006) define a firm's location as the location of its headquarters. The authors claim that this is a reasonable choice, given that corporate headquarters are not only close to corporate core business activities but also the center of information exchange between the firm and its suppliers, service providers, and investors.

In a study investigating the role of local market makers in providing liquidity and improving the quality of a dealer market, Kedia and Zhou (2011) classify dealers as geographically proximate or local if they are in the same Metropolitan Statistical Areas (MSA)[1] as their clients. According to the authors, there are two advantages of using MSA as a unit of analysis: (1) It provides a more natural unit of geographical analysis compared to an arbitrary cutoff of 100 or 250 km. (2) The tight social and economic interaction within an MSA is precisely what facilitates information transfer and generates information advantages. Local share for a firm is defined as the fraction of the firm's market makers that are located in the same MSA.

Das (2011) defines a firm and mutual fund manager as local if located in the same MSA in his study examining the influence of geographical proximity on mutual fund proxy voting decisions. In analyses, he uses a dummy variable (*local*) that takes the value of 1 if the fund and firm are located in the same MSA.

In another study exploring familiarity bias in the geographic context by focusing on the individual's decision to purchase utility stocks, Nofsinger and Varma (2012) use a dummy variable that takes the value 1 if a household is local to utility i. In order to explore whether households overweigh their local (in-state) stocks as a proportion of their entire utility stock portfolio, both in terms of the number and value of stocks, they firstly divide all households into four regions, based on the 1990 US Census classification: midwest, northeast, west, and south. Then, they compute a household's observed local utility allocation according to value (or number of stocks) by averaging the percentage of the total value (or number of stocks) of its utility portfolio invested in local (in-state) utility stocks over the number of months in which it held utility stocks.

A non-US study in this field, by Jacobs and Weber (2012), uses a sample consisting of the common stocks of all firms headquartered in Germany, which have been listed on a German stock exchange. They use a firm's headquarter as a proxy for its location. In a similar way, Feng and Seasholes (2008) compare the investment behavior of men and women in the People's Republic of China, and they define as local a stock of a company whose headquarter is located in the same province as the investor.

[1]Metropolitan Statistical Areas (MSA) of the headquarter. MSA is a geographic entity defined by the US Office of Management and Budget. An MSA consists of a core area that contains a substantial population nucleus, together with adjacent communities that have a high degree of social and economic integration with that core. MSAs include one or more entire counties, and some MSAs contain counties from several states. For example, the New York MSA includes counties from four states: New York, New Jersey, Connecticut, and Pennsylvania.

Grinblatt and Keloharju (2001), document that investors are more likely to hold, buy, and sell the stocks of Finnish firms located close to the investor. In order to measure the influence of distance on the behavior of Finnish investors, they use the ratio of the firm i's shareowner weight for investors in the municipality of its headquarters to the firm i's shareowner weight among all investors in Finland. They give as an example the shipping firm Birka Line, which has 3,299 household shareowners, 1,669 of whom live in its headquarters city of Mariehamn. Summing the number of household shareowners over all firms, they find that Mariehamn has 14,440 household shareowners, while Finland has 1,157,783 shareowners. The numerator for Birka Line's ratio is thus 1,669/14,440, and the denominator is 3,299/1,157,783, making Birka Line's ratio 40.56. In the absence of distance effect, this ratio is one.

2.2.3. *Local investment defined as a computed distance and measurement of local bias*

In many studies, the distance between the invested firm and the investor has been computed before measuring local bias. In their pioneering study, Coval and Moskowitz (1999) investigate whether investors have a preference for geographically proximate investments, and to this end they develop a test statistic. Since this test statistic has been regarded as valid in the literature, we quote the test procedure used by the authors in Box 1.

Zhu (2002) follows a 3-step procedure for measuring the individual investor local bias. Firstly, following Coval and Moskowitz (1999), he calculates the distance between an investor and the market portfolio. In order to calculate the location of the market portfolio as the value-weighted average of the location of all stocks in the market, first of all, he obtains the latitude and longitude of the centroids of all 3-digit zip codes and calculates the total market value of companies headquartered in each. The latitude and longitude of the market portfolio is computed as the average of the latitude and longitude of all 3-digit zip codes, weighted by the total value of public companies headquartered in each particular zip code area. The distance between a particular investor and the market portfolio is then calculated as the distance between the zip codes of the investor and the market portfolio. The second step consists of calculating the distance between the investor and their investment by measuring the distance between the zip codes of the investor and the company's headquarter, focusing only on buy transactions. Zhu (2002) then calculates the distance between investor and personal portfolio as the average of the distances between investor and investments, weighted by the value of each transaction as explained in Box 2.

The final step involves two methods for calculating local bias (Box 3):

Dorn and Huberman (2005), following the approach of Coval and Moskovitz (1999), define the local bias of a portfolio as one minus the ratio of the distance between the investor and his portfolio, to the distance between the investor and the market portfolio. A local bias of 0.05 means that the customer holds a portfolio that is 5% closer than the market portfolio. Mutual funds are assumed to have the same distance from the investor as the market portfolio.

In another study, for measuring the proximity between the residence of the investor and the place where the company is located, Massa and Simonov (2006) use two different measures: (1) the logarithm (to base 10) of the inverse of the distance between the ZIP code of the investor and the ZIP code of the closest branch/subsidiary of the company whose stock they consider; (2) the logarithm of the inverse of the distance between the ZIP code of the investor and the ZIP code of the company headquarters. These measures are similar to those used by Coval and Moskowitz (1999). The greater the value of the variable, the closer is the investor to the stock.

Box 1. Computation of the Test Statistic for *Local Bias*

"Suppose there are F different fund managers and n different securities in the economy. Let $m_{i,j}$ represent the portfolio weight on stock j in the benchmark portfolio for which fund manager i is compared. If the market portfolio is the relevant benchmark for all funds, then $m_{i,j}$ is the same across all fund managers i and represents the market value weight of stock j in the economy. Next, let $h_{i,j}$ represent the actual weight that fund i places on stock j. We then compute the distance, $d_{i,j}$, between fund manager i and the corporate headquarters of stock j as follows:

$$\begin{aligned} d_{i,j} = arc\cos\{&\cos(\text{lat}_i)\cos(\text{lon}_i)\cos(\text{lat}_j)\cos(\text{lon}_j) \\ &+ \cos(\text{lat}_i)\sin(\text{lon}_i)\cos(\text{lat}_j)\sin(\text{lon}_j) \\ &+ \sin(\text{lat}_i)\sin(\text{lat}_j)\}2\pi r/360, \end{aligned}$$

where lat and lon are latitudes and longitudes (measured in degrees) of the fund manager and company headquarters locations and r is the radius of the earth (≈6378 km).

Finally, we compute the average distance of fund i from all securities j it could have invested in, by weighting the distances between manager i and

(*Continued*)

(*Continued*)

all n stocks in the economy, by the appropriate benchmark weights. More formally,

$$d_i^M = \sum_{j=1}^{n} m_{i,j} d_{i,j}.$$

With variables defined as above, our test for whether fund i exhibits a proximity preference is stated in Proposition 1.

Proposition 1 *Consider the test statistic,*

$$LB_i \equiv \sum_{j=1}^{n} (m_{i,j} - h_{i,j})(d_{i,j}/d_i^M)$$

which measures how much closer fund manager i is to her portfolio than to her benchmark (as a fraction of the distance she is from her benchmark). If deviations from the benchmark portfolio are unrelated to the distance between manager i and the securities she chooses to hold, then the null hypothesis H_0:$LB_i = 0$ cannot be rejected.

Source: Coval and Moskowitz (1999).

Box 2. Computation of the Distance Between Investor and personal Portfolio

$$\text{Dist}_{i,own} = \sum_{j=1}^{n_{i,j}} w_{i,j}\text{Dist}_{i,j}$$

where $\text{Dist}_{i,own}$ is the distance between investor i and her own portfolio $w_{i,j}$ is the value of j_{th} buy transaction divided by the total value of investor i's buy transactions during the sample period, $n_{i,j}$ is the number of buy transactions that investor i has made during the sample period, $\text{Dist}_{i,j}$ is the distance between investor i's home and the headquarters of the company of her j_{th} buy.

Source: Zhu (2002).

Analogous to the approach of Coval and Moskowitz (1999), Dorn, Huberman, and Sengmueller (2008) calculate the average distance between a trader on a given stock-day and company headquarters by translating investors' and firms' zip codes into geographic longitude (lon) and latitude (lat) by matching them against a list of zip codes and the corresponding geographic coordinates for 6,900 German municipalities. Given the geographic coordinates, the distance between trader i and firm j is estimated as follows:

$$d_{i,j} = \text{earth radius} \,.\, \text{acos}(\sin(\text{lat}_j)\sin(\text{lat}_i) + \cos(\text{lat}_j)\cos(\text{lat}_i)\cos(\text{lon}_j - \text{lon}_i)).$$

Box 3. Computation of Local Bias

The local bias of an investor is calculated in two different ways:

[**First way**]: The absolute local bias LB^{abs} is calculated as the difference between an investor's distance to the market portfolio and the distance to his or her own portfolio.

$$LB_i^{\text{abs}} = \text{Dist}_{i,\text{market}} - \text{Dist}_{i,\text{own}},$$

where $\text{Dist}_{i,\text{market}}$ is the distance between investor i and the market portfolio. $\text{Dist}_{i,\text{own}}$ is the distance between investor i and her own portfolio.

This absolute local bias can be either positive or negative. A positive (negative) absolute local bias indicates that the investors' own portfolio is closer to (farther from) her than the market portfolio.

[**Second way**]: To accommodate the heterogeneity in investors' locations, an alternative normalized measurement of local bias is used. It is defined as the absolute local bias normalized by the distance between the investor and the market portfolio:

$$\text{LB}_i^{\text{norm}} = \text{LB}_i^{\text{abs}}/\text{Dist}_{i,\text{market}},$$

where $\text{LB}_i^{\text{norm}}$ is the normalized local bias of investor i.

If there is no local bias in individual investors' investments, the normalized local bias will have the mean of 0.

The average distance between investors and the market portfolio is measured as both an equally weighted and as a value-weighted average of all investors' distances to the market portfolio.

$$\text{Dist}_{\text{avg.}\,market}^{\text{equal}} = \frac{1}{n}\sum_{i=1}^{n}\text{Dist}_{i,\text{market}}$$

$$\text{Dist}_{\text{avg.market}}^{\text{value}} = \sum_{i=1}^{n}\left(\text{Value}_i \Big/ \sum_{i=1}^{n}\text{Value}_i\right) * \text{Dist}_{\text{i,market}},$$

(*Continued*)

(Continued)

where $\text{Dist}^{\text{equal}}_{\text{avg.market}}$ is the equally weighted average of the distances between investors and the market portfolio, $\text{Dist}^{\text{value}}_{\text{avg.market}}$ is the value-weighted average of the distance between investors and the market portfolio, Value_i is the total value of all buy transactions that investor i has made during the sample period, n is the sample size.

The equally weighted and value-weighted average distance between investors and their own portfolios are similarly defined as

$$\text{Dist}^{\text{equal}}_{\text{avg.own}} = 1/n \sum_{i=1}^{n} \text{Dist}_{i,\text{own}},$$

$$\text{Dist}^{\text{value}}_{\text{avg.own}} = \sum_{i=1}^{n} \left(\text{Value}_i \Big/ \sum_{i=1}^{n} \text{Value}_i \right) * \text{Dist}_{i,\text{own}}.$$

Finally, the average absolute and normalized local biases as equally weighted and value-weighted averages of all investors' absolute and normalized local bias are calculated as follows:

$$\text{LB}^{\text{abs}}_{\text{avg.equal}} = \frac{1}{n} \sum_{i=1}^{n} \text{LB}^{\text{abs}}_i \text{ and } \text{LB}^{\text{abs}}_{\text{avg.value}} = \sum_{i=1}^{n} \left(\frac{\text{Value}_i}{\sum_{i=1}^{n} \text{Value}_i} \right) * \text{LB}^{\text{abs}}_i,$$

$$\text{LB}^{\text{norm}}_{\text{avg.equal}} = \frac{1}{n} \sum_{i=1}^{n} \text{LB}^{\text{norm}}_i \text{ and } \text{LB}^{\text{norm}}_{\text{avg.value}} = \sum_{i=1}^{n} \left(\frac{\text{Value}_i}{\sum_{i=1}^{n} \text{Value}_i} \right) * \text{LB}^{\text{norm}}_i,$$

where $\text{LB}^{\text{abs}}_{\text{avg.equal}}$, $\text{LB}^{\text{abs}}_{\text{avg.value}}$, $\text{LB}^{\text{norm}}_{\text{avg.equal}}$ and $LB^{\text{norm}}_{\text{avg. value}}$ are the equally weighted and the value-weighted average of the absolute and normalized local bias.

Source: Zhu (2002).

The authors set the distance between traders with addresses outside Germany and other traders to 1,000 km., and to make the distance measures comparable across stocks, they normalize these by the average distance between company headquarters and the full client sample.

In analyzing the portfolios of individual investors who have changed their place of residence, Bodnaruk (2009) calculates a measure of proximity for Swedish investors, by using postal codes of the location of the investor's residence and the company's closest establishment. Throughout the analysis, the logarithm of this distance is used to measure proximity to the investment. The logarithm of the distance is taken in order to capture the nonlinearity of the effect.

Cumming and Dai (2010), investigating the local bias in venture capital investments, calculate the geographic distance between the VCs and their portfolio companies as follows:

$$
\begin{aligned}
d_{ij}3963 \times \mathrm{ar} = \cos[&\sin(\mathrm{lat}_i)\sin(\mathrm{lat}_j) \\
&+ \cos(\mathrm{lat}_i)\cos(\mathrm{lat}_j)\cos(|\mathrm{long}_i - \mathrm{long}_j|)],
\end{aligned}
$$

where latitude (lat) and longitude (long) are measured in radians and 3,963 is a constant representing the Earth's radius in statute miles.[2]

Following the formula developed in Coval and Moskowitz [1999], Cumming and Dai [2010] measure the local bias as the percentage difference between the weighted-average distance of the actual investment portfolio for each VC and the weighted-average distance of a hypothetical benchmark portfolio. They estimate equally weighted-average distance for both the actual investment portfolio and the benchmark portfolio. The benchmark portfolio is industry and stage restricted, and it consists of a list of all new ventures available in a certain year that have the same industry and stage as the one in which a VC actually invested that year. Firstly, they categorize all the new ventures into three industry sectors (*information technology, medical/health/life science, and others*) and three stages (*early stage, expansion stage, and later stage*), which represents a 3× 3 matrix, or nine industry and stage specific portfolios. They assume that without distance consideration, the VC could have invested in any other ventures available in the same industry and stage specific portfolio with its actual investment. If all the investments of a VC are in the same industry and stage specific portfolio, then local bias is represented by the percentage difference between the average distance of the industry and stage specific benchmark portfolio and the distance of its actual investments. If the VC had invested in multiple industries and stages, they estimate its actual weight in each industry and stage specific portfolio and then apply this weight to its benchmark portfolio, which consists of multiple industry and stage specific portfolios (Box 4.).

[2]Sorenson and Stuart (2001) use "3,437" as the constant representing the radius of the Earth in nautical miles; Coval and Moskowitz (1999, 2001) use "6,379" as the constant representing the radius of the Earth in kilometers. Adopting these different units does not change the measure of local bias in the study of Cumming and Dai (2010).

Box 4. Computation of Local Bias in Venture Capital (VC) Investments

Suppose there are VCs (M) that have invested in new (N) ventures in a specific industry and at a specific stage in year t. Assuming that VCs are equally likely to invest in a new venture within their industry and stage specialization if there is no location preference, its investment weight in each available new venture thus is $1/N$. Let $d_{i,j}$ denote the geographic distance between VCi and all available new ventures in the same industry and at the same stage that it could have invested in year t is equal to

$$d_{iM} = 1/N \sum_{j=1}^{N} d_{ij}.$$

The local bias exhibited by a VC can be calculated as follows:

$$LB_i = (d_{iM} - d_i)/d_{iM} = 1 - (d_i/d_{iM}),$$

where d_i is the actual portfolio distance for VCi and d_{iM} is the benchmark portfolio distance for VCi. LB_i measures how much closer VCi is to her actual portfolio than to the benchmark portfolio.

If the actual portfolio of the VC consists of more than one industry and/or more than one stage, we estimate d_{iM}^p for each industry and stage specific portfolio following the above method, where p represents one of the all industry and stage specific portfolios. Let $\mathrm{W_p}$ represent the VC's actual investment weight in portfolio p, the average distance of this VC's benchmark portfolio is the following:

$$d_{i,M} = \sum_{p=1}^{p} W_p d_{i,M}^p$$

Source: Cumming and Dai (2010).

3. Review of Empirical Studies on Local Bias

The pioneering study in this line of research, Coval and Moskowitz (1999), represents the first attempt to analyze the impact of distance on domestic portfolio choice. By using a sample consisting of 1,189 investment managers, running 2,183 different US equity funds, for the year 1995, they found that US investment managers exhibited a strong preference for locally headquartered firms, particularly small and highly levered firms that produce nontraded goods. In their succeeding study, Coval and Moskowitz (2001) analyzed the equity holdings of US mutual funds for the period January 1975–December 1994, finding that, despite the gains that can be generated from local investments, the average fund in their sample exhibited only a modest bias toward local stocks. On the other hand, some funds particularly focus on local assets, and exhibit even greater local performance. Finally, they found that the extent to which a firm attracts nearby investors is positively related to its future expected return.

In another study, Huberman (2001) found that the shareholders of a Regional Bell Operating Company (RBOC) tend to live in the area which it serves. This geographic bias of the RBOC investors is closely related to the tendency of households' portfolios to be concentrated and to the employees' tendency to own their employers' stocks in their retirement accounts. The same year, Grinblatt and Keloharju (2001) published their study on Finnish investors. For the period from December 1994 through January 1997, their results showed that Finnish investors tended to invest not only in nearby firms, but also exhibited preference for same-language and same-culture firms, and the degree of these tendencies is inversely related to investor sophistication.

In the following years, many other studies provided evidence for local bias of investors. Following the study of Coval and Moskowitz (2001), Zhu (2002) published his study using a sample of 27,189 US individual investors, for the period January 1991–November 1996, finding that individual investors tended to invest in companies closer to them. The existence of individual investors' bias towards the companies that are close to their residences was detected through various measurements. The study also found that investors holding foreign securities exhibit significantly weaker local bias than those not holding foreign securities. This finding suggests that international home bias and domestic home bias are correlated.

For the same period as that studied by Zhu (2002), using data on the investments of individual US investors, Ivkovic and Weisbenner (2005) showed that households strongly prefer local investments. The findings of Hong, Kubik, and Stein [2008] provided evidence for the local bias of investors in US, for a longer period: 1970–2005. The authors find that in the presence of only few local firms competing for investors' money, share prices of spatially close firms are driven up by the excess demand of nearby residents. In their study investigating whether US investors held value-relevant information about local stocks, Seasholes and Zhu (2010) found that investors' portfolios favored local stocks. Their data, from January 1, 1991 to November 1, 1996, were taken from a large discount brokerage house, and have been extensively studied in the behavioral finance literature.

The study of Cumming and Dai (2010) used a different sample type from previous studies. They investigated local bias in the context of US venture capital investments for the period 1980–June 2009, finding that venture capitals exhibit strong local bias in their investment decisions. They also found less local bias exhibited in more reputable venture capitals (older, larger, more experienced, and with stronger IPO track record) and those with broader networks.

There are also studies that provide evidence for local bias in the countries other than US Massa and Simonov (2006) investigated whether Swedish investors used their investment in financial assets to hedge nonfinancial income, for the period 1995–2000. Based on the investigation of the relationship between investor's nonfinancial and financial income and a portfolio-based index of hedging, findings provided evidence that investors do not engage in hedging, but tend to deliberately concentrate their holdings in stocks to which they are geographically or professionally close, or that they have held for a long period. Bodnaruk (2009) also analyzed Swedish investors and found that after moving, investors abnormally increased investment in companies closer to their new location, providing higher risk-adjusted returns compared to companies in which they kept holdings unchanged, or in which they abnormally reduced holdings. In another study focusing on a country outside the US, Jacobs and Weber (2012) provided evidence that local bias at the individual level materially affects stock turnover at the firm level in Germany, for the period between June 1988 and January 2009. In addition, the stocks of firms located in resort regions were found to be less traded than very similar stocks in non-holiday resort regions.

Only a very few studies report local bias in emerging countries. Feng and Seasholes (2008) carried out an analysis on a data set provided by a national brokerage firm from the People's Republic of China, and consisting of individual investors. Their results indicated that, over the period of analysis from January 1999 to December 2000, investors tended to invest a high fraction of their portfolios locally. More specifically, both men and women were found to over-weight local stocks by 9% relative to the market portfolio. Liao *et al.* (2012) also reached similar results in Chinese stock market, for the period January 2003 through June 2009, suggesting that, in China, retail investors display a strong tendency to invest in stock exchange listed stocks that are geographically close.

Baltzer *et al.* (2013) went one step further, and hypothesized that individual investors' local bias is not limited to the domestic sphere,

Table 2. Empirical Studies Providing Evidence for Local Bias

Authors & Date of Publication	Country	Sampling Period
Coval and Moskowitz (1999)	United States	1995
Coval and Moskowitz (2001)	United States	Jan 1975–Dec 1994
Grinblatt and Keloharju (2001)	Finland	Dec 1994–Jan 1997
Huberman (2001)	United States	1996
Zhu (2002)	United States	Jan 1991–Nov 1996
Ivković and Weisbenner (2005)	United States	1991–1996
Massa and Simonov (2006)	Sweden	1995–2000
Hong, Kubik, and Stein (2008)	United States	1970–2005
Feng and Seasholes (2008)	China	Jan 1999–Dec 2000
Bodnaruk (2009)	Sweden	Jun 1995–Jun 2001
Cumming and Dai (2010)	United States	1980–June 2009
Seasholes and Zhu (2010)	United States	Jan 1991–Nov 1996
Jacobs and Weber (2012)	Germany	Jun 1988–Jan 2009
Liao *et al.* (2012)	China	Jan 2003–Jun 2009

but also determines international investment decisions. Using data from Germans' investing in nine neighbor countries, for the period December 2005–December 2010, they found a cross-border local bias among individual investors.

The empirical studies providing evidence for local bias are listed in Table 2.

4. Possible Reasons of Local Bias

As stated by Aabo *et al.* (2013), although the local bias within and between countries is well established in the empirical literature, the underlying reasons are less clear. Currently, two competing opinions exist in the literature. The first one is that the investors may have *informational advantage* due to their proximity to the companies, while the second assumes the existence of *familiarity*. The supporters of this latter view point out that the investors may not have any extra valuable information; instead, they may rely on their familiarity with these stocks. In the literature, the standard approach to identify the possible reason is to calculate the return performances of local and non-local investments. If the investors earn money from their local investments, it may be inferred that this is due to additional information. This section of the chapter presents a review of the literature about the explanations for local bias of investors (Table 3).

Table 3. Possible Reasons of Local Bias

Information Advantage	Familiarity
Coval and Moskowitz (2001)	Zhu (2002)
Hau (2001)	Pirinsky and Wang (2006)
Ivković and Weisbenner (2005)	Seasholes and Zhu (2010)
Massa and Simonov (2006)	Liao *et al.* (2012)
Ivković, Sialm and Weisbenner (2008)	Baltzer, Stolper and Walter (2015)
Bae, Stulz and Tan (2008)	
Bodnaruk (2009)	

4.1. *Informational advantage*

Several studies claim that investors make better returns from their local investments, as a result of additional information in these equities due to their geographical proximity. The basic premise behind this view is that gathering value-relevant information about companies is easier for local investors. In consequence, if there is a local bias and the reason for it is informational advantage, the level of local bias is expected to be less in equities in which the information asymmetry is lower, i.e., a relatively large amount of information about the company is publicly available to all investors and/or analysts.

Coval and Moskowitz (2001), in their study analyzing the equity holdings of US mutual funds for the period 1975–1994, found that fund managers seemed to earn substantial abnormal returns in nearby investments. Specifically, an average fund manager obtains an annual return 2.67% greater from local investments[3] compared to non-local investments. These returns are strongest among smaller and older funds. Accordingly, they suggested that investors trade local securities at an informational advantage, and pointed toward a link between such trading and asset prices. Similarly, Ivkovic and Weisbenner (2005) found that an average US household generates an additional annualized return of 3.2% from local relative to non-local holdings, indicating that local investors are able to exploit local knowledge. Excess returns are even larger among less widely known stocks, outside the S&P 500 index, for which information asymmetries between local and non-local investors are likely to play a more pronounced role. Ivković *et al.* (2008) conducted further research on the same dataset in order to investigate the role of information asymmetries in individual investors' portfolio decisions.

[3] Holdings within 100km of the fund headquarters.

Their findings indicated that stock investments made by households who concentrate their brokerage accounts in a few stocks outperform those of households with more diversified accounts. Excess returns of concentrated portfolios are stronger for stocks outside the S&P500 index and local stocks, reflecting concentrated investors' capacity to exploit informational advantages.

The role of information advantage in local bias has also been investigated in countries other than US. For instance, Hau (2001) examines informational asymmetries across 756 professional traders located in 23 different cities and 8 European countries, finding that traders located outside Germany, in non-German-speaking cities, show lower proprietary trading profit. Their underperformance is not only statistically but also economically significant, and occurs for the 11 largest German blue-chip stocks. The author finds also evidence for an information advantage due to corporate headquarters proximity in the case of high-frequency trading. In a study on Swedish investors, Massa and Simonov (2006) investigated whether investment in financial assets was used to hedge nonfinancial income, using a portfolio-based index of hedging. Their findings showed that rather than hedge, Swedish investors tend to intentionally invest in stocks which are most closely connected to them. They explain this finding using the concept information-driven familiarity, and showed that familiarity-based investment is a rational reaction to information constraints, as opposed to a behavioral heuristic. Furthermore, this type of investment brings higher returns compared to hedging. The authors observe also heterogeneity in investor behavior. For instance, compared to low-wealth investors, high-wealth investors are more likely to hedge, and for these investors, the impact of geographical proximity and the holding period on profits is lower and less significant. Massa and Simonov believed that, if familiarity is information-based, its importance may decrease as the degree of sophistication of the investors or their relative wealth increases. In another study on Swedish investor, for the period 1995–2001, Bodnaruk (2009) found that individual Swedish investors obtained economically and statistically significant gains from investing locally, and the link between proximity to investment and performance was stronger for more diversified investors, who are able to benefit from the effective collection and processing of information.

In a cross-country study with sample of 32 countries, Bae *et al.* (2008) investigated whether analysts resident in a country are able to make earnings forecasts for firms in that country with greater precision than foreign analysts. Their findings suggest that the earnings forecasts of local analysts are more precise, resulting in the concept of the "local analyst advantage", which, they propose, is due to proximity to the firms under consideration.

4.2. *Familiarity*

Another group of studies argues that local bias does not generate excessive returns and the reason for the existence of local bias is mostly behavioral, i.e., based on familiarity.

Zhu (2002) finds that investors tend to invest in familiar companies, even though such familiarity does not lead to excess returns in their equity investments, compared to non-local investors. In other words, local investors cannot predict earnings better than non-local investors, in contradiction of the "information advantage" hypothesis. Moreover, investors with stronger local bias do not outperform those with weaker one. Consequently, Zhu (2002) argued that advantageous information cannot explain individual investors' local bias, which may be more probably explained by individuals' non-fundamentally-based familiarity with local companies and ready reaction to local information. Consistent with this hypothesis, he found that individual investors are more likely to invest in remote companies that spend heavily on advertising in order to create familiarity. On the other hand, local investors are more responsive than remote investors to unexpected earnings following earnings announcement. Zhu published another paper with coauthor Mark Seasholes in 2010, in which they investigated the distribution of individual US investors' portfolios, for the period 1991–1996. More specifically, they aimed to answer to the following research question: "Do individuals have value-relevant information about local stocks?" Their findings suggest that portfolios of local holdings do not generate abnormal performance, and that individuals do not help incorporate information to stock prices.

Pirinsky and Wang (2006) found that stock returns of firms in the same location exhibited a strong degree of comovement, which, they argued could not be explained by fundamentals. Their approach was different in the sense that they focused on comovement of stocks in the same geography, instead of returns of investors' local stock investments. According to the authors, a word-of-mouth effect, and thus familiarity, is likely to be the cause of this finding, since the comovement is stronger in not only smaller, less profitable firms, but also in firms with more individual investors, and those located in regions with less financially sophisticated residents.

Liao *et al.* (2012) is another study claiming that local bias might be induced by non-information-based familiarity. They found that local bias of Chinese investors appears not to be motivated by information advantage, because investors do not obtain abnormal returns from their trades on local stocks.

In a more recent study, Baltzer, *et al.* (2015) investigated whether familiarity induced by ambiguity aversion may explain the local bias of individual investors. To this end, they used the theoretical framework of investor familiarity developed by Boyle *et al.* (2012), which states that familiarity arises from investors' aversion toward the ambiguous. Boyle *et al.* (2012) argued against the key assumption of traditional models of portfolio choice, which supposes that investors have perfect knowledge about the probability distribution of asset returns. Using geographic closeness as a proxy for investor familiarity, they found that investors disregarded unfamiliar stocks and preferred local stocks during periods of increased market uncertainty. This supports the conclusions of Huberman (2001), suggesting that instead of preferring to optimize along risk-return trade-offs, investors tend to concentrate their portfolios on known stocks (e.g., their own company's stock, stocks of firms that are visible in the investors' lives, and stocks that are reported favorably in the media).

5. Conclusions

This chapter reviews the existing literature on local bias of individual investors. Although home bias phenomenon has been investigated for at least 25 years, local bias, which can be considered as intra-country version of home bias, is a relatively new concept in behavioral finance research.

In this chapter, firstly, the concepts of local investment and local bias and their computations were explained. The different local investment definitions were categorized in three groups defined as: (1) prespecified distance, (2) a computed distance, (3) a specific city or region. In the literature, local bias is measured after selecting a definition of local investment. Then, the empirical evidence on the local bias of individual investors in both developed and developing countries was presented, and it was observed that studies on developed markets dominate this line of research, although there is also limited amount of research on emerging markets. Finally, potential explanations for local bias were presented. Currently, there exist two competing opinions about the underlying reasons behind the local bias of investors. The first is that the investors may have *informational advantage* due to their proximity to the companies, while the second assumes the existence of *familiarity*. If locals have informational advantage, one may expect that they invest earlier than the non-locals, and therefore earn greater profits.

Our general conclusion drawn from this review of the literature is that the geographic location plays an important role in determining investor portfolio choice, and the research findings on local bias complement those on home bias. The findings of the reviewed research studies raise several potentially interesting issues, and suggest a number of directions for further research, including extension to other emerging markets. For the time being, it would be difficult to generalize the findings of these studies due to lack of data showing emerging countries' investment trades. As stated by Aabo *et al.* (2013), taking into account differences in legal, cultural, and economic settings is very important when investigating local bias in a cross-country framework. Furthermore, as expressed by Coval and Moskowitz (1999), investigating local bias of investors in different financial markets may highlight the role of geography/distance in the economy, and may shed light on the various explanations suggested for the international home bias phenomenon. A further interesting avenue is investigating the extent to which existing studies have been affected by different methodologies.

As stated previously, the existing literature on local bias is still immature. However, when the number of relevant studies on the subject, particularly on emerging markets, increases, better implications can be drawn. Yet, if similar findings are obtained in different markets, this may lead to the proposition that policymakers may provide some incentives to facilitate the access of local firms to their local investors and funds. In this regard, policymakers might encourage the establishment of regional stock exchanges as well as regional indexes, which in turn may be conducive to the following outcomes: (1) A more efficient financial intermediation mechanism; (2) Easier access to funds by local firms as well as easier access to information by local investors; (3) Possible increase in the market values of local firms through increase in number of potential investors and trades; (4) Geographically better diversified and less concentrated national market.

This study may be of particular interest to portfolio managers in different countries, who may take into account its conclusions when developing and implementing investment strategies for individuals and institutional investors.

Acknowledgement

This research has been financially supported by Galatasaray University Research Fund (15.102.003). This chapter is based on the ongoing PhD research carried out by Evren Arık and supervised by Ömür Süer at Galatasaray University, Graduate School of Social Sciences.

References

Aabo, T., Pantzalis, C., and Sorensen, M. S. (2013). Game hoarding in Europe: Stock-price consequences of local bias? *Eur. J. Fin.*, 19(4), pp. 318–335.

Bae, K-H., Stulz, R-M., and Tan, H. (2008). Do local analysts know more? A cross-country study of the performance of local analysts and foreign analysts. *J. Fin. Econom.*, 88(3), pp. 581–606.

Baltzer, M., Stolper, O. A., and Walter, A. (2013). Is local bias a cross-border phenomenon? Evidence from individual investors' international asset allocation. *J. Bank. Fin.*, 37, pp. 2823–2835.

Baltzer, M., Stolper, O. A., and Walter, A. (2015). Home-field advantage or a matter of ambiguity aversion? Local bias among German individual investors. *Euro. J. Fin.*, 21(9), pp. 734–754.

Bodnaruk, A. (2009). Proximity always matters: Local bias when the set of local companies changes. *Rev. Fin.*, 13(4), pp. 629–656.

Boyle, P., Garlappi, L., Uppal, R., and Wang, T. (2012). Keynes meets Markowitz: The trade-off between familiarity and diversification. *Manage. Sci.*, 58(2), pp. 253–272.

Chhaochharia, V., Kumar, A., and Niessen-Ruenzi, A. (2012). Local investors and corporate governance. *J. Account. Econom.*, 54, pp. 42–67.

Coval, J. D. and Moskowitz, T. J. (1999). Home bias at home: Local equity preference in domestic portfolios. *The J. Fin.*, 54(6), pp. 2045–2073.

Coval, J. D. and Moskowitz, T. J. (2001). The geography of investment: Informed trading and asset prices. *J. Polit. Econ.*, 109(4), pp. 811–841.

Cumming, D. and Dai, N. (2010). Local bias in venture capital investments. *J. Empir. Fin.*, 17(3), pp. 362–380.

Das, P. K. (2011). Geographical proximity and mutual funds' proxy voting behavior. *Manager. Decision Econom.*, 32, pp. 425–437.

Dorn, D. and Huberman, G. (2005). Talk and action: What individual investors say and what they do. *Rev. Fin.*, 9, pp. 437–481.

Dorn, D., Huberman, G., and Sengmueller, P. (2008). Correlated trading and returns. *The J. Fin.*, 63(2), pp. 885–920.

Feng, L. and Seasholes, M. S. (2008). Individual investors and gender similarities in an emerging stock market. *Pacific-Basin Fin. J.*, 16(1), pp. 44–60.

French, K. R. and Poterba, J. M. (1991). Investor diversification and international equity markets. *The Am. Econom. Rev.*, 81(2), pp. 222–226.

Gaspar, J-M. and Massa, M. (2007). Local ownership as private information: Evidence on the monitoring-liquidity trade-off. *J. Fin. Econom.*, 83, pp. 751–792.

Goetzmann, W. N. and Kumar, A. (2008). Equity portfolio diversification. *Rev. Fin.*, 12, pp. 433–463.

Granger, C. W. J. and Morgenstern, O. (1970). *Predictability of Stock Market Prices.* Heath Lexington Books.

Grinblatt, M. and Keloharju, M. (2001). How distance, language, and culture influence stockholdings and trades. *The J. Fin.*, 56(3), pp. 1053–1073.

Hau, H. (2001). Location matters: An examination of trading profits. *The J. Fin.*, 56(5), pp. 1959–1983.

Hong, H., Kubik, J. D., and Stein, J. C. (2008). The only game in town: Stock-price consequences of local bias. *J. Fin. Econom.*, 90, pp. 20–37.

Huberman, G. (2001). Familiarity breeds investment. *The Rev. Fin. Stud.*, 14(3), pp. 659–680.

Ivković, Z. and Weisbenner, S. (2005). Local does as local is: Information content of the geography of individual investors' common stock investments. *The J. Fin.*, 60(1), pp. 267–306.

Ivković, Z., Sialm, C., and Weisbenner, S. (2008). Portfolio concentration and the performance of individual investors. *J. Fin. Quantit. Anal.*, 43(3), pp. 613–655.

Jacobs, H. and Weber, M. (2012). The trading volume impact of local bias: Evidence from a natural experiment. *Rev. Fin.*, 16(4), pp. 867–901.

Kedia, S. and Zhou, X. (2011). Local market makers, liquidity and market quality. *J. Fin. Markets*, 14, pp. 540–567.

Levy, H. and Sarnat, M. (1970). International diversification of investment portfolios. *Am. Econom. Rev.*, 60(4), pp. 668–675.

Liao, L., Zhisheng, L., Weiqiang, Z., and Zhu, N. (2012). Does the location of stock exchange matter? A within-country analysis. *Pacific-Basin Fin. J.*, 20(4), pp. 561–582.

Lintner, J. (1965). The valuation of risk assets and the selection of risky investments in stock portfolios and capital budgets. *The Rev. Econom. Statist.*, 47(1), pp. 13–37.

Loughran, T. and Schultz, P. (2004). Weather, stock returns, and the impact of localized trading behavior. *J. Fin. Quantit. Anal.*, 39(2), pp. 343–364.

Markowitz, H. (1952). Portfolio selection. *The J. Fin.*, 7(1), pp. 77–91.

Massa, M. and Simonov, A. (2006). Hedging, familiarity and portfolio choice. *The Revi. Fin. Stud.*, 19(2), pp. 633–685.

Mossin, J. (1966). Equilibrium in a capital asset market. *Econometrica*, 34(4), pp. 768–783.

Nofsinger, J. R. and Varma, A. (2012). Individuals and their local utility stocks: Preference for the familiar. *The Fin. Rev.*, 47, pp. 423–443.

Pirinsky, C. A. and Wang, Q. (2006). Does corporate headquarters location matter for stock returns? *The J. Fin.*, 61(4), pp. 1991–2015.

Pompian, M. M. (2006). *Behavioral Finance and Wealth Management: How to Build Optimal Portfolios that Account for Investor Biases*. New Jersey: John Wiley & Sons.

Seasholes, M. S. and Zhu, N. (2010). Individual investors and local bias. *The J. Fin.*, 65(5), pp. 1987–2010.

Sharpe, W. F. (1964). Capital asset prices: A theory of market equilibrium under conditions of risk. *The J. Fin.*, 19(3), pp. 425–442.

Sorenson, O. and Stuart, T. E. (2001). Syndication networks and the spatial distribution of venture capital investments. *Am. J. Sociol.*, 106(6), pp. 1546–1588.

Speidell, L. S. and Sappenfield, R. (1992). Global diversification in a shrinking world. *The J. Portfolio Manage.*, 19(1), pp. 57–67.

Tesar, L. L. and Werner, I. M. (1995). Home bias and high turnover. *J. Int. Money Fin.*, 14(4), pp. 467–492.

Zhu, N. (2002). The local bias of individual investors, Yale ICF Working Paper, No. 02–30.

Chapter 29

Does Geography Matter in Finance? Frontiers, Polarizations, Alternatives and Power Dynamics for Financial Analysis

Silvia Grandi* and Fabio M. Parenti†

* *The University of Bologna, Italy*

† *The Italian International Institute Lorenzo de' Medici — Marist College*

Abstract

This chapter aims at contributing to this Handbook with information, analysis and evidences of the role of geographical factors in examining the financial global system. This perspective is rarely taken into account in mainstream financial publications, whilst patterns of localization, polarization, distribution of population and wealth, distance to financial powers or services, geopolitical institutions and their decisions are all factors that the authors deem important to address for an understanding of the current world financial system. This system, in the last decades, has witnessed important changes following the recent crises. These geographical elements are important not only to understand past and present, but are likely to be fundamental to assess future trends. Providing insights on the evolution of the localization patterns of the global financial institutions and the background of the political theory and powers (shifting from Europe, to the US and to the emerging countries), this chapter shows the difficult path for the setting up of a "new world financial order".

1. Introduction

The analysis of the geographical patterns of a financial system is marginally taken into consideration by mainstreaming finance studies, while patterns of localization, polarization, distribution of population and wealth, distance to financial powers or services, geopolitical institutions and their decisions are all factors that we deem very important in understanding the global finance status, perspectives and frontiers. This topic has received renewed interest and fresh attention from economists and geographers in the light of major technological changes [Grote, 2009; Bassens *et al.*, 2017], corporate strategies transformations [Clark and Wójcik, 2007; Alessandrini *et al.*, 2009; Lucia, 2010; Boubaker *et al.*, 2015; Knight and Wójcik, 2017] and socio-economic and geopolitical events [Elson, 2011; Wójcik, 2013; Dixon and Monks, 2014; Parenti and Rosati, 2016].

In this chapter, we address this challenge by mapping the changing landscape of global financial architecture based on four questions:

(1) What is the institutional global financial architecture as well as the roles of financial institutions?
(2) What are the driving forces and geopolitical power games shaping the world's financial system?
(3) What are the changes in the most significant financial centers' localizations?
(4) What are the new reshaping determinants and phenomena that are transforming the global scenario?

Our analysis draws on geo-elaboration of databases and scientific literature. Additional insight comes from a review of media reports, including a leading specialist trade magazine in finance and economics.

First of all, we observe that the financial globalization that stemmed from the post-second world war era is a political-economic macro process that began in major cities in Europe and in the US. Financial globalization revealed itself in different ways, both in time and space; this phenomenon can be made comprehensible by analyzing the political and institutional development, as well as the changing spatial structure. The recent history of international financial transactions was forged first by the institutions of the two state powers that took turns at the helm of the world system during the course of the last century (the United Kingdom and the United States). Today, however, this power axis is being challenged by emerging countries; in particular, by China and Russia. However, from the 1970s, other cities became financial centers of the global hierarchy: the most important were Tokyo, Hong Kong, Singapore, and, more recently, Shanghai. At a lower level, we also find others, such as Geneva, Amsterdam, Brussels, Chicago, San Francisco, Hamburg, Luxemburg, Toronto, and Sydney (Parenti, 2016). Lately, the so-called Brexit process — the decision of the United Kingdom to leave the European Union — has resulted in significant signs of a potential

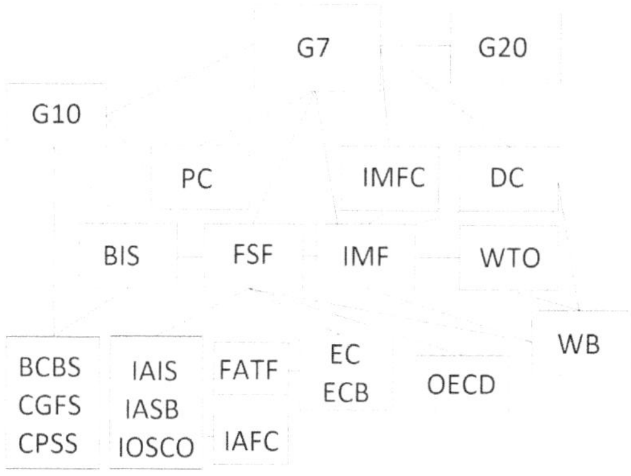

Figure 1. Architecture of the International Institutional Financial System: Elson Model

Notes: (BIS: Bank for International Settlements; BCBS: Basel Committee for Bank Supervision; CGFS: Committee on the Global Financial System; CPSS: Committee on Payment and Settlement Systems; DC: Development Committee; EC: European Commission; ECB: European Central Bank; FATF: Financial Action Task Force; FSF: Financial Stability Forum; G7: includes Canada, France, Germany, Italy, Japan, United Kingdom, and United States; G10: incudes G7 countries plus Belgium, The Netherlands, Sweden, and Switzerland; G20: incudes G7 countries plus Argentina, Australia, Brazil, China, European Union, India, Indonesia, Mexico, Russia, Saudi Arabia, South Africa, the Republic of Korea, and Turkey; IAIS: International Association of Insurance Supervisors; IASB: International Accounting Standards Board; IFAC: International Federation of Accountants; IMF: International Monetary Fund; IMFC: International Monetary and Financial Committee; IOSCO: International Organization of Securities Commissions; OECD: Organization of Economic Cooperation and Development; PC: Paris Club; WB: World Bank; WTO: World Trade Organization).

Source: Elson (2011), p. 20 and Authors' revisions

shift of several financial firms' headquarters from London to Frankfurt, the city where the European Central Bank is located [Parenti and Grandi, 2016].

In light of these few words, it is easy to highlight that the contemporary financial geography can be described as a system with a network-like configuration, where hubs or nodes are financial cities and "edges" can be grouped into two main types:

- Relational ones, which are people-based; i.e., those activities (interactions, agreements, decisions, etc.) occurring through direct contact or using information and telecommunication technologies;
- Spatial ones; these have come about owing to physical elements of real economy (transport systems, business and productive areas, etc.).

In particular, according to Elson's model (Elson, 2011), the geography of the global financial institutions is an architecture that has a reticular structure with a few dominant poles — at least until now — that we can trace in Europe; for instance, Basel and Geneva in Switzerland, Frankfurt in Germany; and in the US, Washington (Parenti and Grandi; 2016).

In this chapter, we summarize the rise and evolution of the global dimension of financial architecture. In the description, attention will be given to the reasons why institutions, events, facts, and effects are place-related and how these configurations have influenced the current global pattern.

This chapter contains arguments on localizations and roles of formal institutions that have had a strong impact on the international financial order, as well as other political networks and think tanks. If the location of a financial center is the result of markets, business communities, power dynamics and localization externalities, the choice of localization of global institutions' headquarters are results of negotiations, diplomacy, and geopolitics, as we report in the following pages.

2. Geohistorical Evolution of the Global Financial Institutional Architecture: The Roots of Current and Future Trends

The geography of the current global finance system traces back not only to what was constituted in the first decades of the 1900s or to the effects of the 2007 global crisis, but also to what was decided at Bretton Woods in 1944 and to what happened in the last 30 years of the 19th century. At that time the world was undergoing a strong developmental stage in various socio-economic fields, namely technology, markets, demography, and politics. These innovative factors created a favorable environment for the expansion of commercial and financial flows, giving rise to a new map of financial centers at the international level: besides London and Paris, cities such as Berlin, New York, Amsterdam, Brussels, Zurich, and Geneva became important financial centers.

The "bank panic" of 1907 and the crisis of 1929 showed the need for greater control and regulation of the financial system. These crises, just like World War I, marked a new pace in the political geography of the world and in the geopolitical approches, as well as in the international diplomatic system. In this regard, the experience from the League of Nations, traced to the 1920s of the 20th century, opened the way to an "intergovernmental cooperation model". In this atmosphere, in 1930 the Bank for International

Settlements (BIS) was created, the first international finance institution to which one could — through convention — retrace the birth of the global institutional financial system.

The interesting fact was the choice of Basel, a toponym that became synonymous with the reforms in the world banking system, i.e., the Basel Accords (Basel I, Basel II, and Basel III) which were widely known by firms as well as citizens (Parenti and Grandi, 2016).

The birth of this institution was the result of a compromise between the founding countries, namely Belgium, France, Germany, Italy, Japan, the UK, and the US. When consensus could not be reached on locating the Bank in London, Brussels, or Amsterdam, the choice fell on Switzerland. This was a state more neutral to the power pressures of the member countries, small and at the same time in a central position and well connected; therefore, it became the localizational solution. Above all, why Basel? Not only for distributive reasons, but also because Geneva had already hosted the League of Nations, Lausanne was considered too small and Zurich "too German". Moreover, Basel also held a winning card in the geography of the early 1900s: its location, with excellent railway connections in all directions, especially important at a time when most international travels was by train (BIS, 2005).

From the 1990s, after the globalization of the finance markets and with the shift of European monetary cooperation from Basel to Frankfurt — where in 1998 the European Central Bank (ECB) started to operate — the BIS started up a new repositioning process by which it became a global institution from being a traditionally European centered institution, covering substantially the central banks of the OECD and the emerging countries.

The latest organizational form of the BIS arose after the Asian crisis of 1997–1998 and the diffusion of the information and telecommunication technologies. In that atmosphere of financial stress in the emerging markets and of euphoria in the USA and Europe, in 1999 the finance ministers and the governors of the G7 central banks founded the Financial Stability Forum (FSF), which in 2009 became the Financial Stability Board (FSB), to coordinate at international level the work of the national financial authorities and develop the implementation of effective regulatory and supervisory policies. It can be observed that the composition of the FSB represents formal global financial governance, with the inclusion of the institutional references of the private system [Parenti and Grandi, 2016].

The birth of the FSB marked an attempt to overcome the fragmentation of global governance, bringing to the discussion table all the finance ministers of the G20 countries, representatives of the related central banks and national

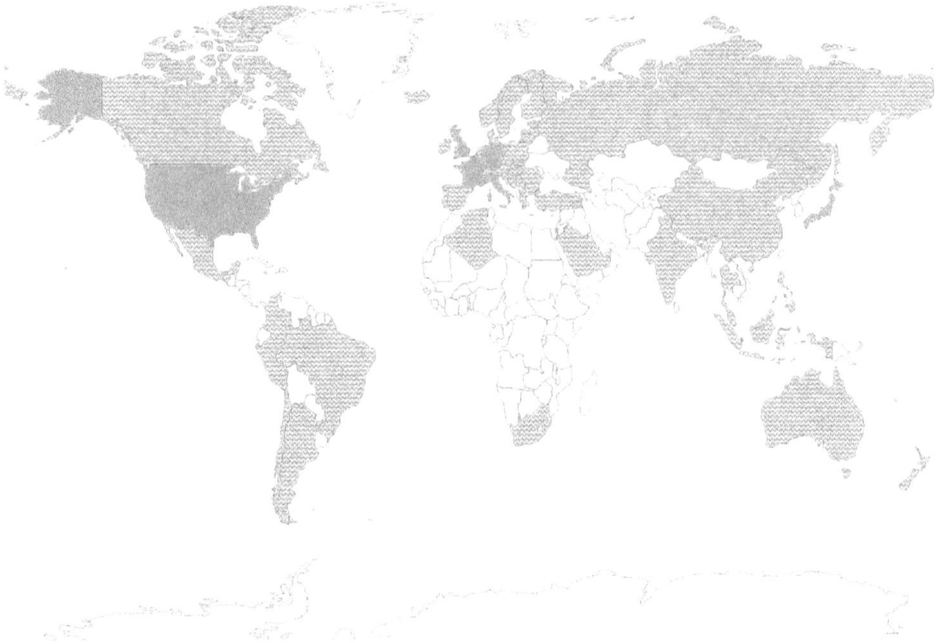

Figure 2. Country Memberships to the Bank of International Settlement (years: 1930 in bold, 2017 in Milled Texture)

Source: S. Grandi elaboration on BIS, 2017 and BIS, 2005 data.

supervisory bodies, and those of the major international organizations (BIS, IMF, WB, OECD) along with other reference organizations in the banking, corporate, insurance, and accounting sectors.

As already mentioned, the institutional architecture that should have reduced the gaps between countries and handled financial crises is not polarized exclusively on the Basel experience, but is Washington-centered as well. The centrality of this location can be linked to the agreements held in Bretton Woods where the leadership role of the United States as *primus inter pares* was set. This created a shift also in the US, as previously Wall Street in New York — creating a dyad or an axis with London — was the center of power [Wójcik, 2013]. As known, during this conference, also known as United Nations Monetary and Financial Conference held in 1944, the post-World War II international monetary and financial order was agreed upon based on setting up a system of rules, institutions, and procedures to regulate the international monetary system. In these accords, the International Monetary Fund (IMF) and the International Bank for Reconstruction and Development (IBRD), which today is part of the World

Table 1. Composition of the Financial Stability Board (FSB) in the Year 2015

Member Jurisdictions		
Country	**Governmental Institution**	**Central Banking Institutions**
• Argentina	Ministry of Economy and Public Finance	Banco Central de la República Argentina
• Australia	The Treasury	Reserve Bank of Australia
• Brazil	Ministério da Fazenda	Banco Central do Brasil — Comissão de Valores Mobiliários-
• Canada	Department of Finance	Bank of Canada Office of the Superintendent of Financial Institutions
• China	Ministry of Finance	People's Bank of China — China Banking Regulatory Commission
• France	Ministry of Economy and Finance	Banque de France Autorité des Marchés Financiers
• Germany	Bundesministerium der Finanzen	Deutsche Bundesbank SAR Bundesanstalt für Finanzdienstleistungsaufsicht (Bafin)
• Hong Kong SAR		Hong Kong Monetary Authority
• India	Ministry of Finance	Reserve Bank of India Securities and Exchange Board of India
• Indonesia	Ministry of Finance	Bank Indonesia
• Italy	Ministero dell'Economia e delle Finanze	Banca d'Italia Commissione Nazionale per le Società e la Borsa
• Japan	Ministry of Finance	Bank of Japan Financial Services Agency
• Korea		Bank of Korea Financial Services Commission -
• Mexico		Banco de México Secretaría de Hacienda y Crédito Público de México
• The Nether-lands	Ministry of Finance	De Nederlandsche Bank
• Russia	Ministry of Finance	Central Bank of the Russian Federation
• Saudi Arabia	Ministry of Finance	Saudi Arabian Monetary Agency
• Singapore		Monetary Authority of Singapore
• South Africa	Ministry of Finance	South African Reserve Bank
• Spain	Ministerio de Economía y Competitividad	Banco de España

(*Continued*)

Table 1. (*Continued*)

Member Jurisdictions		
Country	**Governmental Institution**	**Central Banking Institutions**
• Switzerland	Swiss Federal Department of Finance	Swiss National Bank
• United Kingdom	HM Treasury	Bank of England Financial Conduct Authority
• Turkey	Undersecretariat of the Treasury	Central Bank of the Republic of Turkey
• United States of America	U.S. Department of Treasury	Board of Governors of the Federal Reserve System US Securities & Exchange Commission (SEC)
• European Union	European Commission (EC)	European Central Bank (ECB)
Multilateral Financial Institutions:		
• Bank for International Settlements (BIS)		
• International Monetary Fund (IMF)		
• Organization for Economic Cooperation and Development (OECD)		
• The World Bank (WB)		
International Standard-Setting and Other Bodies:		
• Basel Committee on Banking Supervision (BCBS)		
• Committee on the Global Financial System (CGFS)		
• Committee on Payments and Market Infrastructures (CPMI)		
• International Association of Insurance Supervisors (IAIS)		
• International Accounting Standards Board (IASB)		
• International Organization of Securities Commissions (IOSCO)		

Source: FBS (2017).

Bank Group (WB), were established. The location of the headquarters of these institutions followed the leadership of the United States in the Bretton Woods decision, i.e., Washington hosted them in their role. In particular, while the IBRD, World Bank operated with the aim of furnishing financial support for development and knowledge sharing in the national and international systems, the IMF could be considered an embryo of the global central bank and had been delegated to guarantee the coordination of the monetary policies and harmonization of currency exchange rates. In this Washington-centered system, the US government inevitably played a leading role, even in the recent years. For instance, the Dodd-Frank Act, which is a Wall-Street Reform and Consumer Protection Act, came about in 2010 to reform the national financial system and significantly influenced the new financial order after the 2007 crisis.

In this institutional geography analysis of global finance, another important institutional pillar that stemmed from Bretton Woods is the World Trade Organization (WTO). It was created in 1995 after a long process initiated with the General Agreement on Tariffs and Trade (GATT). In this case, the localization choice followed more the tradition of the League of Nations and therefore is centered in Geneva, having started from the Centre William Rappard. This is a symbolic place conceived as part of the effort to create a League of Nations and other related institutions to encourage multilateral exchanges at a time when international cooperation was still an aspiration rather than a reality. At various points in its history, the building has been home to various multilateral institutions, among which are the Secretariat of the GATT that — prior to the creation of the WTO — had responsibility for the global trading system. Since 1995, it has been the headquarters of the WTO. This institution incarnates, more than others, the implementation of the neoliberal approach in real economy and is deputed to the regulation of transactions correlated to the trading of goods and services according to the free-trade principle. From the perspective of this chapter, WTO has played a tremendous role in shaping financial flows, emerging of new market poles, and creating the current financial and political geography. Financial integration grew also simultaneously with the process of reducing the barriers to international trade.

It is interesting to highlight that the hierarchy of institutional hubs, that we mentioned as poles or centers in this chapter, is getting more complex — as can be seen by the evolution of the opening of regional offices of these institutions. For instance, BIS in the last few years opened two Representative Offices: one for Asia and the Pacific in the Hong Kong Special Administrative Region of the People's Republic of China and one for the Americas in Mexico City. The World Bank Group and the IMF have a wider country and regional offices network, showing the evolution of globalization processes of finance and the widening of the players and their relative importance, especially towards Asia and Latin America.

Next to clearly geolocalized institutions, the locations of which express the results of negotiations, powers, and polarizations, the role of 'networks' should not be overlooked in describing the evolution of major bodies that are shaping the financial architecture of global finance. The Paris Club, the London Club, the G7, G10, and later, the G20 and G77 are deeply rooted in the political composition of the geography of powers that have evolved after World War II in the global arena, thereby creating dynamic centers and peripheries that were able to catch-up (like in China) or completely lose the pace (Parenti and Grandi, 2016).

In this paragraph, we have provided an overview of the institutional global financial architecture and the roles of financial institutions as well as their geography using a diachronic and a classical localization approach. In particular, we can observe that over decades the complexity is growing and polarizations are moving from a bipolar to a multipolar system. This fact suggests the creation of a sense of larger inclusion of emerging countries and a significantly wider span of countries and poles included in the global financial system. This process is still imperfect. Using a geopolitical term, we could argue that despite intentions and auspices, multipolarism is still asymmetric and unstable. The Bretton Woods architecture can no longer adequately cope with the present world of high capital mobility, providing critical assessment to better predict, foresee, and create a safety net to resolve international financial crises or address moral hazards (Eichengreen, 1999; Kanen, 2001; Stigliz, 2010; Kanen, 2010). Thus, in the past few decades, several economists, political scientists, and civil society organizations have called for a stronger attempt in reforming multilateral financial institutions to recreate a simpler, transparent, and efficient global financial architecture. Therefore, next to physiological dynamics that affect localization patterns and organizational development, financial global system governance is moving towards a new stage. However, this process has not been finalized and thus the system is still open to crises, inequalities, uncertainties, and misalignments to significant potential changes. Complexity and weaknesses, paradoxically, affect the reform process adversely; thereby, this process becomes less easy and rapid than desirable, creating a risky spiral and worsening weaknesses.

However, institutions are not the only driving forces of the geopolitical power games shaping the world's financial system, especially when the geoeconomic and geopolitical strategy is based on the socalled Washington Consensus prescriptions.[1] These are rather the places where processes are

[1]The term summarizes commonly shared themes among policy advice by Washington-based institutions at the time, such as the IMF, WB, and US Treasury Department, which were believed to be necessary for the recovery of countries in Latin America from the economic and financial crises of the 1980s. The concept and the names are generally attributed to John Williamson in 1989 who summarized the "receipt" in the following ten points: (1) Fiscal policy discipline, with avoidance of large fiscal deficits relative to GDP; (2) Redirection of public spending from subsidies ("especially indiscriminate subsidies") toward broad-based provision of key pro-growth, pro-poor services like primary education, primary health care, and infrastructure investment; (3) Tax reform, broadening the tax base and adopting moderate marginal tax rates; (4) Interest rates that are market determined and positive (but moderate) in real terms; (5) Competitive exchange rates;

stabilized, analyzed, and regulated, but other significant elements should be taken into consideration as well of these are described in more detail in the following paragraph.

3. Geographical Patterns of the Last Decades of Changes in the Global Financial System from Financial Centers to Frontiers?

Together with the development of the banking and trade system, the unprecedented rise in world population and social policies and the great availability of "petrodollars" have created the strengthening of public and private funds since the 1970s.

Investment funds, management companies, risk capital management companies, institutional and non-institutional investors, sovereign funds, private banking, and other such organizations are also shaping the world map of finance, both in organizational and localization terms. They are creating richer and more fluid geographic layouts compared to the past.

Among these, certainly the more important in terms of capital involved are the pension funds and sovereign funds. At the end of 2011, the global pension assets in the three biggest pension markets, representing 85% of all the funds of this type at global level, were estimated at USD 27,509 billion (Dixon and Monks, 2014). In 2015, according to OECD analysts, private pension assets topped USD 38 trillion worldwide and assets invested through all pension vehicles in financial markets reached USD 36.9 trillion in the 35 OECD countries in 2015; these assets amounted to USD 1.3 trillion in a sample of 45 non-OECD countries. Pension funds were the main investors in these assets worldwide (USD 26 trillion, 68% of the total), followed by banks and investment companies (USD 7.7 trillion, 20.2%), insurance companies (USD 4.3 trillion, 11.3%) and employers through their book reserves (USD 0.2 trillion, 0.5%) (Despalins and Antolín, 2016). A greater portion of the funds are related to public, professional pension funds of the industrialized countries and the biggest among these is the Government Pension Investment

(6) Trade liberalization: liberalization of imports, with particular emphasis on elimination of quantitative restrictions (licensing, etc.); any trade protection to be provided by low and relatively uniform tariffs; (7) Liberalization of inward foreign direct investment; (8) Privatization of state enterprises; (9) Deregulation: abolition of regulations that impede market entry or restrict competition, except for those justified on safety, environmental and consumer protection grounds, and prudential oversight of financial institutions; (10) Legal security for property rights (Bianchi, 2014).

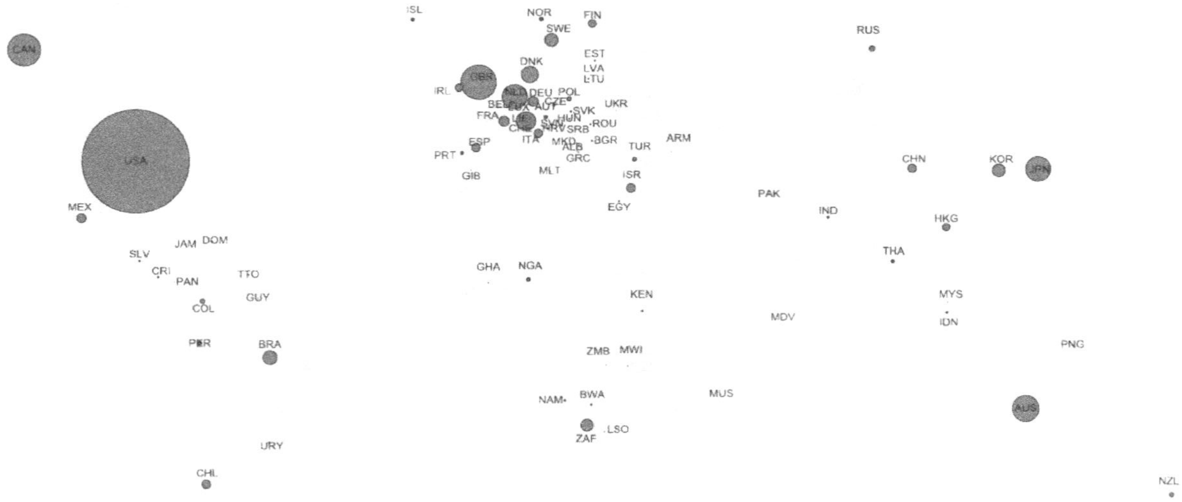

Figure 3a. Size of Private Pension Investments Worldwide, 2015 (a) In USD Terms

Source: Despalins (2015).

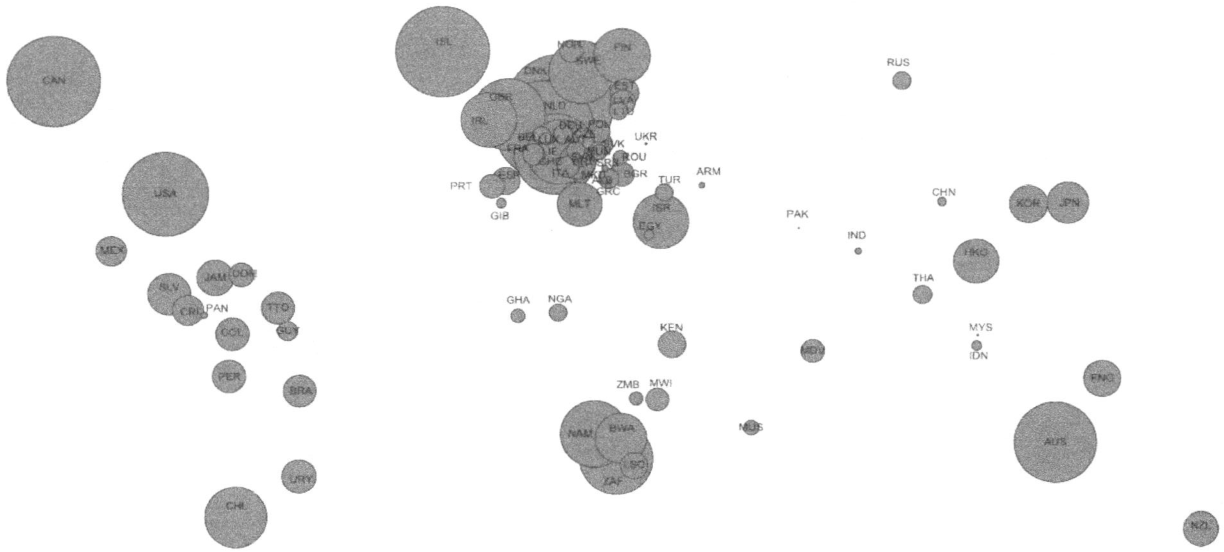

Figure 3b. Size of private Pension Investments Worldwide, 2015 as a Percentage in GDP

Source: Despalins (2015).

Fund of Japan, that manages about 1,400 billion dollars (Dixon and Monks, 2014).

The size of pension providers' investments as well as the number of pension funds in each country varies and it is uneven across countries.

In terms of the number of pension funds, these vary significantly: from a few in Central and Eastern Europe, as well as in Latin America, to thousands operating in Anglo-Saxon countries. Accordingly, in USD terms and relative to GDP, the pension funds' assets in North America, Western Europe and some other countries are the highest, whilst Brazil and Chile have the largest amount of private pension assets in Latin America, as does South Africa among the reporting African countries (Despalins and Antolín, 2016). Overall, in these areas, private pension assets are lower, showing the development process — especially in job policies — that these areas of the world are facing. Thus, a relative marginality in the world financial geography, despite some catching up, has been observed by Dixon and Monks (*ibid.*). However, when considering the potential of world population, these are regions where significant changes can be expected in the future if higher geopolitical stability is reached.

A different geographical pattern can be found in the sovereign wealth funds. These are directly held by the nation-states and created to promote economic, social, and productive development in those countries that had increased their own currency reserves, thanks to the exploitation of oil, other natural resources, or the surplus of trade budgets.

From the 1990s, the sovereign funds remarkably increased in numerical and dimensional terms, so much so that in 2015 their overall capital was estimated at 10,000 billion dollars. Among the countries with great sovereign funds were Saudi Arabia, the United Arab Emirates, Kuwait, Norway, Russia, Brazil, China, Singapore, and India (Dixon and Monks, 2014). Their influential power was enormous, with substantial geopolitical breakthroughs to the point that during the 2007–2008 crisis many of these funds supported the recapitalization of the European banks and industries for about 45 billion dollars.

To understand the complexity and the fluidity of the system, it is important to observe that the operative management of the pension or sovereign funds is often delegated to private companies that operate for profit and are localized in the main global financial centers that, with respect to the objective of stability in the long term, prefer short-term investments with greater yields and risks (Parenti and Grandi, 2016). In a central location, higher opportunities for investment diversification, specialized

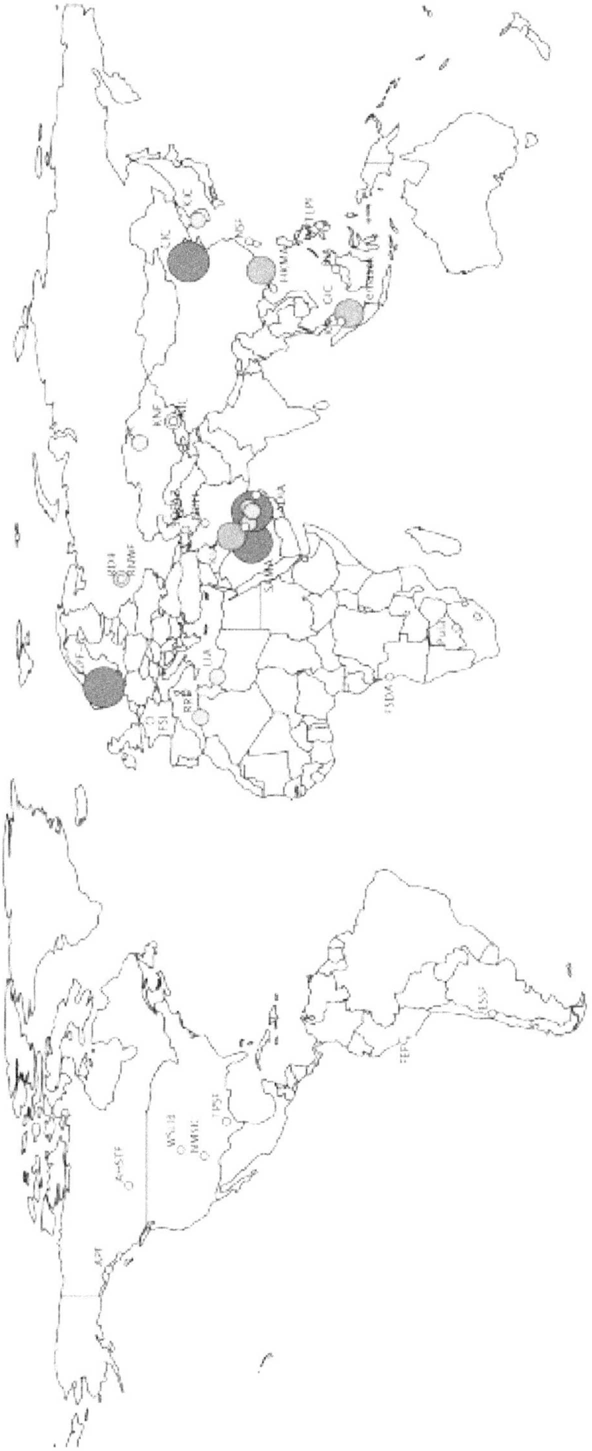

Figure 4. Distribution of the Main Sovereign Funds in the World

Source: Dixon and Monks (2014).

Table 2. List of All Global Systemically Important Institutions (G-SII) Composed of the Global Systemically Important Banks (G-SIBs) and Global Systemically Important Insurers (G-SII) (Nov. 2016 update)

	Headquarter			Headquarter	
Entity	**Country**	**Type**	**Entity**	**Country**	**Type**
Bank of America	*USA*	*Bank*	Royal Bank of Scotland	*UK*	*Bank*
Bank of NY Mellon	*USA*	*Bank*	Barclays	*UK*	*Bank*
Citigroup	*USA*	*Bank*	HSBC	*UK*	*Bank*
Goldman Sachs	*USA*	*Bank*	Standard Chartered	*UK*	*Bank*
JP Morgan Chase	*USA*	*Bank*	Credit Suisse	*Switzerland*	*Bank*
Morgan Stanley	*USA*	*Bank*	UBS	*Switzerland*	*Bank*
State Street	*USA*	*Bank*	Nordea	*Sweden*	*Bank*
Wells Fargo	*USA*	*Bank*	Santander	*Spain*	*Bank*
American International Group, Inc.	*USA*	*Insurance*	ING Bank	*Netherlands*	*Bank*
MetLife, Inc.	*USA*	*Insurance*	Unicredit Group	*Italy*	*Bank*
Prudential Financial, Inc.	*USA*	*Insurance*	Deutsche Bank	*Germany*	*Bank*
Prudential plc	*USA*	*Insurance*	BNP Paribas	*France*	*Bank*
Mizuho FG	*Japan*	*Bank*	Groupe Crédit Agricole	*France*	*Bank*
Sumitomo Mitsui FG	*Japan*	*Bank*	Groupe BPCE	*France*	*Bank*
Mitsubishi UFJ FG	*Japan*	*Bank*	Société Générale	*France*	*Bank*
Bank of China	*China*	*Bank*	Aegon N.V.	*Netherlands*	*Insurance*
China Construction Bank	*China*	*Bank*	Allianz SE	*Germany*	*Insurance*
Agricultural Bank of China	*China*	*Bank*	Aviva plc	*UK*	*Insurance*
ICBC	*China*	*Bank*	Axa S.A.	*France*	*Insurance*
Ping An Insurance	*China*	*Insurance*			

Source: Elaboration of FSB, 2016a and 2016b data.

financial services, and an attractive atmosphere of highly qualified workers can be expected.

Indeed, the global financial system goes beyond just public funds and institutions; commercial and investment banks, stock markets, money mints, investors, businessmen, and credit groups are essential components of the geography of the financial system, creating a complex and fragmented system, where the global players are few and still localized in few countries. Compared to the location of the main governing institutions, in this case the map of the global institutions is larger, with a strong pole in Asia as well. To rapidly understand the distribution of global insurance and bank, the Systemically Important Financial Institutions (SIFIs)[2] can constitute an indicator (see Table 2) (FSB, 2016a, 2016b) despite the focus of the FSB in evaluating risks rather than overall significance.

The analysis of the evolution of the centers considered in the Global Financial City Index[3] (GFCI) (Yeandle, 2015), in harmony with main globlalization trends, shows that the polarizations are changing greatly, reducing the importance of continental Europe in the global scenario. From 2007 to 2015, the first top four global financial centers continued to be London, New York, Hong Kong, and Singapore, while many European cities moved out of the first 40 positions leaving room for the emergence of the Asian and Middle East centers. Osaka, Doha, Shenzhen, Busan, Tel Aviv, Taipei, and Abu Dhabi, in just 10 years entered the global scenario together with Sao Paolo and Johannesburg, certainly with more uncertainty than stability.

Another interesting pattern is related to distances between the higher-range and intermediate centers: these are reducing.

By using the Christaller's Central Place Theory vocabulary, we could ask the following questions, namely are the lower-range centers emerging? How do they compensate for localization disadvantages? Stanford University started up a survey on this theme; moreover, Dixon and Monk [*ibid.*] evidenced that in the last 10 years "frontier finance" hubs have emerged. Financial localities without historical presence of operators, specialized training systems, and labour markets are growing driven by investors eyeing the prospect of long-term investments like sovereign funds, pension funds, foundations, donations and bequests, Islamic finance and family offices, and due to new courses of education in economics and finance (Clark, 2016).

[2]Systemically Important Financial Institutions (SIFI) are identified with a methodological approach based on the works of Basel III. These institutions are called, in general, to greater fulfillments in terms of controls and capitalization.

[3]The GFCI is an index initially developed with the support of the City of London from 2007. It is published every six months, within the think tank "Z/Yen Group" supported by the Qatar Financial Center. It is based on the analysis of assessment questionnaires of the sector operators and fact-checking analysis of secondary localization factors and secondary data produced by the international institutions and organizations [Yendel, 2015].

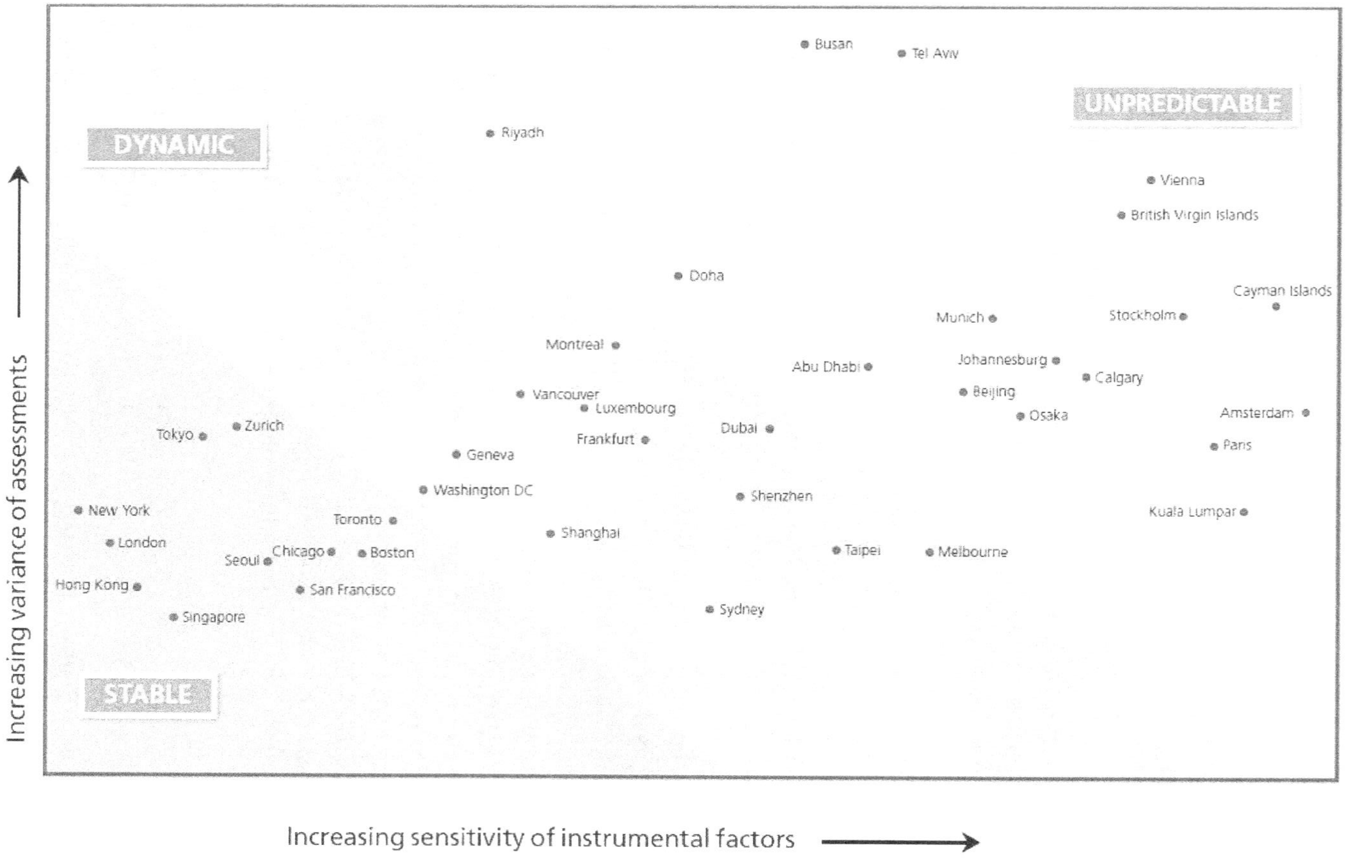

Figure 5. Dynamicity of the Positioning of Global Financial Centers Based on the GFCI-18

Source: Yeandle (2015).

Social aspects can be important to compensate localization disadvantages: more affordable cost of living, less congestion, personal affinity with a place, greater work-life balance for the management of families and the elderly, etc. Examples range from the great centers of Beijing, Shanghai, and Melbourne in comparison to the small cities of Gaborone (Botswana), Dili (Timor-Leste), and Edmonton (Alberta).

Futhermore, we can argue that in the global-local dialogue, the so-called "alternative" economic and financial experiences (microcredit, digital money, ethic banks, etc.) are growing. Despite representing very limited financial flows, these can be a ground for "frontier" hubs to develop alternative financial models and specialized countries and cities. In this last perpective, analyzing the rankings of the top 50 microfinance institutions (Swibel, 2007), we found that most of them were not located in high-ranking financial centers. In particular, the first ranked institution was ASA, whose headquarters are located in Dhaka (Bangladesh), followed by Bandhan in Kolkata (India), Banco do Nodeste in Fortaleza (Brazil), Fundación Mundial de la Mujer in Bucaramanga (Colombia), FONDEP-Salaf Albaraka in Casablanca (Morocco), etc.

Correspondingly, Poon (2016) examines Kuala Lumpur's emergence as a prominent global Islamic financial centre. He argues that its distance from the West and the Middle East offers a frontier positioning that facilitates new social practices from the integration of financial knowledge of Western world cities and Shariah authority claimed by Gulf cities.

Integrating all the above perspectives, "frontier" can be, consequently, a term used with a triple connotation to indicate:

- the particular functions in the financial processes,
- the alternative approach to providing financial services and products,
- the different geographical localizations with respect to historical centers.

4. Conclusion: Reshaping Forces in the Map of Global Financial Centres

In this chapter, we have elaborated the evolution of financial architecture and the localization of its centers. In a geohistoric approach, we have described that at the start of the 20th century the world financial centers were London and Paris, with the addition of Berlin, New York, Amsterdam, Brussels, Zurich, Basel, and Geneva. After World War II, the role of the US rose significantly and Washington emerged as a fundamental institutional location of Bretton Woods organisations: IMF and IBRD-World Bank. From the 1970s the cities of Hong Kong, Singapore, Tokyo, and Frankfurt emerged, as also the so-called peripherical tax havens in the US (Cayman Isles, Bermuda, Bahamas).

The financial globalization that stemmed from the second post-war era is a political-economic macro process whose birth was favored particularly by the governments and corporations of the United States of America and Europe (United Kingdom, France, Switzerland, and their respective financial centers). Geneva, Amsterdam, Zurich, Brussels and Frankfurt, Hamburg, Luxemburg can be considered global-regional hubs like Chicago, San Francisco, Toronto and Sydney that in time have gained momentum. In terms of major international players in global finance, a growing multipolarity can be observed.

On one hand, this creates fragmentation and complexity. Moreover, this creates competition among cities. For instance, this is the case now for the financial cities competing to attract the relocation of headquarters of banks leaving the UK due to Brexit (Knight and Wójcik, 2017). On the other hand, this has positive effects in terms of generation of ideas, flows of professionalism, development of data, good and bad practices, and comparative analyses, which the governments — and their more or less formal groups — could benefit from (Parenti and Grandi, 2017).

In terms of localization analysis, we have noted the following concurrent phenomena:

- the centralization, reinforcement, and consolidation of the big "historical" financial centers (Grote, 2009; Yeandle, 2015) with a potential weakening of London following Brexit;
- the rise of new, medium centers, called "frontier finance" places that are often correlated to the emergence of the new, big, urban areas in emerging countries (Dixon and Monk, 2014; Parenti e Grandi, 2016);
- the rise of new minor centers connected to "frontier finance" phenomena (Dixon and Monk, 2014; Parenti and Grandi, 2016);
- the virtualisation of transactions (Grote, 2009; Parenti and Grandi, 2016), thus the reinforcement of "edges" rather than hubs recalling the network model explained in the first paragraph of this chapter.

The frontier of the geography shows several concurrent phenomena that are reshaping the global distribution of the financial centers and localization patterns. First, the concentration and consolidation of the big "historical" financial centers as well as the rise of new, medium-sized, '*frontier centers*' that are often correlated to the emergence of the new, large, urban cities in emerging countries (Dixon and Monks, 2014). In the last decades, these locations have developed in terms of organization patterns resulting in a new landscape of localized geographical articulation and networks much richer and smoother than ever before.

The virtualization of transactions and FinTech start-ups result in the development of advanced and innovative services (Bassens *et al.*, 2017). 'Big Data' mining, digital money, distributed ledger technology, robo advice, and other FinTech applications might drive radical change in the existing financial sector business practices. Incumbent financial institutions, with their legacy systems and sunk costs, can find it interesting to adopt these innovations that can result sometimes in leapfrogs, first in organizational patterns; eventually, sooner or later, these innovations can spell out the cards on the table and change the existing arrangements of the financial system [*ibid.*]. However, according to Grote (2009), these innovations will not significantly change the tendency of financial activities concentrating in large urban areas. Implicitly, Grote is confirming the intrinsic role of advanced financial services that tend to localize in higher-order places, i.e., major world cities, referring to the evergreen seminal work of Christaller's Central Place Theory.

In this global ecosystem, the foundations for the contemporary financial industry are composed of a large number of players and instrument types over the traditional ones. This system is becoming more complex and significantly difficult to regulate and control. Despite a high level of commitment from the most important official institutions (BIS, FSB, WB, IMF, G7, ECB, G20 etc.), it seems still very vulnerable and open to financial and geopolitical crises. Therefore, in its present form, this system is a potential driver of strong inequalities and instability in the changing world order.

Acknowledgment

This chapter is edited by both authors and they both wrote the first paragraph and the conclusion, however, paragraph 2 has been written by Silvia Grandi and paragraph 3 by Fabio Massimo Parenti.

References

Alessandrini, P., Fratianni, M., and Zazzaro A. (eds), (2009). *The Changing Geography of Banking and Finance*. Heidelberg: Springer.

Bassens, F., Hendrikse, R., and Van Meeteren, M. (2017). The appleization of finance: Reflections on the FinTech (R)evolution, FinGeo — Financial Geography Working Paper n. 2, pp. 1–27.

Bianchi, P. (2014). *Globalizzazione, crisi e riorganizzazione industriale*. Milano: McGraw Hill.

BIS, (2005). *This is the Biz*. Basel: BIS.

Boubaker, S., Derouiche, I., and Lasfer, M. (2015). Geographic location, excess control rights, and cash holdings. *Int. Rev. Fin. Anal.*, 42, pp. 24–37.

Clark G. L. and Wójcik D. (2007). *The Geography of Finance: Corporate Governance in the Global Marketplace*. Oxford: Oxford University Press.

Clark G. L. (2016). The components of talent: company size and financial centres in the European investment management industry. *Reg. Stud.*, 50, pp. 168–181.

Despalins, R. and Antolín, P. (2016). *Pension Markets in Focus*. Paris: OECD.

Dixon, A. and Monk. A. H. B. (2014). Frontier finance. *Ann. Assoc. Am. Geograph.*, 104(4), pp. 852–868.

Eichengreen B. (1999). *Toward a New International Financial Architecture. A Practical Post-Asia Agenda* Washington: Peterson Institute for International Economics Press.

Elson, A. (2011). *Governing Global Finance*. New York: Paigrave Macmillan.

FSB, (2016a). List of globally systemically important banks (G-SIBs), 21 November 2016.

FSB, (2016b). List of global systemically important insurers (G-SIIs), 21 November 2016.

FBS, (2017). FSB Members, www.fsb.org/about/fsb-members.

Grote M. H. (2009). Financial centers between centralization and virtualization. In Alessandrini P., Fratianni M., Zazzaro A. (eds), *The Changing Geography of Banking and Finance*. Heidelberg: Springer Dordrecht, pp. 280–294.

Kanen P. B. (2001). *The International Financial Architecture: What's New? What's Missing?* Washigton: Peterson Institute for International Economics Press.

Kanen P. B. (2010). The substitution account as a first step toward reform of the international monetary system. *Peterson Institute for Int. Econom. Policy Brief*. n. 10–6.

Knight, E. and Wójcik, D. (2017). Geographical linkages in the financial services industry: a dialogue with organizational studies. *Reg. Stud.*, 51(1), pp. 116–12.

Lucia, M. G. (1999). *La geografia finanziaria*. Patron, Bologna: Mercati e territorio.

Lucia, M. G. (2010). *Lo spazio geografico dell'economia finanziaria*, Torino: CELID.

Parenti, F. M. (2018). The international financial system and its evolution. In Parenti, F.M. and Rosati, U. (eds.), Geofinance and Geopolitics. Milano: Egea, 2018, pp. 9–35.

Parenti, F. M. and Grandi, S. (2018). The evolution of global financial architecture: the institutional framework. In Parenti, F.M. and Rosati, U. Geofinance and Geopolitics (eds.). Milano: Egea, 2018, pp. 37–54.

Poon, J. P. H., Pollard, J., Chow J. W., and Ewers M. (2016). The rise of Kuala Lumpur as an Islamic financial frontier. *Reg. Stud.*, doi: 10.1080/00343404.2016.1214254.

Stiglitz, J. (2002). *Globalisation and its Discontent*. New York: Penguin.

Swibel, M. (2007). The 50 Top Microfinance Institutions https://www.forbes.com/2007/12/20/microfinance-philanthropy-credit-biz-cz_ms_1220microfinance_table.html.

Yeandle, M. (2015). *Global Financial Center Index GFCI18*, Z/Yen Group and Qatar Financial Center, September 2015, Z/Yen Group Limited.

Wójcik, D. (2013). The dark side of NY–LON: Financial centres and the global financial crisis. *Urban Stud.*, 50, pp. 2736–2752.

Wójcik, D., Knight, E., O'Neill, P., and Pažitka, V. (2017). Investment Banking since 2008: The Geography of Shrinkage and Shift, FinGeo — Financial Geography Working Paper n. 3, pp. 1–27.

Index

M

N

O

P

Q

R

S

CPSIA information can be obtained
at www.ICGtesting.com
Printed in the USA
BVHW011345030719
551978BV00019B/17/P

9 789813 236646